**Aljian's
Purchasing
Handbook**

OTHER McGRAW-HILL HANDBOOKS OF INTEREST

ALBERT · *The Handbook of Business Problem Solving*
BRADY · *Materials Handbook*
BUELL AND HEYEL · *Handbook of Modern Marketing*
DAVIDSON · *Handbook of Modern Accounting*
DIEBOLD · *Automatic Data Processing Handbook*
FAMULARO · *Handbook of Modern Personnel Administration*
GREENE · *Production and Inventory Control Handbook*
GREENWALD · *McGraw-Hill Dictionary of Modern Economics*
HANCOCK · *Executive's Guide to Business Law*
HEYEL · *The Foreman's Handbook*
HEYEL · *Handbook of Modern Office Management and Administrative Services*
HIGGINS AND STIDGER · *Cost Reduction from A to Z*
JURAN · *Quality Control Handbook*
LEWIS AND MARRON · *Facilities and Plant Engineering Handbook*
MAYNARD · *Handbook of Business Administration*
MAYNARD · *Handbook of Modern Manufacturing Management*
MAYNARD · *Industrial Engineering Handbook*
ROCK · *Handbook of Wage and Salary Administration*

Aljian's Purchasing Handbook

Fourth Edition

Sponsored by the

NATIONAL ASSOCIATION OF PURCHASING MANAGEMENT

Coordinating Editor

Paul V. Farrell, C.P.M.

Formerly Edited By

George W. Aljian, C.P.M.

Vice-President of Purchasing, Packaging, and Traffic (Retired),
California and Hawaiian Sugar Company, San Francisco, California
Formerly Lecturer in Industrial Procurement, School of Business Administration,
University of California, Berkeley, California
President, National Association of Purchasing Management

McGRAW-HILL BOOK COMPANY

New York   St. Louis   San Francisco   Auckland
Bogotá   Hamburg   Johannesburg   London   Madrid   Mexico
Montreal   New Delhi   Panama   Paris   São Paulo
Singapore   Sydney   Tokyo   Toronto

Library of Congress Cataloging in Publication Data
Purchasing handbook.
    Aljian's Purchasing handbook.

    Bibliography: p.
    Includes index.
    1. Purchasing—Handbooks, manuals, etc.   I. Aljian,
George W.   II. Farrell, Paul V.   III. National Associa-
tion of Purchasing Management.   IV. Title.
HF5437.P795 1981   658.7'2   81-8350
                                           AACR2

 234567890   KPKP   89876543

ISBN 0-07-045899-5

The editors for this book were Harold B. Crawford and Olive H. Collen,
the designer was Blaise Zito Associates, and the production supervisor was
Sally Fliess. It was set in Baskerville by University Graphics, Inc.

Printed and bound by The Kingsport Press.

*The purchasing profession offers numerous opportunities for men and women
alike. Thus the pronouns "he" and "his" have been used only in a generic
sense in this book, to avoid awkward grammatical constructions.*

*To all men and women who by competent
purchasing performance on their day-to-day
assignments are contributing to the
advancement of purchasing as a career
in management*

Contents

Contributors

Wayne D. Adams, C.P.M. Corporate Director of Purchases, J. M. Huber Corporation, Houston, Texas

Nick M. Alex, C.P.M. Director, Corporate Purchasing, NCR Corporation, Dayton, Ohio

American Bar Association Model Procurement Code Staff, principally Michael K. Love and Herbert H. Ferguson, Project Directors

Ralph L. Andreas Retired Director of Purchasing and Traffic, Amoco Oil Company, Chicago, Illinois

Richard T. Arnott Vice-President and Managing Director, Kellogg Continental, B.V., Amsterdam, Netherlands

John J. Bennett Former Director, Federal Acquisition Institute, Office of Management & Budget, Washington, D.C.

Solon A. Bennett, C.P.M., CPPO, CPCM Director of Purchases and Stores, City of Austin, Texas

Eric H. Bergman, C.P.M. President, Eric Bergman & Associates, Seattle, Washington

Edward J. Bierman, Ph.D. Director of Certification and Professional Activities, National Association of Purchasing Managment, New York, New York

C. B. Bishop Specifications and Standards, Mechanical Engineering Department, Lawrence Livermore National Laboratory, Livermore, California

James A. Black, C.P.M. Vice-President, Specialty Materials, Eagle-Picher Industries, Inc., Miami, Florida

Ted Black Quality Control Engineer, Varian/Eimac Division, San Carlos, California

C. L. Blue, C.P.M. Manager of Procurement, Supply, and Business Services, University of California, Lawrence Livermore National Laboratory, Livermore, California

Jay H. Bolton Former Deputy Commissioner, Federal Supply Service, General Services Administration, Washington, D.C.

Robert E. Booton Director, Contract Placement, Office of Defense Research and Engineering, Department of Defense, Washington, D.C.

R. G. Bradyhouse, C.P.M., C.V.S. Manager, Value Analysis Services, Black & Decker (U.S.), Inc., Towson, Maryland

Ronald G. Brown, C.P.M. Buyer, Tektronix, Inc., Beavertown, Oregon

D. B. Carmody Manager, Engineering Construction and Equipment Purchases, Union Carbide Corporation, New York, New York

Robert C. Carson, C.P.M. Director of Purchasing, Federal-Mogul Corporation, Detroit, Michigan

D. O. Corvey, C.P.M. Staff Vice-President, Materials, RCA Corporation, Cherry Hill, New Jersey

James Coughenour Buyer—Metals, Carrier Air Conditioning Company, Syracuse, New York

Mary R. Crowell Librarian, Purchasing Information Center, National Association of Purchasing Management, New York, New York

Bruce B. Curtis (Retired) Director of Purchasing, International Harvester Company, Chicago, Illinois

Herbert C. Damron, C.P.M., CPPO Director of Purchasing, St. Louis Community College, St. Louis, Missouri

John J. Davin, C.P.M. Vice-President, Materials and Facilities, GTE, Stamford, Connecticut

Peter H. Denning, C.P.M. Manager of Purchases, Koppers Company, Inc., Baltimore, Maryland

Thomas F. X. Dillon, C.P.M. Senior Editor, *Purchasing,* Boston, Massachusetts

Richard L. Dunn Editor, *Purchasing World,* Barrington, Illinois

Donald F. Fair Vice-President and Director of Purchases, Corporate Office for Research and Technical Services, W. R. Grace & Company, New York, New York

Joseph E. Flannery, C.P.M. Corporate Director—Transportation (formerly Director, Purchasing), Armco Inc., Middletown, Ohio

Homer A. Foerster, C.P.M., CPPO Executive Director, Texas State Purchasing and General Services Commissioner, Austin, Texas

Gailon C. Fordyce, C.P.M. Assistant Purchasing Director, The American Tobacco Company, A Division of American Brands, Inc., New York, New York

Roger R. Frank, C.P.M. Corporate Director of Purchasing, Baxter Travenol Laboratories, Inc., Deerfield, Illinois

Gary L. Fratilla, C.P.M. Manager, Corporate Contracts, NCR Corporation, Dayton, Ohio

Bernard J. Frey Manager, MIS/DP, Bailey Controls, Wickliffe, Ohio

Myron E. Frye Vice-President, Corporate Purchasing, Maremont Corporation, Chicago, Illinois

Roger Gano Executive Manager, *Oregon Purchasor,* Portland, Oregon

Arthur A. Gibson, C.P.M. Director of Purchasing, Glass Containers Corporation, Fullerton, California

K. Paul Graham, C.P.M. Purchasing Agent, City of San Leandro, California

Charles T. Haffey, C.P.M. Vice-President, Corporate Purchasing Division, Pfizer Inc., New York, New York

J. Douglas Hall, P.P. Former National Director, Region VIII, Purchasing Management Association of Canada, Toronto, Canada

Kenneth W. Hartwell, C.P.M. Associate and Technical Procurement Engineer, Overseas Advisory Associates, Inc., Detroit, Michigan; retired Director of Purchasing, The Detroit Edison Company

S. R. Heath, Jr., C.P.M. Vice-President, Division General Manager, Filtration & Minerals Division, Johns Manville Corporation, Denver, Colorado

Floyd D. Hedrick, C.P.M. Chief, Procurement and Supply Division, The Library of Congress, Washington, D.C.

W. L. Hertenstein Manager of International Purchasing, Caterpillar Tractor Company, Peoria, Illinois

John H. Hoagland, Ph.D., C.P.M. Professor of Management, Graduate School of Business, Michigan State University, East Lansing, Michigan

H. W. Hutchison, C.P.M. Director, Governmental Procurement Programs, RCA Corporation, Cherry Hill, New Jersey

John J. Huzar, C.P.M. Chief Purchasing Agent, City of Detroit, Michigan

Glenn W. Inman, C.P.M. Vice-President, Purchasing and Materials, Clow Corporation, Oak Brook, Illinois

Robert L. Janson, C.P.M. Manager, Management Consulting Services, Ernst & Whinney, Cleveland, Ohio

Caleb L. Johnson, C.P.M. Director, Materials, Plumbing & Specialty Products Group, Kohler Company, Kohler, Wisconsin

J. Edward Johnson, C.P.M. Manager, Purchasing (Retired), Amoco Oil Company, Atlanta, Georgia

Tom Lang General Manager, Corporate Procurement, Control Data Corporation, Minneapolis, Minnesota

Allen J. Levy Quality Assurance Office, Lawrence Livermore National Laboratory, Livermore, California

Al J. Manthos, C.P.M. Manager of Purchasing, Varian/Eimac Division, San Carlos, California

James H. McDowell, Jr., C.P.M. Assistant Director, Division of Purchasing, Tennessee Valley Authority, Chattanooga, Tennessee

Paul E. Merchant Corporate Manager, Purchasing, The Bendix Corporation, Southfield, Michigan

W. P. Mitchell, C.P.M. Manager, Regional and Technical Purchasing, Hunt-Wesson Foods, Inc., Fullerton, California

Robert M. Monczka, Ph.D., C.P.M. Professor of Management, Graduate School of Business Administration, Michigan State University, East Lansing, Michigan

David L. Morgan Field Purchasing Manager, Carrier Air Conditioning Company, Syracuse, New York

R. L. Morton Quality Assurance Office, Lawrence Livermore National Laboratory, Livermore, California

Daniel J. Murphy Manager of Planning and Economics, Rio Blanco Shale Oil Company, Denver, Colorado

Len B. Neubert, C.P.M. (Retired) Vice-President, Purchasing and Transportation, Aluminum Company of America, Pittsburgh, Pennsylvania

Richard H. Olson, C.P.M. Group Materials Manager, Lighting Products Group, GTE Products Corporation, Danvers, Massachusetts

Robert C. Parker, C.P.M. Vice-President, Purchasing, Transportation & Facilities Service, International Harvester Company, Chicago, Illinois

John D. Peters, C.P.M. Vice-President, Purchasing & Traffic, Dravo Corporation, Pittsburgh, Pennsylvania

John E. Pughe, C.P.M. Corporate Director, Purchasing, The Bendix Corporation, Southfield, Michigan

Anne D. Repko, C.P.M. Director of Material, Howmedica, Inc., Subsidiary of Pfizer, Inc., New York, New York

Rosemary Schoenberger, C.P.M. Director of Purchasing, UIP Engineered Products Corporation, Elk Grove Village, Illinois

C. L. Scott, C.P.M. Director of Procurement, Defense & Space Systems Group, TRW Inc., Redondo Beach, California

Clifton L. Smith, C.P.M. Manager, Worldwide Purchasing, Construction Equipment Group, International Harvester Company, Schaumburg, Illinois

Lewis E. Spangler Executive Vice-President, National Institute of Govermental Purchasing, Inc., Arlington, Virginia

Mike L. Stone Former Attorney, Johns-Manville Corporation, Denver, Colorado

Robert B. Stone Vice-President, Materials Management Staff, General Motors Corporation, Detroit, Michigan

A. J. Stryck, C.P.M. Senior Specialist, Purchasing System, Standard Oil Company (Indiana), Chicago, Illinois

J. Andrew Sutton, C.P.M. Director of Purchasing, W. R. Grace & Company, Cryovac Division, Duncan, South Carolina

George Tateosian Vice-President, Metal Traders, Inc., New York, New York

John Thorn President, Gulf Consolidated Services Piping Group; Chairman of the Board, Gulf Supply Company, Houston, Texas

D. Michael Tonti Director of Purchasing, Black & Decker (U.S.) Inc., Hampstead, Maryland

Alex J. Vallas, C.P.M. Director of Materials Management, Magee-Women's Hospital, Pittsburgh, Pennsylvania

J. B. Van Dusen, C.P.M. President, Ecclestone Chemical Company, Inc., Detroit, Michigan

M. L. Vyenielo Reliability and Quality Control, Electronics Engineering, Lawrence Livermore National Laboratory, Livermore, California

Joseph J. Warnas, C.P.M., CPPO, CPCM Director of Materials Management, Maricopa County, Arizona

Lee A. Wells, Jr., C.P.M. Purchasing Manager (Retired), Carrier Air Conditioning Company, Syracuse, New York

Norman M. Weltmann, C.P.M. President, Marley's Inc., Syracuse, New York

Susan K. Williams Senior Systems Analyst, Tennant Company, Minneapolis, Minnesota

A. D. Wilson   Manager, Overseas Purchasing, Warner-Lambert Company, Morris Plains, New Jersey

Daniel S. Wilson   Assistant Administrator for Commercial, Office of Federal Procurement Policy, Office of Management & Budget, Washington, D.C.

Frank J. Winters, C.P.M.   Executive Vice-President (Retired), National Association of Purchasing Management, New York, New York

Peter E. Woodger   Former Executive Vice-President, Purchasing Management Association of Canada, Toronto, Canada

Stanley D. Zemansky, C.P.M., CPPO, CPCM   City Purchasing Agent, City of Baltimore, Maryland

Preface

The foreword to the first edition of the *Purchasing Handbook* was written by George A. Renard, the first executive secretary of the National Association of Purchasing Agents. (The name was changed to the National Association of Purchasing Management, N.A.P.M., in 1968.) In that 1958 edition, Mr. Renard stated: "The *Purchasing Handbook* is a milestone in the development of purchasing as a major management responsibility for profitable operations."

He further stated: "The National Association of Purchasing Agents recognized this need and listed a purchasing handbook as a necessary educational objective for its members twenty years ago. It further upgraded the importance of that need, and the requirements to meet it, with the years, as purchasing continuously increased in management recognition and profit importance. This progress in purchasing and the need for a handbook were fully and very agreeably reaffirmed with the development of this project.

"George W. Aljian is the logical person to serve as the Editor-in-Chief. With a practical knowledge of purchasing, plus a standing in purchasing circles and organizing ability second to none, he has gathered a staff of editors, contributors, and reviewers representing a virtual "who's who" in purchasing. The usefulness and practicality of the book reflect the combined knowledge of this editorial group.

"Although the NAPA does not sponsor any commercial publications, it does believe in and actively supports competitive commercial enterprise. That policy has proven to be sound in the organization for the development of the *Purchasing Handbook*. With the publication of this handbook, purchasing executives can personally applaud and approve this satisfactory completion of one of the Association's major professional objectives."

Just as the completion of the original edition of the handbook was a "milestone" more than 20 years ago, so is the fourth edition. Paul V. Farrell assumed the role of coordinating editor for this edition. As the recent director of publications and editor of the *National Purchasing Review* for N.A.P.M., Paul Farrell possesses an unequaled knowledge and understanding of today's purchasing profession. Using the format and principles originally employed by George W. Aljian more than 23 years ago, the fourth edition provides an up-to-date version of the handbook.

George W. Aljian identified the basic objectives for the handbook in the preface of the first edition, and they remain today.

Its objectives were permanently blueprinted by the leaders of purchasing when this handbook was only a dream. The primary objective of the handbook is to serve as a guidebook or manual. It is intended to provide practical, dependable reference information to assist in answering the day-to-day "how to do it best" concerns of the men and women engaged in purchasing activities for small, medium, and large organizations in industry and government, as well as in other nonprofit organizations. It should be particularly useful to management people responsible for procurement in their organization whether or not an established purchasing department is part of their company. It is directed also to students of schools and colleges, to clarify and illustrate principles and practices referred to in purchasing textbooks.

The original *Purchasing Handbook* and each edition thereafter have continued to reflect currently accepted purchasing policies and procedures. This handbook is especially valuable today, as we face the challenges of the decade of the eighties. The need for practical solutions to specific job-related problems remains basically unchanged from the date of that first "dream" of publishing a handbook, to November 1958, when the first edition was released, and to today with the fourth edition.

Certainly the topics of concern and the methods have changed since 1958, and so has the content of the handbook. Several sections have been completely revised to reflect major changes in the profession. These include:

The sections on purchasing organization, ethics in purchasing, inventory management, electronic data processing in purchasing, public purchasing, purchasing in international markets, evaluation of purchasing performance, and traffic and transportation management. Moreover, completely new sections on materials management and on the N.A.P.M. Certified Purchasing Manager Program have been added.

It is the use of practicing purchasing professionals as editors, contributors, and reviewers that makes each edition so valuable, whether the reader is one of the new breed of purchasing professionals, eager to find the answers to that question "how to do it best" and to learn from those who have already experienced similar challenges, or whether it is the established buyer or purchasing manager looking for better ways to find solutions to organizational needs. Associate editors and anonymous reviewers are what makes the handbook a viable and workable document. Without their contributions, the advances made in purchasing management would have never reached the broad acceptance that they enjoy today. We, the users of the handbook and the members of the National Association of Purchasing Management, express our appreciation to all those professionals.

N.A.P.M. is and will be eternally grateful to George W. Aljian and his wife, Mary Lou, for their contributions to the profession and N.A.P.M.

Through the years many individuals have contributed to the handbook; we look forward to continued support from these important contributors in the years to come.

It is also important to recognize the contributions made by many members of the N.A.P.M. staff. Without the "dream" of Frank Winters, N.A.P.M. may not have been involved in this edition. Without the able contributions of Dr. Edward Bierman, Joseph Stagg, and Harry Wada, the updated information about N.A.P.M. programs would not have been included. Finally, without the tireless effort of Mary Crowell, the project would never have been completed.

R. Jerry Baker, C.P.M.
Executive Vice-President
National Association of Purchasing Management

**Aljian's
Purchasing
Handbook**

Purchasing Management

EDITOR

D. O. Corvey, C.P.M. *Staff Vice-President, Materials, RCA Corporation, Cherry Hill, New Jersey*

ASSOCIATE EDITORS

J. B. Van Dusen, C.P.M. *President, Ecclestone Chemical Company, Inc., Detroit, Michigan*

H. W. Hutchison, C.P.M. *Director, Government Procurement Programs, RCA Corporation, Cherry Hill, New Jersey*

THE IMPORTANCE AND SCOPE OF THE PURCHASING FUNCTION

The most significant factor in the success of any business is management of the company as a whole. This involves coordinating the maximum contribution from each major function of the business for the success of the entire company.

These major functions commonly include:

Engineering
Research and development
Purchasing and/or materials management
Manufacturing and assembly
Marketing and sales
Distribution
Industrial relations
Finance and accounting

This handbook devotes itself primarily to the purchasing aspects of the business enterprise. This includes the interrelation of purchasing with other functions and the ultimate effect that it has upon them.

The philosophy, techniques, and methods described in the following 31 sections are directed primarily toward industrial, governmental, and institutional purchasing managers who buy for manufacture, consumption, and conversion. However, those who buy for resale or speculation also will find many ideas beneficial in their type of buying.

Definition of Purchasing

Purchasing is the term used in industry and management to denote the act of and the functional responsibility for procuring materials, supplies, and services. In a narrow sense, the term *purchasing* simply describes the process of buying; however, in a broader sense, the term involves determining the need, selecting the supplier, arriving at proper price, terms, and conditions, issuing the contract or order, and following up to ensure proper delivery. In simple terms the basic elements involved in performing the purchasing function are obtaining the proper equipment, material, supplies, and services in the *right quality,* in the *right quantity,* at the *right price,* and from the *right source.*

Buying the Right Quality   The term *quality,* as used in the field of purchasing, carries a meaning quite different from that usually associated with this word. In common usage, when the term *quality* is not further modified, it refers to the excellent features of the subject. In purchasing, this term refers to the suitability of a product for its intended use. Concern for safety features and the useful life of products has introduced a requirement for reliability which today is often used in conjunction with quality. Quality and reliability are often used interchangeably and both are the concern of purchasing.

It should be pointed out that determination of the quality of materials, parts, and supplies purchased by the industrial concern is not the sole responsibility of any one department. In general, the engineering, research, and design departments of a company will prepare the bill of specifications or listings of parts which are incorporated into the finished product. In doing this, such departments will prescribe the quality levels of components. Many organizations have a quality control activity responsible for designating the quality levels of component parts as well as the final product. Quite often this same activity defines the testing procedures for determining whether or not the specified quality levels have been attained. The testing may be done by the supplier or by the buyer. The purchasing department, however, has a major responsibility for raising questions at any time when its information indicates that changes in quality should be considered. Purchasing departments do not, on their own, change the specifications of requisitions made by using departments; however, their responsibility for securing the right (most suitable) quality obligates purchasing personnel to question at any time when possible economies seem indicated.

Purchasing managers are in an excellent position to contribute to company profits in the area of quality. This is so because they can bring to bear their broad knowledge of materials, markets, market trends and conditions, and the reliability of sources of supply. As a result of this knowledge, the purchasing executive is able to equate material requirements with the market availability of those requirements, their prices, possible substitutes, and reliable suppliers who can meet the quality-level requirements. If this equating is not done, the company is sacrificing profits by not using the managerial capabilities of its purchasing department personnel in properly carrying out the objective of securing the right quality.

Buying the Right Quantity Frequently, as much as one-half of a company's total expenditures is in the form of inventories of raw materials, parts, and supplies. The purchasing department will be either directly or indirectly involved in the control of this inventory. It can contribute significantly to a company's profit by sound management of the quantity and timing of purchases.

There is but one right quantity to purchase for any given transaction, but, since there are many different kinds of transactions, the determination of the correct quantity is a complicated matter. Similarly, there is only one right time to purchase this right quantity. The issue is an important one because, if too small a quantity is purchased, the unit cost will usually be higher, shortages may increase, expediting work will necessarily be greater, and the relationship between vendor and purchaser may suffer. On the other hand, if too large a quantity is purchased, the excess inventory will raise costs, obsolescence may become a serious problem, and the probable need for additional storage facilities may create investment problems. Placing orders at the wrong time can be costly in the same manner.

Just as the term *quality* has the special meaning of suitability for the intended purpose, so has *quantity* a special meaning of quantity at a given time. Because of variations in price levels, delivery schedules, demands, and sales forecasts, today's correct quantity may be quite different from the correct quantity tomorrow.

Purchasing departments have developed a number of mathematical tools that can be utilized in helping to determine the right quantity to buy. None of these tools is a substitute for the judgment of the purchasing manager, but they do provide invaluable assistance and guidance in his decisions.

Many larger companies use a materials requirement planning (MRP) system that handles quantity logistics with the aid of a computer. Responsibilities are usually those of a production planning and control activity, but even in these cases, inputs from purchasing are important to efficient planning. (For further discussion of MRP, see Section 12.)

Buying at the Right Time Proper buying involves buying to meet production schedules without loading warehouses with inventory. It also involves buying judiciously so as to minimize the unfavorable effects of price-level changes. The need to meet production schedules is self-evident. It involves not only a knowledge of a buyer's own company's production plans, but also an understanding of the lead-time requirements of the various alternative suppliers to produce and deliver orders placed with them.

Timing orders in connection with price changes involves study of the present supply-and-demand situation in the market and forecasts of future conditions. Since markets are dynamic, purchasing personnel must be constantly studying all the varied factors which affect the markets for materials and supplies in order to buy at the right time.

Buying at the Right Price   The right price is that price which is reasonable and fair to both the buyer and the seller. Buying personnel have always been insistent on paying a fair price for any item bought. This insistence has been incorporated into the policy manuals and codes of purchasing practice of most well-run purchasing departments.

The right price is not necessarily the lowest price. The lowest price may not provide the proper quality for the intended purpose, or it may not secure the proper service from suppliers. Even where it does meet these requirements, the lowest price may be offered for buying a substantial quantity in advance of needs, thus reflecting added costs that do not appear in the initial lowest price.

The three basic factors in any purchase decision between alternate suppliers are the quality, the service, and the price. The quality must be right if the purchase is to be made at all. Therefore, this is the first consideration. Second in importance, most purchasing executives believe, is the service consideration, which involves securing the goods that were ordered, at the proper quality and quantity levels, and at the proper time and place. Price is the last consideration because of the basic premise that it does no good to secure a right price but have everything else wrong.

Basically, what purchasing executives do is to take a broad and objective view of their company. They must determine which price, in combination with the quality features of the product and the service aspects of the relationship with the supplier, will afford their company the greatest ultimate value.

Buying from the Right Source   The selection of the source of supply is the acid test of sound purchasing. A purchaser may describe the quality of the desired product accurately and completely, may establish the precise quantity needed, may estimate the exact price that will be demanded, and may clearly determine and specify the exact time and place of delivery. All this careful planning can be jeopardized, or even nullified, by a poor selection of a prospective supplier. Some suppliers will not be capable of producing to the desired quality specifications; others will not be able to furnish the amounts needed at the time when they are needed; while still others, who may be able to meet the quality and quantity requirements, will not sell at the right price. The purchaser must find the supplier who will furnish the *optimum combination* of these factors.

There are a wide range of policy decisions in connection with selecting suppliers. Purchasers must resolve such issues as whether to concentrate purchases with local suppliers or to ignore geographical considerations; they must determine whether to concentrate their purchases or split them up among competing suppliers; they may have to determine whether to buy direct from producers or through wholesalers, representatives, or distributors. In recent years, buyers have been required, by company or institutional policy or government regulation, to consider a number of socioeconomic factors before selecting suppliers. These relate to buying certain percentages of their requirements from small businesses, minority suppliers, employers of handicapped persons, suppliers in labor surplus areas, and more recently from businesses owned by women. The effect of such constraints on purchasing policies and operations is discussed in several other sections of the handbook.

Selecting the right source of supply is a complicated decision; but it is a challenge which is one of the major attractions of a career in purchasing. It is in connection with selecting the right source of supply that the purchaser is in contact with a wide range of people and companies other than his own. No other employee, with the possible exception of a salesperson, has as many outside contacts as does the purchasing manager of a company. To many outsiders, he is the only contact with his company. On his actions will depend the public relations attitudes that are generated toward his company.

Over a period of time purchasing has evolved from being little more than a clerical function to its present stature as a part of management. Likewise, the term *purchasing* has evolved to encompass much more than the concept of *buying*. Today's purchasing managers or agents are involved in the planning, organizing, and controlling of every aspect of materials acquisition and utilization.

Procurement Management

With the new responsibilities that this evolution added to purchasing, it became desirable to use a term which more accurately describes these wider areas. Hence, the term *procurement* rather than *purchasing* is used by many, and in government, *acquisition management* is used, to describe the combined functions of procurement planning, purchasing, inventory control, traffic, receiving, incoming inspection, and salvage operations.

Materials Management

Further evolution of the purchasing function to meet the growing complexity of the industrial structure has brought about the use of the term *materials management*. Progressive modern management has expanded the traditional scope of purchasing and procurement to encompass the entire materials management process. This change has been accelerated through the adoption by many companies of the systems concept.

Definition of Materials Management   *Materials management* is that aspect of industrial management which is concerned with all the activities involved in the acquisition, handling, storage, and use of all materials employed in the production of the finished product and in some cases even the storing and distribution of finished goods.

These activities may include production control, inventory control, purchasing, expediting, traffic, materials handling, warehousing, receiving, shipping, scrap and surplus disposition, and customer services. However, the term *materials management* is frequently used when only some of these functions are included. With the exception of production control and customer services, all these activities are defined and explained in one or more sections of this handbook.

The materials management concept is based on the theory that more effective control over an important aspect of a company's operations and faster reaction to external change can be obtained by the group action of all departments involved in any way with the materials used by the company. Under this concept all the aforementioned departments are included. These are the departments which handle different aspects of the same basic problem, namely, the efficient and economical planning, scheduling, and handling of the materials used in the manufacturing process. (For more details on materials management see Section 19.)

The Scope of Purchasing

Each and every business enterprise develops a purchasing requirement. The volume of work, the dollars expended, and the degree of sophistication affecting purchasing will vary considerably with the type, size, and nature of the product and the complexity of the business enterprise. Regardless of this wide divergence, demands placed upon modern business by the free enterprise system dictate that the procurement process be accomplished in the most professional and capable manner possible.

U.S. manufacturing and associated industries purchase materials and services costing hundreds of billions of dollars annually. The magnitude of these expenditures emphasizes the importance to the U.S. economy of performing the procurement function in the most effective manner possible.

Another measure of importance of the procurement function in U.S. industry is the relationship between cost of purchased materials and services and the sales dollar. Table 1-1, based on the Department of Commerce 1976 Survey of Manufactures, shows the percentage of the sales dollar of U.S. manufacturing firms spent for the purchase of materials and services from other companies. Table 1-2 shows the percentage of sales increase needed to equal a 2 percent savings in the cost of purchases in companies with various aftertax margins on sales.

The percentage distribution of the sales dollar in the 100 largest U.S. manufacturing concerns in 1974 indicates clearly that a relatively small improvement in purchasing costs improves the profit of a concern more than considerable improvement in any other type of cost. A dollar saved by purchasing increases the profit by a dollar, whereas a dollar increase in sales may add very little to profit because of the increased costs in making additional sales.

In addition to the cost of materials and supplies, other costs that may offer opportunities for reduction are labor and overhead. Reductions in labor costs are very difficult to bring about in today's economy without automation. Cutting overhead costs is also difficult to attain without eliminating essential services unless

TABLE 1-1   Purchasing's Share of the Sales Dollar

All Manufacturing	57%	Asbestos	49%
Durable goods	53%	Abrasives	47%
Nondurable goods	62%	*Primary Metal Industries*	64%
Food	71%	Steel mills	65%
Meat products	83%	Steel pipe and tube	62%
Grain products	71%	Iron and steel foundries	45%
Sugar products	65%	*Primary Nonferrous Metals*	69%
Tobacco	53%	Primary copper	78%
Textiles	61%	Primary lead	78%
Cotton weaving mills	56%	Primary zinc	71%
Synthetic weaving mills	57%	Primary aluminum	60%
Knitting mills	60%	*Secondary Nonferrous*	81%
Finishing mills	64%	*Nonferrous Rolling/Drawing*	73%
Floor covering mills	69%	Copper rolling/drawing	75%
Apparel	52%	Aluminum sheet late/foil	80%
Lumber and Wood	58%	*Nonferrous Foundries*	49%
Millwork	61%	*Fabricated Metal Products*	50%
Wooden containers	52%	Metal cans	62%
Wooden pallets	52%	Plumbing/heating	50%
Furniture and Fixtures	49%	Handtools/hardware	40%
Household furniture	50%	Fasteners	44%
Office furniture	42%	Forgings/stampings	51%
Paper	58%	*Engines and Turbines*	55%
Paperboard mills	54%	*Machinery*	46%
Paperboard containers	60%	Farm	54%
Corrugated boxes	63%	Construction	52%
Folding boxes	58%	Mining	56%
Setup boxes	42%	Conveyors	45%
Commercial Printing	43%	Hoists, cranes, monorails	45%
Industrial Chemicals	48%	Industrial trucks/tractors	58%
Plastic materials	62%	Special industrial	44%
Synthetic rubber	71%	General industrial	44%
Synthetic fibers	63%	Office/computing machines	41%
Drugs	29%	*Electric/Electronic Equipment*	44%
Paints	58%	Transformers	48%
Agricultural	59%	Switchgear	50%
Adhesives	59%	Motors/generators	43%
Petroleum Refining	86%	Industrial controls	40%
Paving/roofing materials	63%	Household appliances	53%
Lubricants	67%	Lighting/wiring	42%
Rubber	50%	Radio/TV receivers	57%
Tires	52%	Telephone/telegraph	47%
Hose/belting	44%	Electronic components	40%
Leather	51%	*Transportation Equipment*	61%
Footwear	48%	Motor vehicles	69%
Luggage	50%	Aircraft and parts	43%
Stone, Clay, Glass	46%	Railroad equipment	57%
Flat glass	39%	Shipbuilding and repairs	44%
Glass containers	40%	*Instruments*	36%
Cement	45%	Scientific/Engineering	35%
Concrete/gypsum	54%	Optical	33%
		Medical	40%

Source: U.S. Commerce Department, Annual Survey of Manufactures.

new and innovative methods are employed. Computer-generated purchasing systems will often increase productivity and decrease costs at the same time.

Thus, it can be seen that competent purchasing is one of the basic opportunities for a company to cut costs and thereby increase profits.

When one contemplates the fact that for every sale there must be a buyer, and that the other side of the sales coin is purchasing, one begins to realize the significance and magnitude of purchasing. In fact, the difficulty in spending large amounts of money wisely, coupled with unlimited opportunities to contribute to

TABLE 1-2   Sales Increase Needed to Equal a 2% Procurement Cost Savings

Company's aftertax margin on sales	Percentage of sales spent on material procurement									
	35%	40%	45%	50%	55%	60%	65%	70%	75%	80%
3%	12.60	14.40	16.20	18.00	19.80	21.60	23.40	25.20	27.00	28.80
4%	9.45	10.80	12.15	13.50	14.85	16.20	17.55	18.90	20.25	21.60
5%	7.56	8.64	9.72	10.80	11.88	12.96	14.04	15.12	16.20	17.28
6%	6.30	7.20	8.10	9.00	9.90	10.80	11.70	12.60	13.50	14.40
7%	5.40	6.17	6.94	7.77	8.49	9.26	10.03	10.80	11.57	12.34
8%	4.73	5.40	6.08	6.75	7.43	8.10	8.78	9.45	10.13	10.80
9%	4.20	4.80	5.40	6.00	6.60	7.20	7.80	8.40	9.00	9.60
10%	3.78	4.32	4.86	5.40	5.94	6.48	7.02	7.56	8.10	8.64
11%	3.44	3.93	4.42	4.91	5.40	5.89	6.38	6.87	7.36	7.85
12%	3.15	3.60	4.05	4.50	4.95	5.40	5.85	6.30	6.75	7.20
13%	2.91	3.32	3.74	4.15	4.57	4.98	5.40	5.82	6.23	6.65
14%	2.70	3.08	3.47	3.86	4.24	4.63	4.01	5.40	5.79	6.17
15%	2.52	2.88	3.24	3.60	3.96	4.32	4.68	5.04	5.40	5.76

the profitability and growth of a business, presents a most demanding, exciting, and rewarding challenge to those engaged in or seeking a career in purchasing.

Accordingly, the significance and importance of the purchasing function in many companies have elevated it to top management level and beyond a perfunctory activity of business. A *Purchasing* magazine survey revealed that, of the purchasing managers reporting, 78 percent report directly to top management, 76 percent enjoy increased authority, and 58 percent head enlarged staffs.

In a survey conducted by the National Association of Purchasing Management, 5539 responding members reported that one or more other functions were supervised by the purchasing department. Many of the functional areas cited were those commonly associated with purchasing in some form of materials management organization. Also included were others which are not normally associated with purchasing.

The clerical order placers have given way to value-conscious purchasing personnel, skilled in price and cost analysis, product reliability, economic order quantity determination, learning curves, purchasing research, economic forecasting, supplier selection, contract negotiation, evaluation of supplier performance, value analysis, material studies, and the logistics of supply management.

With the development of faster and better means of communication, time sharing, real-time processing, information retrieval and visibility, and greater data storage capacity, the modern purchasing-materials function has become a significant user of the data processing equipment and other business tools. No longer is the purchasing function the last to be considered when setting up a data processing system.

RESPONSIBILITY OF PURCHASING

The purchasing executive is the custodian of the firm's purse. Therefore, his first and foremost obligation is *integrity* in spending its funds. The purchasing department acts as the legally authorized representative of all others in the company in dealing with every firm supplying or aspiring to supply materials and services. *Professional competence* in representing them intelligently, honorably, and forthrightly is a mandatory responsibility.

The materials and services purchased represent the largest single element of cost in the business process; therefore, the exercise of prudence and good judgment in securing the best possible ultimate value for the money expended is perhaps the purchasing man's heaviest burden of responsibility.

Limitations in Responsibilities

In the small single-proprietorship business, the owner may decide whether or not to purchase an item, the specifications and quality level desired, how many to buy and when it will be needed, where to buy it, how it should be packaged and delivered, and how to store it pending actual use, as well as the terms he can afford in payment of his commitment. However, as a business increases in size and complexity, it becomes essential that the owner delegate the function of purchasing. This delegation of authority creates a legal agency, and the person receiving the authority becomes the purchasing *agent*. Because the purchasing agent has the legal authority to obligate the company for purchases, any limitation on that authority should be clearly established to make certain it will be recognized and observed.

The overall limitation is that all purchases must be for necessary requirements of the company. Buying for speculative purposes is not usually within the authority of the purchasing agent. Acquiring plants and subsidiary companies is not considered a necessary requirement.

Within the usual authority there may be certain specific limitations. Many companies state a *dollar value* at which point approval from higher authority is required. Other companies limit the purchasing authority to a particular commodity or class of items. Some companies limit the type of contract that may be approved by purchasing. Top management approval of budgets and production schedules also limits purchasing authority. In other companies reciprocal agreements limit the freedom of purchasing to exercise its usual prerogatives.

Regardless of limitations, it is the responsibility of the purchasing executive to keep his management, his requisitioners, and his associates constantly informed and advised of the right quantities to buy, the most economic quality to specify, and the most practical schedule to follow. It is his obligation to insist that proper policies and procedures be followed unless there are overriding contrary considerations.

Interdepartmental Relations

One of the intangible benefits of a career in purchasing is the close relationship developed with so many other departments within the company. No other department can provide its personnel such a broad exposure. There are obvious advantages that are gained in terms of training and familiarity with all aspects of the company's operations and, thus, of qualification for general management consideration.

Purchasing and General Management   All members of the purchasing department are contributing directly and daily to the operating results of a company and, thereby, to its profits. The general results obtained in the day-to-day operations of the business concern are the major responsibility of members of the general management group.

Thus, management expects and has the right to expect a great deal from its buying personnel. Management, with its prime interest in profitable operations, must closely control the efforts of purchasing, which spends the largest percentage out of every dollar taken in by sales. Management will look to purchasing to use judgment in developing its training and experience so as to realize greater savings from the day-to-day buying efforts of the department.

Purchasing and Sales   No company can stay in business for very long unless its products can be sold at a profit. The purchasing department assists the sales department by buying at as low a cost as is possible so that the company can maintain a competitive selling position.

At the same time, the sales department can assist the purchasing department to schedule its purchases effectively by apprising the purchasing department of sales quotas and sales expectations. The sales department can be particularly helpful by giving the purchasing department as much advance information as possible during negotiations with customers for special orders and nonstock items.

Material costs, in many instances, are greatly affected by the amount of procurement time available to a purchasing department. If time is short, costs will tend to be higher, since the buyer cannot make as complete a search of the market. However, if purchasing participates with sales in the early planning stages of new programs, definite and tangible monetary advantages may be gained that can actually strengthen the impact of the new sales program on the company's customers. During such planning sessions, purchasing can contribute not only information on current material costs, sources of supply, and other price considerations; it can also advise and counsel on possible substitute materials which lower cost without impairing quality.

Purchasing and Production Control   It is necessary for the two departments to have a complete exchange of information in order to ensure a smooth, well-adjusted control over materials. Production control informs purchasing of its requirements and plans, with sufficient lead time to allow for finding a supplier, negotiating a purchase, securing delivery, and passing the purchased material through inspection. Purchasing must keep production control informed of lead-time requirements for all major categories of purchases and of any changes in lead times as they occur. Purchasing is expected to keep production control informed of the results and expectations disclosed through the follow-up and expediting process. It is important that there be a clear understanding of responsibility in connection with the expediting function so as to avoid duplication of effort between the two departments. In general, purchasing should have complete responsibility for all expediting, since it is the department which is regularly in contact with the suppliers in the course of placing purchase orders.

Purchasing and Quality Control Buyers must work closely with the quality control personnel in their companies. Many of the quality standards developed by quality control departments cannot be defined on the engineering drawings in the same manner as dimensions and tolerances are defined. Buyers must be familiar with these quality standards so that they can pass them on to their suppliers. Buyers, because of their contact with vendors, assist the quality control department in establishing inspection standards that can be met by the vendor and that can easily be measured by the control department inspectors.

Another area in which these two departments should work closely is in connection with plant visitations or inspections of vendors' facilities. The basic purpose of such inspection trips is to ascertain the acceptability of a vendor. Since one of the most important criteria in determining whether a given vendor should be awarded contracts is the vendor's ability to produce to desired standards, it is quite appropriate that a member of the quality control department be included in the visitation team.

Purchasing and Production Purchasing furnishes the materials needed for production to function, and production must rely on purchasing for this service. Thus, there is a basic common interest between the two departments.

There is a basic difference in the philosophical outlook of the two departments. Production people tend to emphasize protection against shutdowns due to out-of-stock conditions, whereas purchasing people are more likely to tend to lower inventory levels in order to minimize investment costs. This basic difference must be continually evaluated in order to reach the proper compromise between the two valid but different viewpoints. However, management should not permit one department to dominate the other.

Another area in which the two departments must closely coordinate their efforts is in the development of specifications for purchased parts and materials. Production must not set standards that are too high, relative to actual need; and purchasing must be on the watch for the opportunity to suggest standard in lieu of special-order items.

The *make-or-buy* decision is generally handled by the general management group. However, both purchasing and production furnish the basic information upon which such decisions are based. Purchasing secures bids from outside suppliers; but, in addition—by the compilation of cost information most of which comes from production departments—it is also securing bids for making (manufacturing in house).

Purchasing and Engineering The engineering department is primarily responsible for the design and specifications of the products a company uses, although in some businesses the development of specifications may be the responsibility of quality control, research and development, or other departments. Engineers in such departments have positive ideas about the physical and chemical properties required in the end product and know what materials have the desired properties. However, since there frequently are several materials possessing suitable properties, it is important for someone to determine which material can be purchased most advantageously. This is a proper responsibility of the purchasing department. Present-day concerns over the use of materials that meet the requirements of the Environmental Protection Agency and the Occupational Safety and Health Administration—as well as concerns about consumer protection—make the need for engineering specifications much more urgent than in the past. These requirements also restrict the flexibility of purchasing to substitute alternate materials or products.

The two departments complement each other. Purchasing must not overemphasize price to the point that it interferes with sound engineering requirements, and engineering must not be so exacting in its demands that price and market considerations are neglected.

Probably the greatest area for mutual cooperation and assistance is that of value analysis/value engineering (VA/VE).

Value Analysis Value analysis is the organized and systematic study of every element of cost in a part, material, or service to make certain it fulfills its function at the lowest possible cost. Value analysis employs techniques which identify the functions the user wants from a product or service; it establishes by comparison the appropriate cost for each function; and it then causes the required knowledge, creativity, and initiative to be used to provide each function for that cost. The terms *value analysis* and *value engineering* are used synonymously in this handbook (see Section 8.) Since value analysis or value engineering is strictly a team effort, both engineering and purchasing should have freedom of suggestion or proposal in their respective spheres. Many companies have organized VA/VE teams made up of representatives from purchasing, engineering, and production, who work together on specific projects to maximize value on every dollar expended.

Purchasing and Stores If the stores department is independent of the purchasing department, the relationship between the two is closer and more continuous than that between any other two departments. On stock items, the stores department generally initiates the purchase requisition. The buyer's action in connection with this requisition is based on such factors as rate of use, number of defective parts, and trends in the rate of use. This is the type of information that is readily available in the records of the stores department. Generally, the buyer establishes the minimum stock and reorder points which guide the storekeeper in initiating requisitions. Many mathematical formulas have been devised to determine economic ordering quantities (EOQs) to support decisions necessary to keep inventories at a desired level.

Purchasing and Traffic   In many smaller companies this function is assigned directly to purchasing; in other companies, it may be a separate department reporting to the head of the purchasing department or the material manager, and in still other companies it may be entirely separated from purchasing and materials. The basic function of traffic is to secure delivery of materials and parts at the right time and place at a minimum of delivery costs. It is, in a sense, a highly specialized form of purchasing—the purchase of transportation. The traffic group usually supplies the buyers with shipping routes and carriers which are included as a part of the purchase order. This service can be extremely useful in keeping transportation costs under control, and too often, is not fully used by the purchasing department.

Purchasing and Accounting   Every purchase transaction initiates a chain of accounting transactions, from charging the transaction to the proper account to the final payment of the invoice. In many companies, a part of this work may be assigned to the purchasing department, as in the case of the invoice audit. Regardless of where the particular accounting task is performed, close cooperation of the departments is essential, since company funds and significant discounts are involved.

Purchasing and Legal   Every buyer for industry should have enough knowledge of law to be able to understand the relationship between the buyer and his company and to understand the legal consequences of the activities which the buyer performs in the company's name. Unless he knows and possesses some competence with respect to the essential legal concepts, he may unconsciously do things which could cost his company substantial sums of money or result in lengthy litigation.

Purchasing and Public Relations   As has been noted earlier in this section, purchasing has more contacts with people from outside the organization than any other department in the company, including the sales department, and therefore, in a sense, a purchasing employee is a public relations employee. The attitudes and actions of this employee will have a distinct bearing on the attitudes held by suppliers and others toward the firm. In the company which has a separate public relations department, it is important that there be close communication between the two departments in order to present the best possible image to the many publics of the company.

PURCHASING FUNCTIONS

The purchasing system includes all the functions involved in the procurement of material from the time a need or possible need is first known until the material is received and approved for use. Types of activities, tasks, and functions on a broad scale include:

1. Requirement determination: Functional coordination with manufacturing, engineering, marketing, finance, and quality control.

2. The procurement decision: Make or buy, standards, vendor certification, value analysis, market trends (forecasting), schedule, cost and budget considerations, capacity, control, and opportunity alternatives (return on investment).

3. The procurement process: Source selection, soliciting bids, schedule, cost-price analysis, negotiation, contract, expediting, terms and conditions, specifications, and contract administration.

4. Materials management: Traffic and receiving, economic order quantity determination, inventory requirements and control, material handling, scrap disposal, and stores.

Determining Factors

The basic purchasing function, combined with related ones supervised by the purchasing department, spells out the total responsibilities of any purchasing department. Translating them into specific areas for any one organization is not possible because of the endless variations in company size, character of the business, and the capacity of the executive heading the department.

Administering these responsibilities or activities requires a wide variety of detailed routine and managerial assignments. Many fall under the exclusive jurisdiction of purchasing, whereas some may be shared with other departments.

Typical specific responsibilities or activities of the average purchasing department are listed in Table 1-3. These are particularly applicable to the small and medium-sized departments in industry or government. A list of functions for the larger, more sophisticated organizations could show more areas of responsibilities, as outlined in the remaining sections of this handbook.

It is well to repeat that standard functions and responsibilities cannot be specifically itemized. The main purchasing function, plus related ones and the routine or specific responsibilities in Table 1-3, constitute established patterns that are intended to be used as basic guidelines or spheres of influence.

OBJECTIVES OF THE PURCHASING FUNCTION

Creation of a purchasing department represents a recognition of purchasing as an organized activity. Organized activities are characterized by their discernible objectives. Purchasing activities, in order to make an effective contribution to the institution of which they are part, must be attuned to and oriented toward the overall objectives of the organization.

Contribution to Profit and Cost Effectiveness

Purchasing is an economic function. While some nonprofit organizations, such as hospitals, schools, and government agencies, may not stress profit, purchasing in an industrial organization must have profit as one of its prime objectives.

To perform the economic function of contributing to profit and to serve his organization efficiently, a buyer must exercise professional competence. To

TABLE 1-3   Specific Responsibilities or Activities of Typical Purchasing Department

Records, Data, and Basic Information
  Maintaining general purchase records
  Maintaining price records
  Maintaining parts history records
  Maintaining stock and consumption records
  Maintaining records of vendor performance on price, quality, and service
  Maintaining specification files
  Maintaining standards file, including MIL/JAN specifications
  Maintaining catalog files
Purchasing Research, Analysis, and Studies
  Conducting market studies and trends
  Conducting material studies
  Conducting make-or-buy studies
  Conducting price-cost analysis
  Investigating supply sources
  Conducting supplier-plant visits and inspections
  Developing new supply sources
  Developing alternate materials and sources
  Participating in value analysis studies
  Developing computer-oriented purchasing systems
Purchasing
  Checking authorized requisitions
  Obtaining capital appropriation approvals
  Issuing requests for bids
  Determining bidders list
  Preparing request for bids
  Conducting pre-bid briefings
  Receiving all bids
  Analyzing quotations and/or proposals
  Determining nonresponsive bids
  Evaluating suppliers
  Selecting suppliers
  Determining quantity to buy
  Scheduling purchases and deliveries
  Determining mode of transportation and carrier
  Interviewing salespeople
  Determining type of contractual instrument
  Negotiating contracts
  Writing and issuing contractual agreement (purchase order, subcontract, blanket order, lease,
    rental agreement, etc.)
  Developing legal conditions of contracts
  Determining applicable federal, state, and local taxes or foreign duties
  Following up for delivery, i.e., expediting and updating open-order status reports
  Checking receipt of materials
  Checking and approving invoices
  Corresponding with suppliers
  Negotiating adjustments with suppliers
  Negotiating contract changes
  Terminating contracts
Inventory Management
  Developing inventory classifications
  Maintaining minimum stocks
  Establishing economic order levels
  Maintaining inventory balance
  Improving inventory turnover
  Establishing stock and parts numbering system
  Transferring materials

TABLE 1-3   Specific Responsibilities or Activities of Typical Purchasing Department (*Cont.*)

Consolidating requirements
Avoiding excess stocks and obsolescence
Declaring surplus inventory
Standardizing packages and containers
Accounting for returnable containers
Accounting for demurrage charges
Making periodic reports of commitments
Maintaining property records
Managerial
Preparing and updating purchasing manuals
Assisting in department audits and reviews
Evaluating purchasing performance
Evaluating personnel performance
Performing merit reviews and salary determination
Making reports to management
Conducting training and job enrichment programs
Conducting cost improvement programs
Participating in quality and zero defects programs
Shared with Other Departments
Contracting for services
Purchasing consultants' and special services
Purchasing construction contracts
Determining whether to make or buy
Negotiating leases for real property and equipment
Purchasing vehicles, trucks, and off-the-road equipment
Operating garage and fleet maintenance
Operating janitorial and custodial services
Operating and maintaining record archives
Supervising reproduction equipment
Purchasing exhibit and advertising material
Conducting scrap and surplus sales
Establishing employee purchase program
Operating cafeteria, in-plant feeding, and vending services
Purchasing computer time sharing and special outside test facilities
Operating and maintaining company aircraft

become professionally competent, the buyer must strive to increase his knowledge in many fields. As a professional buyer such an individual must wear many "hats" and wear them effectively. A measure of professional competence is how well a buyer can secure the willing cooperation of users and others in the company who have special knowledge of the factors that determine the value of a given purchase. The purchasing department must weigh all factors involved in a purchase by bringing together the experience and judgment of all parties concerned to achieve the profit objective.

Many companies have developed formal profit improvement or cost reduction programs which set out savings objectives and measure performance against those objectives.

The Service Objective

An important objective of purchasing is to serve the entire organization. This is accomplished by supporting its operating programs. In the long run, cooperation between operating departments and purchasing can result in maximizing purchasing's contribution to the company. However, purchasing may have to forgo some of its immediate goals in order to secure this long-run cooperation.

In the nonprofit institutions, government agency, or research establishment, the opportunity to be of service represents an even greater challenge to purchasing personnel. Saving the time and attendant cost of scientific, engineering, or medical personnel and making them more effective by allowing them to do what they are best skilled, trained, and educated to do can increase creativity and bring the organization to a new level of productivity.

The Socioeconomic Role of Purchasing

In recent years purchasing personnel have been urged by top management to assume a new service role by contributing to the solutions of the socioeconomic problems of the nation. In addition to awarding contracts, these involvements have included professional assistance and business advice to small disadvantaged groups and minority entrepreneurs.

Purchasing's Role in Minority Business   Purchasing personnel have been prominent in the work of the National Minority Supplier Development Council (NMSDC; formerly the National Minority Purchasing Council) since its founding in the late 1960s. Affiliated associations of the National Association of Purchasing Management (a charter member of NMSDC) have regularly sponsored or cosponsored seminars and workshops designed to guide corporate buyers in developing business relationships with minority-owned firms and assisting such firms with their marketing and production problems. More recently, buyers purchasing under government contracts must meet the requirements of Public Law 95-507, which requires subcontracting plans and goals for both small businesses and small businesses operated by disadvantaged groups.

Purchasing's Role in Ecology   Along with the recognition of the need for environmental protection and the proliferation of regulations at the federal, state, and city levels aimed at improving the quality of our environment has come the recognition of the purchasing role in ecology. Purchasing people must now concern themselves with the cost of low-sulfur fuel and pollutant-monitoring equipment, as well as the ultimate use and destination of plant refuse and plant processes that may contaminate the atmosphere or the water supply.

A newly emerging ecological industry is that of recycling waste products. Purchasing people must look to the recycling market as a source of raw material supply and as a source for the sale of scrap and surplus.

Purchasing's Role in Consumerism   Just as the socioeconomic and environmental protection problems have become important areas for purchasing, so has protection of the consumer become an area of paramount consideration. Purchasing has an outstanding challenge to improve the quality performance of their suppliers and subcontractors, to promote zero defects, and to contribute to the acceptability and quality standard of their company's products.

As a result of greater governmental and consumer vigilance against items considered to be health or safety hazards, the number of product recall situations has risen annually. Purchasing has a definite role when a product recall situation arises; for example, arranging the return of faulty material (including packaging, transportation, etc.) and assisting in the rectification of the specific problem and return of the product to the customer.

This kind of activity can become increasingly complex when the product is an integral part or a component of another product or when the product is repackaged and sold under a different name.

Purchasing's Contribution to Safety   Purchasing has always been concerned with the suitability and safety aspects of products purchased. Enactment of the federal Occupational Safety and Health Act (OSHA) of 1970 has imposed broad and significant new standards. Therefore buying personnel must now assure that new products purchased comply with the OSHA, and they will become increasingly involved with upgrading, modifying, and replacing existing equipment and facilities that fall short of the regulations.

Advice and Assistance to Management

Besides the day-to-day purchasing services such as obtaining technical information and prices, expediting orders, and conducting vendor surveys, *skilled purchasing personnel have unlimited opportunities to be of service and assistance by making an impact upon the more meaningful problems of industry,* such as make or buy, acquisition and merger, plant location, lease or buy, and foreign opportunities. While many of these purchasing efforts and services are not directly measurable in dollars and cents, the resultant effects upon the enterprise can be invaluable. Such information, assistance, and advisory service to management and other departments have earned respect for and enhanced the reputation of purchasing.

Corporate Image

Every corporation, company, agency, institution, and governmental body zealously guards its reputation. An image is created through continued relationships with customers, suppliers, stockholders, employees, and the general public. Goodwill is an intangible asset of every enterprise.

The importance of purchasing as a projector of the corporate image cannot be underestimated. Purchasing portrays the public relations image to:

1. Other departments within the company
2. Sales representatives and suppliers
3. The general public
4. Business and professional contacts

Failure to project the proper image or to conduct business without regard for reputation, goodwill, and the larger community could be ruinous.

Purchasing activities must be conducted upon a strong foundation of honesty, integrity, and fairness to all. Ethics and good taste are paramount.

ORGANIZATION OF THE PURCHASING FUNCTION

Purchasing organizations are usually identified as centralized, decentralized, or departmentalized. Although these terms are sometimes used to refer to physical location of purchasing people, their more common usage is concerned solely with the location of purchasing authority.

Centralized Organization

Centralized purchasing exists when the responsibility for the entire purchasing function is assigned to a single individual. This person is accountable to management for proper performance of the purchasing function regardless of where the actual buying may take place.

A company which has a single operating facility readily recognizes the efficiency and profitability of centralizing the control of, as well as the responsibility for, its purchasing. But with the scattering of plants and the diversification of products, the problems of purchasing organization, as with other vital functions of the company, become increasingly complex. Centralized purchasing can be entirely satisfactory in a multiplant organization if the plants are manufacturing the same products from the same materials. However, companies with considerable diversification of product may find it necessary to employ some other type of organization structure.

Decentralized Organization

In a single-plant company decentralization of purchasing exists when production, sales, finance, engineering, or other functional area personnel do their own buying or perform any other purchasing function. This type of decentralization tends to produce duplication of effort, inefficiency, and outright waste.

There are, however, conditions and situations that tend to cause a certain degree of decentralization to be desirable. If the company uses a single, natural raw material in very great quantities, it is common to have that material bought by a group not a part of the purchasing department. A multiplant company with diversified product lines may find decentralized buying to be most appropriate. Research and development areas of a technically oriented firm may be permitted to do their own purchasing until specifications become firm. Recent organization trends toward *profit center decentralization* make it desirable to assign purchasing to the profit center.

Departmentalized Organization

Neither completely rigid centralization nor loose decentralization of purchasing seems to meet the needs of all companies. Although there are advantages to both methods of organization, many disadvantages exist. The solution to the problems presented by either extreme centralization or extreme decentralization is to be found in a centralized executive, or in corporate staff control of purchasing policies and administration, with decentralization of purchasing operations.

A large company may have a vice-president, a director, or a manager of purchasing, and a number of division or plant purchasing agents. The variations in responsibilities at the different levels are numerous, but a compromise between centralization and decentralization is usually employed in an attempt to utilize the advantages of both and to minimize their disadvantages.

For a more extensive discussion of purchasing organization see Section 2.

REPORTS TO TOP MANAGEMENT

It is essential that top management receive reports from the various departments in order to have information to use in planning, organizing, and controlling operations. An enlightened management who appreciate the importance of purchasing will actively seek and plan the reports that will be of most help to their activities. There are, however, top executives who do not understand the real contribution that purchasing may make to the overall success of the firm and consequently do not ask for reports from the purchasing department. In that case it is essential that purchasing report on its activities to keep management informed of purchasing's contribution to the entire company operation.

In reporting to top management it is desirable that certain basic principles be followed. Purchasing should be *selective* in choosing what is included. It is not necessary to report everything. Reports that collect dust and are never read are of no value to anyone.

Purchasing should *summarize* rather than try to give all the details. It should be possible for the reader to get to the point without having to sort through unimportant statistics.

Purchasing should also *compare* current performance with previous performance, with other companies, with standards, with forecasts, and with the entire industry. These comparisons, as a guide to management and as a measure of purchasing performance, are much more valuable than isolated statistics.

Purchasing should *interpret* the facts given in the report. Although the report should be so well prepared that many conclusions are obvious, purchasing is in the best position to interpret certain data and to make recommendations for action. And management should welcome such recommendations if they are made for the benefit of the company and not simply to aggrandize the purchasing department.

There is no uniformity as to the frequency with which written reports by purchasing are required to be made; it may run all the way from weekly to annually. As the time between reports lengthens, the information contained in a report may tend to become a somewhat detailed review of the department's activities and include comparative statistics related to earlier estimates and actual budget performances.

Where the company policy calls for written reports to be made at fairly long intervals, it is customary to supplement them with interim memorandums which present timely information and market conditions, as well as any purchasing problem which should have attention.

Below is a partial listing of subjects that a survey by the National Association of Purchasing Management indicated might well be included in a purchasing department's report to top management:

- Analysis of general business conditions and how they affect the company
- Budget
- Charts—to illustrate graphically a particular condition
- Changes in department organization—benefits to accrue
- Commitments, including current forward buying policy
- Cost reductions through securing new sources of supply, changing of specifications, value analysis, etc.
- Estimates of yearly requirements of main materials—availability—recommended policy
- Inventories—control methods, turnover, short supply, etc.
- New sources for major commodities
- Price trends—commodities—indexes
- Purchase orders—number issued—value
- Procurement problems—those resulting from internal conditions
- Recommendations
- Supplier relationship
- Transportation—effect of rate changes—strikes—weather
- Future plans

When there exists a close relationship with top management, when information is needed promptly, when unusual conditions arise that should be known immediately, or when it becomes necessary to obtain a quick decision, the report may be made orally. Consequently, although periodic written reports may be the rule, occasional oral reports to top management may be required.

The preparation of written reports to management provides an opportunity for the staff to review regularly all of the purchasing department activities. The review may suggest the need for a change or improvement and should result in more effective operations and administration.

EVALUATION OF THE PURCHASING FUNCTION

The measurement of purchasing performance is a recognized responsibility of management. Both purchasing and management executives alike have given a great deal of time and effort trying to develop some reliable yardstick by which purchasing could be evaluated. However, despite all that has been written on the subject, no such yardstick for measuring performance has been agreed upon.

Many measures of operating efficiency have been developed that clearly indicate how well the department is being administered. There is great danger, however, that these efficiency measures will be mistaken for measures of how well the department actually does the job of procurement. In fact, it is entirely possible for a department to improve many of the measures of efficiency by actually doing a poorer job of purchasing.

Successful purchasing is not a matter of a magic formula that enables one to buy the *right commodity* at the *right time,* in the *right quantity,* and at the *right price.* Continuing study, analysis, and application by competent personnel and organization are required to attain that objective.

A much more important and likewise more difficult factor to measure is that of purchasing proficiency. This measure would indicate how well the real job of buying is being done and not simply how well the department is processing paper work. Buying proficiency clearly contributes greater savings for the company than does buying efficiency. Efficiency is a worthwhile goal but not at the expense of proficiency.

In evaluating purchasing performance, emphasis frequently is placed upon how well it has developed supplier relationships through which the company may not only obtain its specific requirements at competitive prices but also benefit from the research facilities and technical services which the supplier places at the disposal of the firm.

The practice in some companies is to evaluate the purchasing function almost exclusively by the overall success of the company, in the belief that its performance will be a reflection of the objectives, plans, and policies of the management.

Because cost savings are brought about by the performance of all departments, it is extremely difficult to separate and measure the exact contribution of purchasing. Excessive claims of cost savings by purchasing may alienate other departments and thus hamper the cooperation which is essential to the proper performance of purchasing as well as of these other departments.

Because evaluation of purchasing is not a simple process in which a single measure gives the necessary rating, proper measurement requires detailed consideration of many factors which provide a composite picture of overall performance (see Section 27). Evaluation may be performed by the purchasing department or it may be done by an outside audit firm. Such an outside audit is frequently used by large firms, but for smaller companies this method is employed only when known problems exist.

CONCLUSION

This section has presented an overview of the purchasing function. Each of the following sections elaborates in detail practically every idea expressed here. Collectively, they demonstrate that there is no magic formula for buying the *right commodity* at the *right time,* in the *right quantity,* and at the *right price.* A continuing project of study, analysis, and application by competent personnel and organization is required to attain that objective.

It is recognized that purchasing has come a long way since the days when it was merely a mechanical job of obtaining a few competitive bids and affixing a signature to a purchase order to the lowest bidder. In those days, purchasing did very little in challenging specifications, suggesting substitute material, participating in the acquisition of plant and capital equipment, or participating in top management decisions.

It is also recognized that the purchasing function, as outlined in this handbook, will not remain static.

Purchasing, because of the very varied nature of the work, the wide exposure it gives to all aspects of a company's operations, and its obvious relationship to total costs and profits, is itself a training program that fits the purchasing executive for higher responsibilities. Those seeking a career in purchasing need not fear that they will be entering a field that is a dead end. Purchasing offers at least as many pathways to the top management group as do the other major functional areas in the business concern.

There are organizational changes inherent in the materials management concept which will have an effect on the scope of a purchasing executive's job and advancement opportunities. Electronic data processing will have an increasing influence on some aspects of the job. The value analysis concept is being adopted by more and more companies on a formalized basis. These trends in purchasing may be but the forerunners of still other changes that cannot even be conceived of at this time. Purchasing is definitely a dynamic field and a distinct challenge to those who would keep abreast of the changes that are taking place in business.

NOTE: For further information on subjects covered in this section see the list of references in Section 30.

Section **2**

The Purchasing Organization

EDITOR

Charles T. Haffey, C.P.M. *Vice-President, Corporate Pur-chasing Division, Pfizer Inc., New York, New York*

ASSOCIATE EDITORS

S. R. Heath, Jr., C.P.M. *Vice-President, Division General Manager, Filtration & Minerals Division, Johns-Manville Corporation, Denver, Colorado*

Len B. Neubert, C.P.M. *(Retired) Vice-President, Purchasing and Transportation, Aluminum Company of America, Pittsburgh, Pennsylvania*

Alex J. Vallas, C.P.M. *Director of Materials Management, Magee-Women's Hospital, Pittsburgh, Pennsylvania*

The basic objective of any purchasing department is to provide those materials and services procured outside the company when and where needed and at the least cost for the function or service required. When this objective is achieved, the enterprise is kept competitive and a major contribution is made toward healthy profitability.

Purchasing is a functional staff aid and is a profit contributor of major import in the business. In an era of inflation, top management has given increased scrutiny to the management of the purchasing function and its effect on profits. With an increased percentage of the sales dollar or institutions' revenue being spent for materials, supplies, and services,[1] managements have come to the realization that purchasing has tremendous leverage with respect to the success of the company.

[1] See Section 1.

One dollar not spent for a needed item converts, dollar for dollar, into the pretax profit column.

Whether a company is in a profit squeeze, or is growing rapidly, effectiveness can be enhanced through increased managerial emphasis on a more efficient purchasing operation. Of prime importance are the organizational structure and its effect on the channels of communication so vital to effective procurement. Reporting relationships determine who sets the criteria for objective measurement of performance. Since purchasing affects all areas of business, it must be integrated into the company organizational structure so as to optimize and ensure its contribution to the success of business strategies.

RESPONSIBILITY, AUTHORITY, AND ACCOUNTABILITY

The chief executive of a progressive company normally delegates full responsibility and the necessary authority for the purchasing function to a capable purchasing officer. *Responsibility* means accountability for the performance of duties. *Authority* is the formal right to require action of others or to act oneself. *Functional authority* is a recognized right to require the *necessary* actions of others or to act oneself to ensure that the function will be performed. To fulfill his or her responsibility, the purchasing officer must be given functional authority to discharge that responsibility. This is because delegation of responsibility without commensurate authority is, in effect, no delegation at all.

Problems often arise, especially in decentralized companies, in reaching a clear understanding of functional authority. The purchasing department itself in this type of organization is often unclear as to its authority to discharge its responsibilities. Line managers are hesitant to accept the fact that purchasing will meet its responsibilities or that it has the same sense of urgency that they do because of their accountability (responsibility) for bottom-line results.

Functional Authority

The *functional authority* of the purchasing department is the authority necessary to see that purchasing activities carried on in the corporation and its divisions are conducted in accordance with the resolutions of top managers. The purchasing department will set policies, standards, and procedures for all purchasing employees to follow.

The purchasing department must approach its job of enforcing these policies, standards, and procedures in a spirit of exercising its responsibility. These policies, standards, and procedures must be responsive to effective functional performance and supportive of line department objectives and goals, thus gaining acceptance and enforcement from line management.

The purchasing department should possess the necessary knowledge and technical expertise to perform these functions for the overall benefit of the corporation and its divisions, and it must exert every effort to convince division management of the efficacy of its proposed actions. At the same time, it acknowledges that the final authority for the commitment of funds rests with the president and division general managers in any operating company.

For effective operation of the purchasing department, in either a centralized or decentralized organization, responsibility and functional authority are inseparable. In its written policies, both purchasing responsibility and functional authority must be clearly defined. The limits of purchasing authority must be clearly set out and its functional authority established.

As a basis for these policy statements, top management must put in writing a statement of purchasing responsibility and functional authority. Such a statement, sometimes called a *charter,* avoids overlapping of functional authority with the authority of line functions and with other staffs and their concomitant functional authority. An excerpt example of such a written charter statement follows:

> 1. It will be the responsibility of the Purchasing Department to conduct negotiations and make all final commitments for materials, supplies, and services as required at the headquarters location. Additionally (as outlined in detailed purchasing procedures), the Purchasing Department is charged with the responsibility to ensure that, prior to final commitment of the company, proper legal and financial reviews are made as necessary. Compliance with existing and future purchasing rules and regulations will also be monitored by the purchasing organization.
>
> 2. Purchasing will negotiate for, and make the commitments on, all of those commodity groups and/or individual part numbers for remote plants, whenever it is to the cost or other business advantage to do so. For example, whenever combining purchasing volume will result in a better price, the central department will act for the company as a whole.

Statements such as those in the second paragraph excerpted above sometimes lead to major uncertainty in the distinction between central and decentralized authority and responsibility, or between line and functional authority. It may be advantageous for top management to clearly state the broad functional authority of purchasing in the charter, and to hold purchasing responsible for results under such a charter statement. Figure 2-1 is an example of such a charter.

Alternate or supplemental methods of delegating responsibility and authority toward the accomplishment of the purchasing objectives are numerous. Most commonly, a policy manual (discussed in Section 3) is used. As the organization increases in size, greater complexity mandates that the purchasing officer clarify responsibility and authority. Purchasing management must pay greater attention to the articulation of clear policies and effective planning, organization, administration, coordination, and functional control.

Great emphasis must be placed on purchasing's relationship to the business managers, departments, and divisions in any organization. Teamwork and cooperation are essential to the proper discharge of purchasing responsibilities.

Purchasing is not an end in itself. Since it exists to supply the company's material, energy, and service requirements, purchasing must contribute to the achievement of business goals through the execution of understood business strategies,

SUPPLY CHARTER

By resolution of the management committee dated July 23, 1973, and reaffirmed in their resolution dated March 29, 1976, the vice-president, supply has been delegated the authority for supply activities of the company. This authority encompasses negotiation with vendors, solicitation of adequate competitive bids, execution of purchase transactions establishing purchasing policy and procedures for the corporation, and applies to the general office and all divisions and field operations.

Supply will execute its purchasing authority throughout the corporation as a service to the operating divisions. Supply is responsible to operating divisions to meet established specifications for purchased goods and services in quantity, quality and price when it executes purchase transactions. The approval authority of the vice president, supply is limited by definition of transactions, monetary value of the transaction, and duration of the contract resulting from the transaction.

As used herein, purchase transactions mean transactions, whether evidenced by purchase orders or other contract documents:

1. For the purchase of supplies, including but not limited to, raw materials, energy, maintenance, repair and operating supplies and packaging materials and office equipment to be used in the manufacture, production and sale of products by the company at any operating location, and in the performance of services incident to such manufacture, production and sale

2. For obtaining services, including but not limited to, services of independent contractors, such as maintenance services, construction services, temporary labor services, and advertising production services, the need for which is incident to the manufacture, production and sale of products by the company

3. For purchase transactions for land improvement, buildings, machinery or equipment, as called for in approved authorization for capital transactions

As used herein, purchase transactions do not include the purchase of real estate, insurance, transportation services, commitments to advertising agencies or professional consultants, capital stock of another corporation, or the lease of real or personal property to the Company or to a subsidiary or affiliate of the company.

For purchase transactions, the vice-president, supply is delegated the authority to execute such purchase transactions as defined by duration of contract as follows:

1. For transactions extending 18 months or less, in amounts in excess of $5 million provided the vice-president, supply delivers a written abstract of the proposed purchase transaction to the president and executive vice-presidents and receives the approval of one or more of them; for any amount up to and including $5million under such system of review as might be established for each division by each respective divisional vice-president and general manager

2. For transactions which are to extend for a period in excess of 18 months, in amounts in excess of $2 million provided the vice-president, supply delivers a written abstract of the proposed purchase transaction to the president and executive vice-presidents and receives the approval of one or more of them; and in amounts up to and including $2 million under such system of review as might be established for each division by each respective vice-president and general manager

With respect to purchase or capital transactions which require payment in excess of $200,000 prior to delivery of goods or rendering of services, the vice-president, supply shall execute the contract or issue the purchase order only after delivering a written abstract of the proposed purchase transaction to the vice-president and treasurer, and receiving no objection from him within 5 calendar days after delivery of the abstract.

The vice-president, supply may delegate to company employees in the supply department and/or field locations authority to negotiate and execute contracts and to issue purchase orders on behalf of the company with respect to purchase and capital transactions as defined above provided the appropriate divisional vice-president and general manager have approved in advance of the person or persons to whom such authority is to be delegated, and written advice of the identity of any person to whom such authority was redelegated and the maximum amount of such authority has been sent to the vice-president and general manager and the vice-president and controller in advance of any approvals by such person.

For purchase transactions for foreign operations, the vice-president, supply will ensure that commitment authorities are established in line with corporate purchasing policy, and consistent with limitations established herein, and will work through and with the officer of each division responsible for foreign operations to ensure appropriate purchasing procedures are followed in those foreign operations.

Fig. 2-1 Supply charter.

which purchasing plays a part in formulating. Purchasing must assist other departments—and be given latitude, communication, and assistance by those departments—as a recognized member of the management team.

The Purchasing Line Concept

It is essential for the purchasing department and the departments it serves to grasp the full concept of the *purchasing line*. When this line is clarified to all who interact with the purchasing function, and when responsibility is assigned across the purchasing organization, purchasing's functional authority will be understood, and accountability will be fully perceived.

This line of purchasing authority is diagrammed in Fig. 2-2, which conceptualizes where purchasing responsibility falls in executing the discrete acts of:

- Specification and requisition
- Procurement
- Distribution of supply
- Receiving
- Stores control
- Distribution to work-in-process
- Production
- New orders

Whether centralized or decentralized, purchasing must execute those basic responsibilities along the purchasing line which are listed below each action point. Depending upon the form of organization or the mix of other functions, other responsibilities may exist for those other functions, but the responsibilities listed in Fig. 2-2 must be executed by purchasing, which must be given the necessary authority to do so.

Coordinating Channels of Communication

The organization chart is a useful approximation of the interactions of people. It represents the formal right to reward and discipline and to hire and fire but informational flow, the lifeblood of an organization, may not follow the formal channels.

While the organization chart defines lines of responsibility, authority, and accountability, it neither indicates fully nor limits channels of contact or flow of information among members of the organization. Since the best and most productive efforts of the staff cannot be obtained unless staff persons are kept currently informed of all developments with which they are concerned, it is the responsibility of each member of the organization to take such steps as may be necessary to inform those associated with any project or problem of developments. Common sense and good judgment are expected in determining the best channels of contact at all organization levels for expeditious handling of company work. Information must flow to those with a need to know.

Contacts and flow of information between members of the organization should

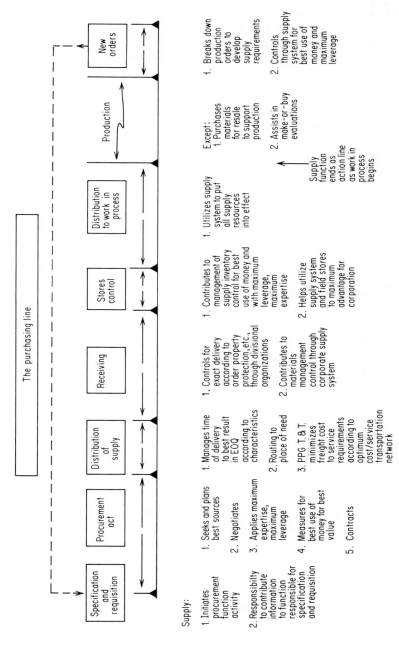

Fig. 2-2 The purchasing line.

be carried out in the simplest and most direct way practicable—by face-to-face or telephone communication. Another means is by distribution of copies of memorandums and letters when a written record is desirable. However, each member of the organization has the duty to keep his superior promptly informed regarding any matters discussed in such contacts:

1. For which his superior may be held properly accountable by others
2. Which are likely to cause disagreement or controversy, particularly between different departments of the organization
3. Which require the advice of his superior or coordination by his superior with other components of the organization
4. Which involve recommendations for change in, or variance from, established policies

To Whom Purchasing Reports

Where the purchasing manager in any sizable company has executive or policy-making status, the trend today is toward having the head of the purchasing function report to the president (chief operating officer) or to an executive vice-president or corporate vice-president. There is also a trend to recognize the function by assigning direction of the management of the function to an officer as shown in Fig. 2-3.

Purchasing officers are increasingly recognized as authorities on general eco-

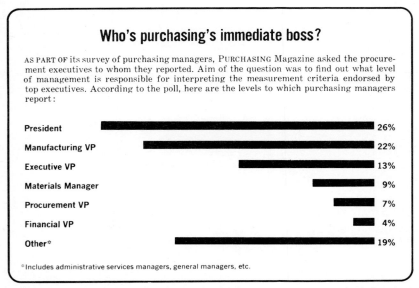

Fig. 2-3   To whom purchasing reports. *(Reproduced by permission from* Purchasing *magazine.)*

nomic trends, competitive market conditions, and price trends. Their timely words of caution, their hedging on commodities or volume-sensitive inventory, or their suggestions for revising material dates or production schedules can have a direct effect on company profitability. Value analysis, management of inventory levels and of the subsequent data in building data analysis, and development of the management tools to accomplish these operations are primary contributions of a purchasing manager.

When he has direct contact with top management, the purchasing department head has access to advance information, which enables him to alert the department to future changes, thereby saving lead time to incorporate such changes. The purchasing manager's participation and alert judgment (and the opportunity to apply

TABLE 2-1   To Whom Purchasing Reports, Based on Company Size

	Under $5 million, %	$5 to $50 million, %	Over $50 million, %	Total, %
President	56.1	30.8	19.0	34.7
Vice-president	15.8	20.5	41.3	25.4
Executive vice-president	5.3	10.2	27.6	13.9
General manager	8.8	13.0	1.7	8.3
Treasurer (or secretary and treasurer)	1.7	5.1	...	2.6
Others	12.3	20.4	10.4	15.1

it) make the company as a whole more flexible in the face of changing economic or marketing conditions.

The purchasing manager, operating from a strategic vantage point in the management hierarchy, should be in an optimum position to make overall contributions for the good of the company through use of purchasing volume leverage. Purchasing supports not only functions involved with material, energy, and equipment supply, but also other vital operating segments—the engineering search, plant operations and expansion management planning, cost predictions and control, profit improvement, and the like.

In the case of decentralized operations, district or plant purchasing usually reports to a local chief executive, such as the general manager or plant manager.

As shown in Table 2-1, based on an earlier research study of 350 respondents made for this handbook, the reporting relationship is affected by company size. Dollar figures represent annual purchases.

There has developed a growing awareness by operating top management that the purchasing department must be free to act on its own initiative without working through, as opposed to working with, some other department or division that may not be cognizant of the market conditions or appreciative of the problem or of the opportunities for purchasing department contributions.

External Communications and Working Relationships

Communication is essential to purchasing management, which depends completely on its input of information from external or internal sources.

First, consider external communication with the hundreds—or thousands—of vendors who furnish supplies. This vendor network is an integral part of the business operation, with whom communication must be kept timely and up to date. Information must be sought on market conditions, sources of supply, supplier capacity, materials and energy supply position of suppliers, labor contract status and conditions, tax matters, prices, traffic costs, and product availability.

External communications are often very difficult to control. In many companies, various other departments feel that they have a responsibility to communicate directly with vendors—quality control likes to make contact on quality matters, engineering on design matters. When the variety of possible contacts between vendors and a buying company is considered, the enormity of the coordination problem is evident to the purchasing manager.

The seller seeks generally to eliminate competition, and the purchasing manager seeks to create it. The seller normally coordinates his sales approach through the sales representative, and when members of the buying company make contact with the seller, communication is normally channeled, or at least acknowledged, back through the sales office. With this kind of coordination and control, the seller may tactically play off various departments of the customer company against each other to its disadvantage.

In contrast to the seller, the buyer can lose control. The buying company is frequently dissected if the buyer cannot coordinate the various contacts between his organization and those of the vendors.

The buyer's job is unusual in that he has to coordinate or control one, two, three, or more users of influences to achieve a balanced result in a purchase decision. Yet, the buyer has little or no direct authority over any one of the other participants in the buying decision. Their input is essential along the purchasing line (Fig. 2-2) if the optimum buying decision is to be reached. It is no surprise that the seller often wonders who speaks for the buying company when there is no coordination of the various inputs. The purchasing manager must participate in conversations between the seller and the several interested functions of his company to the extent that he is sufficiently knowledgeable to influence and control what he deems strategically desirable. But he cannot be a party to every discussion, technical or otherwise, that can take place in the intricate buyer-seller relationship. It is good managerial practice for the purchasing manager to insist that contacts with the buyer be initiated through his office. How effectively the purchasing manager controls his external communications is a major determinant in accomplishing the purchasing job in an effective manner.

Internal Working Relationships and Communications

Internal communications greatly affect the confidence others have that the buyer represents their interest fairly and accurately. While external communications affect the company's image in the eyes of the seller and are important for control in purchasing negotiations, internal relationships and communications affect management's confidence in how the purchasing job is being handled.

Internal relationships and communications constitute a most difficult area for the purchasing manager and one which is most often neglected. It is in this area of integrating purchasing work within the organization that perhaps most purchasing managers and buyers are deficient. Internal communications include: stores and inventory status; adjustment of material costs; production needs; engineering design and changes; material specifications; new product development; quality control methods and standards; finance involvement; business forecasting; tax matters; purchasing contribution to the business strategy and long-range plan; and a host of functional relationships with users and with quality control, inspection, and others in an organization.

To complicate matters, purchasing frequently must take the vendor's side on certain conflicts that naturally arise in the conduct of business between buyers and sellers. The purchasing manager has to interpret the seller's position and work toward an equitable solution with the using departments. Users frequently are impatient, and fail to understand why the purchasing manager simply does not take their side and fight for their desired objective. In a turnabout, the purchasing manager often must execute vigorously a claim with the same seller to achieve equity in a supply matter. Internal management often cannot understand why this is not *always* the purchasing manager's approach to the seller.

This gap in understanding within a company comes from a lack of involvement in the interchange between buyer and seller. The purchasing manager is often the person in the middle in a friction situation. Unless he works very diligently at his in-house communications so that it is understood why he takes certain actions, his image may suffer unreasonably.

It is a truism that the purchasing manager has as much authority as others within the organization will allow him to have. His peers must recognize and understand his buying strategy—and see its interconnection with and support to their respective business strategies—before they can accept his proper exercise of functional authority.

Organizational attempts to overcome the internal relationships and communications problems can be creative and useful. Accountabilities should be reviewed by the business team to perfect their interrelationships. Purchasing should contribute to the formulation of 1-year operating plans by reviewing its resource requirements with each business manager since they will contribute to the achievement of those plans. Purchasing should contribute to the definition of long-range business strategies and integrate its long-range plan with that of the business. Purchasing should participate in operations meetings to determine its input to support of longer-range strategies. Increased use of specialists, such as the purchasing planning manager, purchase engineer, purchase analyst, and value analyst, will assist in improved communications with management and with vendor specialists. The purchasing management task is to integrate these new approaches to achieve enhanced business results—and optimum purchasing results.

PURCHASING OBJECTIVES

Purchasing management should articulate its overall purchasing objectives and publish them widely among internal management personnel. These objectives should flow from an analysis of corporate objectives and business strategies. They set the tone of the environment in which the purchasing function must perform and achieve. They are the basis for the establishment of accountabilities for each

---

PURCHASING OBJECTIVES

1. Ensure adequate dependable sources of supply for materials, supplies, equipment and designated services procured by supply while maintaining an optimum balance of quality, utility and cost.

2. Maximize purchasing strength in the marketplace to obtain most favorable terms and conditions of purchase.

3. Contribute to maximum corporate profitability through judicious and ethical buying of raw materials, equipment, supplies, and designated services.

4. Develop and apply sound purchasing principles, practices and techniques to the supply functions.

5. Develop and maintain a competent purchasing staff and manage companywide procurement activities to achieve the lowest cost to adequately carry out the function.

6. Contribute to improved management decision making through development and maintenance of information services in the areas of:
   a. new items and services
   b. market demands
   c. new sources
   d. price fluctuation and trends
   e. equipment design changes
   f. new materials and methods

7. Promote a positive image among vendors, and the general public.

8. Establish and maintain equitable and mutually profitable relationships with suppliers.

9. Cooperate with other departments to promote the overall best interests of the corporation.

10. Develop and implement contractual safeguards which clearly establish responsibility for the warranting of design, materials, workmanship, performance and patents for all purchased materials, goods and services.

11. Optimize investment in purchased material inventories through cooperative and supportive activity with operating departments.

12. Minimize total delivered costs through management and control of inbound transportation, in cooperation with the traffic and distribution department.

13. Utilize internal sources of supply when this is to the best overall advantage of the company.

14. Maximize investment recovery through judicious scrap and surplus disposal.

15. Contribute to the orderly development and implementation of a materials management concept in the company.

Fig. 2-4   Purchasing objectives.

purchasing manager and buyer. They, and purchasing management's charter, are the credentials against which purchasing management credibility will be established throughout the business. They should be established and published early in the life of the purchasing organization. Figure 2-4 is an example of purchasing objectives for a purchasing organization within a multiplant company.

THE PURCHASING ORGANIZATION

Just as there is a strategy to the business, there is a strategy to the development of an efficient purchasing organization. The basic objective in the organization of purchasing should be a structure that facilitates the motivation of purchasing personnel, and effects the coordination of their professional efforts toward the common goals of the business. It should be a structure that does not get in the way of the various business managers' approach to their business strategies but on the contrary assists in the integration of purchasing in this process.

Very few businesses have adopted organizational structures for purchasing that are exactly alike. The structure a business will adopt will usually represent a compromise designed to accommodate the business environment and the various operating problems in the business. Purchasing organization is so varied because of its importance to profit leverage, yet there is little unanimous top management opinion as to how it is best or ideally structured. Purchasing organization is usually tailored to a particular situation. The imprint of the personalities within the business cannot be forgotten in organization design. Enough flexibility must be built in to accommodate the dynamics of change. Market environment is one of the greatest single influences in shaping the final organizational design. Organizational structure will have to adapt to the changing supply environment. The organization design process must be thought of as dynamic and a managerial art of balancing numerous trade-offs.

Accordingly, the choice of organizational structure should evolve from a thoughtful study of the various factors within and without the business that must be addressed in the application of purchasing management skills. A timely and thorough analysis of these aspects of the business will have a high return in management results if properly done.

When the job to be done is known and the factors in the business environment have been identified, the purchasing organization should be fitted to the job to be done. The scope of responsibilities within the organization will vary not only from industry to industry but from company to company within an industry.

In the last few years, one trend has evolved among the numerous reorganizations that have been announced: it seems essential that purchasing be stationed at the highest possible level in the organization in order to speak to vendors with as large an economic voice as possible as a member of top management. Yet it must be structured to be an organic part of the company and to work closely with those who consume the materials. Achieving this top-level role and yet being an integral part of the company it serves is the objective of sound purchasing organization.

Department Organization for a Single-Plant Facility

The basic single-plant facility organization is the foundation of practically all purchasing departments, regardless of the type and size of the corporation, the number of plant facilities, the types of products manufactured, the services offered, or the geographical spread of the plant facilities.

Simplicity Desired in Purchasing Department A purchasing department should not be established merely for the sake of having an organization but to best achieve the stated objectives as efficiently as possible. An example of this type of department is shown in Fig. 2-5.

The main function of the purchasing department is to fill the company's requirements for materials, supplies, and services. Other services and goals of the purchasing department are established to assist in this main mission. Red tape and procedural complexity should be held to the minimum required for orderly buying procedures and adequate control of dollars spent by the function. The responsibilities and duties of the various members of the basic department will

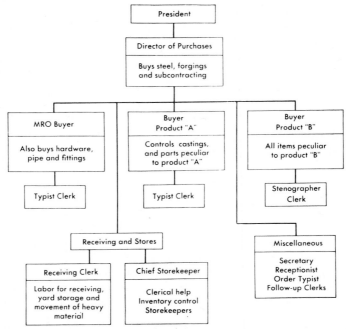

Fig. 2-5 Purchasing department for a company with sales volume of $10 to $15 million annually manufacturing two basic products, each of high value.

remain essentially the same as the members and their department grow. The growth of the department remains directly under the control and direction of the purchasing executive who has the responsibility for the department's activities. With diversification and/or expansion can come the organizational modification, enlarged expertise, and specialization that evolves in a dynamic organization to make it function more effectively.

Expansion and contraction should be possible without disrupting a basic organization. There is a capability to withstand boom or depression. Good basic purchasing organization has a measure of flexibility. Even with forward planning, there may come a time when the department should be reorganized to meet changing conditions. Evolutionary changes occurring frequently in the department are preferable to radical changes long overdue.

Purchasing Department Must Be Functional   An organization, if it is to be flexible, quick to react to change, and competitive, must be completely functional, with the accent on the job to be done.

In some organizations, specific responsibilities are assigned on the basis of the peculiarities or the personality of an individual or individuals. Allowances must naturally be made for some outstanding individuals, but only those positions should be established that are essential to the overall success and efficiency of the department and of the company.

Simplicity should be the goal in setting up the organization, in writing procedures for its operation, in developing the required printed forms, and in making contact with others within and outside the company. Figure 2-6 is a basic schematic of an organizational approach to purchasing (supply) in either a large or a small company. Regardless of the size of the department, its work force, or the value of its purchases, the same end results are expected. The goal—optimum purchase results—is the same, although the manner of achievement will vary depending upon the size of the department and the type of product or products purchased and manufactured.

So basic is the buying job that the procedures and policies developed at great expense by large corporations are usually available, and adaptable at least in part, to the smallest company.

Purchasing departments in larger corporations may be practically self-sustaining for many services, such as engineering, inspection, and records, while smaller purchasing departments must secure those services from other departments or individuals. Naturally, the smaller the company or plant, the more versatile its personnel must be to successfully combine functions that are the responsibilities of individual specialists or, in some cases, even of sections or departments in the larger corporations. The smaller organization needs a generalist manager to handle several different responsible functions within the purchasing line, while the larger organization can employ specialists on each function or on subfunctions of purchasing responsibility.

Also, in the small company or plant, it may be necessary to seek information from or borrow personnel on a temporary basis from other departments, such as the inspection, engineering, manufacturing systems, or planning department, in order to complete the functions of the purchasing department.

Scope of Job Determines Size of Department   Volume of purchases determines, to an extent, the size of the organization and the types of supplemental personnel, as well as the number of buyers, required.

The complexity of the materials purchased and the end products produced also will affect the size of the department, as well as the choice of service peronnnel, such as purchasing engineers and quality control people. The greater the complexity, the greater the need for more specialized or expert buyers and the smaller the output of orders per buyer. There are a number of other variables, such as geographical location and scope of responsibility, which affect the size of a partic-

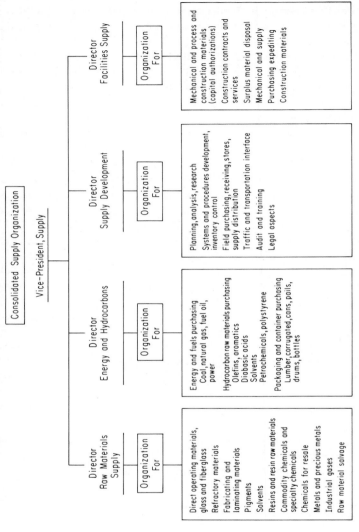

Fig. 2-6 Consolidated supply organization.

ular department. It is practically impossible to compare intelligently different purchasing operations unless all factors are known.

Purchasing should be sufficiently flexible even in its planned organization to meet changing conditions or new demands. For example, the availability or nonavailability of the right type of personnel may force compromises in establishing the anticipated ideal organization. It may even be desirable to revise the intended organizational structure to best utilize the unusual abilities of an available outstanding individual who may not exactly fit the job description.

The type of material to be purchased, how often material is required (whether the purchase order covers a day's supply or a year's supply), and similar factors affect the ratio of buyers to service and clerical personnel (e.g., in times of material scarcity, expediting is of relatively greater importance).

Managers of smaller departments may wish to concentrate on a higher ratio of skilled buyers (who do their own expediting, specification analysis, etc.) to clerical personnel. An organization of this type can rapidly expand its capacity for work through the addition of inexperienced clerical personnel. This approach would be in direct contrast to the time-honored "one-man department" with one high-salaried individual who makes all decisions and uses clerical support.

Such a policy of being relatively long on buying and technical talent anticipates greater growth potential; better servicing of manufacturing facilities; more contributions in value analysis; added production aids through improved materials, supplies, methods, and equipment; and further continuing cost reductions for materials procured. Such a policy also retains the flexibility to reorganize so as to better optimize use of computer systems, approaches to strategic and tactical purchasing, and evolution into materials management and materials requirements planning modes.

Department Organization for a Multiplant Company

In a multiplant company, purchasing may be either decentralized or centralized, with many variations. Except for the requirements of better controls and coordination between headquarters purchasing and geographically dispersed plant units, the internal structure, rules, and regulations are practically indentical with those of a single-plant purchasing department.

To eliminate any misunderstanding relative to the word *centralized*, in the following pages use of the term indicates that a company has centralized all its purchasing activities under one department head. Figure 2-7 illustrates such an organization.

In contrast, in those plants where decentralized purchasing is the policy, plant purchasing is usually handled by local independent purchasing departments. In practice, most multiplant companies are neither purely centralized nor purely decentralized in organization but represent combinations of the two extremes.

In many multiplant organizations, purchasing is highly centralized, with the home-office purchasing department buying all productive and high-dollar items and the local purchasing departments allowed to make only emergency purchases.

CENTRALIZED SUPPLY (PURCHASING) DEPARTMENT

Vice-President, Supply
  Director, Raw Materials Supply
    Manager, Supply Glass Materials & Fiber Glass Batch Materials
      Senior Supply Agent
      Senior Supply Agent
    Manager, Supply C&R Materials
      Senior Supply Agent
      Senior Supply Agent
      Senior Supply Agent
    Manager, Supply Chemical Materials
      Senior Supply Agent
    Manager, Supply Metals & Fiber Glass Binder Materials

  Director, Energy and Hydrocarbons Supply
    Manager, Hydrocarbons Supply
      Senior Supply Agent
    Manager, Fuel Supply
      Supervisor, Liquid & Solid Fuels Supply
      Senior Supply Agent, Utility Fuels Supply
    Manager, Packaging & Container Supply
      Senior Supply Agent
      Assistant Supply Agent

  Director, Supply Development
    Manager, Supply Planning & Analysis
    Manager, Field Supply
      Supervisor, Field Supply
    Manager, Supply Data Systems
    Manager of Distribution Development, Supply
      Supply Transportation Analyst
      Trainee, Distribution & Transportation

  Director, Facilities Supply
      Buyer / Supervisor Secretarial Services
    Manager, Construction Services Supply
      Senior Supply Agent
    Manager, Capital Equipment Supply
      Senior Supply Agent
      Senior Supply Agent
      Senior Supply Agent

    Manager, Mechanical Supplies
      Senior Supply Agent
      Senior Supply Agent
    Manager, C&S Supply
      Senior Supply Agent
      Senior Supply Agent
    Manager, Contracted Procurement Services

Field purchasing offices report on a dotted line to the manager, field supply.

Fig. 2-7 Centralized supply (purchasing) department.

Other companies allow the local offices to procure all maintenance, repair, and operating (MRO) supplies, and some allow all follow-up functions to be performed locally. Some companies allow local procurement of all parts or materials peculiar to a particular operation. An example of this type of organizational planning is shown in Fig. 2-8.

The tightly centralized purchasing department at the home office with little

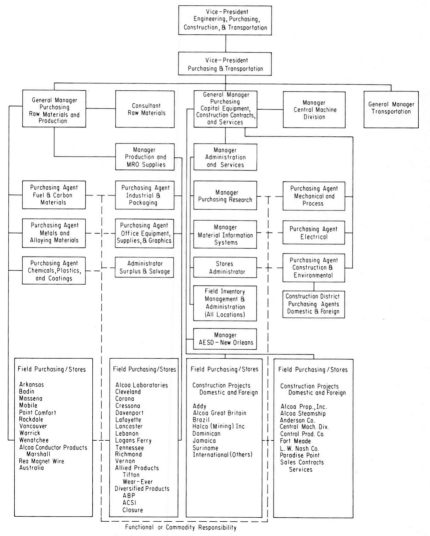

Fig. 2-8 Purchasing department organization chart.

local-plant freedom of action is at the other extreme from complete local autonomy.

The choice of a centralized or decentralized purchasing organization or a combination of the two types should be based on ultimate rather than temporary benefits and should take into consideration all relevant facts and unusual conditions. Major factors to be considered are:

1. The organizational pattern of the corporation, i.e., profit centers, functionally organized or highly centralized
2. The similarity of products produced in the various plants
3. The profit leverage of purchases on company performance
4. The managerial attention required or desired for the purchasing function
5. The geographical distribution of the plants
6. The overall size of the company and the volume of purchases in total and by major commodity or product categories

In most recent times, the evolution of purchasing management philosophy has been such that the more strategic planning and control aspects of purchasing management are being moved upward in the organization, while day-to-day mechanics of purchasing—releases against contract, purchase order and file maintenance, and purchasing aspects of stores control—are being delegated to the buyer and plant purchasing manager. Regardless of the size of the organization, this leads to far greater centralization of policy making, procedure issuance, contract negotiation, purchase strategy and long-range purchasing planning, purchasing research, market analysis, cost reduction, inventory control, functional reviews, systems design, and purchase price forecasting and budgeting. These functions can be carried out more effectively and thoroughly under the specialization available with centralized purchasing.

Plants Producing Similar Products at Relatively Close Distances   Centralized purchasing permits greater buyer specialization and expertise. Buyers can concentrate on fewer duplications of effort in similar categories of materials. Particularly when new products are to be introduced, for purposes of value analysis or cost control, and for evolution of integrated purchasing strategy, this specialization is of inestimable value. This type of organization is shown in Fig. 2-9.

Each year this company has added a new product to its line. With an organization of the type shown, new items that were similar to those already purchased were delegated to the buyers who had the experience to recognize and immediately apply value analysis to the component parts before the engineering was completed. Such buyers were able to call upon known and proven suppliers for engineering, styling, and even marketing assistance. As a result, new products reached the market faster, and were more competitively priced, and production had fewer interruptions.

Centralized purchasing retains strict authority and control at the home office without sacrificing (where plants are closely concentrated) the advantages of local purchasing.

In lieu of centralized purchasing, one multiplant electrical product manufacturer channels all copper buying through a plant purchasing manager who is acknowledged as an expert in that field. Textile requisitions go through a different plant purchasing manager, and similarly for other supplies. This system is acknowledged by the company to be a substitute for a central organization and

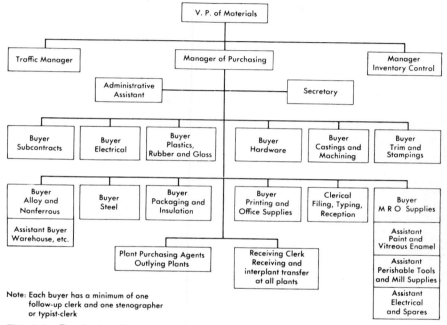

Fig. 2-9   Purchasing department of a major appliance manufacturer with annual purchases of $50 million.

came about through a series of mergers in which a few top-quality purchasing managers of equal ability were absorbed within a short time. Each manager thus employs his administrative ability in his local plant while having overall responsibility for some material or materials for the entire company. Such a system has obvious pitfalls and is mentioned because this company represents a successful exception. Its continued success calls for close cooperation and understanding.

Centralized purchasing, without any real sacrifice in authority or control or any loss of effectiveness, can permit MRO, emergency, or uncommon items to be purchased by the local-plant purchasing department. This type of local buying has the twin advantages of allowing the local plant some necessary flexibility and of helping to improve its community relations. With such a system the home office would still buy a large proportion of productive materials and components and place all high-value orders. Home office staff would also generate national purchase agreements to capitalize on purchasing leverage.

Centralized purchasing should encourage local buyers to shop their areas for productive parts that may be the specialties of some local producers in their areas, regardless of where the parts are used in the company. Quotations developed from local sources should be summarized in competition with those secured by the central buyer, and the resulting orders should be placed by the central buyer or whoever has the preassigned responsibility for making the purchase.

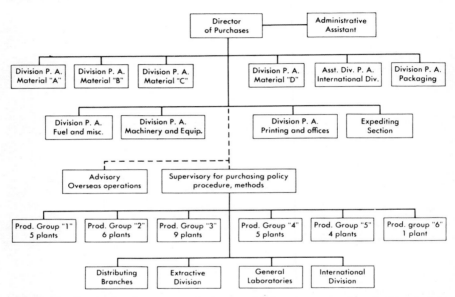

Fig. 2-10   Purchasing department of a large multiplant company where basic materials are centrally purchased for decentralized operations.

It may be advisable to decentralize the follow-up function for "on-the-spot" expediting. The advisability of this step would depend on the nature of the products produced, the geographical proximity of the various plants to each other and to the sources of supply, and the seriousness of the delivery problem.

Plants with Dissimilar Products or Geographical Dispersion   Companies whose plants produce unlike products, or which are widely separated geographically, will often resort to decentralized procurement, with each plant being practically autonomous as to purchasing organization. In such cases, the general or home office will still prescribe and issue policy—and in some cases even detailed procedures. In this type of organization, the home office usually employs commodity or product specialists to advise purchasing departments.

In recent years, this type of organization has consolidated and recentralized purchasing management by grouping purchases of items or materials in general use in order to gain maximum discounts. It has further centralized the management of energy procurement, facilities supply (capital equipment and contracted services), packaging, and even raw material purchases. An example of such a national organization is shown in Fig. 2-10.

Other companies may choose to treat all problems as local problems and in no way dictate even policies and procedures.

Decentralized purchasing gives the local-plant organization close control over its material and components. The plant purchasing manager, being closer to his suppliers, can better operate with smaller inventories and better meet emergency requirements.

Where plants are widespread geographically, decentralized purchasing avoids possible problems due to transportation, loss of time, and poor communications between the local organization and the supplier.

Where plants produce dissimilar products from unlike components, specialization in the buying function may not be practical above the individual-plant level. In such an organization, a decentralized purchasing organization, under overall managerial direction from the responsible local line officer or manager, does not seriously hamper buying efficiency.

Widespread Decentralized Organization with Central Control   In large corporations with operating units spread throughout the country, decentralized purchasing has often been the policy regardless of products produced. However, there is now a tendency for closer corporate control of these outlying units, aided by data processing and newer communication devices.

In decentralized purchasing organizations with strong plant purchasing departments, certain characteristics of value are shown:

1. The purchasing departments make particular purchases best handled at a plant level in accordance with *divisional* policies established by general office divisional organizations.

2. Plant purchasing systems operate within the *operating* entity, the plant, where the manager is charged with providing efficient and economical operations:

    a. The departments purchase particular materials and supplies and seek divisional help for strength, coordination, and specialization.

    b. The departments coordinate, expedite, and operate within the *materials management chain* as follows:

Engineering or planning	Materials specified
	Materials bought
	Materials received
Materials administration	Materials stored
Manufacturing	Materials fabricated
Quality assurance	Product inspected
Shipping	Product shipped
Shipping	Product shipped

    c. The purchasing departments maintain a community and public relations functional assist, and handle special local problems such as those involving transportation facilities, storage facilities, climatic conditions, local laws and customs, and special suppliers locally.

In these situations, divisional centralized purchasing organizations seek to assure for the division:

- Structure of relationships
- Assignment of specific job responsibilities
- Assignment of specific authorities and chains of command
- Development of job specifications
- Development of policies which define and permit routine subordinate decisions.

These divisional organizations specifically aim for directing operational activities so as to achieve the following:

- Maximum profit-impact results
- Optimized supplier relationships
- Maximum business impact from the purchasing function inside and outside the business
- Maximum coordination with other materials functions serving within the division (inventory control, production control) and from corporate direction (traffic)

In recent years corporations have asked if purchasing would be more effective if it were performed on a corporate-centralized basis rather than on a divisional or departmental-centralized basis.

Certain benefits of centralization have been recognized:

- Under accountabilities management, the company is best managed to meet objectives, and there is power when functions can be managed as if the company were an entity. The materials program could be so coordinated.
- Economics of scale should be recognized—centralization moves in this direction.
- Centralization is an organizational move which can avoid duplication of effort and working at cross purposes between divisions on items of common concern.
- Centralization is a move toward consolidation of orders for material commonly used by more than one division, greater buying power, and more favorable national contracts and trade agreements.
- Centralization permits and enhances establishment of and adherence to unified purchasing policies, practices, procedures, and product standards.
- Procurement and materials management is recognized as a major function.
- Centralization permits correlation of each division's resource acquisition cycle, resulting in improved companywide material flows (including interdivision flows).

• Centralization permits eventual development of greater knowledge and concentrated skills by materials managers specializing in materials management for all divisions.

• Development and effective utilization of relations with suppliers are facilitated.

• Volume buying through national agreements reduces ultimate material, energy, and equipment costs.

Decentralized purchasing with central control permits local release and sometimes purchase of supplies and services peculiar to each plant, while the central office normally has the responsibility of purchasing construction, equipment, and supplies for a new plant during its construction period. If lead time makes such a step necessary, the central office may also procure all materials needed to commence production. The central office frequently negotiates national contracts for common production materials and MRO supplies used in quantity by more than one plant, allowing local plant purchasing managers to release orders against these contracts. It assists local plants, at their request, in locating materials and in expediting deliveries against open orders. It also advises the plant purchasing manager of changes in government regulations and secures legal approval for agreements incorporating unusual terms or conditions. It may also handle long-term purchase contracts and purchases above a given stated dollar level.

Central control generally has responsibility for interplant transfer of machinery, equipment, materials, and supplies; for the disposal of surplus; for the standardization of tools, equipment, and supplies; and for the overall inventory position of the company. It advises management and the plant purchasing departments on general business conditions, commodity price trends, and unusual conditions that may influence future operations of the company.

Some large companies with far-flung and even diversified operations have developed regional purchasing offices. These regional offices do all buying in their assigned regions that is not handled at the home office and thereby replace or at least greatly reduce the size of the local-plant purchasing departments.

Companies using regional purchasing offices should consider assigning a purchasing representative at plants served by such regional offices. The total elimination of purchasing coverage at medium- and large-sized plants may cause considerable dissatisfaction and friction between the regional office and plant management. A plant purchasing representative has solved this problem very well for a number of companies.

The plant purchasing department normally conducts all purchasing activities except those expressly retained by the central purchasing department. It keeps the central purchasing department advised of local conditions, unusual aspects of vendor performance, and any developments that may affect the plant's or the company's welfare or future planning. It normally procures supplies and disposes of locally generated scrap within limits defined by central procurement or company policy. Even when plant purchasing managers report to the local plant managers, they conduct all purchasing activities in accordance with policies established by the central procurement department. This procedure allows the realization of maximum discounts through the grouping requirements for largest-quantity purchases.

Central Authority in Decentralized Organizations   How far the authority of the home-office purchasing executive should extend into other plants in multiplant organizations should be carefully determined by:

1. The degree of centralization or decentralization established in the company's policy

2. The specific responsibilities of central and of plant purchasing, which should be spelled out in practical detail to avoid overlapping functions and possible confusion within the company organization and among the vendors

3. Plant purchasing managers reporting to their general managers except for overall purchasing policy, versus item 4 below

4. Plant purchasing agents reporting to the home-office purchasing executive except for strictly local problems, such as working hours

When the authority, duties, and responsibilities of the home office and of each of the local-plant purchasing organizations are clearly spelled out, they must be understood by all who are affected by such policies.

Particularly in corporations where decentralization is the rule, local management is usually strong and independent and may resist apparent home-office pressure unless the authority, duties, and responsibilities of each are clearly defined, understood, and agreed upon. Understanding and acceptance of such purchasing policies are necessary for the company to guard against a claim of a plant purchasing department that it is too restricted to function effectively, or against the complaint from headquarters that individual plants have too much freedom of decision and action.

The lines of communication between the home office and the local-plant purchasing organizations must be kept open—both ways—at all times. This permits the free exchange of buying information between the home office and the local purchasing organizations.

The local purchasing manager should be conversant with all local conditions and problems relating to his activity. He should keep the central purchasing executive apprised of unusual local developments affecting purchasing.

The home office should make available to the local purchasing managers whatever information has been developed or is available to help the plant purchasing managers to improve their functions. It is imperative that home office and plants cooperate and assist each other.

Intracompany cooperation can assist the promotion of worthy personnel from plant to plant and the staffing of new plants. It will also spread the experience among the divisions and reduce the tendency to overstaff at the local plant level.

The home office is normally the clearinghouse or court of appeals, regardless of its degree of authority, on such basic matters as: the compilation, with the assistance of plant purchasing managers, of the volume of purchases by suppliers and a list of acceptable bidders or vendors; the maintenance of a record of the location of common tooling; the issuance of national contracts; the establishment of staff functions such as market analysis, vendor analysis, and comparative quality studies; the supplying of credit rating information; and the solution of legal questions.

General Considerations of Centralized versus Decentralized Purchasing   The degree of decentralization of the purchasing department should normally parallel that of management responsibilities, so that there is a prompt, free, and on-the-spot interchange of information or ideas in the solution of normal and emergency problems. However, the advantages of combining the total volume of purchases and of the use of buying specialists should not be overlooked. No organization should be centralized to the degree that local productive operations can be paralyzed or that cooperation is lost because of the distance between procurement and production.

In the early 1960s the trend was toward decentralization, i.e., toward getting the job done by those who were sufficiently close to it—those who had a primary interest in getting it done. The purpose of this was to avoid loss of local perspective by routing through the home office, which added to detail and necessitated cooperation of many people who did not have the local problem as a primary interest. Decentralization of an activity develops personnel by spreading responsibilities and giving more growth opportunities, while making possible quicker recognition for achievements.

The trend toward decentralization reversed itself in the 1970s. Today, the move to combine the advantages of closer centralization with local autonomy is apparent. The advantages of establishing profit centers of control have not measured up to the advantages realized with central control, which allows the use of buying specialists and secures the savings of larger-volume purchases. So, many hybrid organizations have developed.

An example of a *centralized-decentralized* department is shown in Fig. 2-11. The department, spending well over $500 million annually, is centralized at its main location. While other locations are decentralized, central purchasing monitors all purchases and contracts for total volume where doing so economically results in better purchases.

It is recognized that a change to decentralization means the duplication of many charges that could quickly liquidate the savings effected by the change. Some of these are:

1. Fixed charges carry on.
2. There is a tendency to overstaff outlying units.
3. With duplications, a lack of specialization normally follows.

So important is the coordination between headquarters and plant purchasing that many companies use specialists bearing such titles as: Purchasing Services

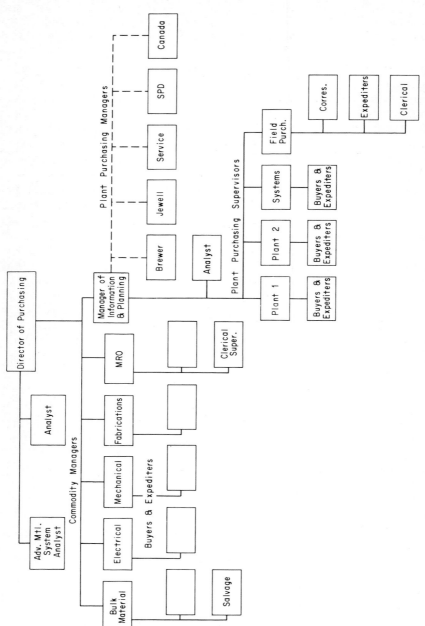

Fig. 2-11 Example of an actual centralized-decentralized purchasing department made up of 70 individuals.

Manager; Manager of Information and Planning; Coordinator, Procurement Policies; Manager, Field Supply; and Director, Supply Development.

OPERATING WITHIN THE MATERIALS MANAGEMENT CONCEPT

Materials management is an important function, and its implementation is a significant factor in the struggle for improved earnings. The clearest definition of materials management is the *localization or bringing together under one organizational component the responsibility* for:

1. Determining the manufacturing requirements
2. Scheduling the manufacturing process
3. Procuring, storing, and disbursing materials on time within allocated costs to complete the process

Materials management provides the centralization of authority and the resulting coordination and control to overcome the shortcomings of conventional organizations by improving coordination and providing cohesion in the materials flow area. Just as manufacturing, sales, and finance are basic activities, materials management is a basic activity responsible for balancing *all* related variables, including cost of materials procured, cost of investment and inventory and cost of maintaining inventory, concomitant administrative expenses, cost of delays in manufacturing owing to lack of materials of specified quality, and—most important of all—contribution to profit.

The current reasons for adopting materials management in industry are many. This concept will certainly enable the company adopting it to better utilize control tools, to cut across functional lines, and to enhance interdepartmental coordination in the materials area. It will make a profit contribution that is measurable because of the direct management of inventory, production control, purchasing, and traffic or distribution, and it has a clear potential to contribute cost reductions in all these areas. Most importantly, with proper authority given to the function, it will be the most direct means of reconciling conflicting objectives in the performance of materials subfunctions because decisions *must* be made with the *total* materials position in mind.

Materials management is such an important concept that a separate section, Section 19, has been devoted to it within this handbook.

PROPER ORGANIZATION ESSENTIAL TO EFFICIENT OPERATIONS

Effective company organization eliminates friction, duplication of effort, and noncoverage by defining responsibilities and authority. Job descriptions ensure the better utilization of personnel.

Procedures and Job Analysis

The development of understandable and workable procedures and job analysis is the first step in organizing and standardizing the efforts and activities of the purchasing department.

Published procedures or manuals, such as those illustrated in Section 3, spell out the procedures and systems within the department. They also define the relationship of the department to other departments or divisions of the company. They cover all routine situations and the operations of the department, and they provide for meeting the unusual conditions or problems that so frequently face purchasing.

In setting up or revising the organization of the small purchasing department, it is helpful to study the organizations and procedures of larger departments. While it may be natural to ignore large-company organizations as being too dissimilar, the knowledge and responsibility that are required to develop a successful purchasing department are found in equal proportion in the large and the small company.

Except for the volume of purchases, many small and medium-sized purchasing departments handle as many and diverse commodities as the larger departments. Some small departments must also procure thousands of separate items per year. Their solution to their problem is to specialize in a limited number of major purchases and to investigate improved buying procedures for the smaller commitments through experience on the job, through contacts with fellow buyers, and finally through the services of professional purchasing associations.

Title of the Purchasing Executive

The titles of the department head and his subordinates are secondary in importance to the authority exercised by the executive and that delegated to his subordinates. The department head may be an officer of the company, such as Vice-President, Purchasing, or the position may be titled either Director of Purchasing or Manager of Purchasing where the department head reports to the president and chief operating officer or to a vice-president of the firm.

For many years, the top position in smaller or medium-sized purchasing departments was often titled Purchasing Agent. In recent years most companies have recognized the true importance of devoting managerial attention to the purchasing function and this title has practically disappeared. It is recommended that the top positions in smaller departments or subpositions in larger firms be entitled Purchasing Manager. The office of the purchasing manager views the purchasing process from the managerial perspective. Recognition of this revised concept was unquestionably responsible during the mid-1960s for the shift from Agent to Manager in the titles found in professional purchasing associations as well.

In larger companies the department head will generally concern himself primarily with policy and administration of the function. In medium-sized companies he may buy a few commodities or products because he is expert in those fields, or because the time required for his other duties does not preclude buying. The head of the department is primarily an administrator and is mostly concerned with personnel selection; the training, development, and supervision of personnel; forward planning; and coordination with other departments. He is secondarily a buyer. He should have a general knowledge of all the items purchased and of their ultimate use, but he should not be expected to have detailed technical knowledge of all fields. His responsibility is to manage the organization of specialists who handle these responsibilities.

The smaller the company, the more buying will be done by the department manager, until in the so-called one-man department he will obviously perform all purchasing tasks. In a small company, he may even have duties beyond the normal scope of the purchasing function. It is recommended, however, that managements of businesses in operation in the supply field today give strong consideration to maintaining the job of purchasing manager as an integral job, with 100 percent of its time allocated to the purchasing function.

Title of the First Assistant

In larger companies the executive may have one or more direct assistants, variously titled in accordance with their different duties. They will supervise the people performing certain phases of the procurement function, such as commodity buying, inventory, or material control; planning, specification, or value analysis; expediting; quality control or purchasing engineering; facilities purchasing; and an array of clerical functions that include filing, maintaining of records, typing, and material allotments. A representative highly centralized purchasing department employing more than one assistant is shown in Fig. 2-12.

The first or only assistant is usually so designated by the job title, such as Assistant Vice-President for Purchasing, Assistant Purchasing Manager, Assistant Director of Purchases, or Director of Purchases.

All Purchasing Department Managers—Example of Job Descriptions

All purchasing department managers have certain responsibilities and authority regardless of their specialty. Figure 2-13 is a job description for the head of a purchasing function in a large corporation, the vice-president, supply. Not all job descriptions are written in the same manner, and the purpose of any job description is to reflect the basic management tenets needed for the person who fills the position to handle the specific responsibilities as defined by the company.

Beyond the example given in Fig. 2-13, job descriptions should in general cover the managerial tenets listed below by category.

GENERAL DUTIES AND RESPONSIBILITIES.   Within the limits of company policies, approved programs, and control procedures, assume responsibility for and have commensurate authority to accomplish the fulfillment of duties as set forth in the organizational manual. Delegate appropriate portions of responsibilities to subordinate personnel if desired, together with proportionate authority for their fulfillment—but do not delegate or relinquish overall responsibility and accountability for results.

PLANNING AND REVIEW.

• Plan near- and long-term programs compatible with major company objectives and policies, seeking advice and counsel of immediate superiors as necessary.

• Keep immediate superiors currently informed of major plans and programs and of the progress and the problems of operations for which they are responsible.

• Develop for approval of immediate superiors such budgets as are necessary or are requested to maintain departmental functions at lowest possible cost consistent with quality and to operate within the limits of the approved budget.

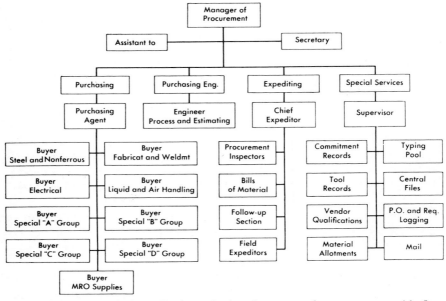

Fig. 2-12 Completely centralized purchasing department for a company with five plants manufacturing identical products with only MRO supplies purchased locally.

ORGANIZATION.

• Maintain a sound plan of organization, and propose for approval of immediate superiors modifications in and deviations from the basic plan of organization as may be required by changing circumstances to best facilitate management control and coordination of purchasing activities.

• Subject to approval of immediate superiors, select immediate subordinates— and approve, in turn, selection of their immediate subordinates.

• Ensure that competent employees are available at all times and in training for effective conduct of operations directed, and that subordinates concerned are kept sufficiently informed on current activities so that they are qualified to take over effectively in a superior's absence.

Date:		Incumbent:	
		Position:	Vice-President, Supply
Written by		Reports to:	
Approved by:		Department:	
		Division:	Corporate
		Location:	General Office

ACCOUNTABILITY OBJECTIVE

Direct the materials management supply activities of company, including procurement and all procurement aspects of material and inventory control, and to develop, issue and direct company policies and procedures for supply to support the management of the various businesses of the company.

DIMENSIONS

Purchase dollars (approximate):
   U.S., Foreign Plants
   All Other

Forty-six field, manufacturing, and research facilities, 200 branch facilities, 450 retail facilities, and the general office. Five major divisions, and the corporate offices; direct functional relationship with wholly owned subsidiaries, and a consulting relationship with paritally owned subsidiaries.
Annual operating budget of $_____ developed and administered for the corporation.

PERSONNEL

Direct:	Director, Raw Materials Supply
	Director, Energy & Hydrocarbons
	Director, Facilities Supply
	Director, Supply Development
Indirect:	(Through Direct Reporting) 57 personnel in the supply function
Functional:	Responsibility for 46 field purchasing units with 140 exempt and non exempt personnel.

NATURE AND SCOPE

The incumbent is one of six reporting to and taking his principal direction from the vice-chairman of the board and chief administrative officer. Others reporting to the vice-chairman of the board and chief administrative officer are: vice-president, law; vice-president, distribution and transportation; vice-president, finance; vice-president, marketing; and vice-president, employee relations.
The incumbent is responsible to procure for the company, at that point in the company where it is needed and economically useful, the company's requirements of raw materials, energy and hydrocarbons supplies, purchase parts, facilities equipment, packaging and containers, operating supplies, and all other purchased materials and services at the lowest possible cost consistent with accepted and necessary standards for efficiency, effectiveness, quality, and service, and thereby to maximize the profit contribution from the function under the most optimum conditions.
The incumbent shall be responsible to direct the energy supply activities of the company, and to contribute to the development of the policy positions of the corporation with respect to energy requirements. This includes long-range planning for energy and hydrocarbons supply; direction and development of strategies and successful negotiation for multiyear contracts for fuels, hydrocarbon materials, coal and electric power. The vice-president, supply is responsible for the total company needs of fuels, energy materials and purchased power to properly maintain and optimize operations. A detailed knowledge and understanding of alternate fuel capabilities, supply sources, costs and process economics is essential, as well as familiarity with federal and state government laws and commissions. The vice-president, supply must represent the corporation effectively to supply sources, utilities, industry groups and governing bodies as the officer in charge of energy procurement.
The incumbent will develop for the approval of the vice-chairman and president, and put into effect approved policies and programs, which will assure maximum effectiveness of the supply function throughout the corporation at all company plants and offices at all times. This can include the interpretation of the policies and procedures for the major operating units and locations within the Company. It is the responsibility of the vice-president, supply to administer these matters and to control compliance as necessary.
The incumbent is responsible to direct the audit of general practices, and internal procedures of mjaor operating units with respect to supply.

Fig. 2-13   Job description for vice-president, supply.

The incumbent will make available to operating organizations across the corporation, as requested, the services of supply specialists to assist in solving operational and supply problems.

The incumbent has the responsibility to approve, prior to placement, all purchase contracts up to $5 million and up to and including eighteen months duration. Reviews all contracts over $2 million or 18 months duration with the vice-chairman and president, and may delegate responsibility but always directs all supply functions in proper administration of those contracts under $2 million or 18 months duration.

The incumbent will submit timely reports to the vice-chairman and general managers of the operating divisions concerning the supply function, its level of performance, cost of its performance, and will submit to operating management reports concerning price trends, availability and recommendations for the development of substitute materials.

The incumbent is responsible to direct the supply activities such that negotiations will achieve appropriate contracts to maximize the opportunities for better service, prices and leverage for the materials, equipment and facilities supply and services needs of the corporation.

The incumbent will direct the maintenance of records of purchases and contracts sufficient to meet the requirements of the corporation in the analysis of records of purchases to optimize opportunities to improve sources, distribution of business, prices, and terms and to assure compliance with the current supply contracts. In support of this, incumbent shall direct the development, implementation, and maintenance of such systems and procedures necessary and ensure their compatibility with other corporate and divisional systems.

The incumbent will ensure the direction of a program of training and audit of field supply operations across the corporation, in line with the goals of supply, and in keeping with the general policies of the corporation in the highest standards of accounting, finance and law.

The incumbent is responsible to develop policies governing the disposal of surplus inventories, scrap materials, surplus and obsolete equipment, and excess facilities throughout the corporation.

The incumbent shall be responsible to direct the facilities supply activities in the corporation; to effect the interfaces with all operating and engineering units to provide services as required in regard to facilities supply; to evolve coordinated specifications with engineering, research, and operations input; to negotiate contracts for services; and to negotiate purchase contracts, license contracts, confidentiality agreements, and other requirements for facilities supply for all major machinery, equipment, tooling, and construction services throughout the world across the corporation.

The incumbent shall develop an interface between the distribution and transportation function and the supply function at all levels of operation, and direct the supply activities related thereto to the overall materials management benefit of the company.

The incumbent shall assure that competitive, promotable people are selected, trained, and developed in supply organizations throughout the corporation, and shall review the selection of proposed transfers of such supply personnel.

The incumbent shall collaborate with all standards groups in other activities across the corporation to promote standardization of common items throughout the corporation.

The incumbent will develop and direct programs for supply profit improvement and value engineering activities across the corporation.

The incumbent shall direct the management, development, and presentation of the supply five-year plan and supply operating budgets of the corporation.

The incumbent shall direct supply compliance with corporate policy and government regulation in the areas of Equal Employment Opportunity (EEO), small businesses, minority enterprises, Occupational Safety and Health Administration (OSHA), and product liability.

ACCOUNTABILITIES

1. Contribute to achievement of corporate and divisional profit objectives by directing the corporate supply function in the purchase, distribution, and inventory control of raw materials, energy and hydrocarbon supplies, facilities, equipment parts, supplies and services, negotiating and executing contracts that are within specifications and standards of quality and service while optimizing cost-inventory relationships.

2. Ensure energy coverage, supply, and development to meet the corporation's short and long-range needs through understanding of the total energy situation, its changing environment, and governmental restrictions affecting that environment.

3. Ensure corporate growth and vitality through the development and implementation of plans to introduce new techniques to improve the effectiveness of the supply function and to improve the measured value of the supply function in divisional operations throughout the corporation.

4. Develop effective organizational structure and dynamics by providing for the optimum number, kinds, and structures of jobs and through the selection, development, motivation, and maximum delegation to key supply executives in a manner that will contribute effectively to the profit of the operating divisions.

Fig. 2-13   (*Continued*)

5. Maintain managerial relationships of the highest order by encouraging and providing a timely, two-way flow of the information required for effective decision making by superiors, peers, and subordinates.

6. Contribute to the corporate and divisional images with their public of a dynamic, profitable, professionally managed, socially responsible business by establishing open, positive communication channels within the sphere of influence, both internally and externally, and taking positive steps to ensure this image.

7. Establish, implement, and maintain corporate policies, procedures, and communications which will ensure that the supply function is carried out legally, efficiently, and professionally throughout the corporation.

8. Keep personal achievements in tune with total corporate operation and continue personal growth and development for managerial effectiveness in all accountability areas through involvement in appropriate on-job and off-job activities.

Fig. 2-13   (*Continued*)

PERSONNEL.

• Establish high standards of performance for purchasing personnel and require performance in accordance with standards established.

• Regularly appraise the performance of immediate subordinates, measuring such performance against established goals and making necessary recommendations thereon.

• Maintain satisfactory personnel relations to assure just and equitable treatment of all personnel in accordance with the policies and contracts of the company and to promote cooperation through the department and stimulate all employees to their best efforts.

OPERATIONS.

• Through proper direction, control, coordination, and delegation, put into effect and ensure the implementation of approved departmental policies, plans, programs, and assignments and the attainment of approved objectives.

• Approve detailed operating programs and procedures recommended by immediate subordinates which fall within the framework of established divisional or departmental objectives and policies.

• Review progress against approved programs and consult with departmental personnel on means of improving the operation of the division or department.

• Coordinate the work of directly responsible department or section heads or group leaders and interpret and delegate to them their responsibilities for effecting approved objectives, policies, and programs.

• Assist in promoting the acceptance and installation of modern management techniques, with the objective of promoting efficiency, economy, and teamwork.

• Consult with other department heads to coordinate department programs and collaborate with other departments in such activities, projects, and programs as are of mutual interest and concern.

• Serve, as required, on regular or special committees and execute assignments connected therewith.

• Conduct such relationships not elsewhere specifically defined which are necessary to the accomplishment of company functions.

Purchasing Department Positions

Many types of purchasing positions have been established in recent years to handle some of the increasing responsibilities of purchasing organization. Persons in many of these positions have considerable influence on the activities and decisions of purchasing personnel in the department. Rather than a detailed job description of each, a brief discussion of the general area of responsibility will be given. A job description for each position would reflect the basic tenets of purchasing management suggested before and the specific responsibilities within the particular company.

Manager of Purchasing   This person would normally report to the head of the purchasing department, such as the director of purchasing or vice-president for purchasing, and would have responsibility for departmental, administrative and materials investigation activities within the scope of the purchasing department activities.

Manager of Purchasing Planning   All prominent planning activities associated with commodity groups or specialists and decentralized purchasing groups would be the responsibility of this person. Centralized or pooled purchasing projects and the establishment of national or corporate contracts would be directed by this executive, who would normally report to the head of the department.

Commodity Manager   In companies where major commodities have significant impact upon the profitability of the organization, commodity groups made up of commodity specialists are frequently established. The commodity manager would be responsible for supervising and coordinating the work of this group. This executive would ensure that the group developed purchasing programs for the most effective and economical purchase of the particular commodity. Normally the commodity manager would report to the head of the department.

Manager of Purchasing Development   This position would handle field purchasing relationships; functional audits; training, development, and promotion of personnel; and other administrative functions necessary for the development of the people comprising the organization.

Need for Experienced Buyers

Those members of the department who, through proper training and experience, can study markets, forecast trends, chart economic conditions, analyze values, and review new materials, new techniques, and new equipment should specialize in buying and be freed from time-consuming clerical duties. Each buyer should be backed with adequate clerical help to assist him or her and to allow time for the more technical phases of the assignment.

The buyer's primary function is to buy the categories assigned to him by reviewing specifications; locating potential suppliers; securing and analyzing quotations; selecting the suppliers; negotiating price, delivery, and any unusual conditions; signing the purchase order; and discussing quality, acceptance, and replacements. Buyers are responsible for the completeness and the accuracy of purchasing orders that carry their signatures.

Specialization by Buyers

In larger companies the buying function is normally divided, on the basis of categories of material or products, into sections which are assigned to buyers. In some companies, groups of buyers may be under the supervision of senior buyers or purchasing managers, who in turn report to the department head or to his assistant. There is a trend in some companies to employ buyers who work specifically for particular departments—such as engineering, research, parts, and advertising—which make specialized purchases.

Buyers are usually given assignments based on their abilities and interests or degree of specialization, with recognition of the fact that they can best perform in assignments that they like.

Frequently in large organizations, buyers operate as section supervisors, with other subordinate buyers, follow-up clerks, and all necessary clerical help reporting to them. This procedure gives strength to the department, as the follow-up clerk, buyer's secretary, and order typist concentrate, as does the buyer, on only a phase of the purchasing department job, and in consequence they become more expert in that phase. The education of the group is more rapid through concentration. The group may substitute for the buyer in his absence and may relieve him of the more time-consuming duties, allowing him more time to do a better job of the actual buying with all its attendant intangibles.

Because of the large amount of paperwork normally associated with MRO items, techniques such as stockless procurement, word processing, preissued checks, and systems contracting techniques are being used to free the buyer of the clerical tasks. These techniques relieve the buyer not only of his paperwork burden, but also of receiving, order typing, and accounts payable responsibilities, as well as often reducing inventories.

Typical Buyer Job Description
Reports to: Purchasing Manager

GENERAL FUNCTION. Performs buying assignments of a complex nature requiring substantial experience in assigned commodities and purchasing policy and procedure. Purchases items at the most favorable price consistent with quality, quantity, and specification requirement. Considerable independent judgment is required.

SPECIFIC DUTIES.

1. Maintains good company image and supplier relations through many daily business contacts.

2. Searches continuously for improved and/or less costly materials and supplies within the classifications assigned to him. Recommends to the engineering and development departments new or different materials and revised designs which he feels are of better quality or greater procurability or which can be obtained at lower cost.

3. Is responsible for selecting and maintaining sources of supply, using progressive purchasing techniques and methods.

4. Advises other departments of any changes in price or procedure and of restrictions on materials which would prohibit purchase. Also keeps interested departments advised with respect to lead time required to obtain critical materials.

5. Works with engineering, standards, and cost improvement groups for new designs, materials, or suppliers.

6. Visits vendor plants to analyze facilities and capabilities.

7. Completes each requisition by selecting the vendor, setting the proper price, and studying the terms, f.o.b. point, and other buying considerations. Calls to the attention of the purchasing manager when and in what quantities materials should be purchased to meet market conditions.

8. Expedites deliveries and, where necessary, gets engineering approval for alternate methods or materials if delivery is not available when required.

9. Interviews salespersons promptly and courteously to assist in accomplishing all the foregoing functions.

10. Corresponds tactfully with sources or potential sources of supply to overcome any misunderstandings, complaints, etc., or to secure further pertinent information regarding purchased material.

11. As required, reviews invoices which the invoice audit department refers for approval, particularly where price or other items do not agree with the purchase order.

12. Negotiates vendor rejections and advises vendor of reasons for rejections and cost incurred as a result of defective material.

13. Approves expense orders charged to defective purchased materials and negotiates settlement with vendor.

14. Issues debit memorandum to vendors on charges resulting from returned material and labor performed.

15. Issues credits under circumstances that require cancellation of debits or where adjustments are necessary to settle disputes.

16. Supervises the maintenance of current and potential source information in connection with materials under his jurisdiction.

17. Performs miscellaneous assignments as required.

18. The buyer is expected to use good judgment in consulting with his superior on all matters in which he is uncertain of the proper application of company policy. This is true regardless of the amount of money involved. However, all orders which commit the company to an expenditure of $XXX,XXX or more must be reviewed with the buyer's direct supervisor.

PURCHASING DEPARTMENT POLICIES AND PRACTICES

Policies and Functions

The responsibility and authority of the purchasing executive should be spelled out and thoroughly understood by top management and all department heads as a matter of good company planning and effectiveness.

However, this responsibility must be extended into basic policies and practices that must be understood by everyone in the organization who has direct or indirect dealings with the purchasing department. These persons must know, for example, the specific policies concerning vendor relations; negotiation of price and other conditions; issuance of the purchase order; and discussions of all related points, such as delivery, quality, and price, after the order is in force. Among the media for communicating this information to the company employees are (1) published regulations, (2) company informational booklets, and (3) departmental manuals, as described in Section 3.

One company in the nonferrous metals industry has defined its policies and procedures through the following published regulations.

GENERAL POLICY.   The authority and responsibility for purchasing rests with the Purchasing Department. This places the responsibility on those who have the interest and the skill to do the work properly and whose primary concern is in the performance of this special task. It permits the setting up of uniform policies with respect to seller relationships. It facilitates in prescribing the procedure, records, and routing, and also expedites inspection and approval of materials. It promotes economy by consolidating requirements and by setting up material standards for inventories.

PROVISIONS.

1. All requests for prices or for repair service, and all purchases, must be made by the Purchasing Department.
2. Salespersons should be received in other departments only with the approval of the Purchasing Department.
3. If necessary to interview salespersons regarding special details of their products, other departments should request such visits through the Purchasing Department.
4. In interviews with salespersons, no one who is not a member of the Purchasing Department should commit himself on preference for any product, the company's source of supply for any product, or give any information regarding performance or price which might in any way embarrass the Purchasing Department or the company.
5. All correspondence with suppliers should be through the Purchasing Department, except in special cases where the technical details involved make it advisable to delegate authority to others. In such cases, the Purchasing Department should receive copies of all correspondence.
6. With the exception of freight adjustments which are handled by the Traffic and Accounting Departments, the Purchasing Department should conduct all adjustment negotiations.

7. The Purchasing Department has full authority to question the quality and kind of material asked for, in order that the best interests of the company may be served.

8. It is within the province of the Director of Purchasing to delegate to representatives of the different departments authority to select material, but the actual purchasing can be done only on the company's approved purchase order through the Purchasing Department.

With the official rules and regulations in writing, all departments will understand the authority and the responsibilities of the purchasing department. This will also make known why vendor relations must be conducted or at least initiated through the purchasing department. If vendors look to others than purchasing personnel for business, the purchasing department becomes ineffective and company policies are weakened. Purchasing needs the complete cooperation of all management to maintain its responsibilities. However, it must be recognized that this cooperation must be earned through professional purchasing performance within the company. If employees of other departments insist on interviewing salespeople without the approval of purchasing, this situation should be resolved with the department head or, failing that, through the chief officer of the company or plant.

Conversely, if purchasing is to be maintained as the only door between the company and the fulfillment of its needs, the door must open two ways. Purchasing must be ever ready to bring in new ideas to the organization. It should see that vendors' representatives who offer worthwhile contributions for the company's welfare obtain prompt audiences with the proper people in the organization.

Functions Frequently Assigned to Purchasing

Many functions related to but not a part of purchasing fall under the supervision of the purchasing manager by inclusion in his title (e.g., Manager of Purchasing and Stores, Director of Purchasing and Packaging, or Manager of Materials) and sometimes by assignment on the company organization chart or in a statement of company policy. Such exceptions are based on the peculiar nature of the business or grouping of related activities, or on the unusual talents of the manager or his staff. Other companies may assign these extra functions or duties by implication or probably through their understanding that such functions, being closer to purchasing than other departments, are as much a part of the purchasing duties as is the actual buying function. Some assignments vary widely in their scope, including in rare cases probably every function performed in business.

There are, however, certain activities that are included fairly frequently in the overall purchasing function. The wide range of these functions is best illustrated by the results of a 1971 survey by N.A.P.M. Of the total responding members, 30 percent reported that one or more other functions were supervised by purchasing.

Expediting or Follow-up   The expediting or follow-up function is usually assigned to the purchasing department. It may also be assigned to production, operations, stores, or even the requisitioning department, possibly through material control. The expediting function may be set up in the purchasing department as a unit reporting separately as a subdepartment, or the follow-up clerks may work through and report to the separate buyers, functioning as assistant buyers as well as follow-up clerks.

The follow-up duties normally begin with the receipt of the requisition in the purchasing department. Then, with the mailing of the purchase order, sufficient time is allowed for the return of the signed acknowledgment. In some companies this is required only on significant orders. On failing to receive the acknowledgment, the expediter must see to it that the acknowledgment is forwarded, without alteration, to ensure that the contract exists as originally intended.

It may even be necessary to determine that the supplier has his orders placed with his subcontractors for adequate delivery and that production is properly scheduled. The reputation of the supplier and the condition of the inventory will have much to do with the degree of expediting effort required.

Once the follow-up clerk has assurance that the material has been shipped, he should work with the traffic department to ensure its receipt. There should be adequate controls to ascertain that the material is acceptable before the purchasing job is considered complete.

Traffic While traffic is the subject of Section 23, the survey cited in Section 1 shows that this function is supervised by 35 percent of purchasing departments. If outgoing transportation costs are much greater than incoming costs, traffic often is made a part of marketing or distribution.

Inventory Control Inventory control or management is the subject of Section 12. It is frequently within the province of purchasing (in 56 percent of the cases covered in the survey), as discussed in Section 1. Usually it is part of the production department, as a function of either production or material control. Or it may be part of materials management, as described earlier.

Stores keeping—the physical control, storage, and disbursement function—frequently is broken into two responsibilities, productive and nonproductive stores, which because of their nature and frequency of use may call for separate organizations.

Checking Invoices The purchasing department occasionally shares the responsibility for checking invoices in some companies; however, the trend is to relieve the buyer of this accounting function. Many companies feel that the responsibilities for purchasing and for invoice approval should be handled by separate departments as a matter of good internal control. Only invoices with discrepancies are referred to purchasing for the buyer's corrective action.

Traveling Inspectors The employment by purchasing departments of traveling inspectors who visit vendors' plants is an excellent step in the direction of guaranteeing timely receipt of high-quality materials when the volume of purchases can substantiate the expense. The traveling inspector should survey the plants, equipment, quality of workmanship, and the like of possible vendors to determine whether they should be seriously considered by the buyer as potential suppliers. Such traveling inspectors may also double as field expediters when necessary, as many of the problems of nondelivery are traceable to unsatisfactory quality. As representatives of purchasing, they should be briefed to handle almost any problem in geographical areas covered by their itineraries.

Purchasing Engineering   Purchasing engineers are employed by some of the larger companies. They have a variety of responsibilities, most of which are included in the following:

• *Specification analysis*, i.e., reviewing and translating current specifications and working with buyers, value analysts, and vendors on specification substitution for product availability, cost reductions, or quality improvements.

• Processing and estimating new purchased parts or changes in parts to supply the buyers with benchmarks to check vendors' quotations for new parts or to check vendors' estimates of cost increases due to authorized changes. May set target cost objectives for cost of new items.

• Reviewing with the buyers the equipment and facility lists submitted by potential vendors to be certain that they can qualify as suppliers prior to the issuance of requests for quotations.

• Liaison between purchasing and engineering on technical problems when requested by buyers or by the purchasing manager.

Specifications   In the many types of purchasing transactions, specifications are not only desirable but often necessary to ensure that the commodity required by the purchaser is correctly purchased. Specifications identifying or describing the purchase may be for physical or chemical characteristics, material and method of manufacture, performance, or standard.

Purchasing personnel have the responsibility to review purchase requirements to ensure that any necessary specifications are included in the purchase transaction. Usually these specifications are defined by the requisitioning department. Frequently the purchasing manager (or organization) is responsible for drawing up specifications, especially in terms of performance. Governmental purchasing organizations usually have a specification or standards group.

Value Analysis   *Value analysis* (covered in Section 8), the study of functions, has the goal of determining that every element of cost—whatever it may be—contributes in proportion to its value.

There is some question as to whether the purchasing department should have a separate value analysis section, whether the function should be left to the buyers to work out detailed plans with progressive vendors, or whether the value analyst should work closely with the buyers as the coordinator of the program. As the coordinator, the value analyst would be a consultant to the buyers or to their vendors and the moving force to keep the program in operation. The answer would vary according to the type and volume of products manufactured.

It has been generally agreed that the buyer is a key person in the value analysis program. He knows what items lend themselves to improvement, in what area the high dollar amounts are spent, what vendors can assist in the program, where the new ideas originate, and when to inject changes developed in the program. On the other hand, because of the pressure of keeping production flowing, the buyer can too easily set aside a cost improvement program unless there is some organized effort to keep him on target. The third possible arrangement, wherein value analysis is a staff service for the buying personnel, is therefore normally most successful in achieving results when the bulk of the company's purchases are high-volume repetitive orders.

Disposal of Obsolete Material and Equipment   Disposal of surplus and obsolete material and equipment is covered specifically in Section 24. This function is usually assigned to the purchasing department in order to obtain the best price fairly and to ensure effective disposal.

Purchasing personnel are in constant contact with the sources of material and equipment. Consequently, it is natural for the purchasing organization to have complete knowledge of arrangements for disposing of the same material or equipment when it becomes scrap or obsolete. Additionally, it is recognized that the purchasing organization is in a better position to have knowledge of prices, possible users of material or equipment, etc., than other departments in the company.

In order to ensure the effective disposal of suplus or obsolete material or equipment, the purchasing person must ensure that his efforts are effectively coordinated with those of the other departments in the company. Production, maintenance, and engineering usually have responsibilities in the disposal process.

Clerical Operations

Though often taken for granted, clerical operations are just as important as any other function of the purchasing department. The ratio of clerical help to buyers normally increases with the size of the company and the volume of materials and equipment purchased. Such clerical functions usually include typing, filing, reporting, record keeping, logging, operation of business and communications machines, and reception.

A well-organized, smoothly operating department expresses itself by promptly processing paperwork, having accurate, necessary records readily available, and seeing that buyers and others do not encounter roadblocks in the performance of their duties through delays or because information is misplaced.

The central filing section usually includes the requisitions, numerical purchase order files, vendor purchase order files, and any current informal data generally referred to.

Miscellaneous Services

Central order typing, wherein all orders are channeled through a typists' pool, is frequently used in larger departments. This has the advantage of spreading the workload from various buyers over the available typists and theoretically evens out the work flow. It has the disadvantage of having different typists, who lack a secretary's knowledge of a buyer's activities, working on that buyer's orders. This is frequently a training position with frequent turnover. The preparation of "requests to quote" forms is on some occasions similarly routed through general typing but normally is the responsibility of the buyer's secretary or of whoever handles the buyer's general correspondence.

Stenographic pools are used in some purchasing departments. However, because of the involved nature of purchasing correspondence and the fact that research, gathering of documents, and background are frequently required in the purchasing department, pool assignments usually do not prove as successful as assignments to individual buyers. With the latter arrangement, the stenographer will have better opportunity to learn the habits, routines, and commodities of the individual buyer and by performing more of his clerical work can extend his value to the company.

There is a trend toward the use of computerized equipment for the preparation of purchase orders or releases. The benefits of this procedure are reduction in clerical personnel and increased accuracy in preparation. (This subject is discussed in greater length in Section 15.)

NOTE: For further information on subjects covered in this section see the list of references in Section 30.

Section **3**

Policy and Procedure Manuals

EDITOR

Clifton L. Smith, C.P.M. *Manager, Worldwide Purchasing, Construction Equipment Group, International Harvester Company, Schaumburg, Illinois*

ASSOCIATE EDITORS

Donald F. Fair *Vice-President and Director of Purchases, Corporate Office for Research and Technical Services, W. R. Grace & Co., New York, New York*

W. P. Mitchell, C.P.M. *Manager, Regional and Technical Purchasing, Hunt-Wesson Foods, Inc., Fullerton, California*

Effective and efficient purchasing performance requires that policies and procedures be clearly understood by all company personnel. Company policy should define the responsibilities of the purchasing function, the character of that function, and the nature of specific constraints imposed by governmental laws and regulations and other company policies.

Purchasing policy and procedure manuals should be written to ensure that all company personnel, not just those assigned purchasing responsibilities, understand the "rules of the game." Purchasing manuals, whether of policies, procedures, or instructions, should be established as the recognized authority on the particular subject, easily understood and adaptable to all situations. Availability of a written purchasing policy and of a purchasing manual has come to be recognized as one of the hallmarks, or criteria, for identifying a mature, competent, and professional purchasing organization.

PURPOSE AND USE OF MANUALS

Purchasing manuals may take many forms. It is necessary to differentiate clearly among policies, procedures, and instructions. It is conceivable that all three might be needed in order to ensure clarity of purpose.

It is important to recognize that all company personnel understand the purpose of a company purchasing manual. An example of such a statement is shown in Fig. 3-1.

In large multilocation, worldwide companies, and in particular those with highly decentralized control, a purchasing policy manual is essential. Such a manual, normally developed and maintained at the corporate purchasing executive level, must communicate the vital areas of concern in broad terms. Such policies should provide for and require that the decentralized operation(s) comply with stated corporate policy. This is usually done by means of a procedure or instruction manual which the decentralized functional responsibility develops and maintains. That manual should implement in specific detail the purpose, definition, criteria, and procedural instructions to be followed by all personnel having any procurement responsibility.

Purchasing manuals for smaller companies may include any or all of the poli-

W.R. Grace & Co.		PURCHASING MANUAL
SUBJECT: PURPOSE OF MANUAL	Issued by: Corporate Office for Research & Technical Services	

	Page:
	    1 of 2
		Date Approved:
		    9/15/

I. THE PURPOSE OF THIS MANUAL IS:

    A. To inform Purchasing personnel of the general policies.

    B. To instruct Purchasing personnel in the application of standard purchasing practices and procedures necessary to effectively contribute to an efficient and profitable division operation.

    C. To assist personnel engaged in the purchasing function to attain a high degree of proficiency in their procurement activities.

II. THIS MANUAL IS DESIGNED TO:

    A. Provide those persons who work in Purchasing Departments with an understanding of their responsibilities, objectives, limitations and duties within the framework of the overall company organization.

    B. Acquaint all employees of W.R. Grace & Co. with the purpose and functions of the Purchasing Departments.

    C. Convey to our employees, and through them to our vendors and our customers, a clear understanding of our purchasing policies and objectives.

    D. Outline the practices, principles and procedures to be followed in the performance of the purchasing function.

    E. Provide a sound basis of conduct and performance for the guidance of purchasing personnel and to provide a fund

Fig. 3-1 Statement on the purpose of a company purchasing manual.

cies, procedures, and instructions. Each organization must determine its own best way to provide the required instructions for clarity of understanding and control.

All purchasing manuals should include a foreword which establishes the authenticity and requirement for adherence thereto. In larger companies, such as W. R. Grace & Company, the corporate purchasing manual may appear to be

W.R. Grace & Co.		**PURCHASING MANUAL**
SUBJECT: PURPOSE OF MANUAL	**Issued by:** Corporate Office for Research & Technical Services	
	Page: 2 of 2	**Date Approved:** 9/15/

of information that will be invaluable in the training of new purchasing employees.

F. To gain benefits of standardization in practice and procedures and to insure uniformly proper conduct of our purchasing activities.

G. To establish reasonable standards against which the Financial Group's Internal Auditing Department and the Outside Auditors can measure the performance of the divisions' purchasing functions.

H. To be adapted in whole or in part or used as a guide in the preparation of a purchasing manual for division purchasing departments.

Fig. 3-1 (*Continued*)

one of policy, including standards of performance, which requires the groups, divisions, and other lower organization levels to implement corporate policy by issuing their own operating instructions (see Fig. 3-2, from W. R. Grace & Company's purchasing manual).

An example of a foreword used in a purchasing manual made up of procedures

---

W.R. Grace & Co.		PURCHASING MANUAL
SUBJECT: FOREWORD	Issued by: Corporate Office for Research & Technical Services	
	Page: 1 of 1	Date Approved: 11/15/

This Corporate Purchasing Manual contains instructions regarding the basic policy, procedure and practice for procurement in W.R. Grace & Co.

These instructions are for the guidance of all personnel who participate in the actions and decisions relating to procurement and for all other personnel in order to give them a more complete understanding of purchasing policies, procedures and practices.

This Manual is not intended to provide operating instructions for the Groups or Divisions, but is to serve as a continuing reminder of the duties and responsibilities involved in W.R. Grace & Co.'s relations with the companies that supply the goods and services that are required for the development, manufacture and sales of its products.

It is good business to establish purchasing principles and to live up to them. Well-defined statements of objective, responsibilities and limitations can be of great value in carrying out the procurement function.

Recommendations for improvements or additions to this Manual's content will be appreciated.

K.G. Scheye
Corporate Vice President
W.R. Grace & Co.

Fig. 3-2   A foreword for a manual that establishes corporate policy.

and/or instructions is that shown in Fig. 3-3, from Hunt-Wesson Foods, Inc.'s purchasing manual. You will note the variance between this foreword and that of the W. R. Grace manual, which reflects the difference in philosophy between the two manuals. The manual of W. R. Grace is more of a policy manual; that of Hunt-Wesson Foods is more of a procedure or instruction manual.

Purchasing management should not avoid the much needed effort of preparing a purchasing manual for lack of understanding of the difference between policies, procedures, instructions, methods, etc. The important thing is that written documentation, regardless of its title, should be available and in use to ensure adherence to the standards desired. The following is a series of definitions which may

---

FOREWORD

In order that Hunt-Wesson Foods, Inc. might have a means for assuring continuity and uniformity in its purchasing practices, the following pages have been prepared. As an added benefit, these procedures provide bases for proper auditing both of the *function* within the corporation, and the Purchasing *department* as an entity.

Most of the procedures which follow are basically descriptive of practices and forms which already exist, having evolved over the years as being most practicable. In many cases, however, no written summarization existed, which oftentimes created difficulty when enforcement became necessary. There are, in addition, a number of comparatively new procedures—such as major work-contract provisions, and packaging development purchasing—which, because they may represent a noticeable shift from previous company practice, should be carefully studied.

Any procedures manual is meaningless unless it derives its authority from corporate policy. In the case of the purchasing function, such authority is found primarily in corporate administration policies numbered A-1 through A-14. There are, in addition, references to required Purchasing involvement to be found in various policies and procedures issued by other departments, particularly Finance and Legal. Such references are noted in appropriate sections of the following pages.

It is hoped that issuance of this manual will serve a twofold purpose: first, as a basis for uniformity and efficiency in the company's procurement of goods and services; and, second, as groundwork for proper training of Hunt-Wesson personnel, both within Purchasing and outside it.

Fig. 3-3 A foreword for a manual that establishes procedures.

---

assist in a better understanding of the type of information included in a purchasing manual:

Directive. A general instructional order issued by central office normally indicating that a specific activity is to be performed.

Instruction. Knowledge, information, etc., given or taught describing the methods to be used.

Method. A prescribed way of doing anything; mode; procedure; process; especially a regular, orderly, definite procedure or way of teaching, investigating, etc.

Policy. A stated governing principle, plan, or course of action which normally establishes general parameters for the organization to follow in carrying out its responsibilities.

Practice. A stated method or procedure to do, exercise, or perform frequently or usually; to make a habit or custom of.

Procedure. The act, method, or manner of proceeding in some process or course of action. Usually, a series of related tasks that list chronologically the sequence to be followed in performing the work to be accomplished.

Regulation. A course of action, or a rule, ordinance, or law by which conduct, etc. is regulated in an authoritative manner.

Rule. An established guide or regulation for an action, conduct, method, arrangement, etc. that must be followed. Usually, a fixed principle that determines conduct, habit, custom, etc.

Standard. A level or grade of excellence, attainment, etc., regarded as a goal or measure of adequacy which aids planning, contributes to efficiency, and expedites control.

NEED FOR AND VALUE OF MANUALS

A number of writers have clearly stated the value of the purchasing manual.

> Employees need manuals to expedite their training and indoctrination. Salesmen request statements of policy and procedures to help them in their sales effort and to promote good supplier and customer relations. Auditors recommend manuals as a point of measurement of approved procedures against which to audit; methods analysts and computer programmers need this kind of work-flow information to develop improved purchasing systems.[1]

Needs for a purchasing manual are summarized as follows:

1. Define purchasing authority and procedures
2. Clarify and improve relationship with other functions
3. Develop improved policies and procedures
4. Standardize and communicate approved practices
5. Train new personnel and guide others
6. Promote supplier understanding and cooperation
7. Fulfill management and/or government requirements
8. Provide standards for evaluating performance
9. Elevate and improve purchasing function

Corporate Policies

Development of any departmental manual is dependent solely on established corporate policies. The following is taken from The Pillsbury Company's *Policies Manual* and is intended to set the guidelines for the issuance of policies within its divisions and departments.

> Corporate policies will be issued by the Executive Office to establish fundamental and basic requirements for the foreseeable future which will govern the actions and decisions of all levels of management. They will pertain to corporate reasons only and will be widespread, involving all or most segments of the corporation.
>
> They will be restricted to obligatory actions which limit the freedom of the operating companies and the corporate staffs to the extent specified, whether they be stated in a restrictive or permissive context. They will reflect the concept that the operating companies are free to conduct their business within legal and ethical limitations in all areas and to all degrees except when restricted by corporate policy. Policies will not be issued to instruct operating units and corporate staffs on how to conduct their business or on what course of action or approach should normally apply.

---

[1]*Guide to Purchasing,* 1.7, "Purchasing Policies and Manuals," National Association of Purchasing Management, New York, N.Y., 1968.

The form of corporate policy may be specific or general, broad or narrow, depending upon the subject and limitation imposed. Reasons and procedures will not be incorporated in policy statements. In the event it is necessary to issue instructions or specify procedures, Standard Practice Instructions will be issued by the Corporate Offices.

Policy Manuals

This type of manual explains the company's purchasing policies and usually consists of an 8½- by 11-inch binder or booklet. It is distributed to other departments within the company as well as to purchasing personnel, and it is often made available to vendors to acquaint them with the company's policies.

Procedure Manuals

As procedures change frequently, while policies, if sound, rarely change, some companies issue, for internal distribution, separate procedure manuals which include samples of the various forms used and explain their usage in detail. Manuals vary in size and content according to the company involved and the complexity and number of the forms used. Companies engaged in government contracts, for example, find it advisable to prepare procedure manuals which include government forms that are necessary in the company's area of responsibility.

Policy and Procedure Manuals

In many companies, particularly smaller ones, the purchasing manual combines both policies and procedures in one volume. Figure 3-4 shows a typical index page from such a manual used by A. B. Dick Company.

Tailoring Manuals to Individual Needs

There is no standard concept of the contents of a purchasing manual, and thus variations will be noted from one company to another. As a whole, manuals incorporate such matters as organization, responsibility, authority, functions, company policy, department policy, procedures, references, specifications, and specific instructions regarding company purchase orders and acceptances. Possibilities are limitless, as shown by Fig. 3-5. The individual manual, however, is tailored to the needs and requirements of its own organization.

Even the style of the manual must be tailored to the individual needs. Memorandums may suffice in some companies. Irrespective of style, manuals are usually indexed and placed in standard looseleaf binders so that amendments can be made easily when necessary. Purchasing is not static. It is alive. As changes in policies or procedures become advisable, they should be made without delay. A purchasing manual is as necessary to a modern purchasing department as a sales manual is to the sales department, an accounting manual to the accounting department, or as any manual is to a department where a definition is required of what is to be done and how it is to be accomplished.

Suggestions on manual structure and content are given in the following pages.

ABDICK®   PURCHASING MANUAL

SUBJECT		NO.
INDEX TO PURCHASING MANUAL INSTRUCTIONS		

NO.	SUBJECT
P-5	Personal Purchases
P-6	Purchase Requisition Approval
P-7	Purchasing Auditing Practices
Q-1	Quotation Request Practice
Q-2	Quotation Analysis
Q-3	Quality Control/Quality Assurance
R-1	Receiving
R-2	Releasing Methods
R-3	Receiving Inspection
R-4	Requisitioning Methods
R-5	Relations with Other Company Functions
S-1	Sub-Contracting
S-2	Surplus/Scrap Disposal
S-3	Standard Costs
S-4	Supplier Relations
S-5	Supplier Suggestions

I N S T R U C T I O N

ISSUED BY:	DATE ISSUED	SUPERSEDES ISSUE DATED
Clifton L. Smith		10/28/
MANAGER - PROCUREMENT	4/19/	PAGE 4 OF 5

71-1

Fig. 3-4   An index page from a purchasing manual.

Since some larger company manuals run to as many as 200 pages, it would be impractical to attempt to publish an entire model manual. The excerpts that are included in this section, however, should provide basic material that can be adapted by companies of any size to their particular needs. The editors of the section are indebted to the following companies for permission to use material from their purchasing manuals: Aluminum Company of America; A. B. Dick

WHAT DO MANUALS COVER?

The ground covered by a purchasing manual will of course depend on its size and its audience— for example, a small pamphlet used as a handy reference for buyers will rarely go into as much detail as a full-scale policy manual distributed to suppliers and other departments. But the scope of topics touched upon in manuals today is virtually limitless. *Purchasing* Magazine's survey turned up over 100 areas that respondents have included in theirs. Here, in alphabetical order for checklist referral, are many of them.

A-B-C analysis	Job descriptions
Acknowledgments	Leadtimes
Adjustments	Learning curves
Association memberships	Leasing
Back-orders	Legal aspects of purchasing
Bid evaluations	Letters of intent
Blanket orders	Licensing
Books and periodicals	Linear programming
Buyers' assignments	Long-term agreements
Buyers' authority	Make-or-buy
Cancellations and claims	Material review boards
Capital purchases	Negotiation
Cash discounts	Organization of purchasing
Catalogs	Overs and unders
Change orders	Patents
Classified material	Personal purchases
C.o.d. orders	PERT/CPM
Commodity coding	Petty cash orders
Competitive bidding	Plant visits
Conflict of interest	Pooled orders
Consignment purchases	Production control
Construction purchases	Progress payments
Consulting services	Public relations
Contracting with employees	Purchase orders
Cost/price analysis	Quality control
Cost reduction	Receiving
EDP methods	Relations with other departments
Engineering change notices	Releasing methods
EOQ methods	Requirements contracts
Ethics	Requisitioners' authority
Expediting	Requisitioning methods
Filing systems	Research and development purchases
Fleet purchases	Royalties
Foreign buying	Rush orders
Government regulations	Samples
Household moves	Sealed bids
Incentive contracts	Security
Inspection	Service agreements
Insurance	Services purchases
Interplant transfers	Short-order methods
Interviewing	Sole sourcing
Inventory control	Specifications review
Invoice approval	Speculative buying

Fig. 3-5 "What Manuals Could Cover," *Purchasing,* Jan. 11, 1972. *(Reproduced by permission.)*

Standard costs
Standardization
Strike procedures
Subcontracting
Supplier certification
Supplier coding
Supplier contacts
Supplier evaluation
Supplier relations
Supplier selection
Supplier suggestions
Surplus/scrap disposal
Taxes
Terms and conditions

Time and material orders
Tooling and patterns
Trade relations
Traffic
Training and development
Travel & entertainment
Trial orders
Unpriced orders
Value analysis
Vending machine agreements
Verbal orders
Warehousing
Warranties

Fig. 3-5   (*Continued*)

Company; Hunt-Wesson Foods, Inc.; and W. R. Grace & Company. The length and style of the excerpts are intended as guides for readers who wish to develop purchasing manual sections on any of the other subjects discussed in this handbook.

PROGRAM FOR PREPARING A PURCHASING MANUAL

The program for preparing a manual, as outlined in Fig. 3-6, may appear to be time-consuming and elaborate. However, experience has shown that manuals are necessary and minimal. The assignment of developing a manual can be the responsibility of one member of purchasing or the responsibility can be shared. When one company switched to a material-management type of organization, it was necessary to completely rewrite its purchasing manual. Each member of a four-member team was given specific assignments based upon special abilities and background. Some sections were made joint efforts by two or more team members. Most of the work was accomplished outside office hours and to an exact time schedule. A manual prepared for circulation in a purchasing department only, for example, is not effective beyond that department. Thus other departments were consulted. Consequently, these other departments felt they had a part in the development of purchasing policy and would cooperate with it. After suggestions agreed upon have been incorporated in the proposed manual, copies should be distributed by the head of the purchasing department to the chief executive officer of the company, to each department head, and to the assistants and buyers in the purchasing department.

A reasonable length of time should be allowed for purchasing personnel to familiarize themselves with the contents of the manual. Then the head of the purchasing department should meet with his group and discuss the manual's contents chapter by chapter. He will thus learn whether or not the contents of the manual are understood and will be able to correct any existing misunderstandings. He should also make certain that his employees understand, appreciate, and use the purchasing manual policies and procedures in their dealings with others within the company, as well as in their outside contacts. The manual will then be an effective tool for improved interdepartmental relations with vendors and for more successful and outstanding purchasing performance.

Program for Preparing a Purchasing Manual

1. Do your own thinking. Decide what you want, why you want it.

2. Get permission of top operating executive to cross department lines in exploring and formulating policies. (Policies to be submitted again for final approval.)

3. Collect and compile material:
   a. Start a tentative index of subjects.
   b. Jot down unwritten policies carried in minds of old-timers or observed by company custom.
   c. Record information already appearing in company bulletins, letters, or pamphlets that concern purchasing.
   d. Collect other information defining purchasing subjects from organization charts, job descriptions, procedure manuals, correspondence, reports, etc.
   e. Collect manuals issued by other companies. Request information on their development.

4. Evaluate this material. Are existing policies compatible with stated objectives of the company or those of other departments?

5. Select and edit retained material so evolved policy has companywide applicability and value for frequent and permanent reference.

6. Make a draft of policy manual.

7. Circulate draft to other department heads and associates in purchasing department. Ask for suggestions, confer personally with each man. Try to reconcile all possible points of controversy.

8. Rewrite and resubmit on basis that document now reflects participation by all concerned.

9. If manual is also intended for vendors, submit it to a few of them for comment and review at this point.

10. Submit document to chief executive officer. Include summary of all expressed comments secured for or against policies.

11. If top executive approves, get his foreword and signature to make it an official company statement of purchasing objectives and policies.

Fig. 3-6   Program or steps for preparing a purchasing manual. (*Reprinted by special permission of* Purchasing Week.)

MANUAL STRUCTURE AND CONTENTS

The basic contents of a comprehensive purchasing manual will vary widely, as has been noted, depending on the size and nature of the purchasing organization. The suggestions and the sample manual sections that follow should, of course, be adapted to a department's special needs. The sample sections on interdepartmental relationships from the Alcoa manual, for example, represent a large company's approach to the subject, but may be somewhat formal for the small company. Nevertheless, the principles enunciated are applicable to both.

Index or Table of Contents

The illustration in Fig. 3-7, taken from the W. R. Grace purchasing manual, extensively covers subjects for a suggested index or table of contents to be included in any purchasing manual. Whether the organization chooses to refer to it as a

W.R. Grace & Co.		PURCHASING MANUAL
SUBJECT:	Issued by: Corporate Office for Research & Technical Services	
TABLE OF CONTENTS	Page: 1 of 5	Date Approved: 9/15/

Fig. 3-7 Table of contents for a purchasing manual.

W.R.Grace & Co.   PURCHASING MANUAL

SUBJECT:	Issued by: Corporate Office for Research & Technical Services
TABLE OF CONTENTS	Page: 2 of 5	Date Approved: 9/15/

Fig. 3-7   (*Continued*)

W.R. Grace & Co. PURCHASING MANUAL

SUBJECT: TABLE OF CONTENTS

Issued by: Corporate Office for Research & Technical Services

Page: 3 of 5

Date Approved: 9/15/

PAGE NO.

Fig. 3-7 *(Continued)*

W.R.Grace & Co.		PURCHASING MANUAL	
SUBJECT: TABLE OF CONTENTS	Issued by: Corporate Office for Research & Technical Services		
	Page: 4 of 5	Date Approved · 9/15/	

Fig. 3-7   (*Continued*)

W.R.Grace & Co.	PURCHASING MANUAL

SUBJECT:	Issued by: Corporate Office for Research & Technical Services
TABLE OF CONTENTS	Page: 5 of 5 — Date Approved: 4/1/

Fig. 3-7   (*Continued*)

policy or procedure manual is immaterial. The range of coverage will depend upon the nature and size of the organization.

The Foreword

This should contain a signed copy of a letter from the president of the company, or the chief executive officer, addressed to the company's executive staff, general managers, and purchasing managers. It gives official approval to the policies and procedures that follow. One such foreword has already been shown in Fig. 3-2.

EXAMPLES FROM PURCHASING MANUALS

Organization

This part contains an organization chart of the titles and names of personnel in the purchasing department and often indicates to whom the head of the purchasing department reports.

The manager of purchasing (or the purchasing agent, depending on the company organization) has various functions and responsibilities. Usually included in his accountability are that he:

1. Provide a continuous purchasing organization of qualified personnel.

2. Develop company-wide purchasing objectives, policies, programs, and procedures for the negotiation and acquisition of materials, equipment, supplies, and services.

3. Delegates purchasing assignments and related activities as necessary, including many of the following functions:

- Coordinate purchasing procedures throughout the company.
- Act as company spokesperson on all matters pertaining to purchasing.
- Institute the reports necessary to permit analysis of purchasing department performance.
- Develop and administer a program for the development of personnel suitable for promotion with the company.
- Disseminate to other departments information designed to promote efficient operation of their function.
- Negotiate and approve term contracts and leases with suppliers to the best interest of the company.
- Consolidate purchases of like or common items to obtain the maximum economic benefits.
- Purchase all equipment, supplies, and services for company use in such a manner that the maximum value will be obtained for the money expended. Purchases shall be made from qualified manufacturers whose reputations, financial positions, and price structures are sufficiently adequate for consideration as logical sources of supply.

- Arrange for the disposal or negotiate the sale of surplus materials and equipment, including obsolete stock, scrap, and turnings.
- Cooperate with other departments of the company to maintain inventories at a satisfactory operating and dollar-value level.
- Study markets to analyze prices paid for materials and equipment, generally define how to obtain savings through improved specifications and supervision of supply sources, and recommend changes in quantities to be ordered when conditions warrant.
- Utilize known contacts and sources to expedite deliveries of needed material and equipment.
- Work with other departments of the company to promote better customer and supplier relations.
- Work with the standards committee in establishing standardization of materials and supplies used throughout the company.
- Provide liaison with government agencies for handling requests for information concerning the company's ability to handle contracts which may be proposed in the event of mobilization.
- Prepare and submit for approval annual purchasing department operating budgets. Control budget expenditures by before-the-fact authorizations and after-the-fact approval of such expenditures.

For use in companies having more than one plant:

- Conduct periodic audits of division and subsidiary purchasing departments to ensure compliance with approved policies and procedures as outlined in the purchasing manual.
- Purchase or assist in the purchase of materials, equipment, supplies, and services for divisions or subsidiaries when requested to do so.

For use when purchasing and traffic departments are combined:

- Establish and administer policies and procedures related to the use of carrier or transportation facilities, including agency to be employed, rate compliance, expediting action, liability protection, filing of claims, etc.
- Protect company's interest in all matters involving freight rates, freight classifications, transportation costs, and transportation services. Represent the company before carrier rate committees and individual carriers in the negotiation of transportation rates.
- Maintain adequate rate tariff files and follow proceedings of regulatory bodies and carrier rate committees on matters affecting rates on the company's traffic as well as on the traffic of competitors.
- Arrange travel accommodations for employees and secure transportation tickets when requested to do so.

Purchasing Policy

This is one of the most important sections of the manual because it places the authority and responsibility for purchasing in the purchasing department. Purchasing is one of the most common of business activities. It means the acquisition of some kind of property and the giving of an accepted price or consideration in return.

Every transaction between a buyer and a seller involving the transfer of property is a contract. Some contracts are of the simplest form, while others are made the subject of lengthy written agreements defining in technical terms the nature of the material, the method of payment, and other contractual conditions.

From the inception to the consummation of a transaction between a buyer and a seller, many important problems are involved, and the proper handling of these and the administering of the business features connected with them are vital factors in the successful operation of the company.

For these reasons, the authority and responsibility of purchasing rest with the purchasing department. This places the responsibility on those who have the interest and the skill to do the work properly and whose primary concern is in the performance of this special task. It permits the establishing of uniform policies with respect to seller relationships. It assumes adequate controls over expenditures.

The purchasing department is to establish and administer purchasing policies, institute reports necessary to permit analysis of purchasing performance, negotiate and approve term contracts, consolidate purchases of like or common items, analyze prices paid for materials and equipment, and generally define how to obtain savings and to coordinate purchasing procedures.

Additional policies are summarized briefly:

1. All requests for prices or for specified services and all purchases must be made by the purchasing department. In some instances, authority to request prices may be delegated to others.

2. If it is necessary to interview salespersons regarding the details of their products, other departments should request such visits through the purchasing department.

3. Only purchasing personnel should discuss prices and quantity with supplier representatives.

4. All correspondence with suppliers is to be through the purchasing department, except in special cases where the technical details involved make it advisable to delegate authority to others. In such cases, the purchasing department must receive copies of all correspondence.

5. With the exception of freight adjustments when handled by the traffic department, the purchasing department will conduct all adjustment negotiations.

6. The purchasing department has full authority to question the quality, quantity, and kind of material asked for, in order that the best interests of the company may be served.

7. In cases of extreme emergency, and only in such cases, an exception to the above rule may be made with the understanding that the head of the department placing the emergency order personally assumes the responsibility of immediately

following up the verbal order, given by himself or his representative, with the proper department requisition.

An example of a brief but clear outline of purchasing policy is that of Hunt-Wesson Foods, Inc. Its policy is divided into twelve broad, but briefly stated, categories:

1. Purchasing policy and objectives
2. Supplier contacts
3. Negotiations with suppliers
4. Matters of security relating to purchasing
5. Suppliers' quotations
6. Purchase commitments
7. Selecting sources of supply
8. Purchase order specifications
9. Purchasing contracts
10. Vendor relations
11. Trade relations
12. Gifts and gratuities

The company's purchasing policy and objectives are briefly stated as follows: "Planned growth for any Corporation requires profitable results in all management areas. Therefore, Policy Objectives have been formulated to outline the responsibilities and duties of the Purchasing function within our corporation. The expressed goal herein is to provide for both profitable expenditure of Company funds and efficient service to requisitioning departments."

The purchasing department has as its basic goals the following:

• To seek, develop, and maintain reliable sources of supply that will create and encourage a competitive buying atmosphere
• To secure materials, equipment, services, and supplies in accordance with the quality, quantity, and delivery requirements of the requisitioning department
• To obtain on all items the lowest cost that quality, quantity, delivery, and safety permit
• To organize and use our total buying power in a manner that will yield maximum benefits to the company
• To maintain good supplier relations to promote the company's reputation for fair dealing
• To recommend standardization or substitution of materials, equipment, or supplies whenever practical and to the best interest of the company
• To develop and maintain a qualified purchasing staff by selective hiring, planned training, and continued evaluation and performance

The scope of all purchasing policy includes all areas of acquiring goods and services for the company, excepting those of field buying, commodity buying, advertising/graphics. It is intended that this policy work in harmony with and supplement recorded policies of all other departments. Whenever apparent conflict or contradiction arises, the corporate director of purchasing shall consult with the vice-president of administration for guidance and clarification.

Hunt-Wesson's policy on supplier contacts states briefly: "All contacts with suppliers regarding negotiation of price, quantity, delivery, etc., are handled by purchasing. When the needs of a particular group (e.g., R&D or engineering) are for information of a technical nature and where discussions with a supplier may continue over a considerable period of time, it is not necessary for a buyer to become involved in these preliminary discussions with a vendor. However, there must be no commitment to buy on the part of these other departments, and purchasing is to be kept informed, by copies, of all written communications between other departments and suppliers."

Product Purchasing Responsibility In general, product purchasing responsibility is determined by the nature of the material or fabricated part in question, the attempt being made to see that all identical, similar, or closely related items are handled in the same buying office. This allows for substitutions to be made of one material or part for another when desirable from a price or delivery standpoint.

1. Scrutinize requisitions, letters, memos, and quotations for correctness and clarity.

2. Keep interested departments informed on proper lead times required and on all unusual supply situations.

3. Follow up and expedite delivery as deemed desirable or necessary after issuance of purchase orders.

4. Cooperate to adjust deliveries up or down when necessary.

Relations with Other Departments

This subject is covered in the *Standard Procedure for Purchasing* of the Aluminum Company of America.[2]

> The Purchasing Department supplies the purchasing needs of all departments of the Company. In performing this function it is charged with optimizing the combination of quality, service and economy in the purchase of goods and services. How well it does the job in the area of service is reflected, to a great extent, by the attitude of the other departments in their daily relations.
>
> The Purchasing Department is in constant contact with other departments, and cooperation and mutual confidence are absolutely essential. The Buyer should be knowledgeable of and must be in sympathy with the particular requirements of the various users of material or equipment and must exercise tact, discretion and diplomacy to establish and maintain harmonious relations with these users.
>
> The Buyer is the real link between the other departments in the Company, and its potential and existing suppliers. How well the Buyer coordinates and performs his duties as the liaison in eliminating the bottlenecks, errors and inefficiencies in the satisfying of needs has a great influence on the performance of other departments, and the overall profitability of the Company.

[2]Reprinted with permission.

If, at any time, there is any question of the work overlapping that of another department, the duties of each should be clearly defined and arranged on the basis of the best interests of the Company.

Engineering Department The Aluminum Company of America defines the role of an engineering department as follows.[3]

The Engineering Department is responsible for the design and successful operation of the special machines and equipment which are built to order, either in the Company's shops or elsewhere. It is also responsible for the efficient layout of equipment and for results obtained from standard machinery and equipment purchased for construction and operation. The engineers have definite materials requirements expressed in terms of strength, rigidity, toughness, hardness, ductility, or other physical properties. They also have a good working knowledge of the various materials available which embrace these desired properties. In determining which of the materials can be obtained most advantageously, however, the Purchasing Department's training and experience are required.

The members of the Engineering Department should not be too exacting in their specifications. They should recognize that such considerations as price, economy, and convenience in production should be weighed along with those of design, and that the Purchasing Department should have reasonable latitude in making purchases. The engineer does his best job when he allows for plenty of competition, as competition brings out the best in latest developments as well as the best prices. On the other hand, the Purchasing Department should not push the matter of price or supplier to the point where it interferes with real engineering requirements.

The functions of the two divisions are complementary and supplementary, and close cooperation is essential if the best results are to be obtained. It is always important to incorporate in design every possible advantage that can be derived from intelligent purchasing. Good design can suffer tremendously if it is not backed up by intelligent selection and purchase of materials and parts.

The Engineering Department cannot be expected to know all about prices, size and quantity extras, time required for delivery, or extras for special conditions like tolerances. The Purchasing Department should advise of any change in specification or substitute material which in its opinion would lower the cost without sacrifice of results.

The Engineering Department should request information on engineering materials, supplies, and equipment through the Purchasing Department. No major engineering service should be accepted from any company without the Purchasing Department first determining whether that company would be acceptable as the supplier. The Purchasing Department should refer salesmen and information regarding engineering matters to the Engineering Department when there is something which may be of advantage to the Company. The Purchasing Department, however, should not waste the time of the engineers by having them do interviewing which should properly be done by the Purchasing personnel.

Legal Aspects of Purchasing

This section of a manual is not intended to be an exhaustive study of the legal principles having to do with the purchasing function. Only general principles should be discussed and interpreted, in the hope that with some basic understand-

[3]Reprinted with permission.

ing of their rights and liabilities, buyers may at least avoid serious controversy and litigation.

The legal section of any purchasing manual should always be written in cooperation with legal counsel to assure that buyers are fully informed of the legal ramifications of their acts and clearly understand in what situations they should consult legal counsel.

Following a general outline of the law of agency and the law of contracts and sales, the manual could cover appropriate parts of the Uniform Commercial Code. (Legal considerations in purchasing are covered at length in Section 4.)

Various laws that have special relevance to purchasing have received special attention in some larger company manuals.

Law of Warranty   Warranties are of two sorts, expressed and implied. An *expressed warranty* is one that is defined and negotiated into a mutually satisfactory contract between the buyer and supplier. In the absence of expressed warranties of quality, fitness, or performance of product, if the buyer makes known to the seller the particular purpose for which the supplies or equipment are required, relying on the seller's judgment and skill, there is an *implied warranty* that the goods shall be reasonably fit for that purpose. The inclusion of an expressed warranty covering any of these points renders the implied warranty void, since the latter cannot exist when the supplier expressly guarantees his merchandise.

The purchaser is under obligation to take action as soon as a deficiency of goods, or a breach of warranty, is determined. Many sales contracts for goods that are capable of inspection upon receipt place a limit on the time in which such claim may be made, usually 30 days. These limiting clauses have been judged valid.

Law of Patents   A *patent* is a monopoly created by law. There are five classifications or bases for patents: mechanical, process, composition, articles of manufacture, and design. The patentee for a limited period has the sole right of making, using, and selling the patented article, and he may control its use by others.

A person (or company) may be liable for infringement of a patent if he uses it, or if he makes it for his own use, or if he purchases and resells an infringement device, although the purchase is made in the belief that the seller had a license from the patentee to sell or use the device. The owner of a valid patent is privileged to sue for infringement either the manufacturer, the seller, or the user of the invention, or all of them.

In view of the heavy liability that may be incurred through patent infringement without knowledge or intention on the part of the purchaser, a precautionary protective clause should be included in the terms and conditions of purchase orders whereby the patentee or seller agrees to assume full responsibility for losses sustained by the purchaser as a result of infringement suits. Such clauses, normally referred to as patent indemnification, are valid.

Not only should purchasing personnel be concerned with protecting their company from infringement, but they should also be instructed to gain rights for their company whenever possible. An invention can become a valuable asset to a company. Accordingly, the purchasing department should consider each purchase thoroughly, prior to the award of a contract, in order to decide whether or not rights to a by-product invention is a subject to be negotiated. It should be made a policy that the company receives all rights, title, or interest in any invention or process which was discovered by the supplier with the use of company funds.

Robinson-Patman Act   The congressional intent in enacting the Robinson-Patman Act was to provide a tool whereby sellers could more ably resist pressures from large-volume buyers who were seeking more favorable prices, terms, or conditions of purchase than those available to competing buyers. Hence, under the law, the buyer who knowingly induces or receives a discriminatory price in his favor can be held equally liable with the seller who has granted such an unjustifiable price difference.

Both direct and indirect price discriminations are prohibited. A direct discrimination is simply a large discount or a lower price. Indirect discrimination includes especially beneficial terms of sale, special allowances connected with or in some way related to the sale, services not generally provided other buyers, etc.

A rule of thumb which should be applied by each buyer in applying the provisions of the Robinson-Patman Act is that buyers are prohibited from exerting pressure on a seller for lower prices, knowing full well that there is little, if any, likelihood of the seller being able to justify the price discrimination on the basis of his comparative costs.

This law should not be interpreted, in any sense, as prohibiting the solicitation of sellers' competitive quotations and selecting those of greatest advantage to the buyer.

Additional legal-oriented topics include the following:

Agency
Contracts for sale
The Uniform Commercial Code
Nonconforming goods
Acceptance
Antitrust

Relations with Vendors

This deals with all those purchasing activities which extend beyond the company itself and, as such, defines the responsibilities of purchasing personnel and reflects the resulting public image of the department. The purchasing department has as many contacts with the public as any other department in the company, and the greatest public is that vast group of vendors serving even the smallest of companies. Relations may include any or all of the following:

Public Relations   The purchasing department maintains regular contact with many persons and companies in the course of its day-to-day activities, and the manner in which these contacts are carried out can and does reflect on the company's name. Thus, purchasing must accept responsibility for the public image as it is viewed by vendors and others with whom purchasing interacts. In carrying out these duties, purchasing must consider:

FAIRNESS. The company's reputation for dealing in a fair manner always must be upheld and promoted by treatment of salespersons in which competition is kept open, by cooperation when not to the company's detriment, by consideration of another's difficulties, and by other factors of a similar nature.

INTEGRITY. Purchasing must, at all times, maintain its integrity and that of the company by observing strict truthfulness in every transaction; by respecting the confidence of each vendor, and by keeping free from any personal obligation to a vendor.

COURTESY. The members of the purchasing department cannot conduct the company's business in a satisfactory manner unless all relationships, regardless of personal feeling, are maintained in a courteous and polite manner. This does not suggest that any purchasing employee should be less than firm in representing the company's interests, but, even in the most difficult of vendor relations, there can be no excuse for discourtesy.

GOODWILL. Each of the above, like public relations itself, is a factor in promoting the goodwill of the company. This goodwill is a valuable asset, and purchasing's actions, more so than those of many others, can develop and expand it and, conversely, can destroy it.

Relations with Salespersons Salespersons represent one of purchasing's major areas of contact with the company's vendors, and for this reason cultivation of a satisfactory relationship is essential. This is not to suggest the need for a personal friendship, but rather to encourage a mutual feeling of trust in all business dealings. The salesperson can be a source of information concerning both his company and his industry, an effective liaison in representing you to his company, a problem solver, an expediter, and a provider of innovative ideas. He should be treated courteously, fairly, and openly. He should not be imposed upon or antagonized. Above all, purchasing's authority should not be flaunted to the salesperson in an effort to take advantage of a position. He should be given time to present his story. As in other factors of relations, however, none is to suggest that purchasing's role is more than a businesslike representation of your own company, but rather that, in the final analysis, it is your company interests that must prevail.

Gifts and Entertainment Company policy prohibits the acceptance by any of its employees of gifts, either in kind or of money or of excessive entertainment, from a vendor or a potential vendor. Gifts would include any items offered to you or your immediate family which are not obviously in the nature of advertising. "Excessive" entertainment shall include, but not be restricted to, transportation of other than a business nature beyond that of an intracity nature and overnight accommodations. It is not intended that this restriction include the bona fide business lunch. It is recognized that there is a place for such meetings and that, if correctly structured, they have a beneficial purpose. However, caution should be taken to be certain that such lunches do not become a regular occurrence with selected vendor representatives or that the impression is given that such lunches are a requirement for doing business with your company.

Trade Relations (Reciprocity)   *Reciprocity* may be defined as the direct trading of unlike products on a fixed ratio or basis in a buy-sell configuration. It implies coercion of either the buyer or seller and tends to restrain trade. This practice is illegal and will not be condoned. Accordingly, the following policy will apply:

POLICY REGARDING PURCHASES AND SALES.

It is the policy of (Company Name) that its purchasing and marketing departments bear in mind that profit from the sale of its products, on their merits, is (Company Name)'s ultimate objective.

(Company Name) policy is to sell its products on the basis of quality, price, service, and reliability. It is (Company Name) policy to make purchases on the same basis. It has long been (Company Name) policy that under no circumstances is there to be any threat or pressure on any present or prospective vendor that (Company Name) will withhold or will not continue to make purchases unless such vendor buys from (Company Name), nor will the fact of past, present, or prospective purchases be used to coerce or pressure any vendor or customer to do or refrain from doing business with anyone, including (Company Name).

Nothing in this policy should be construed:

1. To require any diminution of competitive efforts to sell (Company Name) products in any market or to any customer, including those vendors who deal with (Company Name).
2. To have any application to transactions in the nature of exchanges or barter arrangements.

Confidential Information   In the course of many business transactions, it is inevitable that some confidential information must be given to the other party. In those cases where purchasing must divulge such information to a vendor's representative, it clearly should be labeled as such. Any verbal revelations also should be prefaced by a word of caution to the recipient. In those cases where the information divulged is considered more than confidential, i.e., secret, the use of a secrecy agreement may be desirable. This should be prepared by a member of the legal staff, after consultation with your management.

Purchasing representatives often receive information from vendors which is considered confidential. If it is clearly labeled as such, then care must be taken so that it will not be divulged to unauthorized persons, particularly representatives of competing vendors. If the information is not classified as confidential, judgment must be shown as to what may be revealed and what may not. In every case, this judgment should be based on the effect which the action taken will have on your company, considering economics, integrity, good will, etc. Generally, any special price offering from a vendor should not be discussed in specifics with others outside the company.

Ethics   Although mentioned later, ethics is included here as a reminder that the ethics as accepted by the purchasing department have an important effect on any vendor relations. Without a firm policy on purchasing ethics, relations with others can be impeded seriously.

Samples   Acceptance of samples on a gratis basis should be discouraged unless the sample has little intrinsic value. If a sample is paid for, it tends to encourage the vendor to provide a product from more representative production and removes any requirement that the buyer handle it in a special manner, report results of tests, or feel any obligation to the vendor.

Interviewing Hours   Individual company policy varies widely, and wording for such a section here is omitted so that it can be made to conform to the company's policy. However, several considerations follow. It has been suggested that to limit the hours of interview restricts the effectiveness of a salesman, thus, theoretically, increasing vendor costs and finally raising prices. Conversely, failure to limit the time has a similar effect on buyers. The premise that it is beneficial for buyers and sellers to meet together is a true one. Because of this an effective compromise has been worked out by many companies. This starts with the policy that, if at all possible, every salesperson will be interviewed at least for a time sufficient to determine that he has something to offer. Regular interviewing hours then are established, but with the provision that salespersons will be seen outside of these regular hours by appointment only. This permits both buyer and seller to plan their time more effectively.

Vendor Evaluation   Evaluation of the company's vendors is considered an effective tool for improving their ability to serve more satisfactorily and as a basis for making future purchasing decisions. This evaluation will be done on a periodic basis but at least annually for all regular vendors and prior to completing any term commitments covering a period of 6 months or more. It will include written evaluation relative to quality, service, price, etc., and will be obtained from the buyer, using unit, and any other interested departments such as engineering and quality control.

United States versus Foreign Purchases   Company policy provides that, where possible, requirements for use in a specific country be purchased in that country from manufacturers domiciled there. Deviations with value in excess of $5000 must be approved by the vice-president of purchasing.

Vendor Selection and Development   A purchasing manual should include a section covering this subject. It may appear in any one of several sections. Rather than attempt to word a sample paragraph here, the reader is referred to Section 6 of this handbook for a complete discussion of the subject.

Obtaining Proper Quality

This part sets forth procedures and suggests policies required to ensure that the right quality will be purchased to fulfill, but not exceed, the requirement for which the goods are intended. Essential subjects have been covered, but some amendment may be necessary to conform to specific company situations. The sections follow.

Purchase Specifications   Complete specifications help to obtain proper quality.

Definition: A *specification* is no more than an accurate description of the material to be purchased. A good specification should be:

- Identified, when possible, with some brand or specification already on the market. Special goods are expensive.
- Capable of being checked. It should describe the method of checking which will govern acceptance or rejection.
- Reasonable in its tolerances. Unnecessary precision is expensive.
- Capable of being met by several vendors for the sake of competition.
- Clear.
- Flexible. Inflexible specifications defeat progress. Invite vendors to suggest cost-saving alternates or substitutes.

Who Provides   Production and/or engineering personnel will be responsible for providing specifications for all requirements. Purchasing has the right to question any specification if it is written so as to result in apparent excess cost to the company.

Review of Specification and Modification   Purchasing is required to review all specifications upon receipt and at least once a year thereafter to be certain that:

- More than one vendor *can* offer.
- It is reasonable in tolerances.
- It is clear.
- Previous standard items have not become specials.
- Unnecessary details do not add another delay in delivery or increase the cost.
- New technology has not made the present specification obsolete.

If any of the above situations develop, the specification should be returned to the originating department for review with suggested changes if possible.

Inspection   Buying proper quality means also the checking of material purchased against the specifications. The specification itself is not satisfactory unless the product delivered can be reasonably checked against it. Purchasing is not usually responsible for inspection but must develop a procedure whereby it can be advised of the results of any inspection of materials purchased. These inspection results should become a part of the supplier evaluation report.

Determining Proper Quantity

Even though purchasing is not normally responsible for developing demand numbers, other factors necessary to determine quantity are a function of purchasing. Thus the following sections should appear in a complete manual.

General   Any purchase must originate with a requirement, and determination of this demand is the responsibility of the operating department. Communicating this demand to purchasing is handled by purchase requisition, as discussed later. However, purchasing should keep informed about operating conditions so as to be able to move rapidly when changes occur. The determination of proper quantity consists of more than just demand, and purchasing is responsible to apply such factors as inventory on hand, lead time, cost of acquisition, volume pricing, and the safety factor. The following sections discuss these in detail.

Inventory   For every requirement there must be some consideration of a working inventory—that is, the volume of material required to sustain operations until a new order can be placed and received. Inventory has a cost element: the cost of money not available for other things (interest charges), the cost of the storage facility itself, and the cost of obsolescence. These costs are balanced against the penalty of not being able to operate a facility because of lack of material or parts. A judgment factor is involved.

Lead Time   This is the time elapsed between the receipt of a requisition and the receipt of the goods required. It includes time to obtain quotations, time to place an order, time for the vendor to manufacture, and time for transportation from vendor's plant to destination. Caution must be taken to be certain that both the requisitioner and purchasing do not add volumes to cover lead times. Excessive inventory will result.

Cost of Acquisition   These costs usually include the administrative aspects of procurement. They include cost of placing an order, cost of processing an invoice, cost of expediting, etc. While normally small in relation to the value of the material purchased, they represent expenses which must be weighed in determining the optimum order quantity.

Volume Pricing   Part of the manual should define various elements to consider in evaluating price. Here, though, in determining proper quantity, discounts for volume must be considered. If the addition of one or more units to an order will result in a lower price for all, the various other cost factors must be evaluated against this lower price, and it is purchasing's responsibility to do so.

Safety Factor   The success of the inventory control system can be evaluated largely on the basis of two factors, stockouts and excessive inventory. Both of these are the result of poor planning or, stated in another way, of incorrect application of the *safety factor*. This safety factor is the volume nominated for inclusion in an inventory to take care of contingencies in the system. Determination of this volume is a judgment made on the basis of knowledge of the company's operations, of your supplier's abilities, of industry conditions, and of the general economic situation.

Formula for Order Quantity   A simple formula is: Net demand, less stock on hand, plus demand during lead time, plus a safety factor. This formula makes no allowance for possible minimum charges per order or possible savings through ordering larger quantities. These are judgment factors.

Determining Proper Price

The price of an item may, at first glance, appear to be the most elementary of determinations, but, in fact, it can be extremely complicated. Any complete purchasing manual should cover the subject thoroughly and include most of the following phases:

Price-Value Relationship   The price for any item may be defined in the simplest terms as the value applied to that article by the seller. But value to the buyer should include things other than quality, such as delivery and service. The buyer is expected to obtain for the company the best total value and thus to consider price as only one element, although price is often the only finite measurement of value. It is the buyer's responsibility to relate this price to the other elements of value and to analyze each purchase so as to secure the best total value.

Types of Prices   There are many different types of prices in use today, and knowledge of them is essential.

Price Knowledge   It is important that the buyer be familiar with the pricing basis for most if not all of the items for which he is responsible. He should be familiar with the price history, price trends, and, if possible, reasons for change. At times he should forecast future prices to advise other company personnel of the impact of price action on future company activity. All of this calls for maintaining a record of price history.

Cost-Price Relationship   An essential responsibility of the buyer is the determination of the fairness of a price. Many factors must be considered, and the importance of each varies by product and timing. For example, in an extremely tight market, the seller sets the price and it must be accepted. Quite often, though, the buyer is in a position to accept, reject, or negotiate some change in the seller's price. In such instances a knowledge of costs is desirable. It permits the buyer to know more about the limits to which he might negotiate. Such knowledge also is useful as a means of combating proposed price increases. Accordingly, each buyer should attempt to determine a cost basis for major items of purchase. In so doing he should utilize the knowledge and experience available in the company's own engineering and research departments and from outside the company where possible.

Discounts   To determine the net price, the applicable discounts must be deducted.

Transportation Costs   The price of a purchased commodity must be the price delivered to point of use. Thus a price available at the vendor's producing location is not a complete price. Therefore, the buyer must consider only delivered prices in any comparison. This means that transportation costs often must be added to a vendor's price to ascertain the delivered price. Costs of transportation should be obtained from the traffic department. It is desirable, too, to consult the traffic department as to possibilities of reducing costs on any regular freight movements. Traffic is in a position to improve both rates and routes.

Total Cost   It is imperative that commitments be made on the basis of the best total value. This implies optimum delivery, service, and quality. It also assumes that not only price but total cost has been considered. *Total cost* includes the selling price and also items covered above, such as discounts and transportation. Other elements of cost include: the cost of replacement parts, special inventory required, the cost of maintenance or service, the cost of obsolescence, and possibly others related to specific commodities.

Contracts

The purchasing department is one of the few corporate departments that deal regularly with contracts, and for this reason any purchasing manual should include a section covering them. However, every company's legal adviser will have his own ideas and opinions on many aspects of a contract. Thus, the following should be used as guides only. Before including them in a manual, each point should be approved by company legal counsel. The following are suggested:

General   A contract is a legal obligation between a buyer and a seller to perform certain duties. It may be verbal or written, and the purchase order itself is one form of written contract. The legal aspects of procurement are considered elsewhere in this manual, and the following sections relate to formal agreements other than the purchase order.

When to Use a Formal Contract   Generally a formal contract will be used when the terms and conditions involved in a commitment are such that a standard purchase order is not adequate. In addition, the formal contract will be used when:

1. The purchase period extends beyond 1 year.
2. The value of the commitment exceeds the limits of authority granted the purchasing manager.
3. (Other restrictions may be added as appropriate.)

Factors to Be Considered When Preparing or Reviewing a Contract   In most instances it is common for the seller to prepare the contract. Purchasing therefore has the responsibility to review the document to assure that:

1. The buyer receives protection equal to that given the seller.
2. The commercial aspects are as agreed to during negotiation.
3. Every clause is definite to the point of making any misunderstanding unlikely.
4. All necessary provisions have been included in the contract.
5. Any revisions by either party must be confirmed in writing.
6. Finally, *that the document itself is reviewed, approved, and initiated by a member of the company's legal staff.*

Terms and Conditions   Every contract will be somewhat different from any other, but certain sections should be included, such as:

1. QUANTITY OR VOLUME.   From the buyer's standpoint, the least restrictive quantity clause usually is the most desirable. If a minimum or more fixed quantity is included, the penalty for failure to meet this quantity should be included.

2. PRICE.   To be binding, a specific price must be fixed or a means must be spelled out to accurately determine the price.

3. ESCALATION.   If it is necessary to permit the seller some means of escalating the price, provision should be made for de-escalation. If escalation is permitted, the basis should be well defined and testable. If a price is increased, the buyer should have the right, with at least 30 days' notice, to cancel the contract if the increase is not acceptable.

4. PRICE PROTECTION.   The optimum for the buyer is to have the contract price as a ceiling, with the seller being required to meet other lower-priced com-

petition if it develops. Even without the ceiling, though, a clause requiring the seller to meet competition, if available, is almost mandatory.

5. FAVORED NATIONS CLAUSE.   This clause stipulates that if the seller makes a sale of similar quantity and quality to the same category of buyer at a lower price, that lower price will be applied to your purchases. It is difficult for a seller to refuse to include such a clause and still warrant good faith.

6. EVERGREEN CLAUSE.   A clause often requested by the seller. It provides that a contract will renew automatically for a like period if not specifically canceled by the buyer by a date usually 60 days before intended expiration. There are both advantages and disadvantages to this type of clause, and it should be considered carefully before accepting it.

7. WARRANTY.   Every seller's contract will contain a warranty clause, one which usually will restrict his liability more than the Uniform Commercial Code does. It should be meticulously reviewed to assure acceptance.

8. FORCE MAJEURE.   With rare exceptions, contracts should contain a provision which will permit nonperformance *by either party* if it is the result of fire, war, labor difficulties, etc., beyond the party's control.

9. SPECIAL CONDITIONS.   There may be many other items covered, such as penalties, liquidated damages, inspection, testing, etc. These must be analyzed to assure compliance with the commercial aspects of the agreement.

Releases against Contract   Releases against purchasing contracts may be made by use of either a release notice or a standard purchase order. In either case, reference will be made to the contract number in the body of the release document, for example: "Apply to Contract No. H-345."

Specific Types of Contracts

1. NATIONAL AGREEMENTS.   A contract covering the company's requirements of a specific commodity on a national basis.

2. BLANKET ORDER.   A contract covering one or more commodities for one or more use points but usually formalized by a purchase order.

3. CONSTRUCTION CONTRACTS.   A contract drawn to cover the construction of a plant or unit of equipment; it usually includes a labor factor.

4. SYSTEMS CONTRACTING.   Also known as *vendor stocking*. This type of contract usually covers a plant or department's requirements for maintenance, repair, and operating supplies. It generally provides for the supplier to carry inventory and to make regular, timely deliveries; usually it reduces paper work.

Purchase Requisition

A purchase requisition serves as a written communication transmitting the needs of the requisitioner to the purchasing department. It provides a record of the request to purchase and approves the commitment of funds by noting the signature of properly authorized personnel. The requisition also serves as a reference document for the typing of the purchase order.

The purchasing department should be responsible for checking the accuracy and completeness of information received on the requisition. All purchase orders should be supported by a properly executed purchase requisition. Requisitions should be retained and filed in the purchasing department for use and reference as required.

Quotation Requests

The purpose of a quotation request is to inform the supplier of the work to be performed if a contract is awarded to him. It provides a sound basis for the preparation of a bid or proposal by the supplier and analysis of it by the purchaser. Purchasing departments that make numerous requests for quotations should give consideration to the advantages of using a multiple-copy preprinted quotation request form. The printed form offers a uniform method for preparing quotation requests and assures that all prospective suppliers are given complete information regarding a purchase requirement. Standard terms and conditions and instructions for preparation of bids can be included in the form. This avoids unnecessary typing and reduces the chances for omission of information. Special terms and conditions and additional instructions to suppliers that are unique to a given request can be incorporated into the typed portion of the request.

Quotation Analysis

Purchasing procedures should provide for the use of a quotation analysis record in the review and appraisal of competitive bids of major importance. The form will provide an adequate record of bids and aid in the evaluation of them when a source or sources of supply are being selected. Such a record will promote a better analysis of several factors which must be considered in making a selection. It will provide a record of the considerations which were recognized by the buyer and will serve as a basis for the selection of other than low price when such action is in the best interest of the buying company.

It may be desirable for purchasing to obtain the assistance of personnel from other departments in making the analysis and appraisal of the quotation. This helps to ensure that the purchase agreement to be made will represent the best effort of the company.

The department head should establish a level above which expenditures will require the use of a quotation or bid analysis form.

Pricing Methods

All charges from suppliers which are nonrecurring or are of a special or unusual nature and not a part of the ordinary unit price should be described and priced separately on the purchase order.

The term *special or unusual charges* means, but is not limited to:

Special tooling
Setup
X-ray and testing
Test bars or samples

Use of oversize material

Development or startup charges

Correction of discrepant parts furnished by the purchaser

Rework or revision of goods caused by changes initiated by the purchaser

There are times when it is appropriate to authorize payment of premium charges to accomplish improved delivery. In order that payment of such charges may be appropriate, the purchaser should, by its actions, impose some requirements upon a supplier which are clearly over and above those which were included in the existing agreement between the purchaser and the supplier. The purpose of premium charges is to afford the supplier an incentive to meet a requirement that is not encompassed in the existing purchase agreement. Therefore, purchasing should make payment of additional charges for premium performance contingent upon supplier's actual delivery of the performance agreed upon. Premium payment should not be granted for failure to meet the objective. Authorized premium charges should be described and priced separately on the purchase order.

Purchase Order

A purchase order is the supplier's authority to ship and charge for the goods specified in the order. It is the purchaser's commitment for the value of the goods ordered. It is essentially a legal document. When the order is written as an acceptance of a quotation or an offer, a contractual relation is established upon its issuance. This does not hold if the supplier quotes on his own form and its conditions differ from those on the purchase order. When there is no proposal from the supplier, or if he has made an offer under different conditions, the purchase order itself is an offer to a contractual relation, which is completed by an acknowledgment or acceptance by the supplier.

While it is unnecessary to employ intricate legal phraseology in the text of the order, the importance of the purchase order as a legal document should not be slighted. It should clearly and precisely cover the essential elements of the purchase to be made in a manner which will render future misunderstandings impossible and which will minimize the necessity of additional correspondence.

The purchase order should be in writing to provide a written record of the purchase agreement and to provide information to other departments concerned with the purchase transaction.

The purchase order should be a preprinted form. It should contain general instructions and standard terms and conditions and should provide space for information necessary to define the agreement between the purchaser and the supplier. Special terms and conditions covering a specific procurement can be incorporated in the purchase order by reference.

Purchase Order Amendment

Any change which is significant to the negotiation or administration of a purchase order should be incorporated into the order by use of a purchase order amendment. The amendment serves as a record of the action taken by purchasing and provides a notice of the change to the supplier and to all departments that have a copy of the order.

A change which is significant to the negotiation or administration of the purchase order means a change which must be made known to and agreed upon by both the purchaser and the supplier during the performance of the order.

Minor deviations from the quantity and/or price shown on the purchase order can be handled by a less detailed and expensive means. Notice of the change can be limited to only those departments that are directly interested in and affected by the change.

Purchase Order Acknowledgment and Acceptance

Purchase orders issued that are not in direct response to a firm quotation must be accepted by a supplier before they become contracts. The supplier may accept an order by written acknowledgment either on the purchase order copy provided for this purpose or on his own form, or by performance of the order. It is most desirable to have a written acceptance. The buyer placing the order should be responsible for obtaining it if this is a requirement.

The buyer should attempt to obtain an unqualified acceptance of the terms and conditions of the purchase order. Each acknowledgment should be reviewed to be sure it is acceptable to the buying company. Minor variations should be approved by the buyer as a matter of practical business conduct.

Any disagreement regarding significant terms and conditions should be resolved promptly. Purchasing's failure to take action on a supplier's proposal for change may cause acceptance of terms and conditions that are not desirable to the buying company.

In any event, the buyer should obtain acknowledgment of orders from suppliers in the form that is suitable for the transaction to be handled. These should be retained in the purchasing department files or recorded in a suitable manner.

Trial Orders and Samples

It is sometimes desirable to obtain material or equipment on trial to determine whether it is satisfactory for a specified need. This may be handled as: (1) free sample or trial; (2) trial order bought outright; or (3) trial order subject to approval.

A free sample should be accepted for trial only when the value of the sample is insignificant. Even when no money is involved, it is a good practice to record the matter by a purchase order which outlines all terms and conditions. The buying company is under an obligation when a free sample is accepted. This is especially true if the supplier furnishes a sample which is unsatisfactory and he spends additional money, time, or effort in an attempt to meet the requirements.

Some trial commodities may be bought outright. This leaves the purchaser free to make tests as it sees fit and to use the results of the experiments in any manner it wishes.

Trial orders are sometimes placed on the condition that the material or equipment will be accepted only if it meets certain requirements. Under no circumstances should such an arrangement be made unless a purchase order is issued, outlining all terms and conditions of the trial. When such a purchase order agreement is made and the material fails to prove satisfactory, the supplier should be formally notified before the termination of the trial period. Otherwise, the purchaser may be compelled to pay, as acceptance can be implied from the fact that possession is retained after the trial period has expired.

Petty Cash Orders

Petty cash procurements are most frequently considered for the purchase of small-quantity general supply items which do not require formal inspection. Petty cash may also be used for making emergency buys.

The major advantage of a petty cash order is the immediate payment to the supplier, which avoids the cost of processing purchase orders, receiving records, and invoices.

The petty cash order is nothing more than a properly executed purchase requisition. The requisition must be for a small value and must satisfy other requirements, and the purchasing department arranges for a cash purchase. The supplier's sales receipt serves as a receiving record and invoice. The sales receipt and a copy of the purchase requisition are submitted to accounting for audit and reimbursement.

Normally, petty cash orders are limited to low-dollar purchases. A popular limitation is $25 per order.

Blanket Orders

When economically appropriate, repetitively ordered supplies can be purchased through the use of blanket-type purchase orders. Such orders can provide discounts for volume buying and can reduce the number of purchase orders, administrative costs, and paper work.

A *blanket order* is a term contract or basic agreement between the purchaser and the supplier for a stated period of time. It establishes certain terms and conditions under which material is delivered upon issuance of orders in the form of releases. The releases can be either verbal or written. The basic order is established to cover specific items with stated prices, or it can include items of a general category that are covered by a published price list.

Release orders and necessary instructions are given to the supplier by an authorized person of the buying company. A release number is assigned to identify each release placed against the basic order. Internal documentation and processing can follow normal procurement procedures or they can be simplified to whatever degree desirable.

Blanket orders should not be considered for requirements which involve special conditions, complexities of shipping, or excessive follow-up.

Paperless Purchase Orders

Most blanket orders can be established in such a manner as to provide a paperless purchase order. This is accomplished by placing the burden for paper work on the supplier. After establishing a blanket order, specific administrative conditions are incorporated in the basic agreement. These conditions establish the procedures for the administration of the order and include the following types of limitations and controls:

1. No items can be shipped incomplete.
2. All releases are to be expeditiously processed.
3. Preprinted forms for administrative control are supplied by the buyer. The supplier must complete the form in accordance with applicable instruction and forward four copies with each shipment of material ordered. The following information should appear on each packing slip:
    a. Purchase order number
    b. Item number
    c. Quantity
    d. Description of service or supplies furnished
    e. Unit price and extended price
    f. Total price—including discounts and taxes
    g. Name of buyer issuing the release
    h. Purchaser's part number (when applicable)
4. The purchaser must specify the names of personnel authorized to initiate releases. The supplier shall not accept requests from unauthorized personnel.
5. Not-to-exceed dollar values must be established per line item, per individual release, and for total dollar value of all releases per month.
6. Invoices should not be issued. All payments are made by utilizing the priced form accompanying the delivered material.
7. The buyer's authorized personnel must sign all copies of the preprinted form, acknowledging receipt of the material covered by the packing slip.
8. Copies of the executed preprinted forms should be distributed to accounts payable, purchasing, the requisitioner, and receiving.
9. The supplier should provide a monthly report to the buyer showing the total number of releases and the total dollars for the month, and cumulative total dollars of all purchases against the blanket order.

Receiving Record

The receiving record serves as notification to interested departments that material ordered has been received. These records should be prepared in such detail as is necessary to properly show the quantity and description of the material reported. The receiving record is an important part of a company's records. It should be prepared accurately and distributed promptly.

Departments that normally require notice of receipt of material and their use of this information are shown below:

Department	*Use of Report*
Purchasing	To record delivery status on purchase order
Accounts payable	To verify receipt of material invoiced by supplier
Material control	Record of receipt of material requisitioned
Receiving inspection	Notice of material requiring inspection
Chemical and metal laboratory	Notice of material requiring inspection and test
Receiving department	Record of material received on purchase order

General Information

1. Invoices are approved for payment on the basis of the information in the receiving record.

2. Production plans and schedules are set up on the record of material on hand.

3. The activity of the receiving inspection department is based upon the notice of delivery of material.

4. Follow-up and expediting efforts are based upon the reports from the receiving department.

Inspection

The purpose of inspection is to ascertain that the supply of service delivered meets the standards of quality required and conforms to the drawings, specifications, or other data used to describe it in the purchase order. When practical, all supplies and services purchased should be inspected before they are placed in stock or used in production. This inspection should be performed by the department responsible for the control of the quality of the item received from a supplier.

The method of inspection should be established by the department responsible for quality control. Purchasing must be knowledgeable concerning this method and be responsible for informing the supplier of the type of inspection that will be used to evaluate his product.

If the supplies or services are not subjected to formal inspection, purchasing should obtain an evaluation of the quality of the items furnished by making inquiry directly to the department that uses them.

Payment of Invoices

Control of payments to suppliers should be established in the accounting department. Accounts payable should make payment to suppliers in accordance with established payment schedules if the description and price shown on receiving record and invoice agree with those shown on the order, except in those cases wherein the order calls for approval of the invoice by the buyer and/or some other person before payment. These approvals should be obtained before payment is made.

If the description or price is not in agreement with that on the purchase order, the invoice should be referred to the buyer for correction or approval before payment is made to the supplier.

Price extension, discounts, etc., should be checked before an invoice is paid.

Records

Purchase History Record   Purchasing should maintain a record of purchase of commodities which are used by the operating departments. The record should include information regarding sources, usage, prices, competitive bids, and other data which are useful in negotiating for the purchase of current requirements. A purchase history record can be useful for purchases of repetitive or continuing requirements regardless of whether they are standard or special items. It can acquaint the person handling the current requirements with the details of negotiations that have been conducted on prior purchases and assist him in the selection of a source and in pricing a new order. There are several methods used to maintain information for a purchase history record:

1. A traveling purchase requisition form
2. A parts history card
3. A purchase history folder
4. Electronic data processing records

Vendor Record   A file record of all active suppliers should be maintained in the purchasing department. An alphabetical record can be maintained in a looseleaf binder or card file.

The file should include the supplier's name, address, and telephone number, name of sales contact and sales manager or owners, terms of payment, f.o.b. points, and other information pertinent to the specific supplier.

List of Approved Suppliers   The purchasing department should consider the advantages of maintaining a list of approved suppliers for the guidance of personnel in the selection of sources of supply. This listing should be prepared in the manner and detail that are suited to the needs of the department. If a record is to be maintained, it should contain the names of suppliers who have been approved for use on the basis of past performance or upon specific review or survey of the supplier's facility. The record should be supported by information consisting of, but not limited to, reports on quality and delivery performance and financial and facility capabilities.

Miscellaneous Records   The importance of various other reports will vary with the nature of the business and other factors involved in the operation of a purchasing department. Other reports to be considered are:

1. National contract agreements
2. Record of pattern location
3. Company tooling in the possession of suppliers
4. Sale or disposition of surplus material or equipment

5. Record of returnable containers
6. Trial or testing of sample material

Administrative Records and Reports to Management

The reports and records normally maintained by a purchasing department fall within two major categories:

Administrative   Reports and records used by the head of the purchasing department as aids in organizing his department and supervising the activities of his employees.

1. PURCHASING ORGANIZATION CHART.   The department head should maintain an up-to-date organization chart for his department. This should show the title and name of his immediate supervisor and the personnel under his supervision.

2. JOB DESCRIPTION.   The department head should maintain job descriptions for the personnel under his supervision. The descriptions should provide the following general information:

   a. Job title
   b. Reports to
   c. Basic function
   d. Responsibility and authority
   e. Relationships
   f. Qualifications

3. COMMODITY ASSIGNMENT SCHEDULE.   The department head should maintain a schedule showing the commodities which are assigned to each buyer in his department. This schedule should also show the work assignments of other personnel, analysts, expediters, and clerical employees. The schedule should include the employee's name, title, and list of commodities or general work assignment. These assignments should be described in the detail necessary to advise personnel in other departments whom they should contact for information relating to purchasing.

4. DEPARTMENT BUDGET REPORT.   The department head should prepare an expense budget for the cost of operating his department. Budget expense figures should be established on a monthly basis and should be listed in accordance with the account numbers and descriptions prescribed by the company's accounting system.

Operating   Records and reports which provide information regarding the purchase transactions that are performed by the purchasing department.

1. COMMITMENT REPORT.   A monthly commitment report should be prepared summarizing the department's buying activities. The report can be generated from individual reports from each buyer or compiled from a central data center. The main function of this report is to establish the total dollar value of

commitments made by purchasing that will result in a liability to the company. A secondary use of a commitment report is the recording of buying activity for each buyer. Individual records can be kept of the number of purchase orders placed by each buyer and their value. This information can be used by the department head for work load leveling and performance reviews. The commitment report can be as simple or as complex as desired. It can include information for such items as: performance to standards, make/buy changes, replacement orders, amendment activity, and small and large business reports.

2. SUPPLIER QUALITY PERFORMANCE.   One of the most important responsibilities of purchasing is to select suppliers that can deliver supplies and services that meet quality requirements of the purchase order. It is equally important that internal operating procedures be established which measure and report the actual performance of suppliers in meeting quality requirements. The department head should obtain the cooperation of the department responsible for control of quality to furnish such a report to the purchasing department.

3. COST PERFORMANCE.   The accounting department, with the agreement of purchasing, should establish a base for comparing purchased material cost performance. The most popular base is the use of standard costs, but the material cost estimate used in quoting company sales is sometimes used. Each purchase order commitment should be compared with the established base for the given item. Major variance should be explained and approved by the department head prior to the commitment. The posting of the data for individual orders can be included in the commitment report.

A monthly report summarizing all cost performance activity for the department should be generated. This report will provide the department head with cost trends that can be helpful for forecasting purposes. Also, the listing of activity by buyer can provide additional information for employee performance review.

4. SAVINGS REPORTS.   More and more emphasis is being placed on purchasing's effect on profitability. Good purchasing performance can make significant contributions to company profits as a result of savings ensuing from activities, such as:

   a. Lower prices obtained by developing new sources of supply.

   b. Price reductions, other than normal market fluctuations, made through negotiations.

   c. Price reduction resulting from the development of nonrestrictive specifications, resulting in increased competition.

   d. Savings from the use of standard items by eliminating special designs and sizes.

   e. Savings from the utilization of new or substitute materials.

   f. Negotiations of improved discounts—cash, trade, and volume.

   g. Utilization or salvage of surplus and obsolete supplies and equipment.

   h. Improvements in purchasing procedures and lower departmental operating costs.

It should be considered an important function of purchasing to compile a savings report. The report should list actual measurable savings. It should include only those savings developed through deliberate effort of the purchasing department.

Special Instructions

A separate section of the policy and procedure manual covers instructions relating to:

1. Travel expense and charge accounts
2. Employee relocation expenses
3. Electronic data processing for purchasing
4. Tax policies
5. Accounting policies
6. Surplus and obsolescent materials
7. Special instructions relating to specific types of orders

NOTE: For further information on subjects covered in this section see the list of references in Section 30.

Section **4**

Legal Aspects of Purchasing

EDITOR

S. R. Heath, Jr., C.P.M. *Vice-President, Division General Manager, Filtration & Minerals Division, Johns-Manville Corporation, Denver, Colorado*

ASSOCIATE EDITOR

Mike L. Stone *Former Attorney, Johns-Manville Corporation, Denver, Colorado*

This section of the handbook is not intended as an exhaustive study of the legal principles having to do with the purchasing function. Only the general principles are discussed and interpreted in the hope that, with some basic understanding of his rights and liabilities, the buyer may at least avoid serious controversy and litigation.

It is the sincere hope of those who have worked on this section that the necessarily short presentation as given will induce the reader (the buyer) to seek further information as to the nature and application of legal principles involved in the day-to-day duties of a purchasing manager.

The buyer should avail himself of legal counsel whenever and to the extent necessary. He will recognize that a sound sense of ethics is by far the most potent tool of his profession. Without it the law is powerless to aid him in the proper and effective discharge of his responsibilities.

PURCHASING AND THE LAW OF CORPORATIONS

The modern businesses that buyers generally come in contact with are corporations, partnerships, and single proprietorships. The single proprietorship is owned and managed by a single person who receives all profits and is personally liable for all losses. The partnership is merely an enlargement of this way of doing business. Each of the partners is personally liable for the losses or debts of the business, if any. In order to get away from the unlimited personal liability that proprietors and partners have, and to restrict or limit this liability to a fixed, known amount, the concept of a corporation was developed. The only certain way for an individual to get limited personal liability is to do business only through a properly created corporation.

The accompanying table compares a corporation with a partnership.

	Corporation	Partnership
Legal entity separate from its owners	Yes	No
Approval of government	Yes	No
Death of member	No effect	Terminates
Disposal of member's interest	No effect	Terminates
Property	Corporation owns; stockholders do not	Partners own
Individual partner or stockholder	No direct control	Direct control
	Not a manager	May manage
	Not an agent	Is an agent
	Not liable for debts	Is liable for debts
	Not liable on contracts	Is liable on contracts

Management of the Corporation

A board of directors manages the corporation, the members being elected by their stockholders. The board of directors has a fiduciary responsibility to the stockholders to conduct the business of the corporation in their best interest. The board appoints the chief corporate officers and, ordinarily, delegates to them the responsibility of conducting the day-to-day operations. Neither the members of the Board, nor the shareholders, nor the officers or employees of the corporation are personally responsible for the liabilities of the corporation unless that liability is created by an individual acting outside the scope of his authority. Only the corporate entity itself is liable. When dealing with a corporation, therefore, look to its financial resources and not to the wealth of the president or the officer with whom you may be dealing.

PURCHASING AND THE LAW OF AGENCY

Business long ago ceased to be a one-person affair. The professional buyer, in discharging the responsibilities of his position, is not buying goods and services for his private use. He is buying them for someone else: the company. And what about the salesman from whom the goods are purchased? Chances are, the supplies or services he is selling are not his own; rather, he is selling them for someone else, the company. The buyer and salesperson, under these circumstances, are performing roles for their respective companies which have one thing in common: they are both agents. As such, it is important that each understand his relationship to his company and to each other. The professional buyer should particularly understand the law of agency sufficiently well to determine what authority he has and to recognize the importance of determining what authority the salesperson with whom he is dealing has.

Creation of Agency

There are many ways by which an agency may be created. Most frequently it is created by express agreement between the principal and agent. It is accomplished when an employer hires the buyer or when an employer hires a salesperson.

Elements of an Agency

Agency is the relationship which exists where one person acts for another person with the latter person's authority. This relationship may arise gratuitously, from a contract, or by operation of law. The person for whom the agent acts is the *principal.* The person undertaking the performance of the act is the *agent.*

It is the general rule that every person able to act in his or her own right and own behalf may act through an agent. The converse is also true, that a person who is unable to act in his own right and in his own behalf cannot act through an agent. One cannot do by an agent what one cannot do in person.

The agent acts merely in a representative capacity for the principal and exercises authority delegated by the principal. Almost any person, except a lunatic, imbecile, or child of tender years, may be an agent.

The word *authority* as used here means the power of the agent to obligate the principal to third parties.

When Agency Must Be in Writing

There are some situations where the appointment of an agent must be done in a specific way. These situations are usually covered by a statute, called a *statute of frauds,* which requires the authority to be conferred in writing. The buyer's most frequent contact with the effects of such a statute probably would be in the area of contracts dealing with real property, which, generally, must be in writing. In any event, if the appointment of an agent is made in writing, the document should be complete. It should cover all the terms of the agency, including the purpose for which the agency was created, the duties of the principal as well as of the agent; payments to be made, if any; the duration of the agency; and any other matter which might later give rise to misunderstanding.

Other Ways Agency May Be Created

The principal may expressly say the words that establish the agency. For instance, the president of a company may say to a buyer, "You are hired as purchasing manager for this company to purchase the materials, supplies, and services we will need. Your authority to commit the company is limited to $100,000." If the purchasing manager agrees with the president of this company, the manager becomes the agent for the company for the purpose and with the limitation specified. The manager under this arrangement may obligate the company in dealings with suppliers.

Words alone, whether written or oral, are not the only way the authority of an agent can be given. The acts and conduct of the principal may be such that the authority of an agent may be inferred from such acts or conduct.

Authority of Agent—Express and Implied

A newly formed company may hire a person as the president with the express authority to "run the business." The president then does those acts ordinarily done in running a business. He borrows money; he acquires more facilities, machinery, and equipment; he hires people; he authorizes the procurement of materials and supplies; he establishes a manufacturing operation; he sells the products manufactured; and, if possible, he makes a good profit for the company.

But let us look at the president as an agent—when he has the express authority to run the business. All the acts he has done are incidental to and necessary for the running of the business. Although he was not expressly authorized to borrow money or hire people, such authority is implied by the act of the company in establishing the person as the president or head of the company and telling him to run the business.

The agent has the authority to do everything necessary or proper and usual in the ordinary course of business for effecting the purpose of his agency. This authority might be called *customary* authority. A salesperson with express authority to sell a principal's goods and who has possession of the principal's goods may by implication have the authority to deliver the goods or receive payment for the goods. However, mere possession of goods alone does not by implication give the holder authority to sell or deliver goods.

Apparent Authority

The authority may also arise by implication where the principal makes no overt act but merely acquiesces to an act being done by another. This may best be illustrated by the following factual situation: A person who had no authority to do so claimed to be a salesperson for a certain company and solicited orders from a buyer. The buyer from time to time gave the salesperson orders in the name of the company the salesperson claimed to represent. The so-called salesperson took the orders to the company; the company filled the orders without indicating to the buyer that the salesperson was not an authorized agent of the company. By continuing to fill orders, knowing the salesperson had obtained the orders by posing as the company's agent, there is acquiescence by the company to the salesperson's acts. This acquiescence then creates the agency relationship. It is this act of acquiescence by the company, the principal, not the acts of the salesperson, that creates the agency. Although a salesperson is a representative of his company, as an agent the authority he possesses may be somewhat limited. Courts long have regarded a salesperson as an emissary to solicit business for his employer, not a duly authorized agent possessing authority to obligate the company.

Another illustration of *apparent authority* is the situation in which a company permits its purchasing manager to buy materials beyond his express or stated authority as to type and amount involved. Or the company may allow others in the company outside of the purchasing department to make purchases without any stated agency authority. If the company accepts the material and pays for it, third persons would have a right to consider that the purchases were made with authority.

The general rule of law is that whenever one person has (1) held another person out as the first person's agent authorized to act for the first person in a given capacity or (2) has knowingly and without dissent permitted such second person to act as though he were the first person's agent, or (3) where the first person's habits and course of dealing have been such as to reasonably warrant that such second person was the first person's agent, it will be presumed that there is an agency so far as it may be necessary to protect the rights of anyone who has relied upon the actions of the first person.

Proof of Agency

As most agencies are contractual arrangements, the agent must be notified of the appointment and must accept the appointment. No particular method of acceptance is required. The agency must be proved by the facts by which the authority was conferred, and those facts must be acts of the principal with acceptance by the agent. The authority may not be proved by the agent's statements or admissions.

Ratification

Ratification is the subsequent adoption and affirmance by one person of an act which another, without authority, has previously assumed to do for him while purporting to act as his agent. Generally, any act which might previously have been authorized may be ratified, and any person who might have authorized an act may ratify it. Ratification requires that all the following conditions be met.

1. A principal must have the present ability to act.
2. A principal must have been identified or identifiable by the person doing the act at the time the act was done.
3. The act must have been done by a person allegedly acting as an agent.
4. A principal must have been in existence when the act was done. (This is important when one is dealing with corporations.)
5. The principal must have knowledge of all material facts.
6. The principal must ratify the whole act or none of it.
7. The transaction must still stand.
8. The ratification may not cut off intervening rights of third parties.

Generally, the legal effect of ratification is that the act becomes the act of the principal, with its benefits and detriments, from the beginning, as though he had previously authorized it to be done, except that if the rights of third persons have intervened between the act and its ratification, such rights cannot be cut off by the ratification.

Delegation of Authority of Agents

Generally an agent may be authorized to appoint other agents. A purchasing manager usually is authorized to hire buyers for his company. The buyer becomes the agent of the company, not the agent of the purchasing manager.

Usually an agent may not delegate authority to a subagent without the expressed or implied consent of his principal. A subagent is a person to whom the agent delegates, as his own agent, the performance of an act which the agent is obligated to do. A buyer is obligated to make purchase contracts for his company. He is not permitted to appoint someone else to perform his job for him without the expressed or implied consent of his company.

Termination of the Agency

An agency once created comes to an end in one of two ways: either it is terminated by an act of the parties or it ends by operation of law. The most common way of ending the agency relationship is by completing the original agreement. This may be done by accomplishing the object. Or, if the agency is, by its terms, to last only for a certain period of time or until an agreed event occurs, it terminates upon the expiration of that time or upon the happening of the agreed event.

Revocation

Acts of both parties or either party may also terminate an agency. The principal may revoke the authority granted at any time provided that the revocation has no effect on any acts the agent may have already done and that the authority was not originally granted by way of security or coupled with an interest.

Revocation may be by any method which clearly manifests the intention to do it. Notice of revocation to the agent must be given and is effective when the agent receives it or has knowledge of it. Notice of revocation of the agency to third persons must be actual notice to those who have relied on the authority, i.e., former customers, in the case of the revocation of a sales agency. It may be in the form of an advertisement in the case of notification to the general public.

Operation of Law

An agency may come to an end by operation of law. Death, bankruptcy. or insanity of either the principal or the agent would terminate an agency. Likewise, war between the countries of the principal and agent ends the relationship. Loss, destruction, or sale of the subject matter of an agency would also terminate the relationship. A change in the law which makes the subject of the agency illegal would also automatically end the relationship.

Duties of an Agent

It is the duty of the agent to conduct himself with the utmost loyalty and fidelity to the interests of his principal. The agent must not place himself, or voluntarily permit himself to be placed, in a position where his own interests, or those of any other person whom he has undertaken to represent, may conflict with the interest of his principal. *Any confidential information given the purchasing manager by his company must be kept in complete confidence and not divulged. This duty applies even after the purchasing manager leaves the employ of the company.*

The agent has the duty to obey the lawful instructions of his principal. Good faith is no excuse for an agent disobeying the instructions of his principal.

The agent has a duty not to exceed his authority. Although the agent has the *power* to exceed his authority, if he does so, he breaches his contract with his principal. If a purchasing manager acts outside the scope of his authority—either expressed or implied—he becomes subject to potential liability. If his company is forced to honor a contract which he negotiated that was not within the scope of his authority, his company may hold the purchasing manager personally liable for any loss which it may sustain. The company may, of course, elect to ratify and accept the actions of the purchasing manager, in which case the purchasing manager will be relieved of personal liability for his unauthorized acts.

The agent is ordinarily not personally liable to third persons on a contract properly made within the scope of his authority in the principal's name. However, the agent does make himself personally liable to third persons in the following situations:

1. When he makes a contract for a principal without the authority to do so
2. When the contract is made in the name of a principal having no legal existence (this is important when one is dealing with new corporations)
3. When, although the agent is authorized to bind his principal by contract, the agent pledges his personal responsibility for performance of the contract
4. When the agent has received money from the third person for his principal
5. When the agent has received money from his principal for the third person

It is essential for a buyer to remember that a buyer is personally liable for contracts he makes with third parties in the name of his principal if he exceeds the authority granted him by his principal.

The agent has the duty to exercise reasonable care in the performance of his undertakings. He must do what any reasonable, prudent person would do under similar circumstances. The purchasing manager, in addition to exercising reasonable care in his own actions and judgments, is responsible for the successful operation of his department. This does not mean that the purchasing manager insures his company against all losses occasioned by the commission of errors and mistakes in judgment. It merely means the exercise of ordinary care in selecting employees, in training them adequately, and in supervising them properly.

PURCHASING AND THE LAW OF CONTRACTS

Almost every action a buyer takes has some legal significance, and it is imperative that the buyer have a grasp of the essentials of commercial law. He need not be an attorney, but he does need to know the consequences of his actions, understand sufficient contract principles to protect his company's interests at first hand, and be able to recognize problems requiring expert legal assistance in time to permit his company's attorney to take appropriate action.

Nature of a Contract

A *contract* is a promise or a set of promises, the performance of which the law recognizes as a duty and for the breach of which the law provides a remedy. To fit the definition, the promise or promises must be of a certain character. Only promises which are made with contractual intent and which are binding are enforceable.

The contract may involve an exchange of promises or it may involve the exchange of a promise for an act. The former case is called a *bilateral* contract and the promises become binding upon the making of the promises. The latter case is a *unilateral* contract and the promise becomes binding upon the performance of a required act.

The contract may be *executory* or it may be *executed*. In the case of the executory contract, one or more of the promises are not fully performed and either party may avail itself of all remedies and defenses related to any aspect of the contract. In the case of the executed contract, all of the promises are fully performed and, generally, in the absence of fraud, the law will not examine the circumstances of formation of the contract or irregularities related to the general requirements for contracts.

The contract may be *express* or it may be *implied.* In the express contract, the parties have agreed, either orally or in writing. In the implied contract, the contractual relationship results from acts of the parties which indicate an intent to create a contract even though they have failed to express themselves either orally or in writing on the matter.

General Requirements

Four elements must be present in any contractual situation, whether the resultant contract is express or implied and whether it is unilateral or bilateral. A failure or absence of any one of these elements will prevent the creation of an enforceable contract, no matter what the intent of the parties.

Capable Parties   All persons are considered to have contractual capacity except those who are, by the law, either partially or completely disabled. Although there are some variations from state to state, the insane, the drugged, and the intoxicated are totally incapable of entering into contracts during the period of their disability, and minors and corporations have limited capacity. The insane, the drugged, and the intoxicated are considered to be unable to understand the significance of their acts and are therefore unable to give consent. The minor is only partially disabled since he or she has capacity to enter into contracts for *necessaries* based upon the so-called *station in life* test. The corporation has limited capacity since it is a fictitious person created under the sanctions of the state for the limited purposes set out in its charter. Its contractual capacity is limited to those purposes and such others as are necessary to permit it to operate within those limits.

Mutual Assent (Consent)   The contractual relationship is a voluntary relationship. Force, coercion, and duress prevent the creation of an enforceable contract. *Economic* pressures, short of actual duress, do not prevent the creation of a contract as long as the contractual act is the free will of the contracting party, no matter how reluctant he is. The mechanism of mutual assent is offer and acceptance, which we shall examine at length shortly.

Lawful Objective   The purpose or subject matter of the contract must not be criminal, immoral, or otherwise unlawful or against public policy. The proscribed objectives are both those which are bad in themselves *(malum in se)* and those that are bad only because they have been made so by some statutory enactment *(malum prohibitum)*.

A Sufficient Cause to Contract   This means the reason the parties entered into the contract—the consideration. It does not necessarily mean a commercial or monetary purpose. It means merely the *quid pro quo,* the "something for something" each hopes to get. In effect, it is the price of the bargain.

Formation of the Contract

The offer and the acceptance define the promises which constitute the contract and are the evidence of the mutual assent of the parties. The contract can come into being only if these are properly made and if the promises become binding by the existence of legally sufficient consideration.

The Offer An *offer* is usually defined as an act on the part of one person whereby he gives to another the legal power of creating the obligation called contract. A promise may be such an act. The offer must be carefully distinguished from preliminary negotiation. An offer can be accepted and can thereby become a contract. Preliminary negotiations may lead to the making of an offer. The distinction is extremely important in purchasing, for it determines the point at which the bargain is struck. While in practice the *invitation to bid* and the *request for quotation* are usually preliminary negotiation and the *purchase order* is usually the offer, there is no rule of law which makes this distinction. The intent of the parties, as expressed in their communications, is controlling. Requests for quotations should clearly state that they are not offers and cannot be accepted. Under the Uniform Commercial Code[1] as adopted in all the states except Louisiana, agreement on quantity may be sufficient to form a contract, and it is possible that a poorly drawn request for quotation may be construed as an offer.

In order to be legally sufficient, the offer must exhibit a present contractual intent by communication to the other party and by the certainty and definiteness of its term. The secret thoughts or mental reservations of the party making the offer are immaterial. His apparent intentions, as viewed by a reasonable person in the position of the one to whom the offer is made, are controlling. As between persons in the same trade or business, the usage of the words in the trade will be given effect. While the courts will attempt to resolve ambiguities by the application of certain rules of law, they will not remake a contract if the offer is unintelligible as to significant elements. Similarly, uncertainty in a contract cannot be waived. A contract based upon a poorly drawn offer may fail for uncertainty even after it is executed.

The offer begins to run at the time it is received by the person to whom the offer is made, unless otherwise stated in the offer. It continues in effect until it is accepted or rejected by the recipient, until it is revoked by the offerer, or until it lapses. The offer lapses at the end of a stated time or after a reasonable time if no time is stated in the offer. As between merchants, the Uniform Commercial Code provides that a written assurance signed by the offerer that the offer will not be revoked will be effective for a period not to exceed 3 months, even though the assurance is not sufficient as an option. The 3-month period may be renewed by another signed writing. In most states, the revocation of the offer is effective upon receipt by the person to whom the offer was made. Under certain circumstances the revocation may become effective upon transmission.

Once an offer is terminated, by whatever means and for whatever reason, it cannot be revived. An identical offer may be made by either party thereafter, but it is a new offer, and the timing, the relationship of the parties, the character of the offer, and the rights of the parties are a function of that new offer and not of the terminated offer.

---

[1]Copy available from the American Law Institute, 4025 Chestnut St., Philadelphia, Pa. 19104.

The form of the offer is important. All documents intended to be incorporated must be expressly referenced and made a part of the offer. Mere attachment to or enclosure with the offer will not be sufficient. Nor will words preprinted on a letterhead serve the purpose without express reference in the body of the offer.

Between merchants, unless the offer expressly limits acceptance to the terms of the offer, exceptions taken by the acceptance may become part of the contract, if they do not materially alter the offer or if the offerer fails to give notice of objection within a reasonable time.

The Acceptance   *Acceptance* is the exercise by the recipient of the offer of the power conferred by the offer. Acceptance occurs by the performance of an act, remembering that a promise may be an act.

If the offer requires the performance of an act other than a promise, nothing less than the full performance of that act will suffice. If the offer requires the making of a promise, the act of performance will not create a contract. Only the making of the promise will constitute an acceptance. The distinction is an important one, since upon it rests the determination of whether or not anything further remains to be done to consummate the contract. If the offer calls for the performance of a series of separate and distinct acts, the offer may be a continuing offer from which a series of individual contracts can be made. Each one stands on its own, and the recipient of the offer is at liberty to accept, reject, or ignore each offer as he chooses.

To be legally sufficient, the acceptance must satisfy four distinct criteria. First, it must be voluntary. The offer is gratuitous, and the acceptance is likewise at the free will of the one to whom the offer is made. Economic pressure short of actual duress does not destroy the voluntary character of an otherwise valid acceptance.

Second, there must be mental assent—some overt act on the part of the one to whom the offer is made evidencing a subjective intent to accept the offer. No special formalities are required, however, except as may be required by the statute of frauds. It is enough that the act indicate that at least one of the motives of the actor is to accept. Mere performance of an act which is repetitive, routine, or otherwise indistinguishable from normal behavior of the actor does not qualify that act as an acceptance. Subjective intent should not be confused with secret motives. The party need make no disclosure as to his motive for acceptance unless he is under a duty to disclose as a result of the existence of some confidential, fiduciary, or statutory relationship. Intent is nothing more than wanting to do the act, whatever the reason.

Third, the acceptance must be made by the recipient of the offer. Offers are personal, and even indirect knowledge is not enough to form the basis for an acceptance. Where the offer is made to an agent acting as an agent, the acceptance can be made by the principal himself, for he was in fact intended to be the ultimate recipient. Where the principal is undisclosed, the resulting contract is normally enforceable unless the undisclosed principal is one that the principal and the agent knew would be unacceptable to the offerer. The agent does not cease to be a party even after disclosure of the identity of the principal. He may sue or be sued on the contract, and he may even assume the rights and obligations of the contract if his principal chooses not to perform.

Fourth, the acceptance must be unequivocal or unqualified. Except under the special conditions for merchants set out in the Uniform Commercial Code, a qualified acceptance is no acceptance. It is, rather, a counteroffer and an implied rejection. The test as to whether the acceptance is qualified or not is whether it injects a condition which is not part of the offer or not implicit in the offer. As long as the offer and the acceptance coincide, it is immaterial that it is a "grumbling" acceptance, which is a request rather than a demand for a change in the offer. Often successive exceptions to the offer and objections to the exceptions develop during the course of negotiations and may extend even into performance. This contest of wits and half-wits is sometimes known as the "battle of the forms," and in fact is no battle at all. The Uniform Commercial Code has come to the rescue.

A definite and seasonable expression of acceptance or a written confirmation which is sent within a reasonable time operates as an acceptance even though it states terms additional to or different from those offered or agreed upon, unless acceptance is expressly made conditional on assent to the additional or different terms.

The additional terms are to be construed as proposals for addition to the contract. Between merchants such terms become part of the contract unless:

(a) the offer expressly limits acceptance to the terms of the offer;
(b) they materially alter it; or
(c) notification of objection to them has already been given or is given within a reasonable time after notice of them is received.

Conduct by both parties which recognizes the existence of a contract is sufficient to establish a contract for sale although the writings of the parties do not otherwise establish a contract. In such case the terms of the particular contract consist of those terms on which the writings of the parties agree, together with any supplementary terms incorporated under any other provisions of this Act.

The resulting contract may be something other than the buyer intended if a dispute develops.

The acceptance becomes effective when communicated to the offerer. Where the offerer fails to say how acceptance is to be communicated back to him, it is he, the offerer, who must assume the hazards of the means of communication he has selected. In such a case the rule states that the acceptance of an offer for a bilateral contract is effective when *properly dispatched* by an *authorized means* of communication. *Properly dispatched* means correctly addressed, delivery charges prepaid, properly enclosed, and acceptable to the intermediary, and deposited in the normal place for pickup or delivery. The *authorized means* is one which is either requested expressly by the offer or implied by the means selected to communicate the offer, that is, the same means as the offer. It is important to note that an acceptance which is not properly dispatched or does not use an authorized means is not ineffective. Such an acceptance takes effect upon receipt, rather than upon dispatch. If the offer requires a stated means of communication as the only one acceptable or specifies that the acceptance will not become effective until received, no other means will be acceptable.

Finally, since the offer is gratuitous, the recipient cannot be forced to act. He may ignore the offer completely, unless he has a duty to respond, as in the case of a confidential, fiduciary, or statutory relationship. The offer may not require silence as the means of acceptance. Silence can constitute acceptance only in the very limited case where the prior conduct of the parties indicates that silence was intended for acceptance.

Consideration   As mentioned before, *consideration* is one of the necessary elements of a contract—that which binds the promises and makes them enforceable. It is the element which binds the promises and so has meaning in relation to those promises. It must always be examined in terms of particular promises in a particular contract and of the parties who make and receive the promises. In legal parlance, the party who makes the promise is called the *promisor* and the one to whom the promise is made is called the *promisee*.

In the usual bilateral purchasing situation, the seller promises to deliver something in return for payment by the buyer, and the buyer promises to pay in return for delivery by the seller. There are two distinct promises, and each party's promise is consideration for the promise by the other. In the absence of any other circumstances, each one is agreeing to do something he is not otherwise obligated to do—the seller to deliver and the buyer to pay. Each is also receiving something he is not otherwise entitled to receive—the buyer his parts or services and the seller his payment.

When one of the promises in a contract is unenforceable for lack of consideration, the other promise is also unenforceable. The essence of contract is that both parties must be bound. If one is not bound, neither party is bound. We have, then, the second significant element in the subject of consideration. The consideration passing between the parties must result in *mutuality of obligation*. If either party reserves for himself the right to withdraw from the contract for any reason without providing for a means for payment for services performed to that time by the other party, his promise is illusory and the contract falls. Where the consideration for a promise is in the alternative, and one of the alternatives is insufficient as consideration, the promise which the consideration purports to bind is unenforceable. The promisee may elect to exercise that alternative which is insufficient as consideration and suffer no legal detriment. Whether he elects to do so or not is immaterial. The sufficiency of consideration is measured at the time the promises are made and not at the time of performance. The contract is defective at the outset and the action of the parties cannot cure the defect.

Consideration must be bargained for. Bargaining need not be extended or even conscious, but it must be present. In the absence of bargaining, it is apparent that the parties intended only a gift, and gifts are enforceable only within the limits set by statute in the particular jurisdiction. The element of bargaining is provable from the action of the parties.

Courts will not examine the value of consideration, though it must have some value, no matter how slight. It need not have the same value to both parties and, indeed, it need not have the same value to the promisee that the promisor intended.

If consideration is present, it will serve to bind all of the promises made by the promisor simultaneously as part of the same contract. Separate consideration need not be found or recited for each individual promise.

Statute of Frauds

The law related to the necessity for a writing in order to make a contract enforceable is a combination of statutory and common law. The original statute was passed by the English Parliament in 1677 and was called An Act to Prevent Frauds and Perjury.

Although the name has been shortened to the *statute of frauds,* the purpose remains the same—to *prevent* frauds and perjury by memorializing the agreement of the parties in writing.

It is most important to note that the statute does not require every contract to be in writing. Only those specifically set out in the local statute need be written. The great majority of contracts are enforceable even though they are oral.

Also significant is the fact that the statute of frauds is a defense which must be raised by the party against whom enforcement is sought. That is, an oral contract will be enforced, even though the statute requires that it be in writing, if the defending party fails to raise the issue and claim the defense of the statute. The oral contract is voidable only and not totally void from the outset.

Kinds of Contracts Needed to Be in Writing   They fall basically into two categories—"pure" contracts and contracts of sale. The first category is normally covered in general statutes of the jurisdiction, while the second is essentially within the purview of the Uniform Commercial Code. Each will be examined separately.

Contracts Other Than Contracts for the Sale of Goods   The following are the most common and the most important of the categories of such contracts which have the protection of the usual statute.

1. An agreement which *by its terms* is not to be performed within one year from the making thereof. It must appear that there is no possibility that the contract can be performed in less than a year in order to fall within the requirement for a writing.

2. Contracts which *by their terms* are not to be performed within the lifetime of the promisor. Any possibility that it can be performed within the lifetime of the promisor will take the contract out of the statute and an oral agreement will be sufficient. If death ends performance under the agreement (using words such as, "Until I die"), the contract is within the statute and will require a writing.

3. Agreements for the sale of land or an interest in land and leases for *more* than one year. Note that the lease must be for more than one year and that the time does not start at the making of the lease, as in paragraphs 1 and 2 above. The term *interest in land* can include future interests, reversions, remainders, fixtures, and the like. Some states consider an option to buy land to be an interest in

land within the meaning of the statute. Other states consider it merely a contract to keep an offer open. The safest policy is to put the option in writing.

4. Special promises to answer for the debt, default, or miscarriage of another. Normally the buyer is not concerned with this provision of the statute.

5. Various local statutes contain the provisions requiring a writing for agreements which are of little concern to buyers.

Contracts for the Sale of Goods   The necessity for a written contract with respect to the sale of goods is controlled by the Uniform Commercial Code. The appropriate section (2-201) has three distinct parts.

1. Contracts for the sale of goods for the price of $500 or more must be in writing signed by the party to be charged or his authorized agent or broker. The writing will be considered sufficient even though it omits or incorrectly states a term agreed upon, but it will be enforceable only for the quantity shown in the writing. This has been taken to mean that a writing which evidences agreement on nothing more than the quantity can be an enforceable contract. The courts will supply the rest of the contract, using tested legal principles of reasonableness, equity, trade customs or usages, market conditions, and prior course of conduct of the parties. This potential danger further strengthens the need for the buyer to indicate clearly in his invitation to bid, request for proposal, and other preliminary negotiations that such prior conduct does not constitute an offer. Failure to do so may result in premature creation of a contract under conditions less than favorable to the buyer.

2. Between merchants, a written confirmation of a prior oral agreement, received within a reasonable time after the oral agreement, will be construed as satisfying the requirement for a writing if the recipient has reason to know its contents, unless written notice of objection is given within 10 days after it is received. Under the code, the failure of a merchant to repudiate a confirmation sent to him by another merchant is treated the same as if the silent merchant had signed the written confirmation. The buyer must take positive action if he has any objection, and he may not delay beyond the 10-day period.

3. Even if the contract is for the sale of goods valued at $500 or more and there is no writing, or if the writing is insufficient, an oral contract may still be enforceable under the third part of Section 2-201. If the goods are to be specially manufactured for the buyer and are not suitable for resale to others in the normal course of the seller's business *and* the seller has made a substantial start to manufacture or to commit himself for procurement, no writing will be required. An oral agreement will be sufficient. If the goods are accepted by the buyer, an oral agreement will be enforceable, but only to the extent of the quantity of goods accepted by the buyer.

What Kind of Writing Does It Take to Satisfy the Statute?   Any writing attempted to be enforced as a contract must be signed by the party to be charged, that is, the party against whom enforcement is sought. Note carefully that both parties do not have to sign the agreement—only the party to be charged.

Beyond those general requirements, a writing evidencing agreement on the *quantity* of goods will be sufficient under the statute in a contract for the sale of goods.

In contracts other than for the sale of goods, the writing must further describe the subject matter, recite the consideration, and set out any other significant terms and conditions.

Other Considerations in a Written Contract   Some jurisdictions have other statutes which provide that a written contract is presumed, either conclusively or rebuttably, to contain all of the terms of the agreement. If the presumption is conclusive, no evidence may be offered to show otherwise. If the presumption is rebuttable, evidence may be offered to show the variance between the writing and the intent.

Conditions

Our definition of a contract said, in part, that it was a promise or a set of promises which the law recognized as a duty. Most of the promises in a contract are not absolute. They are *conditional.* The terms in which the conditions are expressed are determinative of the extent of the duty of the promisor and of the manner in which he must perform.

A *condition* is defined as a fact or event, the happening or nonhappening of which creates or extinguishes an absolute duty to perform on the part of the promisor.

One way to classify conditions is by the manner in which they are created. In this classification, they may be created either by action of the parties or by being constructed by the law. In the former case, they are *express*—set out in the contract—or *implied in fact*—i.e., resulting from obvious understandings of the parties, even though not stated in the contract, or from the very nature of the contract. Express conditions are set out in the contract, and as long as such conditions are not illegal, immoral, or otherwise against public policy, the courts will not disturb them, but will use them to gauge the performance of the parties. Implied-in-fact conditions exist by virtue of the circumstances and the relationship of the parties even though not expressed. They can be construed by answering the question, "What did the parties reasonably expect when they entered into the contract?"

Conditions constructed by the law are called *implied in law* or *constructive* conditions. These are such that the law will impose them regardless of the intention of the parties where fairness demands it. The subject is complex and beyond our purpose here.

Another method of classifying conditions is by the time of the fact or event taking effect—that is, the time of the happening or nonhappening of the event which creates or extinguishes the absolute duty.

Conditions Precedent   A *condition precedent* is one which must be fulfilled or satisfied *before* the promisor becomes liable to perform his promise. The most common such condition in purchasing relates to the buyer's obligation to pay. *In the absence of an express provision to the contrary,* the buyer's promise to pay is conditioned on delivery by the seller. The buyer is not obligated to keep his promise of payment until the seller has made delivery and the buyer has had a reasonable opportunity to examine the goods to verify that they conform to the contract.

If the seller is required to submit certain documentation for the buyer's approval and the seller's delivery of goods is dependent upon such documentation (drawings, test procedures, etc.), the failure on the part of the buyer to approve the data in a timely fashion may constitute a condition precedent and excuse delivery by the seller at the stated time.

If the contract provides that the buyer will furnish certain tooling or raw materials as the basis for performance by the seller, such provision is a condition precedent to performance by the seller.

Conditions Subsequent   A *condition subsequent* is one in which the occurrence of an event *extinguishes* a duty to perform. If the seller promises to deliver a given quantity of merchandise periodically for the stated period of performance *unless* there is a strike which affects his ability to perform, his duty to deliver is absolute until such time as a strike occurs. Upon the happening of that event, his further duty to deliver is cut off.

Conditions Concurrent   Where performance by the parties is mutually dependent and capable of simultaneous or almost simultaneous performance, the conditions are deemed *concurrent*.

The usual cash sale is an example of conditions concurrent. The salesperson is under no obligation to deliver until the buyer pays or tenders payment, and the buyer is under no obligation to pay until the seller delivers or tenders delivery. The events are capable of simultaneous performance and usually occur as such.

In contracts for personal services, the law will construe conditions as concurrent whenever possible. Once personal services are performed, they can rarely be recalled, and the burden for payment ought to be as close to simultaneous as possible.

Special Cases of Conditions

Impossibility of Performance   This concept says simply that if performance is or has become impossible, performance is excused. Whenever the buyer believes he has this situation, he should consult his attorney.

Frustration of Purpose   This concept is also called *economic frustration* and provides that where, as a result of unforeseen and fortuitous circumstances, the promisor, through no fault of his own, will not get what he expected when the contract was made, his further performance will be excused. In such a case the buyer should again consult his attorney.

Ambiguity and Mistake

If neither party knows or has reason to know of the mistake or ambiguity, there is a contract only if both parties attach the same meaning subjectively to the words.

If both parties know or have reason to know of the mistake or ambiguity, there is a contract only if in fact both attach the same meaning to the words.

If only one party knows or has reason to know of the mistake or ambiguity, there will be a contract based upon what the innocent party intended.

The real problem is not with the rules but with determining whether the parties knew or should have known. The purpose of the law is to look for the intent of the parties in their writings and their actions. The courts first search the "four corners of the document"—the contract. That is, they will read the instrument as a whole rather than the single provision in dispute. If an ambiguity still remains or the intent of the parties is not clear, the courts will look to extrinsic evidence— evidence outside of the contract. Such evidence includes preliminary negotiations, prior course of conduct, usages of the trade, communications between the parties prior to and during the course of performance, conduct during performance, and any other circumstance from which the intent of the parties can be derived. It is for this purpose that the buyer should keep complete and clear minutes of his negotiations and exercise care in communications during the course of performance.

Warranties

A *warranty* is simply a promise given by the seller to the purchaser that the goods are of a certain quality and will conform to certain standards. The standards may be expressed by description or by reference to a sample or model or written criteria such as a specification or an industry standard. A time period may be specified or not. The parties may choose to be totally silent on the subject.

Statutory Warranty   In the absence of express exclusion by the parties in their contract, the Uniform Commercial Code provides certain minimum requirements. It defines how express warranties may be created, which warranties are implied by law, and how the parties may disclaim or exclude warranties from their contracts.

1. SECTION 2-312. WARRANTY OF TITLE AND AGAINST INFRINGEMENT; BUYER'S OBLIGATION AGAINST INFRINGEMENT.   This section provides that in every contract of sale, unless expressly excluded by the parties, the seller promises that he will give good title to the buyer for the goods sold, that he has the right to sell, and that the goods will be be delivered free from any lien, security interest, or other encumbrance of which the buyer has no knowledge. Such promise may be excluded only by "specific language" or by circumstances which give the buyer "reason to know" that the seller does not claim title or is selling only such title as he or another person may have, if any. Finally, and of special significance in purchasing, the section requires that "a buyer who furnished specifications to the seller must hold the seller harmless" against claims of infringement by third persons "which arise out of compliance with the specification."

2. SECTION 2-314. IMPLIED WARRANTY: MERCHANTABILITY; USAGE OF TRADE.   This section provides that there will be implied by the law in every contract for the sale of goods a warranty that the goods will be "merchantable" if the seller is a merchant with respect to goods of that kind. The section defines *merchantable* as able to "pass without objection in the trade under the contract

description" and "fit for the ordinary purposes for which such goods are used." There are further requirements that the warranty shall apply equally to each unit of all the units involved, that they be adequately contained, packaged, and labeled *as required by the agreement,* and that they conform to the promises of fact on the container or label. Such warranty may be excluded or modified only expressly by the parties, as may implied warranties arising "from course of dealing or usage of trade."

Thus, under this section, a hammer must be fit for the purpose of driving and removing nails, since this is the ordinary purpose for which a hammer is used. While it may serve occasionally as a doorstop or a crowbar, those are not its ordinary uses, and the warrant of merchantability is not applicable if it fails in such use.

3. SECTION 2-315. IMPLIED WARRANTY: FITNESS FOR PARTICULAR PURPOSE. Again, unless expressly excluded or modified by the parties, there is implied in every contract of sale a warranty to the effect that the goods will be fit for a *particular* purpose if, at the time the contract was made, the seller had reason to know that the goods were intended for that particular purpose and that the buyer was relying on the seller's skill and judgment to select or furnish goods suitable for that particular purpose. Here it is immaterial what the ordinary use of the article is.

4. SECTION 2-316. EXCLUSION OR MODIFICATION OF WARRANTIES. This section is quite long and complex. From the buyer's standpoint, the significant elements are that the implied warranties may be disclaimed or excluded *only* by a conspicuous writing and that the words of exclusion are contained in the section itself. The word *conspicuous* has been taken to mean that the disclaimer should be carried in boldface type in order that it shall stand out from the surrounding words.

The section contains three separate exceptions to the above requirements. First, that all implied warranties are excluded by use of words such as *as is, with all faults,* and other language which in their common understanding call the buyer's attention to the exclusion. Second, that implied warranties may be excluded or modified by usages of the trade or by a course of dealings or by the course of performance between the parties. Third, that "when the buyer before entering into the contract has examined the goods or the sample or model as fully as he desired or has refused to examine the goods there is no implied warranty with regard to defects which an examination ought in the circumstances to have revealed to him."

Express Warranties While the Code leaves the parties free to establish whatever standards they choose by way of warranty, it does identify the three ways in which express warranties may be created. First, by "affirmation of fact or promise made by the seller," and the goods must conform to such affirmation or promise. Second, by "description of the goods," and the goods must conform to the description. Third, by "sample or model," and all the goods involved must conform to the sample or model. In all three cases, the affirmation or promise, the description or the sample or model, must become "part of the basis for the bargain."

The section goes on to say that words such as *warranty* and *guarantee* need not be used, and that the seller need not have a specific intention to make a warranty in order to create one. Merely affirming the value of the goods or giving his opinion of the goods does not constitute an express warranty by the seller.

Patent and Latent Defects   The buyer has a reasonable time to inspect the goods to assure himself that they conform to the contract. Under the Code, the expenses of inspection must be borne by the buyer but may be recovered from the seller if the goods do not conform and are rejected. The buyer has the options to accept the entire lot of nonconforming goods, to reject the entire lot, and to accept any indivisible unit or units and reject the rest. The seller may "cure" the non-conforming delivery by giving notice of his intention to do so and by making a conforming delivery if the contract time for performance permits. The buyer may surrender his right to reject if he fails to give notice of the nonconformance within a reasonable time or if he fails to "particularize" the reasons for rejection upon request and in time for the seller to "cure" by a timely and conforming delivery. These are the general rules, but the subject of remedies is complex, and the buyer should seek legal assistance immediately in the event of nonconformance of the goods or in the event of refusal by the seller to deliver.

Defects giving rise to the buyer's right to reject goods are normally defined as either *patent* or *latent*. The patent defect is one which is visible upon reasonable examination appropriate to normal receiving-inspection acceptance procedures. The failure of the buyer to inspect does not change its character. If the defect is not discoverable by examination, it is a latent defect. The mere fact that the article fails in performance and that the defect was not visible on examination does not mean that there was such a "latent" defect as to warrant rejection by the buyer. In order to qualify, the defect must have been present *at the time of delivery*. Once the fact of the defect is established, it is immaterial that it is either patent or latent, and the buyer's rights and obligations depend on his actions in accordance with the general rules set out above.

Of course, if the warranty provision in the contract sets out a specific period during which the buyer may reject for nonconformance, he has only that time to give notice of the defect. In the absence of any expression of time, he has only a reasonable time.

Economic Considerations   It is a common belief among buyers that warranty is exclusively the province of the attorney. Nothing could be further from the truth. To be sure, it is the attorney's function to assure that the express warranty contained in the contract accurately reflects the coverage agreed upon. It is the buyer's function to determine how much warranty his company needs, how much his company wants, and the extent to which the cost is worth the protection his company will get.

Express warranties may cost money. A warranty is a contingency which is included in the price of the goods purchased. The extent to which it is expressed or separately stated in cost breakdowns or included in overhead rates is a matter of the seller's accounting practices. The cost per unit, or the rate if it is a function of overhead, is dependent on the seller's statistical experience with the item if it is part of his standard line, or on his confidence in the design if it is being developed especially for the buyer. If his experience has shown that 1 out of 20 of his items has been returned for repair under warranty provisions, his price will somewhere include a 5 percent factor to cover the contingency that a similar ratio will occur in the future. The percentage factor may be greater or less for sales of greater or lesser quantities than the statistical 20. Time is another factor in his experience which becomes an element in assigning a part of the purchase price to the contingency. If failures and rejections occur at the rate of 5 percent within 3 months and 10 percent within 6 months, the buyer who requires a 6 months' warranty will pay twice as much for such a warranty.

The buyer must, of course, consider the economics from a different point of view. If his experience indicates that failures have occurred at the rate of only 1 percent, he is wasting his company's money to pay 5 percent. If experience shows that failures always occur within 3 months of delivery, it is similarly uneconomical to buy a 6 months' warranty. How much time does he need to cover the warranty given by his company to its customers? How long will the goods be on the shelf before they are consumed? How much can his company afford to pay and still remain competitive? Would it be cheaper in the long run to become a self-insurer? The buyer *must* make this kind of analysis, expecially where the subcontractor or supplier has taken exception to the buyer's "boiler plate" warranty provision. He must determine why the exception is taken. Will an increase in the purchase price eliminate the exception? Is it an indication of the seller's lack of confidence in the goods? The buyer should draw on all of the information available to him—the opinions and experience of his manufacturing, engineering, and sales people, as well as management—in making the necessary trade-offs and the ultimate decision. Only then can he approach his attorney to assure that the final warranty provision affords the protection he bought and does not conflict with some overriding company philosophy.

Survivability of Warranty Rights   Since under the Code the buyer has the right of reasonable inspection and may reject goods if they fail to conform to the contract, warranty will survive for an additional period only to the extent that the contract expressly provides for survival or to the extent that the Code permits. Under the Code, the buyer's rights are conditioned on *acceptance*. Section 2-606 states that acceptance occurs when the buyer "(*a*) after a reasonable opportunity to inspect the goods signifies to the seller that the goods are conforming or that he will take or retain them in spite of their non-conformity; or (*b*) fails to make an effective rejection . . . ; or (*c*) does any act inconsistent with the seller's ownership. . . ." Section 2-607 states that the buyer must pay at the contract price for any goods accepted, and "acceptance of goods by the buyer *precludes* rejection of the goods accepted and if made with the knowledge of a non-conformity *cannot be* *revoked* because of it." Section 2-608 provides that the buyer may revoke his acceptance if goods "whose non-conformity substantially impair its value to him if he has accepted it (*a*) on the reasonable assumption that its non-conformity would be cured and it has not been seasonally cured; or (*b*) without discovery of such non-conformity if his acceptance was *reasonably* induced either by the difficulty of discovery before acceptance or by the seller's assurances." The section goes on to require that the buyer make known his revocation of the acceptance within a reasonable time after discovery of the nonconformity or after he "*should have discovered* the grounds for it and before any substantial change in condition of the goods which is not caused by their own defects." Revocation is not effective until notice is received by the seller.

The net effect of the Code, in the absence of any express time period for rejection contained in the contract, is to put the burden on the buyer to inspect the goods upon receipt, to force him to make an election of remedies if a nonconformity is discovered on receipt of the goods, and to take positive action if a defect is discovered after the goods are originally accepted as conforming to the contract. Nothing less will afford him any protection.

Breach of Contract

Actual Breach   An *actual breach of contract* is simply a failure to perform at the time and in the manner required by the contract. The innocent party expected performance, was entitled to receive performance, and did not get it from the other party.

Anticipatory Breach   In the *anticipatory breach of contract* there has not yet been a failure of performance. There is reason to believe, however, that performance will not be forthcoming from one of the parties. It can occur in one of two ways. A party may repudiate the contract, stating that he will not perform when performance is due, or he can disable himself by doing something which will eliminate his capacity to perform. Under the old rule of law, which is still in effect in a few jurisdictions, the injured party could not take action until the time for performance had passed and the promisor had failed to perform.

Under the modern, majority rule an action for anticipatory breach will be allowed except on promissory notes, bonds, and other financial paper. This rule is based upon the theory that there is implied in every contract to perform in the future a promise that neither party will do anything to prejudice the rights of the other inconsistent with the contract and that the promisor will not decrease the value of the original bargain. Repudiation and disablement are breaches of that implied promise. In order to prevail, however, the aggrieved party must show convincing evidence of the anticipatory breach and compelling reasons why he must go elsewhere for performance or take some other course of action. There must in fact be evidence of a *need to decide* on the part of the injured party.

Measure of Damages   Although this subject is properly the province of the attorney acting for the buyer, certain general considerations should be known to the buyer. The general rule is that recovery will be allowed for the value of the bargain lost as a result of the breach. No punitive damages are permitted except in situations involving fraud and deceit. Nor will the buyer in the usual purchasing situation be given specific performance, that is, a requirement that the defaulting party perform as required by the contract. Money damages only will be given except in very unusual circumstances.

Courts will not enforce provisions which impose a penalty or a forfeiture upon the defaulting party. In the case of provisions for liquidated damages, that is, provisions which set out a fixed amount as damages for a breach, such provisions will be enforced only where damages were uncertain and difficult to ascertain at the time the contract was created, where there was an intent on the part of the contracting parties to liquidate damages in advance, and where the amount is reasonable, looking back to the time the contract was made.

Arbitration

Most purchasers and sellers dislike disagreements about performance under purchase or sale agreements and do all that is possible to prevent court action. If the buyer and seller cannot reach agreement, it may be well to refer the dispute to an arbitrator or a group of arbitrators, with agreement in advance to abide by their decision rather than to resort to the courts. A contract provision for arbitration should be specific and should set up the manner of selection of arbitrators and the entire mechanism for arbitration. Such a contract may adopt by reference the rules of the American Arbitration Association. In foreign procurements, the arbitration rules of the International Chamber of Commerce are available.

Identification of Sales

Under the Uniform Commercial Code, Section 2-106, a *sale* is defined as a transaction consisting of the passage of title from the buyer for a price. A *present sale* is defined as a sale which is accomplished by the making of the contract.

Bailment Distinguished from Sale   Buyers are frequently required to furnish suppliers with tools or materials from which to fabricate parts, or to warehouse merchandise. This transaction is a *bailment* and not a transfer of title. Adequate insurance and a careful selection of contractors should be the rule.

Consignment, Sale or Return, and Sale on Approval   A consignment should not be confused with a sale. A *consignment* refers to goods entrusted to another for sale. The relationship is that of agency, and title remains in the consignor until the sale is accomplished.

Under Section 2-326 of the Uniform Commercial Code, if the delivered goods may be returned by the buyer even though they conform to the contract, the transaction is a *sale on approval* if the goods are delivered primarily for use, and a *sale or return* if the goods are delivered primarily for resale.

Conditional Sales   A *conditional sales contract* is one in which the buyer is given possession of the goods but legal title remains in the seller. Normally full title passes to the buyer upon final payment, if payment is the condition. Most states have provision for recording conditional sales contracts.

Transfer of Ownership   Section 2-401 of the Code states that "title to goods cannot pass under a contract for sale prior to their identification to the contract." In the absence of any agreement to the contrary, therefore, the buyer acquires no rights to goods on the shelf until they are taken off and assigned to his contract, or to growing materials until they are cut and assigned to his contract. The section further states that "unless otherwise explicitly agreed title passes to the buyer at the time and place at which the seller completes his performance with reference to the physical delivery of the goods."

Questions of passage of title in a sales contract are usually resolved by reference to an *f.o.b.* (free on board) point. The buyer gets title when the goods are delivered to that point. If the delivery is f.o.b. the seller's plant, the goods must be delivered to the carrier by the seller and packaged and labeled in a manner acceptable to the carrier, and it is the buyer's obligation to insure it against loss or damage during transit. If the delivery is to be f.o.b. the buyer's plant, the insurance obligation is on the seller. The parties are free to select any point by agreement in their contract.

C.o.d. (Cash on Delivery) Sales   A *c.o.d. sale* provides for payment by the buyer immediately on delivery. The seller may be in doubt about the buyer's credit, he may have a company policy that all sales under a certain amount must be c.o.d., or he may have a policy of making no sales on credit. Under this kind of sale, if the buyer fails to make payment at the time of delivery, the seller or his carrier agent need not, and probably will not, leave the goods in the buyer's possession. In addition, the buyer is in default of his promise to pay on delivery and will undoubtedly be required to pay an additional amount for redelivery.

General Legal Considerations

Applicable Statutes   In addition to the Uniform Commercial Code, the local statute of frauds, and state statutes relating to periods of limitation and other procedural elements, the following federal statutes have varying degrees of application to purchasing activities:

Anti-Kickback Act
Armed Services Procurement Act
Buy American Act
Contract Work Hours Standards Act
Davis-Bacon Act (minimum wages for public works employees)
Miller Act (bonds of contractors for public buildings)
Walsh-Healy Act (minimum wages and maximum hours of work)
Renegotiation Act of 1951
Small Business Act
Sherman Anti-Trust Act
Truth in Negotiations Act
Vincent-Trammel Act (profit limitations)
Wunderlich Act (government contracts judicial review)

Which Law Governs   Where the laws of two or more jurisdictions involved in a business transaction are in conflict, it becomes important to determine which law governs. Generally, the formation of the contract and the interpretation of its provision will be governed by the law of the jurisdiction in which the last act that brings the contract into existence is executed. However, the legal rules relating to delivery of goods and their acceptance are determined by the laws of the jurisdiction in which the delivery is to be made or accepted, unless the parties have agreed to the contrary. The question of conflict of laws in such cases is an entire branch of the law in itself, and it may be desirable to specify by contract provision that the laws of a particular state shall govern the purchase transaction. Even if this is done, however, it is advisable for the buyer to make certain that nothing in the seller's acknowledgment or acceptance is in conflict with such provision. If such conflicts are discovered, the problem should be resolved immediately so that both parties understand which laws are to apply.

Unpriced Orders   It is sometimes necessary to issue purchase orders without a definite price being shown for the items ordered. This may occur when time does not permit lengthy cost calculations on the part of the supplier before beginning work, or because some emergency requires immediate purchase without advance negotiation. If the parties fail to agree on a price thereafter, the courts will determine the price based upon the *reasonable value* of the goods and services furnished. What is reasonable may vary from time to time and from place to place for the same goods and services, depending upon market conditions, past course of conduct of the parties, usages of the trade, and other factors. Section 2-305 of the Uniform Commercial Code confirms that principle, with the additional provisions that:

1. If the parties fail to fix a price through fault of one of the parties, the other may treat the contract as canceled or himself fix a reasonable price, at his option.

2. Where the parties intend not to be bound unless a price is fixed, there will be no contract if a price is not fixed. In that case, the buyer must return any goods received or pay their reasonable value at the time of delivery and the seller must return any part of the price paid on account.

Proprietary Information

Proprietary information is defined as any information which is not generally known to competitors and which provides a competitive advantage. Such information may be technical in nature or may be of a business nature. Matters of public knowledge or general knowledge cannot be proprietary information. The terms *trade secret* and *confidential information* are often used interchangeably with the term *proprietary information*. Proprietary information may be known by a limited number of others and still be proprietary provided such others also treat it as proprietary. It is not necessary that proprietary information be patentable, but it appears that it should constitute something which is not readily obtainable by other means or obvious in nature. Unrestricted disclosure of proprietary information, of course, places it in the public domain, where it can no longer be represented to be proprietary. For example, information which is readily obtainable from a product sold in the open market cannot be argued to be a trade secret or proprietary, at least from a proprietary information or trade secret standpoint. The term is sometimes broadly used to designate patented items, and therefore it could properly be stated in this sense that a patented article, although sold in the commercial, open market, is still proprietary. The words *confidential disclosure* or words of similar import seek to establish that information is trade secret or proprietary information. When information is submitted with the express provision that "this information shall only be used for the purpose of . . . ," a proprietary relationship or a confidential relationship is sought to be established.

It is customary, of course, when receiving bid information or proposals, and the like, that prices and technical proposals not be disclosed to bidding competitors. This is a legally binding obligation deduced from the circumstances of the situation and also from the custom in procurement. Such obligation between the parties is implied even though there are no express words between the parties as to that aspect.

Rights in Data

In view of the possibility of data, or other information which is being purchased, being proprietary, trade secret, or confidential information, where particular use is intended to be made of the data or where particular rights are desired in the data, they should be procured with the necessary rights in order to preclude the possibility of not being able to use the data for the desired purpose. Legal counsel is ordinarily required in such matters in order to assure the obtaining of adequate rights.

Patent Liability

In the procurement of work or supplies, it may be that patents of others are infringed in carrying out the work or furnishing the supplies. In almost all procurement situations, there is a question as to who will stand such potential patent liability to others. If the parties are silent on the subject, ordinarily the liability is the seller's. The warranty against patent infringement is deemed to be one of the warranties of title. However, where the seller is merely conforming to what is specified by the buyer, the liability is the buyer's. The Uniform Commercial Code makes note of such situations.

Ordinarily in the procurement of commercial work and products, express patent indemnity is sought from the seller. The contingent patent liability is then, of course, an element of cost in the sale price.

Patentable Inventions

It may be that in the performance of work under a purchase order an invention will be made. This is particularly true where research, experimentation, development, or design is called for. A clear understanding should be arrived at as to the ownership of inventions made in the performance of work under the contract. If no express language is found, it is likely that the inventions made in the performance of such work will belong to the buyer. Such a situation could prove embarrassing to the seller where he intends to continue to exploit the development. As stated previously, matters in these areas should be discussed with legal counsel, particularly a patent lawyer. Generally, a nonexclusive license for the buyer to use any such information and to sell to others is sufficient from his standpoint.

NOTE: For further information on subjects covered in this section see the list of references in Section 30.

Section **5**

Purchasing Systems

EDITOR

Arthur A. Gibson, C.P.M. *Director of Purchasing, Glass Containers Corporation, Fullerton, California*

ASSOCIATE EDITORS

Richard H. Olson, C.P.M. *Group Materials Manager, Lighting Products Group, GTE Products Corporation, Danvers, Massachusetts*

James H. McDowell, Jr., C.P.M. *Assistant Director, Division of Purchasing, Tennessee Valley Authority, Chattanooga, Tennessee*

A good purchasing system will include a network of information flow which includes forms and records that enable the people involved in the purchasing cycle to communicate and control the what, when, where, and how of the purchasing process. The developed system should facilitate purchasing's daily work with other people and departments while maintaining good control of the purchasing decision process. Section 1 discusses the interdepartmental relationships, but the following are perhaps the people and departments most often involved with the purchasing cycle and the systems that support it.

1. Requesting individual
2. Approving authority
3. Buyer
4. Vendor
5. Accounting department
6. Receiving department
7. Inspection department

The purchasing department should design and utilize forms and records which enable the foregoing people and departments to quickly and accurately perform their functions. This section explains various types of purchasing forms, records, and files and how they are used.

FORMS

There is no such thing as a standard form which will apply to all purchasing departments regardless of company size. While the forms covered in this section

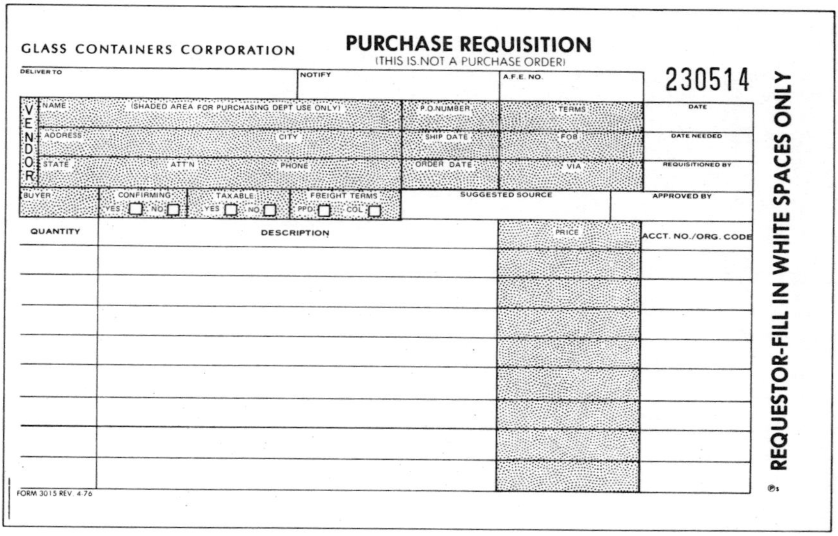
GLASS CONTAINERS CORPORATION

PURCHASE REQUISITION

(THIS IS NOT A PURCHASE ORDER)

230514

DELIVER TO | NOTIFY | A.F.E. NO.

VENDOR: NAME (SHADED AREA FOR PURCHASING DEPT USE ONLY) | P.O. NUMBER | TERMS | DATE

ADDRESS | CITY | SHIP DATE | FOB | DATE NEEDED

STATE | ATTN | PHONE | ORDER DATE | VIA | REQUISITIONED BY

BUYER | CONFIRMING: YES ☐ NO ☐ | TAXABLE: YES ☐ NO ☐ | FREIGHT TERMS: PPD ☐ COL ☐ | SUGGESTED SOURCE | APPROVED BY

QUANTITY	DESCRIPTION	PRICE	ACCT. NO./ORG. CODE

FORM 3015 REV. 4-76

REQUESTOR-FILL IN WHITE SPACES ONLY

Fig. 5-1 Purchase requisition. *(Glass Containers Corporation.)*

are basic, the printed matter may vary according to the type of business involved, company policy, and laws in different states.

For some companies, forms might involve some type of mechanization, such as is described in Section 15. Also not included in this section are procedures in governmental purchasing, which may be covered by special legislation, as discussed in Section 20. The basic forms and records presented here should apply to most other situations, however.

Purchase Requisition

The purchase requisition is the prime document authorizing the purchasing department to purchase specific materials, parts, supplies, equipment, or services. A more or less standard format is illustrated in Fig. 5-1; a more elaborate form is shown in Fig. 5-2.

Requisitions can originate from any department. However, from a control standpoint, the fewer originating locations the better. Most companies issue instructions over the controller's or general manager's signature, defining who may issue and approve purchase requisitions and the limitations of such authority. Some departments keep specimen signatures of authorized approvers on file.

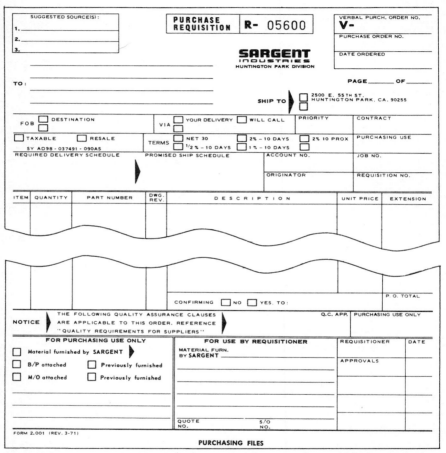

Fig. 5-2 Purchase requisition form—the prime document from which the purchasing department makes purchases. *(Reproduced by permission of Sargent Industries.)*

Generally there are two types of requisitions: (1) for purchase on a one-time basis (*nonrepetitive*), and (2) for purchases made on a regular basis, such as stores commodities (*repetitive*). Regardless of the requisition type, certain basic information is required if the purchasing department is to do an intelligent job of buying. These data usually are filled in on the requisition by the originator or by the person authorized to approve it.

A requisition should include the following basic information:

1. Requisition number and individual (department) issuing requisition
2. Quantity of material required
3. Complete description of the part, goods, or service, with specification number, blueprint reference, or catalog number, so that there will be no misunderstanding of what is required
4. Date the material is required to be in the plant or at the site
5. Delivery information to show which plant, department, or individual is to receive the material
6. Account number or authorization number to be charged, when required by company procedure
7. Special instructions (any deviations from normal or standard procedures)
8. Affidavits or material certifications required
9. Authorization or necessary approvals

As a further guide, some companies require that additional information be furnished, such as quantity on hand and usage for a given period of time.

To speed the procurement function, the requisition should be accompanied by at least one set of all applicable prints, specifications, and manufacturing data sheets required by the buyer in his evaluation of the requirement and for the solicitation of bids.

It is as easy to prepare a requisition properly as it is to prepare it improperly, and the purchasing manager can do much to lighten his load by issuing written instructions for its preparation—and then insisting that they be followed. Requisitions should be written uniformly, and material call-outs should follow industry practice for that commodity, saving rewriting or transposition of terms by the buyer.

To facilitate completion of the purchase requisition for issuance of the purchase order and to provide a clear audit trail, the requisition form may provide spaces for the buyer to add:

1. Shipping destination
2. Vendor's name and address
3. Purchase order number
4. Date delivery is promised (or ship date)
5. Order date
6. Terms of payment
7. F.o.b. point
8. Routing instructions (via)
9. Buyer's initials
10. Whether purchase order is confirming
11. Tax status
12. Freight terms (prepaid or collect)
13. Complete price information
14. Any special terms or conditions

All the above information should be in logical sequence for the typist to transpose it to the purchase order.

Nonrepetitive   Nonrepetitive requisitions (Fig. 5-1) are usually designed to fit the needs of individual companies. At least two copies are needed: one for the person requesting the material, and one for the purchasing department. A third

ITEM:										STOCK NO.	
USE:										UNIT	

DELIVER TO				NOTIFY	INSPECTION		TAXABLE	ACCOUNT		ORG. CODE	
					YES ☐ NO ☐		YES NO				

MAX.	MIN.	OK	DATE	VENDOR NAME – TERMS, F.O.B., VIA, LEADTIME
				1.
				2.
				3.
				4.

USING DEPT.

			%		%		%		%		%

	REQUISITIONED				PURCHASED						
DATE	ON HAND	NEED QUANTITY	DATE	BY	DATE	VEND. NO.	P/O NO.	QUANTITY	PRICE	BUYER	DATE PROM.

	YEAR	JAN.	FEB.	MAR.	APRIL	MAY	JUNE	JULY	AUG.	SEPT.	OCT.	NOV.	DEC.	TOTAL
USAGE RECORD														

TRAVELING REQUISITION
FORM NO. 434 (REV. JULY 70)   *Physical Inventory Must Be Taken Prior To Forwarding To Purchasing Dept.*

Fig. 5-3   Traveling requisition. *(Glass Containers Corporation.)*

copy is needed for the person requesting the material, indicating with whom the order was placed and the date delivery is promised, if a copy of the purchase order is not provided to this person. As discussed elsewhere, the purchase requisition can be designed to create a copy for use as a purchase order to the supplier.

The old question of single-item versus multi-item requisitions is still debated. There are advantages and disadvantages to each, and each purchasing manager must resolve this within the context of his own needs.

Repetitive   Many items are repetitive; hence the same information must be written again on a new requisition. Rewriting can be excessive and wasteful. This is handled through the use of a *traveling requisition* (Fig. 5-3). Normally it is a single-part form or card on which is written or typed all the information that remains constant from purchase to purchase. The requisitioner merely indicates the variables: new quantity required, date required, etc. This form "travels" to the purchasing department, where the purchase order is issued, and then it is returned to the requisitioner. This form has the added advantage of providing a record of previous purchases right on the requisition. Different colors can be used to indicate the department requisitioning the material, a practice which guards against the form being returned to the wrong department.

With the advent of tape-punching and -reading typewriters, some firms employ a pocket on the back of the traveling requisition to house the prepunched tape or card which is used to receive the constant data. The purchasing department can then rerun the tape or cards when preparing the purchase order and have all constant data written in automatically. This not only saves time, but eliminates the need to check for typing errors.

Request for Quotation (RFQ)

Inquiry Form   An invitation to bid or a request for quotation (RFQ) conveys to vendors a requirement for materials or services that the purchaser intends to buy, and it is a means of inviting a bid or bids from prospective suppliers.

There are three types of RFQ: verbal, letter, and bid forms. A verbal RFQ usually is used for minor purchases. Normally these are obtained in an interview or by telephone conversation (Fig. 5-4). Otherwise, an RFQ should be handled by a written request in letter form or on a specially designed request form (Fig. 5-5).

This request form is normally sent out in duplicate, with one copy to be returned to the buyer with the quotation. Some vendors return quotations on their own form, with their own terms or conditions of sale. This is an area in which extreme care should be exercised, as terms and conditions vary from company to company.

A well-designed RFQ form should provide space for the following pertinent information (filled in by the purchasing department):

1. Request number
2. Date of request
3. Return deadline

	G. C. C. TELEPHONE QUOTATION	
	Item: Quantity: Need Date:	Date: Taken by:
Rank	Source: Address: Quoted by: Price: (List) (Disc.) (Net) Terms: (Payment) (F.O.B.) Delivery Method/Ship Date:	
Rank	Source: Address: Quoted by: Price: (List) (Disc.) (Net) Terms: (Payment) (F.O.B.) Delivery Method/Ship Date:	
Rank	Source: Address: Quoted by: Price: (List) (Disc.) (Net) Terms: (Payment) (F.O.B.) Delivery Method/Ship Date:	
	Form No. 8815 (Rev. A 9-76)	

Fig. 5-4 Telephone quotation. *(Glass Containers Corporation.)*

4. Name of buyer or purchasing agent
5. Quantity required and complete description
6. Delivery dates
7. Tooling and/or pattern available
8. Any other special information (such as packaging) that would affect price
9. Shipping destination

Space should be provided for the vendor to fill in the following information:

1. Unit price
2. Total cost of contract (optional)
3. F.o.b. point
4. Lead time required
5. Payment terms and cash discount
6. Tooling charges (separate item)
7. Date of quotation
8. Signature

This form is more likely to obtain all the necessary information than the letter invitation. Since the invitation form is designed and printed with copies for three sources, it also takes less time to prepare. Careful blanking and carbon selection are necessary to keep each source anonymous to the others, however.

When a purchase requisition is received, purchasing determines whether or not a quotation will be sought from different suppliers. However, the purchasing department does not necessarily wait until requisitions are received before request-

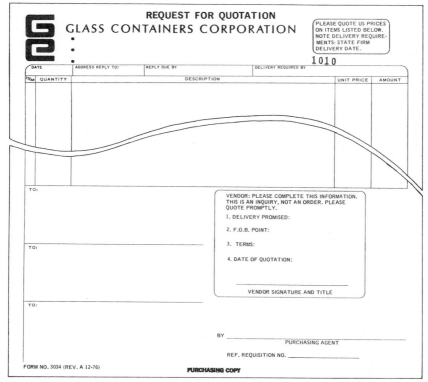

Fig. 5-5   Request for quotation. *(Glass Containers Corporation.)*

ing quotations. Production materials and items that are ordered on a regular basis should be checked constantly.

Bid Evaluation Form   To facilitate quotation analysis, particularly when several items or vendors are involved, a quotation summary sheet or card can be prepared (Fig. 5-6). This may be done by listing the essential information from the quotations of all vendors for ready comparison.

GLASS CONTAINERS CORPORATION
BID EVALUATION
CONSTRUCTION OR EQUIPMENT

Job/Item _____   Date _____

GCC Estimate _____

CONTRACTOR/VENDOR				
Bond Included (yes/no)				
Past Performance/Rating				
Complies w/spec. (yes/no)				
Spec. Exceptions				
Start-up svc./Cost				
Brand Name (Equip.)				
Guarantee				
BASE PRICE				
+ Freight/F.O.B. Pt.				
+ Tax				
− Discounts				
Payment Terms				
T & M Work				
Labor Rate/Mark-up				
Material Mark-up				
Other Charges				
Delivery				
Cost Over Low Bid				
NET PRICE/NOT TO EXCEED				
REMARKS (Basis for Decision):				

Fig. 5-6   Bid evaluation. *(Glass Containers Corporation.)*

Form Requesting Recommendations to Reduce Cost or Improve Product   When requesting quotations from vendors, their recommendations for reducing costs or improving the product involved can be solicited by the form shown in Fig. 5-7. To make the request meaningful, the vendor is provided additional information which allows him to determine how the part or subassembly is used and to submit realistic recommendations. This is one technique of value analysis in purchasing. Other means and procedures are included in Section 8.

Purchase Order

The purchase order is a written contract between the buyer and the seller for the purchase of items or services at an agreed price and delivery date.

Types of Contracts   To begin with, a variety of purchase-order contract types have been developed over the years to define the particular needs of parties entering into purchase agreements. They were created to reflect varying degrees of risk and responsibility assumed by the parties and were directly related to the pricing arrangement under the agreement. At one end of the scale is the firm fixed-price agreement, which in effect places the highest risks of performance upon the sup-

NORTH AMERICAN ROCKWELL CORPORATION
Pittsburgh, Pennsylvania

Quote No. _____

Date _____

Vendor   Name: _____   Address: _____

We Value Suggestions

We look for your suggestions on substitution, design changes, etc., that could reduce our costs and/or improve our product.

To assist you in making suggestions we provide the following check list, and ask that you supply the information, if applicable, for the items covered by the attached Invitation to Bid.

Please Return To My Attention

Part	Drawing
Name	Number

Check List:

1. Can you suggest any design changes that will lower the cost of this item?   ____yes ____no

2. Is there any part of this item that can be more economically produced by another method? (casting, forging, heading extruding, etc.)   ____yes ____no

3. Do you have a standard item that can be satisfactorily substituted for this part?   ____yes ____no

4. Can you recommend a substitute material?   ____yes ____no

5. Are there any other ideas that might save weight, simplify the part, or reduce the cost?   ____yes ____no

6. Would a relaxation of any tolerance result in a lower cost?   ____yes ____no

7. Would relaxation of the finished requirements make any appreciable reduction in cost?   ____yes ____no

8. Are there tests or qualification tests that appear unnecessary?   ____yes ____no

9. Can material handling, packaging, and transportation changes be considered that will reduce costs?   ____yes ____no

10. Other   ____yes ____no

If your answer was "yes" to any of the above questions, please give us your suggestions.

| | Unit Cost | |
Description of Changes	Present	Suggested

Signature _____   Date _____

Fig. 5-7 Form requesting vendors to recommend changes that will reduce costs or improve product. Two parts: original returned with suggestions; copy retained by vendor. *(Reproduced by permission of North American Rockwell Corporation.)*

plier, who agrees to do the work for a set price. On the opposite end of the scale is the cost-plus agreement, wherein the supplier performs on a "best efforts" basis. Cost-plus agreements place the greatest risk on the buyer. These two types of agreements and those falling in between, in terms of risk potential, will be discussed later in greater detail.

The increased requirement for high-value, sophisticated products and components has made the proper choice of purchase documents in today's competitive environment more important than ever before. The right selection can have a direct bearing on the profit objectives of the company. Effective supplier relations and performance are heavily dependent upon an agreement that achieves the best balance of the buyer's and seller's interests.

Among other things, the proper agreement will: (1) clearly define and direct supplier performance requirements under the agreement; (2) effect a well-defined distribution of the risks involved between buyer and seller; and (3) provide complete and clear instructions for fair and reasonable payment for work performed.

Obviously, there are no easy rules that will always ensure a successful purchase agreement. Each transaction requires careful analysis and sound judgment. Important factors to be considered include:

1. Nature and complexity of the item
2. State of development of the item
3. Urgency of the requirement
4. The relative importance of different performance parameters desired by the buyer
5. Period of contract performance and the length of the production run
6. Degree of competition
7. Difficulty of estimating costs because of such factors as the lack of firm specifications, the lack of production experience, and the instability of design
8. Availability of comparative price data, or lack of firm market price or wage rates
9. Prior experience with the supplier
10. Extent and nature of lower-tier procurement contemplated
11. Assumption of business risk
12. Technical capability and financial responsibility of the supplier
13. Cost of administering the purchase agreement
14. Compatibility between supplier's accounting system and the proposed form of agreement
15. Total dollar value involved
16. Special requirements of buyer's customers

Discussions and/or typical examples of the various types of agreements that follow are also included in Sections 10, 11, 17, and 18.

FIRM FIXED-PRICE AGREEMENT.   Under this form of agreement the supplier agrees to supply goods or services for a firmly committed amount that is not subject to adjustment by reason of unforeseen costs experienced by the supplier in the performance of the agreement. The most stringent incentive is placed upon the supplier to effectively manage his performance under this type of agreement.

This is by far the most preferred form of purchase agreement for the buyer because it is simple to administer, exposes the buyer to minimum financial risk, and provides the supplier with a profit incentive to control the costs of performance. Firm fixed-price agreements are particularly suited for procurements such as catalog or off-the-shelf commercial items, where reasonably definite specifications are available, price competition exists, production experience is present, and costs can be predicted with reasonable certainty. Such agreements should be avoided where design or other features are so unstable that significant changes may be required during the course of performance.

AGREEMENTS WITH REDETERMINATION PROVISIONS.   Fixed-price agreements with redetermination provisions, sometimes referred to as *repricing agreements,* provide a contractual method for shifting certain risks from the seller to the buyer in order to eliminate or minimize the inclusion of contingency allowances in the purchase price. Although repricing may be up or down, such agreements normally establish a ceiling price and may be written to provide for redetermination or repricing at different points in time on either a retroactive or a prospective basis. For example, an agreement may be written to provide for a firm fixed price for an initial period of performance. A repricing point is then established, which may be based upon a percentage of completion, a production quantity point, or a period of time. Upon reaching that point, actual costs are reviewed and cost estimates of the remaining work are developed to arrive at a firm price for the entire order.

This type of agreement is suited for procurements calling for quantity production or services where it is possible to negotiate fair and reasonable firm prices for an initial period but not for the entire period of required performance.

Another variation of a redetermination provision provides for retroactive repricing upon completion of work. This form of agreement should be avoided, as it offers little incentive for effective cost control by the supplier during performance. This type of agreement may be appropriate for short-term research and development programs, which do not lend themselves to other forms of agreement. However, under government contracting regulations such an agreement may also be considered a violation of the prohibition against cost-plus-a-percentage-of-cost (CPPC) contracting.

AGREEMENTS WITH INCENTIVE PROVISIONS.   Still another means of facilitating proper pricing under varying circumstances is the use of fixed-price incentive provisions. Such provisions provide for the initial negotiation of a target cost, a target profit, a ceiling price, and a final-profit formula which allows the supplier to participate in any cost savings that accrue below target costs. Its objective is to give the supplier a built-in incentive to reduce costs of performance, since his profit is increased thereby.

Care must be exercised by the buyer to keep the targets and ceiling price reasonably low or realistic to benefit from the advantages inherent in this provision.

For this reason the incentive provision should make it possible to determine a realistic base or target price.

In addition, the supplier's accounting system must be adequate for price revision purposes and must permit satisfactory application of the price adjustment formula. Further, a sufficiently long period of performance is required in order to permit achievement of substantial cost reduction.

For maximum effectiveness the incentive arrangement should be as simple as possible and negotiated early in performance, preferably at the time of award. Dollar-incentive provisions may also be used to maximize technical performance and to provide delivery incentives.

AGREEMENTS WITH ESCALATION PROVISIONS.   An *escalation provision* provides for the upward or downward revision of the stated price upon the occurrence of certain contingencies which are specifically defined in the agreement. Escalation provisions are frequently insisted upon by suppliers who are bidding on a product or service to be delivered some time in the distant future. Buyers who agree to such provisions in a contract should make sure that they allow for downward as well as upward price adjustments.

Escalation provisions are not meant to allow for price increases that are the result of a supplier's failure to estimate accurately the costs of fulfilling a contract. Instead, such provisions are meant to make the final price reflect any changes in the cost of labor or materials used by the supplier. The escalation provision is thus often linked to some correlative index published by the U.S. Bureau of Labor Statistics or some other federal agency. Normally, price changes should apply only to the portion of items undelivered at the time of the price change.

COST-REIMBURSEMENT   AGREEMENTS.   Cost-reimbursement-type   agreements provide for reimbursement of allowable costs incurred during performance and, except when suppliers are nonprofit organizations, normally provide for the supplier to receive a fixed or incentive fee for work performed. This form of agreement is suitable for major procurements where the cost of performance cannot be estimated with sufficient reasonableness to permit the use of a fixed-price-type agreement. To be effective such agreements require: (1) a clear and complete definition of cost for purposes of allowance and reimbursement; (2) an appropriate formula for computing cost and profit; and (3) the exercise of stringent surveillance and approval of supplier costs.

The two most common forms of cost-reimbursement agreements are the cost-plus-incentive-fee (CPIF) agreement and the cost-plus-a-fixed-fee (CPFF) agreement.

The CPIF agreement assures the supplier a minimum fixed fee and permits the fee to be increased within specified limits if the supplier performs the work for less than the estimated cost. Under this type of agreement the parties agree at the time of negotiation upon the target cost of performance. The target fee is then determined in relation to the target cost. Also established are minimum and maximum fees and, finally, a fee adjustment formula similar to that used under a fixed-price incentive agreement. Upon completion of performance the fee payable to the supplier is determined in accordance with the formula. The formula provides, within limits, for an increase in fee above the target fee when the total allowable costs are less than target costs. Conversely, it provides for decreases in the fee below the target fee when the total allowable costs exceed target costs.

This type of agreement is normally used for development, test, and prototype work where there is a probability that its use will result in lower costs to the buyer than would be experienced under a CPFF-type agreement. Other performance characteristics can also be incentivized in addition to the incentives on cost performance.

The CPFF agreement provides for the payment of allowable costs incurred in the performance of the agreement plus a fixed dollar profit for doing the work. The fee (profit) dollars change only when the scope of work required by the agreement changes.

In practice, this type of agreement is quite unlike the firm fixed-price agreement, where price is fixed and every dollar of cost incurred by the supplier means one dollar less profit. Under a CPFF agreement, each dollar of added cost does not change the amount of profit dollars.

This type of agreement provides a minimum incentive for cost reduction, and for obvious reasons its use is normally discouraged. Such incentives as it contains are the result of (1) the urge to maximize the relation or percentage of fee to ultimate actual cost; (2) the need to use labor and facilities effectively on CPFF business so that more resources can be devoted to other business; and (3) the desire to demonstrate efficient and economic operations as a means of encouraging additional business.

TIME AND MATERIAL AGREEMENTS. Time and material agreements provide for the procurement of supplies or services on the basis of payment for (1) a composite hourly rate or rates which include all elements of cost, factory burden, general and administrative (G&A) expense, and the supplier's profit and (2) material at cost. Alternatively, labor and material may be incorporated in the agreement as base labor rates and material invoice costs plus a negotiated percentage to cover expenses, overhead, and profit. In either case, all cost elements must be carefully scrutinized. Sometimes G&A or material handling expenses on materials are provided as part of the material at cost. *Labor-hour agreements* are similar in operation except that materials are not furnished under such agreements.

Once again, this is not a preferred method of procurement, from the buyer's standpoint, because it does not encourage effective cost control and it requires constant surveillance by the buyer to assure that inefficient or wasteful methods are not being used.

Time and material agreements are frequently used to purchase (1) precision machine work; (2) the manufacture of dies, jigs, fixtures, gauges, and special machine tools; (3) repair, maintenance, or overhaul; (4) work to be performed in emergency situations; (5) work scheduled to relieve periods of peak or excessive workload forecast by shop and engineering departments; and (6) minor construction where time is of the essence and specifications are sketchy.

The types of agreements discussed above are those most frequently used by industrial firms today. Extensive study and experience are necessary to understand

and employ the many variations and subtleties inherent in each type. Use of a particular type of agreement in an individual pricing situation that it was not designed to meet would not produce the desired result and could cause severe problems. On the other hand, when the proper type of agreement is selected and skillfully negotiated, the chances for a successful agreement are greatly enhanced.

Purchase Order Terms and Conditions   The purchase order may take many forms: from a simple verbal, unconfirmed commitment to large, exceedingly complex procurements supported by voluminous instructions and terms and conditions. In every case, however, the procurement is supported by terms and conditions, either expressed or implied.

Purchase order terms and conditions are somewhat like a life raft: something one gives little thought and attention to on a daily basis, but they can be comforting to have on hand in case of a legal storm. In a society of increasing complexity and wide-flung business activities, and where a simple verbal statement of intent often no longer suffices, a well-conceived and well-executed purchase order with the appropriate terms and conditions is a business essential.

Over the years a great deal of attention has been given to the desirability of adoption of standard terms and conditions by the purchasing fraternity. While there is considerable sentiment for it, there is probably little likelihood it will ever come about. There is little agreement among those who wish it; and those who feel standardization to be impracticable point to the wide divergence in the size, complexity, and needs of the various companies.

Terms and conditions are generally in written form, appearing on the purchase order form itself. However, it should be pointed out that in industry all contracts are supported by a whole body of common law and, in all states except Louisiana, by the Uniform Commercial Code (see Section 4). The courts will also apply these laws to the most complex procurement if needed to fill a void in the contract.

WRITTEN TERMS AND CONDITIONS.   Written terms and conditions may take a number of forms:

1. The simplest of all are to be found on the preprinted purchase order form carried in most stationery stores and used by many small shops. Here, the terms and conditions are reduced to the essential items of quantity, description, and price of the item purchased; the purchase order date and number (if any); seller's name and address; delivery rate; terms of payment; and the buyer's name and address.

2. On custom-printed purchase order forms the standard legal terms and conditions applicable to all procurements are most generally printed on the reverse of the order and are commonly called the "fine print" or "boiler plate" (see Fig. 5-8.) It is often advisable to type on the face of the order specific references to certain of the fine-print clauses when they have particular significance in a given procurement. This highlighting will give them added weight in the event of legal dispute.

3. There are certain standard and general instructions which are usually printed on the face of the order. These concern such matters as the identification

of shipping containers, submission of invoices, taking of cash discounts, and limitations on changes.

4. Many procurements require special terms and conditions peculiar to that specific transaction, such as liability insurance or liquidated damages for nonperformance. These are frequently spelled out on the face of the order.

5. Some procurements, particularly for special-purpose machinery, research and development, etc., may require a comprehensive set of terms and conditions which largely or completely replace the standard terms and conditions printed on the reverse side of the order. These may be drafted as a completely separate set of documents consisting of several exhibits which, collectively, may be made a part of the purchase order by reference to them as exhibit A, exhibit B, etc.

6. Under some conditions, and this is particularly true under government contracts, procurements must be made under contractual "flow-down" requirements which take precedence over the buyer's own terms and conditions. Many purchasing managers find it advantageous under these conditions to create an exhibit containing all the flow-down clauses. These are then made a part of any purchase order by appending the exhibit to the order and invoking the applicable clauses by referencing their numbers on the face of the order, as: "The following numbered clauses of Exhibit A-Supplementary Terms and Conditions (Rev.) are hereby made a part of this order as though printed thereon: clauses 1, 2, 4 through 20, 27, and 30."

7. All government procurements are made under certain rules and regulations. The Department of Defense, for instance, procures under the Armed Services Procurement Regulation (ASPR), and certain sections of ASPR are applicable to all DOD procurements. Many firms print a listing of the titles of these sections, together with their identifying numbers as they appear on the boiler plate on the back of the order, with a heading which states that in the event a government contract number appears on the face of the order, the sections following automatically become applicable. Additional sections of ASPR peculiar to that specific procurement must, of course, be spelled out on the face of the order.

It is not the function of the terms and conditions to gain for the buyer a temporary or lasting advantage over the seller by imposition of unusual terms; rather, it is to clearly define the buyer's rights under the contract, based on the law and good business and industry practice. They should afford the seller the same protection, for unless the terms and conditions are generally palatable to him, the buyer will be entering into a ceaseless round of negotiations.

It is well to observe that the buyer can achieve more restrictive clauses on an exception basis through negotiation, and they can be incorporated on the face of the purchase order, where they will take precedence over the printed terms and conditions.

CHECKLIST OF TERMS AND CONDITIONS.   It is beyond the scope of this handbook to do more than give cursory consideration to this very broad subject. Every industry has its own special requirements, as do the various public jurisdictions. *The purchasing manager faced with the need for a set of terms and conditions can*

TERMS AND CONDITIONS

1. Acceptance. No acknowledgement, or other document written or executed by Seller or forwarded by Seller to Purchaser after date of this purchase order, containing terms or conditions other than those specified herein, shall be binding on Purchaser unless any such instrument shall be signed by the person who signed this purchase order on behalf of Purchaser, and such instrument shall have been delivered to Seller. In the absence of the execution and delivery of any such instrument by Purchaser, as aforesaid, all deliveries of goods and/or the rendering of services by Seller to Purchaser shall be delivered, rendered, and accepted upon price, terms, conditions, and shall be delivered, rendered and accepted solely upon price, terms, conditions, and shall conform to specifications, set forth in this instrument.

2. Quality, Quantity, Deliveries, and Packing. In the event no quality is specified on the face hereof, the goods delivered and/or services rendered hereunder must be of the best quality. The quantity of goods indicated on the face hereof must not be exceeded without written approval of Purchaser. Seller shall ship and deliver goods and render services hereunder on the date or dates specified on the face hereof, unless prior written approval of any change in such date or dates is given by Purchaser. No charge will be paid by Purchaser for packing, boxing, or cartage, unless specified on the face hereof. Loss of or damage to any goods not packed in such a manner as to insure proper protection to same shall be borne by Seller. Each package of goods shipped must contain a memorandum showing shipper's name, contents of package, and the purchase order number on the face hereof.

3. Inspection. Notwithstanding prior payment and/or inspection by Purchaser, all shipments of goods and/or all services rendered hereunder shall be subject to inspection by and approval of Purchaser after arrival of such goods at the delivery point specified on the face hereof and/or after such services have been rendered, taking into consideration, if there be delays in inspection, the seasonal nature of Purchaser's business.

4. Rejected Shipments and Purchaser's Remedies. If the goods shipped or to be shipped and/or services rendered or to be rendered hereunder are rejected, in whole or in part by Purchaser by reason of Seller's failure to comply with any of the terms, conditions and/or specifications contained herein, Purchaser, after so notifying Seller in writing, may: either return the rejected portion of such goods and/or the

8. Responsibility and Indemnification. All work to be performed by Seller hereunder shall be performed entirely at the risk of Seller and Seller shall defend, indemnify, and hold harmless Purchaser, its agents, servants, representatives, and employees from and against any and all loss (including without limitation, loss of use), liability, damage, claims, demands, actions, and/or proceedings and all costs and expenses connected with any thereof (including, without limitation, attorneys' fees) of whatsoever nature on account of any and all damage to or loss or destruction of any property (including, without limitation, property of Purchaser), or injury to or death of any person (including, without limitation, employees of Purchaser) arising directly or indirectly out of or in connection with the performance of Seller of such work. Without limiting the generality of the foregoing, Seller agrees to indemnify and hold Purchaser harmless from and against all claims and liens of any and all persons based upon the furnishing of labor and/or materials in connection with the goods sold and/or services rendered by Seller hereunder.

9. Equal Employment Opportunity. Seller hereby agrees to comply with the provisions set forth in paragraphs (1) through (7) of section 202 of Executive Order 11246 and all similar orders, rules, registrations and laws prohibiting discrimination in employment, and further agrees that it will not discriminate on the basis of Race, Creed, Color, Sex, National Origin or Age.

10. Illegal Pickets. Seller shall promptly exercise all legal rights and remedies afforded by applicable law to remove and suspend illegal pickets.

11. Continuing Guaranty Under Federal Food, Drug and Cosmetic Act. If the material furnished hereunder is a food, drug, cosmetic or device (as such terms are defined in the Federal Food, Drug and Cosmetic Act), such material comprising each shipment or other delivery made hereunder by Seller to, or on the order of the Purchaser, is hereby guaranteed as of the date of such shipment or delivery, to be, on such date, not adulterated or misbranded within the meaning of the Federal Food, Drug and Cosmetic Act, and not an article which may not, under the provisions of Section 404 or 505 of such Act, be introduced into interstate commerce.

12. **Compliance With Law.** Seller shall comply with all applicable federal, state and local laws, regulations and orders, and Seller will furnish Purchaser with a warranty in a form satisfactory to Purchaser to such effect if requested by Purchaser.

13. **Warranty.** Seller warrants the material furnished hereunder (a) to be free from defects in title, labor, material or fabrication, (b) to conform to applicable specifications, drawings, samples or other descriptions given, (c) to be suitable for the purpose intended, (d) to be of merchantable quality, and further warrants that material of Seller's design will be free from defects in design.

14. **Insurance.** Seller shall carry insurance protection sufficient to meet all the liabilities that are mentioned herein.

15. **Events Not Within Control of Purchaser.** If by reasons of fire, earthquake, flood, explosion, accident, difference with or inability to secure workmen, shortages of energy or raw materials, equipment, labor or transportation, production shutdown, or curtailment, lack of facilities, act of God, or of any public enemy, voluntary or involuntary compliance with any valid or invalid, law, order, regulation, request, or recommendation of any government agency or authority, or other cause beyond the immediate and direct control of Purchaser, whether or not of the kind or nature hereinbefore specified, Purchaser shall be delayed in whole or in part in taking any delivery or deliveries of goods and/or accepting the rendering of services as herein specified, Purchaser may, by giving written notice to Seller:

a. Cancel this purchase order in whole or in part as to any undelivered portion of such goods and/or unrendered portion of such services; or

b. Suspend, in whole or in part, deliveries of goods and/or the rendering of services during the continuance of and to the extent of such cause.

rejected portion of such services to Seller at Seller's expense or hold the same for such disposal as Seller shall indicate, without invalidating the remainder of this purchase order; or Purchaser may reject the entire shipment of such goods and/or reject the entire services and cancel this purchase order for any undelivered balances of goods and/or unrendered services.

If goods shipped or to be shipped and/or services rendered or to be rendered hereunder are rejected, as hereinabove provided, Purchaser may purchase like goods and/or services elsewhere and charge Seller with any loss or damage (either direct or indirect) sustained by Purchaser (including, but not by way of limitation, any difference between the price paid by Purchaser for such like goods and/or services and the price specified on the face hereof) plus all costs of collecting the same (including, but not by way of limitation, attorneys' fee and court costs).

Purchaser shall not be obligated to pay for any goods shipped and/or services rendered which are rejected by it.

5. **Invoices.** No invoice will be paid by Purchaser unless it carries the following certificate: "Seller represents that, with respect to the production of the goods and/or the performance of the services covered by this invoice, it has fully complied with the Fair Labor Standards Act, as amended.

6. **Patents.** Seller warrants that the goods furnished hereunder do not infringe any United States or Canadian patent; that it will defend any suit that may arise in respect thereto; and that it will defend, indemnify and hold Purchaser harmless from and against any and all loss which Purchaser may incur (including, but not by way of limitation, attorneys fees and court costs) by reason of the assertion of any patent rights with respect to the goods furnished hereunder whether by reason of Purchaser's purchase, use, or otherwise.

7. **Health and Safety.** All items to be supplied hereunder by Seller shall conform in all respects to the requirements of applicable insurance and governmental health and safety regulations, including regulations administered by OSHA

Fig. 5-8 Conditions of purchase.

be best advised to consult competent legal sources for assistance in their drafting.
Much help can be found by reviewing the terms and conditions of major concerns
within his own field—particularly of firms known to have their own legal staffs,
as these are most apt to be tailored specifically to their own industry problems and
conditions.

However, there are certain fundamental subjects which should be considered,
based upon the company's size or field of endeavor. These are listed below as a
guide or checklist, with no attempt to recommend specific wording. Some of these
may be combined or omitted, or may appear with different emphasis according to
the needs of the business:

1. Purchase order is exclusive agreement
2. Conditions of acceptance—bidding procedure
3. Compliance with purchase order specifications (quality)
4. Quantity tolerance on overshipments and undershipments
5. Packaging and crating charges
6. Change in delivery date
7. Right of inspection by buyer and customer
8. Disposition of rejected material and rights of buyer
9. Pricing conditions—payment of invoices
10. Guarantees and warranties
11. Responsibility and indemnification for worker or property injury
12. Insurance levels for on-premises work
13. Conditions of use, protection, and liability for buyer's material and
equipment
14. Rights of buyer to discoveries and developments arising from research and
development work
15. Disclosure of information
16. Buyer to be held harmless in the event of patent and copyright infringement
17. Default
18. Force majeure
19. Right of change of order by buyer
20. Government contracts
21. Limitation on subcontracting
22. Conformance by seller with legislation such as Equal Employment Opportunity Act or OSHA
23. Taxes
24. Disputes procedures
25. Assignments
26. Order of precedence of documents and terms and conditions
27. Termination
28. Any additional supplementary terms and conditions for engineering and
design service, performance of service, or requirements under government contract. A specially imprinted Continuation Sheet is at times used for this purpose.

Occasionally certain of the standard terms and conditions may not be adequate under a given set of circumstances, in which case the purchasing manager should consult with legal counsel for modification or substitution. This may be particularly true as regards insurance liability, patents and copyrights, and those cases where government contract provisions are applicable.

Figure 5-8 represents typical terms and conditions usually printed on the back of purchase orders.

The Purchase Order Form—Systems   The purchase order form, of course, is the basic instrument by which the buyer reduces to writing the agreement between buyer and seller (see Figs. 5-9 and 5-10.) It describes the item purchased and the circumstances under which it is to be produced and delivered, as well as the legal considerations under which the contract is to be performed and paid for. The purchase order form becomes a contract when it is accepted by the seller—either through acknowledgment or performance.

The purchase order may assume one or more forms, depending on the size and complexity of the business firm, the nature and value of its purchases, the fiscal controls required, the basic procurement system, the sophistication and ingenuity of the purchasing manager, and even the requirements of the company's customer—as in the case of procuring for government contracts.

Again, it is beyond the scope of this section to treat these several forms and their many variations in detail, but the more important purchase order formats are discussed briefly. With the exception of commercial preprinted forms, the first discussed below, all printed forms are assumed to be custom-designed and printed, as applicable.

COMMERCIAL PREPRINTED.   These are offered by many firms dealing in standard business forms, are simple in format, and are quite adequate for many small users. The lack of printed terms and conditions forces reliance on the Uniform Commercial Code.

CUSTOM SNAP OUTS.   Perhaps the most common format of all is the multicopy snap-out form with one-time carbon paper interleaved. It is relatively inexpensive and easy to use. It may be handwritten or typed. The copies are generally of different colors to aid in distribution. The carbon sheets may be die cut to control printouts on the various copies. Additional copies, when required, may be a problem unless a duplicating machine is available. The snap out is limited as to number of legible copies which can be produced. Electric typewriters will produce the most copies. It is designed and printed to the user's requirement.

SPIRIT MASTERS.   A master is prepared, and from it the required copies are run. The blank forms are generally printed in different colors and collated in reams. This system is slower than the snap-out form, but it can furnish basic sets of any number of copies and the operator can furnish additional copies by feeding in extra copies, printed for the purpose, when the standard set does not suffice. This is frequently required when purchasing for government contracts, although as electrostatic copy costs come down, this method is used less for the multiple-copy requirements.

COPIES FROM ELECTROSTATIC COPIERS. A whole range of copying equipment is available for reproduction. This approach, under some circumstances, can be used in the purchase order system. Some machines print copies on stacked sheets of any kind of paper, while others utilize rolls of coated paper stock. The former equipment makes quite acceptable purchase order copies when printed on colored paper collated to meet the requirements of the system. It is not as versatile,

▼	▼	Speediset ® Moore Business Forms, Inc.		▼		
DELIVER TO		REQUESTOR	REQUISITION NO.	A.F.E. NO.	INSPECTION YES | NO	

GLASS CONTAINERS CORPORATION   **PURCHASE ORDER/RELEASE**

BUYING ADDRESS

No. ____ 33617

THIS NO. MUST APPEAR ON ALL INVOICES, PACKING SLIPS, ETC.

BILLING ADDRESS

BLANKET ORDER NO.

SHIP TO:

SUPPLIER

THIS IS A:
- [ ] PURCHASE ORDER
- [ ] RELEASE

BUYER

CONFIRMING
- [ ] YES [ ] NO

TAXABLE
- [ ] YES [ ] NO

FREIGHT TERMS
- [ ] PPD [ ] COLLECT

ATTENTION   PHONE

RESALE NO.

SHIP DATE	ORDER DATE	TERMS	F.O.B.	VIA		
ITEM	QUANTITY		DESCRIPTION		PRICE	ACCT. NO. & ORG CODE

ACCEPTANCE OF THIS ORDER IS EXPRESSLY LIMITED TO THE TERMS AND CONDITIONS HEREIN (SEE BELOW & RR REVERSE SIDE)

THIS IS <u>NOT</u> A PURCHASE ORDER OR RELEASE UNLESS SIGNED BY AUTHORIZED AGENT. **ACKNOWLEDGE IMMEDIATELY -**

SIGNED

▶ BY _____

TYPE

SPECIAL INSTRUCTIONS:
1. SHIP CHEAPEST WAY UNLESS OTHERWISE STATED.
2. BUYER RESERVES THE PRIVILEGE OF CANCELLING ALL OR ANY PART IF SHIPMENT IS NOT MADE WITHIN SPECIFIED TIME.
3. PLACE ORDER NUMBER AND RELEASE NUMBER (WHERE APPLICABLE) ON ALL SHIPMENTS, INVOICES AND CORRESPONDENCE.
4. PACKING SLIPS MUST ACCOMPANY EACH CASE OR PARCEL SHOWING OUR NUMBER AND RELEASE NUMBER (WHERE APPLICABLE, ITEM NUMBER AND A COMPLETE DESCRIPTION OF CONTENTS.

FORM 3022 (REV. A 5-77)

ORIGINAL

Fig. 5-9 Purchase order release. *(Glass Containers Corporation.)*

nor can as sophisticated forms be devised with it, as with the snap-out or spirit forms. The continuous-roll type is nearly useless for this purpose.

EDP PRINTOUT. This is a whole subject in itself and is treated in detail in Section 15. However, it is mentioned here because the resultant printout may take many forms, from the size of the standard punched card to full 8½- by 11-inch format, complete with all copies.

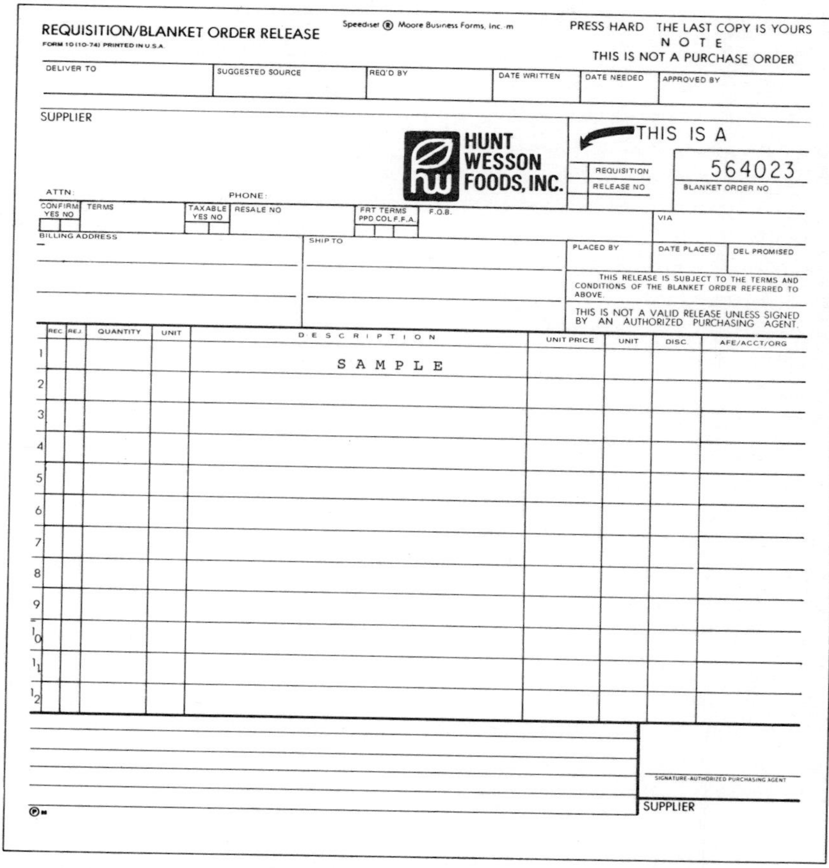
REQUISITION/BLANKET ORDER RELEASE
FORM 10 (10-74) PRINTED IN U.S.A.
Speediset ® Moore Business Forms, Inc.
PRESS HARD THE LAST COPY IS YOURS
NOTE
THIS IS NOT A PURCHASE ORDER

DELIVER TO	SUGGESTED SOURCE	REQ'D BY	DATE WRITTEN	DATE NEEDED	APPROVED BY

SUPPLIER

HUNT WESSON FOODS, INC.

THIS IS A
REQUISITION
RELEASE NO
564023
BLANKET ORDER NO

ATTN: PHONE:

CONFIRM YES NO | TERMS | TAXABLE YES NO | RESALE NO | FRT TERMS PPD COL F.F.A. | F.O.B. | VIA

BILLING ADDRESS | SHIP TO | PLACED BY | DATE PLACED | DEL PROMISED

THIS RELEASE IS SUBJECT TO THE TERMS AND CONDITIONS OF THE BLANKET ORDER REFERRED TO ABOVE.

THIS IS NOT A VALID RELEASE UNLESS SIGNED BY AN AUTHORIZED PURCHASING AGENT.

	REC	REJ	QUANTITY	UNIT	DESCRIPTION	UNIT PRICE	UNIT	DISC	AFE/ACCT/ORG
1					SAMPLE				
2									
3									
4									
5									
6									
7									
8									
9									
10									
11									
12									

SIGNATURE-AUTHORIZED PURCHASING AGENT

SUPPLIER

Fig. 5-10 Requisition/blanket order release. *(Hunt-Wesson Foods, Inc.)*

LETTER CONTRACTS. Here the entire agreement is contained in either a preprinted form or a typed document specially tailored for the contract at hand. It may be originated by either the buyer or the seller.

CONSTRUCTION CONTRACTS. These are frequently covered by contract forms developed by the American Institute of Architects and the Association of General Contractors and may be used for engineering services, for general contracting, or for construction. They are also designed for fixed-price or cost-type contracts. They are well conceived and are constructed to protect the owner, the architect, and the builder. It is generally necessary to modify certain standard provisions and to append supplemental instructions and conditions. See Section 18 for examples.

LEASE-RENTAL AGREEMENTS. In some companies leases and rentals of machinery and real property are the responsibility of the controller; in others, of the purchasing manager. These are often better handled on standard lease or rental forms, although satisfactory agreements can be tailored to the purchase order as mentioned in Section 16.

MAINTENANCE SERVICE AGREEMENTS. Most office equipment and some shop equipment and instrument manufacturers and distributors offer service agreements covering the maintenance of equipment they sell. For this they usually offer their standard service agreement contract forms. Many purchasing managers, while not objecting to the conditions set forth on the forms, object to their use as their control document. Their feeling is that such agreements are outside their standard procedure and tend to lose their identity. A simple solution is to issue a purchase order for the required services for the period and charges agreed on but to make it subject to the applicable terms and conditions of the supplier's service agreement by reference. See Section 17 for further details.

REQUISITION-PURCHASE ORDER FORM. Some companies have found it advantageous to use a copy of the purchase requisition as a confirming copy of the verbal order to the supplier. It has the advantage of eliminating typing of the purchase order, although it does pose difficulties when items on a single requisition must be procured from more than one source. Also, if the requisition is hand-written, there may be problems of interpretation. The usual corrections and additions by the buyer due to poorly written requisitions often result in a document of dubious value.

THE VERBAL ORDER. This, while not resulting in a printed form, deserves a listing here because in its verbal form it has equal validity with the written order under certain conditions. In recent years this buying technique is finding increasing favor with the beleaguered purchasing manager in his endless battle to stem the mounting flood of paper and to reduce his departmental operating expenses. Under the Uniform Commercial Code, verbal contracts between merchants are enforceable at law up to a maximum of $500. In its general application this is not a real handicap, as most purchasing managers favor written contracts for production parts and material, services, major purchases of capital equipment, and the like. The verbal order is an excellent device used in conjunction with a series of blanket or supply-type contracts to handle those myriads of small purchases made each year of supply-type items, maintenance, repair, and operating supplies (MRO), and engineering lab requirements. Between them they can nearly eliminate the typing of nonproductive supply orders.

The mechanics of the verbal order are simple. The purchase requisition, in whatever form it may be, is the authority for the procurement, which is made by phone. The supplier is given an identifying order number and informed that no confirming written order will be forthcoming. For the sake of both internal and external control, such orders should be identified either by their own series of numbers or by a unique prefix designator to the order number, such as V for "verbal" or NC for "nonconfirmed."

In smaller purchasing organizations simple logs or registers are maintained to track and control orders. In larger organizations EDP systems may come into play.

The purchase requisition form may be modified for this use. This may be as simple as adding the identifying order number and providing a copy to accounting

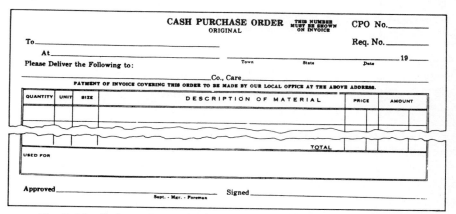

Fig. 5-11   Cash purchase order form, used for local small-dollar purchases.

and perhaps to receiving. By way of illustration, one such simplified system utilizes a three-part requisition prepared by the requisitioner. Two copies are forwarded to accounting for appropriate assignment of charge numbers and subsequent transmittal to purchasing. Purchasing then selects the supplier, adds the order number to the requisition, and telephones the order. After the order is recorded in a purchase order register, one copy of the requisition is sent to accounts payable and the other to receiving.

WIRES.   Telegrams, TWX, and TELEX messages serve as purchase orders in some instances.

PURCHASE-ORDER-DRAFT SYSTEM.   A few companies have found it advantageous to use the purchase-order-with-check-attached system, wherein the supplier detaches and cashes a preprinted check before shipment of material. (Section 10 describes this system.)

CASH PURCHASE ORDER.   Some companies have a policy of purchasing supplies from a petty cash fund. This is used to pay authorized local service bills as well as to make small-value purchases of materials and supplies (see Fig. 5-11).

CONSIGNMENT PURCHASE ORDER.   Consignment purchase orders are issued to cover work done on a buyer's material which is physically in the possession of a vendor. In such a situation, the regular purchase order could be used with a notation similar to the following:

> *Consignment Purchase Order. Attached conditions become part of this order. Please read carefully.*
>
> Material to be repaired, machined, treated, etc., on this purchase order will be shipped to you on a consignment basis and remains the property of (company name) and you agree to return said material, etc., upon request. Material found to be defective on account of error in design or for other causes for which we may be responsible should immediately be returned for credit. A packing ticket applicable to the material so returned against this purchase order should accompany shipment and such material should be invoiced to us on a no-charge basis. At the completion of this contract, we reserve the right to deduct from your account the value of all material shipped you to apply against this purchase order which has not been returned to us as a part of this purchase order.

BLANKET PURCHASE ORDER.   Blanket orders generally are issued for parts, commodities, or services for which the quoted price is on an "any quantity" or "annual requirements" basis. Blanket orders can be issued on productive or nonproductive items purchased on a quantity price schedule, provided proper safeguards are established and maintained to check the invoice price.

The grouping of several nonproductive parts or commodities of a like kind is investigated and a quotation based on estimated requirements is requested from a supplier who can furnish the entire package (or the major portion of it) for a set period of time. This should make it more attractive to a supplier and, in the long run, result in lower prices. A blanket order also, in some cases, has the advantage of reducing the amount of paper work handled.

After negotiation and execution of a blanket order, ordering items covered thereunder becomes merely a matter of notifying the supplier as requirements arise. Notification may be accomplished by telephone or by issuing an authorized release form to the supplier.

Depending upon the type and value of materials covered by such orders and the existence of appropriate internal procedures, the requisitioner is often permitted to contact the supplier directly to place orders under blanket agreements. This is the case in many companies with respect to the procurement of MRO items. The authorized releaser should be identified in the blanket purchase order or by change notice and any dollar limitations should be noted.

When the requisitioner makes the telephone release, he should obtain the price from the supplier, who is held responsible for pricing according to the blanket order agreement. Then the requisition copies are forwarded to purchasing, where a spot check for accuracy is made and the buyer signs approval. The copies are then distributed internally.

Blanket order agreements take on a variety of forms to meet the needs of purchasing. Some are designed to offer quantity price breaks by pegging prices to predetermined cumulative quantities. Under this method the prices to be paid will be revised as the predetermined cumulative quantities are achieved. Another form of agreement establishes unit prices on the basis of estimated usage for the contract period. If the estimated requirements do not materialize, the buyer is reinvoiced at a higher rate; conversely, if actual procurements exceed the estimate, the supplier credits the buyer accordingly. Yet another variation provides for firm scheduled deliveries at specified prices. This is essentially a type of forward buying intended to minimize inventory costs and gain the advantage of current pricing conditions.

The blanket agreement has been recognized by all levels of purchasing as one of the most effective means of eliminating paper work. There are, however, other significant advantages to be gained:

1. Increasing procurement volume by combining requirements usually offers substantial savings over individual purchase.

2. The important task of selecting vendors and negotiating prices is centrally controlled by purchasing.

3. Prices are protected for the term of the agreement. This feature could, however, favor a supplier if general market prices soften during the term of the agreement unless appropriate deescalator clauses are included in the agreement.

4. Items are ordered only as needed, which, in effect, establishes the supplier's facility as a warehouse.

5. The supplier's knowledge of projected requirements provides him with substantial opportunities for planning and reducing operating costs, which saving can be passed along to the buyer in the form of lower prices and quicker deliveries.

Blanket orders are normally written on the standard form mentioned above. However, it is generally agreed that additional terms and conditions, other than the standard ones appearing on the purchase order, are required in the issuance of a blanket purchase order. Examples of these additional terms and conditions follow:

PRODUCTIVE PARTS OR COMMODITIES:
This blanket order is issued to cover such portion of Buyer's requirements of the parts or commodities listed below, for the period beginning _____ and ending _____, as Buyer may from time to time specify in shipping schedules to be furnished to Seller, deliveries to be made only in the quantities and at the time specified in such schedules. Such schedules may also authorize Seller to acquire raw materials necessary to fabricate a specified quantity of the parts. Buyer shall have the right at any time and from time to time to cancel, in whole or in part, the quantities specified or raw material authorizations contained in any shipping schedule. In such event, Buyer shall be under no obligation to Seller for parts completed or partially completed, or raw materials acquired by Seller, unless the delivery or fabrication of such parts or the acquisition of such raw materials was specifically authorized in a shipping schedule delivered to Seller by Buyer.

NONPRODUCTIVE PARTS OR COMMODITIES:
This blanket order is issued to cover such portion of Buyer's requirements of the materials or services listed below, for the period beginning _____ and ending _____, as Buyer may from time to time specify in releases to be

furnished to Seller, deliveries on materials to be made only in the quantities and at the times specified in such releases. Under no circumstances shall Buyer be under any obligation to Seller for materials or services not specifically released.

The length of the wording of these terms may require a separate page. This should be attached to the purchase order, and reference should be made on the face of the order to the attachment so that it becomes a valid part of the blanket purchase order.

DATA-PHONE.[1]   The DATA-PHONE is an electronic data communication service developed by the Bell System which permits a fast mechanical means for ordering materials under blanket orders, as discussed in Section 15. Items covered under the order are recorded on punched cards that are normally prepared and maintained by purchasing. Upon receipt of a requisition, the data from the prepunched card, along with the required quantities and other variable data, are transmitted via the DATA-PHONE unit, sometimes directly to the supplier's computer. The receiving unit at the supplier's plant simultaneously duplicates the data card, and the order is filled. Copies of the data cards may be used as shipping documents by the supplier. A duplicate deck of cards may be furnished to the requisitioner for him to use as a purchase requisition by indicating the quantity required. This ordering system has not been embraced wholeheartedly by purchasing managers because of some inherent limitations—namely that too few suppliers have such receiving units and that the system does not encourage the buyer to seek out the most competitive bid.

SYSTEMS CONTRACTING.   Many of the blanket order and other techniques discussed in preceding paragraphs have been adopted and formalized into a procurement system used by Carborundum Corporation called *systems contracting*. In its simplest form, it is a stockless system providing for direct ordering by the requisitioner of catalog items generally bought from distributors.

Under this system, the buyer selects the supplier, negotiates prices for the items to be ordered, and awards the purchase order. Items covered under the order are identified and priced in a catalog which is furnished to approved requisitioners. The system further calls for a four-part requisition form which is completed by the requisitioner. Copy 4 is retained by the requisitioner and the original and two copies are sent directly to the supplier. The supplier assigns the order number, prices the items, and ships the material. The original and copy 2 accompany the shipment, serving as shipping documents.

After receipt and verification by the receiving department, the material is forwarded to the requisitioner with copy 3. Accounting receives the original copy for price verification and accumulation for payment on a periodic basis.

Although systems contracts have found widest acceptance in the procurement of materials such as stationery, pipe valves, fittings, bearings, and other general industrial supplies of this nature, they are beginning to be used for high-volume

---

[1] Registered service mark of American Telephone and Telegraph Company.

production parts made to specification. Under the latter application, it is generally understood that the buyer will share in any losses which occur as a result of obsolescence or design changes. The advantages to be derived from systems contracting and stockless purchasing are similar to those listed above for telephone orders and regular blanket orders.

General Requirements of the Purchase Order Form   As noted, the purchase order is the vehicle by which the buyer formalizes his contract with the seller. It is a legal document and must therefore contain all the elements of the contract. In the interest of uniformity and of saving time, the buyer uses a printed form providing spaces for variable instructions and with a body of standard, printed information and terms and conditions. The purchase order form itself may be simple or complex, but it must accommodate certain basic information to adequately describe the purchase agreement (see Fig. 5-9.) These basic requirements are listed below with comments.

EXPRESS LIMITATION.   With increasing frequency, court interpretations of the Uniform Commercial Code have negated "boiler plate" terms and conditions unless they are prominently visible. To meet this need and ensure a contract on the best terms possible, the buyer should place on the purchase order in bold and/or colored type a notice such as the following: "Acceptance of this order is expressly limited to the terms and conditions on the face and reverse sides thereof."

THE MASTHEAD.   This is the printed area, generally at the top of the form, giving the precise name of the buyer's company, its address, zip code, phone number, and its TWX and TELEX numbers. The seller will automatically invoice in accordance with this information unless the purchase order form gives separate billing instructions.

SHIP TO.   Unless contrary instructions are given, the seller will ship to the buying address as shown in the masthead.

PURCHASE ORDER NUMBER.   Almost without exception, purchase orders are serially numbered as a means of tying together all paper work and elements of the purchase transaction. Purchase order forms may be prenumbered or assigned numbers by the individual buyers as issued. Prenumbered-order advocates—usually company controllers—fear unauthorized use of unnumbered forms and require accountability for all voided prenumbered forms. The unnumbered-form partisans point to elimination of the above control operation and to greater flexibility in use of purchase order numbers in program control, buyer evaluation, material delivery, etc., by use of the order number as a control method. The uses of the purchase order number are limited only by the ingenuity of the purchasing manager and the length of the number. A few typical uses:

1. Orders can be identified with specific programs by a prefix or suffix dash number.

2. The buyer can be similarly identified.

3. The year of placement of the order is designated by one company by the first digit (0 = 1980, 1 = 1981, 2 = 1982, etc.,) which is followed by additional digits

(10001, 10002, etc.) The cycle is repeated each 10 years. This facilitates filing and quick interpretation of pricing records.

4. A suffix can be used to designate the requesting department. This is particularly valuable for the verbal purchase order and serves as "deliver to" instructions to the receiving department. Care should be taken to avoid lengthy, complicated numbers because of possible verbal and transcription errors.

PURCHASE ORDER DATE.   There are essentially two schools of thought here. The first holds that the date under the purchase order number should be the date the order is actually typed, with date of verbal placement shown in the "confirming to" area. This is to show the date the order actually enters the paper work system. The other school holds that the correct date should be the date of verbal placement, regardless of the time taken to work out details of the order or the time taken to issue the order because of typing load. This dilemma may be partially resolved by placing the day-of-typing date inconspicuously near the bottom of the form.

TERMS OF PAYMENT.   Cash discounts are offered by the seller as an incentive to the buyer to make prompt payment. While cash terms are generally uniform within an industry or trade group, they are usually negotiable (particularly during periods of tight money) and form an integral part of the contract. Cash discounts taken which exceed the cost of using such money represent pure profit to the company. While the buyer should strive for the largest cash discount, he must be wary of negotiating a large cash discount on a custom-built item, only to have it added to the basic cost of the item, thus inflating the real cost of the order and perhaps the sales tax. See Sections 10 and 11.

Cash terms are generally based on 10 days from date of invoice (although buyers should insist on dating from receipt of invoice.) To avoid almost daily pay periods to meet the 10-day terms, many companies pay on regular schedules, such as on the 10th, 20th, and 30th, or on the 10th and 25th of the month, starting the 10-day cash discount at the beginning of the next regularly scheduled pay period. A *net 30 days* term is variously interpreted by different buyers. The buyer usually defines his pay schedule somewhere in his terms and conditions, and most frequently on the face of the purchase order form itself. The term *net cash* and similarly vaguely worded terms should be avoided. In case of doubt, the use of *net 30 days* is generally safe.

F.O.B. POINT.   This is an abbreviation for "free on board" and refers to the point of delivery of goods by the seller, at which time title usually passes to the buyer. In the absence of agreements to the contrary, damages sustained prior to that point in time are the responsibility of the seller, while those after that time belong to the buyer, and each must file claims for damages accordingly.

The f.o.b. point is a negotiable item, and whether the buyer or the seller pays for the cost of delivery can be significant. However, it can sometimes be to the buyer's advantage to accept goods f.o.b. seller's plant in order to control routing because of favorable transportation arrangements, pool cars, or simply the need for expedited, premium shipment. F.o.b. can take several forms, as listed below.

1. F.o.b. Destination (or Delivered).   This creates the fewest problems for the buyer, as the seller pays transportation charges and must file all claims for damages. Unless the mode of transportation is negotiated and spelled out on the order, it is the shipper's prerogative to select the carrier—and usually this will be the cheapest available. The buyer may find this plan incompatible with his needs.

2. F.o.b. Shipping Point (or Freight Collect).   As the term implies, the seller turns the shipment over to the common carrier or the buyer's truck, and his responsibility ceases. This is the most common f.o.b. condition, except for local shipments where the seller has regular delivery service.

3. F.o.b. Shipping Point, Freight Prepaid.   Here title passes upon delivery of goods to the carrier, but the shipper prepays the freight, which charges are billed to the buyer.

4. F.o.b. Shipping Point, Freight Allowed.   Here again title passes upon delivery of goods to the carrier. However, in this case the seller reimburses the buyer for transportation costs.

F.o.b. terms are explained in more detail in Sections 10, 11, and 23.

SELLER'S NAME AND ADDRESS.   It is important that the seller's name and address be accurately set up in a purchasing index and used uniformly on all purchase orders. This is particularly critical in companies using EDP, as each variant will usually turn up in EDP printouts as separate-line items, creating considerable confusion in matching records, in payment of invoices, and in the compilation of statistical records and reports.

SHIPPING INSTRUCTIONS.   In conjunction with establishing the f.o.b. point, the buyer should clearly define the routing and mode of transportation if he is to pay the freight charges. For purchasing departments without traffic managers to advise them, routing is not always a simple problem. Frequently, when the buyer is in doubt as to the best routing, the seller can offer helpful advice, as he has probably had many occasions to ship into the buyer's area. Such terms as "best way" and "fastest way" are too indefinite and provide no control or quick means of tracing shipments and are to be avoided. Detailed discussion of the traffic function, routing, and selection of carriers will be found in Section 23.

DELIVERY DATE.   Frequently the promised delivery date is a negotiated compromise between a required date and a normal lead-time date. To highlight this and to provide a reminder to the seller of the buyer's true requirements, many companies show both a required date and the promised date on the order. This is also a useful tool in follow-up activity.

SIGNATURES.   There are many schools of thought concerning who should sign and approve purchase orders.

1. In most cases the buyer will sign the order.
2. Some companies variously require the purchasing manager to approve and/

or countersign all procurements; those over a certain dollar value; blanket orders; term contracts; or when unusual conditions or circumstances are involved.

3. A few require the purchasing manager rather than the buyer to sign all orders.

4. In large companies with multilevels of purchasing supervision, each level may be charged with responsibility for approving procurements of increasing value or complexity.

5. Most companies have policies requiring the general manager, controller, and/or president to approve (as opposed to signing) orders for capital equipment, orders of certain dollar value, when unusual terms and conditions form part of the order, and when the order is let under unusual circumstances. In any event, the name of the placing buyer should be typed somewhere on the order to provide the seller with a name to contact relative to the order.

CONFIRMING TO.   It is always advisable to show the name of the person with whom the order was placed verbally and the date of placement, or to check a "nonconfirming" block when the order is forwarded without verbal placement.

RESALE OR TAXABLE.   Many states and cities have a sales tax, and it is vital to the seller to know whether the items sold are subject to the tax. This is most easily indicated by checking either of two boxes titled Resale and Taxable. The resale certification number should be printed on the order form.

REQUESTED BY.   The name of the requester is of interest to the various departments handling the material or processing the order.

DELIVER TO.   It is obviously important to the receiving department and others to have delivery instructions.

DESCRIPTION OF ITEM PURCHASED.   It should be self-evident that a full, complete description is necessary to the proper filling of an order. Far too many erroneous shipments are due to incomplete or inaccurate descriptions. The wise purchasing manager will establish written instructions for describing the various items and will insist that they be followed by ordering departments. Below are a few guidelines.

1. *Machinery Repair Parts.*   Give machine name and model number, year of manufacture, serial number, and manufacturer. Use part numbers from manufacturer's catalog or parts list together with the catalog number. If these are not available, a sketch of the part and/or location in the equipment is often more accurate than a name of the part as defined by shop personnel.

2. *Raw Material.*   Describe material by size, shape, name, form, alloy, or grade and specification in exact order and conformance with the industry's practices. Other considerations should not be overlooked, such as increments of length, minimum/maximum lengths, random lengths, surface finish, heat treatment, quality standards, and other items not always spelled out in referenced specifications.

3. *Items Purchased to Manufacturer's Part Number.*   Because many such numbers are often long and a combination of numerals and letters, verbal and

transcription errors are easily made. In addition to the part numbers it is usually advisable to give the full description of the part rather than just the generic name: thus, "bearing, double row, double thrust, Class I," rather than just the term "bearing." This gives the seller as well as the buyer's own inspection department a double check against the part number.

QUANTITY.   Care must be exercised to clearly show the unit of measure, in order to avoid receiving six dozen of something when only six are wanted. Metal bars are generally ordered by the foot but sold by the pound. It is always good to show the calculated weight in parentheses under the footage ordered. This serves as a double check to the seller and also assists the accounting department in the processing of invoices.

PRICE.   It is wise to price the purchase order at the time of order to avoid misunderstandings, perhaps save a change notice, and provide accounting and other concerned departments with the information on a routine basis.

It is important to price orders in relation to the ordering unit measure. Usually these are the same; however, there are exceptions, as in the case of metal bars, which are ordered in feet and sold by the pound. Always show the pricing unit (pound, hundredweight, ounce, dozen, etc.) if other than "each," or if it differs from the ordering unit.

The use of *TBA* (to be advised) or *advise price* is to be generally avoided. However, in the interest of eliminating delay in procurement where pricing is not immediately available, as in machine repair parts, it is often customary to release orders with prices to be advised. Small, out-of-town orders are better released on this basis than held for pricing before release because the risk of loss through uncontrolled prices is less than the cost of extra handling of the order. It is common under these circumstances for the buyer to incorporate in the order a phrase limiting the price which may be charged without prior approval, or including a phrase such as: "In accepting this order seller warrants price charged shall not be in excess of lowest prevailing market price."

Some purchasing managers extend prices, while others do not. This is a decision to be made based on their use in compiling commitment or activity reports by purchasing or the use to which they are put by accounting. To reduce typing and provide more space on the face of the order, extensions may be made on the purchase requisition, with only the unit prices and order total shown on the face of the order itself.

SUPPLIER NUMBER.   This is most generally used when purchase orders or accounting records are set up on EDP.

REQUISITION NUMBER.   To tie the purchase transaction to specific requisition numbers for benefit of the requisitioner.

VARIOUS CONTROL NUMBERS.   These include account numbers, job numbers, and program identification numbers.

ITEM NUMBER.   Frequently EDP identifies material by purchase order item number rather than by description; also used for quick reference in discussions concerning purchase order.

Distribution of Copies   The number and distribution of purchase order copies are dictated by the needs of each individual company and can run as high as 20 or more for multidivision corporations engaged in government work.

In addition to the original purchase order sent to the vendor, copies ordinarily are necessary for purchasing, receiving, and accounting. These may be color-coded for departmental identification. Purchasing must have a record of every purchase order. The receiving department is often furnished a copy of the purchase order for use when material is received. The accounting department is furnished a copy when that department is responsible for checking the invoice to see that it is in accordance with the purchase order. Following is a list of copies that may be needed:

1. Purchasing department copy
2. Acknowledgment copy
3. Follow-up copy
4. Accounting department copy
5. Inspection copy
6. Requisitioner's copy
7. Inventory control copy
8. Receiving department copy

Once a year the purchasing manager and his management should take a hard, uncompromising look at the number and distribution of copies, for purchase order copies have a way of proliferating if not controlled with an iron hand. It is not that the cost of the extra form is significant, but it has to be delivered; someone has to look at it; it is filed; it takes up file space. All these cost money. On the other hand, the purchase order is a vital tool to many people and it is essential that their needs be met—in which case the cost of the extra form is insignificant. The most common copies are those described briefly below.

SUPPLIER ORIGINAL AND ACKNOWLEDGMENT.   These are sent to the supplier, with the acknowledgment copy to be signed and returned to buyer.

PURCHASING COPIES.   Practice here varies widely, but most small to moderate-size departments seem to favor the use of two copies: the *purchasing file* and the *numerical file* copies. The purchasing file copies are usually filed alphabetically, by supplier, in an open file and when completed are transferred to a closed file. Some purchasing managers attach all relevant documents, such as receiving reports, quotations, requisitions, correspondence, and rejections, to the referenced order; others file supporting documents separately from the order. Sometimes the file copy is used for follow-up, whereas others may utilize a separate copy for this purpose. A numerical file containing a copy of every order issued is particularly valuable for quick reference. Related copies of change notices should be filed with the purchase orders. To prevent their going astray, these copies may be bound.

ACCOUNTING COPIES.   Usually accounts payable requires a copy, as does cost accounting, although in many cases they may share a single copy.

REQUESTER.   The requester usually requires a copy, although he may work instead from a returned completed copy of the purchase requisition.

RECEIVING. Many companies use the spirit duplicator master system for writing purchase orders and/or receiving reports, in which case the master is usually sent to the receiving department for use in creating receiving reports. In this case a separate copy of the purchase order is not required. In some companies the receiving department is purposely not furnished a copy of the order, leaving it, rather, to the receiving department to write receiving reports based on the packing slips received.

RECEIVING INSPECTION. Copies are usually furnished directly by purchasing if the receiving department does not forward an exact copy of the order with the material, whether by the spirit duplicator or by other reproduction method.

The above covers the essential requirements, but, as indicated before, many diverse uses of purchase order copies can be found in the various companies, and the purchasing manager must design his system and its support forms and procedures to meet the needs described above.

Forms Security   Purchase order forms still to be used should be kept in locked storage. This will help prevent unauthorized use. Blank purchase order forms should not be left on desk tops during the workday. It is advisable that typed purchase orders and correspondence be removed from visual range of sales people and other visitors to the Purchasing Department. Purchase order forms should be treated as accountable documents. They can be controlled through the use of pre-printed sequential numbers that will provide control through stores issues and the purchase order log record.

Purchase Order Change Notice

Purchase order adjustments require change notices or revisions to cancel, alter, change the price, or otherwise modify the purchase order as originally issued. This can be accomplished by use of a purchase order change notice form, as illustrated by Fig. 5-12.

Space should be provided on the change notice form for the following:

1. Vendor's name and address
2. Date
3. Reference to order number and date
4. Details of change desired—effective date
5. Signature
6. Change number (consecutive, in case of multiple change notices)

Where semiautomatic typing or other types of control require the use of a continuous perforated form, frequently the purchase order form can be used for a change order. In this case, it is necessary to type the words *Change Notice* directly above the words *Purchase Order*. If the volume of change orders is small, a rubber stamp may serve the purpose. However, it is still best to have a specially printed form with the words *Change Notice* in bold or color type; such an attention-getting device will ensure that the change will get prompt attention.

All departments receiving copies of the purchase order should also receive copies of the purchase order change notice.

The purchase order change notice sent to the vendor should contain an acknowledgment form for the vendor to sign and return, indicating receipt of the change notice and what effect it will have on the original order.

A follow-up file should be used to ensure prompt replies.

The purchasing manager who makes it a hard-and-fast rule with his suppliers

SARGENT INDUSTRIES
HUNTINGTON PARK DIVISION

PURCHASE ORDER
CHANGE NOTICE

2533 EAST 56TH ST., HUNTINGTON PARK, CALIF. 90255
TELEPHONE: (213) 583-4161
TWX: (910) 321-2849
TELEX: 67-4403

PURCHASE ORDER NO.	
REV. NO.	
DATE	
ACCT. NO.	

TO:

CHANGE FROM:

TOTAL PRICE

CHANGE TO READ:

REASON FOR CHANGE:

CONFIRMING TO:

NON-CONFIRMING ☐

TOTAL PRICE

NET CHANGE

1. The "General Provisions, Terms and Conditions" as printed on the Purchase Order apply equally to this CHANGE NOTICE as though printed hereon.
2. No revision to this Purchase Order is binding on Buyer unless confirmed in writing by Buyer.

SARGENT INDUSTRIES
HUNTINGTON PARK DIVISION

BY ______________________ – BUYER

______________________ – PURCHASING MANAGER

FORM NO. 2.051 (REV. 11-72)

Fig. 5-12 Change order form, which amends the purchase order. *(Reproduced by permission of Sargent Industries.)*

that no change to the order is valid (regardless of who makes it) unless and until it is confirmed by a purchase order change notice has eliminated a major source of trouble.

Changes in larger companies, originating in other departments, are normally initiated by means of a purchase order change request form (see Fig. 5-13).

PURCHASE ORDER CHANGE REQUEST/NOTICE

(FOR INPLANT USE ONLY)

P.O. _____

DATE _____

REQ'N. _____

INV. _____

SUPPLIER _____

TO: PURCHASING

PLEASE CHANGE REFERENCED PURCHASE ORDER AS NOTED BELOW:

BY _____ DATE _____   APP. _____ DATE _____

REQUESTER – DO NOT WRITE BELOW THIS LINE

☐ SHORT FORM (TO: ACCOUNTING DEPT.)   ☐ LONG FORM (TO TYPIST)   CN. NO. _____

REFERENCED PURCHASE ORDER IS CHANGED AS FOLLOWS:

CHANGE FROM		TO READ
	ITEM	
	QUANTITY	
	DESCRIPTION	
	PRICE	
	TERMS	
	RESALE	
	TAXABLE	
	F.O.B.	
	VIA	
	SCHEDULE	
	OTHER	

CONFIRMED (SUPPLIER) _____ DATE _____

TO ACCEPT ☐ OVERSHIPMENT   ☐ UNDERSHIPMENT

ITEM IS ☐ COMPLETE   ☐ INCOMPLETE

DIST.: ACCOUNTING   (WHITE)
PURCHASING   (CANARY)
REQ. TICKLER   (GREEN)
REQUESTER   (GOLDENROD)
EXTRA   (PINK)

BY _____ DATE _____

APP. _____ DATE _____

Fig. 5-13 Change request notice form requesting the purchasing department to amend purchase order. Normally initiated in plant. *(Reproduced by permission of Sargent Industries.)*

Some purchasing managers completely rewrite an order, incorporating the newest revisions and assigning a revision identification to the purchase order number. This is not generally considered good practice, as it can make for duplicate orders and shipments if the supplier fails to recognize it as a revision.

Some companies divide the working portion of the change notice into Changed From and Change To sections for greater preciseness. It is the practice of some companies to insert at the bottom a Reason for Change statement, to eliminate ambiguity and problems of interpretation.

Cancellation, termination, and rework charges often result from purchase order change instructions, and the date of notification can be important in determining the time of effectiveness as well as associated costs and charges; this is particularly so should the matter result in legal action. The buyer should make it a rule to reference the initial date, mode, and contact's name on confirming change notices.

The simpler the wording and the more clearly the actual changes are highlighted, the fewer the opportunities for errors in transcription and interpretation.

There are, it should be noted, basically two types of change notices: those required to give instructions to the seller, and those affecting only the buyer's own operations. For the sake of easy identification these may be called *full distribution* and *restricted distribution,* respectively. Most purchasing managers make this distinction, restricting the latter to in-house distribution. It is used for changes in account numbers, as a vehicle for closing orders over or undershipped, to add or change prices to agree with invoices, and such matters. They should carry separate and distinct serial numbers to avoid confusing either suppliers or employees with gaps in the number series upon possible receipt of subsequent change notices.

A different form may be developed for changes to construction contracts. The principles to be followed would be the same as for the purchase order change notice, except that all construction contracts require extra effort on the part of the buyer to control price extras and deductions (see Section 18).

Purchase Order Acknowledgment

The copy of the order provided to serve as an acknowledgment by the vendor is of special design, with space provided for the vendor's signature and promised shipping date. The acknowledgment copy must contain the same printed information as appears on the original. The acknowledgment copy returned with the vendor's signature makes a legal contract between the two parties (see discussion of Uniform Commercial Code in Section 4 and in the following paragraphs).

It is expected the seller will return the buyer's acknowledgment copy of the purchase order, duly signed, acknowledging receipt and acceptance of the order as written, but many do not.

Many sellers, such as distributors, do not worry much about terms and conditions, provided their customer's credit rating is good. Generally the merchandise ordered consists of stock items which will be delivered and accepted before the formal order is received. In fact, the verbal, nonconfirmed order which today is used so broadly in the procurement of supply-type items generally ignores the written terms and conditions factor, relying on protection under the Uniform Commercial Code. These sellers rely on the integrity of their customers to adhere to ethical business practices, and this trust is seldom misplaced.

Many larger concerns carefully examine customers' terms and conditions.

When a supplier determines he cannot accept a buyer's terms, either because of company policy or because certain of the clauses are unacceptable, he can do one of several things:

1. Reject the order and not perform
2. Present his standard conditions of sale as a counteroffer
3. Offer to negotiate the offensive clauses
4. Offer to commence work subject to concurrent negotiations to resolve the problem areas

The buyer then has the options of withdrawing his order and going elsewhere or accepting one of the above alternatives. The buyer is frequently at a disadvantage, for if he must purchase a proprietary unit from a sole source, his options are few. On the other hand, most sellers are not completely insensitive to the effect of their actions on future business.

When the buyer mails an acknowledgment copy of the order to a seller, he will find one of several things happening:

1. It will be returned signed, with no exceptions, and the contract is formed.
2. It will be returned signed, but with corrections or exceptions made thereon. The buyer must decide whether the changes are acceptable. If they are, he may file the copy without further contact with the seller, signifying acceptance by silence, and a contract is formed. If the buyer disagrees with the changes, he must immediately reconcile differences with the seller and should confirm any revisions in writing. (In this and items 3 and 4 below, a review of the Uniform Commercial Code Section 2-207 is advisable. The form and character of changes in terms and conditions can alter the effect.)
3. The seller may return the acknowledgment either signed or unsigned with a copy of his sales agreement which bears the notification which reads substantially: "We are entering your order as shown hereon. Please ascertain its accuracy and notify us at once of any variance with your order." This is a devious ploy by the seller of issuing a counteroffer, of assuming the buyer's acceptance, and absolving himself of any transcription errors. The buyer is well advised to carefully examine the sales contract for its accuracy and for any conflict of terms and conditions with his own before filing it away. Each purchasing manager has to determine for himself the conditions or circumstances under which he will enter into the foray commonly called the "battle of the forms." For the average purchasing manager, when dealing with large concerns with legal staffs, the battle can be nearly impossible and, unless the circumstances are unusual, seldom worth the effort. So often the intent is not so different as the wording of the conflicting terms and conditions.

If the buyer elects, he may notify the seller that there is no contract until the buyer's terms are accepted or the differences are negotiated.

Or it may be agreed that the seller will commence performance under certain limitations while the buyer and seller work out an agreement. This is often the circumstance under which Letters of Intent are issued. (A letter of intent usually involves a limited contracted liability. It should be carefully written to explicitly limit in terms of time and money the buyer's commitment—that minimum required to obtain the desired action by the seller—pending a further decision or the issuance of a purchase order.)

4. The seller may commence performance without either returning the acknowledgment or forwarding his own sales contract. This may be done because of the nuisance factor or because the seller does not have the time or legal staff to review the myriad buyers' terms and conditions he receives. If he determines the sale is routine, the seller signifies his acceptance by performance, taking the position that a signed acknowledgment contributes nothing when the written order conforms to the verbal commitment.

There is a widespread lack of agreement on the value and use of the acknowledgment copy of the purchase order. Some purchasing managers look upon it as "just another piece of paper," contending that performance against the order and the absence of verbal or written exception to the purchase order give them all the protection they need. On the other hand, there are those who feel that a signed acknowledgment copy provides the buyer with more than just legal protection: it offers confirmation that the buyer and seller have a common understanding of the procurement. Also, it gives the seller an opportunity to note any errors on the acknowledgment, such as in description, quantity, price, terms of payment, f.o.b. point, or delivery promise. Confirmation of order entry can be of great importance to the buyer on long-lead-time purchases.

Retention of acknowledgment copies of both purchase orders and change notices varies, depending on the policy of the individual purchasing manager, that of his company, or legal requirements. The following is a suggested guide for retention:

1. Retain acknowledgment of all orders over a given dollar value—perhaps $2500.

2. None for orders for standard, off-the-shelf production items.

3. None for orders for MRO, shop supplies, stationery, and miscellaneous low-cost items.

4. All change notices.

5. All acknowledgments with qualifications, corrections, or alterations by seller.

6. Orders with unusual, nonstandard terms.

7. Orders with other than fixed prices.

8. All service-type contracts.

9. All term-type contracts.

10. All capital equipment orders.

In any event, the buyer must decide when and under what circumstances he will insist upon return of acknowledgment copies and must establish the necessary mechanism to ensure their return.

Under certain circumstances signed acknowledgments of change notices can be particularly valuable, as they may be used to establish the time or point of effectiveness of a change when termination, cancellation, or engineering changes are involved—factors which should be clearly defined in the change notice itself.

Follow-Up (Expediting)

Follow-up is a process as well as a form. The process may be *internal* or *external*. The form for external expediting, discussed here, can be a two-section, single-page form or a two-section postal card form, with perforations between the sections (see Fig. 5-14). The top section is addressed to the vendor and signed by the purchaser. Purchasing requests the vendor to use the bottom section to provide definite shipping information on the items specified. The bottom section, addressed to the purchaser, provides space for on how and when shipment has been, or will be, made. Signature space is provided for vendor. This form is a timesaver, as it can be completed quickly for mailing.

Some companies use an extra copy of the purchase order known as the *tracing copy* or *expediting copy* to record the expediting effort and to prevent disturbing the file copy of the order until completion. Others place telephone and other expediting notes on the file copy itself in lines provided at the bottom. The tracing copy should be filed to come up for attention on a specified tracing date. Alternatively, a variety of tabbing procedures may be used including preprinted check dates for marking for follow-up on the tops of order file copies. The expediter must work closely with the buyer and stores and/or manufacturing departments.

Receiving Report

This form shows that the listed item(s) have been received from the vendor (Fig. 5-15). It is required for matching to the purchase order and the vendor's invoice as a basis for payment. It is essential information to purchasing as the basis for transferring the purchase order from the Open File to the Closed File and to signal that follow-up for delivery is no longer needed.

A copy of the purchase order may be used for the receiving report. The receiving department enters date received, packing slip number, quantity, carrier/car number, collect freight charges or prepaid, condition of shipment and receiver's initials. A verified count for each item is required.

To save paperwork and the employee-hours necessary to fill in forms, many companies today are using the packing slip from the shipment as a material receipt form. A rubber stamp provides blocks and direction for entering required additional information.

Regardless of the form or system used to record receipt of material, the receipt record should contain sufficient information to satisfy all departments having a need to know of material received.

J. M. HUBER CORPORATION
PURCHASING DEPARTMENT
BOX 831
BORGER, TEXAS

Date .... Our Order No. .... Dated .... Your Order No. ....

ATTENTION: EXPEDITING SECTION

Gentlemen:

We are particularly interested as to the deliveries of the following items on the above order. We must know immediately when, and how the contents of this order will be shipped.

Please fill out, detach, and return the lower half of the form giving complete details. We will appreciate your immediate reply to this request.

Yours very truly,

_____
Purchasing Department

PLEASE DETACH AND MAIL

J. M. Huber Corporation
Box 831   Date ....
Borger, Texas   Attn: Purchasing Department

Gentlemen:

  (have not)   (partial shipment)
We   (have)   made   (shipment)   of your order No. ....

ITEMS NO.   **BRIEF DESCRIPTION**   **SHIPPING INFORMATION**

ENTIRE ORDER _____   _____

          (will go)   (Express) (Parcel Post)
Shipment (went)   forward by (Carload) (L.C.L.)   on (date) ....
          (Pkg. Frt) (Motor Frt.)

and routed via ....

REMARKS: ....

Yours truly,

By: ....

Fig. 5-14   Follow-up form. Sent to vendor to trace delivery of material on order. Purchasing department fills out upper portion and sends to vendor; after detaching and filling out, vendor returns lower portion to purchasing department. *(Reproduced by permission of J. M. Huber Corporation.)*

One procedure uses a simple 5- by 8-inch serially numbered snap-out form. Under this system the receiving clerk never receives a copy of the purchase order. He creates a receiver for each packing slip, listing the supplier's name, purchase order (PO) number, and quantity and description of material, plus any documentation received. Distribution of copies may typically be to: (1) purchasing, (2) pro-

RECEIVING REPORT		GLASS CONTAINERS CORPORATION		NO. 609323

RECEIVED FROM		RECEIVING LOCATION	DATE RECEIVED	P.O./B.O./AUTH. NO.
RECEIVED FOR		IS ORDER NOW COMPLETED? ☐ YES ☐ NO	PACKING SLIP NO.	RELEASE NO.
VIA		CAR/TRUCK NO.	BILL OF LADING NO.	FREIGHT CHARGES ☐ PREPAID ☐ COLLECT

QUANTITY	UNIT OF MEASURE	DESCRIPTION / REMARKS

COPY DISTRIBUTION	WHITE	YELLOW	GREEN	PINK	RECEIVED, COUNTED, INSPECTED BY:
☐ PURCHASES	ACCOUNTING	PURCHASING	REQUESTOR	RECEIVER	
☐ RETURNED WARE	ACCOUNTING	ACCOUNTING	REG. SALES	RECEIVER	
☐ ALL OTHER TRANS.	ACCOUNTING	PURCHASING	REQUESTOR	RECEIVER	ABOVE RECEIVED IN GOOD CONDITION EXCEPT AS NOTED IN REMARKS

FORM 17 (REV. JUNE 76)   PRINTED IN U.S.A.

Fig. 5-15   Receiving report. *(Glass Containers Corporation.)*

duction or material control or requester, (3) accounts payable, with packing slips attached, and (4) receiving inspection, with material and with reports and certifications attached, if production material; or with material to the requester, if an individual; or to a nonproduction supplies stockroom.

This system has two advantages. First, it forces the receiving clerk to write the receiver to cover the material actually received, and not just as an item on a purchase order. Misshipments are thus quickly identified when purchasing receives its copy. But the greatest advantage is that of speed. Material can be written up and sent on its way without being held up by a backlog of typing in purchasing. This, or a similar system, is a must for the nonconfirmed verbal order system where no purchase order form is created.

Disadvantages are lack of information by the receiving clerk on items ordered, possible receipt of wrong material, no information on completion quantity and misdirection of material internally.

A variation of the above is where the receiving clerk, referring to a copy of the purchase order, creates a snap-out form for distribution in the normal fashion. This has the disadvantage of having to wait for a copy of the order from purchasing.

When a snap-out purchase order is used, a copy may be sent to receiving. The receiving copy provides a space for entry of receipts, and after each entry a set of receiving documents is made on an electrostatic printing machine. On the other hand some firms may be able to provide receiving with all the copies needed pre-typed as part of the purchase order typing, except for the partial receipts.

The use of electronic data processing (EDP) usually requires a completely different approach in the supporting paperwork and is described in detail in Section 15.

The above are only the more popular, basic systems. There are numerous variations and combinations of these which can be devised and used by the purchasing manager to serve his own particular needs.

Returned Materials

This form covers anything being returned, e.g., rejected material, damaged material returned for repair, or overshipments on an order. It is preprinted with fill-in spaces and checkoff boxes for the common reasons for return and instructions to vendor and would be used in conjunction with a shipper-debit form in place of an individual letter to the selling office. Most companies should be able to avoid using this form through careful design of the shipper-debit form with a copy for sending to the selling office as well as one accompanying the shipment.

Where material flow is heavy and procedures require written authorization from the seller before a return is made, several functions may be combined in one form. Figure 5-16 illustrates such a multi-use form; it may be a snap-out with as many as seven copies for the required distribution.

Advance Work Authorization

A useful form is the advance work authorization (see Fig. 5-17.) It is used as a combination shipping instruction-work authorization when material and tooling are sent to a supplier for processing or fabrication. Full instructions are given on the face of the form, so that work may be performed and perhaps even returned before the formal order is typed and mailed. It is not necessary to repeat those terms and conditions appearing on the purchase order except by reference. Processing instructions, due date, and return shipping instructions, plus, of course, the purchase order number and "confirming to" name, if any, will suffice. There is usually no reason why the form cannot be written by hand by the buyer—or by production control personnel—if the work is covered by a blanket order.

By adopting a format similar to that of the purchase order, the advance work authorization form may also be made to serve as a purchase order, provided the supplier is notified that his shipping copy of the work authorization form will be the only document he will receive, and a method for price authorization is devised.

It is important to remember that buyers must exercise their judgment about those situations in which they should *not* make use of the advance work authorization. If the price for the work will be very high or if the terms or conditions are likely to be unclear or subject to dispute, the buyer should avoid using the advance authorization.

The advance authorization form is generally a three-part snap-out set consisting of an original, which remains in purchasing, plus two copies sent with the mate-

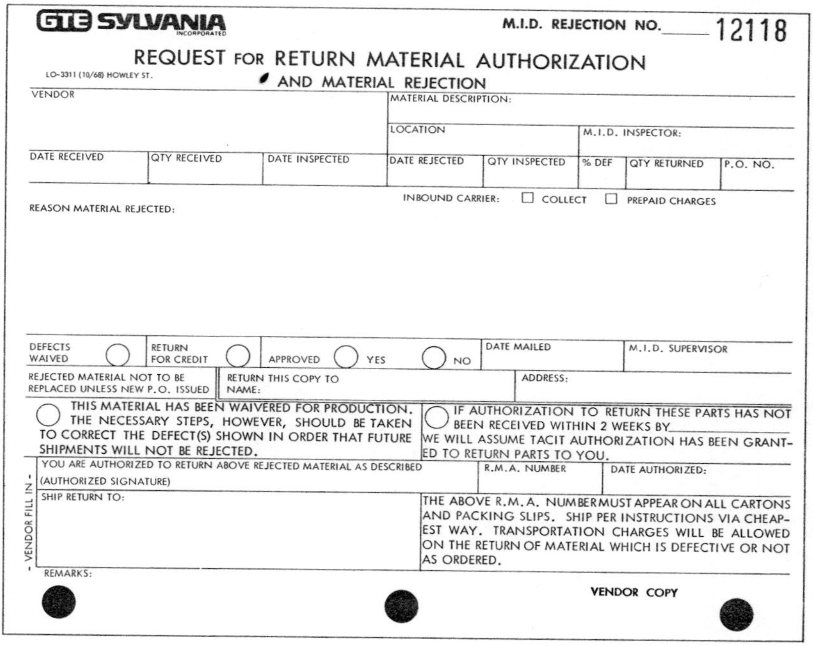

GTE SYLVANIA INCORPORATED

M.I.D. REJECTION NO. 12118

REQUEST FOR RETURN MATERIAL AUTHORIZATION AND MATERIAL REJECTION

LO-3311 (10/68) HOWLEY ST.

VENDOR | MATERIAL DESCRIPTION:

LOCATION | M.I.D. INSPECTOR:

DATE RECEIVED | QTY RECEIVED | DATE INSPECTED | DATE REJECTED | QTY INSPECTED | % DEF | QTY RETURNED | P.O. NO.

INBOUND CARRIER: ☐ COLLECT ☐ PREPAID CHARGES

REASON MATERIAL REJECTED:

DEFECTS WAIVED ○ | RETURN FOR CREDIT ○ | APPROVED ○ YES ○ NO | DATE MAILED | M.I.D. SUPERVISOR

REJECTED MATERIAL NOT TO BE REPLACED UNLESS NEW P.O. ISSUED | RETURN THIS COPY TO NAME: | ADDRESS:

○ THIS MATERIAL HAS BEEN WAIVERED FOR PRODUCTION. THE NECESSARY STEPS, HOWEVER, SHOULD BE TAKEN TO CORRECT THE DEFECT(S) SHOWN IN ORDER THAT FUTURE SHIPMENTS WILL NOT BE REJECTED.

○ IF AUTHORIZATION TO RETURN THESE PARTS HAS NOT BEEN RECEIVED WITHIN 2 WEEKS BY____ WE WILL ASSUME TACIT AUTHORIZATION HAS BEEN GRANTED TO RETURN PARTS TO YOU.

- VENDOR FILL IN -

YOU ARE AUTHORIZED TO RETURN ABOVE REJECTED MATERIAL AS DESCRIBED (AUTHORIZED SIGNATURE) | R.M.A. NUMBER | DATE AUTHORIZED:

SHIP RETURN TO: | THE ABOVE R.M.A. NUMBER MUST APPEAR ON ALL CARTONS AND PACKING SLIPS. SHIP PER INSTRUCTIONS VIA CHEAPEST WAY. TRANSPORTATION CHARGES WILL BE ALLOWED ON THE RETURN OF MATERIAL WHICH IS DEFECTIVE OR NOT AS ORDERED.

REMARKS:

VENDOR COPY

Fig. 5-16 Request for return material authorization. (*GTE Sylvania, Inc.*)

rial. The supplier keeps one copy and receipts for the material on the other and returns it to the buyer. A fourth copy may be provided for production or material control. If the form also serves as a purchase order; as noted above, the distribution should include accounting.

These forms may or may not be serialized; if so, numbers may be preprinted, but they can be hand-serialized as release 1, release 2, etc., against specific orders. This form is not used as a debit; that function is more properly handled by more formal means.

Shipper-Debit

Purchasing departments have occasion to return material to suppliers for credit or for replacement or correction of rejections. It is customary, and generally advisa-

WORK AUTHORIZATION/SHIPPER

P.O. NUMBER MUST APPEAR ON ALL PACKAGES, PACKING SLIPS, INVOICES AND CORRESPONDENCE.

SARGENT INDUSTRIES
HUNTINGTON PARK DIVISION

2533 EAST 56th ST., HUNTINGTON PARK, CALIF. 90255

TELEPHONE: (213) 583-4161
TWX: (910) 321-2849
TELEX: 67-4403

PURCHASE ORDER NO.
DATE
BUYER

TO:

SHIP TO: ☐ 2500 E. 55TH ST. HUNTINGTON PARK, CA. 90255
☐

INSTRUCTIONS TO SARGENT SHIPPING DEPT.
SHIP TO ABOVE ADDRESS VIA:
☐ OUR TRUCK
☐ UPS ☐ OTHER
☐ WILL CALL
☐ CALL FOR PICK-UP PHONE

SHIPPING INSTRUCTIONS TO SELLER
RETURN TO SARGENT VIA:
☐ YOUR DELIVERY
☐ UPS ☐ OTHER
☐ OUR TRUCK
☐ CALL EXT. 271 FOR PICK-UP

REQUIRED DELIVERY SCHEDULE | PROMISED SHIP SCHEDULE | M/R NO. | JOB NO. | ORIGINATOR | REQUISITION NO.

ITEM	QUANTITY	PART NUMBER	DWG. REV.	DESCRIPTION/WORK AUTHORIZED

ATTACHMENTS:
REFERENCED ☐ BLUEPRINT(S) ☐ M/O(S)
CONFIRMING ☐ NO ☐ YES, TO:

NOTICE THE FOLLOWING QUALITY ASSURANCE CLAUSES ARE APPLICABLE TO THIS ORDER. REFERENCE "QUALITY REQUIREMENTS FOR SUPPLIERS"

PURCHASING USE ONLY

WORK AS SPECIFIED AND AUTHORIZED ABOVE SHALL BE PERFORMED IN ACCORDANCE WITH THE TERMS AND CONDITIONS OF THE PURCHASE ORDER REFERENCED HEREON.

SARGENT INDUSTRIES
HUNTINGTON PARK DIVISION

By ______________ BUYER

ROBERT N. HUNTOON – PURCHASING MANAGER

FORM NO. 2.018 (8-71)

PURCHASING DEPT. FILE COPY

Fig. 5-17 Advance work authorization form instructing supplier to process or fabricate buyer's materials. *(Reproduced by permission of Sargent Industries.)*

ble, to handle such transactions formally via the debit-and-credit route in order to permit accounts payable to track the transactions with a minimum of difficulty. Multiple-item orders with multiple receipts and rejections can lead to a staggering tangle of paper work, which can become virtually impassable unless each form is carefully prepared at each step of the way.

Many purchasing departments prepare shipping orders with one copy going to accounts payable, which prepares the necessary debits, and one copy to stores-shipping, which prepares the shipment and bill of lading. This is a wholly satisfactory procedure, but it is just as easy to devise a multipart snap-out (or spirit form) which permits preparation of the debit concurrently with the shipping order. This procedure has the advantage of eliminating separate typing of the debit with its possible transcription errors. Identical shipping orders and debits make for easy matching of paper work by both buyer and seller. It is advisable to forward the debit portion of the set to accounts payable for review and processing and for eventual actual mailing to the supplier.

A typical combination set may consist of the original copy as the file copy which is retained by purchasing, a two-part debit memo (for accounts payable and the supplier), and a two-part shipping order (one to be retained by the supplier and the other to be signed and returned to the buyer). These forms should be serially numbered by preprinting. The top file copy and the debit memo copies are printed with a *DM* preceding the serial number, while the shipping copies carry the prefix *S* (see Fig. 5-18).

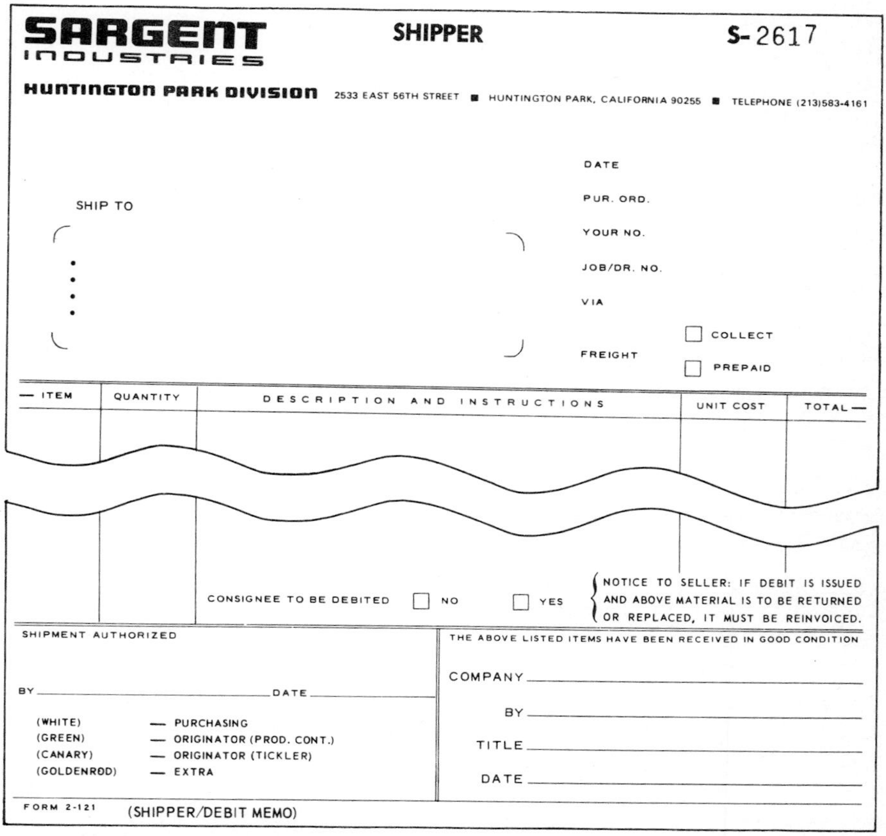

SARGENT INDUSTRIES

SHIPPER

S- 2617

HUNTINGTON PARK DIVISION 2533 EAST 56TH STREET ■ HUNTINGTON PARK, CALIFORNIA 90255 ■ TELEPHONE (213)583-4161

SHIP TO

DATE
PUR. ORD.
YOUR NO.
JOB/DR. NO.
VIA
FREIGHT ☐ COLLECT ☐ PREPAID

ITEM	QUANTITY	DESCRIPTION AND INSTRUCTIONS	UNIT COST	TOTAL

CONSIGNEE TO BE DEBITED ☐ NO ☐ YES

NOTICE TO SELLER: IF DEBIT IS ISSUED AND ABOVE MATERIAL IS TO BE RETURNED OR REPLACED, IT MUST BE REINVOICED.

SHIPMENT AUTHORIZED

BY ______ DATE ______

(WHITE) — PURCHASING
(GREEN) — ORIGINATOR (PROD. CONT.)
(CANARY) — ORIGINATOR (TICKLER)
(GOLDENROD) — EXTRA

THE ABOVE LISTED ITEMS HAVE BEEN RECEIVED IN GOOD CONDITION

COMPANY ______
BY ______
TITLE ______
DATE ______

FORM 2-121 (SHIPPER/DEBIT MEMO)

Fig. 5-18 Returned material form sent to supplier requesting credit, replacement, or correction of rejections. *(Reproduced by permission of Sargent Industries.)*

A credit memo can be created by lining out the *DM* and substituting *CM* with the typewriter. The shipping portion of the set is not used in this application.

Processing of Invoices

An integral part of the procurement cycle consists of the approval and payment of invoices. Speedy payment of invoices makes for better buyer-seller relations and can have a distinct bearing on pricing. Slow payments often result in the loss of discounts. Also, they may force the seller into short-term borrowing, the cost of which is usually passed along to the buyer in the form of higher prices. Better delivery and quality usually result from prompt payments, with the buyer being placed in a preferred-customer status.

Accounting is responsible for the actual payment of invoices, although there is a difference of opinion as to whether accounting or purchasing should approve invoices for payment. Some companies require purchasing to review and approve all invoices, while others ask purchasing to deal with invoices only on an exception basis, when the invoice, receiving report, and purchase order fail to agree in all particulars. There seems to be little real benefit to be derived from having purchasing approve all invoices, other than shifting the work load from accounting to purchasing. It then becomes a management decision as to where the task can be done more economically.

Purchasing is almost universally charged with the responsibility for reconciliation of invoice discrepancies, and this is as it should be. Only the buyer knows all the circumstances surrounding the original transaction and is thus in the best position to resolve any problems with the seller.

For accounting to pay an invoice, a careful check must be made of the purchase order, the receiving report, and the invoice to determine that they all agree, thus verifying that the purchase transaction was consummated as contemplated by purchasing. The form of these documents may vary from company to company, but the basic requirement of matching the three documents will remain unchanged.

Some firms pay invoices upon receipt of material; others pay only after its acceptance. The advocates of the former point out that by not having to wait for inspection, accounts payable is able to process invoices on a smooth, routine basis and to take the proffered cash discounts in virtually all cases. They recognize that a certain percentage of material is returned for rework or replacement after it has been paid for, but they usually find the actual cash losses to the company to be no higher than by the other system if purchasing utilizes reputable suppliers. Usually offsetting unpaid invoices are in the buyer's accounts payable cycle awaiting routine payment dates. Working together, purchasing and accounting can spot potential problem suppliers and remove them permanently or temporarily from the routine processing schedule.

Where there is a transportation department, it should be charged with approval of freight bills. Proper classification of freight and the interpretation of freight tariffs require a highly specialized knowledge generally beyond the skill of the invoice clerk. In the absence of a traffic manager, the purchasing manager is usually responsible for such approvals. Very often the traffic function comes under the purchasing manager. Having periodic audits of freight bills made by an outside freight audit organization can pay dividends, as they will process claims for any overpayments for a fee of about one-half the savings.

Because of the methods of preparing invoices, frequently there is no recogniz-

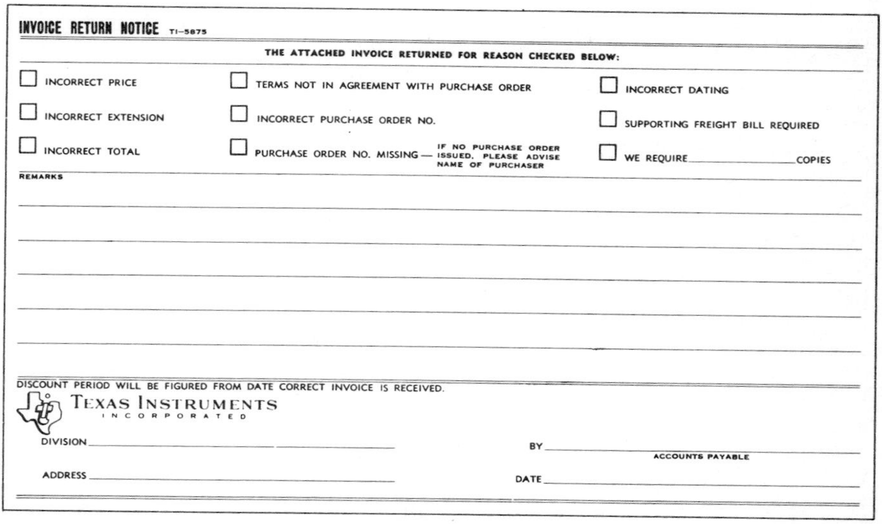

INVOICE RETURN NOTICE TI-5875

THE ATTACHED INVOICE RETURNED FOR REASON CHECKED BELOW:

☐ INCORRECT PRICE
☐ TERMS NOT IN AGREEMENT WITH PURCHASE ORDER
☐ INCORRECT DATING
☐ INCORRECT EXTENSION
☐ INCORRECT PURCHASE ORDER NO.
☐ SUPPORTING FREIGHT BILL REQUIRED
☐ INCORRECT TOTAL
☐ PURCHASE ORDER NO. MISSING — IF NO PURCHASE ORDER ISSUED, PLEASE ADVISE NAME OF PURCHASER
☐ WE REQUIRE ______ COPIES

REMARKS

DISCOUNT PERIOD WILL BE FIGURED FROM DATE CORRECT INVOICE IS RECEIVED.

TEXAS INSTRUMENTS
INCORPORATED

DIVISION ______ BY ______
ACCOUNTS PAYABLE
ADDRESS ______ DATE ______

Fig. 5-19 Invoice return notice form. *(Reproduced by permission of Texas Instruments Inc.)*

able original copy. A rubber stamp should be prepared by accounts payable with the word *Original* at the top and with spaces reflecting:

1. Date invoice received
2. Date material received
3. Receiving report number
4. Quantity O.K.
5. Price and extension O.K.
6. Terms O.K.
7. F.o.b. O.K.
8. Account number

All checking and payment activity should be restricted to the original copy, for, with the initials of the invoice checker, it becomes a certified document.

Invoice Return Notice

The purchasing department should handle all corrections of errors on invoices directly with the vendor. The accounting department, if auditing invoices, may make minor corrections. The use of an invoice return notice (see Fig. 5-19) is

FORM 5361-A   (DO NOT DETACH)
                                               (FROM INVOICE)

To: Purchasing Agent
Invoice does not agree with Purchase Order in the following particulars:

| ☐ Price | ☐ Cash Discount | ☐ Freight Terms | ☐ Quantities |

COMMENTS

Please indicate on which basis vendor should be paid:

☐ Purchase order is correct. Please take action noted below:

   ☐ Pay invoice; issue debit memo for difference.

   ☐ Pay invoice; Vendor will submit credit memo.

   ☐ Hold invoice   Pending reply to correspondence attached.

   ☐ Hold invoice; Vendor will submit corrected invoice.

☐ Purchase Order is correct but overlook small difference and pay according to invoice.

☐ Invoice is correct and should be paid as submitted.
A change order is not required.

☐ Invoice is correct and should be paid as submitted.
A change order is attached.

COMMENTS

P.A. APPROVAL: _____

Fig. 5-20 Internal form between accounting and purchasing departments. Directs action to be taken; invoice does not agree with purchase order. *(Reproduced by permission.)*

helpful in handling the majority of details involved. Since the form normally is attached to the invoice and both are returned to the vendor together, it is not necessary to repeat invoice information on the form.

Space should be provided on the invoice return notice for the following:

1. Incorrect price
2. Incorrect extension
3. Incorrect total
4. Terms not in agreement with purchase order
5. Incorrect purchase order number
6. Purchase order number missing
7. Incorrect date
8. Supporting freight bill required
9. We require _____ copies
10. Remarks

The Remarks portion of the form is used whenever an explanation of unusual circumstances is required or when the error is other than one of those listed. The form illustrated does not have a box for quantity differences because when quantity variance occurs, the buyer must negotiate with the vendor.

In addition to the invoice return notice, a company can utilize an internal form which documents corrective action (see Fig. 5-20) for communication between accounting and purchasing. Such a form, of course, is not required where purchasing audits the invoice for payment.

Telephone Quotation

With the increased necessity of executing purchases quickly, more and more orders are being placed verbally. At the same time, however, it is important to maintain as much competition as possible among suppliers. These factors, along with the need to control and audit purchasing proficiency, make the telephone quotation sheet an important record-keeping document and management tool. Buyers who frequently work on the telephone can use a pad of telephone quotation forms to make sure that they are getting all the necessary competitive data, and completed forms can be used to confirm orders and to review how well telephone purchasing is being managed (see the discussion under Request for Quotation earlier in this section).

RECORDS

Records are valuable only if they serve a particular purpose and can be made readily available for future use. Before adopting the use of a particular record, careful consideration should be given to whether the effort involved in maintaining it will be less than would be necessary without the record. If effort is saved or an essential purpose is served, certain records can be very useful. All records need to be purged periodically so that the files do not become unwieldy. In purging their files, however, purchasing managers should make sure they are not destroying anything that they are required by law to keep.

Price and History Record

The price and history record form (see Fig. 5-21) serves to tabulate purchases of a particular item or material. It is useful to the buyer in marking the purchase

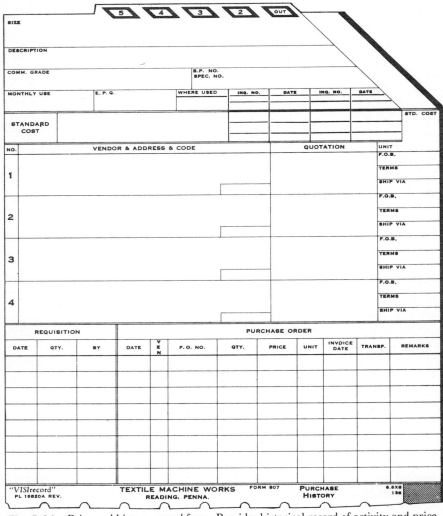

Fig. 5-21 Price and history record form. Provides historical record of activity and price. *(Reproduced by permission of Textile Machine Works, Reading, Pa.)*

requisition for preparation of the purchase order. It is also useful in checking on future bids on like materials. It can furnish information for developing price trends and for setting standard material costs.

The successful bidder's quotation is recorded on the form, and as orders are placed, the order number and date are entered.

Price record forms usually are filed by item or commodity in visible record filing equipment of the cabinet type, or in looseleaf binders in manual systems. The commodity or item designation is listed at the top or bottom of the form, or both, so that it may be readily visible when the usual lapping method of filing is used.

In automated systems a record is initiated with the first purchase of an item, commodity, or service. The record is then updated with each subsequent issuance of a requisition or purchase order. An automated purchasing record system can provide an almost instantaneous price history for an item, and in many cases a history of vendor performance as well. (What the system provides of course depends on the program and what has been put into it. See Section 15.)

Price record forms should provide space for the purchasing department to insert the following essential information:

1. Item or commodity designation
2. Price and discount, and price unit
3. F.o.b. point
4. Vendor's name and address
5. Order number and date
6. Comments which may be pertinent to a particular item, commodity, or transaction

Tool, Die, and Pattern Record

Many companies have no need for this type of record. However, this record is essential to those firms purchasing items that require the building of special tooling (tools, dies, patterns, jigs, and fixtures).

Who owns the tooling is a point that must be clearly understood at the time the contract is made. Payment of a tooling charge does not always indicate ownership.

A record of special tooling owned by the purchaser should be maintained, listing location, age, type, and insurance coverage.

A pictorial record, or photograph, of the tooling is an excellent method of recording tooling details.

Commodity Record

Each major material and service purchased repetitively should have a record that lists market and materials information as well as specifications. This record, which complements the price and history record and the vendor record, needs to be kept only on those major commodities and services that are vital to a company's operations.

Union Contract Status Record

To protect the supply of materials, the purchasing department should keep informed of termination dates of labor contracts of critical vendors. A critical vendor is one who supplies material or services which cannot be obtained readily from another supplier.

A simple chronological filing system can alert the buyer prior to the date of critical-vendor labor contracts. The situation can then be reviewed with the vendor and appropriate action taken to protect the delivery of material.

Order Index

There is an advantage in having a record of purchase orders issued, i.e., a numerical listing. (It is sometimes also called a *purchase order log* or *numerical order record*.)

The numerical listing can be a looseleaf form. The pages should have columns to provide for order number, vendor name, date ordered, and buyer. Some companies use a copy of the purchase order which is bound in a permanent book. An alternative to binding is microfilming the copies. The advantage of either system is that a permanent file by number is available, giving all the original information on a purchase order.

Contract Record

If there are several long-term contracts for materials or services, it is helpful to have a consolidated listing showing order numbers, supplier names, brief descriptions, and expiration dates. (Blanket purchase orders can also be made a part of this contract record.) A contract record helps a buyer plan ahead for upcoming contract negotiations—the negotiating workload can then be staggered so that contract expiration dates are not missed. The record is also especially useful for checking on and complying with time-period notices in contracts.

Vendor Record

An accurate, up-to-date listing of all vendors is a very helpful purchasing tool. Many firms keep such a record on a rotary card file that is convenient to the buyer and the order typist. An expanded vendor record that is in a separate file should be used to keep information on vendor ratings, financial data, and capabilities. As mentioned before, all this information can be adapted to data processing systems.

A complete vendor record should contain all the following information:

1. Complete company name and address
2. Name of representative calling
3. Main office contact
4. Terms and f.o.b. point
5. Shipping method and routing
6. Type of operation or product line
7. District office (address, telephone number, and contact)

Tests on New Products and Materials

With many new materials coming on the market, it is often necessary that these materials be put through a test period to determine their usefulness. A record of such test results should be kept for future reference.

FILES

Obviously a purchasing department's files will contain all the materials discussed under Records on the preceding pages. They should also contain such things as general correspondence, catalogs, vendor insurance certificates, projects under way or proposed, and manuals, etc., which are discussed here. It is always important to keep in mind, however, that the purchasing department's filing system will be valuable only if it provides ready access to important information and is not crowded with useless and outdated material. For example, advertising materials in the form of unsolicited brochures, flyers, and catalogs should be discarded unless the purchasing manager believes they are or will be of direct interest to the department. Obviously, the purchasing manager's good judgment is essential in keeping the files uncluttered and up to date.

Many firms now microfilm many of their records to save space and provide for easier records retrieval. Suppliers of these types of equipment can provide information on potential uses, costs, and legal status.

Two fundamental objectives for files are to support and identify the purchase decision and to guide purchasing personnel in their decisions and actions. Irrespective of the filing system selected, simplification should be an important factor. Filing should be kept current. A large number of files are referred to regularly in a purchasing department, and the efficiency of that department can almost be judged by its filing system.

Open and Closed Orders

Basic to every purchasing department is an *open-order file* and a *closed-order file*. The open-order file is a temporary one, pending receipt of the materials or services ordered; when delivery is accomplished, the order is transferred to the closed file. For many purchasing departments the portable tub-type file is used to hold open orders; it can be moved about to various work stations—e.g., to a buyer who is checking on an order by telephone.

Completed orders that are transferred to the closed file are usually arranged alphabetically by supplier, and within each supplier category by date. At the end of a calendar or fiscal year, these closed orders can then be transferred to storage. It is a good idea, however, to have one previous year's closed purchase orders easily accessible; they are often very valuable in disputes and negotiations with suppliers.

Correspondence

Much general correspondence which has no direct bearing on a purchase order, contract, or purchase requisition is received daily. This correspondence generally will fall into two classes, open and closed. Open correspondence, on which answers are desired, is the most active of the files. When correspondence is completed, it is transferred to the closed file, in accordance with company record retention policy.

The permanent files are the archives of the purchasing department. While seldom referred to, if they have probable future value, they should not be destroyed. To minimize use of filing space, care should be exercised so that only essential material is placed in permanent files. Such files are often placed on microfilm.

Suppliers' Catalogs, etc.

Probably the most difficult filing in a purchasing department concerns suppliers' catalogs and pamphlets and correspondence with noncataloged suppliers. There is no standard format for catalogs and pamphlets; they come in varying sizes and thicknesses. To be of value, these must be filed and cross-indexed so as to be readily available when needed. (See also Section 30.)

Many catalogs contain classifications of items that are not suitable for filing by any specific class of commodity. Each catalog should have a number applied on the back. This number should be visible when the catalog is on the shelf. An alphabetical cross index should be maintained for all catalogs in the library. The index should show the commodity classification and the vendor's name, and each listing should have the same number as that on the back of the catalog to which it refers. This index may be preserved in a looseleaf binder with alphabetical guides.

Obsolete catalogs and pamphlets should be eliminated; filing space is expensive and should not be maintained for useless catalogs and pamphlets. They take up space and make it more difficult to locate the proper catalog or pamphlet. Purging the catalog file can be made an annual event.

Various communications are received from suppliers who do not publish a catalog. These may pertain to specific items regularly used by the purchaser, may cover new items considered as substitutes for items currently in use, and may cover items not currently used but for which there is a possible future use. It is desirable to keep much of this correspondence, and it should be filed for ready future reference. These and pamphlets and brochures can be hole-punched and placed in binders or simply placed in indexed file drawers.

One fairly recent development is a microfilm system produced by the Thomas Publishing Company (One Pennsylvania Plaza, New York, N.Y. 10001). The system can reproduce one hundred 8½- by 11-inch industrial catalog pages on one 6- by 4-inch microfilm card. This system makes it possible for many purchasing departments to cut down drastically the bulk of their catalog files.

Purchase Requisitions

A good method of filing requisitions is by numerical sequence or with the vendor purchase order file. This is a matter of purchasing department preference.

Request for Quotation

Request for quotation forms should be filed together, with the successful bidder form on top. These would be filed alphabetically, by classification, by project number, or with the purchase order.

Retention of Records

There is no quick-and-easy solution to the problem of what records to retain. The basic factors to consider involve: (1) legal requirements, (2) administrative requirements, (3) historical requirements, and (4) administrative discretion. A booklet *Retention and Preservation of Records with Destruction Schedules* is available from Record Controls, Inc., 209 South LaSalle Street, Chicago, Ill. 60604. This publication contains information on organizing a records retention program and a summary of state laws as well as federal laws and regulations.

For detailed federal regulations on what records must be kept, who must keep them, and for how long, refer to *Guide to Records Retention Requirements,* available from Superintendent of Documents, Washington, D.C. 20402. Ask for catalog number GS 4.107/a:R245.

Some definite plan of retention should be established and formalized. Uniformity of practice will be established and personnel will be able to discard obsolete files in an orderly fashion.

FORMS DESIGN AND PROCUREMENT

Factors in Forms Design

When adopting a form, the following three considerations should be kept in mind:

1. Will the purpose for which it is intended be better or more economically served by utilizing a form than by other means? Perhaps a letter, memorandum, or telephone call will do the job more quickly and at less cost. Forms cost money to buy and use.

2. If a form is to be used, is there a standard one available? Most printing vendors or stationery supply houses carry in stock some standard forms which are adaptable to use in any company, and since these are printed in large quantities, they may be much more economical to use than a custom-printed form.

3. If a custom-printed form is to be used, what is the best size, style, and type and the essential printed matter needed to do the job and be consistent with other company forms?

In general, forms which will be sent outside the company should be of good quality and appearance. Those for internal use should emphasize utility and economy. All should be simple and easy to use.

Repetitive information should be printed on the form, but care must be taken to avoid including items that frequently must be crossed out or changed. To avoid this, use of the box-check method, such as that employed on Fig. 5-19, may be advantageous.

Spaces to be filled in should be large enough to accommodate the maximum volume of information that may be entered, to avoid crowding. Vertical spacing of headings should correspond to standard typewriter spacing. Headings should be placed in the same order in which information will logically be entered, whether by machine or hand. Consideration should be given to folding for insertion into window envelopes. This saves addressing the envelope. If handwritten entries are to be made, supply lines on which to write.

If copies are to be made, consideration should be given to whether plain or printed copies are necessary. The plain copy is obviously the most economical and may serve the purpose as well as the printed one. When several copies are necessary, such as of the purchase order form, utilization of specialized forms may be more economical or more expeditious. Among these are (1) the carbon-interleaved type of form which incorporates single-use snap-out carbon paper and (2) the continuous folded type used with a carbon-paper-holder attachment on the typewriter. Many multicopy forms use no-carbon-required paper; this is a great advantage over the messy carbon-interleaved form.

The economical printing of complicated forms requires specialized machinery, and some printers specialize in their production. Furthermore, there are companies which make a specialty of designing and producing business forms to fit the need. Such specialists should be consulted when designing and procuring forms for the purchasing department.

Cost of Forms

The cost of forms is materially affected by paper quality and size. Design should incorporate the minimum weight and quality of paper suitable for the purpose.

Standard sizes should be used to avoid the extra costs resulting from the necessity of cutting paper to special size, with attendant trimming wastage. Booklets on standard qualities, weights, types, and sizes of paper are available from paper vendors.

Usually the lowest unit price obtainable for printed material is for the largest quantity. To obtain low unit cost and yet keep quantity to a realistic figure based on actual or anticipated usage, it is well to ascertain prices on quantities representing 6, 9, or 12 months' requirements. On large quantities, some vendors will offer to print as much as a year's needs and permit withdrawal from their stock as needed, with payment being made for the quantity drawn. On a newly adopted form it is well to have only a small quantity printed initially, since after it is placed in use revisions may be necessary. All forms should be checked periodically for updating and revisions.

There are several printing processes, two or more of which may do the same printing job well, but one may be more economical. Discussion with printing vendors can be very fruitful.

Checklist of Forms Design

The following checklist may be helpful in verifying that the factors outlined above have been considered before adopting a form:

1. Is a form actually needed?
2. Is a standard form available?
3. Is a special form, with a few changes, adaptable for other uses?
4. Does the form meet your requirements in terms of:
   a. Size and style
   b. Appearance
   c. Spacing and location of headings
   d. Preparation of copies that may be needed
   e. Utilization
   f. Printed matter
   g. Allocation of space
   h. Paper stock
   i. Carbons
   j. Printing process
   k. Overall economy of production and use

Procurement and Control of Forms

Control of the inventory of forms and initiation of purchase requisitions usually are best handled in the stores or purchasing office. It is preferable to treat forms as a regular stock item to ensure that replenishment requests will be initiated far enough in advance of stock depletion so that replacement stock can be ordered, produced, and received. As such, each should be assigned a discrete form number. Form revision numbers should also be used to avoid confusion when reordering.

The same purchasing procedures utilized for other materials should be employed in purchasing forms and printing service. Combining two or more forms of the same style, size, and paper into one purchase and printing frequently result in lower printing costs because the printer can then double up on a single press run. This is value analysis in its simplest application.

NOTE: For further information on subjects covered in this section see the list of references in Section 30.

Section **6**

Selecting Sources of Supply

EDITOR

Glenn W. Inman, C.P.M. *Vice-President, Purchasing and Materials, Clow Corporation, Oak Brook, Illinois*

ASSOCIATE EDITOR

Rosemary Schoenberger, C.P.M. *Director of Purchasing, UIP Engineered Products Corporation, Elk Grove Village, Illinois*

Selection of the supplier is the pivotal responsibility of the purchasing function. Without final authority in this decision, the purchasing department is essentially clerical. If other departments are allowed to choose suppliers, purchasing is stripped of the one function that distinguishes it from other acquisition activities.

Supplier selection is the most important milestone in the purchasing process. The ultimate success of a new product, the profitability of a product line, and the timeliness of delivery to the marketplace may depend upon this decision. Moreover, the selection must be reviewed periodically to see that it remains valid as time alters circumstances.

The selection decision is always a part of the purchasing process. It may be an almost unconscious decision, made in a fraction of a second, as the buyer reaches for the catalog of a particular distributor. It may, at the other extreme, require an extensive analysis of complex, competing proposals for something as sophisticated as a major weapons system, or an offshore oil drilling platform. Such decisions may take as long as a year and require the funding of several million dollars. At either end of the scale, a decision must be made.

This section will describe the major steps in the selection process. It will review what must be known about the material and its application, the determination of the essential characteristics of prospective sources, the assembling of a bidders list, and the gathering of needed information concerning the bidders. It will then summarize techniques for analyzing bid data and suggest guidelines for making the final award. Finally, considerations such as trade relations and the achievement of social objectives are reviewed in terms of their impact on supplier selection.

THE MATERIAL: WHAT IS IT?

It is necessary for the buyer to know precisely what he plans to purchase. This knowledge depends, in the first place, on how adequately the requisitioner has described the requirements. Conversely, the buyer must know when the requisitioner has not adequately described the required purchase.

The need to know precisely what must be bought does not necessarily mean the buyer needs to know a great deal. Generally, the end use of the material will determine the amount and kind of information that must be assembled for a knowledgeable procurement.

An extensive list of factors, relating to material, that may have a bearing on the selection decision may be helpful. The buyer is cautioned to be concerned only with those that are important to the requirement at hand.

Specifications[1]

Descriptive information may state required physical characteristics, desired performance, essential manufacturing processes, or special packaging requirements. Whatever the nature of the information, it provides the buyer with a specification to be met.

---

[1]Also described in Section 9.

Industry Standard   This is one of the simplest specifications available. By common consent all like items made to an industry standard are identical, regardless of manufacturer. Consequently, a simple designation of standard will always result in the acquisition of the proper item. A further advantage is that an industry standard is generally the least expensive alternative.

Manufacturer's Standard   This standard also has the advantage of a simple designation allowing procurement of an identical item repeatedly. Generally such items are made in quantity for stock, are based upon the manufacturer's particular expertise or manufacturing equipment, and are readily available on short notice. The manufacturer's standard item, however, does not enjoy the universal availability of an industry standard. In addition, it is not normally as good a value as an industry standard, although it is clearly a better value than a specially designed item.

Brand Name   Such an item is nearly the equivalent of a manufacturer's standard. Usually the composition of a brand name item is provided through labeling, but broader tolerances and less consistency from item to item can be expected as compared with a standard item. Other manufacturers may provide a nearly identical item under their own brand name, so there may be some freedom of choice. The use of a brand name generally indicates that the manufacturer has established a recognizable market preference for that name. The buyer may, therefore, obtain better value through brand name purchasing, but he should clearly establish superiority by comparing the branded item with the industry or manufacturer's standard items on the basis of composition or performance.

Standard Grade   In some industries material is completely described by standard designation. For example, No. 2 white pine completely describes a quality of white pine lumber to persons familiar with the lumber trade. Such a grade designation has, however, fairly broad parameters, and is subject to the judgment decisions of a knowledgeable person within the industry. The buyer nearly always must depend upon the supplier to select and furnish the grade ordered. Since price is based upon grade, the use of a reputable supplier and the occasional verification of grade by an impartial agency are recommended.

Buyers are urged to promote the use of standards by requisitioners to the maximum extent possible. This practice will foster the accurate choice of required material with a minimum of description and reduce delays in delivery due to misunderstanding of requirements by suppliers. Most important, cost of material is reduced and cost of acquisition is minimized.

Part Drawing   Material to be acquired may also be described by a part drawing in which the requisitioner pictorially describes the needed item. Part drawings are sometimes used to designate simple requirements, such as fasteners, within the parameters of the requisitioner's engineering identification system, but the addition of corresponding industry standard identification of the part is to be encouraged. Usually part drawings portray an item that must be made to the special needs of the requisitioner. The drawing should indicate all necessary dimensions, tolerances, and other information, including identification of critical requirements.

It is helpful if the buyer has the ability to read such drawings so that he can ascertain whether they are sufficiently clear and complete to enable the supplier to produce the part as desired.

Part Specification   This is nearly the same as a part drawing in that a specific item is completely described. The difference is that the description is narrative, with no drawing to aid the supplier. Such a specification has limited value and should be accepted only when the requisitioned part can be clearly described by this method.

Tolerances   When appropriate, tolerances of dimensions should be specified. If tolerances are not important, this fact should be indicated, since the maintenance of tolerances is costly. Tolerances are particularly important when purchased parts are to be assembled. Tolerances may also be designated for a range of color shades, performance characteristics, and other material requirements.

Finishes   Like tolerances, finishes should be specified when important but omitted when unnecessary. The cost to produce smooth finishes goes up very rapidly, so requirements should be assessed very carefully. While the designation of mechanical finishes follows an established standard, description of finish for cosmetic purposes is quite difficult. Generally, it is helpful to furnish a sample of the finish required in the latter case.

Material Specifications   A refinement of part drawing or part specification designation is the use of material specification. This should be used when the precise composition of material for the part is important. Care should be taken to see that the material specified is available in the market, and that quantities needed justify asking for special processing. In simple instances, an industry standard, such as SAE 1040 steel, can be used. In more complex material applications, complete chemical and metallurgical composition may be combined with instructions for heat-treating the base metal. The more rigid the material specifications, the more costly it will be. In addition, expense will be added for monitoring the material composition. A more subtle risk is the shifting of responsibility for performance of the part from the supplier to the buyer as the buyer eliminates the seller's right to choose the appropriate material.

Manufacturing Process Specification   This further refinement directs the supplier to make the item according to precise instructions. Such instructions may include machine tool feeds and speeds, stress relief cycles, curing cycles, injection pressures, cleaning methods, and other process requirements. This type of specification is often used in conjunction with a material specification. It is useful primarily when the manufacturing process has a demonstrable effect on the performance of the part. Again, overzealous inclusion of this kind of specification will add to the cost and will shift performance responsibility to the buyer. However, when it must be employed, the buyer should make certain it is understood and is part of the supplier's contractual obligation.

Quality Control System Requirements   There is increasing use of the specification of quality system standards to ensure that material furnished will meet requirements. While requiring the supplier to maintain a quality control organization may increase his costs, there may be such an improvement in the number of usable items shipped that there is a net cost decrease. In addition, there is an increase in the confidence level of reliability, which is important to ultimate cost. Quality control requirements, as described in Section 9, may vary from a random sampling for acceptability of important characteristics to the complete quality system requirement described in the Department of Defense Specification MIL-Q 9858A.

Acceptance Tests   A variation of the specification of quality control requirements is the use of acceptance tests. The quality control system is not specified, but the material must pass tests of characteristics selected as important to performance. The tests may be as fundamental as dimensional checks or color matching. They may, on the other hand, be designed to stimulate ultimate performance with a requisite percent achievement rate. Acceptance tests are usually designed to be nondestructive, but they may take the form of performance to failure. Destructive testing can establish safety margins, detect hidden flaws, and reveal inadequate design. Test requirements must be clearly understood, acceptance criteria agreed upon, and an allowance for waste provided in the case of destructive testing.

Packaging Specifications   These may be necessary to provide protection against the elements, particularly for overseas shipments. They may also be necessary to provide special protection against shock, abrasion, or other damaging exposure. Reusable packaging is sometimes prescribed as a cost-cutting technique whereby material is shipped to the customer in the same package in which it is received. Packaging or palletizing may also be specified to provide ease of handling at the receiving dock, in the storeroom, or to the production floor. Occasionally packaging specifications may include the use of printed material for advertising purposes.

Performance Specifications   A form of specification used more often with capital equipment than with material or components is the performance specification.[2] In its simplest form this type of requirement does not direct the supplier to furnish a carefully described item, but requires that he furnish an item that will perform a specific task. Performance may be described as pieces per hour, inches per minute, or some other measurable output. Such a specification can become quite complex. It should set forth clearly the desired operating parameters, as well as limitations of weight or dimensions if such are necessary. Supplementing output requirements, a performance specification may also indicate that the item must function normally in a hazardous atmosphere, under shock conditions, when exposed to weather, or in some other abnormal state. Further, it may be necessary to describe the conditions under which, or frequency with which, maintenance can be performed without interfering with normal operation.

Warranty Provisions   Key components that can affect the performance of the end product should be put under warranty provisions. The supplier should be called upon to warrant performance of his product in support of his customer's

---

[2]Also see Section 16.

warranty, when the end product is normally sold with such protection. The supplier may also be called upon to provide warranty service or to reimburse the buyer in lieu of providing warranty service.

Distributor Provisions Occasionally the supplier may be asked to agree to special terms of distribution. This will normally occur when spare parts support of service centers is necessary. Sometimes the supplier will have a more suitable distribution system than the buyer for parts or product, in which case distribution can become an important element in the purchase.

Field Service Requirements Field service for warranty purposes, as mentioned above, or for installation, maintenance, or operation may be a very necessary part of the procurement of large items of equipment.

Resale Requirements A purchasing situation in which marketing considerations play a major role is procurement for resale. The kind of market the product is to be sold into, warranty provisions, distribution provisions, and service provisions required of the supplier have a very direct bearing on the success of the buyer's firm with its customers. The buyer must, therefore, assure himself that his supplier has both the desire and capability to treat the ultimate consumer as though he were the supplier's own customer.

Availability

Quantity Not only is it necessary to know precisely what material is required, but it is also important to know and understand the required availability characteristics of the material to successfully meet the requisitioner's needs. The most obvious piece of information needed is the quantity, discussed in Section 12. The number of pieces or pounds or feet ordered should be sufficient to allow for shipping damage, inventory shrinkage, scrap rates, or manufacturing yield and still make the necessary quantity available at the point of use.

Usage Rates Information regarding rate of usage may be important in scheduling deliveries. Availability without excessive investment in inventory is always a desirable goal. Therefore, a comparison between the scheduling of partial shipments as contrasted to the specification of a single shipment may be profitable.

Lead Time Procurement lead time has an important bearing on sourcing decisions and, therefore, must be known. Comparison of user requirements with market availability can alter the choice of suppliers, the type and cost of transportation, and the decision between partial and complete shipments.

Long-Term Requirements Consideration of long-term availability is important for continuing requirements. Short-term price advantages may be forgone when long-range supply is required. Continuing harmonious relationships with suppliers may be of overriding importance to the long-range market plans of the buyer's firm. Obviously, those considerations are unimportant for a one-time requirement.

Transportability This characteristic can limit availability in unusual circumstances. Availability of alternate methods of transportation as protection against strikes or catastrophes can be comforting. Shortages of rail cars or trucks must be monitored. Unusually heavy or large or odd-shaped items must be checked for route clearances, both physical and legal.

Chronic Short Supply   When the raw material of which the purchased item is made is in chronic short supply, the buyer must take protective action to assure himself of availability. He may choose suppliers who are vertically integrated, who are in a strong inventory position, or who are known to be in a strong supply position. He may choose to take a position in the raw material market to protect the supply of material to his source—a practice called *tolling*. He must, in any event, consider the problem as crucial to his supplier selection decision.

SOURCES: WHAT TO CONSIDER

Once the material requirement is clearly understood, the buyer can turn his attention to an understanding of the supplying market. This step will identify the characteristics of appropriate suppliers, thus enabling the buyer to select a bidders list of comparable, capable competitors more easily.

Quantity

When the quantity required is small, the normal channel of distribution is a distributor. The quantity that marks the boundary between distributor and manufacturer varies from industry to industry, as do the units of measure of such quantities. Distributor quantities of electronic components are measured in number of pieces, whereas in steel the measurement is in tons. The quantity may vary within an industry by product line. Distributors in some instances perform a limited number of operations upon material normally processed by the manufacturer and may thereby increase their quantity. Further, the quantity may vary with time—permanently, as industry practice changes, or temporarily, as business conditions rise and fall. The buyer should determine whether his required quantity dictates purchase through a distributor or direct from a manufacturer. While the latter is often considered the most desirable alternative, the true economic function of the distributor should be recognized and supported.

The buyer should also determine whether the quantity of the immediate requirement approximates the quantity that will usually be ordered. If he will normally be ordering in distributor quantities, he may be well advised to always order from a distributor to establish lasting rapport. On the other hand, if he will usually be ordering in mill quantities, he may ask without embarrassment for mill service on an occasional distributor quantity requirement. If the number of transactions at both quantity levels will be substantial, he may wish to establish both distributor and mill suppliers.

In major product lines wherein long-term availability requirements are coupled with a need for large quantities, it may be prudent to establish a raw material position. The buyer can purchase raw stock outright, maintain a reasonable inventory position, and furnish it to his fabricating source. Since this course of action requires abnormal inventory investment, it should not be taken lightly, but it will provide assurance of supply for quantity requirements that may be out of the reach of the fabricating supplier of limited resources.

Availability

Among the important characteristics of a qualified supplier is an ability to make the required quantity available to the buyer as often as necessary. Suppliers selected to bid should be large enough to satisfy this characteristic with the added ability to perform either above or below the probable requirement quantity without undue strain on capacity.

Not only might it be risky to depend upon a supplier whose capability would be strained by peak needs, but also it might be just as risky to acquire too large a share of the capacity of a supplier. Long-term stability is reduced when a company becomes overly dependent on a single customer, and assurance of supply suffers.

When either the component or the material from which it is made has a tendency toward long-term or recurring scarcity, it becomes important to invite bidders who enjoy a relatively strong position with their sources of supply. This position may be a result of size, long-standing relationships, long-term contracts, or vertical integration. For whatever reason, some assurance of the bidders' ability to furnish needed material continuously in periods of shortage is important.

Availability of reliable and appropriate means of transportation is occasionally a problem. Remote sources may require special service which is not always available and is often expensive. Better suppliers will have both adequate carrier equipment and alternative means of transportation as backup.

Distribution

The buyer should ascertain normal industry marketing practices before deciding upon his bidders list. Although industry practices are not inviolable, deviations from normal patterns are usually permitted only under very unusual circumstances. Some products are sold by the manufacturer's own selling force directly to the user, with shipment from either a factory warehouse or strategically placed regional warehouses. Others sell through manufacturer-owned but separately operated marketing and warehousing organizations. Custom products tend to be sold directly by the manufacturer, while standard products tend to be sold through separate selling organizations.

Products are also sold through independent distributors who provide a stocking service, application engineering services, or final manufacturing operations. Manufacturer assistance for unusual application engineering or other problem solving is often available, even though ordering must be done through the distributor.

Manufacturers' representatives are similar to independent distributors, but do not provide any stocking service. Typically, a "rep" will not take possession of material at all, but acts as a broker between seller and buyer. A manufacturer's representative normally provides a very useful service to the seller who cannot afford full-time marketing representation and to the buyer who wishes to secure a line of complementary products from one source.

Industries are generally made up of companies that can be characterized as broad-line suppliers but with a few relatively narrow specialists. The broad-line suppliers may not cover all product lines, but they tend to cover several, with no single line particularly outstanding. The specialists, on the other hand, have become proficient in one or two lines, make no attempt to compete beyond their own field, and may even be higher-priced on a unit cost basis. However, they can provide their product with above-average assurance of performance, knowledgeable assistance in application problems, and complete coverage of a narrow field. The specialist is a highly desirable supplier in many instances because he must maintain superiority in his chosen field to compete with his larger, broader-based rivals.

Although there is a strong tendency to prefer to deal directly with a manufacturer, indirect purchasing can be equally satisfactory. Every alternative method of distribution is justified by the special service it provides. The buyer must decide which services are needed, if any, before deciding which channel of distribution to select, if, indeed, he is provided a choice by the supplying industry.

SUPPLIERS: ASSEMBLING THE BIDDERS LIST

When the buyer has determined the precise material requirement and the appropriate characteristics of potential suppliers, he can assemble a list of prospective sources. While it may be difficult to know as much about the suppliers as the buyer would like at this stage, if a reasonably good analysis has been made, a number of sources who can probably meet the requirements may be listed. It may be satisfactory to identify as few as two or three to generate adequate competition for a generally available part or raw materials. However, it may be wise to identify as many as a dozen potential suppliers when the nature of the competition will probably extend beyond price to design support, field service, special raw material inventories, or other complex criteria.

Published Sources

There are a large number of sources for published information concerning prospective suppliers. The following list is comprehensive but not all-inclusive.[3]

1. General industrial registers or directories
   a. *Thomas's Register of American Manufacturers*
   b. *Conover-Mast Purchasing Directory*
   c. *MacRae's Blue Book*
   d. *Sweet's Catalog*

[3]See Section 30.

    e. Metropolitan and regional directories provided by chambers of commerce and industrial development agencies

2. Industry sources
    a. Industry associations
    b. Trade associations
    c. Trade papers and journals
    d. Professional associations
    e. National and regional association publications
    f. Industry buyers' guides
3. Classified telephone directories
4. Professional source services
    a. Microfilm libraries
    b. Data retrieval services
    c. Inquiry services
5. Manufacturers' catalogs and sales literature

Random Sources

There are also a large number of sources for supplier information that depend upon alert documentation of information provided by others. Some of these are listed below.

1. *Interviews with Salespersons.*   This should be a primary source of supplier information, but the quality of data varies considerably and the salesman can be expected to display bias.

2. *Interviews with Other Buyers.*   Data accumulated by others, both factual and judgmental, when properly organized can be helpful. A file of other buyers known to the purchaser, organized by field of experience, is particularly useful.

3. *Trade and Product Shows.*   Such exhibits may provide useful source and product information.

4. *Interviews with Personnel from Other Functions.*   Design engineers, plant engineers, manufacturing personnel, and others develop much information regarding the particular segment of industry that interests them.

Foreign Sources[4]

Information regarding potential foreign sources is of increasing importance, since world markets have become as available to the buyer as domestic markets. Information regarding foreign companies can be obtained from the following sources:

1. U.S. Department of Commerce.
2. Commercial attachés of foreign missions.
3. American chambers of commerce in foreign cities.
4. *Trade Directories of the World,* Croner Publications, Inc., 211-05 Jamaica Ave., Queens Village, New York, N.Y. 11428.
5. *Made in Europe,* 27 Unterlindau, 6 Frankfurt/M., West Germany, lists

[4]Also see Section 22.

sources of foreign-made goods. Two publications are available. One lists consumer products and the other, technical equipment.

Special Data System Sourcing[5]

In the larger international type of purchasing operation—particularly in dynamic industries in which technology is changing rapidly—quick access to sources of supply is essential. Use of the typical purchasing department technical library in such situations, however, can be excessively time-consuming. Moreover, the cost of the space required to store a large amount of technical information is significant, and sometimes prohibitive.

The International Civil Aviation Organization (ICAO) in Montreal, Canada, has overcome these obstacles with a computerized-microfilm suppliers and equipment information retrieval system (SEIRS). ICAO is a regulatory organization that includes among its services to 153 member nations assistance in aviation development work. SEIRS gives ICAO missions throughout the world ready access to data and specifications on approximately 17,000 items used in the aviation industry.

The heart of the system is a data bank containing details of equipment items, each of which is referenced by a unique identifier. Details include year of data entry; indication of whether the item is "basic," i.e., is in frequent and common use in diverse locations; equipment description; location of additional information—on microfilm or in the purchasing library; manufacturer's name and location and, if applicable, name of agent or distributor; price; weight; and miscellaneous information highlighting main specifications and features.

Since it is unrealistic to consider the information stored in the data bank as being comprehensive, the design of the system includes a microfilm element. Data sheets or catalog entries are microfilmed, with each entry bearing the same reference carried by the identifier in the data bank.

There are two essential stages in the operation of SEIRS: (1) interrogation of the data bank by specifying the group and subgroup covering the equipment specifications required and visual scanning to single out items that appear to meet specifications; (2) study of those microfilm frames that relate to the equipment selected. (The computerized entries are supported by about 30,000 microfilm frames.)

When missions submit requests for information (usually by telex) to Montreal, ICAO personnel search the data bank and reply by sending either a printout of the appropriate entries or a microfiche of the printout. The missions then select items from the printouts or microfiches and ask for full specifications on them, since the data bank carries only basic specifications. In response, ICAO sends a microfilm copy of the data, which can be read on the inexpensive microviewers that the missions have at their disposal.

[5]This portion of the handbook was written by A. C. J. Everard, Chief, Procurement Supply and Contracts, Technical Assistance Bureau, International Civil Aviation Organization, Montreal, Canada, who devised the system described.

Full details on all aspects of SEIRS, including preparation of the input data, was published in the April 1977 issue of *National Development* magazine, published by Intercontinental Publishers, Inc., 15 Franklin St., P. O. Box 5017, Westport, Ct 06880.

Restrictions

There may be restrictions imposed on the buyer's freedom to assemble a bidders list other than those implicit in the requirement. It may be the policy of management to place as many orders as possible in the area surrounding the plant to enhance community relations. Some procurements are restricted to domestic sources by the terms of the Buy American Act. Others, particularly those related to government contracts or subcontracts, may require the use of a special segment of industry, such as small business firms or minority-owned enterprises, to further the government's social objectives. The placement of purchase orders pursuant to the fulfillment of a government contract requires the determination of mandatory *flow-down* clauses. Reciprocal agreements, to the extent they are legal, between countries or companies may narrow the buyer's choices. Desire to exploit a particular technology or the resources of an affiliate may also be restrictive.

There are occasionally restrictions on the free selection of bidders as the result of legal factors.[6] Warranty requirements, patent rights, license agreements, or other obligations may prevent either buyer or seller from attempting to purchase or market.

The vast majority of purchases are made from companies which the purchasing department has been using. Exceptions that require unusual sourcing research efforts include purchases for research laboratories, new product lines, cost improvements, redesigned products, capital equipment and construction, and complex systems. But most of the time the buyer will be in familiar territory. Therefore, it is recommended that published supplier information be kept in a well-organized, carefully maintained, properly codified source library. It is good practice to maintain a vendor index file for repetitive purchases to lessen the burden still further. Data obtained through personal contacts should be carefully recorded and included in a central file, or they are soon lost.

SUPPLIERS: ASSEMBLING REQUIRED INFORMATION

Once the prospective bidders list is established, it is necessary to assemble information about each source to judge properly its ability to fulfill the requirement. The buyer should not attempt to accumulate more data than needed, since doing so generally takes valuable time and may be expensive. However, too little data may prove to be very costly in terms of supply failure or cost, so the buyer is cautioned to be somewhat overzealous in preference to being too superficial.

[6]For a more complete discussion, see Section 4.

Request for Quotation (RFQ)

The request for quotation illustrated in Fig. 6-1 will provide a prospective supplier's price, his agreement to furnish the required material, and any other information requested. However, the RFQ will not provide any judgmental information concerning the supplier's ability to do what he promises. The RFQ may be important in establishing the terms for a contract, but it is of little value in providing the buyer with basic information regarding probable performance.

VENDORS — NOTES

1

2

3

CLOW — CLOW CORPORATION

No.
Request For Quotation
Date

SUBJECT TO THE TERMS AND CONDITIONS ON THE FRONT AND REVERSE SIDE HEREOF.

1. Please insert net unit price opposite each item and mail copy properly signed to this company.
2. All dies, patterns and tooling charges, if required, must be quoted separately, and are to be Clow Corporation property and subject to removal by it at any time unless Clow otherwise agrees in writing.
3. Negatives & positives prepared by you or furnished by Clow remain the property of Clow.
4. We reserve the privilege of either accepting or not accepting any part or all of your quotation which is to be a firm price for 30 days after receipt of your reply.

Your Bid must reach us no later than
Material Destination
Requisition Number

RETURN TO
Attention: Purchasing

QUANTITY	DESCRIPTION	LIST UNIT PRICE	DISC.	NET UNIT PRICE	TOTAL PRICE
	THIS NOT AN ORDER				

PLEASE COMPLETE THE FOLLOWING:

Cash Discount	F.O.B.		Shipping Point
10th Proximo	Del'd	Your Plant	

NOTICE TO VENDOR

1. If unable to quote, please advise at once and return all prints, specifications etc.
2. Itemize all unit prices, discounts, terms, & charges.
3. Attach complete specifications for any substitutions offered.
4. Sign and return copy.
5. We invite cost saving or quality improving substitutes or alternates. If you recommend any change from our specifications, please describe adequately.

Date
Vendor
Signature

CP 3/78

Fig. 6-1 A typical request for quotation form of four-part snap-out construction. *(Courtesy of the Clow Corporation, Oak Brook, Ill.)*

Management Capability

The buyer may conclude that an assessment of management capability will be germane to the probability of successful performance. A contract requiring complex coordination of development and production, coupled with state-of-the-art design, obviously will require management skill. Management ability is also important in the smooth operation of a distributor's warehouse to prevent stockouts, to provide inventory backup, and to provide consistent delivery schedules. For many reasons, the ability to control a particular organization in a suitable manner can influence successful performance.

Technical Capability

Clearly, technical capability is a factor when expertise in a particular field is the prime objective of the purchase. This may be as specific as the established scientific knowledge of a few individuals in a supplier's company or as broad as the general expertise of a specialty producer. Contribution to the design of elements of the buyer's product may be sought, or application engineering of the supplier's product may be the goal. Tool design or value engineering of components may be desirable. For whatever reason, a legitimate objective is the extension of the buyer's engineering resources to include the technical capability of the supplier.

Manufacturing Capability

Even more obvious is the need to consider the manufacturing capability of prospective suppliers. The better supplier will have suitable equipment, reasonably modern, and enough of it to meet quantity requirements in the time available. Further, such equipment should be available for the production of the buyer's needs and not already scheduled for other work. The supplier should be capable of controlling his production and should be able to provide a realistic schedule. Efficient shop operations will keep costs low and prevent unpleasant surprises regarding delivery. He should have sufficient manpower of the right skills. He should be capable of consistently producing material of the required quality and will probably have a quality control system to accomplish it.

Labor-Management Relations

The buyer will often find it beneficial to understand labor-management relations at suppliers' plants. Historically poor relations will often result in erratic delivery performance and inconsistent quality of product. Good relations, on the other hand, may provide the buyer with lower-priced components in addition to good quality and delivery. It is well to determine the timing of union agreements, if any, and to be prepared to consider alternatives at contract termination time. For keeping abreast of termination dates, a two-part, self-addressed postal card is used by many firms.

Past Performance

Of course, past performance provides excellent insight into probable future success. The buyer would do well to consider his own experience with those suppliers he knows. He should not, however, necessarily equate past success in one product line with probable success in another. The experience of other buyers with prospective suppliers, especially those as yet unknown to the buyer, should not be overlooked.

Financial Strength

The financial strength of suppliers can be of crucial importance in preventing supply interruption. It is routine to obtain the financial background of an unknown source. But it is also prudent to review the financial strength of current suppliers from time to time to avoid unpleasant surprises. Financial failure can ruin the buyer's production schedule completely and may cause the temporary loss of tools and molds. It is also important to evaluate a supplier's ability to finance a large work-in-process inventory to avoid funding him through progress payments. It may be wise to estimate the supplier's ability to grow in financial capability in parallel with the long-term growth of the buyer's requirements.

There may be other specific areas of importance in a particular acquisition. The supplier's field service capability, his warehouse network, or his access to scarce raw materials may be critical. The buyer should identify special criteria such as these and seek accurate information about them.

Ethics

It is unwise to risk dealing with suppliers who are known to have questionable ethics. The buyer who knowingly associates with such firms exposes himself to the probability of being "known by the company he keeps." Such a reputation, however unjustified, can drive away valuable, reliable, competitive sources.

In addition, the buyer may expose his company to a number of serious business risks. An unethical supplier may reveal proprietary information to competitors or use it himself. He may knowingly bid low to buy in, only to raise his price later at a crucial point in the schedule—in effect performing blackmail. He may knowingly promise a delivery that cannot be made in order to get an order. He may claim the ability to produce a product that is beyond the capability of his firm, fully intending to "shop" the order to other firms. He may even resort to commercial bribery in an attempt to achieve a supply position that is not warranted by his firm's real ability.

Even though there may appear to be short-term advantages to special deals with unethical sources, it is poor policy to succumb to the temptation, since long-term objectives will often be jeopardized. In fact, it is seldom that the supposed short-term advantages actually materialize.

Other considerations on this very important subject will be found in Section 7.

Information Sources

There are many sources of information concerning specific companies which may be tapped. Some of these are:

Annual Reports Company product and financial data, although self-generated, can be quite informative. Comparative year-to-year information is especially useful, and the financial notes should not be overlooked.

Trade and Industry Information Many trade associations provide information on the manufacturing capabilities of member companies. Information on technical competence and other areas may also be provided, but is usually less informative.

Field Survey A buyer team can develop a great deal of factual information and can assess intangible capabilities through a plant visit. The team should include purchasing, engineering, manufacturing, and accounting personnel for comprehensive evaluation. A useful survey form is illustrated in Fig. 6-2*a* and 6-2*b*.

Beckman® INSTRUMENTS, INC.

BECKMAN USE ONLY	
APPROVED	
APPROVAL WITHHELD	

CAPABILITIES SURVEY

NOTE: Please return this form with equipment brochure to:
Purchasing Manager, Beckman Instruments, Inc. __________ Division
Address __________

TO BE FILLED IN BY SUBCONTRACTOR: Date __________

Full name of company __________

Office–Street address __________ Telephone __________

City __________ State __________

Person to be contacted __________ Position __________

Plant–Street Address __________ Telephone __________

City __________ State __________

Person to be contacted __________ Position __________

Type of business: (check one) Proprietorship ☐ Partnership ☐ Corporation ☐

Subsidiary of __________

PRINCIPAL OFFICERS: (OF FACILITY TO BE SURVEYED)

NAME	TITLE
NAME	TITLE
NAME	TITLE
NAME	TITLE
NAME	TITLE
NAME	TITLE

Please attach total organization chart

TYPICAL CUSTOMERS

NAME	ADDRESS	BUYER
NAME	ADDRESS	BUYER
NAME	ADDRESS	BUYER

Financial Information:
Name and Address of Bank __________

NAMES AND ADDRESSES OF THREE CREDIT REFERENCES: (Concerns from whom you have purchased materials)

NAME	ADDRESS
NAME	ADDRESS
NAME	ADDRESS

Financial Statement attached for year ending __________

Length of time company has been in continuous operation __________

PAGE 1 OF 2

Fig. 6-2*a* Front side of a vendor capability survey form. To this basic form can be added special survey forms covering quality control, manufacturing, and other functions of special interest. *(Courtesy of Beckman Instruments, Inc., Fullerton, Calif.)*

SHOP INFORMATION (A survey team will call on you to discuss some of the following in more detail)

Type of work company is best prepared and well equipped to do (specify capabilities and tolerances)

Survey Team Use Only

1. _____

2. _____

Other work company can do:

Special skills possessed by company personnel:

TOTAL NUMBER OF EMPLOYEES	COVERED AREA		UNCOVERED AREA	
		SQ FT		SQ FT
NUMBER OF QUALITY CONTROL EMPLOYEES			NUMBER OF SHOP EMPLOYEES	
NUMBER OF SHIFTS BEING WORKED			AVAILABLE PLANT CAPACITY	
PERCENTAGE OF WORK FOR PROPRIETARY ITEMS				
TYPE OF PRODUCT UNDER CONSIDERATION				
OTHER TYPES OF PRODUCTS AVAILABLE				

SIGNATURE _____ TITLE _____

FORM DO-13 72   FEBRUARY 1968   18TW200   PRINTED IN U.S.A.

Fig. 6-2b   Reverse side of vendor capability survey form shown in Fig. 6-2a.

Quality Survey   A quality survey to determine the supplier's ability to meet specification requirements is quite common. This can be done by buyer company personnel or through a professional service that is now available. The quality survey will often provide insights into other areas.

Salespersons   Sales representatives should be eager to provide information the buyer seeks. They have direct access to whatever data can be made available. Obviously, they will be biased in evaluating intangible capabilities, but they should be heard nevertheless.

Other Customers   It may be somewhat difficult to obtain much factual data from other customers of prospective suppliers, but impressions and assessments are usually available. The buyer should be careful not to solicit information, such as pricing, from other customers that can be considered as contributing to illegal restraint of trade.

Credit Reports   Credit reports can tell an impartial and sometimes eloquent story on current and potential vendors. Such reports are available from various agencies, one of which is Dun & Bradstreet, Inc., with offices at 99 Church Street, New York, N.Y. 10008.

Figures 6-3 to 6-7 illustrate such an analytical report on Allied Devices, Inc.,

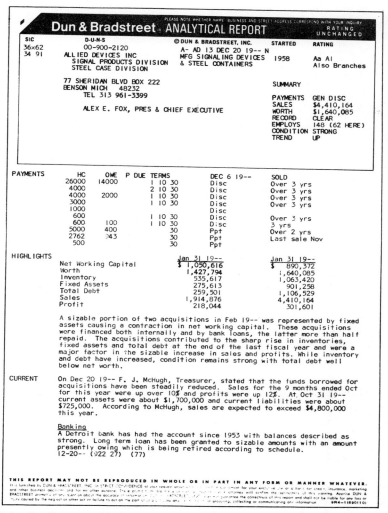

Fig. 6-3   Credit report showing payments, highlights, and current information regarding fictitious supplier. *(Courtesy of the Dun & Bradstreet Corporation.)*

a fictitious firm. This report covers five basic areas of information, each of which has its special use to the buyer. The key elements of the credit reports, and uses buyers make of them, follow:

1. PAYMENTS.   This section of the credit report shows how the supplier pays his bills. If a supplier is soundly financed and pays his bills according to terms, it

```
ALLIED DEVICES INC                                    A CD PAGE  I
BENSON MICH                                           12-20---

Figures of Jan 31 19-- were prepared from a balance sheet signed by Frank J. McHugh,
Treasurer.  Mitchell and Mitchell, CPA's, accountants.

                                    FINANCIAL STATEMENTS

                         Jan 31 19--      Jan 31 19--      Jan 31 19--

Cash                  $    396,666    $    393,818     $    301,802
Marketable Securities      189,128         201,340
Accounts Receivable        154,011         179,342          356,116
Inventory                  452,616         535,617        1,063,420
                      -----------     -----------      -----------
TOTAL CURRENT ASSETS     1,192,421       1,310,117        1,721,338

Fixed Assets               202,171         275,613          901,258
Investments                 92,000
Prepaid-Deferred             4,916           8,622           38,407
Other Assets                 9,725          92,942           85,611
                      -----------     -----------      -----------
TOTAL                    1,501,233       1,687,294        2,746,614
                      ============    ============     ============
Accounts Payable            44,456          66,587          117,913
Accruals                                    38,301          136,040
Taxes (Exc Fed Inc)                         12,572           18,601
Federal Income Taxes       161,644         126,542          383,412
Long Terms Liabs (curr)                                     175,000
Other Curr Liabs            43,210          15,499
                      -----------     -----------      -----------
TOTAL CURRENT LIABILITIES  249,310         259,501          830,966

Long Term Liabs                                             275,563

Common Stock               190,000         190,000          210,100
Capital Surplus             11,313          11,313           11,313
Earned Surplus           1,050,610       1,226,480        1,418,672
                      -----------     -----------      -----------
TOTAL                    1,501,233       1,687,294        2,746,614
                      ============    ============     ============
NET WORKING CAPITAL        943,111       1,050,616   •      890,372
CURRENT RATIO                 4.78            5.02             2.07

TANGIBLE NET WORTH       1,251,923       1,427,794        1,640,085

At Jan 31 19-- accounts receivable shown net less undisclosed reserves.  Inventory
valued at cost on first in-first out basis.  Fixed assets shown net less reserve for
depreciation $235,612.

                                                    (CONTINUED)
```

Fig. 6-4   Continuation of credit report shown in Fig. 6-3.

is reasonable to assume he can get the materials he needs when he needs them. On the other hand, often the first sign of approaching difficulty is the inability to meet bills as they fall due. If the trend is toward tardiness, the possibility arises that the supplier will be unable to get prompt shipment of materials he needs to meet delivery schedules.

2. FINANCIAL INFORMATION.   This part of the report, including sections identified as Highlights, Current, and Supplemental Data, usually shows a recent financial statement, the sales volume, and a summary of recent trends. From this section of the report the buyer can tell which suppliers have capital enough to handle his requirements—information which can be just as important as knowing

whether the equipment at their disposal can effectively handle the necessary volume. This section is an important factor in assigning the credit rating.

3. HISTORY.   The history section of the report describes the background of the business. When it was started, by whom, starting capital, authorized and paid-in capital, when present management assumed control, and many other pertinent facts are outlined.

```
         ALLIED DEVICES  INC                              A CD Page  2
         BENSON MICH                                      12-20---

                    INCOME STATEMENTS AND SURPLUS RECONCILIATION

                         JAN 31 13--      Jan 31 19--      Jan 31 19--

Net Sales               $ 1,825,171     $ 1,914,876     $ 4,413,164
Cost of Goods Sold          922,930       1,129,964       2,932,205
Gross Profit                902,241         784,912       1,477,959
Expenses                    485,933         401,399         763,112

Net Income on Sales         416,308         383,513         709,847
  Other Income                6,427          46,100          19,255

  Other Expenses             37,010                          42,501
  Federal Income Taxes      210,014         119,369         395,000

Final Net Income            201,666         218,044         301,601
                        ===========     ===========     ===========

SURPLUS START               900,925       1,050,610       1,226,480
  Add:  Net Income          201,666         218,044         301,601
  Deduct:  Dividends         37,981          42,172         109,409
SURPLUS-END               1,050,610       1,226,480       1,413,672
                        ===========     ===========     ===========

SUPPLEMENTAL DATA Footnotes appended to the Jan 31 19-- statement showed no contingent
               debt.  Annual rent shown at $62,000, lease expiring 1985.

According to management, the item other assets represents (1) $50,000 cash held in
escrow by the landlord who pays interest on that sum.  (2) Balance consists mostly
of a mortgage receivable on property in Edison Township, Mich. which was sold in 1964.
Management states that more than $2,000,000 in fire insurance is carried on inventories
and fixed assets.

Feb 19-- the company acquired for an undisclosed cash consideration the outstanding
capital stock of Signal Products Corporation and Steel Case and Tube Co. both of which
were established and profitable.  A bank loan of $1,000,000 was obtained at that time.
A portion of the loan was voluntarily prepaid and was reduced to $450,563 at Jan 31
19--.  $175,000 of that amount is due this year, payable quarterly and the balance is
due over the next two years.

Records show a financing statement entered Feb 15 19-- naming Allied Devices Inc. as
debtor and Saginaw Machine Tool Co. as secured party.  Collateral:  Specified Machinery
File #108761.  According to F. J. McHugh, Treasurer, the company purchased 2 high speed
Turret lathes at a cost of $28,500 payable over 36 months.

                                                          (CONTINUED)
```

Fig. 6-5   Continuation of credit report, showing supplemental data.

4. OPERATION.   This section of a Dun & Bradstreet report is the one the buyer probably scrutinizes most closely. It lists the physical facilities of the business, including size and location of plants and warehouses; proximity to transportation facilities such as rail sidings and docks; machinery and equipment, in instances when considerable volume is under contract or made to individual specifications; number of employees; active seasons; and usual selling terms. In addition, other aspects of the business needed for a complete understanding of the company's operations are described.

5. MANAGEMENT BACKGROUND.   This section describes the previous experience of the owner, partners, officers, and directors. The section also lists outside

```
ALLIED DEVICES INC                          A CD Page 3
BENSON MICH                                 12-20---

HISTORY     Incorporated Michigan laws June 30 1920 as Railroad Devices Corp.  Name
            changed to present style Feb 1 1960.

Authorized Capital Stock:  1,000 shares no par value common stock, increased to 4,000
shares latter part of 1958.
Outstanding Capital Stock:  $210,000 at Jan 31 19--.

Control:  The General Holding Corp., New York City owns 35% of the outstanding capital
stock which is held in voting trust by the Detroit National Bank, Detroit, Mich.  40%
acquired by A. E. Fox in 1958.  Balance owned by Sanborn, Caputo and McHugh.

In early 19-- the company purchased the outstanding capital stock of Signal Products
Corporation, Fairdome, Ky. and Steel Case & Tube Co., Minneapolis, Minn. for an undis-
closed cash consideration.  Late in that year these corporations were merged into
Allied Devices Inc. and their activities are now conducted as divisions.

General Holding Corp., New York City, is an investment and holding company.  It was
formed under New York laws 1900.  At Dec 31 19--, that company had a net worth of
$20,816,112, and a strong financial condition.  According to McHugh there are no inter-
company loans, guarantees, endorsements or merchandise transactions between the two
companies.

OPERATION   Products:  Manufacturers electric signaling devices including crossing
            gates 60% and steel containers 40%.

Distribution:  Sales made to railroads throughout the United States to approximately
100 active accounts.
Terms:  1 10 Net 30 days.
Seasons:  Fairly steady throughout the year
Salesmen:  Six on commission basis.  A. E. Fox and J. S. Caputo are active in sales.
Employees:  148

At headquarters Benson Mich., leases 20,000 square feet in a 3 story brick building
where signal devices are manufactured.  62 employed.

Branches are located at FAIRDOME, KY., MINNEAPOLIS, MINN. and branch sales offices at
New York, N.Y. and Los Angeles, Calif.

Signal Products Division, Fairdome, Ky., leases 12,000 square feet in a 1 story
frame building where railroad crossing signal gates are manufactured.  39 employed.

Steel Case Division, Minneapolis, Minn., leases 15,000 square feet in a 2 story brick
building where steel enclosed containers are manufactured.  47 employed.

                                                           (CONTINUED)
```

Fig. 6-6   Continuation of credit report, showing history and operating information.

```
ALLIED DEVICES INC                          A CD Page 4
BENSON MICH                                 12-20---

ALEX E. FOX, PRES                    JOHN S. CAPUTO, V PRES (SALES)
FRED W. SANBORN, V PRES (PROD)       FRANK J. MC HUGH, TREAS
HARRY K. LITTLE, SEC                 MARY (MRS. GERALD) LOY, ASST TREAS

DIRECTORS:  A.E. Fox, F.J. McHugh, Edward Raines and P.J. Walsh.

MANAGEMENT BACKGROUND

FOX born 1908, married.  Employed by the Pennsylvania Railroad latterly as Freight
Operations Manager from 1925 to 1958.  Since 1958 has been with this company as Chief
Executive Officer.  Life is insured for $200,000 with this corporation as beneficiary.

SANBORN born 1913, married.  Princeton graduate 1934 BA Degree.  1935 to 1943 employed
by Ford Motor Company in production control.  Joined this company in 1944, became
General Manager 1951 and elected Vice President in 1958.  Life in insured for $100,000
with corporation as beneficiary.

CAPUTO born 1916, married.  1940 to 1955 employed by Steel Case and Tube, latterly was
General Sales Manager.  Joined this company as a divisional sales manager and elected
a Vice President in 1958.

MC HUGH born 1909, married.  Employed by this company since 1939 as an inside account-
ant.  Elected Assistant Treasurer in 1948 and Treasurer in 1958.

LITTLE born 1932, single.  Served U.S. Army 1951 to 1953.  Employed by this company and
elected Secretary in 1960.

MRS. LOY employed here since 1959 and elected Assistant Treasurer in 1963.  Her husband
is an Associate Professor of Mathematics, University of Detroit.

RAINES is a practicing attorney in Detroit and general counsel.  WALSH is Executive
Vice President of Detroit National Bank, Detroit, Mich.
12-20--- (922 68)
```

Fig. 6-7   Conclusion of credit report, showing management background.

business interests of partners or officers and the subsidiary and affiliated companies of a corporation. Knowledge of such relationships can forestall collusion on competitive bidding.

PICKING THE SUPPLIER: ALTERNATIVES

The most important step in supplier selection is the analysis of the information assembled regarding the alternatives available to the buyer. The key to a successful analysis, no matter the technique, is to identify the important characteristics of the procurement. This identification has probably taken place to a large extent if the material requirement was carefully researched and the profile of appropriate suppliers was established properly.

Choosing the Criteria

The buyer should choose only the important features, to simplify his analysis. Things that are "nice to have" but will not significantly affect the outcome have no place in the evaluation. If the sole consideration is truly price, then nothing else need be examined. If price and long-term availability are the determining factors, then only these need be weighed. The buyer must carefully and deliberately choose the factors of significance, which will usually range in number from two or three in a simple purchase to a dozen or more in a complex procurement.

In addition, the buyer must decide the importance of each factor. For example, if delivery is more important than price because of a penalty clause in the customer's contract, he must decide how much more important it is.

Having identified the significant factors and graded their importance, the buyer can complete his analysis. It should be kept as simple as possible, but it may become complex. If it is complex, some disciplined approach is recommended. There are a number of techniques that may be useful.

Vendor Evaluation

Each competing supplier is evaluated on quality, price, and service. Quality evaluation is simply the supplier's record with respect to meeting required specifications and is measured as the percent of rejections to total material shipped. The quality control function often keeps factual data that can be used directly. Price evaluation in its simplest form is the figure quoted in each instance for conforming material as compared with the prices quoted by others. Consistency of success and integrity in price behavior would provide measurement criteria. Service evaluation includes prompt submittal of data, response to inquiries, delivery performance, special service rendered, and other intangibles. Aside from delivery performance, most measurement of service is quite subjective, but it is nevertheless valuable.

In ordinary purchasing situations, comparisons of prospective suppliers' current standing on these factors properly weighed should be sufficient. The majority of decisions should not require consideration of more than these basic elements.

Matrix Analysis

If there are more than three suppliers in competition and more than three significant factors to be considered, matrix analysis may be the best analytical tool. Suppliers are listed on one axis and the factors on the other, as shown in Fig. 6-8. Each factor is graded for each supplier. The grade may be numerical, such as 96

		DISTRIBUTORS							
NO.	CONSIDERATION FACTORS	ASL HOUSE	BARON ELECT.	CARVER ELECT.	JEFFERSON ELECT.	ACTIVE DEVICES INC.	SILICON VALLEY SALES	SWITCH-OUSE INC.	HILL-TRONIX INC.
1	PRICE PROPOSAL	B	B	A	F	B	D	D	B
2	PRODUCT LINES APPLICABLE	B	B	B	B	B	D	B	D
3	KEY FRANCHISE EXCLUSIVES	YES	NO	YES	NO	NO	NO	NO	NO
4	INVENTORY POSITIONS (APPLICABLE LINES)	B	B	A	F	C	C	C	C
5	FINANCIAL SOUNDNESS	OK	OK	OK	OK	?	OK	OK	OK
6	MEANTIME TO DELIVER STOCKED PARTS	6 HOURS	6 HOURS	12 HOURS	24 HOURS	48 HOURS	72 HOURS	6 HOURS	24 HOURS
7	MANAGEMENT RATING	OK	OK	BEST	POOR	POOR	OK	OK	OK
8	DELIVERY PROMISE INDEX (%)	85	92	95	80	50	60	50	90
9	TECHNICAL SERVICE CAPABILITY	YES	YES	YES	YES	NO	NO	YES	YES
10	SPECIAL SERVICES	WIRE STRIPING	CAP. BRIDGE	ROM PROGRAM	ROM PROGRAM	XISTOR MATCH.	CONN. ASSY.	NONE	CONN. ASSY.
11	INFORMATION PROCESSING SYSTEMS (• INVENTORY CONTROL • OPEN ORDER STATUS • CUSTOMER REPORTS	YES	YES	YES	YES	NO	YES	YES	NO
12	OBSOLETE INVENTORY PROPOSAL	NO	NO	NO	YES	NO	YES	YES	YES
13	SPECIAL INVENTORIES PROPOSAL	NO	NO	YES	NO	NO	YES	NO	NO
14	ACCEPTED LOTS/TOTAL LOTS RATIO (%)	75	78	72	76	90	60	80	50
	COMBINED FACTORS - RANK	2	3	1	8	7	6	5	4

Fig. 6-8 Matrix analysis applied to a complex distributor agreement. *(Courtesy of the Raytheon Company, Lexington, Mass.)*

percent acceptable material in the past 12 months, or it may be yes—no, such as whether or not a distributor's stock is controlled by EDP. The supplier with the best combination of grades usually is apparent.

Categorical Plan

This calls for continuous, disciplined evaluation by all members of the buying staff. Each buyer keeps a listing of his major suppliers at hand. As events occur, he notes them against the list. A monthly meeting is held at which each seller is reviewed, with the intent of weighing the plus notations against the minus, each seller being then assigned to a preferred, neutral, or unsatisfactory category.

This plan is easy and effective. It does not permit corrective action with a vendor, since provable data do not exist. However, it provides a continuous record of conscious judgment on the part of professional buyers and can be quickly referenced for a simple sourcing decision.

Weighted-Point Plan

Quality, price, and service are given *weights*. Sellers are rated for quality and service in terms of percentage of good performance to the total performance; in the case of price, rating is in terms of delivered total cost to the buyer.

The resulting ratings are then changed to a composite one, which becomes a portion of 100 percent. There will emerge a seller with a composite nearer 100 percent than the others. The decision will be supported by factual data which can be used for corrective action with the faltering suppliers.

				QUALITY		
(Insert drawing & part no.)	Lots received	Lots accepted	Lots rejected	Percentage accepted × Factor		Quality control rating
Supplier A	60	54	6	90.0	40	36.0
Supplier B	60	56	4	93.3	40	37.3
Supplier C	20	16	4	80.0	40	32.0

Note: To rate lots closer, a system of fractional lots can be used. Thus, if an unacceptable lot is only half or one-tenth bad, it could be said 0.5 or 0.1 lots were unacceptable, etc. This would distinguish between suppliers with a total lot unacceptable and those with only a small part of a lot unacceptable.

Fig. 6-9   Quality rating under the weighted-point plan. *(Reproduced by permission of the National Association of Purchasing Management.)*

With the approval of the National Association of Purchasing Management, Figs. 6-9 through 6-12 are reproduced to illustrate the use of this approach. In the example, weights have been assigned to the factors as follows:

Quality . . . . 40 points
Price . . . . 35 points
Service . . . . 25 points

Figure 6-9 shows the relative simplicity of arriving at the quality portion of the rating.

In Fig. 6-10, the price factor is illustrated as being more complex, since one must first determine delivered cost, as shown in Part A. Then the buyer must convert this into a merit value, as shown in Part B. Here the lowest cost is rated as 100 percent and the others are rated relative to the lowest cost.

In Fig. 6-11, the service factor (promises kept, in this illustration) has been tabulated as in the quality rating.

By combining these factors, as in Fig. 6-12, an optimum choice of suppliers can be made, in this case Supplier A.

Part A   PRICE

	Unit price	— Discount	+	Transportation charge	=	Net price
Supplier A	$1.00	10%	($ .90)	$.03		$ .93
Supplier B	1.25	15%	($1.06)	.06		1.12
Supplier C	1.50	20%	($1.20)	.03		1.23

Part B

	Lowest price	÷	Net price	=	Percentage	× Factor	=	Price rating
Supplier A	$.93		$ .93		100%	35		35.0
Supplier B	.93		1.12		83%	35		29.1
Supplier C	.93		1.23		76%	35		26.6

Fig. 6-10   Price rating under the weighted-point plan. *(Reproduced by permission of the National Association of Purchasing Management.)*

		SERVICE	
	Promises kept	× Service factor	= Service rating
Supplier A	90%	25	22.5
Supplier B	95%	25	23.8
Supplier C	100%	25	25.0

Note: As in the quality factor, a closer or finer evaluation of service can be used. Fractional lots delivered on time can be so reported; for example, the final percentage might be based on 11.5 lots of 14 received on time, etc.

Fig. 6-11   Service rating under the weighted-point plan. *(Reproduced by permission of the National Association of Purchasing Management.)*

	COMPOSITE RATING		
Rating	Supplier A	Supplier B	Supplier C
Quality (40 points)	36.0	37.3	32.0
Price (35 points)	35.0	29.1	26.6
Service (25 points)	22.5	23.8	25.0
Total Rating	93.5	90.2	83.6

Fig. 6-12   Composite rating under the weighted-point plan. *(Reproduced by permission of the National Association of Purchasing Management.)*

Cost-Ratio Plan

This plan assumes a flow of cost and time data to purchasing, probably from an electronic data processing system, but possibly from a manual data collection system. The net price is set down for each seller. All other activities concerned with the seller's performance are valued in dollars and cents. Letters, telephone calls, visits, and other occurrences are charged to his account. The total cost of purchasing an item from any vendor can be accumulated in this manner. Frequently, items such as number of days of lateness are assigned penalty points per day, which are in turn assigned a real dollar value. Items like transportation, whether planned or of premium variety to cover lateness, can be charged at actual value.

It is intended that the flow of information to this record be on a continuous basis. Purchasing can then select suppliers on the basis of lowest current net cost. The real cost of the same item from several sellers will vary with the skill and dependability of the seller. It is good practice to notify suppliers of their ratings periodically.

If the buyer's organization is able to provide data on rejection percentages and delivery delinquencies, and to segregate overhead cost factors to vendor accounts, the cost-ratio plan of vendor control is even more desirable because of its reasoned nature.

The majority of buyers will probably be satisfied with the simple but effective weighted-point plan modified to suit specific conditions. But it is important to repeat that all the techniques illustrated, and others that might be devised, involve the arbitrary assignment of importance to the pertinent factors. In the previous illustration, 40, 35, and 25 points were chosen as the weights for quality, price, and service, respectively. Figures 6-13 and 6-14 illustrate the use of weights of 50, 35, and 15 percent for the same factors. The effect is to remove price as a significant factor in the overall rating. The actual weights assigned to factors should be a measure of (1) the importance of that factor to the buyer and (2) the difficulty in achieving that factor.

Sole Source

The buyer must decide whether to place all his requirements with one supplier or to award the requirements to two or more sources. The situation in which all the requirements, for whatever reason, are placed with one supplier is generally distasteful to a buyer. Competition is either minimized or eliminated, a catastrophe at the supplier's plant will halt deliveries abruptly, the motivation to supply technical or other assistance is diluted, and the ability to change rates of delivery rapidly is severely limited.

However, there are circumstances in which sole sourcing is the proper course. Concentration of purchases may produce a lower price or lower transportation costs. Unusual arrangements, such as systems contracts or consignment stores, work on an exclusive basis. Spreading requirements too thin or awarding very small shares to some suppliers will weaken the buyer's clout in the market. Particular technical expertise or proprietary material may be available from only one source, or it may be too expensive to tool more than one supplier. The buyer must decide whether to use one or several suppliers, along with his decision on whom to select.

VENDOR EVALUATION RATING SYSTEM

VENDOR EVALUATION – DELIVERY FACTOR
PER CENT ALLOWABLE OF FACTOR RATING OF 35 MAX. POINTS

0 DAYS LATE EXCELLENT		ONE DAY LATE GOOD		TWO DAYS LATE FAIR		THREE DAYS LATE QUESTIONABLE		FOUR DAYS LATE UNSATISFACTORY	
100	35	85	29.75	70	24.50	55	19.25	40	14.0

DAYS LATE FIGURED AFTER FIVE DAYS FROM VENDOR'S AGREED SHIPPING DATE
FIG.= PERCENT OF POINT VALUE.
.FIG.= ACTUAL POINT VALUE.
*% OF ACCEPTABLE LOTS BY Q C

VENDOR EVALUATION – QUALITY CONTROL FACTOR
PER CENT ALLOWABLE OF FACTOR RATING OF 50 MAX. POINTS*

	EXCELLENT		GOOD		FAIR		QUESTIONABLE		UNSATISFACTORY	
MAXIMUM	100	50	99	49.5	94	47.0	89	44.5	84	42.0
AVERAGE			97	48.5	92	46.0	87	43.5	82	41.0
MINIMUM			95	47.5	90	45.0	85	42.5	80	40.0

```
QUALITY   = 50
DELIVERY  = 35
PRICE     = 15
          ———
           100
```

QUESTIONABLE - CAUSE FOR IMMEDIATE REVIEW

UNACCEPTABLE - CAUSE FOR REMOVAL FROM BIDDER'S LIST

VENDOR EVALUATION – COMPOSITE RATING

	EXCELLENT		GOOD		FAIR		QUESTIONABLE		UNACCEPTABLE	
QUALITY	100	50	97	48.50	92	46.0	87	43.50	82	41.0
DELIVERY	100	35	85	29.75	90	24.50	55	19.25	40	14.0
PRICE	100	15	100	15	100	15	100	15.00	100	15.0
		100		93.25		85.50		77.75		70.0
SPREAD			99 - 92.25		92.24 - 84.50		84.49 - 76.75		76.74 - 69.0	

PRICE- ALL VENDORS WILL RECEIVE 15 POINTS IN COMPOSITE RATINGS UNLESS THE RATING IS BEING APPLIED TO A CURRENT BID COMPARISON.

Fig. 6-13 Vendor evaluation showing effect of different weights. *(Courtesy of GTE Products, Inc., Stamford, Conn.)*

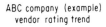

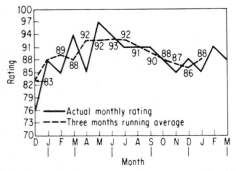

ABC company (example) vendor rating trend

Point range:
100 – excellent
99.00 – 93.25 – good
93.24 – 85.50 – fair
85.49 – 77.75 – questionable
77.49 – 70.00 – unacceptable

—— Actual monthly rating
--- Three months running average

Fig. 6-14 Vendor evaluation showing trend of performance with time. *(Courtesy of GTE Products, Inc., Stamford, Conn.)*

Multiple Sourcing

Using more than one supplier has many advantages, provided there is enough business to keep all genuinely interested. Multiple sources provide a broader technical base to the buyer. Competition is kept alive, as suppliers seek to increase their share of available business. The buyer is protected against failure at one supplier's plant and has provided himself with options should requirements rise or fall suddenly.

When using more than one source, the buyer must decide how to divide the business. A 50:50 split is quite different from an 80:20. When things are really equal, 50:50 may be the sensible answer. When a second source is desired, but a premium must be paid, 80:20 or some other lopsided share may provide the protection sought at minor cost. The small share should, however, be large enough to keep the supplier interested.

MAKING THE AWARD

Telling the Winner

The supplier or suppliers chosen should be told promptly of their selection so that they can plan immediately for fulfillment of the purchase contract. They should be told no later than the announced award date, if one has been established, so that there can be no question of the fairness of the evaluation. If more than one supplier is chosen, all should be told at the same time. When delivery schedule agreements are part of the basis for award, notification timing must be planned so that the "clock is started" neither too soon nor too late.

In many cases, it will be important to tell the winner why he was chosen. If his delivery promise was the key to his victory, he should know that failure to ship on time will receive more than passing attention. If prospective technical contribution was important in the decision, he needs to brief his company's technicians on what will be expected. It is to the buyer's advantage to advise the successful vendor of the important considerations influencing his selection so that the supplier will concentrate on performing in accordance with the buyer's wishes.

In some instances, usually in highly technical procurements or awards with important logistical features, it will be wise for the buyer to warn the winner of the hazards the buyer foresees. When the buyer has suffered from an uncomfortable history on a difficult purchased part, it will be prudent to tell the new supplier so that preventive measures can be taken from the start, rather than to maintain silence and hope that by changing sources the problem will disappear. Open, free, and complete communication of all known or potential hazards is an integral part of the philosophy that the supplier's operation is an extension of the buyer's facility.

In addition to telling the winner the key points in his successful competition for the award, the buyer should also point out any critical features of the requirements. For example, ability to achieve consistency in cosmetic quality may not have been an element in making the award, but it may be a pivotal factor in the success of the final product. Mechanical fit with mating parts, electrical characteristics vis-à-vis other circuit elements, interchangeability, and many other such characteristics can be essential and should be stressed to the successful supplier, even if they have already been highlighted in the pre-award competition.

Telling the Losers

Practice varies widely on the need to tell the losers that they have lost the competition. As a practical matter, it is neither expected nor necessary that unsuccessful vendors be informed on minor, repetitive, low-value purchases. On the other hand, it is clearly good practice to advise losing bidders on major awards such as complex technical systems, capital equipment, construction, term agreements, major blanket orders, and high-dollar-value purchases. Bidders may well be reserving capacity against potential success and deserve notification so that they can release it for other opportunities. As a matter of courtesy, notification is expected on major bids and should be granted to preserve live competition on future bids. It is difficult to draw a line at the appropriate point between nonnotification and notification of losing bidders, particularly since it may change with time. But the buyer should attempt to draw the line nevertheless, making a conscious and sincere effort to anticipate the expectations of the bidders for the sake of enhancing his own professional image and building goodwill for future competition.

The buyer should not disclose the successful price to the losers. There is a strong moral case to be made for the confidentiality of all data, including price, submitted to a buyer by a bidder. Revelation of price to another party is as much a betrayal of confidence as would be the revelation of a trade secret or proprietary technical data. Even if the buyer does not agree with the moral argument, it is in his own self-interest not to reveal the low price. When the winning figure is made known, a firm floor is established for the next set of bids. The buyer then may never reach the lowest available competitive price.

Without revealing confidences, the buyer should advise the losing bidders of the reasons for their loss of the business. This will enable them to become more responsive the next time and enable the buyer to maintain a truly competitive group of bidders. Good suppliers are anxious to know the reasons for failure so that they can improve performance, whether it is in cost, delivery, quality, technical capability, assurance of availability, or any other factor. Such improvements rather clearly operate to the advantage of the buyer.

The buyer may sense a need, when telling losers of their loss, to make certain that the basis for the competition was clearly understood. A partly nonresponsive bid will provide an indication that this aspect of the bidding should be explored. The main purpose is to make certain that there are no lingering doubts as to the fairness of the evaluation and no question of the basis for future competition.

OTHER SELECTION CONSIDERATIONS

Reciprocity[7]

Reciprocity, or trade relations, as it is often called, should never be the primary basis for source selection. It is a factor of interest for many firms, but only when all other conditions are unmistakably satisfied should it be considered. The buying professional bases his judgment on economic and logistic elements. He will have an extremely difficult time justifying an uneconomic procurement on the basis of reciprocal relationships, and he should resist such a decision.

Reciprocity is under increasing attack from federal authorities who have pursued cases in which reciprocity is merely implied by the presence of sales and purchases data. To the extent that reciprocity is demonstrated to cause restraint of trade, it violates the Clayton Act. Authorities have liberalized their definition of *restraint of trade* to the point where nearly all reciprocity-related activities have come under fire.

Reciprocity is not a sound basis for the selection of a supplier unless all other pertinent factors are clearly and unmistakably satisfied. Even then, current legal interpretations of activities that create restraint of trade make decisions based on reciprocity, however sound otherwise, hazardous at best.

Social Objectives

The use of the power of procurement as a tool in the achievement of social objectives is not new, although it has been in the spotlight only recently. Supplier selection, or the selection of the bidders list, may well be influenced by community pressure for social reform or by regulations that restrict freedom of choice.

The most common practice in this area is the deliberate use of local suppliers to improve relations between the plant and the community and to support the local economy. Usually such purchases are restricted to supplies and other relatively minor items, except in the rare case where another large potential supplier shares the same community. In any case, there are usually demonstrable advantages, both tangible and intangible, to the practice.

On a national scale, the practice is called the Buy American Act. This piece of legislation does not prevent buying from foreign suppliers, but provides a legal percentage advantage to the domestic supplier when his price is compared with that of the foreign source. The legislation is applicable only to purchases made in support of government contracts. Several states have adopted similar legislation for purchases against state requirements.

For quite some time there has been legislation encouraging the use of small businesses as suppliers to government prime contractors. These large contractors are measured quarterly with regard to their success in flowing government work

---

[7]Also discussed in Section 7.

down to small firms. The purpose of this particular law is to encourage small businesses to flourish, since they are considered by the legislators to represent the essence of free enterprise.

More recently there has appeared a combination of legislation and regulation which encourages the use of minority-owned suppliers by prime government contractors. The social objective, of course, is to support minority groups in their effort to obtain a proportionate share of the available business.

Similarly, there are both legislation and regulation encouraging the placement of subcontracts in areas of labor surplus. The obvious objective is to aid in the alleviation of severe unemployment in particular communities or entire regions.

The newest limitation on source selection in accordance with social objectives is the requirement that the buyer procure material that will not pollute. For example, the choice of fuel oils must be restricted to those that will not produce sulfur pollutants above a prescribed level. Similarly, buyers are restricted from free choice in that some suppliers must either close polluting facilities, thus restricting available sources, or install pollution control devices that raise cost and price.

Other artificial restrictions are to be found in state and federal procurement regulations. Fortunately, most such regulations do not require the payment of premiums, but encourage competitive procedures. Further, they are aimed for the most part at legitimate objectives that society has come to accept as desirable and necessary. The buyer should be aware, however, that his freedom of choice of supplier may be restricted by the pursuit of social objectives, and that the price he pays, while competitive, may reflect the cost of the achievement of social goals.

Documentation

The need to document the basis for selecting suppliers varies considerably. At the one extreme, the Armed Services Procurement Regulations and government audit procedures demand detailed and precise accounting of the decision making process. Extensive purchase order records are often necessary to support post-award audits of this type.

On the other hand, sufficient records should be kept at least to allow the buyer to reconstruct his decision at a later date in order to make the next decision easier. Good records are valuable for efficient operation and can save extensive supplier research in future competitions.

Many large firms employ internal auditors to examine the record-keeping function in purchasing departments which are responsible for a large share of company revenues. Impartial judgment of the quality of purchasing records is to be welcomed.

Supplier Relations

Goodwill   Marketing people devote much time, effort, and money to the development of goodwill in the attitude of the customer toward the seller. For a great many reasons, it is just as important for the buyer to develop and cherish goodwill in the attitude of the seller toward his customer. The advantages are largely intangible, but they are nonetheless important.

There are many difficult occasions when the buyer needs something more personal than a satisfactory but cold business relationship with his supplier to solve a problem. A sudden surge in orders may call for a sharp increase in the rate of supply, a change beyond that contemplated at the time the original order was placed. Conversely, a sudden change in the market may call for a large reduction or even cessation of production. An emergency breakdown of machinery may require special service for the supply of spare parts. In any of these situations, it is important to have the friendship and confidence of the supplier if the problem is to be solved rapidly and effectively at least cost to the buyer.

In addition, there are many nonemergency circumstances in which goodwill can play a part. If the buyer has been consistently fair, truthful, accurate, and considerate, a supplier is much more likely to be cooperative in his appraisal of rejection claims, rework compensation, termination problems, and other situations calling for negotiated settlements.

Furthermore, when the buyer is clearly trying to provide the supplier with as much information as possible concerning total-requirement quantities, usage rates, and application problems, the supplier can be expected to respond wholeheartedly to requests for technical support, inventory backup, and other voluntary services. Giving the supplier all data possible regarding his responsibility to maintain the buyer's manufacturing operations will be rewarded with much more than perfunctory performance.

In one sense, the buyer is the representative of the seller in the buyer's own plant, making sure that the supplier is treated fairly and honestly in internal discussions.

When goodwill exists between supplier and customer, it is a great deal simpler to conduct necessary business. Negotiations will be shorter, terms will be simpler, disputes will be at a minimum, and communication will be better. So long as the supplier has confidence in the buyer, the buyer's task will be done more effectively. And as a final bonus, the buyer's company will have a better image, not only as a good customer, but also as a good company with which to do business.

Treatment of Salespersons   Perhaps the single most important relationship in the development of goodwill between seller and customer is that between the salesperson and the buyer. The salesperson is the primary link to the supplier's organization. It is the salesperson who discusses the behavior of the buyer and other customer personnel and communicates the total impression of company character. It is also the salesperson who knows the supplier personnel who can solve problems, as well as contribute to the success of the buyer's company.

The salesperson is the buyer's basic source of information regarding the company the salesperson represents. He knows of product changes, new product applications, scheduling problems, management changes, acquisitions, and other data affecting his company's ability to be a creative supplier. He also carries a wealth of information regarding his industry, from gossip to price trends and from foreign competition to imminent mergers. He is, therefore, to be treated with not only courtesy but also respect.

At the superficial level, it is well to provide a comfortable reception room equipped with a telephone and a receptionist, if possible. Information regarding the organization of the purchasing department, commodity assignments, telephone extensions, and other pertinent factors should be provided. It is a nice touch to add information regarding nearby accommodations, travel directions, airline and rail connections, and restaurants.

It is even more important to grant a prompt interview, especially for those salespersons with appointments. Visiting hours should not be restricted unless absolutely necessary, to allow the visitor maximum flexibility with his complicated schedule.

The buyer should conduct each interview in an efficient manner. He should tell the salesperson everything he needs to know to serve the buyer's need. He should be truthful, complete, and accurate—and never misleading. He should grant access to technical personnel when their expertise is needed to exchange required information adequately. Perhaps above all, the buyer should be a good listener in order to learn all the salesperson has to tell, but in a minimum amount of time.

Cultivating good salespersons can be the key to successful procurement. It is undoubtedly an important key to good supplier relations.

NOTE: For further information on subjects covered in this section see the list of references in Section 30.

Section **7**

Ethics in Purchasing

EDITOR

Robert C. Parker, C.P.M. *Vice-President, Purchasing, Transportation & Facilities Service, International Harvester Company, Chicago, Illinois*

ASSOCIATE EDITOR

Gailon C. Fordyce, C.P.M. *Assistant Purchasing Director, The American Tobacco Company, A Division of American Brands, Inc. New York, New York*

K. Paul Graham, C.P.M. *Purchasing Agent, City of San Leandro, California*

CONCEPT OF ETHICS

The noun *ethics* comes from the Greek word *ēthikos,* meaning "moral." The plural *ēthika* became the title "Ethics" in a number of early treatises on the subject, the most famous of them being Aristotle's "Nichomachean Ethics." The basic word in Greek is *ēthos,* meaning "character, disposition, or characteristic spirit." The adjective *ethical* can then easily be seen to mean moral, decent, virtuous, upright, fair, just, proper, straightforward, aboveboard, fitting, and correct.

While the philosophical theory of ethics must be distinguished from the everyday task of making moral decisions, it has usually been held by moral philosophers that the chief test which can be applied to an ethical system is to ask if it can be harmonized with what is often called "common-sense" ethics, i.e., with those ethical judgments which at our best we feel constrained to make, apart from philosophical argument, in our ordinary ethical thinking.[1] This begins to sound as though it might apply to the buyer as he makes decisions from day to day. Such a conclusion becomes even more likely when you consider one of the main premises in Kant's *Critique of Practical Reason*, namely that a person should ask not what the particular consequences of his action will be, but what would happen if everybody acted in the way he proposes to act. Kant's reasoning may sound faintly like a rebuttal to the frequently heard argument that a given action must be all right because it doesn't hurt anyone.

From the above carefully considered philosophical arguments, we may reasonably conclude that the Golden Rule is a greatly condensed statement of logical ethics. And it may follow that a good philosophy for the buyer to pursue would be one which causes him to treat sellers in the manner he would consider just, proper, fitting and correct if the situation were reversed. What follows, then, is an attempt to articulate the minimum ethical standards which the vast majority of our profession[2] would consider just, proper, fitting, and correct, and to provide some simple insights into the application of those standards.

APPLYING ETHICAL CONCEPTS IN PURCHASING

Toward the Employer

The buyer is expected by his professional peers to apply his undivided energies and intellect to the benefit of his employer. This requires him to avoid without

---

[1] *Encyclopaedia Britannica,* vol. 8, 1971, p. 752.

[2] Thomas L. Martin, Jr., President of the Illinois Institute of Technology, home of the Center for Study of Ethics in the Professions, has said, "The characteristic which distinguishes a professional from a technician is the ability of the professional to bring considerations of professional ethics into the application of his technical skills in the solution of problems."

fail all situations wherein he might gain personally from acts by a supplier or any other party which might work in any way to the detriment of his employer. He must safeguard all proprietary information learned in the performance of his duties and turn his full efforts toward achieving the goals of his employer. Should the goals or practices of his employer ever conflict with the ethical standards of his profession, he has only three honorable courses of action open:

1. Achieve a change in his employer's goals or practices which eliminates the conflict.
2. Resign his position.
3. Withdraw from his professional association and relinquish any professional recognition.

Toward the Supplier

The buyer must treat the supplier fairly in all matters, starting with a prompt and courteous reception, then proceeding through a sufficiently detailed inquiry, fair competition, and an accurate and comprehensive purchase order to the prompt and equitable settlement of all problems growing out of the business done. The most effective buyer will encourage his best suppliers to bring their latest ideas and newest technology to bear on the customer's product, and will recognize the value of such contributions when awarding business. He will also take care to protect the proprietary ideas which come to him in this manner, recognizing they are a valuable competitive asset of the supplier and will be entrusted to him only as long as he treats such ideas and innovations with proper respect. The farsighted buyer will search for those areas of common ground which will allow both the buyer and seller to maximize their benefit from the transaction while avoiding demands on the supplier which only diminish his return without improving the value to the buyer's employer. And the buyer will not knowingly take advantage of an error in a quotation without providing the supplier one last opportunity to reexamine his bid for accuracy and thoroughness. In all the above, the buyer is expected to strive diligently to develop the very best *long-term* value for money for his employer, discarding any short-term gain in favor of the best long-run position. (See Fig. 7-1 for Georgia-Pacific Corporation's vendor relations policy as stated in the company's purchasing manual.)

Toward the Profession

The buyer is expected to contribute to the development, recognition, and application of the formal ethical standards established by his profession, the most notable of which are the Principles and Standards of Purchasing Practice issued by the National Association of Purchasing Management (N.A.P.M.). He must profess his belief in and adherence to these Principles and Standards of Purchasing Practice before he can become a member of any of the local associations of the N.A.P.M. or be recognized by that organization as a certified purchasing manager (C.P.M.). His membership or his certification, or both, may be revoked by the board of directors of N.A.P.M. for proved unethical behavior or malpractice.

	GP	
	GEORGIA-PACIFIC	
Effective: _____8/1/71_____	CORPORATION	*Section:* _____6_____
Supersedes: _____None_____	**PURCHASING**	*Page:* _____1 of 2_____

<u>VENDOR RELATIONS</u>

PURPOSE: To inform the new and inexperienced buyer and/or Purchasing Agent of a common purchasing philosophy, recognized by industry and supported fully by Georgia-Pacific, concerning the importance of good relations between the Corporation and its suppliers <u>and</u> to reaffirm that philosophy to seasoned purchasing personnel as Georgia-Pacific's basic purchasing policy for day-to-day relations with salesmen.

GENERAL: Goodwill, like good people, is a valuable asset to the Corporation and, over the years, has contributed significantly to the success and growth of Georgia-Pacific. You, as members of the Purchasing Department, have a real opportunity and major responsibility for the reputation of the Corporation and the goodwill which it commands.

The Purchasing Department's relations with salesmen provides a contact through which the good name of Georgia-Pacific may be enhanced or it may be injured. Keeping in mind that his daily contacts with suppliers form much of the basis for their opinion of the Company, the Purchasing Agent should do everything possible to maintain and promote Georgia-Pacific Corporation as an organization noted for fairness, integrity, service, progressiveness, and friendliness.

The Purchasing Agent can and should exercise these attributes of

FAIRNESS: 1. By giving all salesmen a full, fair and courteous hearing on any subject that is justified by the nature of the product and the needs.

2. By keeping competition open and fair.

3. By declining to take advantage of a seller's errors.

4. By discouraging revision of bids after submission and insisting on receiving the best price first and holding the bidder to it.

Fig. 7-1 Vendor relation policy in the purchasing manual of the Georgia-Pacific Corporation.

SOME PRACTICAL GUIDELINES

There should be no room for doubt that every act of the buyer is dedicated to the long-term best interest of his employer. He should know who are the best sources, from his employer's point of view, in each supplier industry, and he should conduct the employer's business in a way which keeps those best sources interested in giving his employer their very best efforts and ideas in order to share in the

	▲ GP ▲ **GEORGIA-PACIFIC** CORPORATION **PURCHASING**	
Effective: ____8/1/71____		*Section:* ____6____
Supersedes: ____None____		*Page:* ____2 of 2____

INTEGRITY:
1. By observing strict truthfulness in all verbal and written transactions with salesmen.

2. By respecting the confidence of the salesmen or his company regarding quotations or other confidential information.

3. By stating the reasons for rejection of bids or for awarding business elsewhere as fully as possible without betraying confidential information.

SERVICE:
1. By receiving salesmen promptly or, if impossible, explaining and making a definite appointment. Remember - his time is also valuable.

2. By answering letters promptly.

3. By an efficient follow-up system.

PROGRESSIVENESS:
1. By keeping an open mind on new products and materials offered.

2. By visiting, when advisable, sources of supply and keeping informed regarding their methods of doing business.

FRIENDLINESS:
1. By maintaining a friendly, but businesslike approach, in all dealings with suppliers. Friendship is a matter apart from money. It has been and always will be an important factor in business. On a proper plane, it is to be encouraged between buyer and seller, for it can be of great advantage to both parties. To confer with business friends when a new item is suddenly required is the quickest and surest way to find the best market and best price. When it is difficult for a Purchasing Agent to secure an article quickly, a seller, for sake of friendship, will undertake to supply it and will put himself to much inconvenience to do so.

It is the duty of the Purchasing Agent to procure the best possible products for a given service and at the best possible prices, regardless of the source of supply from which they may be obtained. All questions of policy should be referred to the Director of Purchasing, Portland, Oregon.

Fig. 7-1   *(Continued)*

available business. The buyer then should make sure that there is open and fair competition among those best sources, with the business being awarded to the firm offering the best long-term advantage to the employer. Any activity or involvement between the buyer and active or potential suppliers which in any way diminishes, or even appears to diminish, the above process is to be strictly avoided. This necessarily precludes any equity or financial dealings between buyer and supplier, and in most cases it will preclude or at least discourage the forming of any close personal relationships between the buyer and supplier personnel which could give the impression of diminishing the chances of fair and vigorous competition against that particular supplier. And under fair and open rules, everyone profits in the long run, with the greatest good being done for the greatest number. This was recognized at least as far back as biblical times when Moses told the Israelites after their deliverance: "Wherefore it shall come to pass, if ye hearken to these judgments [God's law], and keep and do them, that the LORD thy God shall keep unto thee the convenant and the mercy which he sware unto thy fathers: And he will love thee, and bless thee, and multiply thee: he will also bless the fruit of thy womb, and the fruit of thy land, thy corn, and thy wine, and thine oil, the increase of thy kine, and the flocks of thy sheep, in the land which he sware unto thy fathers to give thee."[3] In modern parlance, Moses seems to be saying that good ethics is good business.

International Harvester Policy
on Conflicts of Interest
and Ethical Business Conduct

International Harvester Company and each of its subsidiaries and affiliates (together referred to as *the Company* in this restatement of policy) expects from each of its employes complete and undivided loyalty and business conduct consistent with the highest ethical standards. The company's business has always been carried out in accordance with those standards, which reflects the clear understanding of the company's policy at all levels. This restatement of policy describes briefly the company's conflicts of interest policy and touches upon other matters related to ethical business conduct which are discussed in greater detail in several of the company's corporate policy statements. It will be distributed each year to all managerial employes.

All conflicts of interest and other unethical business practices cannot be listed. The best guidelines are individual conscience, common sense, and a careful and unwavering compliance with the law, domestic and foreign.

Conflicts of Interest: No employe (which in this restatement of policy includes members of his immediate family) may directly or indirectly benefit personally from his position or connections as an employe or from any sale or purchase or other activity of the company. For example:

a. No employe may seek or accept from, or offer or provide to, directly or indirectly, any individual, or public or private organization, or governmental entity, or any representative of the foregoing, which is seeking or doing business with the company any services, payments, loans (except with banks or other financial institutions), excessive entertainment or travel, vacation or pleasure trips, gifts of more than nominal value, or gifts of money in any amount.

b. No employe may have any interest, direct or indirect, in any organization which is seeking or doing business with the company or which is a competitor of the company, except when such interest comprises securities in a widely held corporation which are traded regularly in recognized security markets, and such interest is not in excess of 1 percent of any class of securities of such corporation, or except when such interest has been fully disclosed to the chief executive officer of the company for a determination as to the substantiality of such interest and the propriety of retaining it.

c. No employe may serve as an officer, director, employe or consultant of another company or organization which is a competitor of the company or which is seeking or doing business with the company, except that with the knowledge and written consent of the chief executive officer of the company such employe may serve as a director of a corporation which is doing business with the company, where no competitive situation is present.

Fig. 7-2 International Harvester Company policy is distributed annually to all managerial employees.

---

[3]Deut. 7:12,13.

d. No employe may without proper authorization use or reveal any confidential information received in a company capacity, or use or permit others to use company property or services for personal purposes. The purchase or sale of securities in reliance on inside nonpublic company information is prohibited.

Illegal or Improper Payments: No personal payments of any kind, whether of money, services or property, may be offered or made directly or indirectly to any domestic or foreign public official (including employes or agents of or consultants to governmental organizations) or to any employe, agent or representative of any organization seeking or doing business with the company. Bribes, kickbacks, or the giving of anything of value to obtain business concessions to any individual or organization are prohibited. Normal and properly authorized business expenses such as reasonable business travel and entertainment, non-cash gifts of nominal value provided openly and according to established business practice and product demonstrations or visits to company operations, are permitted. Specific policies contained in the corporate policy manual set forth requirements to authorize payment of commission agents or fees (corporate policy no. 05-05), payments into numbered bank accounts or to persons other than the person to whom payment is due (corporate policy no. 05-06), and payments outside the country of residence or place of business of the person to whom payment is due (corporate policy no. 05-07). Employes who authorize such payments on behalf of the company must be familiar with each of the policies and comply fully with all of their requirements.

Political Contributions: All domestic and foreign contributions by or on behalf of the company directly or indirectly, of money, services or property to any candidate for or holder of federal, state or local office or to any political organization, party or committee are prohibited, including the purchase of tickets to dinners or other fund-raising events or the purchase of advertising space in programs.

Accurate Accounts, Invoices, Documents and Records: All company accounts, invoices, memoranda and other documents and records must be prepared and maintained with strict accuracy and completeness. All assets, liabilities, revenues and expenses must be recorded in the regular books of the company.

Interpretation: Each employe is urged to consult with his supervisor and, if appropriate, with the law department if he has any question about the applicability of company policy in a given situation.

Board of Directors, International Harvester Company.
Originally Adopted: January 19, 1961.
Revised and Reaffirmed: March 16, 1977.

Fig. 7-2 (*Continued*)

Conflict of Interest

Figure 7-2 constitutes an example of a modern corporate statement on conflict of interest by International Harvester Company. Figure 7-3 illustrates an equally modern statement on conflict of interest by General Telephone and Electronics, which also contains a number of remarkably helpful examples of its intended application to everyday ethical questions. Figure 7-4 is a brief, well-written policy statement on purchasing ethics issued by Xerox Corporation.

Gifts and Favors

Buying and selling are two sides of the same coin—held firmly together by the substance of the transaction between them, but equally firmly held apart by the fact that they are unalterably located on opposite sides of that transaction. Either side may at times be immensely sharper in detail and more pleasing than the other, but there can be no coin at all without *both* sides.

Selling, then, can be viewed largely as the process conducted by the prospective supplier by which he hopes to convince the buyer to join with him in creating a transaction favorable to his side of the coin. There are immense pressures on the seller to use any means at his disposal to accomplish this end.

II. RELATIONS WITH CUSTOMERS

A. PROVIDING GIFTS OR ENTERTAINMENT

1. Gifts—*No employee shall offer or give any gift, gratuity or money to a customer or prospective customer when the offering may be reasonably construed as resulting from the business relationship. An employee may, however, offer advertising novelties that are widely distributed.*

Example: A GTE Lenkurt salesperson gives a potential customer a $500 set of golf clubs for Christmas.

Such a gift would not be permissible under ordinary circumstances, as it is excessive, would not generally be reimbursible under normal expense account procedures, and would have the appearance of causing the customer to select GTE Lenkurt products.

2. Entertainment—A GTE representative may provide entertainment to customers if all the following conditions are present:

    a. Management would approve it and the employee can be reimbursed under normal expense account procedures.

    b. The purpose is to develop a better understanding of and closer relationship with customers in order to improve communications with them.

    c. The entertainment is reasonable in nature, frequency and cost.

    d. The entertainment does not have the purpose, effect or appearance of causing customers to select GTE products or services solely because of the entertainment.

    e. The entertainment will not violate the customers' own rules against receiving entertainment.

Example: A GTE Sylvania salesperson invites a prospective customer to dinner and an evening at the ballgame.

Such an invitation in the above example is acceptable in the absence of unusual circumstances that would cause one of the conditions not to be met.

3. General—It will not always be possible to distinguish readily between what is and is not proper to provide to a customer. Such decisions must always be made responsibly and with sensitivity to the total circumstances. If there is a possibility that the gift or entertainment is of such a lavish nature that the customer might feel constrained to act based on the gift or entertainment alone, the gift or entertainment should not be provided.

B. RECEIVING GIFTS OR ENTERTAINMENT FROM CUSTOMERS

1. Gifts—*No employee shall solicit or accept from a customer gratuities, compensation, gifts of more than token value, advances, loans (except from established financial institutions), lavish entertainment or other substantial favors.* Gifts of more than token value, lavish entertainment or substantial favors should be considered those which the employee would not normally be in a position to reciprocate under normal expense account procedures.

2. Reporting Gifts—*All gifts offered to or received by employees shall be reported by them to their superiors.* If a gift is received but may not be accepted under this guideline, the superior should instruct the employee to return it to the customer or, in the case of a perishable gift, give it to a local nonprofit charitable organization.

3. Discounts—*An employee may accept discounts on personal purchases of the customer's products if such discounts are generally offered to others having a similar business relationship with the customer.*

Example: The customer, an automobile parts supplier, allows its employees to purchase parts at a 20 percent discount. It also has an agreement with the local telephone company and others to supply parts at the same discount. The customer generally extends this same benefit to others who work on its premises from time to time. The customer offers this benefit to GTE telephone installers.

The telephone installers may accept this benefit from the customer because they are within the class normally offered this benefit by the customer. Such benefits must never be sought, requested or expected.

4. Accepting and Giving Gifts—The accepting and giving of gifts from or to customers are not just matters of business ethics. Violations of these policies will almost necessarily lead to employees being put in a position where they must compromise the best interests of GTE and this may in turn lead them to commit some wrongdoing and jeopardize their employment.

Fig. 7-3 Extracts from a statement of policy on ethical business conduct by Theodore F. Brophy, Chairman and Chief Executive Officer, General Telephone and Electronics.

C. FINANCIAL AND OTHER INTERESTS IN CUSTOMERS

These are covered in Sections IV and V below.

III. RELATIONS WITH SUPPLIERS

A. GENERAL

GTE *employees must avoid any interest in or benefit from any supplier that would in fact or in appearance cause them to favor that supplier over others.* Our suppliers will retain their confidence in the objectivity and integrity of our companies only if each employee strictly observes this guideline. Financial and other interests in suppliers are covered in Sections IV and V below.

B. RECEIVING GIFTS OR ENTERTAINMENT FROM SUPPLIERS

1. Compensation or Gifts—*No employee shall solicit or accept from a supplier or prospective supplier any compensation, gifts of more than token value, advances, loans (except from established financial institutions), lavish entertainment or other substantial favors.* Gifts of more than token value, lavish entertainment or substantial favors should be considered those which the employee would not normally be in a position to reciprocate under normal expense account procedures.

2. Reporting Gifts—*Gifts received or offered shall be reported by employees to their superiors, who should instruct the employees to return the gift if already received or, in the case of a perishable gift, give it to a local nonprofit charitable organization.* In any event, the superior should contact the supplier by letter explaining GTE's guideline on the subject. A gift does not include advertising novelties such as calendars or paperweights. However, employees who have contact with outsiders, should not keep advertising novelties at their work stations.

3. Discounts—*No employee shall solicit or accept any discount on personal purchases of the supplier's products if such a discount could be construed as being offered because of the business relationship, nor shall an employee accept any personal benefit for dealing with a supplier.*

Example: A supplier offers trading stamps to a GTE buyer on all GTE purchases from the supplier.

The buyer may not accept this offer because it is being extended as a result of his position as a buyer and the same offer is not publicly extended to all other GTE employees.

Discounts made available to all employees of the GTE company as well as employees of other companies as a general practice may be accepted.

Example: A department store makes available to all employees of a GTE company a discount on any purchases whether for personal or business use.

Employees may accept the discount, even though they buy items for their own personal use.

4. Entertainment—*No employee shall solicit or accept any entertainment offered by a supplier unless it is incidental to and commensurate with a business meeting.*

Example: A GTE Sylvania buyer attends a trade show on electronic testing equipment. One supplier maintains a hospitality suite in the hotel to which all customers and prospects are invited for afternoon refreshments.

The buyer may go to the hospitality suite for refreshments.

Example: Two GTE telephone company engineers attend a training seminar on central office equipment put on by the supplier of such equipment their company has on order. An afternoon of golf is included for the second day of the three-day seminar.

The engineers may participate in the afternoon of golf.

Example: A supplier of office equipment invites three employees of a GTE company who purchase such equipment as part of their responsibilities and their spouses to dinner and an evening of entertainment at an exclusive night spot.

The employees should not accept the invitation because it is not incidental to a business meeting and it could appear to competing suppliers that getting the GTE company's business depends more on "wining and dining" the proper people than on offering the best product.

5. Services—*Services offered by a supplier may be accepted by an employee when the need for the services is associated with a business relationship and the supplier provides the services to other customers and prospects as a normal part of its business.* Examples of such services are transportation to and from the supplier's place of business, lodging at the supplier's place of business and business lunches and dinners for business visitors to the supplier's location. The services should generally be of the type normally used by GTE employees and allowable under normal expense account procedures.

Fig. 7-3 *(Continued)*

IV. FINANCIAL INTERESTS IN OTHER ORGANIZATIONS, INCLUDING COMPETITORS, CUSTOMERS OR SUPPLIERS

A. GENERAL

No employee or member of his or her immediate family shall have an investment or other financial interest in a competitor, supplier or customer which could create a divided loyalty or the appearance of one, or could cause speculation or misunderstanding. Because of the wide range of businesses in which GTE is engaged and because companies continually change the way they do business, it would be virtually impossible to compile a list of competitors, customers or suppliers which would be accurate at all times. The following factors should be considered in determining whether an investment or other financial interest violates this guideline:

1. The position held by the employee.
2. The dollar amount of the investment or interest. (An investment or interest amounting to less than 1 percent of the securities of a publicly owned corporation which are listed on a national exchange would not ordinarily constitute a breach of this guideline. Securities traded over the counter are not considered to be listed on a national exchange.)
3. The relative importance of the investment or interest to the employee.
4. The nature and extent of the relationship between the employee's company and the other company.
5. The manner in which and time when the investment or other interest was acquired.

B. EMPLOYEES WITH PURCHASING AUTHORITY

No employee who has any authority to purchase goods or services or is in a position to influence decisions in any way with respect to GTE purchases shall be employed by, hold any position with, serve as a director of, or have a financial interest in or business relationship with any outside concern which is a supplier of goods or services to GTE. This would include employees who establish specifications for, recommend, evaluate, test, or approve a supplier's product or service, or who participate in the selection of, or arrangements with, a supplier. As stated in factor 2 above, an investment or interest amounting to less than 1 percent of the securities of a publicly owned corporation which are listed on a national exchange would not ordinarily constitute a breach of this guideline.

C. QUESTIONABLE SITUATIONS

Each situation must be considered on its own facts. If there is any question whatsoever as to the propriety of an investment or other financial interest in another company, the employee should consult GTE counsel for a written determination.

D. REEXAMINE AND REPORT INVESTMENTS

Since companies may modify their operations or add to their product line, employees should reexamine their investments periodically to avoid becoming involved in a conflict of interests where no such conflict previously existed. Each employee who owns more than 1 percent of the securities of a publicly owned corporation listed on a national exchange or who owns securities in any amount in any other corporation supplying goods or services to GTE is required to report such holdings to GTE counsel for a determination as to the propriety of retaining such holdings.

E. INFORMATION ABOUT OTHER COMPANIES

Employees whose professional or managerial responsibility involves working with information about another corporation should refrain from buying and selling stock in such corporation.

V. OTHER RELATIONSHIPS WITH COMPETITORS, CUSTOMERS, OR SUPPLIERS

A. GENERAL

Apart from financial interests, other relationships which could cause employees to be interested in the success of another organization and thereby compromise their loyalty to GTE must be avoided. Such relationships include serving as a director, officer, or employee of, or adviser to, a competitor, customer, or supplier. Under these circumstances, the employee's sense of duty and priorities would tend to be divided between GTE and the other organization.

An exception to the policy enunciated in this Section V is made in the case of membership on the boards of directors of GTE and its subsidiaries of members of the banking and investment banking community. One of the major activities of GTE and its subsidiaries is to secure financing upon the most advantageous terms. Thus, it is essential to have available on a continuing basis expert advice in this area and one of the best ways to accomplish this objective is to have dis-

Fig. 7-3 *(Continued)*

tinguished bankers and investment bankers on the boards of directors of GTE companies. Any possible conflict-of-interest problems should be avoided by assuring that directors refrain from voting upon matters in which they have a personal interest. Moreover, most state corporation laws have provisions specifically covering these situations. It should be obvious that both the letter and spirit of these statutes should be scrupulously observed.

B. EMPLOYMENT OR SERVICES

1. General Rule—*No employees shall be employed by, or perform any services for, any competitor or supplier of GTE, whether or not they receive any compensation, or be otherwise employed or render services where it might cause embarrassment or jeopardize the interests of a GTE company, interfere with their work schedules or adversely affect their productivity or that of fellow employees.*

2. Gainful Employment—*No employee shall engage in gainful employment supplementary to company employment, involving sales, operation, maintenance, repair, design, construction or installation of customer-owned or leased equipment that is interconnected with GTE company lines and/or central offices, and/or which provides a service, feature or facility that a GTE telephone operating company has or may have available through its tariff offerings.* The term *gainful employment* includes personal work effort, direction or training of other persons, or consultative advice for any form of remuneration for services rendered.

3. Discouraging Potential or Actual Customers—*Any advice by any GTE employees, solicited or unsolicited, for the intended purpose of discouraging any potential or actual customer from utilizing service offerings or products of a GTE company to aid another company will be considered as an act of serious disloyalty and subject the employees to discharge.* This activity is improper because it diverts a business opportunity from the GTE company to another company for the employee's personal gain. Such diversion is improper whether or not the employee believes the GTE company would not have been able to obtain the business anyway. The GTE company's loss of business might have occurred only because the employee seized the opportunity for himself or herself.

4. Managerial or Consultation Services—*No employee shall render any managerial or consultation services to, or work on goods or services being provided by, any outside concern which does business with GTE or is engaged in the same business as the employee's company except with the consent of the board of directors of the employee's company and of General Telephone & Electronics Corporation or where such work or service is required as a part of the employee's job responsibilities.* This principle applies whether or not the employee receives compensation from such outside concern.

5. Moonlighting—*Not all outside work or moonlighting is improper.* Work unrelated to GTE business would not ordinarily be improper, nor would most charitable work even though related to GTE business.

Example: A GTE Sylvania engineer tutors high school dropouts in the fundamentals of television as a favor two nights a week.

While such outside activity would ordinarily be all right and even laudable, many cases are not so clear and should be discussed with GTE counsel. Even in the example, for instance, the employee should avoid misleading the students into believing that a GTE company will hire them.

C. TRANSACTIONS WITH FIRMS IN WHICH AN EMPLOYEE IS INTERESTED

1. General Rule—*No employee shall purchase, lease, rent or otherwise acquire for GTE, products, goods, services, supplies, accommodations, or the like from an employee or from a firm in which an employee has any financial interest.* When it is necessary to deviate from this section of this instruction for sound business reasons, authority to do so shall be obtained from the board of directors of the GTE company after obtaining written approval of GTE counsel.

Example: A GTE employee has a financial interest in a firm which does office maintenance and cleaning for a number of companies, including the GTE company for which the employee works.

Example: A GTE employee has a financial interest in a building which the employee desires to lease to GTE.

It would be inappropriate in either case for the GTE company either to permit the concern to perform the cleaning service or to lease the building because it creates the appearance of impropriety— namely that the relationship was established because of the employee's affiliation with GTE.

Fig. 7-3 (*Continued*)

The Ethics of Buying for Xerox

When you're selling, life can be hard.

When you're buying, everybody's your buddy.

When you're Xerox, you buy a fierce lot of things before you can sell anything at all.

Those three simple propositions add up to a continuing corporate hazard.

Every sort of influence, inducement and sales strategy is brought to bear at one time or another on those of us involved in buying for the company.

And how Xerox buys is basic to our costs, our product quality and performance, our competitive strength. To our personal and company integrity. To immediate profit and long-term growth.

You can't get much more serious than that.

This policy statement could not be more serious.

It is designed to keep the smallest trace of buddyism forever out of the buying process at Xerox. To forestall any smallest chance of unethical behavior. To ensure that the only ultimate influence on the buying decision is the good of the company.

It is designed to speak not just to Xerox people who are professional buyers, but also to the many others who influence what's bought, and from whom.

It is designed to set out with utmost clarity the ethical standards Xerox expects of anyone concerned in any way with buying decisions.

And, for the benefit of those of us who are not professional buyers, it cites the business goals that guide the work of our purchasing department people.

Our objective is a very distinct Xerox climate. People who do business or wish to do business with us must not only respect our insistence upon high standards of performance—but must expect and respect our unfailingly ethical, considerate and fair treatment of every current and potential supplier.

Are you involved?

You're a new-product engineer, specifying certain electronic components purchased on the outside. Maybe you have a choice of sources, maybe you don't—but you know which supplier's devices are acceptable when you write your specifications.

You're involved.

You're a quality assurance engineer continually surveying present and potential suppliers for quality control practices and procedures that meet Xerox requirements. Your survey report can result in a supplier being approved or disapproved.

You're involved.

You're a lawyer, and you need some highly specialized advice; you know just the person. Your work has to do with advertising, sales promotion, maybe public relations—and hardly a day goes by that you don't farm out work to artists, writers, photographers, printers you select. You're in product distribution, picking freight carriers and riggers and staying on top of them every working hour.

Involvement.

You manage a data center, and you want the extra capability offered by company A's disk drives even though B's are lower priced. Purchasing signs the PO's—but you know they're going to be strongly influenced by what you say.

You're a branch manager who helps real estate find you better space. Again, influence.

In these and dozens of similar situations, Xerox people outside the purchasing department help the system work.

For better or for worse.

And even if you in particular don't, your friends seem to think you do. Amazing how many of them are with a business that would like to have Xerox as a customer, and are sure a word from you in somebody's ear would do the trick.

Fig. 7-4 Clear policy statement on ethics of buying of the Xerox Corporation is addressed not only to professional buyers but to any others who influence the buying decision.

The code

Xerox requires and expects that any employee who buys any goods or services for Xerox, or who influences such buying in any way or to any degree, will maintain the highest standards of ethical conduct.

That applies to choosing suppliers. Negotiating prices, terms, conditions, quality. Monitoring performance and securing fulfillment.

Maintaining that standard is, for Xerox, a condition of your continued employment.

That's good and clear—but could it be more specific? Yes indeed.

In any activity involving outside suppliers, your only interest can be the best interest of Xerox. You must
show no favor or preference to anyone at the expense of the company and its ability to serve its customers most effectively.

You do nobody any favors. Nobody.

Neither do you accept any.

You know, certainly, that accepting kick-backs is criminal—morally and legally. And about the fastest
way to find the way out of Xerox. But there are many forms of favor short of that extreme.

Gifts, free services, discounts on personal purchases—whether to you or anyone in your family or household—are just as offensive. Trips, entertainment, special considerations of any kind are equally wrong,
equally actionable. That includes those that are unsolicited.

Favors must be declined, gifts returned. Pleasantly, diplomatically— but firmly.

The supplier sitting beside your desk offers you a cigar. Do you have to turn it down? You go to lunch
with a man who sells you packaging, and he reaches for the check. Do you have to fight him for it?

Of course not.

Our relationships with all our suppliers are friendly, or should be. Totally objective and strictly business,
to be sure—but friendly. We work with the people who meet our needs. We are not adversaries.

The small courtesies, the pleasantries, the kindnesses that occur between people who get on well and
respect each other are all to the good. They help keep simple humanity in our business dealings.

Then where do you draw the line? About here:

A gift or service or consideration of any kind with a value over $10 must always be refused.

Lunches with suppliers should not be encouraged. Go when you think you have to, but try to take turns
with the bill, particularly when you're on your home ground.

Dinners and other forms of evening or weekend entertainment should be avoided. If for some reason you
think it's in the best interest of Xerox to make an exception, ask for approval in advance from your
manager.

There are two other major areas of ethical conduct in our supplier relationships.

First: there can be no conflict of interest between your personal affairs and those you conduct for Xerox.
Specifically, you may not have a significant financial interest in any company with which you do business
as part of your work for Xerox.

A significant interest means anything substantial enough to color your judgment, to interfere with your
concern for the best interests of Xerox. Ten shares of stock in General Electric won't cause a problem—
or would they? What's at issue here is not one share or ten shares or a hundred. It's you.

It's also your immediate family—your wife or husband, children, or any relative. Any significant financial
interest in their name is a conflict under yours.

Conflict of interest can occur in other ways as well, or seem to. You may have a family or personal
relationship with a supplier, or with his salesman or someone on his staff. In such cases you should talk
to your manager about it as soon as you become aware of it.

Second: ethical behavior includes safeguarding the security of confidential business information.

Certainly you reveal nothing relating to Xerox that should remain inside the company. Patentable and
secret processes, production schedules, product information, pricing—any information that is proprietary to Xerox must stay that way. And in your dealings with a supplier this would include prices, quotations, contract terms from—and possibly even the names of—other sources of supply.

You have an absolute obligation to protect the confidential information offered to you by any supplier or
would-be supplier. He, too, makes his way in a coldly competitive world. Often he must divulge to you

Fig. 7-4   (*Continued*)

information as proprietary to his business as ours is to us. It is essential that we respect his confidences—for his sake, of course, but in the long run for our own, too.

Finally, Xerox observes without fail all the laws and regulations that apply to purchasing in a locality, in a state, in a country. Normally you'll be kept informed about them by your manager. If not—or if you have any doubt about the legality or propriety of a course of action—check with your manager or the appropriate Xerox attorney.

That initiative is a vital part of your conformance with the law. For Xerox, as always, this is a matter of spirit as well as letter. There are no corners to cut, no thin edges to skate on.

There is only a straight and solid path: the highest standards of ethical conduct in purchasing.

The guidelines.

In purchasing for Xerox, or influencing the process, you've been charged with acting in the company's best interest. What exactly does that mean?

Our professional purchasing people define it as *balanced value*—a concept that has four critical parts.

The first is *optimum quality*. The goods or services must be the best obtainable for the purpose to sustain the quality level Xerox is determined to deliver to its customers.

Note the words *for the purpose*. You wouldn't spend your own money on a bulldozer for a job you could do with a shovel. No more should you specify a switching device engineered for ten million operations when the product only demands one million. It may be less convenient and it may demand more technical competence to select a lower-cost device with confidence—but that's part of what Xerox is paying you for.

Second is *reliability* on the part of the supplier. Has he the capacity? Does he meet delivery schedules? Is his performance consistent? Does he have reserve capacity or would he be stretched to the limit?

Third is *service*. A supplier to Xerox is, in a sense, a full partner in our business. He must have something more than technical expertise, production efficiency, and good intentions. Things like commitment—and a willingness to do everything necessary to get his part of the job done.

Finally, there is *minimum final cost*. This is a figure that only begins with quoted unit price. It seeks to factor in all the other aspects of cost that represent expense to Xerox: design and application features, transportation, taxes and duties, installation, storage, handling, packaging. And all of those things in varying combination from different potential suppliers.

This is no attempt to make you an instant expert in purchasing. Rather, it should tell you that purchasing is a professional discipline in its own right. A business capacity grounded, like any other, in skill and training and experience.

Take it seriously, any time you're part of the process. Ask the professionals for help or advice; they'll be happy to give it.

Above all, keep your involvement where Xerox has to find it: at the highest standard of ethical personal and business conduct.

Fig. 7-4 (*Continued*)

It follows that the seller will study the other party as carefully as the business in question warrants in order to determine which of the many things he might do would have the greatest probability of success. If he concludes that a gift or a particular entertainment would greatly enhance his prospects, there is ample incentive for him to offer such a gift or entertainment to the buyer, engineer, supervisor, or anyone whom he perceives to have an influence on the buying decision. It is becoming clear that the intended recipients send out subtle signals regarding their attitude toward such gifts and favors. Some clearly invite such offers, others give little signals that they would be highly offended. The experienced salesperson can read these signals reasonably well, and seldom makes an offer which is received as offensive.

A carefully conducted survey of active buyers and purchasing managers[4] recently concluded that "it seems that the more ethical respondents (to the anonymous survey) are less likely to be offered these gifts by salespersons in the first place." This same survey also noted that firms which reviewed the ethical practices of their employees more often than the average also produced a higher proportion of the individuals judged to be "more ethical." This suggests a strong and direct correlation between the actions of management and the frequency with which gifts and favors are offered. Put simply, management *can* reduce the degree of temptation put before its employees by vigorously reviewing their ethical activity. Put even *more* simply, managers *can* manage, even in the field of ethics.

A consensus is beginning to emerge from the extensive work currently being done in the specific field of purchasing ethics which suggests that the buyer who follows three rather simple rules of thumb will not be likely to find himself in trouble over the matter of gifts or entertainment. These rules are:

1. *Keep Job and Private Life Totally Separated.* The buyer (or any other employee for that matter) should never use his position of influence over suppliers to enhance his standard of living, except through his paycheck. More and more firms are saying it's all right for a buyer to attend a ball game when invited, but they would fire him the instant he *asked* for tickets because of the totally different perspective that would place on the buyer-seller relationship.

2. *Keep Relationships with Suppliers in Balance.* Some employers prohibit their buyers from accepting even the simpler social interchanges such as lunch at supplier expense. The greater majority, however, recognize that there are social amenities between seller and buyer personnel which are useful to the customer, and the more farsighted of these are insisting that the buyer be the host when the occasion warrants it. And this provides a useful guide in determining whether or not to accept a particular gift, favor, or entertainment being offered: If the buyer could offer it to the seller when the occasion warrants and charge it to his employer, the gift, favor, or entertainment is probably all right to accept. If, however, there is no conceivable circumstance in which the buyer would reciprocate in this manner, then it is almost certainly not wise for him to accept such a gift, favor, or entertainment in the first place. It is worth noting that President Carter raised from $25 to $50 the long-standing limit on the value of gifts permissible for the President of the United States to receive for personal use. Anything above $50 must be returned or placed in a public institution such as the Smithsonian Institution.

3. *When in Doubt, Ask the Boss.* It is at last becoming fashionable to talk openly about the ethical questions which arise in business. More and more firms and institutions are telling their employees to ask their superior for guidance on ethical matters exactly as they would ask for guidance on technical, commercial, legal, or other matters. And if your boss mistakenly advises you to proceed with

---

[4]*Midwest Purchasing,* October 1977, p. 25.

something which later raises questions, it is far better to have him in your corner helping to give the answers than sitting on the other side challenging your ethical judgment.

It is clear that the buyer is subjected to more frequent and probably greater ethical hazards and temptations than are persons in most other occupations. It is equally clear that the means are available for dealing effectively with these hazards, and that the means are neither particularly mysterious nor particularly incompatible with the standards by which traditionally ethical people lead their lives. N.A.P.M. offers strong guidance in this regard (see Fig. 7-5), and its permanent Ethical Standards Committee is available to anyone in the profession who wants specific counsel, or who wishes to learn how others have handled the problems he faces. The reader is encouraged to make use of this resource whenever it can be of help in this sometimes sensitive area.

OTHER ETHICAL ASPECTS OF PURCHASING

Reciprocity

Since the beginning of selling and buying, the question of reciprocity has been one of controversy. Its practice has been cussed, discussed, and debated. As a way of business life, it has been used, misused, and abused to some extent. Some buyers and sellers bitterly oppose its use. Others accept it as good common sense. In most instances their feelings on the subject simply reflect the policies of their managements.

Right or wrong, reciprocal relations expanded substantially after World War II—especially after the wartime shortages eased. Through the years reciprocity has been deemphasized during periods of shortages. In the postwar period many large and reputable companies organized their reciprocal efforts by setting up elaborate trade relations departments, customer relations departments, and a variety of other departments. By whatever name, their objectives were the same— the promotion of sales through use of purchasing power.

A brief but inexact definition of *reciprocity* is: Reciprocity is the practice of giving preference in buying to those vendors who are customers of the buying company as opposed to vendors who do not buy from the company.

Government Interest

As early as 1931 the Federal Trade Commission was looking sternly at the many abuses of reciprocity when it charged Waugh Equipment Company with the coercive use of reciprocity. In other cases the FTC ruled that it was illegal "to abusively use large buying power to restrict competitive market opportunities." In the early 1970s many major companies entered into settlement agreements with the FTC which forbade reciprocal dealing and required the elimination of trade relations departments. Companies that have not been cited have seen the light. If the present trend continues, it is not likely that reciprocity will be a major concern to purchasing people in the years ahead.

Purchasing Responsibilities with Regard to Reciprocal Buying

Because reciprocal purchasing involves many company functions, it is a management problem. Where purchasing is centralized and is fully a part of top man-

N.A.P.M. Standards of Conduct

Officially adopted June 1959

FOREWORD

"WHAT MAKES A PROFESSION"

"If there is such a thing as a profession as a concept distinct from a vocation, it must consist in the ideals which its members maintain, the dignity of character which they bring to the performance of their duties, and the austerity of the self-imposed ethical standards. To constitute a true profession, there must be ethical tradition so potent as to bring into conformity members whose personal standards of conduct are at a lower level, and to have an elevating and ennobling effect on those members. A profession cannot be created by resolution, or become such overnight. It requires many years for its development, and they must be years of self-denial, years when success by base means is scorned, years when no results bring honor except those free from the taint of unworthy methods."

— Author Unknown

When a group of people engaged in the same profession get together to form an Association, the aims and purposes are carefully outlined for all to heed and follow. This brings about unity of action and the results will be accumulative and reflect the ability and accomplishments of the membership. This is taken care of in the Constitution and Bylaws.

If the Association is to prosper and receive the desired degree of respect by society, a Standards of Conduct is essential. Just what does the phrase "Standards of Conduct" mean? Standards of Conduct for those engaged in the field of purchasing are simply a code of ethical behavior which practically all of us would live by even if they were not in existence. They are set up not because it is assumed that we would act improperly without them, but primarily to help us recognize an appropriate action from an inappropriate one. Since the decisions involved entail the use of judgement, a Standards of Conduct Manual should help up as members of the National Association of Purchasing Management and the profession it represents, to evaluate, the factors in a similar manner and help us arrive at uniform conclusions. The underlying principles of these standards are based on common sense, courtesy, and moral codes that are essential for us to govern our official conduct in a manner to reflect our profession in the most favorable manner to society.

Purchasing people are engaged in activities which come under the continuing scrutiny of our superiors, our associates, our suppliers and prospective suppliers, the public and the press. In our contacts with individuals, and the suppliers with whom we have business dealings, it is necessary for all of us to exercise a strict rule of personal conduct to insure that relations of a compromising nature, or *even the appearance* of such relations be scrupulously avoided.

How we ourselves judge our personal actions is essential to *us*, but we must be ever mindful of the impression made on the public, for it is by them our profession is judged. Hard and fast rules applicable to every incident and situation which may confront us cannot be laid down. Holding, as we all do, positions of trust dictates that our actions must be governed by the highest standards of conduct.

The National Association of Purchasing Management many years ago established "Principles and Standards of Purchasing Practice" and "Standards and Ethics of Buying and Selling" for the guidance of all in our daily conduct.

Principles and Standards of Purchasing Practice

Loyalty To His Company
Justice To Those With Whom He Deals
Faith In His Profession

From these principles are derived the N.A.P.M. standards of purchasing practice.

1. To consider, first, the interest of his company in all transactions and to carry out and believe in its established policies.

2. To be receptive to competent counsel from his colleagues and to be guided by such counsel without impairing the dignity and responsibility of his office.

3. To buy without prejudice, seeking to obtain the maximum ultimate value for each dollar of expenditure.

4. To strive consistently for knowledge of the materials and processes of manufacture, and to establish practical methods for the conduct of his office.

5. To subscribe to and work for honesty and truth in buying and selling, and to denounce all forms and manifestations of commercial bribery.

6. To accord a prompt and courteous reception, so far as conditions, will permit, to all who call on a legitimate business mission.

7. To respect his obligations and to require that obligations to him and to his concern be respected, consistent with good business practice.

Fig. 7-5 Comprehensive standards of conduct adopted by the National Association of Purchasing Management include principles and standards of purchasing practice, as well as standards and ethics of buying and selling, established in the early days of the association.

8. To avoid sharp practice.
9. To counsel and assist fellow purchasing agents in the performance of their duties, whenever occasion permits.
10. To co-operate with all organizations and individuals engaged in activities designed to enhance the development and standing of purchasing.

Standards and Ethics of Buying and Selling

Unnecessary sales and purchasing expense is an economic waste—a tax on legitimate industry. Its elimination will assure satisfactory profits to the producer, economy to the consumer, and greater efficiency in commercial relations.

We recognize that the concern which buys must also sell, that buying and selling are companionate functions, that sound commercial transactions must be mutually profitable, and that cooperation between buyer and seller will reduce the cost to purchasing, sales, and distribution with consequent benefits to industry as a whole.

In furtherance of these principles, we subscribe to the following standards in our buying and selling:

1. To buy and sell on the basis of value, recognizing that value represents that combination of quality, service, and price which assures greatest ultimate economy to the user.

2. To respect our obligations and neither expressly nor impliedly to promise a performance which we cannot reasonably expect to fulfill.

3. To avoid misrepresentation and sharp practice in our purchases and sales, recognizing that permanent business relations can be maintained only on a structure of honesty and fair dealing.

4. To be courteous and considerate of those with whom we deal, to be prompt and business-like in our appointments, and to carry on negotiations with all reasonable expedition so as to avoid trespassing on the rights of others to the time of buyers and salesmen.

5. To avoid statements tending to injure or discredit a legitimate competitor, and to divulge no information acquired in confidence with the intent of giving or receiving an unfair advantage in a competitive business transaction.

6. To strive for simplification and standardization within the bounds of utility and industrial economy, and to further the development of products and methods which will improve industrial efficiency.

7. To recognize that character is the greatest asset in commerce, and to give it major consideration in the selection of customers and source of supply.

8. To adjust claims and settle disputes on the basis of facts and fairness, to submit the facts to arbitration if a mutual agreement cannot be reached, to abide by the decisions of the arbiters and to resort to legal measures in commercial disputes only when the preceding courses prove ineffective.

9. To provide or accept no gifts or entertainment in the guise of sales expense, where the intent or effect is to unduly prejudice the recipients in favor of the donor as against legitimate competitors.

10. To give or receive no bribes, in the form of money or otherwise, in any commercial transaction and to expose commercial bribery wherever encountered for the purpose of maintaining the highest standards of ethics in industry.

We are going to elaborate on a few principles which are mentioned rather briefly and which have come in for considerable discussion in Association meetings. We believe we should maintain our standards on an even higher plane than that generally accepted by society. This is the true test of greatness.

Gifts and Gratuities

This is a subject of increasing concern to all clear-thinking purchasing people. There is a lot of precedent involved and it is difficult to reconcile the philosophy of a Purchasing Department which does not desire to receive gifts with that of a Sales Department in the same company which makes it a regular practice to present gifts. However, a firm and understandable attitude on our part will go a long way to attain the position of dignity and repute for which we are striving. Time and concerted action will eventually bring about the desired results.

There is nothing that can undermine respect for the purchasing profession more than improper action on the part of its members with regard to gifts, gratuities, favors, etc. People engaged in purchasing should not accept from any supplier or prospective supplier any money, gift or favor which might influence, or be suspected of influencing their buying decisions. We must decline to accept or must return any such gift or favor offered us or *members of our immediate family.* The declination of these gifts or favors must be done discreetly and courteously. Possible embarrassment resulting from refusals does not constitute a basis for an exception.

The term "Gifts, Gratuities and Favors" includes, but is not limited to, monies, credits, discounts, seasonal or special occasion presents (Christmas, birthday, weddings, etc.) edibles, drinks, household appliances and furnishings, clothing, loans of goods or money, tickets to sporting events, theaters, etc., dinners, parties, transportation, vacations, travel or hotel expenses and various forms of entertainment. In any case, where the return of a gift is impracticable because of its perishability, disposition may be made to a charitable institution, and the donor informed of the disposition.

Fig. 7-5   (*Continued*)

agement, its participation and responsibilities are very different from where purchasing is decentralized. Under the conditions, purchasing has definite responsibilities it must perform. It is incumbent upon purchasing to be knowledgeable of laws covering reciprocity and to fully inform the chief executive of the company in this regard. When purchasing is decentralized, conditions change and purchasing can only advise its superiors of the law. It would be doubtful that purchasing would know when laws are violated, let alone participate in reciprocal buying policy. For example, in a huge, multidivision company, the divisional purchasing manager may be told to buy from a particular supplier. He carries out an

Personal business transactions with suppliers or prospective suppliers should be scrupulously avoided. Personal loans must not be accepted from such companies on any basis. Offers of hospitality, business courtesies, or favors, no matter how innocent in appearance, can be a source of embarrassment to all parties concerned.

We should not allow ourselves to become involved in situations where unnecessary embarrassment may result from an offer or refusal of a hospitality or a business courtesy from our suppliers or potential suppliers. It is generally the best policy to decline any sort of favor, hospitality or entertainment, to insure that all relationships are above reproach at all times. Situations requiring common sense and good judgment will develop such as a company-provided luncheon during the course of a visit to a supplier's plant located in some remote area. Another example is the case of a buyer or a purchasing expeditor-inspector accepting free company-provided automobile transportation on a temporary or emergency basis where other means are not available.

A purchasing man may ethically attend periodic meetings or dinners of trade associations, professional and technical societies or other industrial organizations as the guest of a supplier where the meetings are of an educational and informative nature and where it is considered to be in the best interest of buyer-seller relationships. The repeated appearance of an individual at such regularly scheduled meetings, as the guest of the same company, is the type of situation which should be tactfully avoided.

The simple casual luncheon or cocktail with a supplier's representative is merely a normal expression of a friendly business relationship or a time-saving expediency. It would be prudish to raise any serious question on this score. The purchasing man himself is in the best position to judge when this point has been exceeded. It is the time-saving expediency which makes up the great majority of such instances and, since the buyer's company prestige is also involved, there is every reason why an adequate expense account should be available to the buyer. It is a small price for maintaining a position free from any taint of obligation.

Mature purchasing people know that they are quickly classified among the sales' fraternity by the amount of entertainment they expect or will accept. Salesmen usually speak with real respect of the buyer who pays his share of entertainment expenses. The purchasing expense account is the most effective answer to this ethical problem.

Outside Business Affiliations

Since we are engaged in the administration and expenditure of funds of the company we represent, our conduct must necessarily be subject to more restric-

tions and to higher standards, not only on the job, but in our outside activities as well. We should not be involved in purchasing transactions with any companies in which we, our family or relatives, are owners or have a substantial financial interest. We should not engage in business and professional activities from which we might derive financial profit or other benefits resulting from our employment as a buyer.

Ethical Responsibility of Groups

If we will concede that it is important for purchasing people to conform to high ethical standards as individuals, then it will inexorably follow that it is more important that purchasing people in groups do so. The impact of group deviation from the highest of ethical standards will be infinitely greater than deviations of a single individual. And this is true if only for the fact that more people are involved. A single person can be guilty of unethical conduct and this does not necessarily reflect discredit upon the organization nor upon purchasing generally. But, when a group commits an error of this kind the charge can justifiably be made that someone in the group should have known better. And, the next step by someone who is so inclined would very likely be to generalize and say they're all alike.

It is quite possible for an individual who personally observes the highest degree of ethical conduct to accede to the majority opinion or remain silent when a questionable act is being considered by a group. The individual may hide behind the cloak of anonymity provided by the fact that action is being taken as a group. He may also feel that criticism which might be justly directed toward an individual act would be withheld in the case of a group. Lack of respect and vocal criticism do not necessarily go hand in hand. We can well have the former without the latter. And, if we are to engender that respect for our profession, which we so earnestly desire, then we must be extremely careful that group action is such that the highest order of respect is commanded—that our actions are above criticism.

In most organizations, there are developed over the years habits and patterns of action which tend to be taken for granted as being perfectly natural and in conformance with the aims and ideals of the group. Newcomers into the group and, particularly, newly appointed or elected officials of the group, tend to automatically continue these action patterns. Periodic scrutiny to determine conformance with current aims and ideals is minimized. Minor changes from year to year, although insignificant in themselves, can cumulatively distort the action pattern so that it no longer represents the ideals of the group.

It is necessary, therefore, to take stock periodically to see that programs are consistent with the high ideals for which we strive. Each element of the pro-

Fig. 7-5 (*Continued*)

order with probably no knowledge of why. This places him in an awkward position, for he cannot explain his action to possible suppliers without opening a Pandora's box. If he tells a disappointed supplier that he acted on orders, he invites the supplier to go over his head, which probably will displease his superiors.

Management Responsibilities with Regard to Reciprocal Buying

Policies prohibiting reciprocal buying practices must stem from the very top management. As a prerequisite, a management policy statement should be written and gram should be subjected to a searching examination to determine whether it does or does not conform to the highest of standards. And, if it does not, it should be discontinued. It will probably be well to consider here some group actions which may be considered to be at least questionable. This is not to say that those practices discussed below are all-inclusive. Rather, it is the intent that they should be considered as examples.

There has grown up among groups of purchasing people and particularly local associations of the National Association of Purchasing Management, the custom of holding periodic joint meetings with sales organizations, such as local affiliates of the National Sales Executives' organization. This can be an estimable practice and can be beneficial to both groups. Quite frequently, a "hospitality hour" becomes part of the program. And, more than likely, the entire meeting can be enhanced by a custom of this kind. However, consideration should be given to each organization acting as host on an alternate basis. In this way, there is no obligation incurred by anyone and no one is penalized.

The temptations are many and sometimes the pressure is great to let a salesman's organization or a supplier company provide the cocktail party, the prizes for the Christmas party or the golf outing or the annual picnic. There is frequently the implied if not the direct offer to provide more than the proper degree of hospitality during a plant visit. But those in authority on the purchasing side of the coin will think twice before departing from the strictest interpretation of the highest standards of conduct.

Purchasing organizations which publish magazines or other periodicals containing advertising must be especially conscious of the proprieties. Here, again, the temptation (admittedly with only the good of the organization in mind) is great to subject the advertiser or prospective advertiser to pressure.

In this area of association activities it is well to conform to the "Standards of Practice" established by the Editors' Group of the National Association of Purchasing Management, which are:

We, the publishers of magazines, published by, and/or for Associations affiliated with the National Association of Purchasing Management, pledge ourselves to the following Standards of Practice:

1. To disseminate information relative to and to promote the welfare of industry in general and the purchasing profession in particular.

2. To promote a better understanding of the ethics and functions of purchasing.

3. To decline any advertisement that has a tendency to mislead or that does not conform to business integrity.

4. To establish and maintain suitable contacts with Association members.

5. To establish contacts with, and arouse interest of prospective members in our local Associations and the National Association of Purchasing Management.

6. To maintain our editorial pages in accordance with the highest journalistic practice . . . to maintain balanced publications . . . to publish nothing that will reflect upon the good name of an individual, an association, a firm, or the purchasing profession.

7. To accept advertising solely upon the basis of value of the medium to the advertiser . . . to accept no advertising given as a favor to any purchaser or group of purchasers . . . to recognize a definite responsibility to the advertiser . . . to keep our reading columns independent of advertising consideration.

Actions of all purchasing people on ethical questions must not only be meticulous at all times and under all circumstances, but must also be constant and consistent. Relations of a compromising nature, or even the appearance of such relations must be scrupulously avoided.

Fig. 7-5   (*Continued*)

made known to all parties of concern. The policy should state, "No laws are to be broken; any customer who is a potential vendor is welcome to solicit for business; the fact that a person is a customer will not influence a deviation from the written purchasing procedure in awarding orders." In other words, being a customer will open the door, but, just like any other supplier, the customer must win by competition any business he receives. This kind of policy builds the loyalty of all vendors; it creates confidence and loyalty in purchasing whether centralized or decentralized; and all other company departments and people know and understand exactly how reciprocal buying is to be conducted.

When purchasing controls reciprocal buying, the morale of purchasing personnel is kept high, with the realization that good purchasing is foremost. Also, the skilled purchasing manager will not lead his company into a costly legal entanglement just to satisfy a reciprocal buying whim.

Example of Letter Prohibiting Reciprocity

Some companies have taken the position that the federal antitrust laws prohibit reciprocal buying and selling and have issued policies prohibiting its practice. Their position has been upheld by the courts. The U.S. Department of Justice and the Federal Trade Commission have been active in searching out and prosecuting where such violations are detected. The Bendix Corporation has issued the following letter to all its officers, divisional general managers, sales and marketing managers, purchasing managers, and attorneys:

> Attached are notices received from two corporations advising us that they are now under court orders which prohibit reciprocal buying or selling arrangements. By receipt of these notices, Bendix is obliged not to engage in such reciprocal buying or selling arrangements with these particular companies. But we are also under an obligation to refrain from such activities with all of our customers and suppliers in any event. As you know, under the antitrust policy statement promulgated by our Chairman on January 15, 1969, "I will buy from you if you will buy from me," or similar sales arrangements are absolutely prohibited. All purchases and sales by Bendix are to be made solely on the basis of price, quality, service and similar considerations, without regard to the status of the supplier or customer as an actual or potential supplier or customer of Bendix. If these simple principles are applied to your purchase and sales arrangements, we will not become involved in any unlawful reciprocal dealing practice, including any of the arrangements referred to in the attached notices. If you have any question about any specific sales or purchase agreement or proposed agreement, you should immediately call the facts to the attention of the Legal Department.

PERSONAL PURCHASES FOR EMPLOYEES

In some states, laws have been enacted which prohibit personal purchases by purchasing department personnel. Certainly, in states which prohibit the practice, it should not be allowed. In the other states, there is considerable controversy as to whether or not personal purchasing is ethical. The statutes prohibiting personal purchases for employees are most commonly called *trade diversion laws*. These laws make it illegal to sell to employees material which is not manufactured by the employer or not handled by him in his normal course of trade. Certain exceptions are usually made, such as meals, cigarettes, tobacco, and articles sold from vending machines. Other things required for the health or safety of the employee are also exempt. These would include, but not be limited to: safety shoes, safety gloves, other safety equipment and clothing, such as uniforms, work clothes and hats, and even special tools required to perform a job but not furnished by the employer. The employer can maintain much better quality control by purchasing this type of material for the employee. When such is the case, the articles purchased are usually charged at cost, or, sometimes, the company may pay part. Trade diversion laws are not enforced generally, but, regardless, buyers should not engage in such a practice when a violation of the law is known. One of the most difficult problems for the purchasing agent is to have a company superior ask for such purchases and further complicate the matter by requesting that the invoice be rendered to himself and not to the company.

Trade Diversion Laws

Illinois, Ohio, Michigan, Minnesota, Pennsylvania, and Wisconsin have trade diversion laws which prohibit a company from selling to its employees any item which it does not usually procure or otherwise handle. It is possible that other states may pass such laws in the future.

The Illinois statute is an excellent example of this type of law.

> No person, firm or corporation engaged in any business enterprise in this state shall, by any method or procedure, directly or indirectly, by itself or through a subsidiary agency owned or controlled in whole or in part by such person, firm or corporation, sell or procure for sale or have in its possession or under its control for sale to its employees or any person, any article, material, product or merchandise of whatsoever nature not of his or its own production or not handled in his or its regular course of trade.

Similar prohibitions relating to such sales by state agencies, municipalities, or other local subdivisions are also included in the statute.

Personal Purchases as a Fringe Benefit

Where no laws prohibit personal purchases for employees, the question of whether or not it is ethical becomes clouded. Thus, one must examine various facets of the problem before drawing a conclusion as to when it is ethical and when it is not.

Many companies treat personal purchases as a fringe benefit for employees and actively encourage the use of the purchasing department's facilities. When the labor market is tight and good workers are hard to find, this is used as a selling point in recruiting employees. It is also widely practiced when the company is in a remote location where it is difficult for employees to make their purchases. Certain industries tend to encourage this activity—in particular, very old industries where company management has a paternalistic attitude toward employees. Many industries which are notable for lower wages often foster personal purchases. The vast majority of companies, however, have not adopted this practice as a part of the company policy. For the most part, in fact, personal purchases are discouraged for a variety of reasons. Members of the corporate hierarchy usually consider themselves exempt and often request special treatment.

Methods used in carrying out personal purchasing bear greatly on the judgment of whether the activity becomes unethical. There is little doubt the practice is unethical if the corporate purchasing position is used to force any special concession from the vendor. This could include price concession, special packing, delayed billing, special shipping, added free extras, or any other treatment not consistent with the seller's normal *modus operandi.*

Setting Procedures and Standards for Personal Purchases

No matter what standards are set, there is virtually universal agreement by most purchasing professionals that the practice of personal purchases when carried on too long becomes subject to censure. In view of this, the burden falls on the purchasing department buyers, as masters of the marketplace, to be thoroughly knowledgeable of trade and marketing procedures and thus be the final authority concerning the ethics of each and every purchase. A buyer must judge all transactions after considering the purchasing code of ethics, his company loyalty, normal trade practices, and the guidance of his own conscience.

Under no circumstances is it ethical to employ a subterfuge in making personal purchases. A vendor, when he receives and fills an order, naturally assumes he is furnishing material for the buyer's company. Should the company order form be used for personal purchases, it is incumbent upon the buyer to make this fact known to the supplier.

LEADERSHIP FROM PURCHASING

Purchasing in the last two decades has made greater strides than at any other time. Purchasing has emerged from its clerical status and moved into the management structure. In so doing, it has established itself as a profession. Having achieved this status, purchasing is now looked to for guidance, and one of the areas where purchasing can show true leadership is in the field of ethics. There is little doubt that purchasing is one of the most sensitive areas of a company, subject to all types of pressures and influence. From experience in this atmosphere, the purchasing manager has much to offer.

Most top management is willing and ready to accept guidance from purchasing in the total-company ethical concept. This is not only a challenge to purchasing, but a responsibility—one that cannot be ignored without loss of status. The purchasing manager must meet this challenge in a number of ways.

First and foremost, he must ensure that proper ethical conduct exists in his own department. Next, he must become the leader in seeing that the same high standards adopted by his department in dealing with suppliers are also in effect throughout the whole company for anyone who has dealings with vendors. Suppliers, naturally, have contact with many people in the company not directly subordinate to purchasing. These people or functional activities vary from company to company, depending upon the organizational structure. Examples might be: designers, quality control people, production people, salespersons, public relations personnel, advertising people, and many others who use purchased material and supplies. The company cannot afford to have a double standard or multiple standards of conduct established by separate departments. The effects of such an approach brand the company with an unenviable reputation. The purchasing manager must remain ever alert to ensure proper ethical treatment of suppliers by all. He and his department should stand ready to detect unethical practices and be prepared to correct any that do occur.

Conveying to the rest of the company the proper ethical approach to supplier relationship is a matter of great concern to purchasing. A statement of policy developed by purchasing and issued as a management proclamation is very useful in setting parameters. Such a statement should not attempt to spell out in detail how to handle all the various possible situations that might happen, for it would necessarily become too lengthy and cumbersome and could not be all-inclusive. The policy will be far better if it is written in broad terminology, but is concise and pointed enough to be readily understood by everyone throughout the company. It should stress that purchasing is always available for consultation and guidance in coping with any particular problem. Purchasing should further take the initiative and hold seminars or workshops on this subject. These could be part of normal employee training and should be continually updated, with all employees who deal with suppliers participating in the sessions. Seminars of this sort should be conducted at least once a year and more often if required.

The example set by purchasing in its ethical conduct will, of course, be the obvious guide to the rest of the company. Proper ethical conduct is as much good judgment as anything else, and here others turn to purchasing to see how to conduct themselves. They lean on purchasing, for they feel that purchasing people are skilled in this area.

Elevating the Purchasing Profession

A buyer dedicated to sound ethical standards can do much to raise the stature of his employer, himself, and the purchasing profession. A buyer should be honest, courteous, cheerful, fair, capable, morally responsible, tactful, friendly, respectable, dependable, energetic, and able to handle his own financial affairs capably. By perseverance and hard work these objectives can be approached, to the great credit of all those in purchasing. It must be remembered that one cannot buy an ethical reputation; it must be earned. Once earned, it must be zealously maintained. One bad move can destroy a reputation that it has taken years to build.

NOTE: For further information on subjects covered in this section see the list of references in Section 30.

Section **8**

Value Analysis

EDITOR

D. Michael Tonti *Director of Purchasing, Black & Decker (U.S.) Inc., Hampstead, Maryland*

ASSOCIATE EDITOR

R. G. Bradyhouse, C.P.M., CVS *Manager, Value Analysis Services, Black & Decker (U.S.) Inc., Towson, Maryland*

The true measure of worth applied to the purchasing department by modern business is its contribution to profit. Ensuring delivery on time of specified items of proper quality and at a satisfactory price is only a part of purchasing's total responsibility, and the achievement is no longer acceptable to progressive management as functional effectiveness. Spending, as they do, approximately half of the company's sales dollars, purchasing executives are charged with the responsibility for making certain that maximum value is obtained for every dollar spent—whether it be for raw material, components, equipment, services, or supplies. A proven technique for obtaining maximum value is value analysis, which is the subject of this section.

VALUE ANALYSIS: TOOL FOR FUNCTIONAL EFFECTIVENESS

Definitions

Value Analysis Value analysis is the organized and systematic study of every element of cost in a part, material, or service to make certain it fulfills its function at the lowest possible cost; it employs techniques which identify the functions the user wants from a product or service; it establishes by comparison the appropriate cost for each function; then it causes the required knowledge, creativity, and initiative to be used to provide each function for that cost.

Before it was widely accepted, value analysis was often referred to as just another fancy name for the type of cost reduction program that had been common in industry for many years. The comparison is completely inaccurate.

Value Engineering The terms *value analysis* and *value engineering* will be used synonymously in this section, although some authors prefer to define value engineering as the application of value analysis techniques in the engineering sphere of responsibility, and value analysis as the application of value analysis techniques in the materials procurement sphere. Since value analysis or value engineering is strictly a team effort, freedom of suggestion of proposal in both spheres should be accorded both functions. Purchasing must question engineering specifications; engineering must question purchasing practices, such as sourcing and award decisions based on price.

Functions—Primary and Secondary This section will accent the functional characteristic of value analysis, because it is a study of function. The *function* of a part, material, or service is the job it does. It is frequently defined as "something which makes an item work or sell." It can usually be defined with a verb and a noun, viz.:

Knife—cuts materials
Thermometer—indicates temperatures
Paint—protects surfaces

Defining the function by using just two words, the verb and noun, prevents the attempt to define more than one simple function at one time and makes the identification of the function as specific as possible. There may be a secondary function in addition to the primary, or basic, function.

Examples:

	Primary Function	Secondary Function
Cigarette package	Protect cigarettes	Sell cigarettes
Refrigerator	Preserve food	Make ice

Main interest in this section will be the *primary* or *basic function*. A design engineer, however, must consider the secondary functions, which are the creation of eye appeal to help sell the product and certain added features which will appeal to the buyer but really add nothing to the accomplishment of the basic function.

Value   Since this section is dedicated to the analysis of value, a clear understanding of what is meant by *value* is essential. Value may be defined as the lowest end cost at which the function may be accomplished at the time and place and with the quality required. Value has no direct relationship to cost. Some items which cost less than a similar product accomplish the function in a superior manner. For example, a premium paid for overtime labor increases the cost of a product or service but does not add anything whatsoever to its value. Value cannot be determined exclusively by an examination of an item being evaluated. The value of any service, material, or product is established by the minimum cost of other available alternatives, materials, products, or services that will perform the same function.

Value is a relatively broad term, which may be categorized as value of use, of cost, of esteem, or of exchange.

USE VALUE.   Use value is based on the properties and qualities of a product or material in relationship to the purpose of the item. Use value is objective.

Examples:	Compass	—to mariner
	vs.	to housewife
	Bolt	—in airplane wing
	vs.	in a lawn chair

COST VALUE.   This is based on cost of product, always expressed in money.

ESTEEM VALUE.   This is based on properties or features or attractiveness involved in pride of ownership of the item. Esteem value is subjective.

Examples:	Gold watch band
	Mink coat
	Masterpiece paintings

EXCHANGE VALUE.   This is based on properties or qualities which make the product exchangeable for something else.

Examples:	Real estate
	Money
	Bonds

The main concerns in value analysis are use and cost values. To achieve high value, emphasis must be placed on obtaining high *use value* at the lowest possible cost.

SYSTEM NATURE OF VALUE ANALYSIS

Value analysis is a system—a system requiring the organized application of specific techniques, designed and arranged in a rational sequence, to accomplish the end objective of enhancing total value.

This should not be construed to mean that the value analysis techniques are entirely new. On the contrary, purchasing managers applying some techniques of value analysis will recognize many procedures that have been successfully used in other effective management disciplines for many years. A closer examination, however, will reveal that these well-known systems may be used "as is" or may be modified, refined, and, more importantly, organized in a logical sequence to produce a specific result. Some new ones may be added to this overall system. The logic of this statement can perhaps be supported by a simple analogy regarding the use of wood, steel wire, and ivory.

Scholars tell us that the use of wood has been understood since prehistoric times. Primitive people found that the branch of a tree could be used to provide the function of a club. The club provided a means of protection against natural enemies and also a means of obtaining the food necessary to sustain life. Moreover, wood used in fires could warm the caves used as habitations. It could also be used to cook food and make it more palatable.

For many years, steel wire has been used in many forms and fashions. For example, wire can be used as a snare to trap animals. Used as a fence, it can confine animals to a desired area and/or prevent intruders from entering certain areas.

Admirers of primitive art have long been fascinated by the tools, household implements, and objects of art that have been fashioned from ivory with the very crudest of tools. Examples of this art may be found in northern regions where for hundreds of years Eskimos have so utilized the ivory tusk of the walrus. Similar items made of ivory obtained from elephant tusks may be found in primitive villages in Africa.

Although each of these items was known and used for many years in its own individual applications, it was not until early in the eighteenth century that Bartolomeo Cristofori combined these three basic ingredients into a single system which resulted in a stringed percussion instrument commonly known as the piano. What startling difference in the result!

VALUE ANALYSIS TECHNIQUES

As illustrated by this simple analogy, the techniques comprising the system of value analysis have been carefully blended into an organized system to present a completely different end result. Although any note on the piano will produce sound when struck, the keys must be touched in proper sequence if the end objective is music. So the necessary techniques of value analysis must all be used and must be applied in proper sequence if the desired end result is to be achieved.

The system of value analysis is a method by which value is brought into proper perspective This can be illustrated by the definition of method given by René Descartes, French philosopher and mathematician of the seventeenth century. "Method," said Descartes, "consists entirely in the order and arrangement of those things upon which the powers of the mind are to be concentrated in order to discover some truth."

The value analysis system provides the necessary techniques in their rational order of dependence. This approach will enable the practioner to:

1. Accumulate facts
2. Identify areas of knowledge required
3. Provide efficient knowledge search
4. Apply creative skills
5. Apply precise evaluation techniques

The combination of these techniques will in turn provide the means of placing functions and their values in their proper relationship.

The procedure which accomplishes these five things logically and in proper sequence is known as the *value analysis job plan* and will be fully covered later in this section.

Ten Tests for Value in a Product or Service

Value analysts usually apply the following tests to a part, material, product, or service to determine whether maximum value is being obtained for each dollar spent in accomplishing the function:

1. Does its use contribute value?
2. Is its cost proportionate to its usefulness?
3. Does it need all its features?
4. Is there anything better for the intended use?
5. Can a usable part be made by a lower-cost method?
6. Can a standard part be found that will accomplish the function as well at a lower cost?
7. Is the product made on proper tooling, considering the quantities that are used?
8. Do material, labor, overhead, and reasonable profit equal its cost?
9. Will another dependable supplier provide it for less?
10. Is anyone buying it for less?

Selecting Items to Be Value-Analyzed

To maximize results, particularly at the beginning of a program, it is essential that certain important considerations be given attention in the selection of products to be value-analyzed. Specifically, a part should be selected for improvement.

1. With a large annual dollar volume
2. Purchased in large quantities
3. Complex in design
4. With high scrap or rework costs
5. Which involves many operations
6. That is part of an assembly that offers possibilities for part combinations (see Fig. 8-1)

7. That is relatively difficult to make
8. That appears to offer possibilities for standardization
9. That is not competitive as the result of changed market conditions

NEED FOR FORMAL PROGRAM TO ANALYZE VALUE

There is hardly an industry or plant that is not searching for new or better materials or more sophisticated machinery or processes which will make their products more competitive in the marketplace and improve product performance. In the relatively recent past, innovations in manufacturing processes and development of new materials and products materialized slowly, and one could keep abreast of them by traditional means. To be effective in this rapidly changing economy where 25 percent of today's sales come from products unknown 5 years ago, business must constantly update its skills and knowledge and match or best competition in the improvement of the function-accomplishing ability of its products, along with the maintenance or improvement of the products' sales appeal, quality, and normal maintenance costs. Unfortunately this is usually done on an informal, temporary, cost reduction–accented basis. Such approaches are not as effective as a formal program and often result in cheapening the product at the expense of less efficient operation and increased maintenance costs.

A *formal* program is vital to the accomplishment of maximum benefits. The formal program involves purchasing, engineering

Fig. 8-1 A typical example of applying value analysis technique. Result: an over 50 percent reduction in cost. The fitting originally was an elbow, made of two pieces at a cost of $0.11. The first attempt to make the part in one piece pushed the cost to $0.12. The value analyst and the supplier then set $0.05 as their target and found the only way to meet it was to make the part straight. Further investigation showed that the necessary bend could readily be made in the part to which the fitting was connected.

(product, plant, and industrial, as required), manufacturing, accounting, and perhaps others in varying degrees. The formal program establishes targets and measures progress.

The formal program should include:

1. Pre-production value analysis
2. Value analysis of existing company products—both those purchased and those manufactured internally
3. Value analysis of maintenance, repair, and operating supplies
4. Value analysis studies of office systems and purchasing procedures, etc.
5. Continuing value analysis studies of products after they reach the market

MANAGEMENT UNDERSTANDING OF VALUE ANALYSIS

The cooperation and participation of other departments—marketing, engineering, production, etc.—are important to the success of any value analysis effort. Understanding and support from management are even more important, since indifference and lack of enthusiasm at the top are quickly reflected in the lower echelons of a company.

Top management must be convinced that value analysis will maintain or improve quality while reducing costs. Thus it is incumbent on the purchasing manager or value analyst to stress to all levels of management the relationship of value analysis to those product characteristics so important in a competitive economy: quality, performance, marketability, maintainability, and reliability.

Quality

Quality is measured in several ways. In some cases, *durability,* or long life, is a major consideration. In others, efficiency of operation may be paramount. Easy maintenance may be another quality criterion.

For example: A reentry space rocket engine must be completely reliable. The portion of its life which is longer than the relatively few minutes during which it is required is of no concern or value.

A decision as to suitable quality must involve *technical quality* and *economic quality.* No matter the degree of technical suitability, the item must be procurable, at a satisfactory cost, and on a continuing basis. So, economic quality includes technical quality but also includes cost factors and availability as well. Reappraisals of the material, product, and process selected are necessary from time to time because applications, competition, and customer expectations do change. Technological developments and savings in market prices may affect a company's ability to meet actual requirements. For instance, if copper rises in price and aluminum holds relatively stable, a reappraisal may be made along the following lines.

Aluminum has roughly two-sevenths the weight of copper. Aluminum has only 60 percent the conductivity of copper, so 2 pounds of copper will carry an electrical load equivalent to roughly that of 4.2 pounds of aluminum. So when the price of aluminum is less than 2.1 times the price of copper and the element of conductivity is considered, aluminum constitutes the proper choice.

It should be apparent, therefore, that the engineer, the production specialist, and the buyer must work closely together if they are to reach a sound decision as to the best buy.

Performance

No matter how attractive in appearance or solidly built, if the product does not function efficiently, it will not sell. In value analysis the goal is equal or improved accomplishment of the function at a lower cost. In some cases, costs may be increased to achieve better *performance* or to lower maintenance costs and thereby improve product marketability.

Marketability

The primary aim of business is to produce supplies, equipment, or services which find a ready market and provide a reasonable profit. All items must have the necessary degree of sales appeal, whether it be in

- Efficiency of operation
- Low operating costs
- Low repair and maintenance costs
- Esteem value

Value analysis recognizes that *marketability* must be maintained or improved.

Maintainability

Maintainability is a most important feature affecting the customer's total end cost of an item or product. Regardless of initial quality of components and initial marketability of the product, if the value analysis study resulted in increased maintenance costs for the customer, any savings realized would sooner or later be wiped out by decreased sales and loss of goodwill.

Reliability

It is equally important that the required *reliability* of the product be preserved or improved by the value analysis recommendation. Suppose an electrical relay performed perfectly for half its expected life and then malfunctioned and shut down a production line. Suppose a commercial water heater functioned perfectly 98 percent of the time! What would happen to sales, to goodwill, and to profits?

OVERCOMING RESISTANCE TO CHANGE

The selling of value analysis runs head-on into the natural tendency of individuals to resist change. Overcoming resistance to change has always been a difficult task.

Resistance can be overcome in a value analysis program if facts are marshaled into a logical and challenging program where profit contributions can be made and factually documented and wholehearted support of all levels of management obtained.

Citing of actual accomplishments by other companies always proves helpful in convincing the skeptical or those who show some form of resistance that formal value analysis programs can be great profit contributors. Professional and technical magazines and bulletins are replete with examples of profit improvement and product improvement through value analysis. For instance, a major mechanical-sweeper manufacturer formerly used on its sweepers metal wheels which had rubber tires molded on. Through value analysis, the wheels were redesigned to plastic, which not only reduced the cost approximately 20 percent but gave an added sales feature: the new wheels do not mark the floor as rubber did.

Another interesting example involved the fabrication of hay-rake teeth or tines by a major farm equipment supplier. They were made of spring-steel coil springs. Metal fatigue caused the teeth to break off in the field. Not only was the tooth loss objectionable, but cattle died from consuming the broken teeth. With the supplier's assistance, the design was changed to insert a rubber ball joint between the metal teeth and the metal mounting fixture. This boosted the tooth life ten times, with only a slight increase in cost. If teeth fail now, they remain on the rake and are not left in the field to cause the cattle-killing "hardware disease."

A major electric refrigerator manufacturer eliminated $0.5 million in excess costs by a value analysis program and, as a result:

- Refrigerators are provided at a lower cost per cubic foot of space.
- They have added features, such as thinner walls and corrosion-resistant interiors.
- They sell for considerably less than 20 years ago—despite increasing costs of material and labor.

THE BASIC STEPS OF VALUE ANALYSIS

In recognizing that value analysis is a systematic approach to acquiring the basic function at the lowest cost, it cannot be emphasized too strongly that logical sequencing and application of the techniques and job plan must be followed in order to achieve greater value at lower cost. The logical systematic approach is known as the *job plan*.

Value Analysis Job Plan

The Information Phase In this phase it is necessary to gather all the factual information required to make an intelligent study of the project or component, as illustrated by Fig. 8-2.

First, the basic value question should be asked:

What is it?
What does it do? What is its function?

All products or services have a prime function and many secondary functions. A pump for domestic use may have to operate at a low noise level; a clock or watch may need to provide attractiveness. Where possible, the parts and costs of a product or service should be broken down into functional areas, and the costs of each area should be obtained. For instance, an electrical switch can be broken down into electrical function, mechanical function, enclosing function, etc.

PRELIMINARY INFORMATION CHECK SHEET

1. Functional Information
a. Can this function be eliminated? ☐
b. Does this do more than is required? ☐
c. Is it over-designed? ☐
d. Can it be simplified? ☐
e. Can something do the job better? ☐

Comment: _____

2. Design Information
a. Is a severe environment involved? ☐
b. Must this be highly reliable? ☐
c. Is there an installation problem? ☐
d. Will this be difficult to operate? ☐
e. Can a standard be used? ☐
f. Is there a strength problem? ☐

Comment: _____

3. Special Requirement Information
a. Are special platings required? ☐
b. Are special finishes required? ☐
c. Are special procedures required? ☐
d. Does this require special quality? ☐
e. Are special safety considerations
   required? ☐

Comment: _____

4. Materials Information
a. Can special materials be eliminated? ☐
b. Will a special material do it better? ☐
c. Are materials difficult to obtain? ☐
d. Are these materials hard to process? ☐
e. Is material treating a problem? ☐

Comment: _____

5. Specification Information
a. Are the specifications unrealistic? ☐
b. Will modification simplify design? ☐
c. Does design do more than specifications require? ☐

Comment: _____

6. Processing Information
a. Is this difficult to manufacture? ☐
b. Is there a less costly method? ☐
c. Does this require special tooling? ☐
d. Is special equipment required? ☐
e. Can a specialty vendor do this at
   less cost? ☐
f. Are processing requirements too
   strict? ☐

Comment: _____

7. Supplementary Information
a. Are there particular packaging
   problems? ☐
b. Are there other supply problems? ☐
c. Does this require costly accessories? ☐
d. Will this be difficult to transport or
   handle? ☐
e. Will maintainability be difficult? ☐
f. Are instruction manuals required? ☐

Comment: _____

8. Value Summary
a. Is this function unimportant? ☐
b. Does this cost more than it is worth? ☐
c. Does it cost more than the total of
   reasonable labor, overhead,
   material, and profit? ☐
d. If it were your money, would you
   refuse to buy it? ☐

Comment: _____

9. Purchasing Summary
a. Should larger quantities be ordered?
b. Could smaller quantities be ordered
   to advantage?
c. What changes would the present

Comment: _____

vendor suggest to reduce the cost
and price?
d. Should the shipping method or the
   shipping container be changed?

Fig. 8-2   Outline of the information phase of the value analysis job plan.

What does it cost?

All available and applicable costs should be compiled. Hidden costs—scrap, reject rate, warranty cost—must be searched out. Every element of cost must be questioned and documented as to costs to perform the function. Actual shop costs must be obtained—not standard costs. It is most important that all information be obtained from reliable sources inside and outside the company.

The source from which the item is obtained, the cost, and the ordering quantities must be determined. Necessary drawings, samples of the item, specification sheets, manufacturing methods, data, and assemblies should be obtained where possible.

The Speculative Phase   When all the information has been gathered and the necessary understanding is achieved, various techniques are applied to obtain the fullest benefit.

This is where the question is asked: What else will do the job? Then the analyst or group should *speculate* freely. Such elements as brainstorming and vendor know-how enter the picture. Creativity comes into full play. The function is evaluated. The item, material, or service is evaluated by comparison. A feeling of confidence and the use of one's own judgment are vital during this phase.

The techniques of *blasting, creating,* and *refining* should be employed at this point.

Nitpicking should be avoided. The basic functional areas should be tackled with the idea of cutting out over 50 percent of the cost. The more obvious, overengineered components should receive prime consideration. This will lead into new and previously overlooked areas.

The Analytical Phase   This is where the last value question is asked: What will that cost? Estimate the dollar value of each exposed idea.

Investigate thoroughly those ideas with a large dollar value to objectively determine their good and bad points, and then seek to eliminate, overcome, or minimize objections to those ideas which appear good.

Specifications must be examined to be sure they are essential to accomplishment of the function.

For instance, when value-analyzing a productive part, the analyst should:

Find out:	*Then decide:*
What stresses the part is subjected to	How strong the part should be
What uses it is put to	How the part should look
What features the customer wants	What its characteristics should be
How the present part is performing	What should be changed
How many repair parts are sold yearly	

Remember: too many parts are made much better than they need be.

Neither the supplier nor the customer gains from overdesign. The waste represents false value.

The design should be analyzed to determine answers to:

- Is it properly designed for its function?
- Does it have all the characteristics it needs but no special characteristic it doesn't need?
- Is it serving its purpose well?

Considering	*Is the Part Adequate?*	*Is the Part Too Adequate?*
Stress	Strong	Excessive material or heat treatment
Impact	Sufficiently resistant	Overly constructed
Corrosion	Decorative only	Excessive material or finish
Wear	Hardened and lubricated	Excessive heat treatment or material
Operation	Protective design, human-engineered	Too many features
Maintenance	Accessible, easily adjusted and maintained	Life well beyond use

Industry specialists and in-plant engineering should be asked to consider carefully the utilization of a standard part or parts. Slight design modifications can be made sometimes to accommodate a standard component at a considerable saving, particularly on high-production items.

Throughout this phase the analyst should avoid generalities and get down to specifics.

He should put a dollar sign on the main idea and find out what the key tolerance is costing. Each item should be checked thoroughly in the relationship of its value to its cost and to its function. The whitewash brush should not be used to evaluate new methods, materials, or processes. Roadblocks must be expected—some real and some for personal reasons. The analyst must have the courage of his convictions and pursue promising solutions until a satisfactory answer is achieved.

To maximize results, the best vendors should be selected for consultation and should be given full information.

All recommendations selected by the analyst or value analysis committee as having potential should be in written form and accompanied by all pertinent comparative data.

The Program Execution Phase   The best ideas should be selected and the job broken down into functional areas, e.g., electrical contact function, enclosing function, supporting function, etc. The various ideas must be carefully evaluated and pursued diligently and thoroughly. The analyst or committee must stay with the job until difficulties or roadblocks are overcome and tangible, usable results are obtained or the objections are justified.

Appropriate value analysis techniques should be applied.

Remember: This is the final *action* phase.

The Summary and Conclusion Phase   Many different methods can be used to summarize the project. That method which will gain the necessary attention to secure the necessary action should be used. Here it is well to "let the dollars do the talking" as much as possible by:

- Accenting the lower net cost which would be available by following the value analysis recommendation
- Pointing out the better marketability and resultant higher profits because of lower maintenance costs
- Showing the features making for greater sales appeal, such as improved appearance and better functioning of the product

The following should be considered:

Booklets
Flip charts
Transparencies
Interoffice correspondence
Suggestion sheets

The language of the manager must be used. The report must reflect the enthusiasm of the value analyst or value analysis committee. It must be short but to the point, with necessary supporting data.

THE WORKSHOP APPROACH TO VALUE ANALYSIS

The organization through which value analysis principles can be applied to actual products will vary according to the size of the company and the number and complexity of its products. The smaller the company, the more likely it is that the purchasing manager or the buyer of the product will be a one-person value "team." The more common approach, however, is to create a value analysis committee composed of representatives from each of the functions involved in the design, production, and marketing of the product (or its components) that is subject to analysis. Larger companies may have specialized staff groups of value analysts or value engineers, assigned either to the purchasing department or the engineering department but in either case working closely with the other department.

Whatever the organization, it operates most effectively when it employs the workshop method in reviewing possible value analysis opportunities—i.e., encourages free discussion and exchange of ideas on how the functions of particular parts, materials, or services can be performed as well or better at lower cost. Even the individual buyer-analyst employs an adaptation of the workshop method in informal discussion with counterparts in other departments such as engineering and production.

Value analysis workshops have led to a number of refinements of the basic principles and procedures described earlier in this section. Four that have been used successfully by the value analysis committee at a leading manufacturer of electrical tools are described below.

Function Analysis System Technique (FAST Diagramming)

FAST diagramming is a means of graphically showing the functions of a mechanism (see Fig. 8-3). By diagramming the functions in a manner similar to that

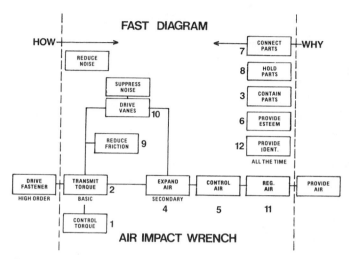

Fig. 8-3 Function analysis system technique (FAST) diagramming enables value analysis committee to understand functions and relative costs of those functions in a product and helps identify high-cost areas subject to improvement. (In the actual analysis, specific dollar figures were used in place of the 1–12 ratings.)

used in the program evaluation and review technique (PERT), which is described in Section 18, committee members can:

Increase their understanding of a system and its functions as a preliminary to considering feasible alternatives

Allocate all costs in a unit to the appropriate function

In the air impact wrench example used in Fig. 8-3, the relative costs of the functions have been indicated by the numbers 1 to 12. The control torque, number 1, is the most expensive function in the unit. The least expensive is the name plate, number 12. (In an actual analysis the monetary costs are also posted.) The chart then enables an analyst to evaluate cost-function relationships and identify high-cost areas subject to improvement.

Creative Brainstorming

Creative brainstorming is the process of stimulating an uninhibited flow of ideas, however outlandish they may seem at first, from members of the value analysis team. In such sessions "negative thinking," i.e., expressing skepticism or derision about another team member's ideas, is not permitted. The theory behind the rule is that nothing keeps a person's mouth shut so much as the fear of being laughed at. Another rule is to record all ideas, no matter how foolish they may seem at first, and defer judgment until the later phases of the analysis.

Hitchhiking

Hitchhiking is a by-product of brainstorming. Team members' ideas that are expressed and recorded may not be the solution to a problem, but they may trigger second thoughts in other members that ultimately lead to the solution.

Leapfrogging

Leapfrogging is a technique of value-analyzing comparable products in the company's line to identify their best features and design. These are combined into a hybrid product that, in turn, is value-analyzed to bring additional creative ideas from the team. This process has, in some cases, enabled the company to enter a new market with a superior product which is priced competitively.

MAJOR AREAS FOR VALUE ANALYSIS

Many areas will provide rich rewards for value analysis efforts. A few of those with the greatest potential are briefly reviewed below. There are many other areas where costs are not commensurate with value.

Design and Specifications

The value analysis approach is inherent in efficient design. Design should begin with a clear statement of function expressed by means of a requirement specification. The function and value of each component should be established. Good design will ensure that actual costs approach, or are even less than, the assigned value.

Good requirement specifications are essential for functional design. Sufficient time should be allowed for value engineering. Parts should be designed with the complete assembly under consideration. Since the manufacturing method and material affect the design, they must be a part of the design rather than be chosen afterward. Overdesign is not in accordance with value analysis principles, which require that costs must be justified.

Specifying smaller tolerances and a finer finish than required will increase costs significantly. Figures 8-4 and 8-5 show the magnitude of cost increases that occur as tolerances are tightened or smoother finishes called for. Both charts are reproduced by permission of The American Society of Mechanical Engineers.

Drawing dimensioning can contribute to needless manufacturing, inspection, and rejection costs. Critical dimensions should not be referenced from noncritical locations so that they too become critical. Cumulative tolerances should be avoided (see Fig. 8-6). True-position dimensioning should be considered where savings will result.

Material should be conserved. Casting wall sections should be no thicker than the design and production method require. Thinner-gauge material might suffice for stampings and roll-formed parts. Tubing might be substituted for rod. Scrap generated in making one part might serve as raw material for a second part. Design ingenuity can eliminate parts or simplify tooling (see Fig. 8-7). This shows how holes perpendicular to the die-opening directions were produced without slides in a die casting.

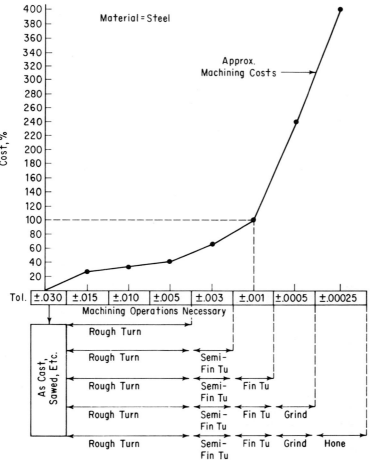

Fig. 8-4   Cost and value of small tolerances and smooth finishes, ASME Paper 61-MD-12. *(Courtesy of American Society of Mechanical Engineers.)*

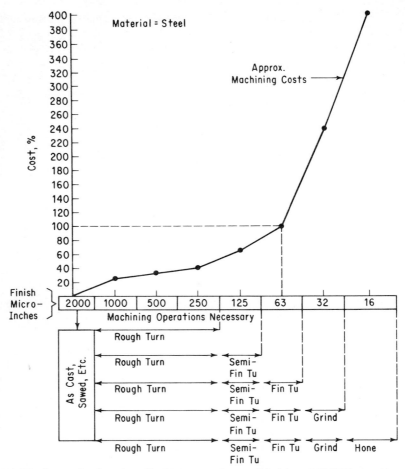

Fig. 8-5 Cost and value of small tolerances and smooth finishes, ASME Paper 61-MD-R. *(Courtesy of American Society of Mechanical Engineers.)*

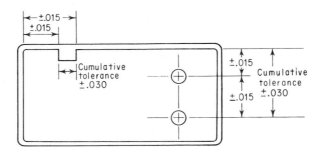

Fig. 8-6 Pool tolerancing procedure costs money.

Specifications should be written clearly and with full understanding of actual requirements. Industry and association standards, such as those of AISI, NEMA, SAE, and ASME, should be employed wherever possible. Specifying by trade name may be a simple means of ensuring that necessary requirements are met, but may result in higher costs.

Standardization

Potential savings resulting from standardization must not be overlooked. Products sold, components, materials, supplies, tools, methods, and procedures all can benefit from standardization in the value analysis program.

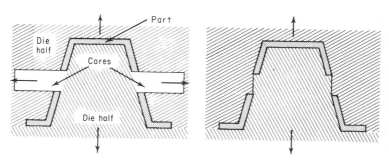

Fig. 8-7   Part and tooling design can reduce costs.

Standardization may be defined as the process of establishing a definite agreement upon a product, design, size, and quality and physical and chemical characteristics. This type of standardization is sometimes called *industrial standardization,* as contrasted with *managerial standardization,* which deals with procedures, processes, methods, etc. Both afford significant potential for value analysis savings.

Savings from standardization result in numerous ways. Purchase of fewer items in larger quantities means greater discounts. Savings also result from the lower costs to purchase, receive, inspect, stock, and pay the bill. It is less difficult to control inventory and prevent outages when fewer items are involved. Attractive possibilities for standardization are lubricants, cutting oils, hand tools, tops, drills, stationery supplies, and miscellaneous MRO items.

Standardization of design specifications is important. It can be very costly to satisfy a nonstandard call-out for a dimension, angle, flatness, etc. Not only may the item be expensive to produce, but it may require extraordinary time and equipment to inspect. Rejects may be needlessly excessive.

The standards of vendors and the industry should be adopted whenever possible. Unique requirements will cause costs to increase and availability to decrease.

In the designing of a product, maximum use should be made of the same parts throughout the product line. Utmost consideration should be given to the use of the company's own production facilities when designing, particularly when a standard item can be used on several products.

Reduction in the variety of components and materials stocked and available for use by designers can result in major savings. A designer should not select from vendors' catalogs but from a listing of those items standard to his company. Only after justification should a nonstandard item be used. Prime items for standardization include fasteners, packaging materials, bearings, finishes, sheet and coil gauges, bar stock sizes, and wrought and cast alloys.

Standardization programs are set up differently in many companies. Some have a *standards engineer* who works closely with design and product engineering. Others have a *standards committee* which may be made up of

- Product engineering
- Industrial engineering
- Purchasing
- Safety engineering
- Manufacturing engineering

There may be considerable variation in the committee's makeup in various companies.

The advantages of standardization are:

- Lower pattern or tooling expense
- Lower initial and continuing costs
- Lower inventory required
- Reduction of procurement time
- Lower price from the vendor if the purchase order permits fabrication when the vendor's workload is low and delivery from stock as required
- Diversity in selection of sources

Among the disadvantages sometimes cited are:

- Lessened competition if the standard is a one-source item.
- Tendency to sacrifice originality of design, special features, market innovations, etc., in favor of lower costs, which, in turn, can affect sales appeal.
- The danger of restriction of desirable or necessary design changes because of the likelihood of cost increases.
- Loss of profit on original equipment manufacturer's (OEM's) repair parts if a standard, easily obtained part is used. (*Note:* It is the practice of most manufacturers to price repair parts with an extremely high profit margin, and therefore the company may be reluctant to lose the very profitable repair part segment of its business.)

It should be remembered that the specification of one company's product as standard to reduce parts in inventory or because of a favorable volume price is not standardization in the true sense of the word.

Materials

Materials should be chosen because the properties they possess best satisfy the needs of the part in performing its function. These properties may include strength, corrosion resistance, appearance, ductility, conductivity, weight, transparency, dimensional stability, or machinability. Price is important, but only after essential property requirements are met.

Materials are bought by the pound but are used by the cubic inch. Plastics may be more expensive per pound but the piece price may be less. A pound of alumi-

	Specific gravity	Relative parts per pound
Osmium	22.7	1.0
Silver	10.5	2.2
Yellow brass	8.5	2.7
Steel	7.8	2.9
Titanium	4.7	4.8
Aluminum	2.8	8.0
Magnesium	1.7	13.0
Acetal	1.4	16.0
Nylon	1.14	20.0
A B S (acrylonitrile-butadiene-styrene)	1.07	21.0
Polyethylene	0.95	24.0

Fig. 8-8   Effect of materials weight on parts per pound.

num gives nearly three times as many parts as does a pound of brass. The relative number of pieces per pound for some materials is shown in Fig. 8-8.

A material is sometimes chosen to satisfy surface requirements—appearance, reflectivity, corrosion resistance, etc. A low-cost material with a suitable finish added may suitably replace a more expensive material. The finish might be provided by means of electroplating, galvanizing, painting, chemical dips, vacuum metallizing, etc. Plastics generally do not require a finish, whereas metals often do.

The form and condition in which a material is obtained can affect costs. Hot-rolled steel is considerably less expensive than cold-rolled steel. Parts with a hole through the center might be made more economically from tubing rather than from rod. Welded tubing is less expensive than seamless tubing. If a part should require a profile through its length, it can usually be made least expensively from extrusions made with that profile. It is sometimes possible to make stampings from electrogalvanized stock rather than to zinc-electroplate the stamped parts. Stampings are lower in cost when made from automatically fed coil stock rather than from sheared sheet or blanks.

Considerably higher production rates can be realized when the optimum material for the process is used. The free-machining alloy of a metal will probably be best if parts are to be machined. The slight additional material cost is more than offset by lower machining costs. Forging brass allows greater forging productivity than all other copper-base alloys. Aluminum alloy 380 has die-casting properties generally superior to those of other alloys.

Heat treatment of castings can sometimes be avoided by using natural-aging alloys. Heat-treated bar stock and sheet metal can be used to make some parts, thereby eliminating the need to heat-treat the parts.

The scrap generated in making parts has value. The scrap can be sold or perhaps used as raw material for the making of other parts.

Production Methods

There is generally one optimum process for the manufacture of a part, depending upon its configuration, the quantities required, properties, material, tolerances, and finish. Common metal-part manufacturing methods are briefly described and the advantages and limitations of each given in Figs. 8-9 and 8-10.

Sometimes during the lifetime of an item, the optimum production method changes because of changes in the quantities required. A change of production method or of the tooling may well be warranted by piece-price savings. Sand castings might be made as die castings. Short-run stampings might be made in a progressive die. Loose piece patterns for making sand castings can be replaced with a match plate. Powder metallurgy might be used to make small parts which previously required several machining operations.

Consideration of manufacturing methods generally involves make-or-buy decisions. Special consideration should, of course, be given those processes which can be done in-house with known, inherently lower costs and with greater control. Questionable items that might be run on high-production equipment by a specialty supplier should be candidates for make-or-buy decisions.

Assembly Methods

The primary function of assembly is to secure components. It is an essential function but inherently one of low value.

An attempt should be made to eliminate parts and the need for assembly. Not only is the assembly cost saved, but also the costs of the part, fasteners, stocking, handling, etc.

Conventional fasteners include screws, bolts, studs, threads, keys, cotter pins, wire forms, and clamps. Special-purpose fasteners can be money savers in locations of limited access, where several parts must be secured, and where other secondary functions can also be performed by the fastener. Push-on nuts save the use of threaded fasteners and speed up assembly. Self-tapping or thread-rolling screws save tapping of holes. Mating parts made with matching studs and holes can be secured after assembly by flattening the stud as shown in Fig. 8-11.

Metal components can be secured into a single fabrication by means of soldering, brazing, and the many welding techniques. Press and shrink fits are common

Process	Description	Materials	Advantages	Limitations
Sand casting (green sand)	Most sand is packed around a pattern, pattern is removed, and molten metal is poured into cavity. Mold is broken to remove casting.	Iron, steel, heat and corrosion resistant alloys, aluminum, magnesium, nickel, copper, lead, tin, zinc.	Low tooling cost, almost no limit on size or shape.	Close tolerances difficult to achieve, rough surface finish, long, thin, projections not possible.
Sand casting (dry sand)	Same as green sand casting except core boxes are used instead of patterns. Sand is bonded with a binder that sets when core is baked in oven.	Same as green sand casting.	Same as green sand castings, except that long thin projections may be formed.	Limited to smaller parts.
Shell mold casting	Sand coated with plastic resin packed around heated pattern which cures plastic. Shell halves are stripped off, reassembled. Shell is broken away from finished casing.	Iron, aluminum, copper, steel, heat and corrosion resistant alloys, nickel.	High production, good dimensional accuracy, smooth surfaces, uniform grain structure.	Patterns, equipment and mold materials are expensive.
Full mold casting	Sand packed around a foamed plastic pattern. Plastic vaporizes when molten metal is poured.	Iron, steel, nickel, heat and corrosion resistant alloys, aluminum, copper, lead.	Similar to green sand and dry sand casting, but no draft, no flash.	Patterns are expendable.
Permanent mold casting	Molten metal is fed into cavity in metal die blocks. Dies are reusable.	Aluminum, magnesium, iron, steel, copper, lead, nickel, tin, zinc.	Good surface finish and accuracy. High production rate, molds reusable many times.	Initial mold costs are high. Cannot handle high melting point metals, such as steel. Casting intricacy limited.
Die casting	Molten metal forced into a closed steel die at high pressure.	Aluminum, lead, magnesium, zinc, copper, tin.	Good surface finish, high dimensional accuracy, high production rate.	Initial die costs are high. Limited part size.

Fig. 8-9 Parts are made better at less cost when the optimum production method is selected. (*From Materials Engineering, September 1968. Reproduced with permission of Reinhold Publishing Company.*)

Process	Description	Materials	Advantages	Limitations
Plaster mold casting	Slurry mixture containing a special gypsum is poured over a pattern. After setting, pattern is removed, mold is baked. Casting removed by breaking mold.	Aluminum, copper.	High dimensional accuracy, smooth surfaces, intricate parts, low porosity.	Limited to small parts.
Ceramic mold casting	Mold is formed from ceramic powders, binder and gelling agent. Sand break-up can be used, or mold can be all ceramic.	Iron, steel, heat and corrosion resistant alloys, precious metals, copper, aluminum, nickel, zinc.	Close tolerances, intricate configurations.	Limited to small-moderate sizes.
Investment casting	Refactory slurry is cast around a wax, plastic or frozen mercury pattern. When slurry hardens, pattern is melted or baked out.	Steel, aluminum, copper, heat and corrosion resistant alloys, magnesium, nickel, precious metals.	Close tolerance, good surface finish, intricate configurations, no flash.	Limited sizes. Patterns are expensive. Labor costs high.
Centrifugal casting	Mold is rotated. Molten metal introduced in center of mold is thrown to mold wall and held there by centrifugal force until it solidifies.	Iron, steel, heat and corrosion resistant alloys, aluminum, copper, nickel.	Dimensional accuracy. Produces large cylindrical parts.	Limited shapes. Expensive equipment.
Open die forging	Heated metal stock is hammered into required shape. Little or no lateral confinement involved.	Steel, heat and corrosion resistant alloys, aluminum, copper, magnesium, nickel, refractory alloys, titanium.	Tools are simple and inexpensive. Economic for small quantities. Improves strength.	Limited to simple shapes. Difficult to hold close tolerances. Production rate slow. High skill required.

Process	Description	Materials	Advantages	Limitations
Closed die forging	Compressive forces produced by hammer are applied over entire surface of heated metal stock, forcing metal into die cavity.	Steel, heat and corrosion resistant alloys, aluminum, copper, magnesium, nickel, refractory metals, titanium.	Improves mechanical properties, good dimensional accuracy, high production rate, good reproducibility.	High tool costs; machining often necessary.
Upset forging	Matching dies compress material to shape.	Steel, heat and corrosion resistant alloys, aluminum, copper, magesium, nickel, refractory alloys, titanium.	Fairly intricate parts; good dimensional accuracy, high production rate.	Limited to cylindrical shapes. Limited sizes, high cooling cost.

Fig. 8-9 (*Continued*)

Process	Description	Materials	Advantages	Limitations
Cold heading	Similar to upset forging, except metal is cold. Raw material usually is wire up to 1 in. in dia.	Steel, aluminum, copper, heat and corrosion resistant alloys, lead, nickel.	High production rate. Good surface finish. No scrap loss.	Limited sizes and shapes. Leaves residual stresses.
Impact extrusion	Backward extrusion—metal blank in die cavity is struck with punch at high velocity; metal is forced back through space between punch and die. Forward extrusion—blank is struck with punch and moves forward through die opening.	Aluminum, copper, lead, magnesium, tin, titanium, zinc.	High production rate. Good dimensional accuracy. Good surface finish, Low scrap loss. Low tool cost. Good strength characteristics.	Tubular shapes only. Length to diameter ratio is limited. Also, limited part size.
Blanking	Metal is sheared by stressing above ultimate strength.	Steel, aluminum, copper, nickel, heat and corrosion resistant alloys, magnesium, precious metals, refractory alloys, titanium, zinc, virtually any metal.	High production rate. Good surface finish. Wide variety of shapes and sizes.	High tool costs. Limited to thin sections. Sheared edges are rough and subsequent finishing often required. Often involves high materials waste.
Stamping	Metal is stressed beyond its yield strength and permanently deformed.			
Drawing	Special forming operation in which flat blank is pressed into a dished shape.			
Explosive forming	Impact of high pressure waves created by detonating explosive deforms metal blank to required shape.	Steel, heat and corrosion resistant alloys, nickel, titanium.	Suitable for extremely large parts. Low tooling costs. High strain rate believed to improve formability of some materials.	Skilled labor required. Low production rate. Usually limited to symmetrical shapes.

Fig. 8-10 Comparison of advantages and limitations of additional production methods. (*From* Materials Engineering, *September 1968. Reproduced with permission.*)

Process	Description	Materials	Advantages	Limitations
Electromagnetic forming	Electric currents induced in metal workpiece interact with strong magnetic field to produce forces that deform workpiece or force it into a die.	Copper, aluminum, precious metals, steel.	Materials can be worked in hardened condition.	Equipment costs high. Configurations limited.
Electrohydraulic forming	Similar to explosive forming except shock wave is generated by electrical discharge instead of a chemical explosion.	Titanium, aluminum, steel, nickel.	Good finishes, Good dimensional accuracy. Handles parts too large for conventional machinery.	Skilled labor required. Production rate low. Specialized equipment required.
Spinning	Rotating metal disc is drawn over male form by applying pressure from a simple round-ended tool.	Steel, aluminum, copper, nickel, refractory metals, heat and corrosion resistant alloys, lead, magnesium, precious metals, titanium, zinc.	Low cost. Good surface finish. Short lead time. Strength improved through cold working.	Low production rate. Limited to symmetrical shapes. Low tooling costs. Skilled labor required. Limited part thickness.
Powder metallurgy	Metal powders are placed in a die and compressed. Part is sintered in controlled atmosphere.	Iron, steel, stainless steel, copper, refractory metals, aluminum, nickel, precious metals.	Control of density and porosity. High production rate. Low scrap losses. Close tolerances.	Limited shapes and sizes. Not practical for small quantities.
Electroforming	Metal is electroplated to the required thickness on a mandrel which is subsequently removed.	Iron, copper, nickel, precious metals, aluminum, lead, tin, zinc.	Good dimensional accuracy and surface finish. Large and small parts of considerable intricacy.	Low production rate. Skilled labor required. Some limitations on configurations.
Extruding	Heated metal is forced through a die with an aperture of desired shape.	Steel, aluminum, copper, lead, magnesium, nickel, refractory metals, tin, titanium.	Produces a large variety of complex shapes. Low die costs.	Limited size. Parts must have uniform cross section. Close tolerances are difficult to achieve.

Fig. 8-10 (*Continued*)

Process	Description	Materials	Advantages	Limitations
Roll forming	Metal fed through successive pairs of rolls is formed into shapes similar to those obtained by extruding.	Steel, aluminum, copper, magnesium, titanium, zinc.	High production rate. Good dimensional accuracy and surface finish.	Large production runs required for economy. Tooling costs high. Cross section of parts must be uniform.
Continuous casting	Molten metal is continuously fed into a mold, rapidly cooled and withdrawn.	Steel, aluminum, copper, lead.	Low cost. High production rate. Handles alloys that cannot be easily worked.	Uniform cross sections only.

Fig. 8-10 (*Continued*)

means for securing wheels to shafts and rims to wheels. Adhesives available can satisfactorily bond many similar or dissimilar materials. Joints must be designed, however, so that stresses are properly distributed.

Special techniques have evolved for assembly of plastic parts. With proper design, plastic parts can be made to snap-fit together. Solvent bonding and various adhesives can be used. Ultrasonic welding employs high-frequency energy to cause localized melting and bonding of plastic components.

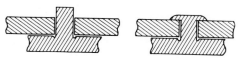

Fig. 8-11   Assembly savings via design or mating of components.

VALUE ANALYSIS IN NONMANUFACTURING OPERATIONS

Since production parts and materials account for the great bulk of purchasing expenditures, value analysis has scored its most dramatic successes in the manufacturing sector. Value analysis can, however, be used effectively in almost any organization or company function in which purchase costs are substantial. Value analysis is practiced in governmental and institutional purchasing departments, public utilities, commercial establishments, etc. It is applied to various nonmanufacturing elements in industry: packaging, transportation, office forms and systems, capital equipment, scrap and surplus disposal, and maintenance, repair, and operating (MRO) supplies.

The process of describing a function, putting a price tag on it, determining if the cost is justified, and suggesting alternatives does not always have to be carried out in the relatively sophisticated manner described earlier in this section. Applied to less complex products in an informal way, it can often produce substantial savings or improvements—or both—in a nonproduction item. Analysis of a multipart office form, for example, might be done informally along the following lines:

What is the function of the form—of each of its multiple copies?

What does the form—and each copy—cost? (An important consideration when forms are used by the thousands or tens of thousands each year.)

Is each necessary—or does it simply duplicate a record that is readily available elsewhere?

Is all the copy on the form necessary?

Can the form be redesigned to simplify typing, thereby increasing the typist's productivity?

This type of creative thinking, or brainstorming, can be employed on an almost endless range of products and services—from audiovisual products to zippered equipment covers. There must, of course, be some probability of savings, and the savings should be proportional to the time and effort required for value analysis. Thus it is important in value analysis, as in other purchasing operations, to select targets from among the 20 percent or so of items that generally account for about 80 percent of the dollars expended. In the greatly simplified range of products just mentioned, a university, for example, probably would be spending more money on audiovisual supplies than on equipment covers, so the former would be a more logical candidate for value analysis.

ESTABLISHING A VALUE ANALYSIS PROGRAM

A prime essential to the establishment of a good value analysis program is that top management completely understand the scope and merits of the value analysis approach to profit improvement and give full and enthusiastic support to it.

With management's support and concurrence, resistance of certain functional areas which must provide the assistance and information vitally necessary to the success of the program will be overcome. Top management support should be in the form of a policy statement, reinforced by written and verbal communications, such as staff meetings, house organs, letters, and special bulletins.

Its Place in the Organization

It is most desirable to have a value analysis team report to a top officer of the company rather than to a functional manager. This will enable the team to cross functional lines in their pursuit of total value. It must be mentioned, however, that in the majority of cases the value analysis team or value analyst does report to a functional manager.

The ideal team or task force will consist of representatives from the following functional areas:

Engineering
Purchasing
Industrial engineering
Quality control
Manufacturing

Functional Areas Involved

The following functional areas should have personnel available for assistance and consultation:

Financial
Marketing
Maintenance
Research and development

Below in outline form, are the responsibilities of the various departments and other interested parties in a successful value analysis program.

Who Is Responsible for What?

Management—Provides Top-Level Support

Defines value analysis/value engineering (VA/VE) goals
Sets up organizational structure
Ensures plantwide cooperation
Establishes priorities
Develops return on investment targets
Coordinates with other programs

Purchasing—Collects and Disseminates Information

Searches for new materials, technologies, and suppliers
Projects market trends of materials and components
Checks availability and lead time
Provides cost comparisons
Works with other departments on standardization
Outlines company goals and requirements to suppliers
Spurs suppliers to participate in VA/VE
Provides guidance for suppliers' VA/VE programs

Marketing—Studies Effect on Sales

Analyzes customer acceptance
Defines optimum price range
Studies packaging advantages
Consults on styling changes
Reviews field service and maintenance factors
Contributes competitive market data

Design Engineering—Evaluates Performance

Defines function
Sets quality standards
Establishes engineering standards
Reviews alternate specifications, materials, and processes
Checks effect of VA/VE changes on other parts
Analyzes tolerances

Industrial Engineering—Evaluates Production and In-Plant Handling Methods

Performs time-motion studies
Evaluates material handling and material flow
Compares manufacturing and assembly processes
Analyzes scrap generation and costs and reviews them with production management

Supplier—Proposes Available Alternatives

Reviews customer's specifications
Studies quality requirements
Submits specific ideas on materials, products, and processes
Gives counsel on industry standards
Analyzes packaging methods
Reports on changing lead times and availability
Provides information on new technical developments

Production—Evaluates Impact on Manufacturing

Provides data on labor: costs, rates, and availability
Defines capital equipment needs
Checks proposed alternate materials from production standpoint
Checks effect of VA/VE changes on other manufactured parts
Coordinates standardization program
Analyzes scrap costs
Acts to overcome line workers' resistance to change

Quality Control—Establishes Quality Criteria

Provides testing program
Sets up acceptable quality levels
Maintains quality standards
Evaluates suppliers' quality control (QC) facilities
Studies suppliers' production reliability
Inspects first-lot samples

Maintenance—Reviews Maintenance and Operating Efficiency

Compares machinery reliability and serviceability
Studies maintenance methods
Defines effect of value analysis changes on maintenance labor hours
Reviews changes and possible improvement in maintenance MRO inventory disbursement techniques and control methods
Reviews and compares suppliers' technical assistance in capital equipment start-up and maintenance

Traffic—Assesses Inbound and Outbound Freight Costs

Compares shipping modes, rates, and distances
Studies containers and containerization
Analyzes materials handling equipment with assistance of accounting
Reviews packaging materials and methods
Evaluates returnable and reusable packaging
Reports on suppliers' shipping facilities

Selecting Proper Personnel

In selecting personnel for participation in the value analysis program, it is a good idea to choose individuals with sufficient expertise to contribute, who in addition are not biased and do not have preconceived opinions which would inhibit constructive action toward total value at the lowest cost. They should be given sufficient authority to request and get assistance and information from both within and outside the company and from suppliers.

Care should be exercised and instructions should specify that the persons selected not make any commitments or imply that they are acting as agents; they are basically coordinators of information. It is imperative that purchasing coordinate all activities with outside sources. Proprietary information, both internal and from suppliers, should be handled with the greatest care to protect all parties concerned.

Personnel in the value analysis task force must be carefully selected. They must practice good human relations, yet be diligent enough to overcome roadblocks. The task force should always have targets established by mutual agreement with management. It should be required to report periodically on all projects.

It has been proven that a properly trained value analysis team, given the opportunity to perform and the necessary organizational support, will justify its existence many times over through savings achieved. Additionally, the existence of the value analysis team will create an atmosphere conducive to achieving total value at the lowest possible cost.

SELECTING, TRAINING, AND DEVELOPING THE VALUE ANALYST

Perhaps most important in selecting potential value analysts are desirable personal traits. It is very difficult, if not impossible, to affect personality characteristics that are not really one's own. Given reasonable intelligence, time, and opportunity, the candidate can obtain the knowledge required, but usually he cannot change his personality and inherent traits to suit the requirements of a situation.

Successful analysts generally possess a high degree of initiative and perseverance. They are self-starters—not easily frustrated by the difficulties they encounter. They are not always extroverts, but they must work well with others. Other desirable characteristics are the ability to organize, creativity, imagination, concern about costs, and maturity—a sense of balance.

Many value analysts are graduate engineers. A lesser number have degrees in business administration. Past work experience may be in design, industrial engineering, manufacturing, purchasing, or estimating. It would be desirable, of course, but not likely, that a prospective analyst have some experience in each.

A knowledge of basic design principles is desirable for an analyst and should include basic physics, part layout, and strength of materials. Some basic knowledge of materials is certainly also desirable. Production methods represent a third important field. The manufacturing capabilities, processes, and procedures of one's own company are important to know. Knowledge of the company product line and customer applications is extremely valuable. Other helpful knowledge areas include packaging, transportation, quality control, and cost accounting.

Value analysis is a specific activity with definite procedures and techniques. These may be learned through reading articles, taking courses, and attending seminars and conferences. It would be well for the trainee to gain some on-the-job training under an experienced value analyst.

Continued development of analysts can be realized through their gaining greater knowledge in the outlined areas. Development is fostered by interchange of ideas and experience between value analysts at seminars and conferences.

MOTIVATING SUPPLIERS TO CONTRIBUTE TO THE VALUE ANALYSIS PROGRAM

Among the strongest and most valuable members of a successful value analysis team are suppliers or vendors. They represent a virtual gold mine of ideas. Their knowledge of their products can save lengthy trials and testing of materials or products which they know, from past experience, will not accomplish a certain function reliably and economically. Vendors appreciate the opportunity to join the value analysis team. Often, when requested, they will utilize their research and development group to supplement the customer's engineering effort.

To justify the extra effort and expense, the vendor may expect some tangible reward or justification for the expenditure of funds and effort. He may expect to be a sole source or at least a major supplier of the item for a period of time. If his company is not competitive on the item value-analyzed, additional business in some other products his company can furnish at an attractive price may be in order.

Some feel that the savings from any implemented value analysis changes should be shared with the supplier as a proper motivator. This was done with government contractors during the Vietnam war and produced some substantial savings. Some companies have also used the sharing of savings with suppliers to good effect, but the practice is controversial and can present some problems, so it should be carefully considered before adoption.

There are many ways suppliers can be motivated to contribute to a company's value analysis program. Among those methods which have been tried and have proved successful are the following.

Lobby Displays

The products which appear to have potential for value analysis savings are attractively displayed. Fact sheets are provided for visiting salespersons, showing the primary function, the material of which the product is made, the approximate annual usage, the usual ordering quantity, and the name of the buyer. An attractive, neat sign in the display area invites participation.

Vendor Clinics

A commodity group, such as packaging, fasteners, and cutting tools, is selected by purchasing. Existing and prospective suppliers are invited to the clinic. Purchasing opens the clinic with an explanation of the objectives and format of the meeting, with assurance that vendor ideas will not be divulged to competitors. The product's function is discussed in detail with the group. The parts are available for inspection by the attendees. A *fact sheet* is attached, or supplied separately, showing pertinent information. Vendor quotations are submitted later in writing. Prices are not discussed at the clinic. Such clinics have proven successful where carefully planned and well run.

The problem of leaving out good prospective suppliers is always present, but where a complaint is received, that vendor may be permitted to quote from the fact sheets which can be supplied.

Invitation to Attend Value Analysis Meetings

Many major companies have found it advantageous to have Vendor Days, to which potential contributor salesmen and engineers are invited. They are asked to suggest better ways to accomplish the function of the products under study. The vendor representatives are permitted to show other items which they feel would be of interest to the host company and to make a very short explanatory talk.

Direct Invitation from the Buyer

The buyer may choose to invite a vendor representative to join a current value analysis study of a specific product or products. He may also invite the appropriate engineer from a vendor company. This is done on an informal basis and may involve a new product, an item or items currently supplied by the vendor invited, or similar items being supplied by a competitor.

Invitation on Requests for Quotation

Some companies print on their quotation request or an addendum sheet attached to the request a suggestion that the prospective vendor recommend changes in material, specifications, or method of manufacture which, in the supplier's opinion, would accomplish the function at a lower net cost (see Fig. 8-12).

All the above means of obtaining supplier help in the value analysis program have proven successful. Each should be reviewed by the value analyst or value analysis committee and selectively utilized, depending upon the company's particular situation or need.

KEEPING THE VALUE ANALYSIS PROGRAM GOING

One of the most important and difficult problems associated with value analysis programs is the maintaining of enthusiasm and keeping the program going after the first year of usually spectacular savings. Initially, management's attention is

REQUEST FOR QUOTATION ADDENDUM   JOHN SMITH COMPANY

VENDOR VALUE ANALYSIS SUGGESTIONS

PART NUMBER OR DESCRIPTION

Note: It is *important* that this form be returned with your quotation, showing your recommendations or indicating that you have no suggestions.

QUESTION	YES/NO	BRIEF DESCRIPTION OF SUGGESTION	Approximate savings if suggestion is approved
1. Would a relaxation of any toler-ances result in lower manufac-turing costs?			
2. Can you suggest any design changes that will lower the cost of the item?			
3. Is there any part of this item that can be produced as a cast-ing, forging, or extrusion, in lieu of machining?			
4. Can you suggest any material substitute?			
5. Are there any finish require-ments that could be eliminated or relaxed?			
6. Are there any test requirements that appear unnecessary?			
7. Have you any other suggestions which might save weight, sim-plify the part, or reduce the cost?			
8. Do you have a standard item that can be satisfactorily sub-stituted for this part? What is it?_____ What does it cost?_____ Is it qualified?_____ What would a qualification test cost? _____			

The above information submitted by
Company name
Signature
Date

Fig. 8-12   Form requesting value analysis suggestions from suppliers often accompanies requests for quotations.

focused on its profit-contributing potential through workshops, seminars, special reports, etc. Manufacturing and engineering select projects for study, a committee is established and meets regularly, and it is assumed that the program will continue from the initial momentum. It will not! Management must not assign a value analyst to the program and then remove him every time engineering experiences a heavy workload. Regular committee meetings must not be discontinued because some members feel that other work is more important. Stimuli must be regularly injected into the program and arrangements made to assure sufficient projects for study.

Here are some proven methods of maintaining enthusiasm and keeping the program's effectiveness at a high level.

Publicity and Reports

Utilize a purchasing department publication, containing reports of successful projects, editorials slanted at value analysis, cartoons, and personal items of interest regarding personnel doings. Monthly reports of actual accomplishments against targets for all participating plants or divisions are very effective. They stimulate participants to greater effort and keep the responsible executive advised as to how his plant's or division's performance compares with that of others.

Lobby Displays

Lobby displays may be utilized to invite suppliers to participate in the value analysis program. They will keep vendors' interest high. A display board with actual successful examples of contributions by suppliers serves to stimulate other vendors to participate.

An award, or Certificate of Achievement, is sometimes awarded to those vendors who have made outstanding contributions to the program. The vendor is proud to receive this award, which may prove helpful in his sales efforts with other companies.

Workshops, Seminars, and Group Meetings

Company value analysis workshops can be very effective. The plants or divisions bring suitable purchased or self-manufactured parts for value analysis study. These parts—or components—should be either fairly complex, used in high volume, or of high dollar cost. The small companies may find group discussions and reviews of projects with the buyers or committee members very effective. Individuals select items as value analysis projects and set a target for the amount of cost reduction they expect to achieve and the date the project is to be completed. Progress or completion is reported at regular monthly meetings.

All these methods will prove helpful in keeping the value analysis program going. In addition, a considerable amount of creative thinking or ingenuity is called for in publicity, program format changes, and program name changes, such as to Value Achievement, Value Assurance, or possibly Value Improvement. Planned maintenance of the program is imperative or it will "die on the vine."

Ingenuity in soliciting suppliers' ideas and a fair system for rewarding the sources that come through are key factors in making the most of suppliers' value analysis know-how.

COMMON PROBLEMS IN VALUE ANALYSIS PROGRAMS

There are a few common problems experienced by both large and small companies in their value analysis program, and it is well to know what they are so that plans may be made to overcome or minimize them:

Obtaining approval on projects by engineering or the approving functional group after completion by the value analyst or committee.

Overcoming objections of the sales department to the design change of a part in current production which would also affect all replacement parts for units in the field.

Keeping the top-caliber purchasing specialist or engineer on the job when the current workload of regular business in the plant greatly accelerates. (Too often, in such cases, a poor replacement is placed in the job.)

Convincing the skeptical that value analysis is not "buying a cheap item"—that it will in some cases mean paying considerably more to achieve a lower end cost.

Overcoming the natural tendency of many people to resist change.

Determining what should be included in value analysis programs versus cost reduction programs.

SUMMARY

Utilization of value analysis techniques and the job plan as detailed in this section may be summarized by the following sequential steps:

Examining the function of each part of the product in terms of what it is and what it does—analyzing the reasons for using present material, manufacturing processes, components, and other factors—and determining exactly how much each costs.

Accumulating as many ideas as possible for reducing costs without sacrificing the essential function—the more ideas, the better the chance of increasing value—calling on all available sources of specialized information, both inside and outside the organization.

Evaluating the ideas coldly, realistically, and objectively, and eliminating those that fail to measure up to such yardsticks as: Is it too expensive? Is it too complicated? Will it create more problems than it solves?

Studying carefully the ideas that remain—measuring them in terms of cost, application, availability, and other pertinent factors—and checking with specialists for further information and data.

Programming for implementation and making formal recommendations—weighing such alternatives as make-or-buy decisions—helping suppliers solve problems that the changes may create for them—seeing that everyone concerned has a clear understanding of the recommendations.

Following up to make sure that recommendations are put into effect, promptly and properly.

Results to be expected from a successful value analysis program strongly supported by top management and involving materials, products, procedures, and services are:

Reduction in costs resulting from accomplishment of the function at a lower cost

Greater sales because unnecessary costs will be removed, thus keeping a company's products more competitive in the marketplace

Better customer acceptance because of the concentration of more attention on the maintenance or improvement in quality and function accomplishment of products and product components

A desirable atmosphere of questioning costs and improving products and services within the company which motivates greater participation at all levels

NOTE: For further information on subjects covered in this section see the list of references in Section 30.

Section **9**

Buying the Right Quality

EDITOR

C. L. Blue, C.P.M. *Manager of Procurement, Supply, and Business Services, University of California, Lawrence Livermore National Laboratory, Livermore, California*

ASSOCIATE EDITORS

Al J. Manthos, C.P.M. *Manager of Purchasing, Varian/Eimac Division, San Carlos, California*

Ted Black *Quality Control Engineer, Varian/Eimac Division, San Carlos, California*

C. B. Bishop *Specifications and Standards, Mechanical Engineering Department, Lawrence Livermore National Laboratory, Livermore, California*

R. L. Morton *Quality Assurance Office, Lawrence Livermore National Laboratory, Livermore, California*

Allen J. Levy *Quality Assurance Office, Lawrence Livermore National Laboratory, Livermore, California*

M. L. Vyenielo *Reliability and Quality Control, Electronics Engineering, Lawrence Livermore National Laboratory, Livermore, California*

What is quality? Why it is necessary? How is it obtained? The quality of a product is a measure of the degree to which the product meets the requirements of the immediate purchaser, the intermediate fabricator or assembler, the distributor, and the ultimate consumer of the end product.

BASIC FACTS ON QUALITY

Quality requirements may include, but are not limited to:

Dimension	Finish
Weight	Appearance
Chemical analysis	Design
Physical properties	Value for the price
Performance characteristics	Reliability

Quality is necessary for user satisfaction whether the user is the immediate purchaser, an intermediate processor or handler, or the ultimate consumer.

Quality is obtained:

By accurately specifying the requirements
By selecting vendors who have the capabilities and know-how
By mutual understanding of the purchaser's needs
By the exercise of adequate quality control in the producer's operations

Quality specifications cannot be written in detail into every purchase order or purchase agreement, but a quality specification is a necessary part of every purchase agreement. This may be accomplished by reference to:

Established buyer specifications
Established vendor specifications
Blueprints
Catalog references
Trade names
Engineering association specifications
Industry association standards
Government specifications

Selection of vendors may be made: [1]

By a specific investigation involving one supplier and a single transaction
By a choice from an established list
By a routine selection based on experience
By use of a well-established, well-known company

Mutual understanding of the purchaser's quality needs is an essential element of good vendor-user relationships and is accomplished:

Through adequate and accurate specifications
Through education of vendor by visitations of qualified purchasing personnel
Through review of the vendor's performance to ensure compliance
Through prompt contact on quality problems through established channels

Quality control in its broadest sense includes:

The organization and procedure through which a producer measures and controls the quality of the product manufactured
The specifying of purchase requirements
The on-site surveillance of the manufacturing process where appropriate
The inspection and acceptance of incoming parts
The assurance of compliance on the part of the supplier with specified quality levels by education, including field representative reviews
The contacting of vendors on quality problems
The handling of rejected items
The financial and accounting aspects of rejections

[1] Also see Section 6.

Quality control is the responsibility in some degree of all of the following functions or departments, whether separately organized or in combination:

Sales	Purchasing
Engineering	Technical
Manufacturing engineering	Receiving
Production	Incoming inspection
Quality control	

However, the purchaser (buyer) has the basic responsibility of adequately and accurately specifying the quality requirements. In turn, the supplier has the basic responsibility of satisfying the quality requirements in conformance with the mutually agreed-upon price and time schedule.

QUALITY DEFINITIONS

The definition of the word *quality* and the meaning of *quality control* have gained much significance in connection with modern manufacturing needs. These help in the close control of necessary requirements of material analysis, dimensions, makeup, and performance specifications. From the buyer's standpoint, an acceptable definition of quality is that established by the American National Standards Institute (ANSI Z1.7) and the American Society for Quality Control (ASQC A3), i.e., *the totality of features and characteristics of a product or service that bear on its ability to satisfy a given need.*

From this it will be seen that, as far as the buyer is concerned, the mere fact that an article is good, or best, or highest priced does not necessarily mean that it has the required *quality*. From the standpoint of the purchase order specification, an item is not of adequate quality unless it does the required thing in the needed manner.

It may be assumed from this that job specifications or performance requirements must be written into every purchase order agreement. To attempt to do so on every order is impossible from a practical standpoint and is too time-consuming and costly for the benefits it may bring.

What it does mean is that the *quality specification* is a necessary part of every purchase transaction. The purchase order must state what the item is required to be and/or do. The quality specification may be expressed in terms of size, weight, dimension, color, kind, reliability, or performance, or in any other terms necessary so that the vendor supplies what the buyer needs. To assist in the use of the information which follows, please keep the following definitions in mind. They will help to avoid confusion with terms which are sometimes used to describe different activities not covered here:

Quality.   Quality refers to the power to accomplish; the capability of doing a certain thing; or the establishment of a specification of capability of doing a certain thing.

Quality Control. For the purpose of this handbook *quality control* is meant to apply only in the area of purchased items obtained from suppliers. It is not to be confused with the quality control of items produced within the buyer's own plant or business. See also Responsibility in the Quality Control Department, later in this section.

Necessity and Benefits of Quality Control

There are many reasons for the control of quality on purchased items, all of which will add up to profit dollars for the buyer's company. One important reason is that it avoids confusion between buyer and seller in determining what is required, etc.; correct understanding will result in improved supplier relationships.

The legal aspects of the quality control program are important. Without a clear statement of needs on the purchase agreement and without full understanding of the needs by the vendor, there can be legal responsibility on the buyer's part if the vendor ships under an honest misunderstanding. The buyer may than find himself responsible for all or for a part of the defective goods if the quality requirement on the purchase order was incomplete or not clear.

It should be noted that losses incurred by the ultimate customer (the user) which are traceable to defective quality may be recoverable through lawsuits against the purchaser and/or the supplier.

Production requirements are met in time and in the needed quality by material or parts which meet the quality specification. High costs always result from:

Rejection of shipments
Resultant production delays
Extra rework costs
Excessive quality specifications
Extra handling of rejections and replacements
Extra inspection of rejections and replacements
Lowered quality of finished items made from or with poor-quality components
Increased production time in buyer's plant

Lowered costs will result from the right thing (the specified quality) at the right time for the buyer's needs. As in the case of all purchases, a lower price may also result when the vendor is able to produce well and continuously material and parts which meet the buyer's quality specifications on delivery.

Traceability

Included in the quality control concept is a new quality requirement which is being termed *traceability,* meaning that a part is completely traceable in all of its handlings and processings—sometimes even to the basic raw material (metals as they come from the mine, etc.).

Although traceability is not a feasible characteristic for ordinary commercial products, the alert purchaser should be aware of this highly technical quality requirement, as the impact of such programs may well have an effect on many of our commercial and industrial activities.

RESPONSIBILITY FOR QUALITY CONTROL

The need for quality control, broadly speaking, makes it the responsibility of everyone in the buying company and the selling company. Its cost benefits are so great that every good employee of both buyer and seller will do everything possible to ensure good material and parts on the first delivery.

From a practical standpoint, however, it is well to pinpoint some of the areas of responsibility. These will vary from industry to industry and may be different within companies in the same industry, depending on conditions and products and sometimes on organizational setup. It may be necessary to examine several plans and company setups and to alter them to suit the particular problem or industry. It is essential, however, in every organization that management delegate to the purchasing department the responsibility to question and challenge quality requirements.

The following ideas work in some instances. One of them, a combination of several, or parts of them may give the most workable setup for effective quality control.

Responsibility in the Purchasing Department

Quality is a prime responsibility in the purchasing department regardless of where the quality specifications actually originate. The buyer's job is not finished with the placing of a purchase order; the purchased item must be delivered on time and be of the correct, specified quality.

Where quality specifications are not severe and where the purchase requisition may be originated in the purchasing department, the quality specification is often established or coordinated with the issuance of the requisition.

Where the quality specification may be complicated, and particularly where performance is expressed as a function of the purchased item, the quality specification may be the responsibility of other departments within the buyer's company.

There are several departments and activities where the prime responsibility of quality specification of purchased materials may be placed. Some of these are discussed under appropriate headings.

Whether or not the purchasing department has the responsibility of originating or coordinating the quality specification, it is accountable for seeing that the quality specification is part of purchase agreements.

The purchasing department *must:*

1. Know what is wanted and pass the information on to the bidders and to the vendors
2. See that the vendor performs according to the purchase quality specification

3. Take necessary steps to protect the buyer's company against financial loss from material or parts which do not meet the purchase specification

4. Utilize suggestions from the vendor where they promote desirable quality and reliability

To accomplish the above, it will be necessary for the buyer on occasion to enlist the assistance of others (both inside and outside the buyer's company) to develop and make workable the purchase quality specification.

The buyer does not start negotiations or ask for bids on an item of purchase (the nature of which requires a quality specification) without having available to him sufficient information to permit the prospective supplier to submit an intelligent and realistic bid. Under such circumstances the buyer sees to it that a proper specification is developed so that the buyer's company, and the prospective vendor, may be protected from financial loss which can result from poor-quality material or defective parts or from claims arising out of lack of understanding of what is required. In some instances the vendor may be given an opportunity to review and participate in establishing the quality specification.

In spite of all preliminary precautions, material may be rejected by the buyer's receiving inspection as not meeting the purchase quality specification. The purchasing department is then responsible for the negotiations leading to the disposition of any extra costs which may have been incurred.

The vendor notification of rejected items and the subsequent negotiations regarding the disposition, credit, etc., involved should be the responsibility of the purchasing department. It is desirable that these negotiations be handled with the vendor by the same buyer who handled the original purchase. The person who does the buying is in a better position to negotiate rejections of materials than others in the buyer's company for several reasons, among which are the following:

1. The buyer was instrumental in the negotiation of a mutually acceptable agreement; i.e., the purchase order was placed by him, and he is familiar with the entire picture.

2. Vendors will be more receptive to resolving quality problems and negotiating quick turnaround and/or replacement if they are dealing with the person responsible for placement of new business with their company.

The purchasing department is the focal point for the buying company's procurement quality control program and will enlist all the help necessary from within the company to make it function effectively on purchased items.

Responsibility in the Engineering Department

The establishment of the purchase quality specification is in many instances the responsibility of the engineering department because of the technical complexity of the item involved. In order to fulfill this responsibility, the engineering department must document the specification in terms of performance, characteristics, reliability, mechanical strength, chemical composition, size, weight, etc. Additionally, the engineering department must work in conjunction with the purchasing department to select a qualified vendor.

Direct contact between engineering representatives of the buyer and the vendor will greatly aid in the clarification of the specification. Such contact with engineering may be more appropriate during formulation of the specification and in evaluating a potential vendor's capabilities. Whenever possible, however, such contact should be made with the knowledge of the purchasing department.

Responsibility in the Production Engineering Department

In some industries, production engineering is responsible for the quality specification of purchased items. This duty may be prime; i.e., the production engineering department may originate the specification or may coordinate it with the material requirement (such as on the bill of material, etc.) so that the quality specification appears on the requisition to purchase. Where it is not the originator, the production engineering department should, at a minimum, review the quality specification for completeness, accuracy, and suitability for production use.

Responsibility in the Production Department

In some instances it is advisable to have the production department establish or cooperate in the development of the purchase quality specification. This is especially true in the case of capital equipment intended for production use and for facilities used by, or under the control of, the production or operating department.

It is also customary for the purchase quality specification on supply items (such as expendable tools, wheels, bits, etc.) to be originated by or controlled by the production or operating department.

Where the production department is not primarily responsible for the origin of the purchase quality specification for raw materials or components parts, it is important that the needs of the production department be carefully established and reflected in the development of the quality specification. The purchasing department's cooperation with the production or operating departments at this point, as well as after receipt and during use of purchased items, pays big dividends in lowering production costs and increasing profits.

Responsibility in the Quality Control Department

Sometimes it is useful to have one group responsible for checking on quality problems and the maintenance of quality control by the vendor. Where such a function exists in the buyer's company, it may be advisable, and it is frequently the custom, to charge the quality group with responsibility for quality of items purchased as well as for quality of items to be produced or processed in the buyer's plant. Where this is the case, the quality control department may have the prime responsibility for issuing the purchase quality specification. In other cases it is desirable to leave this prime duty in other departments (as in engineering, etc., as before mentioned), with the quality control department acting in an advisory capacity in the preparing of this specification.

The on-site involvement of representatives of the quality group at the vendor's facility to perform in-process and end-item inspections will greatly enhance the assurance that the quality specifications have been complied with. Such involvement will also afford more expeditious resolution of problems and will in many instances result in significant reduction in the degree of inspection or test required upon receipt at the buyer's facility.

Where a quality control group exists within the buyer's company, it is desirable that such group have responsibility for incoming inspection in order to:

1. Capitalize on the information available through on-site inspections
2. Provide the positive link between the buyer's shop operation and the purchasing department

The quality control group can, as well, be utilized to conduct surveys of potential vendors in conjuntion with the purchasing department.

Responsibility in the Receiving Department

This is the point at which deviations from the purchase quality specification may become evident. Adequate inspection facilities (of people, space, and tools) are a prime requisite of receiving and of receiving inspection functions. When possible, the inspection activity should be carried on in or closely adjacent to the receiving area. When it is necessary to perform one or more of the inspection checks at a point removed from the receiving area, an in-transit check should by controlled by the receiving department until the incoming shipment has been accepted or ejected. When rejections are made, the receiving department will see that proper notification is forwarded to the purchasing department with sufficient details as to the reason for the rejection so that the vendor may be notified. The receiving department will continue to have physical jurisdiction over rejected material until disposition is received from the purchasing department; or in some cases the receiving department will release the material to some department that has been agreed upon, which in turn will retain the shipment until such disposition. (Among the latter will be the segregated area which is designated for rejected materials awaiting disposition and the so-called material review board (MRB) which has become popular in metalworking industries such as the aircraft industry.) Regardless of how the organization may be set up (i.e., wherever the quality specifications may originate), it appears that the following items are a necessary part of the receiving department's contribution to a smooth-working quality control program

1. Incoming shipments must be checked immediately on receipt for possible shipping damage and to see that the weight, count, etc., agree with the shipper's forwarding documents and appear to be substantially within the quality or amount specified on the buyer's purchase order.

2. Receiving inspection must be performed as soon as possible to determine whether the quality specification on the purchase order has been met and the received item is within the specified quality limits. (See Determination of Quality later in this section.)

3. Where unacceptable parts (or material) have been received, the shipment must be segregated and notification forwarded to the purchasing department of the reasons for rejection.

4. Adequate records must be maintained for the purpose of material-vendor identification in the event latent defects arise during operations at the buyer's facility subsequent to receipt.

Responsibility in Other Departments

There will be other departments in many companies which will have an interest in and some responsibility for the quality specification for purchase and for the quality control program with respect to purchased items. These will vary with the industry, the company, and sometimes the product, but a few of the activities which have some interest are listed here.

Matériel or materials division
Material control
Production control
Production scheduling
Research
Technical

Often activities such as these will have the responsibility of originating purchase requisitions against which the purchasing department issues an order. Some of these may have the prime responsibility of the purchase quality specification and may operate from a central specification file. Where they do not have the prime responsibility for the purchase quality specification, it is necessary that they be accountable for coordinating the quality specification so that it appears on the requisition at the time of issuance or that reference is made in such a way that the quality requirement becomes an integral part of the requisition to purchase. The buyer's sales department also has an interest in proper quality control, although perhaps on a more general basis. For example, it may be desirable (or even necessary) that sales departments obtain from customers their needs in the form of definite and acceptable quality standards. These quality requirements will be passed on to other departments within the buyer's company so that these departments in turn can incorporate these requirements in the buyer's quality purchase specification.

EFFECTIVE QUALITY CONTROL PROGRAM
REQUIREMENTS

An effective quality control program is generally comprised of a detailed system of checks and balances. The buyer need not be knowledgeable in every facet of the program, but he should at a minimum be aware that the quality control program includes the following:

1. Specifications of quality which may develop from
   a. The needs of buyer's own products of production
   b. Customer
   c. Those within buyer's company who design, plan, schedule, control, purchase, etc.

2. Responsibility for the establishment of the quality specification by such departments as engineering and production engineering, as already enumerated

3. Responsibility for passing the quality specification to the vendors

4. Responsibility for adequate incoming inspection to be assured of receiving the required quality

5. Responsibility for checking and reporting to the purchasing department any items rejected for quality deviation

6. Responsibility for negotiation for the return and replacement, for credit, etc., of rejected materials

HOW QUALITY IS EXPRESSED

Quality may be expressed in various ways, but it is important that it be done in a manner which will clearly show what the item is intended to be or to do and what the buyer expects to receive. It is important not to overspecify, and it is not necessarily true that the highest-priced material is the best quality for the intended use. Methods of expressing the purchase quality specification follow.

By Blueprint or Dimension Sheet

This is a common way of establishing the quality specification in metalworking, building, or other industries where dimensional limits are required. When using these, the information must be clear, the dimension completely specified, the tolerance (if any) expressed, and the language or terminology not ambiguous. Blueprints or dimension sheets may originate from sources such as the following:

1. Customers' drawings or specifications.

2. Central specifications file. (Some purchasing departments have their own or a duplicate of their engineering department's specifications file.)

3. The engineers or others in the company who prepare the requisition for the purchasing department.

The blueprint of dimension-sheet method has the advantage of inviting competition and establishing the buyer's right to inspection and rejection on agreed standards. Its disadvantages include the cost and time of preparing specifications.

By Industry Standard

Particular requirements of certain industries and industry groups have developed a type of need which has come to be expressed as an industry standard. Such standards are frequently outlined in sufficient detail and with enough exactness to make it satisfactory to refer to them as part of the purchase quality specification. An industry standard may also be an American Standard.

In addition to industry or company standards, various common-use standards are frequently used as an American Standard issued by the American National Standards Institute. These include:

MS—Military Standards
ASME—American Society of Mechanical Engineers
ASTM—American Society for Testing and Materials
NEMA—National Electric Manufacturers Association
SAE—Society of Automotive Engineers
USP—United States Pharmacopoeia
Federal and state specifications

Standards such as the above, and many others which are not listed, are the outgrowth of much experience in use and represent an accurate and understandable quality specification. Where they fit the buyer's needs, or when the needs can be adjusted to take advantage of an existing industry standard item, important savings of time and money can often be made, because such items are quickly available at lower cost, and with better-quality acceptance, than are many tailor-made products or materials.

By Brand or Trade Names

Continued manufacture and merchandising of a product or material to consistent quality standards over a long period of time will often establish the brand or trade name as an effective and dependable standard of quality. Where such a brand or trade name has been found satisfactory, the buyer is often safe in specifying it as his purchase quality specification. Often it may be satisfactory to specify a brand name or trade name "or equal." At other times, however, it may not: even within a brand name, manufacturers have a way of introducing small changes in their products without notifying buyers. If such is the case, purchasing by brand or trade name will not be adequate.

There are many brand or trade names of industrial and commercial products which have been well established through long usage and which can be used as acceptable quality standards. The buyer may establish a list of his own which will provide an effective and convenient way of transmitting the purchase quality specification to bidders and to suppliers. Using brand names has the advantage of simplicity but may limit buying to a single source for a particular product and thus destroy the competitive element desirable for sound procurement. Therefore, whenever the cost of preparing a specification is deemed advisable in order to stimulate competition among brand manufacturers of a like item, the procurement should be made by specification rather than brand name.

By Chemical or Physical Specification

In the case of chemicals, metals, etc., it is sometimes necessary or desirable to specify composition of purchase materials.

Companies in the chemical business and firms that compound purchased items for resale frequently have their own chemical specifications on the material which they purchase. Where such specifications exist, they should be attached to the purchase order to establish the quality specification desired. Another way to handle this is to furnish the bidders and vendors with a master copy of the specification which is coded or identified in such a way that a purchase order reference will clearly establish the quality specification desired. (An example of this might be a paint company which specified on its purchase order "our XYZ specification aluminum bronze" to a supplier who had a copy of XYZ specification.) Where metal alloys are purchased and industry standards do not cover the necessary requirements, the chemistry of the alloy should be specified to make sure that the vendor will furnish the correct quality.

By Performance

On occasion the function of performance of a purchased item is a significant portion of the quality specification. Where performance is specified, it is important that the required behavior be as simply expressed as possible, with the performance limits of variables (where such exist) clearly specified. It is not unusual for the purchaser to disregard completely the appearance or the composition of a purchased material and simply specify work which is expected of the purchased material. The purchase order may specify a metal as follows:

Example Must be suitable for forming 90-degree bends by drop hammer without rupturing and must withstand operating temperatures of 1100°F without appreciable surface oxidation evident after 72 hours of such temperature.

In this case it will be seen that appearance does not have any bearing on the quality specification, and that the purchaser does not care about the chemical makeup of the metal as long as it meets the performance requirements.

Similarly, in the electronics industry, the purchaser may specify the input signals available and the outputs desired from a black box, leaving the internal circuit design to the supplier. Here again the purchaser has no interest in the internal makeup of the black box, as long as the unit meets the quality, reliability, and performance specifications.

By Sample

Where the quality specification cannot be established clearly or satisfactorily by any of the previously mentioned means, it is well to furnish a sample of the item desired to the vendor for duplication. In using the sample for quality specification, the following points are important:

1. The sample must be of sufficient size or quantity to permit easy matching.
2. The limits within which acceptance can be effected should be specified. (As an example, color samples are often furnished in textiles, paints, etc. Wherever possible, the color variation permissible should be expressed in relation to a common factor of whiteness, such as magnesia, and to a color-rating scale, such as that furnished by Keuffel & Esser. Paint color should be rated both wet and dry.)

Combination of Specifications

Where the needs (the quality specifications) cannot be clearly expressed by any one of the means covered, a combination of two or more may be used to advantage. The quality specifications should be as short and as concise as possible but should not sacrifice exactness or clearness for brevity. In whatever manner quality is specified, the buyer should know what he wants and needs, and the vendor must also know what the buyer expects to get. Any compromise with these requirements means the possibility of shipments which will not meet the quality specifications and which will result in expensive rejection.

Brand X or Equal

Occasionally the design engineer will specify "Brand X or equal," particularly where he is cognizant of several suppliers producing the identical desired commodity, i.e., identical in terms of quality, reliability, performance, price, and delivery. To the layman such a specification would seem to simplify the buyer's task. To the experienced buyer, however, such a specification presents a greater challenge. He must now make more detailed comparisons between potential suppliers in order to ascertain which one is most suitable to his company's needs. Consideration of freight rates, financial terms, and the supplier's reputation will become significant factors. In the final analysis the buyer's task is to identify the difference factor which is of benefit to his company and consequently influences his selection.

In the purchasing environment, "or equal" is an inadequate specification, and as such it should alert the buyer to search out those factors which make apparent equals become unequals for his company's benefit. When the "or equal" designation is used and an alternate product is offered, the relevant characteristics (such as size, weight, performance, etc.) must be evaluated. A buyer may also specify that interchangeability with an old product is one of the requirements of the new product he is purchasing.

The Buyer's Quality Primer

> **Q**uestion the requirements
> **U**nderstand the requirements
> **A**ssure conformance
> **L**isten to the vendor
> **I**ntegrate quality, cost, and schedule
> **T**hink, for
> **Y**ou are responsible

THE APPROVED BIDDERS' LIST[2]

Where an item or material is substantially a tailor-made one for a particular purpose, an approved bidders' list may be established by the buyer. The list will consist of those vendors who can satisfactorily supply the product to the buyer's

---

[2]Also see Section 6.

quality specification. The problem involved in establishing an approved bidders' (or vendors') list are too numerous to allow a complete coverage in a quality specification or quality control discussion. However, it is not possible to establish such a list without carefully appraising vendors from the quality standpoint.

As an important and effective tool of the quality control program and its contribution to lower costs, it is necessary that alternate sources be established on all purchased items. At least two sources should be maintained at all times, and where possible it may be desirable to have more than two vendors on the approved list of suppliers. In having an alternate source, the buyer will be able to maintain production within his own plant pending resolution of any problem which is a development of a quality rejection of purchased materials or parts. In addition, the availability of a number of qualified sources will enhance the price competition, a factor which is always of benefit to the purchaser.

DETERMINATION OF QUALITY

Assurance of quality is, of course, an essential consideration in planning for the evaluation and selection of qualified vendors. Once a supplier has been selected, however, determining compliance with the required quality is perhaps the most involved and probably one of the most important parts of a good quality control program. To function effectively, quality determination should be made immediately on receipt of the shipment. For this reason the receiving inspection function should be located in the receiving area or as close to it as possible. This will avoid expensive handling and rehandling and save time in releasing correct material or parts to the production department or to production stores. The physical layout, the personnel, and the equipment of receiving inspection are not often the responsibility of the purchasing department, but the purchasing department will have a substantial interest in the workings of this group and will cooperate closely with it in quality determination efforts and in developing standards, as well as in the prompt handling and disposition of rejected shipments. The starting point for receiving inspection is a copy of the purchase order with the quality specification clearly spelled out or supported by referenced standards or attached documents. Figure 9-1 shows a typical purchase order attachment dealing with reliability test requirements.

Receiving inspection provides for the verification of materials with the purchase order to determine whether they meet the quality specification on the order. Such determinations might include (but may not be limited to) quality, weight, size, count, appearance, odor, dimension, color, performance, and composition. With some components, inspection may be destructive, e.g., with fuses, flash bulbs, or matches.

Such verification is not always completely possible within the geographical area of receipt and will be supplemented by additional or supplementary checks performed by engineers, chemists, production personnel, etc., at points which may be far removed from the receiving area itself.

RELIABILITY TEST REQUIREMENTS

GENERAL

This purchase order attachment requires that parts manufactured for _____ as specified on this order be tested to the requirements on Form 3260. These tests are performed periodically on sample units taken in accordance with the instructions contained herein. Performance of these tests prior to shipment of the lot shipments sampled is not required but should be completed as promptly as possible after the end of the manufacturing period. Although double sampling and testing is permissible, _____ will pay only for first sample tests and for the units destroyed in these tests. Payment for these tests is subject to acceptance by _____ of the certified test results reported on Form 3260. These test results should be sent to _____ Receiving Department.

1.   GROUP C TESTS

1.1   Testing to measure the reliability of a component, or to test the conformity of the design, construction, and materials shall be conducted by the seller at periodic intervals. The Group C tests shall be performed in the order listed on Form 3260.

1.2   Units of the same general construction shall be grouped for the purpose of Group C inspection. Classification of units for such grouping is supplied by the buyer. Sample size to be tested will be governed by the sampling table referenced on Form 3260. An exception to grouping shall be made when the part is first produced or production is resumed after a lapse of more than four months. In this case samples from the parts produced will be subject to Group C tests in accordance with test requirements of Form 3260.

1.2.1   Those characteristics which assure conformance to the procurement specification and which measure the conformity to design, processes and material shall be designated as Group C.

1.2.2   Life tests shall be designated as Group D.

1.2.3   The list of Group C and Group D characteristics shall be supplied to the seller on _____ Company Form 3260 (Reliability Test Certification).

1.3   All units withheld for Group C inspection shall have successfully passed Group A and Group B inspection.

1.4   A portion of each week's production shall be randomly selected during a three-month or other specified manufacturing period and held as samples for Group C tests. The number withheld shall be proportional to the rate of production and be sufficiently large to provide for both the first and second sample. The samples selected shall be as evenly distributed and as representative as possible. At the end of the manufacturing period as specified in Section 1.4 or 1.5, the seller shall perform, or have performed by a testing laboratory approved by the buyer, all required tests listed on Form 3260. At the completion of the testing, the results shall be immediately forwarded to _____ Company Receiving Department.

1.5   The sampling interval set forth in Section 1.4 shall be increased to four months when three successive lots have successfully passed Group C tests.

1.6   If an outside testing laboratory is used, so indicate in the proper column and supply the name and address of the laboratory on the form.

1.7   All units manufactured for the buyer shall be identified with a unique mark or code to identify manufacturing period. This mark or code shall be supplied to the buyer on Form 3260.

1.8   If any sample unit fails any of the Group C tests, the seller shall immediately notify the buyer and furnish a written record of the cause of failure and proposed corrective action. The buyer will reply as promptly as possible as to whether the proposed corrective action is acceptable or whether additional information or alternative steps will be required.

1.9   No further shipments of the type represented by the sample shall be made until authorized by the buyer.

Fig. 9-1   Specimen purchase order attachment on reliability test requirements.

1.10 Units which have been subjected to Group C inspection shall not be shipped to the buyer, unless specifically requested.

1.11 If, in the manufacture of a unit, seller proposes a change in (a) materials used, (b) manufacturing process, (c) construction, (d) place of manufacture, the buyer is to be notified in detail. However, changes shall not be binding upon buyer unless evidenced by a purchase order Change Notice issued and signed by buyer.

2.0 GROUP D INSPECTION:

2.1 Where the item is of a type that requires life testing, details of the test will be supplied by the buyer on _____ Company Form 3260 (Reliability Test Certification). Group D testing need not be performed prior to shipment.

2.2 Sample size shall be in accordance with the sampling table referenced on Form 3260. The sampling interval shall be the same as provided for Group C inspection unless otherwise specified.

2.3 Samples for Group D testing shall be selected in the same manner as set forth in Section 1.4. Samples shall have passed Group A and Group B tests, but shall not have been submitted to Group C tests.

2.4 Group D test results shall be forwarded in accordance with Section 1.4.

2.5 Failure to pass Group D inspection shall be handled as established in Sections 1.8 and 1.9.

2.6 Samples which have been subjected to Group D tests and second set of samples not requiring testing shall be shipped to the buyer only on issue of a Change Notice to the purchase order. Overshipments against production orders will not be accepted.

2.8 Questions concerning these requirements or need for additional copies of instructions, forms or sample tables should be referred to the responsible _____ Buyer.

THIS ATTACHMENT, WITH ITS TERMS AND CONDITIONS,
IS AN INTEGRAL PART OF THIS PURCHASE ORDER.

NAME OF COMPANY   PURCHASE ORDER ATTACHMENT

Fig. 9-1   *(Continued)*

Where such verification must be performed at another point and in another department, it is important that the responsibility for the material being tested remain with the department performing the receiving inspection.

Sampling

Where material or parts are received in large volume, it is expensive and time-consuming to inspect 100 percent of the material or parts so received. Several shorter methods of determining quality have been found satisfactory in some industries and for some products or materials. As an illustration, the custom of physically counting small parts will often give way to an agreed weight-quantity determination between the vendor and buyer. (For example, miniature bearings may be sold and accepted on the agreed basis of 1 pound avoirdupois being equal to 10,000 bearings. This eliminates the herculean task of physically counting, which may not be worth the time and expense involved.)

Among the methods of quality determination the *statistical sampling method* is quite popular. This method operates on the basis of taking samples of a predetermined size or quality, inspecting them, and accepting or rejecting the entire shipment on the basis of the quality evaluation of the sample. Mathematically it has been proved that statistical sampling will operate satisfactorily within predictable limits, and savings of inspection time and money can be realized without adversely affecting the accuracy of quality determination. Statistical sampling operates on the basis of published mathematical tables. It is not necessary to understand the mathematical background of these frequency tables to be able to use them successfully. Tables such as those in *Computation of Sampling Inspection Tables*,[3] by H. F. Dodge and H. G. Romig, have successfully replaced haphazard selection or the arbitrary selection of any given percentage with a method of predictable success.

When we sample, we acknowledge that we are willing to tolerate a proportion of defects in the accepted lot, and that we may accept a lot that has a higher percentage of defects than had been specified.

Terms frequently referred to in the discussion of acceptance sampling are *acceptable quality level* (*AQL*) and *lot tolerance quality* (*LTQ*). When assurance is sought regarding the percent defective, the latter becomes *lot tolerance percent defection* (*LTPD*).

AQL is defined as the poorest quality, or the highest percent defective, that will be considered acceptable. When it is associated with a given sampling plan, it may be inferred that a large percentage of the lots will be accepted if the process average equals or is better than the AQL. The risk of having a lot rejected from a process of AQL is called *producer's risk*. In many sampling plans producer's risk is about 5 percent.

LTPD specifies what the consumer considers to be barely tolerable quality. It is usually specified when the consumer is concerned with a particular lot rather than a stream of lots. The consumer desires the risk of accepting lots of barely tolerable quality, or worse quality, to be low. This risk, called *consumer's risk*, is frequently set at 10 percent.

Types of Sampling Plans   Sampling plans can be classified in two categories:

- Attribute plans: A sample is taken from each lot, and each unit is classified as good or bad. The number of bad units is then compared with the allowable number stated in the plan, and a decision is made to accept or reject the lot.
- Variable plans: A sample is taken, and a measurement of a specified quality characteristic is made on each unit of the sample. These measurements are then summarized into a simple statistic (e.g., sample mean), and the observed value compared with an allowable value defined in the plan. A decision is then made to accept or reject the lot.

The success or failure of the various techniques suggested here and others which may be in use will depend on using samples of the proper size and distribution so that sufficiently accurate results are obtained. Where heavy product mortality occurs suddenly with an old and established vendor on an item which he has been

[3]Published by John Wiley & Sons, Inc., New York.

producing successfully, it will be desirable to "back up" on inspection techniques by increasing the size or frequency of sampling. This remedial action may take the form of 100 percent inspection of all shipments until the cause for the discrepancy has been determined and the remedy made effective. Samples must be random. Each item in the lot should have an equal chance of being selected. If there are 10 boxes of an item, a sample should be taken from all 10 boxes. If there is only one box, samples should be selected from all layers and all corners rather than from the top layer only.

Among other receiving inspection techniques will be those required by special products or requirements, particularly where performance checks must be run prior to acceptance. In those instances the gauges or instruments utilized in the measurement of the performance by the vendor and the purchaser should have a common standard of calibration to preclude measurement inaccuracies.

The prime standards for physical measurements (dimension, voltage, current, temperature, etc.) are maintained and controlled by the National Bureau of Standards, Washington, D.C. 20234. It should be mentioned as well that for a nominal fee the Government Printing Office will supply a copy of *Sampling Procedures and Tables for Inspection by Attributes* (Apr. 29, 1963), which is most useful in establishing various acceptable sampling plans.

REJECTIONS

Rejections should be handled promptly and with good judgment. There are many sound reasons for such action, a few of which follow. The protection of the buyer's production needs and the cost factor which is so quickly affected by poor parts and material are probably the prime reasons for handling rejections quickly and carefully. The matter of public relations with suppliers and the obtaining of maximum cooperation in speed of remedy of the trouble causing the rejection—as well as reducing the costs of rejections—are also important aspects of this activity.

The mechanics of rejection should be such that notification and complete details are given to the purchasing department as soon as possible after the rejection. The paperwork phase of this procedure is quite important in some companies, and it is not uncommon to use a copy of the rejection notice for the vendor's notification after proper approval by the purchasing department. See Fig. 9-2 for a sample rejection form, which also serves as vendor notification of rejection.

It is important that the purchasing department get the rejection notice promptly with full information for cause of rejection. The vendor should have full information at once so that he can take the necessary steps to replace the defective shipment with proper parts or material which will meet the purchase quality specification.

The responsibility for actual rejection of material lies within the department that performed the receiving inspection. The responsibility for resolving the rejection (disposition of the material) lies within the purchasing department. For reasons previously stated it is advantageous to have the buyer who originally negotiated the purchase handle the rejection with the vendor.

Promptness in determining the quality of a shipment is the first requirement. The second requirement is immediate notification of the purchasing department, with full details as to the reason for rejection. After these two requirements are

Form 6301-1

UNION PACIFIC RAILROAD COMPANY Order No. ____

REPORT OF OVER, SHORT, REJECTED OR DAMAGED MATERIAL

Report No. ____

Firm Name ____ ____ (Location) Date ____ 19__

Street ____

City ____ State ____ Order No. ____ Date ____ 19__

MATERIAL ORDERED		MATERIAL RECEIVED Shipping Notice No. ____ Date ____ 19__	
QUANTITY	DESCRIPTION	QUANTITY	DESCRIPTION

REMARKS:

Rejected Account ____

Nature of Defect ____

or Damage ____

What does waybill cover? ____ (No. & kind of containers)

Were all items shown on waybill received? ____

MATERIAL PREVIOUSLY RECEIVED

Over ____

Short ____

Receiving Sheet No. ____ Date ____ Car No. ____ W.B. ____ Date ____

Seals (Side) ____ (End) ____ Condition of Container when received ____ F. B. ____ Date ____

Weight Gross ____ Tare ____ Net ____ Whose Scale? ____

ACTION TO BE TAKEN AS INDICATED IN SPACES MARKED (X) BELOW:

1. ( ) Make immediate shipment {of material reported short / to replace rejected material} {transportation charges prepaid / transportation charges collect}
2. ( ) Furnish disposition together with return goods tags for material to be returned to you {transportation charges collect / transportation charges prepaid}
3. ( ) Render credit memorandum for incorrect or rejected material promptly upon receipt of return shipment
4. ( ) Excess or incorrect material will be retained
5. ( ) Adjust charges for material retained
6. ( ) Form {5805 / 5846} No. ____ Date ____ has been rendered reporting loss or damage in transit

Above rechecked and found to be correct ____ Storekeeper ____ Stockman

NOTE: All correspondence, return goods tags and other pertinent data pertaining to this report should be mailed to the undersigned promptly showing action taken. Please show reference to the order number as well as number and date of this Form 6301-1 on Invoice, Credit Memorandum, and all Correspondence.

Yours very truly,

Fig. 9-2 Combination rejection form. Also serves as vendor notification of rejection. *(Reproduced by permission of Union Pacific Railroad Company, Los Angeles, Calif.)*

met, the buyer will have several choices of action in the disposition of the rejected shipment.

The action selected by the buyer will vary, depending upon the circumstances, but will include the following:

1. Notify the vendor of the cause of rejection so that corrective action may be taken on future shipments and on work in process at the vendor's facility.

2. Explore (with the help of others within his company) the possibility of salvaging the shipment by:

   a. Diversion to another less critical use within the buyer's plant.

   b. Taking corrective action on the rejected shipment in the shape of rework procedures which may make it comply with the purchase quality specification. (This rework may be performed by the buyer, the seller, or another, based on an agreement which should be reached with the vendor in advance of the work and the rework expense.)

  3. Reject the shipment and ask the vendor for disposition and credit.

The investigation of salvage is always a sound one. It will not only save time in getting the correct item into the buyer's production, but is also keeps the seller's cost at a minimum. Rework or diversion to another less critical use will often save much, if not all, of the cost of items which may otherwise have only scrap value. When a vendor's costs are kept at a minimum by such a common-sense approach to the rejection problem, relations with the supplier will most certainly improve.

Cost of Rejected Shipments

The cost of rejected shipments will not prove to be entirely the worry of the vendor, even if he credits in full or replaces at no charge the particular item which is rejected. The vendor's own overall cost, upon which his price to the buyer on future orders must be based, will be affected by expensive rejections. It will be to the buyer's interest to work closely with the supplier on rejections and on the remedy which will be desirable following such rejections (see Vendor Quality Rating and Vendor Quality Education in the following pages of this section).

During the period of time in which the rejection is under discussion and prior to the time when disposition of the rejection shipment is determined, it is desirable to segregate the rejected shipment. Unless this is done, there is the possibility of loss or damage during the time in which the return or replacement is being negotiated. There is also the possibility that the material or parts may be placed into the buyer's production or production stores by mistake if it is not segregated and clearly marked with rejection tags, etc. In order to preclude loss, damage, or inadvertent use, it will be beneficial to provide a separate controlled area for rejected material until disposition can be determined.

The policy of segregation of rejected shipments has several advantages in addition to the protection against unauthorized usage by the buyer's production department. One advantage is that it provides an "as is and where is" location where the vendor can physically inspect the rejected material. If there is a discussion on quality and on quality determination, the buyer should arrange for the meeting and conduct the proceedings in order to ensure proper control of the negotiations. During such discussions, it is often possible to determine the possibility of rework either by the buyer or by the seller.

Minor differences can often be adjusted by work which the buyer can conveniently perform at his plant. Where this can be done, the expense of boxing, transportation, handling, etc., for return to the seller can often be saved. Where such salvage is not possible, the vendor may be able to make the necessary adjustments on the rejected items, or will replace the shipment with items meeting the purchase quality specification. When determining the method of diversion, rework, or return, the buyer will keep in mind the relative cost of the method and the possibility of providing from it an acceptable item under the purchase quality specification.

Establishing Rejection Costs   Under whatever method is selected or whatever combination of methods that fit the case, the buyer should determine as soon as possible the vendor's responsibility and the amount of the costs involved which the vendor is expected to assume. In establishing the financial basis on which rejected shipments are returned, it will be useful to determine the following:

1. The point of shipment of the rejected item and with what identification, so that it can be quickly handled in the vendor's plant.

2. Whether shipment is to be made collect or prepaid, the method of shipment, and/or the carrier. (When a vendor is paying this bill, he may want to select his choice of these items.)

3. Whether the incidental costs of transportation, packaging, handling, etc., are for the vendor's account on both the original and the replacement shipment (if there is a replacement).

Among the steps necessary in connection with adjustments will be the following (the selection of any one or any combination will depend on the circumstances of the rejection and on other factors which will influence each particular case):

1. Withhold payment of invoices for items received until after acceptance by receiving inspection.

2. Where a bill has been paid and rejection made after payment, debit the vendor's account with the value of the rejected shipment or withhold payment of a like amount in other billings of the vendor.

3. Arrange for replacement shipment (if there is a replacement) or an even exchange for the returned shipment, or bill the rejected shipment to the vendor and instruct him to invoice for the replacement shipment.

4. Instruct the vendor as to whether he is to make the replacement shipment on the original purchase order or whether a new purchase order will be issued to cover the replacement.

5. Agree with the vendor on the procedure to be followed in the settling of any other financial details, which may include items such as the following:

    a. Transportation

    b. Packaging charges and handling

    c. Cost of extra inspection time

    d. Cost of lost production time

    e. Loss of associated parts or materials

    f. Any other loss or damage which may have occurred

In most cases, the rejection of shipments and the settlement for them are simple and clear-cut; however, the matter of contingent liabilities may be quite involved. Where contingent costs are involved, the original purchase order with a clearly stated purchase quality specification will be found invaluable.

With a complete and clear understanding at the time of purchase, and with a written record of the purchase quality specification, it is usually only a question of mechanics and careful handling on the part of the buyer to effect a speedy and fair settlement with any good supplier. In large companies, where there is usually a large volume of paperwork in the purchasing, receiving, and accounting functions, it is common practice to debit the vendor for rejected material and to have him remit, or the buyer will deduct on the basis of the vendor's credit memorandum. A replacement shipment can then be billed in the regular manner by the vendor and any difference in count etc. which may occur will be a matter of written record.

VENDOR QUALITY RATING [4]

A valuable purchasing tool is a vendor rating based on the quality of material or parts which he delivers to the buyer. Often this can be included with the vendor's performance rating insofar as delivery schedules are concerned. Receiving inspection records (where the results can be tabulated and watched over a period of time) will soon show the purchasing department whether the vendor is a good one and whether the buyer is buying at the lowest cost when the quality of the vendor's shipments and his performance over a period of time are taken into account. Many types of analyses and reports can be developed from a study of a vendor's performance, and most of them will be tailored to the needs of a particular company or to a particular product or material.

An arbitrary determination of unsatisfactory performances based strictly on a flat percentage of failures may be unfair to vendor and buyer alike. As an example, where the major or minor type of discrepancy is the basis for rejection or acceptance, the proper weight and evaluation should be given to the vendor who is heavy in one or the other. It is unfair to penalize a vendor who has a high percentage of deviations in the minor range, but it may be necessary to take decisive action against a vendor who has a relatively low percentage of rejects that are all in the major category.

Samples of such vendor performance rating charts are shown in Section 6. Although differing by company and by item, such charts generally include the following:

1. Vendor's name
2. Material or part identification
3. Period of time covered
4. Quantity delivered
5. Quantity accepted, rejected, or both

In some cases the above list will be expanded to show the number of items in the total requiring inspection. In other cases it will be desirable to show the major and minor (see Determination of Quality, earlier in this section) performance of the vendor. Other variations will suggest themselves, but it is important that the

[4]Also see Section 6.

conclusions drawn from such evaluation be arrived at with care and with complete and up-to-date information. It may be possible to obtain a vendor performance check very simply, such as by accumulation of copies of rejection notices against particular vendors and making calculations from the totals which these show. Before developing a form for purchasing department use, the receiving and receiving inspection forms should be examined to see whether the information is not already being accumulated on a form which can be adapted to purchasing department use.

Since quality determination is so much a community responsibility and activity, it is recommended that the purchasing function work closely with all related functions which have interest in or information to contribute to the vendor quality performance rating chart.

VENDOR QUALITY EDUCATION

A sound quality control program for purchased items begins with the following rules:

- The vendor must know what the buyer wants.
- The vendor must know how to meet the buyer's quality requirements.
- Specification must be covered in the purchase negotiation and by the purchase order.

Earlier discussions cover the matter of telling the vendor what is wanted. How to meet such requirements is equally important. Primarily, it can be considered the vendor's responsibility and in his interest for him to know how to produce properly the item on which he bids and for which he accepts orders.

It is the buyer's responsibility to select vendors who by their experience, facilities, and knowledge (as well as their past performance) are fitted to fill a purchase order in accordance with the buyer's purchase quality specification. The buyer will select alternate sources of supply, each vendor being considered capable of supplying in a satisfactory manner the items required by the buyer. On such a basis the vendor education phase of a buyer's responsibility starts with the selection of the bidders, each one of whom should be potentially a satisfactory supplier from the standpoint of the purchase quality specification.

In purchasing standard items which require only superficial inspection, much reliance can be placed by the buyer on sources which have supplied satisfactory products over a long period with no appreciable difficulty insofar as quality is concerned. Where the item is new, where the application is new, or where the specifications take on new significance because of the new use, a new selection of vendors is frequently indicated.

The selection of new vendors should be approached with care. The buyer should enlist the help of engineers, production people, quality department personnel, and any others who can help in the factual analysis of prospective suppliers. Often the basic requirements of a good vendor will be summarized on a check or rating sheet similar to that shown in Fig. 9-3. Such a preliminary analysis of a

---

FIELD LIAISON REPORT ON
PROSPECTIVE SUBCONTRACTOR

NAME OF COMPANY _____

ADDRESS _____

TELEPHONE NUMBER _____

ACTIVITIES ENGAGED IN _____

NAMES AND TITLES OF EXECUTIVES

_____

I GENERAL INFORMATION

1. STATE NUMBER OF PRODUCTION EMPLOYEES _____

2. STATE NUMBER OF EMPLOYEES BOTH PRODUCTIVE AND NON-PRODUCTIVE _____

3. HAS COMPANY PREVIOUSLY DONE SUBCONTRACT WORK FOR RYAN? _____

4. IS COMPANY INTERESTED IN DOING SUBCONTRACT WORK FOR RYAN? _____

5. IF SO, WHAT CLASS OF WORK? _____

6. TOTAL FLOOR SPACE AVAILABLE _____

7. TYPE OF BUILDING OR BUILDINGS _____

8. CONDITION OF BUILDINGS AND OFFICES _____

9. GENERAL HOUSEKEEPING CONDITIONS _____

10. ARE LIGHTING FACILITIES ADEQUATE? _____

11. DOES THIS COMPANY UNDERSTAND THAT IF FOR ANY REASON RYAN WORK IS FARMED OUT, THE RYAN LIAISON INSPECTOR MUST BE NOTIFIED IMMEDIATELY?

II INSPECTION FACILITIES

1. DOES THIS COMPANY HAVE A SATISFACTORY INSPECTION ORGANIZATION? _____

2. NAME OF CHIEF INSPECTOR _____

3. CHIEF INSPECTOR'S PAST EXPERIENCE _____

4. TO WHOM IS THE CHIEF INSPECTOR RESPONSIBLE? _____

5. DOES THE CHIEF INSPECTOR HAVE FINAL AUTHORITY TO ACCEPT OR REJECT WORK? _____

6. ARE INSPECTORS RESPONSIBLE TO ANYONE OTHER THAN INSPECTION SUPERVISORS OR THE CHIEF INSPECTOR?

7. IN THE EVENT THAT THIS COMPANY DECIDES TO ACCEPT SUB-CONTRACT WORK FROM THE RYAN AERONAUTICAL COMPANY WILL IT AGREE TO MAINTAIN AN INSPECTION ORGANIZATION ACCEPTABLE TO THE RYAN QUALITY CONTROL DEPARTMENT?

8. THIS FACILITY HAS BEEN ASSIGNED CLASS RATING* _____

GENERAL COMMENTS

*CLASS   A   LIMITED ONLY AS TO TYPE OF WORK
              B   QUALIFIED WITH LIMITATIONS LISTED IN GENERAL REMARKS
              C   NOT APPROVED BY INSPECTION DEPARTMENT

DATE _____ PREPARED BY: _____

Fig. 9-3 Preliminary check sheet used to rate a prospective vendor. *(Reproduced by permission of Ryan Aeronautical Company, San Diego, Calif.)*

prospective supplier will help the buyer in establishing a good, dependable source insofar as the vendor's potential production of quality items is concerned. The preparation of such charts or rating sheets will follow the needs which are indicated by the buyer's business and by the products which are to be purchased. Care should be exercised that all the critical items, the potential trouble spots, be recognized and covered thoroughly in the survey.

The vendor survey is the opening part of the buyer's vendor quality education. In the survey the buyer's requirements, his method of operation, and frequently his manufacturing and inspection methods are covered in enough detail so that the vendor knows what will be expected when he gets a purchase order.

Further education may be necessary after a vendor has been placed on the approved list, and this will be governed by the items which are to be furnished and the quality specification to be applied. When further education is needed, it should be apparent to the buyer at the time the requisition is received, and the buyer should then prepare to assist, where necessary, the vendor's efforts to meet the quality specification of the purchase order. Such education may take several forms (as discussed below in Methods Used in Vendor Quality Education), and the type of education, as well as the extent of the effort expended by the buyer's company, is something which will be varied with the buyer's judgment of the benefit to be gained. It is not wise to attempt to lead vendors by the hand in quality education matters. It is better to carefully select sources which have the knowledge and the facilities to produce the quality specified by the buyer. The buyer should interest his own company in vendor quality education and in quality supervision of a vendor's production only to the minimum extent necessary to provide a quality product at the lowest possible cost. A vendor who requires constant supervision, even though his quality performance is good, may be leaning too heavily upon the buyer for technical support, and for that reason he may be a costly supplier. The buyer should keep his education and technical advice efforts to suppliers at a minimum in order to protect the buyer's own cost.

METHODS USED IN VENDOR QUALITY EDUCATION

Some of the education required by the vendor is basic and must be supplied by the buyer no matter how simple the quality specification. To take care of this basic information need, the following actions by the buyer are frequently found helpful:

Explain the quality specification.

Show the vendor the buyer's plant, operation, or use of the purchased item.

Discuss the quality specification and/or the use of the item with other members of the buyer's company, such as engineers, production specialists, and inspectors.

Demonstrate to vendor any special tools or procedures to determine quality of incoming items

Visit vendor's plant, possibly accompanied by technical people from the buyer's organization who can help in vendor evaluation and vendor operations insofar as they affect quality of parts to be furnished to buyer.

The purchasing department, with the support of technical help from within the buyer's company, should establish the extent and the method of the vendor's education. Where such education, and particularly vendor supervision, is required in any substantial amount, other sources of supply should be established.

Where necessary or desirable, particularly in the beginning of production of a new part or material (or one which is tailored to the buyer's specification), the purchasing department should request the help of engineers, production quality personnel, etc., in whatever efforts are necessary. In some cases this may result in the vendor having the buyer's technical personnel stationed in the vendor's plant during initial production of the item.

QUALITY AND PRODUCT LIABILITY

In respect to quality, the old concept of *caveat emptor* is dying. The emphasis now is in the opposite direction: manufacturers and suppliers are being held responsible when products fail to perform as intended, advertised, or warranted. A broad base of product liability cases involving settlements in favor of end users has been established. Some settlements have been great enough to bankrupt the supplier defendants.

It is imperative for producers to satisfy precisely the requirements of the purchase order or applicable contract. Purchasing managers, in turn, have a responsibility to monitor supplier performance insofar as quality is concerned, to minimize the possibility of liability claims against their own companies.

Manufacturers who control their quality assurance systems and whose products are designed and manufactured to meet the requirements of a standard or a customer specification are in a position to issue a certification to that effect. When such a certification is based on adequate records, there is reasonable protection against product liability. The records referred to may consist of, but not be limited to:

1. Chemical and physical analysis of the materials used in the manufactured product
2. Detailed operator instructions describing methods and use of tools and inspection methods
3. Detailed procedures describing the various processes used such as brazing, welding, plating, fastening, and cleaning
4. Flowcharts illustrating the manufacturing steps involved in fabrication of the product
5. Routing sheets describing each of the steps in and locations of the manufacturing operations

6. A complete set of drawings with critical dimensions and related notes for each part and assembly that make up the product

7. Close control over materials and parts when being moved about and when stored in stockrooms

8. The ability to identify the materials used in each finished assembly and to trace the material back to the supplier of the material

With all the government and private agencies constantly placing additional demands upon industry and business—agencies such as the Occupational Safety and Health Administration (OSHA), Fire Prevention and Control Administration (NFPCA), Environmental Protection Agency (EPA), National Athletic Injury Reporting System (NAIRS), Food and Drug Administration (FDA), Consumer Product Safety Commission (CPSC), National Electronics Injury Surveillance System (NEISS), Government/Industry Data Exchange Program (GDIP)—close attention must be paid to meet these requirements to avoid costly court cases.

SUMMARY

A good, effective quality control program has the following objectives:

Quality and reliability consistent with the requirements of the purchased items
Lowest possible cost consistent with delivery of the required quality to the buyer's production point with minimum handling and supervision

The responsibility for a good quality control program is a wide one and probably rests in some degree on everyone in both the vendor's and the buyer's organizations. Pinpointed responsibilities are necessary to make a good quality control program work. These will vary from industry to industry, from company to company, and even within the same company, depending on the products involved.

The responsibility of the purchasing department in a good quality control program is usually in the category of transmission of specifications to, and negotiation with, the vendors. In some companies the purchasing department may have other responsibilities, including the creation of adequate quality specifications. If departments other than purchasing have the responsibility of originating the purchase quality specification, they have the responsibility of transmitting that specification to the purchasing department along with the purchase requisition.

Quality and the purchase quality specification may be expressed in several ways. It is important that a clear and unmistaken expression of the buyer's needs be part of every purchase order. Among the ways in which quality can be expressed are the following:

1. By blueprint or dimension sheet
2. By industry standard
3. By brand or trade name, by catalog number
4. By chemical or physical specification
5. By performance

6. By sample
7. By an approved bidders' list
8. By combinations of the above

The determination of quality and the comparison of items received from various vendors are usually a function of the receiving department and/or the receiving inspection activity, which should be closely located and allied with the receiving area. This inspection group should be required to furnish a rejection notice and rejection details to the purchasing department.

When an incoming shipment is rejected as not meeting the purchase quality specification, the purchasing department should be so notified with sufficient information so that the vendor can be contacted. Negotiations with the vendor on the points of replacement costs should be the responsibility of the purchasing department and should preferably be handled by the buyer who negotiated the purchase. The buyer, with the aid of others in his organization, will carefully explore all possibilities of diversion or salvage by rework, etc., where this results in lower cost than outright rejection and return. The buyer will protect his company by negotiating cost settlements with the vendor and will establish the method of handling such settlements with a minimum of confusion and paper work.

Vendor performance ratings on quality will be found useful in reducing the buyer's cost by eliminating vendors with a high rejection record.

The buyer will take whatever precautions are necessary to ensure that the vendor has the necessary education and know-how to produce items to the buyer's quality specification. Such education will be simple or involved as the circumstances may dictate and will include others in the buyer's organization who can assist the vendor in meeting the purchasing quality specification.

The broad aspects and the substantial benefits of a successful quality control program are many, and the buyer will carefully and intelligently approach all angles of this problem, beginning with the time and purchase requisition is received, so that the purchase order when issued has a complete and easy-to-understand purchase quality specification.

NOTE: For further information on subjects covered in this section see the list of references in Section 30.

Section **10**

Price Considerations

EDITOR

Myron E. Frye   *Vice-President, Corporate Purchasing, Maremont Corporation, Chicago, Illinois*

ASSOCIATE EDITORS

Wayne D. Adams, C.P.M.   *Corporate Director of Purchases, J. M. Huber Corporation, Houston, Texas*

Gary L. Fratilla, C.P.M.   *Manager, Corporate Contracts, NCR Corporation, Dayton, Ohio*

The basic responsibility of the procurement function is to obtain the greatest value at the lowest cost. Value is determined by numerous factors, but primarily by quality and the function to be served. Cost is the actual amount of money expended to deliver a commodity to the buyer's point of use. This cost principally consists of the base price, applicable discount, terms of sale, and transportation cost. Other factors to be considered include applicable taxes and insurance, the ease of handling—involving packaging, palletization, or bulk handling—legal restrictions, and usually numerous miscellaneous additional costs.

The buyer must be diligent in searching out any special factors which could influence the net final cost of a purchased item. Some of these unusual pricing considerations can be very obscure and difficult for the buyer to identify, particularly in dealing in an unfamiliar marketplace such as a foreign country.

In a highly competitive market where there are numerous suppliers, all producing materials of equal quality and offering the same services and reliability, price considerations usually become the dominant factor. Price as it relates to cost of manufacture, or as it is affected by supply-demand conditions, will be covered in Section 11. Price from the standpoint of the value of the article to the buyer is the subject of Section 8.

This section examines the various factors that must be considered to arrive not only at the right price but, of more importance, at the net final cost to the buyer. How to arrive at the latter, i.e., final cost, is covered by the following Section 11. Also recorded in this section are sources of information from which a buyer can obtain pricing information in his particular field of interest. No attempt is made to set forth specific trade or industry practices, because these vary widely with industry and geographical location. This information must be developed by the buyer.

PRICING TYPES

To establish a binding contract, a definite consideration must be set forth in the purchase order. This may be either a specific price or a basis for determining a final price.

Under the Uniform Commercial Code, explained in Section 4, there is a binding contract through the purchase order even though there is no price or other definite consideration set forth in the body of the purchase order. This is particularly true on standard items that have an established market price. It is therefore important to avoid misunderstanding and possible lawsuits by inserting either a specific price or a basis for determining a final price in the body of the purchase order.

The most commonly used types of pricing will be discussed in the following paragraphs.

Firm Price

This is the most commonly used pricing in day-to-day purchasing transactions. It simply means that the price agreed to by buyer and seller when the order is placed or the contract executed will not change until the material is delivered and the transaction completed. This agreed price may apply to a specific quantity of material for delivery on a set date schedule or even to an undetermined quantity within a set time period. Generally speaking, the establishment of a firm price should be the basic goal of the buyer for each order unless extenuating circumstances in the market indicate that it would be to his advantage to make other provisions which could result in a lower net final cost.

Price in Effect at Time of Shipment

This means that the price paid by the buyer will be that charged by the seller on the date shipment is actually made. This type of pricing is usually requested by the seller for two reasons:

1. Major raw materials are obtained on and subjected to a public commodity exchange-type market. Examples are raw materials based on agricultural products, such as vegetable or animal oils, tallow and grease, and imported material such as cocoa and castor beans and oil, or on minerals, particularly imports which are subject to world market pressures and fluctuations in money rates of exchange.

2. Wage and material costs are increasing rapidly during periods of strong inflationary pressures and heavy consumer demand in a particular industry or the economy as a whole. During such periods, it is difficult for the manufacturer to determine his costs over an extended period of time. Generally, the price to apply

at time of shipment can and should be tied to published market prices or to the manufacturer's published market price on the date of shipment.

Whenever a seller quotes *price at time of shipment,* it behooves the buyer to investigate carefully the effect this pricing term may have on his cost and to determine if the price he will ultimately be charged is fair to both the buyer and the seller. Relative bargaining power and market conditions are involved. Many times, if the buyer resists this method of pricing, a firm price can be established. If this is not possible, the buyer should make every effort to tie the price at time of shipment to a published price schedule or establish a fair escalation based on applicable published indices for labor and material.

Price with Escalation Clauses

Such clauses are usually employed in a contract to reflect changes in the cost of labor and/or materials involved in the manufacture of the product. Escalator clauses are generally used in long-term raw material contracts of several years' duration. Under certain economic conditions, they may also be encountered in the procurement of major capital equipment requiring an extended period of time for manufacture. Changes in material and labor costs are generally tied to the applicable costs as determined by published indexes such as those of the Bureau of Labor Statistics, *Iron Age,* and the American Iron and Steel Institute. They also may involve changes in transportation costs, taxes, and fixed costs.

To develop an equitable escalator clause, the buyer and seller must first agree upon the proportion of the total price represented by materials and labor. They must next agree upon published indices which fairly reflect material and labor cost changes over the time period involved. A typical escalation clause for both material and labor would be:

> Twenty percent of the base price shall be adjusted by an amount in proportion to each increase or decrease from the base value in the average of the final monthly indexes for Industrial Commodities, as published in the monthly booklet entitled *Wholesale Prices and Price Indexes,* issued by the Bureau of Labor Statistics, U.S. Department of Labor, for the 12-consecutive-month period ending on September 30 of the calendar year immediately preceding the then current calendar year, such adjustment to be calculated to the nearest $\frac{1}{100}$ of $0.01 per pound. The base value referred to above shall be the average of the final monthly indexes for industrial commodities as published by the Bureau of Labor Statistics, U.S. Department of Labor, for the period October 1, 19—, through September 30, 19—.
>
> Ten percent of the aforementioned price element shall be adjusted by an amount in proportion to each full $0.01 increase or decrease from the base value in the average of the final monthly index of average hourly earnings for the Manufacturing Group, Chemicals and Allied Products as published in Table C-2 entitled "Gross Hours and Earnings of Production Workers," issued by the Bureau of Labor Statistics, U.S. Department of Labor, for the period October 1, 19—, through September 30, 19—.

Escalation clauses can easily be developed for equipment which may take a year or more to manufacture. For such items, the main concern is usually the increase in the cost of labor. The buyer should be wary of escalating the cost of materials or component parts because the manufacturer has usually included a contingency factor in his bid and figures he will be able to purchase such materials and components more cheaply than at the price used in the bid. Usually the seller will be able to commit for most of his material requirements at fixed prices as soon as he gets the equipment order. If the seller insists upon escalating materials, he should be made to set forth in his bid the base price for the major materials and components, and the buyer should pay only the actual increases in cost experienced by the seller for such materials.

Cost-Plus Pricing

Cost-plus agreements are most frequently encountered not only in construction or service contracts but also in the procurement of major items of capital equipment which require extended periods to manufacture. Such contracts contemplate reimbursement to the contractor or supplier for the actual cost of the work involved plus a specified compensation.

Such pricing is justified only when there is a high degree of risk in the work to be done, so that costs are difficult to estimate accurately. Under such conditions demanding a firm price would result in all bidders including a high "insurance" factor in their quotations. In accepting a cost-plus contract, the buyer is willing to accept this risk, assuming that he has found a reputable supplier and can help to control the costs of the project.

Cost-plus contracting is generally considered in private industry as the least desirable method of contracting if there are any alternatives. Certain types of cost-plus contracts are either prohibited or their use is severely restricted in government procurement. Buyers directly or indirectly involved in government work are advised to thoroughly familiarize themselves with the regulations governing the use of such contracts.

The term *cost* usually includes the following:

1. Cost of all material, labor, and services directly applicable to the job
2. Taxes applicable to the job payroll and insurance premiums or bonds specified in the contract
3. Cost of hand tools and rental of special equipment necessary for the job
4. Other overhead costs as defined in the contract

The compensation to the contractor can be either a fixed amount or a percentage of the actual cost as defined above. Several variations of this pricing term may be used, so that it is important for the buyer to understand the differences among such variations. In all cases, the compensation usually includes an agreed share of the contractor's general overhead, administrative expenses, salaries, and expenses of executive offices, plus profit. See also Section 18.

Cost Plus a Percentage of Cost

Under this arrangement, the supplier receives as his compensation a predetermined percentage of the total cost of the project. See also Section 18.

Guaranteed Maximum Cost Plus Fixed Fee

Under this arrangement, the supplier sets a guaranteed maximum cost for the project and a fixed fee as his compensation. See Section 18.

Estimated Cost Plus Fixed Fee with Underrun Incentive

To provide an incentive, when the owner and supplier arrive at a mutually agreed estimated cost, in addition to the fixed fee, the buyer may agree to split with the contractor any savings effected by efficient work such that the actual cost of the project is less than the estimated cost. See Section 18.

Detailed Factors in Cost-Plus Contracts

In a cost-plus type arrangement, there are many factors which must be carefully detailed in the contract because they have appreciable effects on the ultimate cost to the buyer. The following factors are very important in their effect upon the final cost.

1. The scope of the project must be carefully defined, as well as what constitutes a change of scope. In a fixed-fee or a guaranteed-maximum-plus-fixed-fee contract, the method of adjusting the fee for a change of scope must be carefully detailed.

2. Taxes and insurance required by law should be reimbursed only in the amount actually paid by the contractor.

3. Overtime work should be performed only with the approval of the owner. If the contract is a cost-plus-percentage-fee, the fee percentage should be calculated only on the straight-time portion of the overtime work.

4. What tools and supplies are to be furnished by the contractor and what by the owner and who is responsible for tool pilferage, loss, or breakage should be defined.

5. A basis and schedule for the rental of equipment necessary for construction operation should be established.

6. Who pays for miscellaneous expenses such as telephones, office equipment and supplies, preparation of payrolls, and mailing and duplicating expenses should be defined.

7. It should be specified that the owner has the right to review and approve all purchases made by the contractor.

8. Define payment schedules for work done and, particularly, for any fee involved. This should provide for a retention by the owner of a certain portion of the fee and/or of the costs involved until final acceptance of the project.

9. If possible, there should be a definition as to who is to pay for mistakes or poor-quality work performed by the contractor. This can be a particularly difficult point to negotiate.

10. It should be provided that the owner has the right to audit all records of the contractor involved in the project.

Before entering such a contract, it is particularly important to investigate the financial condition of the supplier. If there is any concern that the supplier may experience financial difficulties during the term of the contracting, it is advisable to consider the performance bond. This, however, adds to the buyer's cost. It is generally desirable to deal only with contractors who have a sound financial condition; therefore, a performance bond should not be required.

Recapture Clause

Recapture clauses are sometimes included in equipment rental contracts. This permits the lessee to purchase the equipment for an agreed-upon amount at any time during the rental period. A percentage of the rentals paid may be applied against the purchase price.

Renegotiation

Certain governmental contracts are subject to renegotiation provisions which provide for a reopening of the contract where the final profit margin falls outside limits considered to be reasonable.

Price Protection Clause

In the purchase of raw materials and other goods which are bought on a recurring basis throughout a period of time, the buyer usually desires more than one source of supply. It is common practice to sign contracts with several vendors, with the base price on all contracts being at the same competitive level. In order for the buyer to take advantage of competitive market situations which may develop during the contract period, a price protection clause should be incorporated in the contract which allows the buyer to take advantage of a lower price offered by a different vendor, either by being released from his existing contracts or by forcing his contract suppliers to meet the lower competitive price. A typical example of a price decline clause is as follows:

> If buyer is offered material of equal quality by a responsible domestic manufacturer for delivery to the same destination in similar quantities and on like terms as herein provided at a lower delivered cost to buyer than the delivered cost hereunder, seller, upon receipt of written evidence of same, shall either meet such lower delivered cost or permit buyer to purchase elsewhere at said cost the quantity so offered, which quantity, if so purchased from others, shall be deducted from the quantity covered by this contract.

Favored Nations Clause

Another price protection clause, commonly known as a *favored nations* clause, protects the buyer against the possibility that the seller will offer a lower price to another customer. A typical example is:

> Should seller, during the term of this agreement, sell this material to any other domestic consumer at a lower price, determined on a delivered basis, than that in effect hereunder, then buyer shall receive the benefit of such lower price on all shipments made while such lower price is effective.

Internal Pricing

As industrial structures become more complex and conglomerates become more common, buyers frequently find that a manufacturing facility within their own corporate organization can be a potential supplier. In such situations certain unusual pricing considerations must be taken into account. These considerations are related to the make-or-buy decision discussed in Section 11.

When dealing with his own factory or another division of his company as a potential supplier, the buyer should be extremely careful in performing good cost-price analysis. Assuming that the internal supplier is quoting competitively, the buyer has a vested interest in knowing the chances of a profit or loss on the job, since these will have a direct impact on the results of his own corporate enterprise.

The buyer should be able to get a more complete cost analysis from an internal supplier than from an external supplier. He should also recognize and identify all the indirect cost factors related to this type of buying decision, such as: personnel and equipment utilization, material volume purchases, labor relations, and new-process training. Moreover, he must be fully prepared to discuss all of these considerations with the appropriate corporate management people.

The buyer should always strive to evaluate internal sources of supply on the same basis as outside vendors, i.e., with respect to delivery performance, conformance to quality specifications, resolution of problems, etc., before any consideration is given to overall company impact and/or contribution of an internal source.

It is also more likely in internal pricing arrangements that renegotiation either upward or downward will be involved if serious cost errors are discovered after the work begins.

PAYMENT TERMS

Terms of payment usually specified by the seller fall into two general categories:

1. Those terms which designate the method of payment
2. Those terms which influence the ultimate delivered cost

Such terms as *net 30 days* or *net 10th prox.* merely designate the time period in which the seller expects his invoice to be paid and do not affect the actual cost of the material. Cash discount terms such as *2 percent 10 days* allow the buyer to effect a savings of 2 percent of the invoice price if payment is made with 10 days from date of invoice. Payment terms may also require cash on or before delivery or may extend credit in some form. As noted above, the establishment of payment terms is usually the prerogative of the seller; but it is a factor which can affect the buyer's delivered cost and therefore is a subject for negotiation by the buyer. It is generally best, however, to negotiate for favorable payment terms or cash discounts after the base price has been established; otherwise, the seller may add the discount to his price before quoting the buyer.

Cash Discount

Payment terms which allow a cash discount are rather common in certain industries and are usually offered by the seller as an incentive to the buyer to make payment of invoices promptly. To the buyer, a cash discount represents a reduction in the cost of the goods purchased. However, whether the discount should be taken really becomes a financial decision—the value of the discount as related to the cost of money. As interest rates go up and the cash position of the buyer company becomes tight, financial officers will encourage buyers to negotiate longer terms of payment—60 days or more—unless discounts of at least 2 percent are offered.

The most commonly used payment terms are:

Net 30 days. Payment of the entire invoiced amount is to be made within 30 days from the invoice date.

Net 10th prox. Payment of the entire invoiced amount is to be made by the tenth of the month following the month of the invoice date.

2 percent 10/net 30. Payment made with 10 days from date of invoice may be discounted 2 percent. The invoice becomes overdue 30 days from the invoice date.

Annual Inducements for Cash Discounts The value of increasing cash discounts justifies aggressive negotiation. For example, 2 percent 10 days/net 30 days gives the buyer 36 percent a year, since there are 18 periods of 20 days each, which might be anticipated if he were having shipments made constantly each year. For the typical range of cash discounts, the annual inducements are shown below:

$$\frac{1}{2}\% \ 10 \ \text{days/net} \ 30 \ \text{days} \ = \ \ 9\% \ \text{per annum}$$
$$1\% \ 10 \ \text{days/net} \ 30 \ \text{days} \ = \ 18\% \ \text{per annum}$$
$$1\frac{1}{2}\% \ 10 \ \text{days/net} \ 30 \ \text{days} \ = \ 27\% \ \text{per annum}$$
$$2\% \ 10 \ \text{days/net} \ 30 \ \text{days} \ = \ 36\% \ \text{per annum}$$

Protection Clause for Delayed Invoices If the supplier is responsible for delay in invoice payment through submitting incorrect invoices, etc., a clause can be included on the purchase order permitting payment after the normal discount period has expired. One example follows:

Cash discount periods will be computed either from the date of delivery and acceptance of the goods ordered, or the date of receipt of correct and proper invoices, prepared in accordance with the terms of Buyer's Order, whichever date is later.

Prepayment Discounts and Deferred Terms

These terms are payment methods which extend credit in recognition of the seasonal nature and/or frequent short cash position inherent in the nature of some businesses. They are similar to normal cash discount payment terms except that they allow more time for payment, generally 2 to 3 months, and the discount rate is generally a more realistic 6 to 9 percent per year. Examples of prepayment discount terms are:

Net 10/60 extra. Invoices are due 70 days after invoice date, and the buyer is given the opportunity to prepay, discounting at the rate of 6 percent per annum. Payment before 10 days yields a 1 percent discount. Payment in 40 days entitles the buyer to ½ percent.

Net 90 days, ½ percent per month anticipation. The invoice is due in 90 days and may be discounted ½ percent for each 30 days' prepayment, permitting a maximum discount of 1½ percent.

Cash at Time of Purchase

Payment terms which require payment with the order, payment in advance of shipment, or payment on delivery protect the seller from bad credit risks. This type of payment can also be used on small orders to avoid costly invoicing and collection procedures. These terms, however, place the buyer in a difficult position in adjusting the settlement of claims.

Consignment Terms

Consignment terms most frequently used in merchandising activities defer payment until the goods are resold or used by the buyer. They are used by the seller as an inducement to promote sales and to obtain the use of buyer's space for inventory. Title to the materials shipped on consignment is retained by the seller and payment is made only after the goods are resold or used by the buyer. There are seldom any cash discount terms offered for consignment buying.

Progressive Payment Terms

Progressive payment terms are usually encountered on construction contracts. They may also be requested by the seller in the purchase of major capital equipment requiring appreciable operating capital and a lengthy period of time to manufacture. This type of payment is discussed in detail in Section 18.

LEGAL RESTRICTIONS ON PRICING

Effect of Certain Laws on Price Schedules

It is not the purpose of this section to treat legal matters as such; however, there are several laws which have a direct effect on commercial pricing practices. These include the Sherman Antitrust Act, the Federal Trade Commission Act, the Clayton Antitrust Act, the Unfair Trade Practices Act, and the Robinson-Patman Act. These statutes are intended to protect what is essentially a competitive economy and to eliminate unfair competition. Section 4 furnishes further details of these laws.

Robinson-Patman Act

The act which is of particular interest to buyers is the Robinson-Patman Act. This was intended as an anti-chain-store law, having been enacted during a period when there was considerable feeling against chain-store operations. The pertinent part of the Robinson-Patman Act which deserves mention in this connection has to do with that part which amended Section 2 of the Clayton Act. These two acts are referred to in this connection as one.

Section 2(a) outlaws direct and indirect discriminations in price. Mere differences are not unlawful, but they become so when the effect of such differences may be to substantially lessen competition, may tend to create a monopoly, or may injure, destroy, or prevent competition. Price differences which make only due allowance for differences in cost of manufacturing, sale, or delivery resulting from differing methods or quantities in which goods are sold or delivered are not prohibited.

Section 2(b) provides that a seller may escape the prohibitions of the section if he can prove "that his lower price or the furnishing of services or facilities to any purchaser or purchasers was made in good faith to meet an equally low price of a competitor, or the services or facilities furnished by a competitor."

Section 2(c) prohibits "a commission, brokerage, or other compensation or any allowance or discount in lieu thereof" to or for the benefit of the other party to a transaction. Such payments can be made by a seller only to one who represents him and only for services actually rendered. It is unlawful for a buyer or intermediary to accept such prohibited payment.

Section 2(f) provides "that it shall be unlawful for any person engaged in commerce, in the course of such commerce, knowingly to induce or receive a discrimination in price which is prohibited by this section."

In summing up, it is important to recognize that the buyer is liable for "knowingly" inducing or receiving price discrimination which is prohibited under Section 2(a) or for receiving, with or without knowledge, brokerage payments or allowances prohibited under Section 2(c).

TRANSPORTATION COSTS

All elements of cost which must be paid before the purchased goods are available at their point of ultimate use represent important price considerations to the buyer. A major such element is transportation cost. Whether it is paid directly by the buyer or is included in the seller's price, this transportation element should be separately identified and examined by the buyer.

Both seller and buyer have obligations with respect to transportation costs, liabilities, and procedures involved in delivering goods sold at one location to the buyer's point of receipt. These obligations affect the ultimate cost of the goods.

Detailed discussion of the many trade practices that pertain to the consideration of transportation modes and methods and their effect on the quotation and ordering of goods may be found in Sections 22 and 23.

TAXES AFFECTING PRICING

Among the multiplicity of taxes levied by the national, state, and local governments there are certain ones which, for special reasons, become price considerations to the purchasing agent.

Those which do so are, in general, taxes where the sales transaction as such provides the measure of the tax. It is also important to know precisely on whom the tax is legally levied and the legal provisions for collection.

Because of the complexity of tax laws and their interpretations, this discussion is limited to an outline of certain fundamental principles. The buyer must have a working knowledge of the tax laws applying to his area of operations. However, he must then rely on guidance by his own legal counsel.

One of the first things to consider is on whom the tax is legally levied. Certain governmental units do permit some taxes to be absorbed by the seller, and consideration must be given to whether the tax is being absorbed (as a cost component) or passes on to the buyer as an addition to the price.

A second consideration concerns the legal procedure for collecting the tax. This becomes a procedural matter for the buyer which may be settled because of legal requirements or which may be handled by mutual agreement with the seller where the law so permits.

The procedure for collecting state use taxes is one example. For instance, all states employing use taxes require the ultimate consumer to pay the tax. This is the only way the state can collect where goods are shipped from another state by suppliers not doing business in the using state. In all states the law provides that the seller is to collect the tax if he is licensed by the state to do so, but it falls upon the buyer as user to recognize that he may need to establish a procedure to accumulate such tax charges and report to the taxing unit directly.

Another instance of this procedure involves the collection of gasoline taxes. Many state gasoline taxes are legally levied on the consumer but provide for the collection of these taxes by the service station that makes the sale. Taxes collected on gasoline used for nonhighway purposes may be subject to a refund upon filing of the proper claim forms with the appropriate taxing agency.

Gasoline purchased for nonhighway use is wholly or partially exempt from state gasoline taxes in some states.

Likewise, in many states, while a sales tax is levied on the seller from whom it is legally collectible, the law may permit the seller to absorb the tax as part of his price or pass it on and collect it as such from the buyer. In the former instance, absorption of the tax or adding it to the quoted price on the invoice may become a trade practice.

Taxes on Tangibles

Taxes on the manufacture, sale, and use of tangible personal property generally divide into three categories: sales taxes, use taxes, and excise taxes.

Sales Taxes   Sales taxes in general are imposed either upon the seller for the privilege of selling tangible personal property or upon the sale itself. The law may be mandatory or permissive as to the seller passing the tax on to the buyer.

Use Taxes   Use taxes are levied against the storage, use, or consumption within the taxing unit (usually a state) and are primarily designed as a compensating tax in connection with sales taxes for the purpose of reaching property used in the area but purchased elsewhere. The user is in all instances required to pay the tax whether it be to the seller or directly to the taxing agency.

Practically all states and endless cities, counties, and districts impose sales and use taxes on purchases, including labor in some area. Percentages vary and are rising at an alarming rate. Up-to-date data are available from Commerce Clearing House, Inc., 420 Lexington Avenue, New York, N.Y. 10017.

Excise Taxes   Excise taxes are taxes levied on the manufacture of specific items. They are levied at both the manufacturing and the retail level by the federal government as well as by many states and local taxing units.

Many counties and cities levy sales, use, or gross receipts taxes, and some states collect such local taxes. For information concerning such local problems, the buyer may refer to one of the current tax service publications.

Taxes on Services

In addition to the above taxes there are certain other taxes which become pricing considerations.

Transportation Taxes   These are the taxes levied on the transportation of materials and persons. Where applicable, they are generally paid by the carriers, which issue the freight bill or sell the tickets, and are shown as a separate item to be added to the tariff.

Taxes on Labor   Buyers who purchase services involving labor on a cost-plus basis need to consider the social security taxes which are levied on wage payments as such. These taxes are the federal old-age and survivors' insurance tax and the federal unemployment tax; under the latter all states have established their own unemployment insurance acts.

As pointed out at the outset, because of the complexity of tax laws and their interpretations, it is essential that the buyer have a working knowledge of the laws which are applicable to his area of operations. Among the best-known services which are available on the subject of taxes are those published by Commerce Clearing House, Inc., 420 Lexington Avenue, New York, N.Y. 10017 and Prentice-Hall, Inc., Englewood Cliffs, N.J. 07632.

Import Duties

An import duty or tariff is a tax levied on certain goods entering a country. The United States began levying import duties in 1789, primarily to produce revenue for government operation. This has changed somewhat. The tariff act of 1930 listed four reasons for our import duties:

1. To provide revenue
2. To regulate commerce with foreign countries
3. To encourage the industries of the United States
4. To protect American labor, and for other purposes

The last two, encouraging U.S. industries and protecting American labor, are now the most important.

Not all goods entering this country are dutiable. Coffee, natural-rubber, sulfur, cocoa beans, fertilizers, rough and uncut diamonds, wood pulp, newsprint paper, and many other materials enter duty free. The goods which are dutiable are assessed for duty in three different ways:

1. *Specific* duty is a fixed charge per unit of material. *Example:* $0.10 per pound; $0.03 per gallon; $2 per ton.
2. *Ad valorem duty* is a percentage of the value of the product.
3. *Compound duty* includes both a specific and an ad valorem duty. *Example:* $0.035 per pound and 15 percent ad valorem.

Although there are nine different bases of valuation in the U.S. customs laws, the primary method utilized in arms-length transactions is *export value*. This is generally the purchase price. There are other methods for special products and buyers should contact their local Customs Service to identify these.

Under an international agreement, the United States has granted duty preference covering approximately 2200 products, to a substantial number of less developed nations. For example, Hong Kong, Taiwan, most South American and other Latin American countries, as well as many African countries, receive this preference treatment. There are limitations on the applicability of a preference, and local customs officials should be contacted to determine if it applies to the product and country involved. There are strict documentation requirements.

The rates of duty applied to articles imported into the United States are listed in the Tariff Schedules of the United States, Annotated (Title 19, U.S. Code), revised periodically by the U.S. International Trade Commission, Washington, D.C. 20220.

For articles not specifically listed in the tariff schedules, an answer as to what the duty might be may be obtained from the Customs Service, Treasury Department, Washington, D.C. In contemplation of importation, an application for a formal ruling from the Customs Service on the classification provision which will be applied will be given priority.

Further information on import duties will be found in Section 22.

INSURANCE REQUIREMENTS—BONDS

It has been generally assumed throughout this section that the goods or services under consideration are available and/or will be delivered according to the terms of the contract. However, consideration of prices is meaningless unless performance is to be carried out in accordance with needs.

It is important, in some instances, to consider protection against exposure to risks or liabilities which may arise out of the performance by the contractor or supplier. The cost of such protection becomes a pricing consideration.

Contract Bonds

Occasions may arise, generally in contracting for services but occasionally covering the delivery of goods, where it is desirable to ensure performance by requiring a contract bond. Such bonding is a common requirement in procurement by governmental bodies but is generally discretionary in private business. Thus the cost of such a contract bond, if such bond is deemed advisable, becomes a pricing consideration in appraising the proposals of individual bidders.

Worker's Compensation—Public Liability Insurance

The property owner, when contracting for services, is concerned as to whether he is adequately protected against liabilities which may arise during the performance of such services. It is common practice to require contractors to provide evidence of insurance coverage of sufficient limits, effective for the duration of the contract, to afford adequate protection for the owner. Usually these include such coverage as workmen's compensation and occupational disease (under the laws of the state in which work is to be performed), bodily injury liability, and property damage liability. Many other insurance coverages are available. In selecting suppliers or contractors, the cost (or additional cost) of providing sufficient insurance coverage is a price consideration.

Cost-plus contracts offer a special case. The premiums for the coverage mentioned above are based on hours worked; the cost of the insurance is usually included as an item of cost. Rates charged are usually based on a contractor's casualty experience, so that contractor's experience variations may introduce a pricing consideration.

Another important factor on cost-plus contracts is that unsatisfied claims arising out of the work may be held to be items of cost and charged to the owner by the contractor. As the risks involved frequently have little relationship to value of the work, this is an important consideration.

All-Risk Insurance (Transportation)

This is a special case involving shipment of extremely large or valuable items. The carrier is normally responsible for the safe delivery of goods, but under various tariffs the carriers' liabilities are limited to certain values and to certain causes of loss or damage. Insurance coverage is available to cover cases exceeding the carrier's liability, the cost of which is a pricing consideration.

PRICE INFORMATION

Development of reliable current price information is important in all purchasing activity. Knowledge of prices is essential to many engaged in other functions of company activities. Determination of prices and the maintenance of adequate company price records are therefore an important function of the purchasing department. Price information generally falls into six categories:

1. Prices published by vendors in their catalogs and price sheets.
2. Prices submitted by vendors upon direct request for bids.
3. Prices developed during negotiation.
4. Prices developed by the operation of open commodity markets, such as the grain market operated by the Chicago Board of Trade.
5. Prices of commodities not traded on exchanges but which, largely because of the breadth and activity of the market, are reasonably uniform and are published on a daily basis. This category for the most part is represented by raw and semifinished materials such as metals, lumber, and basic chemicals.
6. Price indexes designed to be generally representative of widely traded materials but which because of variations within the market do not represent specific item prices or the price of a given material in a specific market. These indexes form a very valuable source of widely published pricing information. They are developed and published by government agencies, industry groups and associations, and private organizations engaged in the sale of economic services and counseling services.

Maintaining a current catalog and price-sheet file is difficult if it is to be complete. Catalogs and price sheets are printed in a multitude of sizes, shapes, and arrangements and do not lend themselves to shelving and filing in an orderly and economical way. Most companies develop and maintain pricing information designed to meet their own needs. Consequently, many such price files are selective, relying on past purchase records and local vendor representatives for price information when desired.

The buyer should make full use of the salesperson as a continuing source of price information. During every visit some time should be spent discussing price trends in specific commodities, broad industry areas, and the general economy. Obviously, information obtained from salespeople must be carefully checked against other sources of information to guard against pricing comments being made a part of the negotiation process. When the proper rapport is established with certain salesmen, their information on pricing can be very valuable.

The buyer must learn by experience which salespeople are well informed and therefore can offer constructive information regarding price trends. This help is especially useful during the stage of estimating when there is not time or it is not desirable to obtain formal quotations.

The good salesperson is very helpful in analyzing price quotations by identifying the major cost elements. Therefore, it is possible to quickly identify those specifications which add undue cost to a material and to eliminate such requirements before they become firmly fixed. For example, if specification changes are being considered, a good salesperson can estimate from his experience the approximate cost of each change, thereby permitting quicker decisions regarding the value of the changes.

It must always be understood that this exchange of pricing information with salespeople seldom represents a firm quotation because the salesperson seldom has this final authority. It can be most helpful when it is fully understood that unfair advantage will not be taken on either side and that proper competition will exist before final commitments are made.

A widely used method for securing prices for major nonrepetitive purchases is to secure competitive bids from several logical suppliers. For a simplification of the bid procedure, many purchasing departments use a request for quotation form as shown in Section 5.

Obtaining formal bids requires time that can usually be justified only for purchases of some magnitude. Often for purchases of small and intermediate value, the use of the telephone to obtain quotations from several suppliers is a satisfactory substitute for the formal bid. If a record is desired, it may be simply notes on the requisition form.

When the issuance of a formal request for quotation is indicated, it is necessary to exercise the same care in its preparation as in the writing of a purchase order. The request should specify the material in detail and spell out the quantity, delivery requirements, and terms under which the bid will be considered. It may also be desirable, although not necessary, to state whether the bids should be itemized, whether partial bids will be accepted, and the date and time at which the bids must be received.

Bids may be obtained verbally, by letter, or, as is common practice in government purchasing, by advertising in newspapers and posting on the bulletin board of a public building.

Tabulation of bids is the first step in bid analysis. Incorporated in the request for quotation form is a section for summarizing the bids. In the case of very complex proposals, a more elaborate analysis sheet may be needed to suit the specific situation.

The bidding, to be fair and useful, must be on identical goods or services, and any variations should be shown on the summary sheet. If the variations are significant, it is best to reject all bids. When the transaction is complete, the summary provides an important part of the department's price records and pricing information.

While the industrial buyer is under no obligation to purchase from the lowest bidder and uses the request-for-bid technique as a convenient method for securing price information, the buyer for a governmental agency must under normal circumstances award the business to the lowest bidder. Public purchasing is discussed in detail in Section 20.

A third method for securing prices is by negotiation. This approach is particularly suited to the purchase of nonstandard materials or materials which can be made to order at a saving to the buyer and/or the seller. Techniques of negotiation are described in Section 11.

A variation of negotiated prices is *contract buying* or *stockless purchasing,* previously discussed in this section. Bids are requested for all, or a substantial part, of a plant's or company's requirements of a particular category of goods or supplies for a given period of time. In addition to the advantages mentioned in the preceding paragraphs, contract buying allows a company to reduce substantially its investment in storeroom facilities and stocks and to reduce its payroll as well. Furthermore, it establishes definitely the maximum price for a given future period. These agreements usually contain downward escalator clauses.

The profit the seller shall make is also a subject for negotiation, and this in turn requires a consideration of the risks involved in the seller's manufacture and the buyer's use. The buyer can combine a competitive bidding with a detailed discussion of the factors which make the price. This discussion often leads to opportunities for price reductions, which are developed mutually by buyer and seller. A detailed discussion of price analysis and price negotiation is covered in Section 11. Mention is made here only because negotiated prices become an important division of pricing records to a company.

Many materials which are produced in large volume, by a large number of manufacturers, and/or sold to a large number of buyers are bought and sold on commodity exchanges, or so widely as to produce an effectively free open market. Prices of many such commodities are widely reported in the press and in a number of daily and weekly publications.

Most daily newspapers publish commodity market prices for their own locality, besides covering national markets. The U.S. government, through the Department of Commerce, publishes certain pricing information which forms a valuable source of such information for the use of the buyer. The Department of Labor also publishes data concerning labor costs and price indices which are useful to the buyer in price analysis. Many of these periodicals are listed in other sections of this handbook, particularly Section 30.

In addition to these public sources, there are many sources available to the buyer privately. Trade associations collect and disseminate market information for the use of their membership. In this category also are the large number of economic services which furnish their clients with information on prices and price trends. Probably the most readily available source to the buyer is that furnished by suppliers on a regularly published basis.

NOTE: For further information on subjects covered in this section see the list of references in Section 30.

Section **11**

Price Evaluation

EDITOR

Myron E. Frye *Vice-President, Corporate Purchasing, Maremont Corporation, Chicago, Illinois*

ASSOCIATE EDITORS

Wayne D. Adams, C.P.M. *Corporate Director of Purchases, J. M. Huber Corporation, Houston, Texas*

Gary L. Fratilla, C.P.M. *Manager, Corporate Contracts, NCR Corporation, Dayton, Ohio*

Price is ordinarily defined as the money value set by the seller for a lot or unit of goods or services. This simple definition is useful as long as the buyer is aware that mere comparison of prices will not support a buying decision if there are other competitive factors which affect value.

For the buyer, a more useful definition of price is the total value of the right goods or services delivered to the point of use. The objective of price evaluation, then, is to make a valid comparison of the value of competing materials or services in terms of need. The seller's price must be modified by differences in quality, service, reliability, cost of transportation, inventory requirements, yield, and other factors to arrive at a true value. The comparison of these values provides the basis for a sound purchasing decision, often quite different from what the initial comparison of prices alone would indicate. The preceding Section 10 lists the many factors affecting price which must be considered in arriving at value.

The purpose of Section 10 is to define all factors affecting price. Section 11 recapitulates not only those price considerations in Section 10 but also many others requiring effective evaluation by the buyer. Thus some repetition is demanded in this section to minimize reference to Section 10.

INFLUENCES ON PRICE EVALUATION

Price versus Cost

Any study of price evaluation or pricing influences must of necessity place the element of price in its true perspective in relation to cost. Price should be regarded as only one of the elements in the formula for cost. It must never be overlooked that such factors as transportation, receiving, handling, recording, and storage are in themselves expenses to the purchaser which must be added to the price to determine the ultimate cost. Still other factors —among them quality, as related to the function to be performed, service, obsolescence, and spoilage—also must be considered in determining the ultimate cost, although they may be more difficult to evaluate and convert to dollars and cents.

It should be noted, too, that buying at a lower price is not necessarily a criterion of good procurement and, in fact, may be a very easily attainable objective. The buyer who sets as his objective the attainment of a lower ultimate cost has, however, established a solid basis for an intelligent job of purchasing. For example, the purchase of a grinding wheel at a higher price than others on the market may well be justified if tests indicate that under the user's conditions it will remove more metal over a longer period of time than competing wheels.

None of this is intended to minimize the importance of price in the buying decision, but rather to call attention to the many other considerations vital to the determination of the ultimate cost of the goods purchased.

Another interesting facet is the influence of the supplier's cost in the establishment of his selling price. While every producer must eventually recover his costs plus a margin of profit if he is to remain in business, it is primarily the marketplace which will determine the selling price of his product.

The Right Price

There are three basic methods of pricing: (1) published price lists (with quantity and other discount setups); (2) bids on individual specifications; and (3) negotiated prices on specific jobs or lots of material.

Published Market Price Lists   Many suppliers publish price lists which represent the prices charged to all customers. This standard list does not mean that all customers will pay the same price, but only that all customers who qualify for a certain category as described in the list will be charged the same price.

This so-called one-price policy has considerable backing among major national manufacturers. It is the easiest to administer, as it relieves the pressure of price selling on the part of the sales force. Selling can concentrate on service and quality, and differences between the price schedules of competitiors will be rationalized on those factors.

Under this method of pricing, retailers, wholesalers, and manufacturers each may have an appropriate price list, and quantity-price brackets also may be shown. A quantity discount may also be available to each class of purchaser, based on annual volume or dollar value of material purchased. The purchasing manager should know the several categories into which the price schedule is organized and should assure himself that he is obtaining the prices applicable to his company for each class of purchase. Combining purchases of all plants within the same company is recommended so that the company may become eligible for a higher discount.

An aggressive buyer will go beyond this point and attempt to assess the economic justification for differences in prices between the classes of customers. Original equipment manufacturers (called OEM) are usually entitled to special discounts on standard products incorporated into a finished product. The purchasing manager for an OEM is negligent if he is not obtaining this benefit for his company. The purchasing manager for a large user of similar items, but not for incorporation into final product, should attempt to have his own category accorded equivalent price treatment.

Where price lists are not available, it is the responsibility of the buyer to negotiate if his purchases indicate an economic and legal basis for special treatment.[1]

Prices of many items in the raw material or semifinished categories are published daily for well-established market grades. While these are not price lists, as such, they are effectively used in business as published price information. These prices usually are a reflection of the demand and availability, or apparent availability, of the commodity. They tend to fluctuate as the result of factors which control output or availability, such as weather, labor conditions, strikes, and floods. If the future supply appears to be shorter, users of the product will buy heavily, and the price may advance quickly. The condition of surpluses in these markets also may occur quickly with the consuming industry finding itself committed for large stocks of commodities at inflated prices. The purchase and sale of futures and hedging are devices used to minimize fluctuations that may occur in the production and price of some of these commodities, as described in Section 13.

Bids on Individual Specifications This approach to pricing really involves two methods:

1. Bids on individual detailed specifications
2. Competitive bidding on standard items

Some materials and parts are made according to the buyer's detailed specifications and are bought on the basis of bids by producers. This is the most competitive form of pricing, since many economic forces can be brought to bear and the price

[1]See Sections 4 and 10 concerning the Robinson-Patman Act and other applicable laws.

level may be determined by the supplier's need for the business. In this method of pricing, careful and complete specification, good bidding procedures, and careful bid analysis are essential.

Suppliers from time to time will vary prices even when they have published price lists. Among the many reasons are: to maintain volume, to clear inventories, to gain additional volume so that they can buy in more economical quantities, and to meet competition. Purchasing will frequently request bids on the basis of performance specifications or other less detailed specifications to obtain benefits from these temporary conditions in the market, in effect, inviting the bidders to quote standard items at the best price available.

Negotiated Prices   The two previously discussed basic methods of determining the right or fair price depend largely on the existence of a competitive market or the ability to set forth the exact, detailed specifications of the equipment or materials to be purchased. Very often, however, these and other criteria are lacking or totally absent, and the buyer must then resort to negotiations with the supplier to secure the best advantage he can for his company.

Sometimes when certain kinds of equipment or materials are to be purchased, or when a specific job is to be done, direct competition may not be present because the offerings of the various bidders are not identical. Different pieces of equipment have individual features, although they may be intended to do the same job. Technical assistance may be required to evaluate the bids.

When a construction or installment project is to be accomplished, the ability of all interested contractors to perform may be questionable to the point that only one is considered qualified. Familiarity with plant facilities, specially trained employees, or a record of previous accomplishment may favor one contractor to the exclusion of all others. In such circumstances, negotiations may be used to establish the scope of the project and the right or fair price.

While this section concerns itself primarily with pricing matters, the area of negotiations with suppliers will often involve other matters, such as transportation, tooling, scrap disposition, tolerance, or any of the host of considerations that are part of a procurement decision.

THE ART OF NEGOTIATION.   The art of negotiation provides the purchasing executive with perhaps his finest opportunity to improve his company's profits and to obtain the recognition not usually accorded one who merely checks price lists or bids. His knowledge of value analysis and learning-curve techniques, discussed later in this section, will strengthen his negotiating skill. As with any art, the practitioner must develop and refine his skills through repeated exposure.

Negotiations involve the psychology of persuasion. Nothing contributes more toward successful negotiations than advance planning of objectives and strategy. The purchasing manager should enter the session with a positive attitude toward achieving his objectives, as well as having decided upon the maximum extent of his potential concessions. All pertinent facts should be collected and studied before the meeting so that the buyer will be ready to answer promptly and speak with determination on any points the opposition may bring up to weaken his position. An agenda should be developed and be made known to all participants.

Selection of those who are to participate is a vital consideration of planning. Quite often the purchasing manager will be the sole negotiator for his company. At other times when technical or other considerations predominate, he may ask qualified persons from engineering or other departments to join him. While he will derive certain advantages from the presence of these experts, there is also the danger that one of them, if not experienced in negotiating strategy, may expose a weak point in the buyer's position or prematurely commit the buyer with a thoughtless remark.

An appreciation and understanding of the emotional factors are important to the successful conducting of negotiating sessions. A personal contact between buyer and seller is involved, with both presumably dealing in good faith and each having his company's and his own best interest uppermost in his thoughts. The buyer should learn all that he can about those with whom he is to negotiate and appraise the position they are likely to take on the issues involved. Displays of temper or generation of anger by the purchasing manager will generally avail him little and may even be a handicap to logical, clear-headed thinking.

Even the physical environment of the negotiating session is an important consideration. Pleasant surroundings make it easier to successfully complete negotiations. Inadequate ventilation, lighting, or space may present unnecessary obstacles to an otherwise pleasant and fruitful discussion. Recess periods may be desirable, both for a change of pace and for a review progress.

THE PROCESS.   The negotiation process provides a legitimate and ethical means for the buyer and seller, through give and take, to eliminate unjustified or unnecessary increments of cost. It should not be construed as a means for stripping the vendor of a fair profit or an opportunity for extracting unreasonable concessions. In reality, the most successful negotiations are those which produce results satisfying to both sides and which provide the framework for a long-term, mutually beneficial relationship.

It should be remembered that the conditions on which an agreement has been based may well change over a period of time. Therefore, the prudent purchasing manager will not file away and forget a contract or agreement he has just negotiated but will regard his responsibility as one of continuing administration. He will remain alert not only to his company's and the vendor's observance of all provisions, but also to the possibility of reopening negotiations if and when it is to his company's advantage to do so.

DOS AND DON'TS.   One author offers several dos and don'ts which may be helpful in negotiation sessions.[2]

Don't:

1. Tip your hand too early. Withhold something for later concession in return for a point.

2. Get so bogged down in details that the overall objectives are lost. A sug-

[2]Victor H. Pooler, Jr., *The Purchasing Man and His Job,* American Management Associations, New York, 1964.

gestion: After close scrutiny to details, give way relatively generously to a compromise which is still satisfactory.

3. Try to prove the vendor is wrong. You may win the point, but you won't reduce the price and leave him room to back off gracefully from a stated position.

Do:

1. Negotiate at home when possible. Isolate members of the selling team by seating buying members between them to break up their attack.

2. Negotiate with those who can make concessions. It is useless to attempt negotiations with a salesman on items such as mill steel, where prices are set at the home office—although it will help if his sales reports back up your position. Many salesmen, however, have a range of prices to submit, and they may be able to drop a figure 5 percent without contacting management.

3. Remain silent at times. Often greater concessions result from a seller's fear of losing business. Vendors may talk themselves into a better settlement than expected.

4. Know what you can expect to gain by negotiating and keep your target in mind. Analyze the amount of "give" the vendor can reasonably be expected to have.

5. Plan ahead. Prepare the agenda to your advantage and brief team members beforehand to be sure none of them tip your hand or give in on a point before you do.

6. Negotiate for the long pull—not the short-sighted advantage which may backfire at the first turn of economic conditions.

7. Be confident of facts presented. Don't use information that you may have to acknowledge as wrong.

8. Use new techniques such as the learning curve and price-cost analysis.

9. Divert attention if the negotiation hits your weak points. Shift the strategy of attack to minor points which you may later concede.

10. Call a recess if talk hits a snag, or arrange for a lunch break. Set the meeting for a time that will allow the vendor to relax at lunch with company people (at the buyer's expense, of course).

11. Enlist the aid of specialists in manufacturing, methods, finance, and engineering to help evaluate tooling and other special costs. Purchasing research will help supply basic data for negotiating in depth.

12. Always be fair.

All the above indicates clearly that no other skill or responsibility is more basic to the universal description of the purchasing manager's function than the requirement that he negotiate in the interest of his company.

NEGOTIABLE AREAS AND EFFECTS

A few of the many specific items to be negotiated and those that have a significant effect on the realized cost to the buyer are: quantity purchased; size, frequency, and mode of shipment; specified quality levels; required packaging or containerization; timing; and commitment versus intent.

Price Variation with Order Size

The size of an order governs the economics the seller can effect in production, packaging, billing, and sales expense. The larger the order, the lower these costs become per unit of product shipped. Price schedules for virtually all commodities reflect numerous price breaks as the quantity ordered increases. In order for the buyer to take full advantage of the quantity-price relationship, he should be familiar with the pricing schedules applicable to the commodities he purchases and relate these schedules to the economic order quantity which his requirements justify.

Quite often lower prices are offered for large orders as an inducement to obtain a greater share of the buyer's business and, therefore, may not be a reflection of lower cost to the seller. However, quantity is probably the greatest lever the buyer possesses for negotiating advantageous prices. If his requirements are measured in millions of pounds or gallons or units, he is in an excellent position to negotiate a price appreciably below the seller's published market price schedule.

Price-Quantity Relationship to Distribution Costs

The quantity which a vendor can handle on a single order has an appreciable effect upon his storage and handling costs per unit of product. Orders for large quantities permit the vendor to turn over his inventory faster, utilize his warehouse and storage space to greater advantage, and schedule his material handling labor more efficiently. For example, it is considerably cheaper for the seller to store large quantities of bulk materials, particularly liquids, in large outside storage tanks and load directly into tank cars than it is to load the same material into drums and store, handle, and load the drums onto carriers. Common carriers also recognize the efficiencies of large movements, and freight rates are appreciably cheaper for full carload, truckload, or bargeload shipments than they are for less-than-carload or less-than-truckload movements. These economies are usually reflected in appreciable differences in the price schedules for various-size quantites covered by a purchase order.

For many products, freight rates further reflect an additional savings for quantities above the minimum carload or truckload limits. For example, steel pipe may be shipped in 40,000 or 80,000 pound minimum carloads. Bulk chemicals reflect progressively lower freight rates for 10,000- 20,000- or 30,000-gallon and larger tank cars. Bargeloads reflect still lower rates.

Today, it is common practice to combine several materials in a single shipment so that the total quantity makes up a full truckload or carload. These are known as *mixed-car* or *mixed-truck* shipments. The buyer must be certain, however, that the total weight meets or exceeds the weight requirements for the product with highest minimum-weight provisions, or excessive freight charges may result. Sometimes when the quantity ordered is less than a full carload or truckload, it is more economical to pay the full truckload or carload freight rate than to ship as an LTL (less-than-truckload) or LCL (less-than-carload) quantity at the rate which applies to the order's actual weight.

Price Variation with Packaging Requirements

Today a buyer may have his purchased commodities packaged in virtually any type of package or container suitable for holding the material. The type and design of container or package used and its size, however, have a considerable effect upon the seller's packaging costs. They may also have an appreciable effect on the buyer's costs of handling and storing the commodities at his plant.

A liquid product sold in a 1-gallon metal, plastic, or glass container may cost as high as $1 per gallon for packaging. The same product shipped in a standard 55-gallon steel drum would involve a container cost of about $0.15 per gallon, and the drum may have salvage or reuse value. Shipping the same material in a 20,-000-gallon tank car would reduce the container cost to less than $0.005 per gallon. When the mileage allowance paid by the railroad for the use of a seller's or buyer's tank car is considered, the tank car itself may cost the user virtually nothing.

The buyer should also be conversant with Interstate Commerce Commission (ICC) and Department of Transportation (DOT) rules and regulations with regard to packaging requirements for the particular items he buys. He also needs to be aware of the DOT regulations on packaging items such as bags, cartons, and containers that he purchases for shipping his company's products. This is especially important in the area of packaging and transporting hazardous materials.

The buyer should also carefully consider his requirements from the standpoint of the economic order quantity and the protection which must be afforded to the materials purchased in storage, transit, and handling in order to achieve the lowest possible cost with respect to container size and type.

Price Effect of Quality Restrictions

Price schedules for many materials show a variation in price for different levels of quality. The higher the quality, the higher the price, because to achieve the higher quality level usually means that the seller must use additional refining steps and/or more costly quality control methods. For example, many chemicals are sold in industrial, technical, USP (United States Pharmacopeia), or reagent grades.

Many materials are sold at a price which varies in direct relation to the concentration of the desired ingredient. Sulfuric acid, for example, may be purchased at 93 percent, 95 percent, or 98 to 99 percent concentration. The price increases in direct proportion to the amount of sulfuric acid contained.

The important point for the buyer to remember is that the lowest quality which will serve the function required in his manufacturing process is usually the most economic quality to purchase. To buy at a higher quality level usually means paying a premium price for quality that is not required.

Commitment versus Intent

A key and critical point which in most cases impacts both price and cancellation terms during negotiations is the nature of the commitment. It is essential that a mutual understanding exist between buyer and seller on this point in order to assess and address costs and risks.

Typically, a *hard* contractual buyer commitment in terms of quantity over time will elicit best possible pricing. This is due to the fact that the vendor is better able to plan production scheduling, be assured of sales volume, and reduce overhead per sales dollar associated with the buyer's account. In turn, such efficiencies and related economies are passed along to the buyer in the form of lower prices.

This is especially true when dealing with custom or special parts and with most forms of capital equipment. It is here that genuine economies can be realized by vendors in the manufacturing processes.

On the other hand, contractual expressions of intent to buy such as blanket purchase agreements carry specific and sometimes extreme uncertainties. Serious doubts exist as to quantities actually to be ordered. These conditions manifest themselves in the form of contingency costing by vendors and ultimately higher prices. Unless the buyer and seller have successful past experiences together in this mode, or standard, high volume product is involved, pure purchase intentions will often not provide sufficient inducement to the seller to offer his very best price terms. It will, however, normally afford the buyer improved terms and benefits over buying requirements on a *spot* or *as needed* basis.

Timing

Another method by which the buyer can ascertain his relative negotiating position is to consider his purchase volume leverage as well as market conditions. It is important that these be examined from both an existing position and probable future situation. Further, such appraisals should progress from general information to the point of specifics. For a study, industrial capacity as a whole may not be indicative of a trend for a specific segment of the industry itself. For example, an increase in building capacity within the semiconductor electronics industry should not be construed as appropriate for all electronic families classified under the general heading as semiconductors.

Once the buyer examines those external factors impacting costs and assesses their present and future role, he is in a position to superimpose his volume requirements. From this comparison, the buyer can discreetly determine where his best optimum negotiating position lies. This may indicate the need to stall negotiations for long-term contracts in anticipation of near future market softening which would strengthen his negotiating position. Or, buyer's purchase forecasts may be minimal and have little, if any, appreciable effect upon garnering better prices. In this case, the buyer may set aside the project for the time being, buy on a spot basis, and remain alert for a change in those factors which could enhance his bargaining position. Once the trend is on the upswing and more suitable, the buyer would reinstate negotiations under more favorable conditions.

Summary

Many purchases involving list price items of standard design require no decision except the selection of the lowest price. However, the buyer must be aware that the printed price list does not give assurance that the prices are the best available. For the infrequent purchase they may suffice. But even price lists complete with quantity discounts may be inadequate if the buyer can use the techniques of combining purchases through use of blanket orders or systems contracting to seek further discounts.

Also, price is a variable in terms of general or local market conditions. Knowledge of underlying conditions may be acquired through the reading of books, periodicals, and the like. Knowledge of a particular industry can be gained through reading its trade journals, handbooks, and texts and intelligent questioning of its representatives. Physical inspection of specific plants will increase familiarity and provide further insight. In addition, knowledge of a particular vendor's physical conditions, financial situation, and company policies provides invaluable background for judging its price offering.

In summary, price properly evaluated in relation to the particular end use is the most important decision the buyer makes.

BASIC AREAS OF CONSIDERATION IN PRICE EVALUATION

Quality

Once the need has been established and transformed into a request to purchase, the quality of the requirement becomes the most important and difficult single aspect of the many-phase function of price evaluation. *Quality* in purchasing has a twofold meaning. Dictionaries refer to it as "that which makes something what it is." In its use in purchasing it is coupled with the degree to which something satisfies the function for which it is intended.

Well-planned specifications, carefully worked out in terms of generally accepted industry standards, are prerequisite to price determinations. Many companies are penalized unduly in buying because of highly restrictive specifications or because of quality factors emphasized far beyond the point of necessity. The purchasing manager must be aware of the cost factors built into the specification used. He should seek management assistance in buying materials of suitable quality and not materials that are of far higher quality than necessary. Specials of any sort increase the price considerably and cause other procurement difficulties because they have to be worked into production schedules and are not stocked either by manufacturers or by their jobbers. Ambiguous or omitted parts of a specification will make it impossible to negotiate from a firm basis.

Once quality standards are established, a buyer should develop and maintain contact only with firms that have the facilities and that demonstrate an ability to deliver consistently merchandise of the quality that meets those quality standards.

These all-important quality standards must be maintained from the outset by the use of clearly outlined specifications. Specifications, as far as is possible, must not be so restrictive as to limit the number of potential suppliers to so few that the element of competition is destroyed. Specifications must be broad enough to give equal opportunity to qualified bidders, and yet stringent enough to ensure the maintenance of quality standards and the exclusion of offerings that may be undesirable from a quality standpoint. A good specification will tell a qualified bidder the characteristics which he must include in his product or service to produce the results desired by the buyer.

The buyer should avoid buying more quality than is needed. Quality is determined by balancing two major considerations:

1. The technical consideration of suitability
2. The economic consideration of price and availability

The using department is usually responsible for the suitability determination of materials, and the purchasing department is responsible for the economic consideration of quality. In the area of quality most progressive companies give their purchasing department a management responsibility along with its economic responsibility. This management responsibility is the right to challenge the quality requirements on all requisitions. The right to challenge is not the right to change. To challenge means to request reconsideration of the technical decision for economic reasons.

For instance, corrugated packaging sometimes presents such opportunities. One situation deals with the grade and type of outer liner. Typically, it boils down to a matter of esthetics. The astute buyer of corrugated boxes will be familiar with the various types of linerboard available. Correspondingly, the buyer is knowledgeable about the product packaged as well as his company's methods and sources of distribution and marketing. Armed with this, the buyer is in a logical position to oftentimes solicit, propose, and seek changes to material specifications which result in more standard, readily available, and less costly material while still satisfying his company's packaging requirements.

Very often the application of a quality specification brings out the need for modification and amendment, both from a cost and a practical standpoint. For example, a buyer in one company challenged a requisition for 500,000 pounds of crystals of a specified chemical. The requisitioning department agreed that the same chemical in the form of flakes could be used. This change resulted in a $30,000 annual savings.

A buyer who is familiar with the quality standards of his company should constantly encourage his suppliers to offer substitute materials, new materials, and recommendations that offer potential savings to the buyer and maintain his quality standards.

There will always be some item which must be purchased from one source and for which only one quality or grade is available. In such cases, price cannot be the determining factor, although the buyer should do his utmost to negotiate the lowest possible price under such conditions. Machinery repair parts fall into this category, and in some cases the decision or determination of the best price becomes one of *make or buy* discussed near the end of this section. Where repair parts purchased from a proprietary source are prohibitively high, and the cost of making the same parts in the buyer's plant is equally high, there is a good opportunity for the buyer to recommend purchase of machinery which does not offer such an expensive handicap in terms of parts replacement.

In the case of a patented process or article, the manufacturer is entitled to a fair and legitimate profit. But if, by manipulation or opportunism, an unwarranted price is quoted, the buyer should try to find a substitute or should negotiate with the vendor toward a fair price. All legitimate steps should be taken to get a fair price.

Quantity

Quantity purchases generally represent a saving over smaller purchases, and rightfully so. But there are many facts to be considered before seeking price reduction through quantity alone. One of the chief factors to be considered is the cost of possession, or carrying charges.

Cost of Possession   The following, for quick reference, are elements of cost associated with the possession of inventory:

CAPITAL COSTS.

Interest on money invested in inventory
Interest on money invested in land and building to hold inventory
Interest on money invested in inventory handling and control equipment

STORAGE SPACE COSTS.

Rent on building
Taxes and insurance on building
Depreciation on building
Depreciation on warehouse installation
Cost of maintenance and repairs
Utility charges, including heat, light, and water
Salaries of security and maintenance personnel

INVENTORY SERVICE COSTS.

Taxes on inventory
Labor costs in handling and maintaining stocks
Clerical expense in keeping records
Employee benefits for warehouse and administrative personnel

HANDLING-EQUIPMENT COSTS.

Taxes and insurance on equipment
Depreciation on equipment

Fuel expense
Cost of maintenance and repairs

INVENTORY RISK COSTS.

Obsolescence of inventory
Insurance on inventory
Physical deterioration of inventory
Losses from pilferage

Range of percentages for these and other inventory carrying costs are listed in Section 12.

Obsolescence   This is one of the gravest dangers to which inventories are subjected and should receive foremost consideration where quantity purchases are contemplated. For example, if the shelf life of an item is 90 days, it would be unwise to buy in excess of a 90-day supply for the sake of price reduction. Also, if the particular item is susceptible to obsolescence due to design changes or other factors, it would be unwise to stock beyond normal lead time plus a safety factor.

Quantity purchases, as all other purchases, should be made on the relationship of the dollar value of the item to the ratio of its turnover, and not on the possible price reduction of a given quantity.

In most purchases, in addition to the purchase price, there is the cost of owning. This cost of getting versus the cost of keeping is of utmost importance. For instance, if a buyer can save 3 percent by purchasing in larger quantities, and yet the carrying charges amount to 6 percent, he obviously loses money rather than saves on the large-order price. The cost of possession is of such importance that it is usually advisable to consult with the finance department.

Consolidation of Quantities   One of the easiest ways to secure lower prices is to consolidate quantities. This is one basic reason why central purchasing departments in multiplant companies were established. By consolidating quantities and by having proper stores-inventory facilities and controls, the materials required by the company can be on hand at the time needed without an excessive investment in inventory scattered through numerous departments of a plant. This invites standardization of products, parts, and raw materials to the highest degree feasible.

The grouping of orders into larger quantities and into classifications commonly sold by vendors requires that the purchasing manager have a voice in the planning of production and also have at least partial control and responsibility of stores and inventory.

The purchasing manager must be aware also of new developments within his own company involving design and engineering changes so as to prevent overstocking items that soon will not be used. He must become an effective member of the management team and must devote the time necessary within his own company in order that purchasing considerations, as well as manufacturing considerations, can be determined when products are in the planning stage.

In no case can all small or emergency orders be eliminated. The purchasing manager, however, should constantly strive to see that their impact is minimized and that the large, important orders in terms of dollar value or production significance are not lost in the shuffle of servicing many numerous small and rush requisitions. Attention can then be given to doing a better job in commodities used in large quantities which involve large sums of money. Procedures should be formulated to consolidate small requirements into larger and fewer orders.

Service

This is an element that must be considered in price evaluation. *Service* can mean many things; generally it consists of one or more of the following:

Deliveries made on time
Packaged or crated according to specifications
Routed properly for speed in delivery as well as possible freight savings
Vendor technical or value analysis assistance
Prompt response to emergency requests
Willingness to make satisfactory adjustments for misunderstandings or clerical errors
Furnishing regular reports from supplier's quality control laboratory

Some elements of service may constitute an additional expense which can be avoided if proper technical and professional personnel are available within the buyer's own company. Conversely, whether or not such personnel are available, it may well be that the supplier is in a position to provide certain services at lower cost to the buyer than if they were to be performed within the buyer's own organization.

The determination of service required is important because great numbers of businesses have added technical personnel, equipment, and other means of furnishing their own services during critical periods. This type of service is often reduced by sellers and many times eliminated entirely. Survival of the purchaser's company may depend upon its being able to provide the service from within. Technological development in new materials has spread at such a rapid rate that all industries must be in constant contact with all markets in order to remain abreast of the advantages which new developments may offer. It should be noted that sellers' services in these fields will often outweigh the price paid for materials.

Of necessity, certain industries must emphasize service at the sacrifice of price savings. A manufacturer operating a production line must have consistent schedules, deliveries of the specified quality, with immediate attention to the purchaser's emergency requirements. Any delivery or service failure which would hold up a production line would cost much more than an initial reasonable difference in price. For this reason, buyers in many industries are reluctant to take a chance with suppliers who do not have proven ability to provide service, even though such suppliers may have offered a price advantage.

In such circumstances, a buyer's continued efforts should be directed toward improving the price of the supplier whose service ability has been proved, while he continues to study and develop the service ability of the new or potential supplier who offers lower price.

Beware of the seller whose staff consists merely of production personnel and salesmen. Even though the buyer maintains his own laboratory, conducts his own inspections, and renders all the necessary services at his own expense (thereby paying a lower price), he still must rely on the vendor to conduct research toward product improvement. In other words, the buyer cannot rely on a source that is not constantly endeavoring to offer a better product in the marketplace. This is not to say that such a vendor should be scorned and turned away. At any given time, this vendor can well be the most advantageous source for his product, and the intelligent buyer will use him. Good ethics and good business sense demand that he be warned that progressive competitors may gradually diminish his advantage.

PRICE-COST ANALYSIS

The objective of analyzing prices and costs is to determine whether the price paid is a reasonable one in terms of the market, the industry, and the end use of the material bought. In addition, price analysis is a means of isolating and possibly eliminating items of unnecessary cost.

Sources of Published Price Data

Vendors Many materials traditionally are priced on the basis of published price lists; this procedure normally involves a *list* price for each item, which is then subject to a scale of trade discounts for either various quantity brackets or for various classes of customers. In utilizing vendors' price lists, a buyer should assure himself that he:

1. Uses the right price list that applies to his kind of business (e.g., on a given commodity, such as tires, there can be several price lists—retail, distributor, fleet user, OEM, etc.)

2. Applies the proper trade discount that is normally extended to his type of trade

Trade Publications There are numerous trade publications that periodically publish current price information. Such periodicals normally are specialized for a particular industry or group of related industries; in addition to specific price information, these trade journals often include material written by experts, which can cover price influences, market conditions, and probable price trends.

Some examples are:

Chemical Marketing Reporter—chemicals
American Metal Market—metals
Official Board Market—paper board

Government Both the Bureau of Labor Statistics and the U.S. Department of Commerce issue a wealth of price information on commodities and manufactured goods. While the data are of value in assessing both historical and future trends, it is difficult to reliably ascertain current prices of specific items from these reports. The buyer should realize that the government data are compiled from thousands of sources and are published as *averages*; therefore, he must use great care and judgment in attempting to relate general data to his specific procurement problem.

Quotations

In a period of fluctuating market conditions and changing prices, competitive quotations are probably one of the most reliable means of determining the going price of a material. The buyer should assure himself that each bidder is capable of supplying goods of the proper specification with regard to quality, delivery requirement, packaging, etc., and should solicit quotations from only those firms with whom he is prepared to do business.

The rare practice of soliciting bids merely to check prices is to be discouraged; in many cases, it is costly for a vendor to prepare a quotation, and it would not be ethical to ask him to do so merely for exercise or for the sole benefit of the buyer.

Negotiations

In some procurement situations, it becomes apparent to the buyer that he is "wired in" to one particular supplier. This could be the result of a restrictive material specification or it could be due to the fact that a supplier has some unique capability to fill the customer's need.

Such a situation lends itself to negotiation of a mutually satisfactory price. The negotiation procedure involves the effort of buyer and seller to arrive at an equitable price, balancing on the one hand the costs and profit of the vendor and, on the other hand, the value of the product for the buyer's intended use.

Price History

Historical records are invaluable as a tool for checking current prices against prices previously paid, as well as for establishing price trends and as a basis for forecasting prices.

Many companies prepare their own price indexes for selected groups of items, finding these to be more relevant to their affairs than the published government indexes.

In the implementation of its planning function, top management must consider the price trends of purchased materials because such items constitute a major portion of manufacturing costs; therefore, the purchasing department must be prepared to furnish such data on a regular basis.

Fundamentals of Costs

A knowledge of costing procedures and terms is essential to the buyer in understanding the vendor's approach to pricing. In some instances the buyer armed with knowledge of the vendor's costs will be able to detect a possible savings based on increasing his volume or changing order quantities or other conditions of purchase.

Even partial information on the vendor's costs can be used to counter requests for price increases based on labor rate increases, raw material price rises, or other factors.

In some instances complete information on costs can be obtained by requesting it as a condition of bidding. In most cases the information will be partial and must

---

Name of Supplier _____   Analysis of Cost as of _____ 19 ____

Address _____   Quantity _____ at _____

Article _____   Net Total of Quotation _____

1. MANUFACTURING COST

  Raw Materials . . . . $_____

  Purchased Components . . . .   _____

  Total Material Cost . . . . $_____   _____

  Direct Labor . . . .   _____   _____

    Total Variable Cost . . . .   _____   _____

  Overhead Cost . . . .   _____   _____

    Total Manufacturing Cost . . . .   _____   100%

2. SHIPPING COST

  Materials . . . . $_____

  Packing & Shipping . . . .   _____

  Total Shipping Cost . . . .   _____

  Total Factory Cost . . . . $_____

3. SELLING, GENERAL, AND ADMINISTRATIVE EXPENSE

  _____% × Total Factory Cost _____ =   S G & A   _____

  Total Product Cost . . . .   _____

4. PROFIT

  _____% × Total Product Cost _____ =   Profit   _____

                 Selling Price = $_____

Fig. 11-1   Cost analysis work sheet—a format used by purchasing to evaluate pricing by vendors.

be supplemented by general information from industry sources, trade journals, company annual reports, and other media. In any event, it is essential that the buyer understand the terms and have an organized approach to the recording and use of whatever data can be obtained. A cost analysis work sheet (Fig. 11-1) is shown as an example of this approach. This must be adapted by the buyer to his particular need, the type of material being purchased, the number of potential suppliers, the make-or-buy possibilities, and other factors. The retention and updating of such a record will provide valuable knowledge of the material, vendor, and industry being analyzed.

Definitions of the terms itemized in Fig. 11-1 follow.

Manufacturing Cost

RAW MATERIALS.   The delivered cost of raw materials. Much price information on this important element of cost is available from industry sources and competitive suppliers. Usage may be more difficult to obtain, as factors of formulation, waste, and obsolescence must be considered.

PURCHASED COMPONENTS.   Many raw materials may appear in the form of purchased subassemblies. The same sources of information may be available as for raw materials, and the same caution as to allowance for losses must be observed.

DIRECT LABOR.   If direct information is unavailable, unit labor cost may be deduced from the number of employees on the manufacturing line times wage per person, divided by production speed.

VARIABLE COST.   This is the cost which can be directly assigned to the output and will vary directly with the number of units produced.

OVERHEAD COST.   This is the portion of factory cost which is not associated with the product itself. Examples are depreciation, property taxes, maintenance, and managers' and office salaries. This is an area where the additional volume may have a decided effect on unit costs. This knowledge can be used to advantage in negotiating a purchase that is large in relation to existing volume.

Shipping Cost   This ordinarily comprises variable costs but may have elements of overhead which can be large enough to be considered separately.

Selling, General, and Administrative Expense   Includes the salaries of the executive management and staff plus selling expenses. This element is almost separated from volume considerations. It is commonly expressed as a percentage of factory cost or sales and in many instances is available through annual reports and other sources of financial data.

Profit   May be arrived at directly but may more commonly represent the margin between the seller's price and the costs derived from various sources. Profit represents the return on investment for the owner or owners of a business; it is unreasonable to expect any company to operate without a profit.

Analysis through the use of such a simple form as Fig. 11-1 is a powerful tool for the buyers to use in evaluating:

1. Reasonableness of pricing by a single vendor
2. Comparison between vendors of varying sizes and capabilities
3. Requests for price increases based on changes in the vendors' costs

The Learning Curve

When a supplier asks for a price increase, his main argument—higher labor and material costs—is often difficult to counter. But there is one force that offsets increasing costs: manufacturing progress itself—the process that permits costs to go down as experience and improved techniques increase. Properly used, this force can result in lower or static prices.

The learning curve is a mathematical device that can be used for predicting manufacturing progress. From a purchasing standpoint, it provides a basis for introducing manufacturing progress as a factor in price negotiation. In addition, it can be useful in other activities, such as scheduling and make-or-buy analyses.

Analyses in various sophisticated industries, but primarily in the airframe and aerospace fields, have shown a reduction in direct labor hours as a greater number of units are produced. These studies, reduced to mathematical statements, define this inverse relationship called the *learning curve.*

These statements concerning progress curves or *improvement curves,* as they are sometimes called, cannot by themselves effect a reduction in direct labor costs; they require the assistance of design, methods, tooling, and managerial reinforcements.

The concept is based on the premise that a learning factor is injected into the repetitive production of a new item and that a worker gains in speed and efficiency as he acquires experience in the operation. With this technique of evaluation, both sides—buyer and seller—gain additional bonuses, such as:

Better scheduling
Higher quality
More efficient overall management

Benefits of evaluation to the buyer are:

Develops information needed in make-or-buy decisions
Gives data necessary to make progress payments when called for in purchase contracts
Supplies buyer with knowledge of delivery time
Acts as a bargaining tool in negotiations when supplier's performance slips
Assists buyer in establishing estimated costs to be used in future products

Frequently, a discussion on the subject refers to a 90 percent learning rate. It could be 85 percent, 80 percent, or a number of other percentages determined by the peculiarities of the industry. What is referred to, in this instance, is the determination that when labor costs decline 10 percent on a particular item each time production is doubled, the learning rate is 90 percent. The rate is always expressed as a percentage calculated on the basis of units produced. The learning curve can be reproduced graphically either on regular graph paper or on log-log paper, as shown in Figs. 11-2 and 11-3.

Examination of the two charts shows the same 90 percent learning curve; however, the one used most frequently by analysts is the log-log method. Here the log scale converts the curve to a straight line, which is easier to read. Since it is a straight line, buyer forecasting is made simple and quick by extension of the line or "eyeballing" an enlarged chart.

Utilization under Specified Conditions   It should be emphasized that in arriving at a fair price with cooperative suppliers, the learning or improvement curve is useful only when certain conditions exist, such as the following:

1. When a nonstandard part is being manufactured
2. When the amount of money involved justifies the use of the theory

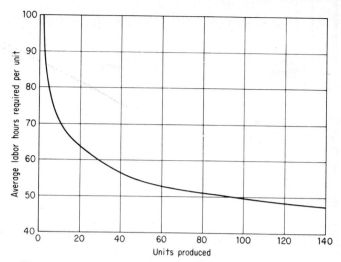

Fig. 11-2 The 90 percent learning curve on regular graph paper. (*Reprinted by special permission from L. Lee and D. W. Dobler,* Purchasing and Materials Management, *3d ed., McGraw-Hill Book Company, 1976.*)

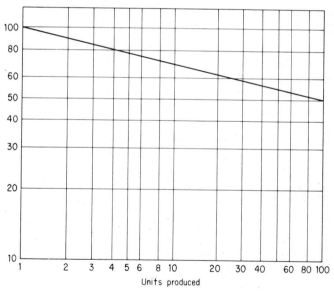

Fig. 11-3 The 90 percent learning curve of Fig. 11-2 plotted on log-log paper. (*Reprinted by special permission from L. Lee and D. W. Dobler,* Purchasing and Materials Management, *3d ed., McGraw-Hill Book Company, 1976.*)

3. When free competition is prevented by such factors as proprietary items, expensive or complicated tooling, specialized equipment, specialized know-how, or patents

4. When the direct labor increment is a substantial proportion of the costs

It is under these conditions that the learning-curve concept becomes an extremely useful tool.

Common Misuses   Although the learning or improvement curve is a very useful buying tool, it can easily be misused to the detriment of the supplier, the purchaser, and other companies that may purchase from the supplier at a later date. The most common misuses of the curve are:

1. Applying a curve to an estimated price, which tends to magnify any errors in the original estimate.

2. Attempting to apply a curve to standard items and acting as if the first article purchased were the first article produced, even though many thousands of similar or identical parts may have been manufactured in the past.

3. Attempting to apply the curve in fields different from those in which the statistics were originally developed, e.g., in modification work.

4. Attempting to apply one percentage curve universally. Good judgment is needed to select the proper slope to be applied.

The success of any buyer in using the theory for negotiating prices is directly dependent upon his ability to convince the supplier that the basic figures used are correct and that his costs will follow the improvement shown by the curve.

POSSIBLE PITFALLS IN PRICE EVALUATION

Many factors that influence evaluation of prices cannot be measured precisely in terms of price.

Reciprocity

Reciprocity is a common situation, and the best approach is also the simplest—a vendor's status as a customer will be considered only when evaluation shows all other factors are equal. A firm corporate policy on this subject will avoid many lost opportunities for purchasing savings. Recent strong activity by federal antitrust agencies has discouraged the practice of reciprocity and tends to place it in its rightful status as a secondary consideration.

Application of Law

Application of law is a frequent source of confusion, particularly the Robinson-Patman Act. Recent application of the law makes the buyer who knowingly solicits an illegal price equally guilty with the seller. Because the buyer is entitled to the best price available, he must ask and insist on it. Paradoxically, knowledge of prices available to a specific competitor may place the buyer at a disadvantage.

His best interests are served by his general knowledge of prices in the specific field, the offerings of competing vendors, and his knowledge of a particular vendor's strength or vulnerability to price concessions. See Section 4 for particulars.

Pressures

Pressures by large stockholders, customers, and relatives likewise can be overcome by firm policy directives that are enforced uniformly. In the case of governmental buying, this interference may be political. Strong statutory legislation has increasingly been enacted to minimize this problem.

Services or Advice

Services or advice offered as an added inducement is another factor that often is difficult to evaluate. In many cases these services offer a real inducement. In the case of market-type commodities, offered at uniform price from many sources, the product services may well be the determining factor. Volume in a commodity such as heavy chemicals is frequently divided among suppliers to take advantage of multiple sources of information.

Often product services are offered as a part of the price package but may be purchased separately as needed. Periodic maintenance service usually should be purchased separately, on a per-call or per-hour basis, so that a realistic comparison can be made of the basic price of the equipment itself.

Inventory Carrying Costs

Inventory carrying cost is a factor that may vary widely among vendors. Transit time, vendor loading facilities, switching service, production capacity, and other factors affect the ordering quantities and the amount of inventory to be carried out. These costs, more fully evaluated elsewhere, must be added to each vendor's price.

For production materials, delivery by pipeline of liquid materials offers practically inventory-free delivery for the buyer. Conversely, purchases by truckload, carload, and tanker require increasing amounts of inventory to ensure a steady supply.

For general stores items, many companies now are benefiting by purchasing from conveniently located supply houses which offer systems contracting—again virtually inventory-free. Supplies are transferred from the vendor's shelves directly to point of use. Carefully evaluated savings in inventory may justify a higher unit price from the contract vendor as contrasted to one who delivers in a conventional manner.

Spare parts on production equipment can add considerable amounts to inventory dollars. To eliminate the excess, many companies buy equipment from well-established manufacturers who agree to carry a stock of replacement parts for a number of years after purchase. After a time limit, the parts are offered to customers at reduced prices.

Labor

Labor history and projections for the future are important to the buyer as indexes of reliability of the source. These ordinarily would be difficult to evaluate quantitatively but might be a deciding factor in close competition.

Government Regulations

Government regulations frequently impose restrictions on sources that may disqualify them. Failure by a vendor to adhere to fair employment standards could disqualify a source with an otherwise attractive price.

Good Records

Good records of price should form the basis for the buyer's knowledge of general trends, but, more specifically, they will illustrate the trend for a particular commodity. Price trends for a basic raw material often will indicate future prices of the product. Rapidly advancing energy costs will indicate possible future price increases in commodities requiring high energy input. An increase in sulfur costs will generate predictable increases in sulfuric acid and, in turn, in a chemical such as alum.

Distress Bids

Distress bids require the utmost caution. Knowing that "there is one born every day and two to take him," many so-called hustlers have appeared on the scene in recent years to dupe unsuspecting purchasing departments into bidding on distress merchandise. Their product areas cover such items as stationery, janitorial and cleaning supplies, and solvents. The telephone caller claims he or she has been referred to the buyer by a top corporate executive, somebody whose name the buyer is very familiar with but someone with whom he generally has very little contact.

The pitch is to tell a tale of woe. No matter what the story is, the end is the same: the caller is in a desperate situation and wants to liquidate a family business fast. To do so he is offering his wares at very low prices.

The clincher comes when the merchandise arrives. Often it is not what was agreed upon, the price is different, quantities are much higher than ordered, and quality is inferior. Such pitfalls can be avoided by purchasing department procedures stressing the value of dealing only with known and reputable suppliers.

Unusually Low Price

Unusually low prices should be examined carefully. The price may offer perfectly legitimate savings even though the material may be old inventory or surplus. However, the buyer must realize that it is not a commitment for long-term supply, and he should be aware of this in evaluating such a price against competition from regular sources.

"Get-Foot-in-Door" Price

These are vendors' bids to attract new customers with unusually low prices. The buyer may test this intention and possibly improve his savings by requesting a long-term commitment at the favorable price.

VENDOR CAPABILITY

The price paid for a product or service is predicted upon the vendors' costs. The difference between this figure and the selling price (the profit) usually is a percentage of the costs that is common to the trade or established by the manufacturer as what he needs to make his business prosper. For standard competitive articles this aspect of evaluation is not susceptible to searching study, but for special products and construction services detailed cost studies may be required. In large competitive bidding, the buyer usually is equipped with an estimate to compare with the bids received. If the buyer's estimate differs from the competitive bids, discussions with the bidders may be held, and these will be concerned with generalized figures not usually in great detail. Sufficient information should develop to assure the purchasing manager that he has at least closely approximated the fair price.

Failing to achieve such assurance, he can either accept the most favorable bid, reject all bids and submit his request to a new bidders' list, or select a limited number of suppliers and negotiate with them on a *negotiated price* basis.

A negotiated deal entails a detailed study of the supplier's capability and his past performance record. At its completion, the buyer has the tools to sit down and negotiate a fair and equitable price.

In considering vendor capability, there are eight essential points to be covered:

1. Management
   - Does the vendor have the depth of management to run the business?
   - Are the accounting procedures according to generally accepted trade practice?
   - Is the procurement function an efficient operation?
2. Plant inspection
   - Is the shop kept in an orderly manner—good housekeeping—efficient handling of materials?
   - In what condition is the equipment?
   - Is the labor force being utilized to its potential?
3. Financial position
   - Does the supplier meet its commitments to suppliers?
   - What is its credit rating?
   - What is its reputation in the banking community?
4. Production capacity
   - Does it have the tools, labor, and equipment to produce your requirements?
   - If not, is it going to be a problem to expand present production facilities?

5. Quality control
   - Are updated quality control techniques being used?
   - What type of equipment is used to accomplish quality control?
   - What is the average reject rate?
6. Experience
   - What is the supplier's previous experience?
   - How long has the vendor been in business?
   - What is the average length of service of its employees?
   - Does the company have the knowledge to perform your particular requirement, or is it going to have to learn an entirely new operation?
7. Labor conditions
   - Is it a union shop?
   - Has the area a history of labor strife?
8. Industry contribution
   - Is the company a leader in its field?
   - What reputation does the supplier have among its competitors?

Completion of all the reference material is only an assist to the buyer. It is his evaluation of such information, together with knowledge and judgment, that ultimately must prevail.

MAKE OR BUY (OR LEASE)

Make-or-buy decisions must be based on a considerable number of factors, many of which are not susceptible to straight cost analysis. Such decisions, except when concerning relatively minor matters, cannot be the responsibility of any one department. In owner-operated enterprises, the owner may presume to make his own decision, but unless he has the counsel of others, including purchasing, he is only guessing.

To buy is generally the easy way out. The cost can usually be determined in advance and included in the selling price. Unfortunately, if everything is bought and assembled, the product may not be salable because of the lack of quality control in manufacture, or the final selling price may be too high.

To make everything would also be an easy decision, and for certain products this is done for all items except standardized operating supplies, standard production and processing equipment, and materials not entering directly into product or production. In cases where this is practical, the final product is new, highly complicated, and of relatively high monetary value.

To Make

To make requires production equipment, personnel, material, space, supervision, and, in varying degrees, overhead, maintenance, taxes, insurance, management attention, and other indirect or hidden costs.

To make returns immediate control of quality. It also may provide work for idle equipment or personnel, utilize scrap material, shorten delivery time, permit use of a part which outside suppliers are not able to produce, permit experimentation, promote flexibility when dimensions are variable, ensure continuity of supply, train personnel for more complicated operations, cost less than purchased items, and keep design information secret.

To Buy

To buy permits lower investment in facilities, smaller labor force, lower plant cost for building and upkeep, and less overhead for taxes, insurance, supervision, etc.

To buy permits specialization, manufacture by the most efficient equipment, lower inventories, scheduling of material deliveries as required, change of design without loss of investment in equipment or inventory, obtaining lowest real cost by competitive bidding, and obtaining best price and product by suppliers' more varied experience.

Arriving at the Decision

In arriving at the decision, purchasing generally will be best equipped to counsel in regard to the buy side of the decision-making process. Since purchasing is the contact with outside suppliers, purchasing should have knowledge of suppliers' capabilities and reliability. Purchasing effort should be directed toward obtaining all necessary information in this regard and should concern itself not with the details of costs of make but only that the appropriate departments have given adequate attention to them.

Depending upon the production level at which the company is operating in comparison with the general level of economic activity, each of the various advantages of make or buy will assume varying importance, as will each of the disadvantages. If the company is producing at a maximum level, buy will be more attractive in order to permit the company to utilize personnel and equipment to produce the maximum for sale. At lower levels of operation it may be desirable to make as much as possible, to spread fixed costs over as wide a range as possible, to produce the best product through direct quality control, and to maintain the work force with minimum layoffs. In either level the decision may be made even though the other alternate might have resulted in a lower actual cost for the particular item.

When producing *at normal levels of operation* it becomes more difficult to reach make-or-buy decisions. True costs to make a particular item are difficult to determine. Cost accounting necessarily makes arbitrary assignments of various overhead factors, which in a particular instance may miss the actual cost by a wide margin on either the high or the low side.

Use of existing production equipment may not actually be free, because it wears the unit, uses power, requires heating of the space, dilutes supervision, and may require special costs. Purchase of new equipment may not be justified, because it dissipates working capital, involves depreciation which may continue after product changes make the part obsolete, requires floor space, and may involve new personnel.

Buying the item is indicated if satisfactory sources are available and can meet quality, delivery, and service requirements at a satisfactory price. If the reliability of suppliers is not good, inspection costs may be increased even though the supplier stands the costs of rejects. His labor difficulties become the buyer's too, and transportation to buyer's plants opens opportunity for transit damage or delays.

If a capital purchase is under consideration, the further avenue of lease versus buy should be considered. The ramifications of this approach are discussed in Section 16.

Positive Approach to Make or Buy

The foregoing has tended toward the negative side of the decision-making process. In practical application the negative approach tends to encourage continuity of past practices. Aggressive companies have determined make or buy on the basis of positive thinking after examination of the disadvantages of each as applied to specific problems.

One world-known manufacturer is reputed to follow a policy of making one-half of the required quantity of each component and buying the other half. The basis of the policy is said to be to ensure continuity of supply in the event of labor difficulties in either plant. This has a further benefit in that both plants act as cost checks on each other.

Shortage of skilled personnel has tended to encourage buying in recent years. Many technical experts have formed small companies and offer new or improved products which are advantageous to incorporate into other goods and which the buyer cannot make himself for want of personnel to design or manufacture.

Conversely, automation tends to encourage making insofar as automobiles and other large products are concerned. The high cost of some of these automated machines prohibits any but the largest companies purchasing them. Small manufacturers have neither sufficient money to purchase nor enough output to justify these units.

Other types of automated equipment do encourage buying by the average purchasing manager. These machines produce at lower costs than conventional equipment, but must be kept busy to be justified. Prices quoted by specialists in these fields are so much more attractive than the buyer's costs that in many instances companies are closing certain departments and utilizing space, personnel, and facilities to increase production of final product.

PRICE HISTORY

Countless numbers of articles are bought by the purchasing department, and it is not supposed that their prices can be remembered. Proper records of previous purchases must be kept and used for price checking and to assist in analyzing price.

The purchasing executive must be constantly aware of prices and price trends, certainly on major items which he purchases. A good inventory system may incorporate price information. In many cases, this can be used without duplicating records within the purchasing department itself. The purchasing department, however, must keep track of prices, quantities, and sources of supply of major items in order to evaluate properly its own performance in terms of general economic trends and to evaluate sources of supply with whom it deals.

Price information must be timely and must be accurate. Trends of prices gathered from all sorts of sources, including weekly commodity price indexes, Bureau of Labor Statistics, charts and forecasts from financial papers and magazines, and even the intelligent reading of a magazine and the proper evaluation of current events, all must be kept up to date. Many markets fluctuate rapidly. The trend may be more important than the spot prices of any particular day.

Many purchasing managers have found it worthwhile to develop charts or other visual aids to cover price trends on items that are of major importance to their company. Here the trend becomes very apparent and graphical. Such visual aids are of interest and assistance to top management as well as to purchasing department personnel.

Price records are a basic tool in analyzing price. They are essential for the buyer to make a fair and adequate comparison of price among vendors. How extensive price records will be is a matter requiring considerable judgment. "You can't see the forest for the trees" if too much effort is made to keep detailed records on items of small value. A carefully indexed record of prices and quantities purchased should be kept for all important, repetitive items. These records may be in price books, card files, or visible-tray indexes. They may be filed alphabetically by commodity or numerically by code.

With the growth of integrated data processing, more and more companies of all sizes are utilizing tabulating and computer equipment. One particular company, among many others, has adopted the use of punched-card control of all stores and materials. Thus, every item is assigned a code number, and all receipts, issuances, and changes are handled mechanically by tabulating equipment. In this company's purchasing department, a set of these material cards is maintained, filed numerically by code number. Basic information, including the code number, item description, and standard cost, is automatically printed by the tabulating machine.

Actual purchase prices, quantities bought, and vendor information are clerically recorded on these cards. The numerical filing actually speeds up location of the cards for most users of this file, since all purchase requisitions must bear the code number. Numerical location is considerably faster than alphabetical location, as cards can be arranged numerically by the tabulating machine.

The disadvantage of this system comes when one is searching for an item without knowing its code number. Of course, code numbers are systematically assigned and cross reference is relatively easy. An important advantage of this system is its utilization of cards which are mechanically printed, thus eliminating the considerable clerical job of preparing a card for each item.

In summary, the extent to which price records are kept is a matter of judgment—the ability to draw the line at that point where the value of the record justifies the cost of keeping it. High dollar-volume materials certainly justify careful, complete price records. The actual system of record keeping must be adapted to the nature of the business, the organization of the department, and the commodities purchased.

NOTE: For further information on subjects covered in this section see the list of references in Section 30.

Section **12**

Inventory Management

EDITOR

Caleb L. Johnson, C.P.M. *Director, Materials, Plumbing & Specialty Products Group, Kohler Company, Kohler, Wisconsin*

ASSOCIATE EDITOR

Susan K. Williams *Senior Systems Analyst, Tennant Company, Minneapolis, Minnesota*

Responsibility for the management of inventory is often shared by most of the operating functions. Marketing sometimes has responsibility for finished goods, and manufacturing often controls work-in-process inventories. More and more companies have embraced the materials management concept and assign all inventories—raw materials, work in process, finished goods, and operating supplies—to this organization. Where purchasing is an independent function, it often carries the responsibility for the control of certain classes of inventory, usually raw materials, purchased parts, and supplies. Organization responsibility for inventory will vary from industry to industry and, more particularly, with the size of the company. Regardless of which organization has responsibility, purchasing will exert a certain amount of influence on inventory decisions.

Today top management is very aware of the importance of inventory and its impact on the financial investment required to operate a business. Good management of inventory by maintaining the required balance among customer service needs, manufacturing efficiencies, and financial resources plays a vital role in meeting the objectives of the business enterprise. On the other hand, poor management of inventory can be disastrous, resulting in lost customers because of poor deliveries, labor problems because of interrupted production, and skyrocketing costs which erode profits and result in unhappy managers and stockholders.

It is important to realize that moneys invested in inventories in many companies represent 30 to 50 percent of the assets of the business. On this investment the business pays taxes, insurance charges, storage costs, and interest, while it also assumes risks of obsolescence, damage, deterioration, and devaluation. It is also important to realize that some investment in inventory is necessary, although too much is not good. Funds tied up with too much inventory may not be available to purchase new equipment, pay stockholder dividends, develop new products, etc. This situation may also necessitate the borrowing of funds by the business, on which it is required to pay interest charges. In this world of rapidly changing technology, overstocks of inventory may be subject to obsolescence due to product design improvements.

Insufficient inventories lead to other problems for management—including higher costs of operations because of work stoppages, uneconomical production runs, increased personnel turnover, etc.—which result in irate customers.

It is, therefore, incumbent upon management of a business to determine and maintain an adequate level of inventory in the proper mix for a given level of business which will yield the optimum return on its total assets. This is inventory management in its fundamental meaning.

Management must weigh the demand for funds required for inventory against other demands for those same funds, as resources in most companies are limited. In making a decision regarding inventory, management normally asks one or more of the following questions:

1. Why is it required?
2. How much should be ordered?
3. When should a quantity discount be taken?
4. When is it required?
5. When should it be ordered?
6. How much should be purchased when advised of a price increase?
7. How much of a speculative risk item should be purchased?
8. At what minimum price should surplus inventory be sold?
9. How much is on hand now?

PURPOSE OF INVENTORY

Inventory is created for two general purposes:

1. To provide sufficient material to meet demands for the particular raw material, fabricated part, or finished product with a minimum of delay (i.e., *protection*)

2. To effect lower product costs by realizing the savings resulting from longer manufacturing runs and from purchasing larger quantities per order (i.e., *economy*)

Although there may be a variety of individual reasons for creating inventory under a given set of circumstances, these reasons, if closely examined, will all fall into one of the two categories mentioned above.

In almost all manufacturing companies there are conflicting objectives that managers must face. Three of these are efficient plant operation, customer service, and minimum inventory investment. It is the responsibility of management to keep these objectives in balance to serve the best interests of the company.

This balancing requires decisions that fall into four major categories:

1. What balance is desired between inventory investment and customer service? Where effective inventory control exists to execute management policy, there is a definite relationship between the amount of inventory carried and the service that results. The lower the inventory, the more back orders and stockouts; the higher the inventory, the better the service.

2. What balance is desired between inventory investment and costs associated with changes in the production level? Higher costs will be incurred for excess equipment capacity, overtime, idle time, the hiring, training, and laying off of employees, and related items if production must fluctuate in response to changing sales rates.

3. What balance is desired between inventory investment and the cost of placing inventory replenishment orders? Low inventories can be maintained by setting up jobs frequently or by placing a great many purchase orders for small quantities. These practices result in high setup costs, purchasing costs, lost quantity discounts, and other excessive operating expenses.

4. What balance is desired between inventory investment and transportation costs? Providing the work force and materials handling equipment so that jobs in production can be moved hourly, for example, requires a greater expenditure than would be required if jobs were moved daily.[1]

FUNCTIONS OF INVENTORY

If inventory is to be controlled, a manager must understand the functions that it serves. They are:

Anticipation Inventories

Anticipation inventories are built in anticipation of future demand. Many firms have seasonal periods of high sales, and the work force cannot keep up with customer demand during this period. Therefore, inventories are built prior to the seasonal increase to satisfy customers and to maintain a stable work force. Pro-

---

[1]G. W. Plossl and O. W. Wight, *Production and Inventory Control,* Prentice Hall, Inc., Englewood Cliffs, N.J., 1967, pp. 48–49.

motions and new products normally require the building of anticipation-type inventories. Possible labor strikes and vacation shutdowns are other reasons for building this type of inventory.

Fluctuation Inventories

These inventories are necessary when there are fluctuations in demand and supply. Safety stocks are typical examples of *fluctuation* inventories. Customer demand is not constant but will vary from one time period to the next. Work centers in a manufacturing plant do not produce at the same level. This normally results in the buildup of queues in the work-in-process inventories.

Lot-Size Inventories

Most manufacturing companies do not produce or purchase items exactly at the rate they are used or sold because of setup charges for manufactured items or ordering costs for purchased items. Items in excess of immediate needs provide an example of *lot-size inventory*.

Transportation Inventories

These inventories are necessary because materials are moved. Most manufacturing companies sell on a regional or national basis. Where regional warehouses are used or where product is transferred between plants prior to or during the selling process, the inventory required to support the delay in transit time is known as *transportation inventory.*[2]

CLASSES OF INVENTORY

Inventories are also classified according to condition during processing. These classes are:

Raw Material and Purchased Parts Inventory

This is recognized generally as the stock of raw materials (such as steel, copper, etc.) and purchased parts and components awaiting processing or assembly.

Work in Process

Work in process includes parts in progressive stages of completion, such as raw material just issued from stores, material in various stages of processing, and parts or assemblies awaiting final acceptance as finished stock.

Finished Stock

Finished stock comprises units of the manufactured or completed product awaiting sale or consignment.

[2]O. W. Wight, *Production and Inventory Management in the Computer Age,* CBI Publishing Company, Inc., Boston, 1974, p. 176.

Supplies

Supplies are the expendable items which are required to manufacture the product but do not become a part of that product, such as tools, cleaning materials, and cutting oils. These are commonly termed *maintenance, repair, and operating (MRO)* supplies. The above classes are not to be considered fixed or all-inclusive, since it is understandable that the broad classifications and the constituents of inventory will vary with the particular industry.

INVENTORY ANALYSIS AND CLASSIFICATION (ABC)

One of the first steps in organizing for more effective control of inventory is the analysis, tabulation, and classification of the characteristics of the commodities being carried in inventory. The comprehensive classification of all items in order of descending dollar activity will permit sound financial control of inventory by directing the attention of the inventory planner to those items which represent the vast majority of dollars. Some of the more important points of consideration in making such a classification or analysis of items in inventory are discussed below.

Classification by Usage

An analysis of *usage* (sometimes called *activity*) has been found to be most useful when prepared as a listing of inventory items in order of descending dollar activity; this is sometimes called the *ABC concept*. This list, when totaled in cumulative fashion, will indicate at a glance which accounts control the bulk of dollars in inventory. It is interesting to note that the curve shown in Fig. 12-1 is typical of a manufacturing inventory. Approximately 10 percent of the items stocked account for 70 percent of the dollar investment; at the other extreme, 70 percent of the items represent only 10 percent of investment, with the remaining 20 percent of the items representing 20 percent of the investment. This relationship is shown in bar chart form in Fig. 12-2.

Here, then, is one of the keys to more effective management of inventory. The control policies and techniques which apply to the few items representing 70 percent of the total inventory value (classification A) would be designed for close supervision through continual review of requirements, stock balances, and scheduled materials deliveries to maintain a minimum of inventory.

The 70 percent of inventory items (classification C) which comprise 10 percent of the dollar value may be con-

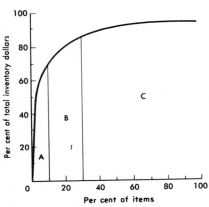

Fig. 12-1 Distribution of inventory items by inventory dollars.

trolled on an automatic basis with sufficient lead times and adequate inventory levels to avoid stockouts.

The 20 percent of inventory items (classification B) which represents approximately 20 percent of the dollars should be reviewed on a periodic basis and scheduled deliveries set up to maintain adequate stock levels.

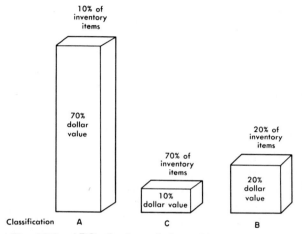

Fig. 12-2 ABC selective technique of inventory control.

Here is one of the keys to better inventory control. This may be illustrated by the simple example, using only 10 items, shown in Table 12-1.

After the list is compiled and a number assigned to rank the items in accordance with descending dollar activity, another listing is made. This time the items are listed according to ranking of highest dollar activity, including cumulative annual dollar usage and cumulative percentage. The inventory classes can be decided

TABLE 12-1

Item no.	Annual usage	Unit cost	Annual $ usage	Rank
301	62,500	0.08	$ 5,000	3
215	5,000	0.09	450	8
418	40,000	0.12	4,800	4
603	20,000	0.14	2,800	5
812	7,000	0.10	700	7
156	4,000	0.07	280	10
806	143,000	0.15	21,450	1
727	8,000	0.05	400	9
938	8,000	0.16	1,280	6
594	420,000	0.04	16,800	2

upon according to the requirements of the individual company. In Table 12-2 class A items make up 20 percent of the total items, class B items represent 30 percent, and class C items make up the remaining 50 percent.

The following examples are typical of the applications of the ABC concept.

Degree of Control

• *A items* require the tightest control possible, including the most complete, accurate records, regular review by top-level supervisors, blanket orders with fre-

---

TABLE 12-2

Item no.	Annual $ usage	Cumulative annual $ usage	Cumulative percentage	Class
806	$21,450	$21,450	39.8	A
594	16,800	38,250	71.0	A
301	5,000	43,250	80.2	B
418	4,800	48,050	89.3	B
603	2,800	50,850	94.4	B
938	1,280	52,130	96.7	C
812	700	52,830	97.9	C
215	450	53,280	98.9	C
727	400	53,680	99.6	C
156	280	53,960	100.0	C

---

quent deliveries from vendors, close follow-up through the factory to reduce lead time, etc.

• *B items* require only normal controls, involving good records and regular attentions.

• *C items* receive the simplest possible controls, such as periodic review of physical inventory with the simplest notations that replenishment stocks have been ordered. Large inventories and order quantities are maintained to avoid stockouts, and scheduling in factory receives low priority.

Types of Inventory Records

• *A items:* Most accurate and complete with frequent audits of accuracy; tight control of scrap losses, rejects, etc.
• *B items:* Normal good records
• *C items:* No records or only the simplest

Priority

• *A items:* High priority in all activities to reduce lead times and inventory
• *B items:* Normal processing with high priority only when critical
• *C items:* Lowest priority

Ordering Procedures

- *A items:* Careful, accurate determination of order quantities and order points; frequent review to reduce, if possible
- *B items:* Good analysis for economic-order-quantity (EOQ) and order-point determinations but with review made only quarterly or when major changes occur
- *C items:* No EOQ or order-point calculations—1 year's supply ordered while there are still plenty on hand[3]

FUNDAMENTALS OF ORDER POINT AND ORDER QUANTITY

Inventory is created for two reasons: (1) to reduce overall operating costs (economy); (2) to provide protection against unpredictable demands (protection). It is usually difficult to isolate these two characteristics when examining a given stock account, but it is necessary to do so if effective methods of inventory control are to be installed.

Economy Function

An inventory of purchased raw material and parts may be created even though a company could operate with no inventory at all. Assume that X Company makes a product whose sales can be predicted, item by item, for long periods, and the finished products which are not sold are put into finished-stock inventory. Each product could be "exploded" into all the required raw materials and parts, and the requirements of each could be pinpointed to the exact day it would be needed. All material could be brought in daily and routed directly to the manufacturing area where it is needed. The only inventory would be work-in-process inventory.

If X Company is assumed to have 5000 different items which are purchased regularly, such a policy would mean scheduling hundreds of incoming shipments daily, with all the associated paperwork. X Company would quickly conclude that it would be more economical to purchase, receive, and store these items *in advance of need.* The creation of raw-material inventory would, of course, result in additional costs associated with the storage of material such as obsolescence, depreciation, etc. These so-called inventory carrying costs, when compared with the previously mentioned costs associated with ordering and receiving, could be used to calculate the most economical policy of ordering and storing the inventory. If it proved less expensive to carry inventory for that period of time than to incur the costs of daily or weekly ordering and/or receiving, inventory would be created.

Figure 12-3 shows the rise and fall of the stock level for a given stock item whose predictable usage is 100 pieces per month. For this particular item, the most economical method of ordering[4] may be assumed to be 300 pieces once every 3 months. The stock controller would place his orders so that each new order

---

[3]Plossl and Wight, op. cit., pp. 60–61.
[4]See calculation under Using the EOQ later in this section.

would arrive just as the stock reached zero. The stock level would fluctuate between 300 and zero, resulting in an average inventory of 150 pieces, or 1½ month's supply.

The inventory which is created by the use of a predetermined order quantity is directly related to that order quantity, provided the same quantity is used on all subsequent orders. Figure 12-3 shows this to be true:

$$\text{Average active stock} = \tfrac{1}{2}\text{ order quantity}$$

In this example, the inventory is composed entirely of active stock, i.e., every piece of stock turns over during the period between receivings. This principle, if applied

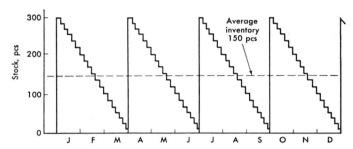

Fig. 12-3   Predictable monthly usage 100 pieces; order quantity 300 pieces.

to every item in the inventory, provides a means of forecasting the total inventory. The total inventory would be one-half the sum of each order quantity.[5]

This illustration has been oversimplified to illustrate how the active stock portion of the inventory is created. Except for companies whose production schedules are 100 percent predictable, most raw material inventories must contain an additional segment of inventory called *safety stock*. This subject is discussed next.

Protection Function (Safety Stock) and Economy Function

A more typical situation than that of X Company is illustrated by Y Company. The latter organization manufactures a product which can be forecast only by general product lines. The individual items within those product lines may be required by its customers upon short notice. This short lead time does not allow time enough to purchase the material for each individual customer's order. Therefore, there is an obvious need for the creation of raw-material inventory to be available for these periodic demands. The stock level of each stock item may be set initially by guess or intention, but after a period of months the issue pattern from the stock record should provide for a more factual approach. That is, past activity may be used to forecast probable future requirements. An example of such a historical record is shown in Fig. 12-4.

[5]This neglects the *safety stock* portion of the inventory. See Calculation of Safety Stock later in this section.

This example is shown to illustrate two points:

1. If the item in question is a stable item, used frequently, so that many demands are made upon it each month, there will be an issue pattern which may be used to forecast future activity. This rate of usage may be expressed as *average monthly usage,* or usage in any convenient time period.

2. Even the most stable of the items will occasionally experience a period of unusually high activity. This may be called *maximum monthly usage* and may exceed the average monthly usage by a significant amount.

January	970
February	850
March	1,010
April	900
May	910
June	980
July	1,770 (maximum monthly usage)
August	910
September	830
October	980
November	910
December	980
	12)12,000
	1,000 (average monthly usage)

Fig. 12-4   Stock issue record.

With these fluctuations in usage because of changing levels in demand, it is necessary to provide extra stock, which will be used in those periods of above-average usage. This is normally called *safety stock.* Once established, the safety stock is reviewed for adequacy on a periodic basis. As long as the fluctuations in demand do not increase, the safety stock level should remain the same. Over a long period, including seasonal or cyclical fluctuations, if the magnitude of the highest period of usage drops, then a lower level of safety stock should be used.

Figure 12-5 illustrates the problem of a stockout occurring in August, using the data from Fig. 12-4. Adding safety stock would prevent this from occurring. It is important to note that the rise and fall of the stock level, on the typical stock item, is not as symmetrical as the ones illustrated, which have been deliberately over-simplified. The safety stock portion of the inventory is, therefore, difficult to visualize. It may be determined, however, by simply measuring the points of minimum stock over a period of months and calculating their average value. The active stock portion of the inventory is then calculated by subtracting the safety stock from the average inventory over that period.

It should be emphasized that the order quantity is not increased to provide protection against periods of unusually high usage. The order quantity is based upon the average usage—in this example, 12,000 pieces per year. Protection is provided by maintaining a safety stock level, through adjustment of the order-point level.

Active Stock—Order Quantity   The *active stock* portion of the inventory is that portion which is created for the purpose of satisfying the *expected* requirements of material. It is directly related to the *order quantity*. The order quantity is simply the expected annual requirements divided by that number of orders which has proved most economical based on the cost of ordering and carrying inventory (see Economic Order Quantity later in this section).

Safety Stock—Order Point   The *safety stock* portion of the inventory is that portion which is created to take care of above-average or unexpected demands on the inventory. It is directly related to the order point. The amount of stock is

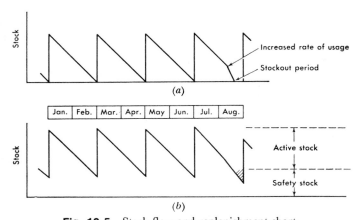

Fig. 12-5   Stock flow and replenishment chart.

determined not on ordering–carrying cost considerations but on the need for protection against stock outages for each stock item under consideration. Some items will need more safety stock than others, depending upon the amount of deviation that has been experienced between the forecast material usage and the actual material usage for any given time period, plus the reliability of the suppliers' deliveries and of the order lead time (the longer the lead time, the more uncertain are the forecast of sales and the resultant material requirements. Those items whose future activity can be forecast with 100 percent accuracy will require, theoretically, no safety stock.)

Protection Function Alone

Items which are stocked for protection most often are classified as MRO types of inventory. The consequence of being out of stock when the item is required is carefully considered in determining the safety stock level. Such items are normally found in maintenance inventories and are items that are subject to wear or have a high incidence of breakage.

Use of the terms *active stock* and *safety stock* does not imply that a given item is to be physically separated into two distinct parts. It does suggest that the two functions be recognized and analyzed separately, so that an inventory policy may be established which will result in the desired amount of protection against stock-outs at the minimum overall cost.

ORDER QUANTITY

Maximum-Minimum System

The first system to be considered, the *maximum-minimum* system, combines order quantity and order point and operates as follows: Two arbitrary levels of

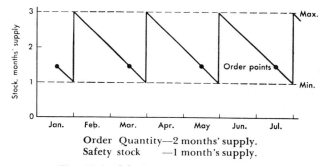

Order Quantity—2 months' supply.
Safety stock   —1 month's supply.

Fig. 12-6 Maximum-minimum system.

stock are selected, usually expressed in weeks' or months' supply. The stock controllers are instructed to order their stock in such a manner that it stays within the two specified limits. For example, in Fig. 12-6, the following conditions have been assumed: maximum stock level, 3 months' supply; minimum stock level, 1 month's supply; supplier lead time, ½ month. To maintain the stock about the 1-month minimum, the stock controller must reorder before the stock drops below 1½ months. He expects the order to arrive when the stock represents about 1 month's supply. He must not order in quantities in excess of 2 months' supply, because this order, plus his minimum stock, must not exceed 3 months. This system has some advantages, as well as some serious disadvantages.

Advantages:

1. The system prevents excessive buildup of stock on any given item because of the 3-month maximum.
2. It provides a level of protection against unusual demands on the stock because of the minimum level.
3. It is easy to explain to operating personnel.
4. Actual performance can easily be checked against the standard.

Disadvantages:

1. The system is not necessarily the most economical one when costs of processing orders and carrying inventory are considered.

2. The minimum stock may give either too much or too little protection for specific stock items.

3. The system tends to be *too automatic*. Repeatedly ordering to raise a minimum stock to a maximum level can lead to an overstocked position automatically; frequently design changes are given too little consideration in the strict compliance with maximum-minimum principles. An appropriate check against future requirements must be made to avoid reorders based only upon past experience.

4. Quantity discounts may be lost because of order-quantity restrictions.

5. The system does not specifically define either the order point or the order quantity.

If any systematic means, other than pure intuition on the part of the stock controller, is to be used to determine the order quantity, there must first be some method for estimating the expected future usage of each stock item. In many cases, the estimates or forecasts may be in error by as much as 25 to 50 percent, but this is not necessarily a deterrent to ordering in large quantities, provided the following is true:

1. The item is not likely to become obsolete in the near future (the product line is not being redesigned).

2. The item does not have a limited shelf life.

3. Large quantities do not present an unreasonable storage problem.

Assuming, then, that there is available an estimate of the annual activity of each item, the stock controller must make a decision as to the quantity of each item to be ordered. (This assumes that he is not operating under a system which limits stock on every item to 2 or 3 months' supply.) The decision which he makes as to his order quantities will, in turn, reflect itself in the inventory level.

In this example, the only restrictions on order quantity are a 1 month's supply minimum and a 12 months' supply maximum. Obviously, some practical limit must be imposed on either extreme. Ordering more frequently than once a month per item will usually result in excessive costs of paperwork, material checking, etc. Ordering more than a year's supply will frequently mean exceeding the limits of predictable future activity.

The item shown in Fig. 12-7 has an estimated annual activity of 1200 pieces and costs $1 per piece. If the entire year's supply were purchased in one order, the active stock[6] would fluctuate from a maximum of $1200 to a minimum of zero, with an average stock of about $600. Alternate methods of ordering this same item may be chosen. If the order frequency is increased, the resulting active stock is

---

[6]That portion of inventory created by order quantity.

reduced. If ordered monthly, in this example, the average active stock would be reduced to about $50. In general, the following rule applies:

Average active stock = ½ order quantity

In this example, an ordering cost of $10 per order and a carrying cost of 20 percent per year are assumed.

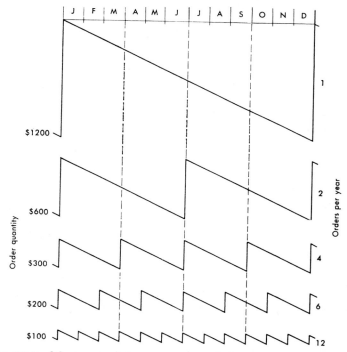

Fig. 12-7 Maximum-minimum system—ordering annual requirements.

The above illustration, which shows five different order quantities, is given to emphasize the point that there are many ways in which the annual requirements of a given item may be ordered. In this case, the resulting inventory could vary from $50 to $600. Given the costs associated with each alternative, however, it is possible to select the most economical method. Without such an analysis, the stock controller must rely on intuition or experience to make these decisions.

Economic Order Quantity (EOQ)

Figure 12-8 illustrates that the costs associated with carrying inventory vary inversely with the number of orders (these costs are reduced from $120 to $10 as

Number of orders	Order size	Average inventory	Inventory carrying cost	Ordering cost	Total cost
1	$1200	$600	$120	$ 6	$126
2	600	300	60	12	72
4	300	150	30	24	54
6	200	100	20	36	56
12	100	50	10	72	82

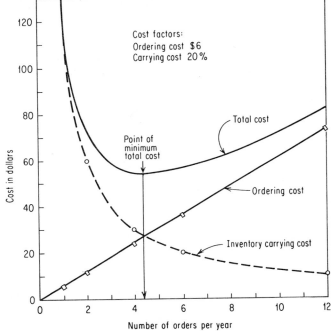

Fig. 12-8   Economic order quantity

the number of orders is increased from 1 to 12). Figure 12-8 also shows that the ordering costs increase directly with the number of orders (going from $10 to $120 in this case). Since the total cost is made up of both the ordering and carrying costs, it is this cost which must be minimized, rather than either of the component costs alone. In this case, the total cost appears to reach a minimum point somewhere between two and six orders per year. If the costs are plotted as curves (Fig. 12-8), it can be demonstrated that the point of minimum total cost is at the point of intersection of the ordering and carrying cost curves. This will always be true, regardless of the cost factors involved.

Other items, having different annual activities, could be analyzed in a similar manner, but this is impractical for a large number of items. Therefore, the following formula may be employed:

$$A = \text{Annual requirements (\$)}$$
$$C = \text{carrying cost, variable (\% per year)}$$
$$K = \text{ordering cost, variable (per order)}$$
$$N = \text{number of orders}$$
$$\text{Average inventory} = \tfrac{1}{2} A/N$$
$$\text{Annual ordering cost} = \text{annual carrying cost}$$
$$K/N = C(\tfrac{1}{2} A/N)$$

Solving for N, which in this case is the most economical number of orders,

$$N = \sqrt{\frac{CA}{2K}}$$

This formula is a general formula, which may be used for any combination of ordering and carrying costs. The specific cost factors which any given company may have developed can be inserted in this formula. In the example shown, these were $6 and 20 percent.

$$N = \sqrt{\frac{CA}{2K}} = \sqrt{\frac{0.10A}{2(6)}} = 0.13\sqrt{A}$$

This formula may be used to construct a table which relates the annual usage of any stock item to its most economical number of orders per year:

Annual $ Usage, A	Number of Orders, N
60	1
240	2
540	3
960	4
2160	6
4860	9
8640	12

Determining EOQs and many other facets of inventory management lend themselves to the use of electronic data processing. Less sophisticated time-saving techniques for calculating EOQs are specialized circular slide rules.

Inventory Carrying Cost (Variable Percentage)

Computation of this cost is based on a period of not less than 1 year. The following data (in percent per year) are needed to establish the value of the C factor in the EOQ formula:

Interest costs	8.0 to 12.0
Taxes	2.0 to 3.0
Insurance	0.1 to 0.15
Obsolescence	2.0 to 8.0
Shrinkage	0.2 to 0.5
Storage costs	2.0 to 4.0
Scrap	0.2 to 0.5
Value of C factor	14.5 to 28.15%

Ordering Cost (Variable per Order)

The following data are needed to establish the value of the K factor in the EOQ formula:

Expenditure	Approximate Cost per Order
Labor	$5.00
Supplies	0.50
Incoming inspection and handling	2.25
Accounts payable procedure	2.25
Value of K factor	$10.00

The characteristics of the EOQ formula are such that the order size is determined partly by the relationship between the relative values of K and C and partly by the value of the annual usage of the item. A K value of $10 and a C value of 20 percent (50:1) will give the same order size as a K value of $5 and a C value of 10 percent (also 50:1).

Extreme accuracy in these calculations is not necessary as long as the relationship between the K factor and the C factor is not disturbed too much. In fact, a distortion of the relationship will affect the order size by only the square root of the distortion. If the relationship were erroneously doubled, the order size would be increased by only 40 percent. At best the EOQ formula gives the buyer only an approximate value which must be adjusted to fit packaging conditions, shipping requirements, and quantity discount considerations.

Using the EOQ

The EOQ table may be made with many increments or with just a few, as shown. If computations are done by the longhand method by the stock controller, it is best that the table be simple and easy to use. The following case shows how the table may be used on a sample item:

1. These facts should be available to the stock controller:
   a. Estimated annual usage, in pieces ... 4000
   b. Approximate unit cost ... $0.50

2. He performs this calculation:

$$\text{Annual usage (pieces)} \times \text{unit cost} = \text{annual usage (\$)}$$
$$4000 \times \$0.50 = \$2000$$

3. He refers to table for correct number of orders per year:

$$A = \$2000 \qquad N = 6 \text{ (approx.)}$$

4. He calculates this order quantity:

$$\frac{\text{Annual activity}}{\text{No. of orders per year}} = \frac{4000}{6} = 666 \text{ pieces or \$333}$$

The calculations described here are simple, and no attempt should be made to carry calculations out to the last decimal place, as this will soon discourage use of the table. By reasonable rounding of his figures, a stock controller should be able to compute his order quantity to within 10 to 15 percent without resorting to tedious calculations.

Order Quantity Relative to Lead Time

The situation may arise where the most economic order quantity is small (say 1 month's supply), but the lead time is longer than the order quantity coverage (say 3 months). In such cases, in order to cover the procurement cycle, it would be necessary to have several orders open at any given time; it may then be more convenient to consider the use of a *blanket order,* with monthly shipments of specified quantities.

ORDER POINT

The *order point* is a predetermined signal which will indicate to the stock controller that he should consider the possibility of reordering the stock item in question. It is expressed in units of material as it is stocked and ordered (pounds, pieces, etc.). Whenever an issue from stock causes the coverage of an item (equivalent to stock balance + open orders) to drop below this predetermined point, the item should be investigated.

The order point must be selected at a figure high enough so that the stock will be sufficient to satisfy the maximum number of expected demands upon the stock during the period when the replacement stock is on order. In brief:

Order point = maximum expected usage during lead time

There are two problems which are inherent in the selection of the proper order point:[7]

1. The lead time cannot always be accurately determined.
2. The usage during the lead time cannot always be accurately forecast.

In those exceptional cases in which both the usage of material and the lead time are absolutely predictable, the order point is simply stated:

Order point = known requirements during lead time

In Fig. 12-9 the lead time is 2 months, and the known requirements are 100 pieces per month. The order point is therefore 200 pieces.

In the more typical situation, however, the material usage can only be estimated, and the lead time is subject to variations. In the previous example, either a late delivery or a period of above-average activity would have caused the stock to reach zero before the new stock arrived. Therefore, when material usage rates and/or lead times are based on estimates rather than firm figures, it is expedient

---

[7]One exception is the case of a local supplier who can deliver on a moment's notice or is carrying buyer's inventory. The order point here might be simply zero stock.

to make an upward adjustment of the order point. This is done through introduction of safety stock. The order point now becomes:

Order point = expected lead time usage + safety stock

In the example given previously, there was no safety factor to absorb unexpected usage or delayed delivery. In Fig. 12-10 the order point has been raised by

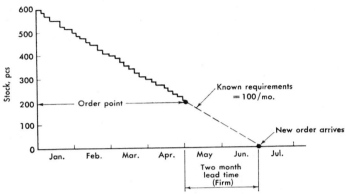

Fig. 12-9   Chart of order-point system.

100 pieces, a buffer stock which can absorb these unexpected demands being thereby provided.

Calculation of Safety Stock

The amount of safety stock necessary to provide adequate protection will vary from item to item. This is true because forecasts can be made with greater accu-

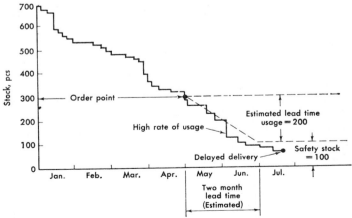

Fig. 12-10   Chart of order-point system with safety stock provision.

racy for some items than for others. Lacking accurate forecasts, the stock controller may examine past stock records for help in estimating the maximum rate of usage which could be expected to occur during the reorder period. He may also determine the longest recorded delivery time for the item. Judgment should be used, however, so that nontypical, nonrecurring situations will be excluded. Based on such an analysis, the stock controller may decide upon an amount of safety stock sufficient to cover those occurrences which are in excess of the average usage and/or lead time.

Lengthy analyses, which may be valuable for an occasional stock item which is critical or of high dollar value, are usually impractical to apply to all items. The problem may be resolved by the use of an across-the-board safety stock. Such a generalized safety stock is often defined as 1 month's supply. It means that the stock controller will order in such a manner that he will always have at least 1 month's supply of stock on hand if conditions remain normal. If not, he will have the extra month's supply of stock to carry him over the period of high usage or delayed delivery.

When the safety stock is expressed in months' supply, it is convenient to use the formula:

$$[\text{Safety stock (months)} + \text{lead time (months)}] \times [\text{average monthly usage (units)}] = \text{order point (units)}$$

Following are three items with different activities and lead times. In each case, a safety stock of 1 month's supply is assumed.

Item	Monthly Usage, pieces	Lead Time, months	Safety Stock, months
1	100	1.0	1.0
2	500	2.0	1.0
3	20	2.5	1.0

The order points are computed as follows:

(Safety stock + lead time) (average month's usage) = order point
Item 1 (1.0 + 1.0) 100 = 200 pieces
Item 2 (1.0 + 2.0) 500 = 1500 pieces
Item 3 (1.0 + 2.5) 20 = 70 pieces

Relationship of Safety Stock, Stockout Rate, and Stockout Cost

An examination of Fig. 12-5a will disclose that the stockout period is reached only after the reorder point has been reached. It therefore follows that if the order size were increased, there would be fewer orders; and consequently there would be less risk of possible stockouts.

This raises an interesting question about the relative costs of increasing the order sizes and decreasing the safety stock. If a safety stock of $1000 and a C factor of 20 percent are assumed, it is costing $200 per year to carry a safety stock that in most cases is never used. If the safety stock is decreased to $500 and the order size is increased by $500, the average inventory will decrease by $250 with an annual savings of $25. The larger order size will decrease the number of orders and will consequently decrease the risk of possible stockouts. The chances are that with the remaining $500 in safety stock, there will still be an excessive amount of safety stock that will never be used.

The logical conclusion of this type of reasoning is that all the safety stock should be transferred to the order size, thus cutting the costs of carrying safety stocks to 50 percent of the present costs. This is a very logical procedure except in those rare cases in which the cost of a stockout exceeds that of carrying a safety stock.

QUANTITY DISCOUNTS[8]

If an item of raw material or a part is being purchased for a special application rather than for inventory, the problem arises of whether or not to increase the requested quantity to take advantage of a quantity discount. An item for which future activity seems unlikely should be purchased in the quantity requested, since there is a known requirement for only the special application. The buyer should check with persons in marketing, design engineering, material control, etc. to determine the likelihood of future use. Given this information the buyer might work with material control to consider increasing the order quantity, provided that the resulting price reduction was justified in light of existing inventory policies.

The two factors which must be considered are the potential reduction in material cost and the increase in inventory. Because the inherent risk of obsolescence is great, in such cases it is advisable that the potential price reduction be significant compared with the increased inventory investment. The ratio of the former to the latter may be expressed as a percentage.

Example:

$$S = \text{requested order quantity (units)} = 200 \text{ pieces}$$
$$S_d = \text{minimum order quantity for discount (units)} = 1000 \text{ pieces}$$
$$P = \text{unit price at requested order quantity} = \$1.00$$
$$P_d = \text{unit price at discount quantity} = \$0.80$$
$$Q = \text{requested order quantity in } \$ = S \times P = 200 \times \$1 = \$200$$
$$Q_d = \text{discount order quantity in } \$ = S_d \times P_d = 1{,}000 \times \$0.80 = \$800$$
$$\text{Material price reduction} = S_d(P - P_d) = 1{,}000 (\$1 - \$0.80) = \$200$$
$$\text{Increase in inventory value} = \frac{Q_d - Q}{2} = \frac{\$800 - \$200}{2} = \$300$$
$$X' = \text{percent return on additional investment}$$
$$= 100 \times S_d \frac{P - P_d}{\dfrac{(Q_d - Q)}{2}} = 100 \times \frac{200}{300} = 66\tfrac{2}{3}\%$$

[8]Terms and conditions are described in Section 10.

Frequently an arbitrary minimum percentage is decided upon below which the discount will not be taken. For example, it may be decided that no item of a certain commodity will be ordered in excess of actual requirements unless a 30 percent return on investment can be realized. Since the actual percent return exceeds the 30 percent minimum, the discount would be taken on 1000 pieces.

A more scientific method is to tabulate a before-and-after price-break chart. If the savings exceed the cost of carrying the additional inventory, the discount is

1	2	3	4	5	6	7	8
Total dollar amount after quantity discount	Total dollar amount *before* quantity discount						
	10	50	100	150	200	500	1,000
20	0.60						
50	2.40						
100	5.40	3.00					
200	11.40	9.00	6.00	3.00			
300		15.00	12.00	9.00	6.00		
400			18.00	15.00	12.00		
500				21.00	18.00		
700					30.00	12.00	
900						24.00	
1,200						42.00	12.00
1,500						60.00	30.00

Fig. 12-11 Added inventory costs.

taken. If the saving is less than the cost of carrying the additional inventory, the lower quantity at the higher unit price would be more economical.

If a (variable) carrying cost of 12 percent is assumed and the average inventory is based on one-half the (additional) order quantity, a sample price-break chart would look like Fig. 12-11. The horizontal column headings (columns 2 through 8) are the total dollar amounts for an item in the required quantity. Column 1 lists the total dollar amounts to be spent if the quantity unit-price discount is to be taken. As an example, take the column indicating a "before" cost of $100. If an expenditure of $200 is required to take the discount, then a carrying cost of $6 is incurred. (By going from $100 to $200, an additional order amount of $100 is committed. Average inventory would be ½ × $100 = $50. Carrying costs of 12 percent produce an inventory cost of $6.)

Example 1 The EOQ for an item is 110 pieces at $0.90 each, for a total of $99. The unit cost reduces to $0.80 in quantities of 250 and up, for a total of $200. Annual usage is 150 pieces. The chart shows that an inventory cost of $6 is incurred by going to the larger quantity. The usage of 150 pieces produces savings of 150 × $0.10 = $15 per year. There is a net gain of $9 on an annual basis, and the discount should be taken.

Example 2 The EOQ for an item is 40 pieces at $5 each, for a total of $200. A reduction of the unit price to $4.70 each is available in a minimum quantity of 150 pieces, requiring an investment of $705. Annual usage of this item is 80 pieces. Reference to the chart shows added inventory carrying costs of $30. The annual saving (80 × $0.30 = $24) is less than the cost of carrying the additional inventory. The discount should not be taken.

MATERIALS REQUIREMENTS PLANNING (MRP)

With the advent of the computer, techniques of *materials requirement planning (MRP)* have been developed which have enabled the material control and manufacturing organizations to plan priorities more effectively. Inventory control systems have been able to go beyond the order launch concept, and the results have been dramatic where formal, workable systems have been developed and used. Inventory turnover has increased and productivity has improved in a number of companies.

MRP is of interest to purchasing personnel as it is a viable tool to use with the *outside shop,* i.e., subcontract vendors, just as material control and manufacturing uses it with the *inside shop,* i.e., the manufacturing or operating departments. MRP techniques have been tested, refined, and improved over the past decade. Software packages are available, and the cost of adopting one has dropped to the level where small companies can afford to use MRP.

The information provided in this section is not intended to make you an expert in MRP but to inform you of some of the basics of this technique and how it works. If it appears that your purchasing operations can benefit from this type of technique and your company is not yet using it, you might want to discuss the matter with your systems, material control, and manufacturing departments. Determine its potential in your particular company. MRP may not be the best technique for every company. Whether or not it is for you deserves investigation.

Concepts of MRP

There are two basic approaches in the release of orders for inventory. The *order-point* technique seeks to replenish depleted inventories; i.e., an order is placed when the balance on hand falls below a predetermined level. The order-point technique is appropriate for independent-demand items, where usage is relatively uniform and predictable and occurs in small increments relative to order size.

The second approach is to calculate specific requirement quantities and due dates for an item based on a production schedule, bill of material, and lead-time backoff. In this, the MRP method, an order is placed just in time to meet a specific calculated date of need, in discrete quantities or lot size as appropriate. In contrast to the order-point technique, it seeks to bring in inventory to satisfy a specific demand rather than to maintain a constant supply. Where demand can be calculated, this approach is appropriate and results in lower inventory investment.

The concept of MRP has been around for a long time. However, the numerous calculations involved for even a moderately complex product make it almost impossible when done manually. With the advent of the computer, not only has MRP become a practical method for inventory control, but because of its capability to replan it has evolved into the basis for managing the manufacturing operation. The term *MRP* has expanded to encompass inventory planning, shop floor control, and capacity planning and control. Operating in a closed-loop mode, all systems are kept in balance by feedback on changing circumstances at every level and by effective, appropriate responses in order to maintain information integrity. The MRP data base is accessed by customer service for making delivery promises and by finance for cash flow projections. As a corporation-wide integrated system, its potential for assisting in top-level management decisions through simulation is yet to be fully realized.

An offspring of the computer age, an MRP system is not as easily controlled or understood as the order-point, order launch, and expedite modes of operation.

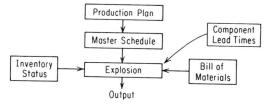

Fig. 12-12   Flowchart of MRP concept.

Its sophistication returns rich rewards to the company capable of achieving and maintaining the discipline and education it requires, but dismal failure to the halfhearted.

ABCs of MRP

There are some ABCs of MRP which are essential to its successful operation. Figure 12-12 and explanations present an overview of the MRP concept.

Production Plan   A *production plan* is the operating standard by which a manufacturing operation is measured. It defines expected production rates by product group, normally in response to forecast demand. Since success depends on cooperation by many departments, it is important that the level of production established be achievable and agreed upon by all functional areas, including production, marketing, and top management. It must be based on a realistic, continual assessment of all production and vendor capabilities. Other considerations are allowance for unique product characteristics, such as seasonality, storage problems, new material availability, etc., and the probability of a significant forecast error.

Master Schedule   The *master schedule* evolves from the order forecast and production plan. It is a schedule by date and quantity of top-level or planning bills of materials, which in MRP terms represent the production plan. Together with a forecast of independent demand requirements, the master schedule feeds the bill of material explosion which is the heart of MRP. An example of input to a master schedule is shown in Fig. 12-13.

Because the master schedule drives the manufacturing game plan, it is essential that it not be overstated. Too often the master schedule is allowed to become a wish list reflecting what is wanted, not what can be produced. This leads to incorrect priorities, to excess capacity requirements, and to the informal system taking over.

Bills of Material   An MRP system requires that the master schedule be stated in bill of material terms. Its planning logic depends on the quantified relationships between end items, i.e., master schedule bills, and their components. It is often the

Week	1	2	3	4	5	6	7	8	9
Product A	50	—	40	80	—	20	30	—	50
Product B	—	40	10	—	40	30	—	40	—

Fig. 12-13   Master schedule.

case that when a company installs an MRP system, its existing bills of material must be restructured. The bill of material structure should:

- Facilitate the scheduling of product options
- Provide for minimal numbers of master-schedule-level bills, as these need manual control
- Support final assembly scheduling
- Support product costing
- Recognize engineering change effectively

While weaknesses in the above areas would probably not render MRP ineffective, there is one weakness that would—inaccuracy. The bill of materials must be valid in terms of part number relationships and in quantity required per assembly.

An example of a three-level bill is shown in Fig. 12-14.

This bill of material states that end item A is made of subassemblies E and B. Subassembly E is made from one each of components F and G and two units of H. Subassembly B is made of one D and one C.

Inventory Status   To make an MRP system work, it is necessary to know exactly what is in stock, both in kind and in quantity. Most companies, when they take a physical inventory once a year, find that the dollar value of the inventory is actually very close to book value. The only problem with the physical inventory is that it is aimed at accountants, who are concerned with the dollar value. To build a product, however, it is necessary to know the precise mix of the inventory, not just that the dollars are accurate.

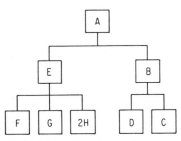

Fig. 12-14   Bill of material structure.

Prior to implementing an MRP system, companies typically find that their inventory accuracy is in the 40 to 50 percent level; in other words, 50 percent of the parts in stock have incorrect balances. In an MRP environment, this would cause tremendous problems, since the amount available in inventory is one factor in determining what will be needed in the future.

To achieve and maintain accurate inventories, most companies utilize a cycle count program, in which portions of the inventory are counted every day. This enables the stockroom to continually monitor the accuracy of its inventory and to take appropriate action whenever necessary to correct problems.

Component Lead Time   The *lead time* on any manufactured or purchased part represents the amount of time required to replenish that item. It begins at the time the paperwork is initiated and extends until the item is received into inventory.

MRP requires that a total lead time value be supplied for each part. Because every day of manufacturing lead time adds to in-process inventory, it is important to keep lead time as lean as possible while yet being practical.

The calculation of the lead time for a manufactured item varies from company to company, but the following items are almost universally recognized as elements:

- Run time (the time actually spent working on that operation)
- Setup time (the time required to get a machine or facility ready to run an operation)
- Move time (the time spent in transporting this job between operations)
- Queue time (the time spent waiting for an earlier job to be completed)
- Other (this can include paperwork time, raw material and tooling pull time, inspection, etc.)

The lead time on a purchased part is almost identical to that of a manufactured part except that the vendor includes the run and setup time as part of the total lead time quotation. The purchasing department then adds transportation time, inspection time, and order process time to the vendor's quoted lead time.

Gross-to-Net Explosion   Once these prerequisites are achieved, the master schedule is fed into the computer and a gross-to-net explosion takes place. This means that the computer combines master schedule production and service part requirements, traces the bill structure, backs off component lead time, and calculates gross requirements by time period. Then by deducting the current balance on hand along with the on-order quantities, it determines net requirements and, using preselected order quantity formulas, generates planned orders. The results of this explosion are typically summarized for each part in a format shown in Fig. 12-15.

Order quantity = 700, Lead time = 4 weeks

Week	1	2	3	4	5	6	7	8	9
Projected requirements	—	—	600	—	—	800	—	—	600
Scheduled receipts	—	—	700	—	—	700	—	—	700
On hand	200	200	200	300	300	300	200	200	300
Planned order release	—	700	—	—	700	—	—	—	—

Fig. 12-15   Exploded master schedule.

As can be seen, assembly requirements are for 600 of the item in week 3, 800 in week 6, and 600 in week 9. Projected on-hand balances are shown along with the scheduled receipts. Backed off by lead time, orders are scheduled for release 4 weeks ahead of requirement dates. The scheduled receipt of 700 units in week 3 represents an order which is currently open. The on-hand value indicates the net inventory projected for each week of the planned horizon.

Ordering Techniques

In the example shown in Fig. 12-15, the order quantity was set at 700. Because of the different factors that relate to specific items, such as setup cost, storage requirements, and item value, there is no one order-quantity formula that is appropriate for all items in inventory. MRP systems usually provide several techniques, which are applied on an item-by-item basis.

Economic Order Quantity (EOQ)   The formula and theory used to arrive at the EOQ were discussed earlier in this section. The EOQ technique is based upon the assumption of continuous and uniform rate of demand. This renders it inappropriate where combined requirements from higher-level assemblies generate lumpy and sporadic demand.

Fixed Order Quantity   The fixed-order-quantity technique is best described as finding the quantity that best fits a unique situation. Determining factors may be excessive storage requirements for a particular part, the number of items that fit on a pallet, the life of a piece of tooling, or relatively high ordering overhead compared with item value. Even though these quantities may not be the most economical, they can be the most practical.

Lot-for-Lot Ordering   The lot-for-lot ordering technique, or discrete order policy, matches order quantity directly to a requirement that the order will satisfy or to the total requirements in a given time period. The main advantage of this technique is that there is no carrying of inventory between lot runs. It is, therefore, very applicable to high-value items.

Updating Methods

One of the significant features of an MRP system is its replanning capability. The most common mode of updating today is *regeneration,* whereby the complete master schedule is reexploded. This approach is rapidly being replaced by the *net change* technique, whereby only changes since the last update are analyzed. Whichever method is used, the computer gives periodic updates as to the actual need date of every open shop and purchase order. In the days of the order-point system, the need date was fixed at the time the order was released. Replanning was rarely considered. However, with an MRP system, orders are continually updated depending on what changes have been made in the part requirements.

An example of such a change is given in Fig. 12-16. The requirements for 600 from week 3 have moved out to week 4. This has the effect of creating excess inventory in week 3, when the on-hand balance becomes 900. This situation triggers a reschedule exception message to the inventory planner. Likewise, the system will flag orders which must be moved in because of a schedule change. Knowledge of what parts are needed and when they are needed on a continuous basis is the foundation for priority and capacity planning.

In a purchasing department, an MRP system provides continuous updating on all open purchase order requirement dates. An elementary example of the type of

Order quantity = 700, Lead time = 4 weeks

Week	1	2	3	4	5	6	7	8	9
Projected requirements				600		800			600
Scheduled receipts			700			700			700
On hand　　　200	200	200	900	300	300	200	200	200	300
Planned order release		700			700				

Fig. 12-16 Updated exploded master schedule.

output a purchasing department might work with is shown in Fig. 12-17. In this example, the purchasing department has elected to specify the date the vendor should ship the product from his plant rather than the due date. The current need date is the key MRP input to purchasing and shows when the parts are needed in the buyer's plant. These data would be reviewed by the MRP system at least weekly and updated whenever requirements change. To illustrate the type of action a buyer would take based on this report, we will examine each entry.

Ship date 10/20, need date 10/25—no action would be taken on the assumption that it takes only a couple of days to transport the parts from the vendor to the buyer.

Ship date 10/30, need date 11/25—in this case the buyer would move out the ship date, probably to 11/20, depending on the value of the part.

Ship date 9/28, need date 9/20—the buyer would try to move the ship date up to 9/15 since a schedule change has occurred, causing the parts to be needed earlier.

Ship date 10/3, need date 10/10—no action necessary.

Using this type of output, the purchasing department can effectively control shortages while minimizing inventories. Depending on the level of sophistication designed into an MRP system, the computer may analyze need versus ship date, considering shipping lead time, the vendor's firm schedule, and present reschedule parameters and highlighting only those changes which are necessary.

Open-Order Status Report Dated 9/10 for Vendor XYZ

	P.O. no.	Part no.	Description	P.O. qty., pieces	P.O. ship date	Current need date
(A)	B2150	38925	Clevis	280	10/20	10/25
(B)	B2150	42986	Mount	100	10/30	11/25
(C)	X3820	91885	Pin	225	9/28	9/20
(D)	C9245	38888	Brush	1000	10/3	10/10

Fig. 12-17 Vendor status report.

Many purchasing departments also have developed techniques for buying vendor capacity and providing vendor production scheduling via the planned orders maintained by MRP. This enables the buyer to drastically reduce lead times and gives extra flexibility in order scheduling.

STOCKLESS BUYING TECHNIQUES

Stockless buying techniques as presented in this section are basically methods of transferring inventory responsibility to the vendor. They can be prepared to cover all types of purchased materials, such as raw materials, fabricated parts, production hardware and supplies, packaging, and MRO items. The advantages of such techniques are reduction in the buyer's inventory investment and warehouse space, better inventory turnover, and purchase savings in lower prices and paperwork simplification.

It is often best to start with a hard look at what is the real purchasing function before discussing stockless buying techniques, such as *contract purchasing* or *consignment purchasing* (other terminology may also be applied). Essentially, the real purchasing function should be charged with the responsibility of securing a quality consistent with the need, at the time required, at the least possible cost. Once this criterion is satisfied, further involvement by a purchasing department becomes more clerical in nature, and these clerical functions should be delegated or at least minimized. The criteria for each transaction should depend upon the contribution to the purchasing function. If a good and valid contribution can be made to individual transactions, it should by all means be handled with purchasing expertise. However, if the contribution would be nothing more than one of processing paperwork, the direct involvement of purchasing should be questioned.

Many of the commodities that any purchasing department buys are repetitive in nature, all the way from the company's prime raw materials to the pencils and typewriter ribbons that are equally essential to the operation of the business. But the buying techniques, the buying controls, and the methods of obtaining these items can and should vary. There is no one good, single stockless system, for either the purchasing department or the company, that can be used as the sole procedure for obtaining the materials and services required for the operation of the business. Every purchasing department, regardless of its size and the complexity and nature of its business, needs to use a variety of systems and techniques for obtaining material and services that will satisfy the requirements of both the supplier's and the buyer's companies. Each supplier, as well as each purchaser, has different requirements, depending upon the materials involved, the controls to be applied, the type of commodity being supplied, and the impact of that particular transaction (or group of transactions) on the business. The documentations must also be geared to the particular transactions (or group of transactions) that are going to take place or, at least, are anticipated at the time the parties arrange a stockless buying program.

When developing stockless buying programs, the buyer should be extra careful in the selection of suppliers. The transfer of inventory responsibility to the supplier conveys a heavy responsibility to the seller, and the buyer must be assured that his suppliers will be capable of meeting the requirements of the stockless plans. Once a buyer has executed a number of stockless buying arrangements, he may lose a certain amount of flexibility to maneuver in the marketplace. Consequently, the competitiveness of any arrangement must be guaranteed throughout its duration.

VENDOR SHELF STOCK PROGRAM

A vendor shelf stock program is basically an obligation on the part of the vendor to maintain selected items of the buyer's purchased materials, in finished or semifinished form, on the vendor's shelf or premises. The program can be a continuous stocking plan whereby each time the buyer releases a quantity of an item from the vendor's shelf stock, it is automatically placed into the vendor's production schedule for replenishment of the quantity released. The program can also be instituted on a make-and-hold type of commitment whereby the vendor will manufacture only a prescribed quantity and hold the material until released by the buyer. In each case, however, the material so processed will remain the vendor's until so released or shipped to the buyer, and it is essentially a technique to reduce buyer's in-plant inventory and lead time.

Applicability

This type of vendor stocking program is most effective for purchased parts or components needed for assembly production. Care should be exercised by the buyer in setting up such a stock program for purchased parts or components for assembly since in many cases these items are designed and manufactured to fit only the buyer's finished product. In such instances, the buyer may elect to have the vendor stock such parts or components in a semifinished condition, in which case further processing is required to complete the item. In this manner, the buyer can minimize possible obsolescence and provide the vendor more flexibility in meeting several finished-product specifications.

Supplier and Product Selection

The selection of a vendor for this type of program should follow the usual principles of supplier selection plus several other factors. The supplier should be a source that the buyer expects to retain, since once a shelf stock program is developed, the buyer is normally obligated to take any unused quantities. The supplier selected should also have good internal controls to keep the program working and be flexible enough to handle an automatic restocking arrangement.

Whereas a contract purchasing plan may cover several classes of materials and many purchased items, the shelf stock program for purchased parts or components is geared to a selected number of key items. A sound approach to the selection of key items is the application of the *80:20 rule*. An analysis of the inventory investment of purchased materials will generally substantiate that 80 percent of the average inventory dollar is represented by 20 percent of inventory items. By concentrating on this 20 percent of the items, the buyer will secure inventory reduction in the area of greatest expenditure. This approach also ensures that the vendor will not be burdened with items of small inventory value and frees the vendor to concentrate on stocking those items representing greatest dollar value to the buyer.

Implementation and Controls

The implementation of such a stocking program can be done in any contractual manner. An agreement may be issued to the stocking vendor indicating the type of program (e.g., self-replenishing or make-and-hold), items, prices, stock quantities to be maintained, etc. By concentrating volume items with several suppliers, a buyer should be able to negotiate lower prices to offset any additional carrying costs to the vendor due to the stocking program. In setting up the stocking program, the buyer should check the following points:

1. Make sure plant inventory levels and lead times are reduced accordingly to take advantage of vendor's stocking program once the program is working effectively.

2. Ensure that only key, high-dollar inventory value items are being carried.

3. Institute a reporting procedure with the vendor so that regular (e.g., monthly) inventory reports are submitted to the buyer indicating the status of each item.

4. Set up a control procedure to review usages on a regular (e.g., quarterly) basis to ensure that there is adequate part movement or adequate shelf stock quantity.

5. Notify engineering, product development, and any other interested department of shelf-stocked items, and request these departments to notify purchasing of any changes which will affect the shelf stock program.

NOTE: Mail this report monthly						
TO: _____ Vendor: _____ Date: _____						
						(Signature of Vendor's Representative)
Buyer's Part No.	Vendor's Part No.	Authorized Shelf Stock Quantity	Current Shelf Stock Quantity	Quantity in Production	Completion Date of Production Order	Remarks

Fig. 12-18 Monthly shelf stock report.

6. Request the vendor to segregate and reserve buyer's shelf-stocked items, so that these items can be used exclusively for buyer's requirements.

7. Spell out responsibility on disposition of any unused shelf-stocked items.

The key to the success of this program is, of course, the vendor's ability to maintain the buyer's inventory. One method a buyer can use to ensure that the vendor is fulfilling his obligation is to request monthly reports indicating the status of each item. Figure 12-18 shows a report to be submitted monthly to the buyer. This report identifies each item on the vendor's stocking program by buyer's and vendor's part numbers, authorized shelf stock quantity, current or actual stock quantity on hand at the time the report is prepared, quantity in production to bring shelf stock level up to authorized quantity, completion date of this production order, and remarks.

ALLOCATION OF VENDOR'S PRODUCTION

The allocation of a vendor's production is a method a buyer may use to schedule his requirements into the vendor's production on short notice. This may involve the vendor's reserving a predetermined number of production hours during a fixed period of time to guarantee a fixed output of items needed by the buyer. Some applications of this method permit the buyer an option to take all or a portion of the production allocation, depending on the buyer's immediate requirements, and at predetermined times during the vendor's production cycle. Other allocations may be based on the vendor's finished output of a purchased item, but regardless of how the allocation is based, the effect is to shorten lead times and reduce in-plant inventories.

This method is most effective on single classes of materials involving significant production quantities. When approaching a vendor to negotiate a production guarantee, the buyer should utilize his purchasing position to advantage in securing a corresponding production allocation or guarantee. For example, if a buyer's total purchases from the vendor amount to 15 percent of the vendor's total output, the buyer should plan on securing at least 15 percent of the vendor's production for his allocation. Vendors who can accommodate buyers in such a program must be flexible in their production scheduling. Another advantage of this method is that it permits the buyer more flexibility in securing items of a priority nature.

CONSIGNMENT PURCHASING

Consignment purchasing normally involves the vendor's maintaining an inventory of his merchandise on the buyer's premises to which title does not pass until the materials are used or withdrawn from consignment stock. Some applications of consignment purchasing can involve the use of an outside or public warehouse to free storage space in the buyer's warehouse, which may involve an extra charge to the buyer for warehousing and handling expenses. Consignment purchasing is a frequently used merchandising technique to promote resale, payment for the consigned goods being deferred until the goods are resold by the buyer. However, consignment techniques have been successfully adopted by industrial purchasing managers to reduce their company's inventory investment and to provide immediate access to required items.

Consignment purchasing can be used to cover all types of purchased materials (e.g., MRO-type items, production parts, and raw materials). However, care should be taken to minimize consignment of products with high obsolescence or short shelf life.

Segregation and Identification of Consigned Inventory

One of the principal reasons why vendors may be hesitant to consign stock is their concern that their merchandise will not be properly accounted for by the buyer. In addition to showing the vendor that he will gain more business through consignment, the buyer must also be able to show the vendor that proper accounting controls will be utilized. Two principal controls on consigned inventories are *identification* and *segregation*. First, the vendor must clearly indicate on the packing list that the items being shipped are for the buyer's consignment inventory, to prevent consigned items being mixed with the buyer's regular inventory. If consigned inventories become a significant portion of a buyer's inventory, separate colored receiving reports and stock identification tags may facilitate identification. The second control involves the physical segregation of consigned inventory from the buyer's own inventory. Since the seller will normally maintain the insurance on the consigned inventory, the buyer must also be able the show the vendor that his merchandise will be stored in a protected warehouse with adequate safeguards against fire and other hazards. In addition to actual physical separation of consigned inventory, the buyer should also be able to show the vendor that his consignment will be lock-protected from unauthorized withdrawals if conditions in the buyer's warehouse require this additional protection. One of the more frequent abuses of consignment inventories is the emergency withdrawal by a using department without the proper entry being made on the accounting record. If the vendor is not reimbursed for items actually used, he will quickly cancel his participation in such a program. Periodic physical inventories should be taken by both vendor and buyer stockroom personnel to ensure accuracy of the records and actual stock levels. The vendor should be paid for all shortages turned up by these physical inventory checks.

Coordination with Controller or Accounting Department

Since the success or failure of a consignment program depends a great deal on the accounting controls assigned to it, the purchasing department must coordinate such programs effectively with the controller or accounting department. Before implementing a consignment program, the purchasing department, in conjunction with accounting, should be able to clearly indicate to the vendor the releasing, receiving, disbursing, and reimbursement procedures. Points to be considered in an overall accounting and inventory control procedure are:

1. The vendor's right of access to inspect consigned inventory should be established.

2. A specific schedule for the taking of consignment inventory should be named.

3. Minimum and maximum inventory levels for consigned items should be set.

4. The internal auditor of the buyer's company should be requested to take an independent inventory and audit of controls on a periodic basis (e.g., once every quarter) and a copy of this report should be mailed to the vendor consigning the inventory.

5. If consignment inventories are significant, the buyer may elect to request his company's accounting firm to prepare an annual audit and report on this inventory.

6. A date should be set for the maximum time an item may be retained in consignment, with any shelf life problems kept in mind.

7. A procedure should be worked out with engineering, maintenance, or product development so that discontinued or obsolete items will not be reordered.

8. Rotation of material should be established, e.g., a first-in, first-out (FIFO) basis.

9. Vendor invoices may be eliminated by using a disbursement report on items taken from consigned inventory.

As part of the regular inventory of consigned items, a report is prepared which will serve several purposes. Such a report will show disbursements which can be used by the buyer's accounts payable department as a basis for reimbursement to the vendor and by purchasing as a means for reordering items falling below the minimum levels. Consignment reports of this type will show, by individual part number, beginning balance, receipts, disbursements, rejections, ending balance, unit price, inventory purchased, maximum and minimum levels, and reorder items. Such reports on consignment inventory should be made available to the vendor consigning the merchandise.

The consignment program should be covered in a written contractual form with the vendor. The following commercial areas are normally covered in such a contract in addition to the buyer's usual purchasing conditions:

1. Listing of items to be consigned, prices, quantities, and maximum and minimum levels

2. Duration of consignment agreement, which should not exceed 1 year

3. Title of consigned inventory to remain with vendor until withdrawn from stock

4. Designation of insurance responsibility

5. Policy on rejects—seller responsible for defects, buyer responsible for any missing or damaged materials resulting from buyer's negligence

6. Termination provisions

7. Provisions for disposition of any unused consigned inventory at end of consignment agreement

In conclusion, consignment purchasing, if properly controlled and administered, can be an effective tool to reduce in-plant inventories and to cut purchased material costs at the same time.

PROCUREMENT CYCLE AND ITS EFFECT ON INVENTORY

One of the reasons for carrying inventories is, of course, to provide time for the procurement cycle to react to the requirements. By the use of some of the stockless purchasing techniques discussed previously, the purchaser is able to cut down on the procurement cycle. Once the purchaser is able to reduce the procurement cycle, the safety factor on inventories (which allows for the procurement cycle) can be eliminated or lowered and the inventory investment can be thereby decreased. The purchasing department may honestly believe that inventories can be reduced in this manner. However, the material control department or the production manager, whose job is to protect his production lines, will not agree unless the purchasing department can actually demonstrate that it is capable of consistently reducing the procurement cycle so that the production manager feels comfortable in decreasing inventories.

Essentially, when a purchasing department develops a lead time, it is generated on the best economics but is not necessarily indicative of the capabilities. For example, a purchasing department may have a lead time of 8 weeks on folding cartons. This allows the supplier to purchase his board direct from the paper mills, cut it to the size required, combine it with other orders (if necessary) to ship in full truckload or carload lots, and process the material through his plant without the use of overtime and without disrupting other setups at the various machine centers.

The material control group's conception of this time period is that the purchasing department could not get folding cartons in less than 8 weeks; hence an inventory of at least 8 weeks should be on hand at all times. In truth, the purchasing department could probably obtain folding cartons (at least in sufficient quantities to bridge the gap) in 2 weeks by the use of warehouse board, overtime, special setups, etc. Yet, the company will consistently keep its minimum inventories of folding cartons at 8 weeks, pay the cost of storage, and tie up capital indefinitely rather than set the inventories at 2 weeks and pay the premiums involved to buy itself out of trouble occasionally (which may be far less in the long run than the cost of carrying the substantial inventories).

Normally, for best economics, inventories should be based on the recovery time of a purchasing department rather than the lead times. *Recovery time* may be defined as the capability of a purchasing department to obtain materials and services at premium costs. It is usually better to pay occasional premiums than to consistently pay the bills associated with protecting against situations that may never arise.

USE OF LOGISTICS

In determining the level of inventories to be carried, the logistics of the system should also be taken into account. Logistics may offer reductions in the amount of inventory physically carried. For instance, material that is in transit by rail for 7 or 8 days represents 1 week's inventory of material that is committed. Expediting and tracing such in-transit inventory become essential if the buyer's plan calls for such material to be delivered in time to meet needed requirements.

It has been a known practice to carry a 4-week inventory of the particular raw material. This inventory may be safely reduced to 3 weeks' supply of material actually on hand if the week's supply that is in transit is also considered. Material actually in storage at a supplier's plant should be used when calculating inventories, or, in the case of distributors, the amount of material actually in transit from the prime manufacturers at a given time may be often used to determine inventory levels.

NOTE: For further information on subjects covered in this section see the list of references in Section 30.

Forecasting, Forward Buying, and Hedging

EDITOR

John H. Hoagland, Ph.D., C.P.M. *Professor of Management, Graduate School of Business, Michigan State University, East Lansing, Michigan*

ASSOCIATE EDITOR

George Tateosian *Vice-President, Metal Traders, Inc., New York, New York*

INTRODUCTION

To analyze and forecast business trends accurately, it is necessary to understand both the magnitude and fluctuations of business purchases. Although numerous books and articles have been written on forecasting methods and techniques, most of them err by overlooking the significant role of purchasing in determining business trends. This chapter focuses on aspects of purchasing which should be understood in forecasting, in forward buying, and in hedging. In addition, various techniques of hedging—a means of minimizing future uncertainties—are discussed.

FORECASTING

Since forecasting is not an exact science, there are numerous theories, computer programs, and written works on the subject. Most of them overlook the power of purchasing and the great advantages of the early availability and reliability of purchasing business surveys. Therefore, this chapter focuses attention on important areas of purchasing as they affect forecasting.

For those interested in government data, a good starting source of information is *Guide to Industrial Statistics,* published by U.S. Department of Commerce, Bureau of the Census, Washington, D.C. This publication is periodically updated.

Importance of Forecasting

Fundamental to forecasting is the analysis of trends and changes in trends. Some data measure trends of activities, while others provide direct measurement of change. The business surveys conducted by the National Association of Purchasing Management and its affiliates are some of the oldest and best measurements of change. Many indexes developed from purchasing business surveys are leading indicators because they show turning points sooner than activity indexes do. Furthermore, data from these purchasing surveys are available sooner than most other monthly business data.

Forecasters should thoroughly examine and understand the composition of any data used as indicators—sources of data, influences on them, seasonal adjustments, frequency of data revision, and reliability of sources for gathering information. It should be noted that even reliable sources sometimes produce unreliable data. Historical examination of the behavior of an indicator at crucial turning points is important. It is always important to watch for changes in legal interpretations or any new discovery which may alter past historical relationships.

In the selection and testing of business indicators, consideration should be given to the impact of various outside events such as political situations, labor, and weather. Of course, the behavior of individual industries and indexes may differ from general trends.

Although business indicators furnish information and bases for decisions, they do not make decisions. It should also be remembered that future business trends may not follow forecasts if appropriate corrective measures are taken. Past experience has proved that time and effort intelligently spent in accurately forecasting business trends is a rewarding personal experience and profitable corporate activity.

Purchasing Surveys as Data Sources

For years, purchasers have provided some of the very best data for analyzing and forecasting business trends through their business surveys. Each month purchasing surveys provide business trend information before government data are available. For almost 50 years, purchasing business survey data have been more reliable, smoother, and less erratic than government data. In addition, purchasing surveys are released as final reports whereas much government information goes through numerous revisions and too often is of questionable validity. The information available through some surveys of purchasing personnel is, has been, and should continue to be some of the best data available for the analysis of business trends. Purchasing business surveys are produced for the nation and for various regions. Some local business surveys have been of excellent reliability, whereas others have provided erratic information, primarily because of small sample size.

N.A.P.M. National Business Survey   Since the 1930s, the National Association of Purchasing Management and various of its local affiliate associations have conducted business surveys of their members. *Purchasing Managers Report on Busi-*

ness, compiled by N.A.P.M., is published monthly from data obtained from replies to various standard and special questions asked of 225 industrial companies. The respondents are diversified both geographically (based on value added by state) and by SIC (Standard Industrial Classification) category (based on industrial contribution to national income). Various local affiliates of N.A.P.M. have for many years conducted reliable local business surveys, such as that of the Purchasing Management Association of Chicago.

Calculation of Change Index An important way to use purchasing business survey data is to calculate the appropriate *change index.* This can be done by taking the difference between the percentages of reported increases and decreases.

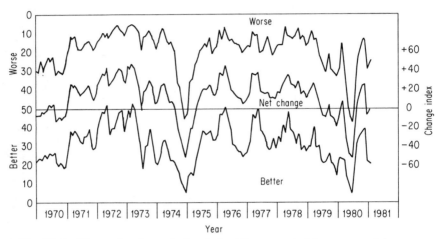

Fig. 13-1 New order change index derived from reported increases and decreases.

An illustration of how this can be done is shown for new orders in Fig. 13-1. The chart depicts survey responses for "better" and "worse," together with the center-line for "net change." Note, the increases (better) are plotted up from the bottom of the graph, and the decreases (worse) are plotted down from the top of the graph by use of the left-hand scale. The change index is the midpoint of these data and is plotted from the zero centerline by use of the right-hand scale.

This type of change-index chart can be useful in detailing the "stalagmite" configurations of the increases, the "stalactite" configurations of the decreases, and the resultant midpoint movement of the change index. Such indexes can be used to compare one business cycle with another, to compare trends over time, and to compare one index with another.

A change index can be produced for most categories in the purchasing business surveys and several can be depicted together to graphically show trends over time. This simultaneous graphing is shown for national monthly change indexes in Fig. 13-2.

Leading Indicators   Purchasing business surveys provide many leading indicators because many of the data measure change. Respondents report through a three-part question, indicating whether an activity has increased, remained the same, or decreased from the previous month. Change indexes derived from these data, like other types of change indexes, fluctuate above or below a zero line. When a change index is positive, it means the activity is increasing; when it is

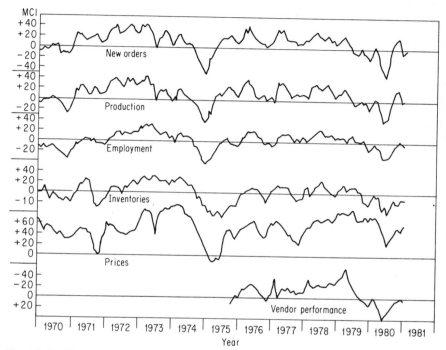

Fig. 13-2   Change indexes of National Association of Purchasing Management business survey data.

negative, the activity is declining. The distance of the change index from the zero line signifies the amount of increase or decrease. Thus, a change index shows by one number both the direction and magnitude of change.

Most other types of change index are derived from an activity index and correspond to the rate of change, or slope, of the activity. The purchasing business surveys, however, provide a direct measure of change.

Any change index has leading characteristics because its turning points occur one-quarter of a cycle prior to the turning point of the corresponding activity index (see Fig. 13-3). Although it is sometimes difficult to visualize or project the peak or trough of an activity index, it is easier to project the point at which a change index is likely to cross the zero line, which signals a peak or trough in the activity.

This characteristic makes a change index a useful forecasting tool. Another advantage of a change index is that it concentrates attention on fluctuations, thus isolating the portion of trends which is often most difficult to analyze and forecast.

A change index is similar to a *diffusion index* except that a diffusion index fluctuates about a centerline of 50 instead of zero.

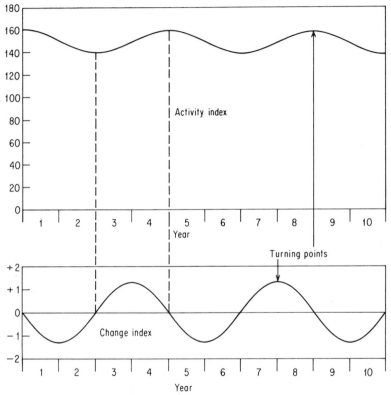

Fig. 13-3 Turning points of change index lead turning points of corresponding activity index.

In addition to the above, purchasing business surveys have the advantage of early availability. Historically, purchasing people have, through their business survey chairpersons, reported monthly results sooner than other comparable business information.

A further advantage of purchasing business surveys has been their ability to measure new elements of business activity. Vendor performance, developed originally as a part of the Chicago Business Survey, has proved very reliable and is recognized as one of the best of the leading indicators. Other more recent measures are the lead time and delivery dependability indexes produced by the Purchasing Management Association of Milwaukee (see Fig. 13-4). These indexes, as well as the purchasing business-survey measures of new orders, order backlogs, production, employment, and inventories, are some of the best indicators of business trends and help in the analysis of past trends and in the forecasting of future trends.

Power of Purchasing

The magnitude of business purchases is very large. For most products, the total amount of prior purchases is greater than the price paid by the final consumer. Shifts in business purchases, often caused by threats to supply, can be of such magnitude that they produce purchasing and inventory waves. These create multibillion dollar false stimulants, which turn into real depressants. Historically,

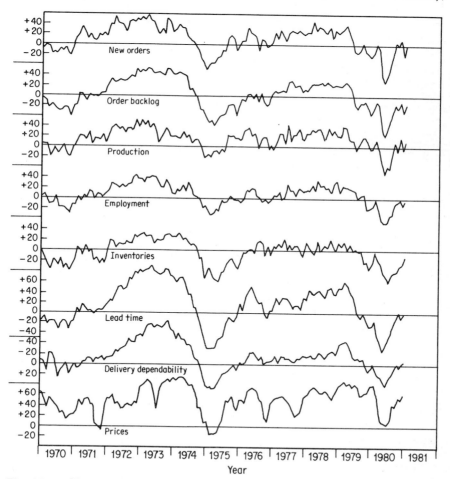

Fig. 13-4 Change index of Purchasing Management Association of Milwaukee business survey data.

most periods of false prosperity and subsequent recession have been caused by business purchasers overbuying and then underbuying as they endeavor to adjust to the dynamics of supply.

Business Purchases Purchases are made in all sectors of business—in retailing, in wholesaling, and in manufacturing. For every dollar of product sold, each average manufacturer has spent about $0.50 for purchases of materials, products, and services to produce that product. The average manufacturing firm's purchases cost *twice as much* as wages and salaries combined. In almost every industry, intermediate input (purchases) is greater than value added. At the wholesale and retail levels of business, purchases represent an even greater proportion of costs. In total, the amount of business purchases is staggering!

Purchase Aggregation The total amount of business purchases can be illustrated by the purchases for an item such as a washing machine. Consider what occurs before a final consumer buys a washing machine from a retail store. The retailer had previously purchased the washing machine from a wholesaler, who had purchased it from a manufacturer. That manufacturer had purchased many materials and products to assemble into the washing machine, including an electric motor. The motor manufacturer had purchased bearings, whose producer had purchased tubular steel and other materials. In dollar figures, the final consumer might have paid $300 for the washing machine, but the retailer had paid $225 to the wholesaler, and the wholesaler had paid $175 to the manufacturer, who had purchased $100 worth of parts and products. The electric motor manufacturer purchased $50 worth of materials, the bearings manufacturer $25, the tubular steel manufacturer $10, and so forth. In this simplified illustration, the total business purchases amounted to $585, while the final consumer paid only $300 for the washing machine.

Similarly, for almost all products the total amount of prior purchases is larger than the price paid by the final consumer. Theoretically, each purchase pays for suppliers' costs of material, labor, overhead, and profit. Costs of prior purchases pass through the business system to be paid for eventually by the ultimate consumer, but the actual flow of materials and products through the system does not move evenly. How and when purchasing is done determines the allocation of resources, business cycles, and inflation or deflation.

Purchases versus GNP Total prior purchases are so large they exceed gross national product (GNP), and even a slight variation in purchases has a considerable impact on the business system. Purchases of just the manufacturing sector are estimated to be approximately equal to GNP, that is, in excess of $2 trillion annually. A mere 1 percent shift in $2 trillion worth of purchases creates at least a $20 billion impact. Also, a 1-week extension (or reduction) in forward buying within this system generates more than a $40 billion stimulant (or depressant).

Business Cycles

An analysis of past business cycles, combined with a study of purchasing and purchasing business surveys, reveals that the primary cause of business cycles has been changes in business purchases brought about by shortages or fear of shortages.

Supply Dynamics   Historically, when normal supply channels were threatened, purchasers extended forward commitments and built inventory stockpiles to protect against threatened shortages. Conversely, when normal channels of acquisition were reestablished, businesses lived off prior purchase commitments and strike-hedge stockpiles. This overbuying followed by underbuying has always been a primary cause of false stimulants which have turned into real depressants. Most business recessions have been preceded by such periods of false prosperity.

Although there are no known measures of the magnitude of shifts in business purchases, the resulting fluctuations in inventories are a revealing consequence of what happens. For example, when conditions changed from scarcity to abundance between 1974 and 1975, inventories went from $17.8 billion worth of accumulation in the fourth quarter of 1974 to $22.2 billion worth of liquidation in the first quarter of 1975. The amplitude of this inventory wave was $40 billion and it impacted many facets of business and government.

Almost all major shifts in purchasing and periods of inventory accumulation and liquidation are the result of supply dynamics and purchasers' protection practices.

Business Forecasting

Most business forecasts can be improved by recognizing the importance of industrial purchasing in determining business cycle activities. Many have not recognized the importance of purchasing because they have been looking at the system from the wrong end. They have looked from the final consumer backward, forgetting that the final consumer lags behind the business system and usually reacts to events and trends within the system.

In forecasting and in government policy decisions, too much emphasis has been placed on gross national product. If comparable attention were paid to gross industrial purchases and gross business purchases, much improvement could be made in forecasts. GNP is primarily final consumption and does not include prior purchases, which are greater and more volatile than final consumption.

To help forecast supply dynamics and the probable impact of purchasing behavior, it is helpful to examine the events which are likely to change supply availability, including such major disruptions as threats of strikes. Furthermore, the interrelationship of many events should be examined carefully. For example, labor strikes often have many political implications, which can be internal to the union or can influence local, national, or international politics. Since political elections are heavily influenced by business conditions, the interrelationships of strikes, purchasers' reactions, business trends, and voter reactions are sometimes of significance.

Whatever the forecasts, many can be improved through an analysis and forecast of actual and potential supply availability. Sometimes supply dynamics will cause only small ripples, but on other occasions, threats to supply of crucial materials will result in large purchasing waves of great significance.

Strikes and War

Historically, strikes and wars have caused major disruptions in the normal availability of materials. They have been a primary cause of dynamic fluctuations in business trends. Even the *threat* of a major strike or war can have great impact. Since most industrial societies are based upon iron and steel, any threat of strike which endangers the availability of these basic materials can trigger false business expansion, as purchasers build strike-hedge inventories. This can lead to subsequent business recessions as strike-hedge inventories are liquidated.

Although threats of strikes and wars have often been major disruptions of multimillion dollar proportions, this does not always happen. For example, the 1974 coal strike threat occurred during a time of supply shortages which caused purchasers to hedge-buy, multiple-source, extend commitments, and stockpile inventories, as they overbought and overcommitted in an effort to ensure adequate supply protection against threatened shortages. After the coal strike settlement, the reversal of these policies and inventory liquidations were a major factor in the 1974–1975 business recession. The coal strike threat of 1977 did not have the same impact, however, because it occurred at a time when there was availability of coal, coke, and steel.

Inventories

Inventory waves created by supply dynamics have been dominant forces in business recessions. Unfortunately, many people have assumed that inventory shifts result from errors in judgment, whereas, in reality, most major inventory shifts are the result of intentional purchasing protection practices.

Furthermore, inventory hedging and liquidation have been important factors in money supply changes because inventories frequently are financed through bank loans. Inventory waves are sometimes so great that they overpower government monetary and fiscal policies.

Although much has been written about companies' maintaining constant inventory-to-sales ratios, many firms do not do this when there is a serious threat of supply shortage or of major price changes.

Purchase Price Forecasting

In addition to trying to forecast general business trends, purchasing managers and buyers must, of course, develop predictions on price trends in the materials, components, and supplies they buy. Traditionally, the forecasting methods used in purchasing have relied heavily on historical price data. In recent years, however, purchasing managers have begun to use more sophisticated techniques in an effort to get more accurate forecasts and to get them more rapidly. Both accuracy and speed are of extreme importance when markets are as volatile as they have been in recent years.

TRW, Inc., for example, has developed an advanced forecasting system that is still flexible enough to be adapted to the needs of the smallest of its 150 divisions.[1]

Some of the major differences between conventional forecasting and TRW's methods are

- TRW forecasts an entire bill of material, not just individual items. This holds true even for a bill of material which covers several plants or divisions.
- Once made, forecasts have purchase prices tracked against them. On a quarterly basis, the price behavior of each item in a bill of materials is examined. Because standard costs vary greatly in times of inflation, it may take several weeks to become aware of variances. But, by tracking prices before the end of the period, purchasing obtains advance information on inflation and can get this information to marketing and accounting departments fast.

Basic forecasting methods used at TRW include the following techniques.

Price Tracking   By periodically monitoring prices actually paid for representative items, indexes can be developed for those items. By choosing the items carefully, such an index can be the basis for a composite index for the entire bill of materials. Price tracking, however, should be considered no more than a preliminary step to forecasting.

Consensus Forecasting   Also helping to create a composite price index for the bill of material is a twice-yearly estimate, by buyers, of price changes that are likely to occur within the following 3 years. These changes are then compared with previous periods and the forecast prices weighted according to their relative importance in the bill of material. Again, this helps to calculate a composite price index.

Forecasting by Regression   Regression analysis is a statistical technique used to forecast future trends of a variable that is also a key component of the bill of material, for example, copper. By taking this variable and determining what is likely to affect its price (for example, demand for copper, copper industry labor costs, shortages due to threatened labor strife), TRW can forecast its future costs (the dependent variable) on the basis of U.S. Bureau of Labor Statistics projections of price indexes (independent variables). Projections are supplied by an outside firm such as Chase Econometrics.

Such forecasts can be of value to purchasing and materials departments. But by combining tracking and forecasting, purchasing can also provide other departments (sales, marketing, accounting, general management, etc.) with information that provides for:

- Faster updating of TRW's own prices, to protect the company's profit margins
- Setting of cost standards and accurate updating of the standards

[1]The TRW system was described in detail in a series of six articles that appeared in *Purchasing World,* January-June 1980.

- Better cash flow planning
- Use of current data in negotiation with TRW's customers

The aim of forecasting by purchasing is not to set up the department as a master section, but simply to keep up-to-the-minute information flowing to others who need it when they need it. An accurate ability to forecast is one of the greatest contributions which purchasing can make to company planning.

Of more immediate value is the use which purchasing itself can make of this forecast information. It helps to:

- Set goals for cost reduction and cost avoidance
- Measure actual performance against established goals
- Evaluate new sources of supply by comparing their prices with those already tracked
- Give an understanding of price trends of commodities
- Negotiate intelligently with suppliers

FORWARD BUYING

It is difficult to establish exactly when buying for immediate use changes to *forward buying*. Most purchases involve some degree of forward buying, the time interval varying from a very short period to many years. Forward buying is the purchase of materials, products, and/or services for future delivery, use, and/or performance under agreed conditions, including a basis for price determination.

Reasons for Forward Buying

There are a variety of reasons for forward buying. A prime reason is to assure continuity of supply. Forward buying can also be used to establish a future price or to safeguard the standard or quality of an item. It is often essential to utilize forward buying for products which are seasonal either in supply or demand. A purchaser can use forward buying to assist a supplier in planning production and, in return, achieve improved service, quality, or price. Vendor lead times require forward buying. Purchasers must alter their forward buying to adjust to actual or anticipated variations in vendor lead times.

One of the most difficult aspects of purchasing is to accurately forecast and plan for future supply situations and to establish requisite lead times. Planning for the future is an essential part of purchasing. A purchasing executive should assess future conditions and project trends in both prices and availability for all items affecting a company's requirements. There should be forecasts of business trends, natural phenomena, political situations, government regulations, and all other factors which might influence supplies and upon which forward buying decisions are made.

Forward buying is the heart of many procurement functions. It should be an important ingredient in a company's financial planning and can make a significant contribution to the profits, growth, and competitive conditions of a company. Forward buying can be practiced in the purchases of almost any commodity, material, component, assembly, or service.

Forward Buying and Speculation

Forward buying can be done to meet the needs of a known production schedule and known lead time requirements or it can be done in excess of this amount as a protection against supply, price, or other uncertainties.

Speculative purchasing generally refers to purchases made for the purpose of making a profit solely through price fluctuations. Most purchases involve some degree of uncertainty or speculation but purely speculative purchasing is not the primary practice of most companies.

Forward buying usually involves more risks than buying for immediate use, but many aspects of business involve calculated risks and require accurate evaluation of alternative courses of action.

Costs of Forward Buying

There are costs of forward buying, but there can also be costs of not forward buying. Some of these costs involve price changes, costs of possession, quantity discounts or charges, and/or stock outages.

Overall costs may or may not rise as the result of forward buying. The time and expense required to research, plan, and execute forward buying can be substantial. On the other hand, potential savings from forward buying can be significant while losses from not forward buying can sometimes be disastrous.

Forward Buying Factors

The collection of background information for making forward buying decisions can be tedious and the results voluminous. The accuracy and relevance of data and information should be carefully scrutinized because some sources either are unintentionally, or purposely, inaccurate or they omit information, which can lead to the making of erroneous decisions. Traditionally, factors examined in arriving at forward buying decisions include the following considerations.

1 Price One of the important factors in all purchasing decisions is price. Past price trends often provide clues to future price behavior. Unfortunately, much published price information consists of list prices rather than actual or transaction prices. An accurate analysis of past price movements and their causality can be indicative of future price trends.

2 Supply and Demand It is often important to have information about production capabilities and product uses. It is also important to ascertain those factors which have been historical threats to supply. Although annualized data can be useful, they frequently hide the dynamic realities of supply and demand. Monthly or weekly data are much more useful than annual data in providing information about dynamics of trends. In studying supply and demand, it is also necessary to consider secondary sources of supply and the suitability of substitutes.

3 Technology and Discovery   When analyzing past trends, it is important to know about important new discoveries or technological changes that disrupt previous historical relationships. In any field of high technology and rapid change, extensive forward buying should be used cautiously because obsolescence is likely to occur frequently.

4 Number and Location of Suppliers   The number, location, and reliability of suppliers strongly influence forward buying decisions. An item with many suppliers close at hand need not be committed as far into the future as one with few suppliers located at greater distances. Size, financial stability, managerial capability, potential disruptions, and other factors should also be taken into consideration.

5 Labor Conditions   Labor unrest, strikes, and threats of strikes are primary reasons for supply disruptions and much forward buying. Protection against possible interruptions in the flow of needed materials can be burdensome and expensive, but the alternative of shutting down operations because of lack of supplies can be even more disruptive and costly.

6 Transportation   Transportation considerations often influence the amount of inventory to be carried and the length of forward commitment. Iron ore, transported through Lake Superior, is a product for which weather conditions (for example, lake freezing) cause considerable forward buying and inventory stockpiling.

7 Government Actions   Possible government actions must also be considered, especially if a commodity is influenced by government stockpiling. Furthermore, changes in governments, which can cause administrative, legislative, or judicial changes in laws or their interpretation, can have considerable influence on forward buying decisions.

8 Costs of Possession   The costs of holding inventories (discussed elsewhere) influence the length of time that inventories can or cannot be profitably held. It is especially important to consider cost of possession when making forward purchases to avoid price increases. Costs of possession are also important when making buying decisions to assure availability of supply. But in these calculations, cost of stockout and operation shutdown should also be considered.

9 International Events   Many products or commodities originate or are derived from sources outside the country and are therefore vulnerable to international political events. The history and potential changes in the political situation of the originating or intermediate countries can be important. Recent problems in Central Africa illustrate the uncertainties that can be produced for such commodities as copper, cobalt, and chromium. For these commodities, the governmental situation in neighboring countries as well as in the originating country has been very significant at times.

COMMODITY EXCHANGES—HEDGING

Commodity exchanges and *hedging* are terms that evoke images ranging from gambling to managed risk. Misconceptions concerning the meaning of these terms and the value of hedging techniques have caused American executives to overlook a valuable purchasing and inventory management tool. In the following discussion, the bare essentials of hedging and commodity trading will be presented. Space does not permit a discussion of the details of sophisticated trading procedures, but qualified metal merchants and commodity brokers are quite able to add "meat" to the "bones" of the discussion presented here.

Hedging Defined

It is important to distinguish between hedging and speculation. Hedging is the minimization of risk and may or may not involve a commodity exchange or futures market. Speculation, on the other hand, involves the assumption of risk. It often involves taking a position in an asset such as land, a security, or a commodity in expectation of making a profit on a change in the market value of that asset. If a broad-based fungible commodity such as corn, cotton, or copper is concerned, it usually but not necessarily involves a commodity exchange or futures market. In reality, almost any investment involves some speculation, and, conversely, speculation involves some investment. A difference between investment and speculation is that an investment seeks a return regardless of a change in market price whereas a speculation relies on change in market price for its reward. Investment may involve a commodity exchange or futures market but usually does not. Speculation frequently does involve a commodity exchange or futures market.

To put these concepts in a different framework, one could say that speculators anticipate price movements and "bet" prices will change in one direction or another. If they expect prices to rise, they will buy today and sell later at a hoped-for higher price. Conversely, if they expect prices to fall, they will *short* the market, or sell today in the hopes of buying back at a lower price on some future date. The speculator serves a useful function. By becoming the hedger's risk bearer through the medium of a futures exchange and futures contracts, speculators help create a mobile and liquid market.

Note that the essential characteristic of hedging is *not* the vehicle used to accomplish its objective but the intent of the operation. Hedging is the minimization of risk. Actions which are designed to minimize the risk either in owning a commodity or in contracting for an item containing that commodity are classified as hedging activities. Hedging may occur in a physical market or in a futures market.

Reasons for Hedging

Ownership of inventory usually entails risk. Rare is the situation in which a business can pass along its prior purchase costs with complete disregard for current market prices. This is particularly true in the case of fungible commodities and most pronounced in products for which there is minimal value added.

An example of this is Romex cable used in residential construction. Prices of this product are sensitive to the day-to-day fluctuations in copper prices; the value added to copper in the manufacture of this building wire is relatively small. In contrast, specialty power cable, which must be bought to a particular specification, has a higher value added. Power cable prices, then, are less sensitive than those for building wire, whose prices are governed more by the conditions of the moment, that is, prevailing market prices on the day of shipment.

Thus, a building wire producer has reasons to hedge. If copper prices fall, the values of raw material, goods in process, and finished inventory will all decline in value. Hedging can offset the financial impact of this decline.

The specialty power cable producer may also wish to hedge, but for different reasons. The sales of finished cable for future delivery at a fixed price were based upon then current copper values. If copper prices rise before the copper purchases are made, the profit margin will be eroded. Hedging at the time of the sale can protect against this erosion of profits.

In a broader vein, hedging can be useful for any product involving a commodity that is subject to price movement, regardless of value added or price practices in the end market. It can provide price protection for purchasing and help ensure orderly business operations and profit planning. Hedging activities can involve either a buying hedge, that is, the building wire producer, or a selling hedge, that is, the specialty power cable producer. Both types of hedges use the physical markets and the futures markets.

Hedging in Physical Goods

When the building wire producer described in the previous paragraph wishes to protect against adverse market movement, copper might be purchased on a deferred pricing basis, that is, the copper will be priced at the point in time when the end product is sold (merchants sell copper on a provisional basis, with the final price to be fixed at a later date). Such future pricing of a copper purchase ensures that the copper in the building wire will have the same base price as the copper in the sales price. Similarly, the specialty power cable producer can protect profits by purchasing copper for forward delivery at a fixed price as soon as the sale is booked. (Merchants sell copper for forward delivery at a fixed price, with no deposit or margin or advanced payment required.) Both types of purchasing involve hedging.

For many reasons, however, it may be impractical for a manufacturer to secure material on a deferred price basis, or to buy forward at a fixed price. But the futures market can be useful in purchase price protection.

THE FUTURES MARKET

There are futures markets covering many commodities. In order to remain with the examples already discussed, the Commodity Exchange, or Comex, as it is known, will be used as an illustration of a futures market, and copper will be used as an illustration of a commodity appropriate for hedging operations.

Generally speaking, futures are *contracts* covering the purchase or sale of specific commodities for delivery in future months. For example, "March copper" refers to a contract for purchase or sale of a specific quantity (25,000 pounds) of refined copper in the month of March. At any point in time, prices are quoted on the Comex market for March futures, as well as for May, July, and so forth.

The reason futures serve as a vehicle for hedging operations is that prices for delivery of a commodity in a forward month usually parallel prices for the spot or cash commodity. If the cash commodity rises or falls in price, usually the price of that commodity for a future month will also rise or fall in price by a similar amount. Thus, the sale of a contract for a forward month (that is, the sale of a futures) will generally protect against a price loss on physical inventory being held. By the same token, the purchase of a contract for a forward month (that is, the purchase of a futures) protects the profit margin in the sale of a product containing that commodity when immediate physical ownership is not desirable or practical at the moment. The building wire producer and the specialty power cable producer can accomplish hedging operations by using the Comex futures market as follows:

> The building wire producer who buys 25,000 pounds of copper today at $0.96 per pound for processing into wire and at the same time sells a forward futures contract has hedged his cash or physical position. If the value of cash copper declines, the price of the futures contract will also decline. Eventually a futures contract can be bought at a lower price and the ensuing profit used to offset the decreased value of the physical copper being sold in the end product.
>
> Or, to take the opposite case, the specialty power cable fabricator who makes a fixed-price sale for delivery at a future date and at the same time buys a forward futures contract has hedged the forward sales position and protected the profit margin involved. If the market price of copper rises before the physical requirements are purchased, the value of the futures contract also rises. Eventually a futures contract can be sold and the profit be applied against the higher price paid for the physical metal.

In theory, it is that simple. But to implement a hedging operation, one should have some knowledge of the mechanics of the futures market and one should be aware of the risks of hedging.

Comex Operations

The purchase or sale of futures contracts on the Comex involves certain costs in the form of commissions, initial margin deposits, and variation margin funds. Trading is governed by a set of well-defined rules covering time of trading, permissible price moves in any one day, size and specification of contracts traded, and so forth. Anyone using the Comex for hedging purposes should be familiar with these regulations and operating rules.

Although space does not permit an exhaustive review of Comex parameters, it would be well to discuss a few of the more important ones as they relate to copper. (Note that Comex also trades such items as gold, silver, zinc, GNMAs, and T-Bills.)

Margin Requirements

To buy or sell a copper futures contract on Comex one must deposit margin with the broker in the amount of $800 per contract of 25,000 pounds (this amount is subject to change) in the form of cash or negotiable instruments such as T-bills. Subsequently, if the market moves against the hedger, that is, if a futures contract was purchased and the market declines, variation margin in cash in the amount of 100 percent of the move must be posted. A $0.10 per pound adverse move would require posting of $2500 for each contract held. Conversely, if the market moved with the hedger, that is, if a futures contract was purchased and the market moves up, variation margin can be drawn back from the broker.

Trading Months

The Comex trades copper futures for every other month, starting with January but skipping November, so that December also trades. In addition, the Comex trades physical copper for the current month and the two subsequent months. Officially, Comex futures trading covers approximately the next 2 years, but actual transactions are concentrated in the nearby months. The Comex operates between 9:50 A.M. and 2:00 P.M. on normal business days, and all trades must be made during those hours.

Trading Limits

Trading limits on physical and futures copper are currently (but subject to change) $0.050 per day for all but the spot month, which has no limit. (The spot month is the current calendar month.) The trading limits are expanded by 50 percent after two successive *limit days* (currently to $0.075 per pound). After this limit move is effected, the limit expands by a similar amount (another $0.025 per pound, for a total of $0.100 per pound, the next day). A nonlimit day reverses this procedure so that two nonlimit days will reduce the trading limit back to $0.050 per pound. For trading purposes, the spot month begins two working days before the calendar month begins and ends two working days before the calendar month ends.

Commissions

Commissions are subject to negotiation. Until recently they were fixed at $35 for each "round trip," or in-and-out trade, for anyone not holding a seat on the Comex. Members pay one-half this fee. Current practice has posted commissions ranging from $70 to $120 per round turn, with exchange members and large volume accounts paying lower rates.

Spreads and Straddles

Spreads and straddles, that is, buying one month's futures and simultaneously selling another's, need not concern the novice hedger. However, they are an essential part of the hedging operation, since all future months do not trade at all times. Implementing a hedge may require an initial position in an actively traded month, with a later switch to the desired hedge month. Also, as will be discussed later, changes in spreads may detract from the effectiveness of the hedge.

RISKS IN HEDGING

There are constraints in practical hedging operations that may interfere with theoretical hedging exercises. A hedge which looks good on paper may turn out to be less than perfect in reality, either because of the rules and regulations surrounding commodity trading or because of other risks in hedging.

Markets do not always behave as anticipated. Furthermore, rules change, distortions occur, and relationships vary. While a hedge often protects the hedger from the consequences of unexpected change, it often does so only to a degree or only at a price. Hedging is not a perfect tool. One obvious hedging risk is margin calls. If the market moves against the hedger, the money tie-up in variation margin may hinder the effectiveness of the hedge. In early 1980, when copper prices climbed $0.40 per pound in the space of 34 days and the prime rate was 16 percent, the money cost of the variation margin on a buying hedge was over $0.005 per pound per month! If that level had persisted, the interest cost alone for a twelve-month hedge would have been $0.064 per pound.

Less obvious are the economic changes or technical conditions that can cause a cash commodity to develop a distorted relationship to the forward month. As was pointed out earlier, the reason futures serve as a vehicle for hedging is that prices for delivery of a commodity in a forward month usually parallel prices for the spot or cash commodity. The forward month usually trades at a premium to the spot month, with the premium, or *contango* as it is called in copper, reflecting all carrying costs including interest charges, storage costs, and insurance.

A case in point: On May 1, 1980, the spot Comex contract for copper closed at $0.863 per pound. The September contract closed at $0.907 per pound. The spread of $0.044 per pound for the 4-month period reflected interest at 14 percent (effective bankers' acceptance rates for 120 days), plus insurance and storage costs of $0.0012 per month per pound.

May contract, closing value	$0.863
Interest through 9/1/80 @ 14%/year	0.0397
Four months insurance and storage	0.0048
Total	0.9075
September contract, closing value 5/1/80	$0.907

When conditions change this spread, the effectiveness of a hedge may be impaired. For example, on December 3, 1979, the December Comex contract for copper closed at $1.080 per pound, while the March contract closed at $1.031 per pound. This was actually $0.0490 per pound lower or a *backwardation* (when the forward month sells at a discount to the spot month), instead of a normal *contango* (premium) of $0.031 per pount (interest plus insurance and storage). The total swing was $0.080 per pound.

A further point can be made vis-à-vis risks. Trading futures contracts usually involves telephonic instructions and rapid decisions regarding price. Both may be quite alien to the normal functioning of the buying office and can result in inefficient trading if not outright mistakes. Orders to buy or sell *at the market* can be expensive, especially in a thin market, since they can place the hedger at the mercy of the bid-and-asked range. *Stop orders* to buy or sell can also be expensive, for they can be triggered by false moves in the market or missed when limit moves occur. The mechanical aspects of trading in the futures markets, while not complex, are best not trusted to the novice.

Other risks are also present. *Limit* moves may prevent orderly hedging operations when the forward months do not trade. About the only way to take a position or liquidate a position in a forward month is to trade the current month and switch to the forward position later. This operation results in additional costs and may be difficult to implement at appropriate spreads.

Many other types of risks are present in hedging operations. While they do not vitiate either the practicality or the desirability of hedging, they do make it a technical operation not to be entered into on a casual basis. Like any other purchasing technique, hedging, if used with discretion, can be a valuable management tool; if used carelessly it can be destructive.

NOTE: For further information on subjects covered in this section see the list of references in Section 30.

Section **14**

Stores Management

EDITOR

J. Edward Johnson, C.P.M. *Manager, Purchasing (Retired), Amoco Oil Company, Atlanta, Georgia*

ASSOCIATE EDITORS

Floyd D. Hedrick, C.P.M. *Chief, Procurement and Supply Division, The Library of Congress, Washington, D.C.*

John Thorn *President, Gulf Consolidated Services Piping Group; Chairman of the Board, Gulf Supply Company, Houston, Texas*

A. J. Stryck, C.P.M. *Senior Specialist, Purchasing System, Standard Oil Company (Indiana), Chicago, Illinois*

The primary function of stores management is to provide for efficient storage and handling of goods to be redistributed to the ultimate consumer. Storage may involve a completed product; a subassembly for completion by another manufacturer; maintenance, repair, and operating supplies (MRO); or raw materials for shipment to other companies for product manufacture. Although stores management is a function of the overall purchasing and stores operation, it is quite specialized. *Inventory management,* discussed in Section 12, deals with inventory control; *stores management* in this section is more specifically concerned with the physical aspects of material storage.

Stores management must take into consideration the purpose for which a stores operation functions—viz., as a holding area for materials until redistributed. It must assure that storage is both safe and adequate, provide for frequent turnover of stock, and maintain the lowest quantity of stock necessary for maximum utilization.

MANAGEMENT AND PERSONNEL

Success of any function lies in the management policies that are established and the quality of assigned personnel. Stores management must recognize the full concept of its responsibilities and must select, train, and upgrade its personnel accordingly. Not only should personnel be well trained in handling stores; they should also be familiar with the total operation to help execute a better job in their own function. Management may use in-house personnel and outside specialists to teach storehouse personnel how to accomplish this objective. If management can get a better job done by teaching people to work "smarter" rather than harder, management has made significant gains.

RELATIONSHIP TO OTHER DEPARTMENTS

Stores management is generally organized as a unit within the purchasing department. This strengthens coordination between the two interrelated materials functions by buying and storing, whether or not a total materials management concept has been adopted. Under a materials management organization, the stores management unit should have equal departmental status with other functions of pur-

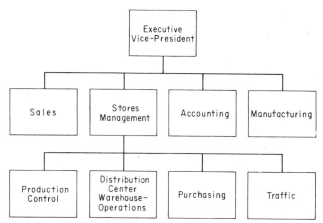

Fig. 14-1 Organization chart of a company oriented toward the distribution center–warehousing concept. In this type of organization, stores management reports directly to a top official of the company and is independent of manufacturing and sales.

chasing, traffic, materials control, and manufacturing or production planning under a single head. In companies which do a large amount of warehousing, the stores management function may be nearly synonymous with physical distribution. In this case traffic, purchasing, and other supply and material control departments may well report to stores management.

Figure 14-1 shows an organization chart of a company strongly oriented toward a distribution center–warehousing concept. An important principle in this type of organization is that stores management reports directly to a top official of the company, independent of manufacturing and sales.

The main purpose of stores management is to provide a service. Its main objective is to operate efficiently in order to provide required services as economically as possible. For stores management to be totally effective, it must coordinate its efforts with those of all departments it serves so that its actions support those departments that form the basic organization of a company.

MANAGING THE FACILITIES

Utilization of Space

Optimum utilization of storage space presupposes that overall foot requirements have been determined from an item-by-item analysis of the total projected maximum inventory. From this study the size, shape, weight, and special features should be converted to bin, box, shelf, and pallet loads and, finally, to the shelves and racks needed to contain them. Space utilization, material handling methods, and material flow patterns are closely related and must be analyzed as a total system. Warehousing consulting services should be considered. Aisles should be adequate to avoid bottlenecks, but not excessive. Receiving and dispersing areas should be designed to provide maximum anticipated activity and no more. Maximum use should be made of all clear overhead space for inside storage. Shelves and rack-decking should be designed with no more unused space above the items stored than necessary for accessibility, movement, and safety. Yard storage should be considered for very large items and any available space at point of use as alternatives to expensive inside facilities.

Design and Layout

To determine proper space utilization, scale drawings and templates are useful at the design-and-layout stage of planning. All logical layouts should be considered and reviewed with the stores operating personnel before a final plan is made. Normally, straight lines and uniformity of arrangement maximize accessibility, orderly flow, and flexibility. Provision for low-position storage near the point of issue of the 20 percent of an item that represents 80 percent of demand may reduce the need for material handling equipment and will speed disbursements. However, a balance must be maintained to avoid stocking common items into too many different locations, which would delay restocking. Maximum use of standard shelf, pallet, and rack dimensions will reduce their acquisition and replacement costs. The completed layout, carefully planned, will minimize material pilferage and facilitate fast and accurate physical counting.

Trade-offs will likely be necessary to attain priority objectives for any particular stores system. For example, accessibility might be sacrificed for greater security of items most subject to pilferage.

Handling Aids

Proper selection of materials handling processes and equipment is necessary. Important goals are to:

1. Eliminate handling wherever possible
2. Reduce travel distance
3. Increase speed of assembly processes, eliminate bottlenecks, coordinate operations, and fill orders rapidly

4. Minimize loss, wastage, and spoilage of materials during storage and handling

5. Reduce chance for physical injury to stores personnel

6. Avoid waste of time caused by customers' waiting for disbursement

To make these selections, one must first analyze and compile data on the scope of the handling requirements and on the equipment available. To be considered are:

1. Type of items to be handled; their bulk, weight, and size; care required in moving; and type of container (if required)

2. Quantity and rate of movement, volume of materials to be moved or handled, and number of times movement will be required

3. Distances material will be moved

4. Direction and variability of travel (horizontal, vertical, or combination of the two) and available routes (floor, overhead, basement, outdoor)

5. Limitations of building: number of floors, ceiling heights, floor loads, elevators, inclines of ramps, and obstructions

6. Available handling equipment: that which is presently in use and that which is available but not being used

Next, one should analyze handling needs on a procedural basis.

1. Study the distribution center layout with the aid of a flow diagram and a flowchart, and arrange facilities for most economical handling of materials. Combine or eliminate operations to reduce handling.

2. Provide definite routes of travel for movement of items. Channeling of the materials flow may permit installation of low-cost, fixed-position handling equipment such as roller or belt conveyors, chutes, or monorails.

3. Eliminate delays due to congestion.

4. Design unit loads of materials and parts to be as large as practical.

5. Coordinate flow of materials to integrate all phases of handling as smoothly as possible.

Following this, the handling method and the equipment best suited to the operating requirements must be selected and integrated in the overall distribution center systems.

1. Use standard handling equipment wherever possible and special equipment for unusual situations.

2. When available, select alternative handling equipment on the basis of suitability for long-run requirements, capacity, ease and reliability of operation, and low maintenance cost.

3. Mechanize handling whenever strenuous and costly manual handling or possible damage to materials can be prevented; mechanization should also reduce loading and unloading time.

The proposed handling system should be appraised by comparing its expected overall performance and cost with those of the existing system or, if new, with a similar operation elsewhere. Finally, it must be determined how long it will take for the proposed system to pay for itself from the savings it will generate.

Location Coding

Since 80 percent of the typical inventory is relatively slow-moving, locator codes should be designed to prevent lost motion and delays in locating items in the inventory. Moreover, a definite *address* for everything stocked is necessary to maintain order and for efficient stowing and order picking. A simple but effective coding system of labeling racks, bins, and shelves with visible letters, numerals, or a combination of both should be developed.

To complete the system, a conveniently placed file of locator cards or a printed catalog listing all items alphabetically (or by stock code) and their stores address must be maintained. This record *must be kept current,* reflecting all changes as they occur. Where electronic data processing (EDP) equipment is available, catalog printing and updating are a relatively simple process and can be programmed for frequent intervals—monthly, bimonthly, or as required. Computer programs and cathode-ray tube (CRT) equipment can replace the locator cards and permit frequent updating of the catalog of items.[1]

MATERIALS IDENTIFICATION—CODING AND CATALOGING

Classification

A stock code to group and identify items with similar physical characteristics in a logical pattern permits simple and precise materials identification as an aid to production, stores, purchasing, and accounting. This stock code should be kept as short as possible, starting with a class designation for like items keyed to major commodity groups, e.g., electrical, hardware, fasteners, pipe fittings, and janitorial supplies. The first two digits should be sufficient for this purpose, followed by a single digit to denote subclass of manufacturer code, and finally three digits to allow for alphabetical sort. Computer analysis of disbursements is facilitated by the use of the first two, or three, digits.

A description should always start with the noun, followed by descriptive adjectives to complete the description. One or more manufacturer's catalog numbers must be included where applicable. Allowance for item addition is accomplished by spreading the number sequence in the alphabetical-sort code.

After all stock codes are assigned, a list of all items by stock classes, subclasses, and item codes in numerical order should be prepared. Every item must be

---

[1]"Stores Control," in National Association of Purchasing Management, Inc., *Guide to Purchasing,* vol. 3, New York, N.Y., 1974, p. 11.

assigned a unit for control purposes; the smallest unit of normal issue, such as foot, pound, or each, is usually best. Finally, one must index and compile the listing in card file or catalog form for distribution to all departments that are actively involved with materials, supplies and equipment. An appropriate price can be indicated to assist in cost-estimating jobs on a gross basis. Figure 14-2 shows an example of a typical catalog page.

Addition of Control Codes

Control codes can also be used to isolate items by activity and/or by reorder groups so that they may be analyzed for inventory policy and control. A simple system is

STOCK CODE	DESCRIPTION	UNIT
	─ Class	
	─ Subclass or manufacturer	
	─ Noun name sequence	
23 5519	Ferrule, copper, for use w/ 2/0 Jumper cable, Kearney #4769-4	EA
23 5867	Terminal, pressure, 2 to 8 wire size, 70 Amp., G.E. #3239	EA
23 5902	Terminal, compression, ring tongue, No. 22-16 wire, No. 3 or 4 stud size, Soli-strand, short barrel, AMP Inc. #34104	EA
23 5903	Terminal, compression, ring tongue, No. 22-16 wire, No. 5 or 6 stud size, Soli-strand, short barrel, AMP Inc. #34105	EA

Fig. 14-2   Sample of typical stores catalog page.

to add alpha (letter) prefixes or suffixes designating selected groups to the established stock code. Some common reasons for using control codes are to identify:

1. Item in regular day-to-day use, controlled by formula; purchases originated by stores

2. Same as above, except purchases originated by operating personnel other than stores

3. Items considered as spare parts, reserved for a special purpose—minimums established by operations and purchases originated by either stores or operations

4. Items not to be recorded

5. Items that have been reconditioned and put into stock for reissue to operations

6. Items to be disposed of through sale outside the company

Protection and Safety

Protection of company investment in stores requires special efforts in a number of areas:

1. Training programs to acquaint employees with established stores procedures and policies

2. Periodic audits to assure that procedures are being followed and corrective measures taken when losses occur

3. Proper maintenance of handling aids

4. Locked storerooms and storage yards

5. Limited access to items subject to pilferage, such as those commonly used in households

6. Repacking or use of preservatives

7. Fire prevention safeguards

8. Housekeeping

9. Adequate lighting

10. Prompt reporting of missing items

11. An atmosphere of order and efficiency

Protection and safety of employees are equally important, and most of the factors mentioned above also apply to the safety of stores personnel.

Management is responsible for developing the overall safety program and for keeping it active through effective communications. A sound safety program provides for frequent safety meetings where both safe and unsafe practices are constantly reviewed and analyzed. Specially trained supervisors and safety engineers should conduct the safety meetings to assure that time allocated to safety is profitably spent.

Pilferage

Pilferage of stores inventory by employees requires constant surveillance and control. Reducing temptation is possible through such procedures as:

1. Caged enclosures or closed cribs with locks for valuable inventories like electronic equipment, pharmaceutical products, automotive parts, and food and beverages. The number of keys issued is limited to the number of authorized personnel.

2. Established checkout system for the use of tools. Such activity shifts the burden of responsibility into the employees' hands.

3. Professionally guarded enclosed and locked areas for precious metals.

4. Regular security patrol for outdoor storage. Outside storage should be kept at a minimum because of the difficulty to guard it.

5. Computer analysis of disbursement records to determine abnormally high usage (and users) of specific items.

Item Placement in the Storeroom

Efficient stores operation depends primarily upon two things: first, movement of materials into and out of storage in the shortest possible time using the minimum amount of labor; and second, proper storage of the material while it is under stores control.

Proper storage requires the correct type of storage system: either racks, pallets, shelving, or bins or combinations of them, and then the most efficient use of that system. To make the proper selection, first study each stores item to determine:

1. Maximum quantity necessary to have on hand to satisfy demands. Study purchasing records to establish probable maximums for each item and add 15 percent as a safety margin.

2. Cube-measure size, shape, and size-weight ratio of each item. These factors determine the best type of storage system for a particular item. For example:

  a. Light, bulky items on shelves rather than in bins. Corrugated bin boxes of various sizes increase the flexibility of shelves and permit addition of similar items to a class or subclass.

  b. Odd-sized or heavy items and case lots on racks or on the floor, either palletized or hand-stacked, rather than on shelves or in bins.

  c. Reserve bins for small, light items.

3. Weight of the maximum amount of each item as well as the weight of individual units. Place heavier items close to the floor and on load beams suitable to support the weight.

Next, one should prepare the plan for placing items in the storeroom. From the cube measurements, one should determine the average bin height and shelf width. A limit on overall height of bins is important for ease, safety, and speed in storing and issuing, particularly with a manual system. If the warehouse system is to be automated, as will be discussed briefly later, bins may be over twice as high for most efficient use of space.

The relative activity of items is important in planning their placement. A-B-C analysis is one good way to determine inventory activity patterns. It can be done manually or on a computer and consists of multiplying the number of units issued in a given period of time by the unit cost. All items are then listed in a high-to-low sequence by total dollar disbursements. Typically, 10 percent of the items will account for 70 percent of the dollars of inventory (Class A—the fast movers); 20 percent will account for 20 percent of the inventory (Class B—the middle class); and 70 percent will account for only 10 percent of the inventory (Class C—the slow movers).

A number of considerations will influence item placement in storage. They depend largely on the materials flow and the physical layout of the particular storehouse or plant operation.

It may be desirable to keep the most active items close to the receiving or shipping point or to shorten the trip to or from storage and to reduce order-picking time. However, if space is limited in the loading areas, items should be placed in general storage, since congestion in loading areas reduces efficiency and increases overall labor costs.

Any items or groups of items that require special storage, handling, or attention, and that will therefore be exceptions to the regular plan for item placement, should be identified and listed. From the earlier analysis of quantity, cube, and weight, consider exceptions, such as:

1. Unusually heavy or bulky items.
2. Hazardous or odorous items, such as certain chemicals.
3. Food products needing protection from possible contamination.

4. Items requiring storage at certain humidity or temperatures, including refrigeration.

5. Items requiring special security to guard against pilferage. (If entire classes are not involved, these items must be in regular sequence, with special bins or fenced aisles.)

The alternative to arranging inventory by activity is arrangement by family groups or by freight classification, if desirable. Often, however, the choice is between making a *permanent place assignment* for each item and random storage of items taking full advantage of cube, leaving no spot vacant.

A permanent place for everything is desirable if space permits. When merchandise comes in, it can be moved directly to easily located stock points. It is more difficult to train new order pickers if there is no fixed location of an item. Disadvantages of random storage decrease with computerized systems, which can sequence items by storage location on the pick list. Marking of item boxes with the warehouse stock code by the supplier speeds accurate restocking and greatly increases efficiency.

Reserve stock must be placed as close to the bin stock item as possible. With bins located in the center, reserve stock can be stored on adjacent racks around the outer edge.

Whether storage is in bins, on racks, or in bulk storage facilities, items must be clearly labeled and, unless readily identifiable, should also be tagged. Sections of the storehouse may also be labeled to facilitate locating material.

ORDERING AND RECEIVING

Regular contact between stores and production personnel makes stores the logical section to originate (or review) all requests for materials and supplies. Stores supervisors, likewise, are frequently authorized to originate and approve local purchases within specified limits and to release orders against purchasing department commitments. Items controlled by the two-bin system mentioned in Section 12 require action by stores when order point is reached. Even with sophisticated computer systems, where purchasing may be remote and highly centralized, alert stores personnel can furnish valuable on-site information for maintaining order and economy in procurement processes.

Receiving—Inspection, a Step-by-Step Process

Receiving, the final step in the purchasing cycle, is a more important stores function than is sometimes recognized. All or most of the following are required in completing a typical receipt:

1. Checking all packages and weights against shipper's manifest.

2. Observing and recording condition of packing or other evidence of rough or faulty handling, with carrier's representative present, prior to acceptance; qualifying acceptance accordingly.

3. Checking all items to ascertain agreement with supplier's packing slip and receiving copy of purchase order.

4. Recording overages, shortages, and damaged and incorrect materials on a form provided for purchasing action and accounting information.

5. Paying (or processing) freight bills.

6. Arranging for detailed inspection and testing of certain instruments, apparatus, etc.

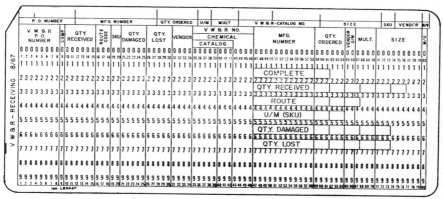

Fig. 14-3 Data processing card used to report receipt of material is processed to prepare a computer printout for each purchase order. *(Courtesy of Van Waters and Rogers Scientific.)*

7. Recording receipt, identified as partial or complete, on receiving copies of the purchasing order or a material received report. Figure 14-3 shows a material received report.

8. Notifying others concerned as to receipt of the shipment and its quantity and condition and arrival time.

9. Marking, labeling, and repackaging as required.

10. Delivering material to proper location for use or for storage.

Further Inspection

Carefully prepared material specification, competitive bidding, negotiation, and internal quality control are valueless if items received do not conform to the quality characteristics specified.

Comprehensive inspection at time of delivery may reveal concealed damages, as well as damage plainly evident. Liability is more easily established then, and such revelations, if the carrier is liable, could mean full recovery rather than the 50 percent maximum allowable if discovered and reported later.

The services of an outside testing laboratory should be considered to verify that quality received is equal to quality ordered.

ASSEMBLY—PACKING—ISSUING

Ways to increase the efficiency and reduce the costs of order filling or dispersal (picking) operations must be reviewed by considering the following:

1. Reducing travel area for pickers
2. Reducing the number of handlings of an order during processing
3. Eliminating bottlenecks
4. Maintaining flexibility to meet variations in volume of receipts or issues
5. Free issue of high-moving, low-dollar-value, low-pilferage items

Alternate pickup processes should be considered to arrive at the best one for a given operation.

Three such alternates are: sequential, batching, and zone picking. The best method relates directly to the size and type of the storeroom operation.

1. *Sequential order picking* gives customer preference on a first-received, first-filled basis. Although apparently desirable, it may be costly, since nearly every order is handled by all pickers.

2. *Batching* of orders provides for the collection of orders for certain time periods and for their release into the picking system. This permits collection of orders for the same items to be picked with fewer trips to the bin or reserve area.

3. *Zone picking,* as contrasted to one-person picking.

Zone Picking.   Personnel are assigned to one area. Orders can be passed from one section to the other. Order pickers should be trained to pick in more than one area as required.

One-Person Picking.   A picker handles the entire order throughout the entire picking area; the plan is useful only if the order does not cover too large a physical area. This also permits carrying out special instructions on individual orders and ensures special attention and handling.

For larger firms, computer-controlled batching and automated order selection are possible. With such advanced systems, management can take the best features from each of the other approaches and reduce handling costs. However, careful studies must be made to show justification for a costly computer-controlled system.

For such studies enlisting the help of specialists, including personnel from outside the company, may be wise. One should look closely at more than one system, observing them in operation and making a thorough cost analysis and systems evaluation of each.

Orders may be assembled by a variety of techniques, using such equipment as four-wheel selection carts, tote boxes of various sizes, and manual or power-driven conveyors, particularly where bin picking is involved. For assembling orders from a reserve inventory stored on racks or on the floor, either forklifts or in-floor tow carts should be used.

Conveyors and power conveyors can be used extensively, following careful study of material flow and personnel movement. Properly installed, they should terminate in a checking and/or staging area where checking can also be performed quickly while material is still on the conveyor.

The general area of packaging for major savings in storing and issuing materials must be explored. New ideas and assistance in packaging are available from trade magazines and from packaging experts on the staffs of carton and container manufacturers.

Disbursements records to establish the most desirable issue unit should be reviewed. Prepackaging can then reflect this established unit.

Materials must be packed as economically as possible without sacrificing protection of product being readied for shipment.

After items have been picked, assembled, and packed, responsibility for their shipment rests with the shipping department, which classifies the items on the bill of lading and makes necessary pickup and delivery arrangements with the carrier.

Careful labeling and marking of the records will assist in preparation for shipping. Mixed orders, such as bulky or heavy floor stock from the reserve area plus bin stock which has been packaged separately, are then assembled and the total number and types of packages clearly marked on the document. This procedure avoids "stragglers" and permits accurate and complete order shipping.

COMMUNICATIONS

Information   Both accurate and timely communications are a must for effective stores management and inventory control. Correct information, reported at the right time, can become entirely inaccurate if delayed.

Records   To keep accurate records, certain paperwork is necessary. Basically this starts with a complete, accurate, and up-to-date stores catalog which informs users of all items and quantities in stores, stock code numbers, and correct ordering descriptions. Other forms that are often necessary are:

1. Requisitions
2. Disbursement record report
3. Receiving reports or receiving copies of purchase orders
4. *Materials out* reports
5. Bills of lading
6. Data process reports (changes)
7. Gate pass-out permits
8. Payroll deduction forms
9. Credit memos
10. Additions to and deletions from the warehouse catalog
11. Vendor reports by commodities for dollar investment purposes and identification of surplus and excess items and money tied up in inventory

Updating Records   It is important to keep stores records up to date. Receiving and disbursement reports should be completed each day. This is particularly true with automated systems using a computer to update records daily based on a critical sequence of input data. Purchasing also must have up-to-date receiving and disbursements reports to order and expedite properly.

Control Documents   Many factors are involved in inventory control. Maximums and minimums are established with thought to lead time, safety stock, material turnover, cost, and importance to plant operation.

Change in the company's economic strategy may well be reflected in maximum and minimum inventory changes.

In automated systems, data from stores and purchasing documents fed into the computer at the proper time can furnish information to control reorder and expediting of materials and other stores and purchasing activities. If a system is not automated, control for reordering is usually a disbursement record card posted until a predetermined minimum is reached. Establishment of maximum and minimum quantities should be a joint effort between purchasing and stores and should have the concurrence of inventory control management.

Reports   Many useful reports can be generated from stores and purchasing information. For example, knowledge of the amount of money spent for any one material or any one category can be used by purchasing in purchase negotiations or by production in investigating nonusage of an item or a possible low-cost substitute for it. Total dollars spent and disbursed by various categories of material can be supplied for management review.

Monthly reports of disbursements, material received reports, material out reports, and gate passes can be used to gauge stores activities and manpower requirements. Reports can be compiled to show low-turnover materials that might be deleted from stock. Other reports can reflect the cost of small tools furnished craftsmen, the cost of special clothing furnished employees, or any of a variety of costs important to management.

COST REDUCTION

The primary reason for the existence of stores inventory is to assure availability of materials necessary to keep the production moving. The cost of carrying inventory must be weighed against the expense of not having it when required or of possibly higher unit prices for spot purchases as needed.

An *open stores system,* where stores personnel maintain a stores operation but items are not controlled by receipt and disbursement records, may be considered. Where a company is involved with a high-production operation, parts and subassemblies flow continually through the plant without the necessity for extensive inventory record keeping.

Stores management must fully understand the company's overall economic and operating policies and the part played by the stores function. Is it an around-the-clock, seven-days-a-week operation? Can a shutdown be allowed, and, if so, how costly would it be? Is an inventory of finished goods maintained to allow sufficient time for parts ordering? These factors influence decisions on maximum and minimum facilities, buy or make, stock or don't stock. Cost of possession balanced against the best estimate of the consequences of not possessing will determine the course to be taken. Stores, purchasing, and inventory management must work closely in making these decisions.

Turnover

Movement of materials should be reviewed regularly. Economic and production changes can quickly affect material flow and inventory policy, and a close scrutiny of flow or lack of flow will help avoid holding obsolete material. Communicating routinely with maintenance on machinery obsolescence is very important. As soon as it is recognized that items are obsolete, they should be removed from stores.

Return

If some material is returned to stores after disbursements to operations, a credit memo must be made to establish that it is in stock again. Credit should be given to the job or cost center originally charged, and the physical and financial inventory record updated.

Money-Making Techniques

Standardization and substitution are recognized ways to mimimize operating costs. Stores management is in a good position to encourage both. A good catalog, properly assembled, will reveal where there is duplication of parts and material. With this visible evidence, maintenance should be encouraged to further standardize on machinery, to reduce inventory and probably also lower procurement costs. Substitution of materials or parts to utilize existing stores stock and extending standardization should be encouraged, but care must be taken to ensure that necessary quality and performance are not sacrificed. Nothing is saved if production suffers or maintenance increases. Parts that can be made by local machine shops for less cost and quicker delivery should be investigated, and a legal check on possible patents is wise.

Inventory Reduction

Reduction of inventory is a proper goal and should be encouraged, keeping in mind that the principal purpose for stores inventories is to assure continuity of operations. Inventory reduction must be offset by procurement arrangements that still meet the basic criterion. Arrangements with vendors to hold stock items in their inventory can be investigated. All duplications of parts and other materials, obsolete materials, and slow-moving items should be removed from inventory. Establishing a committee representing purchasing, stores, production, and maintenance to review current stock and requests for stocking material may be considered. This provides for ample representation from all areas affected, and their group decision can help eliminate stocking items that are not necessary.

COMPUTERIZED MATERIAL MANAGEMENT SYSTEMS

Computer technology, both software and hardware, is now available to provide substantial cost savings in stores management. The opportunity for these savings through computerized materials management systems is usually maximized if inventory management and stores management report to purchasing. This enables purchasing to innovate programs that can reduce or eliminate inventories other than major spare parts and high-value critical items.

The manufacturing industry is adopting the philosophy that inventories are non-revenue-producing assets and is devising programs with suppliers to provide goods only when they are ready to be consumed. In these cases, physical storing of as much as 80 percent of the line items becomes unnecessary and stores management then provides a staging and logistical function. Normally these are low-value, multiple-transaction items, and stores management and purchasing are thus able to devote their talents and energy to the high-value, critical items and to concentrate on eliminating costly functions in the procurement and in-plant distribution of materials. These programs can provide extremely high service levels with no risk to the ultimate function they serve.

STOCK ROTATION

A stock rotation plan can be an integral part of the total storage and handling program if the need for such a plan is paramount. The necessity for rotation does not, however, assure its maximum implementation, because stock rotation depends on conscientious performance by both labor and management personnel. As the number of items and personnel increases, so do rotation problems.

Since rotation has such a high degree of dependence upon the human element for its successful implementation, personal motivations must be stimulated. Stores management should make its interest known by more profound means than the impersonal memorandum, especially if improper rotation can cause a change in the state of the product or its acceptability. Where critical items are involved, 100 percent implementation may be less desirable than concentration on those areas where exposure is greatest.

The concept of rotation is in itself simple, but even under the best conditions, it is affected by situations beyond management's control. Management checks, such as the tabulation of inventory by date of item manufacture, will identify older items. A check might not reveal, however, the legitimate transfer in of old items from other distribution points or from returns by a customer. Then too, in crowded and busy stores operations, older items can somehow get "lost"; they will not appear in the current physical inventory but will often mysteriously appear in the succeeding ones.

This is, however, not a hopeless condition if personnel are adequately trained. The stores operation will manage if the code date on the carton is clearly visible and easy to interpret.

Economy in shipping should also be of concern. Separate requests for individual items should be combined for shipment whenever possible and, in particular, when more favorable freight rates are applicable.

OBSOLESCENCE

In most stores operations there will be obsolete and surplus items from time to time. The only way to operate stores management effectively is to develop a well-organized program for the disposal of unwanted items, sell the program to top management, and then make the program contribute to achievement of company objectives.

Generally, there are four types of operating materials that occasionally become surplus: (1) spare parts for equipment that is obsolete; (2) products that are obsolete because of model or technological changes; (3) spare parts in excess of inventory requirements; and (4) maintenance and operating supplies no longer needed because of changes in operations. The approach to obsolescence and surplus disposal in regard to these items is the same as for idle equipment.

Disposal Alternatives

Many vendors will permit the return of items and issue a credit of 75 to 90 percent of the purchase price. Most have a policy that materials must be in their original condition and cartons to be considered for return. Thus stores management personnel have a prime responsibility to maintain materials that can be returned in good condition.

Although some companies transfer materials to another location, it may be more desirable to return them to the vendor for credit. Unit prices are generally so low that the freight costs involved in shipping them will lower their value to a point below the vendor's credit allowance.

Where products are surplus, many companies dispose of them by selling to employees at substantial discounts, or if large quantities are involved, selling them to discount stores. When equipment is sold, spare parts should be included in the sale price.

SCRAP

Scrap generated in a stores operation is an old problem that often receives very little attention. Unfortunately, stores management has been inclined to be casual in its efforts to dispose of scrap, handling it haphazardly, to say the least.

A few questions need to be answered to determine the highest return for scrap materials. Is too much being spent on the preparation of scrap? Is scrap prepared to a recognized grade or classification that will secure the highest price? Is it segregated at the point of origin? Has a thorough investigation been made of freight costs? Is protection against pilferage adequate? Is weighing correct? And finally, have the best methods for disposing of scrap been investigated?

It is important to note that, in most instances, the scrap dealer does not establish the price. The price of scrap is set by the companies who ultimately use it. Every effort must be made to reduce the cost from point of origin to the point of reclamation for the purpose of increasing the net return.

The place where scrap is generated is obviously the best place to begin controlling cost. There should be boxes on hand for segregating various types of scrap. Mixing scrap and then segregating it only drives up your cost.

Special attention should be given to exotic metals, aluminum, copper, brass, alloy steels, and carbide and diamond tooling. A return is available for data processing cards and discarded computer reports. Do not overlook empty drums not returnable to the vendor.

Finally, seek out all possible competition. It is difficult to outnegotiate an experienced scrap dealer. For additional information on scrap and surplus see Section 24.

NOTE: For further information on subjects covered in this section see the list of references in Section 30.

Purchasing with a Computer

EDITOR

Robert L. Janson, C.P.M. *Manager, Management Consulting Services, Ernst & Whinney, Cleveland, Ohio*

ASSOCIATE EDITOR

Bernard J. Frey *Manager, MIS/DP, Bailey Controls, Wickliffe, Ohio*

INTRODUCTION

The significance of computerization for purchasing and materials management is readily understood when one considers the enormous amount of purely administrative work involved in the procurement cycle of the average manufacturing company. Literally thousands of requisitions, change orders, requests for quotations, purchase orders, expediting communications, receiving records, invoices, and other documents must be processed and recorded every year.

Handling this volume of detail manually not only requires a relatively large staff—buyers, expediters, and clerical personnel—but often leaves the buyers with too little time to concentrate on such basic *managerial* responsibilities as supplier development and evaluation, cost and price analysis, negotiation, and long-range planning.

Much of the paperwork of the purchasing department can, however, be automated. Figure 15-1 shows certain activities in the purchasing cycle that could be done by a computer. This section of the handbook is designed to provide the purchasing manager with guidelines for developing a computer system for purchasing. The approach to computerization of the function, or upgrading of an existing system, is basic and general; since companies vary widely in their procurement procedures and requirements, there is, of course, no one universally applicable system.

PURPOSES OF A COMPUTER SYSTEM

The extensive amount of paper handled by each purchasing person—both buyer and clerical—is one of the main reasons for a computerized purchasing system, but far from the only one.

There are other reasons. Computerization provides a single standard, uniform method of buying and controlling inventories; a method of setting realistic priorities for material; and assurance that checks and balances exist to ascertain whether the department is functioning properly. Purchasing is better able to participate in the company business plan, playing an important role. A computerized system even allows purchasing to demonstrate the benefits of its activities through better reporting and analysis. And since much paper handling is eliminated, all company employees end up with only one "version of the truth."

BENEFITS FROM COMPUTERIZED PURCHASING

Corporations that have successfully installed a computerized purchasing system have reported the following types of benefits:

1. A virtual elimination of filing
2. Easier implementation of volume purchasing and large-scale contracts with resultant savings to the company
3. A 35 percent savings in time for buyers
4. A 40 percent reduction in overall clerical time
5. A great reduction in paperwork
6. Standardization of pertinent data and terminology
7. Ready accessibility of data to all authorized personnel (controlled with built-in security checks)
8. Reduction in time required for all forms of input, retrieval, computation, and response
9. Improved communications and rapport among all purchasing and plant personnel of divisions and plants in the company
10. Adaptability and fast response to changes in priorities, prices, and other variables of purchasing
11. Centralized management without loss of utility of personnel to any outlying departments
12. Savings in equipment and floor space, principally through elimination of files

There are more intangible results. Purchasing is more responsive since expediting is faster and more accurate. Communication with the accounts payable department regarding invoices is more effective. Everyone uses the same files; so-called duplicate data files do not exist. People are more flexible in job assignments resulting from the uniform approach.

After installation, there may be other benefits: a lessening of inventory investment due to the speed and more accurate response time, and a gradual lessening of the department staff through attrition.

One must keep return on investment in mind when planning such sophisticated and costly systems. Installation of cathode-ray tubes (CRTs) and their expensive supporting computer must permit purchasing to "buy smarter," saving enough money to justify the change.

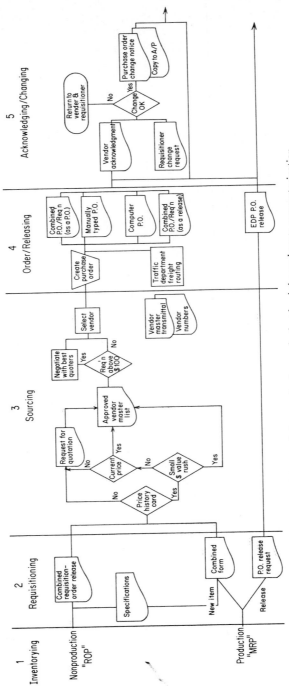

Fig. 15-1 Phases of the purchasing cycle that lend themselves to computerization.

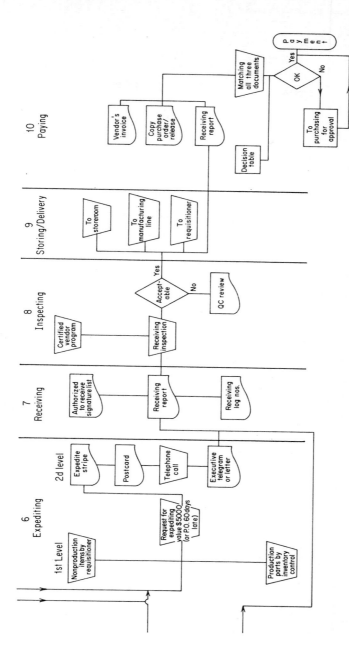

Fig. 15-1 (*Continued*)

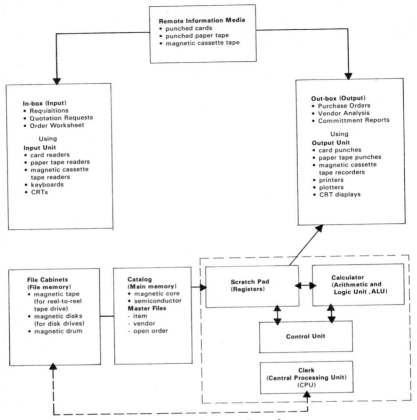

Fig. 15-2 Principal hardware sections of a computer.

THE COMPUTER ITSELF

The central processing unit (CPU) as shown in Fig. 15-2 is the major element in a computer hardware system and has three central sections: the control unit, the memory storage unit, and the arithmetic unit. The illustration shows communications channels between separate sections. Thus input enters the memory unit; output comes from the memory; arithmetical processing is accomplished through communications to and from memory and a direct control mechanism communication with each of the other sections.

EQUIPMENT CAPABILITIES

A widening range of hardware (the physical equipment used in data processing, e.g., the computer and its terminals) is now available.

There are several different types of computer systems, as discussed briefly in the following paragraph.

Batch

In a batch system information is collected during the day and is keypunched, usually at night, in one group or *batch* of information. Not only is the information keypunched at one time, but it is also put into the computer system in the same manner. Controls over the input are based on a *batch number,* and a summary is made of the data contained in each group.

On Line

On-line systems utilize a CRT terminal linked to the main computer (see Fig. 15-3). Using the typewriterlike keyboards that are part of the terminal, authorized

ITEM NUMBER	67391
COMMODITY CODE	14
DESCRIPTION	Bearing
DRAWING NUMBER	A 7861 Chg B, dtd. 6/1/79
MATERIAL SPECIFICATION	1040 Steel
EXPECTED ANNUAL QUANTITY	18,500

VENDOR INFORMATION

| NAME | NUMBER | PERFORMANCE RATING | PRICES PER QUOTATION DATED 7/1/79 | | |
			3,000	6,000	10,000
WILBURN	1691	3.11	26.18	21.79	20.11
R.G. CEPT	0032	2.06	24.16	21.03	19.97
WILEY	0763	3.84	27.11	21.93	20.79

Fig. 15-3   Sketch of cathode-ray tube (CRT), which is similar to a television screen, displaying the type of purchasing information that can be called out from a computer.

personnel can call out a variety of information from the computer data bank. The information appears on the CRT, which is similar to a television screen. The data may have been batch-processed the previous night and therefore may be as current as 5:00 p.m. on the preceding day. In other instances information—receiving reports for example—could be as current as 1 hour ago. Up-to-the-moment calculations of inventory levels, however, are not available.

Data can also be entered in the main computer through the terminals.

Real Time

A real-time computer program also uses a CRT terminal. The information is entered on line into the computer and is updated simultaneously. For example, open or incomplete orders will be updated based on the time the last receiving report was entered into the system, also through a CRT.

Special Terminals

Many special-purpose terminals are available. One model has an optical mark reader, a bar code printer, and an alphanumeric printer. It can be used for processing requisitions by reading optical marks and for translating marks into numbers and letters. It can also be used as a turnaround document terminal to validate the requisition or to supply additional data.

Computer-to-Computer "Conversation"

A computer terminal in a purchasing department at one company can "converse" directly with a vendor's computer at the vendor company's sales department.

DISTRIBUTED PROCESSING SYSTEMS

A more recent development is the use of *distributed processing systems*. In these systems, a major computer processing unit is linked with a smaller computer in another location, such as a purchasing department. The local, smaller computer becomes an extension of the larger computer, which is called the *host*. This system often gives the user greater control of data entry and document preparation. It relieves the host computer of some functions and tends to reduce total operating costs. Sometimes planning functions are done at the host computer while certain operating functions are done at the local computer. A comparison of the activities done by the host and the local computers is shown below.

Preorder Phase

Local Functions	*Host Functions*
Creating and maintaining supplier data	Processing planned-item requirements
Creating and maintaining quotation data	Generating cash requirements reports
Evaluating suppliers	Planning for required-item quotations
Reviewing quotations	Maintaining the master data base
Requesting needed item quotes	Creating original blanket-order records
Creating blanket-order records	

Order-Placement Phase

Local Functions	*Host Functions*
Entering requisition and order data for unplanned item requirements	Creating requisitions from planned orders
Reviewing and approving requisitions	Providing system recommendations for the requisitions
Generating purchase orders	Sending the requisitions to the local computer
Generating releases to blanket orders	

Postorder Phase

Local Functions	*Host Functions*
Posting order acknowledgment data	Providing receiving with open-order data
Processing order changes	Providing quality control with inspection instructions
Altering purchase orders	Closing purchase orders
Answering order inquiries	Updating the history data base
Providing accounts payable with payment approval	
Initiating the closing of a purchase order	

TYPES OF DATA BASE

A *data base* is a collection of information processed by the computer. Creation of a uniform purchasing data base requires standardization of a number of elements. For the requisitioning cycle, for example, there should be standard ordering specifications, nomenclature, ordering units, units of measure, and commodity codes of all repetitively purchased materials and stores items.

Standardization of commodity and purchase data is essential in the procurement cycle because the information is perpetuated in mechanical form for subsequent processing in other functions.

There are normally three computer files or record sources that are used to accumulate data for computerized purchasing operations. These are described below.

Item Master

The *item master* record fully identifies the item that is to be ordered. This record is usually part of a computer bill-of-material file. It contains all the unique item data needed by purchasing:

Stock number–description
Lead time
Costs, units of measure
Inventory
Commodity codes
Ordering policy
Historical and forecast usage
Qualified suppliers

Vendor Master

The *vendor file* contains the following information about each vendor:

Name and address
Contact
Terms
Shipping data
Performance data
Major commodity codes
Purchasing history
All open purchase order numbers

Open Order

The *open-order file* is the key to any purchasing system. In conjunction with the other files, it provides information necessary to initiate and evaluate purchasing activity. The file is created when the order is written and is maintained until the order is received, invoiced, and paid. It contains all updated order information, such as:

Quantity
Prices
Shipping data
Receiving data
Receiving inspection data
Invoice and invoice payment data

PLANNING A COMPUTER SYSTEM

Before moving to convert to or to upgrade a computerized purchasing system, purchasing management must clearly and completely define its objectives in taking the action. Once this is done, the basic steps in planning, justifying, and obtaining a computer system are those listed below. However, one should modify these steps to suit the specific environment in which the company is working. All the steps shown may not be necessary, especially in a small company or when a minor system change is being made.

Before getting involved in the rather elaborate program described below, one should read some basic material on computers, visit trade exhibits, and have preliminary discussions with hardware and software sales representatives to get an idea of current computer literature. Many people also interview users of computers to find out what good experiences and bad problems they have had with the various types of machines.

1. Analyze the Existing System.   Critically evaluate the existing system so that satisfactory procedures, forms, reports, etc., and those that are inadequate or missing are identified. For each of the unsatisfactory items, a recommendation should be made concerning the system improvements necessary.

2. Define the Purpose of the System.   Determine the primary problems and the desired objectives of computerization. Be guided by the company objectives and policy—both overall and for purchasing.

3. Develop a Project Team and a Steering Committee.   A team or committee of purchasing and systems personnel, perhaps assisted by others such as inventory control specialists, should work as a committee, headed by the purchasing manager. A steering committee, consisting of higher-level executives within the company, should review the work of the project team, critique it and approve it, and authorize continuing efforts. Then a tentative work plan should be developed which includes priorities, schedule, and work force.

4. Obtain Information for Preliminary System Design.   Identify what kind of information will be required from the system, when it will be required, and what its unique characteristics are.

5. Develop a Conceptual Design.   Set up a large flowchart of a generalized nature showing the inputs, reference documents, and outputs of the desired system.

6. Prepare a Justification.   List both qualitative and quantitative benefits expected from the investment, including all the elements of the total system. Figure

15-4 gives an example of a cost-benefit analysis that could be used to initially summarize the expected cost and return on the proposed system. Costs are often distributed in about three equal parts—programming, equipment, and operation.

7. Present the Proposal. The entire project team should present the proposal to management via the steering committee, stressing the advantages of the system, the time required, and the expected benefits. Sometimes it is desirable to use visual aids in making the presentation.

8. Design the Necessary System. The desired system design should expand on the conceptual flowchart developed in step 5. It should, of course, be cost-justified as previously described.

			FIRST YEAR	SECOND YEAR	THIRD YEAR

Project Description_____
_____Control No._____
Submitted By_____Date_____
Approved By_____ _____

COST OF PROJECT — DEVELOPMENT
System Design
Programming
Documentation
Testing
Training
Implementation
    Subtotal

COMPUTER
Software Package
Hardware Equipment
    Subtotal
Operating Expense
    Total Project Cost

BENEFITS EXPECTED
Purchased Cost Savings
Cost Avoidance
Supplies reduction
Payroll
Other (Specify)
    Total Benefits Expected

RETURN ON INVESTMENT

$$\text{Return on Investment} = \frac{\text{Total Benefits Expected} \_\_\_\_\_}{\text{Total Project Cost} \_\_\_\_\_} = \_\_\_\_\_ \times 100 = \_\_\%$$

Fig. 15-4 Sample cost-benefit analysis form for summarizing expected cost of and return on a proposed computerized system.

9. Develop System Specifications.   Give the characteristics and explain the technical details of the desired system. These specifications should be prepared with the use of common sense. They should not be restricted to those in any particular package available, nor should they exclude certain desirable features because they might cost too much. Remember to include data-base requirements.

SUMMARY COST BENEFIT RELATIONSHIPS

	1980		1981		
	3rd Qtr.	4th Qtr.	1st Qtr.	2nd Qtr.	3rd Qtr.
A. Development expenses					
1. Design	$ 6,600	$ 6,600	$ 6,600	$ 6,600	0
2. Programming	11,440	11,440	11,440	11,440	0
3. Data center	5,000	8,250	5,000	5,000	0
4. Other	650	1,330	650	650	0
Total development	$23,690	$27,620	$23,690	$23,690	0
B. Operating expense increase					
1. Programming	0	0	0	0	0
2. User personnel	0	0	0	0	0
3. Data center	0	0	$16,375	$16,375	$16,885
4. Other	0	0	0	0	0
Total operating increase	0	0	$16,375	$16,375	$16,885
C. Total A and B	$23,690	$27.620	$40,065	$40,065	$16,885
D. Benefits					
1. Cash discount saving	0	0	$ 500	$ 500	$ 500
2. Inventory reduction	0	0	13,250	13,250	13.250
3. Reduction of small orders placed	0	0	6,250	6,250	6,250
4. Reduction of clerical work	0	0	7,500	7,500	7,500
5. Avoidance of future personnel	0	0	9,500	9,500	9,500
Total Benefits	0	0	$37,000	$37,000	$37,000
E. Total net savings (D − C)	$(23,690)	$(27,620)	$(3,065)	$(3,065)	$20,115

Fig. 15-5   Typical cost evaluation report to management showing savings anticipated from adoption of electronic data processing (EDP).

10. Establish an Estimated Price Breakdown for the Vendor Proposal.   Detail costs of the subcategories of computer equipment, such as hardware and peripheral equipment. Estimate the software required for the computer program. A computer department programmer should also make a cost estimate. Then the trade-off can be studied as suggested by Fig. 15-5.

11. Send Requests for Quotations.   Send a well-prepared request for quotation to at least four hardware and/or software vendors, carefully describing the various items required in the system. Discuss proposals separately with individual suppliers.

12. Develop a Quotation Evaluation System. Using formal documents or large spread sheets, list the various information furnished by the hardware and software vendors to create a comparative matrix evaluation system.

13. Select the Two Best Suppliers. Looking at not just the lowest-priced, but the least-overall-total-cost computer system, invite the two vendors with the best quotes to separate meetings to discuss in depth the details of the quotations. In carrying out this step, keep in mind that the price on the request for quotation is not necessarily the vendor's final price.

14. Select the Best Supplier. Negotiate the final specifications, price, terms, and conditions.

DIVISION									TYPE			
GENERAL MANAGER										DATE		
CHAIRMAN												
COMMITTEE MEMBERS												

CON-TROL NO.	PRO-GRAM NO.	TASK	RESPONSI-BILITY	PURPOSE	PLANNED ACCOMPLISH-MENT	TECHNIQUES TO USE	TARGET DATES		ACTUAL PROGRESS DATES				
							START	FINISH	SURVEY	EVALU-ATE	DESIGN	APPROVAL	IMPLEMENT

Fig. 15-6 Typical form used in setting up a design and implementation schedule for a computerized system.

15. Set Up a Schedule. Begin the implementation phase with a revised design and implementation schedule, as illustrated in Fig. 15-6. Communicate broadly the plan and the rationale for it. Conduct a series of training sessions to brief purchasing personnel and others about the planned revisions.

16. Work on Installing the System. During installation pay particular attention to hardware equipment and the software programming instructions. Perform necessary customizing or tailoring of the programs. Remember to document the procedures in standard operating procedure manuals.

17. Test the Computer Output Reports. Debug as necessary until the programs are as accurate as possible. Be certain that the users in purchasing sign off their agreement on the final format. Make certain the software suppliers continue their assistance; do not accept the system until fully satisfied.

18. Perform a Postaudit. Check the accuracy of the original cost-benefit justification for the new system. Do this at the end of the first full year of use and again at the end of 3 years.

Checklist for Selection

The following checklist covers some of the more important considerations to be kept in mind during evaluation of equipment in the review process described above.

Memory Capacity   Determine how much memory is available on the computer desired, how much additional memory capacity can be made available later on, and at what cost.

Memory Access Speed   Some memory capability is built into the equipment. Access to this memory should be almost instantaneous. Other access time to external (plug-in) memory can vary greatly, however. Thus, analysis of the cost of the equipment should include the memory access via cassette, which is relatively slow yet inexpensive, versus the memory access via diskette, which is faster but more costly. Depending on use, the speed of the diskette could justify additional cost, depending on ultimate use of the equipment.

Central Processing Capability   Determine how big the computer's "brain" is, how much it can do and what its limitations are; and how well it will meet future additional needs.

Programming   The type of program needed will depend on the intended use of the computer. In purchasing, the systems can be relatively simple. Central processing capabilities will be needed. Programming may be obtained through in-house personnel or from outside service companies. In making this make-or-buy decision, obtain figures early. Programming costs may be an unpleasant surprise.

Input Equipment   A standard keyboard may need to be supplemented by other input equipment such as remote terminals or telephonic hookup. Determine whether the price of the basic equipment includes the cost of these external hookup capabilities.

Output Equipment   A CRT is common in purchasing systems, but some kind of printing device will probably be needed. Speed and versatility of the printers have a high bearing on cost. Make sure that the basic equipment is capable of being hooked up to any other output devices that may be needed.

Service and Reliability   A proper warranty is of great importance. Carefully determine what kind of warranty and what kind of service you will have. If the computer breaks down, how long will it take to get service and what will the cost be? Is backup equipment available, and if so, what will it cost?

IMPLEMENTATION OF AN ELECTRONIC DATA PROCESSING (EDP) PROGRAM

Companies have varying operating needs as well as different types of data inputs and desired data outputs. Thus each will use the computer in a different manner. Some basic purchasing functions lend themselves to computerization: preparation of purchase requisitions and purchase orders, automatic follow-up expediting activities, delivery scheduling, quality records by part and by vendor, preparation of various management reports, and invoice checking.

Following is a sample set of purchasing specifications for a purchase order program.

1. Provide purchasing with exception reports from the material requirements plan, indicating receipts that do not agree with required date on a weekly basis
2. Provide for maintenance of files to include ability to process blanket purchase orders
3. Provide purchase order follow-up file by vendor and required date
4. Provide *on requisition report*—requisition open; purchase order has not been placed
5. List purchase order commitment schedule by month over 6-month period
6. Supply receiving documentation, including feedback on receipts, rejections, and items returned to vendor
7. Provide ability to maintain price and delivery information obtained when preparing quotation
8. Allow for option of generating mechanized purchase orders and change documents
9. Maintain vendor name and address file
10. Provide visibility of company-owned tooling at suppliers

COMPUTER APPLICATIONS IN PURCHASING

Types of Reports Available

A computer purchasing system can range from a limited number of reports to 16 or more computer-produced documents. Figure 15-7 illustrates the field headings of a basic set of 12 reports.

A more advanced system could include reports selected from the list below. This list can be used in making the transition from a basic to a more advanced system.

1. *Purchased part history:* Monthly. This report in part-number sequence accumulates all data on a year-to-date basis. On each item all purchase orders, quantity, vendors, unit price paid, date material required, and date material received complete will be displayed.
2. *Purchased material price variance:* Monthly. This report summarizes on an item-by-item basis all purchase orders on which the unit price paid varies from the established standard cost.
3. *Purchased material commodity report:* Quarterly. This report displays the actual dollars committed to each commodity, based on standard cost and invoices paid. This report assists in volume contract identification and negotiations.
4. *Analysis of purchase orders:* Semiannually. This report lists, by vendor number and part number, all items for which prices paid were in excess of the standard purchase cost.
5. *Purchases by vendor:* Annually. Lists the amount of money paid on invoices

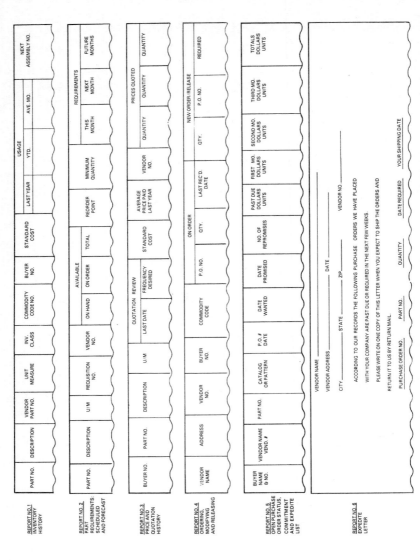

Fig. 15-7 Field headings for a basic set of 12 purchasing reports available in a computerized system.

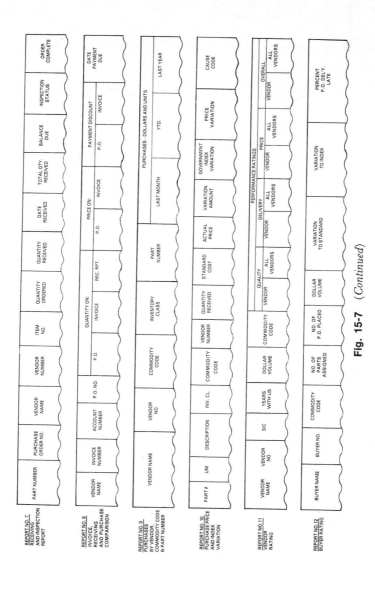

Fig. 15-7 (*Continued*)

by vendor, and is sorted two ways—by vendor alphabetically and by vendor dollars in highest to lowest sequences.

6. *Multiple usage by part:* Annually. Indicates, by part number, if an item is used in only one assembly, or for only one customer, or if used only for spare orders. Is helpful to lessen overbuying.

7. *Vendor delivery record:* Annually. Shows vendor delivery performance, based on percent of late deliveries (against vendor promise) plus number of emergency rush orders provided by the supplier.

8. *Economic indicators:* Semiannually. Measures the prices paid for major commodity groups against the producers' price index, and the actual prices paid divided by the company standard and selected other economic indicators. All measures in percent difference.

9. *Tooling:* Quarterly. Indicates the amount of dollars committed for tooling, the extent of price increases, and the savings achieved through competitive negotiations.

10. *Purchasing backlog:* Weekly. Lists by buyer and by commodity groups the number of requisitions, purchase orders, follow-ups, and requests for quotation to be processed.

11. *Purchasing transaction:* Monthly. Indicates by buyer the number of documents processed, such as orders, requisitions, follow-up cards, letters, and invoices.

12. *On-time deliveries:* Daily. Displays on an office wall Gantt-type chart, the number of late deliveries and of on-time deliveries on the previous work day.

13. *National contract utilization:* Monthly. Explains, for each national contract item, the reason why the available contract was refused, such as better local agreement, wish to use local supplier for small buys, or better service.

14. *Rejection by part by vendor:* Semiannually. Summarizes the rejection rate in percent and in dollars by vendor, listing item detail.

15. *Composite purchasing staff ratings:* Annually. Lists, in ranking order, subjective (opinion) evaluation of staff member by manager, peer buyers, and vendor representatives. Confidential.

16. *Budget, operating costs, and savings:* Annually. Graph of year-to-year trend of dollars purchased, department operating costs, and savings in dollars.

COMPUTER-ASSISTED PURCHASING MANAGEMENT

Certain computer applications can assist management in the measurement of purchasing effectiveness through such means as:

- Commodity commitment systems
- Vendor commitment systems
- Lead-time analysis
- Inventory level and cash flow projection

- Requisition reaction time measurement
- Buyer evaluation systems
- Vendor performance measure
- Entire department measurements

Managers can also evaluate the performance of the vendors, their buyers, and the total purchasing function through the use of the information already in the computer.

Purchase Order Evaluation

While managers have different needs for information, most purchasing executives want to evaluate the performance of vendors, that of individual buyers, and the total purchasing function.

Vendor Evaluation

Purchasing management usually defines its objective in terms of meeting manufacturing's material requirements with the best price, quality, and delivery; therefore, it is obvious that management would like to know how it is doing in relation to its goals.

With respect to price, the computer has captured such information as how the quotations of several vendors compare and the trend of vendor prices.

The delivery data might include the following:

Number of deliveries on time, early, and late
Cumulative number of days early or late
The number of partial shipments, etc.

Within the quality section, data may describe the number of shipments and percent of items rejected, express the degree of the quality problems in relation to an acceptance quality level (AQL), etc. Together, all these factors would yield a composite picture of total vendor performance.

Dollar Expenditures

The computer will be able to give management a detailed picture of how and where the company's money is being spent. This type of information can be of significant use for highlighting potential savings areas and for measuring performance against purchasing expenditure policies. It can provide data on such activities as placement of orders with large versus small business, concentration with a few vendors, and make-versus-buy decisions.

Buyer and Department Analysis

A manager may want to analyze the performance of individual buyers as well as of the total department in terms of such variables as number of orders handled, purchase price variances, percentage of late deliveries, percentage of rejected shipments, number of material stockouts, and number of rush orders processed.

Information for Other Departments

Purchasing can play a part in an overall EDP program for the company. One way involves working with departments in developing a system to use before a requirement comes to purchasing; another involves a system to use after purchasing has completed fulfillment of the requirement. The other areas for development of a total system concept are almost limitless.

A partial listing of what information other departments need from purchasing might include the following:

Sales (through production control): Lead times of purchased parts, cost of a purchased content of end item, inventory levels (anticipated and real)

Production Control: Anticipated deliveries, costs (standard and actual), economical purchase quantity (EPQ)

Receiving, Receiving Inspection, and Stores: Anticipated deliveries

Accounting: Anticipated invoice payment schedule, details for invoice reconciliation, cost distribution instructions

Management: Departmental efficiency reports, individual performance reports, vendor performance reports, accumulative expenditure data

Joint development in these areas is essential so that all departments will receive information in the most efficient manner while, at the same time, not placing any undue burden on purchasing (or the EDP system) to accumulate the data.

The purchasing manager may have to establish a priority rating for the goals he has set for himself. A good rule of thumb is that 10 percent of the total orders usually accounts for 85 percent of the total expenditures. It may be that one purchasing manager may want to get a tighter control on the high-dollar-value items by means of management reports that are not presently available. Another purchasing manager may feel it is more important to direct his EDP activity to the low-dollar-value, highly repetitive items. Mechanizing this area of purchasing activity can give buyers more time to devote to negotiation on the high-priced items.

In the smaller purchasing departments, it may be best to direct attention to mechanizing the purchase of the largest number of transactions, since this will have the effect of freeing up the most hours. The purchasing manager can then utilize such time on other worthwhile projects, for which he never seems to have time otherwise.

BLENDING MANUAL AND EDP PROCEDURES

During the design of an EDP system, it is important to build in maximum flexibility to anticipate probable future advances in equipment and methods without regard to EDP hardware limitations. This flexibility should be limited only by the imagination and ingenuity of those participating in the system's design. The flexibility in design applies to the basic concepts of the system, which in turn determine the logic for programming the computer.

If purchasing is not careful, it is at this point of an EDP program that a computer programmer or systems designer may impose inflexible thinking, which may be based on a desire to achieve simplified or conventional programming. The purchasing manager should not accept as gospel the explanation that technical computer restrictions will prevent his ideas and specific needs from being designed into the system.

As refinements are continually made in the company's EDP plan, however, it is inevitable that some portions must fall by the wayside or be dropped. This will be kept at a minimum if each department head has done a thorough job of pre-planning before sending a representative to the company meetings. It is possible to design and develop a buy-by-computer purchasing system for any department, but it must be tailored to the organization's needs and financial structure and the business objectives of the department. However, the buy-by-computer system seems to be most practical for repetitively purchased items under a computer-controlled inventory system. Materials that are not highly repetitive and are not identified by commodity codes and standard specifications do not lend themselves economically to computerization. The tabulation of purchasing activities below shows which can be done manually and which can be handled by the computer.

Task	Manual	EDP
Enter and control of requisitions		X
Control purchase orders	X	
Secure access to data	X	
Change purchase orders		
Dates		X
Quantities		X
Vendor		X
Track vendor performance	X	
Quality	X	
Delivery	X	
Price	X	
Determine late delivery or wrong quantity	X	
Over	X	
Under	X	
Know when a critical item is received		X
Not overload a particular vendor	X	
Maintain item, order, vendor, quotation, and history data		X
Control and create needed documents		
Purchase orders	X	
Alteration purchase orders	X	
Request for quotes	X	
Expedite orders		X
Answer inquiries from other departments	X	
Provide data to other departments		
Receiving—open order data		X
Quality control—inspection instructions	X	
Accounts payable—payment approval	X	
Close out purchase orders		X
Reduce clerical workload of the purchasing department to allow more time for:		
Evaluation of vendors	X	
Finding new vendors	X	

DATA-PHONE

For highly repetitive items, one of the simplest forms of ordering by EDP is to utilize DATA-PHONE, the Bell System's data communication service.

DATA-PHONE provides direct communication between the purchasing department and the vendor. It carries information on prices, freight terms, f.o.b. points, selection of items, means of transportation, and other pertinent data that are prearranged in a separate agreement before the cards are printed. The only variable that the card does not contain is quantity. The cards originate at the central warehouse and are handled in much the same way as a traveling requisition, except that there is no purchase order to write.

The following outline is typical of the DATA-PHONE transaction:

1. Storekeeper at warehouse sends purchasing department DATA-PHONE card.
2. Purchasing approves the card, and buyer instructs operator to transmit.
3. Operator calls vendor and requests permission to transmit.
4. Operator inserts *item card* into the transmitter and transmission is carried out automatically, with the operator inserting quantity manually.
5. Transmission is now complete.
6. Vendor acknowledges transmission.
7. Purchasing function is now complete, and item card is dated and sent back to the storekeeper.
8. It should be noted that while the vendor is receiving transmission, his receiver is printing out the order on a printer simultaneously.
9. When material is ready to ship, two copies of the printed readout are used as packing slips, with one copy checked by the receiving clerk and forwarded to accounting as a receiving report.
10. Upon receipt of material at the central receiving warehouse, the storekeeper takes the cards from the *on order* file and confirms complete shipments.
11. After the receiving procedure is completed, the cards are filed in the permanent file, where they are ready for the next order.
12. Should any particular shipment be incomplete, the storekeeper notifies purchasing, and the balance is then expedited.

Vendors supply a report (quarterly), listing all purchases for the reporting period. This report is a complete list of:

1. The number of orders placed for a particular time
2. Vendor's item number
3. Vendor's product code
4. Part description
5. Charge number (department buying the item)
6. Original source of requisition
7. Commodity code (pipe, paper, etc.)
8. Unit of measure

9. Total amount of particular items ordered for reporting period
10. Unit price
11. Total dollar value of each type of item, for each classification of items and for the reporting period

A TOTAL PURCHASING EDP SYSTEM

Perhaps the best way to get a picture of the fully computerized purchasing system is to study the office layout depicted in Fig. 15-8. The heart of the system—and

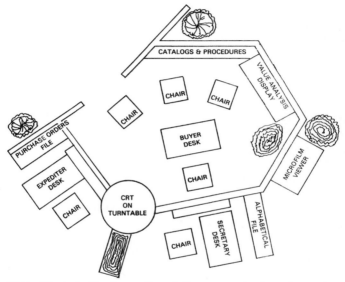

Fig. 15-8   Typical office layout for a fully computerized purchasing system.

the work environment—is the CRT. This device, set up in a real-time, on-line processing mode, eliminates most of the paperwork in the purchasing cycle.

The buyer's day begins with an input into the CRT keyboard, which, in an instantaneous response, shows on the CRT screen a list of all requisitions the buyer has to process. The buyer selects the updated requisitions with the highest priority. For these more important items, the buyer requests another CRT display. Should there not be current competitive quotations, the buyer instructs the computer to prepare a request for quotation (RFQ) to be sent to three vendors already listed for this item, or to add another vendor on an optional basis.

This procedure is followed for each requisition listed on the screen, with the buyer making all the decisions, overriding the computer memory as necessary. The computer can also calculate the most economical purchase order quantity by reviewing the quoted quantity price break. It can also determine the vendor's lead time, based on previous performance.

Once the requisition list has been processed, the buyer may wish to review all quotations. A simple inquiry into the keyboard results in a visual display of selected repetitive parts for which new requests for quotations are required, after review of vendors' recent prices, delivery, and quality. The buyer can delete poor performance and add satisfactory suppliers.

After the vendor has been selected, another instruction to the CRT results in a *hard copy* purchase order being typed on the office computer printer (as was the RFQ).

Expediters can use the CRT to identify past due items. Depending on the severity of the vendor's lateness, the need for the part, the value of the orders, the times repromised, etc. (all of which are indicated on the screen), the expediter chooses the proper course of action. The computer can print a follow-up list or even a specially worded letter (composed in advance but modified at this time) to be sent to the vendor's president, or a telephone call can be made. Any delivery promises obtained are entered into the computer via the CRT.

Purchasing clerks also use the CRT to enter new vendor addresses or changes, delivery acknowledgments, invoice price changes, and part number blueprint revision numbers into the master file memory.

When orders are received, receiving and receiving inspection, using a CRT, can transmit appropriate information to the computer, which is then immediately available to the purchasing department buyer or expediter. Meanwhile, accounts payable can also call up the information on its CRT, so that the purchase order and receiving report can be matched with the vendor's invoice.

Rather than displaying or printing hard copy of reams of report data, this information is exception-oriented, based on the specific demand of the manager. However, in addition to any personnel slow reaction time, the manager can get daily purchase price variation, past due orders, commitment dollars by month, purchases by vendor and commodity groups, number of quotations by buyer, etc.

The CRT system logic uses a series of controls to safeguard information. Purchasing terminals cannot perform the accounts payable function (or access the salary payroll file). A password (frequently changed) is necessary to use a CRT. File maintenance is limited to two specifically trained persons.

Transactions each day are stored for a few more days in a separate computer vault, and all transactions as entered into the CRT are subjected to editing as a check on the validity of the information. Any errors are refused and must be reentered correctly to be accepted.

THE LANGUAGE OF THE COMPUTER WORLD

Data processing systems normally have two major elements: *hardware,* which refers to the mechanical, electrical, and electronic components of the system, and *software,* which refers to the program or set of instructions for the hardware.

Following is a glossary of computer terms.

access time   The time interval from a request by a control unit for data or data storage until the action is completed.

ADP   Automatic data processing.

analog computer   A computer that assigns variable values to numerical data according to the task for which it is programmed, which operates similarly to a slide rule. Contrasted with digital computers.

available time   The time in which a computer may be used by a particular user. Synonomous with *uptime.*

batch processing   Processing of data accumulated in advance so that each batch of data is processed at one time.

binary, or *binary code*   A number system, or code, that makes use of only two numerical characters, usually 0 and 1.

bit   The smallest possible piece of information. The simplest statement that can be made. A specification of one out of two possible alternatives. Usually thought of as a statement of yes or no. Bits are written as 1 for yes and 0 for no. These symbols are the same as those used in binary systems, so a bit is also a binary digit.

bug   A mistake or malfunction.

byte   A binary element, or string of bits worked on as a unit, but usually shorter than a computer word.

calculator   A data processor for performing arithmetic digitally.

cathode-ray tube (CRT)   A device like a television tube used to display electronic data.

central processing unit (CPU)   The unit of a computer that includes circuits controlling the interpretation and execution of instructions.

characters   Letters, digits, punctuation marks, spaces, or other symbols used in data.

closed shop   A computer service in which the client is not permitted to operate the computer equipment and must rely on a specialist to execute his programs.

COBOL   Common business-oriented language. A business data processing language.

computer program   A series of instructions in a form acceptable to a computer prepared to achieve a certain result.

computer word   A sequence of bits or characters treated as a unit.

core storage   Magnetic material of a computer in which data or programs may be stored.

data   Any representations, such as characters or analog quantities, to which meaning is or might be assigned.

data base   A collection of libraries of computerized data.

digital computer   A computer that uses the numerical characters from 0 through 9 in performing arithmetic and logic processes. Contrast with analog computers.

direct access   The process of obtaining data directly from storage only through the position of the data without recourse to an index or a directory of stored data.

display   Visual presentation of data.

downtime   The time during which a computer does not work because of a functional problem.

dynamic storage   Storage in a magnetic drum or disc in which the storage position varies and data can be made available only when in a recovery position.

EDP   Electronic data processing.

flip-flop   A building block having two stable states that stores one bit by means of two gates that are cross-coupled like a latch, with the output of each forming an input to the other. It is capable of changing from one state to the other by the application of a control signal, but will also remain in that state after removal of a signal.

Fortran   A special computer programming language used to express programs by arithmetic formulas.

hardware   The physical equipment (such as the computer itself and its terminals) used in data processing, as opposed to software, or the programs and instructions to tell the equipment what to do.

hybrid computer   A computer in which both analog and digital data are used.

integrated circuit (IC)   A small package with electrical terminals, containing a chip of silicon. The surface of the silicon is processed to form hundreds or thousands of transistors and other devices. These make up an electronic circuit.

interface   A hardware device to link two components, or a portion of storage to which access can be gained by two or more computer programs.

magnetic bubble   A tiny, movable magnetized region formed under certain conditions in a thin film of magnetic garnet crystal fabricated similarly to an integrated circuit. Such bubbles provide very dense, serial-access storage of bits.

magnetic disk   A flat circular plate with a magnetic surface on which data can be stored.

magnetic drum   A cylinder with a magnetic surface on which data can be stored.

main frame   The major part of the computer.

main storage   Storage that can include a program to provide instructions to the central computer.

MICR   Magnetic ink character recognition. A method by which a machine can read specially printed forms, using a magnetic ink. Many banks use these for checks.

MIS   Management information system. A system giving information to management.

modem   A modulator-demodulator. A device that changes the quality or volume of an electronic signal in communications transmission.

module   A component of hardware, usually all in one piece. Several modules together make up a system.

multiplex To transmit two or more messages simultaneously on a single channel.

noise Loosely, any disturbance tending to interfere with the normal operation.

OCR Optical character recognition. A machine that can read on the basis of the shapes or forms of characters, without use of special inks.

peripheral equipment Any equipment distinct from the central processing unit that may provide the system with outside communication or added capabilities.

processor In hardware, a data processor; in software, a program that functions in, e.g., compiling or translating data for a specific programming language.

program Loosely, a routine for the computer.

random-access memory A memory with a number of storage locations, where words may be *written* (stored) or *read* (recovered) in any order at random.

read-only memory A memory unit containing data permanently stored when the unit was manufactured. Usually an IC chip with each bit stored as a permanent electrical connection of some sort, which can be read at random.

real-time processing Manipulation of data that are required by or generated in a process while the process is in operation.

remote access Communication with a data processor from a distant terminal.

response time The lapse of time between the end of an inquiry or demand and the beginning of a response.

run The single performance of one or more jobs or a single computer program.

software Computer programs, procedures, rules, and documentation concerned with the operation of a data processing system. Contrasted with hardware.

terminal A point in a system or communication network, and often the device associated with that point, at which data can enter or leave the system.

time sharing Simultaneous use of a computer system by two or more users.

volatile storage A storage unit whose content is lost when the power is removed.

word A string of characters, or a string of bits considered as an entity.

NOTE: For further information on subjects covered in this section see the list of references in Section 30.

Buying Capital Equipment

EDITOR

Joseph E. Flannery, C.P.M. *Corporate Director—Transportation (formerly Director, Purchasing), Armco Inc., Middletown, Ohio*

ASSOCIATE EDITORS

Roger R. Frank, C.P.M. *Corporate Director of Purchasing, Baxter Travenol Laboratories, Inc., Deerfield, Illinois*

D. B. Carmody *Manager, Engineering Construction and Equipment Purchases, Union Carbide Corporation, New York, New York*

Each year, companies spend large sums of money for new equipment. These expenditures generally result from the need for additional capacity and improved productivity. New developments in materials and technology result in replacement of existing equipment. Increased awareness of the need for energy conservation and protection of our environment has created a whole new generation of equipment.

The equipment that fills these needs typically is classified as capital equipment. Annual spending for capital equipment is a significant component of the gross national product. These expenditures are a major factor in the overall level of business activity. The federal government encourages capital equipment investment as a means of stimulating economic activity and productivity. This concern is further increased by the infrequency of purchase of specific types of equipment. The investor therefore is rewarded via tax credits or accelerated depreciation rates.

Capital equipment purchases are generally complex transactions requiring much planning and coordination throughout both the buyer and seller organizations. Therefore a careful evaluation and study are made of each transaction. The following will provide some insight into the nature of capital equipment and major aspects of its purchase.

WHY BUYING CAPITAL EQUIPMENT IS DIFFERENT

What Capital Equipment Is

The fixed assets of a business consist of long-lived assets not intended for resale in the regular business of the enterprise. Capital equipment is one of the subclasses of the fixed asset category and includes industrial and office machinery and tools, transportation equipment, furniture and fixtures, and others. As such, these items are properly chargeable to a capital account rather than to expense.

Differences from Other Purchases

The long life and high value characteristic of capital equipment purchases differentiate this type of buying from ordinary procurement. Each transaction can require executive-level participation. The procured items are carried on the balance sheet and depreciated over a long period of time. Conversely, operating supply purchases are immediately expensed and considered part of the cost of current production. Raw material buying is often repeat business once the competing vendors have satisfied basic good purchasing criteria. Capital equipment purchases differ considerably. Each transaction usually results in separate and extended negotiation.

The impact of capital transactions is dramatic and often felt throughout the company. A chain reaction can be started with a single major equipment buy. The purchase can be part of the corporate expansion program or an upgrading of manufacturing processes dictated by technology or return on investment. Top management is intimately involved, as are design engineering, manufacturing engineering, production, maintenance, and facilities engineering personnel and, of course, finance officers. This is in sharp contrast to the purchasing of operating supplies and raw materials, which is considered a common, routine business activity, primarily of concern to the using departments. The unique identity of major equipment is preserved through serial numbers, asset tags, detailed accounting, specifications, and statistical records. These procedures are of considerable value for accounting, depreciation, tax, and income determination purposes and can also benefit maintenance, design, and manufacturing engineering groups. This is not the case with raw materials or supply items, where one unit is like another.

Service is the factor which most distinguishes the purchasing of capital equipment from that of other commodities. Should the purchase be made domestically, where immediate service and good communication are available, or in the foreign market, where there is potential for reducing capital outlay? Is the vendor capable of analyzing the buyer's real needs, e.g., chemical and physical properties involved, alloys suited, capacity, overall economics regarding user application? Can the vendor install equipment, provide start-up supervision, do troubleshooting, and train new equipment operators? The effect of capital equipment service—or lack of it—can be critical to the buying company. Most vendors are aware of this and include the cost of their service expertise in the price of the equipment.

Long-Range Planning for Capital Equipment

Since decisions regarding the addition of capital equipment can and do have a significant effect on the future of a company, it is important that tight control on expenditures of this nature be maintained. This is generally done by incorporating in the budgeting process a capital equipment budget. Department heads submit their proposals, which ultimately are reviewed and acted upon. Top management establishes a long-term capital expenditures budget, which serves as a guide for the business. Usually the annual capital budget is approved by the board of directors. The setting up of an appropriation for a project in the annual capital budget usually signifies management's firm decision to commit funds to that project.

Approval procedures may vary for expenditures that are intended to replace worn-out or obsolete equipment (*normal budget*), as opposed to expenditures that are intended to significantly change the operation in terms of its product, capacity, or technology (*special budget*).

Typically, normal, or replacement, budgets maintain current position. Expenditures are planned annually and are made throughout the year as replacement needs are signaled by breakdown and heavy maintenance, or simply as planned replacements. Normal budgets are relatively level from year to year, although some expenditures may be deferred at the cost of heavier maintenance or lower production.

Special budgets provide for a significant change, often involving a major construction project. Planning can be structured in stages which may be identified as follows:

Inceptive stage	Needs identified; long-range plans
Action stage	Initial feasibility studies, task force involvement
Project stage	Engineering studies, projections, costs
Program stage	Final engineering, definitive estimate, board approval
Appropriation stage . . .	Specific purchases approved and scheduled

Each stage is carefully reviewed by management, and participation by functional representatives of engineering, finance, manufacturing, maintenance, sales, and purchasing is provided. As each stage is reviewed and approved, more detailed plans are laid and estimates are refined. An expenditure or project may also be rejected or deferred at any stage as more information becomes available or as conditions change.

Calculating and Evaluating Capital Expenditures

There are a number of methods of calculating and evaluating capital equipment expenditures, some of which are: payback method; return on investment; first-year performance; total life; average rate of return; present worth method; rate-of-return method; and improved Machinery and Allied Products Institute (MAPI) method. Explanations of these various methods can be found in the accounting books listed in Section 30. The most common approach, however, is to calculate the return on investment.

$$\text{Return on investment} = \frac{\text{cash benefits}}{\text{investment}}$$

There are variations in this method, but the common approach is computation of average cash flows (less depreciation) per year divided by average net book value of the assets over the project life. The following will serve to illustrate the method.

A proposal to procure a special baling machine requires a present outlay of $10,000 and has expected cash inflows of $2000 at the end of 1 year and $4000 at the end of each succeeding year for the next 4 years. Straight-line depreciation for the $10,000 investment over its 5-year life is $2000 per year, assuming no salvage value. Cash flows after depreciation are zero in the first year and $2000 in each of the next 4 years ($4000 − $2000 = $2000). The average cash flow therefore is ⅕(0 + $8000) = $1600 per year. The average net book value of the assets is ⅕(8000 + 6000 + 4000 + 2000 + 0) = $4000. The accounting rate of return is 1600/4000 = 40 percent on net book value, if taxes are ignored.

In order to ensure proper decision making, it is important that all costs to be incurred with the purchase of equipment be included to provide a total cost of procurement. Included should be:

1. Engineering and design cost
2. Delivered purchase price
3. Finance cost
4. Performance guarantee considerations
5. Warranty period considerations
6. Parts and service availability considerations
7. Installation and start-up costs
8. Special training costs
9. Operating cost (including energy usage)
10. Insurance and maintenance costs
11. Tax considerations

Involvement of Purchasing

The purchasing manager begins his equipment buying activity with a review of the specifications. This review includes a study of alternative methods, a cost analysis of alternatives, the search for the right equipment to satisfy the need, and a determination of potential savings. The purchasing manager then provides this information on available equipment, its cost, and the delivery schedule to the requesting party. Once the basic equipment has been agreed upon, specifications must be established. The buyer should be alert to control engineering's tendency to insist on unnecessary specifications. Such restrictive requirements can alter the design, increase cost, and delay delivery of originally proposed equipment.

Equipment and Materials Procurement Plan for a Project   On every major capital project a detailed plan for all procurement activities for equipment and materials should be established as soon as an initial major equipment and materials list is available. Such a plan may be appended from time to time after initiation as the equipment and materials lists become better defined, or as the need for change arises.

Purchasing will be responsible for the initial discussions to lay out the format of this plan and assemble the proper people to initiate its preparation. Inputs regarding specific items will necessarily be gathered at later dates from equipment and material purchasing specialists. If a project procurement manager or coordinator has been appointed sufficiently early in the project, he will become responsible for developing, amending, and monitoring the plan within the guidelines established by the project plan.

The equipment and materials procurement plan should include but not be limited to:

1. A listing of major equipment and major materials, with a brief general description of each item and a general approximation of value.

2. The name of the purchasing individual responsible for the purchasing activity for each item.

3. An approximate schedule for the purchasing activity, including issuance of requisition, date of inquiry, bid due date, purchase order date, and date required on site.

4. An overall project bidders list stating those sources of equipment (by type), materials, and subcontract services which are generally acceptable to owner and contractor. At an appropriate time each item listed in the equipment and materials procurement plan shall show the specific bidders lists for such item.

5. Strategies for combining like items or groupings of items for bidding, either as a spot purchase or under a requirements contracting approach. This part of the plan can address itself to the need for scheduling detailed engineering of certain equipment items to accommodate an effective purchasing program. Care should be taken to avoid lengthy delays in issuing inquiries awaiting one or two specifi-

cations for later items, which thereby cause delay in the project. Care should also be taken to avoid leaving items "out in the cold" for late purchase that, by reason of special materials, may be most difficult to procure as single items. It is assumed that most bulk materials will be grouped into classes for requirement ordering.

Involvement of Other Departments

Financial   The financial department is involved with all capital equipment planning and procurement in a number of ways. In planning the capital structure of the company, the financial department must determine how best to finance investment in capital equipment. Funds can be used from gross retained earnings or from sales of stock, or they can be obtained by borrowing and taking on long-term debt.

Taxes and depreciation are indeed very important subjects that have significant effect on capital equipment programs. Tax laws and government policy concerning tax credits, depreciation, and write-offs are dynamic. The financial department must continuously keep up to date on current tax situations. These play a very active role in the planning of capital equipment programs.

Production   The production department is held responsible for achieving improvements in productivity and for realizing established cost and profit objectives. Therefore, production people are continually looking for equipment leading to better methods or better quality and for replacement of worn-out or obsolete machinery and unsafe equipment. They are vitally concerned with the overall capacity of equipment in relation to the needs of the business.

Since the production department is the big user of the equipment, it follows that it will be one of the principal initiators of requests to obtain additional capital equipment. The experience of production personnel and their knowledge of operating conditions automatically give them a strong vote in determining equipment needs.

Engineering   The manufacturing engineering function plays an important part in the acquisition of capital equipment. This group is responsible for preparing processing details when a problem arises, e.g., undue scrap, low tool life, and quality problems, and for developing corrective measures which may result in recommendations for new, improved, or different equipment. Industrial engineering works closely with manufacturing engineering because of their common interest in specific standard methods and time standards. Industrial engineering determines the net economic benefits resulting from improvement in techniques and thus will assist in selecting the most appropriate alternative.

The exact assignment of responsibility within the engineering function may vary by company, but in most cases the preparation of specifications for capital equipment is part of the engineering department's work. The role of the engineering department in the procurement of capital equipment therefore is a substantial one.

TYPES OF EQUIPMENT—DEFINITIONS

Many different situations can and do occur when buying capital equipment. A study of these variations indicates that capital equipment can be classified into the four following types:

Equipment *standard to an industry*
Standard equipment *customized to special needs*
Equipment *unique, built to buyer's specifications*
Equipment *unique or original—no available specifications*

The nature of the procurement task for each of these types of equipment is somewhat different. First, these four types of equipment must be examined in order to understand the similarities and the differences in each of the types. How to buy each type of equipment will be covered later in this section.

Standard to an Industry

Whenever a technology becomes established and a need for a piece of equipment required in that particular field becomes repetitive, this presents the opportunity for someone to develop a product and to offer it for sale. As additional sales are made, this supplier refines his product and then offers it as a standard product. Others, seeing the opportunity to develop and sell this type of equipment, develop their equipment, and soon competition results, with a number of sellers offering equipment to satisfy that need. Although the same basic machine or equipment may be available from each of the competing sources, there will be differences in features or capabilities in each.

In large organizations, where much equipment is purchased, there is likely to be more repetitive buying of machinery. Many such purchases are well defined by standardization in plant practice, for simplification of maintenance, for ease of training machine operators, or for coordination with other existing equipment. The equipment buyer must be fully acquainted with what is available in the marketplace and with advances in equipment being made by suppliers. This is a fertile field for functional and value analysis.

Customized to Special Needs

Frequently the situation faced by the equipment buyer will be one where a basic or standard equipment item is required except that certain modifications are desired. The reasons for customizing could be to increase output, increase efficiency, reduce handling, perform supplementary operations, permit better repeatability, reduce setup time, reduce operator error, or others. Through his intimate knowledge of, and contact with, reliable sources, the buyer can be of great assistance in helping define the actual need. In some cases, it is possible and desirable to secure the cooperation and active assistance of the suppliers in the design and installation of the machinery and in training the user's operatives. Under these circumstances, the buyer has a more complex situation than that described previously, and obviously his responsibilities become much broader.

Unique—To Buyer's Specifications

As business enterprises work at improving their products or services, they will devote considerable time and effort to developing new ideas for conducting their business. Often they will pursue these ideas to the degree that they will actually design special equipment to satisfy their requirements. Considerable engineering time will be invested. Sometimes prototypes will be built and proved out. These prototypes may be built within the company or may have to be contracted for from an outside source. Many special-purpose machine tools have been designed to mass-produce identical parts. Many of these machines cannot be adapted to other work; others can be adapted but only after being rebuilt. The efficiency and the economics of special-purpose machines in the production of numerous identical parts greatly offset the disadvantage of their inflexibility. Aluminum pistons, for example, are automatically polished on their sides, tops, and beveled edges in 15 seconds by a machine specially designed for that purpose. Performing the same operation on nonautomatic machines requires 10 minutes, or 40 times as long. Before investing in a machine tool for a special purpose, a thorough study of the future business should be made. The resale value of unique equipment usually is minimal, and decisions to buy this type of equipment have lasting effects.

Most often in these situations, it is important that information concerning the equipment be treated as proprietary information belonging to the buyer's company. Since the company has expended considerable time and money in developing the design and specifications, it will be most interested in protecting its investment. They will want to assure themselves that their competition does not get the advantage of their efforts. Sometimes the development of special equipment for a special need leads to new business opportunities either in developing the equipment for sale or in developing further the products made by the equipment. The buyer, therefore, in conducting his purchasing activities on this type of equipment, must take the necessary steps to protect his company's interest.

To accomplish this objective of protecting the proprietary information, normally a nondisclosure agreement (also discussed in Section 7) is signed by the prospective supplier before any sensitive information is given to the vendor. The agreement should be developed by the company's legal staff and should contain all of the safeguards deemed necessary.

Unique—No Specifications Available

Occasionally, companies need special equipment to meet their requirements, e.g., better quality, greater energy conservation, or adherence to environmental regulations. If meeting such requirements appears to be beyond existing equipment technology, the companies may design and even build the equipment themselves. If they do not have the in-house capacity to do so, however, they may turn the project over to an outside firm. In either case, the purchasing department should be in a position to comment on the specification and to develop purchasing criteria for the equipment.

CONSIDERATIONS PRIOR TO SOURCING

Preparation of Specification

There are certain definite advantages in the general practice of buying on a basis of specification. It is helpful to the engineer because in preparing the specifications he will recognize exactly what he needs. The supplier will know what his customer's needs are and that they must be met. The buyer will have a detailed equipment description that he can use as a part of his purchase order when negotiating the order. With an equipment specification, the problem is thoroughly analyzed; a speedier understanding and agreement between buyer and seller is reached; procurement time is reduced; delivery is timely; debugging is minimized; and the equipment is installed and turned over to operations on a reduced procurement schedule. This all adds up to significant savings, because the faster an idea is materialized and put into operation, the faster the projected savings are realized.

A *machine specification* may be defined as a documental set of parameters describing the physical characteristics, components and attachments, and functional capabilities of a given piece of equipment. The objective in preparing an equipment specification should be to define what is needed to do what must be done, at the required quality level, in a given time and at a price consistent with the need.

Purchasing participates in preparation of specifications to ensure that equipment is not specified that exceeds the quality, performance, and cost considerations relative to the end use of the equipment. This is also the best time to evaluate the equipment being specified to avoid single sourcing, to evaluate standardization programs of equipment and equipment components, and to investigate availability of the equipment as to standard or unique.

The content of a specification will vary with each piece of equipment. What type of equipment is wanted? Is it standard, does it need modifications, or is a complete new design required? Do not close the door to vendor suggestions for alternate equipment. A good practice is to have vendors bid according to your specification and propose, as a clearly stated alternative, any alternate equipment they would recommend. Whatever the situation may be, there are a number of elements that are common to all. A suggested format which has proven successful is as follows:

Identification and title
General equipment description
Equipment parameters
Components and attachments
Tooling
General information
Conditions of equipment acceptance

Identification   The specification should be identified with a sequential reference number and the date. The company name and address should be included. And last, a brief descriptive title should identify the type of machine in question.

General Equipment Description   A concise description of the equipment and its function should be given. An example of such a description is:

> The equipment in question must be a fully automated system capable of: loading, positioning, inspecting, recording, classifying, and segregating glass lenses.

This could describe a special-purpose inspection machine.

Equipment Parameters   These will vary depending on the situation, but the kinds of information that should be spelled out are:

1. The approximate size of the machine.
2. A description of the necessary motions.
3. The size of the parts that are to be machined and, if possible, the type of holding fixture to be used.
4. The accuracy and repeatability tolerances that must be held.
5. The power requirements, if known.
6. The desired range of feeds and speeds.
7. The machine cycle necessary for meeting the production needs.
8. A brief statement of how the machine is expected to operate. With such a description the vendor not only knows what is wanted, but he also understands how it is expected to be accomplished.
9. A brief request for optional vendor alternate proposals.

Machine Components and Attachments   At times, it is appropriate to spell out specific components. If a standard type of equipment is being specified, the basic components are usually firm and only deviations from the standard should be spelled out. Lubrication is a critical and important factor in determining the life of a machine, and it is important that this be covered in every machine specification. Is it to be manual, semiautomatic, or fully automatic? The desired attachments should be carefully specified as to function and capability. For example, when buying a lathe, the preferred make of chuck should be clearly indicated. A statement as to how it is to be actuated—manually, by air, or by hydraulic power—and what the accuracy and repeatability requirements are, should be given. In addition, the minor attachments, such as good lighting, coolant system, machine way protection, coolant guards, and leveling screws, should not be overlooked, and these should be defined. Safety features are also very important, particularly in view of the impact of the Occupational Safety and Health Act of 1971.

Tooling   Generally speaking, tooling specifications should be written in broad terms. The supplier should have some latitude to design and build the necessary tooling. If, however, interchangeability with present tooling is desirable, or if similar tooling has already been tried and proven, it may be appropriate to be very specific in this matter. Whether the supplier uses the tool design given to him or whether he prepares his own, it is very important to require purchaser approval of tool designs prior to build. Furthermore, it should be stated that purchaser approval of tool design does not relieve the supplier of functional responsibility.

Tooling specifications should be written, if possible, to allow the user the privilege of buying one set of permanent tooling only and of furnishing expendable tools himself. The advantages are to give the buyer an opportunity to manufacture duplicate sets of tooling in his own shop, thus ensuring dependable replacement of jigs and fixtures, and to use standardized items of expendables such as drills, taps, abrasives, cutters, and carbide tools. Frequently, the user can buy such items at a lower cost than if supplied by the equipment manufacturer. Requiring a separate lot price for the tool, jig, and fixtures makes it easier to add or delete units of production without having to debate how much tooling price is in a composite equipment price. Whether or not there is enough competition to allow the choice of make of tool to be purchased, tooling offers the buyer a fertile field for continued cost savings.

Energy Conservation   When it became apparent in the 1970s that the United States had a serious, complex, and long-term energy problem, industry realized that energy efficiency has to be considered whenever capital expenditures are to be made. Many companies adopted formal policies regarding the purchase of the best, most energy-efficient, and yet economically affordable equipment.

As an integral and major part of its policy, a major corporation includes a clear warning to would-be suppliers that they must prove their energy efficiency claims for their equipment or be liable for corrective action or even rejection of the equipment and refund of the purchase price. This information is communicated to potential suppliers by special clauses, one of which is made part of the request for quotation sent out for the equipment. The other is made part of the purchase order sent to the supplier chosen to provide the equipment.

The clause in the quotation request says, in part:

> All pieces of equipment . . . shall be evaluated as to their efficiency in terms of energy conservation, as well as safety, price, durability, maintainability, performance, quality, and delivery.
>
> Seller is to propose the most energy-efficient design to satisfy the enclosed specifications. Seller shall also propose the most economical (lowest initial cost) design to satisfy specifications, should it be different from the most energy-efficient design.
>
> The energy consumption of the equipment is to be specified in appropriate terms, e.g., MMBTU/Hr [million Btu per hour], MLBS/Hr [thousand pounds per hour] steam, KW [kilowatts], HP [horsepower]. The percentage of accuracy of the efficiency data submitted is to be stated. Fuel and/or any other energy input consumption is to be specified. Energy consumption of the specified equipment shall be evaluated at the rate(s) of $_____per_____of bid comparison.

The clause in the purchase order covers verification of the quoted efficiency by a mutually agreed-upon performance test and the dollar rating of energy consumption of the equipment for the purpose of evaluation and/or liquidation of damages. Both clauses spell out buyer's rights and seller's obligations if the equipment fails to meet specifications, standards, and tests defined in the request for quotation and purchase order.

The energy conservation clauses are used primarily for the procurement of major equipment, which is defined as costing at least $50,000 and having an energy consumption that accounts for approximately one-third of its operating cost. The clauses can also be used for less costly equipment if such appears justified.

General Information   There are numerous other general terms that can be incorporated into the specification as required, such as standards, warranties, patent clause, drawing request, operating and maintenance manuals, recommended spare parts list, floor plans, proprietary information, and scheduling. These are discussed later in this section under Special Terms and Conditions. At the risk of being repetitive, a discussion of the more usual terms to be included follows:

1. STANDARDS.   These should be specified for all electricals, hydraulics, and pneumatics. If the company has not established its own standards, the use of N.M.T.B.A. specifications should be considered. (National Machine Tool Builders Association, 7901 West Park Drive, McLean, Va. 22102.)

2. WARRANTIES.   While most suppliers have standard warranties which are made part of their quotations, it is best to safeguard oneself with one's own warranty. A typical warranty statement might be:

> The supplier shall guarantee materials and workmanship for a period of one year from the date of installation. (Installation date to start no later than three months after shipping date.)

3. PATENT CLAUSE.   Protection from possible patent infringement is important when developing equipment that is beyond the standard type of equipment. Assistance from the legal department should be obtained in this regard.

4. DRAWING REQUEST.   Drawings in reproduction form should be obtained for all tooling, hydraulics, pneumatics, and electricals. These drawings should be submitted to the purchaser for approval prior to build, and a set of final prints be obtained with the machine. Ownership and freedom to use drawings for competitive purposes in buying parts should be established.

5. OPERATING AND MAINTENANCE MANUALS.   Operating and maintenance manuals are a must. Copies should be requested for the production department, plant facilities department, maintenance, and any others having a need for this information. Manuals are especially important when the equipment is being installed and put into operation.

6. RECOMMENDED SPARE PARTS LIST.   Time and money often can be saved by procuring and maintaining a supply of critical spare parts. The best time to take care of this is at the time the equipment is being purchased. Machinery manufacturers traditionally make good profits from spare parts business, and for this reason they have established branch warehouses with stocks in areas where a number of machines are in operation. Spare parts, like tooling, divide themselves into two categories. The first consists of major components, which are usually

made from forgings, castings, or fabricated weldments and which are manufactured at the same time as production runs. Sometimes overruns are scheduled, to allow for spoilage in process, and the excess inventory winds up in spare parts at a far lower cost than if the parts were run separately. The second category, expendable parts, includes such items as ball and roller bearings, gaskets, flexible tubing, rubber hose, and grease cups and fittings. The recommended spare parts lists should be studied carefully, however, to ensure that maintenance storeroom inventories are not built up unnecessarily. The buyer should insist that standard items, such as bearings, be listed by bearing manufacturer part number rather than by machine supplier part number, so that bearings can be checked against current storeroom stock or possibly procured from local distributors at a lower cost. At the time of the original negotiations, these identities should be established. Unless the user's plant is in a remote location or there is some other unique situation, he should not tie up capital in spare parts but rather should rely on the vendor's warehouse inventory or a local distributor of the item. A clause could be added stating that the buyer's maintenance and stores operations have the right to order a quantity of parts at prices established in an order for the original equipment up to some reasonable period of time, such as 3 to 6 months after placing the equipment order. In the case of unique equipment, this approach allows additional time for proper analysis of spare parts requirements.

Unless the electric power unit on the machine involved is built in and cannot be furnished separately, many buyers save money by furnishing the unit themselves, particularly when they buy on an original equipment manufacturer (OEM) basis. This also helps standardize their electrical equipment.

It is easier to press warranty claims over defective equipment with each separate manufacturer when the buyer purchases directly from each. There is little advantage, however, if the value of the two pieces—equipment and a component—is low.

7. FLOOR PLAN.   Sometimes it is important that the supplier furnish a floor plan for the installation. Also, if a special foundation or special utilities, such as water, air pressure, or electric power are required, the supplier should be required to furnish sufficiently detailed drawings and specifications for the buyer to make such installations.

8. SCHEDULING.   Time is a valuable commodity. Frequently equipment purchases are made because substantial savings will be realized from the equipment. Every week cut out of the equipment procurement cycle could mean substantial improvement to the company's profits. The final specification should call for a realistic tight delivery date. Most equipment builders are opposed to penalty clauses, however, and will not agree to one. To overcome this, a technique to follow is to include a requirement that the supplier establish a schedule for all critical steps in building the equipment. Such a schedule should identify dates for every important milestone—preliminary design completion and review, final design and approval, placing order for build, assembly of components, tryout, acceptance test, and delivery. This can also be done for special components, attach-

ments, and tooling. Such a schedule provides a series of check points which will make it possible to identify delays early enough to permit appropriate corrective action. On major projects, an early visit to the supplier's plant is highly advisable to establish contacts with the production people who must see that the job gets done.

Conditions of Equipment Acceptance   It is in the best interest of both the buyer and seller to list in sufficient detail the conditions that must be met in order for the equipment to be accepted. Whenever possible, the physical measurement criteria and/or performance should be clearly defined. Any tests required should be run in the supplier's plant if possible, and, if desired, they can be repeated in the purchaser's plant. Obviously, the tests should be witnessed by personnel who have responsibility for acceptance. If it is decided that the equipment is to be received without testing of the equipment at the supplier's plant, there should be a time period established as to when acceptance will be made. Tying receipt of manuals, drawings and spares list into an agreement on an acceptance date and final payment often is the last bit of leverage a buyer has to secure these documents.

BID SUMMARY FORM.   When possible, a bid summary form itemizing specific design requirements, performance parameters, materials of construction, deviations, and any particular commercial items such as price, unit prices of components, and delivery should be a part of the specification package. The completed form should be returned with vendor proposals. This aids proposal evaluation and ensures that vendors have thoroughly considered every item listed on the form.

LEASE VERSUS PURCHASE

Definition of Lease

A lease is a contract by which one party (lessor) gives to another party (lessee) the use and possession of property for a specified time and for fixed payments.

Getting enough money to buy new equipment can be a sizable problem for some businesses. Tight money supply and high interest rates, plus the increasing costs of new equipment, present very real problems to businesses of today. The traditional methods of finance used in capital goods acquisition, such as term loans, conditional sales contracts, debt securities, and equity capital, have not been adequate or desirable in all instances. The result has been a very significant movement toward leasing equipment.

Leaving the title with the original owner is often the best approach when satisfying temporary equipment needs. Leasing can solve temporary service problems while equipment is being repaired or delivered. Some equipment can only be leased. Some special equipment is continually and aggressively being redesigned to the extent that newly purchased equipment quickly becomes obsolete. Leasing leaves the service responsibility with the manufacturer. This can be an advantage when highly sensitive equipment is involved or specially skilled techniques are required. When equipment has a high rate of depreciation, it is best to leave the replacement problem with the lessor. The high unit price of equipment encourages some firms to lease rather than buy, so that a large cash outlay is unnecessary. The entire cost of leasing can be deducted from income. Over the long run however, it is more expensive to lease, since the lessors are charging during the lease period for the risks they have assumed.

Background of Leasing

Leasing has had phenomenal growth over the past 10 years and is a multi-billion-dollar industry. With leasing companies offering a wide variety of services—everything from plant maintenance programs to EDP software—no industrial company can overlook "buying" such intangibles. Just about every type of capital equipment can be acquired on a lease basis. Many leasing firms are broadening the scope of their operations to provide management and technical counsel as well as hardware.

Leasing capital equipment can be done through the equipment manufacturer, a third-party leasing specialist, or a financial house. There are more than 1000 leasing companies in the United States. The bigger companies offer across-the-board leasing and can make available any leasable asset. The medium-size and small companies may specialize in certain lines of plant machinery or equipment. Some concentrate on leasing materials handling or construction or truck and car equipment. Often a small lessor, familiar with local conditions, may perform a better service than a nationally based rival. A number of leasing companies are members of the Association of Equipment Lessors with headquarters at 1700 North Moore Street, Arlington, Va. 22209. Additional information concerning leasing can be obtained by writing there.

Participants in Leasing Decisions

Because leasing decisions can be complex, they require the active participation of other departments of the company. The purchasing department must follow its usual procurement routines: exploring the market, searching for suppliers, establishing various sources, checking financial stability, working out payment schedules and cancellation privileges, etc. The treasurer or controller must assess the financial impact of a lease. The tax managers must evaluate the effect that leasing will have on the company's overall tax situation. The tax manager will undoubtedly ask for counsel from the company's attorney or legal staff. The engineering department must look at the technical matters and review the entire state of the art in the industry in question to make a realistic appraisal. The manufacturing or production department must determine how effectively leased equipment will boost finished goods output and what the effect on overall efficiency will be. There are no cut-and-dried answers on the subject because leasing is a dynamic business. There are, however, fundamental aspects of leasing with which every capital equipment buyer should be familiar.

Advantages and Disadvantages of Leasing

What, then, are the advantages of leasing capital equipment and what are the disadvantages? The more important advantages are:

1. The risk of obsolescence can be minimized or eliminated. Whatever type of equipment a lessee needs—from adaptive controlled machine tools to computers—a cancelable lease can be negotiated under which the lessor will provide the latest and most sophisticated models.

2. Equipment can be made available on a short-term basis for projects that do not justify an immediate capital outlay. A pilot plant production run during a market-acceptance study is an example of this type of project.

3. Maintenance problems can often be transferred to the lessor. This is especially important when the leased equipment is complex.

4. Leasing provides a wider range of options to the buyer and therefore increases his competitive situation.

5. The burden of investment is shifted to the supplier, which means that the buyer's working capital can be used for other, more profitable company opportunities.

6. It can permit a production operation to start or to continue even though capital funds are not readily available at the time.

7. The entire expense can usually be treated as a cost paid from pretax income, if the terms satisfy Internal Revenue Service criteria.

The disadvantages of leasing can be summarized as follows:

1. It will almost always be more expensive than outright purchase and usually will be more expensive than other financing methods.

2. The lessee may be restricted somewhat in his control and use of the equipment.

3. The lessor may require access to the buyer's business place for periodic inspection, etc., and that may not always be desirable.

4. Other disadvantages could arise, depending on the actual terms negotiated in the lease contract. The buyer therefore must be alert to see that the contract does not result in any restrictive or otherwise negative conditions being placed on his company.

Types of Leases

There are basically two types of lease, the *operational lease* and the *financial lease*. The operational lease involves a total financial commitment by the lessee of an amount considerably less than the purchase price of equipment. The basic non-cancelable term of this type of lease varies from hours in some cases to a considerable number of years in others. In general, the lease payments are fixed payments per period, and the term is considerably less than the physical life of the equipment. Such leases stress service rather than original equipment prices. The lessor assumes complete responsibility for replacement parts, taxes, insurance, etc. He also takes over all risks of obsolescence. The charge for this ownership risk is included as an integral part of the lease agreement, and the lessee must evaluate the added premium against his other alternatives. Trucks, automobiles, computers, material handling equipment, and many, many other such equipment items are being leased under this type of lease every day.

The purpose of the other type of lease—the financial lease—is entirely financial in nature. The lessor expects to get back his investment, plus profit, during the term of the contract. The financial-type lease may fall into one of two general categories. The first is the full payout lease, under which the lessee pays the full purchase price of the leased item—plus interest and charges—on a monthly basis. Typical charges include service, maintenance, bookkeeping costs, insurance, etc. The second type of financial lease is the partial-payout variety. This plan gives the lessee credit for the residual value of the leased item after the lease period is completed. In effect, the lessee pays the difference between original purchase price and resale value, plus interest charges.

The financial lease has three component cost parts: (1) the cost of money (interest rate), (2) depreciation rate (determined by length of lease), and (3) lessor's fee. The cost of money or interest rate is determined by the credit rating of the lessee, and thus, theoretically, this cost is no more when leasing than when owning. The depreciation is determined by the length of the lease divided by the principal on a straight-line basis. This will vary according to the type of equipment leased. Thus, in the automotive field, passenger cars run from 36 to 50 months, trucks 60 months as a rule, and machine tools 6 to 20 years; pipelines, for example, may run as long as 40 years. The lessor's fee is generally determined by the type of service offered. For straight financing and nothing else, it is as low as 1 percent, and for full services which involve purchasing, disposal, cost control, etc., it may run as high as 10 percent. This is a gross cost, not a net cost. Leasing companies in the main buy more cheaply than individual companies, as in the case of automotive equipment. On other running stock, such as lift trucks, they get volume discounts based on the volume for all their clients, and this can amount to as much as a 5 percent saving. Sometimes, after equipment is fully depreciated, a nominal lease fee of $1 a month is charged as long as it is in service. This is cheaper than transferring title, with the expenses involved and the loss of the lease tax deduction, which is not available on a deferred purchase plan. Leasing of automobile fleets has had a phenomenal growth, and the automobile manufacturers themselves have entered the field. Many machinery manufacturers have bought out or have established leasing companies for their own volume and in order to offer leasing to customers.

Contract Provisions

Most equipment-leasing companies have their own forms of lease agreement. While there is considerable variation in them, the basic terms are essentially the same. There are, however, special points which can be incorporated into such agreements which can be highly advantageous to the lessee. For instance, what are the arrangements for replacing equipment when obsolete or no longer service-able? Is the lessee in fact free to buy supplies from other sources? Are there any restrictions on the use of the equipment? Are the responsibilities for maintenance and service clearly and completely spelled out? Do rental payments stop while equipment is out of service for certain kinds of repairs?

PURCHASE OF USED EQUIPMENT

One of the first options the buyer has to analyze when considering a major equip-ment requirement is whether to pursue new, used, or leased equipment. The new equipment offers longer life expectancy, incorporates innovative technology, offers limited maintenance, lower spare parts inventory, broader selection available, broader performance guarantees, better terms of sale and the very important aspects of service. These factors stack up against the number one reason for buying used equipment, lower cost. Also used equipment is immediately available. The best areas for this type of buy include: pilot projects, short-life projects, and situ-ations in which the total project is jeopardized by the high cost of new equipment and economizing is in order or in which immediate availability can salvage pro-duction and profit requirements.

Used equipment also has an advantage if duplicate pieces exist in the plant, i.e., no additional spare-parts inventory is required, operator familiarity exists, old design does not adversely affect the balance of the production line, and no addi-tional expenditures to accommodate new equipment design and interface are required. However, it is risky to install a used piece of equipment of uncertain life in a critical area where failure could shut down operations and affect profits. Per-formance guarantees on used equipment are hard to come by and are always for a very limited period. The terms of sale are very restrictive, i.e., "net cash," "as is–where is."

When to Buy Used Equipment

As a fundamental principle, new equipment is to be preferred over used equip-ment. However, there are situations when the purchase of used equipment should be considered. Some of these are:

1. When price is of prime importance and the difference in cost between new and used equipment is significant and/or the buyer's funds are limited.
2. Where equipment will be used for a limited time or where the equipment will be idle much of the time.
3. Where equipment will be used for training or for pilot or experimental purposes.
4. Where equipment is to be for auxiliary operations or services such as maintenance.
5. When better delivery is an essential factor.

6. Where used machines can economically be converted to satisfy the need. There are now companies that will reengineer old equipment, rebuild it with new components, and provide guarantees similar to those available with new equipment.

Used-Equipment Sources

The sources of used equipment are many. When businesses are discontinued, assets usually are liquidated and the used equipment is offered for sale. In addition, nearly all operating companies at some time or other have standby or surplus equipment which is out on the market for sale. Upon completion of large construction jobs, large surpluses of equipment often result. Government agencies are continually offering surplus equipment for sale. There are also many reputable dealers and brokers engaged in the sale of used equipment. (The farsighted buyer accumulates a special file for their names and addresses.) Trade journals and other media are utilized extensively to advertise used equipment. This is especially true of auctions and of liquidations.

Condition of Used Equipment

Used equipment is often sold by the owner or broker on an as is–where is basis. For the most part, no warranty or guarantee of any kind is given and the purchaser buys at his peril. It is, therefore, incumbent on the buyer to make a thorough inspection of the equipment beforehand. If he does that, it is possible that he will be able to see it in operation to test all its moving parts. Moreover, the machine may have a latent defect not observable on inspection, which could cause an early breakdown and costly repairs, all of which the purchaser usually would have to bear without recourse to the seller. The buyer may exercise the option of insisting that he see the equipment under actual working conditions and establish that the machine can produce parts as a new machine can. If the buyer notes that the equipment is marginal, he may negotiate with the vendor to have the equipment refurbished and a guarantee given for a 12-month period. Once suitable equipment is located, the wise buyer will consider whether tooling and spare parts are readily available before proceeding with negotiations to purchase.

Market Value

The used-equipment market is very much a specialty type of business, and it is difficult to be completely up to date as to the market value of used equipment. Many factors will enter into the *determination* of the market value of used equipment—age, condition, supply, demand, and the seller's knowledge of the market. The buyer contemplating buying used equipment must research the market thoroughly and become as knowledgeable as possible before entering negotiations to buy.

Basic Contract Provisions

The purchase of used equipment is often accompanied by an agreement of sale, covering the respective rights of the buyer and the seller. Normally, the buyer should ask the seller to warrant (1) marketable title; (2) the abscence of any liens or encumbrances; and (3) that no litigation or other proceedings questioning the seller's title are pending or threatened. However, in addition, a thorough search by an attorney, to determine if there are any security interests recorded against the equipment, is advisable. A rundown of the provisions that the buyer should include in an agreement of sale is as follows:

1. Acquisition of full legal title and the exclusive right of possession thereto, free and clear of all liens, encumbrances, charges, and taxes.

2. Indemnification against all claims, liens, and rights which may be asserted by any person with respect to the equipment sold.

3. Disconnect of all equipment at seller's expense so it can be easily removed by the buyer. Buyer will normally be liable for any damage caused during his removal of property.

4. Deferred payment under seller's normal credit terms, or in the form of an installment promissory note without any security interests being created. Seller will probably require a security interest for long-term financing.

5. Assurance that risk of damage or loss shall not pass to the buyer until the goods are physically removed by him. If the seller is arranging for shipment of the equipment to the buyer, risk of loss or damage should not pass until the buyer receives the equipment.

6. Warranties relating to the condition and performance of the equipment—if possible. Normally, used equipment will be sold "as is." The seller will not want to give warranties of merchantability and fitness for the intended purpose. But, the buyer should at least get a representation that the equipment is in good workable condition.

7. Indemnification for patent infringement—especially if the piece of equipment was made by the seller in-house. Also, the seller should warrant that the use of the equipment will not constitute patent infringement.

8. Agreement by the seller that he will not compete with the buyer in a particular product line for a period of time if the buyer is purchasing the equipment for an entire product line.

9. Warranty from the seller that he has full authority to sell the equipment in question, and that such sale does not violate any existing law, regulation, or agreement. In all purchases of used equipment, the buyer should insist on receiving a bill of sale, since this document evidences ownership.

GUARANTEED MAINTENANCE

Whether buying or leasing, guaranteed maintenance is a means of placing the responsibility of maintaining equipment during a predetermined active life or life cycle of that equipment on the manufacturer or his authorized service agency.

The award of a guaranteed maintenance contract is based on the sum of two parts:

1. The original cost of the equipment
2. The cost of maintenance for the equipment's predetermined active life

The total of these two costs determines the lowest responsible bid.

A guaranteed maintenance bid allows all vendors to meet specifications and also includes several possible alternatives to produce the lowest total net cost to the buyer. It also gives the purchasing manager a chance to consider all of the costs of the equipment—ownership and maintenance.

The city of Chicago reports large savings with over 700 units under such contracts. These include refuse units, dump-body trucks, diesel engine tractors, refuse collection trailer units, refuse trailers, hydraulic truck cranes, tractor loaders, motor trucks, and rubber-tired tractor loaders.

HOW TO BUY CAPITAL EQUIPMENT

Many of the principles covered in other sections of this handbook with respect to purchasing production materials and supplies are applicable to the buying of capital equipment. The opportunity for the buyer to buy the right equipment at the right price, quality, and service is just as good as it is for any other purchase that the buyer may make. There are, however, special conditions that the buyer must take into consideration when buying capital equipment.

In many large corporations a special central group is set up to handle capital equipment purchases. Other corporations go the opposite route and let the local plants handle the equipment procurement needs. The argument here is that the local operation "knows their needs best." Another approach is to have the local purchasing manager or buyer originate the order but to obtain corporate approval before actual placement of the order.

Regardless of where the equipment buyer reports organizationally, and irrespective of the size of the company or operation, the basic approach to capital equipment buying is the same.

Standard to an Industry

Capital equipment standard to an industry was defined earlier in the section as that which is available from numerous sources serving a given industry. A knowledgeable and experienced equipment buyer can make a major contribution to his company with the proper approach to equipment of this nature. There are many things other than price and shipment that the buyer needs to know and use to make certain that the most satisfactory overall product offering is selected.

One of the first areas of importance for the buyer is to know the general equipment industry serving his company's needs and to be familiar with what other users are doing with this type of equipment. A familiarity with the selling practices of the industry and a basic knowledge of the overall health of the business can be of extreme importance.

A natural follow-on to knowing the industry is to know the specific equipment builders in terms of the product they offer for sale. A thorough knowledge of the equipment builders will ensure the buyer's surveying all available sources and his obtaining the best value.

In buying capital equipment, one of the most important considerations that must be treated properly is the subject of specifications. In this regard, the buyer should first review what is available in the marketplace to meet his specific requirements. With the rapid growth in most equipment industries, there may be standard-designed equipment available. This can be the most attractive from a price and shipment standpoint. Sometimes this is accomplished by selecting standard equipment except with an optional feature. An example of this type of purchase would be a drill press with a numerical control (NC) feature.

Special features contained in the requester's specifications should be reviewed carefully. It is recognized at times that specific features are desirable and can make a contribution to the operation. However, careful evaluation of the special feature is required to be certain that it will give the appropriate payoff. Many times even the simplest of these special requirements will mean substantial increases in dollars of cost and time. A classic example was where a tape reader was specified to be located in a control cabinet a specific distance from the floor. The existing standard design was less than 5 inches off—higher. Redesign of the basic cabinet meant new engineering drawings, an additional charge of several thousand dollars and an extension of six weeks in delivery. Question: Was it necessary?

The major strength that a buyer will have in buying equipment is the utilization of competition. When adequate competition is present, the buyer is in a strong position to get what he wants. Often, in equipment procurement, one specific supplier's equipment is preferred and the requester is not interested in any other equipment. While it may be true that one supplier has better features or will produce more pieces of better quality, it is of the utmost importance in order to conduct a successful negotiation that other suppliers be given the opportunity to quote. The preferred supplier should not feel he has the order in the bag. Remember, the seller is attempting to get the most favorable price, delivery, and other terms that he can. The buyer is attempting to get the best for his company in terms of price, delivery, and other factors. When anyone involved in the procurement cycle indicates that he prefers a certain supplier's equipment and lets the supplier know prior to negotiating the order, he undercuts his company's position.

The subject of negotiation is covered elsewhere in this handbook. There are, however, several points that should be made here. Proper handling of negotiations is extremely important in the procurement of capital equipment. It is important that negotiation sessions be held with someone who has the authority to make decisions. The buyer is trained to use his business and purchasing skills, and therefore he should conduct the negotiations. Technical people are best qualified to handle technical questions regarding equipment needs and should participate in only that part of the negotiations. It greatly facilitates the evaluation of standard equipment when the engineering department can place monetary values on certain parts of the specification—such as tolerable values of defective parts produced, production speed, ease of maintenance, and percentage downtime for repairs. Some of these values should be stated in requests for quotations so that suppliers have an opportunity to furnish a machine that best meets the buyer's needs. To objectively establish these monetary values after quotations are received can be very difficult. When the buyer and the technical people establish a team effort along these lines, this is when the correct equipment is purchased on time, at the lowest possible price.

Customized to Special Needs

In certain situations, a standard commercially available item of equipment can be available to satisfy most of the requirements for a given procurement but yet not fully provide all of them. The missing feature could be beyond the normal options that the equipment supplier provides, and therefore in order to obtain the desired equipment it is necessary to customize a standard piece of equipment. In this situation it is important that the required feature be clearly defined and that it be fully understood by the supplier. In his quotation the supplier should state exactly what the additional feature will consist of and what effect it will have on the operation of the equipment, if any. Further, the pricing should be broken down so that proper evaluation of competitive bids can be made and also so that the net additional cost of the additional feature may be known. A typical example of standard equipment customized to a special need is a punch press with a special transport device.

Unique to Buyer's Specifications

Equipment of this type is of special design and is tailor-made. The need for equipment of this nature arises when the situation is unique and a standard does not exist. The need for clear and complete specifications has been emphasized throughout this section. It is in this situation, however, that the quality of the specification is most important.

Rotary Indexing Machine Tool   A review of the procurement of a special three-station rotary indexing machine tool to machine the finger-type dovetail on a turbine bucket will serve to demonstrate the purchasing considerations in buying this type of equipment.

The first step in the procurement of this special equipment is to survey the market for potential suppliers who can build the type of equipment desired. This will involve preliminary meetings to review proprietary features and information. A formal inquiry on the preliminary specifications should then be issued to the suppliers that are to be considered. Copies of drawings of the parts to be machined and details, including all the desired characteristics of the machine and what it is designed to do, should be included.

When the initial quotations are received, they should be reviewed carefully. The specifications should then be refined and firmed up. It may be that one or more of the suppliers may be dropped—if they have taken an exception to any of the important features of the design or if their prices are completely out of line. A visit to the remaining suppliers who are competitive is suggested as the next step. These meetings will permit the buyer and his technical people to further explain and negotiate definite requirements, secure new quotations, and determine that all sources are quoting on the same specifications. The essential features to be discussed during these visits would be items such as: the table diameter; use of cutter diameters; use of cutter arbors; machine capability for using carbide cutters; machine must have infinitely variable feed ranges without the use of change gears between roughing head and finishing head; the heads must be actuated by feed screws; the spindle speeds to include a range of at least 6 to 73 revolutions per minute; the change gears conveniently arranged for 10 changes; the finishing-head spindle to be stopped during retraction from cut; and the fixtures must be arranged to compensate for variations of $+0.005$ or -0.005 on the fixed locating surfaces. The revised quotation requirements should state that the quotation is to be a package and to include a machine complete with coolant system and electrical equipment.

When the final quotations are received, and even though considerable time and effort may have been spent in discussing and detailing the specifications, it is most important that the final quotations be scrutinized with great care. A detailed analysis of quoted prices and the important features should be prepared to help in the decision of selecting the supplier who offers the best value. While purchasing has the prime responsibility for the commercial aspects of the purchase, it must work closely with manufacturing and engineering and obtain their agreement in the supplier selection. Manufacturing and engineering bear the primary responsibility for the technical aspects of the purchase. Purchases of this type are most successful when there is complete cooperation and agreement between supplier, purchasing department, and other technical and production personnel.

Fabricated Equipment   In process industries such as petroleum and chemicals, many items of production equipment are almost completely specified by the owner. Such equipment includes tanks, pressure vessels, distillation columns, reactors, converters, and heat exchangers. Some of this equipment is manufactured with very stringent codes and requirements. For such sophisticated equipment it is necessary that the owner organization thoroughly evaluate the capabilities of suppliers to be sure that the right suppliers are on the bidder's list. To do this properly requires that suppliers fill out standard qualification sheets and that their facilities are visited by buyer's inspectors and purchasing people to observe supplier capabilities firsthand. New suppliers must receive complete scrutiny before placing an order. Old suppliers should be reviewed periodically to ascertain any changes in capability.

Unique—No Specifications Available

Sometimes the buyer is faced with procuring equipment that has not yet been designed or developed. The company's requirements may be such that there is nothing readily available in the marketplace, and it may be that the company's engineering resources for one reason or another cannot develop the specifications to satisfy the situation. It could be that the company does not have enough engineering manpower, or that it does not have the design expertise to do the job inside. The use of engineering design and development services can be the way to get the equipment specified, developed, and built.

Once it is decided to hire an engineering firm, the buyer should develop a list of candidate firms on the basis of background, experience, and the caliber of the people working for them and their reputation among clients. The qualifications of these candidate firms are compared to the criteria required, and a short list of firms (usually no more than four) is selected to receive a request for proposal (RFP). The RFP should set forth the scope of the work and all the pertinent terms and conditions of the eventual contract that the buyer can reasonably describe. Usually engineering work is best performed on a cost-reimbursable plus a fee basis. Fees may either be fixed at the outset or be a percentage of the reimbursable costs. Some costs may be included in an overhead percentage, and some costs may not be applicable to the percentage fee. All of this must be set forth in some detail so that charges can be properly audited.

The next step is for the engineering company to prepare its proposal. Each proposal should set forth the particulars requested in the RFP. These may include the proposed approach, qualifications, organization, rates, and overhead and fee structure. The firm should also set forth any exceptions it might take to the owner's contract terms and conditions. The request should set the date and time of day that the proposals must be returned to the buyer.

Depending upon the buyer's and the engineering department's knowledge of the engineering firms, or lack thereof, it may be appropriate for the buyer and the requisitioner, while they are preparing the proposal, to visit each of the firms that have received the RFP and rate each firm on the basis of its technical capabilities. Whether or not a visit is made, the technical evaluation of each firm should be prepared prior to the receipt of its commerical proposal.

After the commercial proposal is received, the potential cost of doing the work with each firm is estimated on the basis that each firm is capable of doing the work in the same number of hours. This estimate, which can be called a commercial evaluation, must then be compared with the technical evaluation to determine which firm is the best one to receive the contract.

In preparing the RFP, evaluating the proposals and the engineering firms' technical capabilities, and preparing the contract, the buyer should give prime consideration to the following areas.

Definition of the Problem   This section is the most important in the proposal. Without a clear understanding of what has to be done, design concepts and time and cost estimates are apt to be off base. The definition of the scope of work should include a summary of who will do what. If the buyer is to furnish information, drawings, parts, or materials, this fact should be clearly stated. The extent of the physical output of the engineering firm should also be spelled out. Is the design to include general drawings, detailed or working drawings, breadboard experiments, models, or finished unit?

Proposed Approach   Because of the uncertain and speculative nature of development work, it is usually organized in three phases: feasibility and concept development; design; and the build and problem-solving stage. The first phase will develop the basic concepts—breadboard models if needed—and any design trade-offs necessary to make the basic plan practicable. Normally this phase will include a cost estimate for completing the rest of the project. The development phase commits the program to a definite course of action. It is often the most expensive part, as it requires the services of the engineering firm's most creative and knowledgeable people.

The second phase, design, produces an actual engineering layout which describes the product in detail and gives full dimensions. Usually the buyer's company will have the right to approve each major subassembly and layout as they are made.

The third phase, building, can be the most troublesome. This is the moment of truth: Does the design work, or not? It should be expected that a number of changes will be made in order to make the equipment work.

Qualifications   The proposal should factually describe the qualifications of the engineering company—the nature of its organization, its size, the people working for it, and some of the assignments it has handled successfully. These should be scrutinized and checked thoroughly.

Working Agreement   A good firm respects proprietary matters and will not work directly on competitive projects without the client's knowledge and agreement. The time limit on this sort of arrangement can be negotiated. Service firms customarily grant clients the right to all patentable ideas for a particular application. But they reserve the right to use all ideas, whether patentable or not, in areas other than their client's field of interest.

Organization   A detailed description of how the project will be organized and who will work on it is normally part of the proposal.

Time and Cost Estimate   The cost of a development program will depend on the amount of time spent on it. At best, cost and time estimates are based on the knowledge available at the start of the project. Both time and price can change for a number of intangible factors: unforeseen design switches, problems in building a prototype, or changes in the buyer's company's ideas. Finally—a very important point—an acceptable contract definitely should include a clause that allows the buyer to cancel at any time, leaving the buyer responsible for only the costs incurred up to that point.

The buying of equipment of this type requires a different approach in some ways from that of other purchases, but the fundamental principles of good purchasing are still there. Careful selection of the design and development firm, constant attention to vital details, close follow-up on the progress, and a genuine willingness to work with the supplier can result in the successful procurement of capital equipment despite the lack of specifications or other technical data.

Financing Capital Equipment Purchases

Purchases of high-price capital equipment may present serious financial problems. Special methods of financing are possible, as follows:

1. By the vendor, under an established short- or long-range installment plan.

2. Outside sources, such as loans from banks or insurance companies. Railroads, for example, issue equipment trust certificates, which give a mortgage on the equipment to a financial institution.

3. Rental agreement with a financial institution, at times providing for the application of the rental payments to the purchase price. This actually may prove to be a leasing agreement.

Obviously, the financial officer of the company is responsible for reaching decisions in this area of purchasing capital equipment. Various possibilities, known to the purchasing manager, must therefore be called to his attention.

SPECIAL TERMS AND CONDITIONS

Aside from reference to drawings, specifications, codes, texts, and test reports, which should be made as found necessary with respect to particular types of equipment, there are some other points that are worth attention in preparing the purchase order. They include references to payment for the equipment, approval of drawings, etc., wording of the proposal, inspection and expediting conditions, and installation and initial operating services. Terms such as "standard boiler plate" found on the reverse of nearly all purchase order forms may not be adequate for capital equipment and purchases. The specific requirements should be reviewed thoroughly, and if necessary, the body of the purchase order should be supplemented.

Escalation

In times of heavy demand and/or unpredictable inflation most capital equipment bids consisting of significant monies and lengthy delivery are submitted with a method of escalating cost or a statement indicating final price to be that price in effect at time of shipment.

Government, industry, or company indexes are proposed to reflect changing costs. An analysis of the cost elements involved and knowledge of the indexes' past and anticipated trends are essential in evaluating proposals. The selection of an escalation clause may be made to reduce the risk to either buyer or seller for costs that are beyond their control.

Performance Guarantees

Regardless of the type of equipment, it is good to remember that the fundamental method of purchasing by performance specifications and guarantee often can be employed and should be employed whenever possible.

For the purchase of less complicated machinery and equipment where a statement of definite capacities, ratings, or speeds of operation can be made, a performance guarantee such as the following can be used:

> Vendor guarantees that the equipment supplied hereunder will be capable of the
> performance set forth in the specifications referred to herein, and agrees to make

such changes, adjustments, or replacements as are necessary to meet the guarantee, at no cost to the purchaser.

In the unusual case where more complex machinery and equipment are to be purchased with the requirement that they perform to fit a particular purpose and assure a specified quantity or quality of product, a special performance guarantee should be used. In such cases, engineering and purchasing should collaborate on having the vendor agree beforehand to a performance guarantee providing for the definite results desired and the manner of testing and determining whether the results have been attained. The following is an example of such a performance guarantee:

> The vendor guarantees that the complete equipment sold hereunder will produce at least _____ per hour of finished product _____ from _____ components, the properties and characteristics of each component and each finished product being set forth below. To determine if the complete equipment meets this guarantee, the vendor will submit it to a continuous test of _____ hours and a minimum of _____ samples of said finished product shall be taken at approximately equal intervals and analyzed to determine whether the properties or characteristics of the finished product are as set forth below. If the equipment does not meet said performance guarantee, the vendor agrees to revise, replace, or recondition the equipment in a manner calculated by the vendor to correct the unsatisfactory performance, at the vendor's own expense. Upon completion thereof, the equipment shall again be subjected to a further continuous test of a minimum of _____ hours during which a minimum of _____ samples of said finished product shall be taken at approximately equal intervals and analyzed to determine whether the properties or characteristics of the finished product are as set forth below. Only when the equipment shall meet the full performance requirements shall it be deemed acceptable to the purchaser. If after a reasonable time the equipment has failed to meet the full performance guarantees, then, upon the request of the purchaser, the vendor agrees to dismantle and remove all the equipment at the vendor's own expense and to refund to the purchaser the purchase price paid.

Reference to Payment

It is customary in the purchase of major equipment to provide for a withholding of part of the purchase price (usually 10 percent) until installation has been completed and the equipment properly tested and finally accepted. The payment terms of the purchase order should specifically provide for such retention.

Separate identification on the order and the vendor's invoice of cost components can save tax dollars and affect the amount to be capitalized. Installation labor and supervision, freight, and any special charges may or may not be subject to taxation and/or capitalization. It would be wise to discuss this aspect with the financial department.

Receipt of manuals, drawings, and parts list can be ensured if final payment is contingent upon their receipt.

On specially built equipment—when progress payments are involved and design approval is required prior to manufacturing—the buyer can be assured of vendor performance on the order by requiring the first progress payment to be contingent upon receipt of design drawings. Vendor performance can be further ensured if progress reports of job status are required with each progress payment. In short, progress payments can be a very effective expediting tool.

Reference to Drawings, etc.

The type and number of drawings that the purchaser requires should be set forth in the purchase order. A statement should appear to the effect that fabrication of the equipment is not to start until the drawings have been approved by purchaser. After they have been approved, with or without changes or revisions, the vendor should be called upon to supply certified copies of the finally approved drawings, so that there can be no mistake thereafter as to the full nature and description of the equipment that the purchaser requires or that vendor agrees to furnish.

Reference to Proposal

It is customary to refer to the vendor's proposal or quotation in the order, identifying it by date or number or both. The wording of this reference clause is important because there may be general provisions of the quotation that are objectionable.

Expressions such as "all in accordance with your proposal of _____" or "all the terms and conditions of your proposal of _____ are made a part of this order" will usually incorporate all the terms of the proposal whether objectionable or not. Where the proposal is short, all the acceptable terms can be typed in the order, and an identifying clause such as "refer to your proposal of _____" can be used without too much danger of incorporating unacceptable clauses into the order. Of course, where the proposal contains no objectionable provisions, a simple statement of acceptance can be incorporated into the order.

Where the proposal contains unfavorable provisions or long and involved descriptions of equipment and performance which cannot be typed readily in the order, something along the following lines could be used:

> All material and equipment furnished to us shall comply in all respects with the physical description, specifications, performance characteristics, and warranties contained in your proposal _____, but no other terms and conditions of your proposal shall be a part of this agreement.

The foregoing is all based on the fact that the average purchase order issued in business today is an offer to buy and is subject to the vendor's acceptance.

In those instances where the vendor insists on having a formal proposal executed by both parties, the objectionable terms must be made a matter of negotiation, after which the changes agreed upon can be made in the proposal before signing.

Inspection and Expediting

Vendors usually agree without question to the right of the purchaser to inspect major equipment. This includes inspection as the fabrication work progresses as well as final inspection before acceptance. Where the right of inspection is desired, the order should so provide and the vendor should be required to agree not to ship until inspection has been made or waived.

Arrangements should be made for periodic progress reports to be prepared by the vendor and sent to the purchaser. An understanding should be reached ensuring that the buyer will be advised promptly of any developments likely to affect delivery. The necessary provisions to this effect should be written into the order. Again, terms of payment are an effective expediting tool, as discussed earlier.

Installation and Initial Operating Services

The supplier of major equipment frequently offers to supervise installation or initial operation. The offer is usually made on the basis of the purchaser's paying the vendor's engineer assigned to the work a stipulated per diem fee plus all reasonable transportation and living expenses. Such offers are customarily accepted by the purchaser (although the practice varies, depending on the type of equipment) to expedite start-up, to minimize difficulties connected therewith, and to avoid any conflict of responsibility which might affect vendor's performance guarantees. The purchase order for the equipment should provide that the services will be rendered upon the request of buyer and should set forth the terms of reimbursement. Sometimes the quoted price of equipment includes installation and/or start-up supervision. If buyer prefers that charges for installation and start-up be make on a per diem basis, the cost of the equipment can be reduced by an amount the vendor has in fact included in his price. Again, this approach can affect the amount subject to taxation and capitalization. The order should also provide for the vendor's furnishing the required number of copies of operating instructions. Where a vendor's practice is to issue a guarantee of the equipment after installation is completed and by a separate document, the buyer should make certain he obtains it for protection against future trouble.

Cancellation Clause

One should include provisions and terms of cancellation as part of the order—particularly on nonstandard, unique equipment. The clause and costs related to cancellation should be a negotiated agreement between buyer and seller.

References

Numerous manufacturers' trade associations are good sources for obtaining standard terms and conditions. Standard terms and conditions for machine tools, for example, are available from the Machinery and Allied Products Institute, 1200 Eighteenth Street, N.W., Washington, D.C. 20036.

SELECTION OF VENDOR

What motives or considerations are considered to be most important to the buyer when buying capital equipment? A survey of more than 400 purchasing managers revealed that the primary considerations, in the order of importance, were:

1. Reliability of the seller
2. Cooperation, including technical assistance; ability to provide close liaison before and after delivery
3. Low prices
4. Quick repair service and availability of replacement parts
5. Past services rendered satisfactorily

As is clearly shown by the results of the above survey, the selection of the vendor who shall receive the order is not simply a question of selecting the lowest bid. Competitive bids should be requested only from suppliers who are qualified by competence and experience to furnish the required equipment. On this point, buyers must also consider that bidders often incur substantial costs in bid preparation. However, the selection of the vendor should be made on the basis of which vendor offers the greatest total value, taking into consideration all the important factors. This comparison of vendors may require all the ingenuity of the buyer and frequently calls for the technical assistance of engineers, production, quality control, accounting, and legal personnel. When only one source of supply exists or when, for other reasons peculiar to the transaction, only one vendor may be dealt with, a negotiated purchase is in order.

Sometimes, a buyer finds that foreign sources of equipment must be considered. Great care must be exercised in this area, as practices, terminology, and other aspects of a transaction vary not only from country to country but within nations a buyer may become involved with. Information on these matters can be obtained from U.S. Customs, trading companies, and local customs brokers.

NOTE: For further information on subjects covered in this section see the list of references in Section 30.

Section **17**

Contracting for Services

COEDITORS

James A. Black, C.P.M. *Vice-President, Specialty Materials, Eagle-Picher Industries, Inc., Miami, Florida*

John J. Huzar, C.P.M. *Chief Purchasing Agent, City of Detroit, Detroit, Michigan*

John D. Peters, C.P.M. *Vice-President, Purchasing & Traffic, Dravo Corporation, Pittsburgh, Pennsylvania*

Contracting for services, on or off the owner's premises, is one of the fastest-growing segments of purchasing responsibility. A few years ago, purchasing of services was relegated primarily to maintenance agreements, food catering, consultant or legal expertise, and sales representations. There is now a significant emphasis on automated data processing, data reproduction, plant security, etc. Many services normally performed by a company's own forces are being evaluated against the cost from outside sources. With this shift in emphasis came a spontaneous growth in the buying of services. And the future holds promise for even greater growth.

The U.S. Department of Commerce tabulation of the gross national product for 1980 shows that services accounted for almost half of all purchases made in the United States. And, in 1980, almost seven out of ten American workers were providing services, according to estimates by the U.S. Department of Labor. This rapid growth in the area of services might, in the future, well rank purchasing of service contracting equally with purchasing of raw material, supplies, and capital equipment.

The bidding, negotiating, and contracting phases of service purchasing are more complex than similar features of materials procurement. Many intangibles must often be defined in finite terms. Levels of acceptable performance, for example, should be clearly defined. There is not a substantial body of law or prior practice to define the dos and don'ts of service contracting, and therefore all obligations and liabilities must be spelled out as clearly as possible.

Proper negotiation of a contract for services is essential to ensure desired performance and economies. There is no set standard or even an established preference for contract format or the general terms and conditions in service contracts. The federal government, the largest single buyer of services, has not established any firm guidelines and often purchases services as it would materials or components. The proper rule would seem to be: Use the techniques of materials buying and construction contracting as a baseline, and then expand these techniques to fit the requirements of the necessarily more definitive services contract.

Clear-cut decisions on do or buy, based on purely financial considerations, are not always possible. For example, while contracting for outside services which are available within the company may offer obvious financial benefits (fringe benefit savings, elimination of employee idle time, improved quality), the decision to employ outside help may conflict with labor union interests in a plant by potentially reducing the number of union members. In contrast, a company which desires a defense against unions may deliberately employ outside services, even though the cost may be greater, as a means of reducing the incentives for union organizers.

PURCHASING RESPONSIBILITY FOR CONTRACTING FOR SERVICES

Depending on the nature of the service to be purchased, the knowledge available in the purchasing department, and the significance of purchasing in the corporate structure, purchasing may be involved in various ways when services are to be procured.

In some cases, the department which requires the service will specify the need, select the sources, and evaluate proposals, with purchasing doing no more than negotiating and executing the contract. Ultimately, the degree of purchasing involvement in contracting for services will depend on its ability to make a valid contribution to the contract arrangement.

CLASSIFICATION OF SERVICES

Services may be divided into four broad classifications, as follows:

1. Professional services: legal, engineering, architectural, data processing, programming, testing, consulting, temporary employees, etc.
2. Facilities and equipment-related services: janitorial, equipment maintenance, security, data processing, reproduction, etc.
3. Personnel-related services: cafeteria, clothing and employee personal articles, vending machines, etc.
4. Labor and craft services: construction (see Section 18)

Subsequent paragraphs will discuss each of these classifications, noting common-interest areas as well as dissimilarities. The types of contracts available for service contracting, potential problem areas, and techniques for securing quotations and awarding contracts will be analyzed in terms of suggested usage. Final pages will compare the commercial sector with the government sector, noting the peculiarities of contracting with the government and under government prime contracts.

Discussion of labor and craft services normally purchased from contractors by means of construction contracts is not included in this section, although these are major contracts for services. For information on construction contracts and the terms and conditions that are applicable to other services performed on the owner's premises see Section 18.

TYPICAL APPLICATIONS FOR SERVICE CONTRACTING

Professional Services

The physician who performs employee physicals, the civil engineer who designs the new water-overflow pond, the lawyer who reviews a new reorganization plan, the consultant who assists with packaging requirements or reviews utility contracts—these are all examples of persons who render professional services. The following disciplines are usually associated with professional services contracts:

1. Legal or accounting consultants
2. Advertising consultants
3. Publication services
4. Computer programming
5. Engineering, architectural, or design consultants
6. Personnel or temporary employee agencies
7. Inspection and testing services
8. Management consultants
9. Physician or dental services
10. Mailing of promotional items

Other vocational specialties which may or may not be contracted for include marketing or market development services, abstracting and translation services, professional society agreements, professional services in specialized areas, etc.

In many companies, professional services are contracted for by those departments charged with obtaining the type of service desired. Examples are the advertising department, the legal department, and the engineering department. Furthermore, some types of professional services are not customarily solicited competitively.

When contracting for professional services, the purchasing manager is almost always confronted with one major problem, i.e., how to define, in specific terms, the services to be purchased. A related problem is the necessary association of the ultimate definition with a proper time frame or schedule. Another problem that compounds the difficulties of definition and schedule is that of becoming involved sufficiently early to assure proper selection of contractors or vendors and the negotiation of a realistic price for the task to be performed.

Because of the indefinite nature of many professional service contracts, purchasing should participate in the early or formulative stages. Also, objective competition should be obtained. This step cannot be underestimated for the purchase of services with proper consideration given to all factors involved.

Each contracting situation may be different, but the technicalities and considerations are often similar. Before venturing outside to buy engineering expertise, the buyer should make sure that the capability does not exist elsewhere in the corporation, i.e., in another division, another department, a subsidiary, etc. The make-or-buy (or do-or-buy) procedures should first dictate a thorough research of existing company capabilities.

Consultants—General   In many companies, it is not uncommon for professional services to be contracted for by the department charged with the responsibility for providing a service. Thus, the law department may contract for legal services, the advertising department for advertising and promotion services, or the engineering department for engineering services. The rationale for these actions may lie in the fact that many types of professional services are customarily not solicited competitively.

The need for a consultant in any field should be carefully evaluated. In addition to the common reasons for hiring consultants—to supplement in-house skills or to handle a project which company personnel have no time for—there are two other valid reasons:

1. To carry out a one-time assignment for which the consultant's cost would be lower than the cost of hiring an additional staff member

2. To act as an arbitrator between opposing management points of view, or to provide an independent opinion where management decisions are not seen as satisfactory

Selection of a consultant should be made on the basis of his or her qualifications, resources, and experience and the costs involved. Before contracting for any professional service, the task to be performed or the problem to be solved should be clearly defined by a written statement including a time schedule. Further, criteria should be established to determine the competence of each of the prospective consultants.

Specification for the service to be procured may be established by setting forth:

1. A complete technical description of the problem or work task (ask others to read it and listen carefully to their expressed understanding; use technical people where possible)

2. The objectives of the study or a statement of what is expected to be accomplished

3. Scope of the work, including any mandatory approaches to the problem, or task, specific limitations, questions requiring answers, format for the completed report, and the extent to which assistance from the company's staff will be available to the consultant (and, of course, the conditions for such assistance)

4. Firm or estimated time schedule, including dates for commencement of performance, for submission of progress reports, and for completion

5. Extent to which periodic payments will be allowed and how final payment will be made

6. Understanding for compensation for additional work authorized

It should be a firm requirement that the proposal from the consultant include the following:

1. A description of qualifications, with a brief list of similar types of consulting contracts successfully concluded and a sample of such work when appropriate.

2. A description of the key personnel and anticipated supporting personnel to be employed on the study.

3. An overall description of the techniques by which the consultant intends to approach the problem; amount of time and manpower to be expended; equipment and facilities to be utilized; and, if subcontractors are contemplated, a description of these persons or firms and the portions and monetary percentages of the work to be done by them. The buyer should always reserve the right to approve any subcontractors employed by the consultant.

4. The total cost or price for the study, including a breakdown of how it was computed, setting out any travel and other unusual expenses.

5. Method of payment and terms and conditions.

One should follow the company's standard procedures for advertising for bids, requesting proposals, etc., where possible, to minimize confusion.

If the planned procurement is complex or difficult, the procurement action should be made in a two-step program. First, technical and capability proposals are solicited. These are reviewed, and then independent discussions are held with responsive and responsible bidders. Quotations should then be solicited from those firms best qualified to provide the desired services.

Example 3 at the end of this section presents a selected professional service agreement format. The buyer should always remember that effective dialogue is the key to developing a satisfactory service agreement. Discussions should be open and should cover the requirements both with the requisitioning people and with the vendors. The buyer should encourage discussion, should participate, and, most important, should listen to all questions and answers, so that the final agreement truly reflects what the company requires. Anyone who purchases services must always be thorough. In service contracting for professional services, the thoroughness of the approach will make the difference between a successful contract and a less successful one.

Should time not permit an orderly investigative process, only those firms recognized in the field should be solicited. If the procurement involves a task such as computer programming, the equipment manufacturer should be considered first. Further, working with a local company can have many advantages.

Electronic Data Processing Consultants The advent of computers and electronic data processing (EDP) has brought a new problem area into the arena of service contracting. For years, management had the problem of how best to utilize consultants. Now EDP brings forth a new dimension with a new philosophy, a new language, and a new mathematics with which to contend.

Prior to data processing, consultants with talents in marketing, finance, and production usually related well enough with management because of their general businesslike orientation. They had little difficulty in communicating. In the data processing environment, however, top management is likely to feel much less confident because they are not thoroughly familiar with the art.

Many members of management will admit that the need for consultation in EDP has never been greater. Yet their expressed lack of confidence in EDP consultants continues. The confidence gap may result from what they perceive as consultants' shortcomings:

1. Overreliance on jargon and state-of-the-art technology, regardless of the resulting detriment to effective communication

2. Lack of sensitivity to business problems that may demand a higher priority than EDP

3. Inability to initially confront management with company weaknesses that will eventually conflict with the automation process

Thus, purchasing officials must be very precise in defining the task and/or problems that require consulting assistance. Suggested guidelines are as follows:

1. The buyer should be certain that the EDP consultant understands the scope of the assignment as well as the constraints.

2. A work plan that defines the specific tasks and reviews milestones and time intervals should be requested.

3. The necessary objective liaison should be provided within the company.

4. The buyer should become informed about electronic data processing equipment and techniques where possible.

5. The buyer should keep informed as to progress, be aware of complaints, and act on the problem areas.

Buying time from a computer center or agency should be handled as if the buyer were purchasing services for the company's computer center. Technical people should be used in evaluating the service source.

Temporary Personnel   Temporary personnel services (Office Temporaries, for example) are used by many firms, both large and small, from time to time. Temporary personnel services offer an opportunity to acquire and employ trained personnel for short periods at a minimum cost.

Competition keeps performance sharp in the personnel services field. In purchasing labor services, it is important to know what is needed and the qualifications of the temporary employees who will be assigned to the work. When soliciting temporary personnel services, the buyer should be candid about the requirements. He should request the competence level needed and supporting proof in order to obtain what is required.

Facilities- and Equipment-Related Services

Most purchasing people are familiar with the problem of maintenance. When maintenance is routinely performed in-house, problems do arise associated with the purchase of materials and supplies for equipment breakdown. Many, however, are not familiar with the new maintenance requirements brought about by computers, sophisticated reproduction equipment, recorders, etc. There is a new trend directed at procurement of security services, janitorial services, and warehousing services.

Several categories of service contracts can be grouped with facility or equipment service contracts. Most important of these are:

1. Janitorial services
2. General facility and equipment maintenance
3. EDP equipment maintenance
4. Reproduction equipment maintenance
5. Plant security
6. Warehousing services

Depending on the method selected for contracting for EDP equipment and reproduction equipment, one would associate these contracting specialties with service contracting. However, in acquiring these types of equipment, consideration should be given to a rent or lease agreement. Typewriters, special accounting machines, etc., are also candidates for consideration on a rent or lease arrangement. Section 16 discusses leasing, rental, and similar agreements, and its review would be helpful to a better understanding of the following discussion.

Janitorial services, warehousing services, and plant security services are three business services that are enjoying a better-than-average growth. This trend can be expected to continue through the next decade. Success can be attributed to the disposition of industry, big and small alike, to concentrate on their specialty and to contract for housekeeping and other specialized services to reduce cost and to benefit from professional know-how.

Proper work definition is equally important when contracting for janitorial, plant security, and similar services. However, when purchasing such coverage, it is important also to define the following:

1. Terms of service agency employee contract
2. Times of access to facility (janitorial services and facility maintenance services)
3. Limits of authority (plant security services)
4. Employee clearances (protection of privileged records, machine designs, etc.)
5. Supplies and facilities to be furnished by company
6. Conditions for termination of contract for unsatisfactory performance (individual employee actions as well as overall group actions)

There will be other areas of concern which may come to mind. A good rule to follow is that any contingency should be covered in the agreement where possible.

Office Equipment—General   For electronic data processing, reproduction, and general office equipment maintenance and service agreements, a systematic step-by-step purchase approach as follows is probably the best. Examples 1 and 2 present guidelines for two of the more critical steps. The following suggestions, used with adaptations of these examples, will help ensure proper equipment agreements:

1. Each type of purchased equipment and each equipment manufacturer offers different warranty or guarantee coverage; *the agreement should be read before taking any action.*
2. All rent or lease agreements offer some service coverage; *those agreements should be studied in depth.*
3. A list of all classes or types of equipment which might require servicing, noting model number, manufacturer, and any other pertinent information, should be prepared.
4. The equipment should be segregated into those classes which could conceivably be maintained under a common agreement, e.g., calculators into one class, typewriters into one, reproduction equipment into one.
5. Individual manufacturers should be requested to provide information about

their standard maintenance agreements and about their policy of maintaining other manufacturers' equipment or permitting other manufacturers to work on their equipment.

6. Alternate courses of action may be evaluated, noting the location of the service offices (proximity to equipment location), previous service experience, cost (incremental and total), and compatibility with existing warranties.

7. Independent service organizations should be investigated.

With this information, it should be a straightforward procedure to solicit bids and to award a contract. One point to consider: it may be desirable to divide the contract requirements among two or more firms to assure continued cooperation and competition. Poor response to service calls on out-of-service equipment could result in added cost.

Reproduction Equipment   Reproduction equipment services and maintenance are difficult services to purchase, especially if the requirements are of a large dollar volume. There are many types of equipment available and new versions are introduced continually. Most equipment designs are suited to certain applications, and an equipment mix may be desirable for varying quantities and varying copy qualities. A buyer will usually find after careful study that what appears initially to be the lowest copy price or cost may not be true. Copy quality varies significantly, and therefore it can have a major bearing on the decision.

Factors to consider before contracting for reproduction equipment include the necessity or desirability of copy quality, speed, color, and variety of copy sizes. These should be factored into estimates of volume requirements. The cost of supplies for the equipment can also be a significant factor and should be carefully considered. A chart can be developed from suppliers' proposals which will provide accurate per-copy costs at varying volume levels.

Not to be overlooked when preparing estimates of anticipated volume is the considerable illicit use which will be made of the equipment by company personnel. Secretaries will find it easier to make reproductions of correspondence than to use cheaper carbon paper, and employees will undoubtedly use the machines to reproduce personal papers. Hiring one person to operate the equipment may reduce such use, but the salary of that person must be taken into consideration to offset any savings. A method that many departments have found to reduce illicit use is to obtain equipment that gives low-quality copies. Employees will not then be as tempted to use the equipment.

If a buyer is not thoroughly knowledgeable about reproduction equipment, he would be wise to call for some expert help in arriving at a decision. The company may have an industrial engineering department; if so, a study of this nature will permit a much better opportunity to make the correct decision. If an industrial engineering group is not available, consider engaging a competent independent consultant to perform the study. A dollar spent in a study can repay itself many fold in savings. Dependence on a manufacturer's study should be avoided if at all possible.

The first step in considering the purchase of reproduction equipment is to obtain a profile of actual needs or usage in terms of volume of copies for each location. Needed or desired features—such as quality of copy, speed, color, extended copy sizes—can be imposed on the volume requirements. After that step, offerings can be solicited from suppliers. The price of supplies, which can be significant, should not be overlooked.

A chart can be prepared to serve as a guide in selecting reproduction equipment. Comparative costs per copy at scaled monthly volumes, taken from suppliers' proposals, can be incorporated into the chart. High-volume reproduction is generally more economical, but cost per copy can be exorbitant if the potential of the equipment is not utilized.

Quality of copy is an important cost factor. It is usually controlled by the type of paper and the reproduction process, and greater cost is normally associated with higher quality. For general use, the highest quality is not necessary. (Dont't install a Cadillac when a Ford will do the job.) An interesting aspect of reproduction equipment is that better copy quality usually results in greater unwarranted use of the machines. Bowling scores, cartoons, and other personal items are likely to be copied. And secretaries often find it easier to reproduce originals of correspondence rather than prepare relatively inexpensive carbon copies. Improper use of reproduction equipment can quickly offset anticipated savings.

Some suppliers of reproduction services furnish equipment based on a monthly minimum cost with an added cost per copy based on number of copies produced. There may be a lower monthly cost per copy as the number of copies increases, or it may be a flat charge per copy. The buyer may also find that some companies will sell their equipment for a flat charge and then assess a monthly charge per copy based on the price for the paper and supplies. Example 2 provides a guide for proposal requests that will help assure having reasonably complete information on which to base decisions.

One purpose of the suggested engineering or consultant study will be to determine if it would be more economical for the company to own the equipment, to lease it, or to rent it. A word of caution in making this decision: the buyer should bear in mind that, with technological developments today, many improvements are being made in reproduction equipment. If the decision is to lease or rent, the company can by this means always replace outdated equipment with more modern and up-to-date equipment. Another factor to be considered in reaching a decision to own, or rent, or lease is that all maintenance and repair will be for the owner's account; in a lease, this expense may be the responsibility of the service contractor. Also, the fact that some companies supply all materials while others sell materials as a separate charge should not be overlooked.

Personnel-Related Services

Services with which everyone is familiar are work clothing or uniform service operations, towel and linen services, vending machine services, and cafeteria operations. Of these, the clothing and uniform service and the towel and linen service are usually straightforward, requiring only careful purchasing attention. There is generally sufficient competition in these service areas to keep prices at an acceptable level.

Food Services   Cafeteria operations and vending machine operations require closer attention. For example, these services often become targets in union negotiations and, therefore, are ultrasensitive areas creating both monetary and political concern. In most areas, the cafeteria operations must meet city, county, and state health rules and regulations. It has become established practice to contract for cafeteria services and the related vending machine services from outside firms which specialize in food handling.

Following are several areas of caution which should be recognized and properly resolved prior to executing a formal agreement.

1. Product liability. While it is normally necessary to prove negligence in a liability suit, such is not the case when injuries arise from adulterated food. As a minimum requirement, complete indemnification should be obtained from the contractor providing food services.

2. Liability with respect to injury to contractor personnel working on company property.

3. Conditions of termination in the event of unsatisfactory service (pay special attention to the notice period).

4. Rights of both parties relative to addition to or deletion of services, e.g., change of food or vending machine service locations, special luncheons.

Because of the rather indeterminate nature of food services, it is important that the specification or requirements be stated in as definite terms as possible.

Exposure to liability goes with providing food, either in a cafeteria or in vending machines, even though there are not many instances of absolute liability in law. Normally, one must prove negligence in a civil action to recover damages from another party, but not in the case of harm from tainted food. It need only be proved that an individual became ill from such food, and the party who made the food available is liable. At a minimum, complete indemnification should be obtained from the person providing the food.

In providing food service for employees, a company should also consider the possibility that employees may claim a right to the profit accruing to the company from sales to them. Once a union is introduced into negotiations for food services, contracting and administering the contract become more complex.

To properly evaluate the proposals, it is important that all prospective suppliers of food handling services quote on the same type of services. Any deviations should be determined and a proper evaluation made. Even with the best of specifications, it is easy for the scope of work to be misunderstood.

Before soliciting proposals, a buyer should investigate all prospective bidders, selecting only reliable and dependable companies with which to work. Careful selection among the potential sources will make the analysis of the proposals much easier. It would be well to have the invitations for bid point out any special or unusual circumstances, such as security restrictions and hazardous conditions. The areas to be covered and the areas to be excluded should be spelled out clearly. If the service is to be provided around the clock or at unusual hours, all of this should be stated in the proposal.

Many other conditions should possibly be defined, such as a requirement that the contractor submit menus complete with prices at least one week in advance for approval. It may be desirable to stipulate in the specifications that the contractor is to handle special parties, luncheons, banquets, etc., according to instructions to be provided in each instance and at a cost to be mutually agreed upon.

Specifications should be clear as to company-supplied facilities and equipment for the employee food service program, for example, facilities equipped and ready to operate, including heat, fuel, refrigeration, and utilities, as may reasonably be required for efficient operation. Should equipment of a certain manufacture be necessary or if there are certain functions to be performed by the equipment, these should be listed in the specifications. It should be clearly understood who is to be responsible for repairs to, and replacement of, facilities and equipment supplied as required by normal wear and tear. Also, responsibility as to upkeep of property furnished and responsibility for activities such as cleaning, housekeeping, etc., should be clearly specified to avoid misunderstandings. The buyer should make it clear as to what actions will be taken in the event of unsanitary conditions.

The possibility exists that employees may attempt to claim a right to any profits which the company obtains from vending or food services. And, if a labor union is introduced into any food service negotiations, contracting and administering a contract will also be made more complex. Care should be taken that any contract spells out the extent of employee or union participation and what profits, if any, shall be distributed.

Vending Services   Vending machines are becoming increasingly important in providing in-plant feeding service. The National Association of Purchasing Management's *Guide to Purchasing* contains a number of guidelines for purchasing departments that have, or should have, responsibility for developing and administering contracts for vending service.[1] Among them are the following:

- While responsibility for vending service should generally remain with location management, larger companies with corporate organizations should consider negotiating companywide agreements.
- Specifications should be drawn up immediately following the decision as to what type of vending service and products are required. These should include equipment, product, service, insurance, and financial aspects. New, reconditioned, and existing machines should be evaluated. Type, make, product and coin capacity, number of selections, and uniformity of size and appearance are other considerations. All electrically operated machines should be grounded and meet all other Occupational Safety and Health Act (OSHA) standards.

[1] Charles J. Bates, "Purchasing Vending Services," in *Guide to Purchasing*, National Association of Purchasing Management, New York, 1975, Sec. 3-12.

- Both buyer and seller should know state and local vending sanitation laws and regulations. The National Automatic Merchandising Association (NAMA) in Chicago is a good source for information on existing regulations.
- A standard companywide vending contract should be considered by companies with multiple locations. Duration of such contracts will vary, but sufficient time should be allowed to let operators amortize their equipment investment. A 3-year contract with a 30-day cancellation clause available to either party is generally satisfactory. In the absence of specified time, vending operators have been known to amortize equipment in as little as 1 year and as much as 8 years. Their amortization schedule has a direct relationship to financial arrangements with the buyer of the service.
- Contracts should include all the equipment, product, service, insurance, and financial specifications, as well as provisions for removal, replacement, or relocation of vending machines. Need for additional vending equipment during a contract period should also be anticipated.
- Several guides are available for specifying and monitoring quantity, content, and freshness of vended products. A guide should include measurement aids covering hot drinks, soft drinks, and cigarettes, since these commodities generally represent the majority of sales. All products dispensed from a hot drink vendor may be measured on a gram scale. The amount of drink dispensed is based on the size of the drink and the taste preferences of customers. The Coffee Brewing Center in New York provides, on a fee basis, such services as sample and grind analysis; moisture, color, and acidity measurement; and evaluation of equipment performance. Individual soft drink manufacturers and the NAMA are good sources of measurement data and product specifications.
- Since most vending agreements are based on projected sales for a given period, purchasing should monitor the actual sales against the projected sales. This is particularly necessary where commissions are based on information provided to the vending supplier and where commissions depend on maintaining that volume. As part of the contract, the supplier should be required to supply periodic statements of sales.
- To keep abreast of continuing developments in the vending industry, purchasing departments can subscribe to trade publications such as *Automatic Merchandising* or *Vending Times*.

CONTRACTING AS A COST-REDUCTION TECHNIQUE

It is important to recognize that contracting for services may be an excellent technique for reducing costs—one that is becoming so popular that some unions have moved to prevent the practice. Many services performed by in-house employees can be secured at lower cost from outside sources with greater skills or lower labor and overhead costs.

An extension of the contracting-out concept is the use of services on a long-term basis to avoid investing large amounts of money in construction of facilities to provide those services. This technique may be particularly desirable in considering peripheral facilities, such as those required for environmental protection. When money is tight, it may provide a means of preserving available funds for direct production equipment. Attractive financing of the supplier's facility can be enhanced by means of a long-term "take-or-pay" contract for the services furnished by the facility. Under such an arrangement, the credit of both the purchaser and the supplier forms the basis for extending loans.

TECHNIQUES FOR BID, PROPOSAL DEVELOPMENT, AND CONTRACT AWARD

Effective bidding or proposal solicitations and evaluation techniques are discussed in Section 11. An example of a typical request for bid or proposal on one type of service is presented in Example 2. There are certain rules, however, that apply particularly to service contracting as a specialty. The bidding, negotiation, award, and administration of contracts for services are often complex and difficult because of the more intangible nature of services as compared with goods. Such contracts often involve the obligation of expenditures and the assumption of high risks and liabilities on the part of both the company and the contractor. Particular care in the solicitation and the preparation of service contracts is necessary to minimize monetary, legal, and business risks and to protect the rights of both parties.

Problem Areas Important to Service Contracts

Some of the problems which are not common to other purchasing situations and must be treated accordingly are the following:

1. Contractor's personnel working on the owner's property expose the owner to liability in the event of personal injury or death on the premises.

2. Small to medium-sized contractors usually perform in regional markets and sometimes with minimum or marginal finances.

3. The work to be performed often cannot be fully defined at the time the agreement is negotiated. Consequently the opportunity for obtaining firm prices is often limited.

4. Alterations and additions to the work can be frequent; therefore the methods used to alter the contract price must be carefully defined.

5. Employee goodwill is an important factor, and the service performed must be satisfactory to the employee.

Remember that the basic elements of a service contract must include a description of the work, a time for starting and completing the work, a definition of payment terms for the work, and other customary and legal terms and conditions which must be agreed to by both parties.

In service contracting, the buyer should understand the difference between an *independent contractor* and an *agent* in order to clearly define the relationship between the company (or buyer) and the contractor (or seller) in the contract. This difference is explained as follows:

1. An independent contractor is one who agrees to accomplish a certain result and has full control over the manner and method to be pursued. The person receiving the benefit of the services of an independent contractor is not responsible for the actions of said independent contractor.

2. An agent is someone under the control of and authorized to act for some other person or company known as the *principal*. A special agent cannot bind the company beyond his specific authority. The general agent conducts a series of transactions involving a continuity of service.

Know and understand the status of the bidder when soliciting bids for service contracts.

Before soliciting bids or proposals, the buyer should develop a firm understanding of the exact service to be purchased. One of the most effective ways to accomplish this is through the use of a using department questionnaire. See Example 1 at the end of this section for an illustration. This questionnaire would be submitted to those departments within the plant, division, or corporation which use or will use the equipment.

Invitation to Bid

A letter-type invitation to bid, as illustrated by Example 2 at the end of this section, is usually considered good practice in lieu of the usual purchase inquiry form. The invitation letter should be accompanied by all referenced specifications, drawings, and the general conditions of the proposed contract. The letter invitation should contain:

1. Description and location of the work.
2. References to applicable specifications, drawings, and general conditions.
3. Information as to whom to contact for a site visitation appointment and on what date or dates visitations will be conducted. (The buyer should follow up and make sure these contacts are made.)
4. The date on which the proposals are due.
5. Request for bidders to notify the buyer immediately if they do not intend to bid and to return the complete invitation, including specifications and drawings, to the purchaser.
6. Statement from the contractor declaring that he will employ field labor in accordance with the local trade requirements and will meet the schedule of progress without additional compensation from the owner.
7. The proposed method of reimbursing the contractor, i.e., progress payments, lump sum at completion of work, etc., and when final payment is due.

It is advantageous to include a pre-prepared contract document providing appropriate spaces for the bidders to enter pricing, completion schedules, and other bid information required by the buyer. This document, properly prepared by the buyer and completed and signed by the contractor, can constitute the completed contract upon acceptance and execution by the buyer. Care should be taken to see that all conditions are covered.

A prebid conference to discuss the invitation may be desirable in service contracting. Through the dialogue of the conference, it will be possible to bring most bidders to a common baseline or understanding of the bid requirements. This will reduce the disparities between bids and will simplify bid evaluation and contract award. It also is ever forceful in reminding all bidders about the level of competition being sought.

To assist the various contractors in submitting bids on service contracts, it may be desirable to indicate in the invitation an estimate of the annual minimum and annual maximum value of the services to be purchased—that is, annual sales or annual consumption. This estimate could be secured from previous years' records or from industry experience data. See Example 2 for an illustration. It should be offered as an aid to the bidders, not as a guarantee. Bid specifications should also cover the subject of taxes, right of acceptance of the personnel of the contractor, audit or accounting procedures to be used, identification requirements for the service contractor's employees, insurance limits, hold-harmless provision, patents, assignment and cancellation or termination, proprietary agreements, etc.

The proposal or bid request should require that the potential contractors clearly spell out exactly what they intend to provide for the planned program and the locations at which the services are to be provided. In food handling agreements, it will be necessary to have an understanding as to the size of the portions of food served and the prices to be charged. A suggested listing of menus would be helpful to be sure sufficient varieties are being offered.

The contractor's personnel may be working on the purchaser's premises, and therefore the bid request should state that such personnel must be acceptable to the purchaser and must meet applicable security qualifications. The buyer will want it understood that the successful bidder will have the responsibility of compliance with all federal, state, and local applicable regulations relating to employment and to payment of employees.

TYPES AND TERMS OF CONTRACTS

Other sections in this handbook (refer to the index) explain the various types of contracts and discuss the terms and conditions normally associated with a specific contract type. Because of the constantly fluctuating nature of service contracts, only a very select segment of the available contract types can be successfully applied to a service contract.

The preceding paragraphs have illustrated the variable nature of service purchasing and the difficulty of defining the task within measurable limits. In each case, the specific work to be done or the services to be rendered must be carefully and completely described, and the completion time and the amount and method of remuneration to the contractor must be clearly defined and understood. But how does one cover the variable situation of cafeteria operation, janitorial services, plant security, etc.?

Cost-Reimbursable or Variable-Price Contracts

Cost-reimbursable contracts, regardless of the specific variety, are not generally recommended because of the attendant problems, i.e., high administrative costs, tendency for cost growth, difficulty in auditing allowable costs, etc. There are two types, however, which can be used in the purchasing of services. These are:

1. Time and material contracts
2. Labor or machine-hour contracts

If a cost-reimbursable contract must be used, consideration should be given to these two types. An alternate would be cost plus award fee (where amount of earned fee is directly related to satisfactory performance), but this contract type is somewhat difficult to administer.

In practice, it should be possible to negotiate a labor hour rate (labor cost plus burden cost plus profit) for selective labor categories or for certain personnel. A company representative could then ascertain that the hours charged were reasonable and allocable. Material and sundry costs can be verified by the usual audit techniques. Profit on material is not usually acceptable, but a material handling burden usually is. For reproduction equipment or data processing equipment, a fixed machine rate is the most desirable. Service costs should be defined in quantitative terms, i.e., fixed labor rate per hour plus materials.

Fixed-Price Contracts

Fixed-price contracting is always a preferred method if it does not cost extra money. Its applicability to service contracting, however, depends on the circumstances of the purchase and the service to be procured. Three types of fixed-price contracts are most prevalent in service contracting. These are:

1. Indefinite-quantity contracts (with minimum quantity or level defined and with price ranges for increased quantity purchases defined)
2. Definite-quantity contracts (specific scope of work defined)
3. Consolidated agreements and blanket purchase agreements (these are usually variations of indefinite-quantity agreements)

Fixed-price redeterminable (after completion) and similar fixed-price agreements are not recommended, as they offer little or no advantage over cost-reimbursable agreements.

Terms and Conditions

Caution is needed when selecting both the contract type and the accompanying terms and conditions. The selection could be with you for a long time. Remember these basic rules for contract selection:

1. If it is possible to define the service to be purchased in quantitative terms and to measure (again quantitatively) acceptance of the products or results, use a fixed-price contract.

2. If it is impossible to define the task or product desired or to measure satisfactory performance, select a cost-reimbursable type.

A buyer should not contract on a fixed-price basis when major changes are anticipated unless definite arrangements can be made to handle the changes. If this situation exists, one might consider the possibility of contracting on a cost-reimbursable basis initially until quantitative terms can be established. Then convert to a fixed-price arrangement.

The terms and conditions which generally accompany a standard cost-reimbursable or fixed-price agreement will apply to service contracts. Examples 2, 3, and 4 at the end of the section illustrate the need for special attention to insurance coverage, rights of parties relative to termination or cancellation, labor law compliance, and obligations of both parties with respect to furnished property.

A must provision is that the contractor agree to indemnify and save the buyer harmless from any liabilities which may be asserted against the buyer by reason of acts or omissions of the contractor. Adequate insurance should also be provided with responsible insurance companies. The coverage should be within acceptable limits to both parties and probably would include the following types of policies:

1. Comprehensive general liability (including product liability)
2. Bodily injury—each person, each accident
3. Property damage—each accident
4. Vehicle liability: bodily injury—each person, each accident; property damage—each accident
5. Workers' compensation
6. Employer's liability
7. Federal insurance contributions and all similar requirements of local ordinances

A lawyer skilled in the wording of indemnification and labor agreements should be consulted for specific wording of the proposed agreement. The company's insurance department and an insurance carrier should advise as to specific needs. The personnel department should also be solicited for recent federal regulation requirements on labor.

Before settling on one specific set of conditions, a prudent buyer should take time to be analytical. He should consider what could possibly happen during the contract and then make a list of the answers. Third, he should take the time to make sure that the final agreement covers all points. Opinions of others should be solicited where time permits.

Contract Negotiation and Completion

After the bids have been evaluated and all concerned are in agreement on the contractor selection and award, the successful bidder should be notified by telephone or telegram if time dictates; otherwise, notice should be given by preparing and mailing the contract document. Unsuccessful bidders should be notified promptly that the job was awarded elsewhere, thanked for their cooperation, and requested to return bid drawings and specifications to the buyer.

A contract is considered to be completed when all the obligations contained therein have been fulfilled by both parties. The degree of satisfaction of the obligations to which the contractor has agreed may not be obvious or clear-cut at the time the work is complete because of potential difficulties with technical and legal aspects of the work. Often these problems do not develop until a later date, but some sort of advance warning usually exists. An informed and experienced buyer should have notice of potential problems.

Since one of the contractor's obligations is to satisfy the buyer, the contractor may request the buyer's written acceptance of the work upon completion. A letter of acceptance may be given after inspection and approval by the buyer's inspectors, but such a letter should contain the following statement: "This acceptance is promulgated without releasing the contractor from his continuing obligations under this contract." This will establish that there is no intent to release the contractor from any guarantee, patent indemnification, hold-harmless provision, etc., assumed under the contract.

Before final payment is made to the contractor, a release of liens should always be obtained. These releases usually differ for each state or county; therefore, they should be obtained from a qualified attorney. Once the release of liens has been obtained, the contract is considered closed.

TECHNIQUES TO LOWER COSTS IN SERVICE CONTRACTING

Many methods can be employed in contracting for services, and all of them can be effective when properly used. A few of the most effective techniques will be suggested to demonstrate to the alert purchasing manager some of the more important avenues available for lowering costs of services.

One of the best ways to be assured of spending the service dollar wisely is to thoroughly investigate all potential contractor companies before soliciting a bid or proposal. The buyer should be sure that all selected firms are qualified and that all have the facilities, labor force, and other capabilities to furnish the type of services required. It is not only important but essential that he know and understand the capabilities of those companies which are being considered for contract.

In most cases, including specialty services, there are many qualified providers of the services desired. One of the methods to be assured that the company does not pay for more than is required is to solicit a large number of qualified contractors. By assuring maximum competition, the buyer obtains a representative analysis of the various charges being made throughout the service industry. However, a buyer should remember that source selection is one of his primary responsibilities, and he cannot ignore this responsibility simply by maximizing the number of bidders.

During the course of soliciting bids, a buyer will also find that many companies offer benefits that others do not. These additional services could be of value to the company. In addition, the buyer may find that several companies can, and do, offer certain extra services that were not included in the original bid concept. It may even be desirable to include these services in the final negotiated arrangement.

Specifications should be confined to services required, not desired, i.e., to services that will be beneficial in accomplishing the required objective of the purchase. The specifications should be very carefully reviewed and should include only the necessary service requirements. If unnecessary services are included in contract specifications or bid specifications, the buyer will be paying for such unnecessary services throughout the term of the service contract. Comments should be solicited from all potential using departments or plants. These comments should then be compared with the specification and the required changes made. Only those features that will assure (at a minimum investment or cost) a reasonable quality of service and with the required margin of safety should be included. Equipment that is not needed and not used will only cost the company additional money.

When the bids are received, the buyer would be wise to ask representatives from the principal using departments to assist in the review. He should listen carefully to their comments and recommendations, taking full advantage of the know-how available. Next, the buyer should select two or three bidders for prenegotiation discussions and thank the other bidders for their cooperation. Where possible, one should redefine the specification for the final negotiations, considering all the available information. The buyer should then:

1. Request a final proposal
2. Negotiate the agreement
3. Award the contract

When attempting to develop an agreement on a set of requirements as complex as the typical service contract, a little extra effort on the buyer's part in properly preparing the invitation will pay extra dividends during the contract performance period, as will periodic follow-up to be sure services are being performed in a satisfactory manner.

EXAMPLE 1

TYPICAL USING DEPARTMENT REQUIREMENTS QUESTIONNAIRE

The purpose of this questionnaire is to define the exact equipment and/or services to be purchased. Answer all the questions when possible. Add suggestions for changes and recommendations for additional requirements or improved service.

SURVEY OF CURRENT EQUIPMENT

1. What type of equipment is currently being used in your work area? (Specify make and model, if possible.) _____
2. Are you satisfied with the performance (copy quality, speed, etc.)? _____
_____
3. If not, what have been the problems and how often have they occurred? _____
_____
_____
4. How often do you use the equipment (e.g., once a day, five times a week)? _____
_____
5. How long do you stand in line awaiting use of the machine? _____
_____
   If reproduction center is used, how long do you stand in line before receiving your copies? _____
6. Additional comments or recommendations. _____
_____
_____

SURVEY OF PREVIOUS EQUIPMENT

1. Was there other equipment installed before the current equipment? _____
_____
2. If so, what type of equipment? (Specify make and model, if possible.) _____
_____
3. Were you satisfied with the performance? _____
_____
4. If not, what were the problems and how often did they occur? _____
_____

RECOMMENDATIONS

1. What are your recommendations? _____
_____

USAGE ANALYSIS
(for purchasing use only)

1. Copies per month (last 6-month period)

   Month 1 _____   Month 2 _____   Month 3 _____
   Month 4 _____   Month 5 _____   Month 6 _____
   Average _____   Peak _____
2. Equipment service requirements (breakdowns requiring out-of-plant services)
   Month 1 _____   Month 2 _____   Month 3 _____
   Month 4 _____   Month 5 _____   Month 6 _____
           Average _____   Peak _____
3. Copy cost (per copy produced)
   Month 1 _____   Month 2 _____   Month 3 _____
   Month 4 _____   Month 5 _____   Month 6 _____
           Average _____
4. Service cost (per month)
   Month 1 _____   Month 2 _____   Month 3 _____
   Month 4 _____   Month 5 _____   Month 6 _____
           Average _____

5. Estimated out-of-service time
    Average _____
    Maximum time any machine _____
6. Additional cost (per copy)
    Paper _____
    Toner _____
    Other (specify) _____

EXAMPLE 2

**TYPICAL LETTER-TYPE REQUEST FOR
QUOTATION**

                                                              Date

Company Name
Address
City, State
Subject: Request for Quotation on Reproduction Services
Dear Sir or Madam:

   XYZ Corporation is planning to reorganize and redefine the overall corporate reproduction requirements. Attached are statistics as to number, make, model, location, use,
and various other information on the copying machines located at the various divisions.
As would be expected, since the statistics were compiled, there have been and will continue to be some changes. Using these statistics, however, please quote as follows, based
on rental or lease only at a fixed price per copy.

   A bidders' conference will be held at _____ on _____
_____. Please submit your questions by letter or telephone 2 days prior to the
conference dates. All questions from all bidders will be answered during the conference,
and written minutes of the conference will be forwarded to attendees.

   The following rules should be followed in preparing your quotation:

1. Your quotation must be on the basis of the supplier furnishing all machines, supplies,
   including paper, toner, and all other required supplies, and all necessary maintenance,
   including parts and labor.

1*a.* Complete the following schedule:

Based on approx. total volume of:		In each quantity category in which you choose to quote, show:		Avg. no. of copies per machine	Fixed price per copy
Annual	Monthly	No. of machines	Model no.		

Propose a formula which can be used to establish a price between the annual amounts, e.g., 5 to 10 million copies.

1*b*. With each quantity of machines quoted on in column 3 above, please attach a separate list of machines presently installed at the various divisions which you are proposing to replace under the following headings:

Current model no.		Replaces present machine at:	
	Location	Model no.	Monthly volume

2. It is our desire to conclude an agreement with one concern only. However, the resulting contract cannot be completely exclusive, as XYZ must be free to procure equipment from other suppliers at our option; but XYZ will agree that any machines installed under this agreement will be retained for a minimum period of 12 months, after which time any such machines may be returned upon written 30-day notice.

3. Your quotation should be on the basis of a contract for each of the following periods:
   a.   12 months   *b.*   18 months   *c.*   24 months

4. Include in the quotation provisions that will permit the addition of new and improved models as they are developed and become available, if Buyer so desires.

5. Recommend disposition for machines of your manufacture which XYZ already owns or in which XYZ has a lease-purchase interest.

6. Recommend disposition for all other brands of XYZ-owned and lease-purchase machines.

7. XYZ prefers not more than 30 days' inventory of any paper, toner, or other supplies.
   a. If any item of supply must be stocked in larger amounts, define the item and the proposed stocking period and/or amount.
   b. Explain your emergency supply capability. In other words, how quickly can you deliver emergency requirements at any of our locations?
   c. Assume that any unused supplies, as the result of machines becoming obsolete or for any other reason, remain the property of the supplier.
   d. Define sizes and amounts per package and per carton.
   e. Where supply items, if any, have limited shelf life, so indicate in your quotation.
   f. Where supply items are affected by temperature, humidity, or any other environmental conditions, so define.

8. The following clause or similar wording must be included in your quotation:
   a. "It is agreed by the seller to fully protect, hold harmless, and indemnify the Buyer and stand all expense or loss including counsel fees from any and all suits of law or in equity, and from all damages, claims, and demands for actual or alleged infringement on any United States or foreign patent, trademark, or copyright."
   b. "In addition to all other warranties expressed or implied in law, the seller warrants that the items delivered hereunder will conform to all applicable specifications, drawings, samples, symbols, or other descriptions furnished by buyer, and will be of good material and workmanship and free of defects. In case any such item shall be defective or otherwise not in conformity herewith, seller shall at buyer's option and in addition to all other remedies of buyer, either credit buyer for any such nonconformity or defects, or, at seller's expense replace, repair, or correct any such article."

   c. "Seller shall maintain workers' compensation, comprehensive general liability, and comprehensive automobile liability insurance covering seller's employees who provide maintenance or other service in buyer's facilities. Seller shall carry fire, windstorm, and extended coverage insurance, including vandalism and malicious mischief (broad form) on equipment and machines leased. Certificates of insurance with limits acceptable to buyer must be furnished."

The following information is required for evaluation of your quotation:

1. Service capability:
     a. List locations of your service facilities in relation to our various divisions and subsidiaries.
     b. What is your guaranteed maximum down time at any one time a machine is out of service for any reason?
     c. What is the maximum number of times per month (or other period) a machine must be out of service before it will be replaced with a new machine?
     d. What amount of training will be required for XYZ employees on each of the models of equipment you are proposing?
     e. How much maintenance will be required by XYZ operators on each of the models of equipment you are proposing? (Present experience data.)
     f. Outline your proposed preventive maintenance program.
     g. Your proposal should state that any service necessary during normal working hours to maintain your equipment in good working condition will be supplied and without additional charge to buyer.
2. We will require the supplier to immediately furnish additional machines as they are made necessary by our changing requirements. Please submit your proposed method of handling increases and reductions in number of machines and changes in models.
3. Indicate maximum period of time for completion of installations proposed in your quotation.

Billing must be rendered to each division covering that particular division's total requirements.
     a. By location, showing number of copies and cost
     b. By machines, showing number of copies
     c. List any other billing requirements you may desire

Any local, state, or federal taxes will be the obligation of the supplier. XYZ shall have the option to renew for one additional year at the same prices and conditions. Upon award, any existing leases, rentals, etc., with the successful bidder will be immediately converted to the new quoted prices and other conditions.

   Your quotation is to be delivered to this office in a sealed envelope on _____ _____. Please indicate the name of your account manager and the individual authorized to execute this agreement. The proposal should be valid for 90 days.

   We will consider alternate proposals offering cost economies; however, these proposals must be in addition to your quotation as outlined in this request. Contact _____ _____, Extension _____, or the undersigned if you have any questions or desire any further information.

Very truly yours,

_____

Purchasing Manager

EXAMPLE 3

TYPICAL CONSULTING AND / OR INDEPENDENT
SERVICE AGREEMENT

Agreement No. _____

The ABC Company, a corporation (hereinafter called company), does hereby retain
_____ (hereinafter called contractor) whose
business address is _____ to furnish cer-
tain consulting services upon the following terms and conditions:

I. DESCRIPTION AND LIMITATIONS OF SERVICE AGREEMENT

A. Contractor shall furnish the services described in schedule A to this agreement at the time and place designated by schedule A. Except as listed in
schedule B of this agreement, the consultant will not subcontract or otherwise engage subcontractors to perform the work herein without prior written
approval of the company.

B. The company will provide such working space, equipment, furniture, and
utilities as may be required for performance of said services by the contractor
while on the company premises. Unusual equipment shall be the responsibility of the contractor unless specified in this agreement as company-fur-
nished.

II. PERIOD OF SERVICE AND TERMINATION

A. The period of service hereunder shall be from _____
through _____.

B. Either the company or the contractor may terminate this agreement at any
time by giving the other party written notice of such action at least _____
_____ days prior to the date of termination.

III. COMPENSATION

A. Company will pay fees to contractor for services performed hereunder on the
following basis (specify daily rate, travel expenses, and maximum which will
not be exceeded): _____
_____.

B. The contractor will be compensated for additional work not specified in the
agreement, and approved at a later date, on the following basis: _____
_____.

C. Payment will be made upon submission of invoices by contractor showing
the agreement number and setting forth appropriate charges. The invoice
must show the contractor's taxpayer identification number (social security
number or employer identification number) in accordance with requirements
of the Internal Revenue Service.

D. Final payment will be made after the final report has been delivered and
accepted by the company. An amount of _____% of the monies due the
contractor will be withheld pending final approval of the report.

IV. TAXES

The compensation stated herein includes all applicable taxes and will not be
changed hereafter as the result of contractor's failure to include any applicable
tax, or as the result of any change in the contractor's tax liabilities.

V. REPORTING

In performing the services defined herein, contractor shall report to _____

VI. PATENTS

Whenever any invention or discovery is made or conceived by contractor in the course of or in connection with this agreement, contractor shall furnish the company with complete information with respect thereto and the company shall have the sole power to determine whether and where a patent application shall be filed and to determine the disposition of title to and all rights under any application or patent that may result. Contractor will, at company's expense, execute all documents and do all things necessary or proper with respect to such patent application.

VII. EXAMINATION OF RECORDS

The company shall have access to and the right to examine any directly pertinent books, documents, papers, and records of contractor involving transactions related to this agreement until the expiration of three years after final payment hereunder.

VIII. CONFLICT OF INTEREST

A. Contractor will not hire any employee of the company to perform any service covered by the agreement.

B. Contractor affirms that to the best of his knowledge there exists no actual or potential conflict between contractor's family, business, or financial interest and his services under this agreement, and in the event of change in either his private interest or service under this agreement, he will raise with the company any question regarding possible conflict of interest which may arise as a result of such change.

The ABC Company

By: _____

_____

Purchasing Manager

Date: _____

(Notary Seal and Signature)

_____

Signature of Consultant
Name and Address of Consultant
(Please print or type)

_____
_____
_____

EXAMPLE 4

**TYPICAL TERMS AND CONDITIONS FOR
SERVICE AGREEMENT**

ARTICLE I. The services covered by this order shall be furnished by seller subject to all the terms and conditions set forth in this order, including the following, which seller, in accepting this order, agrees to be bound by and to comply with in all particulars, and no other terms or conditions shall be binding upon the parties unless hereafter accepted by them in writing. Written acceptance or the performance of all or any portion of the services covered by this order shall constitute unqualified acceptance of all its terms and conditions. The terms of any proposal referred to in this order are included and made a part of the order only to the extent of specifying the nature of services ordered, the price therefor, and the performance thereof, and then only to the extent that such terms are consistent with the terms and conditions of this order.

ARTICLE II.—INSPECTION. The services, materials, and supplies furnished shall be exactly as specified in this order, free from all defects in seller's performance, design, workmanship, and materials, and except as otherwise provided in this order, shall be subject to inspection and test by buyer at all times and places. If, prior to final acceptance, any services and any materials and supplies furnished therewith are found to be incomplete, or not as specified, buyer may reject them, require seller to correct them without charge, or require delivery of such materials, supplies, or services at a reduction in price which is equitable under the circumstances. If seller is unable or refuses to correct such items within a time deemed reasonable by buyer, buyer may terminate the order in whole or in part. Seller shall bear all risks as to rejected services and, in addition to any costs for which seller may become liable to buyer under other provisions of this order, shall reimburse buyer for all transportation costs, other related costs incurred, or payments to seller in accordance with the terms of this order for unaccepted services and materials and supplies incidental thereto. Notwithstanding final acceptance and payment, seller shall be liable for latent defects, fraud, or such gross mistakes as amount to fraud.

ARTICLE III.—CHANGES. Buyer may make changes within the general scope of this order by giving notice to seller and subsequently confirming such changes in writing. If such changes affect the cost of or the time required for performance of this order, an equitable adjustment in the price or delivery or both shall be made. No change by seller shall be recognized without written approval of buyer. Any claim of seller for an adjustment under this article must be made in writing within thirty (30) days from the date of receipt by seller of notification of such change unless buyer waives this condition. Nothing in this article shall excuse seller from proceeding with performance of the order as changed hereunder.

ARTICLE IV.—TERMINATION.

A. Buyer may, by written notice stating the extent and effective date, cancel and/or terminate this order for convenience in whole or in part, at any time. Buyer shall pay seller as full compensation for performance until such termination: (1) the unit or pro rata order price for the performed and accepted portion; (2) a reasonable amount, not otherwise recoverable from other sources by seller as approved by buyer, with respect to the unperformed or unaccepted portion of this order; provided compensation hereunder shall in no event exceed the total order price.

B. Buyer may by written notice terminate this order for seller's default, in whole or in part, at any time, if seller refuses or fails to comply with the provisions of this order, or so fails to make progress as to endanger performance and does not cure such failure after written notice within a reasonable period of time, or fails to perform the services within the time specified or any written extension thereof. In such event, buyer may purchase or otherwise secure services and, except as otherwise provided herein, seller shall be liable to buyer for any excess costs occasioned buyer thereby.

If, after notice of termination for default, buyer determines that the seller was not in default or that the failure to perform this order is due to causes beyond the control and without the fault or negligence of seller (including, but not restricted to, acts of God or of the public enemy, acts of buyer, acts of government, fires, floods, epidemics, quarantine restrictions, strikes, freight embargoes, unusually severe weather, and delays of a subcontractor or supplier due to such causes and without the fault or negligence of the subcontractor or supplier), termination shall be deemed for the convenience of buyer, unless buyer shall determine that the services covered by this order were obtainable from other sources in sufficient time to meet the required performance schedule.

C. If buyer determines that seller has been delayed in the work because of causes beyond the control and without the fault or negligence of seller, buyer may extend the time for completion of the work called for by this order, when promptly applied for in writing by seller; and if such delay is due to failure of buyer, not caused or contributed to by seller, to perform services in accordance with the terms of the order, the time and price of the order shall be subject to change under the changes article. Sole remedy of seller in event of delay by failure of buyer to perform shall, however, be limited to any money actually and necessarily expended in the work during the period of delay, solely by reason of the delay. No allowance will be made for anticipated profits.

D. The rights and remedies of buyer provided in this article shall not be exclusive and are in addition to any other rights and remedies provided by law or under this order.

E. As used in this article, the word *seller* includes seller and his subsuppliers at any tier.

ARTICLE V.—LIABILITY FOR BUYER-FURNISHED PROPERTY. Seller assumes complete liability for any tooling, articles, or material furnished by buyer to seller in connection with this order and seller agrees to pay for all such tooling, articles, or material spoiled by it or not otherwise accounted for to buyer's satisfaction. The furnishing to seller of any tooling, articles, or material in connection with this order shall not, unless otherwise expressly provided, be construed to vest title thereto in seller.

ARTICLE VI.—PAYMENT. Seller shall be paid upon submission of acceptable invoices for services rendered and accepted.

ARTICLE VII.—CHARACTER OF SERVICES. Seller, as an independent contractor, shall furnish all equipment, personnel, and material sufficient to provide the services specified expeditiously and efficiently during as many hours per shift and shifts per week and at such locations as buyer may so require and designate.

ARTICLE VIII.—PATENT INDEMNITY. Seller agrees to indemnify buyer, his officers, agents, servants, and employees against liability of any kind (including costs and expenses incurred) for the use of any invention or discovery and for the infringement of any letters patent (not including liability arising pursuant to Section 183, U.S. Code, Title 35 (1952) prior to issuance of letters patent) occurring in the performance of this order or arising by reason of the use of, disposal by, or for the account of buyer of items manufactured or supplied under this order.

ARTICLE IX.—SELLER'S LIABILITY AND
INSURANCE REQUIREMENTS.

A. *General Liability.* Buyer shall not be liable or responsible for any accident, loss, assault, battery, defamation, false arrest, false imprisonment, invasion of privacy, intentional or negligent infliction of emotional distress, injury (including death), or damages happening or accruing during the term of the performance of the work to persons and/or property, and the seller shall fully indemnify and protect buyer from and against the same. In addition to the liability imposed by law on the seller for damage or injury (including death) to persons or property by reason of negligence of the seller or his agents, which liability is not impaired or otherwise affected hereby, the seller hereby assumes liability for and agrees to save buyer harmless and indemnify him for every expense, liability, or payment by reason of any damage or injury (including death) to persons or property suffered or claimed to have been suffered through any act or omission of the seller or any of his subcontractors or anyone directly or indirectly employed by either of them or from the conditions of the premises or any part of the premises while in control of the seller or any of his subcontractors or anyone directly or indirectly employed by either of them or arising in any way from the work called for by this order.

B. *Premiums.* Premiums on all insurance policies shall be paid by the seller and shall be deemed included in his service agreement unless otherwise specified.

C. *Insurance Requirements.* Seller or contractor shall furnish to the buyer a Certificate of Insurance as specified below:

1. Comprehensive automobile liability:
   Bodily injury, $250,000–$500,000
   Property damage, $100,000
2. Comprehensive general liability, with products liability endorsement, $250,000–$500,000
   Property damage, $100,000
3. Workers' compensation and employer's liability insurance in form and amount covering seller's full liability under the Workmen's Compensation Insurance and Safety Act of the State of _____ as amended from time to time. Seller shall require all subcontractors to take out and maintain similar policies of compensation insurance.

D. *Notice of Cancellation or Modification.* Certificate of insurance will require that the seller's insurance carrier shall provide the buyer in writing thirty (30) days prior to the effective date of the cancellation of or change in any insurance provided pursuant to this order.

E. Seller agrees to be responsible for any damage caused to buyer's property including damage caused by other contractors or subcontractors working under control of buyer and to promptly repair any such damage at the seller's own cost.

ARTICLE X.—ASSIGNMENT. This order is assignable by buyer. Except as to any payment due hereunder, this order is not assignable by seller without written approval of buyer. In case such consent is given, it shall not relieve seller from any of the obligations of this agreement.

ARTICLE XI.—AFFIRMATIVE ACTION. Seller agrees to adhere to the principles set forth in executive orders 11246, 11375, and 11598, and to undertake specifically: to maintain employment policies and practices that affirmatively promote equality of opportunity for minority-group persons and women; to take affirmative steps to hire and promote women and minority-group persons at all job levels and in all aspects of employment; with outside recruiting services and the minority community at large; to provide the government on request a breakdown of his labor force by ethnic group, sex, and job category; and to discuss with buyer his policies and practices relating to his affirmative action program.

ARTICLE XII.—WORK ON BUYER'S PREMISES. If seller's work under this order involves performance by seller at buyer's sites or facilities, the following provisions shall apply:

A. *Liens.* Seller agrees to:

1. Indemnify and hold harmless buyer from all claims, demands, causes of action or suits, of whatever nature, arising out of the services, labor, and materials furnished by seller or his subcontractors under this order, and from all laborers', material specialists', and mechanics' liens upon the real property upon which the work is located or any other property of the buyer;
2. Promptly notify buyer, in writing, of any such claims, demands, causes of action, or suits brought to his attention. Seller shall forward with such notification copies of all pertinent papers received by seller with respect to any such claims, demands, causes of action, or suits and, at the request of buyer, shall do all things

and execute and deliver all appropriate documents and assignments in favor of buyer of all seller's rights and claims growing out of such asserted claims as will enable buyer to protect his interest by litigation or otherwise.

The final payment shall not be made until seller, if required, shall deliver to buyer a complete release of all liens arising out of this order, or receipts in full in lieu thereof, as buyer may require, and if required in either case, an affidavit that as far as he has knowledge or information, the receipts include all the labor and materials for which a lien could be filed; but seller may, if any subcontractor refuses to furnish a release or receipt in full, furnish a bond satisfactory to buyer to indemnify him against any claim by lien or otherwise. If any lien or claim remains unsatisfied after all payments are made, seller shall refund to buyer all monies that the latter may be compelled to pay in discharging such lien or claim, including all costs and reasonable attorneys' fees.

B. *Cleaning Up.* Seller shall at all times keep buyer's premises where the work is performed and adjoining premises free from accumulations of waste material or rubbish caused by his employees or work of any of his subcontractors, and at the completion of the work, he shall remove all rubbish from and about the building and all his subcontractor's tools, scaffolding, and surplus materials, and shall leave the work "broom clean" or its equivalent, unless more exactly specified. In case of dispute between seller and his subcontractors employed on or about the structure or structures upon which the work is to be done, as herein provided, as to responsibility for the removal of the rubbish, or in case the same be not promptly removed as herein required, buyer may remove the rubbish and charge the cost to the seller.

C. *Employees.* Seller shall not employ on the work any unfit person or anyone not skilled in the work assigned to him, and shall devote only his best-qualified personnel to work on this order. Should buyer deem anyone employed on the work incompetent or unfit for his duties and so inform seller, seller shall immediately remove such person from work under this order and he shall not again, without written permission of buyer, be assigned to work under this order.

It is understood that if employees of buyer shall perform any acts for the purpose of discharging the responsibility undertaken by the seller in this Article XII, whether requested to perform such acts by the seller or not, such employees of buyer while performing such acts shall be considered the agents and servants of the seller subject to the exclusive control of the seller.

D. *Safety, Health, and Fire Protection.* Seller shall take all reasonable precautions in the performance of the work under this order to protect the health and safety of employees and members of the public and to minimize danger from all hazards to life and property, and shall comply with all health, safety, and fire protection regulations and requirements (including reporting requirements) of buyer. In the event that seller fails to comply with said regulations or requirements of buyer, buyer may, without prejudice to any other legal or contractual rights of buyer, issue an order stopping all or any part of the work; thereafter a start order for resumption of work may be issued at the discretion of the buyer. Seller shall make no claim for extension of time or for compensation or damages by reason of or in connection with such work stoppage.

The safety of all persons employed by seller and its subcontractors on buyer's premises, or any other person who enters upon buyer's premises for reasons relating to this order, shall be the sole responsibility of seller. Seller shall at all times maintain good order among its employees and shall not employ on the work any unfit person or anyone not skilled in the work assigned to him. Seller shall confine its employees and other persons who come onto buyer's premises at seller's request or for reasons relating to this order and its equipment to that portion of buyer's premises where the work under this order is to be performed or to roads leading to and from such work sites and to any other area which buyer may permit seller to use.

To the extent compliance is required, seller shall comply with all buyer's safety rules and regulations when on buyer's premises.

ARTICLE XIII.—PERMITS. Seller agrees to procure all necessary permits or licenses and abide by all applicable laws, regulations, and ordinances of the United States and of the state, territory, and political subdivision in which the work under this order is performed. Seller shall be liable for all damages and shall indemnify and save buyer harmless from and against all damages and liability which may arise out of the failure of the seller to secure and pay for any such licenses or permits or to comply fully with any and all applicable laws, ordinances, and regulations.

ARTICLE XIV.—COOPERATION. Seller and its subcontractors, if any, shall cooperate with buyer and other vendors and contractors on the premises and shall so carry on their work that other cooperating vendors and contractors shall not be hindered, delayed, or interfered with in the progress of their work, and so that all of such work shall be a finished and complete job of its kind.

ARTICLE XV.—WAIVER OF DEFAULT. Any failure by buyer at any time, or from time to time, to enforce or require the strict keeping and performance by seller of any of the terms or conditions of this order shall not constitute a waiver by buyer of a breach of any such terms or conditions and shall not affect or impair such terms or conditions in any way, or the right of buyer at any time to avail himself of such remedies as he may have for any such breach or breaches of such terms or conditions.

ARTICLE XVI.—TAXES. Seller shall pay all contributions, taxes, and premiums payable under federal, state, and local laws measured upon the payroll of employees engaged in the performance of work under this order, and all sales, use, excise, transportation, privilege, occupational, and other taxes applicable to materials and supplies furnished or work performed hereunder and shall save buyer harmless from liability for any such contributions, and taxes.

ARTICLE XVII.—OTHER APPLICABLE LAWS. Any provisions required to be included in a contract of this type by any applicable and valid federal, state, or local law, ordinance, rule, or regulations shall be deemed to be incorporated herein.

NOTE: For further information on subjects covered in this section see the list of references in Section 30.

Section **18**

Purchasing Construction

EDITOR

Kenneth W. Hartwell, C.P.M *Associate and Technical Procurement Engineer, Overseas Advisory Associates, Inc., Detroit Michigan; retired Director of Purchasing, The Detroit Edison Company*

Contracting for construction services requires a double extension of the normal or classical purchasing effort associated with buying goods. Purchasing's birth and development came about in order to satisfy the procurement needs of the producing, manufacturing, or maintenance arms of industries. Purchasing slowly rose from performing the clerical elements of purchasing—through 50 years of development and recognition in the expertise of specifying, soliciting quotations, evaluating offers, making awards, and writing purchase orders—finally to the position of performing professional, scientific buying of the organization's needs of goods.

This has been no natural development or evolution. It has been fraught with most difficult acceptance and growing pains. It was destined to succeed, though, because if a group of buying specialists once sets about to apply its natural and specialized talents and attributes to the art of buying, it is bound to succeed. These specialists, little by little, were given freedom to be innovative, imaginative, and creative about the complex business of buying. They showed their managements that they possessed human characteristics, inherent in successful buying, that could spell added profits to the organization if those who had been doing the buying for years would be willing to exercise their own expertise in engineering, producing, or manufacturing and leave the buying to those possessing these special skills.

It was proved that each dollar saved by purchasing and added to profit was equivalent to the profit from over $4 of increased sales and production.

Now that purchasing has performed so creditably in purchasing goods, there is another field of procurement that presents opportunities for capable, alert purchasing people who want to help those already involved in the procurement of services. Of all the services to be contracted for, that of construction represents the greatest dollar value and opportunity to contribute to the cost-effective, high-quality plant maintenance and expansion needed to meet the organization's schedule. The buyer attributes, the purchasing organization, and effective procurement behavior can readily be applied to buying construction. There are differences that will become obvious as this subject is discussed, but also there are significant similarities. The differences are many and make up the content of this discussion. As an introduction and in broad terms the unique features of construction purchasing are as follows.

- Contractors are gamblers or risk takers in a complex world, trying to win against the odds of adverse weather, undefined or unanticipated physical obstructions, work jurisdictional disagreements, motivations of labor and skilled workers that are obscured by job physical size and complexity, availability of competent workers and supervision, varying levels of drawing and specification quality, and relation of supervisory and project managers of the contractor and owner, etc.
- The communication of the technical requirements through drawings, specifications, and details is extensive and under continual revision.
- The business conditions are extensively described in voluminous general and special conditions and are subject to interpretation.
- The financial terms for payment are completely different from those common in buying goods.
- The terms of payment, including retention to assure performance.
- The warranty provisions.
- The quality sought, which represents the integrity of the work being performed, is not easily described and inspected.
- The contract scope or work quantity of the project changes during the construction.

ROLES OF THE PARTIES

The owner can choose to perform many of the functions of constructing a new facility with his own personnel, or he can contract with others for all the various functions.

The principal elements in the typical construction project are:

- Owner, who establishes the project need and furnishes the funds
- Engineer, architect, designer, and drafter
- Procurement of equipment, materials, and supplies
- Construction management
- General contractorship
- Contractor or specialty contractor
- Subcontractor

The responsibilities, obligations, authorities, and limitations of each of the above is defined in the following paragraphs. It is important to realize that some of these can be combined, and some may not exist in the specific project. The specific situation often dictates just what approach or combination of functions is most suitable. The owner's in-house capabilities, the allowable time to perform the project, the level of uniqueness and technical complexity of the project, and the proximity of the project to the owner's home offices will all have an impact on the decision of just how best to organize the construction contracting, and thus what procurement will be required. Purchasing should be in on the analysis and selection of the best manner to perform the construction.

Owner: Establishing the Need and Furnishing Funds

The analysis of means to carry out the project should begin with a clearly conceived and expressed description of the project, just what need the completed construction will meet and the urgency of the completion date. Monetary considerations may limit or prescribe what can be financed and when. The owner has to be able to furnish all the financing. Where the money comes from—and at what cost—varies with the type of business the owner is in and the current and subsequent credit rating. The financial situation may limit the amount of contractor assistance that can be hired and may establish what functions of the construction will be done in house by owner employees.

The owner-management team, including purchasing, analyzes the following functions to be performed and settles on just who will be hired. This decision sets the pace for specification writing, types of procurement that purchasing will be called upon to accomplish, and the amount of construction management that will be performed by the owner. There is no one way to organize and buy the performance of constructing a project. All the variables must be considered to make the best choice.

Engineer, Architect, Designer, and Drafter(s)

Some qualified, available, and licensed technical staff must take the owner-defined need and put it into working technical specifications, standards, and drawings that, when followed by the constructor, will be what the owner defined as needed. This involves three distinct levels of technical input:

- Conceptual engineering and architecture
- Design engineering and architecture
- Drafting

These segments of effort can each be contracted for or done by in-house employees. It is most common to have all this done by a single contractor called an *architect and engineer* (AE). However, many owners have technical personnel, and they perform the conceptual engineering and architecture with their own personnel and hire only the design engineering–architecture and drafting. If purchasing is going to help management decide what services to hire, then it must be determined just what each of these subfunctions is.

Conceptual Engineering and Architecture   This is the setting forth of what all the technical elements of the project will be, in general but technically sound terms. It defines desired project end results, including capacities, output, appearance, technical limitations, environments, limits, hazards, geographic and topographic conditions, and size parameters that must be met by the design architects and engineers.

Design Engineering and Architecture   This is the effort of interpreting and presenting on drawings the conceptual engineering and architecture in terms of the most modern, technically enlightened, and economic engineering and architecture. The disciplines and drawings involved are usually: civil; structural; mechanical; heating, ventilating, and air conditioning (HVAC); electrical; and safety engineering; and architectural.

Drafting   This is the final pictorial presentation on drawings of the details of all the design engineering and architecture. It includes the checking and presenting of all dimensions, lists of materials, and standards and technical specifications required.

Procurement of Project Equipment, Materials, and Supplies

If the project timing will permit an orderly adoption of sound construction buying methods, it may be to the owner's advantage to have the various contractors and subcontractors purchase the goods involved in their segment of the work. Several contractors can make continuing contracts and develop business relations with their ongoing suppliers of lumber, reinforcing bar, cement, scaffolding, and all materials used in their work. The electrical, mechanical, plumbing, mason, HVAC, roofing, insulating contractors, etc., may all be able to furnish their materials at reasonable prices and on time, since they have their regular suppliers.

There is strong argument, however, for the owner to do the buying. This is especially true if the in-house purchasing staff is adequately staffed with buyers experienced in buying the types of machinery, material, and supplies involved in the project. If the organization is large enough to be continually in the market for the items involved, then the buyers may be able to buy as economically as the contractors. If this condition prevails, then the total project cost may be reduced because the owner would save the 15 to 30 percent markup a contractor puts on all goods he furnishes to a project. A project that includes a great amount of sophisticated or technically complex mechanical and electrical equipment may have as much as 50 to 55 percent of the total project cost made up of equipment, material, and supplies. A 21 percent markup of such a big proportion of the project cost would be appreciable. This is not all profit for the contractors. It has to cover the contractor's costs of writing specifications, sourcing, purchasing, and financing until the owner is invoiced and pays.

Combined contractor and owner purchasing can be very workable, and is often dictated by the overall timing and scheduling of the project. If the project will materially assist the owner to meet production and sales needs and to produce more efficiently, then the earliest possible completion date is mandatory. For this type of situation and others, the entire construction may be done in a more orderly fashion if the owner buys the major installed equipment, machinery, and plant. These, the longest-lead-time items, can be committed and in the supplier's schedule long before all the steps of contracting for the construction can be accomplished. The balance of installed materials, equipment, and fittings and all construction materials can be assigned to the contractors to purchase.

Construction Management

A new function in the chain of construction activities, *construction management,* consists of a construction-capable group managing the construction project. Members of the group do not perform any of the construction, nor do they supervise laborers, artisans, or bosses. They oversee each of the contractor entities that the owner or general contractor has employed. The construction manager's staff is made up of personnel experienced in:

Management (all types including, management by objectives)
Scheduling (including CPM[1] and PERT[2])
Labor relations and labor jurisdiction
Engineering monitoring of plans and drawings
Purchasing and expediting
Personnel management (including hiring, firing, and motivating)
Accounting: supervision of all types of cost records for proper classification, posting, and contractor invoicing, in accordance with the construction contract
Performance measurement

Proponents of construction management point out that it puts a management team in a position to oversee the specialist contractors, even the general contractor. They believe that a general contractor wears blinders when it comes to recognizing the need for improving performance.

Of course, this additional layer of management costs the project an additional 1 to 3 percent of the total project cost, but it may be a real bargain if everyone's performance is improved.

For years general contractors have performed the construction management function along with their general contractorship. This can and often does still happen, but it can be most difficult for a general contracting company to also be its own construction manager—the company is often too wrapped up being a general to discern any mismanagement.

The construction management contractor concept may or may not be *the* way for an owner to go. There are three other means of gaining the advantages that impartial, objective management of construction can accomplish. First, the owner's staff and organization may do it; second, the general contractor may be willing to organize and designate a construction management team that reports to a different part of the contractor's organization than does the physical construction organization; third, the engineering, architecture, and design and drafting contractor may also advocate and carry out construction management.

There is no one best means, but there should be strong, effective construction

---

[1]*Critical path method of planning:* the most suitable approach to performing the project, scheduling and staffing, and monitoring.
[2]*Project Evaluation and Review Technique:* similar to CPM, particularly in shceduling first-of-a-kind project.

management. Who does it should be decided before any solicitation for the general contractor is started. The general contractors believe that the construction management concept will have an impact on them and they want to know, before bidding, if it is being considered.

General Contractor

This is the contractor who customarily accepts the responsibility and obligation to perform all the construction management and administration but also has the capability to properly perform all aspects of the actual construction work not performed by specialty contractors or subcontractors.

Administering and Managing Construction Duties

1. *Master construction schedule:* preparation using construction scheduling and management tools such as CPM or PERT

2. *Requisitioning and purchasing:* including expediting of all equipment, materials, and supplies not furnished by the owner, and obtaining required licenses and permits

3. *Staffing:* to provide adequate supervisory, technical, specialist craft leaders, specialist technicians, and laborers in numbers and with the qualifications needed to complete the job on schedule and in keeping with the specifications

4. *Construction equipment availability:* provided from own inventory, renting, leasing, or hiring

5. *Safety and first aid:* provided along with an effectual program

6. *Security:* designed to include gate and roving guards as required by the job

7. *Field accounting:* to be able always to compare contract billings with project expenditures and scheduled job progress

8. *Field construction; offices availability:* provided and operated to house all the specifications, drawings, inspection reports, and offices of the supervisory, general labor supervisors, and field engineers

9. *Site space assignment:* for specialty contractors' and subcontractors' field offices, warehousing, laydown, etc.

10. *Utilities:* including potable water, sanitary provisions, and electric power as coordinated

11. *Gate house:* provided for vehicle and personnel entrance and exit check

12. *Reporting:* of progress compared with schedule to be prepared periodically for the owner

13. *Site clean-up:* instructions and program

Field Force Construction Work of General Contractor

1. *Laying out site:* to be performed from survey data furnished by owners

2. *Excavation:* including removal of excesses

3. *Filling and grading:* of site to proper elevation and around structures

4. *Site road work:* including building and maintaining

5. *Concrete work:* including forming, reinforcing, rod-bending, and setting, pouring, troweling, and protecting of concrete

6. *Site construction engineering:* as required for site layout, form designs, etc.

7. *Carpentry:* general labor work included

8. *Overall project coordination:* providing general superintendence for administration of all contractors working on the site unless the owner has assigned this responsibility to a construction manager as a separate contract

Contractor or Specialty Contractor

Certain construction work has traditionally been done by contractors who specialize in providing material and technically qualified personnel to install specific types of material. They train the work forces in their specialty if trained personnel are not readily available. If it is desirable for economy in craft employee-hours and for keeping on schedule, they may perform special engineering and graphic drafting of their special work. These contractors' specialties are:

- Electrical
- Mechanical (including piping)
- Plumbing
- Insulation (fire, heating, and cooling)
- Steel erection
- Mason (tile and ceramic flooring)
- Heat exchanger (boiler) erection
- Machinery (turbine) erection
- Instrument or electronic

These companies are referred to as *contractors* or *specialty contractors* because their part of the project represents a significant segment of the work, sometimes even larger in worker-hours than that of the general contractor. In a project that involves setting, installing, and wiring electrical equipment and fixtures, the electrical contract worker-hours could be greater than those of the general contractor. In some instances the owner may agree with the specialty contractors that in addition to their own specialty, they should perform the work of the general contractor. Of course, this could be done; but in deciding, the owner team should perform its appraisal early enough in the master schedule to still permit contracting in the conventional alignment. The study should include evaluating the impact on overall job administration.

Subcontractor

Subcontractors differ from general contractors in that the work they do generally involves less money and is of shorter duration. Subcontractors perform the following types of work:

- Roofing
- Elevator installation
- Window installation
- Cabinetmaking

- Landscaping
- Paving
- Chimney erection

There is no positive demarcation between a specialty contractor and a subcontractor except the foregoing comment. The connotation is that a subcontractor is a contractor subordinate to and paid by the general contractor or by one of the other contractors, but in practice the specialist who furnishes a certain segment of the project can be on the job as a result of being employed by the owner just as the general contractor was. Of course, if the general contractor or one of the other contractors employs another contractor to assist in his work, the name subcontractor fits and is more easily understood.

THE CONSTRUCTION PROCUREMENT TEAM

An organization that is ready to assign or is considering assigning construction buying to purchasing probably has a construction, engineering, manufacturing, or production group concerned with new plants and experienced in the team concept of buying construction. It is important that purchasing realize that if it is going to be responsible for construction buying, the construction buying supervisor, administrator, or coordinator must be the leader of a construction procurement team in addition to supervising his construction buyers and staff. The team is made of representatives of the departments most involved with the new facility about to be contracted for. The usual team makeup is: a representative from the construction-oriented arm or group that has the most actual construction experience; a representative of the engineering group that does all the conceptual engineering and the design engineering or monitors an engineering contractor as dictated by each individual type and size of construction; and finally, a member of the department or group for which the new facility is being built.

The construction procurement team for a project should consider the following activities as its responsibilities.

Planning the Procurement

The team will be instrumental in determining what kind of pricing and contract will be the most suitable to satisfy the prevailing conditions and parameters involved in the particular project at hand. (Types of contracts will be treated in detail below.) The entire team must agree on the type of contract to be used because this decision affects all the engineering, specification writing, amounts of subcontracting, and language throughout *the* type of contract about to be solicited.

Establishing Bidders' List

Establishment of the list of bidders through thorough sourcing techniques requires that the various members of the team be especially alert in investigating their interests. The team should try to establish five or six completely acceptable construction companies that have shown a strong interest in being "in on" the quoting. The construction buyer wants all the directly involved departments to be satisfied, if not pleased, with the list of bidders.

Preparation for Quotation Evaluation

The team will usually be the group that analyzes and evaluates the quotations submitted by the bidding contractors. It is most suitable if each member of the team performs that part of the evaluation that matches his own expertise. The type of contract being bid will have a bearing on how the team will divide up the evaluation effort. Purchasing has the responsibility of analyzing all the commercial or business sections of the quotations. Purchasing should have ongoing data available regarding all the customary construction-contractor remuneration considerations. This should include typical markups on direct labor; direct labor burden and material costs; other overhead markup; general and administrative percentage markup; and markup for percentage fee or the range of suitable fixed fees. Some contracts will require purchasing to be prepared to critique direct costs, indirect costs, construction engineering costs, construction equipment costs, differentiation between reusable and perishable tools, and billing of laborers, artisans, and supervisors. In addition to its all-important evaluation requirement, purchasing should administer the evaluation, collect all the team specialty evaluations, and make up a draft recommendation to present to management.

TYPES OF CONSTRUCTION CONTRACTS

The buyer-seller relationship and negotiation tactics and philosophies in construction buying vary from those common to industrial purchasing. It is most important for the construction buyer to be sensitive to these differences when considering the wide variety of contracts available and perhaps even new ones yet to be explored. Patterning of the bidding, the bidding itself, and the actual performance of the construction work fall under one of two principal construction disciplines or philosophies: *fixed-price* and *cost-reimbursable and fee*. A listing of the more common types of contracts falling into these two categories, with a brief description of each, follows.

Fixed-Price Types

Fixed-price (hard money) construction and building contracts are highly regarded by owners because their engineering, operating, and purchasing arms appreciate being able to present a fairly complete project cost figure which top management needs to assist it in its request to the board of directors and banking institutions for approval to proceed with the project and the award to the selected contractor. Second, the incentive of the contractor to perform well and protect its quoted price or to even lower costs below the price is great, because all the cost savings go to the contractor. This improved performance is good for the owner as well, because it usually means the project is finished on time. Even with the soundness of this theory, there can be occasions when specialty contractors or subcontractors, hired on a fixed-price basis, "poor boy" the job by using small, selected crews, that are too small to finish the job on schedule.

Lump Sum, Firm (Fixed)   This type of contract specifies a single price commitment for paying for all the work defined in the bid specifications and drawings. These can be of varying degrees of rigidness or tightness, which must be clearly defined and understood by the bidders. A very *tight* lump sum would be aimed at allowing only very extreme change in conditions to grant the contractor any additional moneys to the fixed lump sum. Except for minor field changes, the only cause for changing the original contract sum is changes of scope (deleting entire segments of work not in the bid specifications or drawings or adding new segments). These are bid lump sum by the contractor, and if approved increase the contract sum as an order. An *open* lump sum is used if the buyer and team believe that the engineering and design are only moderately complete and correct, the site conditions present too many unknowns, or there are any other aspects of the job that would cause bidding contractors to guess at unknowns by adding contingencies. In this situation it may be best to make the lump-sum price only for the work actually specified and pictured in the drawings. All alterations from that specific base would be cause for contract or field change orders. *Tight* fixed-lump-sum contracts are particularly applicable for small to medium-size construction and large construction when the engineering design is well advanced before bidding.

Lump Sum   This is the same as the preceding lump sum except that any escalation of costs of labor and materials is paid for by the owner in addition to the contract price. It eliminates the contingency the bidders must put in their prices to cover changing costs over which they have no control.

Unit Price   A contract based on remunerating the contractor on a specific price per unit of work is called a *unit price contract.* Each segment of work which is to carry a separate price must be described in detail so that there is complete understanding of exactly what the unit includes and does not include. The total of all quantities of all the units makes up the entire segment, or the whole of the specific segment, or it can include all worker-hours of labor, construction equipment, tools, supervision, material, overhead, and profit. The contractor's price bid for a unit multiplied by the number of the units is the total remuneration the contractor will receive. This type contract can be good for accomplishing a wide range of construction such as furnishing and placing concrete with forms and reinforcing steel, electrical wiring, piping, excavating, backfilling, etc. Unit prices for construction work can also include an extension of the customary dollars per hour for temporary office help, plant protection services, and engineering services.

Cost-Reimbursable (Cost-Plus a Fee) Contracts

While there are many arguments in favor of fixed-price contracts there are other types of contracts to cover work or projects that do not have the proper elements required to properly protect both the owner and the contractor. The name *cost-reimbursable* is a softening of the often disparaged *cost-plus*-type contract. Management or enterprises and corporations, governmental bodies, and individuals contracting for construction are often adamant in their feelings against cost-plus concepts. This feeling is common because of the many experiences in which, both during the course of the work and upon its conclusion, there was a lack of incentive for the contractor to save on labor, materials, and all elements of costs.

The type of cost-reimbursable contract called *cost-plus a percentage fee* left a scar because the more labor, material, tools, equipment, and supervision billed as costs, the greater fee or profit the contractor would receive even if the costs were the result of poor management or even waste. The U.S. Defense Department used this type of contract extensively during World War II because previously prepared and available designs, specifications, and drawings of the requirements were not in existence—everything being contracted for was new, needed in a rush, and lacking a detailed description. During and immediately after those war years there was gross evidence of waste and mismanagement in material, tools, equipment, and labor that gave the contractor profit as a percentage of those excess costs. There appeared to be no incentive for the contractor to manage capably and intelligently and to reduce costs. The federal government has since ordered all contracting officers (buyers) never to subscribe to a *cost-plus a percentage fee* contract. All government construction contracts must be based on some type of incentive for both the government agency and the contractor.

Unfortunately, all this leads those contracting to discount all types of cost-plus or cost-reimbursable contracts. There are numerous construction project situations in which certain cost-reimbursable contracts are structured exactly right and will be by far the best for both the owner and the contractor. The strong argument for this type of contract is that it does not require the administrative work of keeping track of every drawing and drawing revision and any specification modification required in a lump-sum contract with the attendant bidding and issuing of contract change orders. Most important of all, a properly conceived, bid, written, and administered cost-reimbursable contract offers the possibility of the lowest total cost to the owner. If all goes well within the owner's contracting group, and with the construction contractor's responsibility, the project will cost less than with any other type of contracting. The principal reason for this is that the contractor is not being forced to protectively bid all the contingencies due to possible bad weather, bad labor conditions, unexpected site conditions, late and ambiguous engineering, late equipment deliveries, etc.

Cost-reimbursable and *cost-plus contracts* are very similar, and the names will be used interchangeably in this section. Many contend that it is best to discriminate between them and have *cost-reimbursable* mean that the owner pays all direct costs and a fixed fee which covers all indirect costs, administrative overheads, and profit. *Cost-plus* is considered to mean that the owner pays all (direct and indirect) costs and separate markups for overhead and for fee (profit). The typical cost-reimbursable pricing would be *cost plus 25 percent,* where the 25 percent markup on direct costs covers all indirect costs, overhead, and profit. Typical cost-plus pricing would be *cost plus 10 and 10,* where the first 10 is the percentage markup on direct labor and labor burden, materials, equipment and tools, and the second

10 is 10 percent applied to cost and the first multiplier. This second 10 percent covers administrative overhead and profit. Cost plus 10 and 10 is actually a 21 percent markup, and cost plus 15 and 10 is 26.5 percent, because the second 10% is on top of the first percentage.

The various types of cost-plus or cost-reimbursable contracts are as described below.

Cost-Reimbursable and Fixed Fee   The contractor is reimbursed for all costs, overhead, or administration at a percentage of labor costs, but his fee is a lump-sum fixed amount. The fixed fee is altered only if the specifications and scope of the job are changed from the bid documents. This type of contract is suitable for all types of construction for which there are insufficient engineering and specifications to bid a fixed price but enough to avoid a percentage fee.

Cost-Reimbursable, Incentive Fee   This contract permits the contractor to alter his fee if he is successful in performing the work with lower material costs and fewer labor-hours and thus at lower cost for the owner. A target of total manual labor cost or labor-hours or total material, labor, and overhead is established in the bidding. If the contractor performs for less total cost or labor cost or labor-hours than the target, his fee is increased; if he exceeds the target, the fee is decreased in accordance with a formula. If, for instance, the fee is $100,000 and the target of labor cost to the owner is $5 million, the contractor is to earn $0.10 more in fee for every $1.00 over the target. A floor of 50 percent and a ceiling of 150 percent of the original fee govern. These contracts are suitable for all types of construction in which the percentages of drawing and specifications completed prior to bidding are insufficient to fix a price, yet permit the contractor to arrive at and quote a target.

Cost-Plus, Guaranteed Maximum   The contractor is reimbursed for all costs, including labor, materials, equipment, and tools; general or administration expenses are reimbursed by an overhead percentage markup on all costs and percentage markup for fee according to the bid schedule of costs up to a guaranteed maximum total dollar amount for the scope and specifications of the job bid on. If scope and specifications change during the course of the job, the owner and contractor agree on a new guaranteed maximum; otherwise the original maximum remains fixed. A savings below the maximum accrue to the owner, but all costs and markup that exceed the maximum are subtracted from the contractor's fee. These contracts are appropriate for all types of construction in which a reasonable amount of engineering is performed and scope defined. Some contractors consider this to be unfair, because the owner gets all savings and the contractor still has all the risk of overruns.

Cost-Plus, Upset Maximum   The contractor is reimbursed for *all* costs including labor, material, equipment, and tools; overhead or administration is covered by a percentage markup on all costs and a second markup for fee according to his bid schedule of costs. Each bidder is requested to present three lump-sum figures. The principal figure is called the *target* sum, the second figure the *maximum,* and the third figure the *floor*. Contractors are paid for all their costs and a percentage markup for overhead and markup for profit up to floor (if costs plus overhead and profit are below the floor, there can be an owner-contractor sharing of savings). Additional costs are paid plus a percentage markup for overhead only from floor to target. Costs only are paid from target to maximum; the owner pays nothing above maximum. This contract may be used for any type of construction in which the scope or specification definition is too vague for a guaranteed maximum, but sufficient to avoid a lesser type of incentive contract.

		Contractor Receives	
Dollar Billing Amount	*Costs*	*Overhead*	*Fee*
Below floor—savings, split between owner and contractor	x	x	x
Up to floor	x	x	x
Floor to target	x	x	
Target to maximum	x		
Above maximum—no billing to owner			

Cost-Plus, Percentage Fee   Contractor is reimbursed for all costs plus a percentage on material and labor costs for overhead and administration expenses and an additional percent on cost and overhead for fee. This form of contract is to be used for construction in which work cannot be adequately defined to permit incentive bidding or even a fixed fee, or where the schedule is so tight as to defy prediction of work conditions.

Time and Materials   This specialty type of cost contract is based on the concept that an all-inclusive labor rate is charged for every hour of work performed by personnel. This rate is all-inclusive, covering base pay, insurance, taxes, tools, salaries of supervisors, field and home office expenses, and fee. The *material* of time and material is the actual cost of materials billed at the price paid by the contractor less the trade, quantity, and cash discounts. This contract is often used and is preferable when employing specialty consultants and for small construction jobs.

Characteristics of the Various Types of Contracts

The common types of contracts just described have their advantages and disadvantages, not only to the owner but also to the contractor. The term *incentive,* as used in this section, means an incentive for both the owner and the contractor to get the job completed up to quality and as fast as possible. With few exceptions, the earlier a construction project can be completed, the less it will cost the owner. He can save by reducing the stretch-out costs of labor and rental time on equipment and tools, and of administration, and can also reduce the exorbitant cost of money during construction, which cannot be recovered until the project is complete and the economic gains from the new construction can be realized. The incentive to the contractor is usually in the form of more profit on fixed-price contracts and the award of more projects as a reward for good job performance and speedy completion on both fixed-cost and cost-reimbursable contracts. Figure 18-1 is a chart showing the types of contracts arranged under three headings.

The first is arranged by incentive, where the list runs from the greatest incentive to the least incentive. The lump sum, firm is shown as providing the greatest

Incentive (Greatest to Least)	Lowest Possible Dollars of Cost (Lowest to Highest)	Administrative Load Easiest to Most Difficult	
		Engineered 60–70% at bidding	Engineered 90–100% at bidding
Firm (fixed) lump sum (no escalation permitted)	Cost-plus, incentive fee	Cost-reimbursable, fixed fee	Firm (fixed) lump sum
Lump sum (today's price)	Cost-reimbursable, fixed fee	Unit price	Lump sum
Unit price	Cost-plus, guaranteed max.	Cost-reimbursable, incentive fee	Cost-reimbursable, fixed fee
Cost-plus guaranteed max.	Cost-plus, upset max.	Cost-plus, guaranteed max.	Unit price
Cost-plus, upset max.	Cost-plus, percentage fee	Cost-plus, percentage fee	Cost-plus percentage fee
Cost-reimbursable, incentive fee	Unit price	Cost-plus, upset max.	Cost-plus, upset max.
Cost-reimbursable, fixed fee	Lump sum	Lump sum	Cost-plus, guaranteed max.
Cost-plus, percentage fee	Firm (fixed) lump sum	Firm (fixed) lump-sum	Cost-reimbursable, incentive fee

Fig. 18-1 Common types of contracts arranged according to incentive, lowest cost, and administrative load.

incentive because this dollar amount contains contingencies for all anticipated problem areas that might be experienced during the completion of the job. If the contractor can overcome or circumvent any or all of these problems, he can add that amount to the profit he bid into the bid price. His incentive is maximum.

The second type, lump sum, is similar except that there is no incentive for the contractor to resist labor rate increases or to buy materials early to beat price increases, because the owner is paying the escalation.

The third is unit price, which is, in effect, a series of small lump-sum prices and permits the contractor to profit from every performance gain he can effect by getting more units per hour of work completed.

Cost-plus type contracts vary only as to the amount of incentive for making profit above costs afforded to the contractor. At the very bottom of the list is the cost-plus-percentage-fee type of contract, which was a common type of contract during World War II, when both industry and government contracts required crash schedules. Interestingly enough, U.S. Code No. 2304, Section 2306 (A) prohibits the use of this system on government contracts. In the private sector, this is considered the least desirable method of contracting *if there are any alternatives.*

The contractor's incentive to save on materials and labor is low because the more of both he uses, the greater his take for overhead and profit.

The second column in Fig. 18-1 shows these contracts arranged according to what *could be* the lowest possible dollar expenditure for the owner. It may seem contradictory to have the first column indicate that the greatest to least incentive corresponds to something different from the lowest and highest dollar amounts, respectively, but there is a great difference. The second column is arranged with the possible lowest-cost type of contract at the top and the possible highest-priced type at the bottom of the list. The order is reversed for some of the contracts shown in the first column because in a fixed-price contract the price includes, in addition to the known costs of the job to be performed, provisions to cover the following contingencies:

1. All escalation of labor and materials, equipment rentals, and tools
2. Weather conditions
3. Possible labor contract renewals
4. Jurisdictional disputes between labor crafts
5. Site conditions, including laydown space proximity
6. Work conditions, regarding coffee breaks, lunch period, washup time, etc.
7. Type of union cooperation expected
8. Success of supervisors in gaining performance of their crews

Each contingency adds to the contractor's price. If any do not materialize, the owner bears an unnecessary expense. If a contractor on a cost-reimbursable (cost-plus) incentive fee contract could have all the elements of the job go well—good weather, no strikes, no jurisdictional disputes, an effective superintendent, and a happy crew—the owner could probably have the lowest-cost job possible. Since all these good things do not predictably happen, cost-plus contracts are not the only favored type. Owners often tend toward some type of a contract with a high incentive, or some middle ground like cost-plus incentive fee, in which risk is shared in order to balance the benefits of each type of contract.

The third column of Fig. 18-1 shows contracts arranged from the easiest and least costly for the owner to administer to the most difficult and costly at the bottom of the column. This varies according to the amount of engineering completed, as shown in the two divisions of this column. It is difficult to predict where a given contract will fall in this arrangement, but it is important for the owner to consider this matter when choosing a contract.

Cost-plus, fixed fee is easiest to administer because a minimum of change orders and contract revisions are necessary during the course of a job, since the contract is cost-reimbursable, not based on contract changes, and the fee is fixed, not based on any percentage of cost. Other contracts, such as fixed and plain lump-sum, invariably have numerous changes during the course of a job that must be bid by the contractor and change orders that have to be written and added to the contract. Unit-price contracts are burdened with the administration of gathering units at the close of each work period, each day or week. This usually has to be done by both the contractor and the owner. Payment is based upon a successful agreement on the numbers of units of work performed.

Thus each type of contract can very well be the best type for certain work conditions. The selection depends upon: (1) the labor climate; (2) the amount of engineering design accomplished at bid time; (3) the amount of time available for bidding; (4) the complexity and configuration of the work being bid; (5) the amount of owner involvement that can be put into the administration of the contract, and (6) criticality of schedule.

MATCHING CONTRACT TYPE TO THE CONSTRUCTION PROJECT

The numerous types of construction contracts reflect the great variety of construction projects that are carried out under different conditions. There is no one type of contract that is best. The choice depends on all the elements of the project (see

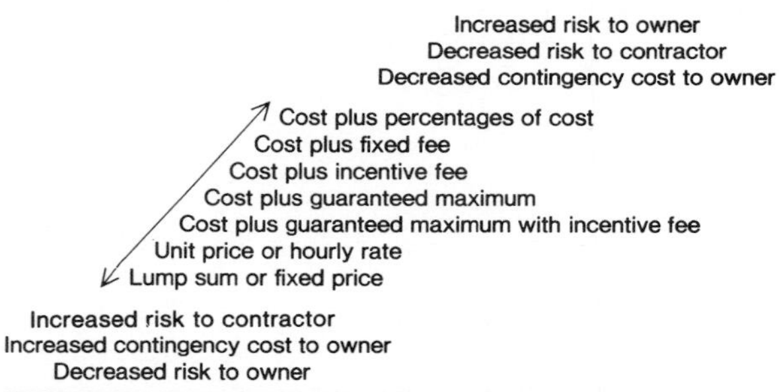

Increased risk to owner
Decreased risk to contractor
Decreased contingency cost to owner

Cost plus percentages of cost
Cost plus fixed fee
Cost plus incentive fee
Cost plus guaranteed maximum
Cost plus guaranteed maximum with incentive fee
Unit price or hourly rate
Lump sum or fixed price

Increased risk to contractor
Increased contingency cost to owner
Decreased risk to owner

Fig. 18-2   Owner and contractor cost risk with different types of contract.

Fig. 18-2). The construction procurement team should list and evaluate all conditions that would call for a specific type of contract. This should be done well before the actual bidding and before or during the very early stages of any engineering specification writing. Many parts of the specifications that will be written by engineering will depend upon the type of contract selected. The very words have to be chosen carefully to relate to the bidding that will be taking place.

An actual incident will demonstrate the importance of this. A clause in the technical specification paragraph dealing with how the thermal insulation on large-size piping was to be finished before painting read, "After completion of the application of the first and second layers of thermal insulation and insulating cement over the joints, a finishing cement is to be applied and the troweling performed so the pipe finish is concentric and smooth." In the general conditions was a clause that read, "Any disagreement as to the acceptable quality of work and level of performance will be settled by the owner's project manager." The solicitation was for a lump-sum type contract, and the contractors read into these two statements a most difficult situation: they visualized having to practically sculpture the troweling, which could be done only by a senior, experienced insulator. During the performance of the work the owner learned that $30,000 had been added to the price by the contractor to cover this contingency. Had it been a cost-reimbursable contract, the contractor would have viewed and bid this entirely differently.

In the prebidding stage the buyer can help the engineers and construction people avoid using expressions in the specifications that would cause the bidders to insert costly contingencies to meet the particular work definition of the specifications. The work conditions under which the contract will be administered are defined under what is termed the general conditions. The technical specifications describe the particular work of the project. It is well to decide on the type of contract to be bid on before either specification is too far along so as to avoid spelling out requirements of the contract in a manner that would jeopardize or compromise the type of contract ultimately to be used.

Of the many important considerations to be weighed when selecting the most suitable type of contract to adopt for the project, some considered as most important are:

1. Have the contract make allowance for the amount of engineering complete at bid time. A project with 90 to 100 percent of the engineering lends itself to fixed-price and fixed-or incentive fee cost-reimbursable if the other job aspects do not conflict.

2. Be sure that the project will be bid and completed on time to meet the owner's desirable, if not mandatory, start-up date. If time is of the essence and the earliest start-up possible is overpowering, then cost-plus with a percentage fee might be the best type of contract.

3. Have the project construction performed under conditions that will assure a very high level of quality that will meet strenuous codes and be trouble-free for years to come. This indicates a cost-plus a fixed fee or cost-reimbursable-upset maximum contract.

4. The administration of the contract should be no more complex and time-consuming than can be satisfactorily accomplished by the owner's forces assigned to the project. Unit price and cost-reimbursable with a fixed fee require less owner bookkeeping and monitoring than other types.

5. Determine whether the project will be broken up into segments with a contract for each or will be kept intact. Some large projects have a *preliminary site work* contract, a *site work with excavation* contract, etc.

6. Decide whether there will be a separate contract for construction management, or whether this will be in the contract being planned.

7. Decide whether the contractor will do all contracting for specialty work over and above the civil engineering work and be general contractor, or whether the owner will do all contracting for electrical, mechanical, insulation, etc.

In addition to appraising such project dictates as the foregoing, there are the variables of the actual construction work that should be carefully considered in selecting the type of contract:

1. Level of uniqueness of the construction
2. Anticipated amount of field (site) irregularities beyond the norm
3. Expectations of a great amount of design and engineering change that will be inflicted on the project by outside dictates
4. Seasons of the year involved and the weather severities likely to prevail
5. Geographic location that would affect labor's travel costs, etc.
6. Amount of owner participation in overseeing, monitoring, inspecting, and patrolling at the site
7. The physical layout of the project—wide area, height of structures, number and distance between separate work centers
8. Amount of involvement of scarce skilled specialty workers

It may appear by now that there are too many considerations to find any one type of contract that would satisfy all the variables. This may be the situation, but having the right type of contract is sufficiently important to be worth considerable study and analysis by the team. Many experienced construction buyers believe that creating *high incentive* for contractor, owner, and all involved in the project is the way to get quality of workmanship, start-up or move-in on time, and a fair and reasonable price. Obviously a fixed-price contract presents great incentive to the contractor—the incentive is to beat the contract price and make more profit. However, even cost-reimbursable with a fixed fee has incentive, because if the contractor can keep costs down, the owner and many who are aware of the project will seek the contractor for future work.

SOURCING FOR ACCEPTABLE CONTRACTORS

Experienced buyers know the methods used and the criteria adopted to source suppliers, so only some aspects of selecting prospective contractors will be dealt with.

It is wise to plan on ending up with five or six contractors on the bidders' list. As in buying goods, three bidders are a minimum that will furnish sufficient competition to let the buyer and his team have sufficient bids to analyze and evaluate. Having only three contractors bid is very risky because any one of them could drop out during the bidding for a variety of reasons not usual with suppliers of goods. Contractors have to be alert to their inability to extend themselves beyond the number of jobs their experienced supervisory staff can handle. Their cash and credit condition may be such that they may be unable to cope with this new project right on top of the new award they just received. Using their own construction equipment may be their "ace in the hole" in bidding this job, but they may have just received another job or had more than normal equipment outages due to need for overhaul, and understandably they may judge your job as undesirable at this time. Because of this somewhat-difficult-to-predict marketplace, it is wise to have five or six completely qualified bidders all anxious to participate in the project.

Including contractors with whom all team members would be completely satisfied is recommended. Search through their capabilities with respect to:

1. Financial condition.

2. Past experience with this particular type of construction under similar conditions.

3. Supervision (by name and résumé) available. A team of about 10 is needed: general superintendent, assistant superintendent and manager, engineer, supervisors for civil engineering work, electrical work, mechanical work, equipment maintenance, accounting and office management, quality assurance, and security and safety supervision.

4. Construction equipment and maintenance availability and reported success.

5. Situation as to labor union affiliation—ability to cope with union or independent. (Certain local pockets and geographic areas have all construction performed with only union members; other areas are open to nonunion workers also.)

6. Does the contractor have a sincere, corporate desire to bid and be awarded the job?

The usual methods of fact gathering should be used. In addition, a team visit to one of the contractor's ongoing, similar jobs would be valuable. Interrogating the owners of a recently completed job can be enlightening. A meeting of the buyer's team with the contractor's home office support personnel is most valuable. There is usually a home office counterpart to every field management person assigned to the project. It is advisable to have a meeting with this person and to learn of the home office support that will be given to the field supervisor in charge of the same discipline. Some contractors, for example, believe that regardless of the limited or great amount of engineering and design presented by the owner's engineer, they want their home office engineering staff to make isometric drawings and specification interpretation for their field staff.

Ask the selected contractors for a letter from their president or a very senior officer to the effect that they know of the project and are very satisfied that all of their staff will turn their best effort to bidding the solicitation, and if awarded the job will perform in an exemplary manner.

BIDDING

When the type of contract has been determined, the specifications have been prepared around the type of contract selected, and the list of construction company bidders fixed, the construction buyer can now put all the bid documents together to solicit quotations from the selected bidders. The bid package usually consists of:

Request for proposal (RFP) or instructions to bidders
General conditions

Special conditions
Technical specifications
Drawings

Request for Proposal (RFP)

This is like a letter of transmittal for all the material to be used in preparing the proposals, but it also defines basic rules to be followed in the quoting:

1. Discussion or recital of what the project really consists of, who the parties involved are, and the construction start-up and completion dates
2. Precise description of what type contract is to be bid
3. Date, time, and place quotations are due
4. Number of copies of the quotations required and if all are to contain prices or only one copy
5. A statement that confidentiality of bids will prevail
6. The premise to be followed is: First bid is the last bid.
7. Sealed bids and a one-time opening after due date
8. Discussion of all the commercial elements that will prevail, such as the payment routine; retention of a percentage of each periodic billing until the project is completed and accepted; advance payment, which can be asked for to assist in mobilizing and equipping the job; material and equipment received ahead of schedule, to be paid for according to some schedule, such as 75 percent; and all invoices to be approved by the owner's site project manager
9. All other advice to bidders not contained in the general or special conditions

General Conditions

This specification is at times referred to as *business provisions,* but is more commonly known as the *general conditions of the contract.* This is a set of behavior guidelines for all parties in the project. It is prepared with great care by the construction buyer, who tries to so structure and define the work conditions that the greatest job compatibility and productivity result. It should be written with great consideration for the contractor's interests, but in each clause or paragraph the owner's best interest is also to be carefully and explicitly protected.

General conditions of projects small in scope, dollars, or duration can be on a single-sheet attachment to the contract form sheet or on the reverse side of the contract form. Having this so standardized precludes having to create these conditions anew for repetitive-type contracts. Since they are used often, they are refined and reprinted from time to time.

General conditions of major construction are usually written for each project. The specification content of the general conditions varies with each project, but there are customary subjects that the following list includes. The list can be expanded or reduced, as the buyer considers most suitable for each specific project:

- Definitions and interpretation
- Contract documents, their precedence and mutual explanatory notes

- Contractor's general responsibilities
- Contract agreement, execution, and governing status
- Duties of the parties and their personnel
- Performance bond
- Site inspection before bidding
- Project management (CPM) schedule to be a project requirement; competent construction management team
- Safety, security, watching, and lighting
- Care of the works
- Insurance of the works: damage to persons and property; indemnity of second party; third-party insurance; insurance against accidents to workers
- Compliance with statutes and regulations
- Patent rights and royalties
- Contractor to keep site clean
- Contractor to hold owner harmless
- Labor relation matters; rules about safety, drugs, disorderliness
- Quality assurance, quality control, and inspection of site work and materials
- Suspension of work by owner
- Uncovering underground cables and marking
- Default of contractor
- Commencement of works
- Possession of site
- Schedule of time and operations delay
- Liquidated damages for delay, if any
- Contract change orders, field change orders, and work change requests
- Scheduled invoicing—Fig. 18-3 shows a typical contractor invoice
- Variations to be in writing and in the contract change made
- Removal of construction plant
- Owner's rights to carry out the work or to stop the work

Some sample articles taken from general conditions are presented below as examples of typical language and tone.

Article 34 LABOR

34.16 DISORDERLY CONDUCT

The Contractor shall at all times take all reasonable precautions to prevent any unlawful, riotous or disorderly conduct by or amongst his employees and for the preservation of peace and protection of persons and property in the neighborhood of the Works against the same but the Contractor shall not interfere with members of any authorized Police Force who shall have free and undisputed access at all times to any part of the Works in the execution of their duties.

34.17 ACCIDENTS

Immediately following the occurrence of any accident on the Site or in connection with the execution of the Works Contractor shall supply the Engi-

APPLICATION & CERTIFICATE FOR PAYMENT

Date _____

To:
Via:

Period From: _____
To: _____

I. **Contract Account Status and Modifications** $ _____

   1. Original Contract Sum $ _____
   2. Contract Change Orders, this period _____   Total $ _____
   3. New Contract Sum $ _____

II. **Billings for This Period**

   A. **Contract and Field Change Orders** (not included in fixed contract sum)
     (details attached) $ _____

   B. **Fixed Price Contract Sum — Monthly Progress Billing**
     1. Total executed work to date $ _____
     2. Add 75% value of material stored (details attached) $ _____
     3. Subtotal — all work and goods to date $ _____
     4. Deduct 10% retention of executed work, line 1 $ _____
     5. Subtotal $ _____
     6. Less previous Certificates of Payment $ _____
     7. Subtotal (billings this period) $ _____
     8. Deduct 20% line 3 (return of Adv. Payment) $ _____
     9. Current payment due $ _____

   C. **Cost Reimbursable Work Billing** (details attached)

	Labor Hours	Cost
1. Work performed:		
a. _____	_____	$ _____
b. _____	_____	$ _____
c. _____	_____	$ _____
d. Subtotal		$ _____
2. Overhead or markup on labor at ____ of line 1(d)		$ _____
3. Fixed fee (pro-rate by work performed this period)		$ _____
4. Total billed herewith		$ _____

   D. **Total Billing this Period** $ _____

The undersigned certifies that the Work covered by this Application for Payment has been completed in accordance with Contract Documents, that all amounts have been paid by him for work which previous Certificates of Payment were issued and payments received from _____ and that the current payment shown herein is now due.

Contractor by: _____

In accordance with the Contract and this Application for Payment the Contractor is entitled to payment in the amount shown above.

Copies to:

By: _____   ☐

                   ☐

By: _____   ☐

Fig. 18-3   Sample of a contractor's invoice form.

neer's Representative with full details thereof in triplicate who will in turn advise the Construction buyer.

34.18 OBSERVANCE BY SUB-CONTRACTORS

The Contractor shall be responsible for the observance by sub-contractors employed by him in the execution of this Contract of the provisions of this Clause.

Article 36 MATERIALS AND WORKMANSHIP

All materials and workmanship shall be of the respective kinds described in the Contract and in accordance with the Engineer's instructions and shall be subjected from time to time to such tests as the Engineer may direct at the place of manufacture or fabrication, or on the Site or at such other place or places as may be specified in the Contract, or at all or any of such places. The Contractor shall provide such assistance, instruments, machines, labor and materials as are normally required for examining, measuring and testing any work and the quality, weight or quantity of any material used and shall supply samples of materials before incorporation in the Works for testing as may be selected and required by the Engineer.

Article 38 FIELD INSPECTION AND EXAMINATION OF WORKS

38.1 No work shall be covered up or put out of view without the approval of the Engineer or the Engineer's Representative and the Contractor shall afford full opportunity for the Engineer or the Engineer's Representative to examine and measure any work which is about to be covered up or put out of view and to examine foundations before permanent work is placed thereon. The Contractor shall give due notice to the Engineer's Representative whenever any such work or foundations is or are ready or about to be ready for examination and the Engineer's Representative shall, with unreasonable delay, unless he considers it unnecessary and advises the Contractor accordingly, attend for the purpose of examining and measuring such work or of examining such foundations.

Construction buyers making up general conditions for a project for the first time would do well to borrow a set used successfully for a similar type of project. The American Institute of Architects has prepared AIA Document A201, *General Conditions of the Contract for Construction,* which can be obtained by writing to the institute (1735 New York Avenue, N.W., Washington, D.C. 20006).

Special Conditions

On occasion, a particularly unique and unconventional type of construction has to be specified, bid, and awarded. This could be for a particularly dangerous waterfront job, on which underwater blasting and considerable diving with air are required of the welders, riggers, and millwrights.

These special conditions are usually written so that the various articles complement or supersede a specific article in the general conditions, and there is no confusion as to which articles are governing.

Special conditions articles often pertain to: strengthening the hold-harmless provision for the owner; more extensive insurance coverage; defining in-depth responsibilities of the parties; special work hours and pay if the project involves working in "off" times regarding public or third-party personnel working in the proximity of the project; renting off-site space for laydown because of the cramped site, etc.

Technical Specifications

The engineering, operating, and maintenance arms of the construction procurement team put into specification form, with supporting drawings, all the mechanical, electrical, civil, architectural, structural, and HVAC requirements of the project. The specifications are word descriptions of what is to be built into the project. The drawings interface with the specifications and show in detail exactly where and how the specification words are translated into plan and elevation and what is the interface relationship. Each amplifies the other and usually requires the other for complete understanding of the effective takeoff of quantities of material and complexity of work.

As discussed previously, the technical specification should have been prepared by individuals who understand exactly what type of contract is to be quoted. Therefore, drafts of the specification should have been shared with the construction buyer and the construction procurement team to assure that the work is adequately described and not made in any way ambiguous enough to permit contingencies to be bid.

Prior to writing the technical specification and making the drawings, the design engineers and drafters must have valid and complete conceptual engineering. If the conceptual engineering is incomplete and still to be fixed, then the bid set of drawings and the accompanying specification will have to become the base, or engineering, bidding freeze, which may be subject to many revisions after the contract award, and these often result in costly contract change orders.

Drawings

The engineering group writes "for quotation only" on all bid drawings, indicating that at that specific time the drawing had a freeze put on it. Copies of the drawings are made from vellums for the bidding, and two additional sets are made for purchasing to keep as a permanent record. These sets are used as *the* evidence of what the quotations were figured on. This is the base for computing and establishing the validity of claims for extras to the contract because of changes. The master or vellum of each drawing is given back to engineering so they can go on with design.

As mentioned previously, the drawings and technical specifications should be in complete agreement and should complement each other so as to avoid any misinterpretation by the contractors when they make up their quotations.

ACTIVITY DURING THE BIDDING PERIOD

The duration of the bidding period is established by the construction buyer in consultation with each bidder. He coordinates this with his knowledge of the allowable time as set up in the project master schedule. While those bidding appear to be pushing for an unreasonably long bid time, it is wise not to make the period so short that the bidders do not have time to make takeoffs, get subbids and material and equipment quotations, and carefully appraise the numerous cost and available personnel issues.

While the bidding is going on, the construction buyer should organize the procurement team to be making up its bid or estimate of what the bids should be when they come in. This helps the team not only to be ready to critique, analyze, and evaluate the bids, but also to become as involved as the bidders are. Many times analysis of owner personnel may show up discrepancies or vagaries that could result in costly contingencies being included in the quotations.

Addendum

If during the bidding period certain errors, additions, or deletions are discerned that are believed to be major enough to bring to the bidder's attention, and it is not too late to deal with them during the bid period, an addendum should be prepared and sent to all the bidders. All items should be numbered so as to be readily identified, and they should show most precisely the modification to the technical specification and drawings involved, as this becomes the new base for the forthcoming quotations and the construction procurement team's estimate.

Assistance to Bidders

The construction buyer will, most probably, be busy assisting bidders in interpreting the general conditions and referring questions on the technical specification to the appropriate engineering or architectural group. This is a difficult and time-consuming matter to deal with conscientiously because all bidders should be treated equally, and if answering these questions makes it obvious all the bidders should know of questions and answers, the buyer has to appropriately handle the notification to all bidders. This can be difficult if the buyer judges the inquiry more as an innovative idea that could be used for the project. In that case the buyer might judge it wrong to bring it to the attention of the other bidders. That is why a mature, rational, experienced buyer is needed to make the judgment.

EVALUATION OF PROPOSALS

The capable evaluation of bids is obviously important. Here again, the construction buyer will call in the construction procurement team. The team has already developed its idea of what the pricing should be, so each member takes on the assignment of analyzing the bold print, particularly the statements pertaining to his or her own specific segment of the project. Each writes up all the questions to ask the various contractors. Each analyzes and appraises in order to select the most complete, responsive, and economic quotation. When all members of the team have completed their individual appraisals, the construction buyer and the team make up a composite appraisal and compare this with the estimate they had made during the bidding period.

If there are unexplained differences, there should be sessions with each contractor to determine the cause of the differences. The unexplained differences of a contractor's bid can be so great that the team practically rules out that contractor's offering. During this period of evaluation and appraisal, the construction buyer has to be strong in his leadership of the team in assuring that unsupported prejudice and favoritism do not get in the way of sound rationality in making the selection.

The buyer has a large assignment in this analysis, since he is responsible for studying the commercial aspects of the offerings. This is an extensive assignment, but because he has been at work estimating during the bidding period, he should be very familiar with the project by now. There are so many tips about construction-bid evaluation to pass on to the buyer that it is best to call out typical ones and encourage buyers to work out their own types of investigation and study.

Elements under Cost-Plus Contracts

Both types of cost items listed below are reimbursable to the contractor by the owner.

Items Usually Subject to Overhead and Profit Markup

1. Taxable wage, the straight-time wages for all labor, both manual and nonmanual (clerical), including fringe benefits (nonmanual employee recruiting, vacations, pension, holidays, educational programs, and educational assistance), based on labor and/or as dictated by the various labor agreements
2. Labor travel and subsistence allowance
3. Wages and wage costs of all contractor's crew bosses (not part of supervision) at the job site
4. Wages and wage costs of contractor supervision, above crew bosses, furnished by craft union
5. Straight-time portion of overtime
6. Rework that has to be performed because the error was not due to contractor negligence (see below)
7. Materials and freight at actual cost, including cash discounts
8. Subcontracts (usually a different single markup applies) covering overhead and fee; no markup in cost-reimbursable contracts
9. Contractor supervision (nonunion at site field office), salaries, including vacations, holidays, pensions, insurance, and taxes (if not included in overhead markup or in profit markup)

Items Usually Not Subject to Overhead and Profit Markup, Reimbursed at Cost

1. Equipment rental at the contractor-quoted rate schedule or the percentage quoted by American Equipment Dealers
2. Light equipment (under $500 purchase price) at quoted rental or AED percentage or percentage of straight-time craft labor, including benefits
3. Consumables and expendables, such as wiping cloths, welding rod, hacksaw blades, and welding gases
4. Field office buildings, furniture, and equipment
5. Light, power, heat, water, and sewer, if not furnished by owner
6. Special vehicles or equipment, such as ambulance and fire truck (in some contracts this can be covered by the overhead markup)
7. Travel expenses of specialist home office personnel to field (job duration)
8. Travel and moving expenses of supervisory personnel on and off job (if not covered in overhead)

9. Sales tax (at times owner pays to state directly)
10. Premium portion of overtime
11. Permits and royalty costs
12. Insurance on all labor *taxable wages* (includes federal and state unemployment, worker's compensation, public liability, property damage, completion insurance, and liability)
13. Taxes, blanket assessment, or percentage of paid wages; includes FICA (and license fees for working in state)

Overhead   Overhead is a percentage markup on all costs to which it is applicable. This percentage is bid and is usually the first number in a bid, such as the 15 percent in cost-plus 15-10. Overhead is paid by the owner to the contractor to cover the owner's expenditures for: home office expenses including nonmanual wages; salaries of home office supervisory personnel even if called to consult at the job; officers' salaries; general administrative (corporate) expenses, such as advertising, and financing, supervision of construction, corporate; supervision of construction, job-site; property-damage insurance and contractual liability insurance; faulty work which has to be redone—specified as a monetary limit in each contract; and recruiting, training, and work certification of craft labor.

Profit (Fee) Percentage Markup   This is percentage markup added to all items of cost to which it is applicable. This percentage is bid and is usually the second number in a bid, such as the 10 percent in cost-plus 15-10. The return to the contractor covers costs of: top executive salaries and expenses; discretionary administrative costs (company plane, advertising, sales promotion, etc.); and profit.

Cost Analysis   Considerable difference in final cost to the owner can result from differences in which items are included in the cost to which overhead and profit apply in cost-plus bids. Careful analysis of all items in costs and of what expenses overhead covers is essential. For example, in a cost-plus bidding two contractors each bid cost-plus 15-10. Contractor A has supervisor salaries as an item of cost subject to markup, and contractor B has supervisor salaries covered by the overhead markup expense and has no such entry as a cost item. If the job has $30,000 of supervisory salaries, the owner will have to pay contractor A the sum of $30,000 plus 15 percent and then 10 percent of this total, or $30,000 $\times$ 1.15 $\times$ 1.10 = $37,950 for these salaries. If contractor B had the same amount for supervisory salaries, since they are covered as part of the overhead percent there would not be such an item billed as reimbursable. Company B's bid is $37,950 less for just this one item.

Billing Elements under Cost-Reimbursable Contracts

Typical items for payment by owner at cost include the following.

Direct Costs   These include items 1 through 9 previously covered under Items Usually Subject to Overhead and Profit Markup; consumables and expendables; sales tax; all insurance and taxes on labor payroll; liability and property damage insurance; completion and contractual liability insurance; jobsite supervision of construction salaries and benefits; and field office buildings, furniture, office equipment, and job utilities (not furnished by owner).

Light Equipment or Tools   These are included at a contractor-quoted schedule of rental rates or at a percent of manual straight-time labor payroll, including benefits. This is for all equipment or tools costing less than $500 new.

Construction Equipment   Equipment above $500 purchase price at AED- or contractor-quoted schedule of rental rates includes, cranes, bulldozers, fire truck, ambulance, trucks, concrete plant, compressors, and welding machines.

Fee   This can be a fixed fee or a percentage markup fee or incentive fee, on direct costs. This covers all contractor indirect costs including: markup on material, markup on labor and fringes, top executive salaries and expenses, discretionary administrative costs, home office and general administrative expenses, and profit.

Elements under Fixed-Price Contracts

Tight Fixed Price   If the instructions to bidders in the request for proposal and the general conditions spell out clearly that it is to be a tight price contract—no price changes due to escalation, and no price increases for minor, obvious, and common omissions or misplacements in the specification and drawings—and there is no project scope change, then the fixed price offered is inclusive. Of course, if there is a scope change, the contractor will bid, and if the price is reasonable, will be awarded the change. Field change orders can be anticipated under any fixed-price contract because there will always be the unexpected field occurrences that were not included in any design—underground obstructions, owner change of direction of door opening after the door is all on, the earth defined in the specification to be available for fill is found to be unacceptable, etc. The analysis of the bids on a tight fixed-price contract is practically a matter of observing the lump-sum prices for the project and determining if there is any reason why the lowest-price contractor should not be recommended. The bidders had all been established as acceptable before the bidding. Of course, if some unit prices have been solicited for field-change-order pricing, then these have to be compared along with the fixed total project price.

Open Fixed Price   If the definition of the contract has not made it a tight fixed-price contract, the appraisal must be different. An open fixed-price contract bidding occurs when the prices sought from the bidders are for only the work positively defined in the technical specification and as shown on the drawings, and any omissions, errors, or even minor changes will be cause for an extra for the contractor. In analyzing open fixed-price bidding, more evaluation and appraising of the expected performance of each contractor must be made.

Exceptions Stated by Contractors

Good requests for proposal stipulate that unless the bidder takes written exception to some parts of the bid documents, it will be judged that all parts of the documents will be accomplished for the price offered. The written exceptions have to be watched for carefully, and each must be appraised to determine whether they can be accepted or whether they cause severe problems in equalizing all the bids. If all those quoting take exception to the same elements, concepts, or provisions of the general conditions or disagree with the technical specifications, the construction buyer may have to clear up the difficulty and possibly ask for rebids.

THE CONSTRUCTION CONTRACT

The makeup of a construction contract can very well follow a general pattern, with the principal segments described below.

The Recital

It is good protection for the owner to describe carefully the parties of the contract, including the company's official location and name. There should also be a fairly comprehensive description of the project of which the contract is a part, whether the contract is for specialty work or is a general contract for the entire job. The recital does for a construction contract what a function description does for the purchase of a piece of equipment or materials and supplies. It puts a burden on the contractor to perform his work in keeping with the owner's overall or project anticipation, whether specifically spelled out in later paragraphs or not.

The Scope

A description of the scope of the individual contract being awarded and the work to be performed by the contractor should include any specifications, drawings, or other official documents, including applicable codes around which the proposal was made and the contract is being formed. It usually includes the technical specification and the general conditions of the contract.

Work to Be Performed by the Owner

To have a complete meeting of the minds of both parties, it should be clear what support the owner customarily and specifically provides for this contract.

Method and Manner of Performance

The status of the supervision and employees of the contractor must be so specified as to indicate that they are not employees, in any sense, of the owner and that the level of competency of the personnel will be subject to the approval of the owner.

The contractor has an obligation to: comply with all laws; conform to reasonable work conditions so that any adjoining property owners are not annoyed by noise, pollutants, or material hauling operations, etc.; establish adequate protection of the work against fire, theft, and storm damage; and establish and rapidly enforce job rules and procedures relating to safety and welfare of the employees on the job, including adequate training programs to assure compliance with all federal, state, and local laws on safety and health.

Contractor must agree to perform the labor relations in keeping with the contractor's labor contract agreement and combined with owner's best interest. The owner should be alert to stating whether he wishes the contractor to limit any behavior with labor that would in any way affect any other owner installations. Any overskill payments or overtime practices or retroactive agreements with unions that would be to the owner's detriment should be limited to only those approved by the owner.

Taxes

A statement regarding the method of handling all taxes to the best interest of the owner is required. Taxation of construction equipment and some materials varies between states and between owner and contractor.

Acceptance by Owner

This section defines the agreed-upon method by which the owner both partially and finally accepts the work. In some kinds of construction the owner needs to take over parts of the job before the entire job is completed in order to start training his operating personnel on segments of the job. Both parties should agree as to what constitutes final acceptance before payment of the retained compensation.

Title to Work—Ownership

A statement satisfactory to both owner and contractor as to where title rests for the work being performed, especially covering the materials and equipment going into the installation, is important. Owner property taxes are levied by many states on the basis of ownership.

Compensation

The methods to be used to compensate the contractor for his work must be completely described. This description should be carefully prepared so as to establish the most workable means of administration, both in the field by the owner's representatives and the contractor's staff and by the construction buyer, who may be called upon to assist accounting in the interpretation of contract regarding the payment of invoices. A sample invoice is shown in Fig. 18-3. This sample includes items not always found in contracts, such as retention advance payment and partial payment for uninstalled but received goods. It is typical and most workable.

Schedule of Payments

The exact timing that the parties have agreed to for submitting the invoices and payment by the owner should be set forth. Sometimes it is desirable to pay for some costs such as materials, tools, and equipment rentals on a monthly basis and the manual and nonmanual labor wages and salaries on a more frequent basis.

Also to be scheduled are the reimbursements by owner for payments to subcontractors.

Contracts with a fee usually define the payment schedule for this fee. Incentive fee contracts should hold back enough fee to make adjustment for contractor performance. A retention of 5 percent on jobs over $1 million and 10 percent on all others is a reasonable schedule. This money is to help supply incentive to the contractor to finish the job as early as possible and to avoid errors or omissions.

The owner should specify any special accounting system the contractor is to follow so the final records will fit the owner's bookkeeping system. The contractor should agree to safeguard the owner's rights regarding waiver of liens against the owner and his property for any unpaid bills of his or any subcontractor or material suppliers.

Changes

There should be a mutually agreed-upon system for establishing the official changes to the contract both in the scope of the change and in any compensation to the contractor.

Assignment of Contract and Subcontractors

Definitely define the acceptability—or unacceptability—of the contractor or subcontractor, assigning any of the rights of the specific contract at hand to another party.

Termination

Give careful attention to the numerous details of physical movement of people and material and the ultimate cost of these in writing a termination or deferment provision to the contract. It is much better to get this done prior to the start of work.

Suspension of Work

It is customary for the owner to retain the right to extend the schedule of work to be performed, or even to cause suspension of this work and expect the contractor to resume the work as directed by the owner, with equitable adjustment of the contract for added costs because of the suspension.

Liability

Suitable indemnification of the owners and the *hold-harmless* provision to be furnished by the contractor should be set forth. If possible, have a provision of this clause include that the need for rework of any portion of the work or any portion of the job, if occasioned by the malperformance of the contractor, is at the contractor's expense. Contractors usually subscribe to this only up to a dollar limit of exposure.

Patent Infringement

The contractor should agree to protect the owner from any patent infringements by equipment suppliers from whom the contractor buys and protect the owner against any suits brought against him because of contractor-created infringements of patents.

Advertising

The owner should reserve the right to approve, prior to release by the contractor, information about a project. This avoids misleading advertising and protects the owner from erroneous statements.

Force Majeure

Since contractors invariably insist upon a protection from job completion defaults occasioned by acts beyond their control, such as riots, strikes, insurrections, or acts of God, it is well to have the exact words of this provision agreed to by the owner and contractor before the job starts.

Arbitration

The owner should have the privilege of directing in this clause his desires about settlement of disagreements by the owner and contractor through the use of courts or through the rules of the American Arbitration Association as then in force.

Governing Law

The contract, and the rights, obligations, and liabilities of the parties, should be construed in accordance with the laws of the state in which the owner resides or the facility is being built.

Equal Employment Opportunity

Be certain to include provisions that the contractor and all subcontractors comply with U.S. Executive Order No. 11246, as amended September 24, 1965, and the rules, regulations, and relevant orders from the Secretary of Labor pursuant thereto.

Binding Effect of Contract

This clause should state that the contract is to be binding upon the benefit of the owner and the contractor and inure to their respective successors, assigns, subcontractors, heirs, executors, administrators, receivers, and other representatives.

Entire Agreement

A statement should be included to the effect that this contract, including any of its appendixes or amendments, constitutes the entire agreement between the parties relative to the subject of the contract and supersedes any previous agreements or understandings. Further, it should be specified that all work performed by the contractor prior to the execution of the written document should be deemed to have been performed under the contract.

Schedule for Performance of Work

It is the contractor's responsibility to find the very fine point where schedule requirements are met without planned overtime and work of marginal quality. Without a realistic, precise schedule for performance of the work, important completion dates may not be met and cost overruns may be experienced.

Progress Reports

Monthly progress reports are required of the contractor. This is to report against the project schedule.

CONTRACT ADMINISTRATIVE GUIDELINES

Much of the management and administration of the contract is performed at the jobsite by the construction forces, but it is important to have the business part of the contract administration positively established so all parties and participants in the project know how to keep financial commitments straight.

Each project has its own specific business management requirements since all the types of contract vary in this particular area. A routine for an open fixed-price contract could be as described in the following paragraphs.

Project Schedule

The project schedule prescribed in the contract is to be established by the contractor.

Price Breakdown

The fixed price is to be broken down by the contractor into the same elements or segments of work as the items in the project schedule (see Fig. 18-4).

Invoice Preparation and Verification

The owner's construction manager or field accountant can work with the contractor on working up the percentage completion of the specific segments of work, and thus that percentage of the money allocated for that piece of work becomes the amount to be billed. At the same time the actual work progress can be compared with the anticipated progress of the project schedule.

Field Change Orders

Changes to the work that arise in the field and must be dealt with immediately are to be handled between the contractor's superintendent, who estimates the cost,

Application and Certificate of Payment
Application Number _____
Project Number _____

Item no. A	Description of work B	Scheduled value C	Work completed		Work completed D + E F	Balance to finish C − F G
			Previous applications D	This application E		
20100	Spare cable	139,653				
20200	Spare electrical material	161,585				
20300	480-V and 13.8-kV distribution system	3,824,758				
20400	Property lighting	88,971				
20500	Radio antenna	33,293				
30100	Fencing	705,441				
30200	Paving and grading	381,827				
30300	Demolition	176,577				
30400	Temporary facilities	420,775				
40100	Wastewater and sewer system	350,983				
40200	Fire and potable water	848,213				
40300	Modifications to G.T.G.	8,459				
40400	Powerhouse ventilation and refurbishing	863,826				
40500	Mechanical spare parts	74,456				
40600	Fountain	121,951				
50100	Bridge crane	41,086				
50200	Gas turbines	476,677				
50300	Generators	512,230				
50400	Turbine and general misc. equipment	663,318				
50500	Relocate water tank	55,953				
50600	Diesel fire pumps	48,542				
50700	Deionizer package	85,688				
50800	Misc. pumps and equipment	168,398				
	Misc. total	10,252,660				

Fig. 18-4 Sample breakdown of contractor's fixed price, containing same items in the project schedule.

and the owner's construction manager. If the costs are under some limit, say $5000, a field change order is issued by the owner (see Fig. 18-5).

Work Change Request

For major changes in the work emanating in the field or in engineering, such as an addendum of considerable drawing and specification revision or just a single change above $5000, a work change request is made out by either the owner's engineering staff or field construction management team. The construction buyer sends it to the contractor for a price estimate (see Fig. 18-6).

Fig. 18-5   Sample of owner's field change order form.

Upon receipt of the work change request, which has been quoted on by the contractor, the construction buyer appraises the quotation in consultation with the involved field and engineering parties. If approved, he issues a contract change order to the contractor. See Fig. 18-7. These major changes above some dollar limit, say $50,000, are added to the cost breakdown, already referred to and then are billed as part of the fixed price. Under $50,000 they are billed separately as the amount for the specific contract change order.

Page ___ of ___   **Work Change Request** _____

Date _____   To: _____

Project   _____

CONTRACT NO. _____

Prepared by   Requested by
_____

Copies To:

                                              _____
                                              Contract Change Order No.
                                              (leave blank until assigned)

Please submit an itemized quotation for changes In the Contract Sum and/or time incidental to proposed modifications to the Contract Documents described herein.
THIS IS NOT A CHANGE ORDER NOR A DIRECTION TO PROCEED WITH THE WORK DESCRIBED HEREIN

1. Description: (written description of the work)

2. Reason for Change:

3. Proposal In Time and Price Revision for Change Requested:
   This revision will ☐   will not ☐ cause changes in the Contract as follows:
   1. Contract sum change (details attached)
      _____
      _____
      _____ $ _____
   2. Contractual program and completion time change
      _____
      _____   _____ days

4. Approved:
                     Contractor _____ Date _____
               Project Manager _____ Date _____
                    1) Approval _____ Date _____
              2) Funds Available _____ Date _____

Fig. 18-6 Sample of work change request form issued by the owner's engineering staff or construction management team.

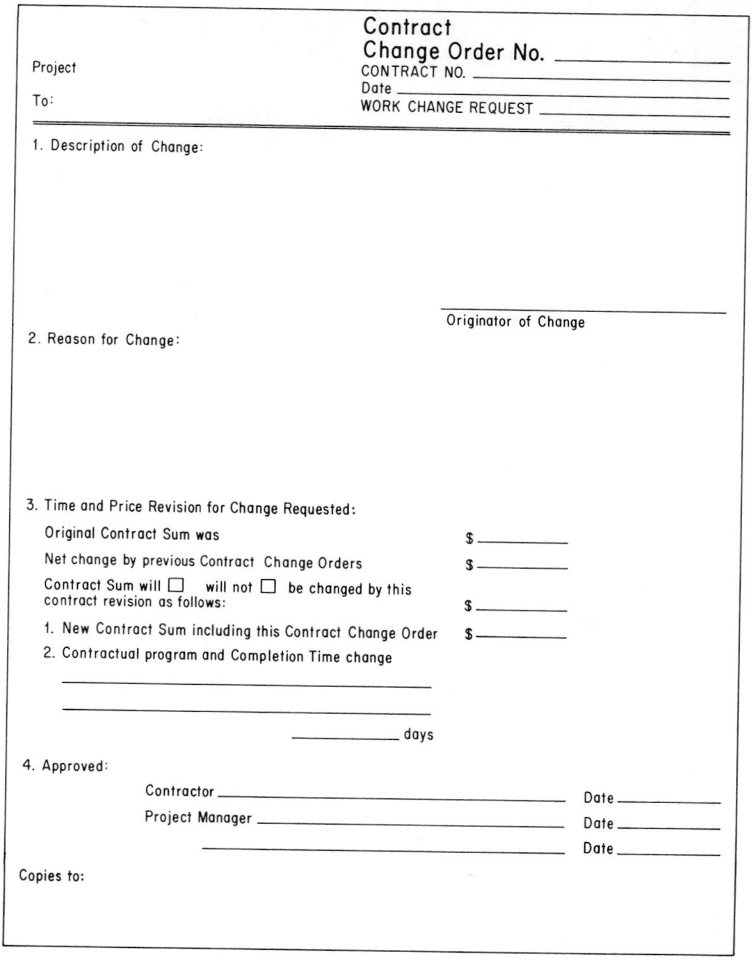

Fig. 18-7 Sample of owner's contract change order form.

CONCLUSION

In conclusion, the entire cycle of construction buying is one of the most demanding purchasing assignments, yet it is filled with gratifying opportunities to be effective and of singular service to the organization.

NOTE: For further information on subjects covered in this section see the list of references in Section 30.

Materials Management

EDITOR

John J. Davin, C.P.M. *Vice-President, Materials and Facilities, GTE, Stamford, Connecticut*

INTRODUCTION

The management of materials has existed as long as goods and services have been required. Under many different names and in many combinations, the management of materials has evolved until currently it unites the functions of purchasing, production control and inventory, and distribution-transportation. The process of buying, making, and moving is universal in scope, but not until relatively recently has the grouping of these functions been a recognized management choice to optimize the synergistic effects of the union. Materials management, then, has become a management option to be contended with and analyzed on its merits. Materials management is primarily a concept that can have many structures; understanding it is of paramount importance to purchasing managers and other professionals in materials-related functions.

Materials are best described as inanimate objects, but decisions that surround their management can hardly be described in those terms. In an area that represents nearly one-half the sales dollars of most manufacturing companies, interests are high and partisan decisions prevalent. Each person responsible for a portion of the material flow tends to skew the issues in the direction that best serves his particular objectives. Without a compromise mechanism in the buy-make-distribute cycle, a crisis can occur which requires management resolution. It is here that the concept of materials management plays its role. Whatever the structure of a materials management organization, its efforts are directed toward the efficient operation of a facility. The results—performance improvement, cost reduction, and work force upgrading—require the understanding and support of management at all levels. To better understand the concept and practice of materials management, some investigation into each of these areas needs to be undertaken. The criticality of material impacting the bottom line has never been greater, and management's attention is focusing on the management of materials as it never has in the past.

Concept of Materials Management

The functions of materials management have been performed for decades, but it is only recently that the form has come into question. Organizations have been traditionally structured along vertical lines (Fig. 19-1): an engineering group, a manufacturing group, a financial group, a marketing group, etc. Each has its vertically focused manager concerned with the operation of the department. However, material does not flow up and down within a specific function; it moves horizontally across the span of an organization.

Decisions are made along the flow by specific functional managers as the material comes under their control. These decisions tend to be limited in scope to the immediate function at hand. The results are less like a flow than a stop-start, hurry-up-and-wait, uneven process, which causes more time to be spent treating the symptoms than correcting the cause. Planning turns into expediting and confusion usually occurs. There can be no doubt as to the adverse effect such a situation has on an organization. Productivity and morale suffer while adversary relationships flourish.

One approach that has been tried to facilitate effective and efficient material flow is the materials management concept. The concept described should not be

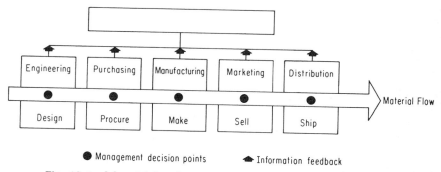

Fig. 19-1   Material flow in a company without materials management.

considered as the answer to all the problems but rather as an alternative that is successfully being applied in appropriate applications throughout industry today.

Functional Integration

The overall concept of materials management is the organizational grouping of the purchasing, production inventory control, and physical distribution-transportation functions under a single manager. That manager is responsible for specifying, obtaining, moving, storing, and planning the use and distribution of materials at the least total cost. It is an association of related functions in which the interrelationship of the buy-make-distribute material flow is emphasized. The emphasis is on the integration of materials functions. While purchasing, production, and physical distribution managers are concerned with the specific requirements of their activities, the materials manager is a generalist concerned with all the functions simultaneously. He is a planner, organizer, integrator, and motivator. The job spans functional barriers and represents a unified input to top management for materials.

Unification of Functions

The materials management job is functional rather than organizational, so it is not always necessary to change organizations to make the concept work. A person with management orientation and the responsibility for the whole spectrum of materials can get things accomplished by the total activity that could not be done by the separate parts. The synergy created by uniting functions is the driving force behind the materials management concept. In its broadest sense, materials management is concerned with material from the time the need is recognized to shipment of the finished goods to the customer. Dean S. Ammer lists the following as "functions typically included in a materials management department: *Hard Core*—inventory management, purchasing, traffic, value analysis; *Other Commonly Accepted Functions*—materials handling, physical distribution, production

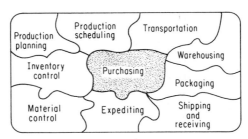

Fig. 19-2   Interlocking functions in the materials management "jigsaw puzzle."

control, receiving, scheduling, shipping, stores, warehousing; *Fringe Areas*—electronic data processing and market research and forecasting."[1] In broader but still definitive terms, materials management is the functional grouping of purchasing, production and inventory control, and physical distribution under one manager. All the functions in Ammer's first two categories fit to some degree into the three headings.

Another way of looking at the materials management picture is a jigsaw puzzle, the interlocking pieces of which form the materials management concept (Fig. 19-2). This association of related functions is the fundamental premise of materials management.

Horizontal Management

Early on it was shown how the vertical focus of organizations can inhibit the material flow through a company without materials management because of functional and personal defenses. The picture changes when the grouping of related functions occurs under one manager (Fig. 19-3). All the functions are still present, but a significant number of barriers have been removed. The results are twofold. First there is greater horizontal control over the material. Management decision points are reduced so that the number of persons with divided vertical control decreases. This smooths the flow of material and reduces the tendency to compartmentalize management. A second benefit that is sometimes overlooked is the

[1]Dean S. Ammer, *Materials Management,* Dow Jones–Irwin, Homewood, IL, rev. ed., 1968.

resultant flow of information back to management. Instead of a chorus of voices there is a single voice speaking for materials across the company structure. Decisions can now be made with reasonable certainty that all aspects of the problem have been fairly presented and necessary trade-offs made. Usually this is done in a shorter period of time because of the unity of control, thereby relieving top man-

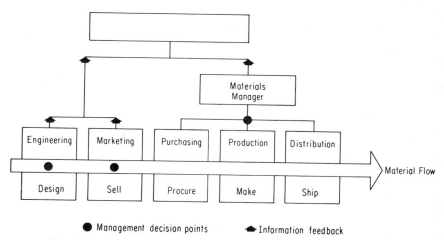

Fig. 19-3 Material flow in a company using materials management.

agement from the sometimes tedious and always time-consuming intrafunctional decision-making process.

THE PRACTICE OF MATERIALS MANAGEMENT

The practice of materials management as a concept is not the panacea for all materials problems. As noted earlier, materials management is a viable option in the management organization. In practice, materials management is a legitimate base for expanded responsibilities with increased control. It is a structure with a potential greater than that of its parts. It is one way to maximize profits while minimizing costs. However, materials management is not right for all companies or industries. It should not be thought of as a solution to specific functional problems, and most important of all, it is not simply a regrouping of existing functions.

Looked at broadly and in terms that encompass all possible functions, the materials manager's span of control is as illustrated in Fig. 19-4.

The materials manager's responsi-

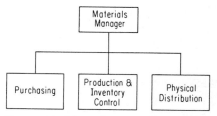

Fig. 19-4 Materials manager's span of control in a total materials system.

bilities go beyond the individuals reporting to him. Along with this expansion comes a concomitant increase in the control of materials. He can make trade-offs within his organization that will benefit the entire company. This is a much more difficult practice when three managers are competing for the same available investment funds and are likely to be more guarded in their generosity. It is difficult to find many other examples in which an expansion of responsibilities brings about a similar tightening of control.

Conflicting Objectives

There is a natural tendency for functional departments—purchasing, production and inventory control, physical distribution—to look inward to accomplish their objectives. The purchasing manager prepares his budget, plans, and objectives each year and is held accountable for his accomplishments. Likewise, the inventory manager is expected to improve turns in order to make his profit contribution. Without coordination, these two managers may end up working against each other—one trying to bring materials into the plant on a volume basis, the other trying to prevent material from accumulating ahead of production. Materials management is a natural solution to the dilemma. Instead of two managers reporting to different supervisors with dissimilar goals, a materials manager becomes the sole decision maker for materials as they flow through the organization. Here is where the potential is greater than if the functions remained separate. Being able to see the entire breadth of a situation, the materials manager will be able to place the correct emphasis in order to accomplish the objective. No longer are lowest purchase price and minimum inventories irreconcilable objectives. The materials manager can work out an optimal solution between volume buying and inventory that would have been practically impossible without the unity of control. This practice is not limited to the cases cited. Production control and physical distribution would lend themselves to similar synergistic effects when managed in a horizontal fashion. This practice is very similar to the program management structure employed by the federal government. The materials manager is the program manager for materials in a company. It is his responsibility from start to finish. In the case of materials, that means from the recognition of the need to the shipment of finished goods to the customer. This practice of horizontal management of materials fits in with the concepts discussed earlier.

Company Characteristics

Materials management is more likely to be found in a decentralized company than in one under strong centralized direction. To be effective in the job, the materials manager must have the freedom to operate within the organization. Critical arbitrary decisions have to be made, and in order to do this effectively the materials manager must have the autonomy to choose from all the possibilities available. Centralized management tends to restrict this independence. While the method and management are factors in materials management, the size of the operation is not. Large or small, staff or operations, materials management as a concept can be applied to any organizational structure. Figure 19-5 shows one possible materials management organization in a large corporation.

To arrive at this structure, the particular characteristics of the corporation must be considered and the department structured to meet corporate needs. The structure encompasses all the major functions of materials management and adds

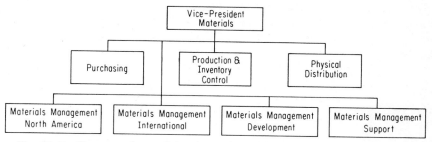

Fig. 19-5   One type of materials management organization in a large company.

another dimension to the practice by having regional material managers in addition to the functional personnel. This matrix is shown in Fig. 19-6. This example shows the flexibility and malleability of materials management in practice. It can be used in most situations to the advantage of the company.

In a small company operating as a profit and loss entity the materials management organization may look like that shown in Fig. 19-7. In this case the department would be more straightforward and functionally oriented. All the functions shown exist to some extent in all companies, and it is their grouping that provides management with those alternatives and possibilities which best suit company

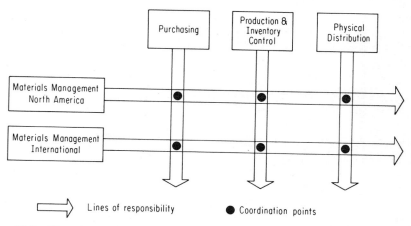

Fig. 19-6   How the organization shown in Fig. 19-5 has been structured to meet needs of a particular corporation by the addition of regional managers.

needs. However, it should be remembered that materials management does not fit all situations and that certain conditions do not lend themselves to the practice of materials management, as discussed.

Single-product-line companies and nonmanufacturing firms are good examples of areas where materials management is least likely to flourish. The key words in the practice of materials management are *unification, coordination, integration, association, and optimization.* Companies with single product lines tend to have routine, repetitive, and well-defined material requirements that can be managed

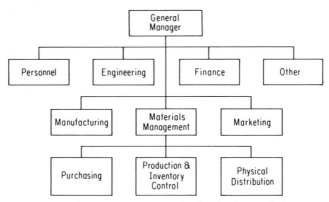

Fig. 19-7   Basic materials management organization in the smaller company is flexible and can be adapted to special requirements.

within existing vertical structures. That is not to say that single-product-line companies are not dynamic and changing but just that their material needs are normally anticipated. However, in multiproduct integrated companies the complexity of material demands is much greater, so that these companies fall into the category where materials management is most likely to be most effective.

Materials management is less appropriate in nonmanufacturing companies. The asset to be managed is the factor determining what a management structure is to be called. In a manufacturing company in which approximately half the sales dollars are material-related, the materials management organization is natural. In a nonmanufacturing company, in which services outweigh goods, the situation is altogether different. If product material cost is minimal but product movement maximum, then the asset to be intensely managed is transportation. The organization controlling this function should be called *distribution management.*

Need to Include Production Control

Many managers, particularly those in operating locations, hold tightly to responsibilities they have acquired over the years. Some argue that production functions are more directly related to manufacturing and should therefore logically be in that area of responsibility. While most concede that purchasing and physical distribution are materials functions, they feel that production control is not. But production control belongs in the materials management organization because of its total impact on materials flow. The manufacturing manager is primarily concerned with the fabrication of piece parts into subassemblies and then into a final assembly. He is oriented toward pieces per hour and labor costs per unit. Material is only a tool for him, albeit a necessary tool to accomplish the job. He is concerned about having the proper amount of material available to support manufacturing requirements. He would also enjoy having additional material available to buffer any manufacturing changes.

On the other hand, material is an asset to be managed by the materials manager. One step in that management process is the planning and scheduling of the material for fabrication. The distinction lies in the fact that manufacturing is physically touching, changing, adding value to raw materials, whereas production control is planning and scheduling the material to be at the right point at the right time so that manufacturing can perform its function. The production planner in fact manages material requirements, not manufacturing functions. Even though there is close interface and interdependence between production control functions and manufacturing operations, the two can and should be separated. This separation allows the materials to be managed by production control according to management's objectives and goals without an internal confrontation with manufacturing.

BENEFITS OF MATERIALS MANAGEMENT

In general, the advantages a materials management organization offers are that it:

- Establishes a single point of responsibility for all materials-related matters and the complete, balanced materials cycle
- Provides one point of resolution for the natural conflicts that can occur between the various materials-related departments
- Allows use of imaginative, organizationwide, total-systems approach for greater efficiency and more innovation
- Provides integrated communications and a mechanism for operational materials system problems
- Provides an effective vehicle for cutting operational costs
- Establishes the basis for creation of specialized organization with a single primary function
- Fixes reponsibility for securing materials at prices commensurate with, or lower than, those of competition
- Results in reduced lead times, fewer parts shortages, more realistic buying policies, and inventory reduction of raw, in-process, and finished goods; leads to lower material prices, better finished-product delivery performance, and total-system cost reduction

A materials management organization also provides specific advantages to individual company functions, as discussed below.

Advantages for Purchasing

Improved Lead Time *Lead time* for purchasing is normally defined as the time between order placement and receipt of goods. However, lead time is greater when internal processing is taken into account. Total lead time is then defined as the time between recognition of a need and receipt of material. In a typical vertically organized company, significant time is lost as the material requisition passes from one functional group to another. Days may go by before purchasing receives authorization to procure material. Under a materials management organization, this internal time can be cut significantly because of the removal of many functional barriers and a single concern for materials flow.

Quantity Flexibility Timely and accurate information about purchased materials needs improves buyers' bargaining positions when negotiating with vendors. How much material to buy is usually the critical factor. In a materials management organization a purchasing manager, using his knowledge of inventories and production, has the authority to make trade-offs, the flexibility to adjust purchase quantities, and the access to longer-term forecasts.

Better Prices When the purchasing manager, production manager, and inventory manager work as a team on the management of materials, the advantages of contract buying and quantity discounts are not sacrificed to inventory control, and vice versa. The purchasing manager can use contract buying and quantity discounts to obtain lower prices and can arrange deliveries according to a schedule worked out with production planners.

Advantages for Production and Inventory Control

Lower Inventories Close coordination between purchasing and production control enables buyers to define accurately current material needs and forecast future requirements. This, in turn, leads to more precise inventory control with resultant reduction in inventory carrying charges.

Faster Turns A reduction in inventory does not in itself produce faster turns, since all things rarely remain equal. Positive, active management of inventories— *a primary objective of materials management organizations*—can reduce internal processing time and thereby increase turns.

Advantages for Physical Distribution

Lower Costs Too often, the cost of transportation is accepted as a given cost of doing business. However, under materials management, physical distribution is treated as a physical asset to be managed. An integrated approach to planning for material requirements allows traffic managers more flexibility in choosing transportation methods. This almost always results in lower physical distribution costs.

Efficient Movement of Goods   In a materials management system, routes will be evaluated with purchasing's vendors in mind. Future transportation needs will be planned so that traffic managers can choose the best means of transportation.

THE FUTURE OF MATERIALS MANAGEMENT

There are many forces working to speed the reception and application of materials management in the decades ahead. Some are internal, i.e., peculiar to a particular company or industry; others are external and reflect the existing economic climate.

Internal Factors

Organizations are becoming more complex as technology advances and the breadth of product lines increases. The day is past when a single owner-manager could directly manage all aspects of a business from one office. From this total horizontal management structure, in which one person did everything, companies have moved toward vertical management, with one person responsible for only a specific aspect of management. Communication lines have multiplied because of this segmentation of the management process. Materials management offers a "back-to-basics" approach to the problem of complexity—a reintegration of related functions. It allows an organization to increase efficiency even though increased demands are being placed on it.

The professional development of managers in the materials-related functions is another internal spur to materials management. Recognizing the need to develop generalists in the materials field, corporations have instituted career programs in materials management. In such programs, recent college graduates work in specific materials functions, thereby gaining experience. Experienced functional experts move into materials management positions on the basis of their general materials background and their management potential. This formalization of education and career development in materials will provide competent managers to staff the materials management organizations.

Computerization and systems application are other internal developments that will advance materials management. As an organization's computer capability and capacity increase, the materials functions fit naturally into the system. Managers of materials must have access to accurate and timely information in order to make correct decisions, particularly since changes in materials requirements are frequent and almost always involve dependent areas. The computer's ability to process and structure large amounts of variables relieves the materials manager of tedious manual burdens and leaves him free to concentrate on the primary role of decision making, based on correct and dynamic information.

Small or medium-sized companies need no longer be restricted by a lack of programming skill. Numerous software specialty houses are creating detailed programs in the materials management field. The commercially available program packages can be tailored to the specific needs and requirements of any size customer. Availability of professional applications will surely increase the number of companies adopting the materials management concept through integrated modular systems application.

External Factors

Increased efficiency and productivity will be necessary in order to survive. Probably the most important stimulus to materials management will be the fact that competitors have done it with favorable results. Economic pressures will skyrocket as margins decrease and management searches for a solution to rising costs. The first place they will look is in the area that dominates costs—materials. Thus, general management's attention will be focused on the management of materials and how to improve its efficiency. Here again, the materials management concept will be thrust into the forefront and its benefits realized.

Development of Materials Managers

Much has been said about the how and why of materials management. The who may be more important than these two combined. Without an effective dynamic materials manager the whole concept and practice may be set back and the benefits lost. The current difficulty in finding the right person is a major obstacle to implementation. Traditionally the materials functions have produced excellent specialized managers, rewarded by being given a more difficult or more responsible job within that same specialty. This practice will have to change, as indeed it has, before professional materials managers can develop. Already mentioned are corporate programs to help launch a career in materials management.

Until the time that formal education catches up to immediate requirements, some thought must be given to who is going to staff the materials management organizations today. The difficulty lies in finding persons who are willing to separate themselves from doing the specific job and spend their time on general topics such as planning, measurement, evaluation, and training. The person most capable of doing those functions today will be the most likely candidate for the materials manager's position. Ideally he will have worked, not in one specific area, but in all three areas, namely, purchasing, production and inventory control, and physical distribution.

As important as specific or general job knowledge are the personal characteristics of the materials manager. He must be able to achieve desired results through the efforts of other people. He must be able to effectively interface with top management, translate its goals and objectives into working policies and procedures, and then direct the efforts of others in accomplishing them.

SUMMARY OF BENEFITS

The concept of materials management is directly in line with the goals of least total costs for materials and contribution to profit by aggressive management. Materials management is not intended to replace or degrade any specific materials functional disciplines. Rather, it integrates and coordinates the existing positions and gives them a unified direction and control. While some may disagree as to the inclusion of certain specific jobs under the control of a materials manager, there is a general consensus as to the overall organizational benefits derived from the practice of materials management. These benefits are summarized below.

Profit Contribution

Management typically views purchasing and physical distribution as expenses of doing business. However, under a single manager these functions can focus on making positive profit contributions through coordinated efforts.

Lower Total Material Costs

The total cost of buying, storing, and moving material can be reduced by coordinated management. Individual managers work in unison to achieve a single goal, thereby eliminating counterproductive efforts and reducing costs.

Optimum Inventory Levels

Inventory management and inventory turnover are becoming increasingly important because of rising carrying costs. Proper inventory levels are the primary objective of a materials manager. No longer is inventory management of secondary importance, behind quantity discounts and "nice-to-have" stocks.

Maximized Materials Movement

The horizontal management of materials places one manager in charge of materials from beginning to end. This unity of control and coordination center reduces time lost through interdepartmental conflict.

Functional Efficiency

Since the purchasing, production inventory control, and distribution managers report to the same person, who is equally interested in each function, they can improve the efficiency of each individual function in relation to the others. There is a general upgrading of the materials functions because of their collective interactive management.

Job Enrichment

The members of the materials management department will experience increased morale and job satisfaction as team members. The elimination of overlapping work reduces conflicts and promotes cooperation. In addition, as members of a multifunctional department, chances for promotion and personal development are greater.

NOTE: For further information on subjects covered in this section see the list of references in Section 30.

Public Purchasing

EDITOR

Solon A. Bennett, C.P.M., CPPO, CPCM   *Director of Purchases and Stores, City of Austin, Texas*

ASSOCIATE EDITORS

Daniel S. Wilson   *Assistant Administrator for Commercial, Office of Federal Procurement Policy, Office of Management & Budget, Washington, D.C.*

Robert E. Booton   *Director, Contract Placement, Office of Defense Research and Engineering, Department of Defense, Washington, D.C.*

Jay H. Bolton   *Former Deputy Commissioner, Federal Supply Service, General Services Administration, Washington, D.C.*

John J. Bennett   *Former Director, Federal Acquisition Institute, Office of Management & Budget, Washington, D.C.*

Homer A. Foerster, C.P.M., CPPO   *Executive Director, Texas State Purchasing and General Services Commission, Austin, Texas*

Stanley D. Zemansky, C.P.M., CPPO, CPCM   *City Purchasing Agent, City of Baltimore, Maryland*

Joseph J. Warnas, C.P.M., CPPO, CPCM   *Director of Materials Management, Maricopa County, Arizona*

Herbert C. Damron, C.P.M., CPPO   *Director of Purchasing, St. Louis Community College, St. Louis, Missouri*

American Bar Association, Model Procurement Code Staff   *principally Michael K. Love and Herbert H. Ferguson, Project Director, Washington, D.C.*

Lewis E. Spangler   *Executive Vice-President, National Institute of Governmental Purchasing, Inc., Arlington, Virginia*

INTRODUCTION

The single most important message that this section will attempt to convey is that public (including federal, state, and local) purchasing and materials management is fundamentally the same as other types, insofar as the essential functional elements are concerned. Many of the problems, procedures, and forms that the public or governmental buyer encounters are found in other sections of this handbook.

This section will assist the buyer in assessing positions and in recognizing certain of the problems common to public agencies, authorities, school districts, and other governmental jurisdictions. In addition, it will cover those activities common only to public or governmental procurement.

The most significant difference between the public and private sectors is that the dollars expended by the public sector are generated and provided by the taxpayers. This difference, particularly at state and local levels, subjects public officials to intense scrutiny and public accountability for all actions. Correspondingly, the legislative requirements, policies, and regulations, as well as the systems and procedures employed, are subject to vigorous internal and external review and adjustments. The flexibility and judgmental factors in the awards of contracts are more available to the private sector buyer than they are to the governmental buyer. The governmental buyer must also operate in a "fishbowl" environment, where actions continually are seen and reported in intimate detail.

The governmental purchasing official, however, does have certain advantages which are not available to those in the private sector. A specific example lies in the complete availability and interchange of information between agencies, a practice which outside the government fraternity may be competitively inadvisable and illegal. The government executive must be constantly alert not only to utilize the approved procedures but also to establish the channels of communication that bring product and pricing information from comparable agencies.

Laws governing governmental procurement are customarily broad. Administrative regulations of varying degrees of complexity are to be found in virtually all agencies.

The basic objectives of governmental procurement can be summarized as follows:

1. To purchase at the most reasonable cost consistent with needs, utilizing a statement of requirements which will attract wide competition
2. To maintain required quality standards
3. To promote standardization and simplification of materials
4. To minimize inventory carrying costs
5. To assure a continuing supply of materials
6. To support the functions of various departments and activities of the governmental jurisdiction
7. To effect cost savings through such techniques as value analysis and life-cycle costing and the use of commercially available items whenever possible
8. To conduct the procurement process in an open, competitive, fair manner and without conflict of interest or the possibility or appearance of improper business relationships

ADVANTAGES OF CENTRALIZED PURCHASING

Centralized purchasing is generally recognized as an important function in good government. Its objective is to achieve savings through the application of efficient management techniques, especially through volume buying. Under centralized procurement procedures, responsibility rests with an authorized specialist and is not incidental to other operating functions. If a specialized effort is devoted to coordinating the requirements of various agencies or departments and inviting widespread competition, maximum value can be expected from dollar expenditures.

Centralization may vary widely in degree according to the size or specialized nature of the governmental unit. Small local governments may achieve reasonable efficiency simply by coordinating and combining total requirements for basic commodities and supplies such as fuel oil, gasoline, stationery items, and office supplies. Larger political units may centralize all material, supplies, equipment, and service requirements. Every government and special authority should periodically review what degree of centralization enables it to function most efficiently. It should be pointed out that the term *centralization* as applied to governmental agencies means the establishment of one separate department for the purchase of goods and services.

Savings Resulting from Centralization

It is not possible to accurately predict savings in particular situations because the potential depends upon the efficiency of the centralized operation. It should be emphasized that successful centralized purchasing requires clearly defined authority, competent personnel, and freedom from political influence. Centralization without a commitment to good business and personnel administration will not produce the desired objective.

Savings may accrue through centralized purchasing in many ways:

1. Combining volume reduces prices.
2. Planned purchases reduce the number of small and emergency orders.
3. Proper planning and coordination result in fewer requisitions, bid invitations, purchase orders, and related paperwork. Costs of legal advertising can be reduced by combining several bid openings in one advertisement.
4. Standard procedures can be set forth in a purchasing manual to help prevent costly, embarrassing mistakes by new or temporary personnel. Coordination and communication are improved, practices are made routine, and efficiency is increased, which, of course, results in increased productivity.
5. Greater value is achieved through improved specifications. Specifications should be continually and objectively reviewed in terms of performance requirements. In some cases savings can be achieved by using higher-priced items which, for quality reasons, actually give a greater value.
6. Specifications for similar items should be standardized whenever possible. It is advisable for the centralized purchasing unit to have the authority to adopt standard specifications relative to items which are utilized by two or more departments.
7. Sales expenses of suppliers are reduced. Sales personnel contact one department and, if necessary, are referred to the using department.
8. Invoice procedures can be standarized and reduced.
9. The sale of surplus materials is centralized, and transfer of excess materials from one department to another is simplified.

PUBLIC AND GOVERNMENTAL JURISDICTIONS

This section briefly reviews the various governmental levels and their purchasing and materials management activities.

Federal Procurement

Federal procurement involves much more than buying. The process is used extensively to promote such social and economic objectives as interests of small business, use of minority business, fair employment practices, payment of fair wages, safe and healthful working conditions, employment of the handicapped, rehabilitation of prisoners, and use of recycled materials.

The scope of federal procurement is over $100 billion annually, plus an estimated $77 billion in federal assistance funds to state and local governments in 1979. More than 100 executive branch organizations award about 50 million contracts annually, with a procurement work force of about 80,000 employees.

Procurement today is governed by more than 4000 fragmented statutes, many of which are redundant and obsolete. Agencies proliferate regulations, procedures, and forms from two basic regulatory systems, the Armed Services Procurement Regulations (ASPR) and the Federal Procurement Regulations (FPR) through multiple levels of implementation. The result is a frustrating array of at least 20 different types of documents that represent a 5-foot shelf of procurement regulations with which a buyer must cope.

Department of Defense   The Defense Department purchases about 4 million items annually. These are commercial, modified commercial, and built to government specifications and drawings. In fiscal year 1976 purchases totaled $46.9 billion.

Department of Defense procurement is effected under the Armed Services Procurement Act of 1947, now codified in Title 10 of the U.S. Code. Title 10, Section 2202, of the U.S. Code provides that the moneys appropriated for procurement and supply can be committed only pursuant to regulations prescribed by the Secretary of Defense. The ASPR primarily implements this congressional directive.

The ASPR has the force and effect of a Department of Defense directive and is issued by the Under Secretary of Defense for Research and Engineering by a directive of the Secretary of Defense. It is coordinated with the Army, Navy, Air Force, and Defense Logistics Agency through the ASPR Committee. Policies are formulated after comments are solicited from representative industry associations and other government agencies, including the General Accounting Office (GAO) and the General Services Administration (GSA).

Actual buying is the responsibility of the military services and the Defense Logistics Agency. The military departments buy a substantial number of items for each other under the single-department procurement program. This program involves the procurement of supplies pursuant to assignment of purchasing responsibility made by the Secretary of Defense. The contracting officer initially determines the method of procurement, i.e., formal advertising or negotiation.

General Services Administration   GSA was established pursuant to the Federal Property and Administrative Services Act of 1949 to provide the government with an economical and efficient system for the procurement and supply of personal property and nonpersonal services, the utilization of available property, the disposal of surplus property, and records management. GSA comprises the National Archives and Records Service, the Federal Preparedness Agency, the Public Buildings Service, the Automated Data and Telecommunications Service, and the

Federal Supply Service (FSS). With headquarters in Washington, D.C., GSA has 10 regional offices.

GSA's principal procurement organization is FSS, which is responsible for supplying common-use, commercial-type items to federal agencies. Additional major responsibilities include operating the GSA Interagency Motor Pool System, administering government-wide excess personal property utilization and surplus donation programs, and managing the government stockpile of strategic and critical matters.

FSS has three primary methods with which to meet agency requirements for supplies and materials. These are stock, nonstock, and federal supply schedule contracts. The first method, stock, involves a supply distribution network for procuring and stocking high-demand or critical items. The nonstock program consolidates procurements for the many agencies and provides for shipment direct from the contractor to the requisitioning activity. The federal supply schedule contracting program, by dollar volume, is the largest FSS procurement program. Schedules indicating successful offerers supplying the same generic type of items at varying prices are distributed to federal agencies. In turn, the agencies are to fill their requirements with the lowest-cost items which specifically meet their needs. This procurement method has received some criticism because the agencies do not always buy the lowest-cost item meeting their needs.

The Office of Federal Procurement Policy (OFPP) in the Office of Management and Budget (OMB) is the central point of control. OFPP is small—24 procurement specialists, with a budget of $1.7 million in the fiscal year 1977. The OFPP was established under Public Law 93-400 in August 1974. The OFPP is responsible for formulating and promulgating procurement policies applicable to all federal agencies. At the direction of OFPP, the Department of Defense and the General Services Administration closely coordinate the issuance of the ASPR and the FPR. In many cases, where conditions permit, identical language is used in both regulations. The OFPP is in the process of considering whether it is feasible to establish a single regulatory system for all executive agencies, either by means of a single regulation or by the use of identical wording in the ASPR and FPR wherever possible. Such a system would contemplate a more direct and active role by the OFPP than previously.

The OFPP with its administrator, three associate administrators, and three assistant administrators, has the following objectives and priorities:

1. Full and effective implementation of OMB circular A-109, which prescribes how major systems will be acquired
2. The development of a new set of regulations to replace the ASPR and the FPR
3. Enactment of a new procurement statute along the lines of S.1264, Federal Acquisition Act of 1977, introduced in the U.S. Senate on April 6, 1977
4. Resolution of the controversy that has inhibited the implementation of the

government's long-standing policy of relying on the private sector for needed goods and services and adoption of procedures that are consistent, fair and equitable

5. Establishment of a national supply system that will minimize duplication and overlap in the acquisition and distribution of common-use items

6. Consolidation of the purchase and inspection of food, including a simplified specification system

7. Increased purchase of commercial products for supply through commercial distribution channels

8. A fully operational federal procurement institute to manage the education, training, and development of a procurement work force (this has been initiated and will be discussed later in this section)

Federal Acquisition Institute   In July 1976 the Federal Acquisition Institute (FAI) was established and the Department of Defense was designated as the executive agency for the institute.

The FAI is committed to the policy of developing the skills, knowledge, and abilities of federal procurement employees through the establishment and operation of progressive and efficient programs and procurement research education, training, and career development, thereby improving public service, increasing efficiency and economy, building and retaining a skilled and efficient work force, and installing and using the best modern practices and techniques in the conduct of the government's business. The creation of FAI is an outgrowth of the recommendations of the Commission on Government Procurement (COGP). In its report to Congress in December 1972, the COGP dramatically documented the need for a procurement institute and for career development programs in the area of procurement. The institute will have the following objectives: (1) develop, conduct, and promote undergraduate and graduate courses, executive seminars, and other academic programs; (2) promote, monitor, and conduct research to develop business methods and management techniques that will advance the state of the art in procurement; (3) develop and implement agency- and government-wide career development programs, which will include the needed education and training; (4) develop and implement plans and procedures for the review and evaluation of programs; (5) articulate standards by which programs can be developed, measured, and certified; (6) monitor and review programs to ensure that they are current and avoid or eliminate duplication; and (7) develop and maintain a system of communication which will ensure identification of and responsiveness to new issues, developments, and needs in the procurement community.

State Procurement

Centralized purchasing is almost universal among the 50 states of the nation. There is no general agreement among the states as to the practical optimum degree of centralized purchasing. In fact, it is impossible to determine what this optimum would be from every viewpoint—social, economic, and political. Centralization cannot exceed the limits established by the statutes of the various states.

Organization   Several types of organizational structures are to be found among state purchasing agencies. These can be categorized basically as follows: (1) a board or commission; (2) a separate agency; (3) a section of an integrated financial or administrative agency; (4) a division of a general services agency.

Purchase Methods   Buying of commodities is one function that all state purchasing agencies have in common. Usually open-end contracts for delivery to all geographical locations are executed for items of common use, such as staple foods, office supplies, paint, janitorial supplies, and tires and tubes. In the majority of the states, the range of commodities involved is much broader—it may include virtually all equipment, materials, and supplies used by the various state agencies. Many states make their contracts usable by a smaller political jurisidiction to allow the smaller jurisdiction to draw from state warehouses.

Services   A number of states have found that considerable monetary savings are possible if the procurement of certain services, such as the moving of furniture and employees, pest control, elevator maintenance, institutional feeding, and, in many cases, the procurement of professional services, is channeled through the central purchasing agency. The functions of a number of state purchasing agencies have been expanded to handle these.

Standards and Specifications, Inspection, and Testing   A major responsibility of a centralized purchasing agency is the standardization of commodities and procedures throughout state government. Many states have a unit in their central purchasing departments which is designated as a standards and specifications section and is headed by an individual designated as a standards engineer or chief standards engineer. A centrally controlled inspection and testing program also ensures compliance with quality requirements in many states.

Stores and Warehouses   Approximately half the states operate central warehouses. Where centralized warehousing is practiced, the purchasing or procurement officer is directly responsible for the stocks and commodities under his or her control until such time as they are issued to the using agency.

Related Functions   The purchasing agency is often required to handle the disposition of surplus materials such as scrap and waste and obsolete or damaged stocks or equipment. In some states the purchasing agency also handles construction contracts, architectural and engineering agreements, and the buying and selling of real estate and of related services such as duplicating or printing, motor pools, equipment repair and rental, communication services, central telephone exchanges, document sales, mail and messenger service, and microfilming.

County Procurement

As counties are major subdivisions of the states, their purchasing operations are an important part of governmental purchasing. Of the 3104 counties in the nation, many have centralized purchasing with different degrees of refinement. As political subdivisions of the state, the counties are usually bound by state statutes, which delineate their purchasing authority. The statutes clearly state such things as what items shall go through a sealed-bid procedure. Where the population and dollar amount of purchases warrant, the county usually operates under a strong centralized purchasing organization, thus achieving maximum benefits.

Organization   It is important that the heads of county purchasing be on the same level as their counterparts in other departments, such as budget, finance and personnel. Only through organization equality can the purchasing function offer the maximum utilization of procurement and materials management skills to other departments and agencies. To establish organizational responsibility and authority, the county may issue a policy statement of the following type.[1]

> It shall be the responsibility of the head of the purchasing department to centralize procurement and establish procedures under guidelines promulgated by the board of supervisors by which materials, supplies, and equipment for all county elected officials and departments shall be purchased; to generate specifications and annual contracts for those items requiring board approval; to issue purchase orders for all materials, supplies, and equipment; to maintain and operate the county's Materials Management Center and inventory control system; and to coordinate the disposal of the county's surplus and obsolete materials and equipment.

Goals of Centralized County Purchasing   These should be: (1) to maintain continuity of supply to meet routine emergency usage requirements with minimal investment and stocking inventory consistent with safety and economy; (2) to maintain usable standards of quality for supplies, equipment, and materials, augmented by ongoing programs of value analysis, cost analysis, total cost bidding, and life-cycle costing to reduce the cost of purchases; (3) to keep the county executive informed of procurement developments which could affect county costs or the county's ability to provide services; (4) to develop and continually evaluate suppliers who can provide efficient services, with emphasis on quality and reliability at the lowest cost; and (5) to inform substandard suppliers they are in danger of being classified as defaulting suppliers from whom no future bids or proposals shall be considered.

Because the agencies and departments, particularly in the large counties, are geographically separate and functionally distinct, centralized receiving should be utilized only for bulk procurement and storage of commonly used items. The county purchasing department can best fulfill this materials management or procurement function by supporting a system of satellite warehouses from one central location which incorporates the purchasing service, inventory control, and warehouse facility. This allows a typical county purchasing department to evolve gradually into a county procurement or materials management center, thereby assuming greater responsibility and enjoying more authority while better coping with the logistics needs of the county's agencies and departments.

Standardization, Receiving, Inspection, and Disposal   Some of the areas of responsibility of a county purchasing department are in standardization of commodities; this can usually be accomplished through a standards committee consisting of major county agency representatives set up to meet the goal of establishing standard specifications for materials, supplies, and equipment.

---

[1]"Purchasing Policy," *Administrative Manual,* Maricopa County, Arizona, Sec. 8-1-A.2, June 5, 1978.

Receiving, inspection, and testing, with use of statistical quality control, should also be the responsibility of the procurement department. Of course, this applies only to merchandise that is centrally received and stored. When necessary, procurement personnel should assist the using agencies in inspecting and testing purchased goods or else should hire a private research laboratory to conduct the tests.

Another area of responsibility is the proper disposal of surplus material. Here county purchasing should have the authority to work with the using agencies in the procurement and disposal of federal and estate surplus property, as well as county surplus property. Regarding cancellation and return of merchandise, the using agencies in every case should be required to handle this touchy area through the centralized purchasing function. The change order responsibility and the signatory authority should be clearly delineated for the purchasing function and for different levels of purchasing responsibility. The use of emergency purchases should be clearly defined and limited. Emergency purchases should be discouraged, as they usually prove to be inefficient and costly.

The head of county purchasing should be conversant with statutes so that he can, with proper authorization, testify in favor of statutory improvements. A case in point is a cash purchase order which has been successfully adopted in Maricopa County, Arizona, through a statutory change, i.e., permissive state legislation empowering the counties to adopt it under the guidance of the state auditor general. Authority to contract must be clearly shown as being delegated to the purchasing head, with a clear statement that elected officials and department heads may not enter into contractual agreements or obligations without risking personal liability. Those purchases which require advertised bid invitations should be clearly called out in procedures implementing the statutory constraints imposed upon the particular county.

Municipal Procurement

Cities, especially the larger ones, are possibly the most numerous among governmental agencies which have centralized purchasing, procurement, or materials management. While dissimilarity of a high order does prevail, the historic existence and interdependence of municipal purchasers have resulted in comparability of operations and interchange of information across state lines and wide geographic areas. The legislative independence of local government in establishing procurement policy has made possible the transfer of ideas between widely separated jurisdictions.

Municipal purchases often include a variety of capital equipment, materials and supplies, and construction. Many departments are also responsible for services, including professional services and leasing. As in the case of states, the municipal purchasing agency often handles inventory management, stores or warehousing and disposals, and buying and selling of real estate and related services, such as repair and rental of duplicating or printing equipment, communication services, central telephone exchanges, document sales, mail and messenger services, microfilming, and building maintenance. This arrangement can be especially effective when operating under a city manager form of government.

In the spring and summer of 1979, the International City Management Association (ICMA) conducted a survey of purchasing practices in municipalities of 10,000 population and over. This survey, and a similar survey conducted by ICMA in 1973, provided data about municipal purchasing practices and what cities are doing to improve their purchasing methods. The conclusion, based on a comparison of the 1973 survey and the 1979 survey, is that municipal purchasing practices are improving. The rate of improvement, however, appears to be slow.[2]

One of the major needs of any city is a purchasing process that assures efficient, cost-effective acquisition of goods, capital equipment, and services. A successful purchasing program requires: a single designated authority to contract for goods and services; a team effort by the purchasing department and user departments; a collection of enough statistical data to know "where we have been and where we need to go"; and a strong sense of integrity.

Central purchasing can produce savings up to 15 percent because of improved specifications and bidding procedures and lower prices through volume buying. The savings can be substantial because approximately a third of governmental operating budgets is spent on the purchase of materials.

Educational Institutions

School districts, as potential purchasing entities, numerically challenge the municipalities, totaling approximately 10 percent more.

School districts that include a centralized purchasing department vary greatly in structure and operation. The observer will recognize that the purchasing function in some districts is responsible for little more than books and school supplies, the remainder of the function being performed by the municipality, county, or state. In other districts, the purchasing function may be responsible for the total logistics function, measured in expenditures that approach $100 million annually.

There are over 3000 colleges and universities in the nation engaged in purchasing a wide variety of supplies, equipment, and services. Annual purchasing volume amounts to hundreds of millions of dollars to provide undergraduate and graduate education for the millions of students enrolled. It can be stated that the educational purchasing agent is responsible for procuring a larger variety of products and services than any other purchasing agent engaged in procurement activities. These items range from books to sophisticated nuclear laboratory equipment. This statement can easily be substantiated by thinking for a moment about the wide diversity of courses offered in college curricula today. Community and junior colleges have further expanded these areas with vocational skills courses in addition to their normal academic transfer courses.

Organization   Educational institutions normally execute their procurement functions in accordance with policies established by a board of trustees or a similar body. These policies, of course, will be subordinate to the state and national legal requirements pertaining to purchasing.

[2]Dan H. Davidson and Solon A. Bennett, "Municipal Purchasing Practices," *The Municipal Year Book 1980*, International City Management Association, Washington, D.C., 1980, p. 209.

Procurement Functions and Methods As mentioned earlier, a broad range of commodities and services must be provided to support the wide range and variety of instructional programs. The larger educational purchasing department is normally responsible for printing, mail functions, insurance requirements, receiving inventory, property accountability, transportation, food service, and disposal of surplus materials. Purchasing departments may also be responsible for supporting several different campuses in different locations throughout city, county, or state. Many educational purchasing agents now have the title of material manager.

Services Obviously, centralized purchasing is practiced to the maximum extent possible. Various types of contracts are utilized to minimize the number of individual orders and transactions. Multiyear contracts are awarded and may be extended under the proviso that funds will be available each year as stated under the contract terms. Data processing equipment is used for analysis of data, supply sources, and bids in addition to preparation of reports, follow-up, and preparation of purchase orders and contracts.

Other Governmental Subdivisions and Authorities

The number of purchasing agents in this category is difficult to estimate. In a single county, they may include such diverse functions as public authorities, water districts, utility districts, mosquito abatement districts, hospitals, universities, and recreational units. Purchasing under rules and regulations of their own development, they may expend hundreds of millions of dollars annually. Purchasing by major utility districts, such as the Los Angeles Department of Water and Power or public authority such as Tennessee Valley Authority, may exceed that of a majority of the states.

Detailed purchasing procedures for political subdivisions are not included in this section. However, many of the procedures found elsewhere in this handbook apply to the procurement function in political subdivisions.

OPERATING ADVANTAGES OF CENTRALIZATION

The specialized knowledge and information available in the centralized purchasing department can be of real assistance to operating departments in the development of proper specifications. Where this knowledge is lacking, departments occasionally rely on specifications supplied by a single vendor and thereby create a prior obligation, or they may obtain specifications which are restricted to a particular manufacturer. Centralized purchasing can make important reports to management which will enable the administration to base policy decisions on accurate and timely information. Standard statistical data reflecting the level and type of purchasing activity engaged in should be reported periodically. Special reports should be used to advise of changing price trends which have an impact on budgets, and reports should be issued to show where savings have been achieved.

Effective planning and coordination are two important attributes of efficient management. Purchases should be planned whenever possible in order to eliminate relatively expensive, rush-type purchases. Judgments must occasionally be made between what constitutes a true emergency and what is merely an operating inconvenience. Emergencies requiring the suspension of usual procedures in the interest of preserving the health, welfare, or safety of citizens are relatively rare. Such emergencies are generally declared by the highest executive office of the governmental unit.

The high cost of rush orders is caused by lack of time to solicit competition, so that low bidders are passed over in favor of those able to make immediate delivery, and by the use of more expensive means of communication and transportation than would normally be chosen.

Planning and coordination should include three basic steps: identification of major purchase categories, establishing bidding timetables, and coordination and incorporation of all department or agency requirements into the bidding timetable.

Commodity Classifications

Purchase categories may be based upon commodities or upon functions. Under a centralized purchasing operation emphasis should be upon coordinating requirements for commodities used by all or many of the operating agencies. Fuel oil, office supplies, and passenger vehicles are examples of commodities which may be required by many or all agencies. Textbooks, athletic supplies, and police supplies are examples of items required by a limited number of departments by virtue of special functions.

Purchase categories can be referred to commodity classifications. The Federal Supply Classification, complied by the Defense Logistics Agency, is a commodity classification designed to serve the functions of supply and is sufficiently comprehensive in scope to merit the classification of all items of personal property. In order to accomplish this, groups and classes have been established for the universe of commodities, with emphasis on the items known to be in the supply systems of the federal government, the largest buyer of materials in the world. The following indexes can be purchased from the Defense Logistics Agency, Defense Logistics Services Center, Battle Creek, MI 49016.

1. Federal Supply Classification, Part 2: Numeric Index of Classes. This is prepared in microfiche and contains the names of items within each class, listed alphabetically under the class number and title. Classes are shown by group in numerical order with the code numbering system.

2. Federal Supply Classification, Part 3: Alphabetical Index. This is prepared in microfiche and contains all names of items which appear in part 2, arranged in alphabetical order. Opposite each entry the applicable code number is shown.

Bidding Timetables

Bidding timetables should be established. Timetables should include single-transaction purchases, as well as open-end contract requirements. All factors which may affect price or delivery should be considered in establishing timetables. Seasonal needs should be considered in the light of off-season discounts if they apply. All using departments should be canvased to determine quantity requirements of the various commodity items. Specifications should be reviewed, refined, and standardized, if necessary, prior to bidding. The purchasing department should have the legal authority to require all agencies to furnish such information or estimates as may be required to effect proper coordination.

Financial and Budget Control

Although financial and budget control is generally the responsibility of other departments, purchasing may participate in the establishment of budgets by providing price information based upon past purchases and projections based upon market knowledge. Section 25 pertains to the single subject of budgeting.

A *purchase-order encumbrance system* is desirable where budgetary procedures establish specific appropriations for departments, categories, or items. Under an encumbrance system, the responsible financial officer certifies that funds are available. The value of each order is charged to the appropriate account prior to releasing the order to the supplier.

There are two advantages to this system. First, overspending can be prevented. This can be particularly important at the end of a fiscal year, when supplementary appropriations may not be available. Second, operating departments should be able to obtain timely information as to the status of their accounts in terms of expenditures, encumbrances, and remaining balances. Where accounting systems are computerized, account status can be obtained quickly and in as much detail as required.

AREAS OF CENTRALIZATION

Legal authority should define functions to be centralized by a particular governmental unit. Areas which potentially may be included under the responsibility of a centralized public procurement or purchasing office are: material, supply, and equipment requirements; stores or warehouse operations; service contracts; disposition of surplus materials; inspection and testing; and other indirectly related operations such as printing, maintenance of buildings, microfilming, and messenger service.

Purchases

As a general rule, all material, supply, and equipment purchases should be centralized. Because there are many highly specialized functions at all levels of government represented by a large number of autonomous or semiautonomous departments, agencies, boards, or commissions, there is a natural tendency for each to think that its material requirements are unique and therefore not included in the concept of centralized purchasing. Centralized purchasing should cross all department or agency lines, however, based upon actual commodity use. Insofar as possible, all uncommon items should be centralized so that the benefits of objectivity and specialized purchasing knowledge and techniques can be realized. Where exceptions are allowed, it may be appropriate to make the purchases subject to approval of the centralized purchasing agency or subject to procedures established by the agency.

Stores or Warehouse Operations

Stores or warehouse operations may be an important part of centralized purchasing, especially in large city, county, or state governments. Local governments may find economy only in the operation of a small stationery storeroom to serve the needs of centrally located administrative offices. This, however, could also be applicable, e.g., to local governments' water and wastewater facilities, where piping, valves, etc., must also be stored.

In order for a centralized operation to be economically successful, the lower cost of volume purchasing must offset the overhead costs of warehousing and distribution. A proper decision on warehousing requires a thorough, detailed analysis of all costs, direct and indirect. Many of the cost advantages that formerly accrued through centralized warehousing have been offset by the increasing use of systems contracting, open-end contracts, or other forms of stockless buying.

Surplus and Scrap

The disposition of surplus materials is logically a function handled by a centralized purchasing or procurement department. In large governmental units, a specialist may be designated as a surplus disposal officer. In smaller units, the function is usually an important part of the overall materials control aspect of purchasing and may be performed by the purchasing manager or one of the buying staff.

After surplus material has been referred to the purchasing department for disposition, a judgment must be made as to the best method of obtaining maximum value for the item. Frequently, equipment can be reduced to less active service, and thus its useful life can be extended. First consideration should be given to transferring the item to another department within the organization for further use.

Obtaining maximum value from the disposal of scrap has always been an objective of an efficient government organization. This activity has received new attention as a result of the emphasis on recycling as a means of preserving natural resources and reducing solid waste. Items which previously were dumped, buried, or incinerated are now being recycled even though there may be little monetary gain. The disposal officer should be alert to new uses for recycled materials and should be able to provide information which will be of assistance in setting realistic policies on recycling by the governmental unit.

Inspection and Testing

Inspection of materials and equipment prior to acceptance is vital in order to ensure that full value is being received. Inspection should be prompt and should take whatever form is necessary, considering the specifications, dollar value, volume, or other characteristics of the order.

Responsibility for inspection rests with the procurement department as part of the overall materials management function. The inspection function is usually delegated to the receiving department, with purchasing taking an active role only when it is necessary to resolve a dispute between the contractor and the receiver.

Small-city or town governments do not have a volume of purchases sufficient to justify a full-time inspection force or the operation of a testing laboratory. In these cases, a brief inspection manual may be useful to define standard inspection procedures and lines of responsibility. Receivers should be cognizant of any simple tests which can be performed without the use of elaborate equipment and should be alert to check for such obvious deficiencies as damaged items, short counts, and short weights.

Where special testing is necessary, local governments may use commercial testing laboratories or other government agencies which have the testing facilities or special technical competence required. The Department of Agriculture, for example, has inspectors available in most areas and inspects meat and produce items at a reasonable cost. Local governments should check with nearby cities, universities, technical schools, the state, and the area office of the General Services Administration (GSA) to determine what assistance may be available in performing tests.

POSITION IN THE ORGANIZATION

The purchasing function should be centralized and positioned in the governmental organization at a hierarchical level which would allow it to effectively carry out its legal responsibilities in a professional manner. To accomplish this, the purchasing head must occupy a management level sufficiently high to deal authoritatively with the requisitioning departments being served and the suppliers with whom contracts are made. Suppliers doing business with a governmental entity should know that the purchasing head has authority to make purchasing decisions and award contracts. Authority in the central purchasing unit should be broad enough to permit delegation of certain purchases to the using department when efficiency and economy are thereby realized.

Consideration should also be given to placing the purchasing function in the governmental organization in such a way as to isolate it from improper political pressures and influences.

Well-defined statutory and regulatory safeguards to preserve the integrity of the purchasing process are not in themselves enough to protect the public interest. The program must be placed within a framework that makes it possible to carry out those well-defined statutory and regulatory safeguards. The report of the National Advisory Commission on Criminal Justice Standards and Goals on community crime prevention (January 1973) made the following observation in its chapter on government procurement of goods and services: "People who are familiar with operation of government recognize that a principal opportunity for personal profit or political funding is to be found in a governmental unit that purchases goods or services."

In many state governments the purchasing activity operates as a separate division within a major department of administration or general services or a similar department of the executive branch. In such structures the department head is often appointed by the elected governor. Such appointed heads often have a tenure no longer than that of the elected official who made the appointment. A state structure which has gained favorable recognition in this regard is made up of a policy board of three citizen members who are appointed by the governor and confirmed by the state senate. Each board member is appointed for a 6-year term, the terms being staggered at 2-year intervals to prevent the possibility of the same governor making all the appointments on the board. The policy board is required by statute to hire an agency head who possesses certain purchasing qualifications as set out in a state statute. This structure was designed not only to isolate the purchasing function from improper political pressures, but also to protect the office of the governor from outside pressures intended to influence purchasing decisions.

LEGAL AND ADMINISTRATIVE REGULATIONS

The statutes governing purchasing are almost as numerous as the agencies they govern. Complete knowledge of these statutes under which a governmental buyer operates is essential. Overlooked, however, is the need for the buyer to be aware of more liberal, more flexible, or more effective purchasing laws so that he may advocate changes to those officials under whom he operates. Here is one of the most cogent arguments for the governmental buyer to participate actively in associations composed exclusively of governmental buyers. The purchasing official— even in the smallest jurisdiction—must be prepared to present his case to the reviewing official who will inevitably be present. His case must factually present the impediments in legislation that prevent effective purchasing performance, as well as the areas in which facilitating legislation is required.

Administrative Regulations

Statutes governing purchasing are customarily broad. Administrative regulations of varying degrees of complexity are to be found in virtually all agencies, and their preparation and revision must be at the top of the work priority list for the governmental purchaser. No line of reasoning is more likely to lead to entrapment than that pursued when the purchasing official leaves the development of this list to the administrator, to the legal counsel, or to other officials not knowledgeable about the purchasing or procurement function.

THE PURCHASING PROCESS

Basic Considerations

The procurement cycle is essentially the same for business and for government or public purchasing or procurement. Requisitioning, quoting or bidding, issuing purchase orders or contracts, receiving, inspecting, testing, and paying invoices are basic procedural elements in any significant procurement operation. Each of these procedural elements is considered in detail in other sections of this handbook, and all public and governmental purchasing officials should be familiar with the information contained therein.

Every governmental agency has various forms for use in the procurement function that have been developed in accordance with the needs and the legal statutes governing the agency. As in industry, forms used in the purchasing cycle vary according to the size and complexity of the governmental agency.

Innovations that can increase efficiency, such as traveling requisitions, preitemized requisitions, and blank-check purchase orders should be noted and adopted wherever possible.

Certain aspects and details of the purchasing process require special emphasis in government because of the public nature of most government transactions and the imposition of controls designed to protect the public interest. Central to most government procurement regulations is the requirement that purchases in excess of a specified amount, usually within the range of $500 to $5000, shall be supported by a written contract, after public advertisement and receipt of sealed bids. Such bids must be opened publicly and award made to the lowest and best responsible bidder. Negotiated purchases are the exception rather than the rule in governmental or public purchasing and are usually specifically limited by regulation to cases of emergency or to other instances in which it is not practical or possible to obtain publicly advertised bids.

Competitive Negotiations

The Council of State Governments in 1974 published a digest on state and local government purchasing. This report was prepared by the National Association of State Purchasing Officials, an affiliate of the Council, and Peat, Marwick, & Mitchell and Company under the sponsorship of the Law Enforcement Assistance Administration of the U.S. Department of Justice. The following comments are taken from this report (pages 22–24).

> Many purchasing laws do not adequately consider purchasing by competitive negotiation. There is a place and need for competitive negotiation in public purchasing; however, negotiation should be allowed only in limited and defined circumstances.
>
> Most purchasing laws provide that all awards for purchases exceeding a stipulated dollar amount be based on formal sealed competitive bids. While this process is and should be the general standard for public purchasing, there are frequent instances in practice in which competitive negotiation can and should be used. For example, when time is a crucial factor, when the procurement involves high-technology items (e.g., data processing hardware, communication systems, complex telemetry equipment), or when the purchase is for professional services, competitive negotiation is advisable. Almost all states reported problems in attempting to apply conventional bidding techniques to the procurement of these types of items because of the difficulty in constructing suitable descriptive specifications, which are necessary so that all bidders can compete on a common and equal basis. To be

most effective, therefore, provision for negotiations should be made in the procurement process.

Contrary to some beliefs, negotiation is in no way synonymous with noncompetitive or single-source procurement. When needed items or services are found to be available from only one source, negotiation can be useful and advantageous. However, the general use of negotiation is not intended to preclude competition; the objective should be to purchase an item or service in the most effective manner and in the best interest of the government, as is the case in a formal sealed-bid process.

Some principles applicable to the competitive negotiation process are the same as those pertaining to the formal sealed-bid process. A bidder's list consisting of qualified offerers should be prepared, public notice of the product or service needed should be made, and all qualified offerers should be solicited. Some of the detailed procedures, however, will differ from the sealed-bid process. A request for a proposal (RFP) is used in lieu of a bid invitation. The RFP should include a description of the item or service to be purchased, the specific criteria which will be used in evaluating proposals, and other pertinent information such as delivery dates or time frames within which the work must be completed. Since these purchases usually involve nonstandard items or complex services, the RFP should also call for additional information such as experience in the line of the work being considered (including references) and staff capability, along with résumés of key individuals who will work on the contract and the cost breakdown of the proposed price. Price is not normally the determining criterion for awards; consequently factors such as the above are used in developing proposal evaluation criteria. These criteria must be carefully developed and a weighting scheme formulated around the most important features of each procurement action. The evaluation criteria should be included in the RFP along with the stated relative order of their importance. Frequently the criteria are divided into three main categories: managerial capability, technical capability, and approach in meeting performance requirements and reasonableness of price.

The proposal evaluation criteria should be looked upon as standards which measure how well an offer or its approach meets desired performance requirements and which permit an evaluation of the differences between desired performance characteristics and what the offerer proposes to do. Moreover, such standards permit the evaluation of proposals against objective norms rather than against each other. A scoring system, once devised, must be impartially applied to each proposal. Any departure from the established plan which is prompted by factors outside the system is proper only insofar as the same treatment is extended impartially to all offerers. Proposal evaluations should include cost or price analysis. Price analysis represents an evaluation of proposed prices without regard to the separate cost elements and proposed profit amount. Techniques such as comparison of proposed prices with each other, with the published price list, and with independent estimates can be used. This type of analysis may suffice when there is adequate competition and prior experience in the item or service being purchased. Otherwise cost analysis is essential. Cost analysis consists of a review and verification of cost data supporting each element of proposed cost.

Negotiation generally involves discussion and bargaining with a view toward reaching agreement on price and other terms of the proposed contract. These discussions should be conducted individually with each qualified offerer. The basic objective is to achieve the contract agreement most advantageous to the government in terms of factors such as period of performance, type of contract, quantity of the items or services being purchased, and price. Proposals submitted by competitive firms are not disclosed to the public or to competitors. However, after a contract is awarded, its terms and conditions should be public record.

Specifications and Standards

Exacting specifications are a requisite for effective bidding. Specifications are clear and accurate descriptions of the requirements for supplies, equipment, materials, or services. Specifications establish minimum requirements for quality and construction of supplies and equipment necessary for an acceptable product. Generally, specifications are in the form of written descriptions, performance requirements, drawings, prints, commercial designations, industry standards, and other descriptive references. Specifications form an integral part of the bid and of the purchase contract. Specifications must be so drawn as to secure fair competition upon equal terms to all bidders. If any public contract entered into with the best bidder contains substantial provisions beneficial to him which were not included in the specifications, it may be voided as not being the contract offered to the lowest bidder by the advertisement. Courts have generally held that awards on bidding must be made by discretion of the awarding body on the basis of common standards made known to all bidders. No such universal standard exists when some of the bidders have approval to depart from specifications as published while others are held to them.

All provisions should be precisely stated to avoid misinterpretation and to ensure that bids can be equitably compared and evaluated. Specifications should be written in a manner which will allow open competition while obtaining the quality of product required. Constant review of specifications is necessary to meet changing requirements and to take advantage of technological advances. There are several types of specifications and standards that can be used in the procurement process. These are: (1) *performance,* wherein function and use of the product needed are the basic definitions; (2) *design,* wherein particular characteristics of the product and their arrangement are the basic definition; (3) *qualified products list,* wherein actual products have been tested or examined and approved prior to seeking prices—this is, in essence, a standard; (4) *or approved equal,* wherein the exact product of one or more suppliers or typical workmanship is designated as the level of quality desired and the purchaser reserves the right to approve any other as equal or acceptable; (5) *questionnaire,* wherein the purchaser prepares a product information sheet which accompanies the request for prices and which each bidder must complete and return as a part of the bid (it should be noted that a questionnaire concept can be combined with a performance or a design specification); and (6) *sample,* wherein the purchaser requires suppliers to furnish representative samples of products offered or compares an evaluation in determining the successful bidder.

Specifications should serve basically as a minimum quality level acceptable to the purchaser. Minor deviations from a specification may receive consideration. Such deviations may provide for an increased or decreased quality level. Minor deviations increasing the quality level at a higher purchase price than the low bid should be considered if the total cost is determined to be lower than that provided by the low bid. Minor deviations from specifications at a lower price than the low bid meeting all aspects of the specification may be waived as an informality or technicality and considered, if it is determined that total cost is lower and overall function improved or not impaired. Major deviations, however, may be considered only prior to bid openings, and all bidders should be advised of same.

One of the most effective means of securing proper quality and economy is standardization of supply items in common use by more than one department or agency. Successful standardization should be developed that utilizes information provided by the using agency's available engineering or technical personnel and the responsible purchasing officer. Multi-use standards should be encouraged and expensive specials eliminated when possible. Standards will reduce inventory because they eliminate duplicate and near-duplicate stock. Also, in stockless purchasing programs suppliers are more willing to stock standard parts than specials. Standard equipment materials and supplies are available from many sources, often from stock, which reduces lead times and assures on-time delivery. Standardization factors to be considered are: (1) design; (2) quality; (3) interchangeability; (4) sizes; (5) grades; (6) colors; (7) methods of manufacture; and (8) material and chemical characteristics.

Government units having sufficient size and purchasing volume may establish a standards and specification division staffed with engineers, chemists, or other technicians who devote their full time to the development of quality standards and specifications. Such a division should normally come under the supervision of the chief purchasing official as a part of the overall materials function.

Considerable time and effort contributed by knowledgeable personnel must be invested in the development of proper specifications. Advantage should be taken of the free exchange of information among governmental units. This can be of particular importance for small government units, which may not employ specialized technical personnel. The federal, state, county, or another local government jurisdiction may have already developed a specification which could be readily utilized.

Federal specifications developed by the GSA cover a multitude of items used by all federal agencies. Although developed for the use of federal buyers, they are also available for general use. The *Index of Federal Specifications and Standards* may be purchased from the Superintendent of Documents, U.S. Government Printing Office, Washington, D.C. 20402. The index and individual specifications are available for reference at GSA regional offices and at some government depository libraries. Federal specifications may be purchased from the GSA Region III Federal Supply Service Printed Material Supply Division, Specification Activity Building, 197 Maple Weapons Plant, Washington, D.C. 20407.

Other potential sources of specifications and standards include the Council of State Governments, American Standards Association, National Institute of Governmental Purchasing, Inc. (NIGP), and American Society for Testing and Materials (ASTM). The interchange between NIGP members is conspicuous.

Where difficulty is encountered in developing specifications in terms of construction details, consideration should be given to the use of performance specifications, which define the end-use performance requirement and which allow bidders relative freedom in terms of design characteristics. In these cases, the use of competitive negotiation is advisable.

Warranties in Specifications   To foster durability it is sometimes stated that the product offered must be guaranteed for a specified period of time or that bidders shall state the extent of such warranty with the expressed intent to consider such warranty in "evaluating the lowest and best responsible bidder." If a definite coverage is specified and some bidder offers a product with a longer warranty, he may claim that on the basis of product life versus price he is the low bidder. On the other hand, the low bidder complying with the limited warranty may insist that he is fully responsive to the proposal as advertised and may claim that he too could offer a longer warranty if the period of coverage had been left to each bidder's determination.

Types of Bids

There are two general classifications of bids in governmental purchasing, formal and informal. *Informal bids* are the telephone quotation and the preferred written quotation whose dollar value is less than the statutory limit. Award is usually signified by issuing a purchase order. *Formal bids* are those which have the following characteristics: public advertising, public opening, and award to the lowest best responsible bidder. Award is usually signified by issuing a contract document.

Formal bids are usually required when the dollar value of the proposed purchase exceeds a statutory dollar limitation. Exceptions to the formal bid requirement should be defined by regulation and include, at a minimum, bona fide emergencies. Procedures associated with formal bids are designed to protect the interest of both the bidder and the government and to reinforce the concepts of openness and impartiality, which should be essential characteristics of all public bidding.

Advertising and Bid Lists

Implicit in the concept of public advertising for bids is an open invitation to all qualified potential bidders to participate. As far as is consistent with the public interest, every reasonable means should be utilized in publicizing the request for bids. Newspaper advertising is a minimum requirement and may be required by law.

The practical limitations of public advertising should be recognized. Advertising, even with wide circulation, cannot be relied upon to reach the best potential bidders. Invitations to bid should, therefore, be sent directly to all responsible interested and prospective bidders.

Bidders' lists for various commodities and services should be established and maintained for the purpose of mailing invitations to bid. Provisions must be made for the addition, removal, and reinstatement of bidders' names on the lists. The criteria used in making these changes should be specified by regulation or policy.

Inclusion on lists may be accomplished by a seller's simple verbal request or by his submission of a formal application supported by an acceptable Dun & Bradstreet report.

Acceptable criteria for removal from a bidder's list would be consistent failure to respond to invitations or failure to perform satisfactorily. In this connection, it is well to keep a performance record for each vendor, listing late deliveries, noncompliance, rejections, etc.

It is essential to assure that bidders interested in providing products or services are placed on the appropriate bidders' lists. One simple means of accomplishing this is to relate bidders' lists to a formal commodity and service classification system. As mentioned elsewhere in this section, the use of the Federal Supply Classification System, in identifying products, and the Standard Industrial Classification System, in identifying services, could be used as a basis. When a prospective bidder indicates an interest in furnishing a particular product or service, the bidder is added to the appropriate bid list. Of course, bidders furnishing several different types of products or commodities would be included on several different bid lists.

When the dollar value of a purchase is equal to or exceeds that value requiring a formal sealed-bid invitation, all bidders appearing on the bid list should be issued a bid invitation. If the dollar value is less, then a proportionally smaller number of bidders should be issued a bid invitation. It becomes uneconomical to issue bid invitations to all bidders for low-dollar-value purchases. In doing this, however, assurance must be had that an equitable opportunity exists for all bidders in all cases.

Bid and Contract Documents

Considerable variation exists in the bid documents utilized by different governmental units. There is no one best set of forms. The important requirements are that they be clear, logical, and as simple as possible and that they produce the desired results.

A complete set of bid documents might consist of the following: (1) a combination invitation and bid, which would include the standard purchase terms and conditions; (2) an addendum used for special instructions, terms, and conditions; (3) a bid sheet upon which the bidder enters pricing to be submitted; (4) an amendment which is used for any changes to be made to the original bid invitation after issuance; (5) a request for quotation—this can be a simple, informal, handwritten form requesting pricing information and used for low-dollar-value purchases; (6) a purchase order, including an acknowledgment to be used in selected purchases, which should be signed and returned to the buyer; (7) and a purchase order change, which should be used to effect any changes to the purchase order subsequent to issuance.

Basic policy information instructions on bid preparation evaluation factors can be included in a basic document provided to bidders when indicating an interest in selling to the jurisdiction. This document would be referred to in all bid invitations and would expressly reserve the right of the jurisdiction to: (1) waive any defect, irregularity, or informality in any bid or bidding procedure; (2) reject or cancel any or all bids; (3) reissue a bid invitation; (4) procure any item by other means; and (5) increase or decrease the quantity specified in the bid invitation unless the bidder specifies otherwise, so that this basic document could include bid evaluation factors and standard purchase terms and conditions, along with sample forms as mentioned above.

Two complete sets of bid documents should be given to each potential bidder. One set is to be returned, properly signed and executed, in a sealed envelope prior to bid opening, and one set is to be retained by the bidder for reference follow-up.

Bid Processing

Formal bids should be submitted in sealed envelopes properly identified on the outside. Some purchasing departments provide bidders with specially colored and marked envelopes for ready identification of a bid submission. The bids should be time-stamped upon receipt, properly segregated, and placed in a locked receptacle until the time specified for the bid opening.

Bid Opening The opening and tabulation of bids should be under the control of a responsible purchasing official, with an additional witness present. Bidders and reporters should be encouraged to attend bid openings, and the bids should be opened and read aloud upon request for the benefit of those present.

Late Bids Many regulations provide a minimum allowable time between the date of a legal advertisement and a bid opening. Late bids are sometimes retained, opened, and filed, but the practice of returning them unopened to the bidder is gaining support.

Some laws require that any local agency which seeks to enter a contract requiring the letting of bids shall specify in the public notice the place where such bids are to be received and the time by which they shall be received. Any bids received after the time specified in the notice shall be returned unopened. While this may preclude situations that can be open to question, there is an advantage in opening all bids even though received late. If only one bid is received on time and several are received late, opening the late bids provides information of use in determining whether or not the price submitted in the lone timely bid is fair and reasonable.

Bids should be tabulated as a summary record and to facilitate making an award. The information on the bid tabulation should be posted or made available to the public upon request.

Bid Errors It sometimes happens that a successful bidder, after the bid opening but prior to award, discovers that he made an error in computing the price quoted and he therefore seeks to cancel his bid on the grounds of unilateral mistake. Usually such situations are amicably resolved by permitting withdrawal or cancellation of the bid without prejudice, with the award going to the next lowest best responsible bidder. However, it is wise to enter this occurrence on the vendor's record, as repetition may indicate a "sharp" bidding practice.

Courts have generally permitted such a bidder to withdraw the offer by cancellation of the bid and have cleared the bid deposit only after determining: (1) that a mistake of a mechanical or clerical nature was actually made—not just an error in judgment, such as underestimating labor and material costs; and (2) that the mistaken bidder was not guilty of culpable negligence in making the error or of delay in communicating the fact to the offeree on discovery.

In instances in which bidders discover a substantial mistake after receiving the award and seek cancellation, the purchasing officer is guided by legal counsel. When such discovery is made before a contract has been executed, courts have allowed cancellation under the same determining factors listed above, provided the parties have not materially altered their positions and no other inequitable consideration has intervened.

Some jurisdictions have inserted clauses in bid forms requiring all contractors to guarantee the accuracy of their bids and to waive all rights to seek relief for clerical mistakes. Even so, courts have still given relief in case of nonnegligent error, stating that no unconscionable advantage taken of a bidder would be permitted to deprive the bidder of equitable remedy or a legitimate action for a unilateral mistake.

The public purchasing officer receiving a bid so out of proportion as to indicate a mistake or obvious error should seek confirmation of the bid from the bidder before proceeding with an award. A bid for a public contract which, in comparison with others, discloses such a disparity as to lead only to the conclusion that, from the viewpoint of the offeree, it is too good to be true may be legally rescinded for a mistake.

AWARDS

Most public purchasing laws specify that the award be made to the *lowest best responsible bidder.* This terminology allows consideration of criteria other than price alone. Basically, awards should be based upon price, quality, and assurance that the vendor will satisfy the terms and conditions of the contract. Impartial professional judgment is crucial, and thorough documentation of reasons is prudent when awarding to other than the lowest-dollar bidder because the notion persists that it is an irregularity to award to a bidder other than the one submitting the lowest price.

Making correct value judgments when considering awards is foremost in purchasing management's responsibility, and this area of decision is particularly vital to the public purchasing official. Award of equally low bids should be governed by a predetermined policy. Factors such as large versus small business, area labor surpluses, the use of locally manufactured products and awards to minority business, and the assurance of better service may be considered. All such factors being equal, the practice of "public drawing of lots" meets the criterion of impartiality.

It should be pointed out, however, that there are no two bids identical in both amount and nature. The difficulty is in quantifying the difference between those bids. If this is possible, then award should be made on that basis rather than the drawing of lots or the selection of the supplier furthest removed, on the assumption that his product cost is actually less but that higher transportation costs resulted in the tie bid.

The fact that only one bid is received should not prevent the awarding of a contract where bids have been solicited in compliance with statutory procedure, provided the price is fair and reasonable. There must, of course, have been a full opportunity for unrestricted competition and a total absence of fraud, collusion, or other dishonest conduct. It would be wise for a jurisdiction to have some legal basis or recourse when it receives only one bid and that bid is determined to be not fair or reasonable. In these cases it should be possible to reject the bid and enter into negotiation with the sole source if, in fact, there is no prospect of additional bidders being available in a rebid situation. In these cases, it would be appropriate for the jurisdiction to request from the lone bidder substantiating cost data to justify or help establish a fair and reasonable price to both the bidder and the jurisdiction.

When the statutory or legal regulations of a jurisdiction specify awards to the lowest best responsible bidder, opportunity is afforded for awards to be based on the *total-cost purchasing* concept. This concept in the evaluation of bids enables the purchaser to take into consideration the initial purchase price, life, output, maintenance or consumption, disposal value, complexity of operation, required training, and other factors contributing to the overall cost of an item. In the purchase of capital equipment, the concept of *life-cycle costing,* which parallels the total-cost purchasing concept, is becoming more prevalent. Including such provisions in the basic document provided to all potential bidders enables the purchaser to make decisions of this type on all purchases. It would be advisable, however, if it is planned to evaluate a bid on that basis, that this should be stipulated in the bid invitation being issued.

Multiple awards are becoming more prevalent in supply-type contracts. Such awards should never be based on the dividing of the award but rather on the basis of, e.g., a 50-30-20 percent split in a contract to provide for incentives and to preclude collusion. Such awards can be made if stipulated in the bid invitation initially.

SURETY REQUIREMENTS

Performance bonds are included in the conditions of certain substantial bids, particularly those for building and construction, where they are required by law.

Bid deposits may be requested for certain bids involving large sums to protect the interest of the public agency in the event the low bidder attempts to withdraw his bid or as a device to make it difficult for financially irresponsible suppliers to bid. Bid deposits in the form of a certified or cashier's check, money orders, or currency are more common than bid bonds, since they represent what the bidder agrees shall be retained to cover liquidated damages in the event of failure to sign the contract or of failure to provide a satisfactory performance bond, if required.

Performance bonds do not always guarantee the faithful performance of a contract. Primarily they provide for responsibility by a third party. Bonds generally increase the cost of bidding and tend to reduce competition. The detail associated with handling checks and bonds also increases the administrative burden upon the purchasing department. Because the costs associated with bonds may outweigh the advantages, the purchasing head should use discretion as to whether they should be required. Moreover, use of performance bonds does not always guarantee a financial recovery. It must sometimes be demonstrated that a financial loss has been incurred by the jurisdiction before recovery of funds on a performance bond is possible.

Failure of a vendor to fulfill a contract in the absence of a bond can frequently be dealt with by aggressive direct action of the jurisdicttion's legal department. This avenue of remedy is sometimes neglected because of an overreliance on bonds for surety.

CONTRACTS

The basic elements of legally enforceable contracts are: (1) offer and acceptance; (2) parties competent to contract; (3) legality of subject matter; and (4) sufficient consideration. These elements constitute the legal foundation upon which all purchasing transactions take place. If the above elements are present, contracts can range in type from oral agreements and written accepted purchase orders to fully documented formal contracts with third-party surety. It should be pointed out that the Uniform Commerical Code requires that all contracts of $500 or more must be in writing to be held enforceable in a court of law.

Formal contracts are employed in public purchasing whenever the statutory dollar limitation for informal purchases is exceeded or a formally documented agreement is required. The two basic types of formal contracts for supplies and equipment are an *open-market-purchase* or *definite-quantity contract* and a *term contract* or *indefinite-quantity contract.* The profusion of names for these contracts, such as *term, annual, blanket, supply, open-end, requirement, price agreement,* and *supply agreement,* refer to some variations of the two basic conceptual types.

Open-market-purchase or definite-quantity contracts may provide for specific quantities of items to be delivered at one time or for specific quantities to be delivered on a schedule over a stated time period.

Open-end or term contracts for indefinite quantities are of wide interest because of their many advantages when the purchasing for multiple government agencies is being coordinated. There are two major advantages to term contracts. First, they permit contracting for total requirements of all departments or agencies on a long-term basis and provide minimum prices in those situations where exact quantity requirements cannot be determined. Second, they have a tendency to minimize the number of items being ordered, since the process of consolidating requirements results in a definite standardization of the best types or qualities of products. The relative simplicity of purchase actions under this type of contract and the elimination of duplicative supply contracts by the various departments or agencies can result in substantial economies and many administrative advantages. In such cases, the operating or using departments can be given authority to release directly to the supplier under the terms of the contract.

Prices under term or open-end contracts may be fixed or subject to the fluctuation of recognized established posted prices, such as those posted for the gasoline or the fuel oil industry. The variety of materials which can be covered and the basis for pricing appear limited only by the ability of buyers and sellers to develop mutually advantageous and legal arrangements. This is covered below under price adjustment contracts.

Contracts for services represent another type of contract because they essentially involve labor. Familiar types include window-washing, laundry, janitorial, or guard service and office machine maintenance. These contracts may result from advertised bidding or negotiation, depending upon the dollar value and the prevailing legal requirement.

SPECIAL CONSIDERATIONS

Contractual Price Adjustment

Escalation or adjustment of contract prices becomes necessary when one or both of two factors are involved. The first is involved when future costs are so uncertain as to make a firm quotation or bid either impossible or, if covering all probable risks, unattractive to the buyer. The second occurs when extremely long-term contracts are involved and it is unrealistic to assume that future economic conditions can be foreseen adequately to enable a seller to establish a firm fixed price based on a fair and reasonable profit. Underlying this is an assumption that costs, whatever they might be in the far-off future, shall be covered. This, of course, greatly reduces for the seller the risk of doing business, which is inherent in our competitive enterprise system. In such cases, the profit margin for the seller should be reduced accordingly.

Uncontrollable Costs

The most significant uncontrollable costs today are those for purchased materials and taxes. Labor costs generally are controllable provided the project or work is adequately defined with minimum changes contemplated. Labor union contracts usually are for three years and, to a great extent, costs inherent in these contracts can be estimated, including those with cost-of-living adjustments based on the consumer price index. Nevertheless, the buyer may in periods of uncertainty be faced with the necessity to adjust labor cost.

Use of Indexes

Generally the use of indexes is preferable to cost reimbursement-type contracts in the purchase of commodities. The use of indexes permits verification without auditing the seller's financial records, which may be objectionable to some sellers. The indexes selected should relate to the seller's cost factors and should closely approximate the cost change. Those indexes should reflect industry averages. If the seller is in transportation equipment, it would be illogical to select a labor index measuring changes and wage rates in the electrical equipment industry.

Published labor and commodity indexes are generally the basis on which changes are agreed to by buyer and seller. For example, the labor rate index could be the average hourly earnings of the transportation equipment industry. Material indexes would include the producer price index for steel mill products. These indexes are included in *Monthly Labor Review* and *Producers Prices and Price Indexes,* published monthly by the Bureau of Labor Statistics of the U.S. Department of Labor. These publications are available by subscription from the nearest regional office.

For certain uses the buyer and seller may agree on a more localized index, such as construction cost information including average prices published in *Engineering News Record* or primary metal prices and scrap prices published in *Iron Age* or *American Metal Market.* This utilizes the impartiality of these sources and bases adjustments on averages in the geographic area in which the seller is operating.

It is essential, of course, to establish that portion of a bid price subject to adjustment that pertains to labor and that portion pertaining to materials. An adjustment on 100 percent of the purchase price which includes overhead and profit should not be accepted. There may be several materials indexes involved in the product; only the major material indexes that are applicable should be used. Adjustments to overhead and profit should not be allowed if they can be avoided. These costs normally can be foreseen, and there is little if any justification for them to be subject to adjustment.

Another form of price adjustment is *price in effect at time of shipment (PTS),* which may be satisfactory if the particular item is a standard self-stock item sold in competition with similar products of other manufacturers at published or established prices. Any price increase incurred is usually based on costs of the immediate past and the projection of future costs. On this basis, the buyer can be invoiced for costs that did not go into the product received. Justification for use of PTS price adjustment is that competitive forces tend to restrict the seller's freedom to change prices at will, assuming adequate competition.

These price increases should be limited to pass-through costs only, and on the increased amount no markup for seller overhead and profits should be permitted. Increases should be verified by comparing the seller's costs at time of bid to the seller's costs of the actual item delivered to the buyer.

Price escalation, of course, is applied to decreases as well as increases. Such price changes should be allowed only up to the scheduled delivery date or the actual shipment date, whichever is the earlier. The PTS should be no higher than the seller's prevailing price. The U.S. Supreme Court has interpreted the prevailing price to be the lowest price for which the items are sold.

If labor is to be subject to escalation over a considerable time period, it is appropriate to take into consideration increased industrial productivity. In its *Monthly*

Labor Review the Bureau of Labor Statistics (BLS), U.S. Department of Labor, publishes productivity indexes and their quarterly and annual percent (%) changes. The BLS Office of Productivity and Technology has information on productivity of certain industries that can be used as an index.

Use of price adjustment clauses and contracts establishes a definite means of arriving at a price. The buyer would be well advised to seek legal counsel in case of doubt since considerable controversy can arise over interpretation.

Small Orders

The need for making small purchases and their proportionately high administrative expense cannot be eliminated entirely. Reducing the number of small or rush-type orders requires a continuing effort to educate requisitioners to anticipate and combine requirements. Purchasing departments—like any others—should operate effectively, as well as efficiently and economically. This requires that purchasing department operating costs be kept in reasonable relationship to the value of the items being purchased. Basically, the alternative means which control this problem are administrative in nature. The primary solution lies in improving purchase policies and procedures.

The following are suggestions on recognizing small orders or handling them efficiently: (1) centralized stores; (2) petty cash fund; (3) telephone requests for quotes; (4) simple handwritten requests for quote "forms"; (5) blanket-type orders or term contracts combining similar dollar-value items; (6) traveling requisitions; (7) combined requisition–purchase order–receiving report; (8) buy schedules and accumulation of purchase requisitions and a one-purchase order; (9) supplier delivery system with daily or semiweekly deliveries; and (10) monthly, bimonthly, or quarterly quotations from supply houses on a variety of items.

Sole Source Items

Sole source items are items performing a certain function for which no other items are known to exist. In a high-technology society such as ours, on occasion a clearly superior product is available to perform a function or patents may limit us to a sole source. If it is to the jurisdiction's economic advantage to use such a product, it would be inappropriate to ignore it. Justification for specifying such items is extremely important and should be clearly stipulated and documented. Sole-source situations, however, can be minimized by use of performance specifications, two-step formal advertising and bidding, and requests for proposals. This conveys to the supplier the performance or results needed or desired. It lets the supplier determine how best and most economically he can meet those needs.

Competitive bidding does not provide a suitable purchase method for sole-source items. Effective competitive bidding requires that at least two responsible bidders, able to satisfy the jurisdiction requirements as to specifications and delivery, independently contend for a contract. In sole-source cases it would be best to advertise for bids on an approved equal basis, and if only one is offered, proceed to negotiate a fair and reasonable price with the sole source. Also, when only one bid is received in a competitive market, it is in effect a sole source situation and is best handled through negotiation if the price is determined not to be fair and reasonable. Some might argue that the jurisdiction makes no provision for negotiated purchases. Obviously in such cases the buyer can keep requesting and rejecting bids from the sole source, but this makes a mockery of the purchase procedure. The jurisdiction's legal officer should be consulted if there is doubt about how to proceed in these cases.

Two-Step Formal Advertising and Bidding

To expand the use of public advertising and bidding under the technical procurement area, a mixed technique referred to as *two-step formal (public) advertising and bidding* was initiated, originally within the Department of Defense. This procurement method is used when existing specifications are inadequate for straight public advertising and bidding procedures. It must be noted that this process is used only as an alternative method.

Two-step public advertising and bidding is appropriate whenever the following prerequisites exist: (1) available specifications are inadequate or are not sufficiently definite to permit full and free competition without technical evaluation or technical discussion to ensure mutual understanding between the buyer and the prospective contractors; (2) definite criteria exist for evaluating technical proposals; (3) two or more technically qualified sources are expected to compete; (4) sufficient time is available to permit use of the two-step method; and (5) a firm fixed-price contract or a fixed-price contract with escalation will be used.

First Step   Procedurally, this process is initiated by the buyer's request for a technical proposal based upon performance or requirement specifications in contrast to *build to* specifications. These proposals are evaluated by the procuring agency and discussed with the proposers to the degree necessary; price is not discussed during this phase. The buyer makes the determination as to the technical acceptability of the supplies, service, or materials offered and may summarily reject unacceptable proposals or make provisions for modification of technical proposals that are marginal in order to raise them to a level of acceptability.

Second Step   The second step of the procedure is conducted as a public bidding or advertised procurement except that it is restricted to those offerers who have submitted technically acceptable proposals during the first phase of the procurement. These offerers then bid on the basis of meeting the performance specifications and providing the exact supply or service as proposed or as modified in discussions with the buyer and approved by the buyer as the initial step. Although the products or services of the bidders may vary, awards are based upon price alone. Competition is equitable in that minimum performance standards must be met and in that terms, conditions, and provisions are applicable to all bids.

Summary   By combining elements of the negotiation process with public advertising bidding procedures, the two-step method provides the opportunity to explore, explain, and clarify the bidder's understanding of and proposed means of providing the buyer's requirements. It encourages innovation and initiative on the part of competing firms to develop new approaches, techniques, and methods in the production of an item by not tying firms to existing processes or rigid specifications. The buyer, in turn, receives the benefit of the industry's best technical efforts and frequently receives a significantly improved item.

The second step of this method creates the competitive conditions of public advertising and bidding. All firms with qualified technical proposals have an equal opportunity for their bids to compete on the basis of price for the buyer's requirement.

Successful application of the two-step method requires both careful planning and a high level of technical competence in the procuring activities. The development of clear statements of performance requirements and the establishment of sound criteria for evaluating proposals against these requirements are crucial to the two-step method. Inadequate attention to either of these elements can create ambiguities as to the nature of the requirement and frustrate the process at considerable cost to firms in the development of technical proposals. For this reason the two-step procedure should normally be used only when the value of the procurement justifies the buyer's undertaking the effort necessary to prepare the bid solicitation and industry's preparing the technical proposal.

Purchase of Services

The purchase of or contracting for services has become one of the fastest-growing segments of procurement responsibility. It covers a broad spectrum from janitorial services and hiring temporary personnel to professional consulting services. Contracts may include both labor and material costs, or they may be for labor alone. Contracts for repairs, maintenance, or laundry rental are examples of service contracts. As a general rule, a contract may be defined as being for service if over 50 percent of the total value represents direct labor costs.

In cases in which skilled workers such as carpenters, electricians, glaziers, painters, or plumbers are not regularly employed as a part of a maintenance department, they should be engaged in accordance with prevailing legal requirements. A few governmental units exempt such services from bidding requirements; others differentiate between services of a professional nature, such as those rendered by architects, engineers, and attorneys, and services performed by skilled craft personnel, exempting only professional services from bidding requirements.

In contracting for services, the best procedure is to plan, specify, and request bids for a particular job in order to establish a competitive total cost. Many service requirements, however, are of an emergency or unplanned nature. When an emergency situation arises, it may be difficult or impossible to obtain competitive bids, particularly if the total value of the work is relatively small.

One solution to this problem is to establish annual contracts based upon competitive bidding. Regular and overtime rates for the various craft personnel can be established, as can markups or discounts on material costs. To be successful, this type of contract must require that performance be subject to inspection during and upon completion of the work in order to verify hourly charges. Charges for materials should be based on an established and agreed-upon price list or pricing service. If such predetermined prices are not available, material charges should be subject to audit.

Where annual service contracts other than centralized contracts for the various trades may be utilized by an agency having a potential need for the specified services, or when one firm cannot handle the total volume of the work, multiple contracts may be required.

Many occupations, including some skilled trades, are often claimed as professions even though this is not the case. One state's procurement agency for goods and services specifies the following occupations in its professional category: (1) architects; (2) engineers; (3) accountants; (4) physicians or related medical practitioners; (5) lawyers; (6) consultants; (7) technical witnesses; and (8) court hearing reporters.

Many jurisdictions have laws or regulations which prohibit competitive bidding for such services. Some professional organizations prohibit their members from providing pricing information to potential customers. They believe submission of pricing information is equivalent to competitive bidding. They hold to this view because they believe price becomes the only evaluation factor and that the "low bid" would be chosen. This is a misunderstanding on the part of the professional organizations, perhaps brought about by inappropriate purchasing actions used in the selection of professional service firms. It must be kept in mind that economics is a basic factor in every procurement transaction. Certainly the selection of a professional service firm should not be based on price alone. Defining a professional service to the extent that materials can be defined, is, of course, extremely difficult and makes a selection based on price alone extremely risky.

The greatest emphasis should be on adequately defining the work or service needed and on adequately evaluating the capability of those firms interested in performing the service. The request for proposal (RFP) method would in many cases be most appropriate.

Request for Proposal

This is prepared and issued by the jurisdiction's purchasing agent or contracting officer and should include: (1) a work statement or performance specification; (2) time frames in which the work is to be completed; and (3) specific criteria to be used in evaluating a proposal. These criteria can cover the offerer's proposed approach to accomplishment of the work, management capability, and price. The RFP should request the offerer to provide the following information: (1) understanding of the problem, work to be done or program, and the approach to be used to achieve the objectives, including detailing of tasks involved in the approach; (2) facility and capability data, including related experience and résumés of key personnel; (3) verifiable milestone list if not specified in the RFP; and (4) pricing, including a bid price breakdown in costs scheduled.

The evaluation of proposals should include a review of the evaluation criteria by an evaluation committee and a meeting with the offerer to achieve a complete understanding of any contract or agreement that may result. This committee can be composed of the purchasing agent or contracting officer, jurisdiction personnel knowledgeable in the discipline being purchased, and key operating department personnel who would be involved in the services purchased. The purchasing agent or contracting officer must be qualified to act effectively as captain of the team. One individual must lead and speak for the committee in the discussions with the offerer regarding the proposal. Any negotiations involved require this expertise—normally a requirement in filling a purchasing agency or contracting officer position. A review of the RFP should cover: (1) general quality and responsiveness; (2) organization and personnel; and (3) price and bid price breakdown or price range and cost schedule.

Three alternatives are available at this point:

1. Select the most responsive proposal and qualified firm for the work, and seek a clear understanding of contract provisions and agreement on a fair and reasonable price if the offerer did not include it in the proposal. If agreement is not achieved, discontinue negotiations and proceed to the next or second most responsive proposal and qualified firms, etc.

2. Select the two or three most responsive proposals and qualified firms for the work, and seek with each firm a clear understanding of contract provisions and agreement on a fair and reasonable price if the offerer did not include it in the proposal. Select the one firm that is judged by the evaluation committee to have submitted the most responsive proposal, price and other factors being considered.

3. This is the same as the second alternative above except that final selection of the successful firm is based on price alone.

There are those who believe that the third alternative is competitive bidding and that this could lead to a deterioration of service, to the detriment of the buyer. On the other hand, others maintain that there are qualified firms with skilled and responsible personnel who can perform high-quality work at a lower cost by virtue of advanced methodology, specialization, and use of modern business practices. Reviewing the qualifications of many firms to select the three or four most qualified assures that the work will be done satisfactorily regardless of any pricing submitted.

Emergency Purchases

Emergency purchases are probably the thorniest to justify and handle. The use of bona fide emergency purchases is justified to protect public health or in the case of unforeseen damage to public property, machinery, or equipment. Poor planning, overlooked requirements, inaccurate usage history, and inadequate forecasting, however, are often responsible for expedited purchases, and are not bona fide emergency situations. The real culprit in these cases is poor management.

In the case of a real emergency, it may be necessary to delegate the purchasing function to an operating department. Control, however, should not be delegated. After the purchase has been made, it would be appropriate to request the governing body's confirmation of the award if the total dollar value is such as to normally require the body's approval. Emergency purchases should be kept to an absolute minimum. It would be most prudent to establish a formal policy or secure adequate legislation or ordinances to govern these purchases.

Emergency purchases will result in higher costs to the jurisdiction. This is because of insufficient time for suppliers to carefully prepare a quotation or bid to provide the lowest possible price, higher transportation costs to expedite shipments, supplier overtime costs, and special attention on the part of purchasing personnel, plus expensive long-distance telephone calls.

Prison-Made Goods

Some states require that, when the need arises, political subdivisions purchase items produced by the labor of prisoners and that such items be given absolute preference. Correctional institutions usually publish catalogs indicating the styles, types, and prices of items available. Public purchasing officials must maintain an awareness of the regulations governing the sale and purchase of prison-made goods in their jurisdiction.

Cooperative Purchasing

Local governmental jurisdictions throughout the United States have learned that they can purchase materials at lower prices if they combine their purchases in cooperative purchasing arrangements. In a 1979 survey of cities with over 10,000 population, the International City Management Association found that of 1364 cities responding, 892 had legal authority to engage in cooperative purchasing and most had established cooperative arrangements with other governmental jurisdictions or institutions.

A public expenditure study committee in the state of Wisconsin in 1966 determined that: (1) a centralized purchasing system is inherently superior to a decentralized system and should be considered by all local subdivisions with populations in excess of 10,000; and (2) where possible, centralized purchasing should be supplemented by cooperative purchasing agreements, both interlocal and state-local, to enable participating units to purchase commodities for less than they could be bought for separately.

Some form of cooperative purchasing by local subdivisions through a state central purchasing agency currently exists in 43 states. Only 2 states make it mandatory, 41 states make it permissible, and 18 states restrict cooperative purchases to certain commodities.

Cooperative purchasing reference among educational institutions has spread nationwide among both public and private colleges and universities. One such cooperative is the Educational and Institutional (E&I) Cooperative, which received its charter in 1934. It began with a small number of schools in the Northeast and today it has spread to every state in the union. Its story is truly that of a highly successful national cooperative program among educational institutions.

In addition to the E&I cooperative, other regional, state, county, and local cooperative programs have been established to effectively supplement the E&I

cooperative nationwide contracts. An example is the Procurement Organization for Educational Thrift (PROFET). PROFET contracts were established for private and public colleges and universities in the city, county, and metropolitan area of St. Louis, Mo. Also participating in the cooperative program were institutions from Illinois located immediately adjacent to St. Louis. Contracts were awarded for common-use items such as data processing cards and forms, lamps, and office supplies. The latest cooperative contract for office supplies exceeds $1 million. Twelve colleges and universities have participated in this cost reduction program.

Cooperative purchasing can be defined as joint purchasing of common or similar commodities and services by two or more jurisdictions. The basic methods by which this can be done are: (1) a special administrative agency composed of representatives from the participating jurisdictions can be established and can solicit bids and award the purchase contract; (2) two or more jurisdictions may jointly request bids from suppliers for certain items and place their purchase contracts either jointly or independently with the lowest best responsible bidder. All jurisdictions participating in the award would be obligated to purchase their needs from the successful bidders unless a rejection for bona fide reasons was in the interest of any jurisdictions. Standardization of materials could be sought where practicable. The jurisdiction with the largest purchase volume of the commodities or items would issue the bid invitation.

Another method is the *piggyback* procedure. The largest jurisdiction merely stipulates in its bid invitation that participating jurisdictions will have the option to purchase materials at the same price available to the large jurisdiction issuing the invitation.

The cooperative bid invitation can stipulate an open-market purchase or a term contract for the individual jurisdiction. It can specify fixed or estimated quantities and provide for common delivery dates. It would be desirable to standardize commodity specifications. While this probably would not be possible on many items, merely including the similar items in a single bidding invitation and increasing the total volume will normally result in lower prices.

Cooperative purchasing should be limited to high-dollar-value commodities such as: antifreeze, auto batteries, auto parts, concrete pipe, construction materials, dairy products, fuels, incandescent and fluorescent lamps, lubricants, medical and drug supplies, office supplies and equipment, printing and copy paper, printing supplies, traffic control paint and sign materials, and standard vehicles and equipment.

Recycled Materials

Since 1971 the GSA has had a viable program to require recovered material in the products it buys, including paper and paper products, packaging and packing materials, and certain building materials. However, the program is being broadened pursuant to the Resource, Conservation, and Recovery Act of 1976, which indicates that federal procurements will promote the use of maximum percentages of recovered material. Specifically, after October 21, 1978, all federal procurements exceeding $10,000 must require maximum percentages of recovered material to the extent that they support competition. Further, it requires that purchase specifications used in such procurement will not prohibit recovered material, will not require virgin material, and will require maximum percentages of recovered material which will not jeopardize the quality of the end item. All federal specifications are being reviewed and revised to incorporate these requirements.

Disposal of Surplus Materials

This function is often assigned to the purchasing and stores department. It should include effective utilization of personal property owned by the jurisdiction, and salvage, reclamation, and disposal of materials.

Surplus materials can be disposed of by relocating, trade-in, return to supplier for credit, sale to dealers and brokers, sale to another jurisdiction, and/or direct sale to the public. Pricing methods include negotiation, sealed-bid invitations, spot bids, auction and retail sale, and donations to nonprofit organizations.

Capital equipment could be renovated or repaired when this can be economically justified by comparing the cost of such work with new equipment costs. The total average annual cost for the equipment in its current state and in a renovated or repaired state should be calculated and compared with the calculated total average annual cost for new equipment. Changing technology, safety and reliability, and anticipated future prices of new equipment should also be considered.

Special Transportation Rates

Interstate Commerce Commission Regulation, Section 22, allows common carriers to extend preferential tariff rates to political subdivisions for the transportation of equipment, materials, and supplies. In practice this has resulted in the carriers' mutually agreeing to and publishing a preferential government rate for many commodities. When no rate has been established, the customer negotiates with the carrier and endeavors to obtain a reduced tariff rate on the item. A check with the local public utilities commission and local carriers will reveal the regulations in any particular area.

Federal Materials Surplus

The federal government has available surplus property that can be applied for or purchased by state or local governments. Public Law 94-519 amends the Federal Property and Administrative Services Act of 1949 to provide for the donation of surplus personal property to any public agency for use in carrying out or promoting for the residents of a given political area one or more public purposes, such as conservation, economic development, education, parks and recreation, public health, and public safety. The law, in implementing regulations of the GSA, requires state and local public agencies desiring to acquire property through this program to establish eligibility for such participation through the state surplus property agency.

Department of Defense surplus material is available to both private firms and governmental jurisdictions. Those wishing to be placed on the national bidders' list for information about upcoming sales or for other information should write to: Defense Property Disposal Service, Attn.: DPDS-MCC-P, Federal Center, Battle Creek, Michigan 49016.

Federal Surplus Personal Property

These programs enable certain nonfederal organizations to obtain personal property the federal government no longer needs. This includes hand and machine tools, office machines and supplies, furniture, hardware, motor vehicles, boats, airplanes, construction equipment, and many other items. State surplus property agencies have been established by each state, the District of Columbia, Puerto Rico, the Virgin Islands, and Guam to distribute personal property designated as surplus by the federal government. Eligible recipients include public agencies, nonprofit educational and public health activities, educational activities of special interest to the armed services, and public airports. For further information contact the regional GSA offices or the Office of Personal Property Disposal (FW), Federal Supply Service, General Services Administration, Washington, D.C. 20406.

Socioeconomic Goals

Pollution, environment, recycling, reused, equal opportunity, and *minority purchasing* are common terms that every purchasing official will be involved with in the 1980s. Many governmental agencies now require an equal employment opportunity clause to be included as part of the specifications for material supplies in equipment or construction contracts. Affirmative action involving minority suppliers is a definite trend at both the federal and state levels of government. The objective is to assist minority business enterprises through procurement preferences and to place governmental procurement contracts with companies in depressed unemployment areas in the country. In this regard, the Office of Minority Business Enterprise has been created under the auspices of the Department of Commerce. Several states and cities have implemented minority business programs.

Intergovernmental Grants-in-Aid

In recent years, intergovernmental grants-in-aid have become a very integral component of the American federal system. State and local governments, finding themselves in the position of having to satisfy the bulk of ever-increasing demands for the provision of new and better governmental services at the state and local levels, have been unable to adequately fund these additional and improved services from their own resources. They have as a consequence increasingly turned to higher levels of government for financial assistance.

The federal government, upon the basis of its perception of needs, has responded to state and local governments with enormous sums of money. According to figures released by the Advisory Commission of Inter-Governmental Relations (ACIR), federal grants-in-aid to states and localities were expected to total over $72 billion in 1977. Federal aid to states and localities rose to its current level from a mere $2 billion in 1949, and in 1976 it accounted for approximately one-quarter of combined state and local expenditures.

In addition, ACIR has estimated that in 1976 state aid to local governments was running at about $50 billion. Together, federal and state aid to local governments had increased from $5.9 billion in 1954 to $68.8 billion in 1976, and in the latter represented 43 percent of local general revenue; this compared with less than 30 percent as recently as 1949. In 1979 it was expected to increase to $77.9 billion.

Obviously the total dollar figures are very general, because they only sum up a wide range of grants-in-aid whose intent and specific forms differ significantly among grants and among governments and their individual grantor agencies. The aggregate figures are indicative, however, of the very important role that "outside" funds play in the daily operation of state and local governments across the United States.

The question naturally arises as to what all this money coming down from the higher levels of government means to state or local government procurement officers. On procurements made with intergovernmental grant funds, in return for the funds they are doling out government agencies have a few minimum requirements that procurement officials or recipients must adhere to in spending the grant money. Failure to comply will result in a slowdown or cutoff of funding.

Standards for Purchases Made with Federal Funds Many aspects of the federal grant process for state and local governments have been relatively standardized and simplified under Attachment O to the Office of Management and Budget Circular A-102. Attachment O establishes standards and guidelines for state and local government procurement procedures for purchasing supplies, equipment, construction, and other services with federal grant funds and provides for federal agency reviews. No additional requirements are to be imposed by the federal grantor agencies upon their grantees unless specifically required by federal law or executive orders. It should not be assumed, however, that Attachment O is the sole governing document with standards for the purchase of goods and services with federal grant funds.

Among those procurement standards prescribed in attachment O are: (1) procurement procedures; (2) selection procedures; (3) method of procurement; (4) contract pricing; (5) grantee procurement records; (6) contract provisions; and (7) contract administration.

In making purchases with funds composed in whole or in part of federal grant money, grantees are permitted to use their own procurement regulations and procedures which reflect applicable state and local laws, rules, and regulations, as long as the purchases made with federal grant funds adhere to the standards set forth in Attachment O.

In addition to complying with the standards set forth in Attachment O, state and local governments, when making purchases with federal grant funds, should ensure that their requirements comply with the minimum standards set forth in the applicable provisions of applicable federal laws, rules, and regulations. Generally speaking, local governments, when purchasing with state aid funds, must comply with those general procedural requirements already set forth by state authorities for use by local governments in making purchases with funds derived from undefined revenue sources. In addition, however, it should be noted that state governments and their agencies may also prescribe specific laws and/or regulations that are to be followed by local governments in making purchases with funds received through a particular state aid program. So-called home-rule local jurisdictions may be exempt in whole or in part from general laws and regulations established by state authorities for local government purchasing.

In principle, the requirements for purchases made by nonprofit organizations with funds received through governmental grants do not differ significantly from those governing purchases by state and local governments with governmental grant funds. However, the details do differ somewhat.

For example, whereas Attachment O A-102 governs purchases made by state and local units of government with federal grant funds, Attachment O of Office of Management and Budget Circular A-110 governs procurements made by institutions of higher education, hospitals, and other nonprofit organizations with federal grant funds. Moreover, there will always be state laws and regulations (separate and distinct from those governing purchases by state and local governments) which specifically govern purchases by those institutions that are in some sense "creatures of the state."

UMTA Grant Funds   When purchases are made by a jurisdiction with Urban Mass Transportation Administration (UMTA) funds in whole or in part, the responsible officials should refer to the Department of Transportation Urban Mass Transportation, Participation by Minority Business Enterprises in Department of Transportation Programs, 49 CFR, Patt 23, March 31, 1980. UMTA circular 1340.2 should also be used.

Tax Exemptions   Governmental jurisdictions are normally exempt from federal excise taxes and from state and local retail sales taxes. These exemptions can vary from state to state and among jurisdictions. The jurisdiction may wish to prepare tax exemption certificates covering such exemptions. These can be based on individual orders or contracts or on blanket exemptions.

PREFERENCES IN PUBLIC BIDDING

Preferences and restrictions in open competitive bidding will only result in higher prices. They can only be considered as subsidies for those allegedly too weak in some phase of their operation to compete on an equal basis. Oftentimes those most vocal about free enterprise are the very ones who advocate restrictions in the system.

In recent years a number of states have passed laws which require that preference be given to bidders who qualify under certain socioeconomic conditions. These provisions generally require that a certain percentage of annual purchases be set aside for small businesses and minority businesses as defined in their statutes. Some organizations have taken the position that there is merit in providing various means of assistance to such businesses but are opposed to allowing preferences of any kind in the competitive bidding process.

PURCHASE AUDIT

How effectively procurement functions are carried out depends on how strong the central procurement authority is. The concept of a central procurement authority does not mean that central purchasing must carry out all functions but rather that there should be a centralization of responsibility and accountability. The following elements comprise a general area of inquiry, but they do not include every audit step that may be necessary to completely satisfy each area of inquiry: (1) authority and responsibility; (2) planning and scheduling; (3) competition; (4) standardization and specification; (5) inspection and testing; (6) property management; (7) professional development; (8) cooperative purchasing; and (9) audit and evaluation.

GOVERNMENTAL VERSUS PRIVATE SECTOR PURCHASING

One important difference between public or governmental and private purchasing is the lack of secrecy in public purchasing. Prices paid and sources of supply are never or only seldom revealed by industry, whereas in governmental purchasing specifications, bids, purchase orders, and other purchasing documents are matters of public record for all interested persons to see. Recent open records legislation has facilitated this. If private management chooses not to divulge who gets what orders and why, it does not have to. Another difference is that public purchasing officials may literally have to turn the other cheek when criticized by dissatisfied suppliers. As long as they do not violate the law, critics may take advantage of the impartiality of the public purchasing official; by contrast, any criticism or public censure of a private official could result in swift retaliatory action.

In public purchasing it is not only necessary to perform with sound business acumen but essential to exercise the function in the manner and form provided by legislation. When a statute prescribes the only mode by which the power to contract for public works or for the furnishing of public materials and supplies shall be exercised, the mode is the measure of the power. On the other hand, private purchasing in most companies is highly flexible. Innovations can be adopted immediately by a private business, whereas the public purchaser may have to wait for an amendment to the statutes before implementing new methods.

Because public purchasing operates in a fishbowl environment, it requires the utmost of professionalism and knowledge. The public purchasing official's actions are in public view and open to review, evaluation, and criticism, which is sometimes unjustified. This requires that the public purchasing official's actions reflect the utmost in professionalism.

Despite some differences between public and private purchasing, the functions are similar. One authority describes this as follows: "In governments as in private business, there exists a necessity of expert handling of all the elements of the supply problem and of complete coordination of effort between the purchasing agent and all other responsible officials having to do with the supply problem."

MODEL PROCUREMENT CODE

State statutes and local ordinances concerning procurement need modernization. They have, for the most part, developed haphazardly over many years. Having been drawn up in piecemeal fashion under pressures from special interests and often in emotional circumstances, they contain provisions that are frequently contradictory and inconsistent.

In particular, three recent developments make the need for modernizing those statutes and ordinances both compelling and immediate: (1) rising expenditures at lower levels of government, (2) increased federal demands on state and local purchasing systems, and (3) rapidly changing technology.

The amount of money which states and municipalities spend for public purchases has risen substantially in recent years. In 1955 the aggregate expenditures for state and local procurement was $14.71 billion. By 1965 that figure had increased to $31.79 billion, and in 1979 it was in excess of $110 billion. This of course includes funding provided by federal government grants, which have increased dramatically under the concept of the "new Federalism."

U.S. Department of Justice Grant

On March 11, 1975, the U.S. Department of Justice's Law Enforcement Assistance Administration awarded a grant to the American Bar Association (ABA) Fund for Public Education to finance the development of a model procurement code for state and local jurisdictions. The grant stipulated that the ABA would raise additional sums from other sources. The project became a joint effort of the ABA sections of Public Contract Law and of Urban, State, and Local Government Law. More than 200 attorneys and public purchasing officials participated in preparing three public review drafts. The House of Delegates of the ABA unanimously approved a final draft on February 13, 1979. The resolution of approval urged legislative consideration of the code by state and local governments.

Code Provisions   A model code offers an example for jurisdictions to compare to existing laws. It is an instrument for examining and revising current laws. Verbatim enactment is not its goal or purpose. The Model Procurement Code approved by the ABA is divided into 12 articles representing 12 substantive areas of government procurement, as follows:

Article Number	Article Title
1	General Provisions
2	Procurement Organization
3	Sources Selection and Contract Formation
4	Specifications
5	Procurement of Construction Architect, Engineer, and Land-Surveying Services
6	Modification and Termination of Contracts for Supplies and Services
7	Cost Principles
8	Supply Management
9	Legal and Contractual Remedies
10	Intergovernmental Relations
11	Assistance to Small and Disadvantaged Businesses; Federal Assistance on Contract Procurement Requirements
12	Ethics in Public Contracting

Public Purchasing Participation and Reservations   The National Institute of Governmental Purchasing (NIGP) and the National Association of State Purchasing Officials (NASPO) participated in the preparation of the ABA Model Procurement Code as members of the advisory board and on various committees that provided input in the preparation of the code. The ABA recognized their efforts as especially helpful. Both NIGP and NASPO have, by resolution, applauded and affirmed their support in principle for the code. They have not, however, endorsed those provisions pertaining to the procurement of certain professional services because the code minimizes, if not eliminates, comparison of prices, which NIGP and NASPO believe should be considered, along with qualifications, in determining the best-qualified offerer.

Paul Shnitzer, formerly associate general counsel for procurement matters, U.S. General Accounting Office, now counsel to the Washington, D.C., law firm of Fried, Frank, Harris, Schriver, and Kampleman, in an article entitled "And Another View" appearing in the National Contract Management Association publication, August 1979 issue, points out that there should be competition on the procurement to be accomplished and that price should be a factor in the evaluation of proposed architectural and engineering services. This is also recommended by a majority of the federal Commission on Government Procurement. While it is obvious that price should not be the significant factor in an architectural-engineering contract, Shnitzer believes that it should not be ignored. Under the procedure emphasized in the Model Procurement Code, there is no opportunity to compare pricing in the procurement of architectural-engineering services.

NOTE: For further information on subjects covered in this section see the list of references in Section 30.

Section **21**

Purchasing in Canada

EDITOR

Peter E. Woodger *Former Executive Vice-President, Purchasing Management Association of Canada, Toronto, Canada*

ASSOCIATE EDITOR

J. Douglas Hall, P.P. *Former National Director, Region VIII, Purchasing Management Association of Canada, Toronto, Canada*

NOTE: Purchasing principles, policies, and procedures in Canada are in general similar to those used in the United States, as enumerated in other sections of this handbook. Major differences that do exist are defined in this section.

Considering the 3000 miles of open border between the United States and Canada and the similarity in language, culture, and economy of the two countries, Canada superficially resembles the United States. Because each is the largest trading partner of the other, there must be harmony in trade agreements. For example, Canada is well on its way toward adoption of the metric system, with completion scheduled for 1983. While the United States has been much slower to go metric, compatibility between the two countries' systems will become a major consideration for suppliers and buyers within a few years.

Yet, there are differences originating in historical background that must be considered in differentiating between purchasing practices in the two countries. Although Canada has been developed by immigrants from all over the world, its constitutional heritage is British. For example, the 10 provincial governments and the central federal government in Ottawa all operate on the British parliamentary system. In addition, while its federal government is autonomous, it retains a tie to Great Britain through the Governor General, who represents the British sovereign. This link to all countries in the British Commonwealth is significant for reasons of import duties, as will be seen later in the section.

Another difference lies in Canada's bicultural heritage. In the early days, many French settlers came to Canada and settled mainly in the province of Quebec. This large French-speaking group strongly defended its cultural heritage and was granted the right to practice French civil law, as well as the right to conduct its business in French. Both rights have implications for the purchasing manager that will be discussed shortly.

Canada differs from the United States mainly in a slower economic development and in lower population. It is rich in natural resources, yet it lacks funds to develop those resources. It knows it must import capital, yet it worries about selling out its resources. Oddly enough, the largesse of agricultural and mineral wealth creates economic problems. For example, Japan buys Canadian wheat, coal, and iron ore and in turn requests Canada to import its finished goods to balance its trade. Thus, in addition to being more exposed to low-cost imports, the Canadian manufacturer also faces the problem of a small home market and the resulting limitations in the scale of production.

The net effect of all these differences is to force Canadian purchasing managers to think in terms of international trade. For example, because Canadian sources of supply, particularly for equipment and machinery, are limited because of the small market, the purchasing managers must search the international markets. A purchasing manager must know not only the exact amount of all cost components associated with importing, but also how they can be modified by action on his part. For example, can he negotiate lower tariffs or lower freight rates? What is the impact of long-range tariff negotiations? Can he buy from a British Commonwealth country at a lower rate of duty? Will exchange rates change, increasing his costs, while his shipment is in transit?

At the same time, knowing that a strong Canadian market is important in the long term, he must constantly encourage Canadian firms to supply his materials and equipment.[1]

LAW IN CANADA

The reader should refer to Sections 4 and 5 for the general implications of commercial law for purchasing. The intention of this presentation on law is to state sources of information and to deal with differences unique to Canada.

For current detailed treatment of Canadian law, the purchasing manager should contact the Purchasing Management Association of Canada for information on the availability of its Commercial Law Seminars.[2] Knowing the fundamentals, the purchasing executive should know when he requires the assistance of legal counsel and when he can rely on his judgment and the goodwill of his supplier.

Sale of Goods in All Provinces except Quebec

The following quotation is from a seminar entitled Performance of Contracts, conducted for the Purchasing Management Association of Canada by Professor Andrew R. Thompson:

> In 1893 the English Sale of Goods Act was enacted as a codification of the common law of sales. It represented a restatement of the principles and rules of the law of sales as they had been formulated by the English courts over several centuries.
> This codification was adopted in the common law provinces of Canada. Consequently, each province has a Sale of Goods Act with almost uniform provisions. In some cases the numbering of sections differs.

It is interesting to note that for most practical purposes the Sale of Goods Act in each province differs little from the American Uniform Sales Act which preceded the present American Uniform Commercial Code. However, the reader would be well advised to obtain a copy of the Sale of Goods Act in the province in which he is purchasing. This may be obtained from the Queen's Printer of the province.

The Law of Sale in the Province of Quebec

The following quotation is taken from *Comments on the Law of Sale in the Province of Quebec,* written from the Purchasing Management Association of Canada by Professor J. J. Gow.

> In Quebec the distinction between the rules of law relating to the sale of goods and the rules of law relating to the sale of other species of property, notably land or real property, does not apply and the law of sale is considered as applicable to all species of property, the primary theoretical distinction, if any, being between

---

[1]See M. R. Leenders, *Improving Purchasing Effectiveness through Supplier Development,* Division of Research, Graduate School of Business Administration, Harvard University, 1965.

[2]Purchasing Management Association of Canada, Suite 1103, 80 Richmond Street West, Toronto, Ontario M5H 2A4, Canada.

the sale of a corporeal thing (land, motor car) and an incorporeal thing (a debt, in the common law a *chose in action*). There is no Sale of Goods Act but the Fifth Title of the Third Book of the Quebec Civil Code of 1866 contains articles 1472–1595 which prescribe rules relating to the *contract of sale*.

While there is little difference in actual practice the purchasing agent should know that the relevant legal concepts and the language describing them differ from the corresponding concepts and language of the common law, e.g., the terms "contract of sale" and "warranty" in Quebec do not have quite the same meaning as the same phrase or word in a common law Sale of Goods Act.

The Quebec purchasing manager is well advised to consult with legal counsel in writing terms and conditions for his purchase order or his tender.

Purchasing managers outside of Quebec would do well to consult with legal counsel before making major, complex commitments in Quebec.

CUSTOMS TARIFF

With the fast transportation available today, alert purchasing managers will survey foreign sources of supply for their major items. They will, of course, know where and how they are made and are used.

Correct purchasing decisions will be made on landed price comparisons that must include selling price, exchange rate, freight, insurance, sales tax, brokerage, dock charges, and customs duty. Knowledge of the composition and end use of his imports will, first, assist the purchasing manager in verifying that the classification for duty is correct and, second, in the case of machinery, help him know when to apply for remission of duty. Customs brokers will assist in the preparation of application for remission of duty for machines and accessories entered under Tariff Items 42700-1 and 42701-1 in cases when the Minister of Industry considers that it is in the public interest and that the goods are not available from production in Canada. The application must be presented within 90 days of the release date.

Knowledge of the underlying principles of the tariff will assist the purchasing manager in requesting a change in the tariff on materials or equipment that play a significant role in his business. The government is particularly interested in maintaining or increasing employment. Discussions with officials of the International Trade and Finance Branch of Finance Canada, Ottawa, are recommended. Trade associations may provide technical assistance. Customs consultants will provide assistance on a fee-for-service basis. Proposals are sent to the Director of Tariffs, Department of Finance, Ottawa.

Importations

Imports into Canada are governed by 24 statutes. The most important of these are the Customs Act, the Customs Tariff Act, the Anti-Dumping Act, and the Tariff Board Act.[3]

---

[3]The various acts and memorandums referred to are available by mail from Printing and Publishing Supply Services Canada, Ottawa, Ontario K1A OS9.

In addition there is a body of reference material known as Department of Revenue Canada Customs and Excise D Memoranda. This sets out procedures, rules, and regulations not contained in the statutes themselves.

Purchasing managers are strongly advised to keep well informed on changes in customs and drawback regulations.

The Customs Tariff Act

This is the statute which classifies goods coming into Canada by tariff item number and provides rates of duty on a three-column basis, namely, British Preferential Tariff (B.P.), Most Favoured Nations Tariff (M.F.N.), General Tariff (Gen) and General Preferential Tariff (G.P.) schedule A.

The rates of duty and the wording of the relevant classifications originate in the Budget of the Minister of Finance, usually presented to Parliament annually. In addition, some changes in the Customs Tariff occur at quarterly intervals throughout the year. These changes are brought about through Orders in Council, which may be looked on as a minor Acts of Parliament, and are usually in the nature of reductions for a stated period of time.

Valuation for Duty

It is essential that the purchasing manager have a good understanding of the basis on which a duty is to be computed. Basically, ad valorem duties, or duties based on value, are assessed on the higher of the fair market value or the purchase price, both converted to Canadian currency.

Where duty is not on an ad valorem basis, it is referred to as a *specific* duty, and such duty is assessed on the basis outlined in a given tariff item, i.e., at so much per pound, per gallon, per ton, per yard, etc.

The procedure for determining fair market value for duty is outlined in sections 35 through 47 (R.S.C. 1970) of the Customs Act. Briefly, value for duty is the price at which like merchandise is sold in the home market at the time and place of shipment to the same class of trade as represented by the Canadian importer, in comparable quantities, and in the ordinary course of trade.

Discounts

The value for duty may allow discounts, only provided such discounts are shown, allowed, and deducted on invoices covering sales for home consumption in the country of export in the ordinary course of trade. Cash discounts are not deductible. However, any internal tax, e.g., domestic sales tax imposed within the country of export or origin and which is exempted in respect to exports, may be deducted from the value for duty. This does not authorize the subtraction of import duties which may be incorporated into a home market price unless so authorized.

Purchasers are urged to become familiar with the foregoing sections in order to fully protect themselves in the determination of the amount of the duty payable.

Customs Invoices

There are two basic customs invoice forms, one for outright sales and one for nonsale transactions, e.g., consignment shipments, identified by letters as follows:

Sales Transactions	Consignment Transactions	Subject to Treatment Under
M	N	General Tariff
MA	NA	M.F.N. Tariff
MB	NB	B.P. Tariff

Four copies are required—three for customs use and one for the importer's use.

The invoice should be completely filled out, and blank forms are usually available from printers and stationers both in Canada and abroad. Lacking the availability of commercially printed blanks, an exporter may use his own billhead, provided it is modified to:

1. Carry the headings on the value columns
2. Record the country of origin
3. Carry the necessary certificates either written, printed, or stamped on the back or front of the invoices but not pasted thereon or attached thereto

Alternatively, the Canadian customs authorities may be requested to approve the private printing of customs invoices. (See Memo D44–5.)

The certificate of origin, where it appears, must be signed in the country of origin stated on the invoice. The balance of the invoice declaration may be signed by the seller or exporter, not necessarily resident in the country of origin.

Invoices covering sales do not have to be visaed as in the case of customs consular invoices required by many countries; however, consignment invoices on forms N, NA, and NB must be attested to in British countries before a collector of customs, justice of the peace, notary public, or other official authorized to administer oaths, and in other countries before a British or other consul, notary public, or other official authorized to administer oaths.

There is a composite form of invoice approved for use on international air movements. When this is used, the international cargo invoice has to include the appropriate certificate associated with either the M, N, MA, NA, MB, or NB form, as the case may be, depending on the origin of the goods. In practice, many exporters simply use the approved regular invoice rather than the international cargo invoice. Further elaboration on the subject of invoices will be found in Memo D43.

The purchaser should advise the seller as to where and to whom the invoices should be directed. In the case of imports by air, and truck shipments from the United States, the importer can if he so wishes have the invoices tendered to the carrier, who will transmit them to the consignee or broker at port of clearance along with the goods.

Imports valued at less than $200 may be processed at customs on the basis of commercial invoices.

Where a Canadian purchaser is buying goods abroad for direct shipment to a third party in Canada, there is provision whereby he can issue a customs invoice to a third party so that such party can clear the goods. Under these circumstances, the Canadian intermediary issues what is known as a *transfer customs invoice* from himself to such third party. This is virtually a duplicate of the exporter's customs invoice and on the same form of invoice except for the usual change in selling price. This transfer invoice must be validated by the collector of customs in Canada.

Entry Requirements

After receipt of customs invoices at the clearance port, goods are released to the importer upon the passing of a customs entry—formal or informal. (See Customs Act Sec. 20, Memo D44-1.)

In order to pass formal entries at Canadian customs, the person processing such entries, be it an employee of the importer or an accredited customs broker, must hold an appropriate power of attorney for this purpose. (See Memo D14.)

Small collection or informal entries not requiring power of attorney are applicable to shipments arriving by parcel post, express, or baggage, or by private automobile when valued at no more than $200. (See Memo D44-1.)

Commercial shipments not falling within the scope of the small collection entries referred to are covered by a regular or formal customs entry, which, when fully processed and checked by the customs appraiser, results in the release of the goods. It should be noted that the law provides that the appraiser may open and examine any package or packages for the purpose of making an appraisal or to verify information given on the entry. (C.A. Sec. 97 R.S.C. 1970.)

Sight Entry Where a customs invoice is not available or has not been acceptably prepared, the importer can pass what is designated as a *sight entry,* under which the appraiser shall assess a deposit in a sum sufficient to pay the full and proper duty and taxes on the goods. A period of three months is usually allowed for the perfecting of such sight entries upon the production of good invoices, at which time a refund claim is also filed to recover any excess duty taken to account by the appraiser at the time of the passing of the sight entry. Where a sight entry is not perfected within the time required, the moneys assessed at the time of the passing of the sight entry will be taken to account and a penalty equal to the original deposit may also be assessed. (See C.A. Sec. 24.)

Later Withdrawal Provision is also made for warehouse entries in respect to goods which are not being cleared but will remain in bonded warehouses for later withdrawal in total or in partial quantities. On shipments entered and warehoused, duties are payable on the quantity and value of goods as entered at the time of warehousing; however, the rate of duty assessed is that in effect at the time the goods are withdrawn from the warehouse. (See C.A. Sec. 68-83, Memo D20 R.S.C. 1970.)

Missing Package   Where one or more complete packages are missing at time of entry, the entry is marked "—packages to arrive," and these packages, when they come to hand, are released on the strength of the original entry.

Emergency Entry   In addition to the aforementioned formal and informal entries, under certain circumstances, *a pro forma entry may be arranged for the immediate release of goods, after examination and before payment of duty. This is accomplished through the use of Form C9, major details being found in Memos D24(19) and D44-2(6).*

While any category of goods is eligible for release in this fashion, it is usually associated with goods which are promptly or urgently required, both during and after authorized hours. It may be on a one-time basis or as standing authority at one or more ports. The use of this service is associated with deposit security in the form and amounts as set out in Memo D44-2.

Goods released under these *regulations* must be duty-paid by a regular or sight entry within 5 days in the case of perishable goods and 3 days in the case of all other goods.

Date of release is date of entry for tariff classification purposes.

Damaged or Lost Goods

Provisions dealing with goods damaged or lost are contained in Sections 60 through 67 R.S.C. 1970 of the Customs Act. Briefly, in the case of damage which has occurred during the course of transportation and before arrival at port of destination in Canada and which is apparent at time of entry, the appraiser can estimate the percentage of such damage and deduction from the original value will be made and duty levied on the reduced value. In the case of breakage to brittle goods, rust to certain iron or steel, deterioration and decay of certain perishable articles, and damage to sugar, certain deductions are taken into account in computing the amount of loss.

In actual practice, it is usually found that importations involving damaged or lost goods are more frequently the subject of refund claims.

Refund Claims

Refund of duty is covered in the Customs Act, partially in the sections referred to above as well as in Secs. 46, 112, 113, 114, and 115. Procedures and regulations for handling refund claims appear in Memo D16-1, with specific aspects covered in Memos D16-2, D44-1, D49-14, 22, 23, complete D50 series and D53, 1E, 16E.

The form required in processing a refund claim is B2. Some of the reasons for application for refund include the following: clerical errors; errors in invoicing; perfecting a sight entry; damage to goods; goods returned that are not the goods ordered; goods which after entry are disposed of in such a manner as to attract a lower rate of duty than that applied at time of importation.

Certain time limits must be observed in connection with various kinds of refund claims; for instance, goods lost or damaged in transit—30 days; invoice errors—

90 days; misdescription of goods on invoices or entry—90 days; reclassification or revaluation—90 days; goods returned as not according to order—2 years; obvious errors in calculations or conversion resulting in overpayment of duty—2 years.

Records

Sections 169–171 of the Customs Act deal with the retention by the importer of records, such as books of accounts, invoices, bills, and correspondence, for a period of 6 years following importation.

Penalties

As might be expected, the Customs Act makes provisions for penalties ranging from seizure to fine and/or imprisonment when its requirements are violated. The areas of particular concern to importers and where caution should be exercised include the following: failure to keep and produce records (C.A. 171 and 241); willful false statements in declarations (C.A. 195); diversion of imports entered at free or low rates for specific purposes (C.A. 105); gaining access to goods while in bond, e.g., breaking car seals before entry (C.A. 214); smuggling (C.A. 192 et seq.); importation of prohibited goods (C.T.A. 12).

Drawbacks

Regulations under which duty drawback is allowed are contained in Memos D17-1–D17-29. Some of these memos deal with stated products, such as spirits exported, Canadian commercial purchases for export, and wireless and telegraph apparatus.

However, importers are probably more interested in the following, which are of more general application:

Memo D17-1 provides for drawback on imported goods used for home consumption, with the drawback rate ranging from 50 percent to 99 percent.

Memo D17-4 deals with perhaps the most widely used drawback regulation, namely, provision for drawback of 99 percent of customs duties and excise and sales taxes paid on goods which are used or directly consumed in, wrought into, or attached to any articles manufactured or produced in Canada and exported therefrom.

To be eligible for drawback, the goods must have been so used and duties and taxes paid thereon within 3 years of the date of exportation of the Canadian article. Claims shall not cover goods exported for a period of more than 12 consecutive months and must be filed within a period of six months from the date of the last export entry covered by the claim.

Memo D17-5 provides for drawback of 99 percent of duty and excise and sales taxes paid on imported goods which are exported, provided the goods have not been used in Canada other than in the development or production of goods destined for export, have been used as plant equipment, or have been damaged prior to export. Time limits are identical to those referred to in D17-4.

Memo D17-13 provides for remission through drawback of 90 percent of customs duty and excise taxes on imported goods where such goods are obsolete or surplus to requirements in Canada and have not been used in Canada for any purpose and are destroyed at the owner's expense under customs supervision. These drawbacks are subject to being filed within 2 years of date of destruction, and will cover duties and taxes paid within a prior 3 year period.

Appeals

The more likely use of appeal action is on decisions about (1) tariff classification, or value for duty, or (2) whether drawback of customs duty is payable and the rate of such drawback.

Appeal under (1) starts with the Dominion Customs Appraiser, and then goes to the Deputy Minister, the time limit in each case being 90 days. Following a decision, (1) and (2) may be further appealed to the Tariff Board within 60 days. Within 60 days any decision of the Tariff Board may be appealed to the Exchequer Court of Canada upon any question of law. The finding of this Court may be further appealed to the Supreme Court of Canada within 60 days.

Advertising

Printed and lithographed matter, such as letterheads, advertising circulars, boxes, cartons, labels, and printed order forms purchased or consigned to Canadian branches or associates at the large-quantity price related to volume purchases by the foreign parent are advanced in value to reflect the value of the smaller quantity shipped to Canada.

The usual advance for nominal imports, e.g., 10 percent of total run, is 30 percent in the case of one-color printing and 35 percent for two or more colors.

Temporary Entry of Articles for Special Use

These regulations are set out in Memorandums D4-1 to -10. Application for the temporary entry of articles should be made to the Collector of Customs.

Varying time limits are applicable, as well as varying duty situations from free to designated monthly payments.

Typical cases under this regulation are:

Goods as listed for entertainment, news coverage, noncommercial lecture material and exhibitions, etc.

Aircraft and foreign railway rolling stock

Molds, dies, patterns, rolls for embossing or printing

Machines and other equipment for temporary replacement of imported units under repair or pending delivery of new units

Equipment of a class or kind not made in Canada for examination, evaluation, demonstration, quality control testing

Travelers' samples for display

The purchasing manager should be aware of the opportunity to temporarily import plastic molds or stamping dies where, for example, one run may satisfy his requirements for a long period of time. This may result in a large saving by eliminating both the importation of finished goods and the investment in tools or equipment.

Antidumping Duty

This represents the difference (margin of dumping) between normal value and a lower export price. Under the Antidumping Act, two basic conditions must apply before antidumping duty assessment is made:

1. The Department of National Revenue must determine that dumping in fact exists.
2. The Antidumping Tribunal must determine that the dumping constitutes material injury to the production in Canada of like goods.

The cycle of action under this statute usually starts by Canadian producers filing with Revenue Canada a complaint alleging that certain goods are being injuriously dumped. Should the Department's follow-up and investigation support the complaint, a preliminary determination of dumping is made and the case is referred to the Antidumping Tribunal for a ruling in respect to material injury. The tribunal has 90 days in which to resolve the issue. During this period, provisional antidumping duty is assessed or security posted for such duty. There is no time limit associated with the Department of National Revenue investigation.

Complaints filed with the Department of National Revenue are usually a matter of correspondence plus, where necessary, personal visits and inquiries made by officers of the Department.

The Antidumping Tribunal usually functions through the medium of public hearings as well as in camera sessions at its discretion.

Antidumping is a complex subject, and persons involved therein are urged to study the act and the regulations associated therewith contained in Memos D41-1 et seq. The Department of National Revenue also issues a summary which covers this subject in further detail.

General Customs Organization

Most contacts are likely to be with local port officers of the National Revenue Department, who administer legislation dealing with imports on a day-to-day basis. Overall jurisdiction rests in the hands of the Deputy Minister of Customs and Excise and the Assistant Deputy Minister of Customs. In Ottawa there is a Director of the Appraisal Division with chiefs reporting to him responsible for areas of valuation, tariffs, and antidumping.

Below this there are unit heads directly concerned with the subjects of valuation and classification, each unit head being responsible for certain specified products.

In Ottawa there is also located a Director of the Customs Drawback Division and a Director of Port Administration.

The Department of National Revenue is further decentralized into regions, as follows:

Name and Location of Regional Office	*For the Regions of*
Atlantic Region: Halifax, Nova Scotia	Nova Scotia, Newfoundland, New Brunswick, Prince Edward Island
Quebec: Quebec, P.Q.	Quebec
Montreal: Montreal, P.Q.	Montreal
Ottawa: Ottawa, Ontario	Ottawa
Toronto: Toronto, Ontario	Toronto
Hamilton: Hamilton, Ontario	Hamilton
Windsor: Windsor, Ontario	Windsor
London: London, Ontario	London
Winnipeg: Winnipeg, Manitoba	Winnipeg
Regina: Regina, Saskatchewan	Saskatchewan
Calgary: Calgary, Alberta	Alberta
Vancouver: Vancouver, British Columbia	Pacific

The purchasing manager will find the Regional Director and his staff most helpful in discussing customs matters, and on occasion he may find it necessary to visit Ottawa to gain information firsthand.

Regional officers communicate with Ottawa where necessary in order to process complex inquiries. Rulings emanating from the regional offices are widely dispersed from coast to coast in order to provide for uniformity of decisions.

Ports of entry staffed with collectors, outports, and other offices are located throughout the country.

Memo D9 gives detailed information with respect to the organization of regions, ports, and outports, addresses, telephone numbers, hours of service, and other useful information.

Other Reference Sources

The purchasing manager will find current information and competent assistance in specific product areas by contacting the head office of related trade associations.

For example, the Customs and Sales Tax Department of the Canadian Manufacturers Association, 1 Yonge Street, Toronto, Ontario M5E 1J9, publishes a circular service on changes, investigations, and appeals for its members. In addition, it offers excellent advice on special problems. The same comments may be made of the Packaging Association of Canada, 10 St. Mary Street, Toronto, Ontario M4Y 1P9.

TAXATION

Sales taxes in Canada are imposed by the federal government and all the provinces with the exception of the province of Alberta. The basic difference between the two sales taxes is the level in the distribution system at which they are imposed. The federal government has the right to impose an indirect tax, i.e., a tax which it is assumed will be passed on in the price of the goods, whereas the provinces must impose a direct tax, i.e., a tax which is imposed on the user of the goods. The federal sales tax is an indirect tax imposed at the manufacturing level, whereas the provincial sales tax is a direct tax imposed at the final-user or consumer level.

The Canadian federal sales tax was first introduced in 1920 as a 1 percent sales tax imposed on all sales by manufacturers, wholesalers, jobbers, and importers. In its original form the tax was a sort of turnover tax applying in some cases more than once to the same goods as they passed through the distribution system. Effective January 1, 1924, the tax was changed to a tax of single application, payable by the manufacturer. That is, the tax applied only once to goods as they passed from the manufacturer or producer to the consumer. The basic form of the tax has changed little since that time.

The first provincial sales tax was imposed by the province of Saskatchewan on August 2, 1937. Since that time all the provinces, with the exception of the province of Alberta, have imposed a provincial sales tax.

The importance of the sales taxes as an element of cost to companies producing goods or importing goods into Canada cannot be stressed too strongly. One has only to look at the tax revenues collected by the federal and provincial governments to realize how important sales taxes are to them. The latest figures available indicate that the federal sales tax provided approximately 17.9 percent of the federal government's tax revenues, and the provincial sales taxes accounted for approximately 24.2 percent of the total provincial tax revenues. The governments in Canada pay a great deal of attention to these taxes, and businesses must do likewise if they are to minimize their costs. A basic understanding of the federal and provincial sales taxes by purchasing managers can assist immeasurably in minimizing the cost of goods purchased.

Federal Sales Tax

A federal sales tax of 12 percent is imposed by the Excise Tax Act on the sale price of all goods (with the exception of those which are exempt) produced or manufactured in Canada and is payable by the manufacturer of the goods. The only rate exception is building materials, where the tax rate is 11 percent. In addition, the Excise Tax Act also imposes a federal sales tax on the duty-paid value of all goods imported into Canada; it is payable by the importer.

The fact that the tax is imposed on the manufacturer and is payable by him is most important. Many manufacturers pay little attention to the fact that the tax is imposed on them and treat it as if it were a tax they were collecting from their customer on behalf of the government. This attitude can result in the manufacturer paying more federal sales tax than is required, with the increase being passed on to the customer. It is for this reason that purchasing managers must familiarize themselves with the basic principles of the federal sales tax and thereby be in a position to know when the sales tax element in the cost of goods purchased is too high.

The manufacturer is required to pay the federal sales tax at the time when the goods are delivered to the purchaser or at the time when title in the goods passes, whichever is the earlier. In the case of goods imported into Canada, the federal sales tax is payable by the importer at the time when the goods are imported or when the goods are taken out of bond. There are some cases where the contract for the sale of the goods provides that the sale price or other consideration shall be paid to the manufacturer or producer by installments. In this instance the federal sales tax is payable by the producer or manufacturer *pro tanto* at the time each of the installments becomes payable in accordance with the terms of the contract, even though the installment may not have been paid.

Since the federal sales tax is imposed on the manufacturer or importer of the goods, it is important that purchasing managers know something of their suppliers' operations. They should at least have some idea of the source of the goods they are buying. For example, are you buying goods which the supplier has manufactured, or are these jobbed goods which he has purchased or imported? This becomes a very important distinction, because the federal sales tax is imposed on the sale price if the goods were manufactured in Canada, but only on the duty-paid value if the goods were imported. If the supplier is selling jobbed goods (goods which he has not manufactured), sales tax should be paid on their cost and not on their selling price.

The selling price of goods produced or manufactured in Canada may be reduced by cash discounts actually taken, volume rebates granted, and the cost of transportation to deliver the goods from the manufacturer's premises to the customer. In addition, Excise Tax Memo ET202 provides for manufacturers to calculate and pay federal sales tax in certain instances on a value less than their sale price.[4] In effect the memorandum permits manufacturers who sell to wholesalers, retailers, and users to calculate their sales tax on sales to retailers and users on the price at which they sell to wholesalers provided they annually sell 15 percent or more of their goods to two or more bona fide wholesalers. There also exists a series of published circulars setting out the basis for tax computation for goods produced in various industries. These circulars normally provide for a discount from sale price which manufacturers may avail themselves of in computing their federal sales tax. It is important that the purchasing manager be aware of these published circulars and make sure that the manufacturer is following the circular in order to reduce the cost of goods being purchased.

It is evident from the above discussion that there can be a difference of opinion between suppliers as to the price on which sales tax will be calculated. It is imperative therefore that purchasing managers always obtain prices which clearly indicate the amount of tax that will be added on taxable goods. If quotations are obtained on a tax-extra basis without the amount of tax being disclosed, it is possible that the lowest quotation could result in a total purchase price that is higher when the tax is added than some of the other prices quoted.

Exemptions   It was previously noted that the federal sales tax is one of single incidence. In order to permit goods entering into the process of manufacture to be

---

[4]Copies of the Excise Tax Act and the memorandums are available by mail from Printing and Publishing Supply Services Canada, Ottawa, Canada K1A OS9, or from the Sales Tax Offices.

purchased exempt of tax, a system of licensing and exemption certificates is used. The Excise Tax Act provides that every manufacturer or producer shall apply for a license if he manufactures goods in excess of $10,000 per year. To obtain a license, the manufacturer applies to the district sales tax office in which he is located. The license is issued free of charge and the license number will be prefixed with the letter S. In certain cases when purchasing goods, it is necessary to quote on the purchase order, in addition to the exemption certificate, the manufacturer's license number. Examples of the most commonly used exemption certificates are as follows:

1. When purchasing raw materials which are to be further processed into taxable goods for sale:

We certify that the goods ordered/imported hereby are to be used in, wrought into, or attached to taxable goods for sale.

License Number S_____   _____
                                                    Name of Purchaser

2. When purchasing production machinery and equipment which are to be used directly in the process of manufacture or production of goods:

We certify that the goods ordered/imported hereby are to be used as outlined in sections 1, 3 and 4, of Part XIII of Schedule III of the Excise Tax Act.

                                             _____
                                                    Name of Purchaser

3. When purchasing materials which are to be consumed or expended directly in the process of manufacture or production of goods:

We certify that the goods ordered/imported hereby are to be used as outlined in section 2 of Part XIII of Schedule III of the Excise Tax Act.

                                             _____
                                                    Name of Purchaser

In some provinces, a manufacturer's license number and certificate of exemption may be preprinted on a company's purchase order forms; otherwise they must be either handwritten, typewritten, or rubber-stamped individually on each purchase order. The purchasing manager should be completely familiar with his company's products and operations so as to be certain that the goods being purchased are capable of being used in the manner in which he is certifying on his purchase order. He must also be careful to place the correct exemption certificate on the purchase order. Failure to use the correct exemption certificate can result in the supplier including federal sales tax in the price he charges for the goods.

Exemptions may be divided into three categories. These are:

1. EXEMPTION OF THE GOODS. Certain goods are exempt from sales tax regardless of the use to which they are put and regardless of the status of the purchaser. An example of this exemption is foodstuffs, which include materials to

be used exclusively in the manufacture of foods. In addition to foodstuffs, there are a multitude of other items which are unconditionally exempt; these include various products of farm and forest, products of mines and quarries, and certain drugs.

2. EXEMPTION BECAUSE OF THE END USE OF THE GOODS. The best example of this important exemption is the exemption for raw materials. *Raw materials* includes partly manufactured goods which are to be incorporated into and form a component part of taxable goods being manufactured for sale. Another important exemption which is dependent on the end use of the product is the exemption for processing materials. This exemption covers materials consumed or expended directly in the process of manufacture or production of goods. It should be noted that the goods must be materials as opposed to articles, and they must be consumed or expended in the manufacturing process.

3. EXEMPTION BECAUSE OF THE STATUS OF THE PURCHASER. Effective October 1, 1977, the federal government and six provinces implemented a system of reciprocal payments of consumption taxes. The six provinces are Ontario, Quebec, New Brunswick, Newfoundland, Nova Scotia, and Prince Edward Island.

The provinces of Manitoba, Saskatchewan, Alberta, and British Columbia are not affected by this change. These provinces will continue to use Crown Funds certificates of exemption, whereby they will be exempt from federal sales and excise taxes on purchases and importation of taxable goods.

On October 1, 1977, the six eastern provinces commenced paying consumption taxes on purchases in the same manner and under the same regulations as any other commercial taxpayer.

On October 1, 1977, the federal government commenced paying the provincial sales taxes of the participating provinces on taxable goods and services, with payment, as a general rule, being made directly to the provinces rather than through individual suppliers. This direct payment arrangement (self-assessing method) was prompted by the fact that the federal government frequently purchases its requirements through a central purchasing agency and then distributes to different locations across the country.

The major exception to the self-assessment method of tax remittance is provincial taxes on fuel. These taxes are to be paid through vendors at the time of purchase.

Manufacturer's License It has been noted previously that all manufacturers must be licensed if they manufacture goods in excess of $10,000 per year. A manufacturer does not elect to be licensed; it is a requirement of the Excise Tax Act. Wholesalers may also be licensed. However, unlike the manufacturer, a wholesaler must meet certain requirements before he will be granted a wholesaler's license. In order for a wholesaler to obtain a license, he must have 50 percent or more of his sales in the three months immediately preceding his application for a wholesaler's license exempt of tax. If this test is met, he will be issued a license number prefixed with the letter W.

In acquiring a wholesaler's license, a wholesaler is required to post security for an amount not more than $25,000 and not less than $2000. The amount of the security is equal to double the amount of sales tax payable on the three largest monthly totals of his taxable sales during the last calendar year. The security must be in the form of certain government of Canada bonds, Canadian National Railway bonds, or surety bonds from an approved guarantee company or chartered bank.

Having obtained a license, the wholesaler must now purchase all goods for resale exempt of federal sales tax. This requires the licensed wholesaler to place on his purchase order an exemption certificate in the following form:

We certify that the goods ordered/imported hereby are for resale.

License Number W_____   _____

                                                        Name of Purchaser

Purchasing managers should make sure when purchasing goods from licensed wholesalers that the sales tax is not being calculated by the supplier as 12 percent on the sale price. This is another example of how the purchasing manager is able to assist his employer in obtaining goods at their minimum cost. It was previously noted that the federal sales tax is a manufacturer's tax imposed on the manufacturer and payable on his sale price. Licensed manufacturers usually operate as unlicensed wholesalers and must obtain goods tax-paid on their cost. However, should the product be sold for a tax-exempt use, a refund may be claimed for the taxes paid.

Tax Refunds   There will be occasions when a company will purchase goods tax-paid and then divert them to a tax-exempt use. When this happens, the company should claim a refund from the sales tax department for the amount of tax included in the purchase of the goods. This refund is obtained by completing forms N15 and N15A and sending them to the district sales tax office for the area in which the company is located. The Excise Tax Act provides, however, that in order to obtain a refund, the claim must be submitted within four years of the date the cause for refund first arose. Since in many cases the company may not recognize that a refund may be claimed until they are close to the four-year time limit and the completion of the forms would take them beyond this time limit, the company should write a letter of intention to submit a refund claim to the district sales tax office. Upon receipt of the letter, the district office will send an acknowledgment to the company stating the period for which a refund claim may be submitted. It is normal for the period to be fixed at 4 years prior to the date of receipt of the letter by the district sales tax office. This then gives the company the required time with which to prepare and submit their formal refund claim.

Revenue Canada issues a *Federal Sales and Excise Tax Manual* which includes excise tax memorandums and the schedules of the Excise Tax Act setting out the items which are exempt from tax. The person responsible for sales taxes should obtain a current copy of this manual and all memorandums issued since its publication date. Additionally, this person should have his or her name added to the appropriate mailing list to ensure receipt of subsequent memorandums.

A more convenient federal sales tax reference would be the *Sale Tax Guide, Canada,* issued annually by the Canadian Manufacturers' Association. Taxation circulars will be issued throughout the year, as required. January 1, 1978 prices— soft cover $17.50, hard cover $22.

This information should be referred to by purchasing managers if they are in doubt as to the exempt status of goods. There may be other cases where a purchasing manager, even after referring to the sales tax manual, is still not entirely

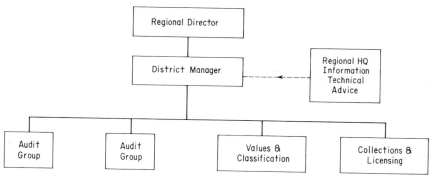

Fig. 21-1   Typical district sales tax office.

certain whether the goods being purchased are eligible for exemption from federal sales tax. Rather than just guessing, he should consult the district taxation office to obtain rulings on the status of these goods. Normal procedure for obtaining a ruling is to write a letter to the district taxation office explaining the nature of the goods being ordered and how they will be used by the company. If, on the other hand, a decision is required immediately, the purchasing manager should telephone the district taxation office and discuss the matter with the values and classifications officer. If the purchasing manager does not agree with the ruling received from the district taxation office, an appeal may be made to the values and classifications officer in the regional office. The organization of typical district and regional sales tax offices is shown in Figs. 21-1 and 21-2.

The Department of Revenue, Canada, Customs and Excise is set up on a regional basis, and within each region there are district tax offices. The district tax offices are responsible for the day-to-day contact with the licensees in their district. It is from these offices that field auditors operate and that rulings are issued in the first instance. The regional office handles complex tax problems referred by the district office and contentious tax matters which cannot be resolved at the district level to the satisfaction of the licensee. The head office in Ottawa is mainly concerned with matters of tax administration policy, procedures, and systems which affect all regions and the districts.

Provincial Sales Tax

In contrast to the federal sales tax, the provincial sales taxes are imposed directly on the consumer or user of the goods purchased. The vendor of the goods is nor-

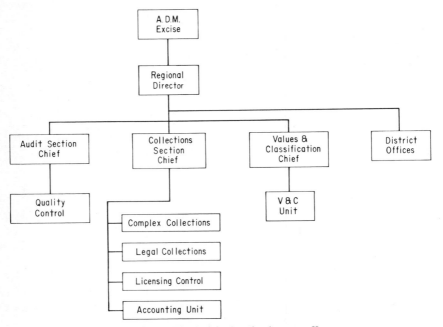

Fig. 21-2 Typical regional sales tax office.

mally appointed an agent of the province for the collection of the tax and is required to remit such tax to the provincial authorities. As mentioned previously, the province of Alberta is the only province which does not impose a provincial sales tax.

The provincial retail sales taxes are of general application. That is to say, like the federal manufacturer's sales tax, they apply to all goods except those specifically exempted. The provinces do not levy a retail sales tax on real property (i.e., land and buildings) but rather confine it to tangible personal property, which is normally thought of as property that can be seen, weighed, measured, felt, or touched, or that is in any way perceptible to the senses. In addition, certain provinces impose a retail sales tax on services such as long-distance telephone calls, telegraph services, and transient accommodation.

The provinces differ in their wording defining the value on which the tax is imposed, but it is normal for the tax to be imposed on the sale price of the goods charged by the vendor to the consumer.

Exemptions   Each province differs in respect to the types of goods which are unconditionally exempt, although they all provide unconditional exemption for drugs and medicines sold on prescription, food products for human consumption (not including prepared meals), and certain goods for use in farming. In order to provide exemption for goods as they pass through the distribution system, the provinces use a form of licensing and exemption certificates. This practice permits goods to be purchased either for further manufacture or for resale exempt of sales tax. It assures that the tax is imposed on the final user or consumer of the goods who is unable to certify whether they are for further manufacture or for resale. The most common exemption certificates used when purchasing goods are as follows:

1. When purchasing goods which are to be further processed:

I/we certify that the tangible personal property ordered herein is to be processed, fabricated into, attached to, or incorporated into, tangible personal property for sale.

_____   _____
Vendor's Permit No.   Name of Purchaser

2. When purchasing goods for resale:

I/we certify that the tangible personal property ordered herein is purchased for the purpose of resale.

_____   _____
Vendor's Permit No.   Name of Purchaser

All the provinces require vendors who have a place where they transact business within the province to be registered as vendors and to obtain a vendor's permit number or license. These permits or licenses are obtained free of charge in each province by making application to the district tax office in which the vendor's place of business is located.

It was previously mentioned that the provincial sales taxes normally apply to the sale price of goods. Some provinces, however, permit tax to be payable on the net amount of the transaction when property is accepted by the vendor as a trade-in. For example, if a company purchased a new machine for $100,000 and was granted a trade-in allowance by the vendor of $25,000 on its old machine, sales tax would be applicable on only $75,000 in those provinces which permit trade-in allowances to be deducted.

It is not possible in a handbook of this type to state all the exemptions which purchasing managers should be aware of for all the provinces. Purchasing managers should be aware that goods which are to be further processed or which are for resale are exempt of provincial tax, while those being purchased for use or consumption are normally taxable. Some provinces also provide exemption for production machinery and equipment to be used in the process of manufacture, whereas others do not. In addition, leased personal property is also taxable—generally based on the rental charge for the property.

In all cases of uncertainty as to whether an exemption can be obtained, the purchasing manager should obtain a ruling from the provincial sales tax authorities.

Tax Rates   Set out below are the rates of tax in effect at the date of publication. Rates do change from time to time, and it is always advisable to make reference to the provincial act under which the tax is imposed to ensure that these rates are still in effect.

Province	Name of Act	Rate of Tax,%
Newfoundland	The Social Security Assessment Act, 1963	10
Nova Scotia	Health Service Tax Act	8
New Brunswick	Social Services and Education Tax Act	8
Prince Edward Island	The Revenue Tax Act	8
Quebec	Retail Sales Tax Act	8
Ontario	The Retail Sales Tax Act	7
Manitoba	TheRevenue Tax Act	5
Saskatchewan	The Education and Health Tax Act	5
Alberta	This province does not impose a sales tax	None
British Columbia	Social Services Tax Act	5

TRANSPORTATION

It is well known that among the nations of the world Canada is second only to the Soviet Union in size of real estate (having about 3,850,000 square miles). Its population of 21 million people, however, places Canada twenty-sixth among the nations in size of population. Its technical status, reflected in a high standard of living, includes a highly developed and generally efficient transportation system that compares favorably with those of most of the nations of the world. This means that the purchasing manager has available to him the most sophisticated transportation facilities to be found anywhere; it remains for him only to select from the various modes the kind of transportation service he needs at a price he is prepared to pay.

The purpose of this section is to describe the kinds of transportation available, the relative merits or intrinsic advantages of each, and some areas of freight transportation that are important to him. Obviously, space limitations preclude a comprehensive treatment of the subject; only experience and reference to texts, trade publications, and tariffs will provide the additional knowledge required.

The reader is cautioned also to realize that, like most things in life today, the transportation scene is dynamic and is changing rapidly. What is observed today is often obsolete tomorrow.

Canada's Transportation Industry[5]

Airlines   There are numerous Canadian airlines serving most locations, including the Far North. The most important to the average shipper to Canadian points

---

[5]Transportation terminology parallels that used in the United States, as explained in Section 23.

are: Air Canada, B.C. Airlines, C.P. Air, Eastern Provincial, Nordair, Pacific Western, Quebecair, Transair, and Wardair.

Shippers to or from foreign points may use Air Canada, C.P. Air, or Wardair, in addition to several foreign airlines that serve major Canadian cities.

Air transport rates are much higher than other rates but may be justified on lightweight-high-value goods and where speed is essential. Other costs, such as packaging, inventory, and documentation, may be reduced by fast air transport. Each purchasing manager should carefully compare total air costs with total surface costs before ruling out the former simply because of freight rates.

Parcel Post   Shippers of small parcels should investigate Domestic Fourth-Class Surface Post Service (Parcel Post). Rates are very reasonable, and shipments may be insured for up to $1,000. The parcel may not exceed 35 pounds in weight and 3 feet in length, and the combined length and girth must not exceed 6 feet; parcels up to 6 feet in length or 10 feet in combined length and girth will be accepted at a surcharge of $2.

Railways   While Canada has but two transcontinental railroads, Canadian National Railways and the Canadian Pacific Railway, there are 20 other Canadian rail companies operating in the country. In addition, several U.S. railroads have lines and terminals serving border cities.

Railways provide low-cost transportation for carload, less-than-carload, express (or merchandise), packaged or in-bulk freight over long distances. Their main competitor is highway transport, although the major Canadian railroads have their own trucking lines which serve as adjuncts to their rail service or in direct competition with the truckers.

Truckers   There are several types of trucking firms offering transportation service: local cartage, intercity, interprovincial, international, and household movers. Their main advantages are specialized equipment, door-to-door delivery, faster service than rail, and competitive rates. For small shipments, bus lines and specialized courier services should be investigated.

Truckers must obtain provincial permits to serve designated areas. As a result, more than one carrier may be involved in an intercity or interprovincial move, as compared with shipment by the transcontinental railways.

Truck lines have acquired highly sophisticated equipment and are now challenging rail transportation, even over long distances.

Water Carriers   Canada's East and West Coast ports are well served by ocean shipping lines the year around. Since 1959 many lines have also been serving Great Lakes ports from April to December. Churchill, Manitoba, is served during a much shorter shipping season, mostly by grain carriers.

In addition, there are numerous inland waterways and coastal water carriers which provide excellent service. The largest and best-known inland waterways carrier is probably Canada Steamship Lines, which operates a large fleet of modern bulk-cargo ships between Sept Isles, Quebec, and the lakehead, and general-cargo ships between Montreal and the lakehead.

Water transportation costs are generally lower than costs of rail or highway, and delivery times are often quite competitive. Purchasing managers located at or near ports should, therefore, familiarize themselves with marine rates and schedules for Canadian or Canadian–United States traffic.

Freight Forwarders Freight forwarders can be divided into two types. Some merely act as agents on behalf of shippers in arranging for the transportation of goods by, for example, booking vessel space, preparing and presenting documents, and obtaining transportation to the port, without necessarily handling any goods themselves.

Others act as carriers in consolidating shipments of less than one carload or one container load, transporting them, and delivering them to the ultimate consignee in Canada or overseas at a single through rate for the door-to-door movement. This rate is generally lower than that applicable if a shipper makes the small shipment without using a forwarder. Within Canada, such freight forwarders are frequently referred to as *pool car operators.*

Private Carriage Companies having a sufficient volume of regular inbound and outbound traffic that requires service not provided by common (for hire) carriers may find that owning or leasing their own vehicles and making their own deliveries is preferable to using a transport company. In fact, in high-volume areas, the purchasing manager may find that, where inbound shipments balance outbound shipments, the inbound shipments may pay for the back haul on outbound shipments and create significant savings in total transportation costs as well as improve the service. This is lawful so long as:

1. The equipment is owned or leased
2. The drivers are on the shipper's payroll or completely under the shipper's control
3. The goods being transported are the property of the shipper during transport

Before selecting private carriage, the purchasing manager should make a careful study of his annual costs using common carriers. The results should be compared with his estimated private-carriage cost, including:

Capital investment (including interest) or lease cost
Wages and supplementals (fringe benefits, uniforms, etc.)
Vehicle operating cost (fuel, oil, repairs, and maintenance)
Garage costs
Vehicle and cargo insurance
Licenses and insurance
Administration

Regulatory Control

Each mode of transport is subject to its own particular brand of regulatory control. This may best be illustrated by Tables 21-1 and 21-2.

Tariffs

The price or freight rate the shipper pays to move his package or carload is based on several factors, including distance, weight, density, value, commodity, volume and the competition of other modes of carriage. Most traffic moves under rates, terms, and conditions set out in tariffs published by agencies established by groups of carriers. Exempt from provisions of the Combines Act, all members of highway tariff bureaus charge the published rates, although they must provide in their by-laws for "independent action" by individual members. Similarly, the railways

TABLE 21-1 Scope of Government Regulation of Carriers in Canada (as of March 1, 1971)

F = Federal   P = Provincial   M = Municipal

Carrier	Permit or franchise	Safety	Rate filing	Rate control	Cargo liability
Airlines	F	F	F	F_1	F
Railroads	F	F	F	F_2	F
Truckers	P	P, M	P_3	P_3	P_4
Water carriers	No	F	No	No	F

Notes: 1. Domestic air rates are filed with the Canadian Transport Commission—no further regulation. International air rates are filed with the C.T.C. after approval by I.A.T.A. (International Air Transport Association) rate conferences.

2. Practically speaking, rail rates are not controlled by regulatory bodies. Shippers who feel they are "captive" to rail may appeal a rail rate that appears too high; in this event, the rate may be established by using a formula set out in the Canadian Transportation Act of 1967. The only other control of rail rates is the stipulation that they all shall be compensatory (refer to the same Act).

3. See Table 21-2.

4. There is no bill of lading common to all provinces that establishes a uniform liability limit per pound of cargo. Short and damage claims are usually filed and settled on invoice value. (A common bill of lading is being developed.)

TABLE 21-2 Highway Common Carrier Rate Control by Provinces (as of March 1, 1971)

Province	Freight rate filing		Freight rate regulation	
	Power	Exercised	Power	Exercised
British Columbia	yes	yes	yes	yes (intra only)
Alberta	no	no	no	no
Saskatchewan	yes	yes	yes	yes (intra only)
Manitoba	yes	yes	yes	yes (intra only)
Ontario	yes	yes	no	no
Quebec	yes	yes	yes	yes (intra and extra)
New Brunswick	yes	yes	no	no
Nova Scotia*	yes	yes	no	no
Prince Edward Island	yes	yes	no	no
Newfoundland	yes	yes	yes	yes

*Carriers operating not more than two two-axle trucks are not subject to the provisions of the Nova Scotia Motor Carrier Act, of which rate filing is a part.

publish rates through the Canadian Freight Association, as do most ocean steamship lines through their conferences (consortia of lines serving the same general route; e.g., Atlantic/Westbound Conference). Airlines and inland and coastal shipping companies publish their own tariffs. Railway express or merchandise freight rates are tending to be published by the individual railroad.

The occasional or small shipper may obtain rates by asking the office of the carrier. Large shippers subscribe for tariffs by ordering from the various publishing offices; the annual cost of such tariffs often amounts to hundreds of dollars. The names and addresses of the major Canadian tariff bureaus for highway and rail traffic are shown below. Basic to all rail rates and applicable to many highway tariffs is the Canadian Freight Classification No. 22, which is issued by the Canadian Freight Association.

Rail:

Canadian Freight Association, 1162 St. Antoine Street West, Montreal, P.Q. H3C 1B5

Highway:

CTTB —Canadian Transport Tariff Bureau Association, 555 Dixon Road, Rexdale, Ontario, M9W 1H8

CHGCTBA —Canadian Household Goods Carriers' Tariff Bureau Association, 4180 Dundas Street West, Toronto, Ontario M8X 1X8

MAC —Middle Atlantic Conference, P.O. Box 10213, Washington, D.C. 20018

NFTB —Niagara Frontier Tariff Bureau, Inc., P.O. Box 184, Buffalo, N.Y. 14221

PITB —Pacific Inland Tariff Bureau, Inc., P.O. Box 4131, Portland, Ore. 97208

QTB —Quebec Tariff Bureau, Inc., 1259 Berri Street, Montreal P.Q. H2L 4C7

WTA —Western Transportation Association, 1116 Centre Street, North Calgary, Alberta T2E 2R2

Demurrage

Demurrage is the name given to the charge assessed by a railroad, under the law, against a shipper who holds a car for loading or unloading beyond the free time allowed. (Demurrage is also charged by a vessel owner on ship charters.) Current Canadian rail demurrage rates are as follows:

Day	Daily Charge, Domestic Shipments*	Daily Charge, Export Shipments †
1 and 2	Free	Free
3 to 5	$10	$30
6 to 8	$25	$50
9 and subsequent	$35	$70

*Free days exclusive of Saturdays, Sundays, and holidays.
†All days exclusive of Sundays and holidays.

Highway Equipment Detention Charges

Charging for detaining highway equipment is not required by law and has been rather uncommon. However, as truckers become more sophisticated in their costing and gather more members into their tariff associations, equipment detention charge provisions are appearing in more and more tariffs.

Privately Owned or Leased Railway Cars

All the railway cars seen on the rails are not the property of the railways. Many cars of a special type, such as tank cars and covered hopper cars, are the property of shippers; these may be owned or leased from the car builders and suppliers. They are identifiable by the letter X appearing in the fourth place of the car number prefix: e.g., CGTX 59000.

Hazardous Materials

It will come as no surprise to learn that there are regulations relating to the transportation of dangerous goods. Dangerous goods are those that are corrosive, explosive, flammable (by flash point definition), poisonous, and/or radioactive. Regulations control handling, labels and placards, packaging, quantities, and vehicle design and equipment.

The party in actual possession of the goods (in this context, the carrier) is responsible for the observance of the regulations, but the shipper must properly identify the hazard by properly describing and labeling his product. In addition, of course, the shipper has a moral responsibility to protect the public from the intrinsic hazards and could become legally responsible if the carrier is not able to pay the total amount of loss resulting from an accident.

The regulations are as follows:

Air   *IATA Restricted Articles Regulations,* issued by the International Air Transport Association, 1155 Mansfield Street, Montreal, P.Q. H3B 4G6.

Rail   *Regulations for the Transportation of Dangerous Commodities by Rail,* issued by the Canadian Transport Commission, Ottawa, Ontario, and distributed by Printing and Publishing Supply Services Canada, Ottawa, Ontario.

Road and Private Railway   *Explosives Act and Regulations (Part VI),* issued and distributed by the Department of Energy, Mines and Resources, Ottawa, Ontario. The road transportation of dangerous commodities other than explosives is subject to the jurisdiction of the provinces. The amount of control exercised is variable and sometimes quite limited. Authorities, such as the respective department of transport, should be checked. Many shippers of such materials other than explosives voluntarily conform to requirements of the Interstate Commerce Commission.

Water   *Dangerous Goods Shipping Regulations,* issued by Transport Canada, Ottawa, Ontario, and distributed by Printing and Publishing Supply Services Canada, Ottawa, Ontario.

The above regulations are accepted by foreign authorities, so that exporters normally need not do more than observe them.

Liability of Carriers

Carrier liability may be discussed under three headings: delivery (place and time), loss, and damage. The extent of liability is covered in the terms of the bills of lading, but it is important to note that the carrier cannot limit his liability beyond what is provided by the law of the land in which the contract to transport was effected.

Delivery Place

Should the carrier not be able to effect delivery at the consignee's address during normal working hours, he shall notify the shipper within the time specified in the bill of lading or the terms of the tariff.

Delivery Time

The carrier shall deliver the cargo within a reasonable time after the shipment is accepted. What is reasonable may be arguable but is nonetheless capable of inter-pretation. If the carrier fails to do this, he is liable for damages. Breakdown of equipment is no excuse for failure to deliver in reasonable time.

Loss

English common law, applicable in all Canadian provinces except Quebec (gov-erned by the Quebec Civil Code), makes the carrier responsible for any loss in transit except when caused by acts of God, war, riot, act or default of shipper, or the inherent vice of the goods (highway robbery or hijacking is *not* an exception). The Quebec Civil Code is similar but includes hijacking as an exception. Carrier negligence is no excuse.

Damage

Liability for damage is similar to liability for loss, except that the shipper must ensure that his packaging and loading are adequate (see Packaging below).

Claims

In the event of loss or damage, file claims early. Precede them, if possible, with a notice of intent to claim. For highway, the limit varies from 10 days after actual or expected delivery in Newfoundland to 90 days in Ontario and Quebec. For rail, notice must be given within four months of actual or expected date of delivery. For both rail-express and intraprovincial rail-owned highway service, notice and claim conform to highway limitations. For interprovincial service, claim for partial loss, damage, or delay requires notice within two months and claim within 12 months; damages for interprovincial nondelivery or complete loss requires filing of claim within 12 months.

Packaging

Cartons, boxes, crates, barrels, drums, bags, and other shipping containers must be manufactured to comply with the Canadian Freight Classification No. 22 or the shipment will be refused or charged a higher rate by the railway and may be treated similarly by highway, air, and marine carriers as well.

Documentation

The basic document for shipments by common (for hire) carriers is the bill of lading or, in the case of express, the merchandise receipt or express receipt. This is completed by the shipper or carrier, signed by the shipper and carrier's agent, and contains a detailed description of the goods, the shipper's name and address, the consignee's name and address, the date accepted, and whether prepaid or collect; on straight and order bills of lading, the conditions of transport (liability, etc.) are printed on the back. A short-form bill of lading may be used; it contains no detailed conditions of transport on the back but contains a statement to the effect that the parties mutually agree to the terms and conditions of the straight or order bill of lading. Copies of the bill of lading are required for the shipper, the carrier, and the consignee (includes one original).

On exports, document requirements vary with the industry, but there is always required, in addition to the bill of lading, a Canada Customs Export Entry (Form B-13). The regulations of the foreign country should always be checked: for example, British Preference countries require a statement showing British content; also, some countries require that an import permit accompany the shipment. In addition, Canada requires an export permit for specific commodities, such as explosives and uranium.

Selecting a Carrier

Perusal of the section Canada's Transportation Industry above will provide guidance in determining whether air, highway, rail, or water transport is required. Within each mode, however, there may be several carriers licensed to serve the shipper. Which one should he choose?

The three areas of concern in this matter, and in this order, are:

Service Can the carrier provide the equipment of the kind required and at the time required? This is of prime importance. Has he a good reputation for picking up on time and delivering on time? Check this with neighboring or similar shippers.

Reliability and Responsibility Are his reputation and resources for accepting responsibility for the transportation, including payment of claims, satisfactory? Check this with neighboring or similar shippers.

Cost What does he charge for his services; that is, what is his rate? If service and reliability are equal among carriers, the shipper will, of course, choose the low-cost carrier. However, "bargain" transportation may be no bargain at all if service and/or liability are lacking.

Shippers interested in doing business on a contract or regular basis with one carrier should satisfy themselves that the rates are remunerative. This is essential to ensure that proper service will continue to be provided. A carrier slowly facing financial failure under too low a rate structure is of no continuing use to a shipper and, ultimately, will become a liability; he should be avoided assiduously.

PURCHASING MANAGEMENT ASSOCIATION OF CANADA

As in other countries throughout the world, purchasing in Canada is represented by a national professional association, now titled Purchasing Management Association of Canada. Organized in 1921, and incorporated under the laws of Ontario in 1931, it was a part of the U.S. National Association of Purchasing Management until 1955, when the present association came into being as an autonomous body. The main objects of this association are: (1) to promote efficiency in purchasing by education and precept so that purchasing managers may discharge their duties better in the interests of their firms; (2) to bring Canadian purchasing managers into helpful association with each other; (3) to provide facilities for the dissemination of information and purchasing literature; (4) to safeguard and improve the professional status of purchasing managers.

This National Association consists of at least 40 districts, each with its own local organization. All are listed in Section 29. The National Association conducts a large number of educational seminars and courses throughout Canada, leading to the professional Purchaser diploma discussed in Section 29.

NOTE: For further information on subjects covered in this section see the list of references in Section 30.

Section **22**

Purchasing Internationally

EDITOR

Peter H. Denning, C.P.M. *Manager of Purchases, Koppers Company, Inc., Baltimore, Maryland*

ASSOCIATE EDITORS

Ronald G. Brown, C.P.M. *Buyer, Tektronix, Inc., Beaverton, Oregon*

W. L. Hertenstein *Manager of International Purchasing, Caterpillar Tractor Company, Peoria, Illinois*

C. L. Scott, C.P.M. *Director of Procurement, Defense & Space Systems Group, TRW Inc., Redondo Beach, California*

J. Andrew Sutton, C.P.M. *Director of Purchasing, W. R. Grace & Company, Cryovac Division, Duncan, South Carolina*

A. D. Wilson *Manager, Overseas Purchasing, Warner-Lambert Company, Morris Plains, New Jersey*

INTRODUCTION

As our world continues to become more complex via changes in technology, political arenas, and limitations of raw materials, our purchasing personnel are and will be affected by the international marketplace. For the experienced international buyer, this section will provide a good checklist. The inexperienced will find an introduction to the myriad problems and exciting challenges of worldwide purchasing. Regardless of experience, it is recommended that the buyer seek suitable counsel for specific details. The Selected Bibliography at the end of this section will provide an excellent starting point.

N.A.P.M.

The National Association of Purchasing Management, Inc. is a member of the International Federation of Purchasing and Materials Management (IFPMM). As a result of this membership, all N.A.P.M. members are also members of the IFPMM. N.A.P.M. appoints two delegates to represent it at the IFPMM. The two delegates and the chairperson of the N.A.P.M. International Group form the N.A.P.M. International Committee.

N.A.P.M. also sponsors an International Group. The group comprises purchasing personnel either working or interested in international purchasing. The goals of the group are:

1. To bring before the members of the International Group knowledge of the selling and purchasing practices of other nations and to encourage better understanding of worldwide differences and similarities
2. To research and communicate better techniques of buying in world markets
3. To provide a clearinghouse for ideas of common interest to members potentially or actively engaged in international markets
4. To pursue the successful solutions of common problems with overseas international buyers' groups
5. To cooperate with the N.A.P.M. International Committee for the advancement of its work and aims with the IFPMM
6. To encourage membership participation in the group
7. To assist local associations in the development of international purchasing groups and seminars

N.A.P.M.'s International Group is an excellent source of information, and one of its members serves as the IFPMM export information service contact for the United States. The N.A.P.M. also publishes a list of export service information for all IFPMM member countries.

Types of International Procurement

International procurement can generally be classified into three types:

Import purchasing: The procurement of goods and services from foreign countries

Export purchasing: Domestic procurement for supplying foreign operations

Foreign purchasing: The procurement of goods or services in one foreign country for use in another

Foreign purchasing will require the greatest amount of detail and knowledge because the buyer is not on his own home ground. The problems of licenses, laws, customs, currency, language, and business ethics are multiplied by the complexity of this type of operation. The novice should seek professional help.

Import and export purchasing are covered further on in this section and are featured in the Selected Bibliography at the end.

REGIONAL PACTS

Successful transactions in international purchasing must be founded on a sound understanding of the many factors affecting such transactions. One factor to consider is the various regional pacts throughout the world. A *regional pact* is an agreement between a group of nations bound to certain trading policies by treaty. They have grown out of, and will continue to grow out of, the self-interest of individual nations and of opposing groups of nations seeking both political and economic advantages over other countries. It is most important that the purchasing manager give warrant to these regional pacts which have economic advantage as their basic objective. However, it is wise to be aware of pacts which are political in nature because they do affect international purchasing.

European Community

The *European Community* imports and exports more than any one country in the world. Its members are Belgium, France, Greece, Italy, Luxembourg, The Netherlands, West Germany, Denmark, Ireland, and Great Britain. The United States is the group's chief partner in trade. In addition, the community has special agreements with more than 20 African countries and several nations in the Middle East.

The European Community comprises three organizations and their treaties. They are the European Atomic Energy Community (EURATOM), the European Coal and Steel Community (ECSC), and the European Economic Community (EEC). Both the EEC and the European Community are sometimes called the *European Common Market.*

In 1968 the European Community abolished all tariffs affecting trade between members. A common tariff was set up on goods imported from other countries into any member country. The goal of the European Community is to remove all barriers to trade between its members on capital, goods, services, and labor.

European Free Trade Association (EFTA)

The European Free Trade Association (EFTA) promotes and regulates free trade between its members—Austria, Norway, Portugal, Sweden, and Ireland—and its associate member, Finland. Like the members of the European Community, the members of EFTA have eliminated almost all tariffs and other restrictions on imports of manufactured goods from one another. The EFTA is the second-largest trade association in Western Europe, the European Community being the largest. Unlike the European Community, EFTA does not regulate its members' agriculture, economy, or trade outside the group.

Benelux Economic Union

This economic union, formed in 1948, predates the EEC, although its free-trade objective is the same. Belgium, the Netherlands, and Luxembourg—from whose names the term *Benelux* is derived—strengthened the alliance by treaty effective in 1960. A completely free labor market has resulted, as well as free trade between the three nations and a common trading unit when dealing with other countries. In 1971 Benelux entered into a trade agreement with the Soviet Union, a first for for any Western European group.

Council for Mutual Economic Assistance (COMECON or CEMA)

This council, founded by the Soviet Union and its satellite iron curtain countries (Bulgaria, Czechoslovakia, East Germany, Hungary, Mongolia, Poland, and Rumania) in 1949, also seeks to promote economic development within its member nations. Albania's participation has been minimal since the early 1960s. Yugoslavia, not an original member although communistic, became an associate member in 1964. Cuba joined COMECON in 1972.

In late 1972 the United States and the Soviet Union acted to increase trade between their countries. The United States, interested in increasing imports from Yugoslavia, made this block of countries a new potential market for the import purchasing manager. Additionally, the Soviet Union and Yugoslavia continue to establish or improve their trading relationships with other noncommunist countries of the world. Thus, these countries will also play a more prominent role as a market for the foreign purchasing manager.

African Markets

Over the past several decades, the African continent has seen the emergence of many new nations. Regional economic and/or political pacts have followed, in connection with attempts to assist these developing nations. Membership in these pacts may be expected to vary over the years, largely in response to the social and political interests of individual nations.

Many purchasing managers will find particular interest in the highly industrialized market of the Republic of South Africa as it moves to increase its exports in the years ahead. The vast majority of the world's output of diamonds, gold, and cobalt, as well as a significant percentage of the world's copper and manganese, comes from Africa. Regional pacts which influence trade with the African nations will require careful research by the international purchasing manager.

People's Republic of China

The economic influence of the People's Republic of China increased substantially in the early 1970s through very attractive Chinese development loans made to African and other nations, to be repaid largely by exports to China. Continuing favorable trade relations are also maintained with the European Communities,

Canada, Australia, and several Pacific nations. Trade in nonstrategic goods between the United States and China began following President Nixon's visit to Peking in 1972.

North and South America

The Organization of American States (OAS), formed in 1948, has broad economic, defense, and political cooperation goals for the nations of the Western Hemisphere. Other regional pacts have since been established by groups of these nations with the more specific goal of common internal and external tariffs.

The Central American Common Market (CACM), established in 1960, essentially met this objective for the member nations—Costa Rica, El Salvador, Guatemala, Honduras, and Nicaragua. A similar regional pact, the Latin American Free Trade Association (LAFTA), also formed in 1960, was initially successful. Argentina, Brazil, Bolivia, Chile, Colombia, Ecuador, Mexico, Paraguay, Peru, Uruguay, and Venezuela (the member nations of LAFTA) and the CACM nations experienced difficulties in the early 1970s in maintaining their common objective. Political and sociological differences have severely strained mutual relationships, upsetting prior successes in reducing tariff barriers.

Other Pacts

World problems are being attacked on a broader front than just economics through such organizations as the United Nations, North Atlantic Treaty Organization (NATO), Southeast Asia Treaty Organization (SEATO), and the Warsaw Pact. These global or regional pacts and the possibility of embargo have direct and/or indirect effects on purchasing internationally. In similar fashion, such financial institutions as the International Monetary Fund, the World Bank, and the import-export financing banks of various countries come into play when one is purchasing in world markets.

MONETARY PROBLEMS

Monetary problems can change a profit-making purchase into a large liability. The problems extend beyond the normal fluctuations of the foreign exchange rates. Such considerations as balance of payments, foreign investments, grants, loans, offsets, and military aid agreements can influence what would appear to be a normal transaction. A country may change its economic policies and regulate or float its currency during the contract period. Most U.S. buyers prefer to conduct their transactions in U.S. dollars if possible. Questions can be addressed to the international sections of major banks.

IMPORT PURCHASING

Rapid industrialization, marked by the spread throughout the world of the most modern technology (particularly in formerly underdeveloped countries), and the "shrinking" of the world through faster means of transportation and communication encourage and facilitate the increase of imports, as well as highlighting the need for their consideration by purchasing executives. As the United States expends its raw materials, it becomes necessary for it to seek other sources. The world is fast becoming one marketplace.

An increase in the volume, quality, and diversity of materials and products available from foreign countries is thus evident. This requires the inclusion of foreign sources of supply in the competitive field of industrial purchasing.

Unusual Aspects

Problems peculiar to import purchasing relate, to a much greater degree than those encountered in domestic purchasing, to the nature and customs of the people abroad, currency and exchange restraints, documentation requirements, payment terms, quality and acceptance, insurance, government controls and restrictions, and transportation facilities. A knowledge of the exporting country's customs, history, political stability, climate, population, principal cities, ports, language, currency, principal products, imports, exports, markets, and problems tends to furnish an insight into the desire and ability of its people to trade, the methodology of their dealings, and their attitudes toward contractual obligations.

There may be both political and economic considerations involved in the importation of certain strategic or critical materials. Certainly there are advantages in supplementing and conserving whatever supplies are available domestically by locating and supporting offshore sources for such materials. Also, an offshore source is desirable for any material not available domestically, either in sufficient quantity or competitively. A technical breakthrough may also be a reason for importing. In addition, it may be advantageous to tie imports to the export sale of the buyer's own products, because the sometime shortages of dollars abroad often may limit opportunities for exporting American products. Initial export sales of machinery, for example, also could create a continuing market for spare parts and replacements; thus, by providing a potential market with the dollars paid for imports, a new outlet may be created or preserved.

With increasing frequency, U.S. business organizations are being confronted with a request or a demand that purchases be made abroad as a condition of exports to a foreign country or as a condition of doing business with that foreign country. Such purchases are commonly referred to as *offset purchases* or *counter purchases*. A condition of the sales (export) contract may require that a certain amount of goods be imported from the country to which the export is being made. A variation of this, depending upon the country and its economic base, may require consideration of a bartering arrangement in which goods instead of currency change hands for at least a portion of the export shipments. Some U.S. businesses, confronted with offsets and barter requests, have formed their own trading companies as a medium for accommodating this aspect of international trade.

Fluctuating Rates of Exchange

The fluctuation of rates of exchange for foreign currencies introduces a hazard for the import buyer that has no parallel in domestic purchasing. The risks include unexpected value changes by government fiat and the possibility of exchange charges, with their influence on methods and costs of payment. Floating exchange rates tend to exaggerate the weakness or strength of currency. For the U.S. buyer, payment for imports in U.S. currency is common and, when possible, is probably the buyer's best option.

The shipment or delivery of commodities or products usually follows the purchase by a considerable interval. In the event that an agreement is made to pay in foreign currency, the buyer should consider the desirability of purchasing foreign currency futures upon execution of the purchase contract—the currency to be available in the amount and at the time needed to make payment for the goods purchased. Most commercial banks are prepared to assist in foreign currency transactions and in preparing strategies to satisfy a buyer's need in foreign exchange. An adverse U.S. balance of payments will influence international exchange, and U.S. buyers will find it necessary to keep abreast of currency fluctuations and to consider their significance in determining methods and terms of payment.

Sources of Supply

There are several reasons why determination of quality at source is important to a buyer of imported commodities. Payment before receipt of goods can place the buyer in a difficult position, should he seek adjustment for failure of the goods to meet his specifications or to conform to the U.S. Customs regulations. In the latter case, there would be delays and perhaps even denial of entry of the goods into the United States. It is necessary to clearly specify the quality required and, if possible, to have the goods inspected at origin by an agent of the buyer or by a reliable commercial or governmental inspecting agency.

The integrity and reliability of the individual supplier, therefore, are of prime importance. The buyer should check carefully on the seller (supplier), to satisfy himself that delivery, weight, quality, and product performance requirements will be met, and that he will be accurately informed of all circumstances affecting the ability of the source to meet agreed contract provisions. It is very important that there be a complete understanding between the importer and the exporter as to just what fees or charges are included in the agreed price in the contract. Usually the price will include such items as export taxes, consular and documentary fees, wharfage, loading, lightering, and similar charges involved in delivering goods into the vessel at loading port. If sampling is required, its cost assumption should be agreed upon between the two parties in advance. Charges for freight and insurance are in accordance with the terms of the contract. The importer normally pays import duty, customs entrance fees, unloading charges at port of discharge, and various fees charged by the banks for handling documents.

Visits to the supplier's place of business in order to evaluate his facilities and trade, though highly desirable in effective procurement, often cannot be made. If there is any possibility that delivery promises will not be met, it may be necessary for the importer to maintain larger than normal inventories of the commodities purchased. Such delays may be in manufacturing or waiting for steamer bookings when delivery is desired at a domestic port not frequently visited by offshore vessels. For purchases involving critical delivery schedules, inclusion in the contract of a penalty or liquidated-damages clause, tied to late delivery, would be advisable. When possible, the import buyer should insist that the purchase contract be subject to U.S. laws and U.S. court jurisdiction.

A common practice for the purpose of minimizing the impact of nonperformance or breach of contract is the use of a bank guaranty. A preferable method is a standby letter of credit from the supplier's bank which spells out penalties for nonperformance under the purchase contract. Performance and payment bonds as issued by a bonding company and which are frequently used in transactions within the United States are not generally used in foreign countries. Upon demand of the buyer, suppliers can turn to their banks to furnish guaranties that provide for redress and penalties in the event of nonperformance. If the supplier cannot get a bank guaranty (local laws) or a standby letter of credit (subject to international law), the buyer should understand the reason and assure himself, to the fullest extent possible, that it is not a reflection on the seller's ability to perform or on his past record of performance. A recommended practice for a buyer to guard against the impact of nonperformance is to ask that the supplier furnish a standby letter of credit, in which case redress by draft is payable immediately if the nature of the nonperformance is correctly dealt with in the standby letter of credit.

Arbitration

Arbitration is a method of settling disputes without resort to judicial process in courts of law. It is normally implemented by inclusion of a provision in a contract by which both parties agree that any disputes or claims arising from the contract will be resolved by designated arbitrators rather than by litigation. Since litigation, especially through foreign courts, is tedious and expensive, it has become common practice in international trade to resolve disputes by arbitration. In transactions with Eastern European nations, provision for arbitration is invariably required.

Because of the uncertainties, expense, and delay attendant to court proceedings (even where U.S. judicial jurisdiction is present), settlement of international trade disputes by arbitration is becoming increasingly common. No judicial process, including arbitration, however, can ever be an adequate substitute for careful contract documentation or a thorough investigation of the supplier's reputation for reliability.

Arbitration is a quasi-judicial proceeding which enjoys several distinct advantages over formal judicial procedures:

1. Arbitration is expeditious, whereas the parties to a lawsuit often must wait years to obtain a court hearing.

2. Arbitral awards can be implemented quickly without having to await the outcome of appeals to higher courts.

3. The costs of arbitration generally are far below those of court proceedings.

4. Arbitration procedures can be more flexible than court procedures, as in respect of the times of sitting, the proper law to be applied, the introduction of evidence, and in ensuring that the arbitrator(s) have personal expertise in the area of dispute.

Arbitration should not be confused with conciliation procedures, which generally are suitable for the resolution of disputes in a long-term relationship such as joint venture and which generally are not enforceable in courts of law.

Available sources of arbitrators and recognized procedures are:

American Arbitration Association, 140 West 51st Street, New York, N.Y. 10020 (regional offices in 22 cities nationwide)

Inter-American Commercial Arbitration Commission, 140 West 51st Street, New York, N.Y. 10020

U.S. Council of the International Chamber of Commerce, 1212 Avenue of the Americas, New York, N.Y. 10036

Court of Arbitration, 38 Cours Albert 1er, Paris 8e, France

Provisions for arbitration can be included in sale and purchase agreements, and are often found in printed foreign-trade sales documentation. The situs of arbitration, the designation of the arbitration tribunal, the rules to be employed, the governing law, and the language of the proceedings—all these are matters for negotiation between buyer and seller. In most cases, an arbitration tribunal in the United States applying U.S. law would be most desirable for the U.S. buyer, although arbitration in another country and application of foreign law in countries such as France, Switzerland, The Netherlands, or Sweden may be equally acceptable. It should be recognized, however, that the laws of different nations do not treat buyers and sellers equally. Although there are as many arbitration provisions as there are standard purchasing agreements from which to choose, such provisions should be prepared by counsel to ensure that the parties' interests are best protected in light of the specific circumstances of any given transaction.

Governmental Regulations

The U.S. government imposes certain controls on the importation of goods, both to implement restrictions applying from time to time (nontariff barriers) and to collect duties (tariff barriers) exacted upon all commodities not specifically exempted under current tariff laws and executive orders. These controls are designed as a protective measure for U.S. manufacturers against unrealistically low-priced foreign products. Governments, moreover, usually require their exporters to obtain export licenses to encourage either certain industries or the production of certain goods. But regulations differ, depending upon the nature and amount of goods exported and, frequently, the country of destination or the currency offered by the buyer.

All imports must comply with U.S. Customs rules and regulations, and there must be exact documentation and correct procedures followed for clearance, as well as payment of applicable import duties. Import duties are of several kinds: *ad valorem*—a percentage of the value of the goods; *specific*—a specified amount per unit of weight or measure; and *compound*—a combination of ad valorem and a specific import duty on one and the same item. Certain items have duty rates which are assessed against an *American selling price,* rather than against the ad valorem. This acts as an equalizer and serves to protect U.S. producers from undercutting or dumping by overseas suppliers, who can capture a majority of the U.S. market by selling well below the U.S. price. Duties, when imposed, may be either *full duty,* i.e., at the rates specified, or *preferential,* i.e., assessed at a stated percentage of the full duty rate depending on the country of origin.

The statutes which control the valuation of merchandise imported into the United States are not easily interpreted, especially as they relate to the dutiable status of buying commissions or of inland charges. In certain situations, the duty is assessed not only against the invoice value, but against a total value including *assists.* Assists apply on some occasions when the buyer has supplied blueprints, unique specifications, or technology to the overseas manufacturer. The buyer should familiarize himself with assist regulations. There are also items originating in territories or possessions of the United States or in other countries similarly favored by treaty which are exempted from duties. *Reciprocal trade agreements* reached by negotiation with any specified foreign country for reduction in U.S. import duties are applicable to many other countries under the provisions of the General Agreement on Tariffs and Trade (GATT) and the favored nations principle. The duty paid on an item may vary greatly depending upon the country from which it is purchased. For example, a given item bought from one country may be duty-free, but from another country a 5 percent and from yet another country a 25 percent duty may be assessed.

There exist, adjacent to certain major U.S. and offshore ports, isolated and enclosed areas known as *foreign-trade* or *free-trade zones* (sometimes called *free ports,* not to be confused with *free cities,* which, because of their location, importance to world trade, and financial importance, often are also referred to as *free ports*). Free-trade zones, when approved by the appropriate customs authorities, permit the loading-unloading, breaking up–repacking, sorting, grading, cleaning, mixing or blending (including with indigenous materials), storing, otherwise handling, and reshipping of merchandise—without payment of duties and without intervention of customs officials. It may be advantageous to use free-trade zones for inspection and reexportation of imports without customs formalities, but in some cases it may be found less costly and simpler to use *bonded* facilities under U.S. Customs supervision.

The exportation of imported goods after they have been released from customs custody does not result in a refund of the duties paid on the goods. However, there are several exceptions, and the possibility of a refund or drawback should be investigated.

The U.S. Customs rules and regulations are complex and subject to frequent changes. It is strongly recommended that qualified and licensed customs brokers be consulted before and at each step in purchasing any commodity for importation into the United States. A good, reliable customs broker will actually handle all details of entry. The broker will know the customs inspectors and can do this part of a buyer's job more cheaply and, in most cases, more efficiently. He is the buyer's *attorney de facto* for customs purposes and is bonded to protect the handling of this work for the buyer. The National Customs Brokers and Forwarders Association of America, Inc., Suite 1109, One World Trade Center, New York, N.Y. 10048, can supply the names of licensed customs brokers. This is the major trade association. Although it includes *freight forwarders* in its title, the organization is composed primarily of customs brokers. Many customs brokers, however, also perform the function of freight forwarding. The classified telephone directories of most major port cities also include extensive lists of customs brokers and freight forwarders operating in such ports.

Documentation

Special documents, not common for domestic transactions, customarily are required on direct import purchases under letter of credit. This is because the seller abroad draws against the letter of credit to obtain payment in the country of origin, or presents his draft on the American buyer to a bank in the United States for payment, sometime before the merchandise is received. Because of the liability to penalty for failure to have proper documents to enter merchandise into the United States, the matter of documentation is of prime concern to the importer. It is the responsibility of the foreign seller to supply the buyer with the proper documentation, but the buyer should be familiar with required documentation. To avoid misunderstandings, the buyer should specify in the purchase order exactly what is required.

Fortunately for those involved in international purchasing, some order has developed out of the chaos of the past. Historically, the world trader has dealt with a multitude of nonstandard forms and documents. Through the efforts of many national and international organizations, the *U.S. Standard Master for International Trade* documentation system (variously called the *U.S. Standard Master* or the *Master*) has been adopted. This system greatly simplifies document preparation and provides a consistency of data and forms acceptable for international trade.

At the time the document order is placed, it is desirable to specify exactly the documents that are required, the number of copies of each, and the destination to which they are to be sent. Those usually required are described below.

Bills of Lading There should be a "clean" *on-board, order-notify bill of lading* issued by the steamship company, accepting the shipment and stating the quantity, description and markings of the goods to be transported. Exact quantity should be specified, not *shipper's load and count,* a term which often appears on domestic straight railroad bills of lading. Title to the materials covered is usually conveyed by endorsement

Invoices   A special customs invoice must be prepared by the seller for each shipment to the United States of goods dutiable at a rate based upon or regulated by the value, when the purchase price or value of the goods exceeds $500. However, for shipments which come within one or more of the provisions exempting certain goods or classes of goods (Customs Regulation 141.83, Section C), the invoice requirement does not apply. Supplies of customs Form 5515, *Special Customs Invoice,* may be obtained free of charge from U.S. consular officers.

A commercial invoice, prepared in the same manner customary for a commercial transaction, is acceptable for customs purposes for goods exempted from the requirements of a special customs invoice. If the required special customs or commercial invoice is not filed at the time the goods are entered, a statement in the form of an invoice (a so-called pro forma invoice) must be filed and a bond given for production of the required invoice not later than 6 months from the date of entry.

Certificate of Origin   As its name implies, this document is a statement for purposes of customs entry, certifying the country in which the goods originated. A certificate of origin is required at times to comply with special restrictions or controls on imports. In some cases, a certificate of origin is required because trans-shipments en route can obscure the identity of the actual country or origin.

Weight Certificate   When the weight is determined by an independent certified weighmaster, government agency, or private party, a weight certificate is used as a basis for determination of the quantity shipped. In some cases a buyer may be willing to accept the seller's own weight certificate, without certification by an independent agency.

Analysis Certificate   Some goods are bought on chemical analysis or quality specifications. If a provision is made in the purchase contract, a certificate of a governmental or commercial analyst or assayer will be the basis for determination of the quality for acceptance or settlement.

Certificate of Survey   A certificate of survey is somewhat similar to, and may include or be incorporated in, weight and analysis certificates, because it identifies the exact material shipped against the other documents or the contract. When the importer or bank desires authoritative assurance that the goods ready for shipment are exactly as specified, an independent cargo surveyor may be engaged to examine the goods and issue a certificate that they are as specified. Examination and certification will be made for those particular qualities which may be authorized, such as chemical or metallurgical analysis, determining specifications, count, weight, and especially identifying markings. This service usually is paid for by the buyer unless other arrangements are specified in the purchase agreement.

Insurance Policy or Certificate   This document is an important part of all import shipping requirements. The type of insurance and the extent of the coverage are in accordance with buyer-seller agreements and the risks specifically covering the particular transaction, including those inherent in the general terms or trade customs.

Markings of Packages   Importers should become familiar with the markings required by port and customs authorities for both inside and outside packages, such as cans, bottles, boxes, crates, rolls, and bags. The importer should transmit this information in detail to the shipper for guidance and inclusion on invoices.

Payments

To obtain the most advantageous purchase, the buyer should have a knowledge of foreign currencies and be familiar with the workings of some of the methods of payment for imported commodities. It is important that he recognize the fact that many countries impose and modify from time to time, for reasons both economic and political, restrictions and controls on the use of their currencies. Trading rates of exchange for various foreign currencies are published daily in the *Wall Street Journal* except for controlled currencies, quotations for which are not available in the market.

The term *free currency* usually is interpreted as meaning that the currency of a specific country is free of all restrictions and can be converted freely into any currency of the world by its owner. *Restricted currency* means that the currency of a specific country is controlled by regulations within that country and may not be converted into the currency of another country without specific approval of the fiscal authorities of the controlled-currency country. The fact that a currency is controlled may be an indication that it is overvalued, or it may reflect governmental efforts to encourage or control particular industries or segments of the economy of the country involved or its trade relationships with a particular country or with various countries.

Wherever currencies are freely convertible, or in free-money areas, it is sometimes found that exchange values of controlled currencies are lower than the controlled rates in the parent country. Anyone engaged in international trade is likely to find that illegal transactions may occur, and he must be continually alert to detect them whenever suspected in his purchase negotiations. Commercial banks with foreign connections keep posted on currency and exchange controls of various countries.

Apart from illegal transactions, there are other devices used by some countries which are perfectly legal and which, if used by the buyer, often can accomplish a more advantageous purchase. One of these is the *compensation deal,* which is a refinement of the original arrangement of simple barter. The compensation deal assumes that:

1. The country is short of foreign exchange, particularly dollars
2. It has an exportable commodity which is not moving too readily
3. It needs an imported commodity which must be purchased with a *hard* currency (dollars or a freely convertible currency)

Under such conditions the government officials controlling the issue of export and import licenses will often consider a compensation deal and authorize the export from that country of a quantity of the slow-moving commodity, the resultant dollars or hard currency being used to import a certain commodity which is needed by that country. The end result is that the imported commodity, which is needed urgently by the exporting country, must be bought at a very high price. In actual practice, one individual in the foreign country usually arranges the compensation deal, obtaining the export and import licenses and currency exchange permits simultaneously. He serves as both the exporter of the indigenous goods and the importer of the needed items, generally in close cooperation with government officials or agencies of his country.

The importer in the United States must decide whether or not he wants to conduct his business operations to make a profit in the handling of the merchandise or to speculate in the exchange markets. A combination of the two objectives is seldom compatible, and the latter is usually an unwise course except for people experienced in international monetary dealings.

Naturally, an importer in the United States is interested in securing the most favorable foreign exchange rate and in taking precautions against loss due to rate fluctuations. He should seek and follow the advice of a reputable domestic bank whose foreign department is engaged actively in exchange transactions and which can advise him on hedging and other strategies. When possible, he should make commitments in U.S. dollars; by so doing, he will be subject to neither loss nor gain by exchange fluctuations.

Methods and Terms of Payment   Methods of payment available to the international buyer are, in general order of preference: open account, consignment purchases, documentary draft collection, letters of credit, progress payments, and cash in advance. Contrary to U.S. practice, many foreign firms do not normally finance their costs incurred for a sales contract. It is common in some foreign countries for the buyer to make a down payment with his order and to make progress payments prior to shipment. This is particularly true for purchases of capital equipment. Thus, the buyer directly bears financing costs which in the U.S. market are usually included in the sales price of the goods. With appropriate leverage, the foreign supplier may be persuaded to absorb such costs, or it may be financially attractive to have the supplier include the finance cost in his price if his cost of funds is lower than that of the buyer. Alternatively, the use of a letter of credit as a preexport financing instrument is common, especially in the Far East. (See discussion later in this section under Letters of Credit.)

Terms and methods of payment are negotiable as in domestic transactions. Terms similar to those used for domestic contracts, including discounts, can be obtained. A firm with solid financial stability may demand terms which could include partial payment against shipping documents and a retention of the remainder of the payment until receipt and acceptance of the goods by the buyer. Continuous, long-term satisfactory transactions between buyer and seller may give rise to sufficient confidence so that letters of credit are not demanded by foreign suppliers except as financing instruments. The most generally used methods of payment are open account, documentary draft collection, and letters of credit.

OPEN ACCOUNT.   The *open account* arrangement is the method of payment most advantageous to the buyer. No instrument other than the purchase order is required. Payment is made after receipt and inspection of goods. In this method, the buyer bears the least risk and the seller the greatest. For that reason this arrangement is often difficult to obtain. It is normally used: when there is a long-standing and satisfactory business relationship between the two parties with a mutual high degree of confidence; when the buyer is a large, well-known firm with impeccable credentials; or when the transaction is so desirable from the seller's point of view, because of dollar value or other reasons, that payment method is of secondary importance.

DOCUMENTARY DRAFT COLLECTIONS.   The method of payment commonly used and specified in the purchase order when the seller is confident of the reliability of the buyer is *documentary draft collection*. Payment must be made by the buyer upon presentation of a draft accompanied by documents required by the purchase contract to confirm evidence of shipment and to entitle him to obtain the goods from the carrier. This method of payment is handled by the seller's bank and its U.S. branch or correspondent bank as a documentary collection. The banks will assure that drafts will be paid and the documents surrendered only in accordance with the terms and conditions of the collection instructions of the seller's bank. Drafts may be *sight drafts,* which require full payment upon receipt, or *time* or *usance drafts,* which permit the buyer to defer actual payment for a specified period, normally 30, 60, 90, or 180 days. A *time draft* is a type of financing and is a negotiable provision of the purchase contract. (Time drafts are also available under letters of credit.) A seller may wish to discount a draft or trade acceptance prior to payment. Unless the buyer and seller have extraordinary financial standings, it is more difficult to discount such drafts than a banker's acceptance created under a letter of credit.

The selection of the method of payment, currency to be used, and drafting of the appropriate contractual language should be made with the assistance of legal counsel, financial people conversant with international transactions, and international trade specialists of an international bank. The buyer should be familiar with the *Revised American Foreign Trade Definitions* (1941) and *Incoterms* (1976), as well as the *Uniform Rules for the Collection of Commercial Paper* (ICC Brochure 254) and the *Uniform Customs and Practices for Documentary Credits* (1974, ICC Publication 290). (For further detail see the Selected Bibliography at the end of this section.)

LETTERS OF CREDIT.   Because of the protection provided both buyer and seller, commercial *letters of credit* are a common method of handling payments for international transactions. In some instances, government regulation in other countries requires the use of a letter of credit before an export license will be issued. Letters of credit are issued by a bank at the request of the buyer. They state the conditions which must be met by the seller and describe the documents which the seller must provide before payment will be made. A letter of credit may be irrevocable, or, rarely, revocable. *Revocable* letters of credit may be canceled, changed, or amended by the buyer, in any way desired and at any time before negotiation has been effected. They are seldom used because they are not generally acceptable to sellers.

Irrevocable letters of credit may not be canceled, nor may their terms be amended or revised without the consent of the seller and all other parties thereto. Since they are irrevocable, the seller may be able to use a letter of credit issued in the United States to establish credit in his own country, something which he may not be able to do with a purchase order alone. Even though the relationship between the buyer and seller is such that an open account arrangement would be mutually acceptable, a letter of credit may be requested by the seller as a preexport financing instrument. It can be seen that the irrevocable commercial letter of credit would be the instrument most commonly used to substantiate the buyer's credit in international purchasing because it gives the foreign seller maximum protection in ensuring reimbursement for goods provided. The importing buyer should be thoroughly familiar with this method of payment and should use his firm's financial personnel and banks with well-established international departments for guidance and assistance.

When the seller meets the conditions of the letter of credit and presents the documents required by the letter of credit to the issuing bank, that bank must make payment irrespective of whether or not the buyer has received the goods or whether or not his need for the goods still exists. It is essential, therefore, that the buyer cover fully in his application for the letter of credit all the conditions which the seller has agreed to meet in order to qualify for payment. If a buyer deals with a small bank not known to the seller's overseas bank, it may be requested that the letter of credit be confirmed by another, larger U.S. bank. The necessity for confirmation of letters of credit issued by prime U.S. banks by an overseas bank is a rare occurrence.

The specimen application (see Fig. 22-1) for a letter of credit indicates the details which are involved and covered by these instruments.

Insurance

Ocean marine insurance includes coverage on shipments of cargo by overseas vessels and domestic shipments by coastal (U.S. Atlantic or Pacific) vessels. Ocean marine insurance, because of its historic background in London and elsewhere, utilizes terms, phraseology, and conditions which are peculiar to itself and which bear specialized meanings and interpretations. Thus, with the increasing importance of foreign trade, an understanding of marine insurance is useful, and its ramifications require early and thorough consultation with an experienced insurance agent or broker on any intended import purchases. It will be discovered also that ocean marine insurance abounds with language which may appear ancient and cumbersome. However, such language on ocean marine cargo forms has been adjudicated over the last 200 years many, many times, and therefore each major word and/or peril has a very clear history behind it in both American and English courts, e.g., "stranding, sinking, and collision."

An adequate *insured value* is of utmost importance. This value usually is computed by adding together the invoice value, freight, all charges (including the insurance premium), and a percentage markup. The markup is to allow for possible market value increase between the date of purchase of the goods and the date of unloading at destination. If the cargo is a total loss, the full insured value, including markup, is collectible. This is the value used for general average purposes, and it is important that the insured value equal or exceed the wholesale market value on the final date of discharge; otherwise, the owner of the shipment is obliged to contribute to the general average on the excess value, if any, as an

---

APPLICATION FOR COMMERCIAL LETTER OF CREDIT

BANK OF AMERICA
NATIONAL TRUST AND SAVINGS ASSOCIATION

_____ _____ , 19___
(PLACE)   (DATE)

L/C No. _____
(For Bank Use Only)

Dear Sirs:

We request you to establish an irrevocable Documentary Letter of Credit on the following terms and conditions by:

☐ Full Text Cable   ☐ Airmail   ☐ Airmail with brief preliminary cable advice

ADVISING BANK (If Blank, Correspondent Bank)	FOR ACCOUNT OF (APPLICANT)

IN FAVOR OF (BENEFICIARY)	AMOUNT
	(EXPIRATION DATE)

DRAFTS TO BE DRAWN AND PRESENTED TO THE NEGOTIATING OR PAYING BANK ON OR BEFORE _____ .

AVAILABLE BY DRAFTS AT (TENOR) _____ ON YOU, YOUR BRANCH OR YOUR CORRESPONDENT AT YOUR OPTION OR YOU MAY WAIVE DRAFT REQUIREMENT.

Documents required: (Please indicate by placing "X" in applicable box)

☐ Invoice in duplicate
☐ Special U.S. Customs Invoice
☐ Marine and War Insurance Policy or Certificate in duplicate.
  Insurance to be effected by _____
☐ Clean Air Waybill Consigned To _____
☐ SOLE ORIGINAL CLEAN   ☐ On Board Ocean   ☐ Railroad   ☐ Truck   Bills of Lading, to order of shipper, blank endorsed, marked:
  "Notify _____"
(If applicant requires more than one original, please indicate number required _____)
☐ Other Documents _____
_____
_____

Covering _____ Invoice value of merchandise to be described in invoice as:
        (FULL INVOICE VALUE UNLESS OTHERWISE SPECIFIED)

(OMIT UNNECESSARY DETAILS AND SPECIFY PRICE BASIS BELOW)
_____

Check one: ☐ C.I.F.   ☐ C & F   ☐ F.O.B.   ☐ Other _____

Shipment from _____ to _____

Shipment latest _____	Partial Shipments	☐ Permitted ☐ Not Permitted	Transhipment	☐ Permitted ☐ Not Permitted

DOCUMENTS MUST BE PRESENTED TO THE NEGOTIATING OR PAYING BANK NO LATER THAN _____ DAYS AFTER DATE OF SHIPPING DOCUMENT (ON BOARD VALIDATION APPLICABLE FOR OCEAN SHIPMENT) BUT WITHIN THE VALIDITY OF THE CREDIT.

All documents to be forwarded in one cover, by airmail, unless otherwise stated under Special Instructions.

Special Instructions: _____
_____
_____

THE OPENING OF THIS CREDIT IS SUBJECT TO THE TERMS AND CONDITIONS AS SET FORTH IN THE SECURITY AGREEMENT (COMMERCIAL LETTER OF CREDIT) APPEARING ON THE REVERSE HEREOF TO WHICH WE AGREE.

_____
(NAME OF APPLICANT)

FX-150 12-75 (REV)

_____
(SIGNATURE AND TITLE)

Fig. 22-1   Form of application for commercial letter of credit. *(Courtesy Bank of America, San Francisco, Calif.)*

uninsured interest. The buyer should be familiar with the definitions of terms including f.o.b. (free on board), c.&f. (cost and freight), c.i.f. (cost, insurance, and freight), f.a.s. (free alongside ship), and others as given in the *Revised American Foreign Trade Definitions,* adopted July 30, 1941. This way, there will be a clear understanding of this aspect of the terms of sale and of just when title to the cargo is deemed to be transferred.

Average Losses   The term *average* as used in marine insurance means "loss less than total." A *general average loss* is one that results when the master of a vessel, in time of stress, takes an action which in his judgment is for the best interest of both ship and cargo. Such action may include jettisoning cargo to lighten a stranded vessel, fighting a fire with resultant damage to articles not on fire, engaging salvage assistance, or putting into a port of refuge for repairs following a breakdown of machinery. From the earliest times, maritime laws have universally held that such loss should be borne by all parties of interest (for whose benefit the sacrifice or expenditure was made), shipowners and owners of cargo alike.

Where a general average loss occurs, the owner of the cargo must sign an *average agreement* under which he binds himself to pay all proper general average which may be assessed against his shipment. If the shipment is insured under an ocean marine policy, the insurance company will file a guaranty as additional security. If the shipment is not insured, the additional security must be provided by the cargo owner and may consist of a cash deposit, surety bond, or bank guaranty for the amount of the assessment against his shipment. As a general average can be very involved, sometimes several years elapse before final negotiations are completed. Without insurance, cash deposits can be tied up for long periods of time.

A *particular average loss* is one that affects specific interests only (those of the owner of a specific shipment which is damaged or partially lost) and is resultant on an insured peril which does not result in a general average loss. Insured perils are described as *of the sea* or *on the sea*. Hazards from natural forces, such as unusually heavy weather, stranding, collision, and sinking are of the sea, whereas fire, assailing thieves, smoke, lightning, steam, water damage from efforts to extinguish fires, and jettison are on the sea. The extent of insurance coverage of a particular average loss is specified in the ocean marine policy in clauses defined as follows.

1. FPAAC—Free of particular average—American conditions. This is the most limited of the average clauses, covering losses resulting from sea perils. Under this clause no loss is paid unless caused by fire, stranding, sinking, or collision.

2. FPAEC—Free of particular average—English conditions. Under this clause losses are paid not only when they are caused by stranding, sinking, burning, or collision, but also when caused by sea perils, irrespective of percentage, if the vessel at any time during the voyage is involved in a stranding, sinking, burning, or collision, even if the loss has no connection with the accident to the vessel.

3. WA or WPA—With average or with particular average. This clause gives protection for partial losses by insured sea perils if the damage amounts to a cer-

tain percentage of the whole shipment of a shipping package. A 3 percent particular average is usual. This clause applies if there is a loss from insured sea perils and the loss amounts to more than 3 percent. In this case the loss is paid in full, as the 3 percent is not a deductible amount but is set as a minimum figure or franchise to eliminate small claims. The minimum is waived if the vessel is involved in a fire, stranding, sinking, or collision. Theft, pilferage, nondelivery, freshwater damage, breakage, leakage, and contamination from other cargo may be added specifically to the WA clause as needed for particular shipments.

4. Average irrespective of percentage. This is the broadest average clause. Under it, losses by insured perils are paid regardless of the loss.

A policy will normally state the percentage (sometimes known as a *franchise*) which must be reached in order for there to be a claim under the policy wording. Marine cargo insurance states certain percentages for specific commodities and in the absence of more specific wording, these percentages would prevail on a policy insured by Lloyds.

Extent of Protection   Protection under ocean marine insurance now generally covers *warehouse to warehouse,* the policy stating when the coverage attaches and terminates. Under the warehouse-to-warehouse clause, the insurance coverage is in effect from the time the goods leave the premises of the shipper, during ordinary transit, until arrival at the premises of the consignee at final destination, or until the expiration of 15 days (30 days if an inland destination), after the completion of discharge overside of the goods insured from the oversea vessel at the final port of discharge, whichever shall occur first. Should cargo be delayed at some point through no fault of the insured, the shipment will remain covered for an additional 30 days for an agreed-upon premium. The insured must advise the underwriter the moment he becomes aware of any deviation or delay.

Marine extension clauses, developed during World War II, continue the coverage during deviation of voyage, delays, reshipment, transshipment, or other variations beyond the control of the insured, and eliminate the 15- or 30-day time limit at destination. While coverage under marine extension clauses is only for interruption and suspension of transit beyond the control of the insured, the insured can secure additional protection upon payment of extra rates to cover interruption in transit within his control and extension beyond the ordinary time limit.

Terms of the purchase contract should be explicit as to the method whereby cargo insurance is affected and by whom. The seller normally assures that insurance coverage protects the cargo while ownership is vested in him, and the consignee often instructs the seller to arrange insurance on his (the consignee's) behalf. Generally, interest in the insurance on the cargo moves with transference of title to the cargo, for the cargo may be owned by a number of different persons during the course of transit. The consignee, who frequently bears the cost of insurance coverage, may arrange for the desired protection. When letters of credit are used as a method of payment, the insurance usually is in the same currency as that in which the letter of credit is issued. A definite understanding should be incorporated in the purchase contract, making clear which party will arrange for insurance and how the costs shall be borne.

The starting point for the setting of insurance rates is known as *base rate.* Unlike most other insurance rates, those for marine insurance are not standardized and may vary among several insurance companies. It will depend upon the relationship between the importer and the insurance company, the amount and type of cargo involved, and the claim experience, if any, which the underwriter may have with the importer or with the type of movement under consideration. Each transaction is an individual matter between the importer and the underwriter. Extras will often be added to the initial base rate depending upon various considerations, such as the flag under which the carrying vessel will sail, age of the vessel, and other conditions of the voyage.

Open Policy   The individual character of marine insurance permits the use of open policies known as *blanket, open-cargo,* or *reporting contracts.* These policies are used extensively and simplify the coverage of repetitive risks. Under an *open policy* an insured may obtain continuous coverage for all shipments for an extended period of time or until the policy is canceled by either party. He has automatic protection, subject to limits and to various conditions stated in the policy, from the time the goods leave the original warehouse until delivered into the consignee's warehouse. It is not necessary that the insurance agent or broker be notified prior to the sailing of each shipment, but the declarations of shipments insured under an open policy should be made monthly, or as soon as practicable after commencement of the transit of the goods. Such a policy, however, normally contains a warranty stating that the insured will declare all shipments coming within the scope of that policy and that failure to do so may give the underwriter the opportunity to serve notice of cancellation.

The open-cargo policy usually carries a limit of liability by any one conveyance or in any one place at any one time. It is most important for all open-policy holders to make sure that their limit of liability is sufficient to cover all the shipments that they may make (or have made for their account and risk). It is quite possible to have an accumulation of goods made up of several separate shipments go forward on the same vessel or conveyance, or arrive at the same pier or customs warehouse, at the same time. An open-cargo policy covering general merchandise is usually written on an *all-risks* basis. The all-risks clause, which is widely used and which is the most complete of the coverages available, reads as follows:

> To cover against all risks of physical loss or damage from any external cause, irrespective of percentage (excepting risks excluded by the F.C.& S. and Strikes, Riots and Civil Commotions warranties, unless covered elsewhere herein).

Under a blanket or open policy, when the amount and the character of each individual coverage have been determined, the details of shipment are reported to the insurance agent or broker by the insured, and (in the case where a negotiable document is required under letter of credit terms) a policy, or a certificate in lieu of policy, is issued. If full information is not known at the time a certificate or policy is required, the insured can bind a specific shipment by submitting to the underwriter a provisional declaration, which is finalized when full particulars are available. The declarations of the insured are the basis for issuance by the underwriter of invoices covering the requisite premiums, either for individual shipments or on a monthly basis, as may have been arranged in the open policy.

When someone who is insured suffers a loss to merchandise insured under a special marine or open policy, it is up to him to notify the nearest agent of the insurance company of the loss and to make a written notice of claim upon the carrier of goods. Policies or certificates of insurance list the names and addresses of representatives of the insurance companies issuing them. If the insurance has been arranged by the importer, he should notify his underwriter through the agent or broker. The insurance company will arrange for a survey and report to permit discussion of all details surrounding the loss and to make the appropriate settlement. The importer may be allowed as part of his claim any charges incurred, such as survey fees, repacking, and reconditioning expenses, subject to the terms and conditions of the policy.

Procedure

The buyer of imported materials may avail himself of many channels of importation, the choice of which, depending upon the size and capability of his organization, the nature of his business, its financial structure and policies, and the practices of the trade, is of vital concern. Thus, a buyer may deal directly with a foreign manufacturer or producer, or he may deal through a foreign export merchant or foreign broker, or through a manufacturer's agent, import commission house, trading company, import merchant, broker, or wholesaler. In considering the problems involved, it is in order to examine the nature of various intermediate channels through which import materials may be purchased.

Import Merchant   The import merchant contracts (in his own name) directly with the domestic buyer, and thereafter buys (in his own name) from the country of exportation, delivers to the U.S. port of entry, and bills the buyer according to the contract. In the same manner, he may buy before he has a contract with the import buyer, on the strength of his knowledge of the market and anticipated requirements. In dealing with an import merchant, the buyer has the advantage— which may not be present in dealing directly with a foreign exporter or agent— of recourse to the U.S. courts in the event of any claim or controversy arising under the contract. He is not concerned with fluctuations in foreign exchange, booking shipping space, or arranging for insurance; and he has the advantage of inspection of the goods in the United States. In addition, he has contact with the other party to the contract, usually an experienced domestic organization which often has warehouse stocks available on short notice in the United States.

Import Broker   The import broker acts as an intermediary between buyer and seller and receives for his knowledge and services a stipulated fee. Insofar as protection to the buyer is concerned, the broker in the United States must, of course, maintain his reputation if he expects to continue doing business. Thus, he is inclined to make certain that the merchandise involved is as good as represented, and he may, in some instances, be in a position to supply technical knowledge acquired in the course of doing business. All this is of value and assistance to an import buyer.

If an intermediary is employed, it is advisable that he understand that you expect disclosure of the manufacturer or principal and that normal correspondence and visitations may be required from time to time with his full knowledge. The understanding is normally requested when establishing a long-term relationship or for items requiring constant and timely replenishment. Such an understanding may not be required for opportunity purchases.

Even though the agent is responsible for quality, delivery, etc., this does not alter the fact that his supplier affects your supply, and therefore his supplier must be evaluated against many of the criteria used for domestic suppliers. The inclusion of progress reports and a clause which describes the intermediary's obligations under unusual conditions such as dock strikes and transportation delays will aid in guaranteeing supply.

If visits are made, one should remember that the purpose is to evaluate the intermediary's judgment in selection of a supplier and not, normally, to negotiate. This is important, since your contract is with the intermediary and may differ from his contract with the supplier.

There are disadvantages in dealing with import agents, of whatever type. They are in business for a profit, and the buyer is one step removed from direct and primary sources of foreign market information. The buyer, in dealing with any import agent, generally must expect to pay a little more for the goods than if he were importing directly. He must be very much aware of the reputation of the intermediary in the foreign country, because by the mere fact of his association, the buyer might at some future time be either helped or harmed in his direct contacts with foreign exporters. The buyer of imported commodities recognizes this and bargains for the insulation from hazards of import purchasing when he deals through an intermediary.

Foreign Agent   In dealing with a foreign agent, a foreign export merchant, or a foreign broker, the buyer has, generally speaking, some advantages similar to those he obtains from dealing with an import house in the United States, namely, grading and sorting of goods, technical knowledge, warehousing and/or stockpiling, booking of steamer space, and arranging for insurance coverage. Just as in the selection of an import merchant, broker, or wholesaler, the choice of such an intermediary in the foreign country depends on the policy of the trade, the commodity involved and its characteristics, and the insulation to be furnished and required against possible loss. There is, however, the ever-present problem of timely communications and a greater potential for misunderstandings in dealing with a foreign agent.

Charter Brokers   Freight charters generally are arranged through ship or charter brokers. This is in part because ocean freight rates customarily are keyed to an agreed time or rate of loading and unloading. It is also because liability for demurrage charges or dispatch premiums is incurred when there is faulty synchronization of the scheduling of arrival of cargo for loading and the handling of the cargo and documentation by the forwarding agent. The demurrage rate normally is twice or three times the rate of dispatch. The charter broker earns for his services (usually paid by ship's owners unless otherwise specified) a commission, which customarily is 1¼ percent of the gross freight revenue and any demurrage. When more than one broker is involved, duplicate brokerage normally is paid, and so most of the current coal, grain, and oil full-cargo charters carry brokerage commissions totaling 2½ percent of the charges paid by the charterer.

For companies having well-staffed traffic departments, it is frequently desirable to make foreign purchases either f.o.b. or f.a.s. the foreign port, so that the buyer can control both the means and the cost of transportation. It is not uncommon for "deals" to be available on transportation, just as on foreign exchange, and on some other portions of importing costs. In cases where the buyer finds it more convenient or customary to buy c.&f. or c.i.f. a U.S. port, he should make sure that he obtains the benefit of any decreases in transportation charges which the seller might obtain, because he certainly will be liable for increases. As an alternate, it is possible to purchase with firm (no escalation) c.&f. or c.i.f. shipping terms.

Air Freight   In the past decade, there has been a significant increase in the use of air freight to move cargo in international trade. The advent of the large jet transports, coupled with reduced air freight rates, has made this method of transportation very attractive for the purchasing manager. Various forms of precontainerization and prepalletizing are used. Roll-on–roll-off features are common. Some carriers will not accept loose-stow shipments on all-cargo aircraft.

For this type of transportation, careful consideration should be given to the employment of a knowledgeable freight forwarder. Because air shipments are completed so rapidly compared with surface shipments, all documentation must be handled efficiently and rapidly. It is preferable that all required documents be attached to the air waybill and thus included with the shipment. If documents are sent separately, or even if those sent with the air waybill or the shipment become detached from it, the shipment will be delayed or set aside until such documents are physically with the shipment. It is also advantageous to airmail a complete set of the documents direct to the consignee at the time of shipment. An experienced freight forwarder may be expected to recognize and cope with this special document problem, which is so critical with regard to air freight.

The importance of proper document handling is also recognized by the International Air Transport Association (IATA), as it has set agency fees. Carrier members of IATA pay an agency fee (*broker's fee*) of 5 percent of the air freight costs to their appointed and authorized agents, such as qualified freight forwarders. In part, this fee is paid by the carrier for proper preparation and handling of all documentation.

Contrary to the practice with surface transportation, the original international air waybill is not negotiable. A statement to this effect is usually printed on the international air waybill form. This fact must be recognized when letters of credit are used to facilitate payment for the goods shipped and freight charges are for the buyer's account.

EXPORT PURCHASING

The foreign policy of the United States involves interest in the economic development and well-being of underdeveloped and developing countries. There has been steady movement of capital abroad, both for the manufacture of products in branch plants and for promoting the sale of American-made goods in overseas markets. The opening of overseas branches has created problems of maintaining quality standards for trademarked items and also of holding down costs, since the economies of mass production and procurement are denied, initially at least, by the smaller demand of the foreign markets. These issues provide added incentives for buying for export.

Financing of exports in an effort to meet foreign policy objectives and improve the U.S. balance of payments is a function of the Export-Import Bank of the United States (EXIMBANK). Financing of exports is also available through the U.S. Agency for International Development (AID) and the International Bank for Reconstruction and Development (IBRD), an agency of the United Nations, also referred to as the *World Bank*. Each of these agencies has programs of various types of foreign development for which financing could be of interest to the export purchasing manager. Information on these agencies is included in the Selected Bibliography at the end of this section.

Purchasing for export involves peculiar problems which require (as for importing) specialized knowledge and handling not common with domestic industrial procurement. An understanding of the distinguishing characteristics, hazards, and sources of information is essential, therefore, to the undertaking of export purchasing. As discussed herein, export purchasing is considered to mean the purchasing of materials in the United States, by an American buyer, for the purpose of exporting such materials from the United States to a foreign country or countries.

Unusual Aspects

Purchasing for export involves considerations for the buyer which in domestic transactions usually are the responsibility of the seller. Such responsibilities include specification of unit of packing, weight and dimensional limitations, and type and adequacy of packing; scheduling and control of inland transportation; booking of ocean shipping; documentation and banking; insurance; and forwarding through port of exportation. Whether such factors will be handled by the buyer, elsewhere in his own organization or through outside agencies, is a question which can only be decided on an individual basis. This decision is dependent upon the circumstances involved, knowledge and experience in export procedure, and the nature, volume, and continuity of the purchasing for export.

Valuable information and assistance are available to the buyer from manufacturers or sellers familiar with or engaged regularly in exporting, and this factor should become an additional consideration in the selection of sources of supply of items being purchased for export. To the extent purchases are made from sellers experienced in export procedure, the complexities of handling can revert to the seller, as is common in domestic trade. It is necessary in every case, however, to reach a clear understanding as to the respective responsibilities of buyer and seller—to a much greater extent than in domestic transactions—because there is no such universally understood and accepted body of practice and law applicable to foreign trade.[1]

For loading and stowage aboard ship, the size and nature of packing of small articles, as well as of bulk commodities, must be given special consideration. The packing must be such as to withstand dock and shipside handling at both ends of the overseas voyage, discourage pilferage, and at the same time be of minimum bulk, since ocean freight rates are influenced by cubic measurement (space occupied in stowage) as well as weight. Differing trade customs and the nature of handling and inland transportation upon discharge at overseas ports also influence the determination of the packing.

The increased use of containerized shipments on a worldwide scale has done much to eliminate some of the packing problems, as well as to reduce pilferage and damage in transit. Special ocean freighters are available to economically handle loading and off-loading gear, thus overcoming some previous problems of limited capabilities of foreign ports. Containers can also be obtained for filling at inland manufacturing plants, with subsequent rapid rail or truck shipment at the port of exit.

Helpful suggestions covering packing for export shipment can be obtained from marine insurance agents or brokers, from various foreign trade associations, and from U.S. government specifications.[2]

For those preferring not to handle the details of packing, there are experienced commercial packing and crating services, listed extensively in the classified telephone directories of major port cities. Freight forwarders and ocean shipping agencies are also readily available and can be found in large numbers in the same telephone directories. It is essential that their services be utilized in this highly specialized field, and much time and expense can be saved if they are consulted at an early stage of export purchasing.

Other sources of information to buyers for export are banks with foreign

---

[1]Codes of practice, however, adopted by various foreign trade groups are available and can be incorporated in contracts by agreement. Examples, cited in the Selected Bibliography later in this section, are *Revised American Foreign Trade Definitions, 1941* and *Uniform Customs and Practice for Documentary Credit.* See also *Arbitration* under Government Regulations in the Selected Bibliography.

[2]Typical pertinent titles include: *PPP-B-621A-Boxes; Wood Nailed and Lockcornered; MIL-P-116-Packaging and Packing for Overseas Shipment, Preservation, Methods of;* and *MIL-B-104-Crates, Wood, Lumber and Plywood Sheathed Nailed and Bolted.* See also listings under Government Regulations in the Selected Bibliography section.

branches or correspondents. The international departments of many commercial banks are experienced in handling details of documentation, shipping, financing, collection, and exchange service. They also can provide valuable information on exchange and import restrictions of various foreign countries, as well as the export regulations of the U.S. government, all of which must be carefully followed in handling export shipments.

U.S. Export Regulations

All exports from the United States, its territories, and its possessions are subject to export controls by the government. In practice, however, the great bulk of exports take place under general licensing. Such exports are made without application to, or specific authority from, the government. The basic document covering export regulations is *Schedule B—Statistical Classification of Foreign and Domestic Commodities Exported from the United States.* It contains classification code numbers used in export documentation for all types of commodities. Specific export controls are covered in the *Export Control Regulations* and supplementary *Export Control Bulletins.* Since all references in the *Export Control Regulations* are in terms of Schedule B, it is desirable to have the latter available when referring to the former.

The Bureau of International Commerce of the U.S. Department of Commerce is the primary export control agency. Complete information and help with export problems relating to controls as well as procedure are available from foreign trade specialists in any of the Department of Commerce field offices (located in major cities throughout the country) or from the Exporters' Counseling Service of the Bureau of International Commerce in Washington. Economists, statisticians, and marketing and other specialists on various areas of the world are located in the Bureau of International Commerce, because one of the responsibilities of the Department of Commerce is to serve business directly in increasing international sales of U.S. goods. The export of munitions, arms, and airplanes is controlled by the Department of State, and current information and regulations governing such exports require direct contact with U.S. Department of State, Office of Ammunitions, Washington, D.C. 20230. The Nuclear Regulatory Commission exercises control of materials under its supervision. Inquiries covering such items as Geiger counters, complete reactors, and various radioactive materials should be addressed to the Director, Division of State and Licensee Regulations, Nuclear Regulatory Commission, Washington, D.C. 20545. The export or reexport of narcotic drugs requires special licenses, issued by the U.S. Bureau of Narcotics, Washington, D.C. 20226.

Special export purchasing opportunities and advantages exist from time to time because of legislation designed to assist certain domestic industries and agricultural groups. There may be available direct government subsidies on the export of certain commodities, usually agricultural products in surplus supply. Restrictions and special taxes on imports of various commodities frequently result in the maintenance of domestic prices for such commodities at levels higher than those prevailing in other countries. In such instances, it is possible either to purchase the commodity in question in the foreign country of origin for shipment to a third foreign country or to purchase from the country of origin (or an American importer) *ex-quota* at "world" prices for reexport from the United States.

By execution of a *surety bond* to the government, involving heavy penalties for default and guaranteeing the reexportation of such imported ex quota items, the items may be permitted entry free of restriction, which usually acts to limit the supply, resulting in the higher prices prevailing in the domestic market. Such bonds cover, generally, commodities which are further processed or entered into the manufacture of other commodities in the United States; therefore, the reexportation may not be of the same identity or form, but may involve only products or commodities containing the equivalent amounts of the materials imported. It is necessary to have paid the scheduled import duties levied on such imports and any special processing or manufacturing taxes, but both these import levies are refunded upon application when the commodities are reexported and the surety bonds are canceled.

The above procedure is not to be confused with transshipment through U.S. ports or retention of imported materials at port of entry *in bond*. In this instance, no import duty has been paid, the materials have never been cleared through U.S. Customs, and, consequently, they have not entered the country officially—merely having been impounded in *bonded storage,* supervised to ensure against release into the country without compliance with governmental regulations and payment of import duties. As the practice of holding imported commodities at U.S. ports in bond is quite common, it often is possible to purchase such materials for export at prices which are below the domestic market by the equivalent of the import duty.

Under certain conditions, imported items upon which the duty has been paid are subject to refund or *drawback* of the duty upon reexportation. Usually, such imports will have been refined, further processed, or incorporated into other products by manufacture. The duty drawback allowed upon reexportation is based upon the item or component of the exported material which had been imported, less any refining or manufacturing loss—not on the entire quantity or amount of duty which had been paid. Prescribed certification is required with application for duty drawback, and purchase agreements covering such materials should specifically include this requirement.

The complexities and the frequency of changes in applicable regulations, only suggested herein, make it almost mandatory for the average exporter, and even many maintaining extensive export departments, to utilize the services of foreign freight forwarders or commercial exporters. In addition to the classified telephone directories previously mentioned, the names of competent freight forwarders operating in most major ports in the United States can be obtained from the New York Foreign World Trade Center Freight Forwarders and Brokers Association, Inc., One World Trade Center, New York, N.Y. 10048. Good freight forwarders are staffed and equipped to comply with all applicable export regulations and to take advantage of any subsidies or refunds available. They also should be able to furnish information in advance as to in bond or ex-quota opportunities and to handle the requisite details covering such purchases.

Foreign Legal Requirements

Many nations have imposed restrictions on the foreign trade of their nationals. In countries other than the United States, regulations are generally more restrictive and more complicated than enumerated herein for the United States. Most foreign countries have specifically limited the importation of merchandise from other countries. These limitations have appeared in the following forms:

1. *Foreign exchange restrictions,* usually requiring licenses for the purchase of exact amounts of foreign currencies for specified purposes

2. *Import regulations,* requiring prior permission for the importation of foreign merchandise, often by exact kind and quantity

3. *Tariffs,* restricting imports of foreign merchandise through high import duties, sometimes selectively by country of origin

These forms, either separately or in combination, for the most part have been the rule rather than the exception.

It is to be presumed that any purchase for export is the reflection of a need originating in a foreign country, and the foreign agent, principal, or ultimate buyer or consignee in the foreign country should be able to furnish detailed information and instructions relating to the governmental controls and documentations required for the particular transaction contemplated. Import permits usually are required, and while obtained by and in the name of the foreign agent or consignee, the U.S. buyer for export should request a copy in order to be fully informed of its terms. Import permits may be expected to include statement of the exchange conversion authorized, commodity, amount, specifications, documentation, payment, and the time limit within which either shipment or arrival is valid.

Careful attention must be paid to the terms of the import permit, because strict compliance is required to avoid penalties, delays, and even revocation of the permit. One of the most frequent difficulties encountered is the exact limitation on both quantity of the goods and the amount of currency available for payment, restricting in advance both price and quantity of the purchase by the exporter in the United States. The time limitation usually included in import permits often presents a problem, particularly if it is based upon arrival date at destination port and shipment is delayed afloat or in leaving the port of exportation in the United States. The multitude of foreign exchange and import regulations prevailing, which differ widely from country to country and are subject to frequent modifications, make it almost impossible for any one person to maintain complete knowledge of the legal requirements existing at any certain time or applying to various commodities being considered for export from the United States. In addition to (or instead of) the foreign agent or consignee of the goods and the suggestions previously included herein, there are several sources of information and simple rules available to assist the purchaser who is faced with these problems. For example, specification of payment in terms of U.S. currency will avoid any risk of exchange fluctuations, and conducting all negotiations and writing the contract in the English language can prevent misunderstandings from errors in translation. Incorporating recognized codes of definitions and practice should make for complete and enforceable agreements.

The major U.S. banks make it their business to keep customers informed of the most important regulations involving trade with foreign countries. They publish informative pamphlets and books on both importing and exporting procedures.

The majority of leading trading nations also maintain consulates in many American cities. Information services, governmental buying agencies, and other offices are maintained in most port cities in the United States and in some inland manufacturing and trading centers. It is the function of such foreign governmental agencies to foster American trade with their respective countries. They can be located readily in telephone directories or through inquiry of the U.S. Department of State in Washington or of any of the field offices of the U.S. Department of Commerce (or directly of the Bureau of International Commerce of the Department in Washington).

SELECTED BIBLIOGRAPHY

The following partial list of references includes descriptions of the contents of representative publications dealing with both importing and exporting. The value of familiarity with the nature and sources of such information cannot be overemphasized, regardless of whether the buyer intends to handle import and export transactions in their entirety or through commercial agents, freight forwarders, or brokers. The best-known current and up-to-date information on U.S. and foreign controls and exchange rates in usable form (other than the daily general and business newspapers) is found in the periodicals listed. Information found in any of these references provides good general guidance but should be checked in every vital particular with authoritative sources because important changes are apt to occur at any time without notice.

It must be emphasized that the exact meaning of the words in general usage in one area of the world may vary considerably from the meaning of the same words in a different area. These differences are further complicated by translation from one language to another. To minimize difficulties and to eliminate, as much as possible, confusion that may arise between the parties to a commercial transaction, several national and international organizations have developed and established multilingual standardized interpretations for most of the terms and references that are essential to a contract.

Reference to these standardized meanings by the purchasing manager as a basis for transacting business is strongly recommended, not only at the time of requesting quotations but especially in composing the text of all instruments of procurement, whether contract, order, or intent to order.

For emphasis, these sources are listed below without regard to stature or acceptance. More detailed information on these publications is also given in the Selected Bibliography which follows:

1. *Incoterms* (1976)
2. *Revised American Foreign Trade Definitions* (1941)

3. *Trade Terms* (1955)
4. *Uniform Customs and Practice for Documentary Credits* (1975)
5. *Glossary of Purchasing and Supply Terms* (1972)

Publications have been grouped according to subject for easy reference. They may be obtained by contacting the publisher of the reference. All U.S. government documents may be obtained from the issuing agency or from the Superintendent of Documents, U.S. Government Printing Office, Washington, D.C. 20402. Many of these publications can be found in public libraries.

A. Export Purchasing

Agency for International Development Procurement Regulations. U.S. Agency for International Development. Basic manual of procurement regulations, with supplements to update it.

Export Control Regulations and *Export Control Bulletins.* U.S. Government Printing Office. Annual. Compilation of official U.S. regulations and policies governing the export licensing of commodities and technical data. Issue is supplemented with *Export Control Bulletins.*

Green, Peter F.: *Exporters' Encyclopedia,* Dun and Bradstreet, New York. Annual. A handbook of information on shipments to all foreign countries and U.S. possessions, including: index of ports and trade centers; index by countries of consular regulations, shipping routes, mail, radio, cable, telephone, exchange restrictions, money, weights, and holidays; radio and cable rates; parcel post, regular and air mail, and air cargo regulations, carriers, and rates to various parts of the world; reference tables of weights, measures, time charts, political and geographical groups; foreign trade organizations in the United States; government agencies, consulates abroad, chambers of commerce, clubs, associations, and organizations; general information covering laws and regulations affecting export trade, insurance, export terms and practice, financing foreign trade, trademarks, and other items; description of export and shipping practices in principal foreign countries, including customs treatment of weights, packing hints, and shippers' export declarations; U.S. licensing system and the Webb Law; steamship companies, ports of the United States, and freight forwarders in principal cities of the United States.

Guidelines for Procurement under World Bank and IDA Credits. International Bank for Reconstruction and Development (The World Bank), Washington, 1977.

B. Government Regulations

Department of Defense Index of Specifications and Standards. Department of Defense. Annual (with periodic supplements). Alphabetical and numerical indexes of Air Force, Navy, and Army specifications. Several (MIL) specifications describing packing materials and methods which affect large-scale international operations are included.

Guide to I.C.C. Arbitration. International Chamber of Commerce, U.S. Council of the I.C.C., 1212 Avenue of the Americas, New York, N.Y. 10036, 1977. Describes characteristics of and information on the ICC's system of international commercial arbitration and its rules of conciliation and arbitration. Contains a list of the members of the court, together with the names of its best-known arbitrators.

Index of Federal Specifications and Standards. Department of Defense. Annual (with periodic supplements). Index provides symbols, code numbers, and brief description of specifications. Federal specifications include information on various shipping containers.

International Commercial Arbitration and the Convention of New York. International Chamber of Commerce, U.S. Council of the I.C.C., 1212 Avenue of the Americas, New York, N.Y., 1960. Describes international commercial arbitration, legal recognition, and enforcement of foreign arbitral awards.

Schedule A, Statistical Classification of Commodities Imported into United States with Rates and Tariff Paragraphs and Code Classifications for Countries. U.S. Bureau of Census. Monthly.

Schedule B, Statistical Classification of Domestic and Foreign Commodities Exported from the United States. U.S. Bureau of Census, 1978. The official schedule of commodity classifications, based on the Standard International Trade Classification revised for international use. Indexed alphabetically by commodity to be used by shippers to fill out the Shipper's Export Declarations.

C. Import Purchasing

Exporting to the United States, Bureau of Customs, 1977. Outlines procedures, documents, restrictions, quotes, and other information necessary to the foreign exporter or U.S. importer to promote a wider understanding of U.S. Customs requirements. Included are lists of collection districts and ports of entry, and a list of senior Customs representatives in foreign countries. Instructions and samples of required forms are also included.

U.S. Imports for Consumption and General Imports: SIC-Based Production Code by Area. U.S. Bureau of Census. Annual. Summaries of U.S. import data for major trading areas. The import data, originally compiled under approximately 10,000 classifications of the Tariff Schedules of the United States Annotated (TSUSA), are consolidated, summarized, and presented in about 2000 commodity classifications based on the Standard Industrial Code (SIC). Includes conversion list of SIC to TSUSA.

D. Insurance, Procedure, and Documentation

Budd, Wm. E.: *American Import and Export Bulletin.* Supplement to the *Customs House Guide.* Monthly. Reports on the latest changes in customs tariffs; newest regulations of various governmental departments and bureaus; post information; import and export opportunities; world trade personalities; and industry news. Port activities, air transportation news, railroads in foreign trade, and steamship notes are included.

Budd, Wm. E., ed: *Customs House Guide,* Customs House Guide, 107 South Tyson Avenue, Floral Park, N.Y. 11001. Annual. Directory containing, for each U.S. port of entry: customhouse brokers, freight forwarders, steamship lines and agents, stevedores, U.S. Customs–bonded truckmen, U.S. Customs–bonded warehouses, general warehouses, foreign consuls, chambers of commerce, port authorities; Canadian customs brokers, freight forwarders, and customs-bonded warehouses; foreign forwarding agents; and customs headquarters of foreign countries. Includes alphabetical index of commodities, showing rate of duty in accordance with the Tariff Schedules of the United States, all revised by GATT, and special and administrative provisions of the U.S. Customs Tariff Act, the U.S. Customs Regulations, and the Internal Revenue Code affecting imports.

Export and Import Procedures. Morgan Guaranty Trust Company, 23 Wall Street, New York, N. Y. 10015, 1977. An informational pamphlet covering background, governmental and intergovernmental agencies, and procedures for both importing and exporting.

Free Trade Zones and Related Facilities Abroad. U.S. Department of Commerce. A listing of more than 100 customs-free ports in 49 countries, including their origins and current trends; discusses advantage of free port usage, transit zones, free perimeters and special customs-privileged facilities.

Winter, William D.: *Marine Insurance: Its Principles and Practice,* McGraw-Hill Book Company, New York, 1952. Discusses the factors which affect marine insurance. The natures, types, provisions, and procedures of marine insurance are described.

Marine Insurance Notes and Comments on Ocean Cargo Insurance. Insurance Company of North America, 1600 Arch Street, Philadelphia, Pa., 1971. A pamphlet describing the natures, types, provisions, and handling of marine cargo insurance. Included is a reprint of the *1941 Revised American Trade Definitions.*

E. International Business Conditions

Commerce America incorporating *International Commerce.* Government Printing Office. Biweekly. Includes summaries of current international business developments and calendar of international business events. Short feature articles are of general interest in any aspect of international trade. Data presented on specific countries.

Factors Influencing U.S. Investment Abroad. U.S. Office of International Trade, 1953. Discusses economic and social factors influencing foreign investment by individual country. Analyzes positions of U.S. companies pertaining to the U.S. government's role in foreign investment.

The Journal of Commerce. Twin Coast Newspapers, Inc. (Eric Ridder, publisher), 445 Marshall Street, Phillipsburg, N.J. 08865. Daily. Latest international transportation developments are addressed, as well as complete international sailing schedule, monetary exchange rates, and world trade updates.

Overseas Business Reports. U.S. Department of Commerce, 1963—Reports provide background data for basic review of international trade position in current markets or entrance into new markets. Single topics on one country are covered in approximately 100 reports per year. Statistical reports on U.S. trade with major world areas are included, along with authoritative information on both developing and industrialized countries. The reports are revised frequently and many of them contain useful bibliographies.

Trade Lists. U.S. Department of Commerce. The lists include names and addresses of firms handling a specific commodity in one country. Lists are issued for importers, exporters, distributors, manufacturers, agents, producers, and refiners. Entries include name, mailing address, chief executive, type of organization, date of establishment, size, and language. Lists are based on *World Trade Directory Reports.*

World Trade Directory Reports. U.S. Bureau of International Commerce. These reports are prepared by the U.S. Foreign Service and can be obtained from the Department of Commerce. Each report describes a foreign firm. A typical report includes information on the firm's method of operation, sales territory, capital, sales volume, general reputation, names of trading connections (including U.S. firms), types of organization, lines handled, and names of owners and officers.

F. Payments

Annual Report on Exchange Restrictions. International Monetary Fund, Washington, Annual. Review preceding year's world payment situation, fiscal and monetary measures, and simplification of exchange controls. A series on country members of the IMF describes their exchange systems, basic exchange rates, authorities administering controls, arrangements applying to settlements with other countries, operation of accounts of nonresidents, and requirements affecting payments of import, export, invisible, and capital transactions. A list of the more significant changes in exchange practices is also included.

International Financial Survey. International Monetary Fund, 19th and H Streets, N.W., Washington, D.C. 20431. Weekly. Items are drawn from published sources, private and official. Explanatory material is sometimes added, but no editorial comment is made by the Fund. Any opinions expressed are taken from the sources quoted and do not necessarily reflect the views of the Fund.

Monthly Foreign Exchange Rates. Board of Governors of the Federal Reserve System, Publication Services, Division of Administrative Services, Washington, Monthly. Rates are issued the first of each month for the previous month. Lists average rates of exchange for various countries, with comparable figures for the preceding 2 months and the corresponding month of the previous year. Based on daily noon buying rates in New York City for cable transfers as certified for customs purposes by the Federal Reserve Bank of New York.

O'Halloran, John L.: *The ABC of Commercial Letters of Credit,* Manufacturers Hanover Trust Company, 350 Park Avenue, New York, N.Y., 10022, 1970. An outline of the fundamental aspects of credit financing includes prodecures for filing of application, handling credit from inception to liquidation, examination in detail of documents, and exhibits of forms.

Uniform Customs and Practice for Documentary Credits. International Chamber of Commerce, U.S. Council of the I.C.C., 1212 Avenue of the Americas, New York, N.Y., 10036, 1975. A compilation of provisions, definitions, interpretations, instructions, and documents designed to simplify and facilitate commercial documentary credit operations, which are now universally adopted by banks and professional associations.

Uniform Rules for the Collection of Commercial Paper. International Chamber of Commerce, U.S. Council of the I.C.C., 1212 Avenue of the Americas, New York, N.Y. 10036, 1975. The main rules applied by banks regarding presentation, payment, protest, liabilities, responsibilities, etc.

Weekly Foreign Exchange Rates. Board of Governors of the Federal Reserve System, Publication Services, Division of Administrative Services, Washington, Weekly. Lists daily noon buying rates in New York City for cable transfers payable in foreign currencies, as certified for customs purposes by the Federal Reserve Bank of New York.

G. Reference Books and Trade Terms

Bureau of Census Catalogue. U.S. Bureau of Census. Quarterly. Complete listing of publications of the Bureau of Census for that quarter. Publications listed are in the areas of agriculture, business, governments, manufacturers, population, housing, and U.S. foreign trade. Subscription includes 12 issues of *Monthly Supplement.*

Foreign Commerce Handbook. U.S. Chamber of Commerce, Washington, 1978. A comprehensive reference to organization services and current published information on all important phases of international trade and investment, procedures, practices, techniques, and policy.

Glossary of Purchasing and Supply Terms. International Federation of Purchasing Management. May be obtained from the National Association of Purchasing Management, Inc., 11 Park Place, New York, N.Y., 10007, 1972. Over 400 purchasing and supply terms have been translated into the various languages of the associations which make up the IFP. A system of numerical coding is used to cross-reference words from one language to another.

How Commerce Field Offices Help Business. U.S. Department of Commerce. A description of Department of Commerce field offices and the services they offer to business firms.

Incoterms. International Chamber of Commerce, U.S. Council of the I.C.C., 1212 Avenue of the Americas, New York, N.Y., 10036, 1976. Twelve standardized trade terms and their international interpretations, listed in both English and French.

Revised American Foreign Trade Definitions. National Foreign Trade Council, Inc., 10 Rockefeller Plaza, New York, N.Y., 10020, 1941. Detailed definitions of trade terms, with general comments and cautions covering their use and outlining the responsibilities of buyer and seller implied in each phrase. The terms were adopted July 30, 1941 by a joint committee representing the Chamber of Commerce of the United States, the National Council of American Importers, Inc., and the National Foreign Trade Council, Inc.

Scott, C. L.: "An Operational Approach to International Purchasing," in *Guide to Purchasing,* sec. 1.11, (Copyright 1975 by TRW, Inc.) National Association of Purchasing Management, Inc., 11 Park Place, New York, N.Y., 10007. This section is a relatively concise and operational guide to international purchasing, outlining the particular problems involved and referencing specialized sources of information for both exporting and importing.

Sources of Information on American Firms for International Buyers. U.S. International Commerce Bureau, 1974. A guide to principal directories, trade and professional associations, trade journals, and local sources of commercial information within the United States.

Trade Terms. International Chamber of Commerce: U.S. Council of the I.C.C., New York, 1955. Comprehensive review of common interpretations of contractual terms used to describe 10 terms and their connotations in 18 trading countries.

World Calendar of Holidays. Morgan Guaranty Trust Company of New York, 23 Wall Street, New York, N.Y. 10015. Annual. A book listing information on bank and public holidays observed in various parts of the world. Includes a schedule of daylight savings time.

NOTE: For further information on subjects covered in this section see the list of references in Section 30.

Section **23**

Traffic and Transportation

EDITOR

Thomas F. X. Dillon, C.P.M. *Senior Editor,* Purchasing, *Boston, Massachusetts*

The responsibility for procurement of materials, supplies, and services by purchasing personnel may include the choice and cost of transportation. It depends largely on the size and type of company. In an N.A.P.M. survey, 35 percent of 5539 responding members reported that the purchasing department was accountable. This percentage is larger for the smaller companies.

The functions of receiving, paying freight charges, and filing claims are important but can be resolved by application of suitable clerical routines. The control of expenditures for *transportation services* lies in routing shipments so as to obtain the maximum efficient service at the lowest possible cost.

Many types of carriers offer a variety of services, so that the buying of transportation service is a somewhat complicated purchasing activity. Even the traffic terminology varies from that normally used in purchasing departments. Some of the common terms are defined in Section 31. For overseas marine shipments, traffic terminology is explained in Section 22.

In addition to the selection of routes and carriers, there are other technical matters in which knowledge is essential to obtain the maximum value in transportation. Some of these are: establishing the proper rate and classification, design of the shipping container, use of proper material-handling methods, and warehousing efficiently. These considerations require the application of specialized training, experience, and judgment.

Proper performance of the traffic function is an important factor in reducing operating costs and increasing profits. It can help to widen company markets and reduce inventory. Careful analysis may also open up new sources of raw materials.

In the purchase of raw materials, supplies, and equipment, freight costs should be known and considered to determine the total delivered costs. Carriers can assist in properly describing the product to obtain lowest rates. An improper description on the bill of lading can result in a 30 to 50 percent increase in transportation costs.

Freight rates and transportation charges usually vary in inverse proportion to the quantities shipped. Purchases should be in quantities that will provide the lowest delivered cost but not produce excessive inventory. The cost of carrying extra inventory should never exceed the transportation dollars saved.

Often the use of tank cars, bulk hopper cars, open-top trucks, or other special equipment will reduce loading or unloading costs.

In spite of the best efforts of both shippers and carriers, loss or damage sometimes occurs to goods in transit. Loss or damage claims must be filed and collected to avoid undue costs of repair or replacement by the buyer.

Many companies do not have a sufficient volume of transportation to warrant the employment of technically trained traffic personnel. However, no company that buys or sells goods is free from the costs of transportation, and most companies can achieve lower operating costs by giving careful attention to transportation.

As the costs of transportation are closely related to the cost of goods purchased, it seems logical that the purchasing manager should concern himself with transportation. In the absence of a traffic department, he should assume the responsibility for establishing the desired degree of control.

This section is in no way intended to serve as a substitute for the knowledge, counsel, and service that should be available to purchasing from its traffic department, if one exists.

TERMS OF PURCHASE

The f.o.b. terms of purchase are an important and integral part of the purchase contract and have a direct relationship to who can and/or should exercise control over inbound transportation costs and services. While there are many variations, the two most frequently used f.o.b. terms are f.o.b. shipping point and f.o.b. destination.

The following summary of definitions and legal responsibilities of both buyer and seller should prove helpful in avoiding the controversies and uncertainties that occasionally result from the use of these terms.

F.o.b. Shipping Point

When f.o.b. shipping point is used, the title or ownership of the goods passes from the seller to the buyer at the moment of delivery to the carrier. Goods are put into the hands of the carrier or loaded in the carrier's vehicle free of expense to the buyer, with delivery to the carrier constituting delivery to the consignee. Thus, the buyer must pay all freight and incidental charges required to effect delivery and bears the burden of recovering the value for loss or damage incurred after delivery to the carrier.

F.o.b. Destination

When f.o.b. destination, consignee, or receiver's dock is specified, title or ownership of the goods passes to the buyer upon delivery to the consignee's dock, factory, plant, or other designated point. The seller must pay all freight and incidental charges required to effect delivery and is responsible for any loss or damage up to time of delivery.

There are many variations of the above terms, based on mutual agreement or negotiation between the buyer and seller. Some common modifications are *freight collect and allowed* (customer pays the freight charges and they are then deducted from the shipper's invoice), *freight prepaid and charged* (added to customer's invoice), and *freight equalized* (with a named competitive shipping point). Any such special agreement does not change the rule that title passes wherever and whenever designated in connection with the f.o.b. terms.

For this reason some contend it is advisable to negotiate *f.o.b. destination* terms. Others contend it is better to negotiate *f.o.b. origin*. They believe that the shipper is not as interested as they are in his outbound shipping charges since they, not the shipper, will wind up paying them. These companies insist that they have full control over how the goods they buy are shipped, and therefore insist on routing f.o.b. origin. One such company is Western Electric Company.

TRANSPORTATION REGULATION

In 1887 Congress, because of complaints about railroad abuses such as lower rates and better service for favored shippers, enacted the Interstate Commerce Act, which established the Interstate Commerce Commission (ICC). This act has been expanded through the years to include pipeline transportation, except water and gas pipeline transportation (1906), truck transportation (1935), domestic water transportation (1940), and surface freight forwarder transportation (1942). The act also regulates transportation brokers and express agencies engaged in interstate commerce or in foreign commerce to the extent that such transportation takes place within the United States.

The Federal Maritime Commission, established in 1961, regulates domestic offshore carriers and common carriers engaged in the foreign commerce of the United States.

Transportation regulators are required to regulate in such a manner that, as stated in the Interstate Commerce Act, the inherent advantages of each mode of transportation will be preserved; that safe, adequate, economical, and efficient transportation service will be promoted; and that sound economic conditions in transportation and among the several carriers will be fostered.

The Interstate Commerce Act directs the commission to encourage the establishment and maintenance of reasonable charges for transportation services "without unjust discrimination, undue preferences or advantages, or unfair or destructive conpetitive practices." The goal of the act is to develop, coordinate, and preserve a national transportation system by water, highway, and rail, as well as by other means, adequate to meet the needs of the nation's commerce.

The problem is that some of these goals conflict. Should a railroad be allowed to lower a rate if the lower rate may take business away from a barge line? Here is a conflict between the "more economical transportation" mandate and the "preserving the inherent advantages of each mode" mandate. A further problem in administering the act is that all provisions are subject to interpretation. Depending on the philosophies of the individual commissioners, some goals are pushed while others are ignored. Critics of the regulatory commissions contend that overall policy has been to preserve the status quo and is more industry-oriented than shipper-oriented. Recent legislation has encouraged carrier competition.

Another government agency influential in transportation is the Department of Transportation (DOT), established in 1966 at the Cabinet level. It was created to develop national transportation policies and programs and has responsibilities in urban transportation, environment, safety, and security.

Many agencies were moved into the DOT. The U.S. Coast Guard, Federal Aviation Administration, Federal Highway Administration, Federal Railroad Administration, Urban Mass Transportation Administration, St. Lawrence Seaway Development Corporation, National Highway Traffic Safety Administration, and National Transportation Safety Board are now all part of the DOT.

Most states regulate intrastate transportation. Usually this is a function of the state public utility commission.

SELECTION OF CARRIER AND ESTABLISHING ROUTING

When the buyer has the right to specify the routing, he should exercise that important authority in all instances. It is preferable to show the desired routing in a space provided for that purpose on the purchase order. If the purchase order covers a number of shipments or is a blanket purchase order, against which subsequent releases will be made, it should be understood by the supplier that all shipments should be routed in accordance with the routing shown on the master or blanket purchase order.

In choosing the various routes over which freight may be forwarded, the person charged with the responsibility of routing is buying transportation service at specified prices, namely, the freight rates as published in the tariff or price lists of the carriers.

In determining a routing to be used, the first step is to choose the type of service which will best meet the delivery requirements. This might be air, truck, rail, water, pipeline, etc. The second step is to select the specific carrier or carriers via which the shipment is to be routed within the mode of transportation chosen.

Finally, after the routing decisions have been made and shipments are moving, a periodic check of the service should be made. If there is deterioration in a given carrier's service, or if changes in freight rates or other factors make alternate routings more economical, changes in the route should be initiated.

A conscientious buyer is constantly thinking of what can be done to ship materials in a more economical manner. Carriers' representatives, although always alert to selling their own company's services, are valuable sources of information and help.

Traffic Publications and Services

A good starting point in the development of proper carrier selection is a working knowledge of the printed information and general services available in this area. Although subsequent attention will be focused on many other factors, one of the most important is the data available from commercial sources. Purchasing personnel can obtain useful information from traffic publications, carriers, traffic bureaus and consultants, professional societies, and civic organizations. Traffic publications are listed in Section 30.

Each type of carrier will provide point lists and memorandum rate charts which are helpful in routing. Carrier freight sales representatives welcome the opportunity to assist, and through carrier cooperation the buyer has at his disposal an established traffic department composed of skilled traffic personnel.

The transportation department of the local chamber of commerce or the manufacturer's trade association may be another source for routing assistance. This type of organization will often assist the smaller company with routing problems and the development of a routing system.

Routing Record System

An important phase of routing is the establishment of a routing record system. A list should be compiled of the regular sources of supply and their shipping points. From this list an individual routing card can be completed with information pertinent to the commodity trade name, freight classification, rates, tariff authority, terms of sale, and the various weight breakdowns. Figure 23-1 shows a typical example of the kind of information required for a routing card file. The routing cards should be indexed alphabetically by supplier or commodity. Some commercial traffic bureaus will furnish routing cards.

On inbound routings, it is the policy of many companies to apply the routing instructions shown in these records to the applicable purchase order. In addition, standard routing instructions can be sent to each supplier's traffic department. The supplier should be requested to acknowledge these instructions. By following this procedure, the chance of misrouting by the vendor is kept to a minimum. If the vendor should disregard the furnished routing instructions, the buyer has a basis for debiting the vendor for any excess transportation costs incurred as a result of misrouting. Since the carrier's rates and services are constantly changing, the importance of keeping the routing cards current cannot be overstressed.

Services Available

In routing freight, it is necessary to be acquainted with the various services offered by the different forms of transportation, the cost, the tariff provisions governing the freight rate utilized, and the delivery requirements. This knowledge can best be obtained through actual routing experience, reading of traffic publications, and contact with carrier representatives.

INBOUND ROUTING

SHIPPER: Fabric Company   **ORIGIN:** Thomaston, Georgia 30286

MATERIAL

Fabric, Tire

Class	Rate	Minimum Weight	ROUTE
LTL-CR-70	8.90 total	1–100 lb	To 50 lb—United Parcel Service Over 50 lb—Roadway Express, Inc.
	9.95 "	101–125	(*) Roadway, Others T. T. Brooks
	10.95 "	126–150	(**) Volume Shipments
	11.95 "	151–175	
	12.95 "	176–200	Only When Authorized
	12.95 "	201 and over	
	5.25 cwt	201 to 500 lb	0 to 50 lb—Air Express
	3.71 cwt	500 to 1,000 lb	Over 50 lb—Delta Air Lines
	3.25 cwt	1,000 to 2,000 lb	
	3.19 cwt	2,000 to 5,000 lb	(**) Determination of Routing,
	2.85 cwt	Over 5,000 lbs.	Rail vs Truck, on volume shipments should include the cost
TL-CR	1.29 cwt	20,000 lb	of loading and unloading to arrive
	.96 cwt	34,000 lb	at the most economical route.
	(*).96 cwt	40,000 lb	
CL-CR	1.16 cwt	1st 24,000 lb	
	.99 cwt	Excess	
	.90 cwt	40,000 lb	
	.74 cwt	60,000 lb	

TERMS: F.O.B. Our Plant

Tariff Authority: United Parcel Service Zone 4
Item 49355—C & S 125-R MF-I.C.C. 410
Item 1460—T. T. Brooks Tariff MF-I.C.C. 11
Rate Basis 702, Item 886 & 6965 C & S 26-G MF-I.C.C. 421
Rate Basis 702, Item 83004 TL-CTR E/S 2008-J MF-I.C.C. C-728

Fig. 23-1   Example of routing data inbound card.

Also, it is necessary to know many special factors that can influence the routing decision. As an example, in the case of railroads, some points of origin or destination may be serviced by a single carrier. If the consignee has several delivering carriers available, it is necessary to specify the delivery desired, thus eliminating possible extra expense of trucking or switching to consignee's plant.

Congestion and lack of space in the shipping and receiving areas are conditions prevalent with many companies today. Consequently, routings are often limited to one or two carriers in an effort to alleviate a crowded situation. Not only will the limited number of carriers mean more to each carrier who serves the customer, but the customer will be in a better bargaining position for rate adjustments and service improvements. Another advantage: fewer representatives of the carriers will call, saving valuable time previously spent interviewing carrier salespeople. Finally, shipment tracing will be simplified: the customer will be on closer terms with carrier personnel and carriers will be more willing to provide rate information and special services when necessary.

Many types of special equipment are available and might meet a special requirement or reduce shipping costs. Such things as piggyback, bulk handling, containerization, palletization, or other special equipment should be investigated and considered. Other services which can be checked and compared might be contract carriage, private carriage, freight forwarders, and shippers' associations, particularly for smaller shipments.

Transit-Time Requirements

An elementary step in the intelligent selection of the type of service to be used for each shipment is to determine the period of time available for transportation between the expected shipping date and the promised or required delivery date. When this fact is known, the most economical method of transportation, consistent with the predetermined service needs, may be selected. Most carriers have routing guides specifying routes to various points and the service that may normally be expected. By constantly checking the service received, it is possible to eliminate the inefficient and lax carriers.

Nature of Shipment

Bulk liquids should be routed via tank car, tank truck, or pipeline. Volume coal shipments are limited to truck, barge, or rail movement. Perishable products should be routed only over those lines which provide heater or refrigerator services. Often, the choice of routes is restricted because of the inability of many carriers to transport specific items, such as inflammable liquids, dangerous articles, or explosives.

Size of Shipment

There are many ways to move small shipments. These include United Parcel Service, United States Postal Service, bus package express, airline small parcel service, and air and surface freight forwarders. Shipments of heavy machinery with extreme height, width, or length measurements will generally be limited to rail movement, but, at times, special permits can be obtained to permit movement by truck if it is advantageous to the consignee.

Susceptibility of the Commodity to Damage

Many items, such as glassware and precision machinery, have inherent characteristics making them susceptible to damage. Such articles should be shipped via routes requiring the fewest number of carriers to avoid additional handling. A single carrier from origin to destination is always to be preferred. On the other hand, much damage can occur as the result of inadequate or improper packaging. If consistent damage occurs in connection with shipments from certain suppliers, regardless of the routing used, the cartons and inner packaging should be carefully inspected to determine whether or not the supplier is complying with the product packaging provisions as defined in detail in the motor carrier and railroad classification rules tariffs. In the case of certain electronic equipment and computers, special vans are available for transport.

Cost of the Service

This is an extremely important phase of narrowing the choice of carriers. Rates and routes are inseparable. It is most important that the route selected be one over which the rate used for cost purposes is applicable. The factor of cost must be weighed by the buyer and a compromise made as to whether faster service at a higher cost is to take precedence over slower service at a lower cost. Many different types of rates are published by the transportation companies. A working knowledge of the rate structure is essential if one is to be assured of any degree of success in obtaining economical transportation.

Demurrage is the charge for detention of carrier's equipment, railroad cars, trucks, etc., beyond a specified free time allowed for unloading. This can be an important factor in cost if desired receiving schedules are not met for any reason. The use of several routes may assist in staggering the receipt of large shipments consisting of several carloads.

On smaller shipments, consideration should be given to the use of freight forwarders and shippers' associations, who can consolidate for shipment by either rail, truck, or air. A shippers' association is usually a branch or a division of an industry association which functions as a freight forwarder. If such a service is available, its use could result in reduced costs.

Carrier Accessorial Services

Many motor carriers and railroads provide special or accessorial services such as stop-offs to partially unload or complete the loading of shipments en route. Many railroads permit milling, fabricating, and storing in transit. These privileges, however, are not universally granted by all carriers, nor are they permitted at all locations. Sometimes there are charges for these services that wipe out the advantage of their use. If a buyer feels that his company might be able to utilize some of these services in connection with inbound shipments, it is suggested that he contact carrier representatives, preferably the freight traffic manager.

Selection of Adequate and Safe Equipment

The problem of acquiring sufficient equipment and equipment of the correct type is one that confronts every shipper. Special equipment is often needed for shipments of excessive height, width, length, or weight measurements. Certain motor carriers specialize in steel hauling and, consequently, have a large fleet of flatbed trailers. Others are general commodity haulers, with their entire fleet consisting of trailers suited for dry freight. Heated and refrigerated equipment is common. Rigging service for the handling of heavy equipment is available. Power tailgates can be used where loading or unloading docks are not available. A working knowledge of the different types of equipment and the carriers possessing this equipment will simplify the routing problem.

Financial Condition of the Carrier

In routing, the company's interest must be protected at all times. For this reason it is wise to use only sound, responsible, and well-financed carriers. If the carrier were to become insolvent, considerable difficulty would be experienced in collecting any outstanding loss or damage claims.

Quality of Carrier Services

Just as the quality of a product purchased at a competitive price is a yardstick for measuring the efficiency of procurement, so too is the quality of carrier services, at competititve prices, an important yardstick for measuring the efficiency with which one buys transportation and selects one carrier in lieu of another.

Purchasing managers and buyers sometimes forget one transportation fundamental: Carriers are suppliers. They provide a service for a price. The same principles and programs that apply to suppliers of materials apply to carriers. As with other suppliers, carriers can be rated on service, reliability, and price.

Carriers can be rated on their willingness to help solve transportation problems, on their interest in customers' needs, on the frequency with which they come up with innovations to solve those problems, on willingness to negotiate rates, on facilities, on financial stability, and on the quality of personnel. Often freight rates via the same mode of transportation between the same two points are identical—but few other transportation elements are identical.

Many buyers assume all carriers are identical, all rates are the same, and all service is the same. These buyers would not make that assumption about all casting suppliers or all machinery suppliers or all electric motor suppliers, and they should not make that assumption about transportation suppliers.

Of all the elements that influence the choice of a particular carrier, probably the *quality of carrier services* is the most important. Note that the reference is to *services* and not *service*. Often, persons routing freight think only in terms of time in transit and overlook the other important considerations. It is the combination of these other services, consistently rendered, that makes for quality transportation and distinguishes the quality carrier.

The next 10 subheadings summarize some of the important service factors that should be considered. They are not necessarily listed in the order of their importance.

Service at Supplier's Point of Shipment   The buyer should determine whether the carrier makes pickups on the day promised, consistently, and on time. In the case of truckload or carload shipments, the carrier should furnish safe, adequate, and, if necessary, specialized equipment.

Dependability of Information   It is important that information from the carrier be accurate, complete, and reported within a reasonable period of time. This information will cover reports from the carrier's rate, claim, sales, traffic, and operating departments as required by the buyer.

Over-the-Road Service   Time in transit is a very important consideration. Some carriers consistently provide a better over-the-road service than their competitors, even between the same points of origin and destination. Reference is not being made to service via motor carriers versus railroads versus airlines, but to the service of carriers within each mode competing with each other. What is wanted and needed is dependable service with day-in-and-day-out on-time delivery to destination. Consistency of service is needed because, like uniformity in quality of product, it permits more orderly planning and scheduling.

Tracing and Expediting Shipments   Even in those companies which have a competent traffic department, the tracing and expediting of incoming shipments from suppliers are frequently considered a responsibility of the purchasing department. It is advisable to learn the terminology and identification that are considered important by the carriers when tracing a shipment. With the proper shipment identification available, the carrier should be expected to do whatever is necessary to return accurate and prompt tracing information. Some carriers use computers to store tracing information and can give almost instant service.

Loss and Damage Claims   Prevention of loss and damage claims should be one of the goals of the buyer, the shipper, and the carrier. The buyer should be careful to select practical routes, the shipper should be certain that the packaging, packing, and loading are adequate, and the carrier should be responsible for careful handling and protection while the shipment is in transit.

It is inevitable that some loss and damage claims will have to be filed with the carriers. The prompt and efficient handling and payment of just claims are other important carrier services. At best, the settlement of a claim can take from 3 to 6 months. Quality carriers have an excellent reputation for paying claims within a reasonable length of time, depending upon the circumstances and conditions surrounding the shipment and the number of carriers involved.

Overcharge Claims   These are claims for the recovery of excess freight charges collected by the carrier at origin or at destination. They may occur by application of the incorrect rate, by the misinterpretation of a pertinent rule, or because of a mathematical error, incorrect weights, or duplicate collections. Assuming that the claim is in order, the service-oriented carrier will pay such claims promptly, usually within a few weeks.

Insurance   Unlike rail and motor freight carriers, domestic air carriers and air freight forwarders have a limited loss and damage liability. This limit may be inadequate to fully protect a shipment. The buyer should check and, if necessary, give consideration to purchasing additional insurance. International carriers provide greater protection, but the coverage might still be inadequate. It should be noted that this protection is from airport to airport, not from door to door.

Electronic and computer equipment shipped in padded vans is protected to a degree, but here again full-evaluation insurance may be desired.

Household goods moved by furniture vans carry less coverage for intrastate than for interstate movements. Full coverage can be purchased, the rate varying according to the carrier's damage-claim history with its insurance company. If antiques or unusually valuable pieces are included, special packing and full-coverage insurance should be considered, with the specific pieces being described.

Notification   If anything is happening or is likely to happen that might affect the buyer's normal flow of inbound materials, a good carrier will call this to the buyer's attention. Examples are embargoes, strikes, threatened strikes, severe weather conditions in an area, a serious delay to a specific shipment, equipment breakdown, and loss of a shipment because of an accident or a fire.

Handling of Complaints   Even quality carriers, furnishing quality transportation services, will occasionally give a buyer cause for complaint. The carrier that investigates complaints promptly and thoroughly and reports the facts to the buyer and advises what steps are being taken to improve or correct the situation for the future has given that buyer another reason to use his services.

Miscellaneous Services   There are many other services by which carriers are judged, such as fulfillment of promises, the prompt remittance of c.o.d.'s, the docketing and support of rate proposals, and, of course, opposition to proposals that adversely affect the shipper or receiver of freight.

Traffic Consultants

There are companies organized to handle the traffic management activities of smaller businesses. They are known as *traffic consultants* or *commercial traffic bureaus.* In the absence of trained and qualified technicians in the purchasing organization, it is sometimes feasible to have a traffic consultant or bureau establish standard routes on consistent inbound and outbound shipments. Usually these service companies charge a flat fee for each routing and assess a retaining fee for keeping the established routing records up to date.

Help Available from Carriers and ICC

The most important source of transportation information available to the purchasing manager or buyer, other than his own traffic department, is the carrier salesperson. The salesperson is exposed to other shippers' problems, knows how they are solving them, and can pass on tips to reduce transportation costs. The salesperson knows that the more help he can provide his customers, the more likelihood of retaining the business and seeing his share increase at the expense of his competitors.

Carrier salespersons have easy access to others in their company, including the general traffic manager (the key person as far as negotiating lower rates is concerned), the dispatcher, the rate clerk, and the freight claims department. The salesperson can assist the customer in dealing with them. In the salesperson's mind, they are the enemy, the customer is the friend.

In today's transportation industry, salespersons have clout. Because of this clout, they can be strong advocates. A letter or telephone call from the customer may not in many cases carry as much weight as a salesperson's complaint that begins "My account says . . ."

Some examples: Many companies do not bother with the expense of maintaining freight tariffs. Periodically they call carriers and have them draw up rate charts covering their major movements, both inbound and outbound. There is nothing in the Interstate Commerce Act that requires carriers to furnish freight rates. All that carriers are required to do is to maintain a set of freight tariffs covering the shipments they handle from and to the specific area involved, so shippers in the area can check out their own rates.

Some companies, usually large shippers, always have a supply of empty carrier trailers in their parking lots. Technically, if this is done for the convenience of the shipper, a demurrage charge should be assessed by the carrier. If it is done for the convenience of the carrier, no charge should be assessed. Who knows? Actually, it is probably done for the convenience of the shipper, but it also helps the carrier and no charge is assessed. A smaller shipper who wanted a trailer to be immediately available when he was ready to load it would have to make prior arrangements with the trucking company and might be subject to an extra charge.

Some help is available from the ICC, which has its central office in Washington, D.C., and regional and district offices throughout the country. The ICC publishes information concerning shippers' rights and responsibilities, carriers' responsibilities, claims processing, etc.

Help is also available from the DOT, particularly in matters of cargo security and hazardous shipments. Information, including counseling on DOT-area problems and brochures, is available from regional DOT offices throughout the country.

The freight tariff/publishing agencies, which are sponsored by carriers, publish information on rate proposals and action taken by carriers on rate proposals. Freight rate dockets giving this information are available to the public for a nominal annual subscription charge.

There are excellent textbooks on freight transportation and traffic and transportation magazines that can help the shipper obtain information and keep current on freight transportation developments.

There are several shipper groups, all of which publish newsletters to keep members informed of freight transportation developments. Among them are the National Industrial Traffic League, the Eastern Industrial Traffic League, the National Small Shipments Traffic Conference, the Drug and Toilet Preparations Conference, and the Transportation Association of America, a shipper-carrier group. The list indicates that some are more specialized than others. Each maintains a legal counsel whose responsibility it is to see that interests of members are represented before government agencies and carrier groups. It is on such associations that the individual shipper must depend for an effective voice in influencing national freight transportation policy, rates, and service.

For more specific help, shippers can turn to industry associations such as the Chain Store Traffic League, National Retail Merchants Association, Manufacturing Confectioners' Traffic Conference, and National Furniture Traffic Conference. These specialized groups often provide effective leadership in solving industry transportation problems. Traffic consultants can also be hired to assist in solving transportation problems of individual companies, whether they be continuing problems, such as filing freight claims or auditing freight bills, or setting up distribution or freight consolidation programs designed to obtain maximum service consistent with the transportation dollars spent.

Shipper Responsibilities

To the extent that shippers fulfill their obligations to the carrier, they are more apt to obtain satisfactory, claim-free, prompt service.

Shipper responsibilities include the correct description of the shipment. Improperly describing a shipment to obtain a lower freight rate, a not uncommon practice, is a violation of the Interstate Commerce Act as well as a fraud. The more accurately the shipper describes the shipment—preferably in the exact wording covering the item in the freight classification—the less trouble the carrier's rate clerk will have in determining the proper freight rate. A standard rule among carrier rate clerks is: When in doubt, charge the higher rate.

The shipper is responsible for packaging the shipment properly as specified by the freight classification. He must make sure the shipment is packaged and described in accordance with any applicable hazardous-material regulations set forth by the DOT. An estimated 10,000 commodities are governed by these regulations, and failure to package or describe hazardous shipments properly subjects the shipper to criminal as well as civil suits.

The shipper must also provide adequate loading and unloading facilities so that the carrier can pick up and deliver the shipments. Carriers are not required to make unreasonable efforts to fulfill their common-carrier responsibilities.

Finally, all carriers must comply with regulations that limit their ability to extend credit to shippers. This means that when credit is extended by the carrier, payment must be made within the specified number of days, or the carrier is in violation of the law.

Hazardous Shipments

In 1974 Congress passed the Hazardous Materials Transportation Act, which centered the regulation of the transportation of hazardous materials in the Materials Transportation Bureau of the DOT. The act gave the Secretary of Transportation broad authority over carriers, shippers, and the manufacturers of vehicles, containers, and packages used to transport hazardous materials. The act also gave the Secretary the power to regulate any material whose transport poses an unreasonable risk to health and safety or property.

In January 1977, the DOT put teeth into its regulations by providing for civil penalties as high as $10,000 for each violation and criminal penalties up to $5000 and 5 years in prison. The regulations, available from the DOT, cover such items as the proper description of each hazardous material, its hazard class, labels required, how the shipment must be packaged, the maximum quantity that can be placed in one package, paperwork required, and special, more restrictive regulations for transport modes where the danger is greater.

FREIGHT-BILL AUDIT

Freight bills are carrier invoices for transportation services rendered, i.e., the cost of having goods transported from one place to another. Freight bills may be said to have three principal functions, namely, (1) a receipt to the consignor or consignee and as prima facie evidence of payment of freight charges, (2) a receipt to the carrier and as prima facie evidence of the delivery of the goods, and (3) a notice to the consignee of the arrival of the shipment.

In an opinion expressed by the ICC, it was stated that it is a carrier's duty, in rendering freight bills, to state thereon such information as will permit the consignor or consignee with the aid of published price lists to verify the correctness of the charges which he is expected to pay. As a result of this commission report, a uniform freight-bill form generally exists throughout the transportation industry. This form lists the point of origin, date of shipment, weight, route of movement, initials and number of any railroad cars, adequate description of property transported, rate applicable to the service rendered, a separate listing of each accessorial charge (such as stoppage in transit, reconsignment, switching, drayage, car service, or storage), and a total charge for the services provided.

The verification of a carrier's freight bill, or invoice, is extremely important. The correct audit of freight bills is as essential to the profit and loss statement as the audit of any other commercial invoice. The audit of a transportation company's invoice necessitates detailed knowledge and experience in the application of carriers' classifications and freight rate tariffs.

The complexity of the various carriers' tariffs makes it desirable to have freight bills authenticated by people who are trained and experienced in conducting intelligent freight-bill audits. Any company making substantial freight-bill payments should give careful consideration to this operation. Smaller companies can arrange with commercial traffic service bureaus to have the freight bills audited. This service may be obtained on a flat-fee-per-bill basis or on a percentage of the overcharge claims filed and recovered.

The individual performing the exacting task of freight-bill auditing must search for the errors that may occur in the issuance of a carrier's freight bill. One must be alert to discover undercharges or overcharges resulting from mathematical errors in extension; transposition of freight charges in improper charge columns; incorrect shipping points, when different rates apply from the different points; incorrect shipping dates, when rates change upon dates just prior to shipment; variance between shipping and billing dates, when rate changes have occurred between these dates; incorrect car numbers, which may alter freight charges because of higher carload minimum weights applying to larger cars on certain commodities as stipulated in rule 34 of the Uniform Freight Classification; incorrect weights; application of incorrect tariffs; misdescription of commodities; transposition of figures in the weight or rate column; improper description of containers, which in turn alters the applicable freight rating; failure of carrier to protect the lowest-rated route; failure of carrier to protect reciprocal switching agreements; improper addition of connecting carrier charges; application of higher combination of rail rates instead of a lower through rate; charges based on through rail rates which are higher than the lawful aggregate of intermediate rates; failure to allow for dunnage or bracing when permissible; and incorrect delivery arrangements which result in extra cartage expenses.

The freight-bill audit may be accomplished before payment or after payment of the freight charges. Many companies that are staffed with competent traffic personnel may find it advantageous to audit the freight bills prior to payment. If the freight bill is increased or decreased prior to payment, it is imperative that the new charges be placed on the bill and complete tariff authority substantiating the correct charge be furnished the carrier. It is good practice to attach a freight-bill correction form to the purchaser's check when the audit discloses any error. This form lists the name and address of the company filing the correction; the date of the correction; the freight-bill number; the description of the commodity as shown on the incorrect bill; the weight of the shipment as originally billed; the total charges as originally billed; the correct commodity description; the correct weight; the correct rate; the correct charges; tariff authority; the nature of the error; additional remarks; and the signature of the individual issuing the correction. Through the use of such a form, the carrier is able to reconcile instantly any differences in charges existing between the billed and paid amount.

If a company audits the freight bills after payment of the freight charges, a different procedure is necessary in correcting the carrier's error. Any overcharge in freight charges discovered after payment to the carrier must be recovered by the filing of an overcharge claim. This is done by preparing a standard form for presentation of overcharge claims, which lists the name of the carrier to whom the claim is presented; current date; claimant's number; amount of claim; description of shipment; name and address of consignor and consignee; shipping point; destination; route; date of bill of lading; paid freight-bill number; detailed statement of charges paid; statement of charges that should have been paid; tariff authority in support of overcharge claim; and signature of person presenting the claim. This document is attached to the original paid freight bill and forwarded to the carrier for action. In the event a company may be reluctant to release the original paid freight bill, it is permissible to issue in lieu thereof a bond of indemnity agreement which guarantees the carrier full protection against any action taken by anyone who obtains possession of the original freight bill at a later date. As provided in the Interstate Commerce Act, an overcharge claim may be instituted within 3 years of delivery of the shipment.

The fundamental purpose of any freight-bill audit is to detect the legal rates that are applicable to any given shipment. This holds true in the case of undercharges as well as overcharges. It is sheer folly for a company to accept continuously and pay freight charges lower than the legal tariff rate. Over a period of time the undercharges will accumulate and develop into a sizable amount. The same statute of limitations provision in the act, guaranteeing the right of the shipper or receiver to collect overcharge claims within the 3-year period, also protects the carrier in collecting undercharges. To avoid this unpleasant occurrence and the accompanying additional paperwork, it is a wise policy to pay the correct legal charges at all times.

FREIGHT-BILL PAYMENT

The actual payment of freight bills can be accomplished through the issuance of checks by the company's accounting department or through the deposit of funds in a local bank upon which a commercial traffic service bureau is authorized to draw in the payment of a subscriber's freight bills. In either method of payment, caution must be exercised in approving for payment only those freight bills covering freight that has actually been delivered. This can be accomplished through the matching of the carrier's delivery receipt with the corresponding freight bill prior to payment.

One method of payment of freight bills is the *bank freight-payment plan*. This freight-payment plan is originated by and operated through a local bank, and eligibility for membership in the plan is extended to all freight-paying concerns and carriers. Each member company deposits with the bank money which is designated as a freight-payment account. Briefly, the carrier renders to the bank all freight bills outstanding against member shippers or receivers. The bank credits the carrier's account and debits the member company's account in the amount of the freight bills deposited. The bank forwards all paid freight bills to the member company for validation. In the event an incorrect amount is charged or a bill is paid for which a concern is not responsible, the member company can return the paid freight bill with an explanatory correction form and receive prompt credit for the amount of the overcharge. For the member company, this plan is designed to eliminate costly check writing and signing, simplify accounting, reduce check filing and record keeping, and eliminate the need for a petty cash fund to pay small collect shipments. The carrier benefits from the elimination of numerous statements, credit risk, double handling of freight bills, and the provision of immediate cash. In most bank freight-payment plans there is no charge for this service to the member company and only a minor fee per freight bill assessed against the carrier for the convenience of immediate collection.

Some shippers have a payment voucher attached as part of the shipping documents. This voucher covers the cost of transportation and can be completed and cashed promptly upon delivery of shipment. Kaiser Aluminum and Chemical Corporation originated the procedure.

Some carriers have organized transport clearinghouses. Under a transport clearings arrangement, the carrier sends the freight bill to a clearinghouse for collection instead of sending it to the customer. The clearinghouse, initially funded by carrier members, pays the freight bill immediately and then bills the customer, sending the bill from that one carrier along with the bills it has received for that customer up to the time of billing. All the bills are included on one statement, which the customer pays to the clearinghouse.

The advantage to carriers is that they get their money right away. The advantage to customers is that they receive only one statement from the transport clearinghouse instead of statements from each carrier serving it. The customer has to issue only one check to pay all bills instead of sending a check to each carrier.

EXPEDITING AND TRACING

The term *expediting* means clearing the way and making arrangements for fast transportation service. By making contact with the carrier in advance of shipments, the way can be paved for fast, efficient handling of the shipment.

Tracing, on the other hand, is the locating of a shipment after it has entered the transportation process. Tracing is the following or pushing of a shipment, whereas expediting is the act of clearing the path for obtaining the fastest possible delivery service.

Tracing is a voluntary service provided by the carrier, and it is a wise policy not to abuse the privilege. Ordinarily, before a tracer request is instituted, an opportunity should be given the carrier to make delivery. However, if prompt delivery is imperative, it is not always possible to wait. It should be understood that tracing is nowhere near as effective a means of speeding delivery as expediting. The sole purpose of tracing is to establish a record of movement and to locate the shipment. Then the decision can be made as to whether expediting from that point on is worthwhile.

It is important for successful tracing and expediting to understand the meaning of such terms as *pro, waybill, carding point, merchandise car, division, reconsignment, classification yards, relay stations,* and *manifest.* Also, one must acquire a fundamental understanding of the various methods of handling freight used by the different types of carriers.

While tracing and expediting generally follow a similar pattern among the different kinds of carriers, there are a few differences to be explained. A brief résumé of tracing by the various carriers follows.

Rail

In carload shipment, the shipper loads a full carload of material and, when finished, applies a car seal. A bill of lading is furnished the railroad, and the loaded car is removed from the company's private siding or public team track, as the case may be. At the railroad's classification yards, the car is assigned to an outbound train and routed, either by shipper or railroad, to its destination. The selected route may be via the originating railroad exclusively, or it may require transfers to many connecting railroads en route. The efficient tracing of carload shipments requires a knowledge of the shipping date, car initial and number, consignor, consignee, origin, destination, commodity, and the route of movement. Also, it is helpful if the junction points to be used in the route are known. With this information, one may ask the originating or delivering carrier to locate the car and advise the shipper or consignee of the approximate delivery date. Routing tracing or expediting may be handled through the local tracing clerk of the carrier, who frequently will have access to a computer, where car information is readily available.

Truck

With the exception of terminology, the tracing and expediting of truckload or less-than-truckload shipments are similar to the procedure followed for rail shipments. Truckload shipments are loaded into a trailer at the origin and unloaded at the destination, and unless repairs are necessary to the trailer, the material is not transferred en route. Trailers are interchanged by the trucklines just as the railroads exchange their equipment. In tracing a truckload shipment, one must possess the usual shipping data, such as date of shipment, consignor, consignee, origin, destination, and weight. The originating truckline will know the *pro* (freight-bill number), tractor-trailer number, and destination of the trailer. Often the originating truckline's office can estimate accurately when delivery will be made. By furnishing the above acquired forwarding information to the destination terminal of the delivering truckline, the expected arrival and delivery date can be learned.

In locating less-than-truckload shipments, the tracer is faced with a different situation. Numerous transfers of freight may be involved in forwarding small shipments. Each time a new truckline transports the material, a new freight-bill number is issued, and it is imperative that the tracer know the correct freight bill to trace the shipment properly. This is especially true in the movement of goods via two or more trucklines, or in the movement via a single carrier in cities receiving less frequent service than the others.

Freight Forwarders

In tracing this type of shipment, one must remember that freight forwarders do not own any equipment which operates intercity. They may possess a fleet of trucks performing pickup and delivery service, but in the physical movement of the goods the freight forwarder utilizes the established facilities of the rail, truck, water, or air carrier. It is the practice of the freight forwarder to accumulate numerous small-lot shipments from different consignors and consolidate them into one volume shipment, which is tendered to the carrier on a truckload or carload basis. The consignor or consignee can obtain from the origin terminal of the freight forwarder the freight-bill number assigned to the shipper's portion of the volume shipment, the manifest number (a packing list showing the contents of the car or trailer), the car initial, number, and carding point when forwarded via rail carrier, and the trailer number and destination when forwarded via truck. With this information, the destination terminal of the freight forwarder will advise the tracer in regard to the expected arrival and delivery date.

Air Freight

Most airlines operate their own air cargo service. The cartage agent of the airline picks up freight at the consignor's plant and delivers it to the airline at the originating airport. The airline uses only its own flights in transporting the freight to the final destination unless, of course, it is necessary to turn it over to a second airline in order to reach the destination city. The originating airline will furnish, upon request, the airbill number and flight on which the shipment was forwarded. If the shipment requires movement via more than one airline, in order to trace it

---

In reply refer
To our Tracer No. 237

TRACER

1/14/

States Freight Forwarding
Youngstown
Ohio 44511

Shipment described below has not been received in its entirety by our customer and immediate tracer is hereby requested for proof of delivery. It is important that a COPY of the FINAL DELIVERY RECEIPT (written advice only will not suffice) be sent directly to our Tracing Division as soon as possible.

Date of shipment 12/23/   Consignee All Industries, Inc.

Your Pro/Waybill SFF - 1632   Destination Cleveland, Ohio 44101

Shipper John Doe Company, N.Y.C. 1001

Our Order No. CH-81333   District Cleveland

Note to carrier: In the event clear delivery receipt is not furnished claim is hereby filed against you for loss involved in the amount of $200.00 more or less. In order to avoid unnecessary claim filing please allow us delivery receipt at once.

☒ Customer acknowledgment. _____

☐ Field acknowledgment. (Does not apply)   1510-B No.   of

Reference is made to your inquiry of 1/11/   , Just as soon as reply is received from the carrier you will be advised the results of this tracer permitting you to close your files.

All Industries, Inc.

Tracing Division

Fig. 23-2 Tracer request form.

one must call each airline to determine the flight on which it forwarded the shipment. Shipments consigned to destinations outside the delivery limits of an airport city are flown to the nearest airport city and released to surface transportation for movement to destination.

Parcel Post

Once a parcel has been mailed, there is no way of expediting or immediately tracing it. If the addresser has insured the package and it is undelivered after a reasonable time has elapsed, it is possible to initiate a tracer by requesting the proper form from the U.S. Postal Service. Such tracers are handled by the origin and destination postmasters, and it is a relatively slow and tedious process to get a reply. If the addresser failed to insure the parcel, there is no recourse against the Postal Service for the addresser or addressee.

Most industrial traffic departments assign the tracing and expediting work to one or two key employees who are skilled in this phase of traffic management. In developing a sound and efficient tracing and expediting program, one must avoid superfluous tracing and expediting, furnish accurate and complete shipping data to the carrier, develop good public relations with the carrier's representatives, and maintain written records of all tracing and expediting requests. To assist in incorporating these points into the tracing and expediting program, many traffic and purchasing departments utilize a tracer request form similar to the one shown in Fig. 23-2. On this form is recorded all pertinent information necessary to trace the shipment. Upon delivery of the shipment, the tracer form is completed and filed for later reference.

SMALL PACKAGE SERVICE

Although the small-shipment problem has received much attention, there is no service problem and rates are not excessive if the shipment is small enough. The "small" shipment that poses a problem is the one that weighs from around 70 to a few thousand pounds. Here rates are high and service is often not as good as that available for much smaller or much larger shipments. Yet, even in this area, some shippers have found a solution through shipper associations.

Airline Parcel Service

The fastest-growing airline freight service offered is for small packages. Its growth was sparked by, and may have contributed to, the bankruptcy of REA Express and its Air Express service. The service is offered under various names to denote speed, such as *Sprint* (Eastern Air Lines), *DASH* (Delta Air Lines), *Priority Parcel Service* (American Airlines), and *EPS—Expedited Package Service* (Northwest Airlines).

Generally—there are exceptions—packages are limited to 25 pounds or less and 90 inches in length, width, and girth *combined*. Packages must be delivered to and picked up at the airport. The airlines guarantee that the shipment will be sent out on the next available flight, with all or a portion of the charges refunded if it is not. The airlines will, if requested, make arrangements (for an extra charge) to have packages picked up or delivered.

Express Mail Service

In addition to regular parcel post service, the U.S. Postal Service offers *Express Mail Service* between major metropolitan areas and some 900 communities. It is a guaranteed, expedited delivery service for items (letters, merchandise, business records, etc.) weighing up to 70 pounds. Items delivered by 5 p.m. to an express mail post office—not all post offices are in the express mail network—are available for pickup at destination post offices no later than 10 a.m. on the next day the post office is open. For an extra charge, the customer can request delivery to the addressee. Delivery will be made by 3 p.m. of the day after mailing, any day of the week.

Postage will be refunded if the delivery schedule is not met, unless the delay was caused by strike or work stoppage. During its 7-year test period, 95 percent of all express mail shipments were delivered on time, and over 99 percent were delivered within 24 hours.

Variations of express mail include a customized program for frequent shippers, a same-day airport-to-airport delivery service, and an international service available to specified countries. Express mail rates are computed on a per-pound basis and vary with the postal zone and type of service—post office-to-post office or post office-to-addressee.

United Parcel Service

United Parcel Service (UPS) is both a small package surface carrier and an air freight forwarder. It sometimes uses the long-line facilities of other carriers to provide the intercity segment of its service. In recent years, because the company has been able to expand its operating authority, its operations have changed significantly and it now provides much of its own long-line service. It provides its own pickup and delivery service. UPS gathers thousands of small shipments daily, sorts them, and combines those destined for the same direction into larger shipments. The UPS destination facility then segregates and delivers the individual shipments.

Shippers can arrange for daily pickup service. When this is done, each day a UPS driver will stop by to determine whether any shipments are ready for pickup. There is a small charge for this service.

UPS delivers packages up to 50 pounds and up to 108 inches in length and girth *combined.*

The company also offers a two-day air freight service for shipments moving 750 miles or more. Called UPS Blue Label Air, it combines the speed of air freight with the convenience of UPS pickup and delivery service. It is the lowest-cost air package service available.

Bus Package Express

One of the best transportation buys is *bus package express,* a service whose annual volume is expanding dramatically as more shippers find out about it. Rates are reasonable and service is excellent. It is often the fastest service available, and in most places is offered 7 days per week, 24 hours per day.

Here, as with airline small-package service, there are size and weight limits, and the package must be brought to and picked up from the bus terminal. Major bus lines, however, have established satellite freight stations around some cities. The packages can be picked up and delivered at these satellites, and the customer can avoid having to travel to the center city for the service. Greyhound Bus Lines sets up temporary service centers at major shopping centers during the Christmas season. Here gifts can be wrapped and packaged for shipment as well as turned over to the bus company.

Shipper Associations

The Interstate Commerce Act regulates *surface freight forwarders,* transportation companies whose function it is to group shipments from several shippers, consolidate them into larger shipments destined for the same area, and arrange for transportation to common destinations via common carrier. The advantage is obvious: the forwarder handles a few large shipments rather than many small ones. The freight forwarder earns income from the spread between the higher rates per hundredweight assessed for smaller shipments and the lower rates per hundredweight assessed for larger shipments. The individual shipper pays the freight forwarder the less-than-carload or less-than-truckload rate that is normally to be paid. The shipper benefits because of the better service afforded volume shipments—less handling en route and more expeditious service.

The Interstate Commerce Act provides that shippers can associate and form groups to accomplish the same thing—without an intermediary—as long as their activities are not designed to make a profit. The result has been the formation of nonprofit shipper associations, whose activities are not subject to ICC regulation. Major shippers as well as smaller ones join these associations and are able to chalk up sizable freight savings. They operate as regulated freight forwarders in that they hire a manager and staff to arrange for the transportation and maintain records, but they are different in one important respect: shipper associations can handle only the shipments of their members. They cannot serve the general public, as regulated freight forwarders can.

There is a gray area in this concept, and because of it, regulated carriers object to some of these associations. They question at what point the manager is an employee and at what point an entrepreneur who, in fact, is operating a business for a profit disguised as his salary. The business, say the carriers, is that of a common carrier operating without the required certificate of public convenience and necessity. Because of this, legitimate shipper associations are most careful to make sure that their operations are not subject to this type of criticism.

The money saved by combining freight and shipping it as a unit is used to pay the expenses of operating the shipper association. The remainder is distributed to members on a pro rata basis, usually in proportion to the amount of freight each member shipped via the association during the period. Freight savings can be substantial. It is not unusual for members to save 25 to 35 percent of the freight charges that would apply if shipments moved via common carrier.

These associations are among the major users of piggyback rail transportation, and one of their shortcomings is that they are generally limited to traffic moving between major metropolitan areas.

CLAIMS FOR LOSS AND DAMAGE

The loss or damage of goods in transit is a problem of major importance to any manufacturer. Because of the controversial nature of loss and damage claims, their preparation, filing, and collection can be very time-consuming and expensive. A basic step in the efficient handling of loss and damage claims is determining when to file a claim. The terms of sale applicable to each purchase order must be studied thoroughly in order to interpret the effect on transportation. Whenever material is purchased f.o.b. buyer's plant, the purchaser should take full advantage of these terms and debit the seller for invoice value of the goods damaged or lost. The buyer should forward all supporting data and documents applying to the claim (delivery receipt, original bill of lading, carrier inspection report, photographs, etc.) to the vendor for actual presentation against the carrier. On the other hand, under f.o.b. seller's plant terms, delivery to the carrier specified by the buyer is comparable to delivery to the buyer. It must be remembered that the risk in transit and the responsibility for filing a claim in the event of loss or damage accompany the passage of title.

The *bill of lading* is as fundamental to the shipper-carrier relationship as the purchase order is to the buyer-seller relation. On the face are stated the specific arrangements and complete description of the shipment, plus routing and rates that apply. On the reverse side the Contract Terms and Conditions, which apply to all shipments, are printed. The *short-form bill of lading* covers the same items on the face but does not carry the printed contract terms and conditions. It is understood, however, that these standard terms and conditions apply even though they do not appear on the document.

Companies making many shipments will have their own printed bills of lading carrying the company name. For those companies making only a few shipments, the carrier will supply blank bills of lading.

The bill of lading is a legal contract between the shipper and carrier, a receipt to the shipper for the goods, documentary evidence of title to the goods, and, in the case of the order bill of lading, a negotiable instrument. Since this document defines the duties, rights, and responsibilities of the shipper and carrier, it is of special import in the just settlement of loss and damage claims. In receipting the bill of lading, the carrier becomes responsible for the goods and is entrusted with their safe and reasonable dispatch. Exceptions to this responsibility are covered next.

Conditions beyond Carrier's Control

The exceptions for which a carrier may be relieved of responsibility in the event of loss or damage to the goods while in transit are as follows: an act of God, act of public enemy, authority of law, act or default of shipper, and nature of the commodity. If such an event should occur, it would be advisable for the purchasing manager to have legal assistance in determining carrier liability.

Types of Claims

Claims may be divided into known loss, concealed loss, known damage, concealed damage, and loss or damage by reason of delay.

A *known loss* refers to any freight which the carrier fails to deliver to the consignee. Such failure to deliver may be attributed to the destruction, disappearance, or conversion of the goods, or to its being so damaged by the carrier as to render it worthless to the consignee. This is the simplest of claims. The carrier has contracted to provide carriage for a definite quantity of freight and at time of delivery there exists an apparent shortage of material. At the time of delivery, the consignee should request the carrier's agent to acknowledge the shortage by endorsement on the original freight bill. This action will expedite the settlement of any loss claim filed and, in addition, immediately place the burden for locating the shortage on the carrier.

A *concealed loss* means a loss that is not apparent at the time of delivery by the carrier but is discovered by the consignee upon later opening of the containers and inspection of the contents. The material received does not agree with the quantity invoiced by the seller. It is imperative in this type of loss that the carrier be contacted immediately and the cartons and inner packing be set aside for later inspection. If the appearance of the package indicates the goods were packed therein, or if it bears evidence of tampering, pilfering, or rifling, every opportunity should be extended to the carrier to make a thorough inspection.

Known damage is defined as damage that is apparent and acknowledged by the carrier at the time of delivery to the consignee. Such evident damage to containers or contents should be noted on carrier's receipt and copy before receiving signature is applied. A meticulous inspection of the damaged goods should be completed by the consignee, and a notation specifying the extent of the damage should be applied to the carrier's original freight bill. The consignee should not refuse damaged freight, since it is his legal duty to accept the property and to employ every available and reasonable means to protect the shipment and minimize the loss. Acceptance of a damaged shipment does not imperil any legitimate claim the consignee may have against the carrier for damage. If the consignee fails to observe the legal duty to accept damaged freight, the carrier may consider it abandoned. After properly notifying the consignor and consignee of his intentions, the carrier may dispose of the material at public sale. This procedure is in accordance with the disposition of abandoned shipments as outlined in Section 4 of the contract terms of the bill of lading.

Concealed damage means damage to the contents of a package or container which is not readily visible at the time of delivery by the carrier. The goods are received in apparent good order and a clear delivery receipt is given the carrier, but upon later opening of the packages breakage or damage is found. Carrier inspection is of extreme importance in facilitating the settlement of the concealed-damage type of claim.

Rules Governing Loss or Damage Claims

In an effort to avoid charges of discrimination and to maintain fair and just practices in the settlement of highly controversial loss or damage claims, the carriers and the National Industrial Traffic League have prescribed a set of rules to govern the inspection of freight and the adjustment of claims for loss or damage thereon. Even though these regulations have no legal status and are not binding on shipper, consignee, or carrier, they furnish the purchasing manager an excellent set of guidelines, and he should become familiar with them. Through observance of these regulations, much can be accomplished in removing the suspicion and doubt surrounding any concealed loss or damage claim.

The final category of loss and damage is by reason of delay. The deciding factor in this type of claim is the length of time in transit. Loss or damage may be suffered by the consignor or consignee as a result of the goods declining in market value when delivered at destination or by actual physical deterioration of the commodity through reason of delay. In loss or damage by delay claims, the transit time provided is compared with the normal movement of goods over the same route, and if the transit time is excessive, the carrier must determine whether or not the delay was beyond its control. Although one of the bill of lading contract terms stipulates the carrier does not guarantee to transport a shipment by any particular train or vessel, or in time for any particular market, the carrier is obligated to forward a shipment with reasonable dispatch. If a carrier can be proved negligent in this duty, claim can be filed for reimbursement of the damages suffered.

Filing Claims

A claim for loss, damage, injury, or delay will not be paid unless filed in writing within the proper time limits and as otherwise required by the contract terms and conditions of the bill of lading or other contract of carriage, whichever may apply. There should be a communication in writing from the claimant to the carrier, within the time limits specified in the bill of lading or other contract of carriage, containing sufficient facts to identify the shipment or shipments involved and asserting liability for alleged loss, damage, injury, or delay. This is considered sufficient compliance with the provisions of the bill of lading or other contract of carriage. Claims on intrastate shipments are governed by applicable state laws. These rules may be obtained by contacting the public utility administration of the state involved.

In preparing a claim against a carrier, the claimant should know that he is entitled to indemnification for full actual loss or damage. Because of the controversial nature of claims and the fact that final recourse if the carrier does not agree lies with the courts and not with the ICC, it must be stressed that claims of a doubtful nature are not to be filed. Once a claim is filed, however, there should be no compromise, and it should stand on its own merits. In the case of a concealed loss or damage claim, if more than one carrier and possibly a warehouse have handled the shipment, each may be liable for its pro rata share of the total claim. Ample time should be given the carrier to investigate the claim fully, since a carrier may be cited by the Commission for rebating in the event of payment of loss and damage claims not justified by the facts. Generally speaking, either a check in full payment or a letter of refusal will be forwarded to the claimant within a period of 1 to 2 months. If a legitimate claim is declined, the claimant has full access to the courts for establishing the carrier's guilt.

The claim file to be presented to the carrier should include a standard form for presentation of loss and damage claims, certified copies of original invoices, carrier inspection report, original paid freight bill and bill of lading, or, in lieu thereof, a bond of indemnity agreement, and copies of correspondence applicable to the claim. Samples of these claim forms are shown in Figs. 23-3 and 23-4.

Claims for loss or damage must be filed with either the originating or the delivering carrier during a period of 9 months from date of delivery or, in the case of loss, after reasonable time for delivery has elapsed.

Loss, damage, and delay exist because of the innumerable unforeseeable incidents which may affect the transportation of goods. Despite the prevalence of loss, damage, and delay, there should be no relaxation on the part of the shipper, receiver, or carrier in the maintenance of an effective claim prevention program. Since goods destroyed are lost forever, the payment of loss and damage claims by the carrier is economic waste. In establishing its rates the carrier must consider the risk element pertaining to loss or damage of property in transit. If claim payments continue to rise, the inevitable result is an upward revision of the rates. In the final analysis, the prevention of claims is of far greater benefit to the shipper, receiver, and carrier than the monetary reimbursement actually received.

One shortcoming of the present freight claims system is that often, if the carrier declines the claim, the amount involved does not justify legal action by the claimant. There is a limbo of small claims, the amount of which may run into hundreds of dollars, with the claimant at the mercy of the carrier.

One organization helping to solve this problem is the Transportation Arbitration Board (TAB), sponsored by the Shippers National Freight Claims Council

(Huntington, N.Y.) and the National Freight Claims Council of the American Trucking Associations (Washington, D.C.). A rotating panel of arbitrators, with both shippers and motor carriers as members, reviews each claim submitted to it for arbitration and renders its decision. Both parties must agree to be bound by a unanimous decision of the two-person team assigned to the claim. If a unanimous

---

Standard Form for Presentation of Loss and Damage Claims

Approved by the Interstate Commerce Commission, the National Industrial Traffic League,
Freight Claim Division, Association of American Railroads.

Freight Claim Agent   1341 E. 222nd St., Cleveland, Ohio 44117
(Name of person to whom claim is presented)   (Address of claimant)

394
(Claimant's Number)‡

X Truck Line, Inc.   10/15/
(Name of carrier)   (Date)

Broadway & Vine Sts., Lima, Ohio   45801
(Address)   (Carrier's Number)

This claim for $ 5,313.60   is made against the carrier named above by ABC Products, Inc.
(Amount of claim)   (Name of claimant)

for Loss and Damage   in connection with the following described shipments:
(loss or damage)

Description of shipment   Electric Motors

Name and address of consignor (shipper) Motor Electric Co., Lima, Ohio   45801

Shipped from Lima, Ohio   , To Cleveland, Ohio
(City, town or station)   (City, town or station)

Final Destination Cleveland, Ohio   Routed via X Truck Line, Inc.
(City, town or station)

Bill of Lading issued by Motor Electric Co. Co.; Date of Bill of Lading 10/1/

Paid Freight Bill (Pro) Number 34870   ; Original Car Number and Initial

Name and address of consignee (Whom shipped to)ABC Products, Inc., 1341 E. 222nd St.,

If shipment reconsigned en route, state particulars: Cleveland, Ohio 44117

DETAILED STATEMENT SHOWING HOW AMOUNT CLAIMED IS DETERMINED
(Number and description of articles, nature and extent of loss or damage, invoice price of articles, amount of claim, etc.)

Costs incurred at ABC Products, Inc., inspecting all motors,	
repacking and reshipping motors to be repaired	$361.80
Freight charges on returned motors to Lima,	
Krause Pro C-800576	21.30
5 Motors lost - A35A 9064-2 at $76.30 ea. (Invoice attached)	381.50
Motor repair charges (copy of invoices attached)	4,549.00
Total Amount Claimed	$5,313.60

IN ADDITION TO THE INFORMATION GIVEN ABOVE, THE FOLLOWING DOCUMENTS ARE
SUBMITTED IN SUPPORT OF THIS CLAIM.*

( ) 1. Original bill of lading, if not previously surrendered to carrier.
( ) 2. Original paid freight ("expense") bill.
(x) 3. Original invoice or certified copy.
x 4. Other particulars obtainable in proof of loss or damage claimed:

Remarks Bond of Idemnity, issued in lieu of original paid
freight bill and bill of lading.

The foregoing statement of facts is hereby certified to as correct.
ABC Products, Inc.
(Signature of claimant)Traffic Mgr.

‡Claimant should assign to each claim a number, inserting same in the space provided at the upper right hand corner of this form.
Reference should be made thereto in all correspondence pertaining to this claim.
*Claimant will please place check (x) before such of the documents mentioned as have been attached, and explain under "Remarks"
the absence of any of the documents called for in connection with this claim. When for any reason it is impossible for claimant to produce
original bill of lading, or paid freight bill, claimant should indemnify carrier or carriers against duplicate claim supported by original
documents.

Fig. 23-3 Standard form for presentation of loss and damage claims.

decision cannot be reached by the first team, the claim is turned over to a second two-person team. The cost of arbitration is $25 for each party, and average time for processing a claim by the TAB, based on a recent survey, is 54 days. Although organized by shippers and motor carriers, the TAB has invited representatives of other transportation modes to participate in its program.

Standard Form for Presentation of Overcharge Claims

Approved by the Interstate Commerce Commission; Freight Claim Division, Association of American Railroads; National Industrial Traffic League, and the National Association of Railway Commissioners.

Freight Claim Agent   1341 E. 222nd St., Cleveland, Ohio 44117   56-1062
(Name of person to whom claim is presented)   (Address of claimant)   (Claimant's Number)‡

All Freight, Inc.   10/15/
(Name of carrier)   (Date)

P.O. Box 7036, Akron, Ohio 44306   (Carrier's Number)
(Address)

This claim for $ 62.00 is made against the carrier named above by ABC Products, Inc.
(Amount of claim)   (Name of claimant)

for Overcharge in connection with the following described shipments:

Description of shipment 3 Skids Machines (Drilling) NOIBN

Name and address of consignor (shipper) Special Machine Co.

*Shipped from Simsbury, Connecticut , To Cleveland, Ohio
(City, town or station)   (City, town or station)

Final Destination Cleveland, Ohio Routed via All Freight, Inc.
(City, town or station)

Bill of Lading issued by Shipper Co.; Date of Bill of Lading 10/1/

Paid Freight Bill (Pro) Number 16-100390 ; Original Car Number and Initial

Name and address of consignee (Whom shipped to) ABC Products, Inc. 1341 E. 222nd St.

If shipment reconsigned en route, state particulars: Cleveland, Ohio 44117

Nature of Overcharge Rate
(Weight, rate or classification, etc.)

DETAILED STATEMENT OF CLAIM.

Note—If claim covers more than one item taking different rates and classification, attach separate statement showing how overcharge is determined and insert totals in space below.

	No. of Pkgs.	Articles	Weight	Rate	Charges	Amount of Overcharge
Charges Paid:	3 Skids	Machines (Drilling) NOIBN	15,470 as 20,000	1.40	$280.00	
		Total			$280.00	
Should have been:	Same	Same	15,470 as 20,000	1.09	$218.00	
		Total			$218.00	$62.00

Authority for rate or classification claimed EC-15, Simsbury takes Hartford rates; Item 6757
(Give, so far as practicable, tariff reference [I. C. C. number, effective date and page or item].)

IN ADDITION TO THE INFORMATION GIVEN ABOVE, THE FOLLOWING DOCUMENTS ARE SUBMITTED IN SUPPORT OF THIS CLAIM.*

( ) 1. Original paid freight ("expense") bill.

( ) 2. Original invoice, or certified copy, when claim is based on weight or valuation, or when shipment has been improperly described.

( ) 3. Original Bill of Lading, if not previously surrendered to carrier, when claim was prepaid, or when claim is based on misrouting or valuation.

( ) 4. Weight certificate or certified statement when claim is based on weight.

5. Other particulars obtainable in proof of Overcharge claimed:†

Remarks Bond of Indemnity issued in lieu of original paid freight bill and bill of lading. Interest demanded on this claim at the rate of 6% per annum from date of collection until paid.

The foregoing statement of facts is hereby certified to as correct.

ABC Products, Inc.
(Signature of claimant) Traffic Mgr.

---

‡Claimant should assign to each claim a number, inserting same in the space provided at the upper right hand corner of this form. Reference should be made thereto in all correspondence pertaining to this claim.
*Claimant will please place check (x) before such of the documents mentioned as have been attached. and explain under "Remarks" the absence of any of the documents called for in connection with this claim. When for any reason it is impossible for claimant to produce original bill of lading if required, or paid freight bill. claimant should indemnify carrier or carriers against duplicate claim supported by original documents.
†Claims for overcharge on shipments of lumber should also be supported by a statement of the number of feet, dimensions, kind of lumber and length of time on sticks before being shipped
Claims based on rates quoted in letters from traffic officials should be supported by the original or copies of such letters.

Fig. 23-4 Standard form for presentation of overcharge claims.

SHIPPER GROUPS

Shippers who want to have any influence on the major issues and forces that shape transportation—or who merely want to keep informed about what the major issues are—have found their most effective instrument to be membership in one or more of the transportation groups organized by and serving shippers. Some, such as the National Industrial Traffic League (Washington, D.C.), cover broad national issues. Others, such as the Eastern Industrial Traffic League (Arlington, Va.), cover national issues also but focus mainly on regional transportation problems. Still others, such as the National Small Shipments Traffic Conference and the Drug and Toilet Preparations Traffic Conference (both also headquartered in Arlington, Va.), focus on problems of interest to specific types of shippers.

All these associations have legal counsel and staffs actively looking out for the interests of their members. They are in the forefront of opposition to rate increases and tariff changes that may harm their members. They regularly testify before regulatory agencies and carrier groups, e.g., at rate-making conferences, to state the position of their members lucidly. Unfortunately, most shippers are unaware of these groups. A relatively small handful of the nation's shippers, often major industrial companies, support these associations, even though their work benefits all shippers.

NOTE: For further information on subjects covered in this section see the list of references in Section 30.

Section **24**

Scrap and Surplus Material Management

EDITOR

Lee A. Wells, Jr., C.P.M. *Purchasing Manager (Retired),*
Carrier Air Conditioning Company, Syracuse, New York

ASSOCIATE EDITORS

Norman M. Weltmann, C.P.M. *President, Marley's, Inc.,*
Syracuse, New York

James Coughenour *Buyer—Metals, Carrier Air Condition-*
ing Company, Syracuse, New York

David L. Morgan *Field Purchasing Manager, Carrier Air*
Conditioning Company, Syracuse, New York

Whether the incentive be conservation of natural resources and concern for the environment or the recovery and reduction of idle investment, the recycling of surplus, obsolete, and scrap materials back into productive channels is an important multibillion-dollar, worldwide business. A well-managed reclamation operation is important to the industrial concern because it is a direct source of added revenue by the reclamation of otherwise nonproductive assets. An efficient and knowledgeable reclamation operation is essential to an effective and profitable recycling process. It must, in the ultimate analysis, return a profit by striking a favorable balance between the use of available resources of surplus, obsolete, and scrap material and the cost of human and financial resources.

GENERAL CONSIDERATIONS

To achieve this objective, the business enterprise must establish clear lines of responsibility for its reclamation program and a means for evaluation and control. The system should provide continual evaluation, both of the return on money and manpower expended in the operation and of the comparative value of alternatives for greater or lesser intensive efforts. It must provide the necessary control to prevent loss, or opportunity for collusion, without excessive paperwork. It must also clearly vest legal authority for the transactions with outside parties, which, as a disposition of assets of the business, will require delegation from the owner or board of directors.

The reclamation program must further give recognition to the differing aspects of the handling and the aftertax value between surplus materials, obsolete materials, and scrap materials, both in inventory accounts and in depreciable capital asset accounts. Consequently, these are treated separately in this chapter.

Classification of Reclamation Material

The classifications of reclamation material to be covered in the authority delegations and reclamation procedures manual are:

Surplus Material and Equipment   *Surplus* should be defined as usable material, equipment, or parts, including capitalized equipment, which are in excess of the normal manufacturing, operating, or repair requirements.

Obsolete Material and Equipment   *Obsolete* should be defined as material, equipment, or parts which are no longer usable in the service for which they were purchased or manufactured and which cannot be utilized safely or economically for any other purpose.

Scrap Material   *Scrap* material falls into three classifications:

FERROUS SCRAP.   Usually designated simply *scrap*. Applies to any ferrous material suitable for reprocessing either by remelting after suitable preparation or by rerolling. The latter is called *rerolling-grade scrap,* e.g., railroad rails, rounds.

NONFERROUS SCRAP.   Usually designated simply *metals*. Applies to nonferrous metals and alloys, such as copper, lead, nickel, aluminum and brasses, which are suitable for remelting, re-refining, resmelting, or electrolytic processing.

WASTE. This term applies to nonmetallic material, and includes paper, rags, rubber, and wood which have a salvageable value for recycling, depending on quantity.

Table 24-1 is illustrative of the volume of consumption of ferrous scrap and certain of the metals for which statistics are available. In addition to copper, lead, nickel, and aluminum, substantial tonnages of antimony, tin, zinc, and the precious metals are salvaged.

TABLE 24-1 Consumption of Purchased Metal Scrap in the United States (Nonferrous in Thousand Short Tons, Ferrous in Thousand Long Tons)
(Reported by U.S. Department of the Interior)

| Year | *Nonferrous* | | | | Ferrous |
	Copper	Lead	Nickel	Aluminum	
1964	1513	705	25	712	32,736
1965	1735	748	21	817	36,821
1966	1868	741	25	896*	37,852
1967	1541	726	18	883*	33,914
1968	1662	726	14	1015*	35,235
1969	1891	798	24	1109*	38,999
1970	1750	786	22	973*	35,418
1971	1660	785	26.5	1005	34,208
1972	1781	814	43.9	1152	41,671
1973	1863	868	33	1262	44,711
1974	1778	929	23.3	1206	51,224
1975	1253	909	19.1	1232	36,753
1976	1514	1003	9.7	1465	41,399
1977	1575	1160	9.6	1568	41,933
1978	1811	1171	10.6	1617	46,100

*Calculated.

ORGANIZATIONAL CONSIDERATIONS

General

No salvage and reclamation program is fully successful without the backing of management and the specification by management of objectives, responsibilites, and authorities. A policy statement from the board of directors, or from the executive vested with the authority, should be issued covering these matters for inclusion in appropriate operating or policy manuals.

Objectives

The stated objectives of the reclamation program should include the following:

1. To ensure that all surplus or obsolete material, equipment, and parts, scrap, and recyclable material are timely and properly identified, located, collected, and handled

2. To obtain maximum reuse and economic disposition of such surplus, obsolete, scrap, and recyclable material

3. To assist in minimizing the generation of reclamation and recyclable material by observing sources and by close cooperation with other departments and department heads

Responsibilities and Authorities

The purchasing officer, with his knowledge of materials and how his company uses them, is the logical person to be held primarily responsible for reclamation and salvage disposal. He is familiar with the companies which take various materials and where they are located. He knows how the items his company buys are made and what they cost. In actual practice, 56 percent of purchasing departments are responsible for this function. This is based on 5539 respondents to a survey made in 1971 by the National Association of Purchasing Management.

However, for a reclamation program to be fully effective, depending on the functions involved, responsibilities should be assigned to and shared by both the line management and purchasing management. The following is a condensation of the stated responsibilities in one company.

1. Each department head shall have the responsibility to periodically review material equipment and parts under his supervision to determine which are to be considered surplus, obsolete, or scrap; and he is hereby delegated the authority to so classify such material and initiate the disposal in accordance with procedures established by the manager of purchases.

2. The manager of purchases shall have the responsibility to establish policies and procedures to facilitate the transfer or sale or other disposition of approved surplus, obsolete, and scrap material, and to maintain cognizance over all such dispositions; and he is hereby delegated the authority to effect the sale or other disposition of such material.

3. The manager of purchases and each department head shall have joint responsibility to determine the possible use of surplus through interdepartmental transfers, transfers between locations, and transfers between companies and divisions.

4. Each above executive shall have authority to delegate authorities enumerated to the incumbents of positions under his supervision.

(*Note:* Any procedure should specify review periods, e.g., every 6 months, annually, etc.)

Personnel

Positions Involved Depending upon the divisional organization of a corporation, the purchasing manager of a division would normally have primary responsibility. In a purchasing department of several or more persons, the actual purchasing responsibility would better be delegated to one of the other people. In the case of a large division or company, this position might well be a full-time assignment. A suitable descriptive title should also be assigned, e.g., By-products Coordinator.

Other personnel who report to plant managers will also be required to assist in the clerical work of tagging, record keeping, etc., for their respective plants, as well as the physical transfer of surplus and obsolete items to holding areas. This obviously also requires that people handling material, such as forklift-truck drivers, be available for actual movement of material.

Job Descriptions   Suitable comprehensive job descriptions must be prepared to specify duties, responsibility, and authority for each position. This is obvious if the positions in purchasing and in the plants are full-time, but is even more important when they are part-time assignments with all the distractions that are inherent in such situations. It is important that such job descriptions define authority, e.g., the by-products coordinator has been delegated responsibility for pricing for sales to employees.

Types of People   Since disposition of surplus, obsolete, and scrap materials presents opportunities for collusion between personnel involved directly in purchasing and in the plants, as well as with employees and people on the outside, it is imperative that the integrity of the individual be a major factor in the selection process. In recent years, for example, copper has been quite valuable, to the point that scrap copper has been a very tempting item. Incidents have been reported in which thieves had even removed sections of copper transmission lines in spite of the danger involved.

It is also recommended that the individuals be retained in the assignments a maximum of 2 to 3 years. Too long a time can increase the inevitable outside pressures.

The people selected should have a good knowledge of the company's overall business, part numbers, and company and plant organization and should be able to work well with various personnel, including outside vendors, other buyers, engineers (e.g., those employed in attempting to find other uses for surplus manufactured or purchased parts), and plant management.

Legal Aspects

All possible liability, including environmental regulations and pollution problems, should be reviewed with the company's legal counsel, particularly any liability that might be involved in outside sales, employee sales, and donations. In view of all the new consumer protection legislation, liability for damage could result in expensive litigation. Even the fine print included in sales agreements may not always be effective. Liability can result from causes such as: parts of special nature or manufactured parts being used incorrectly; capital equipment sold to another manufacturing company, either directly or through a broker, that subsequently causes personal injury to an operator and/or property damage; or a gas cylinder thought to be empty that later explodes.

ORGANIZING THE RECLAMATION PROGRAM

The reclamation and salvage program, the operating manual, and assignment of duties should cover the following:

1. Ascertaining, listing, and processing lists of scrap, surplus, obsolete material and equipment, and recyclable material.

2. Collecting, or supervising the collecting of, reclamation and salvage material from various areas of the plant or field locations and, as necessary, taking them to a central location; or setting up a collection area as near the generation points as possible, thereby avoiding contamination and reducing handling costs.

3. Recording and storing all reclamation items until they are disposed of (only when necessary to avoid damage and excessive handling and storage costs).

4. Sorting and, as appropriate, preparing scrap and waste to obtain maximum return through sale. Wherever possible, establish zone loading procedure to avoid extra handling cost and contamination. Only sort where necessary and avoid any preparation unless it is done at the source with special attachments on the machines producing the scrap.

5. Reviewing purchase requisitions before order placement to ensure use of surplus and salvage material and equipment where possible in lieu of purchase.

6. Reclaiming and refurbishing material and equipment to condition it for reuse only after determining that it will be required for production.

7. Seeking out uses for reclamation and salvage material and equipment.

8. Establishing procedure for handling sale of reclamation and salvage material and equipment to outside parties. Include documentation required to cover procedure from beginning to end. Check problems of product liability.

9. Establish procedure for sales to employees.

The Reclamation and Salvage Manual

The purchasing manager should prepare a manual which includes the aforecovered considerations of objectives, responsibilities, authorities, and assignment of duties and which details the operating procedures. The following is a checklist for the preparation of such a manual:

1. Foreword and policy statement by the chief executive officer of the corporation which includes delegation of authority

2. Objectives

3. Organization

4. Organizational division of duties, responsibilities, and authority

5. Definitions of surplus, obsolete, and scrap material and equipment and recyclables

6. Procedure for identifying, listing, reporting, transferring, and disposing of surplus and obsolete material, equipment, and parts

7. Methods of identifying, collecting, handling, sorting, preparing, storing, and disposing of scrap ferrous and nonferrous metals and waste

8. Reclamation and refurbishing procedures

9. Economic evaluation procedures and limitations

10. Procedures for sales to employees

11. Procedures for donation to educational and charitable institutions

12. Handling of return goods and returnable containers

13. Procedures for surplus real estate

14. Procedures for dismantlements

15. Examples and usage of forms

Declaration of Surplus or Obsolete Equipment

In the course of the periodic reviews or plant surveys previously referred to, all material declared surplus or obsolete should be properly tagged and all available source and nameplate-type data recorded on the declaration list. Nothing can be more damaging to a reclamation program than to have the material or equipment advertised for transfer or sale misrepresented or unavailable or unfindable when a disposition has been arranged. Below are a checklist of data that should be obtained and reported, a sample tag form for surplus (or obsolete) equipment, and a sample reporting form:

Checklist of Recordable Data

1. Nameplate data, including model number, serial number, and type of machine

2. Motor data, including horsepower, enclosure, frame number, voltage, cycle, phase, rpm, and other pertinent information

3. A list of standard and special auxiliary equipment and accessories

4. Design changes, if any, that make this machine different from a standard model

5. Parts missing

6. The operating condition, i.e., poor, fair, good, or excellent

7. An estimate of the cost to repair equipment (if it is worth repairing) only if it might be put back into use and not disposed of

8. An estimate of total weight

9. Estimated cost to remove and load on cars, including cost to skid or crate (this information for own use only)

10. An estimate of current scrap value, as scrap (this information for own use only)

11. Asset numbers if assigned

12. Date purchased, new or used, and cost

13. Depreciated value (for own use)

Tagging Surplus (or Obsolete) Items   Figure 24-1 shows a sample form of the type which should be put on all surplus or obsolete items so identified for listing in the periodic surplus or obsolete equipment report.

Reporting Form for Surplus (or Obsolete) Items   Figure 24-2 illustrates a reporting form for surplus or obsolete items on which material or equipment may

SURPLUS | ASSET NO.

○EQUIPMENT

DECLARED SURPLUS ON (DATE) _____

BY (NAME) _____
DO NOT PUT BACK INTO USE OR MAKE ANY DISPOSAL OF THIS

ITEM WITHOUT APPROVAL OF _____
PLANT ENGINEER

Fig. 24-1   Sample of tag to be attached to surplus equipment.

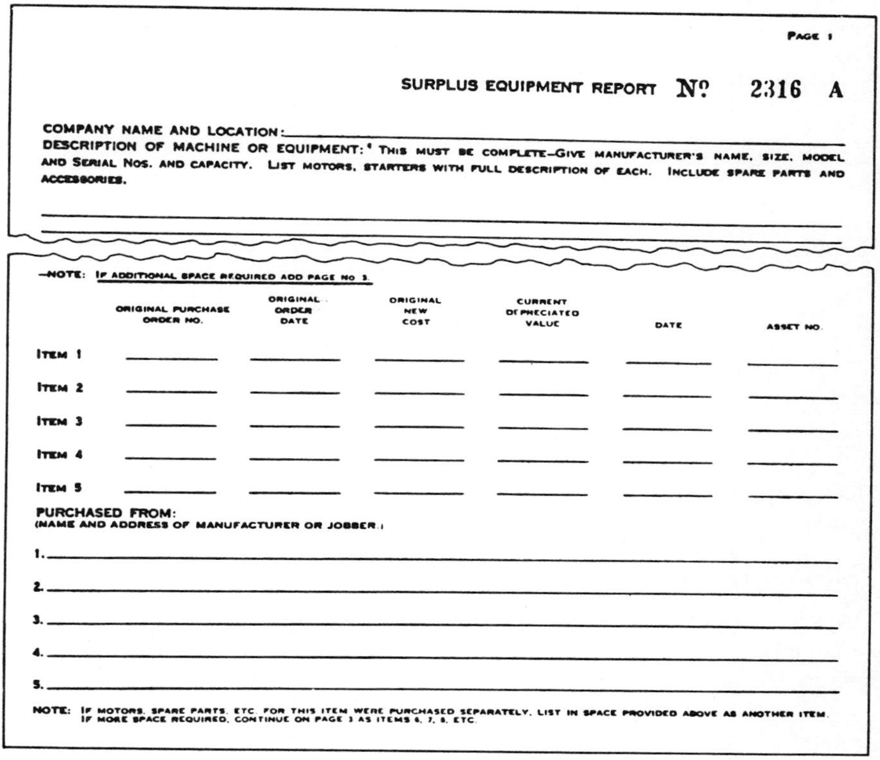

PAGE 1

SURPLUS EQUIPMENT REPORT   N⁰   2316   A

COMPANY NAME AND LOCATION:_____
DESCRIPTION OF MACHINE OR EQUIPMENT: THIS MUST BE COMPLETE—GIVE MANUFACTURER'S NAME, SIZE, MODEL AND SERIAL NOS. AND CAPACITY. LIST MOTORS, STARTERS WITH FULL DESCRIPTION OF EACH. INCLUDE SPARE PARTS AND ACCESSORIES.

—NOTE: IF ADDITIONAL SPACE REQUIRED ADD PAGE NO. 3

	ORIGINAL PURCHASE ORDER NO.	ORIGINAL ORDER DATE	ORIGINAL NEW COST	CURRENT DEPRECIATED VALUE	DATE	ASSET NO.
ITEM 1						
ITEM 2						
ITEM 3						
ITEM 4						
ITEM 5						

PURCHASED FROM:
(NAME AND ADDRESS OF MANUFACTURER OR JOBBER.)

1._____
2._____
3._____
4._____
5._____

NOTE: IF MOTORS, SPARE PARTS, ETC. FOR THIS ITEM WERE PURCHASED SEPARATELY, LIST IN SPACE PROVIDED ABOVE AS ANOTHER ITEM. IF MORE SPACE REQUIRED, CONTINUE ON PAGE 3 AS ITEMS 6, 7, 8, ETC.

Fig. 24-2   Surplus equipment report (front).

· PAGE 2 ·

DESCRIBE PRESENT OPERATING CONDITION. GIVE COMPLETE INFORMATION AS TO BROKEN OR MISSING PARTS, DESIGN CHANGES, CAPACITY LOSSES CAUSED BY DETERIORATED CONDITION, ETC. IF IN YOUR OPINION THIS ITEM IS WORTHY OF REPAIR, ATTACH LETTER DESCRIBING NEEDED REPAIRS AND YOUR ESTIMATE OF COSTS INVOLVED TO PLACE THIS ITEM IN GOOD OPERATING CONDITION.

_____

ESTIMATED PLANT COST TO REMOVE AND LOAD ON CARS $_____

APPROXIMATE SHIPPING WEIGHT LBS. _____

ESTIMATED CURRENT SCRAP VALUE $_____

DO YOU CONSIDER THIS CONDITION TO BE (CHECK ONE) POOR - FAIR - GOOD - EXCELLENT?

WHY IS YOUR PLANT RELEASING THIS EQUIPMENT?_____

DATE EQUIPMENT WILL BE AVAILABLE FOR RELEASE_____?

IN YOUR OPINION WHICH OF THE FOLLOWING METHODS OF DISPOSAL WOULD BE TO THE BEST INTEREST OF THE COMPANY? (CHECK ONE)
          INTER-COMPANY TRANSFER (   )   OUTRIGHT SALE (   )   SELL AS SCRAP (   )

THIS REPORT MADE BY (NAME)_____REPORT DATE_____

EQUIPMENT INSPECTED BY (NAME)_____INSPECTION DATE_____

HAVE SURPLUS SPARE PARTS BEEN INCLUDED? (_____)   STOREKEEPERS (NAME)_____

ALL ASSET VALUES NOTED APPROVED BY (NAME)_____ASSET CUSTODIAN.

RELEASE OF EQUIPMENT FOR TRANSFER OR SALE APPROVED BY:

          DEPT. HEAD OR PLANT SUPT._____DATE_____
                                                    SIGNATURE
          PLANT ENGINEER_____DATE_____
                                              SIGNATURE
          WORKS MANAGER_____DATE_____
                                              SIGNATURE
          DIVISION MANAGER_____DATE_____
                                               SIGNATURE

REMARKS :_____
_____
_____

SOLD OR TRANSFERRED TO_____

M. S. O. No._____DATE_____SALES PRICE_____F. I. No._____

Fig. 24-3   Surplus equipment report (back).

be listed for submission to the purchasing department for disposition. Figure 24-3 represents the back of this form.

The Plant Reclamation and Salvage Operation

Depending upon the size of the plant and the quantity of reclamation and salvage materials produced, the reclamation operation may be part of the plant purchasing duties. Under a materials manager-type organization, both stores and reclamation would be combined with the purchasing department. The supervisor in charge should schedule regular surveys of the plant to turn up dormant surplus and salvage materials and equipment, detect practices which result in excessive waste, develop new possibilities of reclamation, and check performance of reclaimed and refurbished materials and equipment. Consideration should be given to periodic informative meetings with plant personnel to outline the overall purpose of the program and spell out the *who, what, where, when,* and *why* objectives of the reclamation department.

Records   *Records* must be kept to provide as a minimum the following information:

1. Quantities of material, equipment, and parts collected and their source
2. Current listing and inventory of surplus, obsolete equipment, and scrap awaiting disposition
3. Record of sales or other dispositions
4. Inventory and cost records of material, equipment, and parts refurbished for reuse
5. Department operating costs

A simple report on income from sales should accompany a monthly report of operations. This can be in the form of a profit and loss statement if it is possible to determine the true costs accurately. Many employees involved in reclamation and salvage are not assigned to it full time. An example of a brief statement used by one company is shown below.

Sales and Expense
Reclamation and Salvage Department
June, 19—

Sales

Ferrous metals—outside	$ 6.69	
Ferrous metals—plant	54.64	
Nonferrous metals—plant	220.96	
Nonferrous metals—outside	.00	
Miscellaneous sales—plant	.00	
Miscellaneous sales—employees	67.98	
Miscellaneous sales—outside	.00	
Materials returned to stores	.00	
Total sales		$ 350.27

Expenses

Fixed expense	$ .75	
Miscellaneous expense	28.10	
Operating supplies	.00	
Labor	46.74	
Total reclamation expense		$ 75.59

Total sales		$ 350.27
Total expense		$ 75.59
Total profit or loss		$ 274.68
Total sales for year to date (sales)		$12,654.77
Total expense for year to date		$ 1,071.74
Total profit or loss for year to date (net profit)		$11,583.03

Note: This report does not include labor or sales of returned containers.

Controls   *Controls* should be established to keep costs in line and to satisfy the following audit considerations:

1. Is there an effective control over the establishment and representation of the weight of salvage material?
2. Are weights of salvage material property determined?
3. Is accountability soundly and clearly established?
4. Are materials classified for the most profitable returns?
5. Is there any possibility of collusion between employees or with outside persons so as to allow improper dispositions?

SURPLUS MATERIAL AND EQUIPMENT

Definition of Surplus

Surplus may be fully defined as that portion of material, equipment, and parts in excess of maintenance, repair, operating, construction, production, or spare parts requirements at a specific company location. For proper control, it should be further specified that any item not having a foreseeable use within a certain time period—e.g., 1 year—*must* be declared surplus available for transfer or disposition. It may cover items in inventory accounts or in capitalized accounts, and the purchasing manager must recognize the differing economics for disposition of items from the two classifications.

Disposition of Surplus (Economics)

In disposing of surplus, the first determination should be whether the surplus goods can be utilized elsewhere in the plant, or in other plants, since this is normally the most profitable disposition. If the material cannot be used elsewhere within the company, consideration is required of whether to effect disposition through other channels, as outlined later in this section. If the material cannot be used within the company, the fact and the material should be reported to the purchasing manager so he may provide for disposal. The first method for the purchasing manager to investigate is return to the supplier. Many vendors will accept the return of good, salable material at its original cost less a restocking charge.

If this is not possible, the next step will be to offer the material to a dealer, a secondhand dealer, or employees. Sales of this type are usually made on a bid basis or negotiated basis. If the surplus material will have an eventual use within the company, the decision on whether to sell at lower returns or hold it until used at full value, after checking handling and storage costs, will depend on the length of time involved, the company's cost of capital, and the income tax rate. For example, assume material costing $5000 has a salable present market value of $4000 and will be used at full value in 5 years. At a 48 percent tax rate, it has a total present cash flow value, which can be realized by selling, equal to the market value plus tax credits, or $4480. Assuming it will still cost $5000 to replace in 5 years, the $4480 present value in becoming $5000 will earn the equivalent compound interest of 2.2 percent after taxes. If, however, the company's cost of capital is 10 percent, this is an insufficient rate of return and the material should be sold. Figure 24-4 shows the minimum sale values as percentages of carrying value (original cost) based on cost of capital (or inventory carrying cost, if preferred)

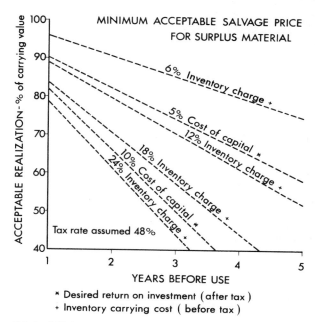

Fig. 24-4 Minimum acceptable salvage price for surplus material.

and the holding period prior to ultimate use. No inflation factor, or obsolescence or deterioration of material, is provided for in the chart reference values. If involved, these factors must be treated separately.

The same type of consideration applies to surplus items from capital investment accounts, but here the purchasing manager must recognize depreciation factors or his evaluation will be erroneous. For example, assume a surplus 2-year-old lathe costing $10,000, with a market value of $9000 and a depreciated book value of $8000 ($1000 depreciation per year, straight-line), will be needed in 2 years and can be replaced in 2 years at the same $9000 market price. The alternatives are:

1. *Sell:*

Sale price $9000

Less tax on gain over book value (depreciation recapture) @ regular
rate of 48%   480

Present cash value after tax $8520

2. *Hold:*

Replacement cost value in 2 years $9000

Plus depreciation cash flow earned, $2000 × 0.48   960

Total value in 2 years $9960

It can be seen that, by not selling, the company has, in effect, increased its asset having a net, aftertax, cash value of $8520 to a total value of $9960. The difference of $1440 represents a 9 percent aftertax return on the $8520 value and may result in a decision to keep, assuming the proceeds of a sale cannot be invested at a higher return, particularly if any inflation factor is added to the replacement cost or if one of the accelerated depreciation rates applies.

The above examples are based on a federal tax rate of 48 percent, which has been in effect for several years. Since this is subject to change by Congress, and since state taxes vary, these should be checked periodically with your financial advisers.

Note: Inventory charge and cost of capital figures shown may not be applicable at the time of your own evaluation. Consult your financial advisers for appropriate values.

OBSOLETE MATERIAL AND EQUIPMENT

Definition of Obsolete

The term *obsolete* should be applied to those items of material, equipment, and parts which are no longer usable in the service for which they were purchased or made and which cannot be utilized safely or economically for any other purpose within the company.

Disposition of Obsolete Items (Economics)

Since obsolete material, equipment, and parts have no use within his company, the purchasing (or reclamation) manager's task is basically one of effecting an expeditious disposition through sale or scrap. There are, however, certain accounting and tax considerations, with which he should be familiar, which will influence the amount of time and effort he should expend.

Inventory Accounts   Obsolete items carried in inventory accounts, i.e., at full value, represent idle investment that should be liquidated promptly. Even if they have no sale value, approximately one-half of the original cost is immediately returned as tax credits, and therefore holding for any length of time seeking a marginal improved sale or use realization is not justified.

Composite Capital Equipment Accounts   Obsolete items in composite property accounts normally will be considered fully depreciated when disposed of and there is no tax consequence of write-off. Disposition in these instances is primarily a matter of good housekeeping, since sale or scrap realization will generally be marginal. Any realization will be treated as an adjustment to depreciation reserve, however, and there will be no immediate tax consequence of the sale.

Individual Capitalized Asset   Disposition of obsolete equipment carried on the books as separate depreciable items (or those which may be lifted from composite accounts as abnormal retirements) will have variable tax consequences, depending on their depreciated tax book value. The portion of any sale realization in excess of depreciated tax book value will be taxable at regular income rates.[1] Otherwise the asset can be considered the same as an inventory item, with a carrying value equal to the depreciated tax book value, and liquidated accordingly.

Disposition of Obsolete Material   See preceding discussion under Disposition of Surplus.

SCRAP

Throughout the United States in most every town, large or small, may be found persons gainfully employed in collecting and processing scrap, metal, and recyclables of every kind. The scrap industry alone is a big business.

Scrap dealers and processors should by no means be compared to the old-time "junk dealer." Most are professional in every sense of the word, maintain their own professional organization (the Institute of Scrap Iron and Steel, Inc., with headquarters in Washington, D.C.), and stand ready to offer the best technical expertise in assisting industry in the most profitable disposal of its scrap, surplus, and obsolete material.

Because of their knowledge of the uses of scrap, referred to below, they are in a position, after making comprehensive surveys of a company or plant's scrap availability, to match this availability to the most advantageous use, depending upon market needs, geography, transportation cost, etc. A professional scrap dealer has the knowledge and experience to provide detailed recommendations to a scrap producer as to handling methods, sorting, pre-processing, etc., that will provide the highest dollar return.

Scrap dealers tend to rate scrap producers as small, medium, and large. This rating is obviously based on the amount of scrap created, but it also relates to the number of plants located in the same geographical area, number of machines actually producing the turnings, chips, etc. A small concern may have to save scrap in small containers for some time to make a worthwhile collection for the dealer to pick up. If the possible payment from the dealer exceeds the cost of storage of the scrap while awaiting collection, and the cost of handling, it obviously is a worthwhile operation. In the case of larger producers, large containers can be spotted at the end of conveyors. When filled, the container is picked up by the dealer, who spots an empty one.

A professional dealer, working with the right people in the plant, can apply his

---

[1] If the obsolete asset has actually appreciated in value, or was acquired prior to 1961, long-term capital gains may apply to a portion. One should thus consult the company's tax adviser, and also investigate the possibility of making a charitable gift, explained later in this section.

experience and available equipment to a survey and recommend the best working arrangement. Obviously, as mentioned below, this can become part of a proposal solicitation to several scrap dealers, if your area supports more than one. In this way, the scrap producer can take advantage of competition and be able to make a selection from more than one recommendation.

Distinguishing Scrap from Rubbish All scrap-producing types of manufacturing also produce *rubbish,* which might be defined as scrap and refuse which has no value but must still be disposed of at some expense. (Some valuable types of scrap, if not sorted efficiently as they are produced but instead tossed into a common bin, then become rubbish and cause the expense of disposal rather than producing a return to the company.)

Do not confuse the rubbish hauler with the professional scrap dealer. Further, if at all possible, do not use a rubbish hauler as a scrap dealer. The two categories should be kept separate and distinct because of the opportunity for accidental or deliberate disposal of valuable scrap as rubbish. In that case, the hauler can do his own sorting and make a profit on the scrap after the company has already paid him once to take it away, supposedly to the local dump.

Sources of Ferrous and Nonferrous Scrap

All scrap and metals that are used in the manufacture of ferrous and nonferrous metals originate from one of two sources: first, that scrap which is known as *home or intraplant scrap* has its origin as a result of the waste or by-product of operations within the mills or foundries and is generally recycled for reuse on the premises from which it originates; second, *purchased scrap,* which further breaks down into (1) prompt, or industrial, scrap, comprising about 40 percent of the total, and (2) obsolete scrap, resulting from wear or obsolescence, which comprises 60 percent of the total.

The source of scrap that is most interesting to the purchasing manager is his own plant. In the majority of enterprises, it is his duty to dispose of these materials to advantage. In order to do so, he must know and understand the various phases of the scrap industries.

Naturally, scrap that has been segregated according to exacting specifications will have a much higher sales value than unsegregated scrap. For these reasons, scrap must be sorted, if economical, according to the use for which it is intended. A practical knowledge of scrap uses will prove to be a definite advantage to those who handle scrap segregation, so that effort will be expended in-house on those preparatory steps that pay off and avoided on those steps which are not recoverable in increased return. Consequently, the industrial purchasing manager must work closely with the scrap processor to find optimum and equitable solutions and to adjust shop practices where warranted.

Uses of Ferrous Scrap

The specification and value of scrap are governed by the type of furnace that will be used in the remelting operation. The size of the furnace is a basic characteristic to be considered.

Use of Scrap in Foundry Gray-Iron Cupola   In past years, most, if not all, foundries used only pig iron and rail scrap. As the years went by, larger foundries were able to reduce the amount of pig iron and rail scrap by the use of machinery castings, structural steel, and plate scrap. Today, most use no pig iron or rail scrap. They are using shortcut automotive steel scrap and shredded automotive scrap with machinery casting, motor (engine) castings, or cast-iron chips.

The electric induction furnaces commonly used in foreign countries found their way into American gray-iron foundries in the 1950s. This furnace uses mostly scrap of high density, including dry cast-iron borings and sheet or crushed fine steel turnings.

Use of Scrap in Blast Furnace   Over the years this furnace has always used fine scrap, such as cast-iron or steel chips or a mixture of both, regardless of analysis, rust, or oxidation. This, together with iron ore and additives to correct the chemistry, is melted in the blast furnace to produce a hot melt for the open hearth or *basic oxygen furnace (BOF)* or pig iron of known chemistry for the foundry.

Use of Scrap in Open-Hearth Furnace   This type of furnace is usually found in the integrated mills where both scrap and hot melt are used. This furnace uses practically all grades of scrap, particularly those of high bulk density.

Use of Scrap in Basic Oxygen Furnace   The BOF, like the open-hearth furnace, can use a variety of grades of scrap, but the percentage of purchased scrap is small, since the in-plant, or home scrap, percentage is high, and a certain amount of hot metal is used to speed up the charge and pouring. It is most important that closed containers or highly volatile scrap of any kind should *not* be included in any charge, so that serious accidents may be avoided. This is because the hot metal is poured over the scrap, and an excessive quantity of gas-forming materials could cause a serious explosion. Billets from basic oxygen furnaces are usually high-grade and suitable for rolling into gauge steel.

Use of Scrap in Electric Furnace   Electric-arc furnaces are completely dependent on scrap. Steelmaking by electric-arc furnace is the fastest-growing method, and its proliferation is being enhanced by direct reduction plants, particularly in remote areas where scrap is in good supply. This, plus the introduction of continuous casting of billets, has created a new type of facility, the so-called mini-mill.

In August 1969 the production of BOF steel exceeded that of the open-hearth furnace for the first time. During 1980 to 1985, the BOF will produce about 75 percent of our carbon steels, the remaining 25 percent being produced by the electric-arc furnace and the open-hearth furnace. Eventually, the open-hearth furnace will become obsolete.

Specifications for Ferrous Scrap

Listed below are some of the more commonly used specifications for scrap as issued by the Institute of Scrap Iron and Steel, Inc., 1729 H St., N.W., Washington, D.C. 20006. They are taken from a booklet that is available on request from the institute. The booklet should be in every purchasing department library. Changes are not often made, but a new booklet should be requested every 2 to 3 years, from the institute or from the local scrap processor. The specifications listed are not all-inclusive but are the ones most likely to be encountered by the average purchasing manager, with the exception of *unprepared, unsorted* and/or *contaminated* material. See below for additional comments.

Every generator of ferrous scrap usually has a grade of *unprepared* or *contaminated,* consisting of materials peculiar to his operation. These grades should be defined as much as possible, as they may well have value.

No. 1 Heavy-melting Steel   Wrought iron and/or steel scrap ¼ in. and over in thickness. Individual pieces not over 60 by 24 in. (charging-box size) prepared in a manner to ensure compact charging.

No. 2 Heavy-melting Steel   Wrought iron and steel scrap, black and galvanized, ⅛ in. and over in thickness, charging-box size to include material not suitable as No. 1 heavy-melting steel. Prepared in a manner to ensure compact charging.

No. 2 Heavy-melting Steel   Wrought iron and steel scrap, black and galvanized, maximum size 36 by 18 in. May include all automobile scrap properly prepared.

The identical designations given for the above two classifications are in accordance with established industry practices in specifying the materials desired.

No. 1 Busheling   Clean steel scrap, not exceeding 12 in. in any dimensions, including new factory busheling (for example, sheet clippings and stampings). May not include old auto body and fender stock. Free of metal-coated, limed, vitreous-enameled, and electrical sheet containing over 0.5 percent silicon.

No. 1 Bundles   New black steel sheet scrap, clippings or skeleton scrap, compressed or hand bundled to charging-box size and weighing not less than 75 lb per cubic foot. (Hand bundles are tightly secured for handling with a magnet.) May include Stanley balls or mandrel-wound bundles or skeleton reels, tightly secured. May include chemically detinned material. May not include old auto body or fender stock. Free of metal-coated, limed, vitreous-enameled, and electrical sheet containing over 0.5 per cent silicon.

No. 2 Bundles   Old black and galvanized steel sheet scrap, hydraulically compressed to charging-box size and weighing not less than 75 lb per cubic foot. May not include tin or lead-coated material or vitreous-enameled material.

Incinerator Bundles   Tin can scrap, compressed to charging-box size and weighing not less than 75 lb per cubic foot. Processed through a recognized garbage incinerator.

Bundled No. 1 Steel   Wrought iron and/or steel scrap ⅛ in. or over in thickness, compressed to charging-box size and weighing not less than 75 lb per cubic foot. Free of all metal-coated material.

Bundled No. 2 Steel   Wrought iron or steel scrap, black or galvanized, ⅛ in. and over in thickness, compressed to charging-box size and weighing not less than 75 lb per cubic foot. Auto body and fender stock, burnt or hand stripped, may constitute a maximum of 60 per cent by weight. (This per cent is based on makeup of auto body, chassis, drive shafts, and bumpers.) Free of all coated material, except as found on automobiles.

Machine-shop Turnings   Clean steel or wrought iron turnings, free of iron borings, nonferrous metals in a free state, scale, or excessive oil. May not include badly rusted or corroded stock.

Machine-shop Turnings and Iron Borings   Same as machine-shop turnings but including iron borings.

Shoveling Turnings   Clean short steel or wrought iron turnings, drillings, or screw cuttings. May include any such material, whether resulting from crushing, raking, or other processes. Free of springy, bushy, tangled, or matted material, lumps, iron borings, nonferrous metals in a free state, scale, grindings, or excessive oil.

Shoveling Turnings and Iron Borings   Same as shoveling turnings but including iron borings.

Iron Borings   Clean cast iron or malleable iron borings and drillings, free of steel turnings, scale, lumps, and excessive oil.

Billet, Bloom, and Forge Crops   Billet, bloom, axle, slab, heavy plate and heavy forge crops, containing not over 0.05 per cent phosphorus or sulphur and not over 0.5 per cent silicon, free from alloys. Dimensions not less than 2 in. in thickness, not over 18 in. in width, and not over 36 in. in length.

Bar Crops and Plate Scrap   Bar crops, plate scrap, forgings, bits, jars, and tool joints, containing not over 0.05 per cent phosphorus or sulphur, not over 0.05 per cent silicon, free from alloys. Dimensions not less than ½ in. in thickness, not over 18 in. in width, and not over 36 in. in length.

Cast Steel   Steel castings not over 48 in. long or 18 in. wide, and ¼ in. and over in thickness, containing not over 0.05 per cent phosphorus or sulphur, free from alloys and attachments. May include heads, gates, and risers.

Punchings and Plate Scrap   Punchings or stampings, plate scrap, and bar crops containing not over 0.05 per cent phosphorus or sulphur and not over 0.05 per cent silicon, free from alloys. All material cut 12 in. and under and, with the exception of punchings or stampings, at least ⅛ in. in thickness. Punchings or stampings under 6 in. in diameter may be any gauge.

Electric-furnace Bundles   New black steel sheet scrap hydraulically compressed into bundles of size and weight as specified by consumer.

Cut Structural and Plate Scrap, 3 Ft and Under   Clean open-hearth steel plates, structural shapes, crop ends, shearings, or broken steel tires. Dimensions not less than ¼ in. in thickness, not over 3 ft in length, and 18 in. in width. Phosphorus or sulphur not over 0.05 per cent.

Cut Structural and Plate Scrap, 2 Ft and Under   Same as cut structural and plate scrap, 3 ft and under, except for length.

Cut Structural and Plate Scrap, 1 Ft and Under   Same as cut structural and plate scrap, 3 ft and under, except for length.

Foundry Steel, 2 Ft and Under   Steel scrap ⅛ in. and over in thickness, not over 2 ft in length, or 18 in. in width. Individual pieces must be free from attachments. May not include nonferrous metals, metal-coated material, cast or malleable iron, body and fender stock, cable, enameled or galvanized material.

Foundry Steel, 1 Ft and Under   Steel scrap ⅛ in. and over in thickness, not over 1 ft in length or 18 in. in width. Individual pieces free from attachments. May not include nonferrous metals, cast or malleable iron, cable, or vitreous-enameled or metal-coated material.

Hard Steel, Cut 30 Inches and Under   Automotive steel consisting of rear ends, crankshafts, drive shafts, front axles, springs, and gears prepared 30 in. and under. May not include miscellaneous small shoveling steel or any pieces too bulky for gray-iron foundry use.

Cupola Cast   Clean cast iron scrap, such as columns, pipes, plates, and castings, of a miscellaneous nature, including automobile blocks and cast iron parts of agriculture and other machinery. Free from stove plate, burnt iron, brake shoes, or foreign material. Cupola size not over 24 in. by 30 in., and no pieces over 150 lb in weight.

Charging Box Cast   Clean cast iron scrap in sizes not over 60 in. in length or 30 in. in width, suitable for charging into an open-hearth furnace without further preparation. Free from burnt iron, brake shoes, or stove plate.

Heavy Breakable Cast   Cast iron scrap over charging-box size or weighing more than 500 lb. May include cylinders and driving-wheel centers. May include steel which does not exceed 10 per cent of the casting by weight.

Clean Auto Cast   Clean auto blocks; free of all parts except cam shafts, valves, valve springs, and studs. Free of nonferrous and nonmetallic parts.

Charging-box Cast   Clean cast iron scrap in sizes not over 60 in. in length or 30 in. in width, suitable for charging into an open-hearth furnace without further preparation. Free from burnt iron, brake shoes, or stove plate.

Unstripped Motor Blocks   Automobile or truck motors from which steel and nonferrous fittings may or may not have been removed. Free from drive shafts and all parts of frames.

Drop Broken Machinery Cast   Clean, heavy cast iron machinery scrap that has been broken under a drop. All pieces must be of cupola size, not over 24 in. by 30 in., and no piece over 150 lb in weight.

Malleable   Malleable parts of automobiles, railroad cars, locomotives, or miscellaneous malleable iron castings. Free from cast iron and steel parts and other foreign material.

No. 1 Chemical Borings   New, clean cast or malleable iron borings and drillings containing not more than 1 per cent oil, free from steel turnings or chips, lumps, scale or corroded or rusty material.

No. 2 Chemical Borings   New, clean cast or malleable iron borings and drillings, containing not more than 1.50 per cent oil, free from steel turnings or chips, lumps, scale, or corroded or rusty material.

Unprepared Ferrous Scrap   Scrap other than that such as black iron, galvanized, galvanealed clippings, which is suitable for hydraulic compression, will have its customary trade meaning as a scrap item that requires processing and sorting suitable for recycling in steel mills and foundries. Contact local area processors and arrange for a special classification.

Specifications for Nonferrous Scrap Metals

The following are definitions for nonferrous scrap published by the National Association of Recycling Industries, Inc., 330 Madison Avenue, New York, N.Y. 10017. The booklet is available on request and should be in the purchasing department library. Changes are not often made, but a new booklet should be requested every 2 to 3 years from the association or from your local scrap processor.

Nonferrous scrap containing lower-grade attachments or contaminants should also be defined for information. It may have value.

Copper

No. 1 Copper Wire consists of clean, untinned, uncoated, unalloyed copper wire and cable, not smaller than No. 16 B & S wire gauge, free of burnt wire which is brittle. Hydraulically briquetted copper subject to agreement.

No. 1 Heavy Copper consists of clean, unalloyed, uncoated copper clippings, punchings, bus bars, commutator segments, and wire not less than $\frac{1}{16}$ in. thick, free of burnt wire which is brittle; but may include clean copper tubing. Hydraulically briquetted copper subject to agreement.

No. 2 Copper Wire consists of miscellaneous unalloyed copper wire having a nominal 96 per cent copper content (minimum 94 per cent) as determined by electrolytic assay. Should be free of the following: excessively leaded, tinned, soldered copper wire; brass and bronze wire; excessive oil content, iron, and non-metallics; copper wire from burning, containing insulation; hair wire; burnt wire which is brittle; and should be reasonably free of ash. Hydraulically briquetted copper wire subject to agreement.

No. 2 Copper consists of miscellaneous, unalloyed copper scrap having a nominal 96 per cent copper content (minimum 94 per cent) as determined by electrolytic assay. Should be free of the following: excessively leaded, tinned, soldered copper scrap; brasses and bronzes; excessive oil content, iron and non-metallics; copper tubing with other than copper connections or with sediment; copper wire from burning, containing insulation; hair wire; burnt wire which is brittle; and should be reasonably free of ash. Hydraulically briquetted copper subject to agreement.

Refinery Brass consists of a minimum of 61.3 per cent copper and a maximum of 5 per cent iron and to consist of brass and bronze solids and turnings, and alloyed and contaminated copper scrap. Shall be free of insulated wire, grinding, electrotype shells and non-metallics. Hydraulically briquetted material subject to agreement.

Copper-bearing Scrap consists of miscellaneous copper-containing skimmings, grindings, ashes, irony brass and copper, residues and slags. Free of insulated wires; copper chlorides; unprepared tangled material; large motors; pyrophoric material; asbestos brake linings; furnace bottoms; high lead materials; graphite crucibles; and noxious and explosive materials. Fine powdered material by agreement. Hydraulically briquetted material subject to agreement.

Machinery or Hard Brass Solids shall have a copper content of not less than 75 per cent, a tin content of not less than 6 per cent, and a lead content of not less than 6 per cent—nor more than 11 per cent, and total impurities, exclusive of zinc, antimony and nickel of not more than 0.75 per cent; the antimony content not to exceed 0.50 per cent. Shall be free of lined and unlined standard red car boxes.

Unlined Standard Red Car Boxes (Clean Journals) consist of standard unlined and/or sweated railroad boxes and unlined and/or sweated car journal bearings, free of yellow boxes and iron-backed boxes.

Light Copper consists of miscellaneous, unalloyed copper scrap having a nominal 92 per cent copper content (minimum 88 per cent) as determined by electrolytic assay and shall consist of sheet copper, gutters, downspouts, kettles, boilers, and similar scrap. Should be free of the following: burnt hair wire; copper clad; plating racks; grindings; copper wire from burning, containing insulation; radiators, fire extinguishers; refrigerator units; electrotype shells; screening; excessively leaded, tinned, soldered scrap; brasses and bronzes; excessive oil, iron and non-metallics; and should be reasonably free of ash. Hydraulically briquetted copper subject to agreement. Any items excluded in this grade are also excluded in the higher grades above.

Yellow Brass Rod Turnings consist of strictly rod turnings, free of aluminum, manganese and composition, Tobin and Muntz metal turnings; not to contain over 3 per cent free iron, oil or other moisture; to be free of grindings and babbits; to contain not more than 0.30 per cent tin and not more than 0.15 per cent alloyed iron.

New Yellow Brass Rod Ends consist of new, clean, rod ends from free turning brass rods or forging rods, not to contain more than 0.30 per cent tin and not more than 0.15 per cent alloyed iron. To be free of Muntz metal and naval brass or any other alloys. To be in pieces not larger than 12 in. and free of foreign matter.

Red Brass Composition Turnings consist of turnings from red brass composition material and should be sold subject to sample or analysis.

Mixed Brass Screens consist of clean mixed copper, brass and bronze screens, and to be free of excessively dirty and painted material.

Cocks and Faucets consist of mixed clean red and yellow brass, including chrome or nickel-plated, free of gas cocks, beer faucets and aluminum and zinc base die cast material and to contain a minimum of 35 per cent semi-red.

Composition or Red Brass consists of red brass scrap valves, machinery bearings, and other machinery parts, including miscellaneous castings made of copper, tin, zinc, and/or lead. Should be free of semi-red brass castings (78 to 81 per cent copper); railroad car boxes and other similar high-lead alloys; cocks and faucets; gates, pot pieces; ingots and burned brass; aluminum and manganese bronzes; iron and non-metallics. No piece to measure more than 12 in. over any one part or weight over 100 lb.

Brass Pipe consists of brass pipe free of plated and soldered materials or pipes with cast brass connections. To be sound, clean pipes free of sediment and condenser tubes.

Admiralty Brass Condenser Tubes consist of clean sound Admiralty condenser tubing which may be plated or unplated, free of nickel alloy, aluminum alloy, and corroded metal.

Mixed Unsweated Auto Radiators consist of mixed automobile radiators, to be free of aluminum radiators, and iron finned radiators. All radiators to be subject to deduction of actual iron. The tonnage specification should cover the gross weight of the radiators, unless otherwise specified.

Manganese Bronze Solids have a copper content of not less than 55 per cent, a lead content of not more than one per cent, and shall be free of aluminum bronze and silicon bronze.

New Brass Clippings consist of the cuttings of new unleaded yellow brass sheet, to be clean and free from foreign substances and not to contain more than 10 per cent of clean brass punchings under ¼ in. To be free of Muntz metal and naval brass.

Yellow Brass Scrap consists of brass castings, rolled brass, rod brass, tubing and miscellaneous yellow brasses, including plated brass. Must be free of manganese—bronze, aluminum-bronze, unsweated radiators or radiator parts iron, excessively dirty and corroded materials.

Machinery or Hard Brass Borings shall have a copper content of not less than 75 per cent, a tin content of not less than 6 per cent, and a lead content of not less than 6 per cent—nor more than 11 per cent, and the total impurities, exclusive of zinc, antimony, and nickel of not more than 0.75 per cent; the antimony content not to exceed 0.50 per cent.

Yellow Brass Castings consist of yellow brass castings in crucible shape, no piece to measure more than 12 inches over any one part; and shall be free of brass forgings, silicon bronze, aluminum bronze and manganese bronze, and not to contain more than 15 per cent nickel plated material.

Yellow Brass Turnings consist of yellow brass turnings, free of aluminum, manganese and composition turnings; not to contain over 3 per cent free iron, oil or other moisture; to be free of grindings and babbitts. To avoid dispute, to be sold subject to sample or analysis.

Aluminum

Mixed Aluminum Castings consist of all clean aluminum castings which may contain auto and airplane castings but no ingots, and to be free of iron, dirt, brass, babbitt and any other foreign materials. Oil and grease not to exceed 2 per cent.

Mixed Low Copper Aluminum Clippings and Solids consist of new, clean, uncoated and unpainted low copper aluminum scrap of two or more alloys and to be free of foil, hair wire, wire screen, dirt, and other foreign substances. Grease and oil not to total more than 1 per cent. Also free from punchings less than ½ in. in size. New can stock subject to arrangement between buyer and seller.

Wrecked Airplane Sheet Aluminum should be sold on recovery basis or by special arrangement with purchaser.

Aluminum Pistons (*a*) Clean aluminum pistons—consist of clean aluminum pistons free from struts, bushings, shafts, iron rings and any other materials. Oil and grease not to exceed 2 per cent. (*b*) Aluminum pistons with struts—consist of clean whole aluminum pistons with struts to be free from bushings, shafts, iron rings and any other foreign material. Oil and grease not to exceed 2 per cent. (*c*) Irony aluminum pistons should be sold on recovery basis, or by special arrangements with the purchaser.

New Aluminum Foil consists of clean, new, pure, uncoated, unalloyed aluminum foil, free from anodized foil, radar foil and chaff, paper, plastics, or any other foreign materials. Hydraulically briquetted material by arrangement only.

Segregated New Aluminum Alloy Clippings and Solids consist of new, clean, uncoated and unpainted aluminum scrap of one specified aluminum alloy only and to be free of foil, hair wire, wire screen, dirt, and other foreign substances. Oil and grease not to total more than 1 per cent. Also free from punchings less than ½ in. in size. New can stock subject to arrangement between buyer and seller.

Scrap Sheet and Sheet Utensil Aluminum consist of clean, unpainted old 25 or 35 aluminum sheet and sheet utensils, free from hub caps, radiator shells, airplane sheet, foil, food or beverage containers, pie plates, oil cans and bottle caps, dirt, and other foreign substances. Oil and grease not to total more than 1 per cent.

Mixed Aluminum Borings and Turnings consist of clean, uncorroded aluminum borings and turnings of two or more alloys and subject to deduction for fines in excess of 3 per cent through a 20-mesh screen and free from dirt, iron, oil, moisture and all other foreign materials. Material containing iron in excess of 10 per cent and/or free magnesium or stainless steel or containing highly flammable cutting compounds will not constitute good delivery. To avoid dispute materials should be sold on basis of definite maximum zinc, tin and magnesium content.

New Pure Aluminum Wire and Cable consist of new, clean, unalloyed aluminum wire or cable free from hair wire, wire screen, iron, insulation and any other foreign substance.

Zinc

New Zinc Clippings consist of any new pure zinc sheets or stampings free from corrosion. To contain no foreign material or attachments. Printers' zinc, such as engravers' zinc, lithograph sheets and addressograph plates subject to special arrangements. Printers' zinc to be free from routings.

Zinc Die Cast Automotive Grilles consist of clean, old or used zinc base die cast automotive grilles, free from soldered material. All foreign attachments and extraneous material are deductible.

Old Zinc Die Cast Scrap consists of miscellaneous old zinc base die castings, with or without iron and other foreign attachments. Must be free of borings, turnings, dross pieces, chunks, melted pieces and skimmings. All unmeltables, dirt, foreign attachments, and volatile substances (such as rubber, cork, plastic, grease, etc.) are deductible. Material containing in excess of 30 per cent iron will not constitute good delivery.

Old Scrap Zinc consists of clean dry scrap zinc, such as sheets, jar lids, clean unalloyed castings and anti-corrosion plates. Borings and turnings are not acceptable. Material must not be excessively corroded or oxidized. All foreign attachments and extraneous materials are deductible.

Mixed Common Babbitt consists of lead base bearing metal containing not less than 8 per cent tin, free from Allens Metal. Ornamental, Antimonial and Type Metal must be free from all zincy and excessive copper in the alloy.

Tin

Block Tin must assay minimum of 98 per cent tin, and to be free of liquids, solder, and brass connections, pewter, pumps, pot pieces, and dirt.

Pewter consists of tableware and soda fountain boxes but should contain a minimum of 84 per cent tin. Syphon tops to be accounted for separately. Material must be free of brass, zinc, and other foreign metals.

Lead

Scrap Lead shall consist of clean soft scrap lead, free of all foreign material such as drosses, battery lead, lead-covered cable, hard lead, collapsible tubes, foil, type metals, zinc, iron and brass fittings, and dirty chemical lead. Free of radioactive materials.

Mixed Hard/Soft Scrap Lead consists of clean lead solids, free of foreign materials, such as drosses, battery lead, lead-covered cable, collapsible tubes, type metals, zinc, iron and brass fittings, and dirty chemical lead. Free of radioactive materials.

Battery Plates. If cells (plates, separators, and lugs) or battery plates, must be reasonably free of rubber. May be bought and sold by assay or as agreed upon between buyer and seller.

Drained Whole Batteries. Batteries to be free of liquid and extraneous material content. Aircraft (aluminum or steel cased) and other special batteries subject to special agreement.

Drosses

Lead Dross should be clean and reasonably free of foreign matter, iron, dirt, harmful chemicals, or other metals. Free of radioactive materials. Assay basis, or as agreed between buyer and seller. Other metals present such as antimony, tin, etc., to be accounted for as agreed between buyer and seller.

Galvanizers' Zinc Dross shall consist of galvanizers' unsweated zinc dross in slabs with minimum zinc content of 92 per cent and shall be free of skimmings. Broken metallic pieces under 2 in. in diameter shall not exceed 10 per cent of the weight of each shipment. Slabs shall not weigh over 100 lb each.

Aluminum Grindings and Aluminum Drosses, Spatters, Spillings, Skimmings, and Sweepings shall be sold on recovery basis or by special arrangements with purchaser.

Prime Zinc Die Cast Dross shall consist of metal skimmed from the top of pot of molten zinc die cast metal. Must be unsweated, unfluxed, shiny, smooth, metallic, and free from corrosion or oxidation. Should be poured into molds or in small mounds weighing not over 75 lb each. Zinc shall be a minimum of 85 per cent.

Nickel-Chrome-Stainless. Nickel and the nickel and chrome ferro alloys are best handled on analysis basis, properly segregated and identified to the prospective purchaser.

Unclassified Nonferrous Items   Items not covered specifically in scrap specifications by consumers should be discussed with local scrap processors and sold by special arrangements between buyer and seller. Contaminated grades should be sold on a negotiated price, based on the recovered basic item of the metal contained in each of these grades.

Specifications for Paper Recyclables

The following are some of the commonly used specifications for recyclables as issued by the National Association of Secondary Material and Industries, Inc., 333 Madison Avenue, New York, N.Y. 10017.

> **Number 1 Mixed Paper** consists of a mixture of various qualities of paper packed in bales weighing not less than 500 lb and containing less than 25 per cent of soft stocks such as news. Outthrows, including a maximum of 1 per cent of prohibited materials, may not exceed 5 per cent.
>
> **Number 2 Mixed Paper** consists of a mixture of various qualities of paper not limited as to type of packing or soft stock content. Outthrows, including a maximum of 2 per cent of prohibited materials, may not exceed 10 per cent.
>
> **Corrugated Containers** consist of corrugated containers having liners of either jute or kraft, packed in bales of not less than 54 in. in length. Outthrows, including a maximum of 1 per cent of prohibited materials, may not exceed 5 per cent.
>
> **Colored Tabulating Cards** consist of printed colored or manila cards, predominantly sulfite or sulfate, which have been manufactured for use in tabulating machines. This grade may be shipped in securely wrapped bales or in bags or cardboard boxes. Outthrows may not exceed 1 per cent. Prohibited materials, none permitted.
>
> **Manila Tabulating Cards** consist of printed manila colored cards, predominantly sulfite or sulfate, which have been manufactured for use in tabulating machines. This grade may contain manila colored tabulating cards with tinted margins but may not contain beater or calender-dyed cards in excess of ½ of 1 per cent. This grade may be shipped in securely wrapped bales, or in bags, or in cardboard boxes. Outthrows may not exceed 1 per cent. Prohibited materials, none permitted.

Sorting and Preparation

While the collecting, sorting, and preparation of scrap metal and waste may be the responsibility of other departments, the purchasing manager should be familiar with all phases of these operations. He should stand ready to advise on current prices of various classes so that optimum return can be obtained and expenditures for unprofitable sorting or preparation avoided.

Sorting is the operation of segregating by type, alloy, grade, size, and weight, i.e., segregating No. 1 and No. 2 heavy-melting grades. *Preparation* is the further processing of material to place it in a higher-priced classification; i.e., scrap which would meet No. 1 heavy-melting classification, except that it is over 5 feet in length, can be sheared to meet this classification.

The reasons for sorting are obvious. If scrap metals or waste are mixed, somebody must sort it if it is to be of any use to the consumer. If a dealer is required to do the sorting, the price he can offer must reflect his cost of sorting. In times when there is excess scrap on the market, mixed scrap may have no market and may incur a net cost for disposal. Few dealers or brokers are willing to do business with plants which consistently mix or misclassify their metals. Only very rarely will it not pay the plant to properly segregate its reclaimable material from the point of production to the point of disposition.

Considering today's in-plant costs, a study may indicate that it could be more economical to sell the scrap as is.

The most economical way of sorting is to use color-coded containers for each type of scrap. In turn, these are emptied into the dealer's large containers, located as near as possible to the generation points. Automation of handling by means of conveyors, directly from the machine tools and other machinery to the containers, trucks, or cars, will save expensive sorting at the source or scrap area.

Processing can be most effectively and economically accomplished at the source by attachments added to the equipment generating the scrap.

Expensive oils found in borings and steel turnings are quite often as valuable, or more valuable, than the scrap itself. A reclaiming process for these lubricants is advisable. In addition, it eliminates what can be a serious pollution problem.

Even in the most efficiently handled places, some mixup is inevitable. This is particularly true in the case of scrap and metal. While there is an almost unlimited number of alloys and grades of ferrous and nonferrous metals, probably less than 100 different alloys and grades make up more than 95 percent of the tonnage produced. Generally, information on the source of the material will limit the number of possibilities so that simple tests will allow identification of the unknown material. Most dealers and mills are equipped with tools and expertise to do some testing and will be glad to aid the salvage manager in developing his own expertise if it is needed. The following is a brief description of tests employed, from the simplest to the most expensive.

Magnetic Testing   Magnetic testing consists merely in determining, with a simple hand magnet, whether or not the material is *ferromagnetic*—iron, nickel, or cobalt. Among the alloys, the iron-base alloys (such as cast iron and plain carbon and low-alloy steels) are most likely to be ferromagnetic, although a few nickel alloys are also magnetic.

Spark Testing   Spark testing employs a high-speed grinding wheel. When iron- and nickel-base materials are ground, the fine particles, raised to incandescence, give characteristic sparks. In alloyed steels, certain elements impart characteristic variations to the plain carbon-steel sparks that the trained operator can readily identify.

Chemical Spot Testing   The chemical tests that may be used for more complete identification of materials range from simple droplet tests to show attack or lack of attack by specific acids to scientifically worked out spot tests to determine the presence or absence of a specific alloying element in a metal. *Spot tests* are based on the formation of characteristic colors or precipitates of the unknown elements when those elements react with various test reagents.

There are two alternate methods for dissolving a minute portion of the unknown metal for these spot tests, the electrographic method and the solution method. In the *electrographic method,* some of the metal is dissolved onto a small piece of electrolyte-moistened filter paper with direct current of dry cell batteries. In the *solution method,* some of the metal is dissolved with a drop or two of an acid or alkali. The resulting droplet of solution is used for spot testing as it lies on the metal, or it is transferred to reagent-impregnated filter paper, spot plates, or test tubes.

Spectrographic Testing   If a complete analysis of a material is desirable, as may be the case with salvage of alloy-content material, the spectroscope or spectrograph is employed. A small quantity of the unknown material is heated to incandescence in an electric arc. Each element in the material can be identified by the color and position of its spectral lines. Since the densities of the spectral lines vary with the quantities of the elements present, quantitative analysis is also possible.

DISPOSITION OF RECLAMATION MATERIAL

As discussed earlier, in the great majority of cases the purchasing department is charged with handling or specifying the handling of reclamation material. Proper disposal procedures can result in one of the most profitable activities of the purchasing manager. Improper disposal procedure not only nullifies any good work done in identifying, reporting, collecting, sorting, and preparing but results in actual loss of profits. *Proper disposal* does not mean just selling by proper classifications to a dealer or broker. When a purchasing officer is considering disposal of material, he will normally consider the following avenues:

1. Use within own company
2. Return to supplier
3. Sale to outside companies
4. Sales to employees
5. Donations to educational and charitable organizations
6. Sale to dealers
7. Use of a commission dealer, broker, or auctioneer

Use within Company

The greatest return will be realized if the material can be used within the purchasing manager's own plant or company. The savings are the difference between the prices of new material and scrap. Some processing may be necessary, but the savings are usually still substantial. A commonly used example is the material remaining when a part has been stamped or punched from sheet or strip material. Often a smaller part can be made from the remaining material.

In the case of a company having two or more plants, often one plant can use the scrap or surplus of another plant. Handling and transportation are the additional factors that must be considered in such instances.

Return to Supplier

Often surplus and scrap are in such condition that they can be returned to the supplier for credit, as an outright sale, or as a deposit on future purchases. Highly alloyed scrap and some nonferrous metals, particularly the semiprecious and precious, fall in this category. During periods of shortage a supplier may require that he be furnished scrap prior to furnishing any new material. Strict segregation of alloys must be practiced if they are to be returned to a supplier.

Nonferrous metals such as copper and aluminum can in some instances be returned to a supplier on a toll basis. In this case the supplier accepts the return of a certain quantity of metal to be reprocessed for a fee or *toll* into new metal. The quantity of new metal returned by the supplier will be slightly less because of melting and fabricating losses. Return of scrap alloy, copper, brass, and aluminum can be arranged with your dealer, who will be responsible for sizing, segregating, and packaging for best results. The dealer's experience can be valuable in these circumstances.

Sale to Outside Companies[2]

Often the refuse of one company is the raw material of another. For example, paper scrap may be sold to a paper mill. Since this type of consumer will pay more than a dealer or broker, the purchasing manager will do well to be constantly alert for sales of this kind. One of the best sources of information regarding such possible sales is the purchasing manager of the other company.

Direct selling has merit when you are a large generator of scrap, capable of shipping full trailer-loads or carloads daily or biweekly. When market conditions soften and steel and paper mills cut back or drop out of the market, it may be costly to find another market for your scrap.

Sale to Employees[3]

Practically every business, large or small, has at least one part-time mechanic, home builder, or do-it-yourself fan among its employees. It has often been said that all scrap has some value. This is particularly true to an individual, since he sets little or no value on his own time and is willing to work many hours putting an object into usable shape. In most businesses surplus equipment, scrap metals, and waste are accumulated where employees can see them at some time during their working hours.

Companies usually sell certain of the materials for which they have no further use to employees as a matter of employee relations. If all factors of cost of selling to employees, such as preparing forms and collecting payment, are taken into account, sales to employees are usually at a financial loss to the company. A min-

---

[2]*Special Note:* It is important that you refer to the discussion of legal aspects presented earlier in this section in regard to sales to outside companies.

[3]*Special Note:* It is important that you refer to the preceding discussion of legal aspects in this section in regard to sales to employees.

imum amount is often set on sales to employees to keep such losses to a minimum. In some cases it may be easier and less expensive to give materials of little or no value to employees at no charge.

Nowhere in the sale of reclamation and salvage materials is uniformity of policy more important than in sales to employees. It is not hard to imagine the effect upon employees' morale in the case where foreman A would let an employee have a discarded piece of rubber hose free while foreman B would charge another employee a nominal sum for identical material. The easiest and only practical solution for the problem is to require that all sales of reclamation and salvage materials to employees be made through one person. This person should be the purchasing representative. Since the price for items of reclamation and salvage being sold to employees is usually set by the company's purchasing manager, it may be well to have another person do the actual selling as a matter of internal control.

All employees should be given an equal opportunity to purchase reclamation and salvage materials. Normally it will not be necessary to publicize materials which are constantly available, such as used dunnage lumber, nonreturnable drums, scrap, and old electrical wire. Materials of this type are generally sold to employees by means of a price list prepared by the purchasing manager; in such cases he should remember to revise such a price list as outside markets fluctuate. One-of-a-kind items or items that infrequently come up for sales to employees should in fairness be brought to the attention of all employees. The simplest way to do this is to post a notice on bulletin boards, allowing ample time before the date of sale for all employees to see it. This type of material is usually sold to employees in one of two ways. One method is to let all employees interested in purchasing the material at a price set by the purchasing department leave their names with the person responsible for sales to employees. The lucky name is then picked at random by such means as drawing it from a hat. The other is to let all employees bid upon the material with the highest bidder getting it.

Donations to Educational and Charitable Organizations[4]

The profit-oriented purchasing manager should be aware that the government encourages corporations to support educational, religious, health, welfare, and other charitable organizations through tax deductions for certain items of property donated to the charitable organizations. This concept of property disposal is many times overlooked as an area for profit potential. Although the Tax Reform Act of 1969 established rules which are less liberal than previously, incentives still exist for donors of surplus real and personal property. Since the rules are complex, the purchasing manager should consult with his tax adviser in all instances. However, he should be cognizant of the fact that a tax or other benefit may accrue by donat-

---

[4]*Special Note:* It is important that you refer to the preceding discussion of legal aspects in this section in regard to donations to organizations.

ing instead of selling certain surplus or obsolete material which has been held for more than 6 months and which is:

1. Appreciated personal property (having a fair market value higher than tax basis)
2. Appreciated real property

The advantage of donating such property in lieu of cash lies in the fact that no tax is levied on the unrealized capital gain. The general rule is that a charitable deduction may be taken for the fair market value less any depreciation taken after 1961 and less investment credits to be recaptured.

However, there are two general situations applying to personal property which diminish the tax advantage:

1. If the property donated is not used by the charity directly in its exempt functions, the charitable deduction must be reduced by 50 percent (62½ percent for corporations) of the potential capital gain.
2. If the property is *ordinary income* property, such as merchandise carried in inventory for sale, the charitable deduction is limited to cost. This applies to any property which would produce ordinary income if sold.

The purchasing manager should also be cognizant of two situations which are often misrepresented. Only in special situations is any advantage obtained by donating (1) items which have been fully expended, such as used supplies and scrap therefrom, or (2) items which as the result of depreciation have a fair market value higher than tax book value but not higher than original cost. In the first instance there is no charitable deduction, and in the second the deduction will be equal to the depreciated book value. In the event it becomes desirable to donate property which has a fair market value less than its tax basis, it is better to sell the property, so as to claim the loss, and then donate the proceeds.

Because of the restrictions mentioned above, there is often a standoff as far as tax benefit is concerned in making charitable gifts of surplus or obsolete property. These situations should not be overlooked, however, because there may well be direct savings in selling expense and commissions, or in effecting disposition of a useful item which does not have a ready market, and there may be substantial intangible benefits produced by the charitable action.

Sale to Dealers

If scrap, metals, and waste cannot be disposed of by the methods listed above, the best outlet is a dealer. Negotiations with dealers are usually carried on by one of the following methods:

Types of Contracts

FIXED-PRICE CONTRACT. Contract to remove scrap metals and waste at periodic intervals. Prices for various classifications are fixed. Prices are established by bid or negotiation.

VARYING-PRICE CONTRACT. Contract to remove materials at periodic intervals. Price to be market price at time of removal less stipulated percentage of dealer's cost and profit. This sum or percentage may be established by bid or negotiation.

BID.   Each lot of one or more classes of scrap metals and waste is offered to dealers, with the high bidder to receive the material.

NEGOTIATION.   Prices for each lot are negotiated with a dealer. A dealer or some other party removes scrap metals and waste at periodic intervals and sells them for the highest price he can find. The method of sale is a function of the type and volume of scrap produced and the personal preference of the purchasing manager. The varying-price contract or bid, however, is to be strongly recommended for materials that fall in standard classifications.

The term of the variable-price contract may vary from a few weeks to a year or more. This type of contract has the advantage to the purchasing manager of taking less time to administer than the bid method. The only duty of the purchasing manager if the contract has been established is to check the price against an agreed source of market prices. The price of the material may be established from one of the following:

1. Market price on specific day to govern for a period of time, i.e., market price on Monday to prevail for entire week. Specify method of determining market price.

2. Average market price for period of time, i.e., average market price for a month to be the price for all material removed during month.

This method has the advantage that the purchasing manager is usually confined to one dealer. When a dealer knows that he is the only outlet for a specific period of time, he is more willing to help and advise regarding sorting and preparation. He will often lend equipment to remove materials and also for other plant operations. In many cases, he will also provide containers for the various grades, relieving the producer of this expense. He may also remove the material which has no value merely as an accommodation to his customer.

Depending upon the circumstances, a yearly *evergreen* contract approach may be advantageous. The variable-price contract is negotiated to cover a minimum of 2 years (the minimum period must be long enough for the dealer to be willing to invest in any special equipment he may need) and then be automatically renewed, if both parties are satisfied with all terms, for 3 additional years. At the end of 5 years or whatever period was originally negotiated, the contract expires and must be rebid. At some agreed-upon time, prior to the end of the first 2 years and prior to the end of succeeding years until the contract expires, either party would have the option of notifying the other party that he no longer wishes to continue, thus causing the contract to expire at the anniversary date immediately thereafter.

The bid method has the advantage of obtaining maximum return to the producer at the time of sale. Sometimes the broker may require large quantities of a particular grade to meet commitments to the consumer. In such cases, he may be willing to pay higher than the market price. This method is also useful for non-standard classification materials which have substantial value.

The bid has the disadvantage that it usually requires more of the purchasing manager's time than the variable-price contract. It is also necessary for the producer to provide all storage containers or bins. Rigid rules should be set up for a periodic issuance of invitations for bid. This may be done on the basis of sending out invitations for bid when certain quantities of material have been accumulated or at periodic intervals, such as the first day of every month. A typical bid form

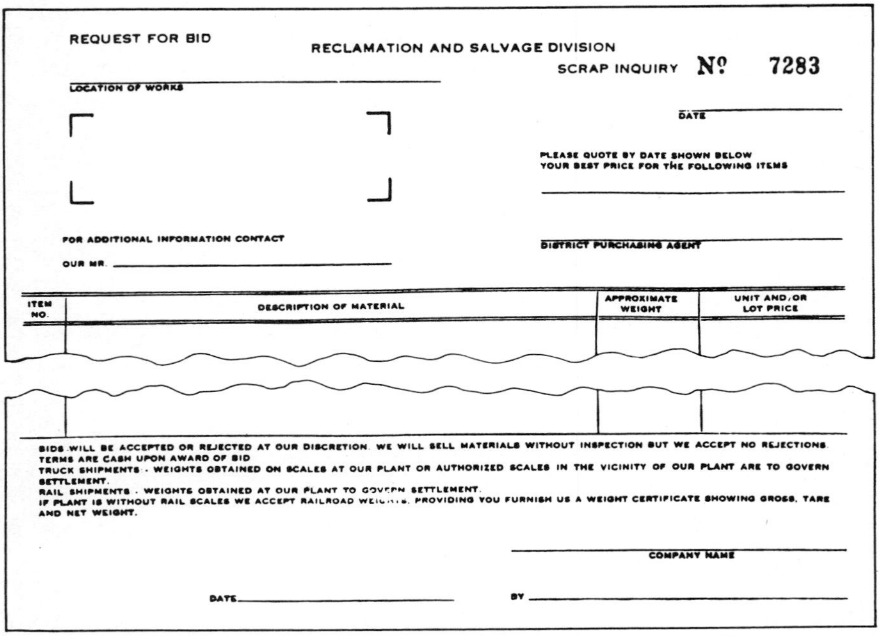
REQUEST FOR BID

RECLAMATION AND SALVAGE DIVISION

SCRAP INQUIRY N° 7283

LOCATION OF WORKS

DATE

PLEASE QUOTE BY DATE SHOWN BELOW
YOUR BEST PRICE FOR THE FOLLOWING ITEMS

FOR ADDITIONAL INFORMATION CONTACT

OUR MR.

DISTRICT PURCHASING AGENT

ITEM NO.	DESCRIPTION OF MATERIAL	APPROXIMATE WEIGHT	UNIT AND/OR LOT PRICE

BIDS WILL BE ACCEPTED OR REJECTED AT OUR DISCRETION. WE WILL SELL MATERIALS WITHOUT INSPECTION BUT WE ACCEPT NO REJECTIONS.
TERMS ARE CASH UPON AWARD OF BID
TRUCK SHIPMENTS - WEIGHTS OBTAINED ON SCALES AT OUR PLANT OR AUTHORIZED SCALES IN THE VICINITY OF OUR PLANT ARE TO GOVERN SETTLEMENT.
RAIL SHIPMENTS - WEIGHTS OBTAINED AT OUR PLANT TO GOVERN SETTLEMENT.
IF PLANT IS WITHOUT RAIL SCALES WE ACCEPT RAILROAD WEIGHTS, PROVIDING YOU FURNISH US A WEIGHT CERTIFICATE SHOWING GROSS, TARE AND NET WEIGHT.

COMPANY NAME

DATE

BY

Fig. 24-5 Request for bid form. Two copies are sent to bidder.

is shown in Fig. 24-5. The normal procedure is to send two copies to the bidder. He will fill out and return one copy and retain the other for his files.

The fixed-price contract is useful in plants producing substantial quantities of scrap, metals, and waste which do not fall into standard classifications and have little value. The main purpose in this case is to have the material removed from the plant site in both good and bad times. While securing bids on each lot may result in a slight increase in revenue, the additional time and expense required may more than offset any gain. The normal period of this type of contract is 1 year. Since the price of standard classification materials may vary over a wide range, the fixed-price contract is not generally used for this type of material.

Negotiation of price with a dealer or broker can be useful in disposing of small quantities of nonrecurring lots of nonstandard classification materials. It can also be used for small quantities of standard classification materials. In either case the value involved should be relatively small. Dealers and brokers are experts on market conditions prevailing for scrap, metals, and waste. Few plants are lucky enough or can afford to have an expert who is equally well informed. Negotiations on price should be carried on only with established dealers or brokers in whom the purchasing manager has confidence.

Where any plant has small quantities of ferrous or nonferrous scrap or other recyclables, it should contact several dealers in the area who offer containerization and select the one best equipped to buy its scrap. This can be sold as an unprepared grade on a monthly price based on prices in trade publications, with deductions to cover handling, freight, and sorting.

The number of dealers with which to deal will depend upon the volume and value of the scrap, metals, and waste involved, the method of disposal, and the number of reliable dealers available in the area. Generally the purchasing manager will find it advisable and more convenient to conduct his negotiations with local dealers. It is usually wise, however, to check dealers periodically in other areas.

The purchasing manager should follow the same rules when dealing with dealers as he would with any important vendor. The dealers are part of a large industry and are usually substantial citizens in their community. A friendly dealer can be of valuable help in any reclamation or salvage program.

The purchasing manager at times may be tempted to outguess the market by holding scrap, metals, or recyclables beyond the normal disposal time, hoping for a rise in a market price. This is risky business. The purchasing manager may be a hero if the market goes up, or he may lose his job if the market goes down. He must remember that he is gambling with money that does not belong to him and must be able to justify his actions at all times. In the long run the disposal of scrap, metals, and recyclables at regular intervals will bring as great or greater return, along with peace of mind for the purchasing manager.

Contracts for Sale   While a given plant may use one or more methods of disposal, the following items should be included in each contract:

1. Price
2. Quantity
3. Delivery time
4. F.o.b. point
5. Cancellation privileges
6. Determining weights shipped
7. Handling shortages and overshipments
8. Terms of payment
9. Weighing specifications (weight determined at certified scales, other than dealer's, when plant has no scale of its own)

Conditions of Contract   The purchasing manager should write the specifications and terms of the contract, and should follow the industry general practice as closely as possible. He should be fair to both seller and purchaser. The National Association of Secondary Material Industries has published suggested contract conditions for some of its standard classifications. The following suggested conditions, taken from *Standard Classification for Non-Ferrous Scrap Metals, Circular NF-50,*[5] are typical and can be used as a guide for disposing of other classes of materials.

a. Delivery of more or less of the specified quantity up to 5 to 10 per cent is permissible.

b. Should the seller fail to make deliveries as specified in the contract, the purchaser has the option of canceling all of the uncompleted deliveries or holding the seller for whatever damages the purchaser may sustain through failure to deliver and if unable to agree on the amount of damages, an Arbitration Committee of the National Association of Secondary Material Industries may be appointed for this purpose, to determine the amount of such damages.

c. In the event that buyer should claim the goods delivered on a contract are not up to the proper standard, and the seller claims that they are a proper delivery, the dispute may be referred to an Arbitration Committee of the National Association of Secondary Material Industries to be appointed for that purpose.

d. A carload, unless otherwise designated, shall consist of the weight governing the minimum carload weight at the lowest carload rate of freight in the territory in which the seller is located. If destination of material requires a greater carload minimum weight, buyer must so specify.

e. A ton for ferrous scrap shall be understood to be 2240 pounds unless otherwise specified. Nonferrous scrap is based on 2000 pounds per ton.

f. If, through embargo, a delivery cannot be made at the time specified, the contract shall remain valid, and shall be completed immediately on the lifting of the embargo, and terms of said contract shall not be changed.

g. When shipments for export for which space has been engaged have been delivered or tendered to a steamship for forwarding, and through inadequacy of cargo space the steamship cannot accept the shipment, or where steamer is delayed in sailing beyond its scheduled time, shipment on the next steamer from the port of shipment shall be deemed a compliance with the contract as to time of shipment.

h. A sworn public weigher shall be employed and weights must be accepted by both parties (cost to be negotiated and specified in contract).

i. When material is such that it can be sorted by hand, consignees cannot reject the entire shipment if the percentage of rejection does not exceed 10 per cent. The disposition of the rejected material should then be arranged by negotiations; no replacement of the rejected material to be made.

Upon request of the shipper, rejections shall be returnable to the seller on domestic shipments within ten days and on foreign shipments within thirty days from the time notice of rejection is received by them, and upon payment by them of 1¢ a pound on material rejected to cover cost of sorting and packing, the seller to be responsible for freight both ways.

Use of a Commission Dealer, Broker, or Auctioneer

In the disposition of equipment, specialty items, real property, and the salvageable items from dismantlements, the use of specialized agents on a fee or commission basis may be indicated. Often the volume of work involved, or the specialized nature of the markets, places the task beyond the buyer's capability or knowledge.

[5]By permission of the National Association of Secondary Material Industries, Inc., 333 Madison Avenue, New York, N.Y. 10017.

The purchasing manager should then solicit a proposal from one of the reputable firms specializing in appraisals, liquidation, and auction. These firms may make one or more of the following offerings:

1. To handle the disposition through one or more market channels or by auction for a fee or commission
2. To guarantee a minimum return in connection with the above
3. To purchase the equipment or facility outright

DISPOSITION OF LAND, BUILDINGS, AND FACILITIES

Surplus real property, be it vacant or improved, may be sold: (1) to obtain cash, (2) to reduce real estate taxes, and (3) to obtain a tax loss.

Sale of Land and Buildings Outright

1. Selecting the Real Estate Agent   In the outright sale of land and buildings, the selection of a real estate broker is important in order to obtain the best results. Naturally such a broker should be one well versed in the value and use possibility of industrial property. He should be in good standing in his community, have a well-organized firm, and be capable of reaching all who may be interested in acquiring properties to be sold.

2. Types of Contracts with Real Estate Agent   An exclusive agency contract with a well-selected broker should bring the best results. The broker is thus protected in his commission and need not hesitate in advertising and letting all who could be interested know that the property is for sale. If not protected by an exclusive contract, he may not feel justified in spending the money and time necessary to bring the best results. Further, a good, reliable broker with an exclusive contract will normally split his commission with a cooperating broker who produces a purchaser. It is also not uncommon for an owner, in order to secure the best results, to agree to pay a commission and a half where an exclusive contract is given and a cooperating broker is involved.

Sale of Buildings Only—for Dismantling

Where improvements are to be sold for removal from the land, care should be exercised in offering the same for sale and in the terms and conditions under which the buildings are to be sold and removed.

1. Making offer for sale
   a. *Description of building:* If construction plans of the building still exist, they should be made available to all bidders. If such information is not available, then a floor plan and perhaps recent photographs should be set up in brochure form for submission to interested parties.
   b. *Provision for insurance by contractor:* One of the conditions under which an offer is made is the insurance requirements to be furnished by the

successful bidder. This insurance coverage should be such as to protect and save harmless the seller and the said lot of land, from any and all lawsuits, judgments, liens, claims, or payments of money which may arise or be made for or by reason of any accident resulting in injury to or death of any person or persons, or in damage to property of anyone, happening in the conduct or through the prosecution of the work of removing, tearing down, filling, or leveling as aforesaid; or for or by reason of the nonpayment of any wages, bills, or charges for anything in connection therewith, or for or by reason of anything happening during the progress of the said work, and until it is accepted as satisfactory by the seller.

   c. *Arrangements for inspection:* In offering the buildings, care should be taken that all interested parties are advised of a specific time when the buildings will be opened for inspection. A definite time should be set forth as to when bids are to have been received and a specific time when such bids will be opened. The owner, for his own protection, should reserve the right to refuse any or all bids. Bids are handled on a closed basis (unless a governmental agency is involved).

   d. *Description of how property is to be left (i.e., condition):*

The successful bidder shall remove within a set period, the whole of each of said buildings from the said lot of land, or tear down the said buildings and remove all materials composing the same from said land, including the cellar walls or foundations; and shall pay all the costs and expenses for or connected with such removal. He agrees:

To obtain, before commencing the work, all permits or licenses required by law in the prosecution of the work; or, if it becomes necessary for the seller to intervene and obtain such licenses or permits, to first pay the fees therefor and all other expenses connected therewith;

To comply with all laws and regulations of the board of health or of any city, county, or state authority that may have jurisdiction of or supervision over the said work, and to assume the risk of loss by reason of the said buildings or any part thereof being destroyed or damaged either by fire or otherwise;

Not to disturb the fences, pavements, or sidewalks, manholes, or other fixtures in said pavements or sidewalks; or, if disturbed, to replace the same and to repair any damage which may be done thereto or thereby.

Within the above-mentioned period, to fill in to the grade of adjacent and surrounding land all cellars, basements, wells, cisterns, vaults, etc., and all other holes or depressions on said lot of land caused by the removal of the building or buildings or material composing the same, by tearing down and utilizing all foundations, chimneys, etc., as a base, the same to be finished and leveled off with _____ feet of clean earth or ashes, first removing all timber, lumber, or other combustible or inflammable matter from such excavations, sloping the surface so that it will not drain onto any adjoining pavement or sidewalk or abutting owner's property; and to leave the said lot of land and pavements or sidewalks in a safe condition both during the progress of the said work and when finished; and to pay all costs and expenses in connection with such filling and leveling.

To plug and seal all sewer and drain openings permanently, and to disconnect gas and water pipes in such manner that same shall remain permanently sealed so that no leakage shall occur, to the satisfaction of the local municipal authorities, utility companies concerned, and the seller.

  e. Lump-sum price versus price per ton of scrap: Where a large amount of scrap is involved and the tonnage indefinite, bids should be obtained based on a price per ton of scrap. Otherwise bids should be requested on a lump-sum basis. There are three alternatives that can be considered: (1) flat price with contractor to retain all materials and scrap; (2) cost of dismantling with all materials and scrap for the account of the seller; (3) lump sum with provisions for certain items to be left for seller's property.

  2. Sales contract   In asking for bids, it is well to furnish prospective bidders with the sales agreement form which the successful bidder will be required to execute.

  a. Deciding award: In requested bids, the time and method of deciding the awarding should be set forth with the further understanding that the seller reserves the right to refuse any and all bids.

  b. Terms of payment: The terms of payment set forth in the sales contract should be such that a substantial certified down payment (not less than 10 percent) is submitted with each bid, with the understanding that such payment will be returned promptly to the unsuccessful bidders. The balance of the bid price should be paid upon execution of the contract, or, where large sums are involved, on a percentage of the work completed as determined by the seller.

  c. Time limit for execution: When requesting bid, one of the conditions is that the successful bidder will execute sales contract within 10 days of receiving such notice or forfeit his down payment submitted with his bid.

  d. Performance Bond. May or may not be required.

Dismantling Facilities to Reclaim Scrap or Usable Materials for Own Use

Where the seller is reclaiming scrap or usable materials for his own use, bids should be secured whereby such scrap and materials are to be turned over to the owner at a specific location and in condition to meet predetermined specifications, the successful bidder to then remove all other materials. It may well be that the materials which the bidder obtains will not be of sufficient value to offset the cost of his obtaining the materials and, therefore, the bids received will in all probability require a payment by the seller to the successful bidder.

NOTE: For further information on subjects covered in this section see the list of references in Section 30.

Budgeting

EDITOR

John E. Pughe, C.P.M. *Corporate Director, Purchasing, The Bendix Corporation, Southfield, Michigan*

ASSOCIATE EDITORS

Robert C. Carson, C.P.M. *Director of Purchasing, Federal-Mogul Corporation, Detroit, Michigan*

Paul E. Merchant *Corporate Manager, Purchasing, The Bendix Corporation, Southfield, Michigan*

For management to fulfill its responsibilities, it must be concerned with controls of its current assets and the planning of the concern's future destinies. One of the manager's most effective tools in fulfilling this responsibility is the use of a vital, responsive budgeting system. This is true whether the concern be a nonprofit organization, a municipality, or one of the group of large and small producers and merchandisers. Budgeting is the beginning step toward responsible management, as management involves planning and control, which are also the essence of budgeting.

Budgeting is a management tool that will be most effective through the actions of responsible individuals. In good business and economic systems, plans are conceived by people, communicated to people, and executed by people. Good use of budgets and their techniques can be realized best through the coordinated efforts of many people at various levels. There should be judicious allocations of the material and human resources. This entails formulating objectives, identifying the problems to meet the objectives, consideration of the alternative solutions to the problems, and, finally, adopting a course of action.

The manner in which this technique of planning and control is handled affects the success of the venture in the organization. After reasonable targets or goals have been generated by the planning executive, the action plan or budget used to reach these goals should be created by the operating people—starting at the lowest responsible level in the company and building up to the corporate budget. Communication and understanding of the corporate or company goals are essential before an action plan can be developed by lower management levels. Budgets should flow up from supervisors and department managers. A budget that has been authored down at the working level will be adhered to, whereas supervisors and even their workers will be inclined to defend themselves from a budget made upstairs or by the accounting and budget staffs.

As the budgeting activity starts with management's direction and the setting of a corporate target, a pace is set that stimulates all divisions to set their individual future goals and objectives. The concern's true economic and profit-making posture can be seen from this pooling of the individual plans of all the segments. Management that looks at short- and long-range objectives and makes them part of its operation gains from the incentive it creates and the discipline it fosters.

BUDGET VERSUS PLAN

Of major significance is the fact that some firms are changing from the term *budget* to the word *plan*. The basic reason for this change is that the latter title more accurately describes the activities which are involved in all areas of management. *Budget* is nevertheless being retained to describe the subject matter of this section, as most practitioners are more familiar with that term. It is believed, however, that more and more companies will understandingly adopt the concept *plan* instead of *budget* during the coming years.

PURCHASING SUPPORTIVE BUDGETING

Purchasing is playing an increasingly vital part in the management process. Its contributions to organization planning can be significant. Purchasing's overall knowledge gained through interfaces with most functional areas provides many opportunities for it to contribute to the organization's profit margin. The process of setting objectives alerts the organization—purchasing specifically—to the matter of financial commitments. For a large number of industrial organizations the amount of money to be spent for goods and services is approximately one-half of every sales dollar. This money becomes the dollars of purchasing power that purchasing is asked to predict and plan in order to obtain optimum value per dollar expended.

The budgeting system is an important part of the overall financial posture and cash flow control, with purchasing right in the thick of it. Various divisions obtain management approval for future expenditures of money required to accomplish their objectives. These approvals are in the form of approved budgets.

Each type of proposed expenditure should be assigned a different work order, account number, or some other unique number. This number is the vehicle for controlling the commitments made for the budgeted item or project. When the engineers or requisitioners prepare their paperwork to send to purchasing, the number of the project must be included. The buyer usually has two responsibilities concerning this number: to verify that the requisition, bill of material, or memorandum has a signature, and to check, through the comptroller or budget administrator, to determine the adequacy of the money in the budget for the project. The budget administrator can then update his record and enter the purchase the buyer is about to award. This recording of the proposed purchase schedules the payments so the cash flow can be predicted by date. Since purchasing is significantly involved in the expenditure budget, purchasing personnel should be involved in the *pricing* of items that are to be included in the budget. See Fig. 25-1.

There are usually three types of budgeting, planning, or forecasting considerations performed by an organization: the production (labor and material) expense budget, the production maintenance, repair, and operating supplies (MRO) budget, and the operating budget (Fig. 25-2). These three budgeting efforts are further refined into short-range, or 1-year, projections and the long-range plans. These apply to manufacturing-type concerns, and therefore they may be broader than the budgeting required for other types of concerns. In those instances the production segment may be replaced. The three broad areas of support planning are:

1. Production or output—raw materials and purchased materials for manu-facturing the organization's product and the labor of production

2. The maintenance, repair, and operating goods and materials to support the entire organization production schedule and changes

3. Capital equipment expenditures to support the production increases or changes in a product and the capital equipment for all other departments' needs

Fig. 25-1 Purchasing involvement in the budgeting cycle. Purchasing assists the depart-ments of the organization in pricing their future plans and then helps monitor them.

Purchasing is involved with all of these because of the contribution it can make in the reporting of current market conditions and predicting these conditions for the months ahead.

Purchasing, with its commodity awareness, its access to and cataloging of the variety of indices and national economic barometers, and its daily contacts with the supplier world, is in a natural position to contribute to the budgeting for numerous departments and divisions of the organization. The three principal areas of budgeting listed are often carried out with the immediate operation of the organization in mind and for a 3- or 5-year prediction. This capability for long-range prediction is particularly applicable in planning the capital expenditures or plant expansion areas. Many long-delivery-schedule items required for plant expansion are subject to an escalation formula and set of indexes that must be forecast. It might be more profitable for an organization to advance its expansion program, if the escalation increase is great enough, to make the advanced building more economical than it would be if deferred until a later date. There will be more detailed discussion of capital equipment budgeting later.

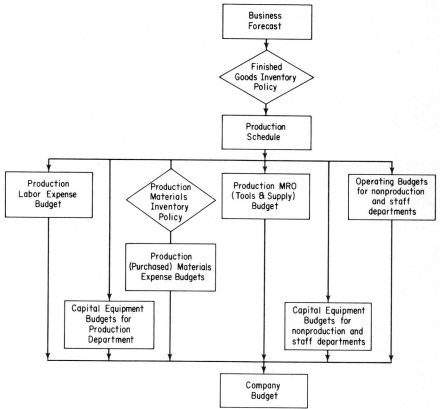

Fig. 25-2   The elements in budgeting. *(Adapted in part from Lee and Dobler,* Purchasing and Materials Management, *McGraw-Hill Book Company, New York, 1977.)*

Purchased Materials Budget in Manufacturing Organizations

Forecasting is an important part of budgeting and is the starting point for establishing the quantities, time, and costs of each raw material and component that will be needed to meet the sales and production forecasts for the year ahead. Generally, forecasting is done 3 months ahead of the year being predicted, but in organizations which have traditionally long delivery on materials or components, the forecasting can be done even earlier. However, budgeting is much more than just forecasting, since a plan is established to accomplish the desired results.

The actual budgeting of purchased materials, components, and raw materials follows the forecasting process and is a planned approach for carrying out the purchasing function. Budgeting makes it possible to gain better control over expenditures for materials and supplies and to correlate these purchases to requirements from the production floor. A good purchased materials budget will help the production control activity in an organization to limit the occurrences of overstocking or running out of items. Helping to minimize total commitment to inventories is particularly important when the cost of money is high and the cost to carry the inventory is also high. Reducing parts shortages can also be critical, especially to an organization with high labor rates and overheads which will continue to be absorbed in part or in full if production lines are forced to shut down.

High inventory turnover is desirable, and budgeting helps accomplish this by keeping the inventory of various material items compatible with the amounts of other items. When some items are either overstocked or slow-moving, there are appreciable hidden losses caused by spoilage and obsolescence.

Intelligent budgeting of purchased materials and supplies helps set a plan of usage that acts as a performance check. Production management has predicted the material usage and can monitor its performance and actual usage against this prediction. This benchmark is a means of spotting wastefulness in the use of the materials when the original prediction is exceeded. It is equally effective in spotting a saving of materials and supplies which makes it possible to identify and further these cost reduction methods.

Finally, the cash flow condition is of utmost importance. The budgeting of purchased materials, including the projection of usage into the future, makes it possible to strengthen the financial side of the organization by being able to anticipate any need for special funding and financing. Although the dollar amounts of money being spent per purchase are not individually as great as the cost of a single piece of capital equipment, collectively they often add up to even greater amounts. Since such expenditures are regular and recurring, they become a base load on the financing of the organization.

Purchased material budgeting comes from the production schedule, which depends on the individual approach of the organization toward its manufacturing for its marketing. The orders already received, the prediction of the sales for a given period, the amount of finished product to be inventoried, plus any long-range predictions, provide the basic data for this budgeting.

A brief description of a typical approach to purchased materials budgeting as shown in part in Fig. 25-2 starts with the business forecast as input to the finished goods inventory policy. This dictates the production or manufacturing schedule, and from this there are often four subbudgets prepared to arrive at the Purchased Materials Expense Budget: (1) Materials Budget, (2) Purchases Budget, (3) Materials Inventory Budget, and (4) Materials to Be Used Cost Budget (Estimate).

Materials Budget   The quantities of each raw material required for production are predicted for each component used in the product, and the date or time when delivery is required and the department responsible for the manufacturing operation are specified. This materials budget contains the combined thinking of sales, production, and management, all working through the production materials inventory policy.

Purchases Budget   The purchases budget is a prediction of quantities of each raw material and component required to meet the materials budget forecast. It also predicts by dates required the cost of each raw material and component. Besides the forecast of the materials budget, it is also necessary to have:

1. An organization policy relating to raw material and component inventory level

2. Determination of the number of units of each type of raw material to be purchased

3. Estimate of the unit cost of each type of material purchased

In the raw material and component inventory policy considerations are given for: (1) maximum and minimum of each item, and (2) turnover ratio or designated month's supply.

Materials Inventory Budget   This is the difference between the materials budget (the need) and the purchases budget (the plan to meet the need). If raw materials requirements are seasonal, purchases parallel usage; or purchases can be planned for at a uniform rate, and the inventory absorbs the peaks of need. Within the inventory budget consideration should be given to:

Timing and quantities of the specific needs of the shops
Economics of quantity discounts
Raw material and components available
Perishability of raw materials
Storage facilities available
Capital requirements to finance the inventory contemplated
Cost of storage
Forecastable changes in the prices of raw materials
Protection desired against material shortages
Risks involved in contemplated inventory

Turnover ratios, maximum-minimum limits, and weeks' or months' supplies of each type of raw material are common terms used in making a standard inventory level that results in the materials inventory budget.

Materials to Be Used Cost Budget   This is significant in manufacturing situations where cost of raw materials and cost of components purchased outside are a major part of the finished product cost. These estimated material costs are tightly bound to the pricing of the product, the financing policies, and cost control. This can only be estimated, since it is a prediction of the future pricing of the raw materials, to which the past pricing history is only an assist. Therefore, top management insists that purchasing supply expected trends in raw material costs that they can predict from their studies of the general economic conditions, specific market trends, unusual demands for commodities, industry production prospects, and current market conditions. This cost estimating includes all the costs of acquiring and delivering the goods at the plants.

Capital Equipment Budgeting

Capital expansion and its procurement vary considerably between industries and between different types of organizations. In some the occasion for any capital plant expansion is infrequent. In these cases the usual manner in which increased production is accomplished is through the innovation and effectiveness of the entire organization's management. Manufacturing provides continuing improvements in its operation with insignificant outlays of capital. Purchasing is continually finding better ways to procure and make reductions through resourcing, making revisions in its specifications, and gaining all the benefits possible from standardization. Even in these situations there can be some new jigs, fixtures, conveyors, and increased-production devices planned and procured.

There are organizations with a fairly steady and secure market that do not need to expand but which find it mandatory to upgrade equipment and processes continually so as to continue or to increase their profit margin. Other organizations have a continuing increase of productive capacity as part of their very existence. The capital or plant expansion planned and budgeted often accounts for up to 20 times as much as the operating or expense budget of the organization. When budgeting for large dollar expenditures, purchasing can perform an important function in helping the planners determine the best schedule to be used to meet the demands for the new equipment and at the same time to expand capital facilities in the most favorable economic period. Escalation that will occur on multiyear lead-time items is best predicted by purchasing and is a significant consideration in the time-frame consideration of the expansion. The cost of money, the cost of construction labor and materials, and the escalation on the major equipment all are reconciled into the scheduling and the budgeting.

Long-lead-time items occasionally require progress payment consideration in budgeting. In these instances, purchasing should predict for the financial side of the organization the amounts and times of the various progress payments required for the duration of the transaction for each undelivered piece of equipment and for the anticipated major commitments.

Maintenance, Repair, and Operating Supplies (MRO) Planning

The planning and forecasting of the numerous items of materials and supplies that have to be inventoried, purchased, and stocked for support of the manufacturing and productive plant or the operating side of the organization are predicated, in part, upon their plans for output. This material consists of more than one type of stock. For example, there can be (1) those items that are standardized, firmly specified, and numbered but which are not inventoried or kept in stock, (2) those items that are standardized and specified and kept in the organization stock, and (3) those that are handled on a special basis where the suppliers furnish a customized stocking service. The prediction of each quantity falling into the *stock* group is usually based on past-usage history plus a safety level and a future use or requirement estimate. For instance, if a large furnace, a multi-operation metal-machining piece of equipment, a steam generator, or a turbine generator is to be overhauled at a specific date in the coming year, purchasing should help predict the lead time required for ordering the materials required in the overhaul. It is necessary to plan for both scheduling the order and predicting the cash on hand that will be needed as a result of placing the order. While performing such budgeting is not a direct responsibility of purchasing, purchasing as the agent can be instrumental in forecasting market considerations that would affect lead-time requirements and stock levels. Purchasing can be most helpful in analyzing the issue of in-house stocking versus stockless contracts with local suppliers and other special stocking considerations. While performing this service for other departments, purchasing should be able to predict the future work load that will have to be supported by its own activities. An accumulation of data from all the divisions it is assisting can provide purchasing with logistics for its own budgeting. This may dictate additional personnel needs or switching of personnel within the department, as discussed later under Personnel Planning—Human Resource Accounting later in this section. It could indicate a need to change to different types of contracts.

Inventory and Economical Ordering Quantities of MRO   Section 12 discusses inventory management in detail; but since this has importance in budgeting, it is also discussed here, although only sufficiently to bring this subject into perspective for the budgeting consideration (see Fig. 25-3).

Those responsible for establishing the level of inventory and the most economical ordering quantity of the various MRO items contribute significantly to the budgeting. In some concerns this function is performed by purchasing. It can evolve in other segments, such as the stores department or materials control department, or as an arm of the materials management organization. Whether it is a direct purchasing responsibility or not, purchasing is in an excellent position. A *lead-time sheet* (see Fig. 25-4) is prepared by purchasing from information furnished by the buyers of the individual items and commodities within the MRO program of the company. Lead time, as shown in this listing, usually includes the complete time elapsed from the moment the requisitioner forwards the requisition to purchasing, through all operations of buying or manufacturing and furnishing of the item and its delivery to the company. This listing can be furnished by purchasing once a year at the time of the company's budgeting or at intervals during the year to assist in short-range delivery planning and budgeting functions.

In preparing the lead-time listing, the buyers must come to grips with the frequent drastic contradiction that exists between the delivery time necessary for a *standard* version of the item and that for a *special*, nonindustry standard of the same item. For these items it is necessary to carry differing lead times—notice the item Paints in Fig. 25-4.

Pipeline Effect on MRO Ordering   In anticipating ordering quantities, there are circumstances when consideration must be given to what is known as the *pipeline effect*, which is the quantity of material used up over the period of time that is

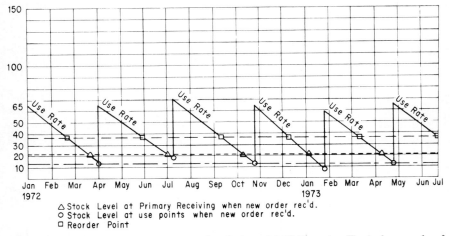

Ordering and Budgeting Facts
Annual usage of item : 208, or 4 per week
Economic Ordering Interval : 4 times per year
Economic Ordering Quantity : 52
To allow for 2 weeks Pipe Line Effect : 8
To allow for 1 month Lead Time Effect : 17
To build up Safety Stock (Initially) : 13

△ Stock Level at Primary Receiving when new order rec'd.
○ Stock Level at use points when new order rec'd.
□ Reorder Point

Fig. 25-3   Budget of inventorying and ordering of MRO stocks. Typical example of how *lead time* and *pipeline* effects couple with *use* to establish a stock budget.

required for the material to be distributed to the actual using address or location. The delivery time from supplier to the organization's principal receiving location is usually included in the lead-time figure. The pipeline effect is the additional time required to get the items to the using point. This can be the time used in the organization's own transport system or that used by a second common carrier. In the case of organizations that have works in many parts of the United States or even the world, the pipeline effect on quantity of materials involved in the furnishing of supplies to the point of use is of significant magnitude that it has to be included when determining the normal reorder date. Those having such widespread delivery points add to the lead time (shown in Fig. 25-4) to cover the pipeline effect to the various points of usage. This time is translated into the quantity of the item that would be used during that period at the usage rate of the item. In the example of Fig. 25-4 this pipeline effect is 2 weeks, which translates into a

PURCHASING DEPARTMENT RECOMMENDED LEAD TIME
Arranged by Stock Class and Lead-time Group

"Lead time" is the total number of weeks required from the origination of the requisition to the receipt of the material. It includes one week of processing time before the requisition is received in purchasing.

Class No.	Buying Div.*	CASP Item	Buyer		Recommended Lead Time (Weeks)			
					12/72	3/73	6/73	9/73
10	M		Davies	Cement	3			
10	M		Davies	Masonry and concrete	3			
10	M		Davies	Masonry (carload)	3			
10	M		Davies	Sewer	3			
10	M		Davies	Tile, glazed	12			
11	M		Devlin	Stone, cut and artificial	4			
13	M		Bohl	Lumber (truck)	3			
13	M		Bohl	Yellow pine	3			
13	M		Bohl	Yellow pine, #1 common creosoted	8			
13	M		Bohl	Fir	3			
13	M		Bohl	Hardwoods (except ash)	3			
13	M		Bohl	Hardwoods, creosoted	10			
13	M		Bohl	Lumber (carloads)	8			
13	M		Bohl	Millwork	4			
14	M		Shannon	Guy wire guards	6			
14	M		Shannon	Poles, Western red cedar—55' and smaller	10			12
				60' through 75'	20			
				80' and up	12			
14	M		Shannon	Poles, Southern yellow pine (dist. sizes)	10			12
14	M		Shannon	Poles, Southern yellow pine (dist. sizes), painted			12	
14	M	X	Shannon	Crossarms (advance notice requirements)	10			
16	M		Manuel	Paints, oil (vendor stock)	4†			
16	M		Manuel	Paints, oil (special)	8			
22	E		Devlin	Springs	9			
35	E		Devlin	Building heater equipment	12			

Fig. 25-4 Estimate of time required for purchasing to process and obtain delivery of an item is the *lead time*; it can best be predicted by purchasing.

quantity of 8 of the item. Therefore, if the normal reorder date based on lead time is 1 month before delivery date, the pipeline effect would push the date ahead by 2 weeks, or the result of 2 weeks' pipeline effect. Payment for the shipments is often made at the time of the end of the lead time, which is the date of receiving at the principal receiving point. This may be prior to receipt at the point of usage by as much as the pipeline effect.

Safety Margin Effect on MRO Stocks   A safety margin of stock running-gear spare parts and similar critical items may have to be maintained to safeguard the dependability of the organization's service and/or the continuity of its manufacturing schedule. This safety margin varies according to certain factors—the number of machines using the same part of its exposure index, level of consequence if the machine is out of service, dependability of vendor as to service and quality of product, and availability of alternate sources for the same type of item. Costs for carrying safety stocks have to be weighed in view of the company's policies on customer service, its competitive position in the marketplace, and costs incurred with production stoppages due to outages of stock of an MRO item. Purchasing plays a vital role in furnishing realistic information to the groups setting the levels of safety stocks; even more important, the more nearly purchasing can have the item coming in the door the moment the need arises, the lower the safety level can be. These stocks do have an effect on the inventory level of a company, which in turn affects the return on investment (ROI).

Variance Prediction

Many aspects of the company's operation require a prediction of just what the variance in cost of goods and services will be for the coming year. Purchasing, because of its market, cost, and price trend orientation, is the logical source for such information. The majority of purchasing departments are organized by commodity groupings. Maintaining records by commodity as well as by vendor establishes a base of information that other departments can readily utilize. Cost accounting, in establishing new standards, manufacturing and engineering in estimating, and estimators in working up costs for quotations, can use these commodity groups as a valuable source of information. Purchasing should identify the major cost reduction projects on which they are working and forecast to the interested departments the lower prices that may be realized as well as any significant increases for the coming period.

PURCHASING DEPARTMENT BUDGET

Budgeting for the purchasing department organization that operates on a budget system takes on many of the same dimensions as the organization's total budget system. In some large corporations this becomes a very sophisticated and extensive operation because it has to fit into the involved cost accounting and bookkeeping system of the organization. In some organizations there is no formal budgeting. Purchasing budgeting in this section is broken down into the two broad categories—budgeting within large organizations and budgeting within small organizations.

Purchasing Budgets in Large Organizations

The dictates of yearly and long-range budgeting within large organizations are so individual and extensive that it is not appropriate in this discussion to pick any one system to describe in detail. Large corporations usually publish their own budgeting manual to be used by all departments in the organization at the time of their budgeting. This discussion will be limited to the elements of purchasing budgeting within any large organization that might be useful as an adjunct to or refinement of the organization-wide budgeting demands.

Lowest-Echelon Budget Responsibility   Purchasing management should be very desirous of assigning budget responsibility at the lowest echelon in its organization consistent with responsible management. If each segment of purchasing is under the direction of a supervisor categorized in the organization as such, this could be the unit of budgeting. Each of these units would then report their budgets to the director, manager, or vice-president of purchases, who would use these to make up the total purchasing budget. A typical division of purchasing budgeting responsibility is:

Production materials buying
Product component buying
MRO buying
Capital equipment buying
Services buying
Purchasing research
Inspection division
Standards division
Purchasing office services
Deliveries coordination
Traffic

These divisions will vary within organizations, and in smaller firms there may be only one or two divisions; but the significant point is placing budgeting responsibility at the lowest echelon possible. Good managing and the motivating of human behavior and performance against projected objectives create a healthy cost responsibility climate.

The budget accounting system used may assign an area code, work order, or responsibility order number to the vice president or administrative head to whom purchasing reports. Within this code number is a series of numbers which can be assigned to purchasing as differentiated from the other areas of the officer's responsibilities. Finally, within the purchasing code number, whether required for the organization's accounting budgeting system or not, there can be assigned a series of subnumbers to this code. One of these can be assigned to each of the individual divisions mentioned previously. This further refinement into low-echelon budgeting within purchasing is best administered when it is part of the corporate accounting budgeting so the monthly reports of actual expenses can go to each purchasing supervisor. If the purchasing subdivision is only an adjunct to the company system, purchasing has to administer within its own organization and come up with its own monitoring or reporting of actual expenses to groups within the department.

Personnel Planning—Human Resource Accounting Work force levels for purchasing should be forecast and planned along with the other facets of budgeting. These levels should be considered for both the short range (within the next 12 months) and the long range (within the next 5 to 10 years). Salaries comprise by far the largest item of expense in most purchasing budgets, so careful planning of personnel is essential. In planning personnel needs, consideration should be given to any additional activities that purchasing may be undertaking. If these new activities or programs require skills not currently available in purchasing, steps should be taken to train and develop existing personnel to meet the timetables and skill levels that are required. Training of one's own personnel in order that they may be promoted as openings occur will materially assist in keeping morale up and employee turnover low, thereby increasing the effectiveness of purchasing. To train and assimilate a well-educated and qualified individual into a purchasing department takes from 12 to 18 months, so training must be planned and budgeted.

Consideration should be given to known coming personnel replacements resulting from retirements and other losses, by year for the next five years. In those industries where the materials management concept exists, planning should include a cooperative exchange of purchasing's most promising personnel with their counterparts in the related functional areas on a job rotation basis. This will give them greater insight into the role purchasing plays in the overall organization structure. The same consideration should be given by those organizations that may be other than industrial. Job rotation in related areas is essential for the development of future supervisors and managers. This type of planning gives a broader base from which to draw when unexpected replacements are required. A program for development should be planned, approvals obtained as required, and the plan executed for each employee in purchasing. This includes clerical as well as management personnel. Moneys should be included in the expense budget to cover the costs of carrying out these programs. This type of activity is readily justified by those firms that maintain a record of personnel turnover. All management is beginning to utilize the concept of human resource accounting, and some are contemplating capital budgeting. This includes the cost of solicitation at colleges and hiring, training, and assimilation of personnel into the organization. While purchasing is not called upon to perform any of this accounting, their personnel have to be budgeted into the organization's human resources budgeting. Purchasing does not normally have as high a turnover as do some of the other functions, yet there is sufficient cost involved to make it imperative to measure the cost and install the necessary policies and procedures in order to keep the rate minimal.

Capital Expansion versus Operating Purchasing Budgeting   Organizations having an appreciable segment of their purchasing activity measured in money spent for and going into capital expansion should segregate their prediction of department costs into an *operating* percentage of their budget and a *capital expansion* segment. The corporation's earnings per share, profit before taxes, and return on investment (ROI) are of great interest to management, particularly during periods of financing for expansion and need to be based on as realistic a segregation of departmental cost into these two cost segments as possible. An organization spending $200 million a year and having a purchasing department budget of $600,000 may have only 40 percent of its purchasing budget spent on the company's procurement for its own operations. The balance is for capital expansion. This gives an entirely different set of figures to be used in the company's financial reporting from those of a company whose entire purchasing budget is spent on operating procurement. In the latter instance, most likely all procurement for capital expansion is done by outside sources as part of a total *turnkey* project where engineering, designing, procuring, and constructing are done by an architect-engineer-construction contractor or a similar outside specialist.

Monthly Monitoring of the Budget   Each segment of the organization, which includes the reporting divisions of the purchasing department, uses its work order and account number for all charges incurred. This includes those charges, for the regular payroll of its employees, of all business-oriented expenses, such as travel, meals charged in the lunchroom, photographs for suppliers, use of pool cars, stenographic help, and computer time. As these charges go into the accounting system, they tally against the individual purchasing department division's budget. These are totaled and compared with its predicted expenditures and submitted to the supervisor of each division within purchasing (see Fig. 25-5). This monitoring and reporting procedure permits supervisors to compare their actual expenditures against their budgets. They can then make appropriate changes within their divisions, if necessary (Fig. 25-6).

Budget Variance Reports   At the end of the first, second, and third quarters, a variance report is desirable as a means of forcing the individual budgeting unit to account for any appreciable variance from its original budget. This permits an adjustment of the budget for the balance of the year, along with an explanation of the variance so purchasing management can concur or remedy the cause of change; thus the organization will be aware of the change and can determine the overall effect of the accumulated changes from all the departments. The occasion for use of such variance reports is usually only when items of the budget have varied, within the particular quarter, more than 5 percent, or some dollar limit such as $250, from those originally budgeted.

Purchasing Department Budgeting in Small Businesses

Budgeting in small-business activities, either manufacturing or nonmanufacturing concerns, municipalities, institutions, and nonprofit organizations may very reasonably be viewed differently by each of these organizations. Some of them feel that budgeting is not a major contributor to their success in managing their activity. However, most studies that have been made of budgeting in these smaller annual dollar endeavors revealed that budgeting is important. Wholesale and retail merchandising concerns as a rule are smaller on the average than manufac-

EXPENSE ACCOUNT STATEMENT MONTH OF			WORK ORDER				JOB		31
SEPTEMBER 1973			821 AB 619						
DESCRIPTION		REFERENCE	DETAILED CHARGES			TOTAL CHARGES			
BALANCE FORWARD		LABOR				57	563	59	
LABOR	825 HR	101 RE10	6	622	78				
		CURRENT-MO				6	622	78	
		TO-DATE				64	186	37	
BALANCE FORWARD		INVOICE					922	40	
COMPANY CASHIER		110 14137							
WILSON LUNCHEON DISCUSS POLE SECTION PROBLEM		110 14137		5	58				
SERV OFF SUPPLY	100066	110 22438		31	56				
		CURRENT-MO					37	14	
		TO-DATE					959	54	
BALANCE FORWARD		J/ENTRY				1	257	36	
REDISTRIBUTION OF COPYING SERVICE COSTS		40 040		44	30				
PHOTOGRAPHIC SERVICES DISTRIBUTED		70 070		22	95				
GRAPHIC ARTS SERVICES	T4455	162 162		8	50				
		CURRENT-MO					75	75	
		TO-DATE				1	333	11	
BALANCE FORWARD		AUTO					567	78	
EMPLOYE CASUAL DRIVING EXP DEPT RE10	000408	48 048		50	59				
		CURRENT-MO					50	59	
		TO-DATE					618	37	
BALANCE FORWARD		F/LABOR					66	17	
FOREIGN LABOR	2 HR	101 RF34		13	45				
		CURRENT-MO					13	45	
		TO-DATE					79	62	
		TOTAL	6	799	71	67	177	01	

ADDRESS INQUIRIES TO GENERAL ACCOUNTING - EXPENSE ACCOUNTING GROUP

Fig. 25-5   Expense account statement. A monthly report of expenses charged against the Labor, Invoice, Journal Entry, Auto, and Foreign Labor accounts permits each group of the company to audit its activity.

turing concerns. However, even in these instances there is no evidence that formal budgeting is any less needed than for small manufacturing concerns. Studies indicate that in the case of nonprofit organizations there is even more budgeting being done than by small manufacturers. The owner-managers or heads of many small concerns that report not having budgets are actually going through the budgeting process on the back of an envelope or scrap paper. Their rationale and behavior are exactly the same as those of a formal budgeting program. The small concerns showing a substantial profit without a formal budget do exist in a fairly significant number, but this does not discredit budgeting in any sense, as there are a significant number of firms of this kind that fail each year because of some management deficiencies.

Among small manufacturers, budgeting within the manufacturing company, whether larger or smaller, performs best when it is based on establishing objectives or goals for the entire company or organization. These goals can be projected earnings per share of outstanding stock, if a stock organization, or returns on investment (ROI), ratio profit margin, or any similar type or unit of corporate performance measurement. Once the organization has established this goal or set of goals, these can be broken down into the goals for the various segments or work groups.

Purchasing plays a vital role in expending practically all moneys and is obligated to evaluate and budget its own cost to operate and to meet the company goals through savings resulting from creative buying. Much of the same budgeting

DEPARTMENTAL BUDGET AND EXPENSE COMPARISON

DEPT. PURCHASING   PURCHASE RESEARCH SUP.   RESPONSIBILITY 619   MONTH OF SEP 73   32

ACCOUNT DESCRIPTION	ACCOUNT NO.	CURRENT MONTH				YEAR TO DATE			
		BUDGET	EXPENSE	VARIATION FROM BUDGET (UNDER-) $	%	BUDGET	EXPENSE	VARIATION FROM BUDGET (UNDER-) $	%
SALARIES SUPPLIES ETC	821 AB								
Responsibility Labor		5 915	6 622	707		64 486	64 186	300-	
Invoices		125	37	88-		1 125	959	166-	
Miscellaneous		150	75	75-		1 350	1 333	17-	
Auto (Travel)		33	50	17		297	618	321	
Overhead		16		16-		144		144-	
Foreign Labor		66	13	53-		594	79	515-	
TOTAL		6 305	6 799	494	8	67 996	67 177	819-	1-
TOTAL		6 305	6 799	494	8	67 996	67 177	819-	1-

Fig. 25-6 Departmental budget and expense comparison. A monthly report of expenses incurred helps the individual groups to monitor their expenses against their budgets.

for purchased materials budgets applies in the case of small manufacturers. Usually the smaller manufacturer buys more components ready to be assembled with the manufactured items. Because of this, purchasing and the sales and production groups budget these purchases as to schedule, inventory levels, and cost estimates. Where the operation of the manufacturer is essentially an assembly activity, the budgeted value of the items being bought by purchasing becomes a dominant factor in the cost of the product, the pricing policy, and the profit level or ROI.

Furthermore, purchasing can make a major contribution to the introduction of a new product. This role can be most dynamic and significant and can be readily accomplished in a small or medium-sized organization. This can be similar to the function performed by the purchasing research group in the automotive industry, where it is subdivided into specialty or commodity groups that specialize in analyzing and costing all segments of their assigned area of the product. The group provides a running source of cost information on the new or redesigned product. For instance, when the new-model car is in its most embryonic stage, each of the research groups evaluates its segment of that car to project for management the cost of the new model. From that moment on, for the next 3 years, while the car is becoming more and more refined, defined, and realistic, they keep upgrading and updating their study of the physical developments of their specific segment of the car and establishing the cost of the segment. By the time each of the many segments is to be purchased, there is a 3-year-old developmental or historical cost figure for each segment. This is ready for use by buyers and all other departments of the company in budgeting and setting the price of the new car.

This important contribution to meeting price goals and budgets can be duplicated in small-business purchasing departments. They can become the vital source of a running cost analysis of important procured segments of the business. Pricing these materials, pieces of equipment, and services provides a vital tool and step toward the organization's forecasting and budgeting.

The second role purchasing can play in small-business budgeting is the setting of purchasing's goal to help meet the organization's goal for the coming year and the years ahead. An example of this would be best shown by taking a hypothetical organization's return on investment picture and then the setting of a goal for improving this through purchasing's improved performance:

1. Current-year sales . . . . $3 million
2. Total assets . . . . $1 million
3. Profit on sales after payment of expenses, interest, and income taxes 3%
4. Portion of sales income spent on purchasing for all goods and services 52%
5. Portion of sales for wages, taxes, debt interest, depreciation, and other costs 41%

From these figures it can be seen that the total cost of operations is 93 percent of each dollar taken in and that profit after taxes is $90,000. This gives a return on investment as follows:

$$\text{ROI} = \frac{\text{profit}}{\text{assets}} = \frac{\$90,000}{\$1,000,000} = 9\%$$

If management sets a goal of improving the return on investment to 11 percent for the ensuing year and wishes everyone in the organization to budget accordingly, there are two principal ways this can be accomplished, and it is herein assumed that both of these become goals. The sales or marketing side of the organization agrees to increase the return on investment by 1 percent by increasing sales. Purchasing agrees to increase return on investment by 1 percent also via the savings they can make in the purchasing of the goods and services. These savings have to be savings over and above the normal good purchasing techniques of low-bid awarding, cheaper-by-the-dozen advantage, and astute negotiations. They should be limited to new, unusual, and not normally experienced savings from value analysis, exceptionally careful sourcing, most advantageous terms of payment and conditions, consolidation of purchases into system contracting, or other innovated actions.

To accomplish this improvement of ROI by 2 percent means an increase of profits of $20,000 (profit increase ÷ 1,000,000 = 0.02). For sales to contribute its $10,000 of increased profit means:

$$0.03 \times \text{increased sales} = \$10,000$$
$$\text{Increased sales} = \$333,333, \text{ or } 11.1\%$$

For purchasing to contribute its $10,000 of increased profit means: 0.52 × new sales, or 52 × $3,333,333 = $1,733,333 (dollars to be spent) — $10,000 ÷ $1,733,333 = 0.0058, or only 0.58 percent savings in dollars spent. If purchasing saved 1 percent of new-expenditure dollars, the ROI would go from 10 percent to 11.73 percent (0.01 × 1,733,333 = $17,333 to be added to profit).

$$\text{New ROI} = (90,000 + 10,000 + 17,333) \div \$1,000,000 = 11.73\%$$

This savings goal can then be broken down and parceled out to the various segments of purchasing to use as part of their goal. Thus the corporate goal is adopted down the line, and the savings goals are established in the lowest sections and fed back to management in the form of a predicted savings by budgeting segments.

Purchasing Department Operating Budget   The A & Z Manufacturing Company is a small, one-plant operation employing about 400 people. Its purchasing department consists of the purchasing director, one buyer, and two office assistants. One of the office assistants, the stenographer-clerk, is used for routine expediting and follow-up in addition to stenographic duties. The other office assistant is an order typist and file clerk. The purchasing director is also responsible for property administration and maintenance and company-chartered air service. There are a janitor and a plant maintenance engineer involved in these functions.

The basic budget factors that will have to be taken into consideration are:

1. Payroll
2. Expendable materials and supplies
3. Miscellaneous expenses
4. Rentals

Under *payroll* one will have such considerations as the salary of each of the four persons concerned as of January 1 of the budget year (for this example, assume a calendar year as a budget year) and any contemplated increases in salaries of any of these persons during the coming year. These salary increases will include such things as normal merit increases, cost of living increases, and annual improvement factors. The entries for payroll costs are shown in the example in Fig. 25-7. Entries for the purchasing director and the buyer are made on a monthly basis, since they are paid monthly. However, the stenographer-clerk, typist, janitor, and maintenance engineer are paid weekly; therefore certain months with 5 weeks in them will have a greater amount budgeted than the other months. Also, since wage increases and other factors affecting pay may take place on a date other than the first of the month, they will have to be computed in parts and will appear in the month in which they took effect. In the example, the purchasing director got a pay increase in July amounting to $100 a month and the buyer got a pay increase in June amounting to $75 a month. The stenographer-clerk got a pay increase in March and another one in August, as well as the annual improvement factor increase that was granted to all hourly workers on July 1 and amounted to $0.08 an hour. The typist, janitor, and maintenance engineer also

ITEM	Jan.	Feb.	(5 wk) Mar.	Apr.	May	(5 wk) Jun.	Jul.	Aug.	(5 wk) Sep.	Oct.	Nov.	(5 wk) Dec.	Code	Total
SALARIES														
Purchasing Director	1,156	1,156	1,445	1,156	1,156	1,445	1,156	1,156	1,445	1,156	1,156	1,445	M	15,028
Buyer	924	924	1,155	924	924	1,155	924	924	1,155	924	924	1,155	M	12,012
Steno-clerk	616	616	770	616	616	770	616	616	770	616	616	770	W	8,008
Typist	464	464	580	464	464	580	464	464	580	464	464	580	W	6,032
Janitor	692	692	865	692	692	865	692	692	865	692	692	865	W	8,996
Maintenance Engr.	768	768	960	768	768	960	768	768	960	768	768	960	W	9,984
														60,060
SUPPLIES														
Purchasing Forms					150							150	C	300
Stationery	40	40	50	40	40	50	40	40	50	40	40	50	W	520
Building Cleaning	35	35	55	35	35	55	35	35	55	35	35	55	W	510
Plant Maintenance	80	80	100	80	80	100	80	80	100	80	80	100	W	1,040
Whse. Equipment	24	24	30	24	24	30	24	24	30	24	24	30	W	312
														2,412
EXPENSES														
Travel													M	500
Tel. and Tel.													M	900
Postage													M	1,000
Periodicals													M	250
Market Services													M	750
Entertainment and Meals													M	1,000
Outside help-vacations							150	150					W	300
														4,700
RENTALS														
Vendor Machines	10	10	13	10	10	13	10	10	13	10	10	13	W	132
Aircraft Services	300	300	375	300	300	375	300	300	375	300	300	375	W	4,000
Elect. Acct. Machines	48	48	60	48	48	60	48	48	60	48	48	60	W	684
														4,816

A & Z MANUFACTURING COMPANY

Purchasing and Services Department 19___Budget Request

Date October 31, 19

Code: C = by Cycle
       M = by Month
       W = by Weeks

Prepared by Purchasing Director

GRAND TOTAL $71,988

Fig. 25-7 Purchasing and services department operating budget. Purchasing departments of small organizations can do their personnel budgeting on a single sheet.

received two small increases during the year, one on March 1 and one on August 1, as well as the July 1 improvement factor of $0.08 an hour. Replacement typing help for relief for the typist and stenographer-clerk during their summer vacations is shown as an expense item for the months of the vacation.

It is important to note that the purchasing director is able to budget fairly accurately what his payroll costs are going to be. In a small company, it is very desirable to make pay increases for such a compact department effective on the same date. This will simplify the preparation of the budget and also the administration of it. The example in Fig. 25-7 is used, however, to show that even if all pay increases for the people in the department do not coincide or do not fall on the same date, it is still not any great chore to prepare the budget estimate.

The next item the purchasing director is going to consider is the budget for expendable materials and supplies required in the operation of the department, as listed in Fig. 25-7. These include such things as stationery, the various requisitions and purchase forms charged against the purchasing department, typewriter ribbons, pencils, and any other expendable items required for the operation of the department. Usually this information is best obtained by looking at past records. Certainly from old invoice records the cost of the various forms used in the purchasing department can be made available. If petty cash funds are used to obtain such things as typewriter ribbons, pencils, and similar items, the purchasing director should be able to find out from the office assistants approximately how much petty cash is allocated for this purpose each year. If these miscellaneous stationery items are drawn on a memo receipt from some central stores facilities such as a stationery storeroom, perhaps these old records will be available to the purchasing director. He will then have some idea of the past history of these expenditures. In any event, when preparing a budget for the first time, a well-thought-out estimate may be accurate enough, since these items are seldom of very great significance in the total budget.

After the installation of a budget system, the purchasing officer will find that he is forced into being more concerned with the amount of money he spends for each of the various phases of his operations and will initiate a system that will enable him to give more accurate estimates in succeeding years. Since the amount spent for expendable materials and supplies is not great in any event, it is common practice to take a year's total figure and divide it by 12, putting an equal amount in each month, or by the weeks in the month, as shown in Fig. 25-7. If more precise budgeting is required, the total amount spent for a year can be divided by 52 and again proportioned according to the months with 5 weeks as against those that have only 4. An even further refinement enters into the consideration when it is known that certain months of the year require heavier cash demands than other months, and these months are so specifically budgeted with larger requirements. There may be some particular cyclical trend or a season of variation that should be shown by budgeting in the appropriate month. Also, a special project might be undertaken that will have an unusual effect on certain months. A good example of this is the practice followed by many small companies that close down the whole plant for a period during the summer when all employees take their vacations at the same time. Also, in some companies the month of December may be particularly heavy while the purchasing department is placing annual contracts or blanket orders for the following year. This activity may draw more heavily upon the supply of expendable materials.

The next consideration for the purchasing director in the preparation of the budget is the matter of miscellaneous expenses. These are shown under the heading Expenses in Fig. 25-7. Here the purchasing director lists all the additional operating expenses he will have or anticipates having during the coming year. (Figure 25-8 lists examples of some of those to be considered.) These expenses, as in the case of the materials and supplies, can be distributed evenly by months or distributed according to anticipated monthly variances.

The best source for this type of information is past experience. If the purchasing director is preparing his first budget, he may have to seek sources for this information outside his own department. The accounting department is always a good place to start. However, if he cannot get detailed information on the various items shown under Expenses, he will have to use his best judgment and make an accurate estimate. Here again, the purchasing director will probably keep a closer record of such expenditures during the first and succeeding budget years, since he will recognize the need to have this information for following budgets. This awareness of the need to know is one of the important arguments for budgeting.

Rentals are the next items to be budgeted, and these are done just as the expense items are—distributed either evenly by months or by 4- and 5-week months.

Expendable Materials and Supplies	Miscellaneous Expenses
Rubber stamps	Meals for business purposes
Personal cards	Travel
Stamps and postage	Reimbursement for use of personal automobile
Pens and pencils	Telephone, telegraph, and teletype
Paper and stationery	Professional association dues and incidental expenses
Market reports and surveys	Conventions and conferences
Purchase handbooks	Flowers and bereavement gifts
Desk calendars	Maintenance of office equipment
Ink and pencil leads	Consultant services
Purchasing department forms	Taxi fares (business)
Dictating machine supplies	Entertainment
Carbon paper	Utilities, heat, light, etc.
Magazines and periodicals	Photographs
Book ends	Parking fees
Filing trays	Air travel insurance
	Pool car expenses (company)
	Plant visits

Note: These are suggested items only. Many others may be added where applicable.

Fig. 25-8 Items for consideration in preparing a purchasing department operating budget.

After all the required entries have been made on the budget request sheet, it is possible to see at a glance what the total expenditures of the department are going to be for any one month (by totaling the columns vertically) or for any one activity or item (by totaling horizontally). The purchasing director needs only to total his expenses for a month and compare the result with his budget to see where he stands. In large companies the accounting department may furnish this information by supplying the budgeted departments with monthly expense statements. This practice relieves the individual departments of the necessity of keeping separate record systems.

If the purchasing director exceeds his budget for any given month, he may be asked to explain this situation to the chief financial officer of the company. By the same token, if he does not spend as much as he budgeted, he will be expected to explain. This is the only budget control necessary.

Review and Modification of the Purchasing Department Budget It is very difficult to budget with any great degree of accuracy as far as a year ahead. Changes in the general economic situation, changes in the company's product line, and employment changes are but a few of the factors which can influence the budget. It is probably a good idea for the purchasing head to check sales and manufacturing regularly to determine changes in business that might affect his operations.

If the A & Z Manufacturing Company had expanded its operations to the point where four people could no longer handle the purchasing operation, it might be necessary for the purchasing director to add another employee or two, say, sometime around the middle of the year. In this event he would also have to increase his budget request for the balance of the year. This can be done in either of two ways:

1. The purchasing director can prepare a revised budget request for the 6 months from July 1 through December 31, increasing each of the various items shown on his budget.

2. He can submit a separate budget for the individual or two he adds to his staff, indicating the increased payroll costs and expenses that will result.

This is called a *budget supplement* and can be stapled or clipped to his regular budget request. In succeeding years, of course, these additions would be integrated into his regular budget.

Budgeting of Inventory in Merchandising Concerns   In this discussion of purchasing's budget assistance in small businesses it is important to realize that these small businesses are made up of the nonmanufacturing as well as the manufacturing interests. Purchasing's successes in the profit making actually make more difference in the small nonmanufacturing concern because there the purchased cost of the goods is of greater significance percentagewise than in a manufacturing concern. The spending margin in merchandising concerns is typically very low and the purchasing function particularly critical. Manufacturing organizations make approximately a 6 to 12 percent profit on sales before taxes, whereas merchandising concerns make from 2 to 5 percent profit on sales before taxes.

Budgeting in the merchandising concern takes on a different complexion, and purchasing is so vital a part that a careful discussion of this is warranted. Often a merchandise budget is established as a first step in the budgeting. This can consist of the following items:

Sales
Stocks—inventory: beginning of the month (BOM); end of the month (EOM)
Reductions
Markdowns
Employee discounts
Stock shortages
Purchases
Gross margins
Investment required to have an adequate assortment of items and adequate quantities of each to optimize the stock-sales ratio for maximum turnover and minimum stockouts

In connection with this merchandise budget, the BOM level of stock inventory is an important consideration, as is the EOM inventory position. The assortment of items and the quantities needed of each, as predicted by the manufacturing and production branch of the company, coupled with the relation of stock to sales that will give a maximum turnover and yet maintain enough stock to keep the stock level of each item complete, is the objective of this budgeting.

Stock-sales ratios are measured in either the value of goods at sales price or the cost price, as follows:

$$\text{Sales } \$ = \frac{\text{average inventory at retail } \$}{\text{net sales}}$$

$$\text{At cost } \$ = \frac{\text{average inventory at cost } \$}{\text{cost of sales}}$$

To discuss this more definitely, a typical pipe valve and fitting distributor in a large city makes an interesting example. In their merchandise budget the following considerations of BOM stock would be typical.

	Projected BOM Stock-Sales Ratio Desired	Planned Net Sales (Feb.)	Planned BOM Stock (at Sales $)
Pipe, carbon	3.0	$175,000	$525,000
Pipe, alloy	1.5	75,000	112,500
Valves, steel	2.0	100,000	200,000
Valves, C.I.	1.3	50,000	65,000
Valves, nonferrous	2.5	125,000	312,500
	2.06 (avg)	$525,000	$1,215,000

The next step toward arriving at the purchases that are to be planned by this concern for the establishment of the planned purchases is shown in Fig. 25-9.

These developed planned purchases are expressed in purchases at sales prices,

Planned Purchases (Sales Dollars) =	Planned Net Sales (Feb.) +	Additions for Planned Reduc- tions * +	Planned EOM Stock (BOM of Following Month) −	Planned BOM Stock (Mar.) =	Planned Purchases
Pipe, carbon	$175,000	$10,000	$ 500,000	$ 525,000	$160,000
Pipe, alloy	75,000	5,000	110,000	112,500	77,500
Valves, steel	100,000	10,000	220,000	200,000	130,000
Valves, C.I.	50,000	0	50,000	65,000	35,000
Valves, nonferrous .	125,000	5,000	320,000	312,500	138,000
	$525,000	$30,000	$1,200,000	$1,215,000	$540,500

* Planned reductions are those sales, donations, or marginal activities that do not net the full return and are just a part of doing business.

Fig. 25-9   Planned purchases. A monthly appraisal of what purchases are to be made can be a great assist to the buyer and controller.

which can be converted to planned purchases cost by applying the percentage markup of the individual merchandising concern which is representative of his own operation in the marketplace. This markup on sales price differs with the various categories of items merchandised, and the price multiplier is the numerical complement to the cost multiplier, as follows:

Item	Planned Purchases (at Sales $)	Planned Initial % Profit on Sales Price	Cost Multiplier, %	Purchases (at Cost $)
Pipe, carbon	$160,000	22	78	$124,800
Pipe, alloy	77,500	27	73	56,575
Valves, steel	130,000	18	82	106,600
Valves, C.I.	35,000	19	81	28,350
Valves, nonferrous	138,000	23	77	106,260
	$540,500	20 (avg)	80 (avg)	$122,585

Those planned purchases are a budget of goods to be bought. Most wholesalers and retailers make definitive purchase budgets from this type of computation. Occasionally buyers desire more explicit information as to amounts to buy during each month. When mid-month calculations are feasible, the purchasing and accounting representatives work together to determine the amount of material that the purchasing department is open to buy at any given time during the month. The open-to-buy amount equals the cost of the planned purchases for a given period minus the amount spent at an instant of the period.

Open-to-Buy Computations (Carbon Steel Pipe for February)

Planned sales	$175,000
BOM inventory	525,000
Planned EOM	500,000
Planned reductions for Feb.	10,000
Actual sales to date, Feb. 20	110,000
Actual reductions to date, Feb. 20	6,000
Merchandise rec'd to date (retail $)	100,000
On order for Feb. delivery (not rec'd)	25,000
Planned initial markup, 10% on sales	11.1% on cost

Open-to-buy is computed thus:

Needed stock:

Planned EOM inventory $500,000

Planned sales for remainder of mo.:

Planned sales	$175,000	
Less actual sales	110,00	65,000

Planned reductions for remainder of mo.:

Planned reduction	10,000	
Less actual reduction	6,000	4,000

Total needed stock $569,000

Open-to-Buy Computations (Carbon Steel Pipe for February) (*continued*)

Available stock on hand at present:				
BOM inventory	$525,000			
Goods rec'd to date	100,000	$625,000		
Less:				
Actual reductions to date	$ 6,000			
Actual sales to date	110,000	$116,000	$509,000	
Stock on order for Feb. delivery			25,000	
Total available stock				$534,000
Open-to-buy at sales $				$ 35,000
Cost multiplier (100%–10%)				90%
Open-to-buy at cost (Feb. 20)				$ 31,500

If available stock were in excess of needed stock, the class of material would be *overbought*.

So it is that a most vital contribution can be made by purchasing, performing so as to help others meet their budget.

EDP Budget Analysis and Projection

Budgeting within small governmental and nonprofit organizations often becomes part of the purchasing officer's assignment. Since the various acts of buying are finance- and economics-oriented, it is a natural extension of his disciplines for him

	COMPANY NAME							
	B U D G E T A N A L Y S I S & P R O J E C T I O N							
		OCTOBER 25, 1972						
								P A G E 1
ACCT #	PROPOSED BUDGET 72-73	PROPOSED BUDGET 73-74	INCREASE DECREASE	PER CENT	PROJECTED BUDGET 74-75	PER CENT	PROJECTED BUDGET 75-76	PER CENT	DESCRIPTION OF ITEMS
001	$15,000.00	$15,000.00	$0.00	0 %	$15,000.00	0 %	$15,000.00	0 %	SALARY OF PLANT MANAGER
002	$6,520.00	$6,520.00	$0.00	0 %	$6,911.20	6 %	$7,325.87	6 %	SALARY OF OFFICE MANAGER
003	$6,800.00	$8,400.00	$1,600.00	23 %	$8,400.00	0 %	$8,400.00	0 %	SALARY OF PURCHASING AGENT
004	$5,500.00	$6,000.00	$500.00	9 %	$6,000.00	0 %	$6,000.00	0 %	SALARY OF SALESMAN
005	$10,500.00	$12,000.00	$1,500.00	14 %	$12,000.00	0 %	$12,000.00	0 %	SALARY OF CHAIRMAN OF BOARD
006	$5,500.00	$6,000.00	$500.00	9 %	$6,000.00	0 %	$6,000.00	0 %	SALARY OF TRUCK DRIVER
007	$12,309.32	$9,600.00	$2,709.32-	22-%	$9,600.00	0 %	$9,600.00	0 %	SALARIES OF OFF. PERSONNEL
008	$69,000.00	$106,586.00	$37,586.00	54 %	$112,981.16	6 %	$119,760.02	6 %	SALARIES OF ASSISTS AND CLERK
009	$337,786.00	$442,301.00	$104,515.00	30 %	$468,839.06	6 %	$496,969.40	6 %	SALARIES OF DIRECT LABOR
010	$16,500.00	$38,000.00	$21,500.00	130 %	$38,000.00	0 %	$38,000.00	0 %	NEW EQUIP FOR PLANT
011	$45,000.00	$51,000.00	$6,000.00	13 %	$51,000.00	0 %	$51,000.00	0 %	GENERAL EXPENSE
012	$14,681.17	$15,000.00	$318.83	2 %	$15,300.00	2 %	$15,606.00	2 %	LABOR PENSION FUND
013	$3,500.00	$4,000.00	$500.00	14 %	$4,000.00	0 %	$4,080.00	2 %	EXPENSE FEEDING ANIMALS
014	$424,208.00	$567,602.00	$143,394.00	33 %	$601,658.12	6 %	$637,757.60	6 %	PLANT EXPANSION
015	$7,500.00	$15,182.00	$7,682.00	102 %	$18,218.40	20 %	$21,862.08	20 %	NEW EQUIP FOR EXPANSION
016	$27,940.00	$39,000.00	$11,060.00	39 %	$39,000.00	0 %	$39,000.00	0 %	GEN EXP FOR EXPANSION
017	$54,011.00	$65,448.00	$11,437.00	21 %	$66,756.96	2 %	$68,092.09	2 %	MGMT PENSION FUND
018	$45,113.00	$43,411.00	$1,702.00-	3-%	$43,411.00	0 %	$43,411.00	0 %	SALARIES OF HEALTH COMM & EMP
019	$500.00	$0.00	$500.00-	100-%	$0.00	0 %	$0.00	0 %	NEW EQUIPT HEALTH DEPT
020	$16,000.00	$16,000.00	$0.00	0 %	$16,160.00	1 %	$16,321.60	1 %	GEN EXP HEALTH DEPT
021	$130,500.00	$138,161.00	$7,661.00	5 %	$138,161.00	0 %	$138,161.00	0 %	SALARIES OF EXEMPT EMPLOYEES
022	$15,000.00	$16,000.00	$1,000.00	6 %	$16,000.00	0 %	$16,000.00	0 %	NEW GARBAGE EQUIPMENT
023	$57,000.00	$60,000.00	$3,000.00	5 %	$63,600.00	6 %	$67,416.00	6 %	GEN EXP GARBAGE DEPT
024	$12,000.00	$12,215.00	$215.00	1 %	$12,337.15	1 %	$12,460.52	1 %	JANITOR SAL & SUPPLIES
025	$10,711.93	$15,000.00	$4,288.07	40 %	$16,500.00	10 %	$17,820.00	8 %	REPAIRS TO PLANT BUILDING
027	$12,000.00	$15,000.00	$3,000.00	25 %	$15,000.00	0 %	$15,300.00	2 %	STAT OFFICE SUPPLIES & EQUIP

Fig. 25-10 A printout of a computer program designed to streamline long-range budgeting.

to be made responsible for the budget. Because of this, a simple but effective electronic data processing (EDP) analysis program that is easily programmed and inexpensive to process is described here.

Figure 25-10 is an example of the printout and results of the program. It is instantaneous and easily interpreted. The program input data furnished by the purchasing officer consist of five entries which are referenced thus:

1. Three-digit department or account number
2. A proposed current-year dollar budget figure
3. Projected following year's budget increase or decrease in dollars
4. The next succeeding years' projected increases or decreases in the budget account are reflected by positive or negative percentage figures
5. The department or account number identification

This information is then ready to be keypunched into a standard 80-column computer card. Everything is now ready to be used in the analysis and projection.

The program determines and prints out the budget amounts for the remaining items.

CONCLUSION

Purchasing and budgeting have more in common than might at first be realized. While their respective contributions to the concern's welfare are different, their mutual involvement in the financial and administrative aspects makes their functions interrelated. Purchasing's participation in budgeting is threefold:

1. Assisting the various segments of the organization in building up their individual budgets for costs of product raw material and components or merchandising inventory and costs of maintenance and repair parts and their planned new capital equipment
2. Assisting in the monitoring of the physical goods expenditures against the individual budgets
3. Building up and monitoring purchasing's own operating budget

These three involvements in the concern's budgeting bring purchasing into close relationship with the total budget and its daily control. In fact, purchasing contributes directly to the monitoring by means of its surveillance of the work order or account number used by each requisitioner. By policing for proper requisition data and signatures, the buyer indirectly administers the budget that has been adopted for the expenditure of funds for goods and services. Purchasing is the last threshold before commitment.

In its own department budgeting and monitoring, purchasing ties in with the company's overall budgeting discipline and sets and monitors its own improvement goals.

NOTES: For further information on subjects covered in this section see the list of references in Section 30.

Selection and Development of Purchasing Personnel

EDITOR

Nick M. Alex, C.P.M. *Director, Corporate Purchasing, NCR Corporation, Dayton, Ohio*

ASSOCIATE EDITORS

Tom Lang *General Manager, Corporate Procurement, Control Data Corporation, Minneapolis, Minnesota*

Myron E. Frye *Vice-President, Corporate Purchasing, Maremont Corporation, Chicago, Illinois*

The image of purchasing as a business activity has changed. Executives are making a new assessment of the role that purchasing should play as a functional activity in their organizations. Today, with increasing interest in managing by objectives and in results-oriented management, purchasing is an emerging profession, especially because of its great contribution in many organizations to product cost reductions.

The question of professionalism is an important one and needs to be examined further. In a study conducted by the American Institute for Property and Liability Underwriters, Edwin Overman suggested that there are seven criteria or components that are generally accepted as a measure of whether a vocation such as purchasing is or is not a true profession. He states:

> (1) There is a need to strive for the ideal of altruistic attitude and behavior (consciously seeking and serving the welfare of others, a lack of self-interest). (2) Necessity for a clear carefully conceived code of Personal Ethics. (3) Importance of a highly unified body of Specialized Knowledge. (4) Significance of a broad educational background containing generalized knowledge (multi-disciplinary not just a single specialty). (5) The role of searching examinations for determining mastery of specialized and generalized subject matter (testing of individuals concerning theory and practice). (6) Functions performed by Professional Societies consisting of those who have been admitted to membership in the Profession (a national society with Professional goals and ethical standards with authority to expel members who fail to adhere to the standards). (7) Respect and status in society (won).

DETERMINING REQUIREMENTS

Determining Purchasing's Role in the Company

Purchasing as a professional activity in business today is an accepted fact. More and more functions recognize the unique contribution purchasing can make to gross profit—to cost prevention—by providing early-entry information when it is pertinent for business decision making. Concurrent with this growing recognition is a greater emphasis on securing better-qualified and professional, management-oriented personnel for the purchasing department.

Most practitioners in the field would agree that, because of its achievement, purchasing has emerged as an increasingly important business activity. It is certainly the chief focal point where business meets the outside world, and it coordinates relationships between the users inside the company and the vendors outside.

In many industrial companies, the typical purchasing expenditure represents at least 50 percent of the product cost. While this may be increasingly true in some companies, purchasing's responsibility starts with a request or requirement generated by other user departments, such as manufacturing, engineering, production, planning, or the financial area, before purchasing can discuss an order with a supplier.

Purchasing acts as an important point of control by giving early-entry information to the engineering department at the design stage of a new product. It is an important input source at the critical decision to make or buy. By developing flexibility, purchasing can suggest alternative, less costly sources of supply. When a competitive edge is needed, purchasing meets the challenge by maintaining a balance between price, quality, and delivery. A company interested in optimizing the performance of its purchasing function can do this, but only if it demands that purchasing search for and obtain a unique competitive advantage in concept, in design, and in its product. See Section 1 for the responsibilities of purchasing and for roles purchasing can be expected to perform.

It is important that purchasing's role be clearly stated and communicated to all concerned within a company. This role will vary widely from company to company.

Determining Types of Personnel Needed to Fulfill Purchasing's Assigned Role

Determining types of personnel needed to fulfill purchasing's assigned role is a challenging task. The types of personnel needed for any purchasing department can vary widely depending upon purchasing's predetermined role in the company.

In a large department, personnel will be needed to function in five main areas as follows:

	Example
1. Management	Vice-president, or director or manager of purchasing
2. Buying	Manager, chemical purchases
	Manager, subcontract
	Senior buyers
	Buyers
	Associate buyers
3. Specialized Staff	Manager, planning and analysis
	Systems and procedures analyst
	Purchasing researcher
4. Services	Manager, services
	Data processing
	Typists-stenographers
	Filing
	Expediters
	Order processing
5. Training and Development . . .	Management trainee
	Procurement specialist
	Materials analyst

The question of how much technical knowledge is needed in a purchasing department has been often debated. Some say a buyer need only be a good business manager and know how to use the technical resources of his own company and the vendor's company. Others insist that technical training is needed. It is a question that each company must answer for itself. There is, however, no question that in order to resolve a quality problem with a vendor, to attempt to reduce the cost of an item by value analysis or by specification and tolerance deviations, or to intelligently discuss other ramifications of the part or item purchased, the more the buyer knows about the specifications, where the part is used and how it is made, the better he can perform in all the aspects of the buying function.

Generally, the lower technology involved in the manufacture of the item, the lesser the need for technical know-how of the buyer. Conversely, in high-technology parts or equipment, a buyer with know-how in that technology has a distinct advantage over a person with little or no technical knowledge of the product. That is why companies engaged in chemicals, electronics, construction, or similar operations usually search for persons with purchasing experience in the same fields.

Setting Job Qualifications

General Considerations   Successful executives who have managed to survive the stressful 1970s, and who manage despite government controls, recognize the increased profit contribution made by the purchasing department.

Although marketing activities have been given more publicity in most companies, progressive management recognizes that profit contribution comes from other sectors of the business, such as the purchasing department, where many firms today spend from 40 to 60 percent of their income securing the goods and services needed by that business.

According to a study of the purchasing function at the Bureau of Research of the University of Wisconsin, the hierarchy of purchasing positions is well established, both in books and periodicals and in company job descriptions. There is rather wide agreement as to the specifics of each position, with slight organizational variations per firm. Buyers are graded by a number and adjective system which designates the ability to procure according to the various degrees of complexity of the task and the supervisory duties performed.

Classification Needed   Once the role of the purchasing department has been agreed upon and it is decided what types of personnel are needed to fulfill this role, the task of setting up job qualifications falls naturally in line. If the role is to contribute to product cost reduction, to profitability, to better control of vendor selection and evaluation, all these things will eventually become part of the job specifications.

Many breakdowns have been made of jobs in the purchasing area, as previously indicated. One broad classification encompasses (1) buying responsibilities, which is a major activity of purchasing, (2) administrative or support jobs, and finally (3) management jobs.

Purchasing Salaries   The results of a recent salary poll have shown that the salary picture for purchasing managers is quite wide, ranging from a low of below $20,000 to well over $60,000.[1]

There is a slight correlation between company size, in terms of sales dollars, and department size and the purchasing manager's pay. The more dollars a company brings in, the more the purchasing department has to spend and the more

---

[1]For latest salary information, check publications such as *Purchasing* and *Purchasing World,* which occasionally conduct surveys and report results.

people the purchasing department needs—all adding up to more responsibility for the department head. As in any profession, increased responsibility brings with it increased compensation.

In most companies, competent, long-term employees do far better than untried newcomers in terms of dollars.

Social Significance of Job Titles   People are very much attracted to job titles, which seem to give their holders a sense of social recognition among their peers. If an organization has been accused of being too impersonal, one of the ways in which more respect for the individual can be shown is by giving more thought to the subject of his job title. One company, for example, successfully changed a job title from maintenance man to sanitary engineer. Likewise, in a purchasing area, the job title associate buyer seems to convey more meaning than junior buyer or assistant buyer.

Job Description

Selection of the right man or woman is largely dependent on the scope of the assignment. The assignment, in turn, is decided by the job description—a definition of the duties and responsibilities and a description of the operation required to perform them. The job description may be a detailed account or a mere outline or list, but, in any case, its existence as a ready reference is necessary for orderly selection and training. The job description will usually include:

1. Title
2. To whom the holder of the job reports
3. Purpose of the job
4. Major responsibilities
5. Supervision of personnel
6. Scope of the job
7. Knowledge and skill needed

Typical purchasing job descriptions (sometimes called *job specifications*) are presented in the examples that follow for a manager of purchasing, a buyer, and a management trainee. Others are listed in Section 2.

Example 1

Job: Manager of purchasing

Reports to: Vice-president, administration

Purpose: Responsible for the coordination of all the company's purchases of raw materials, supplies, capital equipment, and contract services. Exceptions: real estate and transportation

Major Responsibilities:

1. Engage, transfer, promote, administer, and terminate purchasing employees. Actively participate in company's Personnel development program.

2. Initiate purchasing policy for the guidance of personnel in their dealings with suppliers, the public, and other departments of the company and its affiliates.

3. Keep constantly apprised of economic or business situations as they affect purchasing policy; make decisions to adequately meet those changing conditions.

4. Recommend changes in purchasing organization, including personnel, to affiliate and division management; exercise functional supervision over field purchasing personnel; give final approval to purchasing procedures.

5. Initiate and administer manpower development.

6. Give final approval to major purchase agreements for those materials, supplies, capital equipment, and contract services within the responsibility of the Purchasing Department.

7. Make final decision on selection of suppliers in the event agreement cannot be reached at the local level.

8. Determine need and timing for national and/or international purchasing business meetings, and conduct such meetings.

9. Visit vendor plants to observe operations and discuss manufacturing practices.

10. Attend and participate in meetings of functional and trade groups, such as the Conference Board and National Association of Purchasing Management.

11. Coordinate effectively with divisions and departments the financing of large-value purchases.

Scope:

1. General supervision over expenditures in excess of $10 million.

2. Indirect responsibility for materials inventories totaling $2 million.

3. Authorize and sign contracts for purchases not to exceed $50,000 and 3 years.

4. Give final approval or disapproval to claims or expenses resulting from actions of employees or suppliers involving faulty materials, mishandling, or breach of contracts.

5. Annual operating expense budget of $75,000 to $200,000—direct supervision of 10 employees; functional guidance to 20 employees in operating units.

Knowledge and Skill Needed:
B.S. or A.B. degree. M.B.A. desirable. C.P.M. preferred. Proven administrative background in manufacturing, finance, or purchasing desirable. Should be perceptive, analytical, with ability to induce cooperation in complex organizational relationships. Knowledge of manufacturing practices, materials, and their use. Understanding of economic and business situations.

Example 2
Job: Buyer
Reports to: Purchasing manager
Purpose: To promote the most effective use of company funds in the acquisition of assigned commodities. Evaluates market conditions and trends. Plans specific short- and long-range commodity objectives. Develops purchasing arrangements, which are communicated to plant locations. Advises headquarters and plant management of supply sources, arranges for procurement on a pooled basis rather than plant by plant.

Major Responsibilities:
1. Develops specific annual purchasing objectives; creates specific short- and long-range commodity objectives with a view to reducing the cost of materials and improving service to user units.

2. Surveys markets for best source or new supply sources. Contacts potential suppliers and negotiates most favorable proposals.

3. Develops most suitable purchasing arrangement for commodities, including contracts, blanket orders, spot purchase orders, and vendor stocking arrangements.

4. Communicates detail of purchasing arrangements to user units, i.e., prices, terms, and method of handling requirements based on arrangements made in their behalf.

5. Receives requisitions; analyzes each item for quantity, specifications, and delivery requirements; develops and investigates sources of supply; issues request for quotations

for those items not covered by any existing purchasing arrangement. Develops substitutes if commodity is unavailable, or if more economical products might be satisfactory.

6. Receives quotations by mail, by telephone, or through personal representation of bidders; analyzes quotations and checks specifications, quantities, etc.; compares competitive products for desirability and use.

7. Determines best source by evaluating quotations or by application of an existing purchasing arrangement or by approved procedure; prepares information required to process a purchase order.

8. Consolidates annual requirements for commodities common to several use points. Determines adequate definition of commodity; investigates possibility of improving quality without a price increase or of substituting a lower-priced commodity to accomplish the same function.

9. Evaluates vendor performance based on personal knowledge of prices and deliveries and information received from affiliates relative to product acceptability and vendor service. Anticipates and negotiates possible price changes and in general develops thorough knowledge of those commodities assigned.

10. Advises management of industry competitive situations, alternative supply sources, raw material costs, commodity price trends, and supply-demand situations based on knowledge of company's laws.

11. Maintains effective communications between central purchasing and plants.

12. Maintains good relations with supplier personnel, which means courteous, impartial, and objective dealings with suppliers.

Supervision of Personnel:
1. Clerk-stenographer

Scope:
1. Directly procure approximately $1 million annually of materials and equipment and supplies

2. Guide and counsel respective plant and buyers at three plants in the procurement of assigned commodities

3. Assist operations and manufacturing personnel in approximately five affiliates in the development of sources for material and product needs

4. Assist manager in the development of purchasing procedures

Knowledge and Skill Needed:
College degree in either business administration or engineering. Thorough knowledge of purchasing procedures and internal controls; specific knowledge and two years' experience in handling of assigned commodities at a company plant or similar outside experience. Good knowledge of U.S., European, and Japanese sources of materials, supplies, and equipment. General knowledge as regards monetary and customs matters. Ability to represent company effectively in dealings with suppliers is essential.

Example 3
Job: Management trainee
Reports to: Manager, planning and analysis
Purpose: To provide broad exposure for college recruits to a wide variety of purchasing activities during the first 12 to 18 months of incumbent's orientation at development program.

Assigned Duties: The incumbent will be rotated in and out of at least three of the following positions to fulfill the intent of his job classification. Typical positions are as follows:
Expediter
Associate buyer—central purchasing
Systems and procedures analyst

Plant buyer

Administrative assistant—central purchasing

All assignments are to be performed in accordance with approved policies, procedures, and job descriptions. Each assignment will be documented by an employee appraisal by supervisor and a detailed report by trainee.

Job Specifications:

(To be completed by supervisor)

Mental: College Degree. Business administration or engineering preferred.

Skill: None needed. Will be developed during employee's first 12 to 18 months on job.

Responsibility: Will report to at least three different supervisors for development and evaluation purposes. Will be expected to demonstrate extraordinary learning ability and willingness to contribute.

Conditions: Normal working conditions with 40-hour work week.

Additional Information:

Performs work assignments in accordance with specific detailed instructions (oral or written), checked at frequent intervals by immediate supervisor. Refers all situations which deviate from instructions to supervisor.

May receive day-to-day guidance (from someone other than supervisor) in performance of duties. This may be received from a group leader who has no direct supervision other than distributing work and answering routine questions.

Summary

In summary, the job title and description should be appropriate enough to reflect the responsibilities and the authority of the job.

Once the mission of a purchasing area has been established, one successful approach is to develop position specifications for a job, using a given set of job factors; then from these specifications a more comprehensive position concept and detailed list of responsibilities can be written. Of course, the standard technique of using active verbs and short, concise sentences applies here also.

In a small company as well as a large company, the problem of internal and external consistency between jobs becomes a real one. Once the job description or position concept has been written, the next barrier is to evaluate it in relation to other jobs, internally in the company and externally in the community. For example: A buyer's job description needs to be evaluated, using key jobs in relation to jobs in engineering, or in administration, in order to determine its real worth to the company. In terms of the various duties used to describe it, it is possible to determine the price range and the level which should be placed on that job. This establishes the job's internal consistency within the organizational network.

External consistency is established similarly by selecting organizations in the community in relatively the same field and comparing job descriptions, thereby establishing consistency in pay level with those positions in the local community.

For companies which are multinational, the above problems become more difficult. The mission must be established and the description must be written. However, once the job has been described and evaluated in relation to other jobs, the problem is one of giving equal status to that job in all places anywhere in the world. Agreement on the substance of the job and on the progression between jobs assists immeasurably toward the proper organization of the purchasing function and assigns responsibility properly as well, so that the best job can be accomplished in the most effective way.

SELECTION

Search for Talent

Organizing an effective search for needed talent is an important and time-consuming activity.

To illustrate how one might proceed, assume that a buyer of maintenance repair and operating supplies (MRO) is needed for a purchasing department. It will be a new effort for this department, as previously efforts were concentrated on centralized procurement of raw materials. The job qualifications and career paths discussed later in this section have been created. The need is for a nontechnical college graduate with a minimum of 1 year of industrial business experience, preferably within a large plant. Purchasing is growing rapidly in size and scope, and the right person with dedicated effort can expect to progress from buyer to plant purchasing manager to assistant corporate purchasing manager within 7 to 10 years.

The first step in the search should be a discussion with the employment manager, during which the entrant should be furnished with a copy of the job description. Direct initial contact with prospective candidates should be avoided. The employment manager, like a purchasing manager, must understand the requirement. A joint discussion should develop logical internal and external recruitment sources, described later.

It should be made clear that purchasing wants to participate actively in the search and will make the final selection.

The purchasing manager should recognize that he must first communicate the need and then motivate the employment manager to action. The purchasing manager is truly playing the role of a salesperson. If the correct job qualifications and career paths have been defined, a good employment manager will come up with qualified candidates just as a good buyer, when fully informed by a requisitioner, will obtain the right material at the right price.

In selling the employment manager on the purchasing activity itself, the function is described as it really is—an exciting and self-fulfilling place to work. The purchasing manager for one large petrochemical company describes it in his company's college recruitment brochure as follows:

> The Purchasing Department, in more than 25 locations, handles total annual purchases of more than $180,000,000 of equipment, materials, and supplies. . . .
> Duties include working with operating managers and engineers to negotiate with suppliers, forecast price and availability trends, prepare and manage purchasing contracts, and study vendor industries in depth. The purchasing staff member learns almost all areas of the global petroleum and petrochemical business.
> Purchasing employs creative people with diverse talents and educational back-

grounds who use their analytical and decision-making skills to ease the impact of inflation on company costs. Because of its obvious importance to profits, purchasing can be a path to high-level management posts for those with administrative ability.

Incidentally, if a company has a college recruitment brochure, purchasing's role in that company should be delineated. Every function must make a reasonable effort to sell its product—and purchasing is no exception.

Recruitment Sources

In these initial discussions, it should be decided whether potential candidates should be required as part of the screening process to complete aptitude tests geared to measuring the likelihood of their success within purchasing. It is usually a question of whether or not the company believes in the value of such tests. Every company should be gaining some experience in this area, as effective personnel selection is never easy. Reliable aids to selection should be viewed with an open mind.

Next, one considers some of the likely recruitment sources available in the search for the MRO buyer in the hypothetical situation under discussion. Personnel needs can be filled from two major sources—internal and external.

Internal   Progressive companies usually insist that thorough personnel searches be conducted within the company before surveying outside sources of recruitment.

Purchasing, because of its inherent cross-functional nature, should fully support this concept. Company user and staff departments are purchasing's customers, who must first be sold a new product or service before purchasing can negotiate effectively with a supplier.

There are several benefits to internal recruitment by purchasing, such as:

• Providing attractive advancement opportunities for people who have proved their worth in other functions, thus helping to create a better esprit de corps.

• Simplifying the orientation and development process, as the internal recruit will have experience with the company's products, services, and policies.

• Providing purchasing with people who upon entry can see things from the customer's viewpoint. Such people can help make purchasing more aware of its customers' needs and viewpoints.

• Helping to convince a company's general manager that purchasing is a good place to train high-potential employees for eventual promotion into top jobs both within and outside of purchasing.

In the interest of objectivity, one should also recognize that there *can* be disadvantages to internal recruiting, such as:

• Perpetuating current below-grade practice

• Possible reluctance on the part of the employee to become as aggressive with new ideas

• Creating dissatisfaction among employees not selected

Assume, then, that the department is searching internally for an MRO buyer. Some logical functions in which to search for talent would be:

- *Maintenance,* because such people already know both users' service needs and their material preferences.
- *Sales order entry,* since a knowledge of commercial business details within a supplying activity can produce significant benefits when negotiating a blanket order or systems contract.
- *Sales,* for the same reason as above, plus the fact that a salesperson knows sales strategies and comes to purchasing aware of buyers' predominant strengths and weaknesses.
- *Contract administration,* because this experience is invaluable in developing definitive purchasing arrangements and in knowing how to manage a contract once it is executed.
- *Production,* because this experience can give a person firsthand knowledge of how materials are used or misused. It also creates a high regard for materials-required dates and the importance of adequate quality.
- *Employee relations,* because there one has the opportunity to acquire knowledge of people's strengths and weaknesses and the overall importance of human relations factors; also because of interviewing skills acquired, which can be valuable in communicating effectively with and motivating supplier personnel.
- *Engineering,* because such personnel have a knowledge of design requirements and of the advantages of standardization.

An MRO buyer could be effectively recruited from any one of these sources plus a number of others, for example, *auditing,* because this experience develops a broad knowledge of many company activities, and *finance,* because here one builds a pricing and costing skill.

In conclusion, a competent, bright, and willing person from another company function can learn enough about the fundamentals of purchasing to become a fully competent MRO buyer within 6 to 12 months—provided the company has a good buyer development program.

External   While many companies fill job positions from within whenever possible, other companies must fill positions using external sources. The following are the external sources generally used by most organizations:

1. Advertising
2. College placement offices
3. Employment agencies
4. Associations
5. Military
6. Personal referrals
7. Walk-ins
8. Mail-ins

These different sources invariably carry different price tags and produce qualified candidates at different rates of speed. Ultimately, in any recruitment effort, a balance between cost and time must be maintained. One must look at each of these terms, checking the potential advantages for certain kinds of requirements.

ADVERTISING.   Probably the most frequently used method and perhaps the least expensive is the placement of advertising in newspapers. This is also probably the quickest way to obtain immediate candidates. The most common advertisement is the *classified ad* which normally appears in the classified section of the daily newspaper or magazine. *The Journal of Commerce, Chicago Tribune,* and *The New York Times* are examples of this. A very brief description of the job and salary range should be given. Also, the display ad is utilized in the financial sections of newspapers, such as *The Wall Street Journal* and *The New York Times.* This is an expansion of the ad in which a brief description of the job objectives and the qualifications are indicated. The ad is usually larger than those placed in the classified section. Both types of advertisements might perhaps be blind, i.e., they do not identify the company, and a box number is used. This eliminates the need for answering all inquiries of unqualified candidates. Another method is the open advertisement in which the company, generally with a very good reputation and playing on that image to attract quality candidates, indicates its name.

The disadvantage of advertising for candidates in newspapers and magazines is that there is no control over the quality and quantity of the replies. Therefore a very high percentage of unqualified and unsuitable replies are received. Advertising in the specialized publications of the purchasing field, such as *Purchasing* and *Purchasing World,* is the most direct route to reaching experienced specialists of the purchasing field. Not to be overlooked in this area are the local purchasing association magazines published in the major cities of the United States.

COLLEGE PLACEMENT OFFICES.   This is an important source for both graduate and older alumni and surely is the best continuous source for college-trained personnel. Most colleges and universities provide interview days or career days in which industrial firms will grant interviews to any interested student. If there is an interest on the part of the company, an in-house interview is scheduled on the company premises. The college placement director usually arranges for such interviews. The major disadvantage of this source is the fact that, in using it, more interviews must be undertaken to hire one man or woman than with any other source. It is an expensive operation. Many universities maintain centralized alumni placement offices, which is a good source to locate mature candidates who are undertaking specific special graduate programs and are working outside the normal programs. Many studies have been conducted as to the benefits of college recruiting, and surveys have been made which could be helpful in setting up a program for college recruiting. Information on this subject can be obtained through the National Association of Purchasing Management, 11 Park Place, New York, N.Y. 10007, or the Purchasing Management Association of Canada, 80 Richmond Street W., Toronto 110, Ontario, M5H 2A4 Canada. These sources can supply current lists of colleges that offer degrees in purchasing or related subjects, or include purchasing courses as part of their studies. Section 29 contains such a listing.

AGENCIES.   Private employment agencies are an expensive, yet popular recruiting source. Depending upon the location, most employers pay the fee, usually 10 percent of the annual salary. The private agency is a good source for locating presently employed personnel, as opposed to the public employment agencies, which attract unemployed personnel. In the large cities there are agencies that specialize in purchasing candidates. In New York City alone there are three agencies with purchasing specialization. There is a better chance here of selection with definite requirements and a better chance to locate specific purchasing candidates than in general agencies.

The disadvantage is that most employment agencies are local and do not go beyond the local area. They also do a minimum of screening and have a tendency to send out persons with little concern for the specific requirements; therefore the screening has to be done by the company. It is thus necessary to be quite specific in setting the job specifications when dealing with employment agencies. Employment agencies are best at the lower levels for the unskilled and semiskilled and clerical workers or the beginning worker.

EXECUTIVE SEARCH.   Also to be considered in the general category of agencies is the executive search firm. The most expensive and the most successful in recruiting, this source can cost as much as 25 percent of the candidate's first year's salary. The advantages are the screening abilities of this source. It brings candidates who have specific qualifications for the position. Also this search firm will look at people already successfully employed who may not be looking for jobs—a valuable source of recruitment.

ASSOCIATIONS.   Many local purchasing associations maintain placement services similar to employment agencies. The difference, however, is that their services are free. They insert notices in the publications and news bulletins letting members know the availability of positions and individuals. They operate like many of the alumni placement offices. They are an excellent source for specific, unusual, or highly qualified candidates.

The disadvantages are that those who let it be known they are interested in moving may not be the best qualified, and that there may be a tendency on the part of the associations to help those who have been active members, regardless of the candidates' qualifications.

MILITARY.   Relatively few military persons are either old enough or financially secure enough to retire completely after 20 years of service. They are eager to obtain jobs immediately upon their retirement in order to secure continuous income. The imaginative recruiter can capitalize on this valuable experience by contacting individuals before retirement. A person's technical knowledge in the defense industry puts him in a particularly good position to be valuable to those companies in the aerospace and defense-related industries. Two excellent ways to contact military personnel are through: (1) the Retired Officers' Association in Washington, D.C., which maintains an active file on officers soon to be retired and allows industry to review résumés for screening; and (2) the major military installations which maintain counseling service for enlisted personnel and will allow business representatives to visit them and meet and talk with those being discharged. Some centers provide lists that include the name, rank, and specific specialty of each individual. Also to be considered is the local veterans administration as a source for both enlisted and officer personnel.

PERSONAL REFERRALS. While widely used and often an excellent source for recruitment at the lower levels, there is serious question as to the advantages of personal referrals at the upper levels of recruitment. Two of the advantages are that this is an inexpensive method of recruiting and that the prescreening is generally done by the employee. The present employees, as a rule, refer people whom they have been associated with, and they have a personal knowledge of background, habits, etc., of persons they recommend. The disadvantage is that turning away their friends does not have a positive effect on the employees. Another disadvantage is that there is a tendency to settle for less than a completely satisfactory employee when this method is used. Not all the prospects available from other sources are seen, and this has an effect on the quality of the selection.

WALK-INS. A *walk-in* is an applicant who appears at the personnel or purchasing office without an appointment for an interview. It is not unusual for large companies to have thousands of walk-ins a year, depending upon market conditions. It is important here that each walk-in receive a courtesy interview, no matter how brief. If the company is interested, a lengthy interview can be arranged for a later time. If the applicant looks promising, every effort should be made to interview the individual at the earliest convenience.

MAIL-INS. These are another recruitment source because many job applicants send letters through the mail. Depending upon the reputation of the company, the quantity of such applications can be very large and the quality good. This is a very inexpensive and effective recruiting source. But because the applicant normally will write to more than one company, it is important to take fast action if the applicant is promising. Also, if the applicant has typed the letter personally, a personal letter should be sent in answer by the company. The advantage of this recruitment is that the recruiter has an opportunity to read the applicant's background before interviewing him. A disadvantage is, however, that the applicant may not live up to what has been stated in the résumé.

Identify Job Enrichment Opportunities

Herzberg Concept Effective motivation of an employee is difficult but rewarding. Behavioral scientist Frederick Herzberg has developed a concept called *job enrichment,* which is worth considering in assessing the value of a job measured in terms of selection and *development* of a purchasing employee.

Oftentimes a job is structured in such a way as to *minimize* job satisfaction factors, such as achievement, recognition, the work itself, responsibility, advancement, and growth. This makes it difficult to attract and hold employees classified as *high-level input.* Herzberg contends that the factors involved in producing job satisfaction and motivation are separate and distinct from the factors that lead to job dissatisfaction. Job dissatisfaction, he claims, tends to stem from weaknesses in company policy and administration, supervision, relationship with supervisor, work conditions, salary, relationship with subordinates, status, and security.

For purposes of this section, it will be assumed that these job dissatisfiers will not present a problem. It is important, however, to recognize that Herzberg stresses the separateness of *job satisfiers* and *job dissatisfiers*. He contends that the opposite of job satisfaction is *no* job dissatisfaction. Herzberg's experiments have shown that job enrichment can be a valuable tool in increasing a person's motivation. The aim here, then, is to suggest that jobs be structured in such a way as to optimize the job satisfaction factors of achievement, recognition, the work itself, responsibility, advancement, and growth opportunities.

Job enrichment is not job enlargement, and this distinction should be clearly understood. The purpose of job enrichment is to provide an opportunity for the employee's psychological growth, while job enlargement merely makes a job structurally bigger, such as expecting higher output or adding another task. This latter process is called *horizontal loading*.

Buyer Illustration of Job Enrichment Concept   Job enrichment, by contrast, involves a process described as *vertical loading*, encompassing the principles shown below. Under each of these principles, an illustrative example is given of how a buyer's job in a large to medium-size office might be deliberately enriched. For this example, a hierarchy of director of purchases, division purchasing manager, and buyer is assumed.

Job Enrichment Principle	*Illustration*
1. Removing some controls while retaining accountability.	Allow a buyer to sign all or most of his purchase orders. Maintain accountability with *post facto* review by purchasing manager.
2. Increasing the accountability of each individual for his own work.	Encourage purchasing director and others to contact buyer directly in matters concerning his or her assignment.
3. Giving a person a complete natural unit of work (module, division, area, and so on).	Assign buyer complete responsibility for complete management of a commodity group or all the buying for one or more functions of the company.
4. Granting additional authority to an employee in his activity; job freedom.	Allow buyer to schedule and make visits to supplier's facilities on his own initiative. Limits may, of course, be set, if needed.
5. Making period reports directly available to the worker himself rather than to the supervisor.	Encourage director of purchases and user and staff department heads to send reports and other data directly to the buyer.
6. Introducing new and more difficult tasks not previously handled.	Have buyer write monthly accomplishment report for the division, thus forcing him to look at the department or division in broader terms and sharpen his communication skills.
7. Assigning individual specific or specialized tasks enabling him to become an expert.	Assign buyer full responsibility for management of one or more commodities essential to the profitability of the company.

Create a Specific Job Plan for Each Trainee

It is appropriate at this point to review the basic steps in the *selection* process already described. They can be summarized as follows:

- Determine purchasing's role in the company
- Determine types of personnel needed to fulfill purchasing's assigned role
- Set job qualifications
- Search for talent
- Determine what recruitment sources are available
- Identify job enrichment opportunities

Assuming that these steps are clearly understood and properly completed, let us confront the question: How can we create a specific job plan for each trainee?

Summary of Development Needs   First, it must be recognized that training or, more properly, development is needed at several levels, such as:

- New employees at all departmental levels
- Current employees, who must be kept abreast of all improvements and new developments in the function
- All employees, long-range development

Thus, purchasing's training or development needs are open-ended and continuing. A key point, therefore, is that development plans for all employees should be reassessed and reworked at least annually.

Illustration of Job Plan for New Buyer   Focus attention now on *new employees,* such as a buyer. First, recognize the need for proper orientation, a subject which will be dealt with later.

Then provide for orderly development of the *techniques, attitudes, skills,* and *knowledge* needed to perform with optimum efficiency at the buyer level.

Lastly, balance these needs for proper orientation and development with the urgent need in most of our companies to obtain and sustain productive output as quickly as possible.

Avoid in all these steps the blanket approach to training or the outdated school of thought which says, "What's good for one is good for all."

A job plan for a newly appointed buyer could be outlined as follows:

1. *Purpose*
    To create a program which will facilitate development of a newly appointed buyer.
2. *End Result Desired*
    To develop a newly appointed buyer within 12 months of date of hire, such development to provide for adequate training in the TASKs directly related to the job to be performed. This will include *T*echniques, *A*ttitudes, *S*kills, and *K*nowledge components. At the conclusion of the initial development period, the buyer will be expected to perform at a high degree of professionalism. Additionally, the program will be designed to lay the groundwork for further development of the trainee into an experienced buyer who can perform at the excellence level.

3. *Assumptions—Responsibilities*
- Trainee will meet the minimum entry-level job specifications.
- Initial development will be completed within 6 months from date of hire; all requirements will be met by the end of the first 12 months on the job.
- The individual will be expected to provide at least 60 percent of the effort toward successful completion.
- The trainer will provide a specific time schedule, access to key personnel, source material, and opportunities for personal development.
- The trainee will expend at least 5 hours per week in home study.
- The trainee will submit weekly reports of observations, accomplishments, and suggestions for strengthening both the operation and the development program.
- The trainee(s) will make time on a scheduled basis to interview, motivate, and challenge the trainee. Evaluation of trainee's progress will be made at least monthly.

4. *Program Content*

Development through use of a wide variety of development techniques described in later paragraphs should impart the following:

a. Techniques
Systems and procedures
Creating purchasing plans
Processing requisitions
Soliciting quotations
Evaluating quotations
Selecting the supplier
Placing the purchase order or contract
Value analysis—standardization
Cost-price analysis
Make-or-buy
Learning Curve applications
Systems contracting
Inventory minimization

b. Attitudes
Every buyer is a manager
Profit seeking
Objectives
Creativity
Service-mindedness
Diplomacy
Ethics
Flexibility
Social responsibilities

c. Skills
Communications
- Writing
- Listening
- Interviewing
Timing
Time management
Planning
Problem solving
Decision making
Negotiation (introduction to)

d. Knowledge
Company products
Company policies, procedures, and benefits
Company's plans
Company's organization
Key functions interfacing with purchasing
Purchasing's role
Purchasing's organization
Legal implications
Commodities to be purchased
Markets involved
Sources of supply

This same TASK-oriented approach can be used in creating a similar plan for any new employee regardless of the job level or in assessing an old employee's development needs. It is essential that the trainee be totally involved in the effort and that training be job-oriented and not training for training's sake.

Environmental Considerations   A key point to consider in creating a specific job is the *environment* in which a given trainee will have to function.

One illustration of the importance of recognizing *environment* at the job-planning stage is the difference in a large company between a headquarters buyer and a plant buyer. A headquarters buyer is staff-oriented while a plant buyer is line-oriented. Each of their supervisors will have different viewpoints and motivations, as will the general manager. Area differences must also be considered, as well as urban versus rural *environmental* factors.

The person creating the specific job plan must *know,* understand, and reflect these factors in the orientation and development job plan.

Making the Final Selection

Certain steps should have now been completed, as follows:

1. Job qualifications are delineated in a formal job description.
2. Career paths have been identified.
3. Talent searches have produced two or more candidates for interview.
4. A specific job plan has been created and is available in written form.

The next step in the selection process is the job interview. For illustrative purposes, assume one is trying to select the best candidate for the job of a buyer.

The success of the interviews is clearly dependent upon:

- The quality of the planning described earlier
- The skill of the interviewer
- His or her ability to motivate the candidate to be communicative

The candidate must be treated as a competent person and frankness must be encouraged. Each candidate must be given a clear picture of the job and of what he or she can expect *if* selected, as well as what the company wants in return.

The trained interviewer has many aids on which to draw at the time of each interview. If at all possible, a *trained* interviewer should handle the screening of the initial candidates as well as the final candidate. Purchasing personnel should seek competent help here just as they do in legal matters.

If a purchasing person does not have access to a competent interviewer, he should obtain a good textbook on the subject and master the principles involved. Professional interviews are a must if the right choice is to be made. The process can be likened to negotiating a purchase for a valuable item of capital equipment.

People are every company's most valuable asset, and extreme care should be exercised in such long-term investments. The decision to join your firm may be the most important decision the candidate will make in a lifetime. Treat it as such.

DEVELOPMENT

Orientation

Once a person is selected to fill a job, be it purchasing manager, buyer or specialist, expediter, etc., his or her *orientation* and *development* have already been started.

Orientation Starts at the Interview   Training (which includes orientation and development) starts at the interview, when the applicant should be told the details of his or her job.

It is difficult to separate orientation from development. If training is properly handled, the two overlap at several points during an employee's first few months on the job.

As stressed earlier, the effective job plan for each trainee will be unique. It is important that at the end of the training period the trainee understand the *techniques, attitudes, skills,* and *knowledge* needed for success in *his or her* job.

Basic Considerations   For a newly appointed buyer, the early orientation phase could be handled as follows:

1. Accurately define purchasing's role in the company in terms of both its present and future roles. In a progressive company, purchasing's role should be a developing and a changing one. Point out that the buyer can help these plans or dreams to come true.

2. Explain and discuss the *attitudes* a professional-level buyer needs.

3. Next pinpoint the *knowledge*-needed portion of the TASK program for a buyer. In a large company, certain segments of this may be handled in greater depth by a company employee relations or training department. But teach the new buyer (if hired from the outside):
    a. What products or services the company produces
    b. Major company policies, procedures, and benefits
    c. The company's major forward plans, hopes, or aspirations

4. Continuing with the *knowledge* segment of the job, give every newly appointed buyer the chance to learn:
    a. Key functions interfacing with purchasing, emphasizing those functions vital to his job success.
    b. Purchasing's organization chart and where he fits.
    c. Purchasing's major staff and line activities.
    d. Highlight personal growth opportunities and what the buyer should do to attain higher levels of responsibility and authority. Point out job enrichment built into the buyer's job, as described earlier in this section.

5. Explain the "Every buyer is a manager" theme, which includes the obligation to submit personal objectives.

6. Tell the trainee his performance will be evaluated during both orientation and initial development periods and beyond.

7. Review the overall written job plan and give a copy to the trainee.

An ideal job plan for the newly appointed buyer clearly places the above steps into a time frame day by day, hour by hour, week by week, etc. What is more, it indicates what role both trainee and his trainers play. Since the plan is an individual one, it encompasses the trainee's needs for:

- *Orientation* to his or her unique *environment*
- *Development* during the initial training period—the methods to be a combination of those described in later paragraphs

Need to Evaluate and Adjust Orientation Program   In summary, adjust the orientation phase of a trainee's job, when needed. Remember, good planning hinges on flexibility. Naturally each job plan should be an improvement over previous ones.

Career Path Planning

Organizations with clean-cut career paths will probably motivate their people to move upward faster. How fast a person moves up the ladder, however, depends on the job to be done, the person's competence, and his or her desire for improvement.

A cross section of companies reveals rather quickly that there is no one universally accepted definition of personnel planning. The variety of programs is as great as the variety of company situations. What is essentially new today, however, is the growing tendency among companies to integrate all their personnel activities into some meaningful pattern.

This section discusses recruiting, screening, selection, and development of purchasing talent. Not so evident is the fact that all these personnel activities are related to each other. One cannot separate the recruiting and selection process from development. It is a continuous chain of events.

The selection process is really a two-way street. More companies today realize that the applicant selects the company, too, for a number of reasons—chiefly a desire for long-range opportunity and growth.

Why have many attempts at career planning been ineffectual? It is the lack of clearly defined programs, in terms of both clearly defined job descriptions and skills required, and the failure to spell out prerequisites for the next logical assignment. One very interesting approach is found where a major company has established a model for developing various purchasing skills, showing at each level of development the corresponding skills to be acquired.

To see how career path planning works, one should look at a rather typical career route in a manufacturing company.

The entry job must be geared for a trainee coming directly from a university or for a person who has come up through the company ranks. A university graduate may have a degree and no experience; the internal person may have worked as a stock clerk, or expediter in another function. Let us assume that both are interested in a purchasing career. Purchasing has many paths open to each, and either may start as a management trainee (see Fig. 26-1) and qualify almost immediately for purchasing orientation. One company, for example, has a formalized 35-day program that includes specific topics, discussion with various managers, and reading assignments. To give a basic understanding of purchasing, through a programmed self-instructional text the trainee is given an understanding of the basic *funda-mentals of purchasing.* During this 35-day program, the trainee also expedites open orders by telephone, gets acquainted with the various purchasing files, and learns all about the different kinds of activities which take place in the purchasing area. After 6 months, if the trainee shows an interest and has the potential to

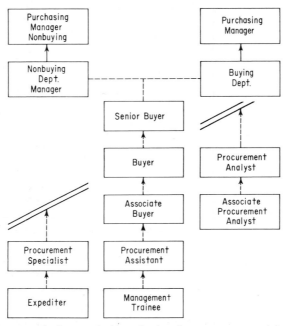

Fig. 26-1   Career paths in a typical purchasing department, geared for personnel from trainee up to and including the purchasing manager.

become a buyer, he may be moved into the buying activity. During this time, he may be placed under the wing of an experienced buyer. He may work in various parts of the buying function: for a few months as an MRO buyer, for a few months as a production plant buyer, for a few additional months as a laboratory buyer, etc. This plan enables him to learn all about buying practices and policies and the procedures that he must follow. He handles the paperwork and may even make some purchases under close supervision. His job title now may change from management trainee to associate buyer or buyer.

Concurrently with this on-the-job training, the new recruit attends a formal educational program entitled New Buyer's School.

Here, in 40 hours, he learns the attitudes, the skills, and the habits a buyer needs. He will also receive briefings about available support activities outside the department. He also learns something about value analysis techniques and may get some exposure to negotiation and cost and price analysis.

As his responsibilities increase and he becomes more specialized in dealing with certain components or commodities, the buyer must know how to get a cost breakdown from a vendor. Thus he needs to know more about cost and price analysis. So he is subsequently sent to Negotiation School, where he learns some fine points of developing a bargaining strategy. One very effective technique used consists of cases that demonstrate the use of various negotiating skills. Training is continuous and simulates real-life situations as much as possible.

Each step in the career path described above clearly spells out prescribed job duties, with each segment of training correlated with job performance.

For the competent person with a limited formal education, there is a similar career path with various checkpoints. He, too, may follow the buying route with progress from expediter to junior buyer to buyer to senior buyer and eventually to buying manager. He also takes part in various educational programs and concurrently handles specific job assignments.

It is essential that career planning be a continuing and companywide effort— one accepted by management. Stop-and-go efforts lose their vitality and creditability with employees as well as manager. On the other hand, sound career-path-planning programs can be a tremendous motivational device in any company.

Traditional Development Methods

There are several traditional methods which can be useful in planning and executing a training program, if tailored to a specific individual. "What counts is what is learned, not how it is taught," says McGeorge Bundy, former president of the Ford Foundation.

Regardless of the method or combination of methods used, the individual gains the knowledge to operate effectively. The best way to monitor the trainee's learning is through interviewing, counseling, and/or actual work assignments.

Traditional methods to be described separately include:

- Manuals
- "Big brother" concept
- On-the-job training
- Buyer rotation
- In-company training program
- Outside instruction or outside agencies
- Staff meetings
- Supplier visits
- Trial and error

Manuals   Many larger companies have developed special training manuals that they give to employees on their arrival. These manuals remain with the employees through their training period.

A specialized training manual should at least include:

1. Company policies
2. Purchasing department policies

3. Objectives of the purchasing function
4. General procedures of the purchasing department
5. Company and department organization charts

For many smaller companies, it may be too expensive to have a manual devoted specifically to purchasing training for newcomers. Any good purchasing operation, however, should have a procedure manual. This can double as a training manual. How? Give trainees assignments to read sections of the manual, putting particular emphasis on subjects they will be involved with immediately. Moreover, it is essential that there be a planned discussion between the trainee and his supervisor or assigned trainer on each section of the manual.

"Big Brother" Concept   A popular training method is called the "big brother" concept or the "sit alongside method." Here a senior employee instructs the new individual in procedures. Just how well can the purchasing veteran teach a new employee? Will he perpetuate many outdated procedures and methods? How much can the new person absorb correctly and coherently to make this method valid? Despite possible weaknesses, this is potentially one of the most effective methods. The teacher's ability determines its success. For this reason, it is important to select an instructor who can teach his job rather than to pick an individual who knows his job. There is a difference.

Under this continuing-learning-experience method, the individual is shown how to perform, is given the opportunity to work under close supervision, and is told what is expected of him and how he is doing.

On-the-Job Training   One frequently used method to train purchasing personnel is on-the-job training. Under this method, the trainee through "learning by doing" acquires the techniques, attitudes, skills, and knowledge he will need once his formal training is complete. He learns in the physical environment that will become his permanent work place. He follows the day-to-day operations and procedures, and he associates during this learning period with his future managers and contemporaries. This method varies, ranging from a simple assignment of a new employee to an experienced worker (the big brother method) to a formal arrangement with professional instructors assigned to guide and evaluate trainees' learning efforts.

On-the-job training may have several definite stages:

1. Orientation—Internal and external work environment and relationships are explained.
2. Instruction—Work is explained and demonstrated.
3. Execution—Work is done by the new person.
4. Discussion—Conferences are held on problems and work.
5. Reports—Evaluation is made of training progress.

Each of these occurs and recurs as the new employee progresses from one station or task to another. A wisely developed program provides the opportunity for sound groundwork to be done in each stage for each assigned task.

Remember, however, that the disadvantage of this method is that the primary function of the purchasing office is not training. So training on the job must take second place to the primary function. Nonetheless, such training can be effective and inexpensive. But it requires careful planning by those responsible to make certain the trainee has the proper learning environment. On-the-job training may include functional rotation, both within the department and in other company departments. The advantage of this functional rotation is that the trainee develops a companywide point of view, which has proven to be very effective in the development of management skills.

Buyer Rotation   Rotation of commodities among buyers, for example, parallels having a new person move from one buying desk to another. Furthermore, it automatically broadens the experience of all buyers, giving them invaluable backup knowledge.

This knowledge usually centers on the technical aspects of various commodities—for instance, when a buyer of fabricated metal parts takes a turn at buying metals in unfinished form. In addition, regular commodity shifts may trigger new ideas on how to purchase a specific item. By observing his predecessor's methods, the replacement may see how to apply the systems to his own specialty or to the next item assigned to him.

Buyer rotation often results in growing use of blanket orders and contract buying, together with increased staff expertise in these purchasing methods. (And the purchasing manager is in a better position to reassign personnel during vacations or illnesses.)

There is no reason why line and staff jobs cannot be rotated as well. This might mean pulling a buyer out of a commodity slot and putting him in an administrative position—replacing him with the former administrator. Purchasing section heads might also be switched in this manner. Large companies, moreover, could temporarily farm out a commodity specialist.

The internal rotation cycle can include these functions:

- Requisition receipt and control
- Source selection
- Securing quotations
- Negotiation of price and terms
- Purchase order preparation
- Expediting
- Invoice checking

Externally, rotation can involve:

- Accounting
- Data processing
- Engineering
- Inventory control
- Production

- Quality control
- Receiving
- Traffic
- Warehousing

Also, a program should be set up whereby a buyer exchanges jobs with somebody involved in the procurement functions outside the purchasing department. Other department managers should be consulted on how the trainee's time should be spent. One large company in the Middle West furnishes the following checklist to each purchasing trainee progressing through the mill or factory:

1. What is the specific end product or products of the department?
   a. What measurements of output are used?
   b. What quantities are being produced at present?
   c. Approximately what quantities of various materials are required per unit of production?
2. What is the principal process or service rendered in the department?
   a. Is it an operating department: manufacturing, converting, finishing, etc.?
   b. Is the department rendering general service: engineering, planning, materials handling, etc.?
   c. What is the nature of the process? If in manufacturing, what is the flow of materials, and what particular function does the equipment play in the manufacturing of the finished product? If in a service department, how does the department contribute to the manufacturing process?
   d. Is a process or department flow sheet used?
3. What are the raw materials used or handled by the department?
   a. What are their specifications, and why are specifications required?
   b. What is the function of each of the raw materials in relation to the finished product?
   c. What operating problems, if any, are created by the quantity of raw materials purchased or the method of purchasing them?
   d. What characteristics of the finished product dictate the type and kind of raw materials?
   e. What raw materials involve storage and handling problems?
   f. Where do they come from geographically?
   g. Which materials are manufactured by another unit of the same firm?
4. Where does the department fit into the general flow diagram of the mill?
5. What are the major pieces of operating equipment?
   a. What function does each perform?
   b. How does the material or product get from one to another?
   c. What is the capacity of each in units of product?
6. How are costs of manufacture determined?
   a. What is the general cost distribution, i.e., labor, raw materials, maintenance, etc.?
   b. How do purchased raw materials and supplies costs affect finished product costs?
7. How do staff services (engineering, research and development, purchasing, traffic, industrial relations department, etc.) assist in operation of mill?
8. Learn organizational structure of mill and its tie-in with staff organization.
9. Become familiar with physical layout of mills and storages.

10. Machine lubrication, plant maintenance, painting, power and steam generation, and laboratory supplies and equipment are major items other than raw materials to be observed during the trainee's progression.

In-Company Training Programs   One increasingly prevalent method of instruction is found in the in-company training programs provided by:

- Professional training organizations
- The National Association of Purchasing Management and its affiliated local associations
- Colleges and universities
- American Management Associations
- In-house education functions
- Numerous combinations of the above

These programs generally hinge on filmed lectures by professionals, case study work, and programmed instruction. This combination permits maximum participation with a minimum cost per individual and eliminates lengthy periods away from work location. Another advantage: programs can be easily scheduled.

The main reason for the growing success of these programs is that the entire training effort is designed to be compatible with each company's specific needs and requirements. Purchasing functions vary with:

- Type of company (commercial, government, industrial, institutional)
- Commodities purchased (raw materials, chemicals, electronics, pharmaceuticals, etc.)
- Structure (centralized or decentralized)
- Varying philosophies (vendor relationships, ethics, vertical integration, make or buy)

In addition to teaching the basics and fundamentals of purchasing, it is also very important to many companies that training programs expound their pertinent business concepts that relate to purchasing. This should indicate that more companies today are requiring their purchasing people to become more business-oriented and not merely a purchasing mechanism.

After completing his assignment in any department, the trainee should write a brief report summarizing his observations, using the questions above as a guide. In this report he should freely evaluate any existing conditions and make suggestions.

In his report, the trainee should also summarize in sufficient detail how the department functions, i.e., listing the organizational relationships and major responsibilities and describing the process flow. The results should be discussed in a meeting with the head of the department.

It is to be understood, however, that such reports will serve as a criterion of the trainee's ability to observe and to express himself.

Outside Instruction or Outside Agencies   Smaller firms which lack the funds needed for formal training programs often turn to outside agencies. Traditionally these consist mainly of either university or college programs; one of the most outstanding is the annual Harvard Seminar Case Study Program. Also becoming increasingly important in this area are the professional training associations; the most prominent are the American Management Associations (AMA) and the National Association of Purchasing Management (N.A.P.M.). Both have expanded their programs to deal with those areas not covered adequately by formal university courses and to increase the professionalism of their members. Instruction by AMA and N.A.P.M. generally falls into the following categories:

1. The *orientation seminar* is primarily an instructional meeting where experienced personnel lecture on basic fundamentals.

2. The *workshop seminar* centers on free discussion among small groups of participants on related experiences and on-the-job situations.

3. *Seminar courses* under the direction of professional instructors use a variety of involvement techniques based on real-life situations.

One major advantage of outside instruction is the benefits that come from association with purchasing people in a wide variety of companies.

A major disadvantage of outside agencies, particularly those of the AMA variety, is that most of the purchasing practitioner instructors, while well equipped to handle their jobs, are not always good instructors.

While outside instruction and outside agencies provide a valuable contribution to training purchasing people, it must be understood that these programs are by necessity very general in order to meet the needs of the broad scope of purchasing trainees emanating from all types of business activity.

By contrast, N.A.P.M. uses a blend of college professors and practitioners in its programs. Second, outside agencies in an attempt to relate to all different types of purchasing operations (commercial, industrial, government, construction, institutional, etc.) by necessity are very general. If tailored to meet a company's specific needs, however, both organizations' programs can be used successfully.

Staff Meetings   Perhaps the simplest training method to organize and run, yet one of the most effective in terms of participative learning, is a staff meeting. These meetings are excellent for discussing interdepartmental day-to-day activities, explaining policy changes, and establishing uniform practices throughout the department. Under this method, a member of the department teaches other department members, using both traditional methods and scientific methods of training, with emphasis on long-term objectives. Sessions may cover:

1. Individual jobs. Individual staff members take turns preparing programs of general interest to the entire department. Through these programs, emphasizing the individual's role in the entire structure, staff members learn to orient themselves.

2. Company operations and continued orientation. Representatives from other departments speak about their specific operations. This improves the understanding of user departments.

3. Vendor operations. Each vendor presents an outline of his company's oper-

ation. This, of course, facilitates communications between the selling and the buying organizations.

For smaller firms, these staff training sessions are particularly effective. They are generally held on a weekly or, at a minimum, a monthly basis. Some companies require all staff members to attend, and business ceases during this time. Others may schedule meetings after business hours or even on Saturdays. Informality is stressed at these sessions.

One way to encourage participation is to have open discussions and allow the staff to suggest other presentations. The individual who makes a suggestion becomes responsible for arrangements. He invites the appropriate speaker, plans the session, and conducts the meeting. Meeting expense is minimal—possibly limited to the rental of film. Such programs are dependent upon the whole staff's involvement and enthusiasm.

Supplier Visits   Training of purchasing personnel must include visits to suppliers. From plant visits trainees gain:

1. Knowledge of vendor's capabilities
2. Industry knowledge

With this knowledge the trainee can evaluate potential use of a supplier's firm for his company's business. Prior planning is important, however, for without a proper attitude such visits can become "just a chance to get away from the office" or "a night on the town" at the expense of the vendor.

Before going on a plant visit, the trainee should know:

1. What and how much the company buys from that supplier
2. What contracts and orders are currently open
3. What methods of shipment are used by the supplier
4. How the supplier's material is handled, etc., and when it is received
5. What use the company makes of the material
6. What specifications are established and why
7. The supplier's financial structure and his credit rating with his supplier
8. The supplier's type of management and principal officers
9. How the supplier rates in size in the industry
10. Methods of distribution commonly used by the supplier
11. Local sales representatives
12. How competitors' quality and prices for the same material compare
13. How supplier has performed for other customers

In addition, prepare the trainee so he will know what to look for, what questions to ask, whom to talk to on the trips, and what information he should obtain. Most companies have a special form, usually entitled Vendor Visit Report, that has blanks to be filled in by the person making the visit. This form serves as a guide as to which questions should be asked and what information and data are required to complete a vendor plant report. A fundamental list of areas that the trainee should investigate includes:

FINANCIAL.   Obviously, the financially healthy supplier is in a better position to serve. He is a better risk than one who has difficulties paying his vendors or whose financial position leaves something to be desired. Careful analysis should be made of the vendor's financial position. This can be done through services such as the Dun & Bradstreet credit ratings. The trainee should be trained to use basic financial analytical techniques.

HOUSEKEEPING.   Inspect plant maintenance and general cleanliness conditions in the vendor's plant. Obvious breakdowns, the state of maintenance, and general cleanliness conditions may indicate other less obvious problems.

PERSONNEL.   Union relationships with company management should be understood, especially the dates union contracts expire. Find out the history of the union and its relationship to the firm. What is the probability of strikes? Who are the key people in the vendor's organization? What are their duties and functions? In the organization itself, what are the average experience and educational levels in each department or group? How would this affect your potential deliveries? Attempt to determine the quality of the personnel and investigate the firm's training and educational programs.

PROCEDURES.   Have vendor explain work procedures and take the trainee through the total order-processing procedure from receipt of order to issuing of invoice.

LOCATION.   Although distribution methods make delivery relatively simple from vast areas in the United States, the supplier's distance from your location is a valid consideration when evaluating vendor potential.

RESEARCH AND DEVELOPMENT.   Trainee should determine the number of people and the amount of money involved in the R&D development process. This gives an indication of the firm's potential to continue innovating and to avoid technical obsolescence.

QUALITY CONTROL.   What are vendor's inspection procedures and controls? How frequently does he calibrate tools and gauges and test equipment for meeting primary engineering standards? How does he control test equipment furnished to subcontractors? Do they have a separate reliability, engineering, or quality control function? Where does it report, and how is it organized? What is the scope of its activities? What are the procedures for in-process inspection and quality control? What is the procedure for receiving inspection? Does vendor require certificates or test approvals from his supplier? If so, on what purchases?

PRODUCTION.   What kinds of planning, scheduling, and inventory control systems does he have? How are requirements released? By job? By lot? By forecast? How is production performance reported, i.e., actual versus schedule? By whom? How frequently? Who is responsible for machine and manpower loading? Does the vendor forecast loads? Is there a procedure for comparing current loads with forecast? What is his system for stock and material control? How does he identify and separate discrepant material?

ENGINEERING.   What are the vendor's design and development procedures? How does he incorporate design changes? How does he integrate tooling and manufacturing techniques with research and development activities? Will he comply with the buyer's engineering standards and procedures on items to be made for the buyer's design? Will he produce drawings in the buyer's format when he requests it? Has the vendor the control to incorporate engineering changes?

MARKETING.   What is the vendor's current projected volume of business? What is the breakdown of his business: military, commercial, or subcontract? Does he employ learning curves in projected labor costs? If so, what grade of learning does he employ?

Because of time limits, the trainee cannot visit all vendors. So he should concentrate on the high-dollar-volume suppliers. Do not send the trainee only to the most efficient vendors. Instead he should see a cross section of the best in the business plus those that have difficulties. Again the importance of preparation prior to plant visits cannot be overstressed. In addition, the trainee should file a formal report on such visits.

Trial and Error ("Sink or Swim")   This method operates this way: Do it, and when you make a mistake, we will correct it. How many costly errors go undetected? How much does the employee actually learn about the entire operation? What about morale and motivation? This method is generally used by small companies that cannot spend more for formal training programs. However, in the long run, this can be more costly than a formal training program.

Summary   In any discussion of training, the purchasing manager should keep in mind cost and profitability. The lecture method of instruction, for example, may seem quite inexpensive because one person prepares a talk in a minimum of time and presents the subject to large audiences. But one must consider also what each individual learns. Is that learning transferred and maintained by the individual on the job? If not, the inexpensive, low-cost lecture can be an extremely expensive training method.

Regardless of the training method or the size of the department, it is generally agreed that people learn best through doing.

Scientific Development Methods

Training versus Development   Scientific management methods focus on the proper utilization of people, since human resources represent the most important asset that any organization has. *Training* and *education* have been used somewhat interchangeably. *Training* has had a very restrictive meaning: to train people has meant to drill them in certain sensorimotor skills. Today the term *training* encompasses many activities, ranging from acquisition of a simple motor skill to development of complex tactical knowledge, learning administrative skills, and the development of constructive attitudes.

Along with its concern for updating of job skills and personnel allocation, management has been developing an even greater interest in such concepts as job enrichment and the general development of people as a resource—thanks to works of behavioral scientists such as Maslow, Herzberg, McGregor, and Argyris.

Formerly in a typical company situation, for example, the training manager

NAME OF ATTENDEE _____
WEEK OF: _____

PURCHASING TOOLS AND TECHNIQUES OF NEGOTIATION
PRE-CONFERENCE QUESTIONNAIRE

Please answer the following questions for the guidance of our instructors.
This information will help them to determine the level of knowledge of class members.
Select one response and place a ($\vee$) opposite your choice.

1. My present age is _____

2. I have been an employee
   Less than 1 year   _____
   1 to 5 years   _____
   10 years or more   _____

3. During this time I have worked in Purchasing for:
   Less than 1 year   _____
   1 to 5 years   _____
   10 years or more   _____
   I have worked in Purchasing before for _____ years.

4. My present job is called _____.

5. During my employment I have spent the following amount of time in negotiation of Contracts:

	0–1 year	5 to 10 years	10 years or more
a. Experienced Negotiator	_____	_____	_____
b. Support for Negotiations	_____	_____	_____

   or never negotiated _____.

6. Regarding the subject of cost and price analysis, check ($\vee$) one:
   a. I have prepared a cost/price analysis   _____
   b. I have some knowledge of cost/price analysis _____
   c. The cost/price analysis was usually made by I.E., M.E., or others _____.
   Note: If you select (a):
      How many cost/price analyses did you prepare in a month?

0–1	5–10	10 or more
_____	_____	_____

7. Regarding the subject of improvement curves, I have:
   a. Prepared an improvement curve myself   _____
   b. A knowledge about improvement curves   _____
   c. Heard about improvement curves   _____

8. Regarding the subject of accounting, I have:
   a. A knowledge of accounting principles   _____
   b. No knowledge of accounting principies _____

9. The subject of Negotiation: check ($\vee$) one:
   a. Is totally new to me   _____
   b. Is partially new to me   _____
   c. Is *not* new to me   _____

10. My knowledge of Negotiations is as follows:
   a. I have taken part as a Negotiation Team Member _____
   b. I have sat in a Negotiation Session   _____
   c. I have heard about Negotiation   _____

11. Regarding the technique of role-playing:
   a. I have played a role in a case situation _____
   b. I have watched a role play   _____
   c. I have *never* played a role in a case   _____
   d. I have *never* watched a role play   _____

Fig. 26-2 Questionnaire to be filled out by employee to determine training needs for improving efficiency or for promotion.

12. During a single week's work I spend the major part of my time in the following tasks:
    (Express your response in percentage of time.)

    Buying activities   _____
    Contacting vendors   _____
    Expediting orders   _____
    Looking for new vendors   _____
    Contacting other functions   _____
    Negotiation with vendors   _____
    Other activities   _____

Fig. 26-2   (*Continued*)

was responsible for developing and implementing training courses. Today, however, this manager functions more as a change agent and an internal consultant to the organization. He assists operating people to accomplish their educational needs and objectives.

Attempts have been made to separate the developmental process from the development of the product, says George Odiorne. But he feels that both activities can take place profitably at the same time. In terms of the individual, education is looked on not as an integrated part of the trainee's work experience, but as something completely unrelated to his job performance. Consequently the support given such programs by management has been marginal.

Determining Training Needs   Today modern industrial educators believe that both functional and developmental aims can be accomplished in the same educational process. The person trained can be productive on his job, and his formal training can also be directly related to his job needs.

Under this approach, management must definitely know what the needs of the individual employee are. Determining needs is one of the manager's most difficult tasks. Most managers have real perception and are interested enough to do a good job, but others perform poorly and need guidance.

There are many methods of determining training needs; some of the more successful have been the use of questionnaires given to students prior to training (see the sample, Fig. 26-2), the in-depth interview, and TASK analysis.

TASK Analysis Approach   TASK analysis, or operations analysis, is a method of coming to grips with the problem of the *content of training*. This principle was illustrated earlier, when attitudes, skills, and knowledge needed for one to perform effectively as a buyer were described. The question is asked: What will the training cover? To answer this, we need a procedure to determine (1) what tasks constitute a job, (2) how these tasks are to be performed, and (3) what behavior is required of an employee to perform the task as specified.

The trainer must first decide what behavior results he wants. For instance, *effective behavior patterns* could include these work characteristics:

1. Set priorities carefully and plan work daily
2. Carefully relate available time to results needed

3. Carefully identify and thoroughly research essential commodities
4. Know and communicate current and long-term availability and price trends
5. Press development of new products and new sources
6. Seek planned profit improvements and cost avoidance
7. Produce purchase plan decisions of high quality
8. Practice value analysis and cost-price analysis
9. Negotiate beneficial purchasing arrangements
10. Vigorously resist proposed price increase
11. Plan communications carefully to promote full understanding
12. Constantly challenge, eliminate, or simplify work routines
13. Motivate salespersons
14. See that formal purchasing arrangements provide protection now and in the future
15. Make certain that timely service is routinely provided
16. Evaluate suppliers continually and replace failures
17. Continue personal development
18. Behave ethically

Modular Approach Another systems approach to education is the creation of specific modules or training units as part of a total package. Each module ties directly into the career path of the trainee. For example, if the entry job in purchasing is that of expediter, a course is developed giving the new candidate background orientation in purchasing, including some knowledge about types of buying activities, the purchasing process, ground rules for purchasing, ethical behavior in purchasing, contracts, etc. Furthermore, as the expediter is promoted into the buying activity, for example, he is eligible for additional training on that new level. Using this modular approach, it is easy for both the trainee and his manager to see both eligibility requirements and progress made, since all prerequisites have been carefully prescribed.

Trainee Involvement Techniques Traditional industrial training methods emphasize the role of the instructor and to some extent deemphasize the trainee's active role in the education process. Lectures seemed to be a reliable way of conveying information and were used extensively. Today, however, behavioral science research shows that the trainee learns best through involvement. The lecture still is valuable and should be used, especially when the course's contents are entirely new to employees and best known by the instructor. It is reliable. However, the value of learning by discovery is important. In other words, if the student somehow becomes part of the training through actual involvement, learning can take place faster. Training methods involving students have been used extensively by schools and colleges for years, the most famous being the Harvard Business School programs.

Some of these involvement techniques used with adults include the buzz group (small-group discussion), the Pigors method (critical incident process), the Harvard case method, the in-basket exercise, sensivity training, brainstorming, the simulation exercises, and various versions of each of these training methods.

In addition to the above involvement techniques, use of audiovisual instruction should be considered. Many studies have been made which highlight the fact that adults learn both by ear and by eye. Therefore many times it is helpful to use a crisp, well-planned audiovisual aid for maximum learning. The visual—a film, a videotape, overhead foils, or colored 2- by 2-inch slides—cannot stand alone, but if well planned, it can be a valuable adjunct to learning. Each visual, however, must be used with discretion. The checklist for the visualizer has been found to be a very valuable aid to instruction (see Fig. 26-3).

---

1. *Is Your Point Worth Making?*
    Is it essential to the understanding of your talk?
    Does it deserve the emphasis which a visual gives?
    What is your objective?
2. *Can It Be Adequately Verbalized?*
    If it can be verbalized, why visualize it?
3. *Does the Verbal Commentary Impart Meaning to the Visual?*
    Does your visual supplement the verbal medium rather than replace it?
4. *Does Your Visual Achieve Unity?*
    Is it free from incompatible and complicating ideas, symbols, art techniques, type faces?
5. *Is It Symbolic or Pictorial?*
    Do you recognize the difference?
    Which treatment is best for the subject?
6. *Is It Visually Fluent?*
    Is the art functional or ornate?
    Is it really one visual or several?
    Are complex subjects presented in comprehensible units (drop-ons)?
    Was the art work designed for *this* medium, or borrowed without modification from another type of presentation?
7. *Is the Visual Honest?*
    Does it plead special interest?
    Have the facts been distorted?
8. *Does It Utilize All Available Techniques Which Will Improve Its Efficiency?*
    Is the color used effectively? What does it contribute?
    Have you considered sequential disclosure or buildup?
    Have you achieved a dynamic presentation?
9. *Is the Visual Intended for the Benefit of the Audience or of the Speaker?*
    Have you avoided "Program Notes" and "Speaker's Outlines"?
    Is your projectible a visualization or a "reading session"?
10. *Is Your Visual Completely Readable by the Entire Audience?*
    Will there be unobstructed view of the screen? Is the type large enough?
    (Minimum $\frac{3}{16}$-in. letters for an 8- by 10-in. transparency)
11. *How Much Effort Did You Put Into the Visual?*
    Is it as good as you can make it?
    Have you sought criticism from others?
    Have you tested the visual?
12. *Has It Achieved Your Objectives?*
    Has your audience understood it?
    Has it changed attitudes and/or behavior?

Fig. 26-3 Checklist used by visualizer in an audiovisual program to determine effectiveness of his instructions.

Importance of Evaluation   Until some type of evaluation or assessment has been made by students and the instructor, the education process is never complete. This feedback mechanism completes the loop in the interpersonal communications process. Ways of getting feedback include giving checklist questionnaires, using after-class interviews, holding the interview with a student's manager, and holding one interview directly after the class and another in 6 months.

Examples of feedback are shown in Figs. 26-4 and 26-5.

Tailoring Development to Meet Individual Needs

Three important types of purchasing training programs are:

1. New-employee training
2. Current-employee training
3. Long-range training for all employees

New-Employee Training   First, consider the new employee. If he has purchasing experience, his training period will be shorter than that of the new purchasing trainee. The time period for the trainee's breaking in probably should be 6 months, whereas that for the experienced purchasing person's training will probably be just long enough for him to familiarize himself with his duties and to complete a company orientation.

The training program for the new trainee will most likely be integrated with the company orientation program and will involve such factors as a variety of work assignments in other departments and factory visits, both within and outside

---

Date _____

VOLUNTARY EDUCATION   MID-COURSE EVALUATION

Subject   Instructor

Instructions: Place an X in the box which indicates your opinion at this time. BE FAIR! BE HONEST! You can perform a valuable service to your instructor by giving a sincere and conscientious opinion of the instruction you are receiving in this course.

The Technique

	Lacking			Adequate			Skillful		
	1	2	3	4	5	6	7	8	9
Presentation and development of objectives									
Creation and maintenance of interest									
Organization and clarity of presentation									
Selection and use of illustrations and examples									
Encouragement of class participation									
Analysis of student's errors and clarification of misunderstandings									

Fig. 26-4   Student's evaluation of program during the schooling.

The Man

	Below Average			Average			Above Average		
	1	2	3	4	5	6	7	8	9
Instructor's management and control of class									
Instructor's knowledge of subject									
Instructor's speech and voice quality									
Enthusiasm of instructor									
Appearance of instructor									

The Material

The material being covered in this course ....
    is less than I need ☐
    is adequate for my needs ☐
    goes beyond my needs ☐

The work required in this course I have found ....
    easy ☐
    requires some effort ☐
    very difficult ☐

The content of the textbook ....
    leaves something to be desired ☐
    is adequate for this course ☐
    includes much additional valuable material ☐

The textbook is ....
    too simple in its approach ☐
    adequate for the course ☐
    somewhat difficult to understand ☐

The homework has been ....
    very burdensome ☐
    reasonable and sufficient ☐
    negligible and lacking challenge ☐

The quizzes and/or exams ....
    skipped much material ☐
    have covered the subject ☐
    have gone beyond the course material ☐

The quizzes and/or exams ....
    did not measure my progress very well ☐
    were adequate gauges ☐
    really showed up my strong and weak points ☐

Fig. 26-40   *(Continued)*

of the company. A typical program for a management trainee could be broken down into two major categories.

1. The *orientation phase,* which includes basic training in purchasing fundamentals and company division and department orientation

2. The *application phase,* which includes the application of the special principles and techniques of the purchasing field

PHASE 1.   The orientation phase follows this pattern:

Weeks 1–2: This time is set aside as an orientation in which the individual learns about objectives of the company, division, and department. Time also will be spent in studying the company's policy and procedures.

Weeks 3–4: Orientation programs in procurement-related departments: traffic, quality control, receiving, inventory control, and shipping. Within the small company, where the individual must immediately begin to be functional, these orientations at a minimum should be interviews with the different departments.

Week 5: An orientational rotation through other departments not directly related to the purchasing department.

Weeks 6–7: Work in the production department. As many companies produce

MANUFACTURING PURCHASING EDUCATION PROGRAM

EVALUATION SHEET FOR THE WEEK
Please place a check (√) on those items which reflect your feelings.
1. My over-all evaluation of this week's program was (check (√) one box)

1. Very good	1	2	3	4
2. Good				
3. Fair				
4. Poor				

2. Of what value for you were the individual topics presented this week:

Topics	Value reached my expectations	Not as useful as I expected	Topic was new to me	Topic not new to me
1. WT Purchasing Organ.				
2. Purch. Responsibilities				
3. Buyer Responsibilities				
4. Interviewing				
5. Practices & Policies				
6. Purch. & Eng.				
7. Purch. & Mfg.				
8. Purch. & Quality				
9. Value Engineering				
10. Purch. & Prod. Cont.				
11. Purch. & Mfg. Plan				
12. Purch. & Finance				
13. Negotiation				
14. Customer Engineering				
15. Legal & Purch.				
16. Purch. Systems				

Other comments about the program:

_____
_____
_____
_____
_____

Your Name _____

Fig. 26-5 Student's evaluation of program on completion of the schooling.

numerous major items, the individual must devote sufficient time to develop a knowledge of the company's products and how they are manufactured.

Weeks 8–9: With user units.

Weeks 10–12: Back in purchasing working with and assisting buyers.

Along with this orientation program phase, the individual could follow a self-study program that involves reading a section from the *Purchasing Handbook* or a current purchasing book. Then he should discuss this reading with senior purchasing people. At the same time, he would be attending in-plant purchasing or staff meetings.

PHASE 2.   The application of purchasing techniques and principles involves:

Week 13: Preparation for and visiting vendor factory and supplier evaluations.

Weeks 14–18: A commodity rotation. Concurrently require the trainee to make a few commodity studies.

Week 19: A negotiation course prepared either by the company or through outside organizations (see Fig. 26-6).

Week 20: Trainee should sit in on all major negotiations.

Week 21: Negotiation projects, with trainee taking an active part.

BASIC NEGOTIATION SCHOOL

Purpose:
- To develop buyer understanding of competence in the use of those negotiation tools and techniques necessary to the procurement of most commodities.
- To correct, improve, and strengthen buyers' negotiation techniques, use of tools, and applications of policy, philosophy, and accepted practice as required in most negotiation sessions when support of other functions in such sessions is minimal.

COURSE OUTLINE:

Monday	• Introduction and administration details
	• Determination of preattendance knowledge level re course content
	• Price and cost analysis
Tuesday	• Contract types
	• Negotiation plan and target
	• Strategy and techniques
Wednesday	• Four case problems
& Thursday	• Critique and discussion
Friday	• Review plan and strategies
	• Testing of knowledge level
	• Opinion questionnaire
	• Closing remarks
	• Testing of preattendance knowledge level re course content
	• Price and cost analysis
Tuesday	• Price and cost analysis (continued A.M.)
	• Contract types
Wednesday	• Contract types (continued A.M.)
	• Negotiation tools and techniques
Thursday	• Negotiation practice
Friday	• Critique re negotiation practice
	• Testing of knowledge level—course termination
	• Opinion questionnaire
	• Closing remarks

COURSE OBJECTIVES
(By Subject)

Fig. 26-6   Outline of one week's schooling on basic negotiation.

PRICE AND COST ANALYSIS
To enable class participants:
1. To differentiate between cost analysis and price analysis by defining each
2. To select, when provided with several procurement situations, which type of analysis should be applied
3. To list and define major elements of cost applicable to their buying activity
4. To recognize and describe the several methods used by industry to allocate overhead
5. To compare estimates with cost breakdowns and to determine areas requiring questioning and / or negotiation
6. To describe, when presented with examples of significant differences between estimated cost detail and quoted cost breakdowns, the limitations imposed by philosophy in the negotiation to resolve such differences

CONTRACT TYPES
To enable class participants:
1. To identify types of contracts by name and to describe how they differ. Given a set of statements concerning applicability, essential elements, limitations, and risk assumptions, the participant will demonstrate his ability to differentiate by matching such statements to contract type.
2. To select the type of contract most applicable to a variety of procurement requirements. Given real-life procurement situations, the participant will demonstrate his ability to choose the proper contract type, stating his selection and giving reasons for his choice.

NEGOTIATION PLANS, STRATEGIES, AND TECHNIQUES
To enable class participants:
1. To differentiate between negotiable and nonnegotiable situations by describing conditions negating or requiring the *use* of negotiation.
2. To describe the desired end results of negotiation.
3. To identify the strategies and basic techniques of negotiation and to describe their function in the total negotiation process.

NEGOTIATION (CASE PROBLEMS)
To involve the buyer directly in planning for and carrying on negotiations
1. In the application of his knowledge of and experience in the use of negotiation tools and techniques, and
2. In his understanding and application of purchasing policy, practice, and philosophy. Given constructed real-life procurement situations requiring the use of techniques, tools, and policy applications (as covered in previous sessions) for analysis and preparation for negotiation, he will, by negotiation with an opposing negotiator, demonstrate the extent of his ability to apply such techniques and tools, and to make policy applications and be able to identify those specific areas where he requires additional skill.

Fig. 26-6   (*Continued*)

Week 22: A value analysis course in the company or through an outside organization.

Week 23: Participation in value analysis projects. Perhaps sit on the value analysis committee if there is one.

Weeks 24–26: Specific task responsibilities within the purchasing department.

At the end of the twenty-sixth week, the formal training for new employees would be over. The new recruit should be prepared to step into the buying operation. Even though his formal training program is ended, it is important to note that the employee's training cannot be terminated here but continues throughout his career.

Current-Employee Training Training for current employees is continuous, with no limit on the time involved. A key factor is identifying employees' needs and utilizing formal company programs where available and those of outside organizations to supplement company programs. Many firms set objectives of at least one outside professional program for each management employee each year. Of course, in-plant staff training is essential to keep buyers up to date on a day-to-day basis. Also involved would be the rotation of commodities between buyers. Continued visits to suppliers' plants are necessary no matter how long employees have been on the job. Also consider requiring buyers to teach or make presentations at staff meetings. These methods, tied in with a strong performance evaluation system, should identify the individual needs and are effective in maintaining training for current employees.

Long-Range Training for All Employees   This must be tied to the corporation's goals. Often large companies train everyone in

- Planning
- Profitability
- Productivity
- Performance
- Personal development

The existence of bold personal development plans which can and should be shown to potential new employees will excite their active interest at the selection stage and provide powerful motivation after hiring.

Prior to structuring plans for continuing training, a careful assessment of the department's strengths and weaknesses is needed—first by overall department needs and then by each individual's unique needs. All problems need not be overcome at once. Priorities must be set, and the program must be continuous. For example, once the new buyer is trained by the company, a course in negotiation techniques, or specialized training in the technology of one or more commodities which the buyer handles, is the next logical step. Conditions are changing constantly both within and outside of most companies. Development programs must be geared to help purchasing personnel meet these needs.

Development programs are directly related to management by objectives—objectives designed to improve purchasing performance in a department for a position that only one person can fill. This is a costly and demoralizing process.

What are the likely needs of the future? Purchasing managers must take this question into consideration. For example, if a firm expects to enter the world market, a manager must consider training people to do their best business internationally and must perhaps even consider language training. Once future needs of the department are identified, training techniques can be selected to meet those needs. Again, this type of training should be continuous, with no time limit involved. This program would also include techniques used before—factory visits, in-plant training, rotation of commodities—and would also stress self-development through career paths. Stronger emphasis would be placed on company management training programs and management subjects, and increased use would be made of outside activities through Harvard Business School or AMA executive-type action courses. An internship program whereby buyers exchange jobs with someone outside of the purchasing department on a one-for-one basis should be considered. Nor should staff meetings be overlooked, with emphasis on management subjects and advanced purchasing techniques which might involve other departments. One very important note: In considering long-range planning, do not forget to provide developmental opportunities for the clerical and secretarial staff.

Certification in Purchasing Encouragement, recognition, and rewarding of those purchasing professionals who successfully meet the requirements of the N.A.P.M. certification program and receive the designation certified purchasing manager (C.P.M.) should be fostered. Purchasing certification is covered in detail in Section 28.

Providing for Measurement of Performance

A trainee's performance should be judged as objectively as possible. The success of each measurement depends on the reasonableness of the performance standards established by the training executive. A person's previous education and work experience must be considered in setting a standard of 12 months' time to develop adequate performance as an associate buyer. By contrast, a trainee new to the company, but with prior purchasing experience, will be expected to reach a professional level in 6 months or less.

Appraisal of Job Performance One vital part of management in purchasing or other areas is the measurement or appraisal of job performance. Some companies use lists of personality traits or other subjective criteria to measure purchasing performance. Far more effective, however, is the management-by-objectives approach. Here objective targets, i.e., planned costs of specific commodities based on historical experience, versus actual costs of procurement for these commodities, gives a real appraisal of the job performance of a buyer.

Much more interesting and time-consuming is the setting of targets for the purchasing manager. First an attempt is made to spell out the list and responsibilities which a manager has to achieve certain desired results. Second, information is obtained by which the manager can assess how well his responsibilities have been performed. Last, a statement of the desired results in a given period of time is developed and agreed to by the manager in a discussion with his superior. This set of objective criteria, once developed, can be revised and used from one performance period to another; it focuses on the result of management effort.

Development Process The *development process* in an organization, according to George Odiorne, cannot be separated from the *functional process*. While keeping an individual productive in his job, you also are developing him as a person. Therefore, a correlation needs to exist between the selection and the development process. Typically the necessary educational experience for the new purchasing person according to each position level is not well defined. In contrast, work experience and performance requirements are well defined for each job, although not always in writing. This is not too surprising, as one would expect most functional business areas to concentrate on entry qualifications, which are largely filled at college. The mature replacement or the recipient of a new management position is recruited largely on the basis of past record, actual work experience, special executive personality, and IQ tests.

More emphasis, however, needs to be given now to the education which is needed along the career path of an individual to build on his strength and optimize his performance on every level of the purchasing operation. Only then can a true correlation take place between the selection of the incumbent and the training of that person on the job to improve present job performance and to increase his potential.

Measurement of Performance   In many books and periodicals on the subject of management, it is fairly easy to identify at least three important phases: first, a planning phase; second, an operations stage; and third, a control phase. The planning phase may be characterized by a procedure for setting target objectives; the operations stage is the carrying out of the objectives; and the control phase is the measurement of performance based on target objectives. Then the process repeats itself with a revision of objectives.

A sound program for measuring the progress of the new employee gives flexibility to the organization when it is needed. Performance measurement is by far the most elusive and neglected of the activities in the purchasing area. Yet the management process is not complete without evaluation of the trainee. Many attempts have been made to automate this measurement process by using various systems of measurement reporting. For example, one system used by one company attempts to measure and report variances to internal cost estimates, new delivery dates, and quality variances of certain projected targets. Included in this measurement is the performance of the buyer, the supplier, and, in fact, the entire purchasing functional area. One example might be a report listing the parts the buyer buys by commodity code and by part number sequence. Comparison is then made with the target costs for these parts based on information about market conditions and information concerning the internal cost estimate for these parts. Costs which are above estimate show the percentage of variance and the code indicating the responsible buyer. This gives an instantaneous appraisal of job performance. In similar fashion, supplier performance may be measured by the prices paid for component parts compared with the internal cost estimate. Again, variances will be reported to management as they are needed, either monthly or quarterly, etc. Delivery-date variances will also be reported in similar fashion, indicating vendor performance in meeting production deadlines.

Another company has a scheme for measuring purchasing performance at three levels of activity. Level one is based on the delivery on time of the required goods. The second level of activity centers on active price negotiation by the buyer with his suppliers. The third level of activity deals with a search for a unique, competitive advantage either in concept, in design, or in product. Under this approach three levels of skill are discernible. Level one involves expediting of product into the shop; level two regards the skill of negotiation, which includes preparation, development of a strategy, cost-price analysis, possibly the use of a learning curve, and other aspects of purchasing. Level three is a highly creative type of activity in which the buyer concentrates on the market for those products which will definitely give his company a competitive edge.

Management by Objectives   Setting target objectives is a prerequisite for effective measurement of job performance. The more subjective approach of judging buyer's performance on the basis of certain personality characteristics has given way to the newer, more scientific approach of *management by objectives*. This is best defined as "deciding on the desired outcome before planning and executing the necessary action to achieve the outcome."

It places more emphasis on results-oriented management and less on the ways and means. It encompasses such traditional areas as planning and control, but it goes beyond these to include the more dynamic aspects of leadership implied by the terms *involvement* and *participation*. There are many approaches to the setting of objectives for various purchasing jobs. A very successful tried and proven method involves the establishment of (1) responsibilities, (2) indicators, and (3) objectives. To better understand the concept and its application to purchasing, these terms must be defined:

Responsibilities are brief titles which identify the major obligations an individual has for achieving results.

Indicators are pertinent information or data which can be considered to determine how well the responsibility has been performed.

Objectives are statements of end results to be achieved within a given period of time.

Notice the emphasis on end results to be achieved within a given period of time. A list of activities to be undertaken is not to be confused with objective setting. Activities may be part of a plan, and this plan is certainly desirable in working toward the set of objectives. Now objectives must be considered, primarily in terms of end results.

With the terms defined, here are some suggestions for preparing each of the above.

RESPONSIBILITIES

1. Make a list of the major responsibilities. Identify each by a brief title. Use nouns instead of verbs.
2. Omit qualifying adjectives.
3. Avoid combining two major responsibilities.
4. Combine minor responsibilities under a single title.

INDICATORS

1. List two or more indicators for each responsibility (four or five indicators are a maximum for a single responsibility).

2. State indicators precisely. If possible, make them measurable. Avoid the use of adjectives.

3. Restrict indicators listed to really important ones. Use critical ones even if difficult to measure.

4. Where budgets, forecasts, etc., exist, reference them. Do not duplicate them.

5. Make indicators easy to use by using your own local terminology and abbreviations, or by using ratios and the exception principle.

6. Include indicators even if all conditions necessary for success are not fully within the control of the individual.

OBJECTIVES.   Obviously objectives can best be set by a specific individual in a specific job. Nonetheless, here are some suggestions that will help in preparing one's own goals:

1. Try to set an objective for an indicator. In some cases you may not be able to do this.

2. State objectives in terms of the results to be accomplished.

3. Set objectives that are difficult to achieve but obtainable.

4. Express objectives as precisely as possible, preferably in measurable terms.

5. State objectives as though all desirable conditions for their accomplishment are not entirely within the subordinate's control.

6. Make objectives practical and usable. They should be restricted to really important results.

Examples of objective setting for the purchasing manager's job and for the senior buyer's job are given in Figs. 26-7 and 26-8.

Purchasing Manager

Responsibilities	Indicators	Objectives
GROUP ONE		
1. Personnel	Overtime	<5%
	Absent ratio	<1%
	Salary administration	Pay according to function
	Administration and clerical progress (promotions)	Once a year
2. Prices	Cost reduction progress	Savings up to 5%
	Internal estimates	Meet estimates ($\pm$ 5%)
	Quotations	Meet procedures
3. Quality	% rejects (receiving)	<2%
	Quality rating system/buyer/part number/vendor	Improvement 10%
	Field returns	None
4. Schedules	No. of overdue orders	<7%
	No. of unplanned shipments	<5%
	No. of claims to vendors	None

Fig. 26-7   Example of objective setting for the purchasing manager's job.

Purchasing Manager

Responsibilities	Indicators	Objectives
5. Relationships	No. of visits to vendors	Twice a year
	No. of meetings with other depts.	4 hours/week
	Claims from vendors (invoices & payments)	None
	Claims from accounting dept.	None
6. Self-development	Seminars	2–3 weeks/year
	Readings	0.5 hours/day
	Exhibitions	2–3/years
GROUP TWO		
1. Personnel	a. Hire	Operating plan
	b. Salary administration	Balance; regular review
	c. Administration and clerical	Meet schedule within 1 year
	d. Job description	Ensure available
2. Supervision	a. Cost conformance	5% under objective by year end
	b. Quality conformance	98% conformance by year end
	c. Delivery conformance	5% 2d qtr; 2½% 3d quarter
3. Objective setting	a. Cost	Operating plan
	b. Quality	
	c. Delivery	
4. Delegation	a. Decision	Survey
	b. Responsibility	
5. Control	a. Purchase order systems tracking (delivery)	
	b. Price-tracking system monthly report	
	c. Internal dept. listing (quality)	
6. Reporting	a. Operating plan	Prepare operating plan
	b. Status reports	Generate cost, quality, & delivery reports for group per qtr.
7. Training	a. Personnel dept. courses	Total group to attend 3 courses
	b. Purchasing dept.-oriented courses	Total group to attend 2 courses
	c. Language courses	½ group to attend 1 course
8. Vendor relations	a. Ethics	
	b. Corporate policy	
	c. Vendor surveys	
9. Self-improvement	a. Courses	
	b. Exhibitions/books	

Fig. 26-7   (*Continued*)

As a measurement tool, setting objectives can be a very profitable activity, for it highlights important tasks and increases objectivity. The buyer has the responsibility to assume continuity of supplier goods into his own house. This means that he must be sensitive to problems of both the supplier and the supplier's subcontractors. As new responsibilities are assumed, an individual should constantly refine and periodically update his objectives. The buyer can include financial requirements such as cost objectives for buying certain commodities, setting delivery and quality requirements; he can set objectives for the use of carriers and transport, and can even use objectives to consolidate work in the event that the work force must be curtailed and duties redistributed.

Objective setting, however, becomes meaningful only when used as part of the annual progress review. In numerous companies, it is now the practice to hold an annual performance review. This appraisal is usually held by the manager for his

Senior Buyer

Responsibilities	Indicators	Objectives
GROUP ONE:		
1. Price	Variance from standard cost	100% of operating plan
2. Quality	Meeting quality requirements	90% +
3. Delivery	Overdues	100% year end
	Zero to five	
	Status report	
4. Contracts	Parts list	Minimum order cost
5. Evaluation	Approved suppliers	Get all suppliers* approval
6. Supervision	Reports on group	Higher performance
7. Interface	Weekly performance reports, new products	Communications
8. Support	Service requests	Vendor education x%
9. Procedure	Corporation manual	Follow-up
10 Education	Career plan	Promotion
GROUP TWO		
1. Knowledge of market	Trends	Monthly reports
	Statistics	Number of visits per given time
	Reports	
	Fairs	
	Visits	
	Literature	
2. Knowledge of in-plant needs	Operating plans	X meeting with users
	Programs	Highlight report (monthly)
	Schedules	
3. Setting priorities	Number of orders	Monthly order status
	Status report	Report
	Claims	X order in process
		Y order to be placed
4. Setting objectives	Lists	Functional
	Reports	Performance rating
5. Vendor evaluation and selection	Number of evaluated vendors	x% evaluation
		New and current
6. Negotiation	Coverage	Coverage 70%
	Results	Rating achievement
7. Functional control	Work load	Record of overtime
	Prices	Planning
	Delivery	
8. Vendor relations	Contacts	

Fig. 26-8   Example of objective setting for the senior buyer's job.

subordinates on a yearly basis. It is generally a discussion between the individual and his immediate supervisor about progress made in achieving the established objectives. These would have previously been discussed by the employee and his manager at a planning session. At the appraisal review, the subordinate can state what objectives he has achieved, what he has not achieved, and why. This review focuses on the end results of effort rather than the means for getting there.

The experience of many managers suggests that a rather thorough progress review should be held at least once a quarter. Indeed, some managers may feel that a monthly progress review with a buyer, for example, is more valuable to them. The time range probably should be between 1 and 3 months. Many progress review sessions probably take place on a day-to-day basis as well as at the formal once-a-year or quarterly review.

Evaluation—Results versus Objectives   A definite relationship exists between the setting of performance objectives and the annual report or review of those objectives. The main difference is one of purpose. Objectives are intended to assist through better management in securing the desired results. The appraisal interview is a development tool. It helps a manager to fulfill a personnel responsibility to "grow people." Either process can exist without the other, however. The objective-setting process using the model described above can contribute greatly to an effective appraisal program. The appraisal becomes an effective communication tool to evaluate objectives and then change those objectives for a subsequent planning period. As such, it is an effective building block in a sound program of workforce utilization.

ADJUSTING PLANS AND METHODS

Good planning must be responsive to necessary changes. Planning of training programs is difficult because, as previously emphasized, it should be:

- TASK-oriented, i.e., train the person to do the job he or she is hired for—not two or three job levels higher
- Tailored to meet the specific needs of the individual involved, taking into consideration prior formal education and work experience
- Structured to use the best-known combination of traditional and scientific development methods

To fulfill these objectives, it is necessary to constantly evaluate both the trainee and the methods involved. For example, the trainee may not be developing as scheduled, which may indicate poor selection or poor training or inadequate plans. Adjustments can and should be made as the schedule unfolds. Alternatively, experience may prove that the training program is too simple for the trainee. Failure to adjust the program or shorten its length may decrease the trainee's motivation.

In conclusion, selection and development of purchasing personnel are a challenging and rewarding effort.

Purchasing activity's long-range success is sharply dependent on a well-planned and strongly managed program. The adage "He who fails to plan, plans to fail" can readily be applied here.

NOTE: For further information on subjects covered in this section see the list of references in Section 30.

Evaluating Purchasing Performance

EDITOR

Robert M. Monczka, Ph.D., C.P.M. *Professor of Management, Graduate School of Business Administration, Michigan State University, East Lansing, Michigan*

ASSOCIATE EDITORS

Robert B. Stone *Vice-President, Materials Management Staff, General Motors Corporation, Detroit, Michigan*

Roger R. Frank, C.P.M. *Corporate Director of Purchasing, Baxter Travenol Laboratories, Inc., Deerfield, Illinois*

Evaluation in purchasing is required to ensure that progress is being made toward objectives according to plan. Evaluation is part of the control process.

Effective purchasing management requires effective control systems. Reporting systems need to be developed, purchasing performance standards established, results measured, corrective actions taken, and rewards provided.

Regular evaluation of the purchasing function is further needed to maintain a professional department. Clear and precisely stated purchasing objectives are a prerequisite to measuring and evaluating purchasing performance. These objectives provide the keys which guide the behavior of people within the purchasing and vendor systems.

WHY EVALUATE?

There are a number of important reasons for evaluating purchasing performance. These include:

- Directing attention to key purchasing performance areas and objectives to ensure that objectives are being met and performance is improving
- Providing data to take corrective action
- Improving purchasing department organization structure, policies, and procedures
- Improving interrelationships between purchasing, other functional areas, and vendors
- Providing guidelines for training
- Documenting and/or justifying the need for purchasing personnel
- Allocating rewards to motivate and reward behavior

Specific illustrations of circumstances under which purchasing evaluation is required include:

1. Executive management wants to assess the overall effectiveness of the purchasing function.
2. Purchase material budgets are trending unfavorably.
3. The administrative cost of purchasing and staffing levels seems too high or too low.

4. The ethical values guiding purchasing actions are questionable.
5. Vendor complaints are received.
6. There is a need to upgrade and professionalize purchasing.

PURCHASING MEASUREMENT AND EVALUATION FRAMEWORK

Purchasing evaluation takes different forms, as illustrated in Fig. 27-1. Three types of measurement and evaluation are identified: (1) purchasing functional reviews, (2) purchasing policy and procedure audits, and (3) short-term purchas-

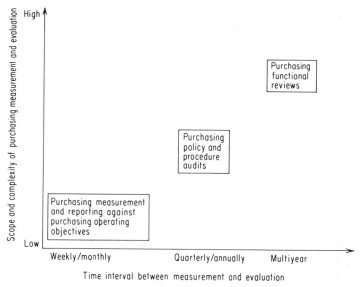

Fig. 27-1   Purchasing measurement and evaluation framework.

ing measurement and reporting. Each type is distinct because of its timing, scope, and data collection approaches.

Purchasing functional reviews are used to evaluate all aspects of the purchasing function, including organization, policies, procedures, personnel, interdepartmental relations, etc. This type of evaluation is the most complex, costly, and time-consuming, and is usually conducted at intervals exceeding 5 years. The major objective is to assess whether the function is performing as effectively as it should be.

Purchasing policy and procedure audits are done more frequently, often once or twice a year. They are used to determine *if* established purchasing policy and procedures are being adhered to. These evaluations are generally less complex and time-consuming than overall functional reviews.

Measurement and evaluation of day-to-day purchasing performance against objectives for key purchasing performance areas is done on a weekly and monthly basis. Monthly reporting of cost-saving performance against plan by buyer, subsection, and department is an example of this type of evaluation. It is characterized by regular data collection and reporting for a number of effectiveness and efficiency indicators.

PURCHASING OBJECTIVES

Clearly stated and well-understood purchasing objectives are prerequisites to purchasing measurement and evaluation. They provide the base against which the various methods of purchasing evaluation will be used to assess performance. Stated purchasing objectives are required to identify the purchasing performance areas that need evaluation. Examples of general purchasing objectives which are typical to many organizations include:

1. Continuous supply of needed materials, supplies, and services
2. Minimum inventory investment consistent with safety
3. Maintenance of adequate quality
4. Lowest total material costs
5. Supplier development
6. Maintaining the organization's competitive position
7. Good interdepartmental and supplier relationships
8. Lowest possible administrative costs consistent with purchasing objectives (productivity)
9. Development of purchasing personnel
10. Meeting legal and social responsibility requirements

Examples of specific company objectives, taken from company documents illustrating these objectives, are presented below.

Company 1

The stated objectives of this purchasing department are both budgeted and nonbudgeted. They include:

Budget

- Realize production bogeys and tooling budgets
- Realize cost reduction budgets
- Realize overhead expense and staffing budgets

Nonbudget

- Achieve and maintain small business procurement ratio
- Realize minority and female employment goals
- Achieve zero over-30-days unresolved consignments
- Improve program to use minority business

- Continue and improve educational program
- Place orders with foreign vendors as required by business commitment

Company 2

The stated purchasing objectives for this organization center around quality, cost, material availability, organization, operations, and cash-flow management objectives. Selected examples from a comprehensive listing include:

Quality

- Redefine quality objectives and measurements
- Analyze critical parts and materials
- Revise and/or validate specifications
- Improve sourcing

Cost

- Establish cost objectives
- Implement material-cost control plans to achieve material variance budget
- Implement commodity-cost teams
- Implement expense-material-cost teams

Material Availability

- Provide required purchased materials and services to meet production schedules
- Meet new model introduction schedules
- Review department-contracted commodities for supply agreements
- Define objectives of key materials program, and
- Implement material availability forecast programs within key materials program

Organization

- Implement professional purchasing program
- Complete organization definition
- Establish and attain equal opportunity and minority recruiting goals
- Appraise present employees

Company 3

- Ensure adequate dependable sources of supply for materials, supplies, equipment, and designated services procured by the supply department while maintaining an optimum balance of quality, utility, and cost
- Maximize purchasing strength in the marketplace to obtain most favorable terms and conditions of purchase
- Contribute to maximum corporate profitability through judicious and ethical buying of raw materials, equipment, supplies, and designated services

- Develop and apply sound purchasing principles, practices, and techniques to the supply function
- Develop and maintain a competent purchasing staff and manage company-wide procurement activities to achieve the lowest cost to adequately carry out the function
- Contribute to improved management decision making through development and maintenance of information services in the areas of
  1. New items and services
  2. Market demands
  3. New sources
  4. Price fluctuation and trends
  5. Equipment design changes
  6. New materials and methods
- Promote a positive company image among vendors and the general public
- Establish and maintain equitable and mutually profitable relationships with suppliers
- Cooperate with other company management to promote the best interests of the corporation
- Develop and implement contractual safeguards which clearly establish responsibility for the warranting of design, materials, workmanship, performance, and patents for all purchased materials, goods, and services
- Optimize investment in purchased material inventories through cooperative and supportive activity with operating departments
- Minimize total delivered costs through management and control of inbound transportation, in cooperation with the traffic and distribution department
- Use internal sources of supply when this is to the advantage of the company
- Maximize investment recovery through judicious scrap and surplus disposal
- Contribute to the orderly development and implementation of a materials management concept in the company

WHAT SHOULD BE MEASURED?

Performance against stated purchasing objectives needs to be measured and evaluated regularly. As shown in Fig. 27-1, different types of measurement and evaluation are conducted at different times. Functional reviews of all aspects of the department are periodically required, while purchasing policy and procedure audits and short-term measurement of performance in key performance areas are done regularly.

Purchasing Functional Reviews

Purchasing functional reviews should provide answers to the following types of questions:

1. What is the scope and authority of purchasing activities at corporate, division, and plant levels, and are they appropriate and clearly established?

2. Are purchasing policies, procedures, and practices up to date, documented, and as effective and efficient as can be?

3. Do the purchasing personnel have adequate knowledge and skills to do business in an increasingly complex purchasing environment?

4. Are there purchasing staff development and education and training plans and programs?

5. What are the roles, relationships, responsibilities, and authority between corporate, division, and plant purchasing activities?

6. How effective is the purchasing organization structure from a company-wide standpoint?

7. Are there adequate purchasing coordination and control mechanisms?

8. How well does purchasing interface with other functional groups, particularly those directly related to the purchasing activity?

9. How is purchasing viewed by vendors?

10. Is full advantage being taken of the company's overall buying leverage?

11. Is there an adequate purchasing performance measurement and control system?

Additional questions of a more detailed nature may also require answers. These include:

- Is purchasing accepted by local management? Why or why not?
- Are there documented purchase plans and strategies?
- Have blanket orders, corporate contracts and/or national buying agreements, and area agreements been fully utilized?
- Are purchased-item inventory management policies, responsibilities, and practices adequate?
- Are expediting systems operating sufficiently?
- Is there a cost-saving program?
- Are competitive bidding practices fully utilized?
- Are purchasing files and records easily accessible?
- Have short- and long-run problems been identified and solutions developed?
- Are there job descriptions?
- Is minority purchasing policy clearly established?

Purchasing Policy and Procedure Audits

Adherence to purchasing policy and procedures requires systematic evaluation. All key areas of established purchasing policy and procedure should be evaluated (see Section 3 for guidelines about what should be included in the policy and procedural manual). Key areas for evaluation usually include:

1. Ethics and gratuities
2. Competitive bidding and source selection practices
3. Proper paperwork documentation and accuracy
4. Responsiveness and fairness with vendors

5. Following authority guidelines and purchasing within dollar authority limitations

6. Cost analysis practices (where appropriate)

Purchasing Performance Measurement and Evaluation

Purchasing measurement and evaluation are needed at regular short intervals for many performance areas. Twelve categories of purchasing performance measures were identified as being regularly measured by various organizations in a major research study[1]. These purchasing performance measures were:

1. Price effectiveness
2. Cost saving
3. Workload
4. Administration and control
5. Efficiency
6. Vendor quality and delivery
7. Material flow control
8. Regulatory-societal-environmental
9. Procurement planning and research
10. Competition
11. Inventory
12. Transportation

HOW TO EVALUATE

Somewhat different data collection, measurement, and reporting techniques are used for purchasing functional reviews, purchasing policy and procedure audits, and regular purchasing performance measurement. Each is discussed below.

Purchasing Functional Reviews

The purchasing functional review process is shown in Fig. 27-2.

A situational analysis provides the starting point for the purchasing functional review. It provides answers to the question: Where are we today? Data are collected about the current situation in a number of areas (earlier discussed) and compared with what should be, or standards of expected performance. Differences

Fig. 27-2   Functional review process.

[1]R. M. Monczka, P. L. Carter, and J. H. Hoagland, *Purchasing Performance: Measurement and Control* (E. Lansing: Michigan State University, Bureau of Business and Economic Research, 1979).

between actual performance and expectations result in recommendations necessary to bring the existing situation into the desired state.

Functional reviews are generally done by a team comprised of both purchasing and nonpurchasing personnel. It may also include a purchasing authority from outside the company to provide an independent viewpoint.

Data are collected by using a variety of techniques such as interviews with purchasing and nonpurchasing personnel; document review of organization charts, policies, and procedures; and review of operating data such as items purchased, dollar value of purchases, purchases by using locations, dollar approval levels, number of purchasing personnel, educational background and experience of purchasing personnel, etc. These reviews often will take 1 to 3 months to accomplish.

Purchasing Policy and Procedure Audits

These audits are usually accomplished by reviewing purchasing transaction files on a sampling basis for a given period of time, for example, the past 3 months. Evidence of adherence or lack of adherence to purchasing policy and procedure is reviewed. Simple counts and percentages are often used to develop qualitative reports to management. Other sources of information about adherence to purchasing policy and procedure, especially in the area of ethics and gratuities, is often obtained by interviewing others in the company and vendors.

The following questions illustrate the kind of monitoring that can be done:

1. Are approval signatures appropriate?
2. For competitive quotations:
   a. Was the date on request for quotation?
   b. Were there the required number of quotes?
   c. Were times of quotes stamped upon receipt?
   d. Was business placed with other than the low bidder?
   e. Was justification for business placed with other than the low bidder documented?
3. Are current quotes on file?
4. Do quote and latest engineering change agree?
5. Is tooling agreement complete?

In addition, some organizations may want to conduct a shortened version of the purchasing functional review as part of a purchase audit. This involves collecting data about a limited number of the factors earlier described and in a less detailed manner.

Purchasing Performance Measurement and Evaluation

Measurements and reporting for the 12 key purchasing performance areas are discussed in the following sections.

Price Effectiveness Measures   Various measures can be used to determine how effectively purchasing dollars are being spent, primarily for production items.

These measures are (1) actual purchase price versus planned purchase price comparisons, (2) actual purchase price(s) compared with a market index, and (3) comparisons of actual-to-actual purchase prices for individual and aggregated items between operating plants or divisions within an organization.

ACTUAL PRICE COMPARED WITH PLAN. Planned purchase prices can be based either on historical cost, historical cost plus a budgeted increase or decrease,

---

Measurements

1. Purchase price variance = actual price − planned price
2. Purchase price variance percentage = actual price ÷ planned price
3. Total purchase price variance = (actual price − planned price) × purchase quantity or estimated annual volume
4. Current year dollar impact of purchase price variance = (actual price = planned price) × (estimated annual volume × percent of requirements remaining)

Units of Measure

1. Dollars
2. Percent

Reported by:

1. Purchase item
2. Commodity or family group
3. Product
4. Project
5. Location
6. Buyer
7. Management group
8. Vendor

Fig. 27-3 Purchase price variance from plan.

or a target price forecast—generally used for new items. Favorable or unfavorable variances from plan can be calculated and used as a measure of purchasing effectiveness. Purchase plans normally are developed, at least for higher-priced purchased items.

Figure 27-3 outlines purchase-price variance calculations, the units of measure, and how these variances often are reported. Actual price, planned price, and variance from plan for each line item can be aggregated by major purchase group or family, by product sold, and by the material budget.

DEVELOPING THE PURCHASE PLAN. The measurement of absolute, percentage, and extended-quantity variances from plan is relatively mechanical. Development of the purchase plan is the most critical aspect of measuring purchasing price effectiveness. Figure 27-4 represents the flow of activities normally making up the purchase material planning and measurement process.

From Fig. 27-4, the first step in the planning process is to determine the purchase requirements. These can be established from a bill of material or other material requirement documents. Next, the operating purchase-price plan for a future time period needs to be developed. This plan is based on: (1) historical price (current or last price paid) modified by documented price changes which have been agreed to and which will take effect before the end of the next planning period; (2) historical price plus forecast price changes; and (3) price forecasts for new purchased items.

In developing an operating plan, price forecasts can be made within the pur-

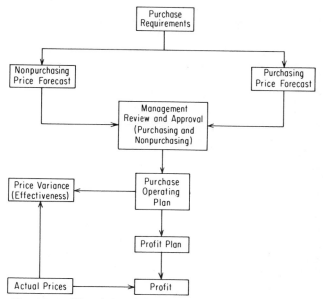

Fig. 27-4   Planning and measurement of price effectiveness.

chasing department by buyers and reviewed by purchasing management 3 to 6 months prior to the planning horizon which was the next budget period. Industrial engineers can also be used to develop independent forecasts of purchase prices by part number.

Other personnel generally involved in the planning process include financial, manufacturing, product, and top management. Whereas buying and staff purchasing personnel develop and review plans at the detail level, financial, manufacturing, product, and top management efforts are concentrated at the commodity, product, and material budget levels.

Approved material budgets become part of the operating plan and are then incorporated into the profit plan. To determine favorable or unfavorable variances, actual prices paid are compared with operating plan prices. These variances are then related to such categories as products being sold, buyers, vendors, and commodity groups.

ACTUAL PRICES-TO-MARKET INDEX.   Purchase price versus market index comparisons are often used to provide information about the relationship of actual prices to published market prices. An index representing the actual cost of items purchased can be compared with the producers price index (PPI)[2], or against an index that included only items in the PPI which the company purchased. Figure 27-5 illustrates how an index reflecting the actual purchases of the organizations can be calculated. Invoiced prices paid are used in these calculations. Comparisons

Purchased Item No.	Purchase Price	Annual Quantity	Annual Value of Purchases	Percentage of Annual Value of Purchases
1	$1.00	100	$ 100	5
2	2.00	150	300	15
3	3.00	100	300	15
4	4.00	200	800	40
5	5.00	100	500	25
			$2000	100

Base period price = $1 × 0.05 + $2 × 0.15 + $3 × 0.15 + $4 × 0.4 + $5 × 0.25

= $0.05 + $0.30 + $0.45 + $1.60 + $1.25

= $3.65 = 100 (Base period price index)

Company Index, Actual		Producer Price Index	Index Based on Selected Items from Producer Price Index Reflecting Actual Purchase
September	105	115	125
October	110	120	140

In this example, weights are assigned to each of the purchased items based on the annual value of purchases in the base year. The base-period price index is calculated by multiplying the purchase price for each item by the weighting factor. In this case the base-period price is $3.65 and the index is 100. Rates of change in the indexes or between the indexes are calculated by dividing the current index by the base or desired preceding period index.

Fig. 27-5   Developing a purchase price index.

of indexes provide information about how the firm is performing compared with the market and indications about the direction and extent of future price changes.

In Fig. 27-5, for example, the PPI and the index based on selected items are both higher than the actual index, indicating a favorable situation of the company with respect to the market. However, the data also show that in the last time period the index of selected items from the PPI was increasing at a greater rate than the overall PPI (140/125, or 12 percent, versus 120/115, or 4.3 percent). By looking at the index based on selected PPI items, the organization could anticipate pressure for more significant price increases than it could expect if only the overall PPI were reviewed. Additional information is available by using more detailed breakdowns of products which make up the PPI, which are available from the U.S. Bureau of Labor Statistics.

PRICE COMPARISONS BETWEEN OPERATIONS.   Actual purchase price comparisons between operating plants and/or divisions buying similar items can also be

[2]Formerly the wholesale price index.

made. This type of measurement provides opportunity to identify purchase price difference requiring justification.

REPORTING PRICE EFFECTIVENESS.   Various reporting formats are used to report price effectiveness. These are illustrated in Figs. 27-6 through 27-8.

Figure 27-6 illustrates approaches typically used to report purchase price effectiveness. After approval of the purchase operating plan, progress toward achievement can be monitored monthly, with reports going to various levels within the purchasing department and to selected nonpurchasing managers.

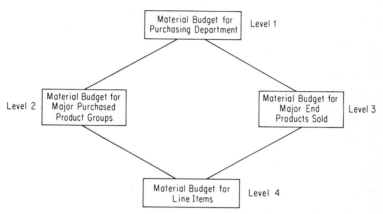

Fig. 27-6   Reporting of purchase variance from plan.

Four reporting levels are depicted in reporting purchase price variances from plan. Level 1 reporting is at the overall purchase material-budget level. The material budget is established and actual-to-planned expenditures are monitored.

Level 4 reporting requires that purchase price plans be established at the part or item number level, which can then be aggregated into major purchase product groups or families. Actual-to-planned purchase price performance can be monitored by buyer, group or section, and vendor. Actual-to-planned performance is usually rolled up into levels 1, 2, and 3.

Level 2 reporting is for major purchases by group or family. Actual-to-planned performance is monitored and reported throughout purchasing. Level 3 control is organized so that actual-to-planned purchase-price performance can be monitored for products sold.

It appears that the most effective control of purchasing price effectiveness requires measurement and reporting at least at levels 1 and 4.

Figure 27-7 represents a typical purchase-price variance (from plan) report. Reports such as this may be sent to purchasing managers and their managers, subsection managers, and to buyers.

The report illustrated is a monthly report and includes a number of measurement factors considered important in managing purchase price. It includes purchases for all products produced.

The relationship between current purchase cost (column 1) and estimated purchase cost (column 2) should be closely reviewed. If the relationship of current purchase cost to estimated purchase cost is trending unfavorably, i.e., approaching 100 percent or more, purchasing management can determine, by line item, which

Month	Current purchase cost (Column 1)	Nonpurchasing estimate of purchase cost (Column 2)	Purchase cost to estimated cost percentage (Column 3)	Actual purchase cost to produce product (Column 4)	Operating plan purchase cost (Column 5)	Actual to plan percentage (Column 6)
January	$ 10,000	$ 12,000	83	$ 9,000	$ 10,000	90
Cumulative	10,000	12,000	83	9,000	10,000	90
February	11,000	12,000	91	10,000	10,000	100
Cumulative	21,000	24,000	87	19,000	20,000	95
March						
Cumulative						
April						
Cumulative						
May						
Cumulative						
June						
Cumulative						
July						
Cumulative						
August						
Cumulative						
September						
Cumulative						
October						
Cumulative						
November						
Cumulative						
December						
Cumulative						

Fig. 27-7   Monthly comparisons report—composite purchase price for major products produced.

purchase prices were trending most unfavorably and then could determine where corrective actions might be taken. This would require analysis of a report with additional detail.

The actual-to-plan percentage (column 6) is calculated by dividing the actual purchase cost to produce finished products (column 4) by the operating-plan purchase cost (column 5), which also is closely monitored. This percentage provides information about whether purchasing is meeting its purchase-cost commitment for final products.

For example, in reviewing Fig. 27-7, the data indicate that a short-term unfavorable trend is developing in the relationship between the current purchase cost and the estimated purchase cost (column 3). The percentage (column 1 divided by column 2) goes from 83 to 91 percent in a 1-month period, indicating unfavorable purchase price changes.

In addition, the data indicate that the actual-to-plan percentage (column 6) is less favorable than in the prior month. Purchasing may need to identify problem parts and take specific actions.

Figure 27-8 represents a typical report for company-to-market index comparisons. This report shows the company index increasing at a more rapid rate than the PPI overall, providing important information to purchasing management.

Cost-Saving Measures   Cost-saving measures can be classified into two basic categories, cost reduction and cost avoidance, which need to be measured and evaluated. *Cost reduction* requires that purchase price be reduced from the last price paid. *Cost avoidance* is the difference between price paid and a higher price that

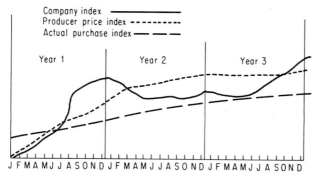

Fig. 27-8   Comparison of company, actual, and market indexes.

might have been paid had purchasing not obtained the lower price. For example, if the price paid was lower than the originally quoted price, the difference could be a cost avoidance.

Figure 27-9 illustrates cost reduction and cost avoidance measures. Figure 27-10 contains an illustration of a return-on-investment measure using cost reduction in its calculations.

Cost reduction measures are measures of how actual costs were reduced by purchasing or by purchasing working with other departments. The following statement from one organization provides a definition of a cost improvement—or a cost reduction.

> A cost improvement is a decrease in operating cost resulting from a change in practice which is brought about by specific individual or group effort aimed at securing such cost decreases. The value of any cost improvement is represented by the annualized value (normally the next 12 months) of the difference between the revised practice and the cost which would have been incurred under normal circumstances without the specific change in practice.

The distinction between cost reduction and cost avoidance is that cost reduction is a reduction from a prior purchase price or practice whereas cost avoidance refers to the difference between what might have been and what is.

Some firms combine cost reductions and cost avoidances into one category,

Measure Examples:

Cost Reduction
Unit cost reduction in dollars = old unit price − new unit price

Annual or quantity dollar
Cost reduction = (old unit price − new unit price) × annual or purchase quantity

Cost reduction variance from budget or target = actual cost reduction (unit or annual) − budgeted cost reduction (unit or annual)

Cost Avoidance
Unit cost avoidance in dollars = vendor requested unit cost − actual unit cost

Annual or quantity cost avoidance in dollars = (vendor requested unit cost − actual unit cost) × annual or buy quantity

Cost avoidance variance from budget or target = actual cost avoidance (unit or annual) − budgeted cost avoidance (unit or annual)

Vendor requested unit cost = average of quoted prices; highest quoted prices; add-on costs not incurred, e.g., free samples, tools

Units of Measure
Dollars
Percentages

Summaries By:
Buyer
Management group
Purchasing department
Commodity group

Location
Purchase item
Project

How Reported
Monthly
Year-to-Date

Fig. 27-9   Cost reduction and cost avoidance measure examples.

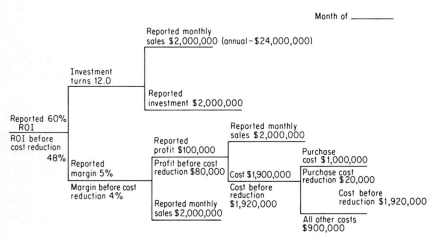

Fig. 27-10   Return-on-investment example.

under labels such as cost savings or cost reduction. The following definition of cost savings from one organization illustrates this:

A savings in the cost of purchased materials or services *is achieved through planned and deliberate action by Purchasing,* often in cooperation with other departments. It results in improving costs for plant, distribution, overhead or capital construction. The savings also reflect that a better way, lower price, less labor, less power consumption, alternate materials, etc., have been achieved through constructive and creative effort that would not have occurred had no such action been taken. It does *not* include cost reductions that may occur without such planned and deliberate action nor those in which Purchasing played no part nor took any role.

Purchasing savings should pass the following basic criteria to qualify for being reportable.

A planned and deliberate action or change must be made by Purchasing which resulted in the reduction of a cost, a value improvement, or an avoidance of a higher cost that would have occurred had the action not been taken.

- *Savings must be identifiable and measurable.*
- *The saving must be an improvement from the cost that would have been incurred if no planned, deliberate action had been taken by the Purchasing personnel.*
- Saving must be *actual,* not *potential,* to be reportable.
- A cost avoidance saving must reduce or eliminate *a new cost which would have otherwise occurred.*

Following are cost reductions that do not qualify as purchasing saving:

- *Windfall saving* which occurs without planned and deliberate action. Example, a price decrease voluntarily offered by a vendor.
- *The routine choice of the lower of two or more bids* that results from routine request for quotations.
- *Saving in "overhead" or allocated cost* between units of Company X when *the total Company X cost will not be directly reduced* by the change.
- Cost saving resulting from *lower requirements* that may be caused by reduced sales, withdrawal from a business, etc.
- Correction of a *previously recognized* error or improper procedure.

Another approach used to measure and demonstrate purchasing cost reductions is shown in Fig. 27-10. Cost reductions in purchasing are shown as contributing to profit as measured by the organization's return on investment (ROI). In this case purchase costs were reduced by $20,000. The rationale used is that if these costs had not been reduced by purchasing, profits for the month would have been $80,000 instead of $100,000 and the rate of return on sales 4 percent instead of 5 percent. If the calculated annualized investment return of 12 had been used, an ROI of 48 percent rather than 60 percent would have been realized.

MEASURING AND REPORTING COST REDUCTIONS AND COST AVOIDANCES. Similarities in collecting, measuring, and reporting cost savings are found in use in many organizations. This process is illustrated in Fig. 27-11. Normally, a cost reduction or cost avoidance is developed by the buyer, who reports it on a cost-saving form. This form usually contains data pertaining to part number, description, purchase order number, supplier, quantity, old and new unit prices, amount claimed as cost reduction or cost avoidance, and supporting justification for the saving. Figures 27-12 and 27-13 are typical examples of cost-saving reports.

Once these cost-saving forms are completed by the buyer, they normally are reviewed by purchasing management and an independent analyst or cost-saving program coordinator. After the cost saving is approved, the forms are included in a monthly measurement report showing progress toward goal on a monthly and year-to-date basis. Reports of cost savings are generally organized by buyer, by management group, by department, and occasionally by product line.

Workload Measures Purchasing department workload can be measured in the following categories:

1. Workload-in—a measure of the new work coming into the purchasing department
2. Workload-current—a measure of the current backlog of work
3. Workload-completed—a measure of the work accomplished by purchasing

Workload measures are used primarily to determine purchasing workload levels and to provide information for staff scheduling, balancing, or justification.

WORKLOAD-IN. Measures in this classification typically are simple counts of work received. Among the items counted are:

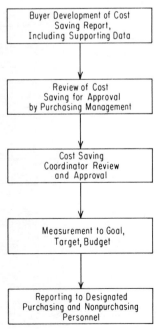

- Purchase requests and/or requisitions received
- Urgent purchase requests and/or requisitions received
- Protests received (public sector organizations only)
- Pricing requests received
- Change notices

Counts usually are reported on a monthly or cumulative year-to-date basis.

Workload-in measures can be reviewed regularly by purchasing management and used to help predict and explain changes in other departmental measures. For instance, increase in workload received would lead to a corresponding increase in purchase administration lead time, if work force size and efficiency stayed the same.

WORKLOAD-CURRENT. Measures in this category typically are counts of the backlog of work within the purchasing department. The most common counts are:

- Open purchase requests and/or requisitions on hand

Fig. 27-11 Typical activity flow of cost-saving measurement and reporting.

					Purchased material cost reduction report				

Originator _____ Report for week of _____ 19 _____

Ref	Order number	Supplier	Part number – noun description	Quantity this buy	Old unit price	New unit price	Total saved this buy

REPORTABLE CONDITIONS

REF   DESCRIPTION

1   New Source –
        A change in the approved, mandated or tooled source of supply at the instigation
        of the buyer
2   Negotiation –
        Includes material cost, payment terms and transportation.
3   Use of residual material on completely different program.
4   Blanket agreements/master orders (report only when order number is issued) –
        Savings in unit prices and estimated reduction in number of orders issued at $25 each.
5   Change in design or specification –
        Acceptance and implementation of change instigated by buyer.
6   Procedural change/simplification of clerical routines.
7   Shipping and handling costs –
        Includes packaging.
8   Reduction in scrap or obsolescence
9   Substitution of standard part for special part –
        Acceptance and implementation of substitution instigated by buyer and accepted by user.
10   Use of repaired, modified, used or salvaged equipment.
11   Return or surplus material for credit.
12   Samples –
        Avoidance of material costs by obtaining samples, savings will equal $25 (order
        cost) or the value of the material involved, whichever is greater.

CONDITIONS WHICH ARE NOT TO BE REPORTED

        Alternate price comparisons.
        Consolidation of requirements for like items.
        Use of residual material on same program.
        Reduced cost due to change in scope unless such change is instigated by Purchasing.
        Economic ordering quantity.

Fig. 27-12   Cost-saving reporting form.

- Line items to be purchased
- Open purchase orders

These are usually reported on a monthly basis and usually compared with the previous year's experience.

WORKLOAD-COMPLETED.   Measures found in this category include:

- Purchase orders placed
- Line items purchased
- Dollars of purchases placed
- Contracts written
- Pricing proposals written

USING WORKLOAD MEASURES.   Workload measures are thought to be valuable in many organizations. Furthermore, a number of workload measures should be used together to most accurately determine work trends.

In most organizations, workload counts are captured from data collected and reported by using a computer system. Reporting frequency of workload varies from weekly to monthly, based on the volume of work and the importance of monitoring changes in workload. In most organizations it seems that monthly reporting is adequate.

Administration and Control Measures Administration and control measures are used to help plan the annual administrative budget for purchasing and to help control administrative expenses during the budget period. The administrative bud-

---

COST EFFECTIVENESS/AVOIDANCE REPORT FORM

_____ Cost effectiveness

_____ Cost avoidance

P/N _____   Date: _____

Mach. type _____   Savings:

Description _____   Category 1. $_____
                                     (Based on gross annual requirement (GAR) at time
PO # _____   of purchase order placement. Use peak year for new
                                     products)

Method code _____
(from CE/CA guideline)   Category 2. $_____
                                     (Based on program requirements)

                                     Other $_____

Brief summary of how cost saving was achieved:

Brief breakdown of financial calculations:

Team contributors:

Name	Dept.	Manager signature

Fig. 27-13 Cost-saving reporting form.

get typically includes salaries, travel and living expenses, training expenses, telephone expenses, office supplies, and miscellaneous. Salaries are by far the largest item.

The major question is: How large should the purchasing budget be? Since salaries are the major item in the budget, the crux of the question is: What should our head count be? Many organizations believe that the answer to this question depends heavily on the workload purchasing is required to complete. This leads to further problems in defining workload and establishing the relationship between workload and head count.

Various methods (discussed below) can be used to plan the budget (i.e., allocate dollars for purchasing administration) and to control actual expenditures against the budget. The following methods for planning and controlling the administrative budget start with the broadest, least complex and proceed to the more detailed and complex.

CURRENT BUDGET PLUS ADJUSTMENT.   The most common method used for establishing a new budget is to start with the current administrative budget and adjust it up or down, depending on the business forecast for the next planning period (usually a year). The adjustment reflects management's views about projected purchasing workload and projected profit margins. Increasing workload, coupled with good or increasing profit margins, often results in a budget increase. Decreasing workload, coupled with poor or declining margins, often results in a budget decrease.

For the firms employing this approach to budgeting, no *formal* methods are usually used to relate workload or business conditions to the budget or head count level. The budget is justified each year by using whatever arguments are currently valid.

CONTROL RATIO.   Where this approach is used, the purchasing administrative budget is established as a percentage (ratio) of another measure chosen to reflect the purchasing workload. The workload measure typically is planned dollar expenditure for direct material. The budget calculation is:

Purchasing administrative budget = ratio × direct material input budget

The ratio is based on historical levels and on negotiations between the purchasing manager and higher management. In good times the ratio might be above the historical average and in bad times below.

The material input budget is based on a projection of material input needed to support final product deliveries for the next year. The implicit assumption is that the purchasing workload is proportional to direct material input dollars.

Once the ratio and budget are set for the year, the ratio then becomes a control figure for actual expenses. That ratio,

$$\text{Monthly ratio} = \frac{\text{actual monthly purchasing administrative expense}}{\text{monthly direct material input dollars}}$$

is calculated and reported on a monthly basis. If this monthly ratio is consistently above or below the negotiated ratio, steps are taken to modify expenditures.

Control of the administrative budget at the departmental level is accomplished in part by controlling the *ratio,* not the dollars. This approach provides a flexible budget (in dollars) that expands or contracts with workload (as measured by direct material input).

A problem with this control ratio approach is that much of the actual work of purchasing is completed before the direct material is received and paid for by the organization. If significant variations in actual purchasing workload and direct material input occur over time, this leads to cycles of over- and underfunding of the purchasing department.

MODELS FOR BUYERS.   Several organizations are using or experimenting with methods for translating projected purchasing workload into a specific head count.

Model 1 Buyer

Buys: New subcontracted systems, new forgings, new castings.

Assumptions: Buyer has 5 to 7 years experience, is working on systems or parts with 30 weeks lead time, and is buying for three programs.

Workload: Buyer can handle 25 active part numbers and 3 new requisitions per week.

Model 2 Buyer

Buys: State-of-the-art products with special testing and data requirements.

Assumptions: Buyer has 3 to 5 years purchasing experience, is working on parts with 24 to 30 weeks lead time and is buying for five programs.

Workload: Buyer can handle 75 active part numbers and 5 new requisitions per week.

Model 3 Buyer

Buys: Special parts made to customer specification without special testing.

Assumptions: Buyer has 2 or more years experience, is working on parts with 8 weeks lead time, and is buying for 10 programs.

Workload: Buyer can handle 340 active part numbers and 30 new requisitions per week.

Model 4 Buyer

Buys: Standard parts.

Assumptions: Buyer has 1 or more years experience, is working on parts with 3 weeks lead time, and is buying for 15 programs.

Workload: Buyer can handle 450 active part numbers and 100 new requisitions per week.

Fig. 27-14   Models of buyers.

There are several variations, but the essence of each is to establish a standard workload per buyer, based on historical performance and/or time studies. The projected workload is then divided by the standard to calculate the total number of buyers required. The projected number of buyers is multiplied by another ratio to get the number of secretarial-clerical workers needed. Finally a fixed number of managers and other staff is added to get a head count for the department.

One organization has developed four models for buyers. The models are shown in Fig. 27-14.

LABOR AND EXPENSE BUDGET REPORTING.   Most organizations need to measure and report actual administrative expenses against budget. Although variations occur in the amount of detail, a representative list of accounts used by most organizations includes the following:

- Labor nonexempt
- Labor exempt
- Benefits
- Clerical
- Purchased indirect labor
- Night shift bonus
- Employee organization expenses
- Education and training expenses
- Office furniture and equipment
- Telephone and telegraph
- Computer time sharing

- Space rental
- Duplication
- Mail service
- Stadium box usage
- Office supplies
- Graphic material and supply
- Purchased services
- Travel expenses
- Books and subscriptions
- Other services
- Other supplies

Expenses generally are reported for control purposes on a monthly and year-to-date (YTD) basis. Representative methods include:

- Actual monthly expense
- Monthly budget
- Year-to-date actual expenses
- Year-to-date budget

Current month expense variance

$$= \frac{\text{Actual monthly expense} - \text{monthly budget}}{\text{monthly budget}}$$

$$\text{YTD expense variance} = \frac{\text{Actual YTD expenses} - \text{YTD budget}}{\text{YTD budget}}$$

The above figures may be reported for the total purchasing department, for groups within the department, and for individual expense categories. Often, labor costs and all other expenses are reported separately and as a total. A sample report form appears in Fig. 27-15.

PURCHASING DEPARTMENT
Actual Expenses through June 30, 19—
Budget through December 31, 19—

Account	19— Actual	19— Budget 6/30/—	19— Actual 6/30/—	19— Budget	19— Estimated Actual	Variance	Comments
Salaries							
Benefits							
Temporary labor							
Total, personnel							
Travel							
Telephone							
Education and training							
Total, expenses							
Total, department							

Fig. 27-15   Example of purchasing administrative budget report.

Efficiency Measures Efficiency measures relate purchasing output, such as line items placed, to purchasing input, such as buyers. These measures range from two-factor measures that have one input and one output to multifactor measures that relate several outputs to several inputs.

Efficiency and *productivity* are sometimes used to mean the same thing. If a distinction between the two terms is made it is that productivity measures effectiveness, i.e., quality of performance, as well as efficiency.

TWO-FACTOR MEASURES. These measures are calculated by dividing a count of some output of the purchasing department by a count of a resource input. A wide variety of inputs and outputs are counted by the purchasing organization, with most using several different measures. Representative lists of outputs and inputs for two-factor measures are:

Outputs

- Purchase orders placed
- Change orders completed
- Line items placed
- Contracts written
- Dollars committed
- Salespeople interviewed
- Average open dollar commitments
- Cost-saving dollars
- Number of releases

Inputs

- Administrative dollars
- Number of personnel
- Actual hours

The more common two-factor measures are listed below. Included in parentheses are some of the variations found. Some of the measures commonly reported as input-output are identified with an asterisk (*).

Two-Factor Efficiency Measures

1. Purchase orders per buyer (per clerk, per total staff)
2. Line items per buyer (per clerk, per total staff)
3. Dollars committed per buyer (per clerk, per total staff)
4. Change notices per buyer (per clerk, per total staff)
5. Contracts written per buyer (per clerk, per total staff)
6. Average open dollar commitment by buyer (per clerk, per total staff)
*7. Worker-hours per line item
*8. Worker-hours per purchase order
*9. Worker-hours per contract
*10. Administrative dollars per purchase order
*11. Administrative dollars per contract
*12. Administrative dollars per purchase dollar (per $100 purchased)

These ratios are often calculated for the whole purchasing department, for various subgroups within the department, and for purchasing departments at various operating sites. Groups and subgroups are compared on the efficiency measures and significant deviations from past, average, or other performances are investigated to determine possible causes. One example of an efficiency report is shown in Fig. 27-16.

PURCHASING ADMINISTRATIVE LEAD TIME. *Purchasing administrative lead time (PALT)* is an efficiency measure that is often tracked. PALT is generally defined to be the elapsed time from the arrival of a purchase requisition in the purchasing department until the requisition is placed with a vendor.

Several approaches can be taken in reporting and controlling PALT. Organi-

Prepared by		Location			
	Average quarter				
Description	previous year	Year 19___			
	19 ___	1st quarter	2d quarter	3d quarter	4th quarter
Purchasing Department actions					
1. Spot purchase orders					
2. Requirement orders					
3. Standing orders/price agreements					
4. Construction/maintenance orders					
5. Leases and rentals					
6. Petty cash orders					
7. Releases made by Purchasing Department					
8. Total actions by Purchasing Department					
Actions by others					
9. Spot purchase orders by EDP methods					
10. Releases made by EDP methods					
11. Releases made by others (storeroom, etc.)					
Purchasing cost and expenditures					
12. Total cost of Purchasing Department (1)					
13. Local dollar purchases (2)					
14. Dollars administered local, purchased by others (3)					
15. Total dollars local, purchased, and administered					
Purchasing savings					
16. Savings reported through area coordination					
17. All other purchasing savings					
18. Total purchasing savings					
Purchasing Department ratios					
19. Cost as a percent of total dollars purchasing, and administration (line 12 ÷ line 15 x 100) (as percent)					
20. Total savings as a percent of total local purchases (line 18 ÷ line 13 x 100) (as percent)					
Purchasing Department personnel					
21. Purchasing					
22. Support personnel					
23. Total Purchasing Department personnel					

Fig. 27-16 Quarterly purchasing statistical summary.

zations establish time limits in which most requisitions should have been placed. Buyers then receive reports listing all open requisitions; those that are over the time limit are flagged to indicate that they are delinquent. This type of report reminds buyers of the age of the requisitions and serves as a basis for an exception report to management, allowing managers to focus on problem requisitions and/ or buyers and to gauge how the department as a whole is doing in the timely placement of requisitions.

Material Flow Control   Many organizations have reports and measures concerning the flow of material from vendors to the organization. These reports can be classified into four functions:

1. Identification of open purchase orders and their due dates

2. Identification of past due open purchase orders, that is, those orders for which the current date is later than the due date, need date, or promise date, and for which material has not been received

3. Identification of material or orders that are needed immediately by manufacturing, i.e., a "hot list"

4. Measurement of how well purchasing, buyers, and vendors are doing in meeting due dates

In many organizations, functions 1, 2, and 4 are included in one report. For example, a buyer might get a weekly listing of all open purchase orders, with overdue orders tagged or identified in some way. A purchasing manager might get only a list of overdue orders, plus the percent of overdue orders to total orders.

A *hot list* in an organization is a separate report generated usually by manufacturing. Items appear on a hot list when manufacturing discovers a shortage in needed parts. Hot lists are generated at least weekly and sometimes more often.

There are many different kinds of material flow control reports. Figure 27-17 is a typical example. On this report are listed all the open purchase orders for a buyer. Included with each open purchase order are (from left to right on the report): part number, purchase order number, item classification (i.e., A, B, C), vendor number, quantity ordered, units of measurement for this item, order placement date, vendor promise date, and description of the item.

Open Purchase Order Status Report
November 12, 19—
Buyer XXXX

Part Number	Purchase Order Number	Item Classification	Vendor Number	Quantity Ordered	Units	Order Date	Due Date	Description
1234	3501	A	9174	40	Each	9/03	10/03	• • •
1249	3502	B	9174	2	Pair	9/20	10/20	• •
2178	3519	C	3135	18	Each	11/04	12/04	
6753	3327	B	2015	1	Each	7/31	10/30	•

Fig. 27-17   Open-purchase-order status report.

The asterisks just before the description identify those items that are overdue and indicate the number of days late. The code is:

No asterisks: item not overdue or 1 to 6 days overdue
One asterisk (*): item 7 to 20 days overdue
Two asterisks (**): item 21 to 34 days overdue
Three asterisks (***): item 35 or more days overdue

In conjunction with this report, a performance report generated for management may summarize the past due performance on a monthly basis. This report is shown in Fig. 27-18. The top curve shows the total number of open orders, and the next curve down shows the total orders past due.

Vendor Performance Measures Various vendor performance measures are being used by organizations. These measures often include vendor quality, vendor delivery, and measures of total dollar purchases from each vendor, from geographical areas, and from other divisions within organizations.

Vendor performance measures are regarded as important to purchasing organizations and are used for vendor selection and to identify problems needing corrective action. Some of these measures also are used to help improve vendor performance or as a justification for dropping suppliers who do not perform adequately. They are also used to evaluate buyer performance. Specific vendor evaluation techniques are discussed in Section 6.

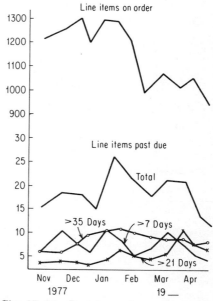

Fig. 27-18 Past due and on order purchasing management report.

Regulatory-Societal-Environmental Regulatory-societal-environmental measures provide information about purchasing's achievement of regulated public policy objectives and/or societal-environmental objectives considered important by organizations. The measures include:

- Purchase dollars placed with small business and a ratio of purchase dollars with small business to total purchases
- Purchase dollars placed with minority business and a ratio of purchase dollars with minority vendors to total purchases

- Purchase dollars and percent of purchases placed in labor surplus areas, that is, areas of high unemployment
- Number and percentage of minority employees in purchasing

Procurement Planning and Research   Various indicators are often used to provide data regarding how much of certain types of planning and research activities is done *or* how accurate planning or research efforts are. These measures include:

- Number of procurement plans established per year, including availability and price forecasts and trends
- Price forecasting accuracy (actual to forecast), based on unit price or percentage differences
- Delivery-lead-time forecasting accuracy (actual to forecast), based on unit time or percentage variance
- Number of make-or-buy studies completed

Competition   Measures which provide information about how purchasing is using its economic power to further competition and possibly improve prices and terms of purchase are used in some organizations. Specifically these measures are:

- Amount and percentage of annual purchases on national or area contracts
- Amount and percent of purchase dollars on annual contracts
- Amount and percent of annual purchases placed with sole source suppliers
- Competitive awards percentage
- Formal advertised awards percentage

Inventory   Where purchasing has direct inventory responsibility for purchased parts and commodities, the following set of inventory measures can be used:

- Dollar value of inventory on hand
- Dollars of inventory issued
- Number of items on hand
- Number of line items issued
- Number of line items ordered
- Percent active items
- Dollars on hand versus number of items
- Dollars issued versus dollars on hand (turnover)
- Dollars issued versus number issued
- Number issued versus number on hand
- Number issued versus number of active items
- Dollars on hand versus number of items and service level
- Number of issues versus number of orders
- Dollars issued versus number of orders
- Number of orders versus number of active items
- Service level, MRO
- Service level, overall
- Number of items versus dollars of gross fixed investment

- Dollars value of inventory versus dollars of gross fixed investment
- Annual inventory dollars issued versus dollars of inventory
- Annual inventory dollar write-off
- Annual inventory dollar write-off versus dollars of inventory
- People in stores versus number of items in stores
- Annual stores functional cost versus number of items in stores
- Annual stores functional cost versus dollars of inventory

Another kind of inventory report that is more frequently seen in purchasing is concerned with inventories consigned to vendors. These reports typically indicate the nature, quantity, and value of the inventory, which vendor currently has physical possession of the inventory, and when it is due back in the manufacturer's plant. These reports are necessary to maintain control over the consigned inventories and to maintain the production schedule.

Transportation   Measures to identify premium transportation costs and detention and demurrage charges on a dollar basis can also be used in purchasing.

EVALUATING PURCHASING PERSONNEL

Purchasing functional reviews, policy and procedure audits, and short-term purchasing performance measurement can all be used to evaluate purchasing activities and purchasing personnel at different levels in the purchasing department. Functional reviews are a primary means to evaluate the overall department and key personnel.

Policy and procedure audits and various short-term performance measurements are used to evaluate subsection managers and buyers on a quantitative basis. These evaluations are normally conducted by purchasing managers throughout the purchasing hierarchy.

In addition to the use of the somewhat quantitatively oriented measures of purchasing performance discussed, personnel appraisal in purchasing also needs to include various qualitative factors associated with purchasing personnel, especially buyers. These factors may include but need not be limited to:

1. Problem analysis capability
2. Decision making
3. Planning-organizing
4. Communications
5. Flexibility
6. Initiative-innovativeness
7. Interpersonal effectiveness
8. Capacity for growth

Valid evaluation of purchasing personnel requires that appropriate standards of performance be established to gauge good, average, and poor performance for key measurement areas. Based on the findings by Monczka et al. in the previously cited study, it is recommended that each organization carefully establish its performance expectations by measure category at various times, reflecting its own situation for the department and for buyers. Continual improvement against these measurement benchmarks should be required.

Not only are there organizational differences in purchasing departments (based on the type of purchases, numbers of people, and many other factors) which work against establishment of industry and overall purchasing standards, but also changes are continually occurring in the purchasing environment affecting purchasing performance expectations. The following list of causes of changes in standards was gleaned from interviews:

- Significant changes in volume
- Market movements or business condition changes
- Introduction of many new items to be purchased
- Increase in late requisitioning
- Purchasing personnel changes
- Design changes
- Inspection changes
- Changes in quality control personnel
- Product mix changes
- Organization changes
- Strikes or other lost time
- Changes in management style
- Changes in technology
- Changes in purchasing systems, methods, and techniques
- New directions from corporate management
- Availability
- Grade escalation

Any of these factors, alone or in combination, can necessitate a revision of specific purchasing performance standards. It appears most reasonable for an individual purchasing department to establish its own expectations and monitor progress over time.

MANAGEMENT SYSTEMS

Many organizations use a *management-by-objectives* system both to incorporate the earlier discussed purchasing measures and as a means of evaluation. *Zero-base budgeting* is another technique being used and considered as a means to review objectives and the resources necessary to achieve these objectives.

Both approaches need to be considered by purchasing for inclusion into the overall purchasing management process, including evaluation. However, detailed discussion is beyond the scope of this section.

CONCLUSION

This section provides up-to-date information about the various approaches to purchasing evaluation. Numerous quantitative measures have also been discussed which are and can be used to measure and gauge the effectiveness of the purchasing department, subsections, buyers, and vendors.

Each company will have to select those measures most appropriate. Furthermore, decisions about the degree of measurement detail and appropriate performance standards will have to be established by the user organizations.

Progressive purchasing departments need to continually improve their measurement and control systems to improve performance. Effective purchasing measurement systems enhance the purchasing manager's opportunity to manage well.

NOTE: For further information on subjects covered in this section see the list of references in Section 30.

N.A.P.M. Certified Purchasing Manager (C.P.M.) Program

EDITOR

Edward J. Bierman, Ph.D. *Director of Certification and Professional Activities, National Association of Purchasing Management, New York, New York*

INTRODUCTION

Qualified individuals in purchasing or materials management were provided the opportunity to move to a new level of professionalism as certified purchasing managers (C.P.M.s) with the establishment of the certification program of the National Association of Purchasing Management (N.A.P.M.) in 1974. Thousands have earned the C.P.M. designation since then, and the program has been widely and enthusiastically accepted in industry, government, and wherever else purchasing is recognized as a separate organizational function.

Since N.A.P.M. has implemented certification, other professional associations, including the National Association of Educational Buyers (NAEB) and the Pacific Northwest Public Purchasing Association (PNPPA) have joined the program. The National Purchasing Institute (NPI), which previously awarded the certified purchasing officer (CPO) designation on the basis of examinations, has also merged its certification program with that of N.A.P.M. Similarly, the California Association of Public Purchasing Officers (CAPPO), which had awarded the certified public purchasing officer (CPPO) designation, has phased its program into N.A.P.M.'s. The CPO and CPPO designations have been replaced by C.P.M. Other purchasing associations still retain their own certification programs.

The brief review of the genesis and development of the N.A.P.M. program that follows provides an insight into the concurrent drive for professional development and the growing recognition of its importance that led to this new level of professionalism. Specific details on the certification process follow this background material.

THE RATIONALE

Certification is the added criterion to professionalism that has always denoted a standard of respectability.

During the mid-1960s, certification advocates promulgated a three-pronged thrust for its adoption. Otto Winter's analysis in the January 12, 1967, issue of *Purchasing* typified the supportive statements that were prevalent then as well as now. They are as follows.

For the individual:

- It will assure professional recognition from his peers. This will create better job opportunities for him.
- It will expedite professional advancement.
- It will serve as a source of information on both the art and the science of professional purchasing.
- It will enhance his value to his employer.

For his company:

- A truly professional purchasing agent can increase corporate profit. The training necessary for certification will teach him how to use modern techniques and methods to obtain the most value from each dollar spent.

For his profession:

- It will tend to tighten loose, haphazard, and arbitrary promotion practices by setting up criteria of knowledge requirements.
- The academic community will begin to take a more active interest and offer courses of study oriented to purchasing certification.
- The purchasing agent will be in a better position to acquire a new, more important status in the corporate hierarchy.
- Purchasing agent standards of performance will improve as a result of the above three factors.

To summarize, a professional certification program is designed to teach purchasing techniques, laws, and procedures to enable an employer to realize the greatest potential from his purchasing agent. Through it, the purchasing agent will be able to make the profession, the industry, and the world more aware of his expertise. A professional designation will be an employer's assurance that the person he is hiring has, in fact, all the tools he needs to do a good job. It will serve to identify the purchasing agent, just as a journeyman's rating identifies the top of the toolmaking trade or as CPA indicates an accountant of proven skill.[1]

THE FIRST CERTIFICATION PROPOSAL

A formal approach to certification was taken in 1966, at which time a proposal for certification was presented to the membership of the National Association of Purchasing Agents (N.A.P.A.). An outline of the proposal was as follows.

The N.A.P.A. Professional Certification Plan

1. This program for professional development was to lead, by examination, to qualification as a certified professional purchaser (CPP).
2. To qualify for examinations, the candidate must:
    a. Submit an application for examination together with a transcript of

---

[1]O. R. Winter, "Philadelphia's P.A. Favors Certification Program," *Purchasing*, Jan. 12, 1967, pp. 174–175.

academic credits and the examination fee of $25. If he fails any portion of his examination, he may reapply and take only that portion for an additional $25 fee.

 b. Not necessarily be a member of N.A.P.A., or any other purchasing association.

 c. Meet the requirements set forth in the business management and the purchasing management syllabi. He may take these two written examinations at different times if he so chooses by the payment of $25 for each examination.

 d. Have acquired 5 years of purchasing experience, of which 2 years must have been in a supervisory capacity. However, there is no minimum or maximum age requirement.

 3. The candidate to be certified must pass two examinations (a two-part written and an oral), conducted separately.

 a. A two-part written examination prepared by N.A.P.A. and graded by university faculty or by an independent agency.

 b. An oral examination conducted by the N.A.P.A. examining board after successful completion of the written examinations.

 4. All candidates must pass the oral examination, even though written examinations may be waived.

 5. Various accomplishments are the bases for waiving one or both of the written examinations.

 a. Examination based on the business management syllabus may be waived for those with the following academic degrees:

  (1) A candidate holding a bachelor's degree with academic credit for at least 7 of the 11 subjects listed in the syllabus; or

  (2) A candidate holding a master's degree with credit for at least 4 of the 11 listed subjects; or

  (3) A candidate holding a Ph.D. degree and credit for at least 2 of the 11 listed subjects.

 b. Waiver of examination based on the business management syllabus through a combination of experience and education, with a high school diploma as the minimum educational requirement, will be granted if the candidate has:

  (1) Eight years of purchasing experience, plus credit in 8 of the 11 listed courses; or

  (2) Ten years of purchasing experience, plus credit in 6 of the 11 listed courses; or

  (3) Twelve years of purchasing experience, plus credit in 4 of the 11 listed courses.

 c. Waiver of examination based on the purchasing management syllabus will be granted:

  (1) To a candidate who has attended an undergraduate or graduate school in which he studied the required purchasing syllabus subjects.

  (2) To a candidate meeting the requirements listed under 5*d* below.

d. Waiver of both written examinations to those candidates with 15 years or more of purchasing experience, including 5 years in a responsible administrative or supervisory position in a purchasing or materials department (and currently employed in an executive or supervisory position). Such candidates are excused from both written examinations, but they are required to pass the oral examination. A review board will approve the candidates to be so exempted. This exemption will expire 5 years from the date this program becomes effective.

6. The level of experience will be established by means of verification of data included on the application and, if necessary, by findings of the review board.

7. Candidates who do not qualify for exemptions may take the examinations based on the business management syllabus and the purchasing management syllabus, either separately or together, upon completion of their studies and payment of the examination fee.

The written examination would be in two parts, covering business management and purchasing management. Subjects to be included in these examinations are:

Business Management

Accounting I, II
Economics I, II
Statistics
Business law I, II
Principles of management

Personnel management
Industrial or production management
Principles of marketing
Finance
Electronic data processing

Purchasing Management

The purchasing function
Organization for purchasing
Policy and procedures in purchasing
Legal aspects in purchasing
Ethics in purchasing
Selecting sources of supply
Quality concepts in purchasing
Quantity determination and control
Pricing considerations in purchasing
Value analysis
Forecasting and forward buying
Automation and purchasing

Make-or-buy concepts
Capital equipment purchasing or leasing
Traffic and transportation
Surplus, salvage, and scrap disposal
Storekeeping
Purchasing budgets
Purchasing internationally
Public purchasing
Personnel for purchasing
Public relations
Performance evaluation

PROFESSIONAL EDUCATIONAL STANDARDS PROGRAM (PESP)

The impetus for the aforementioned was, and still is, to enhance professional growth. The program was rejected by the membership. However, it was replaced by the professional educational standards program (PESP), which was established in 1967. N.A.P.M. had developed the PESP to provide curriculum guidelines to those who desired to pursue additional educational training. This curriculum also provided educational institutions with uniform course outlines for teaching policies, principles, and procedures of purchasing. It was composed of two general bodies of knowledge: general business and the diversified aspects of purchasing. When an individual completed this curriculum and so requested, N.A.P.M. issued a certificate to the individual, certifying his completion of the program, but the certificate was not to be construed as certifying to the individual's professional purchasing competence, as is true of certification programs in certain other associations.

The curriculum for the PESP for individual development included courses in accounting, business law, economics, data processing, management, marketing, statistics, human relations, production management, purchasing management and advanced purchasing, production planning and control, quality control, and traffic and transportation.

THE CONTINUING EDUCATION PROGRAM (CEP)

Concomitantly with PESP, the continuing education program (CEP) was implemented in 1973. While PESP was a formal-credit educational program leading to a certificate of completion for a planned and highly structured curriculum, CEP was concerned with ongoing learning experiences in programs of a wide variety designed to fulfill specific job-related educational needs. Specifically, the CEP objectives were to:

1. Establish broad criteria for recommended noncredit courses, seminars, workshops, and other educational experiences that did not qualify for PESP

2. Stimulate individuals participating in CEP to go on to PESP

3. Provide education guidance and a program for those who cannot or will not participate in PESP

4. Help resolve conflicts of equivalency and other problems of the college-accredited aspects of PESP

5. Help maintain and improve the proficiency of the mature purchasing professional and give initial direction to the new or entry individual

6. Motivate the continual expansion and improvement of local association professional development programs by placing basic administration and control of CEP at the local level

7. Encourage participation in N.A.P.M.-sponsored national and regional educational programs

8. Stimulate the formation of and participation in noncredit purchasing seminars, workshops, short courses, and conferences at universities, colleges, and professional management training organizations

9. Reward and recognize educational efforts by and improvements in purchasing personnel

10. Provide another vehicle to help professionalize the field of purchasing

Within this program, there were two levels of achievement or awards, as determined by a point system (points were awarded various types of seminars, courses, and other educational activities), to measure the candidate's progress. The first level was the continuing education award, with a certificate issued to the individual after he had accumulated 150 points. The second level was the advanced continuing education award, with a certificate issued to the individual after he had accumulated 250 points.

THE ADVENT OF CERTIFICATION

The N.A.P.M. certification program finally came to fruition in 1974, when the first certificates were issued. The program started with a provision which allowed all persons who met the qualifications to be certified up to December 31, 1975. Thereafter, all candidates for certification were required to pass four field examinations.

The examination process went through several changes before its present format was established. The examinations are currently administered through the Educational Testing Service (ETS), Princeton, N.J.

THE N.A.P.M. CERTIFICATION PROGRAM

The Purpose

The process of certification mandates a disciplined learning program, thereby underwriting self-improvement and upgrading professional standards by granting special recognition and proficiency in the procurement field. Certification establishes a standard of competence and quality upon which society can depend. It grants the successful certification candidate new opportunities for professional advancement and offers recognition by his purchasing and management peers. The application for certification is shown in Figs. 28-1 and 28-2. The examination procedures are discussed later.

It is the intent of the certification program:

1. To improve purchasing personnel by giving specific direction to an educational program and to provide a measure of the extent of professional development

2. To provide purchasing people with a goal, motivation, and the assurance that comes from knowing a professional educational standard has been reached

3. To promote the designation Certified Purchasing Manager (C.P.M.) as the recognized standard of proficiency in the purchasing profession

4. To assist employers in selecting qualified purchasing employees

5. To plan and sponsor a program of continuing professional development for the C.P.M.

6. To assert the necessity for professional purchasing personnel to protect the employee and public welfare through safety, health, and other environmental and human relation considerations

NATIONAL ASSOCIATION OF PURCHASING MANAGEMENT

APPLICATION FOR CERTIFICATION AS CERTIFIED PURCHASING MANAGER
(Submit to: Director of Certification, N.A.P.M., 11 Park Place, New York, NY 10007)

Name _____   Date of Application _____

Home Address _____   Tel No _____
    (as it should appear on certificate) No. & Street   City   State   Zip

Employed By _____   / Position Title _____

Business Address _____   Tel No _____

Member of N.A.P.M.?   Regular _____   Associate _____   Non-Member _____

Name of Local Association _____

IMPORTANT

Do not submit
this application
without having
passed all four
field examinations

Years of Purchasing or Related Experience _____
(Minimum 5 years experience in purchasing or a degree from a recognized 4 year college and 3 years of related experience)

Application Fee Enclosed $ _____ or $ _____
(NAPM Member $25)   (Associate or Non-Member $30)

POINTS EARNED TO APPLY TOWARD THIS CERTIFICATION
(Circle Points Earned)

I.   EDUCATIONAL CATEGORY (Attach official transcripts or other documentation)

A.   College Level (Circle points for highest level achieved—Maximum 30 points)—based on highest degree attained. Not on accumulative basis.

DEGREE PROGRAM	NAME AND LOCATION OF INSTITUTION	Course or Major	Year Graduated	Degree Received	Points Earned
Doctors Degree					30
Masters Degree					25
4 Year College					20
2 Year Community College					10

B.   Specific College Courses Taken or Taught (2 points for each purchasing and materials management course, and 1 point for all other college courses. These must be profession related, may be in-residence or correspondence and must not be included in degree progam). Instructors get credit only once for a specific course taught more than once. Attach certificate of completion or other documentation.

COURSE	WHERE TAKEN	DATE COMPLETED	POINTS EARNED
			X2
			X1

C.   Continuing Education Seminars and Courses

TYPE OF ACTIVITY	WHERE TAKEN	DATE TAKEN	POINTS EARNED
2-week Executive Seminar	Harvard University or other		4
1-week Management Seminar	Cornell, N. Carolina, Stanford, or other		3
2-week Management Seminar	Michigan State or other		4
N.A.P.M./Local Association Seminar or Courses (15 hrs. or longer)			X2
N.A.P.M./Local Association Short Seminars (8-14 hrs.)			X1
Seminars & Courses Equivalent to the above sponsored by other recognized organizations			

D.   N.A.P.M. Examinations (all required—total 35 points)

SUBJECT	WHERE TAKEN	DATE PASSED	POINTS EARNED
The Purchasing Function			
The Administrative Function			35
The Organizational Function			
The Continuing Education Function			

Total points in Educational Category (A, B, and C) _____

Fig. 28-1   Application for certification (front).

The Concept

N.A.P.M. is a professional association, dedicated to the motivation and professional improvement of its members and the entire profession of purchasing. Its code of ethics is well known and subscribed to by its members.

Professional certification is defined as a means by which N.A.P.M. denotes that individuals, members and nonmembers alike, have attained a level of qualification

II EXPERIENCE CATEGORY (Circle Appropriate Points and Title and submit verification of employment.)

(Applicant must have at least 5 years experience in purchasing if he does not have a degree from a recognized 4 year college, or 3 years experience with such a degree)

Annual Gross Purchases Responsible for * or Gross Sales Billed by Organizational Group Served by your Purchasing Function * (Mil. $)

		Under 5	5-49	50-99	100 and over	Times Number of Years	Total Points Earned
Class I	(Vice President of Purchases/Materials Mgt. Director of Purchases/Materials Mgt.) Employment from _____ to _____ Employer	4	5	6	7	x	=
Class II	(General Purchasing Agent Materials Manager) Employment from _____ to _____ Employer	3	4	5	6	x	=
Class III	(Manager of Purchasing Purchasing Agent) Employment from _____ to _____ Employer	2	3	4	5	x	=
Class IV	(Supervisory Buyer Senior Buyer Administrative Buyer) Employment from _____ to _____ Employer	1	2	3	4	x	=
Class V	(Buyer Junior Buyer Assistant Buyer) Employment from _____ to _____ Employer	1	1	2	3	x	=

*For position titles and functions not shown use equivalent position as best you can judge and explain in IV below.

Total Points in Experience Category _____

III CONTRIBUTIONS TO N.A.P.M. OR PURCHASING PROFESSION CATEGORY (Submit verification of activities)

Activity	Where Performed	When Performed	Total Points Earned
A. Affiliated Association (1 point per year) Officer, Director, Committee Chairman of professionally oriented standing committee			
B. N.A.P.M. (1 point per year) President, Vice President, National or District Committee Chairman of a professionally-oriented standing committee			
C. Published Articles (2 points each) List title, publication and date			

Total Points in Contributions Category _____

SUMMARY

1. Total Points in Education Category (A, B, C) _____
2. Total Examination Points _____ 35
3. Total Points in Experience Category _____
4. Total Points in Contributions Category _____

GRAND TOTAL OF ALL POINTS (70 required) _____

IV COMMENTS OR EXPLANATION OF ANY ENTRY ABOVE DEEMED NECESSARY FOR CLARIFICATION:

_____
_____
_____
_____

V

I hereby certify that the information submitted above is true and accurate to the best of my knowledge. I further agree to abide by the N.A.P.M. "Code of Ethics" and "Principles and Standards of Purchasing Practice", as listed on the Application for Examination form, whether or not I am a member of N.A.P.M.

Signature of Applicant _____

FOR USE OF NATIONAL OFFICE ONLY

APPLICATION NUMBER _____

APPROVALS _____

Director of Certification _____
Date Certificate Issued _____

Chairman, Certification Board _____

Expiration Date _____

3M Rev. 9-77

Fig. 28-2   Application for certification (back).

considered necessary to establish the individual's competence and proficiency, as described by professional standards. It is, however, recognized that N.A.P.M. cannot certify to a specific individual's actual on-the-job competence and proficiency—only that the individual has met the requirements and standards of this certification program.

These standards represent a minimum level of knowledge required as a basis for certification. The minimum level set forth is high enough so that its attainment represents an accomplishment that has status with the public, business management, and the educational community.

As to the experience requirements, the intent is that the candidate does spend a major part of his time in a procurement position or a materials management or a related activity, and that this position is so identified under the corporate structure of the business or corporation from which the candidate claims experience time.

It is believed that this plan will lead to an acceptance, by business management and by the public, of the professional status of purchasing. It is further believed that certification will lead to increased individual professional competence in the field. Since the N.A.P.M. certification program provides guidelines to individuals as to what is considered a minimum level of professional competence, it will serve as an impetus toward the achievement of that minimum by means of additional study and training. It is a goal toward which men and women can work. It is a great incentive. The professional foundation requirement is the yardstick against which management measures purchasing people when considering hiring, advancing, and promoting individuals.

The C.P.M. designation is a professional one. In addition to establishing that an individual has passed a series of job-related examinations, it indicates that the purchasing man or woman has spent time and effort in preparing to render a professional standard of competence to the employer and will continue to merit the confidence of the employer in his ability to keep abreast of developments in the field of purchasing and the materials management concept.

Above all, it indicates to management that a really effective purchasing person is one who is able to relate his activities to the overall goals and objectives of his organization. This implies that he is aware of the interrelationships of the functional areas, the major strategic problems of competition, and changes in the environment that face his organization. It is this kind of broad comprehension and attitude that is sought in the management point of view.

The Scope

Appropriate recognition for passing the examinations and for various types of experience, education, and contributions to the purchasing association or profession is granted through a point system leading to the certification of the successful candidate as a C.P.M. N.A.P.M. conducts the examinations for eligible candidates in the purchasing field as required.

Those carried in the active registry as C.P.M.s may if they desire use these letters after their names when appropriate for normal business purposes.

CERTIFICATION REQUIREMENTS

A point system is established to provide the means of measuring an individual's qualifications for the designation C.P.M. Seventy points are required and can be earned in any quantity or combination from the listing below. However, it is mandatory that the applicant earn 35 points by passing all four examinations, and he may earn the other 35 required through any mix or combination from the list below.

Educational Requirements

1. Four examinations
   a. The Purchasing Function
   b. The Administrative Function
   c. The Organizational Function
   d. The Continuing Education Function
2. Formal education (highest level attained)
   a. 2-year community college, 10 points
   b. 4-year college degree, 20 points
   c. Master's degree, 25 points
   d. Doctor's degree, 30 points
3. Specific college courses (not included in the degree program): 2 points each
   a. Purchasing (basic, advanced, etc.)
   b. Materials management
   c. Accounting (basic, advanced, etc.)
   d. Management (general, industrial, production, etc.)
   e. Marketing
   f. Computer
   g. Economics
   h. Engineering
   i. Physical sciences
   j. Traffic management
   k. Law
   l. Communications
   m. Finance
   n. Statistics
   o. Behavioral sciences
4. Noncredit seminars and courses
   a. N.A.P.M.-sponsored 2-week executive seminar, 4 points
   b. N.A.P.M.-sponsored 1-week management seminar, 3 points
   c. Local association courses (15 hours and over), 2 points
   d. Short seminars (8 hours and over), 1 point
   e. Seminars and courses equivalent to the above sponsored by other recognized organizations (American Management Associations, universities, etc.): equivalent points to the above as approved by the director of certification.

Contributions to N.A.P.M. or Purchasing Profession

1. Each job assignment per year as local association officer or committee chairman, as listed below, 1 point

President
First vice-president
Second vice-president
Director for national affairs
Alternate director for national affairs
Local director
Secretary
Treasurer
Professional developmment committee chairman
Purchasing techniques committee chairman
Public relations committee chairman
Membership activities committee chairman

2. One point for district committee chairman and for assistant to the vice-president

3. One point for national committee chairman, national group chairman, and district vice-president

4. Two points for each published article

Experience

The following point schedule for the experience factor is designed to reflect management expertise, experience, and responsibility in purchasing on two scales:

1. For persons employed in industry-oriented business which involves manufacturing and/or sales billings.

2. For persons not employed in industry but who have responsibility for purchasing and money commitments. These purchasing people would gain equivalent points based on responsibility for actual dollars committed by themselves or their departments.

The intent of the matrix (see top of Fig. 28-2) is to provide a means of determining how much responsibility in the purchasing field an individual has had. Titles can be diverse; prospective candidates are encouraged to submit appropriate data to substantiate their positions of responsibility.

CURRICULUM IN PURCHASING MANAGEMENT

Objectives

The objectives of the curriculum in purchasing management are:

1. To provide a guide to educators and to student counselors for the advisement of students

2. To provide a suitable academic background for those who are contemplating a career in purchasing

3. To provide the candidate with sufficient expertise to enable him to pass the required examinations for certification as a C.P.M.

Curriculum Standards

An ideal undergraduate program in preparation for a career in purchasing should be a broad program with approximately 50 percent in the area of business subjects; approximately 10 percent in the area of physical sciences, such as chemistry, physics, engineering, and electronics; and approximately 40 percent in other areas of liberal arts and humanities, such as literature, philosophy, psychology, history, and fine arts. It is recognized that some subjects, such as economics, English, and mathematics, can be oriented in either the business or nonbusiness context. Such subjects should be classified according to their content to determine the proper balance between business and nonbusiness subjects.

It is also recognized that in some industries an engineering or physical science education is desirable to equip purchasing people for the technological aspects of their task. Students should, whenever possible, weigh such special considerations in determining the ideal subject mix for them. They may possibly need to supplement their undergraduate work with postgraduate studies to give them both the technological and business management backgrounds desired to enable them to develop competence and proficiency as purchasing and business managers.

Business Core   The business core of the ideal undergraduate program should include the following areas:

Accounting
Business law
Data processing
Economics
Finance
Industrial management
Managerial (cost) accounting
Management and organization
Marketing
Purchasing
Materials management
Physical distribution (traffic and transportation)
Production planning and control
Inventory control
Quality control
Statistics

The balance of the business core should be in the following areas:

Advanced data processing
Advanced purchasing
Advanced materials management
Contract negotiation
Marketing research
Operations research (quantitative methods)

Personnel management
Professional speech
Report writing

PREPARATION FOR CERTIFICATION EXAMINATIONS

At the present time there are no academic prerequisites to taking the examinations leading to certification as a C.P.M. However, an undergraduate degree in business or science is highly desirable.

Each section of the certification examinations is limited to specific areas in the business core.

Examinations

The examinations, as part of the N.A.P.M. certification program, are made up of four modules. Following is a description of the material covered in each module of the examination.

1. The Purchasing Function
   a. Procurement requests
   b. Solicitation of proposals and their evaluation
   c. Vendor analysis
   d. Contract execution and implementation
2. The Administrative Function
   a. The purchasing department
   b. Dealing with personnel
   c. Budgetary concerns
   d. Ancillary functions
3. The Organizational Function
   a. Establishment of an organized purchasing function
   b. Forecasting and strategies
   c. Optimizing purchasing performance
   d. Relationships
4. The Continuing Education Function
   This module is based on extracts from professional literature and case studies to determine what a purchasing manager is doing to enlarge his or her management background.

Appropriate Texts

The following texts are recommended for preparing for the examinations:

Ammer, D. S., *Materials Management,* 3d ed., Richard D. Irwin, Inc., Homewood, Ill., 1973.
England, W. B., H. E. Flaron, and M. R. Leenders: *Purchasing and Materials Management,* 6th ed., Richard D. Irwin, Inc., Homewood, Ill., 1975.

Heinritz, S. F., and P. V. Farrell: *Purchasing: Principles and Applications,* 6th ed., Prentice-Hall, Inc., Englewood Cliffs, N.J., 1980.

Lee, L. and D. W. Dobler: *Purchasing and Materials Management,* 3d ed., McGraw-Hill Book Company, New York, 1977.

National Association of Purchasing Management, Inc., *Guide to Purchasing,* New York, 1976.

G. J. Zenz: *Purchasing and the Management of Materials,* 5th ed., John Wiley & Sons, Inc., New York, 1981.

Study Guide

A comprehensive study guide, prepared by college and university professors and purchasing practitioners and covering all the examination areas, is provided by N.A.P.M. The book includes detailed information under each of the topics covered in the examinations, as well as a bibliography and sample questions.

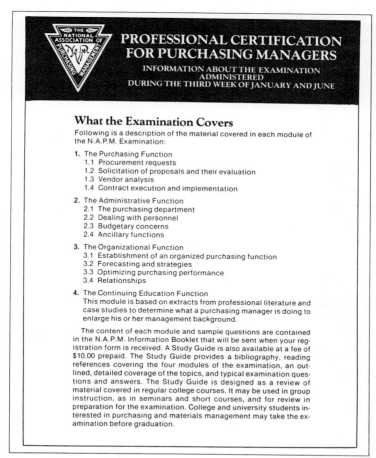

Fig. 28-3 First part of application form, showing what the examination covers.

Examination Procedures

Candidates for certification may take the examinations in January and June of each year at any one of the more than 200 test sites established by the Educational Testing Service in Princeton. Applicants who successfully complete the examinations may then apply for certification.

Data on the certification examination registration are shown in Figs. 28-3, 28-4, and 28-5.

See Instructions on Last Page

National Association of Purchasing Management
Registration Form

1. YOUR NAME — PRINT LAST NAME — PRINT FIRST NAME — MI

2. YOUR HOME ADDRESS — NUMBER AND STREET (FIRST LINE) — NUMBER AND STREET (SECOND LINE) — CITY — STATE — ZIP CODE

3. TEST CENTER — CODE — CITY — STATE

4. TEST DATE FOR WHICH YOU ARE REGISTERING — MONTH — YEAR

5. INDICATE MODULES TO BE TAKEN — 1 2 3 4

6. EXAMINED PREVIOUSLY? — Yes — No — If YES, indicate modules, month, and year. — All 1 2 3 4 — MONTH — YEAR

7. SELF-DESCRIPTION (Optional)
a. Check the block next to the racial or ethnic group that best describes you.
1. ☐ American Indian
2. ☐ Asian American
3. ☐ Black/Afro-American
4. ☐ Caucasian
5. ☐ Chicano/Mexican American
6. ☐ Puerto Rican American
7. ☐ Spanish American
8. ☐ Other ______

b. Check the appropriate block.
1 ☐ M 2 ☐ F

8. COMPANY AND ADDRESS — COMPANY NAME (FIRST LINE) — NUMBER AND STREET (SECOND LINE) — CITY — STATE — ZIP CODE

9. Are you a member of N.A.P.M.?
☐ Yes ☐ No

If yes, type of member
☐ Regular
☐ Associate

______ NAME OF LOCAL ASSOCIATION

10. Total fee enclosed $______

11. SIGNATURE AND DATE — / / DATE — ( ) OFFICE TELEPHONE NUMBER

- After you have completed this registration form, check it carefully for accuracy.
- Attach a check or money order for the fee made payable to: National Association of Purchasing Management (N.A.P.M.). DO NOT SEND CASH. Mail the fee and this completed form to:

National Association of Purchasing Management
11 Park Place
New York, NY 10007

Fig. 28-4 Second part of examination application.

When to Register
You must register on or before May 1 for the examination to be given in June, and December 1 for the examination to be given in January (postmarked by May 1 or December 1).

Who May Register
Anyone engaged in or studying purchasing or materials management may take the examination.

What is the Cost?
The fee for N.A.P.M. members is $25 for each module and for non-members it is $35 for each module.

Where You May Take the Examination
A list of test centers has been provided on page 2 of this flyer indicating the cities where you may be tested. Please reserve the examination week (Monday-Saturday) of January or June. Indicate your preference for a test center on the registration form. Be sure to check the admission ticket when you receive it for the specific date, time and place of your exam.

How You May Register
Complete and detach the registration form and mail it to N.A.P.M., with a check or money order for the appropriate fee, not later than the dates indicated above.

Important Points About Registration
- It is very important that your registration form be completed carefully and accurately. The information you provide on this form will be used by Educational Testing Service to assign you to a test center, to mail your admission ticket to you, and to inform you of your test results.

- Print everything but your signature, which should be written as you would sign a business letter.

- Please note that a response to item 7 is optional. We are requesting this information to obtain comprehensive ethnic group profiles of all candidates applying in order to assure that there is no bias within the examination. If you choose to respond, mark the space next to the racial or ethnic group that best describes you. If your racial or ethnic group is not listed, please mark the space beside "Other" and write it on the line provided. You may omit this item if you wish.

The Examination Schedule
If you are taking all four modules, you will take modules 1 and 2 in the morning of the test day and modules 3 and 4 in the afternoon. If you are taking any combination of only two modules, or only one module, you must take them at the morning session.

Fig. 28-5   Third part of examination application.

RECERTIFICATION

The original certificate authorized under the N.A.P.M. professional certification program is valid for 5 years from the date of issue. To retain the C.P.M. designation, certified purchasing managers must be recertified, prior to the expiration date on their existing certificates, for another 5-year period, or must fulfill requirements for lifetime certification.

Requirements

To be recertified, a certified purchasing manager must have accumulated, since the issue date of the original certificate, at least 6 points in the education or contributions categories of the program. Successful completion of one certification examination is an acceptable method of meeting the point requirement, provided points for such examination had not been earned toward the original certification.

Applications for recertification must be submitted on the official form, together with supporting evidence of point accumulation and the appropriate fee.

Applicants for recertification should proceed as follows:

1. Read the official application form carefully and provide complete and specific information.

NATIONAL ASSOCIATION OF PURCHASING MANAGEMENT, INC.

Application for Recertification or Lifetime Certification as Certified Purchasing Manager

(Submit Application for Recertification to Director of Certification. N.A.P.M. 11 Park Place. New York. NY 10007 no earlier than 120 days and no later than 60 days prior to expiration of original certificate. Applications for Lifetime Certification may be submitted at any time)

Name _____ Date _____
(as it should appear on certificate)

Home Address _____ Tel. No. _____
No. & Street   City   State   Zip

Employed by _____ Position Title _____

Business Address _____ Tel. No. _____

Member of N.A.P.M ? Regular _____ Non-member _____ Fee enclosed (see page 1) $ _____

Name of Local Association _____

Expiration Date of Original Certificate _____ Date of Birth (If applying for Lifetime Certification) _____

NOTE: RECERTIFICATION APPLICANTS CONTINUE BELOW. LIFETIME APPLICANTS SEE NEXT PAGE.

POINTS EARNED TO APPLY TOWARD RECERTIFICATION

Note: All points claimed must have been earned subsequent to the issue date of the applicant's original certificate.

I. EDUCATION CATEGORY

A. Specific College Courses Taken or Taught. (2 points for each purchasing or materials management course, 1 point for all other related college courses). These must be profession-related, may be in-residence or correspondence courses. Instructors get credit only once for a specific course taught more than once. Attach certificate of completion or other documentation.

COURSE	WHERE TAKEN	DATE COMPLETED	POINTS EARNED
			X2 =
			X1 =

B. Continuing Education Seminars and Courses
(Attach Achievement Award or other documentation)

TYPE OF ACTIVITY	WHERE TAKEN	DATE TAKEN	POINTS EARNED
2-week Executive Seminar	Harvard University or other		4
1-week Management Seminar	Cornell, Michigan State, N. Carolina, Stanford, or other		3
N.A.P.M./Local Association Seminar or Courses (15 hrs. or longer)			X2 =
N.A.P.M./Local Association Short Seminars (8-14 hrs.)			X1 =
Seminars and Courses equivalent to the above sponsored by other recognized organizations			

C. N.A.P.M. Examinations (Points necessary for recertification may be earned by successful completion of one examination provided points for such examination had not been earned toward the original certification.)

SUBJECT	WHERE TAKEN	DATE PASSED	POINTS EARNED
Principles of Purchasing			7
Materials Management			7
Principles of Business & Economics			7
Quantitative Areas of Business			7

Total Points in Education Category (A, B and C) _____

Fig. 28-6 Application for recertification or lifetime certification (front).

2. Provide all documentation required: transcripts from institutions, certificates or other evidence of completion of courses, seminars, or examinations; and verification of professional contributions.

3. If further explanation or interpretation is desired after the application has been thoroughly read, address requests to the director of certification.

4. Sign the completed form and send it, with the appropriate fee, to Director of Certification, N.A.P.M., 11 Park Place, New York, N.Y. 10007.

II CONTRIBUTIONS TO N.A.P.M. OR PURCHASING PROFESSION CATEGORY
(Submit verification of activities)

ACTIVITY	WHERE PERFORMED	WHEN PERFORMED	POINTS EARNED
Affiliated Association Officer, Director. Committee Chairman of professionally-oriented standing committee (1 point per year)			
N.A.P.M. President, Vice President, National or District Committee Chairman of a professionally-oriented standing committee (1 point per year)			
Published articles (2 points each) List title, publication and date			

Total points in Contributions Category

SUMMARY: Total points in Education Category

Total Points in Contributions Category

GRAND TOTAL OF POINTS (6 required)

III COMMENTS OR EXPLANATION OF ANY ENTRY ABOVE DEEMED NECESSARY FOR CLARIFICATION:

IV   I hereby certify that the information submitted above is true and accurate to the best of my knowledge. I further agree to abide by the N.A.P.M. "Code of Ethics" and "Principles and Standards of Purchasing Practice", as shown herein, whether or not I am a member of N.A.P.M.
Signature of Applicant _____

INSTRUCTIONS FOR LIFETIME CERTIFICATION APPLICANTS ONLY

Complete top section on the other side of this form. Sign in Section IV above. Send form, verification of 15 years experience in purchasing, and appropriate fee to Director of Certification, N.A.P.M., 11 Park Place, New York, NY 10007.

FOR USE OF NATIONAL OFFICE ONLY

APPLICATION NUMBER _____

APPROVALS _____

_____
Chairman, Certification Board

Director of Certification _____

Date Recertified _____

Expiration Date _____

Fig. 28-7   Application for recertification or lifetime certification (back).

Submission of Applications

All applications for recertification must be submitted no earlier than 120 days and no later than 60 days prior to the expiration date on the original certificate. Applications will be processed as received. Following approval of the application, the new certificate will be mailed directly to the applicant.

LIFETIME CERTIFICATION

Certified purchasing managers who have attained the age of 55 or more and who have 15 or more years of experience in the purchasing materials–management field may apply at any time for lifetime certification. Requests for lifetime certification should be made to the Director of Certification, N.A.P.M., 11 Park Place, New York, N.Y. 10007. Applicant's date of birth and verification of experience must be provided, and the appropriate lifetime certification fee must be enclosed.

Application for recertification or lifetime certification is shown in Figs. 28-6 and 28-7.

REVOCATION OF CERTIFICATION

A certificate may be revoked by the certification board for willful falsification of information on the application for certification or recertification, or for dishonesty in the examination procedures. Failure to recertify shall also be a basis for revocation. Certificates may also be revoked by the N.A.P.M. board of directors for proved unethical behavior or malpractice. Upon revocation, certificates must be returned to N.A.P.M.

NOTE: For further information on subjects covered in this section see the list of references in Section 30.

Section **29**

Professional Purchasing Associations

EDITOR

Eric H. Bergman, C.P.M. *President, Eric Bergman & Associates, Seattle, Washington*

ASSOCIATE EDITORS

Roger Gano *Executive Manager, Oregon Purchasor, Portland, Oregon*

Frank J. Winters, C.P.M. *Executive Vice-President (Retired), National Association of Purchasing Management, New York, New York*

Professional associations, generally organized to draw together individuals in the profession, provide their members with the opportunity for improving themselves and their profession through mutual cooperation, interchange of ideas, educational programs, ethical standards, and other such means.

Purchasing is now becoming recognized as a profession, and purchasing associations are appropriately classed as professional associations (as distinguished from trade associations involving specific industries or civic and social organizations). These purchasing associations, organized in many countries around the world, carry out their objectives in their individual regions of operation through their own efforts and with beneficial interchange of ideas from others. Local groups of interested purchasing people sometimes set up their own associations, local or national in scope, and they may, at their discretion, affiliate with larger associations. They all attempt to serve the same purpose for their members (see Policies and Objectives of Purchasing Associations later in this section for further explanation of these purposes).

While each association operates independently and differently, all provide regular meetings and special programming for their members to get together, exchange ideas, learn new techniques, and engage in real learning experiences. Also, individual members are provided the means and incentives through these meetings for improving their own leadership abilities by participating in committee and officer activities. Through this activity, it has been found, those who participate contribute to their own self-development even more than they do to the fellow members they serve. And through this participation members build valuable experience which they may use individually for job enrichment.

The intent of this section is to provide information regarding purchasing associations around the world for those who desire additional information about specific associations, for those desiring to affiliate with a particular association, and for those involved in purchasing who may desire to use this information irrespective of membership in an association.

PURCHASING ASSOCIATIONS OF THE WORLD

United States

National Association of Purchasing Management   The National Association of Purchasing Management (11 Park Place, New York, N.Y. 10007) was founded as the National Association of Purchasing Agents (N.A.P.A.) in 1915. The name was changed from N.A.P.A. to N.A.P.M. effective June 1, 1968. N.A.P.M. is organized with headquarters staff in New York City and with affiliated associations located throughout the country, which is divided into nine districts. Each district is represented on the board of directors by a vice-president, who is elected by the members within the district. The association may be characterized as a grass roots organization, with the flow of communications and activity coming up from the members as well as down from the national office and national committees and officers.

GROUPS IN N.A.P.M.   Within N.A.P.M. certain industry groups are organized that cut across local affiliated association lines and operate on a national basis, holding periodic meetings, workshops, and conferences. Following is a list of these groups, and further information on any of them may be obtained from N.A.P.M.

Chemical Group
Editors' Group (Purchasing Publications)
Educators' Group
Electronic Industries Procurement Group
Food Industry Group
Governmental, Educational, and Institutional Buyers' Group
Health Industries Group
International Group
Materials Management Group
Office Buyers' Group
Petroleum Industry Buyers' Group
Public Utility Buyers' Group

Rail Industry Group
Steel Buyers' Group

AFFILIATED ASSOCIATIONS OF N.A.P.M. There is a purchasing management
association in each of the following locations:

District No. 1
Arizona
Hawaii
Idaho
Los Angeles
Northern California
Orange County
Oregon
San Diego
Southern Arizona
Spokane
Treasure Valley
Utah
Washington

District No. 2
Austin
Central Texas
Dallas
East Texas
El Paso
Fort Worth
Four States Area
Greater Baton Rouge
Gulf Coast
Houston
Louisiana-Arkansas
New Mexico
New Orleans
Oklahoma City
Permian Basin
Sabine-Neches
San Antonio
Shreveport
Southwest Louisiana
Texas Panhandle
Tulsa
Wichita

District No. 3
Central Illinois
Central Iowa
Central Nebraska
Chicago
Denver
Eastern Iowa
Fox Valley
Illiamo
Kansas City
Lake Superior
Milwaukee

NDM
Nebraska
Ozarks
Rock River Valley
St. Louis
Siouxland
Southern Colorado
Tri-City
Twin City

District No. 4
Central Michigan
Detroit
Eastern Indiana
Evansville
Fort Wayne
Grand Rapids
Greater Lafayette
Indianapolis
Saginaw Valley
South Bend
Southwestern Michigan
Wabash Valley
Western Michigan

District No. 5
Baltimore
Carolinas-Virginia
Central Pennsylvania
Delaware
Lehigh Valley
North Central Pennsylvania
Northeastern Pennsylvania
Old Dominion
Philadelphia
Reading
Washington, D.C.

District No. 6
Akron
Canton area
Cincinnati
Cleveland
Columbus area
Dayton
Erie
Lima area
North Central Ohio
Northwestern Pennsylvania
Pittsburgh
Springfield

Toledo
Tri-State
Western Pennsylvania
Youngstown District

District No. 7
Alabama
Arkansas
Augusta area
Central Alabama
Central Florida
Central Kentucky
Chattanooga
East Tennessee
Florida
Florida Gold Coast
Florida Sun Coast
Florida West Coast
Georgia
Louisville
Memphis
Mississippi
Mobile
Nashville
North Alabama
South Florida
TenneVa
Western Kentucky

District No. 8
Buffalo
Eastern New York
Elmira
New Jersey
New York
Northern New York
Rochester
Seven Counties
Southern Tier—East
Syracuse
Twin Tiers
Utica/Rome—Mohawk
    Valley

District No. 9
Boston
Connecticut
Maine
New Hampshire
Rhode Island
Western New England
Worcester

Governmental

California Association of Public Purchasing Officers, P.O. Box 564, Santa Ana, Calif. 92705

National Association of State Purchasing Officials, P.O. Box 11910, Lexington, Ky. 40578

National Institute of Governmental Purchasing, 1001 Connecticut Ave., N.W., Washington, D.C. 20036

National Purchasing Institute, Inc., P.O. Box 20549, 4189 Bellaire Blvd., Suite 209, Houston, Tex. 77025

Educational and Institutional

American Society for Hospital Purchasing and Materials Management, 840 North Lake Shore Drive, Chicago, Ill. 60611

National Association of Educational Buyers, 180 Froehlich Farms Boulevard, Woodbury, N.Y. 11797

National Association of Hospital Purchasing—Materials Management, 1340 North Astor Street, Suite 2608, Chicago, Ill. 60610

Other

Newspaper Purchasing Management Association.

Canada

In the Purchasing Management Association of Canada (PMAC), the local member associations are called *districts* and the districts are grouped into *regions* (comparable with the N.A.P.M. *districts*). There are currently 29 districts and 5 branches (small pockets of people usually in remote areas not large enough in number to operate as a district).

As the majority of the districts and branches of PMAC do not have fixed postal addresses, they can be contacted through PMAC's national office at 80 Richmond Street West, Toronto, Ontario, Canada, M5H 2A4.

Districts	*Branches*
Atlantic	Halifax, N.S.
Brant-Norfolk	Brantford, Ont.
British Columbia	Vancouver, B.C.
Central Yellowhead Branch	Prince George, B.C.
Thompson Okanagan Branch	Kamloops, B.C.
Calgary	Calgary, Alta.
Central Ontario	Kitchener, Ont.
Eastern Ontario	Kingston, Ont.
The Eastern Townships	Sherbrooke, Que.
Edmonton	Edmonton, Alta.
Essex-Kent	Windsor, Ont.
Georgian Bay	Barrie, Ont.
Hamilton	Hamilton, Ont.
Kawartha	Peterborough, Ont.
Montreal	Montreal, Que.

New Brunswick	Saint John, N.B.
Greater Moncton Branch	Moncton, N.B.
Northern Branch	Bathurst, N.B.
Niagara	Niagara Falls, Ont.
Northwestern Ontario	Thunder Bay, Ont.
Oakville	Oakville, Ont.
Ottawa	Ottawa, Ont.
Quebec	Quebec, Que.
Regina	Regina, Sask.
Saguenay Lac–St. Jean	Chicoutimi, Que.
St. Maurice Valley	Trois-Rivières, Que.
Sarnia	Sarnia, Ont.
Saskatoon	Saskatoon, Sask.
Sudbury	Sudbury, Ont.
North Bay Branch	North Bay, Ont.
Toronto	Toronto, Ont.
Vancouver Island	Victoria, B.C.
Western Ontario	London, Ont.
Winnipeg	Winnipeg, Man.

Mexico

National Association

Confederación Mexicana de Asociaciones de Ejecutivos de Compras y Abastecimiento, A.C. (CONMAECA), Manuel Ma. Contreras 133—512, Mèxico 4, D.F. Tel. 546-1826; 546-7143

Local Associations

Mexico City, D.F., Asociación Mexicana de Ejecutivos de Compras, Abastecimiento y Materiales, A.C. (AMEC)

Monterrey, N.L., Asociación de Ejecutivos de Compras y Abastecimiento, de Monterrey, A.C. (AECAM)

Puebla, Pue., Ejecutivos de Compras de Puebla, A.C. (ECPAC)

Querétaro, Qro., Ejecutivos de Compras y Abastecimiento del Centro, A.C. (ECAC)

Guadalajara, Jal., Asociación Jalisciense de Ejecutivos de Compras, A.C. (AJEC)

Coatzacoalcos, Ver., Asociación Mexicana de Ejecutivos de Compras del Sureste, A.C. (AMECSAC)

Chihuahua, Chih., Asociación de Ejecutivos de Compras y Abastecimiento de Chihuahua, A.C. (AECACHI)

San Luis Potosí, S.L.P., Asociación Potosina de Ejecutivos de Compras y Abastecimiento, A.C. (APECA)

Mérida, Yuc., Ejecutivos de Compras y Abastecimiento de la Península de Yucatán, A.C. (ECAPEY)

Cuernavaca, Mor., Ejecutivos de Compras de Morelos, A.C. (ECOMAC)

All local chapters can be reached through CONMAECA.

International

International Federation of Purchasing and Materials Management   80 Flaming
Roseway, Willowdale, Ontario, Canada M2N 5W8. Telephone: (416) 222-0642.

Argentina: Asociación Argentina de Compradores, Tucuman, 141-6° Piso "O," Buenos Aires.

Australia: Institute of Purchasing and Supply Management, 8 Dernvent Crescent, Banksia Park, 5091, South Australia.

Austria: Arbeitsgemeinschaft Einkauf, Osterreichisches Produktivitätszentrum, Hohenstaufengasse 3, A-1014 Vienna.

Belgium: Association Belge des Chefs d'Approvisionnement, Chemin de Gros Tienne, 36, 1328 Ohain.

Brazil: Associacaõ Brasiléira de Administracaõ de National, Rua Felix da Gumba, 29. Tijuca, Rio de Janeiro CE 20260.

Canada: Purchasing Management Association of Canada, 80 Richmond Street West, Toronto, Ontario, M5H2A4.

Chile: Asociación Chilena de Jefes de Compras, Casilla 161-D, Santiago.

Denmark: Danske Indkøbschefers Landsforening, Charlottenlundvej 26, DK-2900 Hellerup, Copenhagen.

Finland: Suomen Materiaalitaloudellinen Korkeavuorenkatu 25 A3A, SF OU130 Helsinki 13.

France: Compagnie des Dirigeants d' Approvisionnement et Acheteurs de France, 8 Rue du Conservatoire, 75009 Paris.

Association pour le Perfectionnement des Approvisionnements dans les Services Publiques, 2 Rue du Roule, 75001 Paris.

Germany: Bundesverband Materialwirtschaft und Einkauf e.V., 6000 Frankfurt/Main 70, Waidmannstrasse 25.

Great Britain: Institute of Purchasing and Supply, IPS House, Ascot, Berkshire, SL57HU.

Greece: Hellenic Purchasing Institute, Athens.

Hong Kong: Institute of Purchasing and Supply Hong Kong, Box K2241, Kowloon, Hong Kong.

India: Indian Association of Materials Management, Mehta Chambers, Opera House, 13, Mathew Road, Bombay, 400 004.

Ireland: Irish Institute of Purchasing and Materials Management, 90 St. Stephen's Green, Dublin 2.

Israel: Irgun Menahaley Aspaka B'Israel, 6 Sderot David Hamelech, P.O. Box 16524, Tel Aviv.

Italy: Associazione degli Approvvigionatori e Compratori Italiani, Viale Ranzoni 16, 29149 Milan.

Japan: Japan Materials Management Association, Terashima Building, 1, Nihonbashi-Honcho, 2-Chome Chuo-Ku, Tokyo, 103.

Kenya: Kenya Institute of Supply Management, P.O. Box 30700, Nairobi, Kenya.

Mexico: Confederación Mexicana de Asociaciones de Ejecutivos de Compras y Abastecimiento, A.C., Manuel Ma. Contreras 135-5° Mexico, 4, D.F.

Netherlands: Nederlandse Vereniging voor Inkoop-Efficiency, Van Alkemadelaan 700, The Hague.

New Zealand: New Zealand Institute of Purchasing and Supply, P.O. Box 3590, Wellington.

Nigeria: Nigerian Institute of Purchasing and Materials Management, 19 UBUN-EKO Street, P.O. Box 3801, Lagos.

Norway: Norsk Innkjops og Materialadministrasjons Forbund, Trondheimsvn, 80, Oslo 5.

Philippines: Purchasing Association of the Philippines, Inc., Suite 403-A, Campos Rueda Building, Tindalo Street, P.O. Box 1876, MCC, Makati, Rizal.

Portugal: Associaçao Portuguesa dos Chefes de Aprovisionamento e de Compras, Alameda das Linhas de Torres, 201-3°-Dt.° Lisboa 5.

Singapore: Singapore Purchasing and Materials Management Association, 528 Maxwell House, 5th Floor, Maxwell Road, Singapore, 0106.

South Africa: Institute of Purchasing South Africa, P.O. Box 35, 495, Northcliff, Transvaal 2115.

Sweden: Svenska Inköpsledares Förening, Tegnérgatan 1, 111 40 Stockholm.

Switzerland: Schweizerische Einkäufer-Vereinigung, Lorenzenvorstadt 90, Postfach 87, CH-5001 Aarau.

United States: National Association of Purchasing Management, 11 Park Place, New York, N.Y. 10007.

National Institute of Governmental Purchasing, Suite 922, 1001 Connecticut Avenue, N.W., Washington, D.C. 20036.

Venezuela: Associación Venezolana de Compradores, c/o Fabrica de Tinta Olin, C.A., Calle el Empalme, EDF Fedecamaras Piso 2 OHG, Caracas.

POLICIES AND OBJECTIVES OF PURCHASING ASSOCIATIONS

Statements of purposes, policies, and objectives set out by the various purchasing associations more clearly define what they attempt to do for their members and the profession—their reason for existence. Following are several such statements which are representative of most purchasing associations.

National Association of Purchasing Management

Objectives

1. To foster and promote interchange of ideas and cooperation among its members
2. To promote the study, development, and application of purchasing manage-

ment, materials management, improved procurement or purchasing methods and practices and all related matters

3. To collect and disseminate information of interest and benefit to its members, including management, current production and market data, information on business trends, manufacturing methods and practices, products and their uses, and channels of distribution

4. To correct trade abuses and encourage maintenance of ethical standards in buying and selling

5. To encourage and cooperate in the institution and development of courses in the subjects of purchasing management, purchasing, and other subjects related to the procurement functions in colleges and universities

6. To strive by all legitimate means to advance the purchasing management profession

Policies   N.A.P.M. represents a wide diversity of business interests, having members from large and small units of industrial, educational, institutional, governmental, utility, and distribution organizations. On political, social, labor, and even economic problems, the interests and opinions of its members or the policies of their companies would sometimes be divergent.

As a matter of general policy the association does not obligate its members by committing them to be, or representing them to be, for or against any proposal of a controversial nature. The association believes, however, that an exception to this hands-off policy must be made with respect to issues of basic and fundamental importance to the purchasing function. Where legislative proposals or other developments would adversely affect the exercise of purchasing skills in a free economy, or the maintenance of ethical standards in buying and selling, N.A.P.M. will actively oppose such proposals or developments. The association will likewise actively support proposals which would enhance the opportunities for ethical purchasing in a free economy.

N.A.P.M. is strongly opposed to the introduction of politics into the field of public purchasing. The interests of the tax paying public are best served by public purchasing positions being filled only by properly qualified personnel.

N.A.P.M., realizing its social responsibility, cooperates fully in the area of public affairs in providing a program directed toward assisting the handicapped, physically disabled, mentally retarded and mentally restored.

N.A.P.M. also subscribes fully to the minority supplier concept, being a charter member of the National Minority Purchasing Council, with the executive vice-president sitting on the board of directors of that organization. Affiliated associations are urged to encourage members to actively search out and assist minority group small businesses with guidance and help in establishing themselves as viable, competitive business organizations.

In the interest of concern for the rapid and changing ideology and technology of our overall business and culture and environment; and with special interest in and direction toward the procurement function, the members and governing bodies of our organization should willingly offer and solicit the opportunity to provide their expert purchasing knowledge and professional services to those local, state, and federally sponsored institutions, that have the need for such services. However, no individual, local association, district, committee, or group of N.A.P.M. shall offer any services of N.A.P.M. outside of the scope of the responsibilities for which they have cognizant authority. The services of all organizations within the N.A.P.M. will be promptly provided upon the written request of a duly authorized agent or any local, state, or federally sponsored institution.

N.A.P.M., or any of its integral groups or committees acting in behalf of the N.A.P.M., shall not collaborate in the preparation of, endorse, or approve any terms or conditions of sale jointly arrived at with other trade or professional groups. N.A.P.M. does not acknowledge any statements, written or otherwise, past or present, which suggest such endorsement.

The participation by N.A.P.M. members in materials standards determination is a recognized and endorsed function. N.A.P.M. has long cooperated with ANSI, ASTM, and other similar bodies in the establishment of materials and methods standards. ANSI has recognized N.A.P.M.'s participation by honoring certain N.A.P.M. members with the Standards and Howard Coonley medals. It has also awarded a seat on its board of directors to an N.A.P.M. member. N.A.P.M., likewise, established as one of its prime committees a group devoted to standardization. It is, therefore, not incompatible with either N.A.P.M. policy or practice that its members actively participate in standardization activities with such standards-establishing bodies. However, members selected to serve on such bodies will represent their individual companies and not the N.A.P.M.

National Association of State Purchasing Officials

Purpose The purpose of the association is to bring the purchasing officials of the states into an organization through which they can improve the quality of purchasing and procurement, exchange information, and cooperate toward the more effective exercise of the procurement and supply functions to attain greater efficiency and economy in state administration.

Aims and Objectives

To research and recommend improvement in state government purchasing

To develop and promote standards and specifications for state government procurement

To promote and encourage the professional competence of all persons engaged in state government procurement

To strive for better understanding and effectiveness of the purchasing function in the structure of state government

To buy without prejudice, seeking to obtain the maximum ultimate value for each dollar of expenditure

To counsel and assist other state purchasing officials in the performance of their duties

To cooperate with all organizations engaged in activities designed to enhance the development and standing of governmental purchasing

To remember that everything the association does reflects on the entire purchasing profession, and to govern every action accordingly

National Institute of Governmental Purchasing

Organized in 1944 and international in scope, NIGP is a nonprofit educational and technical assistance organization of governmental purchasing agencies of the United States, Canada, and other nations. Chartered in Wisconsin, the institute is affiliated with the Institute of Purchasing and Supply of Great Britain, and is a charter member of the International Federation of Purchasing and Materials Management.

Aims and Objectives

To study, discuss, and recommend improvements in governmental purchasing

To interchange ideas and experiences and obtain expert advice on local, state, and national governmental purchasing problems

To collect and distribute to governmental purchasing officials information on the organization and administration of governmental buying

To develop and promote simplified standards and specifications for governmental buying

To promote effective purchasing structures and uniform purchasing laws and procedures

To promote and foster the professional competence and stature of all persons engaged in governmental buying

To set an academic and professional standard for all such persons and to award diplomas, certificates, and distinctions to any such persons after examination or otherwise

To achieve recognition of the place of public purchasing in the governmental structure, with emphasis on cabinet or top-management status for the public purchasing official

To work for or against proposals affecting the welfare of governmental buying agencies

To give to taxpayers information on governmental buying problems in order to foster interest in public affairs and cooperation between governmental buyers and those they serve

As indicated, the education and professional development of individuals involved in public purchasing has been one of NIGP's primary objectives.

Toward that end, NIGP has developed a comprehensive professional development program which guides the public purchaser to certification as a professional public buyer (PPB) or as a certified public purchasing officer (CPPO). The concept underlying the development of the certification program was to provide a standard by which the qualification of any public purchaser at either the operational or management/supervisory levels could be evaluated.

The PPB and CPPO have been officially recognized by the National Association of State Purchasing Officials (NASPO) as a criterion for selecting and promoting individuals involved in the purchasing activities of state governments. In 1978, NASPO joined with NIGP in the establishment of a Universal Public Purchasing Certification Council which administers the universal certification requirements for public purchasing personnel. The council is composed of representatives of NIGP and NASPO, plus a representative of the Federal Acquisition Institute, Office of Federal Procurement Policy. The U.S. Department of Defense has coded the certification designations into its automated career management system. Several agencies, departments, and local jurisdictions formally recognize the certification designations as a meaningful standard for employment and advancement of public purchasing personnel.

NIGP training courses, which include formal seminars in basic, intermediate, and advanced public purchasing, and seminars/workshops in the specialties of public purchasing are also a part of the educational and professional development program.

California Association of Public Purchasing Officers

Purpose and Objectives   CAPPO was formed, and exists today, for the purpose of exchanging purchasing ideas in an effort to resolve unique, specific, or general problems affecting any of California's public agencies. It is through increased purchasing knowledge, improved techniques, and the exemplary ethics of each individual procurement officer that the various jurisdictions in the state will benefit. CAPPO is thus striving to effect continuing improvement in the purchasing service available to cities, counties, schools, and special districts.

It follows then that CAPPO's objective is to promote good public purchasing practices and to advance our profession through our programs which include:

Educational programs

The certification program

Exchange of information through regular group meetings, and an annual conference

Development of standards and specifications

Review of pending legislation pertaining to governmental purchasing

Dissemination of information to other government officials, vendors, and the general public as well as to members

National Purchasing Institute

NPI is a professional association of public purchasing officials engaged in government, publicly owned utilities, special districts, education, medical, and research, institutions.

This association was founded to:

1. Promote knowledge and understanding of purchasing, its techniques, procedures, and ethics, for the public welfare

2. Provide a forum for the interchange of ideas and information among purchasing professionals working for public trust

3. Prepare policies and programs in support of uniform and simplified laws, regulations, standards, and specifications that affect the public interest

Its purpose is to create general awareness to the field of purchasing for the public sector and enhance, in particular, individual professional development through advocating a universal professional designation, conducting regional seminars and an annual conference, publishing pertinent articles in professional magazines and newsletters, and performing periodic reviews of purchasing literature and legislation to develop an appreciation for the role of purchasing in government.

National Association of Educational Buyers

The National Association of Educational Buyers is a professional association of almost 2000 institutions of higher learning and related organizations, nationwide. Since 1920 it has provided some of the highly specialized information needed by the purchasing professionals it serves.

Objectives

1. To establish and maintain professional standards and cooperation among its members

2. To foster and promote the development and application of efficient purchasing and business methods and practices in educational institutions

3. To collect and disseminate useful product, procedure, and business information to its members

4. To provide the means of carrying out research and to sponsor such other methods and activities as may be useful or necessary in providing its members with facilities for efficient purchasing and business operation

5. To maintain for association members a cooperative relationship with executive offices of various national associations in the field of higher education and with officers of the federal government, whose activities affect higher education

6. To keep its members informed on current national government trends which may affect the purchasing department or the general business management of colleges

National Association of Hospital Purchasing—Materials Management

Objectives   The NAHPMM is an association of professional individuals who are organized to improve purchasing and materials management in hospitals and allied health care institutions and:

1. To foster and increase knowledge and proficiency in the related functions of purchasing and health care materials management

2. To conduct and participate in educational programs and activities concerning purchasing and health care materials management

3. To provide media for the interchange of ideas and dissemination of literature relative to the related functions of purchasing and health care materials management

4. To bring about closer cooperation among individuals of varying disciplines in purchasing and health care materials management and its related functions

5. To develop curricula and supporting materials for use in educational institutions relative to areas of purchasing and health care materials management

6. To cooperate with hospitals and allied patient care institutions and agencies and their related associations, governmental agencies, and other interested groups in matters pertaining to purchasing and health care materials management

7. To establish and promulgate principles relative to purchasing and health care materials management

8. To establish standards of performance for individuals and institutions in various areas of purchasing and health care materials management

9. To collect and disseminate information of benefit to its members regarding:

   a. Fundamental manufacturing, producing, and marketing practices

   b. Various products and their abuses

   c. Sources of supply and distribution

   d. Product research

   e. Inventory turnover rates

   f. Material handling techniques

   g. Distribution, storage, and warehousing techniques

10. To do research in areas of purchasing and health care materials management; to help achieve these objectives through the publication of professional journals and papers

American Society for Hospital Purchasing and Materials Management

The American Society for Hospital Purchasing and Materials Management was established in July 1962 by the American Hospital Association as the American Society for Hospital Purchasing Agents and is one of the oldest personal membership societies affiliated with the American Hospital Association.

Objectives:

1. To bring about close cooperation among hospital purchasing and materials managers in order to promote efficiency in hospital procurement and distribution systems

2. To cooperate with hospitals and allied associations in enhancing standardization and simplification in matters pertaining to purchasing and materials management

3. To encourage and assist members to develop their knowledge and increase their effectiveness in hospital purchasing and materials management

4. To provide a medium for the interchange of ideas and dissemination of information relative to hospital purchasing and materials management

5. To encourage and assist chapters in conducting regular meetings, conferences, and educational programs on hospital purchasing and materials management

The Newspaper Purchasing Management Association

The Newspaper Purchasing Management Association was founded and organized for the following purposes:

1. To promote study, development, and application of improved purchasing methods, practices, and techniques in the newspaper publishing industry

2. To foster and promote interchange of ideas and cooperation among its members

3. To collect and disseminate information of interest and benefit to its membership

4. To encourage and cooperate in the institution of ethical standards in buying and selling

5. To strive by all legitimate means to advance the purchasing profession within the industry

International Federation of Purchasing and Materials Management

The International Federation of Purchasing and Materials Management was founded in London in May 1974 by the merger of two supranational bodies which had for more than 20 years been active in the field of international purchasing and supply management. The federation is an independent, nonprofit, scientific and educational organization. Its specific purposes are to:

1. Further the principles and practices of purchasing and materials management, considered as a basic and distinct function of the management structure of industry, trade, and public undertakings

2. Promote, encourage, undertake, and coordinate the study of all problems affecting purchasing and materials management and to further relevant solutions

3. Ensure the highest standards of business ethics of those engaged throughout the world in the professions of purchasing and materials management

4. Promote and encourage the development of the personal capabilities of all those involved in purchasing and materials management activities

5. Provide a body recognized as the one through which purchasing and materials management can be represented in matters of international interest

6. Encourage and assist those engaged in purchasing and materials management to develop their national associations and their national education schemes bearing on the principles and practices of the profession

7. Assist in founding national associations of purchasing and materials management in countries where such bodies do not as yet exist

8. Promote among those engaged in purchasing and materials management closer relationships and better mutual undertanding

Purchasing Management Association of Canada

Purposes and Objectives

1. To improve procurement and materials management practice

2. To provide service to its members

3. To encourage research and development in the procurement and materials management field

4. To establish and encourage the application of high standards of ethical conduct

5. To further the status of the individuals engaged in purchasing management

6. To promote cooperation among its members and with other purchasing associations

7. To present Canadian purchasing conferences

8. To coordinate the activities of members, with due regard to language and geographic factors

9. To publish information of interest and benefit to its members

10. To establish an educational program that will benefit those employed in the materials field

EDUCATIONAL ACTIVITIES OF PURCHASING ASSOCIATIONS

One of the primary functions of a professional association is to provide educational programs for the benefit of its members. This is typified by the wide range of educational activities carried on by purchasing associations throughout the world. Some have centralized their programs on a national basis; others have decentralized some and centralized others. Following are representative examples of the types of programs available, including information on various educational activities developed by other than purchasing associations but for purchasing students and practitioners. For detailed information concerning any of these or other educational activities in specific associations, contact the association headquarters office at the address shown in the first section of this chapter.

National Association of Purchasing Management

N.A.P.M. has developed a broad program of professional development activities under the overall direction of its educational planning committee. This committee includes three major national committees: academic planning, professional development, and research planning, as well as a committee member responsible for materials management.

Following are the goals and objectives of the educational planning committee, designed to carry out N.A.P.M.'s long-term objective in the field of professional development: namely, to provide the opportunity for, and to motivate, those engaged in purchasing to grow professionally as individuals, each according to his own ambitions, capacity, and effort.

1. To provide the opportunity for the development of the individual as a leader
2. To assist local affiliated associations in their provision of:
   a. Basic purchasing education
   b. Continuing purchasing education
   c. Programs for local meetings
3. To provide aid in planning and programming educational efforts at the district and national level in connection with:
   a. Continuing purchasing education
   b. District workshops
   c. National and district conference programming
4. To cooperate with governmental agencies, management associations, and other organizations in any activities furthering the professional development goals of N.A.P.M.
5. To cooperate with educational foundations, colleges and universities, and faculty members and administrators, in any activities furthering the professional development goals of N.A.P.M.
6. To facilitate the development, expansion, and dissemination of purchasing literature designed to further the educational and professional level of those engaged in purchasing
7. To improve the professional standards of the purchasing function
8. To encourage, implement, and provide long-range guidance to an organized research program for N.A.P.M.
9. To provide a comprehensive and reliable source of information on purchasing and related subjects for the use of members, educators, students, and others interested in the purchasing field

In carrying out these objectives, the educational planning committee and the N.A.P.M. national office personnel are operating a number of specific programs, including those described below. Further information on these activities may be obtained from N.A.P.M.

Doctoral Fellowship Program   A limited number of fellowships are available annually from N.A.P.M. to doctoral candidates interested in pursuing graduate study in purchasing, materials management, management's procurement obligation, and related fields.

Research Grant Program   Purchasing is considered one of the last new important frontiers in business management research. The potential for important discoveries in techniques and management philosophy as well as in the application of known management techniques and philosophies to the purchasing and materials management function is vast. To encourage such research, the N.A.P.M. Research Planning Committee solicits, screens, and recommends worthy research projects to N.A.P.M. and to other sources of funds.

Industry Fellowship Program   This program is aimed at developing purchasing's relationships with universities by arranging for an educator to spend all or part of the summer in a business organization. The educator's primary purpose is to study how the purchasing function is performed and how it relates to the other functions of the business. In this process he acquires valuable background information with which he can enrich his courses and provide better guidance to students.

Program Aids   The various activity committees within N.A.P.M. develop educational package programs and program aids for use by program chairmen, committee chairmen, and officers of the local associations in presenting effective educational programs to their fellow members. These programs and aids can also be used by members and others for in-plant training programs and by college educators to supplement lectures.

Literature   N.A.P.M. has generated a considerable body of literature for its members in order that they may keep abreast of the latest developments in their field and operate their purchasing departments more efficiently. The *Guide to Purchasing* was developed to consolidate in one or more volumes current and future literature produced by N.A.P.M. This *Guide* is furnished to N.A.P.M. members at no charge and is supplemented with new or revised articles on a quarterly basis.

In addition to the literature developed and distributed as a part of the guide, N.A.P.M. created in 1965 the *Journal of Purchasing and Materials Management.* The *Journal* presents concepts from business statistics, economics, engineering, behavioral science, and any discipline which contributes to the advancement of knowledge in business or governmental purchasing, materials management, or related areas. Articles discuss theories, principles, and philosophies; analyze business, economic, and social issues and trends; describe and evaluate techniques and practices; examine legal considerations; and report relevant research. The *Journal* is published quarterly.

Purchasing Management Association of Canada

Education has been one of the chief interests of PMAC throughout its existence. The first professional development program of the association was launched in 1963. At that time the association committed itself to a revision of its program every 5 years to ensure that the program would always reflect the current state of the art of purchasing and materials management. Accordingly, in 1968, 1973, and 1978 the program was revised.

The aim and philosophy of the current program is to supply participants with specialized purchasing and materials courses and seminars as well as a good general management point of view. Specifically, the initial part of the program comprises three materials courses: principles of buying, inventory control and production planning, and traffic and transportation.

Some of the association's seminars are usually taken by participants during the early stages of the program. For those with managerial talent and ambitions, the program continues with a requirement for postsecondary school studies, six general management courses, and finally the association's prestigious advanced purchasing management course.

At the completion of the foregoing requirements, participants are eligible for an interview before the association's board of examiners. If successful, a person is awarded the professional purchaser designation.

The Purchasing Management Association of Canada also offers the following correspondence courses in connection with its professional development program leading to the professional purchaser diploma.

1. Principles of buying
2. Inventory control and production planning
3. Traffic and transportation
4. Advanced purchasing management

Further information on these courses may be obtained from PMAC.

Purchasing Seminars and Continuing Education

National Association of Purchasing Management   In May 1976, N.A.P.M. established a full-time continuing education department with the purpose of expanding the highly successful university seminar program, developing 3- to 4-day seminars cosponsored with district or local associations and initiating specialized seminars required to meet the demand. Assisting members to attain recognition as certified purchasing managers was also an objective, as was the establishment of in-plant training programs using N.A.P.M. programs to assist companies to advance professionalism. The promotion of continuing education on a full-time basis has resulted in solidifying and expanding the university programs. Annual university programs include the following:

1. Purchasing executive seminar—2-week program at Harvard Graduate School of Business, held annually in July or August.
2. Purchasing management seminars—1-week program held annually:

October	Cornell University, Ithaca, New York
November	Houston University, Houston, Texas
June	Michigan State Univ., East Lansing, Michigan
April	University of North Carolina, Chapel Hill, North Carolina
February	Stanford Graduate School of Business Faculty, Palo Alto, California

Program content varies, as attempts are made to schedule outstanding faculty considered authorities in their field.

SUBJECTS COVERED IN RECENT SEMINARS

Purchasing planning and control
Purchasing productivity
Materials requirement planning
Purchasing measurement systems

Negotiation strategies and techniques
Management appraisal
Economic forecasting
Logistics
Price cost analysis
Developing managerial effectiveness
Problem identification and implementation
International purchasing
Use of the computer in purchasing
The psychology of bargaining behavior
Corporate strategy and procurement goals
Legal aspects of purchasing
Materials management
Management perspectives on purchasing
Make or buy decisions

SPECIAL PURCHASING SEMINARS

Three-day seminar on data processing and use of computers in purchasing, Graduate School of Business, University of Texas, Austin, Texas.

Two-day law seminar—conducted by Professor John Murray, Pittsburgh, Pennsylvania.

Three-day seminar for new and experienced buyers—held in different geographic areas of the country annually, established faculty facilitating mobility.

Certification examination review seminars—3 days, each covering specific areas. Held twice a year in different geographic areas.

Several 3-day management seminars, cosponsored with local associations and held annually.

COMPANY IN-PLANT TRAINING PROGRAMS.   In-plant training programs, custom-made to fit the needs of each company, are available. Programs range from 1 day to 1 week and are normally established on a long-range, continuing basis. The advantages of an in-plant program are the much lower costs and long-range programs designed for a company's particular requirements. The interest continues to grow, as evidenced by new sponsors each month. Top management personnel, including the presidents of some companies, have proved their interest by personally auditing segments of the program.

Purchasing Management Association of Canada   The Purchasing Management Association of Canada conducts seminars throughout Canada as a part of its professional development program leading to the professional purchaser diploma. These seminars are designed and taught by Canadian university professors or other experts, and each is devoted to a single topic. Subjects include inventory control, negotiation, forecasting, computers, human relations, law, materials management, supplier development, and others. Seminars are usually 1 or 2 days in length and are held in the daytime.

COLLEGES AND UNIVERSITIES IN THE UNITED STATES OFFERING COURSES IN PURCHASING

In 1968, N.A.P.M. and the N.A.P.A. Purchasing Educational Foundation, Inc., jointly sponsored an in-depth research study of educational activities currently available. This research was carried out by the University of Wisconsin Bureau of Business Research, under the direction of Richard Pinkerton. Pinkerton conducted a survey of courses in purchasing, procurement, and materials management offered by U.S. universities and colleges and junior colleges in 1967–1968.

Updating this survey of purchasing-related courses to the 1977–1978 school year, N.A.P.M. District One's Professional Development Committee Vice-Chairman Ron Aguirre has presented the following list of institutions alphabetically by state.

Alabama
 Alabama Christian College
 Alabama State University
 Auburn University
 Auburn University, Montgomery
 Huntington College
 Troy State University
 University of Montevallo
 University of South Alabama
Arizona
 Arizona State University
Arkansas
 University of Arkansas
California
 California State University of Hayward
 Cerritos Community College
 Coastline Community College
 De Anza College
 Fresno City College
 Fullerton College
 Pasadena City College
 Sacramento State University
 San Diego State University
 San Francisco State University
 San Jose State University
 University of California, Los Angeles
Colorado
 Regis College
Connecticut
 Fairfield University
 University of Bridgeport
 University of Hartford
 University of New Haven
Florida
 Broward Community College
 Hillsboro Community College
 University of North Florida
Georgia
 Dekalb College
Hawaii
 Chaminade College of Honolulu
 University of Hawaii

Idaho
 Ricks College
Illinois
 Danville Junior College
 DePaul University
 Illinois Central College
 Illinois Institute of Technology
 Illinois State University
 Loyola University of Chicago
 Northern Illinois University
 Rock Valley College
 Roosevelt University
 Triton College
 Western Illinois University
 Wm. Rainey Harper
Indiana
 Indiana Vocational Technical College
 Tri-State University
Iowa
 Palmer Junior College
Kansas
 Cowley County Community College
 Friends University
Kentucky
 Morehead State University
 University of Kentucky
Louisiana
 Louisiana State University
Maryland
 Catonsville Community College
Massachusetts
 Babson College
 Bentley College
 College of the Holy Cross
 Tufts University
 Western New England College
Michigan
 Aquinas College
 Davenport College of Business
 Lake Superior State College
 Michigan State University
 Michigan Technological University

Minnesota
 Mankato State University
 North Hennepin Community College
 Southeast State University
 St. Cloud State University
 University of Minnesota
Mississippi
 Itawamba Junior College
 University of Mississippi
Missouri
 Rockhurst College
 Southwest Missouri State University
 University of Missouri
Nebraska
 University of Nebraska at Omaha
New Jersey
 Fairleigh Dickinson University
 Kean College of New Jersey
 Union College
New York
 Bryant & Stratton Business Institute
 Millard Fillmore College
 Niagara University
 Rochester Institute of Technology, College of
  Continuing Education
 State University of New York
 Westchester Community College
North Carolina
 North Carolina State University
 University of North Carolina at Chapel Hill
Ohio
 Bowling Green State University
 Capital University
 Case Western Reserve University
 Clark State Technical College
 Cuyahoga Community College
 Edgecliff College
 Kent State University
 Lakeland Community College
 Miami University
 Sinclair Community College
 University of Akron
 University of Cincinnati
 University of Toledo
 Wright State University
 Youngstown State University
Oklahoma
 American Christian College
 Bethany Nazarene College
 Central State University
 Tulsa Junior College
 University of Tulsa
Oregon
 Lane County Community College
 Mt. Hood Community College
 Portland Community College
 Portland State University
 University of Oregon

Pennsylvania
 Community College of Allegheny County,
  Boyce
 Community College of Allegheny South
 Drexel University
 Elizabethtown College
 Luzerne County Community College
 Mercyhurst College
 Northampton County Community College
 Robert Morris College
 University of Pittsburgh
South Carolina
 Clemson University College of Industrial
  Management and Textile Science
 Furman University
 Trident Technical College
Tennessee
 Chattanooga State Technical Community
  College
 East Tennessee State University
 Jackson State Community College
 Memphis State University
 Middle Tennessee State University
 Motlow State Community College
 Tennessee State University
 Tennessee Technological University
 University of Tennessee at Chattanooga
 University of Tennessee at Martin
 University of Tennessee at Nashville
 Volunteer State Community College
 Walters State Community College
Texas
 Corpus Christi University
 Eastfield College
 North Harris County College
 Southern Methodist University
 University of Dallas
 University of Houston
 West Texas State University
Utah
 Brigham Young University
 L.D.S. Business College
 Utah State University
 Utah Technical College
 Weber State College
Virginia
 Eastern Shore Community College
 George Mason University
 J. Sargeant Reynolds Community College
 James Madison University
 Lord Fairfax Community College
 Northern Virginia Community College
 Paul D. Camp Community College
 Radford College
 Southwest Virginia Community College
 Tidewater Community College
 University of Virginia

Virginia Polytechnic Institute and State
  University
Wytheville Community College
Washington
Edmonds Community College
Lewis and Clark High School
Pacific Lutheran University
Shoreline Community College

Washington, D.C.
George Washington University
University of Washington D.C.
Wisconsin
Marquette University
Milwaukee Area Technical College
University of Wisconsin
Waukesha County Technical Institute

INTERNATIONAL FEDERATION OF PURCHASING AND MATERIALS MANAGEMENT PROGRAMS

The many national members of the federation are at different levels of professional development. Some, founded more than 60 years ago, number their members in the thousands, while others, still in the infancy stages, continue transforming groups of like-minded men and women into an established and recognized professional body. Yet all are moving in the same direction with regard to their professional development concerns.

These national associations, by their own endeavors and by mutual help, are providing more and more facilities for updating those established in their purchasing careers and for training those at the threshold of their professional purchasing and materials management careers. Career prospects in purchasing are improving as the need for skillful management of material resources becomes more widely understood at all levels of industry, commerce, and public service.

While over 20 members of the federation have reported ongoing professional development activities, only 2 are offered below as randomly selected examples of successful professional development programming.

To avoid terminology confusion, the following definitions are used: a *seminar* is a concentrated learning session lasting from 1 to 4 days; a *course* is a series of lectures or classes with a definite sequence and objective, usually lasting longer than the equivalent of 4 full days of work (this could also be available through correspondence); and a *program* is a combination of courses, seminars, and other related activities which together represent a total learning activity. A *one-time* seminar or course is one which is offered once only and not repeated, and a *continuing development program* is one which never really ends, although it may have certification at various stages.

Australia

The objectives of the professional development program of the Institute of Purchasing and Supply Management (I.P.S.M.) in Australia are to foster educational training in purchasing and supply management at all organizational levels. These objectives may be summarized as:

1. To establish purchasing and supply management subjects as core units available in recognized business study courses at mid-levels (certificate) and tertiary levels (diploma degree) of education

2. To provide a continuing program of participative seminars, lectures, workshops, and conferences to enable personnel engaged in all aspects of purchasing and supply to develop their knowledge and skills to the fullest extent to achieve greater personal and professional development

3. To establish postgraduate levels of study in purchasing and supply subjects to encourage higher levels of management skill

Formal education in Australia is controlled by separate government authorities in each state and all education programs are in English. Each state division of the I.P.S.M. maintains close liaison with the education authorities in their respective states and the institute is represented on advisory boards to establish syllabus material as appropriate to the courses concerned.

Certificate or mid-level courses are offered which require an entrance level of fifth-year secondary school (sub matriculation) and comprise 700 to 800 study hours for completion, covering approximately 10 subject units. These courses may be taken on either a full- or part-time basis and are aimed at producing personnel qualified to accept responsible positions at first-level supervisory functions within the purchasing and supply field. Purchasing and supply subject units comprise approximately 20 percent of the course content; finance, business administration, mathematics, and statistics approximately 60 percent; and elective units in other business study fields 20 percent. These courses are offered by a number of technical colleges throughout Australia.

Business management education at the tertiary level is offered at many universities and colleges of advanced education throughout Australia. Business studies or business administration degrees and diploma are generally 3-year full-time courses requiring matriculation standard (university entrance) of secondary education as a prerequisite for admission. Specific subject units in purchasing and supply management functions are not widely offered, but development of syllabus material at this level is making steady progress with full participation by the I.P.S.M.

A postgraduate diploma in physical distribution management containing purchasing and supply management units is offered by the Caulfield Institute of Technology in Victoria. The course is aimed at producing well-qualified graduates capable of meeting the demands of senior management and executive management positions in the supply and distribution fields of industry, commerce, and government.

The I.P.S.M. divisions in each state offer a wide range of seminars and short courses, technical papers, and individual lectures on subjects related to purchasing and supply management.

The geography of Australia and the structure of the state education authorities, which operate autonomously, have made coordination of educational programs difficult. I.P.S.M. divisions are continuing to work closely with state education authorities to accelerate the development of purchasing and supply management units at various levels within the educational systems with considerable success. The National Council of the Institute is continuing to encourage a free interchange of the ideas and developments between all educational areas involved, to ensure the continuing development and improvement of the standards of education available in this field.

Ireland

Professional development for the Irish Institute of Purchasing and Materials Management (I.I.P.M.M.) calls for providing a program of education which will enhance the status of the purchasing and stores management areas of commercial activity.

Management fully recognizes the necessity of good purchasing, but also appreciates that this cannot be realized without formal training in the subjects involved. The various techniques covered in the current education scheme will encourage graduates to expand on an area of business, i.e., purchasing which, when managed properly, only leads to better company efficiency.

The I.I.P.M.M. maintains four areas of continuing education:

1. The ordinary certificate in storekeeping enables storekeeping staff members to carry out their duties with greater interest, comprehension, and initiative by giving them a wider knowledge of commercial and industrial organization and, particularly, the relation of the stores function to the work of other departments.

2. The advanced certificate in storekeeping is an expansion upon the parameters of the ordinary certificate. The function of storekeeping becomes the concept of stores management.

3. The final purchasing diploma–intermediate stage aims at general education in business studies. It consists of fundamental studies in business-related disciplines and seeks to introduce the student to the theories and methods which are valuable in interpreting business situations. No diploma is awarded for successful completion of this stage. The purchasing diploma will be awarded only after successful completion of all subjects in both the intermediate and final stages.

4. The final purchasing diploma–final stage promotes in-depth understanding of the purchasing and materials management function.

Stringent entrance requirements into I.I.P.M.M.'s professional development program include: proposal by members of the institute or by the principal of the institution at which the candidate is studying; sound moral character; commencement or intent to commence a course of studies with the object of obtaining the institute's examination qualifications; to be prepared to present himself for examination every 2 years and for a maximum period of 8 years unless further extended; and to be already employed in some aspect of purchasing or stores activity or if not to be so within a reasonable period of time.

Professional development is an area of the greatest growth in the I.I.P.M.M., and this, it is hoped, will reflect in a large and educated membership in the years to come.

NOTE: For further information on subjects covered in this section see the list of references in Section 30.

Section **30**

Bibliography and Library

EDITOR

Mary R. Crowell *Librarian, Purchasing Information Center, National Association of Purchasing Management, New York, New York*

Purchasing in a modern industrial or governmental organization encompasses a very wide range of knowledge in most fields of endeavor. Every purchasing department, whether small, medium, or large, calls for not only a rudimentary knowledge of all branches of business, but a working familiarity with strategic planning, decision making, professional management, electronic data processing, behavioral science, legal aspects of purchasing, and other subjects.

Procedures used in purchasing today demand knowledge gained from colleges and universities and from actual contact in the field, and also a constant vigil over recent developments that have provided new tools and concepts to further the evaluation of the purchasing function.

The principal source of these new ideas, systems, and applications is published information. This knowledge, found in collections of books, periodicals, government documents, reports, brochures, trade literature, and other material in the purchasing department's library, is incalculable.

There is a wealth of purchasing literature in the United States and other countries. Much is prepared or sponsored by the many professional purchasing associations; much comes from scholars in the field.

PURCHASING DEPARTMENT LIBRARY

The purchasing library should be separate from other company libraries. This specialized library has a unique function. It combines the qualities of a business library with those of a technical one, with the emphasis on the techniques and tools of purchasing and its application to related subjects.

Furthermore, there are special collections that need finer developments as individual files: specifications and standards; the myriad of vendor catalogs and price lists; vendors' annual reports; patents; market research reports; vendor evaluation reports; and many others.

It is an expensive and difficult task to maintain all material needed in a departmental library, and it is strongly urged that purchasing persons rely on the well-staffed and well-stocked libraries of their respective communities, such as those in graduate business schools, the economic and technical divisions of public libraries, and their local purchasing association libraries for both reading material and reference sources.

The needs of the department must be analyzed and decisions made on the extent to which the collection and services will be developed, with plans for the physical layout and furniture following. A central area is preferable, large enough to accommodate the number of users, with shelving, filing cabinets, and tables.

Care must be taken to select someone to execute the services. One person, whether a member of the purchasing staff or a qualified librarian, should be responsible for the supervision of the many diversified tasks.

Retrieval of information is the key to the success of any library. All published material is made available for use by proper classification, cataloging, and indexing. Simple methods for the arrangement of books, periodicals, and related material can be devised for libraries to serve the needs of the smaller purchasing departments. The Dewey classification scheme is suggested for use in larger ones. Catalog cards should be available on all material in the entire collection. A simplified method is to type all descriptive information on a main (index) card and to file the main cards by author. Cross-reference the main cards with title cards and subject cards. One should consult the latest edition of the *Library of Congress List of Subject Headings* or any other authoritative list.

Library supply houses furnish catalogs upon request. Some of the more active ones are the following: Bro-Dart Industries, 1609 Memorial Avenue, Williamsport, Pa. 17701; Demco, Inc., Box 7488, Madison, Wis., 53707; Fordham Equipment Co., 2377 Hoffman Street, Bronx, N.Y. 10458; Gaylord Library Supplies, Syracuse, N.Y. 13201; and Library Bureau, Remington Rand Office Systems, 1 Commerce Drive, Cranford, N.J. 07016.

BOOKS

The aim of this section is to list a wide range of texts, reference materials, and sources of information most likely to be of value to purchasing people. These listings, although not complete, are selected to provide a direction for further research by the individual in focusing on this specific field. Most of the publications are available at public, university, and association libraries; others may have to be obtained from their publishers.

For additional publications, one should request catalogs from publishers and consult the many available book directories, such as the *Cumulative Book Index, Books in Print,* and *Subject Guide to Books in Print.*

Complete names and addresses of most of the publishers mentioned in the following pages will be found at the end of this section under Key to Main Publishers.

Purchasing and Materials Management

Ammer, D. S.: *Hospital Materials Management,* Northeastern University, Publications Department, Boston, 1974.

———: *Profit-Conscious Purchasing,* The Dartnell Corp., Chicago, 1977.

———: *Materials Management,* Dow Jones–Irwin, Homewood, Ill. 1968.

———: *Purchasing and Materials Management for Health Care Institutions,* Lexington Books, Lexington, Mass., 1975.

Bailey, P., and D. Farmer: *Managing Materials in Industry,* Available from the Institute of Purchasing and Supply, Ascot, England, 1977.

———, and ———: *Purchasing Principles and Techniques,* available from the Institute of Purchasing and Supply, Ascot, England, 1977.

Baker, R. J., R. S. Kuehne, D. McCoy, and D. M. Witter, Jr.: *Purchasing Factomatic,* Prentice-Hall, Englewood Cliffs, N.J., 1977.

Baker, R. J., R. S. Kuehne, and L. Buddress: *Policy and Procedure Manual for Purchasing and Materials Control,* Prentice-Hall, Englewood Cliffs, N.J., 1980.

Ballot, R. B.: *Materials Management,* American Management Associations, New York, 1971.

Banks, J., and C. Hohenstein: *Procurement and Inventory Ordering Tables,* Pergamon Press, Elmsford, N.Y., 1977.

Barker, D. E., and B. Farington: *Basic Arts of Buying,* available from the Institute of Purchasing and Supply, Ascot, England.

Barlow, C. W.: *Purchasing for the Newly Appointed Buyer,* American Management Associations, New York, 1970.

Basil, D. C., et al.: *Purchasing Information Sources,* Gale Research Company, Detroit, 1977.

Bierman, E. J.: *N.A.P.M. Certification Program—The New Study Guide,* National Association of Purchasing Management, New York, 1980.

Cantor, J.: *Evaluating Purchasing Systems,* American Management Associations, New York, 1970.

Compton, H. K.: *Supplies and Materials Management,* Cahners Books, Boston, 1968.

Corey, E. R.: *Procurement Management: Strategy, Organization and Decision Making,* CBI Publishing Inc., Boston, 1978.

Dowst, S. R.: *Basics for Buyers,* CBI Publishing Co., Boston, 1971.

———: *More Basics for Buyers: Purchasing Principles and Procedures,* CBI Publishing Co., Boston, 1979.

England, W. B., Fearon, H. E., and M. R. Leenders: *Purchasing and Materials Management,* Dow Jones–Irwin, Homewood, Ill., 1980.

Ericsson, D.: *Materials Administration,* McGraw-Hill, New York, 1974.

Fabrycky, W. J., and J. Banks: *Procurement and Inventory Systems,* Reinhold Book Corp., New York, 1967.

Farmer, D., and B. Taylor: *Corporate Planning and Procurement,* Halsted Press, a division of John Wiley, New York, 1975.

Fearon, H.: *Purchasing Research: Concepts and Current Practice,* American Management Associations, New York, 1968.

Gravereau, V., and L. Konopa: *Purchasing Management: Selected Readings,* Grid Publishing Inc., Columbus, 1977.

Hedrick, F. D.: *Purchasing Management in the Smaller Company,* American Management Associations, New York, 1970.

Heinritz, S. F., and P. V. Farrell: *Purchasing Principles and Applications,* Prentice-Hall, Englewood Cliffs, N.J., 1981.

Henrich, R. R., et al.: *A Study of Purchasing Occupations in Health Care Facilities, Interim Report,* University of California Allied Health Projects, 1970.

Hensel, E., and P. De Vallete: *Purchasing Library Materials in Public and School Libraries: A Study of Purchasing Procedures and Relationship between Libraries, Purchasing Agencies and Dealers,* American Library Association, Chicago, 1969.

Holmgren, J. H.: *Purchasing for the Health Care Facility,* Charles C Thomas, Springfield, Ill., 1975.

Huntoon, Robert N.: *The Procurement Systems Review and the Challenge of Profitable Procurement,* The Huntoon Reports, Redding, Calif., 1979.

Janson, Robert: *Purchasing Agent's Desk Book,* Prentice-Hall, Englewood Cliffs, N.J., 1980.

Kelly, H.: *Food Service Purchasing Principles and Practices,* Chain Store Publishing Corp., New York, 1977.

Kotschevar, Lendal H.: *Quality Food Purchasing,* John Wiley, New York, 1980.

Kudrna, D. A.: *Purchasing Manager's Decision Handbook,* Cahners Books, Boston, 1975.

Lee, L., and D. W. Dobler: *Purchasing and Materials Management: Text and Cases,* McGraw-Hill, New York, 1977.

Manente, M. P.: *Functions of the Purchasing Manager,* American Management Associations, New York, 1969.

McDonald, P. R.: *Government Prime Contracts and Subcontracts,* Procurement Associates, Covina, Calif., 1970. Revised annually.

———: *Negotiation of Government Contracts,* Procurement Associates, Covina, Calif., 1970.

McElhiney, P. T., and R. I. Cook: *The Logistics of Materials Management,* Houghton Mifflin, Boston, 1969.

Menonte, M.: *Functions of the Purchasing Manager,* American Management Associations, New York, 1969.

Monczka, R., P. Carter, and J. Hoagland: *Purchasing Performance: Measurement and Control,* Michigan State University, Graduate School of Business Administration, East Lansing, 1979.

National Association of Purchasing Management, Inc.: *Guide to Purchasing,* vol. 1 (hardbound) 1965–69. vol. 2 (hardbound) 1969–73. vol. 3 (looseleaf) 1973 to date.

New, Collin: *Requirements Planning,* Institute of Purchasing and Supply, Ascot, England.

Orlicky, J.: *Material Requirements Planning,* McGraw-Hill, New York, 1974.

Page, Harry Robert: *Public Purchasing and Materials Management,* Lexington Books (Heath), Lexington, Mass., 1980.

Peckham, H. H.: *Effective Materials Management,* Prentice-Hall, Englewood Cliffs, N.J., 1972.

Pritchard, Robert E., and Thomas Hindelang: *The Lease/Buy Decision,* American Publishing Division, American Management Associations, New York, 1980.

Sambridge, E. R.: *Purchasing Computers,* available from the Institute of Purchasing and Supply, Ascot, England.

Sims, E. R.: *Planning and Managing Materials Flow,* Cahners Books, Boston, 1969.

Spinard, P.: *Best in Purchasing,* American Management Associations, New York, 1972.

Stelzer, W. R.: *Materials Management,* Prentice-Hall, Englewood Cliffs, N.J. 1970.

Stevens, J., and J. Grant: *The Purchasing/Marketing Interface,* Halsted Press, a division of John Wiley, New York, 1975.

Stevens, John: *Measuring Purchasing Performance,* available from the Institute of Purchasing and Supply, Ascot, England.

Tersine, R. J.: *Materials Management and Inventory Systems,* Elsevier North Holland, New York, 1976.

U.S. Department of Defense: *Casebook Life Cycle Costing in Equipment Procurement,* G.P.O., Washington, 1970.

Webster, F.: *Organizational Buying Behavior,* Prentice-Hall, Englewood Cliffs, N.J. 1972.

Willets, W. E.: *Fundamentals of Purchasing,* Appleton-Century-Crofts, New York, 1969.

Zenz, G. J.: *Purchasing and the Management of Materials,* John Wiley, New York, 1980.

Related Fields

Accounting and Finance

Bierman, A. H. and T. R. Dyckman: *Managerial Cost Accounting,* Macmillan, Riverside, N.J., 1970.

Black, H. A., et al.: *Accounting in Business Decisions,* Prentice-Hall, Englewood Cliffs, N.J., 1973.

Christy, G. A., and P. F. Roden: *Finance: Environment & Decisions,* Canfield Press, division of Harper and Row, Pub., San Francisco, 1973.

Curry, J. A. and O. J. Curry: *Cost Accounting Planning and Control,* Southwestern Publishing Co., Cincinnati, 1980.

Dopuch, C. N.: *Cost Accounting, Accounting Data for Management's Decisions,* Harcourt Brace Jovanovich, Inc., New York, 1971.

Fertif, P. E., et al.: *Using Accounting Information,* Harcourt Brace Jovanovich, Inc., New York, 1971.

Fremgen, J. M.: *Accounting for Managerial Analysis,* Dow Jones–Irwin, Homewood, Ill., 1972.

Gordon, K. J., and G. Shillinglaw: *Accounting: A Management Approach,* Dow Jones–Irwin, Homewood, Ill., 1974.

Horngrun, C. T.: *Accounting for Management Control,* Prentice-Hall, Englewood Cliffs, N.J., 1980.

Moore, C. L., and R. K. Jaedicke: *Managerial Accounting,* Southwestern Publishing Co., Cincinnati, 1972.

Neuner, J. J. W.: *Cost Accounting Principles and Practices,* Dow Jones–Irwin, Homewood, Ill., 1973.

Philips, G. E., and R. M. Copeland: *Financial Statements—Problems from Current Practice,* Prentice-Hall, Englewood Cliffs, N.J., 1969.

Soldofsky, R. M., and G. Olive: *Financial Management,* Southwestern Publishing Co., Cincinnati, 1974.

Van Horne, H. C.: *Financial Management and Policy,* Prentice-Hall, Englewood Cliffs, N.J., 1974.

Weston, J., and E. F. Brigham: *Essentials of Managerial Finance,* Dryden Press, division of Holt, Rinehart & Winston, Hinsdale, Ill., 1974.

Budgeting

Chandra, Gyan, and Singhvi Chandra: *Budgeting for Profit,* Planning Executives Institute, Oxford, Ohio, 1975.

Cheek, Logan M.: *Zero-Base Budgeting Comes of Age,* American Management Associations, New York, 1977.

Welsh, Glenn A.: *Budgeting—Profit Planning Control,* Prentice-Hall, Englewood Cliffs, N.J., 1976.

Canada

Businessman's Guide to Canadian Customs Laws and Procedures, Albright's Customs Guide Book, 168 Charlotte Street, Ottawa 2, Ontario, Canada.

Canadian Business Guide, The Bank of Nova Scotia, 44 King Street West, Toronto 1, Ontario, Canada. Furnishes a general outline of taxation.

Canadian Trade Index, Canadian Manufacturers Association, 67 Yonge Street, Toronto 1, Ontario, Canada.

Eaton, K. E., and N. A. Chalmers: *Canadian Law of Customs and Excise,* Canada Law Book Company, Limited, 100 Richmond Street East, Toronto, Ontario, Canada.

Lindsay, Thomas: *Outline of Customs in Canada,* Elgin Publications, Vancouver Printers, Limited, Vancouver, British Columbia, Canada.

McGoldrick: *Handbook of the Canadian Customs Tariff and Excise Duties,* The McMullin Publishers Limited, 417 St. Peter Street, Montreal 125, Quebec, Canada.

Sales Tax Guide, Canada, CCH Canadian Limited, 6 Garamond Drive, Don Mills, 403, Ontario, Canada, and the Canadian Manufacturers' Association, 67 Yonge Street, Toronto, Ontario, Canada.

Capital Equipment

Hanssman, Fred: *Operations Research Techniques for Capital Equipment,* Krieger Publishing Co., Melbourne, Fla., 1974.

Murdick, R. G., and D. D. Deming: *Management of Capital Expenditures,* McGraw-Hill, New York, 1968.

Construction Purchasing

Benson, B.: *Critical Path Method in Building Construction,* Prentice-Hall, Englewood Cliffs, N.J., 1970.

Dand, R., and D. Farmer: *Purchasing in the Construction Industry,* available from Institute of Purchasing and Supply, Ascot, England, 1974.

Hohns, H. Murray: *Deskbook of Construction Contract Law—With Forms,* Prentice-Hall, Englewood Cliffs, N.J., 1980.

Rosen, Harold: *Construction Materials Evaluation and Selection: A Systematic Approach,* John Wiley, New York, 1979.

Economics

Frank, Werner L.: *The New Software Economics,* U.S. Professional Development Institute, Silver Spring, Md.

Galbraith, J. K.: *Economics and the Public Purpose,* Houghton Mifflin Co., Boston, 1973.

Gill, R. T.: *Economics,* Goodyear Publishing Co., Pacific Palisades, Calif., 1972.

Gillis, F. E.: *Managerial Economics—Decision Making under Certainty for Business and Engineering,* Addison-Wesley, Reading, Mass., 1969.

Gordon, D. M.: *Problems in Political Economy,* D. C. Heath, Lexington, Mass., 1971.

Heilbrun, J.: *Urban Economics and Public Policy,* St. Martin's Press, New York, 1974.

Leftwich, R. H., and A. M. Sharp: *Economics of Social Issues,* Business Publications, Inc., a subsidiary of R. D. Irwin Inc., Dallas, 1974.

Lindgren, B. W.: *Introduction to Probability and Statistics,* Macmillan, New York, 1969.

Reichard, R. S.: *The Numbers Game,* McGraw-Hill, New York, 1972.

Samuelson, P. A.: *Economics,* McGraw-Hill, New York, 1980.

Stidger, H. C., and R. W. Stidger: *Inflation Management,* John Wiley, New York, 1976.

EDP in Purchasing

Ditri, A., J. Shaw, and W. Atkins, *Managing the EDP Function,* McGraw-Hill, New York, 1971.

Kollios, A. E., and J. Stempel: *Purchasing and the EDP,* American Management Associations, New York, 1966.

Sambridge, E. R.: *Purchasing Computers,* available from the Institute of Purchasing and Supply, Ascot, England.

Wells, R.: *EDP Applications for the Purchasing Function,* American Management Associations, New York, 1970.

Ethics

Garrett, T. M.: *Cases in Business Ethics,* Appleton-Century-Crofts, New York, 1968.

Kroll, J. B.: *Crimes against Business,* Arno Press, a *New York Times* company, New York, 1981.

Masterson, T., and J. C. Nunan: *Ethics in Business,* Pitman Publishing Corp., New York, 1968.

MacIntyre, Alasdair: *A Short History of Ethics,* The Macmillan Company, New York, 1966.

Forecasting and Futures

Ayres, R. U.: *Technological Forecasting and Long-Range Planning,* McGraw-Hill, New York, 1969.

Clark, J. J.: *Management of Business Forecasting,* St. John's University Press, Jamaica, N.Y., 1968.

Dauten, Carl A., and Lloyd M. Valentine: *Business Cycles and Forecasting,* South-Western Publishing, Cincinnati, 1978.

Gould, Bruce G.: *Dow Jones–Irwin Commodities Trading,* Dow Jones–Irwin, Homewood, Ill., 1981.

Kaufman, Perry J.: *Commodity Trading Systems and Methods,* John Wiley, New York, 1971.
Silk, L. S., and M. L. Curley: *A Primer on Business Forecasting,* Random House, New York, 1970.
Teweles, Richard J.: *Commodity Futures Game,* McGraw-Hill, New York, 1969.
Zenz, G. J.: *Futures Trading and the Purchasing Executive,* National Association of Purchasing Management, Inc. and Merrill Lynch, Pierce, Fenner & Smith, Inc., New York, 1971.

Governmental Purchasing

Jennings, G. W.: *State Purchasing: The Essentials of a Modern Service for Modern Government,* The Council of State Governments, Lexington, Ky., 1969.
Model Procurement Code for State and Local Governments, American Bar Association, Washington, D.C., 1979.
Nicholson, J. W.: *Guide to Government Purchasing,* Lakewood Publications, Inc., Minneapolis.
Professional Development Texts: Basic, Intermediate, Advanced, The National Institute of Governmental Purchasing, Inc., Arlington, Va., 1977.
Ritterskamp, James J., Jr., et al.: *Purchasing for Educational Institutions,* Bureau of Publications, Teachers College, Columbia University, New York, 1961.
State and Local Government Purchasing: A Digest, The Council of State Governments, Lexington, Ky., 1974.
State and Local Government Purchasing, The Council of State Governments, Lexington, Ky., 1975.

International Purchasing

Combs, P. H.: *Handbook of International Purchasing,* Cahners Books, Boston, 1971.
Westring, G.: *International Procurement,* Unitar (United Nations Institute for Training and Research), New York, 1974.

Inventory Management

Baker, R. J., and R. S. Kuehne: *Inventory Factomatic,* Prentice-Hall, Englewood Cliffs, N.J., 1980.
Banks, J., and C. Hohenstein: *Procurement and Inventory Ordering Tables,* Pergamon Press, Elmsford, N.Y., 1977.
Brown, R. G.: *Decision Rules for Inventory Management,* Holt, Rinehart & Winston, New York, 1967.
Brown, Robert G.: *Statistical Forecasting for Inventory Control,* McGraw-Hill, New York, 1959.
Dudick, T., and Cornell, R.: *Inventory Control for the Financial Executive,* Ronald Press, a division of John Wiley, New York.
Enrick, N. L.: *Inventory Management—Installation, Operations and Control,* Chandler Publishing Co., San Francisco, 1968.
Fabrycky, W. J., and J. Banks: *Procurement and Inventory Systems,* Reinhold Book Corp., New York, 1967.
Fuchs, Jerome: *Computerized Inventory Control Systems,* Prentice-Hall, Englewood Cliffs, N.J., 1978.
Greene, J. H.: *Production and Inventory Control,* Dow Jones–Irwin, Homewood, Ill., 1974.
Lambert, Douglas M.: *Development of an Inventory Costing Methodology,* National Council of Physical Distribution Management, Chicago.
Magee, J. F., and D. M. Boodman: *Production Planning and Inventory Control,* McGraw-Hill, New York, 1967.
Meek, J. C.: *Meek's Tables of Economic Order Quantities,* Facts and Comparisons, Inc., St. Louis, Mo., 1977.
Peterson, R., and E. A. Silver: *Decision Systems for Inventory Management and Production Planning,* John Wiley, New York, 1979.
Plossl, George, and Oliver Wight: *Production and Inventory Control: Principles and Techniques,* Prentice-Hall, Englewood Cliffs, N.J., 1967.
Pritchard, J. W., and R. H. Eagel: *Modern Inventory Management,* John Wiley, New York, 1965.
Tersine, R. J.: *Materials Management and Inventory,* Elsevier North Holland, New York, 1976.
Thomas, A. B.: *Inventory Control in Production and Manufacturing,* Cahners Books, Boston, 1969.
Wight, O. W.: *Production and Inventory Management in the Computer Age,* CBI Publishing Company, Boston, 1974.

Leasing

Ferrara W., J. Thies, and M. Dirsmith: *The Lease Purchase Decision,* National Association of Accountants, New York, 1980.

Hamel, H. G.: *Leasing in Industry,* National Industrial Conference Board, New York, 1968.

Metz, Donald: *Leasing Standards and Procedures,* Kaukauna, Wis.

Pritchard, R. E., and T. Hindelang: *The Lease/Buy Decision,* American Management Associations, New York, 1980.

Legal Aspects of Purchasing

American Law Institute and National Conference of Commissioners on Uniform State Laws: *Uniform Commercial Code,* West Publishing Co., St. Paul, 1972.

Anderson, Ronald A.: *Anderson's Uniform Commercial Code.* 4 vols., 2d ed., Bancroft Whitney, San Francisco; The Lawyers Cooperative Publishing Co., Rochester, N.Y., 1970.

Babb, H. W., and C. Martin: *Business Law—U.C.C.,* Barnes & Noble, New York, 1969.

Calkins, Richard M.: *Anti-Trust Guidelines for the Business Executive,* Dow Jones–Irwin, Homewood, Ill., 1981.

Corbin, A.: *Corbin on Contracts: A Comprehensive Treatise on the Rules of Contracts,* West Publishing Co., St. Paul, Minn.

Dillavou, E. R., et al.: *Principles of Business Law,* Prentice-Hall, Englewood Cliffs, N.J., 1974.

Gray, A. W.: *Purchase Law Manual,* J. Lenarth Inc., Pasadena, 1969.

Jennings, G. W.: *State Purchasing,* Council of State Government, Lexington, Ky., 1969.

Keyes, W. N.: *Keyes Encyclopedic Dictionary of Procurement Law,* Oceania Publications, Inc., Dobbs Ferry, N.Y., 1976.

Kintner, E. W.: *Robinson-Patman Primer—A Businessman's Guide to the Law against Price Discrimination,* Macmillan, New York, 1970.

Lavine, A. L.: *Manual on Commercial Law, U.C.C.,* Prentice-Hall, Englewood Cliffs, N.J., 1968.

Lusk, H. F., et al.: *Business Law,* Dow Jones–Irwin, Homewood, Ill., 1974.

Murray, J. E.: *Murray on Contracts,* Purchasing Management Association of Pittsburgh, Pittsburgh.

————: *Purchasing and the Law,* Purchasing Management Association of Pittsburgh, Pittsburgh, 1980.

Vopaw, D.: *Legal Aspects of Business Administration,* Prentice-Hall, Englewood Cliffs, N.J., 1969.

Management

Albers, H. H.: *Principles of Management—A Modern Approach,* John Wiley, New York, 1969.

Basil, D., and C. Cook: *The Management of Change,* McGraw-Hill, New York, 1974.

Blake, R. R., and Mouton, J. S.: *Building a Dynamic Corporation through Grid Organization Development,* Addison-Wesley/W. A. Benjamin, Inc., Reading, Mass., 1969.

Chance, W. A.: *Statistical Methods for Decision Making,* Dow Jones–Irwin, Homewood, Ill., 1969.

Croxton, E. D., J. Cowden, and B. W. Bolch: *Practical Business Statistics,* Prentice-Hall, Englewood Cliffs, N.J., 1969.

Dale, E.: *Management: Theory and Practice,* McGraw-Hill, New York, 1973.

Danial, N. B., and R. J. Jones: *Business Logistics, Concepts and Viewpoints,* Allyn & Bacon, Boston, 1969.

Drucker, P. F.: *Management: Tasks, Responsibilities, Practices,* Harper and Row, New York, 1974.

————: *Managing for Results,* Harper and Row, New York, 1964.

————: *Preparing Tomorrow's Business Leaders Today,* Prentice-Hall, Englewood Cliffs, N.J., 1969.

————: *Technology, Management and Society,* Harper and Row, New York, 1977.

Gellerman, S. W.: *Management by Motivation,* American Management Associations, New York, 1968.

George, C. S.: *Management for Business and Industry,* Prentice-Hall, Englewood Cliffs, N.J., 1970.

Greenwood, W. I.: *Decision Theory and Information Systems,* Southwestern Publishing Co., Cincinnati, 1969.

Hampton, D. R., et al: *Organizational Behavior and the Practice of Management,* Scott, Foresman, Glenview, Ill., 1973.

Hannaford, W. J.: *Systems Selling to Industrial Markets,* National Association of Wholesalers-Distributors, Washington, 1980.

Koontz, H., and C. O'Donnell: *Principles of Management: An Analysis of Managerial Functions,* McGraw-Hill, New York, 1972.

LeBoeuf, Michael: *Working Smart: How to Accomplish More in Half the Time,* McGraw-Hill, New York, 1979.

Linowes, D. F.: *Managing Growth through Acquisition,* American Management Associations, New York, 1968.

Lopez, F. M.: *The Making of a Manager,* American Management Associations, New York, 1970.

Marting, E.: *Creative Planning,* American Management Associations, New York, 1968.

Massie, J. L., and L. Douglas: *Managing—A Contemporary Introduction,* Prentice-Hall, Englewood Cliffs, N.J. 1973.

Musselman, V., and E. Hughes: *Introduction to Modern Business Analysis and Interpretation,* Prentice-Hall, Englewood Cliffs, N.J., 1969.

Odiorne, G. S.: *Management by Objectives,* Pitman, London, 1965.

Odiorne, George: *The Change Resistors,* Prentice-Hall, Englewood Cliffs, N. J., 1981.

Risley, G.: *Modern Industrial Marketing,* McGraw-Hill, New York, 1972.

Sellers, R. C.: *The Executive's Guide to Planning Transition to the Metric–SI System,* National Association of Purchasing Management, Inc., New York, 1973.

Sisk, H. C.: *Management and Organization,* Southwestern Publishing Company, Cincinnati, 1973.

Starr, M. K.: *Systems Management of Operations,* Prentice-Hall, Englewood Cliffs, N.J., 1971.

Steinhoff, D.: *Small Business Management Fundamentals,* McGraw-Hill, New York, 1974.

Terry, G. R.: *A Guide to Management,* Dow Jones–Irwin, Homewood, Ill., 1981.

U.S. Bureau of the Budget: *Standard Industrial Classification Manual (SIC)* G.P.O., Washington, 1967.

U.S. Department of Commerce: *U.S. Industrial Outlook,* G.P.O., Washington (annual).

U.S. Department of Defense: *Zero Defects—Guide to Quality,* 1968.

Negotiations

Calers, H. H., and G. Nierenberg: *How to Read a Person Like a Book,* Hawthorn, New York, 1971.

DeRose, L. J.: *How to Negotiate Purchase Prices,* Management Center of Cambridge, Cambridge, Mass., 1970.

Karrass, C. L.: *Give and Take: The Complete Guide to Negotiating Strategies and Tactics,* Thomas Y. Crowell, New York, 1974.

————: *The Negotiating Game,* Thomas Y. Crowell, New York, 1970.

Kennedy, Benson, McMillan: *Managing Negotiations,* available from the Institute of Purchasing and Supply, Ascot, England.

McDonald, P. R.: *Negotiation of Government Contracts,* Procurement Associates, Covina, Calif., 1970.

Nierenberg, G. I.: *Art of Negotiating,* Hawthorn, New York, 1968.

Nierenberg, J. W., et al.: *Fundamentals of Negotiation,* Hawthorn, New York, 1973.

Pace, D. F.: *Negotiation and Management of Defense Contracts,* John Wiley, New York, 1970.

Pricing

Marshall, A.: *A More Profitable Pricing,* McGraw-Hill, New York, 1980.

Watson, D. S.: *Price Theory in Action,* Houghton Mifflin Company, Boston, 1981.

Production Management

Buffa, E. S.: *Modern Production Management,* John Wiley, New York, 1973.

Fearon, H. E., W. A. Ruch, P. G. Decker, R. R. Reck, V. G. Reuter, and C. D. Wieters: *Fundamentals of Production Operations Management,* West Publishing Co., St. Paul, 1980.

Magee, J. F., and D. M. Boodman: *Production Planning and Inventory Control,* McGraw-Hill, New York, 1967.

Moore, F. G.: *Production Management,* Dow Jones–Irwin, Homewood, Ill., 1973.

Peterson, R., and E. A. Silver: *Decision Systems for Inventory Management and Production Planning,* John Wiley, New York, 1979.

Timms, H. L., and M. F. Pohlen: *Production Function in Business,* Dow Jones–Irwin, Homewood, Ill., 1970.

Quality Control

Dodge, H. F., and H. G. Romig: *Computation of Sampling Inspection Tables,* John Wiley, New York, 1959.

Duncan, A. J.: *Quality Control and Industrial Statistics,* Dow Jones–Irwin, Homewood, Ill.

Feigenbaum, A. V.: *Total Quality Control: Engineering and Management,* McGraw-Hill, New York, 1961.

Hansen, B. L.: *Quality Control: Theory and Applications,* Prentice-Hall, Englewood Cliffs, N.J., 1963.

Vaughn, R. C.: *Quality Control,* Iowa State University Press, Ames, Iowa.
Weinberg, S.: *Profit through Quality,* CBI Publishing Company, Boston, 1970.

Stores and Warehousing

Compton, H. K.: *Storehouse and Stockyard Management,* International Publications Service, New York, 1970.
Jenkins, C. H.: *Modern Warehouse Management,* McGraw-Hill, New York, 1968.
Morrison, A.: *Storage and Control of Stock for Industry and Public Undertakings,* Sir Isaac Pitman & Sons, London, 1967.

Transportation and Distribution

Augello, William J.: *Freight Claims in Plain English,* Shippers National Freight Claim Council, Inc., Huntington, N.Y., 1980.
Barrett, Colin: *Shippers, Truckers and The Law,* Colin Barrett Co., Reston, Va., 1980.
Blanding, Warren: *Blanding's Practical Physical Distribution,* Traffic Service Corporation, Washington, D.C., 1978.
Bruce, H. J.: *Distribution and Transportation Handbook,* Cahners Books, Boston, 1971.
Constantin, J. A.: *Principles of Logistics Management, A Functional Analysis of Physical Distribution,* Appleton-Century-Crofts, New York, 1969.
Davis, G. M.: *The Department of Transportation,* D. C. Heath, Lexington, Mass., 1970.
Fair, M. L.: *Coordinated Transportation Problems and Requirements,* Cornell Maritime Press Inc., Cambridge, Md., 1969.
Magee, J. F.: *Industrial Logistics—Analysis and Management of Physical Supply and Distribution Systems,* McGraw-Hill, New York, 1967.
McElhiney, P. T., and C. L. Hilton: *Introduction to Logistics and Traffic Management,* Wm. C. Brown, Dubuque, Iowa, 1968.
Phillips, C. F.: *Economics of Regulation Theory and Practice in the Transportation and Public Utility Industries,* Dow Jones–Irwin, Inc., Homewood, Ill., 1969.
Taff, C. A.: *Management of Traffic and Physical Distribution,* Dow Jones–Irwin, Homewood, Ill., 1968.
Wentworth, F.: *Physical Distribution Management,* Cahners Books, Boston, 1970.

Value Analysis/Value Engineering

Crouse, R. L.: *Value Engineering/Analysis Bibliography,* Society of American Value Engineers, Dallas, 1969.
Fallon, Carlos: *Value Analysis,* Triangle Press, Irving, Tex., 1980.
Gibson, J. F. A.: *Value Analysis,* Pergamon Press, New York, 1968.
Miles, L. D.: *Techniques of Value Analysis and Engineering,* McGraw-Hill, New York, 1972.
Mudge, A. E.: *Value Engineering, A Systematic Approach,* McGraw-Hill, New York, 1971.
Ridge, W. J.: *Value Analysis for Better Movement,* American Management Associations, New York, 1969.

AUDIOVISUAL TRAINING AIDS

It is said that the mind retains 2½ times more information when it is presented visually and orally than when it is presented only orally. In this section a listing of sources of audiovisual training aids of interest to purchasing personnel is provided. This is a partial listing, as the sources are numerous and are constantly changing.

Many industries, publishers, and national associations have promotional, educational, and entertainment packages available on a rental and loan basis.

The more general subjects may be obtained from the Encyclopaedia Britannica; the New York Public Library, Film Division; Brandon Films, Inc., a subsidiary of Crowell-Collier and Macmillan, Inc.; McGraw-Hill, Webster Division; Pitman Publishing Corp., I.T.A. Division; and Wiley Interscience.

Of particular interest to the purchasing field are the audiovisual training packages available from the following sources (see Key to Main Publishers):

A.A.A. (American Arbitration Association)
A.M.A. (American Management Associations)
A.S.F. (Association-Sterling Films)
A.S.Q.C. (American Society of Quality Control)
B.E.F. (Business Education Films)
IND (Industrial Education Films, Inc.)
N.A.P.M. (National Association of Purchasing Management, Inc.)

N.A.P.M. Audiovisual and Independent Study Programs

The National Association of Purchasing Management maintains a Program Aids Library (PAL). Each year, as recommended by the Professional Development Committee, it produces audiovisual programs consisting of a filmstrip/audio cassette program, a 16-mm film, or a videotape program. In addition to this, N.A.P.M. has produced Independent Study Programs. This activity is still in its initial stage but is steadily growing. The following is a listing of N.A.P.M.'s Program Aids Library and Independent Study Programs. Descriptions of each of the programs and its media are available from N.A.P.M.

N.A.P.M. Audiovisuals

EXPEDITING

| PAL no. 39 | Controlling Vendor Deliveries |

INVENTORY CONTROL

| PAL no. 15 | Principles of Modern Inventory Control |

NEGOTIATION

PAL no. 6	The King Corporation
35	Contract Negotiation Techniques
66	Fundamentals of Negotiation
68	Negotiations in Action

VALUE ANALYSIS-STANDARDIZATION

PAL no. 6	The King Corporation
16	Buyers Can Practice Value Analysis
20	Value Analysis Theory
26	Evaluation of Function, Cost and Worth
69	Value Analysis

PURCHASING MANAGEMENT

PAL no. 27	The "Management" in Purchasing Management
30	Making "Management-By-Objectives" Work
31	Management Expectations

INDIVIDUAL DEVELOPMENT

| PAL no. 11 | Purchasing as a Career |

PURCHASING AND THE LAW

PAL no. 47	Part 1: Warranties
58	Part 2: The Battle of the Forms
61	Part 3: Unconscionability
65	Part 4: The Battle of the Forms Revisited

MISCELLANEOUS

N.A.P.M. Independent Study Programs

PURCHASING AND THE LAW SERIES

Warranties
Unconscionability
Buyer's Remedies for Breach of Contract
The Battle of the Forms
The Battle of the Forms Revisited
Contract Formation
Forecasting
Formula Pricing
Valve Analysis
Price/Cost Analysis

THE MANAGEMENT SERIES

Part 1 Planning
Part 2 Organizing
Part 3 Staffing
Part 4 Actuating & Coordinating
Part 5 Controlling

BASIC PROCUREMENT COURSE

Source of the Contracting Officer's Authority
Elements of the Contract
Choosing the Method of Procurement
Choosing the Contract Type
The Solicitation—Part 1 and Part 2
Evaluating Bids/Offers and Source Selection—Part 1 and Part 2
Preparation for Negotiations
Conducting Negotiations
Contract Administration—Part 1 and Part 2

HANDBOOKS

A handbook is a compilation of data. Since the decisions of the purchasing executive are based on knowledge of properties and qualities of materials and of the techniques of specialized fields, the handbook is indispensable as a working tool. A partial listing is shown below.

American Law Institute and National Conference of Commissioners on Uniform State Laws: *Uniform Commercial Code,* West Publishing Co., St. Paul.

American Society for Metals: *Metals Handbook,* 6 vols., 8th ed., American Society for Metals, Metals Park, Ohio, 1971.

Azad, H.: *Industrial Wastewater Mangement Handbook,* McGraw-Hill, New York, 1976.

Barton, R.: *Handbook of Advertising Management,* McGraw-Hill, New York, 1970.

Bogen, J. I.: *Financial Handbook,* 4th ed. rev., Ronald Press Co., New York, 1968.

Brady, G. S. and H. Clauser: *Materials Handbook,* 11th ed., McGraw-Hill, New York, 1977.

Bruce, H. J.: *Distribution and Transportation Handbook,* Cahners Books, Boston, 1971.

Craig, R.: *Training and Development Handbook,* 2d ed., McGraw-Hill, New York, 1976.

Crocker, S., and R. C. King: *Piping Handbook,* 5th ed., McGraw-Hill, New York, 1967.

Croft, T., C. C. Carr, and J. Watt: *American Electrician's Handbook,* 10th ed., McGraw-Hill, New York, 1981.

Daniels, H. R.: *Mechanical Press Handbook,* 3d ed., Cahners Books, Boston, 1969.

Davidson, Sidney, and R. Weil: *Handbook of Modern Accounting,* 2d ed., McGraw-Hill, New York, 1979.

Davis, C. V., and K. E. Sorenson: *Handbook of Applied Hydraulics,* 3d ed., McGraw-Hill, New York, 1969.

Dean, J. A., ed.: *Lange's Handbook of Chemistry,* 12th ed., McGraw-Hill, New York, 1978.

The Diebold Group Inc.: *Automatic Data Processing Handbook,* McGraw-Hill, New York, 1977.

Fink, D. G., and H. Beaty: *Standard Handbook for Electrical Engineers,* McGraw-Hill, New York, 1978.

Firth, D. et al.: *Distribution Management Handbook,* McGraw-Hill, New York, 1980.

Gray and Ductile Iron Founders' Society: *Gray and Ductile Iron Castings Handbook,* American Society for Metals, Metals Park, Ohio, 1971.

Greene, J. H.: *Production and Inventory Control Handbook,* McGraw-Hill, New York, 1970.

Handley, W.: *Industrial Safety Handbook,* McGraw-Hill, New York, 1977.

Harper, C. A.: *Handbook of Electronic Packaging,* McGraw-Hill, New York, 1969.

——: *Handbook of Materials and Processes for Electronics,* McGraw-Hill, New York, 1970.

Harris, C.: *Handbook of Noise Control,* McGraw-Hill, New York, 1979.

Havers, E., and F. W. Stubbs: *Handbook of Heavy Construction,* 2d ed., McGraw-Hill, New York, 1971.

Holscher, H. H.: *Simplified Statistical Analysis,* Cahners Books, Boston, 1971.

Ireson, G.: *Handbook of Industrial Engineering and Management,* 2d ed., Prentice-Hall, Englewood Cliffs, N.J., 1971.

Johnson, James M.: *Handbook of Depreciation Methods, Formulas and Tables,* Prentice-Hall, Englewood Cliffs, N.J., 1980.

Juran, J. N.: *Quality Control Handbook,* 3d ed., McGraw-Hill, New York, 1974.

Kolb, J., and S. Ross: *Product Safety and Liability,* McGraw-Hill, New York, 1979.

Lasser, J. K.: *Business Management Handbook,* 3d ed., McGraw-Hill, New York, 1968.

Levine, Sumner L.: *Financial Analysis Handbook,* Dow Jones-Irwin, Homewood, IL, 1981.

Lund, H.: *Industrial Pollution Control Handbook,* McGraw-Hill, New York, 1971.

Lyman, T.: *Metals Handbook,* 3 vols., 8th ed., American Society for Metals, Metals Park, Ohio, 1967.

Maynard, H. B.: *Handbook of Business Administration,* McGraw-Hill, New York, 1967.

——: *Industrial Engineering Handbook,* 3d ed., McGraw-Hill, 1971.

Melcher, D., and N. Larrick: *Printing and Promotion Handbook,* 3d ed., McGraw-Hill, New York, 1966.

Merrill Lynch, Pierce, Fenner & Smith, Inc.,: *Hedger's Handbook,* Merrill Lynch, Pierce, Fenner & Smith, Inc., New York, 1971.

Moore, R. F.: *AMA Management Handbook,* American Management Association's, New York, 1970.

Morse, Leon William: *Practical Handbook of Industrial Traffic Management,* The Traffic Service Corporation, Washington, 1980.

Nickerson, C. B.: *Accounting Handbook for Non-Accountants,* Cahners Books, Boston, Mass., 1979.

Oberg, E., and F. D. Jones: *Machinery's Handbook,* 19th ed., The Industrial Press, New York, 1971.

Perry, R. H.: *Engineering Manual,* 2d ed., McGraw-Hill, New York, 1977.

Rydge Publications: *Industrial Businessman's Handbook,* Rydge Publications, Sydney, Australia, 1967.

Society of Plastics Industries: *Plastics Engineering Handbook,* 4th ed., Reinhold Book Co., New York, 1972.

U.S. Bureau of the Budget: *Standard Industrial Classification Manual,* G.P.O., Washington, 1967.

U.S. Chamber of Commerce: *Foreign Commerce Handbook,* 16th ed., U.S. Chamber of Commerce, Washington, 1967.

U.S. Department of Defense: *Procurement Quality Assurance Handbook,* G.P.O., Washington, 1969.

———: *Value Engineering Handbook,* G.P.O., Washington.

Weast, R. C.: *Handbook of Chemistry and Physics,* 1970–1971, 61st ed., Chemical Publishing Company, Inc., New York, 1980.

Wilson, R. M. S.: *Cost Control Handbook,* Halsted Press Division, John Wiley, New York, 1975.

GENERAL REFERENCE TOOLS

Dictionaries and Encyclopedias

Encyclopedia Americana and others.

Encyclopedia of Associations, Gale Research Co., Detroit, 1970.

National Trade and Professional Associations of the United States and Canada, Columbia Books, Inc., Washington, 1981.

Webster's 8th New Collegiate Dictionary; American Heritage Dictionary

Andreano, R.: *Student Economist's Handbook—A Guide to Sources,* Schenkman Publishing Co., Cambridge, Mass., 1967.

Hoffman, P. A.: *Dictionary of Packaging,* International Publications Service, New York, 1968 (polyglot).

Jordan, Philip B.: *Condensed Computer Encyclopedia,* McGraw-Hill, New York, 1969.

Paeson, I.: *Systematic Glossary—English, French, Spanish, Russian—of Selected Economic Terms,* Macmillan, New York, 1963.

U.S. Department of Commerce: *Dictionary of Economic and Statistical Terms,* G.P.O., Washington, 1969.

Specifications and Standards

American Society for Metals: *Book of ASTM Standards,* parts 1–8 and 26–33, American Society for Metals, Metals Park, Ohio, 1971.

ANSI Catalog, American National Standards Institute, Inc., New York (annual).

Military Specifications and Sources, Military Specifications and Sources, Los Angeles.

U.S. Government Purchasing and Specifications Directory, G.P.O., Washington (annual).

Industrial Services

Dodge Building Cost and Specifications Digest, F. W. Dodge Division, McGraw-Hill, New York.

Dun and Bradstreet, Inc., New York (financial ratings).

Moody's Investor Service, New York.

Prentice-Hall, Inc., Englewood Cliffs, N.J. (labor service).

Standard & Poor's Corp., New York (industrial surveys).

Directories of Companies

Fortune Directory, Parts I and II, Time, Inc., New York (annual).
Index of Corporations and Industries, Funk & Scott, Cleveland (annual).
Middle Market Directory, Dun & Bradstreet, Inc., New York (annual).
Million Dollar Directory, Dun & Bradstreet, Inc., New York (annual).
News Front Directory of 25,000 Leading U.S. Corporations, Editors of News Front, New York, 1970.
Poor's Register of Corporations, Directors and Executives of the United States and Canada, Standard & Poor's Corp., New York (annual).

Directories of Associations

Directory of National Trade and Professional Associations of the United States, Canada, Labor Unions, Columbia Books, Washington (annual).
Encyclopedia of Associations, Gale Research Co., Detroit, 3 vols. (annual).
World Directory of Industry and Trade Associations, UNCTAD/GATT, Geneva, Switzerland, 1970.

PERIODICALS

Periodicals and periodical indexes are usually the best sources of current information. The selection of titles for the purchasing department collection requires study of the needs to be met. Periodicals constitute a very important part of a library's resources.

The list of journals useful to the purchasing executive falls ordinarily into three categories: purchasing; material management, business, economic, financial, and general management; and technical and specialized subjects.

The frequency of publication for the periodicals listed under this main heading is indicated by the following:

(a)—annually   (m)—monthly
(bm)—bimonthly   (q)—quarterly
(bw)—biweekly   (sm)—semimonthly
(d)—daily   (w)—weekly

Processing of Periodicals

Periodicals are acquired by subscription, through membership in societies, by gifts, and by exchange. Subscriptions may be placed directly with the publishers, but it is more efficient to place them with an agent, since a majority of the titles required can thus be put on one annual order.

The value of keeping accurate records of each subscription cannot be overemphasized. For all titles the following information should be noted: exact title; where and when ordered; publisher; period covered by order; frequency of publication; current volume number, year, and issue number; indication of receipt of individual issues and index—the date of receipt of each issue should be noted, and also of special issues; record of back issues in the collection; whether bound or unbound; where shelved; period of time held before discarding; names of persons on routing list; name of person who reviews and clips articles for the files.

Journals should be filed alphabetically on the shelves. Interdepartmental arrangements may be shared for subscriptions, routing, and shelving of back issues of journals.

Filing and Indexing Articles

Articles clipped from periodicals and arranged systematically in folders by subject headings are designated *vertical files.* This part of the library collection, which may also include reports, pamphlets, reprints, and other unique material, should be indexed to provide for quick retrieval of a particular piece of information when it is needed, in the most direct procedure possible.

A list of subject headings should be developed by using as a basis official headings from a subject authority list. This may consist of the headings of *Chemical Abstracts* or the *Engineering Index* as modified for the department's particular purpose. With a small collection in the purchasing field, the authority subject heading may follow the headings used in the chapter headings or in the index of a purchasing textbook.

Directories of Periodicals

More complete and detailed information on periodicals may be found in the following directories:

Ayer's Directory of Newspapers and Periodicals (a), N. W. Ayer & Son, Philadelphia.
Directory of Periodicals Published by International Publications, 3d ed., International Publications Service, New York, 1969.
Standard Periodicals Directory, 3d ed., Oxbridge Publishing Company, New York, 1970.
Ulrich's International Periodicals Directory, 14th ed., R. R. Bowker Company, New York, 1971.

Indexes of Periodicals

The following indexes can be used to search for subject headings published in the various periodicals:

Applied Science and Technology Index (m & a), H. W. Wilson Co., Bronx, N.Y.
Business Periodicals Index (m & a), H. W. Wilson Company, Bronx, N.Y.
New York Times Index (sm & a) The New York Times, New York.
Predicasts (q), Predicasts, Inc., Cleveland.
Public Affairs Information Service Bulletin (w & a), Pierian Press, Ann Arbor, Mich.
Readers Guide to Periodical Literature (sm, q & a), H. W. Wilson Co., Bronx, N.Y.
Wall Street Journal Index (a), Dow Jones & Co., New York.
Worldcasts (q), Predicasts, Inc., Cleveland.

Purchasing Periodicals

General Trade

Chemical Purchasing (m), Myers Publishing Co., Inc., Stamford, Conn.
Electronic Buyers News (bw), CMP Publications, Manhasset, N.Y.
Hospital Purchasing Management (m), Lexington, Mass.
Purchasing Administration (m), McKnight Medical Communications, Northfield, Ill.
Purchasing (bm), Cahners Publishing Co., Boston.
Purchasing World (m), Technical Publishing Co., Barrington, Ill.
Utility Purchasing and Stores (m), Pritchard Publishing Co., Durham, N.H.

U.S. Purchasing Association Publications

CAPPO News (m), California Association of Public Purchasing Officers, Los Angeles.
Contract Management (m), National Contract Management Association, Arlington, Va.
Journal of Purchasing and Materials Management (q), National Association of Purchasing Management, Inc., New York.
NAEB Bulletin (m), National Association of Educational Buyers, Woodbury, N.Y.
NAHPM Newsletter (m), National Association of Hospital Purchasing Management, Chicago.
NASPO Newsletter (q), National Association of State Purchasing Officials, Lexington, Ky.
National Purchasing Review (bm), National Association of Purchasing Management, Inc., New York.
Public Purchasor, National Institute of Governmental Purchasing, Washington.

N.A.P.M. Affiliated Association Publications   (For addresses, contact National Association of Purchasing Management.)

Alabama Purchasor (m), Purchasing Management Association of Alabama.
Arizona Purchasor (m), Purchasing Management Association of Arizona.
Baltimore Purchaser (m), Purchasing Management Association of Baltimore, Inc.
Buy Lines (m), Milwaukee Association of Purchasing Management, Inc.
Chicago Purchasor (m), Purchasing Management Association of Chicago.
Cincinnati Purchasor (m), Purchasing Management Association of Cincinnati, Inc.
Connecticut Purchasor (m), Purchasing Management Association of Connecticut, Inc.
Eastern New York Purchaser (m), Purchasing Management Association of Eastern New York.
Florida Purchaser (m), Purchasing Management Association of Florida, Inc.
Golden West Purchaser (m), Purchasing Management Association—Los Angeles.
Heart of America Purchaser (m), Purchasing Management Association of Kansas City.
Hoosier Purchasor (m), Purchasing Management Association of Indianapolis, Inc.
Inland Northwest Purchaser (m), Spokane and Inland Empire Purchasing Management Association.
Kentuckiana Purchasor (m), Purchasing Management Association of Louisville, Inc.
Metropolitan Purchasor (m), Purchasing Management Associations of New York and New Jersey.
Michigan Purchasing Management (m), Purchasing Management Association of Detroit, Inc.
Mid-Continent Purchaser (m), Purchasing Management Association of Tulsa and Oklahoma City.
Midwest Purchasing (m), Purchasing Management Association of Cleveland, Inc.
New England Purchaser (m), Purchasing Management Association of Boston, Inc.
Niagara Frontier Purchaser (m), Purchasing Management Association of Buffalo, Inc.
Oregon Purchasor (m), Purchasing Management Association of Oregon.
Pacific Purchasor (m), Purchasing Management Association of Northern California, Inc.
Philadelphia Purchasor (m), Purchasing Management Association of Philadelphia, Inc.
Purchasing Management (m), Twin City Purchasing Management Association, Inc.
Purchasing Professional, Purchasing Management Association of Rochester, Inc.
Purchasor (m), Purchasing Management Association of Syracuse and Central N.Y., Inc.
St. Louis Purchaser (m), Purchasing Management Association of St. Louis.
Southern Purchasor (bm), Purchasing Management Association of Carolinas-Virginia, Inc.
Southwest Purchasing (m), Purchasing Management Association of Texas, Louisiana, and New Mexico.
Washington Purchasor (m), Purchasing Management Association of Washington, Inc.
Yankee Purchaser (m), Purchasing Management Association of Western New England.

N.A.P.M. Affiliated Association Newsletters

Columbus Area Newsletter (m), Purchasing Management Association of Columbus.
Communicator (The) (m), Connecticut Association of Purchasing Management, Inc.
Dollars and Sense (m), Austin Purchasing Management Association, Inc.
Eastern New York Newsletter (m), Purchasing Management Association of Eastern New York.
Newsletter (m), Fort Wayne Association of Purchasing Management, Inc.
News & Views (m), Purchasing Management Association of Memphis, Inc.
Orange Empire Purchasing Manager (m), Purchasing Management Association of Orange County.
Puma News (m), Purchasing Management Association of Houston, Inc.

Purchaser's Monthly (m), Purchasing Management Association of Dayton, Ohio, Inc.
Purchasing Notes (m), Purchasing Management Association of Nashville.
Rock River P.M. News (m), Purchasing Management Association of Rock River Valley.
South Bend Magazine (m), Purchasing Management Association of South Bend.

Canadian and Foreign Purchasing Publications

ABAM (bm), Associaõ Brasiléira de Administracaõ de Nacional, Rio de Janeiro CE20260, Brazil.
Approvisionnement (bm), Compagnie des Dirigeants d'Approvisionnement et Acheteurs de France, Paris 75009, France.
Action (m), Purchasing Management Association of Canada, Toronto, Canada.
Boletim Do Comprador (q), Associacaõ Portuguesa de Compras e Aprovisionamento, Lisbon 5, Portugal.
Compras (m), Asociación Argentina de Compradores, Buenos Aires 1049, Argentina.
Il Compratore (m), Associazione degli Approvvigionatori e Compratori Italiani, 20149 Milan, Italy.
The Indian Buyer (m), Indian Association of Materials Management, Calcutta, 700016, India.
Innkjøp Materials Administrasjon, Norsk Innkjops og Materialadministrasjonsforbund, Oslo 5, Norway.
Irish Purchasing Journal (bm), Irish Institute of Purchasing and Materials Management, Dublin 2, Ireland.
L'Acheteur (bm), MacLean–Hunter LTEE, Montreal H3R 1K5, Canada.
Materials & Management (q), Indian Society of Materials Management, Calcutta 700001, India.
Materialwirtschaft und Einkauf (m), Schweizerischer Verband fur Materialwirtschaft und Einkauf, 5001 Aarau, Switzerland.
Mexico Compra (q), Confederación Mexicana de Asociaciones de Ejecutivos de Compras y Abastecimiento y Materiales, A.C., Mexico 4, D.F.
Modern Purchasing (m), Maclean-Hunter Publishing Co. Toronto, Ontario, Canada LGH 2R9.
Modern Purchasing (m), W9X2AE, London, England.
New Equipment News (m), Toronto, Ontario, Canada.
The Philippine Purchaser (bm), Purchasing Association of the Philippines, Inc., Manila, Philippines.
Procurement Weekly (w), Institute of Purchasing and Supply, London W.1, England.
Purchasing Journal (q), New Zealand Institute of Purchasing and Supply, Wellington, New Zealand.
Purchasing Management Digest, Clifford Elliott and Associates Ltd., Oakville, Ontario, Canada M5W1A7.
Purchasing South Africa (bm), Institute of Purchasing South Africa, Transvaal 2115, South Africa.
Purchasing and Supply Management (m), Institute of Purchasing and Supply, London, W.1, England.
Purchasing and Supply S'pore (m), Singapore Purchasing and Materials Management Association, Singapore 0106.
Purchasing in Western Canada (m), Purchasing Management Association of Canada, British Columbia District (Gordon Black Publications, Ltd.), Vancouver, B.C., Canada.
Scandinavian Journal of Materials Administration (m), Oslo Institute of Business Administration and the Scandinavian Association for Materials Administration, Oslo 8, Norway.
Shizai Kanri (m), Japan Materials Management Association, Tokyo, Japan 103.
Supply Contact (bm), Australian Institute of Purchasing and Supply Management, Banksia Park 5091, South Australia.
Tidskrift for Inkop, Swedish Federation of Purchasing and Materials Management, S-161 26, Bromma, Sweden.

Business and Professional Periodicals

Newspapers

Journal of Commerce (d), 99 Wall Street, New York.
New York Times (d), 229 West 43d Street, New York.
Wall Street Journal (d), 30 Broad Street, New York.

Scholarly

American Economic Review (q).
Econometrica (q).
Journal of Business (q).
Journal of Economics (q).
Review of Economics and Statistics (q).
Journal of Purchasing and Materials Management.

University

Business Horizons (bm).
California Management Review (q).
Illinois Business Review (m).
Michigan Business Review (bm).
MSU Business Topics (q).

General Business

Business Week (w), McGraw-Hill Publications, New York.
Catalog of U.S. Government Publications (m), G.P.O., Washington.
Dun's Review (m), Dun & Bradstreet, Inc., New York.
Forbes (sm), Forbes, Inc., New York.
Fortune (m), Time, Inc., New York.
Harvard Business Review (bm), Harvard University, Boston.
Nation's Business (m), U.S. Chamber of Commerce, Washington.

Additional Business

Across the Board (m), The Conference Board, New York.
Bank and Quotation Record (m), Wm. B. Dana Co., New York.
Barron's National Business and Financial Weekly (w), Barron's Publishing Co., New York.
Business Abroad (m), Reuben H. Donnelly Corp., New York.
Business Conditions Digest (m), Federal Reserve Bank of Chicago, Chicago.
Business International (w), Business International Corp., New York.
Business Management (m), Crowell, Collier & Macmillan, Inc., Greenwich, Conn.
Commerce Today (bw), Government Printing Office, Washington.
Commercial & Financial Chronicle (sw), Wm. B. Dana Company, New York.
Economic Indicators (m), Council of Economic Advisors, Government Printing Office, Washington.
Financial World (w), Guenther Publishing Corp., New York.
Kiplinger Washington Letter (w), The Kiplinger Washington Editors, Washington.
Marketing/Communications (m), Decker Communications, Inc., New York.
Newsweek (w), Newsweek, Inc., New York.
Survey of Current Business (m), Government Printing Office, Washington 20402.
Time (w), Time, Inc., New York.
U.S. News and World Report (w), U.S. News and World Report, Inc., Washington.

Technical—Industrial

Adhesives Age (m), Palmerton Publishing Co., New York.
American Metal Market (d), American Metal Market, Somerset, N.J.
Automotive Industries (sm), Chilton Book Co., Philadelphia.
Chemical and Engineering News (w), American Chemical Society, Washington.
Chemical Week (w), McGraw-Hill Publications, New York.
Drug and Cosmetic Industry (m), Drug Markets, Inc., New York.
Electronic News (w), New York.
Electronics (sm), McGraw-Hill Publications, New York.
Environmental Control and Safety Management (m), A. M. Best Co., Morristown, N.J.
Food Engineering (m), Chilton Book Co., Philadelphia.
Food Processing (m), Putnam Publishing Co., Chicago.
Foundry (m), Penton Publishing Co., Cleveland.
Good Packaging (m), Reuben H. Donnelly Corp., Chicago.
Hydrocarbon Processing (m), Gulf Publishing Co., Houston.
Industrial Equipment News (m), Thomas Publishing Co., New York.

Industrial Maintenance and Plant Operation (m), Ames Publishing Co., Philadelphia.
Industry Week (w), Penton Publishing Co., Cleveland.
Iron Age (w), Chilton Book Co., Philadelphia.
Journal of Materials (q), American Society for Testing and Materials, Philadelphia.
Lubrication Engineering (m), American Society of Lubrication Engineers, Park Ridge, Ill.
Machine Design (bw), Penton Publishing Co., Cleveland.
Materials Engineering (m), Reinhold Book Co., New York.
Materials Research and Standards (m), American Society for Testing and Materials, Philadelphia.
Mechanical Engineering (m), American Society of Mechanical Engineers, New York 10017.
Modern Manufacturing (m), Morgan-Grampian, Inc., New York.
Modern Metals (m), Modern Metals Publishing Co., Chicago.
Modern Packaging (m), McGraw-Hill Publications, New York.
New Equipment Digest (m), Penton Publishing Co., Cleveland.
Paint and Varnish Production (m), Palmerton Publishing Co., New York.
Plastics Technology (m), Bill Communications, Inc., New York.
Plastics World (m), Cleworth Publishing Co., Cos Cob, Conn.
Product Design and Development (m), Chilton Book Co., Philadelphia.
Rubber Age (m), Palmerton Publishing Co., New York.
Scientific American (m), New York.
Sugar y Azucar (m), Palmer Publications, New York.

TRADE DIRECTORIES

The information published in trade publications is well indexed and cross-referenced by company and subsidiaries, addresses, products, and trade names. Names and titles of officers may also be listed.

This type of literature constitutes one of the most helpful categories for the purchasing executive in search of possible sources of supply.

Guides to Trade Directories

Catalog of City, County, and State Directories Published in North America, Association of North American Directory Publishers, New York, 1969.
Current European Directories, C. B. D. Research Ltd. London, 1969.
Guide to American Directories, 7th ed., B. Klein, Rye, N.Y., 1968.
Guide to Industrial Directories, United Nations Industrial Development Organization (UNIDO), United Nations, New York.
Sources of State Information and State Industrial Directories, Chamber of Commerce of the United States, Washington, 1967.
Trade Directories of the World, Cronor Publications, Queens Village, N.Y.

General Products Directories

Thomas Register of American Manufacturers is the most complete trade directory, published annually by Thomas Publishing Company, One Penn Plaza, New York, N.Y. 10001. The 1981 edition consists of 16 volumes, listing products and services, leading manufacturers, addresses of the main and plant sites, officials, trade names, capital ratings, and company catalogs.

MacRAE's Blue Book is published annually by MacRAE's Blue Book Co., 100 Shore Drive, Hinsdale, Ill. 60521.

Sweet's Catalogs cover the various construction industry products. They are published annually by the Sweet's Division of McGraw-Hill Publications.

U.S. Industrial Directory is published annually by Cahners Publishing Co., 1200 Summer Street, Stamford, Conn. 06905.

Visual Search Microfilm File (VSMF) carries the catalogs of innumerable vendors serving the aerospace, electronic, boating, plant engineering, and other fields, including military specifications. The catalogs are stored on 16-mm microfilm cartridges. They are available from VSMF, 800 Acoma Street, Denver, Colo. 80204.

Specific Product and Area Directories

These types of directories abound in such numbers that no attempt is made here to list them. Many are issued annually as special sections of periodicals; others are published by associations. Reference should be made to Gale's *Executive Guide to Information Sources,* Klein's *Guide to American Directories,* or other reference guides.

The classified telephone directories of major and nearby cities are excellent for source listings. They are available upon request at local telephone offices.

Manufacturing News, Inc. 3 East Huron Street, Chicago 60611, can supply directories of all 50 states in the United States.

Foreign Directories

Foreign product directories are distributed in the United States by International Publications Service, 303 Park Avenue South, New York 10010. These include such directories as the *ABC—Europe Production,* 12th ed., 1971 (polyglot) and the *Japan Chemical Directory,* 9th ed., 1971.

The United States representative of the *Kelly's Directories* is Wire Service Supply Company, Inc., 220 East 42d Street, New York 10017.

Foreign embassies and consulates offer the services of commercial counselors, as do the commercial divisions of international banks.

Fraser's Canadian Trade Directory is available from Maclean Hunter, Ltd., 481 University Avenue, Toronto 2, Canada.

The Iron and Steel Institute, 39 Victoria Street, London S.W. 1, publishes a *Catalog of Books.*

SUPPLIER CATALOG FILES

Trade catalogs can be an excellent source of information for any purchasing department. This collection should be treated as a separate entity from the main library volumes, although the more valuable trade directories will merit full cataloging to place them on the shelves with the book collection. The supplier catalog files, consisting of various trade literature in the form of bound volumes, brochures, pamphlets, folders, circulars, and advertisement clippings, can physically be placed in pamphlet boxes, in lateral-drawer files, or on open-front shelving. It is good practice to date-stamp all material when received, and to add the library or department stamp.

Organization

A system best suited to the individual purchasing department should be applied to and maintained for the acquisition, updating, filing and retrieval, indexing and cross-referencing, routing, loaning, and periodic pruning of this collection. Again, it is best to assign the responsibility to one individual in the department.

Central Files and Variations

A central files system designates the housing of the entire collection of catalogs in one area. All publications are borrowed from and returned to these files. Special catalogs may be marked boldly *Do Not Remove from Files.* A charge-out guide card is inserted in the space of the removed publication. The notations on the guide card should include the title, company name, and year of publication, along with the borrower's name and the date. Sign-out slips or a sign-out book may be used instead, with columns requesting the same information.

Purchasing personnel may require that specific catalogs be charged out to them on a permanent basis, and thus they can accumulate a small collection of their own in their immediate area. This is decentralizing the collection.

In small departments the individual catalog file system is preferable, as it enables the buyer to work more efficiently.

In large departments the buyer can also use a file of this type for the most frequently used catalogs and can refer to the central files for references and other sources of information.

When certain catalogs are in demand, more than one issue should be ordered. Also, the latest edition of a catalog may be assigned to one buyer and the older edition placed in central files with a very obvious notation on it referring to the existence of the newer edition and the borrower's name and location.

Interdepartmental borrowing of catalogs on a permanent basis should be controlled.

Filing and Indexing Systems

The system of filing and the degree to which it is developed are dictated by the frequency of use, the size of the collection, and the time, cost, and space allotted to the plan. Alphabetical filing of catalogs *by company,* using the *Thomas Register of American Manufacturers* as authority for company names, is the most direct approach. Maintaining index cards by company, cross-referenced by product(s), is more involved but rewarding. The company card should include information on title, date, publication number, and shelf location.

Filing catalogs *by product* category or commodity class is more sophisticated and makes for easy reference, since by this means all printed material on the specific product can be found in one location. An updated listing of the contents in each product file also serves as a source selection of manufacturers of that product. Indexes to be referred to for assigning headings are *The Standard Industrial Classification Manual (SIC)* and the *Federal Supply Classification* (FSC), both obtainable from the Superintendent of Documents, U.S. Government Printing Office, Washington, D.C. 20402. Other specialized indexes are issued by organizations such as the National Association of Electrical Distributors and the Electronic Engineers Master. Another system is that of *chronological filing,* in which an acquisition number is assigned to the publication as it is received and the filing of the literature is numerical. This number is added to the company index card and to the product(s) index card. The UNITERM decimal system is an example of this quick indexing and efficient retrieval arrangement.

A wall, stand, or rotary unit with typed information on strip inserts can supply a master list of manufacturers, suppliers, distributors, and vendors and of product catalogs and their location in the files. The strips are easily added or removed as the collection changes. This system allows for the introduction of cross-referencing, which is so important in good catalog filing.

KEY TO MAIN PUBLISHERS

A.A.A.—American Arbitration Association, 140 West 51st Street, New York, N.Y. 10019.
ABA—American Bar Association, 1700 K Street, N.W., Washington, D.C. 20006.
Addison—Addison-Wesley/W. A. Benjamin, Inc., Jacob Way, Reading, Mass., 01867.
A.L.A.—American Library Association, 50 East Huron Street, Chicago, Ill. 60611.
A.L.I.—American Law Institute, 4025 Chestnut Street, Philadelphia, Pa. 19104.
Allyn—Allyn and Bacon, Inc., 470 Atlantic Avenue, Boston, Mass. 02210.
A.M.A.—American Management Associations, Inc., 135 West 50th Street, New York, N.Y. 10020.
   (Representative agent for books, audiovisual material, and so forth, for Europe, Asia, Australia—
   George Allen & Unwin, Ltd., Park Lane, Hemel Hempstead, England.)
Appleton—Appleton-Century-Crofts, division of Prentice-Hall, 292 Madison Avenue, New York,
   N.Y. 10017.
Argyle—Argyle Publishing Corporation. See Metro.
Arno—Arno Press, a New York Times Company, 3 Park Avenue, New York, N.Y. 10016.
A.S.F.—Association-Sterling Films, 600 Grand Avenue, Ridgefield, N.J. 07657.
A.S.M.—American Society for Metals, 9765 Kinsman Road, Metals Park, Ohio 44073.
A.S.T.M.—American Society for Testing and Materials, 1916 Race Street, Philadelphia, Pa.19103.
A.S.Q.C.—American Society of Quality Control, 161 West Wisconsin Avenue, Milwaukee, Wis.
   53203.
Bancroft—Bancroft Whitney Company, San Francisco, Calif.
Barnes—Barnes & Noble, Inc., 105 Fifth Avenue, New York, N.Y. 10003.
Barrett—Barrett, Colin, Reston, Va.
B.E.F.—Business Education Films, 5113 16th Avenue, Brooklyn, N.Y. 11218.
Benwill—Benwill Publishing Corp., Box 211, Medford, N.J. 08055.
Brown—Wm. C. Brown Co., Dubuque, Iowa 52001.
Bureau of Publications, Teachers College, Columbia University, New York, 1961.
Business Publications, Inc., subsidiary of R. D. Irwin, Inc., 13773 N. Central Expressway, Dallas,
   Tex. 75231.
CBI—CBI Publishing Inc., 51 Sleeper Street, Boston, Mass. 02210.
Cahners—Cahners Publishing Company, 1200 Summer Street, Stamford, Conn. 06905.
Canfield—Canfield Press, Division of Harper & Row, 850 Montgomery Street, San Francisco,
   Calif. 94133.
Chandler—Chandler Publishing Company, 124 Spear Street, San Francisco, Calif. 94105.
Chain—Chain Store Publishing Corp., 425 Park Avenue, New York, N.Y. 10017.
Chapman—Chapman & Hall Ltd. c/o Barnes & Noble, Inc.
Chemical—Chemical Publishing Co., Inc., 155 West 19th Street, New York, N.Y. 10011.
Columbia—Columbia Books Inc., Suite 1336, 777 14th Street, N.W., Washington, D.C. 20005.
Commodity—Commodity Research Bureau, 140 Broadway, New York, N.Y. 10005.

Conference—Conference Board, Inc., 845 Third Avenue, New York, N.Y. 10022.
Congressional—Congressional Quarterly, 1414 22d Street, N.W., Washington, D.C. 20037.
Cornell Maritime—Cornell Maritime Press, Inc., Box 109, Cambridge, Md. 21613.
Council—Council of State Governments, P.O. Box 11910, Iron Works Pike, Lexington, Ky. 40578.
Cronor—Cronor Publications, 211-05 Jamaica Avenue, Queens Village, N.Y. 11429.
Crowell—Thomas Y. Crowell, Division of Harper & Row Publishers, Inc. 10 East 53rd Street, New York, N.Y. 10022.
Dartnell—The Dartnell Corp. 4660 Ravenswood Avenue, Chicago, Ill. 60640.
Dow—Dow Jones-Irwin, 1818 Ridge Road, Homewood, Ill. 60430.
Dun—Dun & Bradstreet, Inc., 666 Fifth Avenue, New York, N.Y. 10103.
Dryden—Dryden Press, Division of Holt, Rinehart & Winston, Inc., 901 N. Elm, Hinsdale, Ill. 60521.
Elsevier—Elsevier North-Holland, Inc., 52 Vanderbilt Avenue, New York, N.Y. 10017.
Facts—Facts and Comparisons, Inc., 1100 Oran Drive, St. Louis, Mo. 63137.
Gale—Gale Research Company, Book Tower, Detroit, Mich. 48226.
Goodyear—Goodyear Publishing Co., 1640 Fifth Street, Santa Monica, Calif. 90401.
G.P.O.—U.S. Government Printing Office, Washington, D.C. 20402.
Grid—Grid Publishing, Inc., 4666 Indianola Avenue, Columbus, Ohio 43214.
Groot—A. M. Groot, Santa Ana, Calif. 92700.
Halsted—Halsted Press, Division of John Wiley & Sons, Inc., 605 Third Avenue, New York, N.Y. 10016.
Harcourt—Harcourt Brace Jovanovich, Inc., 757 Third Avenue, New York, N.Y. 10017.
Harper—Harper & Row, Publishers, Inc., 10 E. 53 Street, New York, N.Y. 10022.
Hawthorn—Hawthorn Books, Inc., 260 Madison Avenue, New York, N.Y. 10016.
Heath—D. C. Heath & Co., 125 Spring Street, Lexington, Mass. 02173.
Houghton—Houghton Mifflin Co., One Beacon Street, Boston, Mass. 02107.
Huntoon—The Huntoon Reports, P.O. Box 4245, Redding, Calif. 96001.
I.I.A.—Institute of Internal Auditors, 170 Broadway, New York, N.Y. 10006.
I. Press—The Industrial Press, 200 Madison Avenue, New York, N.Y. 10016.
IND—Industrial Education Films, Inc., 65 Pondfield Road, Bronxville, N.Y. 10708.
Institute—Institute of Purchasing & Supply, IPS House, High Street, Ascot, Berkshire, SL57HU England.
International—International Publications Service, 114 East 32 Street, New York, N.Y. 10016.
Iowa State University Press, Ames, Iowa.
Krieger—Krieger Publishing Company, P.O. Box 9542, Melbourne, Fla. 32901.
Lakewood—Lakewood Publications, Inc., 731 Hennepin Avenue, Minneapolis, Minn. 55403.
Lawyers Cooperative Publishers Company, Rochester, N.Y.
Lenarth—J. Lenarth, 1115 Mar Vista, Pasadena, Calif. 91104.
Lexington—Lexington Books (D. C. Heath & Co.), 125 Spring Street, Lexington, Mass. 02173.
Macmillan—Macmillan Inc., 866 Third Avenue, New York, N.Y. 10022.
Macmillan—Macmillan Inc., Brown Street, Riverside, N.J. 08075.
M.C.C.—Management Center of Cambridge, Box 185, Harvard Square, Cambridge, Mass. 02138.
McGraw—McGraw-Hill Book Co., Inc., 1221 Avenue of the Americas, New York, N.Y. 10020.
Merrill—Merrill Lynch, Pierce, Fenner & Smith, Inc., 70 Pine Street, New York, N.Y. 10005.
Metro—Metromedia Analearn, 56-05 47th Street, Maspeth, N.Y. 11378.
MSU—Michigan State University, Division of Research, Graduate School of Business Administration, East Lansing, Mich. 48823.
N.A.A.—National Association of Accountants, 919 Third Avenue, New York, N.Y. 10022.
N.A.P.M.—National Association of Purchasing Management, Inc., 11 Park Place, New York, N.Y. 10007.
N.A.W.D.—National Association of Wholesalers-Distributors, 1725 K Street, N.W., Washington, D.C. 20006.
N.B.E.R.—National Bureau of Economic Research, Inc.; order from Columbia University Press, 440 West 110th Street, New York, N.Y. 10025.
N.C.P.D.M.—National Council of Physical Distribution Management, Inc., 222 West Adams Street, Chicago, Ill. 60606.
National Institute of Governmental Purchasing Inc., 1001 Connecticut Avenue, N.W., Washington, D.C. 20036.

Northeastern—Northeastern University, Publications Department, Boston, Mass. 02115.

Oxford—Oxford University Press, Box 900, 1600 Pollitt Drive, Fairlawn, N.J. 07410.

Oceana—Oceana Publications, Inc., 75 Main Street, Dobbs Ferry, N.Y. 10522.

P.E.C.—Planning Executives Institute, 5500 College Corner Pike, Box 70, Oxford, Ohio 45046.

Pergamon—Pergamon Press Inc., Maxwell House, Fairview Park, Elmsford, N.Y. 10523.

Pitman—Pitman Publishing Ltd., 39 Parker Street, London, WC2B, 5PB, England.

P.M.A.P.—Purchasing Management Association of Pittsburgh, Inc., Department. P.W., P.O. Box 7316, Pittsburgh, Pa. 15203.

Prentice—Prentice-Hall, Inc., Route 9W, Englewood Cliffs, N.J. 07632.

Procurement—Procurement Associates, 733 North Dodsworth Avenue, Covina, Calif. 91724.

Ronald—Ronald Press, Division of John Wiley & Sons, 605 Third Avenue, New York, N.Y. 10016.

St. John's—St. John's University Press, Grand Central and Utopia Parkway, Jamaica, N.Y. 11432.

St. Martin's—St. Martin's Press, Inc., 175 Fifth Ave., New York, N.Y. 10010.

S.A.V.E.—Society of American Value Engineers, Box 210887, Dallas, Tex. 75211.

Schenkman—Schenkman Publishing Co., Cambridge, Mass. 02138.

Scott—Scott, Foresman & Co., 1900 East Lake Avenue, Glenview, Ill. 60025.

Southwestern—Southwestern Publishing Co., 5101 Madison Road, Cincinnati, Ohio 45227.

Thomas—Charles C Thomas, Publisher, 301–327 East Lawrence Avenue, Springfield, Ill.

Thomas—Thomas Publications Ltd., 724 Desnoyer Street, Kaukauna, Wis. 54130.

Thomas—Thomas Publishing Company, One Penn Plaza, New York, N.Y. 10001

Triangle—Triangle Press, Suite 114, 220 North Story Road, Irving, Tex. 75061.

TSC—Traffic Service Corporation, 1435 G Street, N.W., Washington, D.C. 20005.

UNITAR—UNITAR (United Nations Institute for Training & Research), 801 United Nations Plaza, New York, N.Y. 10017.

U.S.C.—United States Chamber of Commerce, 1615 H Street, N.W., Washington, D.C. 20006.

U.S.P.D.I.—U.S. Professional Development Institute, Inc., 12611 Davan Drive, Silver Spring, Md. 20904.

Univ. of Calif.—University of California Press, 2223 Fulton Street, Berkeley, Calif. 94720.

Univ. of Mich.—University of Michigan Press, 614 East University, Ann Arbor, Mich. 48106.

West—West Publishing Co., 50 West Kellogg Boulevard, St. Paul, Minn. 55201.

Wilson—H. W. Wilson Co., 950 University, Bronx, N.Y. 10452.

Wiley—John Wiley & Sons, Inc., 605 Third Avenue, New York, N.Y. 10016.

World—World Publishing Co., 2231 West 110th Street, Cleveland, Ohio 44102.

Xerox—Xerox College Publishing, A Xerox Education Company, 191 Spring Street, Lexington, Mass. 02173.

Glossary

EDITOR

Anne D. Repko, C.P.M. *Director of Material, Howmedica, Inc., Subsidiary of Pfizer, Inc., New York, New York*

ASSOCIATE EDITOR

Richard L. Dunn *Editor,* Purchasing World, *Barrington, Illinois*

ABC analysis Arrangement of activities—for example, total dollars spent for purchase of particular items—in order of descending dollar value, so that resources (time) can be allocated according to the relative importance of each activity.

abstract of title A condensed history of the title to property, based on the records.

accessorial service A service rendered by a carrier in addition to a transportation service, such as assorting, packing, precooling, heating, storage, or substitution of tonnage.

acceptable quality level (AQL) The percentage of defects in a lot that would be acceptable most of the time.

acceptance number The maximum numbers of defects allowed in a sample for acceptance of a lot.

acceptance of offer The agreement of the buyer to an offer submitted to him by the seller.

acceptance of order The agreement of the seller to transfer the property in goods ordered to the buyer for the price.

acceptance sampling Inspection of a sample in order to predict the number of defects present in the entire lot.

acknowledgment   A form used by a vendor to advise a purchaser that his order has been received. It usually implies acceptance of the order.

acquisition cost   The sum of the ordering cost and the stockholding cost.

acquisition cycle   The departments within a company that directly or indirectly determine what is to be purchased; e.g., company sales, engineering, production control, financial, purchasing. This might vary for each company.

acquittance   A written receipt in full, or discharge from all claims.

act of God   A term used to denote a danger beyond control of or avoidance by human power; any accident produced by a physical cause which is irresistible, such as hurricane, flood, or lightning, and is in no way connected with negligence.

administered price   Price determined by the conscious price policy of a seller rather than by impersonal competitive market forces.

administrative lead time   The time interval between the initiation of a requisition and the placing of the order.

ADP (automatic data processing)   Any combination of EDP (electronic data processing) or IDP (integrated data processing) systems. It is used less often than the more clearly defined EDP and IDP terms.

ad valorem (according to value)   A term usually applied to a customs duty charged upon the value only of goods that are dutiable, irrespective of quality, weight, or other considerations. The ad valorem rates of duty are expressed in percentages of the value of the goods, usually ascertained from the invoice.

affidavit   A written statement sworn to before a notary.

after sight   An expression used on bills of exchange and meaning "after presentation to the drawee for acceptance."

agency   This term signifies relations existing between two parties by which one is authorized to perform or transact certain business for the other; also applies to the office of the agent.

agent   One acting for another, called *principal,* in dealing with third parties.

aggregated shipments   Numerous shipments, from different shippers to one consignee, consolidated and treated as a single consignment.

agreed valuations   The value of a shipment agreed upon in order to secure a specific rating and/or liability.

anticipation   An allowance, usually expressed as a percentage, granted for payment of an invoice in advance of the discount or net due date. It is calculated at the stated percentage rate for the number of days between that of actual payment and the due date, and is allowed in addition to any discounts.

approved list   List of those vendors who have been evaluated and estimated to be capable of satisfactory performance.

arbitration   The investigations by chosen persons and decisions regarding a dispute between parties in controversies.

area code   Numerical identification of geographic telephone calling areas.

arrival notice   A notice sent by the carrier to the consignee advising of the arrival of a shipment.

artisan's lien   The lien of a mechanic or other skilled worker in connection with something on which he has bestowed labor or materials, giving him a right to retain possession of it until paid.

as is   A term indicating that goods offered for sale are without warranty or guarantee. The purchaser has no recourse on the seller for the quality or condition of the goods.

assignment   Transference of some property right or title to another party. This term is frequently used in connection with bills of lading which are endorsed (assigned) over to another party (the assignee) by the owner of the bill (assignor). Such endorsement gives to the party named the title to the property covered by the bill of lading.

attachment   A legal proceeding accompanying an action in court by which a plaintiff may acquire a lien on a defendant's property as a security for the payment of any judgment which the plaintiff may obtain.

average demurrage agreement   An agreement made between a shipper and a transportation line whereby the shipper is debited for the time cars are held for loading or unloading beyond a certain period and credited for the time cars are released by him within a certain period, demurrage charges being assessed by the transportation line, usually at the end of the month, for any outstanding debits.

backdoor selling   The by-passing of the purchasing department by a salesperson who visits the department using his product.

back order   That portion of an order which the seller cannot deliver at the scheduled time and which he has reentered for shipment at a later date.

bailee   A person into whose possession personal property is delivered.

bailment   The delivery of personal property to another for a special purpose, on condition that the property will be returned pursuant to agreement.

bailor   One who entrusts goods to another.

bank(er's) acceptance   An instrument utilized in the financing of foreign trade, making possible the payment of cash to an exporter covering all or a part of the amount of a shipment made by him. Such an arrangement originates with the foreign importer, who instructs his local bank to provide for a *commercial acceptance credit* with, for example, a New York bank in favor of a named American exporter; the New York bank then issues an acceptance credit, in effect guaranteed by the foreign bank, to the exporter, under the terms of which he may draw a time bill of exchange maturing in 60 or 90 days. Supported by the required evidence of shipment, the bill of exchange is accepted by the bank by endorsement on the face of the bill, thus signifying that it will pay the bill at maturity. The exporter may retain the bill until maturity or sell it on the so-called discount market.

bargaining position   Generally refers to the strength or weakness of the parties engaged in negotiation.

barter   The act of exchanging one kind of goods for another, as distinct from trading by the use of money.

basing point   A particular geographic point to which fixed transportation rates are established to be used for the purpose of constructing rates to adjacent points by adding to, or deducting from, the basing point rate.

basing rate   A transportation rate on which other rates are constructed or based. For example, the rates from New York to Chicago constitute the basis on which rates are constructed between western points on the one hand and points in central territory on the other.

biased sampling   Sampling procedures which will not guarantee a truly representative or random sample.

bid   An offer, as a price, whether for payment or acceptance. A quotation specifically given to a prospective purchaser upon his request, usually in competition with other vendors. An offer, by a buyer, to a vendor, as at an auction.

bill   A form used by a carrier as an invoice showing consignee, consignor, description of shipment, weight, freight rate, freight charges, and other pertinent information about goods being transported.

billed weight   The weight on the basis of which charges are assessed by the carrier and shown in freight bill and waybill.

bill of entry   The detailed statement by the importer of the nature and value of goods entered at the customhouse and used for statistical purposes.

bill of exchange   An unconditional order in writing addressed by one person to another, signed by the person giving it, requiring the person to whom it is addressed to pay on demand or at a fixed or determinable future time a certain sum in money to order or to bearer (Uniform Negotiable Instruments Law); in commercial usage, often synonymous with *draft* or *acceptance*. The term is by custom generally confined to an order to pay money arising out of a foreign transaction, *draft* being the term relating to a domestic transaction.

bill of lading (uniform)   Abbreviation: B/L or b/l. A carrier's contract and receipt for goods by which he agrees to transport from one place to another and to deliver to a designated person or assigns for compensation and upon such conditions as are stated therein.

The *straight bill of lading* is a nonnegotiable document and provides that a shipment is to be delivered direct to the party whose name is shown as consignee. The carriers do not require its surrender upon delivery except when necessary that the consignee be identified.

The *order bill of lading* is negotiable. Its surrender, endorsed by the shipper, is required by the carriers upon delivery, in accordance with the terms thereon. The object of an order bill of lading is to enable a shipper to collect for his shipment before it reaches destination.

A *clean bill of lading* is one receipted by carrier for merchandise in good condition (no damage, loss, etc., apparent) and which does not bear such notations as "shipper's load and count," etc.

An *export bill of lading* (through) is one issued by an inland carrier covering contract of carriage from interior point of origin to foreign destination.

A *foul bill of lading* is one indicating that a damage or shortage existed at the time of shipment.

A *government bill of lading* is one supplied by the U.S. government for shipment of government-owned property or of goods being delivered to the government.

An *ocean bill of lading* is one issued by an ocean carrier for marine transport of goods.

bill of materials   A list specifying the quantity and character of materials and parts required to produce or assemble a stated quantity of a particular product.

bill of sale   A written agreement under the terms of which the title or interest in a property is transferred by the seller(s) to the buyer or other designated person(s).

bill of sight   A customhouse document, allowing consignee to see goods before paying duties. Such inspection is made in the presence of a customs officer and is requested by an importer for the purpose of obtaining details which will enable him to prepare a correct bill of entry. This latter document must be completed within 3 days of the bill of sight; otherwise goods are removed to government warehouse.

binder   A tentative but binding commitment, as by the owner of real property, or by a fire insurance company.

blank-check purchase order   Purchase agreement in which vendor is sent a signed blank check. (After shipment, the vendor enters amount due on the check and deposits it.)

blanket order   Sometimes referred to as *master contract* for reducing the number of small orders. It provides for the supplier to furnish special commodities for a certain period of time and at predetermined prices or on the basis of a formula for revising prices due to market or other conditions.

board foot   An area 1 foot square and not more than 1 inch thick.

bond (performance)   A bond executed in connection with a contract and which secures the performance and fulfillment of all the undertakings, covenants, terms, conditions, and agreements contained in the contract.

bonded warehouse   Place owned by persons who have been approved of by the Secretary of the Treasury and who have given guarantees or bonds for the strict observance of revenue laws. Such warehouses are used for the storage and custody of import merchandise, subject to duty, unless the duties are paid or the goods reshipped without entry.

brainstorming   A session involving two or more people during which all ideas generated are scrutinized in order to find a sudden, bright, or harebrained idea that might solve a problem or be creative.

brand-name product   A product whose manufacturer is identified on the product or on the package.

breach of warranty   When the material or product fails to meet the quality or other specification specifically warranted by the seller.

break-even chart   A chart from which effects on costs and profits due to change in volume can be determined.

buffer (safety) stock   A quantity of material kept in store to safeguard against unforeseen shortages. See also *safety stock*.

buyer   A person appointed to purchase on a routine basis in a buying office— usually under the supervision of a section head and generally responsible for a specific range of materials and goods.

buyer's market   A *buyer's market* is considered to exist when goods can easily be secured and when the economic forces of business tend to cause goods to be priced at the purchaser's estimate of value.

buyer's option   The privilege of buying a commodity, security, merchandise, or other property within a given period of time, usually at a price and under conditions agreed upon in advance of the actual sale. A seller usually requires a prospective buyer to pay for an option.

buyer's right of routing   When the seller does not pay freight charges, buyer has option of routing. When seller is to prepay freight, the buyer's right to name the carrier must be made a part of the contract of sale, such right to be exercised before actual shipment of goods. If seller disobeys buyer's orders as to carrier or route, he incurs all risks of transportation.

c.&f. (cost and freight)   A term used when goods are to be conveyed by ocean marine transportation and meaning that the price stated includes both the cost of the goods and the transportation charges to the named point of destination. The seller is liable for the ocean freight charges and for all risks and other charges, until he has received a clean ocean bill of lading from the carrier (either a *received for shipment* or an *on-board,* as agreed between seller and buyer), at which point title passes to the buyer. The buyer is liable for all risks and charges, except ocean freight, after title has passed. The buyer is responsible for arranging for insurance on the goods from the point of ocean shipment.

cargo   The freight transported in a vehicle. The load for transportation as differentiated from things carried as operating equipment and supplies for the conveyance.

carload   Abbreviation: C/L or c/l. (1) A quantity of freight to which carload rates apply, or a shipment tendered as a carload; (2) a car loaded to its carrying capacity.

carload minimum weight   Abbreviation: C/L min. The least weight at which a shipment is handled at a carload rate.

carload rate   The rate applying to a carload quantity of freight.

carrier's lien   A carrier's claim on goods for the collection of freight charges.

car seal   A device to secure against unauthorized opening of the doors of a railroad car. The seal is usually registered and individually identifiable and can be used to identify the place where it was affixed.

cartage   Drayage; a charge for local hauling.

carting   Local delivery by truck of a shipment that was moved by rail, boat, air, or long-distance truck.

caveat emptor   "Let the buyer beware"—the purchase is at the buyer's risk.

caveat venditor   "Let the seller beware"—the seller, in some situations, is liable to the buyer if the goods delivered are different in kind, quality, use, and purpose from those described in the contract of sale.

certificate of compliance   A supplier's certification to the effect that the supplies or services in question meet certain specified requirements.

certificate of damage   A document issued by dock companies in regard to merchandise received or unloaded in a damaged condition.

certified bill of lading   An ocean bill of lading certified by a consular officer to meet certain requirements of his country as to goods imported.

certified check   A check drawn on a bank and accepted by it.

change order   Purchaser's written authority to the supplier to modify or add to a purchase order.

c.i.f. (cost, insurance, and freight)   Similar to c.&f. except that the cost of ocean marine insurance is also for the account of the seller. *War risk* insurance is not for the seller's account unless otherwise agreed upon between the parties.

classification   A publication containing a list of articles and the classes to which they are assigned for the purpose of applying class rates, together with governing rules and regulations.

classification of purchaser   Purchasers are classified by vendors into categories and often are given prices or discounts established by the vendor for such classification. Typical classifications are: ultimate consumer, retailer, wholesaler, distributor, and original equipment manufacturer.

class rate   An article not given a special or commodity rate, and not covered by an exception, comes under the class basis. Such rates are absolute in their nature, and apply to the numbered or lettered groups or classes of articles that are contained in the territorial rating column in the classification schedule.

clearance   A customhouse certificate that a ship is free to leave, all legal requirements having been met. A term also applied to space or measurements above and beside tracks and highways, where they pass through tunnels, or under and over bridges, and which published are known as *clearance tables*.

c.o.d. (cash on delivery)   Payment for purchases on delivery.

collateral   Security placed with a creditor to assure performance of an obligation.

commercial attaché   A representative of a government located in a foreign country for the purpose of assisting and fostering the foreign trade of that government.

commercial law   That branch of the law used to designate the rules that determine the rights and duties of persons engaged in trade and commerce.

commission merchant   An agent, broker, or factor employed to sell goods, wares, and merchandise consigned or delivered to him by his principal, for a compensation called a *commission*.

commodity rate   A rate applicable to an article described or named in the tariff containing the rate, and which applies to, from, or between specific points.

common carrier A person or corporation, licensed by an authorized state, federal, or other governmental agency, engaged in the business of transporting personal property from one place to another for compensation. A common carrier is bound to carry for all who tender their goods and the price for transportation.

common law Law based on precedent expressed in judicial decisions, from the early English days down to the present in this country.

competition, imperfect Competition among sellers of nonhomogeneous products, tending to the same end use, in which the sellers are sufficiently few in number so that each exerts an influence upon the market.

competitive bidding A competitive price offer.

component Any material, ingredient, or part of a subassembly which supplier puts into or assembles with the procured item.

composite sample A sample obtained by mixing together equal portions (sample) from several parts of a lot.

composition of creditors An agreement among creditors and with their debtor by which they agree to take a lesser amount in complete satisfaction of the total debt due.

compromise An agreement between two or more persons, to settle the matters of a controversy without resort to litigation.

computer Equipment used in data processing for developing information. Basically, it performs calculations and stores data on tape and disc files.

concealed damage Damage to the contents of a package which is in good order externally.

concealed loss A loss from a package bearing no indication of having been opened.

conditional sale A sale in which title is retained by the vendor as security for the purchase price, although possession is surrendered to the buyer.

conditions of purchase Terms or provisions in a purchase order.

consideration Something of value given for a promise to make the promise binding. Cf. *binder.*

consignee The person or organization to whom a shipper directs the carrier to deliver goods. Such person or organization is generally the buyer of goods and is called a *consignee* on a bill of lading.

consignment Goods shipped for future sale or other purpose, title remaining with the shipper (consignor), for which the receiver (consignee), upon his acceptance, is accountable. Consigned goods are a part of the consignor's inventory until sold. The consignee may be the eventual purchaser, may act as the agent through whom the sale is effected, or may otherwise dispose of the goods in accordance with his agreement with the consignor.

consignor The person or organization which delivers freight to a carrier for shipment is called a *consignor* or shipper and is the one who directs the bill of lading to be executed by the carrier. If the bill of lading is made to his own order, the person or organization is the consignor-consignee.

consolidation As applied to shipments, consolidation is the act of combining a number of small (less-than-carload) shipments into a carload, generally confined to articles taking the same rating and usually carried on at point of origin.

constructive delivery   Although physical delivery of personal property has not occurred, yet by the conduct of the parties, it may be inferred that as between them possession and title have passed.

consul   A government official residing in a foreign country to care for the interests of his country.

consular invoice   A document in prescribed form required by a foreign government showing exact information as to consignor, consignee, value, description, etc., of a shipment being imported.

consumption   The expenditure of material which results in a loss to the supply system.

consumption rate   The average quantities of an item consumed or expended during a given time interval.

containerization   Shipment of large, sealed containers via rail, truck, or water to reduce transit time, pilferage, damage, packaging, and at times costs through less freight handling.

contingency   A possible future event or condition arising from presently known or unknown causes, the cost outcome of which is indeterminable at a present time.

continuing guaranty   An undertaking by one person to another person to answer from time to time for money to be loaned or goods to be sold to a third person. The term refers to the future liability of the principal for a series of future transactions. It is usually revocable upon actual notice as to all future transactions.

contract   A deliberate agreement between two or more competent persons to perform or not to perform a specific act or acts. A contract may be verbal or written. A purchase order, when accepted by a vendor, becomes a contract. Acceptance may be either in writing or by performance, unless the purchase order requires acceptance thereof to be in writing, in which case it must be thus accepted. A *unilateral contract* is one in which only one party promises performance, the performance being in exchange for an act by the other. A bilateral contract is one where both parties promise performance, each promise being given in exchange for the other.

contract carrier   By motor vehicle, any person or corporation, not a common carrier, who under special and individual contracts or agreements transports passengers or property by motor vehicle for compensation.

contract date   The date when a contract is accepted by all parties thereto.

contracting officer   Any person who, either by virtue of his or her position or by appointment in accordance with prescribed regulations, is vested with the authority to enter into and administer contracts and make determinations and findings with respect thereto, or with any part of such authority.

contract modification   Any unilateral or bilateral written alteration in the specification, delivery point, rate of delivery, contract period, price, quantity, or other provision of an existing contract, accomplished in accordance with a contract clause (e.g., change order, notice of termination, supplemental agreement, exercise of a contract option).

contractor (1) Any one of the parties to a contract. (2) One who contracts to perform work or furnish materials in accordance with a contract.

contracts, types of (1) Firm fixed price-payment of a specific amount when the items called for are delivered and accepted.

(2) Cost reimbursement—contractors are reimbursed for all costs of performance as outlined in the contract. They may be written as:

(*a*) Cost-plus—incentive fee

(*b*) Cost-plus—fixed fee

(*c*) Cost sharing

cost accounting A system of accounting analysis and reporting on costs of production of goods and services, or of operation of programs, activities, functions, or organizational units. The system may also embrace cost estimating, determination of cost standards based on engineering data, and comparison of actual and standard costs for the purpose of aiding cost control.

cost analysis The review and evaluation of a contractor's cost or pricing data and of the judgmental factors applied in projecting from the data to the estimated costs in order to form an opinion leading to a position on the degree to which the contractor's proposed costs represent what contract performance should cost, assuming reasonable economy and efficiency.

cost breakdown Detailed analysis of the supplier's quoted price.

cost estimating The process of forecasting a future result in terms of cost, based upon information available at the time.

cost objective A function, organizational subdivision, contract, or other work unit for which cost data are desired and for which provision is made to accumulate and measure the cost of processes, products, jobs, capitalized projects, etc.

cost plus A pricing method whereby the purchaser agrees to pay the vendor the costs incurred by the vendor in acquiring or producing the goods plus a stated percentage of the cost of the goods or a fixed sum.

cost volume relationship See *break-even chart*.

counteroffer An offer to enter into a transaction on terms differing from those first proposed. It should be noted that vendors' *acknowledgment forms* given to a purchaser in response to a purchase order may be, in fact, a counteroffer.

covenant A promise in writing under seal. It is often used as a substitute for the word *contract*.

CPM (critical path method) Technique for planning and scheduling a project, usually construction, by means of a network program.

currency Lawful money in current circulation. The terms *currency* and *current funds* now seem to include not only coin, silver, U.S. notes, and treasury notes, but also silver certificates, Federal Reserve notes, and national-bank notes.

customs (duties)   Customary taxes, tolls, or duties levied upon goods which pass a frontier, generally upon goods imported.

customs tariff   A schedule of charges assessed by the government on imported or exported goods.

cycle counting   A method of checking inventory levels and records on a routine basis—for example, verifying 2 percent of all stock items each week, with some important items being checked more than once a year. (This approach avoids the disruptive effects of the annual physical inventory.)

cycle stock   The active portion of inventory, i.e., the quantity that is depleted, resupplied, depleted, and resupplied again and again. (Cycle stock does not include the quantity known as *safety stock*.)

damages   Compensation, usually in money, for injury to goods, person, or property.

debt   Any obligation to pay money. Ordinarily the term *debt* means a sum of money due by reason of a contract expressed or implied. Broadly, the word may include obligations other than to pay money, such as the duty to render services or deliver goods.

declared valuation   The valuation placed on a shipment when it is delivered to the carrier.

delivery   The transfer of possession; as applied to shipping, it occurs when lading is surrendered and title to goods passes to the receiver or consignee.

delivery schedule   The required or agreed time or rate of delivery of goods or services purchased for a future period.

demand   A valid requirement for material or supplies placed upon the supply system by an authorized requisitioner.

demurrage   A charge, allowed in tariffs, or by contract, assessed against a consignor, consignee, or other responsible person for delays to transportation equipment in excess of *free time* for loading, unloading, reconsigning, or stopping in transit.

demurrage agreement average   An agreement between a carrier and a consignor (or consignee) whereby delays in excess of the allowed free time, provided in tariffs, or debited against the consignor (or consignee), and delays less than those allowed are credited to the consignor (or consignee). In rail-carrier demurrage agreements charges are assessed by the carrier on the net debits on a periodic basis, usually at the end of a month.

dependent demand   See *internal demand*.

depreciation   Actual or declared decline in value of a capital asset through wear and tear, age, inadequacy, or obsolescence without loss of substance.

destination   The place to which a shipment is consigned.

direct delivery   The consignment of goods directly from the vendor to the buyer. Frequently used where a third party acts as intermediary agent between vendor and buyer.

discount   An allowance or deduction granted by the seller to the buyer, usually when certain stipulated conditions are met by the buyer, which reduces the cost of the goods purchased. However, discounts may be granted by the seller without reference to stipulated conditions. An example of such use of discount is the application of discount to a nominal or *list* price to establish the *net* or actual price.

An *arbitrary discount* is one agreed upon between vendor and purchaser which has no relation to the vendor's usual basis for discount.

A *broken package discount* is one applying on a quantity of goods less than the quantity contained in a vendor's regular package.

A *cash discount* is an allowance extended to encourage payment of invoice on or before a stated date which is earlier than the *net* date. The percent of discount allowed is as agreed between buyer and seller and is often established by industry or trade custom. Usual discounts are ½, 1, and 2 percent, with occasional discount allowances to 10 percent. Typical cash discount terms are shown in Section 10.

A *chain discount* is a series of discounts, the percent of each discount in the chain applying to the amount resulting from application of the immediately preceding percent of discount. A chain discount can be reduced to a single discount by multiplying the complement of each of the discounts and determining the complement of the result. See tables in Section 32.

A *quantity discount* is an allowance determined by the quantity or value of a purchase.

A *standard package discount* is one applying to goods supplied in the vendor's regular package.

A *trade discount* is a deduction from an established price for items or services, often varying in percentage with volume of transactions, made by the seller to those engaged in certain businesses and allowed irrespective of the time when payment is made.

discount schedule   The list of discounts applying to varying quantities of goods or applicable to differing classifications of purchasers.

double-sampling plan   Sampling inspection in which the inspection of the first sample leads to a decision to accept, to reject, or to take a second sample. The inspection of a second sample, when required, then leads to a decision to accept or reject.

draft   A written order drawn by one party (drawer) ordering a second party (drawee) to pay a specified sum of money to a third party (payee). An *arrival draft* is prepared by the seller and, with invoice and shipping receipt for the goods sold, is deposited at his bank for collection. The bank forwards the documents to its correspondent bank at the buyer's city. The buyer secures the invoice and shipping receipt from the bank upon payment or acceptance of the draft, usually at the time when the goods have arrived at destination. A *sight draft* is payable upon presentation to the drawee (as distinguished from an *arrival* or *time draft*). A *time draft* is one which is payable a stated time after acceptance by the drawee.

drawback   A refund of customs duties paid on material imported and later exported.

due bill   A bill rendered by carrier for undercharges.

dunnage   Materials such as boards, planks, blocks, cushions, paulins, straps, etc., used to support, secure, protect, or to facilitate handling of goods loaded in a carrier's transportation equipment.

duty   A tax levied by a government on the importation, exportation, or use and consumption of goods.

e. and o.e. (errors and omissions excepted)   An abbreviation sometimes placed on a quotation or invoice by a vendor to reserve the right to correct the amount charged if this amount is later found to be incorrect.

economic lot size   The number of units put into production to minimize the combined costs of setups and carrying inventory over a specified planning period, usually 1 year.

EDP (electronic data processing)   Application of high-speed electronic equipment in the processing, recording, and printing of information.

endorsement   Writing one's name upon paper for the purpose of transferring the title. When a payee of a negotiable instrument writes his name on the back of the instrument, such writing is an endorsement.

engineering estimate   A cost estimate submitted by the engineering department which enables purchasing to determine a potential purchasing price.

en route   On the way; in transit.

entire contract   A contract which by its terms requires full and complete performance on one side in return for the full and complete performance on the other. The term *entire contract* is used in contradistinction to the term *divisible contract,* wherein a part of the performance required may be set over against a part of the performance on the other side.

entry (customs)   A statement of the kinds, quantities, and values of goods imported together with duties due, if any, and declared before a customs officer or other designated officer.

EOQ (economic order quantity)   Techniques with formula defining the quantity to buy at one time that will achieve the lowest unit cost.

equipment-trust certificate   An interest-bearing document evidencing a part ownership of a trust created for the purpose of purchasing equipment and selling or leasing it to a user. An equipment trust serves as a device for avoiding direct ownership by the user, particularly in the case of railroads, where such ownership would bring the newly acquired asset under existing mortgages and thus make it impossible to have it serve at the same time as security under a conditional sales or installment purchase contract.

escalation   An amount or percent by which a contract price may be adjusted if specified contingencies occur, such as changes in the vendor's raw material or labor costs.

established catalog price   A price included in a catalog, price list, schedule, or other form that: (1) is regularly maintained by a manufacturer or vendor; (2) is published or made available for inspection by customers.

established market price   A current price, established in the usual and ordinary course of trade between buyers and sellers free to bargain, which can be substantiated from sources independent of the manufacturer or vendor.

ethics   The study and philosophy of human conduct, with emphasis on determination of right and wrong.

ex   A prefix meaning "out of" or "from." Used in conjunction with a noun of location, such as, ex-mill, ex-mine, ex-warehouse. *Ex (named point of origin)* means that all charges for transportation and all risks of loss and damage are for the account of the buyer when the goods are delivered to a carrier at the "ex-" location. Where local cartage costs are incurred between the "ex-" location and a common carrier receiving point, such costs are for the buyer's account. On ocean marine shipments the term *ex-dock (named port of importation)*, means all transportation costs, all insurances, risks of loss and damage, export and import duties, taxes, and levies, and consular and entry fees are for the account of the seller. Title passes to the buyer either when he takes possession of the goods at point of import or when the free time allowed on the dock at the point of importation expires, whichever occurs first.

expediting   Maintaining constant pressure on supplier to obtain punctual deliveries. The expression *field expediting* is used when the purchaser has a representative at supplier's plant during the manufacturing period.

express warranty   When a seller makes some positive representation concerning the nature, quality, character, use, and purpose of goods, which induces the buyer to buy, and the seller intends the buyer to rely thereon, the seller has made an express warranty.

external demand   Demand unrelated to the demands for other items produced by the firm; also called *independent demand*.

factor   A factor is an agent for the sale of merchandise. He may hold possession of the goods in his own name or in the name of his principal. He is authorized to sell and to receive payment for the goods.

fair market value   The value of an item as determined by negotiation between buyers and sellers and which value would be acceptable as a basis of a purchase and sale.

f.a.s. (free alongside ship)   The term f.a.s. must be qualified by a named port. The seller is liable for all charges and risks until the goods sold are delivered alongside a vessel at such port or are delivered to the port on a dock which will be used by the vessel. Title passes to the buyer when the seller has secured a clean dock or ship's receipt for the goods. See Section 22.

FIFO   First in, first out; the first put in is taken out first. Applies principally to materials held in inventory.

finder   A person who acts to bring together a purchaser and a vendor and who is not in the employ of either. A finder usually is paid a fee by the party engaging his service.

firm offer   A definite proposal to sell something on stated terms, such offer binding the proposer up to stipulated time of expiration. A *firm bid* is a similar proposal to buy something. Although both are referred to colloquially as firm offers, the distinction between bids and offers is usually preserved in cable codes.

fishyback   Transporting truck trailer on water carriers.

fixed price   Refers to a family of pricing arrangements whose common discipline is a ceiling beyond which the buyer bears no responsibility for payment. In the case of a firm fixed-price arrangement, the agreed-to price is not subject to any adjustment by reason of the contractor's cost experience in the performance of the contract.

fixed-price contract   Contract based on a price that will not differ from that agreed upon or understood to apply at the time of ordering.

floating policy   An insurance policy that covers a class of goods located in a particular place which the insured has on hand at the time the policy was issued, but which goods at the time of a loss may not be the identical items that were on hand at the time the policy was issued. A fire policy covering the inventory of a grocery store is an example.

f.o.b. (free on board)   The term means the seller is required to place the goods aboard the equipment of the transporting carrier without cost to the buyer. The term *f.o.b.* must be qualified by a name of location, such as shipping point, destination; name of a city, mill, warehouse, etc. The stated f.o.b. point is usually the location where title to the goods passes from the seller to the buyer. The seller is liable for transportation charges and the risks of loss or damage to the goods up to the point where title passes to the buyer. The buyer is liable for such charges and risks after passing of title.

follow up   To review a transaction to determine its status. In connection with purchase transactions often synonymous with *expedite.*

f.o.r. (free on rails)   A term meaning that seller will make delivery as far as the railroad terminal named, or, in case of overseas shipment, in harbor at port of departure, name of port stated. To avoid misunderstanding, since term is often considered to be the equivalent of "f.o.b. vessel (   )," or "f.a.s vessel (   )," the phrase is amplified further thus: "f.o.r., cartage to vessel extra."

formal advertising   One of the major methods of procurement (preferred by law when it is feasible and practicable to employ it in governmental procurement). It is used in one of two forms, as appropriate to the requirement: conventional formal advertising and two-step formal advertising. The first involves the procurement of well-defined items or services and the second the procurement of items requiring the submission of technical proposals prior to the submission of prices.

forwarder (freight)   A commercial organization engaged in the business of consolidating less-than-carload, less-than-truckload, or less-than-plane-load shipments and making arrangements for their transportation in carload, truckload, or planeload lots under applicable tariffs.

free goods   Goods not subject to duty.

free lighterage   A privilege accorded export freight shipped in carlots.

free list   A list of articles exempt from customs duties.

free port   A restricted area at a seaport for the handling of duty-exempted import goods, a *foreign trade zone.*

free time   The period allowed to load or unload transportation equipment before demurrage or storage charges begin to accrue.

freight at destination   An expression meaning that freight charges will be paid by the consignee of goods upon their arrival at a specified destination.

freight (customs) bonded   Cargo imported and subject to customs inspections on entry to the United States, which is transported to destination in government-sealed conveyances under surety bond and inspected and released by customs authorities at destination in lieu of initial port of entry.

fungible goods   Fungible goods are goods of which any unit is from its nature of mercantile usage treated as equivalent of any other unit. Grain, wine, and similar items are examples.

futures   Contracts for the sale and delivery of commodities at a future time, made with the intention that no commodity be delivered or received immediately.

general and administrative **(G&A)**   Indirect expenses, including a company's general and executive offices, executive compensation, the cost of staff services (such as legal, accounting, public relations), financial and similar expenses, and other miscellaneous expenses related to the overall business.

good title   A title free from encumbrances such as mortgages and liens.

gross negligence   The want of even slight care.

group (or blanket) rate   Rate covering a large number of related points or a definite section of territory. The blanket system of rate application is very pronounced in cases of long-distance traffic, such as from defined groups to transcontinental and southwestern territories.

hand-to-mouth buying   Purchase of a smaller-than-normal quantity for immediate requirements only, based on anticipated market oversupply or price decrease.

hedge   Any purchase or sale transaction having as its purpose the elimination of profit or loss arising from price fluctuations; specifically, a purchase or sale entered into for the purpose of balancing a sale or purchase already made, or under contract, in order to offset the effect of price fluctuation.

holder in due course   A person who takes a negotiable instrument under the following conditions: (1) that it is complete and regular on its face; (2) that he becomes the holder of it before it was overdue and without notice that it had been previously dishonored, if such was the fact; (3) that he took it in good faith and for value; (4) that at the time it was negotiated to him he had no notice of any infirmity in the instrument or defect in the title of the person negotiating it.

IDP (integrated data processing)   A system for processing business facts into information for several departments without their having to transcribe it.

import   To receive goods from a foreign country.

importer   A buyer or merchant who imports goods.

in bond   The storage or transport of goods in the custody of a warehouse or carrier from whom the goods can be taken only upon payment of taxes or duties to a governmental agency.

independent contractor   The following elements are essential to establish the relation of independent contractor in contradistinction to principal and agent. An independent contractor must: (1) exercise his independent judgment as to the means used to accomplish the result; (2) be free from control or orders from any other person; (3) be responsible only under his contract for the result obtained.

independent demand   See *external demand.*

indorsement   See *endorsement.*

installment payments   A schedule of payment arranged in connection with a purchase transaction requiring periodic payment of a specific sum for each of a stated number of payments.

internal demand   Demand derived from or contingent upon the demand for an end product or other item; also called *dependent demand.*

in-transit privileges   Changes in degree of manufacture, treatment, and other accessorial services provided for in tariffs on commodities between points of origin and destination.

inventory   (1) The amount of property on hand at any given time; (2) an itemized listing of amounts of property indicated as on hand at a particular time. A *physical inventory* is one determined by actual physical count of the items. A *book inventory* is one determined from records maintained in connection with day-to-day business activities.

inventory turnover   Average inventory level compared with issues or withdrawals in a given length of time.

invitation to bid   A request, verbal or written, which is made to prospective suppliers for their quotation on goods or services desired by the prospective purchaser.

invoice   A document showing the character, quantity, price, terms, nature of delivery, and other particulars of goods sold or of services rendered; a bill.

jobber   An intermediary or dealer who purchases goods or commodities from manufacturers or importers and sells them to retailers. Also called *dealer* or *wholesale merchant.*

joint adventure   Sometimes *joint venture.* When two persons enter into a single enterprise for their mutual benefit without the intention of continuous pursuit, they have entered a joint adventure. They are essentially partners.

k.d. (knocked down)   An abbreviation meaning that the article described is supplied unassembled. When an article is shipped k.d., it must be reduced in size by one-third or as specified in the carrier's tariff, to secure the applicable freight rate.

lading   That which constitutes a load, as the freight in a vessel or car.

landed price   A price which includes the cost of the goods, transportation, and other costs incident to ultimate delivery to the location specified by the purchaser.

landing certificate   A document requiring the oath of the foreign consignee, taken before an American consul or merchant or "two respectable foreign merchants," that goods described have actually been delivered to him.

law of agency   (1) Actual authority; (2) specific authority; (3) apparent authority.

lead time   The period of time from date of ordering to the date of delivery which the buyer must reasonably allow the vendor to prepare goods for shipment.

learning curve   A tool of calculation used primarily to project resource requirements, in terms of direct manufacturing labor-hours or the quantity of material (for this purpose, usually referred to as an *improvement curve*) required for a production run. Used interchangeably with the term *improvement curve,* the concept of a learner's curve was adopted from the observation that individuals who perform repetitive tasks exhibit a rate of improvement due to increased manual dexterity.

lease   A contract conveying from one person (lessor) to another (lessee) real estate or personal property for a term in return for a specified rent or other compensation.

legal tender   Currency or coin which a government has declared shall be received in payment of duties or debts.

legal weight   A foreign term denoting the weight of a shipment not including the container.

less-than-carload   Abbreviation: l.c.l. A quantity of freight which is less than the amount necessary to constitute a carload.

less-than-carload rate   A rate applicable to less than a carload shipment.

letter contract   A written preliminary contractual instrument that authorizes the immediate commencement of activity under its terms and conditions, pending agreement on a definite fixed-price or cost-reimbursement pricing arrangement for the work to be done.

letter of credit   A letter containing a request that the party to whom it is addressed pay the bearer or person named therein money, sell him commodities on credit, or give him something of value, with the intention that the addressee later seek payment from the writer of the letter. It is used by a buyer to secure goods without the necessity of having cash in hand.

letter of intent   A preliminary contractual arrangement customarily used in situations where the items, quantities, price, and delivery dates are known, but where the principal contract provisions require additional time-consuming negotiations. It is used to enter into interim agreement, pending a definitive contract, so as to permit the start of construction, production, or delivery of the supplies or materials.

license   A certificate granting permission to do a specific act or acts. An *export license* is granted by a government to ship goods out of the country; an *import license* is granted to permit goods to be received into the country.

lien   A right one person, usually a creditor, has to keep possession of or control the property of another for the purpose of satisfying a debt.

LIFO   Last in, first out; referring to accounting, handling, and pricing of materials held in inventories.

liquidated damages   A sum agreed upon between the parties to a contract, to be paid as ascertained damages by that party who breaches the contract.

lump sum   The price agreed upon between vendor and purchaser for a group of items without breakdown of individual values; a lot price. In construction, *lump sum* means a fixed total price for the complete project, as specified.

make or buy   The decision that determines which components should be manufactured in the buyer's plant and which components should be purchased.

management by exception   Concentrating and directing all efforts toward the problem areas, while allowing the other areas to continue on their natural course.

management by objectives   Establishing specific goals as targets and determining a method of measurement toward attainment of these goals and targets within a given period of time.

manifest   See *cargo (manifest)*.

material requirements planning   See *MRP*.

materials management   Organizational concept in which a single manager has authority and responsibility for all activities principally concerned with the flow of materials into an organization. (Purchasing, production, planning and scheduling, incoming traffic, inventory control, receiving, and stores normally are included.)

metric system   A system of measurements devised in France in 1795 and since adopted by most nations. It is based on factors of 10 for weights and measures. See conversion tables in Section 32.

mock-up   A model, usually full size and constructed of inexpensive material, made for the purpose of studying the construction and use of an article or mechanical device.

mortgage   A lien on land, buildings, machinery, equipment, or other fixed or movable property given by a buyer to the seller as security for payment of the purchase price or given to the lender by the borrower as security for a loan. A *real estage mortgage* applies to lands and buildings. A *chattel mortgage* applies to all other types of property.

MRO   Maintenance, repair, and operating supplies.

MRP   Abbreviation for material requirements planning, a technique providing an integrated approach to scheduling.

mutual assent   In every contract each party must agree to the same thing. Each must know what the other intends; they must mutually assent to be in agreement.

negligence   The failure to do that which an ordinary, reasonable, prudent man would do, or the doing of some act which an ordinary, prudent man would not do. Reference must always be made to the situation, the circumstances, and the knowledge of the parties.

negotiation   In its more general context, a bargaining process between two or more parties, each with its own viewpoints and objectives, seeking to reach a mutually satisfactory agreement on, or settlement of, a matter of common concern. In a purchasing context, the process of arriving at an agreement on the essentials of a purchase contract, through discussion between buyer and seller.

network analysis   A method of planning and controlling projects by recording their analysis in a diagrammatic form which enables each fundamental problem involved to be tackled separately; also provides analyses of the interrelationship of the various problems. This technique is known as PERT (program evaluation and review technique), or CPM (critical path method).

n.o.i.b.n. (not otherwise indexed by name)   An abbreviation indicating an article not specifically included in the list of items named under a general class in the consolidated freight classification.

n.o.s. (not otherwise specified)   An abbreviation indicating an article within a general class in the consolidated freight classification but not completely identified.

OEM (original equipment manufacturer)   A classification assigned by a seller to a purchaser who acquires goods for incorporation into a product which he manufactures for sale, usually without changing the item which he acquires.

open-account purchase   A purchase made by a buyer who has established credit with the seller. Payment terms are usually stated to require payment of invoice on or before a specific date or dates; also, to require payment of invoice in full, or less a certain percentage for prompt payment. Such terms are agreed upon between buyer and seller at time of placing order, or before.

open-end order   Generally specifies price, terms, conditions, and the period covered, but not necessarily the quantity. Shipments are made against buyer's release purchase orders, according to his requirements. See *standing order.*

open-end price contract   Contract to assure a supply of material for some time at the prevailing market price.

open insurance policy   A form of insurance covering shipments for a specified time or a stated value and not limited to a single shipment.

open market price   Price quoted publicly on a daily basis.

ordering costs   Those fixed costs associated with placing a purchase order, regardless of the dollars or number of units represented in the order.

over, short, and damage report (OS&D)   A report submitted by a freight agent showing discrepancies in billing received and freight on hand.

package car   A car containing less-than-carload shipments destined for one or more distant points.

packing list   A document which itemizes in detail the contents of a particular package or shipment.

pallet   A portable platform upon which goods are placed in unit loads to facilitate stacking and handling by mechanical equipment such as fork-lift trucks.

palletainer   A collapsible container designed for transporting and stacking, with its contents, by means of a fork-lift truck. The container's sides and ends fold down to the deck for savings of space of empty units.

palletizing   The loading of supplies and equipment on a pallet.

par value (at par)   The face or nominal value of a commercial paper.

patent   A grant made by the Register of Patents of the United States under the authority of federal legislation to an inventor, which gives the patentee the exclusive right to make, use, and sell the patented article.

penalty clause   A clause in a contract specifying the sum of money to be paid if the contractor defaults on the terms of his contract—particularly in respect of time.

performance specification   Ordering and acceptance of the product on condition that it answers certain performance criteria.

periodic ordering   Orders are placed at regular intervals for amounts needed to bring stocks up to the desired level.

perpetual inventory system   By means of stock cards immediate recording of outgoings, entries, and reorders is provided.

personal purchases   Purchases from a company's suppliers for personal use of its personnel.

PERT (program evaluation and review technique)   Method of planning and scheduling a project, usually construction, by means of a network program.

phased deliveries   Scheduling shipments of material or supplies at specific intervals of time.

piggyback   Transporting truck trailers on rail flat cars.

pilot model   A model, usually handmade, used in production planning for production engineering studies. Cf. *mock-up*.

plant visit   Inspection and evaluation of a vendor's facility, normally done prior to purchase.

pledge   The deposit or placing of personal property as security for a debt or other obligation with a person called the *pledgee*. The pledgee has the implied power to sell the property if the debt is not paid. If the debt is paid, the right to possession returns to the pledger.

point of origin   The station at which a shipment is received by a transportation line from the shipper.

port of entry   A port at which foreign goods and persons are admitted legally into the receiving country. Ports of entry are officially designated by the government.

preclusive specification   Specifications that restrict the number of bidders.

prepaid   A term denoting that transportation charges have been or are to be paid at the point of shipment.

price   A monetary amount given, received, or asked in exchange for property or services, expressed in terms of a single item or unit of measure for such property or services.

price analysis   The process of examining and evaluating a prospective price without evaluation of the separate cost elements and proposed profit of the individual offerer whose price is being evaluated. It may be accomplished by a comparison of submitted quotations, a comparison of price quotations and contract prices with current quotations for the same or similar items, the use of rough yardsticks (dollars per pound, for instance), or a comparison of proposed prices with independently developed estimates.

price maintenance   The price of an item established by a manufacturer or wholesaler below which he will not sell or permit his product to be sold by others.

price prevailing at date of shipment   An agreement between the purchaser and the vendor that the price of the goods ordered is subject to change at the vendor's discretion between the date the order is placed and the date the vendor makes shipment and that the then-established price is the contract price.

price protection   An agreement by a vendor with a purchaser to grant the purchaser any reduction in price which the vendor may establish on his goods prior to shipment of the purchaser's order. Price protection is sometimes extended for an additional period beyond the date of shipment.

private carrier   A transportation line not engaged in business as a general public employment.

procurement   Includes duties performed by purchasing, as well as such additional functions as materials supervision and management, inventory control, receiving, inspection, and salvage operations.

production scheduling   Determination of the sequence and timing of manufacturing activities.

profit   Generally characterized as a basic motive of business enterprise; on occasion referred to as "the wages of risk." In contract pricing, profit represents a projected or known monetary excess realized by a producer or performer after the deduction of cost (both direct and indirect) incurred or to be incurred in the performance of a job, task, or series of the same.

profit center   A discrete, organizationally independent segment of a company, which has been charged by management with profit and loss responsibilities.

pro forma invoice   An invoice prepared by a vendor in advance of a sale to show the form and amount of the invoice which will be rendered to the purchaser if the sale is consummated. Pro forma invoices are often used in export transactions to support the purchaser's request to governmental authorities for import permits and foreign exchange.

progress payments   Payments arranged in connection with purchase transactions requiring periodic payments in advance of delivery for certain stated amounts or for certain percentages of the purchase price.

promissory note   An unconditional written promise, signed by the maker, to pay a certain sum in money, on demand or at a fixed or determinable future date, either to the bearer or to the order of a designated person.

proprietary article   An item made and marked by a person or persons having the exclusive right to manufacture and sell it.

purchase change order   See *change order.*

purchase order   The purchaser's document used to formalize a purchase transaction with a vendor.

purchase requisition   A form used to request the purchasing department to procure goods or services from vendors. Cf. *traveling (purchase) requisition.*

purchasing techniques The manner or method by which procurements are handled efficiently.

quotation A statement of price, terms of sale, and description of goods or services offered by a vendor to a prospective purchaser; a bid. When given in response to an inquiry, is usually considered an offer to sell. Also, the stating of the current price of a commodity; the price so stated.

rebate A sum of money returned by the vendor to a purchaser in consideration of the purchase of a stipulated quantity or value of goods, usually within a stated period.

receiving report A form used by the receiving function of a company to inform others of the receipt of goods purchased. Usually, copies are distributed to the purchasing and accounting departments and the stores room.

reciprocity A policy between two companies by which each makes concessions favoring the purchase of the products of the other.

reconsignment A privilege extended to shippers whereby goods may be forwarded to a point other than the original destination without removal from car and at the through rate from the initial point to that of final delivery. This privilege exists only under the permission granted in a carrier's tariffs and must be exercised only in accordance with the rules and conditions contained therein.

reorder cycle quantity The quantity of supplies required to sustain operations during a specified period of time, e.g. 30 days or 60 days.

reorder point The quantitative point at which requisition action is taken to avoid supply failures.

request for proposals A solicitation document used in negotiated procurements. In governmental purchasing, when an RFP so states, the government reserves the right to award a contract based on initial offers received without any written or oral discussion with offerers.

request for quotation (RFQ) A solicitation document used in negotiated procurements. An RFQ is requested for information. Quotes submitted in response to it are not offers that the buyer will accept without some confirmation or discussion with offerers.

requirements contract A form of contract covering long-term requirements, which is used when the total quantity required cannot be fixed definitely but can be stated with maximum and minimum limits, with deliveries on demand.

requirement objective The maximum quantity of an item to be maintained on hand or on order at any one time to sustain current production.

retention The practice of withholding a portion of the sum due a vendor until the purchase has been finally accepted as fully meeting specifications. The amount or percentage withheld is agreed between the parties at the time of purchase, as is the period of retention. Retention is commonly agreed upon in the purchase of building construction, and occasionally in the purchase of equipment which has to be proved out after delivery.

return on investment (ROI) The ratio between the total capital investment at a given plant (or plants) and the profit return. Normally indicated in percentage. Purchasing personnel can use ROI to determine if it is advisable to purchase larger amounts to receive a better price even though it increases inventories for an increased period of time.

Robinson-Patman Act Federal law requiring that a vendor charge all buyers the same price for the same item purchased in the same quantity.

safety stock That quantity of stock required to be on hand in order to protect against stockouts for each item.

sales tax A tax imposed specifically on a sale made by a vendor.

salvage (1) Property that has some value in addition to its value as scrap, but which is no longer useful as a unit in its present condition and whose restoration of usefulness as a unit is economically not practicable. (2) The act of saving or recovering condemned, discarded, or abandoned property in order to obtain useful parts and scrap therefrom. See Section 24.

sampling Method of obtaining statistics from a large body of data without resorting to a complete census of the data. Two broad methods of selecting samples are *probability sampling,* in which sample units are selected according to the law of chance, and *nonprobability* sampling, in which personal choice, expert judgment, or some other nonprobabilistic rationale is used to select sample units.

scrap Material or part that has no value except for its basic material content.

secured account An account on which liability is evidenced by a negotiable instrument signed by the purchaser at the time the purchase transaction is arranged or at the time of delivery. The usual types of instruments are draft, letter of credit, mortgage, promissory note, bill of exchange, and trade acceptance.

seller's lien The right of a seller to retain possession of goods until the price is paid. Such right does not exist where goods are sold on credit.

seller's market A seller's market is considered to exist when goods cannot easily be secured and when the economic forces of business tend to cause goods to be priced at the vendor's estimate of value.

seller's option The right of a seller to require the buyer to purchase merchandise, or other property, at an agreed price and within a given period of time.

shipping release A form used by the purchaser to specify shipping instructions of goods purchased for delivery at an unstated future date or to an undisclosed destination. Also used to specify quantities to be shipped when the purchase was for an unspecified quantity or when delivery is to be made in partial lots at the purchaser's discretion.

short sale The sale of a commodity for future delivery which the seller does not possess but intends to purchase prior to the required delivery date, expecting that the market price will be no higher or will decline during the intervening period.

sight entry A procedure that must be put through to release goods from customs, occasioned by the use of an incorrect invoice form and particularly applicable to traffic into Canada.

sole source Characterized as the one and only source, regardless of the marketplace, possessing a unique and singularly available performance capability for the purpose of contract award. (Sometimes used interchangeably with the term *single source.*)

specification   A clear, complete, and accurate statement of the technical requirements descriptive of a material, an item, or a service, and of the procedure to be followed to determine if the requirements are met.

   Federal: A specification established in accordance with procedures prescribed by the Federal Specifications Board and approved for use by all government activities.

speculative buying   Purchasing for anticipated future requirements in expectation of shortages or rising prices with the tacit understanding between the purchasing manager and company management that any portion of the purchase not eventually required for production can be sold at a profit for the company.

spotting   The act of placing a car, truck, or trailer to be loaded or unloaded.

standardization   The process of defining and applying the conditions (such as the function, quality, or dimensions of a product or the method of manufacture and testing) necessary to ensure that a given range of requirements can normally be met, with a minimum of variety, in a reproducible and economic manner on the basis of the best current techniques.

standing cost   A cost determined to represent an expected value; a goal or baseline that is used to expedite the costing of transactions, determined from historical experience or contrived from the best information available. Excepting costs attributable to precise and highly predictable operations, actual costs will almost always vary from standard costs because of factors (usually called *variances*) that affect performance, such as employee fatigue, unforeseen interruptions, and other delays.

standing order   Standing arrangement with a selected supplier to deliver goods or to service machinery at prices agreed for a period. See *open-end order.*

station order car   A car loaded by a shipper with several less-than-carload shipments in destination order for different points along the same route. Unlike the trap car or ferry car, this car is placed into a train without its contents being rehandled at the carrier's terminal at point of shipment.

stockout   Condition created when the supply of a commodity in stores is completely exhausted.

stopover   Many carriers allow a *stopover* privilege on carload freight shipments at stations between points of origin and final destination, for the purpose of finishing loading or partly unloading or of taking advantage of transit or other privileges permitted in accordance with tariff rules and regulations.

stopping in transit   The holding of a shipment by the carrier on order of the owner after the transportation movement has started and before it is completed.

storage in transit   The stopping of freight traffic at a point located between the point of origin and destination to be stored and reforwarded at a later date.

store-door delivery   The movement of goods to the consignee's place of business.

s.u.   Setup. An abbreviation meaning that the article described is supplied fully assembled.

subcontractor   A party who contracts with a prime contractor to perform all or any part of the prime contractor's obligations in a particular prime contract.

subrogation   The substitution of one person in another's place, whether as a creditor or as the possessor of any lawful right, so that the substituted person may succeed to the rights, remedies, or proceeds of the claim.

supply review   The process of reviewing a new forecast and comparing that forecast with the present inventory balance for determination of future demands.

systems contract   A method of procurement, affirmed by formal or informal agreement, designed to improve the reordering of repetitive-use materials with a minimum of expense.

tally   To count; the process of counting the pieces of an incoming or outgoing consignment and recording the particular data obtained by visual inspection, such as number of pieces, weight, commodity, and the like. Also, the number of pieces determined by counting.

tariff (freight)   A schedule containing matter relative to transportation movements, rates, rules, and regulations. An *alternative tariff* is one containing two or more rates from and to the same points, on the same goods, with authority to use the one which produces the lowest charge. A *commodity tariff* is one containing only commodity rates. A *class tariff* is one containing rates applicable to classifications of goods as established by the carriers. See also *customs tariff*.

terms of payment   All purchase transactions require a payment for the goods or services received and, excepting in an unusual exchange or barter deal, payment is made in negotiable funds in accordance with the terms agreed between buyer and seller. There are three basic payment terms: cash, open account, and secured account.

tracer   (1) A request for an answer to a communication, or for advice concerning the status of a subject; (2) a request upon a transportation line to trace a shipment for the purpose of expediting its movement or establishing delivery.

track storage   A charge made on cars held on carrier's tracks for loading or unloading after the expiration of free time allowed. The charge is generally made in addition to demurrage charges.

trade acceptance   A non-interest-bearing bill of exchange or draft covering the sale of goods, drawn by the seller on, and accepted by, the buyer. Its purpose is to put into negotiable form an open account having a short maturity. To be eligible for discount it must contain the statement that the acceptor's obligation arises out of the purchase of goods from the drawer, and it may be accompanied by a record of the purchase.

trademark   Generally it is any sign, symbol, mark, word, or arrangement of words in the form of a label adopted and used by a manufacturer or distributor to designate his particular goods, and which no other person has the legal right to use.

trade terms   The broad classification applicable to purchase transactions with reference to understandings between buyer and seller, either as to the meanings of certain abbreviations, words, or phrases or as to customs applicable to transactions or established by agreement between the parties or as established by general usage. *Trade terms* includes agreed or arbitrary classifications of buyers and sellers, or their agents; types and methods of discounts, delivery terms, and allowances; practices peculiar to an industry, etc.

transit charges   Charges made for services rendered while a shipment is in transit.

transit privilege   A tariff provision authorizing a shipper to have specified commodities stopped at some point between origin and destination for processing or storage and later complete their movements to destination at the through rate.

transship   A term commonly used to denote the transfer of goods from one steamer or conveyance to another; the rehandling or transshipment of goods en route.

traveling (purchase) requisition   A purchase requisition designed for repetitive use. After a purchase order has been prepared for the goods requisitioned, the form is returned to the originator, who holds it until a repurchase of the goods is required. The name is derived from the repetitive travel between the originating and purchasing departments.

value analysis   The organized and systematic study of every element of cost in a material, part, or service to ensure that it fulfills its function at the lowest total cost.

variable cost   A cost that changes with the rate of production of goods or the performance of services. As distinguished from *fixed* costs (which do not change with the rate of production or performance), there may be *semivariable* costs (neither entirely fixed nor variable) and *variable* costs as defined here.

variable overhead   That portion of overhead which varies with the volume of manufactured items.

vendor   An outside supplier of raw materials, supplies, equipment, or services needed in the operation of an organization.

vendor's lien   An unpaid seller's right to hold possession of property until he has recovered the purchase price.

visual inspection   A term generally used to indicate inspection performed without the aid of test instruments.

voucher   A written instrument that bears witness to or *vouches* for something. Generally a voucher is an instrument showing that services have been performed, or goods purchased, and authorizes payment to be made to the vendor.

warehouse (bonded)   A warehouse in which goods are held under bond to the government subject to payment of customs duties or taxes on the goods.

warehouse (public)   A place of storage for the use of the general public; usually embracing merchandise and/or household goods, or sometimes limited to certain commodities. In addition to the service of storage, many public warehouses are performing the functions of distributing agent and forwarder.

warehouse receipt   An instrument showing that the signer has in his possession certain described goods for storage, and which obligates the signer, the warehouseman, to deliver the goods to a specified person or to his order or bearer upon the return of the instrument. Consult Uniform Warehouse Receipts Act.

warranty   An undertaking, either expressed or implied, that a certain fact regarding the subject matter of a contract is presently true or will be true. The word should be distinguished from *guaranty,* which means a contract or promise by one person to answer for the performance of another.

waybill   A document prepared by a transportation line at the point of origin of a shipment, showing the point of origin, destination, route, consignor, consignee, description of shipment, and amount charged for the transportation service, and forwarded to the carrier's agent at transfer point or destination. An *astray waybill* is used for freight miscarried or separated from its proper waybill. A *blanket waybill* is one covering two or more consignments of freight. An *interline waybill* is one covering the movement of freight over two or more transportation lines.

weight, gross   The weight of an article together with the weight of its container and the material used for packing.

weight, net   The actual weight of the contents of a container or of the cargo of a vehicle. It is the total weight less the tare weight.

weight, tare   The weight of an empty container and the other material used for packing its contents. *Actual tare* is determined when each cask, bag, etc., is weighed; *average tare,* when one is weighed as a sample; and *estimated tare,* when a fixed percentage is allowed.

Section **32**

Reference Tables

EDITOR

Ralph L. Andreas *Retired Director of Purchasing and Traffic, Amoco Oil Company, Chicago, Illinois*

ASSOCIATE EDITORS

Richard T. Arnott *Vice-President and Managing Director, Kellogg Continental, B.V., Amsterdam, Netherlands*

Bruce B. Curtis *Retired Director of Purchasing, International Harvester Company, Chicago, Illinois*

Daniel J. Murphy *Manager of Planning and Economics, Rio Blanco Shale Oil Company, Denver, Colorado*

TABLES OF WEIGHTS AND MEASURES

TABLE 32-1   U.S. Weights and Measures

WEIGHTS

Apothecaries' 20 grains (gr)	= 1 scruple (s ap. or ℈)
3 scruples	= 1 dram (dr ap. or ʒ)
8 drams	= 1 ounce (oz ap. or ℥)
12 ounces	= 1 pound (lb ap. or ℔)
Avoirdupois 27–11/32 grains (gr)	= 1 dram (dr)
16 drams	= 1 ounce (oz)
16 ounces	= 1 pound (lb)
25 pounds	= 1 quarter
4 quarters	= 1 hundredweight (cwt)
20 hundredweights or 2,000 pounds	= 1 ton (tn or t) or short ton (s.t.)
2,240 pounds	= 1 long ton (l.t.)
Troy 24 grains (gr)	= 1 pennyweight (dwt)
20 pennyweights	= 1 ounce (oz t.)
12 ounces	= 1 pound (lb t.)

MEASURES

Circular 60 seconds (″)	= 1 minute (′)
60 minutes	= 1 degree (°)
30 degrees	= 1 sign
3 signs	= 1 quadrant or 90 degrees
4 quadrants	= 1 circle or 1 circumference or 360 degrees
Cubic 1,728 cubic inches (cu in.)	= 1 cubic foot (cu ft)
27 cubic feet	= 1 cubic yard (cu yd)
128 cubic feet	= 1 cord (cd)
Dry 2 pints (pt)	= 1 quart (qt)
8 quarts	= 1 peck (pk)
4 pecks	= 1 bushel (bu) or 2,150.42 cubic inches (cu in.)
Linear or Long 12 inches (in.)	= 1 foot (ft)
3 feet	= 1 yard (yd)
5½ yards	= 1 rod (rd) or pole (p) or perch (p)
40 rods	= 1 furlong (fur.)
8 furlongs or 1,760 yards or 5,280 feet	= 1 mile (mi)
3 miles	= 1 league
Liquid 8 fluid drams (f ʒ)	= 1 fluid ounce (f ℥)
4 fluid ounces	= 1 gill (gi)
4 gills	= 1 pint (pt)
2 pints	= 1 quart (qt)
4 quarts	= 1 gallon (gal) or 231 cubic inches (cu in.)
31½ gallons	= 1 barrel (bbl)
Mariners' or Nautical 6 feet (ft)	= 1 fathom (f or fm)
100 fathoms	= 1 cable's length (ordinary)
10 cables' lengths	= 1 nautical mile or 6,080.20 feet
1 nautical mile	= 1.1516 statute miles
1 knot	= a speed of 1 nautical mile, or 1.1516 statute miles per hour
Paper 24 sheets (sh)	= 1 quire (qr)
20 quires	= 1 ream (rm)
2 reams	= 1 bundle (bdl)
5 bundles	= 1 bale (B/-)

TABLE 32-1   U.S. Weights and Measures (*Continued*)

Square 144 square inches (sq in.)	= 1 square foot (sq ft)
9 square feet	= 1 square yard (sq yd)
30¼ square yards	= 1 square rod (sq rd) or square pole (sq p) or square perch (sq p)
160 square rods or 4,840 square yards or 43,560 square feet	= 1 acre (A)
640 acres	= 1 square mile (sq mi)
36 square miles	= 1 township (tp)

TABLE 32-2   Metric Weights and Measures

NOTE: United States adoption of the metric system continues to receive broad advocacy. Metric mensuration data and conversion equivalents are given in Tables 32-2, 32-3, and 32-4.

WEIGHT

10 milligrams (mg)	= 1 centigram (cg)
10 centigrams	= 1 decigram (dg)
10 decigrams	= 1 gram (g)
1,000 grams	= 1 kilogram or kilo (kg)
100 kilograms	= 1 quintal (q)
10 quintals or 1,000 kilograms	= 1 metric ton (MT)

LENGTH

10 millimeters (mm)	= 1 centimeter (cm)
10 centimeters	= 1 decimeter (dm)
10 decimeters	= 1 meter (m)
10 meters	= 1 decameter (dkm)
10 decameters	= 1 hectometer (hm)
10 hectometers or 1,000 meters	= 1 kilometer (km)

AREA

100 square millimeters (sq mm or mm^2)	= 1 square centimeter (sq cm or cm^2)
100 square centimeters	= 1 square decimeter (sq dm or dm^2)
100 square decimeters	= 1 square meter (sq m or m^2) or 1 centiare (ca)
100 square meters	= 1 are (a)
100 ares	= 1 hectare (ha)
100 hectares	= 1 square kilometer (sq km or km^2)

VOLUME

1,000 cubic millimeters (cu mm or mm^3)	= 1 cubic centimeter (cu cm or cm^3)
1,000 cubic centimeters	= 1 cubic decimeter (cu dm or dm^3)
1,000 cubic decimeters	= 1 cubic meter (cu m or m^3)

CAPACITY

10 milliliters (ml)	= 1 centiliter (cl)
10 centiliters	= 1 deciliter (dl)
10 deciliters	= 1 liter (l)
10 liters	= 1 decaliter (dkl)
10 decaliters	= 1 hectoliter (hl)
10 hectoliters or 1,000 liters	= 1 kiloliter (kl)

CONVERSION TABLES AND EQUIVALENTS

TABLE 32-3   Metric Equivalents of U.S. Weights and Measures

NOTE: A conversion aid prepared in handy plastic wallet-card form is available from the Superintendent of Documents, U.S. Government Printing Office, Washington, D.C. 20402. It can be ordered as National Bureau of Standards Special Publication 365.

APOTHECARIES' WEIGHT

1 scruple	= 1.296 grams
1 dram	= 3.888 grams

AVOIRDUPOIS WEIGHT

1 dram	= 1.772 grams
1 ounce	= 28.3495 grams
1 pound	= 453.59 grams or 0.4536 kilogram
1 hundredweight	= 45.36 kilograms
1 short ton	= 907.18 kilograms or 0.9072 metric ton
1 long ton	= 1,016.05 kilograms or 1.0160 metric tons

TROY WEIGHT

1 pennyweight	= 1.555 grams
1 ounce	= 31.1035 grams
1 pound	= 373.24 grams or 0.3732 kilogram

LINEAR OR LONG MEASURE

1 inch	= 2.54 centimeters
1 foot	= 0.3048 meter
1 yard	= 0.9144 meter
1 rod	= 5.029 meters
1 furlong	= 201.17 meters
1 mile	= 1.6093 kilometers
1 league	= 4.83 kilometers

MARINERS' OR NAUTICAL MEASURE

1 fathom	= 1.829 meters
1 nautical mile	= 1,853.248 meters

SQUARE MEASURE

1 square inch	= 6.452 square centimeters
1 square foot	= 929 square centimeters
1 square yard	= 0.8361 square meter
1 square rod	= 25.29 square meters
1 acre	= 40.4687 ares or 0.4047 hectare
1 square mile	= 259 hectares or 2.59 square kilometers
1 township	= 9,324 hectares or 93.24 square kilometers

CUBIC MEASURE

1 cubic inch	= 16.387 cubic centimeters
1 cubic foot	= 0.0283 cubic meter
1 cubic yard	= 0.7646 cubic meter
1 cord	= 3.625 cubic meters

LIQUID MEASURE

1 fluid ounce	= 0.0297 liter
1 gill	= 0.118 liter
1 pint	= 0.4732 liter
1 quart	= 0.9463 liter
1 gallon	= 3.7853 liters

DRY MEASURE

1 quart	= 1.1012 liters
1 peck	= 8.8096 liters
1 bushel	= 35.2383 liters

TABLE 32-4   U.S. Equivalents of Metric Weights and Measures

WEIGHT

1 centigram   = 0.1543 grain
1 decigram   = 1.5432 grains
1 gram   = 15.432 grains
1 kilogram   = 2.2046 pounds
1 quintal   = 220.46 pounds
1 metric ton = 2,204.6 pounds

LENGTH

1 centimeter = 0.3937 inch
1 decimeter   = 3.937 inches
1 meter   = 39.37 inches
1 decameter   = 393.7 inches
1 hectometer = 328 feet 1 inch
1 kilometer   = 0.62137 mile

AREA

1 square centimeter = 0.155 square inch
1 centiare   = 1,550 square inches
1 are   = 119.6 square yards
1 hectare   = 2.471 acres
1 square kilometer = 0.3861 square mile

VOLUME

1 cubic centimeter = 0.061 cubic inch
1 cubic meter   = 1.308 cubic yards

CAPACITY

1 centiliter = 0.338 fluid ounce
1 deciliter = 6.1025 cubic inches
1 liter   = 0.9081 dry quart or 1.0567 liquid quarts
1 decaliter = 0.284 bushel or 2.64 gallons
1 hectoliter = 2.838 bushels or 26.418 gallons
1 kiloliter = 35.315 cubic feet or 264.18 gallons

TABLE 32-5   Engineering Units

1 British thermal unit (Btu or B) = 1,055 watt-seconds
                                  = 778 foot-pounds (ft-lb)
                                  = 0.000293 kilowatthour
                                  = 0.000393 horsepower-hour
1 horsepower-hour (hp-hr)   = 0.746 kilowatthour
                                  = 1,980,000 foot-pounds
                                  = 2545 heat units (Btu or B)
1 horsepower (hp)   = 33,000 foot-pounds per minute
                                  = 550 foot-pounds per second
                                  = 746 watts
                                  = 0.746 kilowatt
1 kilowatt (kw)   = 1,000 watts
                                  = 1.34 horsepower
                                  = 737.3 foot-pounds per second
                                  = 44,240 foot-pounds per minute
                                  = 56.9 heat units (Btu or B) per minute
1 megawatt (MW)   = 1,000 kilowatts

TABLE 32-5   Engineering Units (*Continued*)

1 kilowatthour (kwhr)	= 1,000 watthours (whr)
	= 1.34 horsepower-hours
	= 2,654,200 foot-pounds
	= 3412 heat units (Btu or B)
1 watt (w)	= 1 joule per second
	= 0.00134 horsepower
	= 3412 heat units (Btu or B) per hour
	= 0.7373 foot-pound per second
	= 44.24 foot-pounds per minute

TABLE 32-6   Fractions and Their Decimal Equivalents

Fraction	Decimal Equivalent	Fraction	Decimal Equivalent
$\frac{1}{64}$	.0156	$\frac{33}{64}$	.5156
$\frac{1}{32}$	.0312	$\frac{17}{32}$	.5312
$\frac{3}{64}$	.0468	$\frac{35}{64}$	.5468
$\frac{1}{16}$	.0625	$\frac{9}{16}$	.5625
$\frac{5}{64}$	.07812	$\frac{37}{64}$	.5781
$\frac{3}{32}$	.09375	$\frac{19}{32}$	.5937
$\frac{7}{64}$	.10937	$\frac{39}{64}$	.6093
$\frac{1}{8}$	.125	$\frac{5}{8}$	.6250
$\frac{9}{64}$	.14062	$\frac{41}{64}$	.6406
$\frac{5}{32}$	.15625	$\frac{21}{32}$	.6562
$\frac{11}{64}$	.17187	$\frac{43}{64}$	.6718
$\frac{3}{16}$	.1875	$\frac{11}{16}$	.6875
$\frac{13}{64}$	.20312	$\frac{45}{64}$	.7031
$\frac{7}{32}$	.21875	$\frac{23}{32}$	.7187
$\frac{15}{64}$	.23437	$\frac{47}{64}$	.7343
$\frac{1}{4}$	.25	$\frac{3}{4}$	.7500
$\frac{17}{64}$	.26562	$\frac{49}{64}$	.7656
$\frac{9}{32}$	.28125	$\frac{25}{32}$	.7812
$\frac{19}{64}$	.29687	$\frac{51}{64}$	.7968
$\frac{5}{16}$	.3125	$\frac{13}{16}$	.8125
$\frac{21}{64}$	.32812	$\frac{53}{64}$	.8281
$\frac{11}{32}$	.34375	$\frac{27}{32}$	.8437
$\frac{23}{64}$	.35937	$\frac{55}{64}$	.8593
$\frac{3}{8}$	.375	$\frac{7}{8}$	.8750
$\frac{25}{64}$	.39062	$\frac{57}{64}$	.8906
$\frac{13}{32}$	.40625	$\frac{29}{32}$	.9062
$\frac{27}{64}$	.42187	$\frac{59}{64}$	.9218
$\frac{7}{16}$	.4375	$\frac{15}{16}$	.9375
$\frac{29}{64}$	.45312	$\frac{61}{64}$	.9531
$\frac{15}{32}$	.46875	$\frac{31}{32}$	.9687
$\frac{31}{64}$	.48437	$\frac{63}{64}$	.9843
$\frac{1}{2}$	.50	1	1.0000

TABLE 32-7 Temperature Conversion*

General formula: °F = (°C × 9/5) + 32; °C = (°F − 32) × 5/9

C†	value	F	C	value	F	C	value	F	C	value	F	C	value	F	C	value	F	C	value	F	C	value	F	C	value	F
−273.1	−459.4		−17.8	0	32	10.0	50	122.0	38	100	212	260	500	932	538	1000	1832	816	1500	2732	1093	2000	3632	1371	2500	4532
−268	−450		−17.2	1	33.8	10.6	51	123.8	43	110	230	266	510	950	543	1010	1850	821	1510	2750	1099	2010	3650	1377	2510	4550
−262	−440		−16.7	2	35.6	11.1	52	125.6	49	120	248	271	520	968	549	1020	1868	827	1520	2768	1104	2020	3668	1382	2520	4568
−257	−430		−16.1	3	37.4	11.7	53	127.4	54	130	266	277	530	986	554	1030	1886	832	1530	2786	1110	2030	3686	1388	2530	4586
−251	−420		−15.6	4	39.2	12.2	54	129.2	60	140	284	282	540	1004	560	1040	1904	838	1540	2804	1116	2040	3704	1393	2540	4604
−246	−410		−15.0	5	41.0	12.8	55	131.0	66	150	302	288	550	1022	566	1050	1922	843	1550	2822	1121	2050	3722	1399	2550	4622
−240	−400		−14.4	6	42.8	13.3	56	132.8	71	160	320	293	560	1040	571	1060	1940	849	1560	2840	1127	2060	3740	1404	2560	4640
−234	−390		−13.9	7	44.6	13.9	57	134.6	77	170	338	299	570	1058	577	1070	1958	854	1570	2858	1132	2070	3758	1410	2570	4658
−229	−380		−13.3	8	46.4	14.4	58	136.4	82	180	356	304	580	1076	582	1080	1976	860	1580	2876	1138	2080	3776	1416	2580	4676
−223	−370		−12.8	9	48.2	15.0	59	138.2	88	190	374	310	590	1094	588	1090	1994	866	1590	2894	1143	2090	3794	1421	2590	4694
−218	−360		−12.2	10	50.0	15.6	60	140.0	93	200	392	316	600	1112	593	1100	2012	871	1600	2912	1149	2100	3812	1427	2600	4712
−212	−350		−11.7	11	51.8	16.1	61	141.8	99	210	410	321	610	1130	599	1110	2030	877	1610	2930	1154	2110	3830	1432	2610	4730
−207	−340		−11.1	12	53.6	16.7	62	143.6	104	220	428	327	620	1148	604	1120	2048	882	1620	2948	1160	2120	3848	1438	2620	4748
−201	−330		−10.6	13	55.4	17.2	63	145.4	110	230	446	332	630	1166	610	1130	2066	888	1630	2966	1166	2130	3866	1443	2630	4766
−196	−320		−10.0	14	57.2	17.8	64	147.2	116	240	464	338	640	1184	616	1140	2084	893	1640	2984	1171	2140	3884	1449	2640	4784
−190	−310		−9.44	15	59.0	18.3	65	149.0	121	250	482	343	650	1202	621	1150	2102	899	1650	3002	1177	2150	3902	1454	2650	4802
−184	−300		−8.89	16	60.8	18.9	66	150.8	127	260	500	349	660	1220	627	1160	2120	904	1660	3020	1182	2160	3920	1460	2660	4820
−179	−290		−8.33	17	62.6	19.4	67	152.6	132	270	518	354	670	1238	632	1170	2138	910	1670	3038	1188	2170	3938	1466	2670	4838
−173	−280		−7.78	18	64.4	20.0	68	154.4	138	280	536	360	680	1256	638	1180	2156	916	1680	3056	1193	2180	3956	1471	2680	4856
−169	−273		−7.22	19	66.2	20.6	69	156.2	143	290	554	366	690	1274	643	1190	2174	921	1690	3074	1199	2190	3974	1477	2690	4874
−168	−270	−454	−6.67	20	68.0	21.1	70	158.0	149	300	572	371	700	1292	649	1200	2192	927	1700	3092	1204	2200	3992	1482	2700	4892
−162	−260	−436	−6.11	21	69.8	21.7	71	159.8	154	310	590	377	710	1310	654	1210	2210	932	1710	3110	1210	2210	4010	1488	2710	4910
−157	−250	−418	−5.56	22	71.6	22.2	72	161.6	160	320	608	382	720	1328	660	1220	2228	938	1720	3128	1216	2220	4028	1493	2720	4928
−151	−240	−400	−5.00	23	73.4	22.8	73	163.4	166	330	626	388	730	1346	666	1230	2246	943	1730	3146	1221	2230	4046	1499	2730	4946
−146	−230	−382	−4.44	24	75.2	23.3	74	165.2	171	340	644	393	740	1364	671	1240	2264	949	1740	3164	1227	2240	4064	1504	2740	4964
−140	−220	−364	−3.89	25	77.0	23.9	75	167.0	177	350	662	399	750	1382	677	1250	2282	954	1750	3182	1232	2250	4082	1510	2750	4982
−134	−210	−346	−3.33	26	78.8	24.4	76	168.8	182	360	680	404	760	1400	682	1260	2300	960	1760	3200	1238	2260	4100	1516	2760	5000
−129	−200	−328	−2.78	27	80.6	25.0	77	170.6	188	370	698	410	770	1418	688	1270	2318	966	1770	3218	1243	2270	4118	1521	2770	5018
−123	−190	−310	−2.22	28	82.4	25.6	78	172.4	193	380	716	416	780	1436	693	1280	2336	971	1780	3236	1249	2280	4136	1527	2780	5036
−118	−180	−292	−1.67	29	84.2	26.1	79	174.2	199	390	734	421	790	1454	699	1290	2354	977	1790	3254	1254	2290	4154	1532	2790	5054
−112	−170	−274	−1.11	30	86.0	26.7	80	176.0	204	400	752	427	800	1472	704	1300	2372	982	1800	3272	1260	2300	4172	1538	2800	5072
−107	−160	−256	−0.56	31	87.8	27.2	81	177.8	210	410	770	432	810	1490	710	1310	2390	988	1810	3290	1266	2310	4190	1543	2810	5090
−101	−150	−238	0	32	89.6	27.8	82	179.6	216	420	788	438	820	1508	716	1320	2408	993	1820	3308	1271	2320	4208	1549	2820	5108
−95.6	−140	−220	0.56	33	91.4	28.3	83	181.4	221	430	806	443	830	1526	721	1330	2426	999	1830	3326	1277	2330	4226	1554	2830	5126
−90.0	−130	−202	1.11	34	93.2	28.9	84	183.2	227	440	824	449	840	1544	727	1340	2444	1004	1840	3344	1282	2340	4244	1560	2840	5144

TABLE 32-7 Temperature Conversion (Continued)*

C†		F	C		F	C		F	C		F	C		F	C		F	C		F	C		F	C		F
−84.4	**−120**	−184	1.67	**35**	95.0	29.4	**85**	185.0	227	**440**	824	454	**850**	1562	732	**1350**	2462	1010	**1850**	3362	1288	**2350**	4262	1566	**2850**	5162
−78.9	**−110**	−166	2.22	**36**	96.8	30.0	**86**	186.8	232	**450**	842	460	**860**	1580	738	**1360**	2480	1016	**1860**	3380	1293	**2360**	4280	1571	**2860**	5180
−73.3	**−100**	−148	2.78	**37**	98.6	30.6	**87**	188.6	238	**460**	860	466	**870**	1598	743	**1370**	2498	1021	**1870**	3398	1299	**2370**	4298	1577	**2870**	5198
−67.8	**−90**	−130	3.33	**38**	100.4	31.1	**88**	190.4	243	**470**	878	471	**880**	1616	749	**1380**	2516	1027	**1880**	3416	1304	**2380**	4316	1582	**2880**	5216
−62.2	**−80**	−112	3.89	**39**	102.2	31.7	**89**	192.2	249	**480**	896	477	**890**	1634	754	**1390**	2534	1032	**1890**	3434	1310	**2390**	4334	1588	**2890**	5234
−56.7	**−70**	−94	4.44	**40**	104.0	32.2	**90**	194.0	254	**490**	914	482	**900**	1652	760	**1400**	2552	1038	**1900**	3452	1316	**2400**	4352	1593	**2900**	5252
−51.1	**−60**	−76	5.00	**41**	105.8	32.8	**91**	195.8				488	**910**	1670	766	**1410**	2570	1043	**1910**	3470	1321	**2410**	4370	1599	**2910**	5270
−45.6	**−50**	−58	5.56	**42**	107.6	33.3	**92**	197.6				493	**920**	1688	771	**1420**	2588	1049	**1920**	3488	1327	**2420**	4388	1604	**2920**	5288
−40.0	**−40**	−40	6.11	**43**	109.4	33.9	**93**	199.4				499	**930**	1706	777	**1430**	2606	1054	**1930**	3506	1332	**2430**	4406	1610	**2930**	5306
−34.4	**−30**	−22	6.67	**44**	111.2	34.4	**94**	201.2				504	**940**	1724	782	**1440**	2624	1060	**1940**	3524	1338	**2440**	4424	1616	**2940**	5324
−28.9	**−20**	−4	7.22	**45**	113.0	35.0	**95**	203.0				510	**950**	1742	788	**1450**	2642	1066	**1950**	3542	1343	**2450**	4442	1621	**2950**	5342
−23.3	**−10**	14	7.78	**46**	114.8	35.6	**96**	204.8				516	**960**	1760	793	**1460**	2660	1071	**1960**	3560	1349	**2460**	4460	1627	**2960**	5360
−17.8	**0**	32	8.33	**47**	116.6	36.1	**97**	206.6				521	**970**	1778	799	**1470**	2678	1077	**1970**	3578	1354	**2470**	4478	1632	**2970**	5378
			8.89	**48**	118.4	36.7	**98**	208.4				527	**980**	1796	804	**1480**	2696	1082	**1980**	3596	1360	**2480**	4496	1638	**2980**	5396
			9.44	**49**	120.2	37.2	**99**	210.2				532	**990**	1814	810	**1490**	2714	1088	**1990**	3614	1366	**2490**	4514	1643	**2990**	5414
						37.8	**100**	212.0										1093	**2000**	3632				1649	**3000**	5432

Interpolation Factors

C		F	C		F
0.56	**1**	1.8	3.33	**6**	10.8
1.11	**2**	3.6	3.89	**7**	12.6
1.67	**3**	5.4	4.44	**8**	14.4
2.22	**4**	7.2	5.00	**9**	16.2
2.78	**5**	9.0	5.56	**10**	18.0

Note. The numbers in boldface type refer to the temperature (in either centigrade or Fahrenheit degrees) which it is desired to convert into the other scale. If converting from Fahrenheit degrees to centigrade degrees the equivalent temperature is in the left column, while if converting from degrees centigrade to degrees Fahrenheit, the equivalent temperature is in the column on the right. This table, made by Professor Albert Sauveur, is published by permission of the heirs and next of kin of Mrs. Albert Sauveur.

† In common usage, "C" in the above table designates "degrees centigrade." In technical usage the designation "degrees celsius" is increasingly used instead. "Centigrade" or "celsius," the heat value and conversion factors remain the same.

Reprinted from Robert H. Perry et al., *Chemical Engineers' Handbook*, McGraw-Hill Book Company, New York.

TABLE 32-8   Viscosity Conversion

(Approximate)

Gardner Holt	Seconds Saybolt Universal	Seconds Saybolt Furol	Engler degrees	Engler time	Barby	Redwood Standard	Approximate seconds No. 4 Ford cup	Centistokes or kinematic viscosity, centipoises with specific gravity of 1
	35		1.2	60	2,800	32		2.6
	50		1.6	82	880	44		7.4
	75		2.3	102	460	65		14.1
	100	15	3.0	153	320	88	10	20.2
	150	19	4.4	230	205	128	12	31.8
A	200	23	5.9	305	148	170	21	43.1
B	250	28	7.6	375	118	212	24	54.3
B	300	33	8.9	450	98	254	27	65.1
C	400	42	11.8	550	72	338	32	87.6
D	500	52	14.5	750	59	423	37	110
E	600	61	17.5	900	48	518	44	132
F	700	71	20.6	1,050	41	592	51	154
G	800	81	23	1,200	36.5	677	54	176
H	900	91	27	1,300	32	762	57	198
J	1,000	100	29	1,500	29.5	846	63	220
M	1,500	150	42	2,300	19.5	1,270	79	330
P	2,000	200	59	3,000	14.5	1,695	95	440
S	2,500	250	73	3,750	11.5	2,120		550
U	3,000	300	87	4,500	9.6	2,540		660
V	4,000	400	117	6,000	7.4	3,380		880
W	5,000	500	145	7,500	6.0	4,230		1,100
X	6,000	600	175	9,000	5.2	5,080		1,320
Y	7,000	700	205	10,500	4.1	5,925		1,540
	8,000	800	230	12,000	3.7	6,770		1,760
	9,000	900	260	13,500	3.2	7,620		1,980
Z-1	10,000	1,000	290	15,000	2.9	8,460		2,200
Z-3	20,000	2,000	590	30,000	1.4	16,920		4,400
Z-5	40,000	4,000	1,170	60,000		33,850		8,800
Z-6	60,000	6,000	1,750	90,000		50,800		13,200
Z-6	80,000	8,000	2,300	120,000		67,700		17,600

TABLE 32-9 Conversion of Volume, Weight, and Energy Units

Multiply by

To convert from	To cu in.	To cu ft	To cu yd	To fl oz	To pt	To qt	To gal	To grain	To oz troy	To oz av	To lb troy	To lb av	To ml or g	To l or kg	To cu m
Cu in.	1.00000	$0_3$5787	$0_4$2143	.554112	.034632	.017316	.004329	252.891	.526857	.578037	.043905	.036127	16.3871	.016387	$0_4$1639
Cu ft	1728.00	1.00000	.037037	957.505	59.8442	29.9221	7.48052	436996	910.408	998.848	75.8674	62.4280	28316.9	23.3169	.028317
Cu yd	46656.0	27.0000	1.00000	25852.6	1615.79	807.896	201.974	117990_3	24581.0	26968.9	2048.42	1685.56	764556	764.556	.764556
Fl oz	1.80469	.001044	$0_4$3868	1.00000	.062500	.031250	.007813	456.390	.950813	1.04318	.079234	.065199	29.5736	.029573	$0_4$2957
Pt	28.8750	.016710	$0_3$6189	16.0000	1.00000	.500000	.125000	7302.23	15.2130	16.6908	1.26775	1.04318	473.177	.473177	$0_4$4732
Qt	57.7500	.033420	.001238	32.0000	2.00000	1.00000	.250000	14604.5	30.4260	33.3816	2.53550	2.08635	946.354	.946354	$0_3$9463
Gal	231.000	.133681	.004951	128.000	8.00000	4.00000	1.00000	58417.9	121.704	133.527	10.1420	8.34541	3785.42	3.78542	.003785
Grain	.003954	$0_5$2288	$0_7$8475	.002191	$0_3$1369	$0_4$6850	$0_3$1712	1.00000	.002083	.002286	$0_3$1736	$0_3$1428	.064799	$0_4$6479	$0_7$6479
Oz troy	1.89805	.001098	$0_4$4068	1.05173	.065733	.032867	.008217	480.000	1.00000	1.09714	.083333	.068571	31.1035	.031104	$0_4$3110
Oz av	1.72999	.001001	$0_4$3708	.958608	.059913	.029957	.007489	437.500	.911457	1.00000	.075955	.062500	28.3495	.028350	$0_4$2835
Lb troy	22.7766	.013181	$0_3$4882	12.6208	.788800	.394400	.098600	5760.00	12.0000	13.1657	1.00000	.822857	373.242	.373242	$0_3$3732
Lb av	27.6799	.016018	$0_3$5933	15.3378	.958611	.479306	.119826	7000.00	14.5833	16.0000	1.21528	1.00000	453.593	.453593	$0_3$4536
Ml or gram	.061024	$0_4$3531	$0_6$1308	.033814	.002113	.001057	$.0_3$2642	15.4323	.032151	.035274	.002679	.002205	1.00000	.001000	.000001
Liter or kg	61.0237	.035315	.001308	33.8140	2.11337	1.05669	.264172	15432.3	32.1507	35.2739	2.67923	2.20462	1000.00	1.00000	.001000
Cu m	61023.7	35.3146	1.30795	33814.0	2113.37	1056.69	264.172	154320_3	32150.7	35273.9	2679.23	2204.62	1000000	1000.00	1.00000

NOTE: The small subnumeral following a zero indicates that the zero is to be taken that number of times; thus, 0.0_1428 is equivalent to 0.0001428.

Values used in constructing table:

1 in. = 2.540001 cm.

∴1 cu in. = 16.387083 ml = 16.387083 g H₂O at 4°C (39°F)

1 lb av = 453.5926 g
∴1 gal = 8.34541 lb
∴1 lb av = 27.679886 cu in. H₂O at 4°C

1 lb av = 7000 grains
∴1 gal = 58417.87 grains
231 cu in. = 1 gal = 3785.4162 g

When volume and weight interconversions are given, water is the medium the calculations are based upon. By the introduction of specific gravity factors the medium can be changed, giving the weight of any volume of any material, etc.

Table continued on next page.

TABLE 32-9 Conversion of Volume, Weight, and Energy Units (Continued)

To convert from	Multiply by										
	To Btu	To pcu	To cal	To ft-lb	To ft-tons	To kg-m	To hp-hr	To kw-hr	To joules	To lb C	To lb H₂O
Btu	1.00000	.555556	.251996	778.000	.389001	107.563	.$0_3$3929	.$0_3$2931	1055.20	.$0_4$6876	.001031
Pcu	1.80000	1.00000	45.3593	1400.40	.700202	193.613	.$0_3$7072	.$0_3$5276	1899.36	.$0_3$1238	.001855
Calories	3.96832	2.20462	1.00000	3091.36	1.54368	426.844	.001559	.001163	4187.37	.$0_3$2729	.004089
Ft-lb	.001285	.$0_3$7141	.$0_3$3239	1.00000	.000500	.138255	.$0_6$5050	.$0_6$3767	1.35625	.$0_7$8840	.$0_5$1325
Ft-tons	2.57069	1.42816	.647804	2000.00	1.00000	276.511	.001010	.$0_3$7535	2712.59	.$0_3$1768	.002649
Kg-m	.009297	.005165	.002343	7.23301	.003617	1.00000	.$0_5$3653	.$0_5$2725	9.81009	.$0_6$6394	.$0_5$9580
Hp-hr	2544.99	141388	641.327	1980000	990.004	273747	1.00000	.746000	2685473	.175044	2.62261
Kwhr	3411.57	1895.32	859.702	2654200	1327.10	366959	1.34041	1.00000	3599889	.234648	3.51562
Joules	.$0_3$9477	.$0_3$5265	.$0_3$2388	.737311	.$0_3$3687	.101937	.$0_6$3724	.$0_6$2778	1.00000	.$0_7$6518	.$0_6$9766
Lb C	14544.0	8080.00	3665.03	1113150$_3$	5657.63	1564396	5.71434	4.26285	153470$_3$	1.00000	14.9876
Lb H₂O	970.400	539.111	244.537	.754971	377.487	104379	.381270	.284424	1023966	.066744	1.00000

"Pcu" refers to the pound-centigrade unit. "Lb C" refers to pounds of carbon oxidized, 100% efficiency, equivalent to the corresponding number of heat units.

"Lb H₂O" refers to the pounds of water evaporated at 100°C, at 100% efficiency.

Extract from *Chemical & Metallurgical Engineering* magazine.

TABLE 32-10 Wire and Sheet-metal Gauges

Values in approximate decimals of an inch
As a number of gauges are in use for various shapes and metals, it is **advisable to state the thickness in thousandths when specifying gauge number.**

Gauge number	American (A.W.G.) or Brown & Sharpe (B. & S.) (for non-ferrous wire and sheet) *	U.S. Steel Wire (Stl. W.G.) or Washburn & Moen or Roebling or Am. Steel & Wire Co. [A. (steel) W.G.] (for steel wire)	Birmingham (B.W.G.) (for steel wire) or Stubs Iron Wire (for iron or brass wire)†	U.S. Standard (for sheet and plate metal, wrought iron)	Standard Birmingham (B.G.) (for sheet and hoop metal)	Imperial Standard Wire Gauge (S.W.G.) (British legal standard)	Gauge number
0000000	. . .	.4900	. . .	.500	.6666	.500	0000000
000000	. . .	.4615	. . .	.469	.6250	.464	000000 *
00000	. . .	.4305	. . .	.438	.5883	.432	00000
0000	.460	.3938	.454	.406	.5416	.400	0000
000	.410	.3625	.425	.375	.5000	.372	000
00	.365	.3310	.380	.344	.4452	.348	00
0	.325	.3065	.340	.312	.3964	.324	0
1	.289	.2830	.300	.281	.3532	.300	1
2	.258	.2625	.284	.266	.3147	.276	2
3	.229	.2437	.259	.250	.2804	.252	3
4	.204	.2253	.238	.234	.2500	.232	4
5	.182	.2070	.220	.219	.2225	.212	5
6	.162	.1920	.203	.203	.1981	.192	6
7	.144	.1770	.180	.188	.1764	.176	7
8	.128	.1620	.165	.172	.1570	.160	8
9	.114	.1483	.148	.156	.1398	.144	9
10	.102	.1350	.134	.141	.1250	.128	10
11	.091	.1205	.120	.125	.1113	.116	11
12	.081	.1055	.109	.109	.0991	.104	12
13	.072	.0915	.095	.094	.0882	.092	13
14	.064	.0800	.083	.078	.0785	.080	14
15	.057	.0720	.072	.070	.0699	.072	15
16	.051	.0625	.065	.062	.0625	.064	16
17	.045	.0540	.058	.056	.0556	.056	17
18	.040	.0475	.049	.050	.0495	.048	18
19	.036	.0410	.042	.0438	.0440	.040	19
20	.032	.0348	.035	.0375	.0392	.036	20
21	.0285	.0317	.032	.0344	.0349	.032	21
22	.0253	.0286	.028	.0312	.0313	.028	22
23	.0226	.0258	.025	.0281	.0278	.024	23
24	.0201	.0230	.022	.0250	.0248	.022	24
25	.0179	.0204	.020	.0219	.0220	.020	25

TABLE 32-10   Wire and Sheet-metal Gauges (*Continued*)

Values in approximate decimals of an inch

As a number of gauges are in use for various shapes and metals, it is **advisable to state the thickness in thousandths when specifying gauge number.**

Gauge number	American (A.W.G.) or Brown & Sharpe (B. & S.) (for nonferrous wire and sheet) *	U.S. Steel Wire (Stl. W.G.) or Washburn & Moen .or Roebling or Am. Steel & Wire Co. [A. (steel) W.G.] (for steel wire)	Birmingham (B.W.G.) (for steel wire) or Stubs Iron Wire (for iron or brass wire)†	U.S. Standard (for sheet and plate metal, wrought iron)	Standard Birmingham (B.G.) (for sheet and hoop metal)	Imperial Standard Wire Gauge (S.W.G.) (British legal standard)	Gauge number
26	.0159	.0181	.018	.0188	.0196	.018	26
27	.0142	.0173	.016	.0172	.0175	.0164	27
28	.0126	.0162	.014	.0156	.0156	.0148	28
29	.0113	.0150	.013	.0141	.0139	.0136	29
30	.0100	.0140	.012	.0125	.0123	.0124	30
31	.0089	.0132	.010	.0109	.0110	.0116	31
32	.0080	.0128	.009	.0102	.0098	.0108	32
33	.0071	.0118	.008	.0094	.0087	.0100	33
34	.0063	.0104	.007	.0086	.0077	.0092	34
35	.0056	.0095	.005	.0078	.0069	.0084	35
36	.0050	.0090	.004	.0070	.0061	.0076	36
37	.0045	.0085	....	.0066	.0054	.0068	37
38	.0040	.0080	....	.0062	.0048	.0060	38
39	.0035	.0075	....	.....	.0043	.0052	39
40	.0031	.0070	....	.....	.0039	.0048	40
41	.....	.0066	....	.....	.0034	.0044	41
42	.....	.0062	....	.....	.0031	.0040	42
43	.....	.0060	....	.....	.0027	.0036	43
44	.....	.0058	....	.....	.0024	.0032	44
45	.....	.0055	....	.....	.0022	.0028	45
46	.....	.0052	....	.....	.0019	.0024	46
47	.....	.0050	....	.....	.0017	.0020	47
48	.....	.0048	....	.....	.0015	.0016	48
49	.....	.0046	....	.....	·.0014	.0012	49
50	.....	.0044	....	.....	.0012	.0010	50

Metric wire gauge is ten times the diameter in millimeters.

* Sometimes used for iron wire.

† Sometimes used for copper plate and for steel plate 12 gauge and heavier and for steel tubes.

From Dr. Lewis V. Judson with I. H. Fullmer, National Bureau of Standards.

Reprinted from Robert H. Perry et al., *Chemical Engineers' Handbook,* McGraw-Hill Book Company, New York.

TABLE 32-11   Building-material Weights

Asbestos: 153–192 lb per cu ft
Brick:
  Common, 2¼ by 4 by 8¼ in., 5.4 lb each; 2.7 tons per thousand (M)
  Fire, standard, 9 by 4½ by 2½ in., 7.0 lb each; 3.5 tons per thousand
  Hard, 2¼ by 4¼ by 8½ in., 6.48 lb each; 3.24 tons per thousand
  Paving, 2¼ by 4 by 8½ in., 6.75 lb each; 3.37 tons per thousand
  Paving block, 3¼ by 4 by 8½ in., 8.75 lb each; 4.37 tons per thousand
  Soft, 2¼ by 4 by 8¼ in., 4.32 lb each; 2.6 tons per thousand
Cement: Bag 94 lb each; barrel weighs 376 lb
Clay:
  Dry, 63–95 lb per cu ft; 1,700–2,295 lb per cu yd
  Fire, 130 lb per cu ft; 3,510 lb per cu yd
  Wet, 120–140 lb per cu ft; 2,970–3,200 lb per cu yd
Concrete:
  Cinder, 112 lb per cu ft
  Gravel and limestone, 150 lb per cu ft
  Reinforced, 150 lb per cu ft
  Slag, 135 lb per cu ft
  Traprock, 155 lb per cu ft
Crushed stone: 100 lb per cu ft; 2,700 lb per cu yd
Gravel: 95 lb per cu ft; 2,565 lb per cu yd
Lime: 75 lb per bushel; 320 lb per large barrel; 220 lb per small barrel; hydrated, approximately 40 lb per cu ft
Mortar: 103 lb per cu ft
Plaster of paris: 98 lb per cu ft
Sand:
  Dry, 97–117 lb per cu ft; 2,619–3,159 lb per cu yd
  Wet, 120–140 lb per cu ft; 3,240–3,780 lb per cu yd
Shingles: A bundle 24 in. long, 20 in. wide, and 10 in. high weighs 50 lb; approximately 250 shingles per bundle
Slag: 67–70 lb per cu ft; 1,755–1,890 lb per cu yd
Stone riprap: 65 lb per cu ft; 1,775 lb per cu yd

MISCELLANEOUS TABLES

TABLE 32-12 Atomic Weights, 1969 (Based on the Assigned Relative Atomic Mass of ^{12}C = 12)

The following values apply to elements as they exist in materials of terrestrial origin and to certain artificial elements. When used with due regard to the footnotes, they are considered reliable to ±1 in the last digit, or ±3 if that digit is in small type.

Element	Atomic weight	Element	Atomic weight	Element	Atomic weight	Element	Atomic weight
Actinium	—	Erbium	167.2_6	Mercury	200.5_9	Samarium	150.4
Aluminum	26.9815[a]	Europium	151.96	Molybdenum	95.9_4	Scandium	44.9559[a]
Americium	—	Fermium	—	Neodymium	144.2_4	Selenium	78.9_6
Antimony	121.7_5	Fluorine	18.9984[a]	Neon	20.17_9[c]	Silicon	28.08_6[d]
Argon	39.94_8[b,c,d,g]	Francium	—	Neptunium	237.0482[b,f]	Silver	107.868[c]
Arsenic	74.9216[a]	Gadolinium	157.2_5	Nickel	58.71	Sodium	22.9898[a]
Astatine	—	Gallium	69.72	Niobium	92.9064[a]	Strontium	87.62[g]
Barium	137.3_4	Germanium	72.5_9	Nitrogen	14.0067[b,c]	Sulphur	32.06[d]
Berkelium	—	Gold	196.9665[a]	Nobelium	—	Tantalum	180.947_9[b]
Beryllium	9.01218[a]	Hafnium	178.4_9	Osmium	190.2	Technetium	98.9062[f]
Bismuth	208.9806[a]	Helium	4.00260[b,c]	Oxygen	15.999_4[b,c,d]	Tellurium	127.6_0
Boron	10.81[c,d,e]	Holmium	164.9303[a]	Palladium	106.4	Terbium	158.9254[a]
Bromine	79.904[c]	Hydrogen	1.008_0[b,d]	Phosphorus	30.9738[a]	Thallium	204.3_7
Cadmium	112.40	Indium	114.82	Platinum	195.0_9	Thorium	232.0381[a,f]
Caesium	132.9055[a]	Iodine	126.9045[a]	Plutonium	—	Thulium	168.9342[a]
Calcium	40.08	Iridium	192.2_2	Polonium	—	Tin	118.6_9
Californium	—	Iron	55.84_7	Potassium	39.10_2	Titanium	47.9_0
Carbon	12.011[b,d]	Krypton	83.80	Praseodymium	140.9077[a]	Tungsten	183.8_5
Cerium	140.12	Lanthanum	138.905_5[b]	Promethium	—	Uranium	238.029[b,c,e]
Chlorine	35.453[c]	Lawrencium	—	Protactinium	231.0359[a,f]	Vanadium	50.941_4[b,c]
Chromium	51.996[a]	Lead	207.2[d,g]	Radium	226.0254[a,f,g]	Xenon	131.30
Cobalt	58.9332[a]	Lithium	6.94_1[c,d,e]	Radon	—	Ytterbium	173.04
Copper	63.54_6[c,d]	Lutetium	174.97	Rhenium	186.2	Yttrium	88.9059[a]
Curium	—	Magnesium	24.305[c]	Rhodium	102.9055[a]	Zinc	65.3_7
Dysprosium	162.5_0	Manganese	54.9380[a]	Rubidium	85.467_8[c]	Zirconium	91.22
Einsteinium	—	Mendelevium	—	Ruthenium	101.0_7		

ᵃ Mononuclidic element.

ᵇ Element with one predominant isotope (about 99 to 100 per cent abundance).

ᶜ Element for which the atomic weight is based on calibrated measurements.

ᵈ Element for which variation in isotopic abundance in terrestrial samples limits the precision of the atomic weight given.

ᵉ Element for which users are cautioned against the possibility of large variations in atomic weight due to inadvertent or undisclosed artificial isotopic separation in commercially available materials.

ᶠ Most commonly available long-lived isotope.

ᵍ In some geological specimens this element has a highly anomalous isotopic composition corresponding to an atomic weight significantly different from that given.

Atomic weights and footnotes above printed by permission of Butterworths, Scientific Publishers Ltd., N. N. Greenwood, Chairman, IUPAC Commission on Atomic Weights.

TABLE 32-13   Discount Computer 1

Discount, per cent	Equivalent	Net	Discount, per cent	Equivalent	Net	Discount, per cent	Equivalent	Net
2½	.025	.975	25	.25	.75	30, 7½, & 7½	.4011	.5989
2½ & 2½	.0494	.9506	25 & 2½	.2688	.7312	30, 7½, & 10	.4173	.5827
2½ & 5	.0737	.9263	25, 2½, & 2½	.2870	.713	30 & 10	.37	.63
2½, 5, & 2½	.0969	.9031	25, 2½, & 5	.3053	.6947	30, 10, & 2½	.3858	.6142
2½, 5, & 5	.1201	.8799	24, 2½, & 7½	.3236	.6764	30, 10, & 5	.4015	.5985
2½, 5, 5, & 2½	.1421	.8579	25, 2½, & 10	.3419	.6581	30, 10, & 7½	.4173	.5827
2½ & 10	.1225	.8775	25 & 5	.2875	.7125	30, 10, & 10	.433	.567
2½, 10, & 2½	.1444	.8556	25, 5, & 2½	.3053	.6947	32½	.325	.675
2½, 10, & 5	.166	.834	25, 5, & 5	.3231	.6769	32½ & 2½	.3419	.6581
2½, 10, 5, & 2½	.1872	.8128	25, 5, & 7½	.3409	.6591	32½, 2½, & 2½	.3583	.6417
2½, 10, & 10	.2102	.7898	25, 5, & 10	.3588	.6412	32½, 2½, & 5	.3748	.6252
5	.05	.95	25 & 7½	.3063	.6937	32½, 2½, & 7½	.3912	.6088
5 & 2½	.0738	.9262	25, 7½, & 2½	.3236	.6764	32½, 2½, & 10	.4077	.5923
5 & 5	.0975	.9025	25, 7½, & 5	.3409	.6591	32½ & 5	.3588	.6412
5, 5, & 2½	.1201	.8799	25, 7½, & 7½	.3583	.6417	32½, 5, & 2½	.3748	.6252
5, 5, & 5	.1426	.8574	25, 7½, & 10	.3756	.6244	32½, 5, & 5	.3908	.6092
5, 5, 5, & 2½	.164	.836	25 & 10	.325	.675	32½, 5, & 7½	.4068	.5932
5 & 10	.145	.855	25, 10, & 2½	.3419	.6581	32½, 5, & 10	.4229	.5771
5, 10, & 2½	.1664	.8336	25, 10, & 5	.3588	.6412	32½ & 7½	.3756	.6244
5, 10, & 5	.1877	.8123	25, 10, & 7½	.3756	.6244	32½, 7½, & 2½	.3912	.6088
5, 10, 5, & 2½	.2081	.7919	25, 10, & 10	.392	.6075	32½, 7½, & 5	.4068	.5932
5, 10, & 10	.2305	.7695	27½	.275	.725	32½, 7½, & 7½	.4225	.5775
10	.10	.90	27½ & 2½	.2931	.7069	32½, 7½, & 10	.4381	.5619
10 & 2½	.1225	.8775	27½, 2½, & 2½	.3108	.6892	32½ & 10	.3925	.6075
10 & 5	.145	.855	27½, 2½, & 5	.3285	.6715	32½, 10, & 2½	.4077	.5923
10, 5, & 2½	.1664	.8336	27½, 2½, & 7½	.3461	.6539	32½, 10, & 5	.4229	.5771
10, 5, & 5	.1878	.8122	27½, 2½, & 10	.3638	.6362	32½, 10, & 7½	.4381	.5619
10, 5, 5, & 2½	.2081	.7919	27½ & 5	.3113	.6887	32½, 10, & 10	.4533	.5467
10 & 10	.190	.81	27½, 5, & 2½	.3285	.6715	32½ & 20	.460	.54
10, 10, & 2½	.2103	.7897	27½, 5, & 5	.3457	.6543	32½, 20, & 2½	.4735	.5625
10, 10, & 5	.2305	.7695	27½, 5, & 7½	.3629	.6371	32½, 20, & 5	.4870	.5130
10, 10, 5, & 2½	.2497	.7503	27½, 5, & 10	.3801	.6199	32½, 20, & 7½	.5005	.4995
10, 10, & 10	.271	.729	27½ & 7½	.3294	.6706	32½, 20, & 10	.514	.486
15	.150	.85	27½, 7½, & 2½	.3461	.6539	32½, 20, & 20	.5680	.4320
15 & 2½	.1713	.8287	27½, 7½, & 5	.3629	.6471	35	.35	.65
15 & 5	.1925	.8075	27½, 7½, & 7½	.3797	.6203	35 & 2½	.3663	.6337
15, 5, & 2½	.2127	.7873	27½, 7½, & 10	.3964	.6036	35, 2½, & 2½	.3821	.6179
15, 5, & 5	.2329	.7671	27½ & 10	.3475	.6525	35, 2½, & 5	.3979	.6021
15, 5, 5, & 2½	.2521	.7479	27½, 10, & 2½	.3638	.6362	35, 2½, & 7½	.4138	.5862
15 & 10	.235	.765	27½, 10, & 5	.3801	.6199	35, 2½, & 10	.4296	.5704
15, 10, & 2½	.2541	.7459	27½, 10, & 7½	.3964	.6036	35 & 5	.3825	.6175
15, 10, & 5	.2733	.7267	27½, 10, & 10	.4128	.5872	35, 5, & 2½	.3979	.6021
15, 10, 5, & 2½	.2914	.7086	30	.30	.70	35, 5, & 5	.4134	.5866
15, 10, & 10	.3115	.6885	30 & 2½	.3175	.6825	35, 5, & 7½	.4288	.5712
20	.20	.80	30, 2½, & 2½	.3346	.6654	35, 5, & 10	.4443	.5557
20 & 2½	.220	.78	30, 2½, & 5	.3516	.6484	35 & 7½	.3988	.6012
20 & 5	.240	.76	30, 2½, & 7½	.3687	.6313	35, 7½, & 2½	.4138	.5862
20, 5, & 2½	.259	.741	30, 2½, & 10	.3858	.6142	35, 7½, & 5	.4288	.5712
20, 5, & 5	.278	.722	30 & 5	.335	.665	35, 7½, & 7½	.4438	.5562
20, 5, 5, & 2½	.2961	.7039	30, 5, & 2½	.3516	.6484	35, 7½, & 10	.4589	.5511
20 & 10	.280	.72	30, 5, & 5	.3683	.6317	35 & 10	.415	.585
20, 10, & 2½	.298	.702	30, 5, & 7½	.3849	.6151	35, 10, & 2½	.4296	.5704
20, 10, & 5	.316	.684	30, 5, & 10	.4015	.5985	35, 10, & 5	.4443	.5557
20, 10, 5, & 2½	.3331	.6669	30 & 7½	.3525	.6475	35, 10, & 7½	.4589	.5411
20, 10, & 10	.352	.648	30, 7½, & 2½	.3687	.6313	35, 10, & 10	.4735	.5265
			30, 7½, & 5	.3849	.6151	35 & 20	.48	.52

TABLE 32-13 Discount Computer 1 (Continued)

Discount, per cent	Equiv-alent	Net	Discount, per cent	Equiv-alent	Net	Discount, per cent	Equiv-alent	Net
35, 20, & 2½	.493	.507	40, 20, & 7½	.556	.444	45, 20, & 20	.648	.352
35, 20, & 5	.5060	.4940	40, 20, & 10	.568	.432	47½	.475	.525
35, 20, & 7½	.4190	.5810	40, 20, & 20	.616	.384	47½ & 2½	.4881	.5119
35, 20, & 10	.3520	.6480	42½	.425	.575	47½, 2½, & 2½	.5009	.4991
35, 20, & 20	.5840	.4160	42½ & 2½	.4394	.5606	47½, 2½, & 5	.5237	.4863
37½	.375	.625	42½, 2½, & 2½	.4534	.5466	47½, 2½, & 7½	.5265	.4735
37½ & 2½	.3906	.6094	42½, 2½, & 5	.4674	.5326	47½, 2½, & 10	.5393	.4607
37½, 2½, & 2½	.4059	.5941	42½, 2½, & 7½	.4814	.5186	47½ & 5	.5013	.4987
37½, 2½, & 5	.4211	.5789	42½, 2½, & 10	.4954	.5046	47½, 5, & 2½	.5137	.4863
37½, 2½, & 7½	.4363	.5637	42½ & 5	.4538	.5462	47½, 5, & 5	.5262	.4738
37½, 2½, & 10	.4516	.5484	42½, 5, & 2½	.4674	.5326	47½, 5, & 7½	.5386	.4614
37½ & 5	.4063	.5937	42½, 5, & 5	.4811	.5189	47½, 5, & 10	.5511	.4489
37½, 5, & 2½	.4211	.5789	42½, 5, & 7½	.4947	.5053	47½ & 7½	.5144	.4856
37½, 5, & 5	.4359	.5641	42½, 5, & 10	.5084	.4916	47½, 7½, & 2½	.5265	.4735
37½, 5, & 7½	.4508	.5492	42½ & 7½	.4681	.5319	47½, 7½, & 5	.5387	.4613
37½, 5, & 10	.4656	.5344	42½, 7½, & 2½	.4814	.5186	47½, 7½, & 7½	.5508	.4492
37½ & 7½	.4219	.5781	42½, 7½, & 5	.4947	.5053	47½, 7½, & 10	.5629	.4371
37½, 7½, & 2½	.4363	.5637	42½, 7½, & 7½	.508	.492	47½ & 10	.5275	.4725
37½, 7½, & 5	.4508	.5492	42½, 7½, & 10	.5213	.4787	47½, 10, & 2½	.5393	.4607
37½, 7½, & 7½	.4652	.5348	42½ & 10	.4825	.5175	47½, 10, & 5	.5511	.4489
37½, 7½, & 10	.4797	.5203	42½, 10, & 2½	.4954	.5046	47½, 10, & 7½	.5629	.4371
37½ & 10	.4375	.5625	42½, 10, & 5	.5084	.4916	47½, 10, & 10	.5748	.4252
37½, 10, & 2½	.4516	.5484	42½, 10, & 7½	.5213	.4787	47½ & 20	.58	.42
37½, 10, & 5	.4656	.5344	42½, 10, & 10	.5343	.4657	47½, 20, & 2½	.5905	.4095
37½, 10, & 7½	.4797	.5203	42½ & 20	.54	.46	47½, 20, & 5	.601	.399
37½, 10, & 10	.4938	.5062	42½, 20, & 2½	.5515	.4485	47½, 20, & 7½	.6115	.3885
37½ & 20	.50	.50	42½, 20, & 5	.563	.437	47½, 20, & 10	.622	.378
37½, 20, & 2½	.5125	.4875	42½, 20, & 7½	.5745	.4255	47½, 20, & 20	.664	.336
37½, 20, & 5	.5250	.4750	42½, 20, & 10	.586	.414	50	.50	.50
37½, 20, & 7½	.5375	.4625	42½, 20, & 20	.632	.368	50 & 2½	.5125	.4875
37½, 20, & 10	.55	.45	45	.45	.55	50, 2½, & 2½	.5247	.4753
37½, 20, & 20	.60	.40	45 & 2½	.4638	.5362	50, 2½, & 5	.5369	.4631
40	.40	.60	45, 2½, & 2½	.4772	.5228	50, 2½, & 7½	.5491	.4509
40 & 2½	.415	.585	45, 2½, & 5	.4906	.5094	50, 2½, & 10	.5613	.4387
40, 2½, & 2½	.4296	.5704	45, 2½, & 7½	.504	.496	50 & 5	.515	.475
40, 2½, & 5	.4443	.5557	45, 2½, & 10	.5174	.4826	50, 5, & 2½	.5369	.4631
40, 2½, & 7½	.4589	.5411	45 & 5	.4775	.5225	50, 5, & 5	.5488	.4512
40, 2½, & 10	.4735	.5265	45, 5, & 2½	.4906	.5094	50, 5, & 7½	.5606	.4394
40 & 5	.43	.57	45, 5, & 5	.5036	.4964	50, 5, & 10	.5725	.4275
40, 5, & 2½	.4443	.5557	45, 5, & 7½	.5167	.4833	50 & 7½	.5375	.4625
40, 5, & 5	.4585	.5415	45, 5, & 10	.5298	.4702	50, 7½, & 2½	.5491	.4509
40, 5, & 7½	.4728	.5272	45 & 7½	.4913	.5087	50, 7½, & 5	.5606	.4394
40, 5, & 10	.487	.513	45, 7½, & 2½	.504	.496	50, 7½, & 7½	.5722	.4278
40 & 7½	.445	.555	45, 7½, & 5	.5167	.4833	50, 7½, & 10	.5838	.4162
40, 7½, & 2½	.4589	.5411	45, 7½, & 7½	.5294	.4706	50 & 10	.55	.45
40, 7½, & 5	.4728	.5272	45, 7½, & 10	.5421	.4579	50, 10, & 2½	.5613	.4387
40, 7½, & 7½	.4866	.5134	45 & 10	.505	.495	50, 10, & 5	.5725	.4275
40, 7½, & 10	.5005	.4995	45, 10, & 2½	.5174	.4826	50, 10, & 7½	.5838	.4162
40 & 10	.46	.54	45, 10, & 5	.5298	.4702	50, 10, & 10	.595	.405
40, 10, & 2½	.4735	.5265	45, 10, & 7½	.5421	.4579	50 & 20	.60	.40
40, 10, & 5	.487	.513	45, 10, & 10	.5545	.4455	50, 20, & 2½	.61	.39
40, 10, & 7½	.5005	.4995	45 & 20	.56	.44	50, 20, & 5	.62	.38
40, 10, & 10	.514	.486	45, 20, & 2½	.571	.429	50, 20, & 7½	.63	.37
40 & 20	.52	.48	45, 20, & 5	.582	.418	50, 20, & 10	.64	.36
40, 20, & 2½	.532	.468	45, 20, & 7½	.593	.407	50, 20, & 20	.68	.32
40, 20, & 5	.544	.456	45, 20, & 10	.604	.396	52½	.525	.475

Reprinted with permission from the "Personal Record Book for Executives," published by the Dartnell Corporation, Chicago.

TABLE 32-14 Discount Computer 2

To find a net price, multiply list price by the decimal net equivalent of the given discount.
Example. What will be the net price if a discount of 40–10–10–5 is allowed on a list price of $65?
Solution. In the column for Leading Discount 40, and in the horizontal line for Supplementary Discount 10–10–5 at the left, find the decimal net equivalent .4617. Then $65 by .4617 equals $30.01, the net price.

Discount	Leading discount										
	10	20	25	30	33⅓	40	50	60	66⅔	75	80
	Decimal net equivalent										
2½	.8775	.7800	.7313	.6825	.6500	.5850	.4875	.3900	.325	.2438	.1950
5	.8550	.7600	.7125	.6650	.6333	.5700	.4750	.3800	.3167	.2375	.1900
5–2½	.8336	.7410	.6947	.6484	.6175	.5558	.4631	.3705	.3087	.2316	.1853
5–5	.8123	.7220	.6769	.6318	.6017	.5415	.4513	.3610	.3008	.2256	.1805
10	.8100	.7200	.6750	.6300	.6000	.5400	.4500	.3600	.3000	.2250	.1800
10–2½	.7898	.7020	.6581	.6143	.5850	.5265	.4388	.3510	.2925	.2194	.1755
10–5	.7695	.6840	.6413	.5985	.5700	.5130	.4275	.3420	.2850	.2138	.1710
10–5–2½	.7503	.6669	.6252	.5835	.5558	.5002	.4168	.3334	.2779	.2084	.1667
10–10	.7290	.6480	.6075	.5670	.5400	.4860	.4050	.3240	.2700	.2025	.1620
10–10–5	.6925	.6156	.5771	.5387	.5130	.4617	.3848	.3078	.2565	.1924	.1539
10–10–5–2½	.6752	.6002	.5627	.5252	.5002	.4502	.3752	.3001	.2501	.1876	.1501
10–10–10	.6561	.5832	.5468	.5103	.4860	.4374	.3645	.2916	.2430	.1823	.1458
10–10–10–10	.5905	.5249	.4921	.4593	.4374	.3937	.3281	.2624	.2187	.1640	.1312
10–10–10–10–5	.5610	.4987	.4675	.4363	.4155	.3740	.3116	.2493	.2078	.1558	.1246
15	.7650	.6800	.6375	.5950	.5667	.5100	.4250	.3400	.2833	.2125	.1700
15–2½	.7459	.6630	.6216	.5801	.5525	.4973	.4144	.3315	.2762	.2072	.1658
15–5	.7268	.6460	.6056	.5653	.5383	.4845	.4038	.3230	.2692	.2019	.1615
15–10	.6885	.6120	.5738	.5355	.5100	.4590	.3825	.3060	.2550	.1913	.1530
20	.7200	.6400	.6000	.5600	.5333	.4800	.4000	.3200	.2667	.2000	.1600
20–5	.6840	.6080	.5700	.5320	.5067	.4560	.3800	.3040	.2533	.1900	.1520
20–10	.6480	.5760	.5400	.5040	.4800	.4320	.3600	.2880	.2400	.1800	.1440
20–10–5	.6156	.5472	.5130	.4788	.4560	.4104	.3420	2736	.2280	.1710	.1368
25	.6750	.6000	.5625	.5250	.5000	.4500	.3750	.3000	.2500	.1875	.1500
25–5	.6413	.5700	.5344	.4987	.4750	.4275	.3563	.2850	.2375	.1781	.1425
25–10	.6075	.5400	.5063	.4725	.4500	.4050	.3375	.2700	.2250	.1688	.1350
25–10–5	.5771	.5130	.4809	.4489	.4275	.3848	.3206	.2565	.2137	.1603	.1283

Reprinted by permission of the *New England Purchaser* magazine, Boston, Mass.

TABLE 32-15 Greek Alphabet

Alpha	= A, α = A, a		Nu	= N, ν = N, n
Beta	= B, β = B, b		Xi	= Ξ, ξ = X, x
Gamma	= Γ, γ = G, g		Omicron	= O, o = O, o
Delta	= Δ, δ = D, d		Pi	= Π, π = P, p
Epsilon	= E, ε = E, e		Rho	= P, ρ = R, r
Zeta	= Z, ζ = Z, z		Sigma	= Σ, σ = S, s
Eta	= H, η = E, e		Tau	= T, τ = T, t
Theta	= Θ, θ = Th, th		Upsilon	= Υ, υ = U, u
Iota	= I, ι = I, i		Phi	= Φ, φ = Ph, ph
Kappa	= K, κ = K, k		Chi	= X, χ = Ch, ch
Lambda	= Λ, λ = L, l		Psi	= Ψ, ψ = Ps, ps
Mu	= M, μ = M, m		Omega	= Ω, ω = O, o

TABLE 32-16 Roman Numerals

I = 1	L = 50
II = 2	C = 100
III = 3	D = 500
V = 5	M = 1000
X = 10	

Other numbers are created by various combinations of the above nine symbols. If a symbol of smaller value is placed before a symbol of larger value, it is counted negatively to determine the total value of the combination, e.g., IX = 9.

TABLE 32-17 Profits and Markups

Cost per dozen	Each	Profit per cent on selling price							
		20%	23.10%	25%	28.57%	33⅓%	37½%	42.86%	50%
$ 0.12	$0.01	0.013	0.013	.013	0.014	.015	0.016	0.018	0.02
0.15	0.013	0.015	0.016	.016	0.017	.019	0.02	0.022	0.025
0.20	0.017	0.021	0.022	.022	0.023	.025	0.027	0.029	0.033
0.24	0.02	0.025	0.026	.027	0.028	.03	0.032	0.035	0.04
0.25	0.021	0.026	0.027	.028	0.029	.031	0.033	0.037	0.042
0.30	0.025	0.031	0.033	.033	0.035	.038	0.04	0.044	0.05
0.35	0.030	0.037	0.038	.039	0.041	.044	0.047	0.051	0.058
0.36	0.03	0.038	0.039	.04	0.042	.045	0.048	0.053	0.06
0.40	0.033	0.042	0.043	.044	0.047	.05	0.053	0.058	0.067
0.45	0.038	0.047	0.049	.05	0.053	.056	0.06	0.066	0.075
0.48	0.04	0.05	0.052	.053	0.056	.06	0.064	0.07	0.08
0.50	0.042	0.053	0.055	.056	0.059	.063	0.067	0.074	0.084
0.60	0.05	0.063	0.065	.067	0.07	.075	0.08	0.088	0.10
0.72	0.06	0.075	0.078	.08	0.084	.09	0.096	0.105	0.12
0.75	0.063	0.078	0.081	.083	0.088	.094	0.10	0.11	0.125
0.84	0.07	0.088	0.091	.093	0.098	.105	0.112	0.123	0.14
0.96	0.08	0.10	0.101	.107	0.112	.12	0.128	0.14	0.16
1.00	0.083	0.104	0.108	.111	0.116	.125	0.133	0.145	0.166
1.20	0.10	0.125	0.13	.133	0.14	.15	0.16	0.175	0.20
1.25	0.104	0.13	0.135	.139	0.146	.156	0.166	0.182	0.208
1.50	0.125	0.156	0.163	.167	0.175	.188	0.20	0.219	0.25
1.75	0.146	0.183	0.19	.195	0.204	.219	0.234	0.256	0.292
2.00	0.167	0.209	0.217	.223	0.234	.251	0.267	0.292	0.334
2.25	0.188	0.235	0.244	.251	0.263	.282	0.30	0.329	0.376
2.50	0.208	0.26	0.27	.277	0.291	.312	0.333	0.364	0.416
2.75	0.229	0.286	0.298	.305	0.321	.344	0.366	0.40	0.458

TABLE 32-17   Profits and Markups (Continued)

Cost per dozen	Each	Profit per cent on selling price							
		20%	23.10%	25%	28.57%	33⅓%	37½%	42.86%	50%
$ 3.00	$0.25	0.312	0.325	.333	·0.35	.375	0.40	0.437	0.50
3.25	0.27	0.337	0.351	.36	0.378	.405	0.432	0.473	0.54
3.75	0.312	0.39	0.406	.416	0.437	.468	0.499	0.546	0.624
4.00	0.333	0.416	0.433	.444	0.466	.50	0.533	0.583	0.666
4.25	0.354	0.443	0.460	.472	0.496	.531	0.566	0.62	0.708
4.50	0.375	0.469	0.488	.50	0.525	.563	0.60	0.656	0.75
5.00	0.417	0.524	0.542	.556	0.584	.626	0.667	0.73	0.834
6.00	0.50	0.625	0.65	.667	0.70	.75	0.80	0.875	1.00
6.50	0.541	0.676	0.703	.721	0.757	.812	0.866	0.947	1.08
6.75	0.562	0.703	0.731	.749	0.787	.843	0.899	0.984	1.12
7.00	0.583	0.729	0.758	.777	0.816	.875	0.933	1.02	1.17
7.25	0.604	0.755	0.785	.805	0.846	.906	0.956	1.06	1.21
7.50	0.625	0.781	0.813	.833	0.875	.938	1.00	1.09	1.25
8.00	0.666	0.833	0.866	.888	0.932	.999	1.07	1.17	1.33
8.50	0.708	0.885	0.92	.944	0.991	1.06	1.13	1.24	1.41
9.00	0.75	0.938	0.975	1.00	1.05	1.13	1.20	1.31	1.50
10.50	0.88	1.09	1.14	1.17	1.23	1.31	1.40	1.53	1.75
12.00	1.00	1.25	1.30	1.33	1.40	1.50	1.60	1.75	2.00
13.50	1.13	1.41	1.46	1.50	1.58	1.69	1.80	1.97	2.25
15.00	1.25	1.56	1.63	1.66	1.75	1.88	2.00	2.19	2.50
16.50	1.38	1.72	1.79	1.83	1.93	2.06	2.20	2.41	2.75
18.00	1.50	1.87	1.95	2.00	2.18	2.25	2.40	2.63	3.00
19.50	1.63	2.04	2.12	2.17	2.28	2.45	2.61	2.85	3.26
21.00	1.75	2.19	2.28	2.33	2.45	2.63	2.80	3.06	3.50
22.50	1.88	2.34	2.44	2.50	2.63	2.81	3.00	3.28	3.75
24.00	2.00	2.50	2.60	2.67	2.80	3.00	3.20	3.50	4.00
27.00	2.25	2.81	2.93	3.00	3.15	3.38	3.60	3.96	4.50
30.00	2.50	3.12	3.25	3.33	3.50	3.75	4.00	4.38	5.00
33.00	2.75	3.44	3.58	3.67	3.85	4.13	4.40	4.81	5.50
36.00	3.00	3.75	3.90	4.00	4.20	4.50	4.80	5.25	6.00
39.00	3.25	4.06	4.23	4.33	4.55	4.88	5.20	5.69	6.50
42.00	3.50	4.37	4.55	4.67	4.90	5.25	5.60	6.12	7.00
45.00	3.75	4.69	4.88	5.00	5.25	5.63	6.00	6.56	7.50
48.00	4.00	5.00	5.20	5.33	5.60	6.00	6.40	7.00	8.00
54.00	4.50	5.62	5.85	6.00	6.30	6.75	7.20	7.87	9.00
60.00	5.00	6.25	6.50	6.67	7.00	7.50	8.00	8.75	10.00
66.00	5.50	6.87	7.15	7.33	7.70	8.25	8.80	9.62	11.00
69.00	5.75	7.19	7.48	7.67	8.05	8.63	9.20	10.06	11.50
72.00	6.00	7.50	7.80	8.00	8.40	9.00	9.60	10.50	12.00
Per dozen	Each	25%	30%	33⅓%	40%	50%	60%	75%	100%
		Profit per cent on cost							

Reprinted by permission from the "Personal Record Book for Executives," published by the Dartnell Corporation, Chicago.

GENERAL INFORMATION

TABLE 32-18   Geometric Formulas

Area of a circle = half diameter × half circumference
Area of a circle = square of diameter × 0.7854
Area of a circle = square of circumference × 0.07958
Area of a sector of circle = length of arc × one-half radius
Area of a segment of circle = area of sector of equal radius minus area of triangle, when the segment is less, and plus area of triangle, when segment is greater than the semicircle
Area of ellipse = product of the two diameters × 0.7854
Area of a parabola = base × two-thirds of the altitude
Area of parallelogram = base × altitude
Area of a regular polygon = sum of its sides × perpendicular from its center to one of its sides divided by 2
Area of a rectangle = length × breadth or height
Area of circular ring = sum of the diameter of the two circles × difference of the diameter of the two circles and that product × 0.7854
Area of a square = length × breadth or height
Area of trapezium = divide into two triangles, total their areas
Area of trapezoid = altitude × one-half of the sum of parallel sides
Area of a triangle = base × one-half of the altitude
Circumference of circle = diameter × 3.1416
Circumference of circle = radius × 6.283185
Circumference of sphere = square root of surface × 1.772454
Circumference of sphere = cube root of solidity × 3.8978
Contents of pyramid or cone = area of base × one-third of the altitude
Contents of frustum of pyramid or cone = sum of circumference at both ends × one-half of the slant height plus area of both ends
Contents of frustum of pyramid or cone = multiply areas of two ends together and extract square root; add to this root the two areas and × one-third of the altitude
Contents of a sphere = diameter × 0.5236
Contents of segment of sphere = (height squared plus three times the square of radius of base) × (height × 0.5236)
Contents of a wedge = area of base × one-half of the altitude
Diameter of circle = circumference × 0.3183
Diameter of circle = square root of area × 1.12838
Diameter of circle that shall contain area of a given square = side of square × 1.1284
Diameter of sphere = cube root of solidity × 1.2407
Diameter of sphere = square root of surface × 0.56419
Radius of a circle = circumference × 0.0159155
Side of inscribed cube of sphere = radius × 1.1547
Side of inscribed cube of sphere = square root of diameter
Side of inscribed square = diameter × 0.7071
Side of inscribed square = circumference × 0.225
Side of square that shall equal area of circle = diameter × 0.8862
Side of square that shall equal area of circle = circumference × 0.2821
Side of inscribed equilateral triangle = diameter × 0.86
Surface of cylinder or prism = area of both ends plus length and × circumference
Surface of pyramid or cone = circumference of base × one-half of the slant height plus area of base
Surface of sphere = diameter × circumference
Volume of sphere = surface × one-sixth of the diameter
Volume of sphere = cube of diameter × 0.5236
Volume of sphere = cube of radius × 4.1888
Volume of sphere = cube of circumference × 0.016887

TABLE 32-19   How to Analyze Operating Statements and Inventory Figures

Use Ratio Analysis to Gauge Over-All Strength

A sample balance sheet and income statements (sometimes referred to as a "profit and loss statement") are given below. They are oversimplified—with many key items omitted—to emphasize some of the more commonly used financial yardsticks for evaluating vendors.

XYZ Corporation Balance Sheet
on December 31, 1973 (Millions of $)

ITEM	ASSETS		ITEM	LIABILITIES	
	Current Assets			*Current Liabilities*	
A	Cash	$ 6	J	Accounts Payable	$ 5
B	Government Securities	5	K	Accrued Taxes	3
C	Accounts Receivable	4	L	Accrued Wages & Int.	2
D	Inventories	6	M	Total Current	$10
E	Total Current	$21			
	Fixed Assets		N	*Long-term Bonds*	15
F	Building & Eqpt.	$79		*Stockholders' Equity*	
G	Less Accumulated		O	Preferred Stock	12
	Depreciation	20	P	Common Stock	28
H	Net Fixed Assets	$59	Q	Surplus	15
I	*Total Assets*	$80	R	*Total Liab. & Equity*	$80

XYZ Corporation Income Statement
Year Ended December 31, 1973

ITEM		(MIL OF $)
S	Sales	$21
T	Less Cost of Goods Sold	$15
U	Gross Profit	$ 6
V	Less Administrative & Selling Expenses	$ 1
W	Less Depreciation	$ 1
X	Less Interest Charges	$ 1
Y	Net Profit (Before Taxes)	$ 3
Z	Less Income Taxes	$ 1.5
AA	Net Profit (After Taxes)	$ 1.5

The balance sheet presented above gives the condition of the XYZ Corp. as it existed on December 31, 1973. It is not a history of a year's operations, but rather a "snapshot" of the firm on that day. The accompanying income statement gives a summary of how the company operated over the entire year ending December 31, 1973.

All the yardsticks given immediately below can be derived from the figures appearing in these two simple financial statements:

• *Current ratio* (E/M)—This is a commonly used measure which indicates a firm's liquidity (ability to meet current obligations). Defined as the ratio of current assets to current liabilities, it can be obtained by comparing item E to item M in the balance sheet. That would be $21 million compared to $10 million for a ratio of 2.1:1.

Since a figure of 2:1 is generally considered satisfactory, there seems to be nothing to worry about on this score. A firm with a less than 1:1 ratio has a real problem, according to the experts.

• *Quick ratio* $\left(\dfrac{A + B + C}{M} \right)$ —This is another liquidity measure. It is defined as the total of cash, current investments, and accounts receivable to total current liabilities. Inventories are eliminated in the asset section because they cannot usually be converted into cash as quickly as accounts receivable or government securities. For the XYZ Corp., that ratio is determined by adding items A, B, and C and comparing them to item M. That is $15 million compared to $10 million—or a ratio of 1.5:1. A 1:1 ratio is generally considered normal, so that XYZ Corp. also passes this test.

• *Sales-receivable ratio* (S/C)—A comparison of these items aims to show whether customers are paying their bills on time. In the above example, sales are $21 million (item S from the income statement). Assuming terms of net 90 days for the industry, you would not want much more than $5¼ million (the equivalent of 90 days' sales) in receivables. If receivables were more, it might indicate slow payment, difficulties in collection, and a general "aging" of debt. Since the XYZ Corp. has only $4 million in accounts receivable, the firm is again in pretty good shape.

• *Cash flow* (W + AA)—This represents the sum of net income (after taxes) plus depreciation, or how much money is coming in. In many cases, this is as important as the simple profit figures. Reason: With new accelerated depreciation, a reduction in profit figures is often offset by additional cash inflows resulting from lower income taxes. For the mythical XYZ Corp., cash flow consists of item W and AA, or $1 million plus $1.5 million or $2.5 million.

• *Margins* (U/S & Y/S)—A study of gross and net profits (before taxes) relative to sales also provides a lot of interesting information about the vendor. Profits are the lifeblood of the firm, and if they are down, it may spell trouble. A look at profits also gives some guidelines for price negotiations. If a vendor's profits are above the industry average, some questioning on his listed prices might be in order.

Also of particular interest as far as prices are concerned is the gap between gross profit and net profit. This gives information on operating expenses—a factor which often weighs heavily in vendor pricing decisions. In the case of the XYZ Corp., gross profit margin (item U divided by item S or 6/21) comes out to 28.6%. The net profit margin before taxes (item Y divided by item S or 3/21) comes out 14.5%. That is a gap of more than 14%—though, of course, whether it is too large or too small again depends upon the industry. If, for example, the gap is much larger than the industry average, it could mean vendor is padding his payroll or else he might have a relatively inefficient administrative and sales setup.

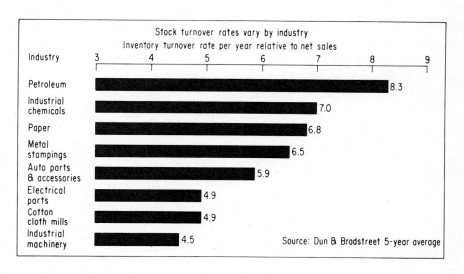

• *Inventory turnover* (T/D)—This figure (cost of goods sold divided by inventories) is designed to show how successful the vendor has been in controlling total inventories. It also can give some hints on the quality of inventories. Thus, if the ratio is relatively low, it could mean that the firm has a lot of obsolete materials or unsalable finished goods on hand—and hence may be in some sort of trouble. It follows then that a high turnover rate is always preferable to a lower one.

But since these figures vary sharply by industry (see chart below), no rule of thumb can be given on what constitutes a high or low rate. Generally speaking, a firm's turnover rate must be compared to that of its industry. In the case of our own XYZ Co., the ratio T over D comes out $15/$6, which boils down to a turnover rate of 2½ times a year.

Review Inventory Methods for Price Strategy

Inventories constitute one of the most important items in financial statements. Considerable emphasis is put on this area by top analysts and accountants because:

• Material costs almost always add up to a large—sometimes the largest—expense item on the income statement.
• Inventories are usually a substantial part of the net assets of a company—and hence figure importantly in any liquidity evaluation.
• Inventories can, and usually are, evaluated in many different ways. For example, whether a firm uses LIFO, FIFO, average costs, etc., can make a big difference in the inventory figures and a firm's over-all profit position.

The whole question of inventory valuation can be illustrated by a simple example. Here is how a merchandising firm (no labor or fabricating expense needed to convert from purchases to sales) might show up, using the three major types of inventory accounting:

Assume the following: The firm has no stocks at the beginning of the year but makes purchases of 50 units at $1 each in January, and another purchase of 50 units at $1.50 each later on in the year. In other words, the actual cost of the year's purchases comes to $125. Further assume that 50 units are sold during the year at $3 each—for a sales volume of $150.

Note from the table below that under FIFO you would charge out as cost the price of the first 50 items purchased (line 3). In this case, it would be 50 units at $1 or a total cost of $50 for the 50 items sold.

Under the LIFO technique you would charge off as cost the price of the last 50 inventory items purchased. In this case, it would be $1.50 per unit or a total cost of $75 for the 50 items sold.

Under the average cost method, divide the 100 units purchased during the year into the total purchase cost ($125) and you come up with $1.25 per unit cost or a total cost of $62.50 for the 50 units sold.

Comparison of Inventory Methods*

	FIFO	LIFO	Avg. cost
(1) Purchases During year	125	125	125
(2) Sales	150	150	150
(3) Cost of Sales	50	75	62.50
(4) Gross Profit [(2)–(3)]	100	75	87.50
(5) Inv. End of Year [(1)–(3)]	75	50	62.50

* Under any of the above methods it is still possible for the current market value to be below the resulting inventory value. If such is the case, inventories are written down to market value to conform to "the lower of cost or market" rule. This is used to prevent overvaluation of inventories on financial statements.

Note that LIFO shows the smallest end-of-year inventory (line 5) and the smallest profit (line 4). This is always the case in times of rising prices, as assumed in the above example. Under such conditions, LIFO generally has inventories which are valued at less than their current market value.

Many companies prefer this method during periods of rising prices because the resulting lower profits mean lower taxes. Therefore over the past decade when prices were generally rising, it is no surprise that many firms switched to this method of valuing inventories. But the government will not allow you to switch back.

Evaluation Guides

There are many other yardsticks used in financial analysis, but they are mostly concerned with evaluation for investment purposes and not for review of a supplier. For a good summary of these measures, get *Understanding Financial Statements*, available free from the New York Stock Exchange, New York City. Another valuable aid is Dun & Bradstreet's pamphlet, *Key Business Ratios in 185 Lines*, which gives typical industry averages for 11 key performance ratios. Single copies are available from D & B, 99 Church Street, New York 10007.

1. How to Get Important Price, Inventory Clues

A close look at financial statements can give some pretty knowledgeable hints on:

• Prices—A low rate of profit in a firm relative to the industry, for example, reveals that costs are too high, or selling prices too low, plant outdated or inefficiently run. In either case, it is possible that prices may be subject to some upward pressures. On the other hand, if the firm's low profit is caused by inadequate volume, it may be willing to negotiate a lower price to build sales.

Conversely, a too-high rate of profit also has some important price implications. It may give the buyer leverage in negotiation. It can possibly be used to put the supplier on the defensive—in that he might be asked to justify the price he is quoting. This may be possible if your requirements are a substantial part of the firm's capacity. You can get an idea of this from the statements, too.

• Inventories—The size of vendor's inventories relative to sales also can give some pretty important clues. For example, a slow inventory turnover rate relative to others in the same industry might indicate that a vendor is overstocked and hence vulnerable to P.A. bargaining pressure.

The inventory figures for companies with few product lines also can give some clues as to how fast the P.A. can get delivery in a pinch. If figures are broken down into raw materials, goods in process, and finished goods, the P.A. may get some idea of any inventory imbalance and distress merchandise on supplier shelves.

How inventories are valued is also an important consideration. Whether last in, first out (LIFO), first in, first out (FIFO), or average cost methods are used can make a big difference in inventories, cost of goods sold, and profits.

• Reliability—The financial condition of a vendor affects quality, delivery, and (as noted above) prices. The solvent firm is more likely to meet its contractual obligations than the firm that is bordering on the brink of bankruptcy. A vendor that is one step ahead of the bill collector is more likely to cut corners on quality, figuring that only by squeezing nickels and dimes can he stay in business. Put another way, it is the creditors rather than the buyers who must get top priority.

2. Where to Go for Information and Comparisons

There are certain standard ways of going about obtaining information on a vendor's financial status: Generally speaking, data for a listed company (a company whose stock appears on the New York or American Stock Exchange) are easiest to obtain. All that is required is a note to the treasurer of the vendor asking for the latest copies of company's financial statements.

For unlisted companies, proprietorships, or family-owned businesses, the situation is more difficult. In some cases, writing to the treasurer of the company might get results. Often, however, these "unlisted" vendors are under no obligation to send this information out and might refuse to do so.

If you do not meet with success, a check with Dun and Bradstreet's credit reporting service might be in order. But this is generally less satisfactory than receiving audited financial statements. That is because the information given to credit rating services comes directly from the corporation—without any audit.

Another information source is the local bank used by the vendor. Since almost all firms need and use credit, the bank that the vendor does business with usually knows a good deal about the firm's financial status. And, generally speaking, they are willing to cooperate. Check directly or through your company's bank.

Finally, there is the time-tested technique of comparing notes with other P.A.'s. While this is the weakest method of all, it is better than none, because chances are if the vendor has performed well before, he will do so again.

For more general information—about an over-all industry—there are several other sources available. Trade associations, for example, very often collect data on sales, costs, and profits of all reporting members. Government sources include the Securities & Exchange Commission and Federal Trade Commission, which put out quarterly financial reports for major manufacturing industries. They are composite financial statements giving assets, liabilities, sales, and profit margins for some 25 industries.

3. But Watch Out for Misleading Conclusions

In any evaluation of financial statements, there are several pitfalls to be avoided. Generally, it is important to check for:

• Reliability—one major question all analysts ask: Are the reports audited by an accredited accounting firm? Generally speaking, an audited report puts the reputation of the accountant behind the statement. It is not likely that these auditors would jeopardize their whole practice to cover up for just one firm. It is a pretty good rule to accept an audited report rather than one that has not been audited.

• Comparability—Do not automatically put one firm's inventory or profit figures up against another's. For individual companies often have different methods of valuing inventories, taking depreciation, etc. And differences here lead to differences in profits and profit margins. The thing to remember: Check the specific accounting methods which underlie each figure in the balance sheet and income statement and read the footnotes to statements.

• Industry differences—Do not compare profit margins blindly. Each industry has its own norm, and it is usually much more important to check against the industry average than any national average.

• Short-run problems—Often a strike or other unusual event can distort operating results because what happened in that year is not a typical occurrence.

Most analysts, however, prefer to look over a firm's history for several years. For in addition to washing out "one-shot" affairs, it helps give a clearer picture of the trend over time—and therefore the basic health of a particular firm.

TABLE 32-20A   Discounted Cash-flow Factors

Time Value of Money. Purchasing decisions often require that the time value of money be considered. By "time value" we mean, for example, that a dollar received today is more valuable than a dollar due one year hence because interest can be earned during the one-year interval. How much interest can be earned? For purchasing decisions in a specific company, the company's rate of return on invested capital is a good guideline. Solving problems involving the time value of money can be facilitated by using Tables 32-20B and 32-20C. These tables list discount factors to apply against cash flows which commute their value to a common reference time—the present. Table A provides factors which can be applied to cash flows which occur instantaneously at some point in time. Table B provides factors which can be applied to cash flows which occur uniformly over a period of time.

Specific Problems. The use of the tables may be illustrated by the following two specific problems:

1. Is it better to pay $250 installed for a higher-quality item with 20 years' life (alternative A) or to replace the item every 5 years with lower-quality merchandise costing $100 installed (alternative B)? All costs are expensed, and the company's cost of capital R is 10 per cent. In the computations that follow, note that R is taken as a whole integer and time T is expressed in years. Solution:

Alternative A

Cash flow	Time, in years	$R \times T$	Factor (Table A)	Present value
−$250	0	0	1.0000	−$250

Alternative B

Cash flow	Time, in years	$R \times T$	Factor (Table A)	Present value
−$100	0	0	1.0000	−$100.00
− 100	5	50	0.6065	− 60.65
− 100	10	100	0.3679	− 36.79
− 100	15	150	0.2231	− 22.31
				−$219.75

A comparison of present values indicates alternative B is $250.00 − $219.75 = $30.25 lower in cost than alternative A.

2. Is it better to make lease payments of $50 per month for 5 years or to pay a $2,000 lump-sum for an item of capital equipment? The lease provides that title cannot be taken, so the monthly payments are expensed. In the other alternative, title is taken and lump-sum payment must be capitalized. The cost of capital R is 10 per cent. Corporate tax rate is 50 per cent, and depreciation is sum-of-year-digits for 5 years. The equipment is of no value at the end of 5 years. As in Example 1 above, R is a whole integer and time T is expressed in years. Solution:

Alternative A

	Cash flow	Time, in years	$R \times T$	Factor (Table B)	Present value
Expense	$-\$50 \times 12 \times 5$	0–5	50	0.7869	$-\$2,360$
Tax savings ..	$50\% \times \$50 \times 12 \times 5$	0–5	50	0.7869	$+ 1,180$
		Net present value of five-year lease costs			$-\$1,180$

Alternative B

	Cash flow	Time, in years	$R \times T$	Factor (Table A)	Present value
Investment ...	$-\$2,000$	0	0	1.0000	$-\$2,000$
Tax savings from depreciation	$\frac{5}{15} \times \$2,000 \times 50\%$	1	10	0.9048	$+\$\ 302$
	$\frac{4}{15} \times \$2,000 \times 50\%$	2	20	0.8187	$+\ \ 218$
	$\frac{3}{15} \times \$2,000 \times 50\%$	3	30	0.7408	$+\ \ 148$
	$\frac{2}{15} \times \$2,000 \times 50\%$	4	40	0.6703	$+\ \ \ 89$
	$\frac{1}{15} \times \$2,000 \times 50\%$	5	50	0.6065	$+\ \ \ 40$
		Net present value of purchase costs			$-\$1,203$

The present value of alternative A is $\$1,203 - \$1,180 = \$23$ less over a five-year period.

Decisions Based on Economic Evaluations. The general method employed in the above two specific examples and other similar problems is as follows:

1. Quantify as many factors involved in the problem as possible, with regard to both their monetary amount and the time of their occurrence.
2. Commute their monetary value to a common reference time—the present.
3. Compare the commuted present values of the alternatives, evaluate other factors which were not quantified, and decide which alternative is best.

Factors which were not quantified in Example 1 include the probability of price rises on the future purchases of the lower-cost item and, conversely, the possibility of technological improvement obsoleting the higher-priced item before the end of the 20-year period. In Example 2, factors not quantified include corporate policy with regard to leasing. Before a final decision is made, consideration must be given to the factors which cannot be calculated.

Those wishing to pursue the subject of economic evaluation in greater depth should refer to *Principles of Engineering Economy,* Ronald Press Company, New York.

Text prepared by D. J. Murphy, Amoco Oil Company, Whiting, Ind.

TABLES OF DISCOUNTED CASH-FLOW FACTORS

TABLE 32-20B Factors for Cash Effects Which Occur at a Point in Time after the Reference Point

R x T	0	1	2	3	4	5	6	7	8	9
0	1.0000	.9910	.9802	.9704	.9608	.9512	.9418	.9324	.9231	.9139
10	.9048	.8958	.8869	.8781	.8696	.8607	.8521	.8437	.8353	.8270
20	.8187	.8106	.8025	.7945	.7866	.7788	.7711	.7634	.7558	.7483
30	.7408	.7334	.7261	.7189	.7188	.7047	.6977	.6907	.6839	.6771
40	.6703	.6637	.6570	.6505	.6440	.6376	.6313	.6250	.6188	.6126
50	.6065	.6005	.5945	.5886	.5827	.5770	.5712	.5655	.5599	.5543
60	.5488	.5434	.5379	.5326	.5273	.5220	.5169	.5117	.5066	.5016
70	.4966	.4916	.4868	.4819	.4771	.4724	.4677	.4630	.4584	.4538
80	.4493	.4449	.4404	.4360	.4317	.4274	.4232	.4190	.4148	.4107
90	.4066	.4025	.3985	.3946	.3906	.3867	.3829	.3791	.3753	.3716
100	.3679	.3642	.3606	.3570	.3535	.3499	.3465	.3430	.3396	.3362
110	.3329	.3296	.3263	.3230	.3198	.3166	.3135	.3104	.3073	.3042
120	.3012	.2982	.2952	.2923	.2894	.2865	.2837	.2808	.2780	.2753
130	.2725	.2698	.2671	.2645	.2618	.2592	.2567	.2541	.2516	.2491
140	.2466	.2441	.2417	.2393	.2369	.2346	.2322	.2299	.2276	.2254
150	.2231	.2209	.2187	.2165	.2144	.2122	.2101	.2080	.2060	.2039
160	.2019	.1999	.1979	.1959	.1940	.1921	.1901	.1882	.1864	.1845
170	.1827	.1809	.1791	.1773	.1755	.1738	.1720	.1703	.1686	.1670
180	.1653	.1637	.1620	.1604	.1588	.1572	.1557	.1541	.1526	.1511
190	.1496	.1481	.1466	.1451	.1437	.1423	.1409	.1395	.1381	.1367
200	.1353	.1340	.1327	.1313	.1300	.1287	.1275	.1262	.1249	.1237
210	.1225	.1212	.1200	.1188	.1177	.1165	.1153	.1142	.1130	.1119
220	.1108	.1097	.1086	.1075	.1065	.1056	.1044	.1033	.1023	.1013
230	.1003	.0993	.0983	.0973	.0963	.0954	.0944	.0935	.0926	.0916
240	.0907	.0898	.0889	.0880	.0872	.0863	.0854	.0846	.0837	.0829
250	.0821	.0813	.0805	.0797	.0789	.0781	.0773	.0765	.0758	.0750
260	.0743	.0735	.0728	.0721	.0714	.0707	.0699	.0693	.0686	.0679
270	.0672	.0665	.0659	.0652	.0646	.0639	.0633	.0627	.0620	.0614
280	.0608	.0602	.0596	.0590	.0584	.0578	.0573	.0567	.0561	.0556
290	.0550	.0545	.0539	.0536	.0529	.0523	.0518	.0513	.0508	.0503
300	.0498	.0493	.0488	.0483	.0478	.0476	.0469	.0464	.0460	.0455
310	.0450	.0446	.0442	.0437	.0433	.0429	.0424	.0420	.0416	.0412
320	.0408	.0404	.0400	.0396	.0392	.0388	.0384	.0380	.0376	.0373
330	.0369	.0365	.0362	.0358	.0354	.0351	.0347	.0344	.0340	.0337
340	.0334	.0330	.0327	.0324	.0321	.0317	.0314	.0311	.0308	.0305
350	.0302	.0299	.0296	.0293	.0290	.0287	.0284	.0282	.0279	.0276
360	.0273	.0271	.0268	.0265	.0263	.0260	.0257	.0255	.0252	.0250
370	.0247	.0245	.0242	.0240	.0238	.0235	.0233	.0231	.0228	.0226
380	.0224	.0221	.0219	.0217	.0215	.0213	.0211	.0209	.0207	.0204
390	.0202	.0200	.0198	.0196	.0194	.0193	.0191	.0189	.0187	.0185
400	.0183	.0181	.0180	.0178	.0176	.0174	.0172	.0171	.0169	.0167
410	.0166	.0164	.0162	.0161	.0159	.0158	.0156	.0155	.0153	.0151
420	.0150	.0148	.0147	.0146	.0144	.0143	.0141	.0140	.0138	.0137
430	.0136	.0134	.0133	.1032	.0130	.0129	.0128	.0127	.0125	.0124
440	.0123	.0122	.1020	.0119	.0118	.0117	.0116	.0114	.0113	.0112

TABLE 32-20C Factors for Cash Effects Which Occur Uniformly over a Period of Years Starting with the Reference Point

R x T	0	1	2	3	4	5	6	7	8	9
0	1.0000	.9950	.9901	.9851	.9803	.9754	.9706	.9658	.9610	.9563
10	.9516	.9470	.9423	.9377	.9332	.9286	.9241	.9196	.9152	.9107
20	.9063	.9020	.8976	.8933	.8891	.8848	.8806	.8764	.8722	.8681
30	.8639	.8598	.8558	.8517	.8477	.8438	.8398	.8359	.8319	.8281
40	.8242	.8204	.8166	.8128	.8090	.8053	.8016	.7979	.7942	.7906
50	.7869	.7833	.7798	.7762	.7727	.7692	.7657	.7622	.7588	.7554
60	.7520	.7486	.7452	.7419	.7386	.7353	.7320	.7288	.7256	.7224
70	.7192	.7160	.7128	.7097	.7066	.7035	.7004	.6974	.6944	.6913
80	.6883	.6854	.6824	.6795	.6765	.6736	.6707	.6679	.6650	.6622
90	.6594	.6566	.6537	.6510	.6483	.6455	.6428	.6401	.6374	.6348
100	.6321	.6295	.6269	.6243	.6217	.6191	.6166	.6140	.6115	.6090
110	.6065	.6040	.6016	.5991	.5967	.5942	.5918	.5894	.5871	.5847
120	.5823	.5800	.5777	.5754	.5731	.5708	.5685	.5663	.5641	.5618
130	.5596	.5574	.5552	.5530	.5509	.5487	.5466	.5444	.5424	.5402
140	.5381	.5361	.5340	.5320	.5299	.5279	.5259	.5239	.5219	.5199
150	.5179	.5160	.5140	.5121	.5102	.5082	.5064	.5044	.5026	.5007
160	.4988	.4970	.4952	.4933	.4915	.4897	.4879	.4861	.4843	.4825
170	.4808	.4790	.4773	.4756	.4739	.4721	.4704	.4687	.4671	.4654
180	.4637	.4621	.4605	.4588	.4571	.4555	.4540	.4523	.4508	.4491
190	.4476	.4460	.4445	.4429	.4414	.4399	.4383	.4368	.4354	.4338
200	.4323	.4308	.4294	.4279	.4265	.4250	.4236	.4221	.4207	.4193
210	.4179	.4165	.4151	.4137	.4123	.4109	.4096	.4082	.4069	.4055
220	.4042	.4029	.4015	.4002	.3989	.3976	.3963	.3950	.3937	.3925
230	.3912	.3899	.3887	.3874	.3862	.3849	.3837	.3825	.3813	.3801
240	.3789	.3777	.3765	.3753	.3741	.3729	.3718	.3706	.3695	.3683
250	.3672	.3660	.3649	.3638	.3627	.3615	.3604	.3593	.3582	.3571
260	.3560	.3550	.3539	.3528	.3517	.3507	.3496	.3486	.3476	.3465
270	.3455	.3445	.3434	.3424	.3414	.3404	.3393	.3384	.3374	.3364
280	.3354	.3344	.3335	.3325	.3315	.3306	.3296	.3287	.3277	.3268
290	.3259	.3249	.3240	.3231	.3221	.3212	.3203	.3194	.3185	.3176
300	.3167	.3158	.3150	.3141	.3132	.3123	.3115	.3106	.3098	.3089
310	.3080	.3072	.3064	.3055	.3047	.3039	.3030	.3022	.3014	.3006
320	.2998	.2990	.2982	.2974	.2966	.2958	.2950	.2942	.2934	.2926
330	.2919	.2911	.2903	.2896	.2888	.2880	.2873	.2865	.2858	.2850
340	.2843	.2936	.2828	.2821	.2814	.2807	.2799	.2792	.2785	.2778
350	.2771	.2764	.2757	.2750	.2743	.2736	.2729	.2722	.2715	.2709
360	.2702	.2695	.2688	.2682	.2675	.2669	.2662	.2655	.2649	.2642
370	.2636	.2629	.2623	.2617	.2610	.2604	.2598	.2591	.2585	.2579
380	.2573	.2567	.2560	.2554	.2548	.2542	.2536	.2530	.2524	.2518
390	.2512	.2506	.2500	.2495	.2489	.2483	.2477	.2471	.2466	.2460
400	.2454	.2449	.2443	.2437	.2432	.2426	.2421	.2415	.2410	.2404
410	.2399	.2393	.2388	.2382	.2377	.2372	.2366	.2361	.2356	.2350
420	.2345	.2340	.2335	.2330	.2325	.2319	.2314	.2309	.2304	.2299
430	.2294	.2289	.2284	.2279	.2274	.2269	.2264	.2259	.2255	.2250
440	.2245	.2240	.2235	.2230	.2226	.2221	.2216	.2212	.2207	.2202

NOTE: For further information on subjects covered in this section see the list of references in Section 30.

Index

Also refer to Section 31, in which many words, terms, and symbols not included in this index are defined. The glossary is in alphabetical order and thus is an index in itself on purchasing management, materials management, and allied subjects. Reference to the table of contents at the beginning of each section may also prove helpful.